KIMBERLEY

SIEGE ACCOUNT AND MEDAL ROLL

KIMBERLEY

SIEGE ACCOUNT AND MEDAL ROLL
FOR THE QUEEN'S SOUTH AFRICA MEDAL
1899–1902

By

David J Biggins
BA (Hons) MBA BSc (Hons)

Token PUBLISHING

2010

First published in Great Britain, March 2010

by

Token Publishing Ltd, Orchard House, Duchy Road, Honiton, Devon, EX14 1YD

Telephone: 01404 46972   Fax: 01404 44788

e-mail: info@tokenpublishing.com Website: http://tokenpublishing.com

© 2010 David J. Biggins and Token Publishing Ltd

British Library Cataloguing in Publication data:

A catalogue for this book is available from the British Library

ISBN 978 1 870192 040

No part of this publication may be reproduced, stored in a retrieval system or transmitted in any form or by any means, electronic, mechanical, photocopying, recording or otherwise, without the prior permission of the publishers

Printed in Great Britain by JF Print Ltd, Sparkford

Foreword

At the start of the Anglo Boer War in 1899, the Boers needed to make some early gains before the British had time to ferry to South Africa the number of troops needed to overcome the Boer republics. Top of their list of strategic goals was the capture of the diamond centre of Kimberley. The town was situated a provocatively short distance from the Orange Free State border and its early capture would generate a powerful message to the world announcing the capability and prowess of the young republics. As if this wasn't sufficient reason, Kimberley held within it that symbol of British colonial expansionism much hated by the Boers, Cecil Rhodes. The scene was set for an epic conflict.

This book is about the siege of Kimberley and of the 50,000 inhabitants who were surrounded by the Boer forces for 124 days and survived bombardment and privation before relief came in February 1900. It is the story of resourcefulness, bravery and internal political intrigue. The main events of the siege are recounted from the hurried and insubstantial preparations, through the early engagements and battles, to the diminution of supplies and finally to a rushed relief by the Imperial forces before the town would have been forced into capitulation.

There are several notable books that focus on the social aspects of the siege or cover the whole siege in all its facets, chief amongst these being the excellent *'Summer of 1899'*. This book however has a different aim. It concentrates on the military aspects of the siege and the personnel (both Imperial and Colonial) who took part in the defence. The creation of the defences, enrolment of the citizen soldiers, military strategies and tactics, as well as the main engagements, are set out and explained. Battles were fought with the Boers outside the defences and there were notable exchanges between Cecil Rhodes and the military authorities within the walls that were equally, if not more, of a threat to the defence of Kimberley.

A major part of this book is devoted to a list of the men and women who took part in the defence of Kimberley. The alphabetical list records the name of each individual, their medal entitlement and biographical details.

The account and medal roll is supported by 35 appendices which provide more detailed information on various aspects of the siege. Included in this part of the book are biographies and portraits of the notable personalities, casualties for both sides, honours and awards, information on the main artillery pieces, the military medals issued, the role of De Beers and the little recorded participation of blacks in the siege.

Photographs and maps appear throughout the book. Many of the photographs have been taken from the book *'The Siege of Kimberley'* which was published around 1900 in Kimberley.

The information in this book is largely based on contemporary records that are now over a century old. Reliance is vested in those people who recorded the events as they happened or who wrote about them in later years. The historical records for the period that have come down to us range from the very precise and accurate to information that is misleading, dubious and, sometimes, factually wrong. However much work is put into a book of this type, the chance of error or omission is a continual and palpable concern. Charting a completely successful course through this sea of uncertainty, choosing only the correct information, is an impossible task. As a result, it is certain that some inaccuracies are contained within these pages and for these the author takes full responsibility.

While inaccuracies in the printed book will prevail, there is no reason why the error should go unresolved. Therefore, updates to the information in this book will appear on a website, the address of which is:

> http://www.angloboerwar.com

This site contains much of the background information on which this book is based. It is also possible to send information to the author about errors in the book, the siege itself, the existence of QSA medals etc. Please use the email address:

> kimberley@angloboerwar.com

For now, read on and discover more about the siege and the 5,458 gallant men and women who risked their lives to defend the Diamond City in its hour of need.

For my family

Acknowledgements

To have reached the stage where this book is ready for publication is due largely to the immense amount of support that has been provided by a large number of people. I am pleased to be able to acknowledge the contribution and assistance that I have received.

The majority of data in this book has been gleaned from the medal rolls and other documents held in the National Archives. This is my favourite of all places and the staff who work there are excellent.

Other information has been collected from a range of sources. Pre-eminent amongst these are the McGregor Museum and Africana Library in Kimberley. Kokkie, Brigit, Sunet and Robert could not have been any more helpful in assisting me with my research, answering innumerable questions and supplying me with information. Both the McGregor Museum and Africana Library are wonderful places to be able to conduct research. The staff of De Beers were also very helpful in providing images for use in this book. I must also mention Elmarie Malherbe at the Bloemfontein Anglo Boer War Museum for her help with portrait pictures.

The internet-based British Medal Forum has been a great help. The willingness of the members of this forum to freely share their knowledge and expertise is wonderful. Their depth of knowledge and helpfulness seem to have no limits. Books have been a great source of information in the compilation of this work. My thanks go to the British Library for providing access to many rare publications and to my local library in Verwood, Dorset for sourcing books from around the country for me. Sue, Julie and Rosemary are deserving of special mention. Cam Simpson extracted from his extensive archive the details of anyone who had a link to the siege and to him I extend my sincere thanks for his willingness and generosity to share the information he has collated.

Mark Reid and Brian Conyngham have been very helpful in finding details of Kimberley QSAs. Philip Skingley is owed a debt of thanks for making available the archives of Spink where I spent many a pleasant visit.

My thanks go to the Royal Logistics Corps Museum for granting the permission to reproduce Captain Gorle's account of the siege. The excerpts from Colonel Kekewich's diary are reproduced by kind permission of the Queen's Lancashire Regiment Museum. MacInnes' account of the siege and his plans of the defences are reproduced by kind permission of the Royal Engineers' Museum. Extracts from the *Diamond Fields Advertiser* are reproduced by permission of the editor. Lieutenant Braine's account of Carter's Ridge are reproduced by permission of Bill Braine.

My thanks to the staff at DNW for their permission to reproduce images from their catalogues. The image of the group to Blundell is courtesy of the James Ellis Collection.

The following individuals have contributed to this book: Ieuan Adlam Hill, Carol Archibald, Paul Baillie, Jeffrey Bates, Tony Beach, Peter Beighton, Alexander Biggins, Cathryn Biggins, Chris Biggins, Edward Biggins, Derek Bird, Richard Black, Charley Bolt, Gordon Brown, Sue Brown, Helene Butler, Brigit Carlstein, John Chidzey, Mike Clare, Mike Claxton, Robin Clay, Steve Corbitt, Peter Counsell, John Coward, Ryan Darby, Jane Davies, Ed De Santis, Clive Dicks, Peter Digby, Chris Dixon, Johan du Plessis, Kokkie Duminy, James Ellis, Chris Elmy, Vicki Fawcett, Helen Fields, Stuart Forbes, Paul Galton, Louise Gordon, Gordon Gould, Celia Green, G Griffin, Robert Hart, Carol Hartman, Ingrid Henrici, Phil Hill, Caroline Holmes, Charlotte Hughes, David Humphry, Natalie Jaffe, Shirley James, Celeste Jones, Michael Kaplan, Brian Kieran, Terry King, S R Kingston-Turner, Geoff Klass, Sam Kremer, Ian Linney, David Lloyd, Henk Loots, Roy Lowe, Elmarie Malherbe, Stephen Malpass, Joan Marsh, Alastair Massie, Charmaine McClean, David McLennan, Gareth Mears, Rob Mitchell, Sue Mitchell, Irv Mortenson, Jim Murray, Phil Mussell, John Mussell, David Owen, Antony Pamm, Robin Pelteret, Audrey Portman, George Pradarits, Fiona Pyle, Ashley Reed, Rory Reynolds, Nicole Riches, Jeff Ritsick, David Rockingham-Gill, Colin Roe, Steve Rosbotham, Mike Rowan, Brian Seward, Carly Simmons-Sadler, Brian Simpkin, Martin Smith, Tim Stankus, Pete Starling, Sunet Swanepoel, Brian Taylor, Emma Truelove, Katie Truelove, Lynne Truelove, Barry Turk, Ann Walker, Catherine Walker, J V Webb, John Welch and Michael Young.

Finally, there are several members of my family who have helped in a wide range of activities from encouraging, proof-reading, entering and checking information to undertaking primary research. I think I must have asked everyone for their opinion on the handwriting on the medal rolls at some time too! My wife and two sons have lived with my interest in the siege of Kimberley for the five years since work on this book started and have provided enormous support. My brother has been a constant source of encouragement and contributed a lot of time, suggestions and improvements. My nieces contributed their time and a diverse and amazing range of skills. I count myself very fortunate to have such a supportive family.

Contents

Introduction
- Foreword vi
- Acknowledgements vii
- Abbreviations viii
- Kimberley's location and history 1
- The origins of the Boer War 5
- Preparations for a siege 6

The siege
- The siege begins 31
- November 1899 38
- December 1899 56
- January 1900 63
- February 1900 70
- The relief 83

Medal roll
- Analysis of the medal roll 91
- Medal roll 97

Appendices
- Appendix 01 – Chronology of the siege 280
- Appendix 02 – Photographs of Kimberley 284
- Appendix 03 – Garrison strength 287
- Appendix 04 – Officers involved in the siege 289
- Appendix 05 – 50th Anniversary reunion (15th February 1950) 292
- Appendix 06 – Plans of the defences 293
- Appendix 07 – Troops involved in engagements 323
- Appendix 08 – Honours and awards 333
- Appendix 09 – Biographies 337
- Appendix 10 – Portraits 359
- Appendix 11 – Military casualties 367
- Appendix 12 – Memorials 377
- Appendix 13 – Organisation of the defence 384
- Appendix 14 – Kekewich's despatch of 15th February 1900 395
- Appendix 15 – Proclamation of the state of siege 418
- Appendix 16 – Kimberley Town Guard 419
- Appendix 17 – Nominal roll by location 423
- Appendix 18 – Unit photographs 450
- Appendix 19 – Photographs of the defences 493
- Appendix 20 – Queen's South Africa medals 499
- Appendix 21 – Non-standard Kimberley QSAs 508
- Appendix 22 – Commemorative medals and awards 516
- Appendix 23 – De Beers Consolidated Mines Limited 524
- Appendix 24 – Long Cecil 529
- Appendix 25 – Long Tom 533
- Appendix 26 – The armoured train 535
- Appendix 27 – Diamond Fields Advertiser 537
- Appendix 28 – The Kimberley Club 542
- Appendix 29 – The Sanatorium 543
- Appendix 30 – The Town Hall 544
- Appendix 31 – The Postal Telegraph Department 545
- Appendix 32 – Despatch riders 547
- Appendix 33 – The involvement of Black people in the siege 553
- Appendix 34 – A Supply Officer's view 555
- Appendix 35 – How Kimberley was relieved 561

References
- Bibliography 567
- Index 569

Abbreviations

14H	14th Hussars	DBMB	De Beers' Maxim Battery
2D	2nd Dragoons	DCM	Distinguished Conduct Medal
2nd	Second	Dec	December
A	Acting (rank)	DFA	Diamond Fields Artillery
ACD	Army Chaplains' Department	DFH	Diamond Fields Horse
ALH	Ashburner's Light Horse	DH	Damant's Horse	Diamond Hill (QSA)
APC	Army Pay Corps	DM	Defence Medal
APM	Assistant Provost Marshal	DMR	District Mounted Rifles
Apr	April	DMT	District Mounted Troops
AR	Army Reserve	DMU	Discharged medically unfit
Arm	Armourer (rank)	DoK	Defence of Kimberley clasp (QSA)
ASC	Army Service Corps	DoM	Defence of Mafeking clasp (QSA)
ASM	Africa Service Medal	DOW	Died of wounds
Aug	August	Drie	Driefontein clasp (QSA)
AVC	Army Veterinary Corps	Drum	Drummer (rank)
Band	Bandsman (rank)	DrS	Driscoll's Scouts
Bas	Basutoland	DS	Dennison's Scouts
BBP	Bechuanaland Border Police	DSO	Distinguished Service Order
Bech	Bechuanaland	Dvr	Driver (rank)
Belf	Belfast clasp (QSA)	Ed VII	King Edward VIIth
BoH	Border Horse	Emp	Employee (rank)
Bombdr	Bombardier (rank)	ETG	Edenburg Town Guard
BQMS	Battery QMS (rank)	Excl	Excluding
BR	Bechuanaland Rifles	FAM	Frontier Armed & Mounted
BrH	Brabant's Horse	Farr	Farrier (rank)
BS	Border Scouts	Feb	February
BSACM	British South Africa Company Medal	FID	Field Intelligence Department
BSAP	British South Africa Police	FLH	Frontier Light Horse
BSM	Battery Sergeant Major (rank)	FMR	Frontier Mounted Rifles
BTG	Beaconsfield Town Guard	FS	Fraserburg Scouts
BWM	Great War British War Medal	GDC	Griquatown Defence Corps
c	Circa	GeS	Geoghegan's Scouts
Capt	Captain (rank)	GFC	Gorringe's Flying Column
CB	Companion of the Bath	Gnr	Gunner (rank)
CC	Cape Colony clasp (QSA)	GOC	General Officer Commanding
CCCC	Cape Colony Cyclist Corps	GSM	General Service Medal
CCOD	Cape Colonial Ordnance Department	GSWA	German South West Africa
CGH	Cape of Good Hope	GV	King George Vth
CGR	Cape Government Railway	Hd	Head (rank)
CI	Cape Infantry	HE	His Excellency
CinCBG	Commander in Chief's Body Guard	Hon	Honorary
Cl	Class (rank)	HW	His Worship
CMG	Companion of St Michael & St George	IDMT	Indwe District Mounted Troops
CMR	Cape Mounted Rifles	IGS	Indian General Service Medal
CMSC	Cape Medical Staff Corps	IHL	Imprisonment with hard labour
Co	Company	ILH	Imperial Light Horse
Col	Colonel (rank)	Colour (rank)	IMR	Imperial Military Railways
Cond	Conductor (rank)	Inc	Including
Const	Constable (rank)	Ins	Instructor (rank)
CP	Cape Police	Insp	Inspector (rank)
CP1	Cape Police, District 1	Int	Intelligence (rank)
CP2	Cape Police, District 2	IY	Imperial Yeomanry
Cpl	Corporal (rank)	IYS	Imperial Yeomanry Scouts
CPS	Cape Police, Special Contingent	Jan	January
CQMS	Company QMS (rank)	JMR	Johannesburg Mounted Rifles
CRS	Cape Railway Sharpshooters	Jnr	Junior
CSM	Colour Sergeant Major (rank)	Joh	Johannesburg clasp (QSA)
ct	Carat	JTG	Jagersfontein Town Guard
CTH	Cape Town Highlanders	Jul	July
CuH	Cullinan's Horse	Jun	June

x

KDF	Koffiefontein Defence Force	RHQ	Regimental Headquarters
KFS	Kitchener's Fighting Scouts	RoH	Roberts' Horse
KH	Kimberley Horse	RoK	Relief of Kimberley clasp (QSA)
KIA	Killed in action	RoM	Relief of Mafeking clasp (QSA)
KitH	Kitchener's Horse	RQMS	Regimental QMS (rank)
KLH	Kimberley Light Horse	RR	Rand Rifles
KMC	Kimberley Mounted Corps	RSM	Regimental Sergeant Major (rank)
KRV	Kimberley Regiment of Volunteers	RSO	Railway Staff Officer (rank)
KSA	King's South Africa Medal	Rwy	Railway (rank)
KStar	Kimberley Star	S	Staff (rank)	Shoeing (rank)
KTG	Kimberley Town Guard	SA	South Africa
KWTTG	King Williamstown TG	SA01	South Africa 1901 clasp (QSA)
L	Lance (rank)	SA02	South Africa 1902 clasp (QSA)
LG	London Gazette	SAC	South African Constabulary
LNLR	Loyal North Lancashire Regiment	SAGS	South African General Service Medal
LS&GC	Long Service & Good Conduct Medal	SAI	South African Infantry
Lt	Lieutenant (rank)	SAMC	South African Medical Corps
Maj	Major (rank)	SAMIF	South African Mtd Irregular Forces
Mar	March	SAMMH	South African Museum Military History
Med	Medical	SAMR	South African Mounted Rifles
MH	Marshall's Horse	SANLC	South African Native Labour Corps
MI	Mounted Infantry	Sapr	Sapper (rank)
MID	Mentioned in Despatch	SAVR	South African Veterans' Regiment
ML	Muzzle-loading	ScH	Scottish Horse
MLA	Member of the Legislative Assembly	Sdlr	Saddler (rank)
MoTG	Montagu Town Guard	Sep	September
MSM	Meritorious Service Medal	Sgt I G	Sergeant Instructor of Gunnery (rank)
Mst	Master (rank)	Sgt I M	Sergeant Instructor of Musketry (rank)
Mtd	Mounted	Sgt	Sergeant (rank)
Nat	Natal clasp (QSA)	Sig	Signaller (rank)
NH	Nesbitt's Horse	Snr	Senior
NLC	Native Labour Corps	Sp	Special (rank)
Nov	November	SQMS	Squadron QMS (rank)
NS	Nursing Staff	SRG	Scott's Railway Guards
Oct	October	StH	Steinaecker's Horse
Off	Officer (rank)	Surg	Surgeon (rank)
OFS	Orange Free State (state | QSA clasp)	TFWM	Territorial Forces War Medal
OR	Orderly Room (rank)	TG	Town Guard
ORC	Orange River Colony	Tmptr	Trumpeter (rank)
ORCP	Orange River Colony PMP	Tpr	Trooper (rank)	Troop (rank)
ORS	Orange River Scouts	Tr	Transvaal (QSA)
Paar	Paardeberg clasp (QSA)	Trans	Transkei
PAGMI	Prince Alfred's Guard MI	TSM	Troop Sergeant Major (rank)
Pion	Pioneer (rank)	UpTG	Upington Town Guard
PMP	Provisional Mounted Police	UTG	Uitenhage TG
POC	Post Office Corps	UVR	Uitenhage Volunteer Rifles
psc	Passed Staff College	VC	Victoria Cross
PTC	Provisional Transvaal Constabulary	VM	Great War Victory Medal
Pte	Private (rank)	VMR	Vryburg Mounted Rifles
QIB	Queensland Imperial Bushmen	VTG	Vryburg Town Guard
QM	Quartermaster (rank)	Witt	Wittebergen clasp (QSA)
QMS	Quatermaster Sergeant (rank)	WLH	Western Light Horse
QSA	Queen's South Africa Medal	WMI	Warren's Mounted Infantry
RA	Royal Artillery	WO	Warrant Officer (rank)
RAMC	Royal Army Medical Corps	WPMR	Western Province Mounted Rifles
RE	Royal Engineers	WS	Warwick's Scouts
Rev	Reverse	Reverend (rank)	WWDMT	Windsorton & Wedberg DMT
RGA	Royal Garrison Artillery	WWTG	Windsorton & Wedberg TG
Rhod	Rhodesia clasp (QSA)		

Kimberley's location and history

Kimberley is located in Cape Colony. In 1899, it was the capital of Griqualand West.

It has an elevation above sea level of 4,012 feet (1,220 m).

Distances to other South African towns:

- Bloemfontein 109 miles (175 km)
- Cape Town 597 miles (960 km)
- Durban 525 miles (845 km)
- Johannesburg 292 miles (470 km)
- Ladysmith 351 miles (565 km)
- Mafeking 217 miles (350 km)
- Vryburg 124 miles (200 km)

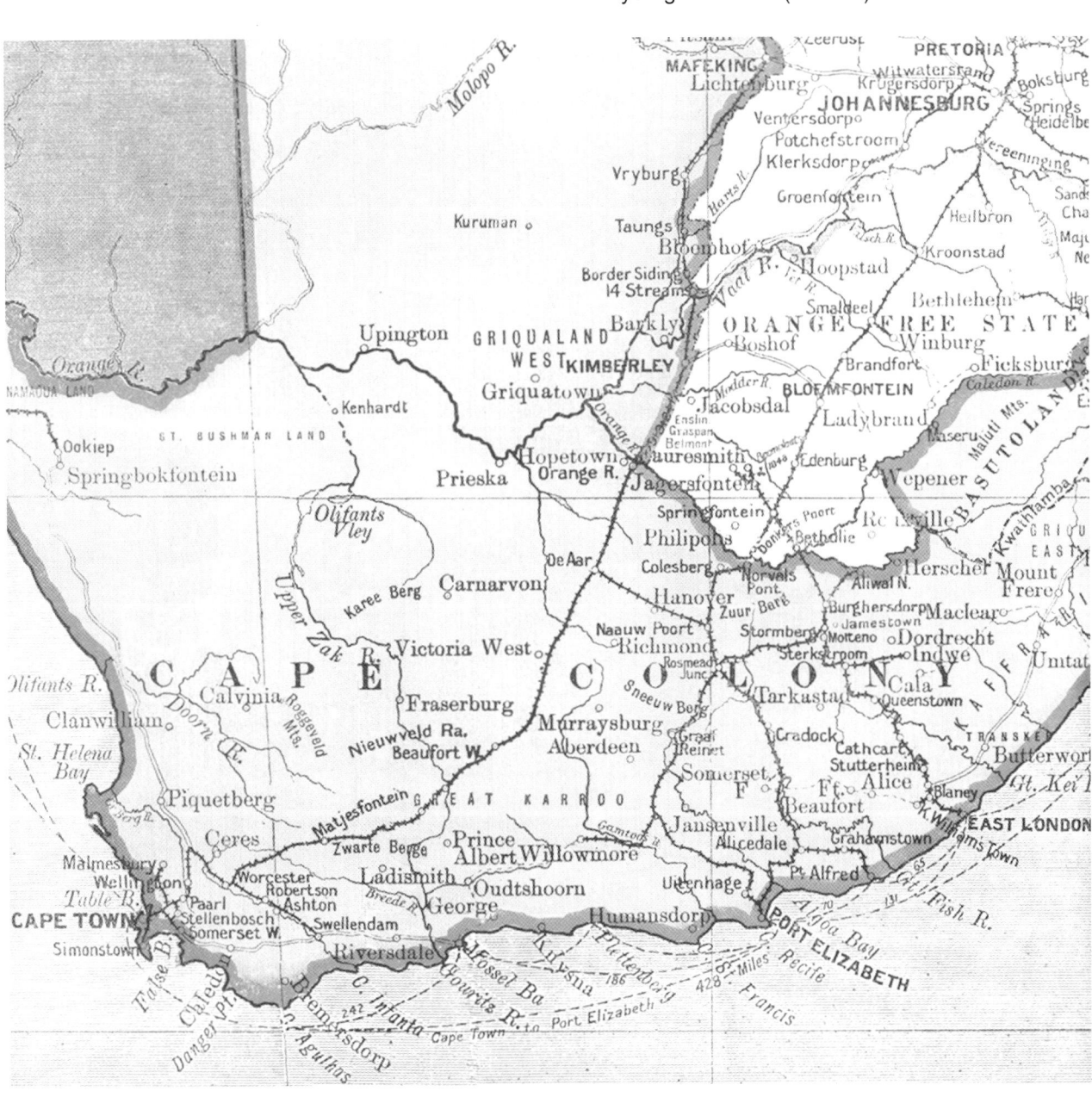

A contemporary map showing Cape Colony

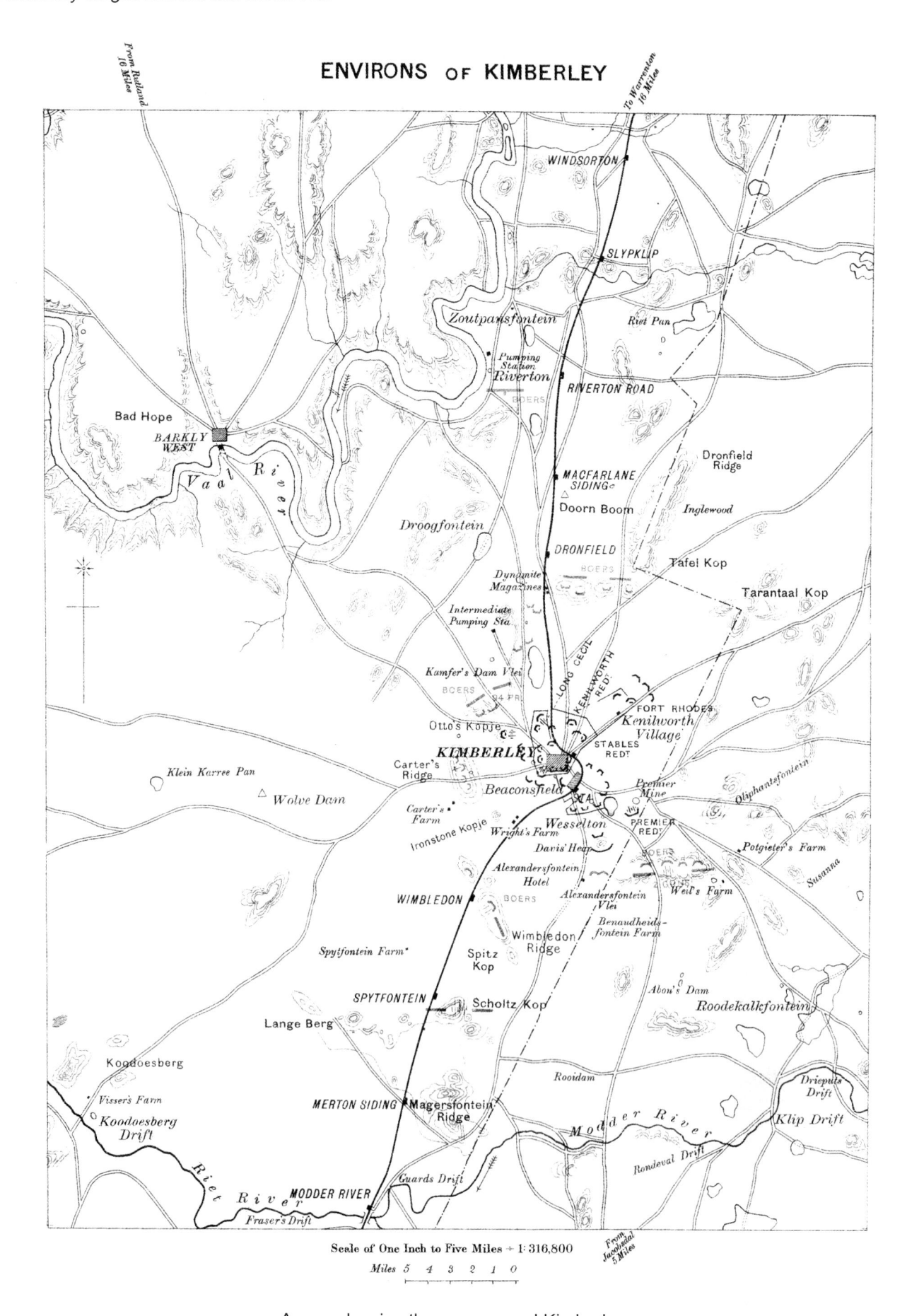

A map showing the area around Kimberley

Kimberley's location and history

The origins of Kimberley

When it was first settled, the city we now know as Kimberley was called New Rush and later Colesberg Kopje. The name of Kimberley originated from the Earl of Kimberley who was the Secretary of State for the British Colonies in the 1870s.

A photograph of Kimberley from the year 1870 shows no more than a thorn tree, a Bushman and a kopje. There was little or nothing to go there for but this was soon to change. Around 1867 a trader by the name of John O'Reilly obtained a stone that had been found by a farmer who lived north of the Orange River. Inspection of the item by Dr W Atherstone of Grahamstown revealed that it was a very high quality diamond. It was soon purchased for £500 by the then Governor of the Cape, Sir Philip Wodehouse. Records do not show what proportion of this huge sum made its way back to the original finder.

News of the discovery spread very quickly and brought a rush of men to the Vaal River. Within a short period, alluvial mines covering over 100 square miles (258 km^2) had been created. The level of excitement was boosted by the discovery of dry diggings at Du Toit's Pan, at Bultfontein, and then at De Beers. The area now known as the Kimberley mine was discovered on 16th July 1871. The banks of the Vaal were soon deserted as the fortune hunters, now joined by a much greater number of prospectors, descended on the Kimberley area. Within a few months the number of prospectors had exceeded 50,000.

The discovery of precious minerals caused the Republic of the Orange Free State to stake their claim of dominion over the area. A local Griqua Chief, Nicholas Waterboer, made a similar claim based on the disputed boundary to his territory. Through negotiation, the matter was soon resolved for on 27th October 1871 the area was proclaimed a British Province, under the name of Griqualand West. The British did pay out compensation of £90,000 to the Orange Free State and granted an annual pension of £1,000 to Nicholas Waterboer.

Vooruitzigt, which translates to 'looking forward' was the name of the farm on which the Kimberley Mine and the De Beers Mine were later located. The farm was sold by Mynheeren De Beer on 19th October 1871 to Dunell, Ebden & Co, of Port Elizabeth, for the lowly sum of £6,000. The new owners realised its value and sold it to the Government of Griqualand West for £100,000 on 19th October 1875.

Nicholas Waterboer

Proclamation Number 22, dated 5th July 1873, circulated in a Government Gazette Extraordinary on 18th July 1873, stated that "… the encampment and town heretofore variously known as De Beers New Rush, the Colesberg Kopje number two, or Vooruitzigt, shall henceforth be designated the town of Kimberley."

The diamond market at the end of the Mine

Whilst the population had grown extraordinarily, there was almost no infrastructure to support the mass of people. The broad, mostly flat land was covered in tents that stretched as far as the eye could see. A hierarchy based on wealth was soon established with the more affluent miners preferring to lodge at Du Toit's Pan or De Beers where the population density was lower. There was a good trade to be made from providing transport for the miners with vehicles of all descriptions pressed into service. Night time brought an end to the mining activity and the camps and thoroughfares were thronged with people. Accounts of the time marvel at the spectacle, public houses sprang up in response to the demand and trade was good.

Kimberley Siege Account and Medal Roll

Despite the multitude of people who made Kimberley their temporary home and the temptations that must have abounded in the unguarded and unsecured tents and wagons, it was reported that crime was low. This may be in part attributable to the fact that the journey from the coast to the Diamond Fields that had to be undertaken by most prospectors cost in excess of £20. This barrier prevented many of those with less means from making the journey.

The lack of artificial light meant that maximum use was made of daylight. Daybreak heralded the sounds of picks, shovels, pulleys, buckets, animals and humans as the prospectors began their day. Life in these early days was hard and not a little dangerous. There were frequent collapses and cave-ins and reports tell of the excited calls that arose from time to time. This was sometimes the result of a valuable find but more often "it would be a cart with a couple of mules or oxen which had toppled over and fallen into the mine, the side of a roadway between the claims having unexpectedly caved in."

Kimberley Mine in 1872

In the early days, a major problem was the scarcity of water. Local supplies were totally incapable of supplying the population. Water sold for 2s 6d per bucket load. The unsanitary conditions caused by the men and animals made disease a constant threat to life and flies and fleas were a regular annoyance. The death rate was abnormally high.

The growth of Kimberley resulted in an eclectic array of buildings. A survey in 1871 noted that corrugated iron structures existed but so did 'houses' made from tin and packing case wood. At the end of that year there were two main streets in the town. On one there were six shops, four hotels, butchers' and shoemakers' shops, a billiard-room, and a saloon. On the other, three hotels, several diamond merchants' offices, provisions stores, confectioners' and pharmaceutical shops and places to eat and play billiards.

The Market Square that exists today in Kimberley had its origin in these early days. The Square would be crowded each morning with wagons loaded with produce from the Orange Free State, wood from the country and game from the veldt.

The discovery of gold in the Johannesburg area in 1885 led some prospectors to leave Kimberley for the new mines and they took with them the experience they had gained from those early days. A 'Mayor's Minute' from the time concluded that "Although the glory of Kimberley for the time being may be dimmed as compared with the dazzling prospects of wealth in more favoured parts in the north - secured to us by the enterprise of Kimberley men and money - I firmly believe that Kimberley will continue to hold its own as one of the most important centres in South Africa."

Kimberley was certainly to come back into the spotlight only a few years later.

Ledges in the Kimberley Mine

The origins of the Boer War

The Boer War took place between 1899 and 1902. Its origins are complex and have roots stretching back into history. Cape Colony was established by the Dutch East India Company in 1652 with the founding of Cape Town. It was initially settled by Dutch people, the forebears of the Afrikaners. In the 1690s, the settlers started to spread out in search of new lands to farm. These nomadic European farmers were known as Trekboers, a term later shortened to Boers. 'Boer' is the Dutch word for 'farmer'.

During the Napoleonic Wars in January 1806, the British took control of Cape Colony to prevent its use and control by the French. The Boer settlers in the Cape disliked British rule and migrated away, first to Natal, until it was annexed by the British in 1843, and then further north where two independent Boer states were established; the Orange Free State and the South African Republic (also known as the Transvaal). The British recognised the two Boer Republics on 17th February 1854 and 17th January 1852 respectively but this did not bring about harmony between the British and the Boers. The attempted annexation of the Transvaal by the British in 1877 led to the First Boer War, 1880-81. The British underestimated the resilience and ability of the Boers and failed to subdue them. After suffering some heavy losses and unwilling to commit the forces necessary to win the war, William Gladstone negotiated a peace treaty with President Paul Kruger and independence was restored.

The Berlin Conference of 1884-85 attempted to define trade, colonisation and the boundaries between the European powers' African possessions. This was not wholly successful as territorial struggles continued and the 'scramble for Africa' was intensified. Germany annexed Namaqualand in 1884 and Britain annexed Bechuanaland in 1885. Within less than 20 years, in 1902, 90% of Africa was under European control.

The discovery of gold in the Transvaal in 1885 paved the way to future conflict by re-igniting British interest in the area. People rushed to the Transvaal in search of their fortunes and the discovery offered the Boer states the opportunity of being the richest and most powerful in Africa. Many of these foreigners or uitlanders as the Boers called them who went to the Transvaal, originated from Britain. The Boers tried to control the political and economic upheaval brought about by the gold. They feared they would soon be outnumbered by the uitlanders and not just in the gold mining areas. The Boers sought to maintain their control by the establishment of new rules that required lengthy residence to gain voting rights, new licences, taxes and administrative bureaucracy.

Disputes grew between the uitlanders and the Boers, political rights were demanded and the situation deteriorated. An uprising by the uitlanders in Johannesburg was organised but this failed miserably. The British troops sent to support the uprising were captured and sentenced in a public trial. Known as the Jameson Raid, this was an embarrassing episode for Britain.

The continuing demand for rights for the uitlanders masked the underlying intention of the British government to control the two republics and to gain control of their economic wealth. The Boers, faced with continuing uitlander immigration, recognised that their independence was under serious threat. If the Boers offered the franchise to the uitlanders, the unintended but ultimate result would be the loss of their own sovereignty. Negotiations were attempted but were never likely to succeed. In September 1899, Joseph Chamberlain, British Colonial Secretary, demanded full equality for the uitlanders in the Transvaal. President Paul Kruger saw no option but to issue a counter ultimatum demanding the withdrawal of British forces from the Transvaal border within 48 hours. The British rejected the ultimatum and war was therefore declared by the two Boer Republics on Britain.

The Second Boer War had begun and was to last until May 1902.

Preparations for a siege

The attractiveness of Kimberley to the Boers

To the Boers, Kimberley must have presented such an attractive and easily attainable target as to be irresistible. Lying just 5 miles (8 km) from the Orange Free State border, 45 miles (72 km) from the Transvaal border and on the open veldt with little in the way of natural defences, the town offered the Boers a most useful supply base with an established railway terminal from which to launch and sustain their attacks deeper into Cape Colony. The reputed wealth of Kimberley and the long-standing grudge that it was incorporated into British territory only worked to strengthen the decision to move against Kimberley[1]. As if this was not reason enough, Kimberley held within its boundaries a personality the Boers would have dearly liked to capture or eliminate, Cecil Rhodes. To have been able to wrest Rhodes from his base of power and source of wealth would have brought an end to the many troubles that this man had caused for the Boer republics and would have been the ultimate prize.

A postcard depicting a situation the Boers would dearly like to create,
a caged Cecil Rhodes in Kimberley

As a first victory so soon after the commencement of the Boer War, the capture of the 'Diamond City' would have presented a fabulous boost to Boer morale and provided an early demonstration of the resourcefulness and ability to their Imperial adversary. There was also the effect the fall of Kimberley would have on the Dutch in Cape Colony who might have been encouraged to throw in their lot with the two republics.

Given all the reasons why Kimberley posed such a target for the Boers, the question needs to be asked whether it would have been a good strategic decision? Would the time, men and resources it would require be justified? The Boers certainly believed so. Like the diamonds it produced, Kimberley was a jewel the Boers meant to acquire for themselves.

Cape Town's view

The location of Kimberley was not chosen for its defensive potential. Indeed when diamonds were first discovered, the possibility of future attack never occurred to the thousands who streamed to the town in search of their fortunes. Over time, the established town and its leading inhabitants were all too aware of its dangerous position and these feelings were exacerbated by the worsening relations with their neighbours and the threat of more serious conflict looming on the horizon.

Major E A Altham, Royal Scots, was sent to Kimberley in 1896 by Lieutenant General Sir W Goodenough (then GOC in South Africa), and in August of that year wrote:

---

[1] Mafeking was a target for the Boers for the similar reason that it too had been incorporated into Cape Colony. There was also the further reason that the Jameson Raid had originated in Mafeking.

"The Government of the South African Republic have a strong feeling against the De Beers Mining Company, and against Mr. Cecil Rhodes, who owes his wealth to that company. The Free State, on the discovery of the diamond mines, claimed Kimberley as within its borders, and received comparatively but a small sum for the relinquishment of that claim. Kimberley is by far the most important place on the line of communications with Mafeking and, through Mafeking, to the north. Even if it should be thought impracticable to maintain that line of communication, the strategic value of Kimberley as a point from which it can be re-opened later in the campaign is very considerable; but, in addition to these considerations, which may have a direct strategic bearing on the conduct of the campaign, there are others connected with Kimberley which would have an indirect but far-reaching effect. Except perhaps Cape Town, Kimberley is the richest prize which the enemy could capture, and lies at a tempting distance from his grasp. Its loss and any damage which might ensue to the mines would not only be a heavy blow to the Cape Colony, but would also be most injurious to Imperial prestige throughout South Africa and, while disheartening the loyalists, would greatly influence the waverers to take active part against us."

The only troops stationed in Kimberley in 1896 were two local Volunteer corps, the Diamond Fields Horse, with a strength of 367 men, including an artillery troop armed with four 7-pounder muzzle-loading (ML) guns, and the Kimberley Rifles, about 400 strong. The protection of the town and the mines necessitated a defensive cordon of 10 miles (16 km). To support a defence, Major Altham proposed to increase the local Volunteer forces, to re-arm and re-form the Diamond Fields Horse, and to provide the white miners with rifles and training in their use. Altham's suggestion was to submit a scheme for the defence of Kimberley to General Goodenough. While he understood the need for action, Goodenough had two problems: he had no Imperial troops that could be sent and the troops that were available, the local Volunteers, were controlled and administered by Colonial Staff officers acting under the direct orders of the Colonial Government in Cape Town. Goodenough had little choice but to forward Altham's report to Sir J Gordon Sprigg, then Prime Minister of the Colony, and also to the members of a Commission which had been formed by the Governor, Lord Rosmead, to look into the organisation of the Colonial forces. One recommendation was carried out with the arming and training of the white miners but, other than that, no action was taken.

In 1896, Colonel David Harris, a Kimberley member of the Cape Assembly, persuaded his colleagues on the Board of the De Beers Company to take the precaution of procuring arms and ammunition. It may seem strange that a commercial company such as De Beers should possess so much military capability. The main sources of these armaments have their roots in the Jameson Raid nearly four years before the siege. Harris explains their motivation and subsequent actions:

"To sit down and do nothing meant disaster to the diamond mines, and ruination to the commercial community of Kimberley. Could war be averted? I debated the matter in my own mind, and came to the irresistible conclusion that some measures must be taken to protect the town. At a special meeting of the Directors of De Beers Company held on the 26th March, 1896, I pointed out to my colleagues that owing to the proximity of Kimberley to the Free State and the Transvaal, and to the hostile feeling exhibited there, there was considerable danger of an attack being made on our town, and more especially on De Beers. It was therefore decided at that meeting to purchase 500 Lee-Metford rifles, 500 regulation bayonets, 4 Maxim guns and 500,000 rounds of ammunition. On April 10, 1896, Mr. Advocate Richard Solomon, … Mr. C. P. J. Coghlan … Mr. W. P. Mallett, solicitor, and Dr. Fuller, met the directors of the company for the purpose of consulting them on the advisability of approaching the Government with a view to obtaining permission to procure and store arms and ammunition for the protection of Kimberley. It was pointed out that the company was specially likely to be an object of attack, and in the event of the volunteer regiment being called away from Kimberley, there would be neither any organised force, nor weapons with which to arm any force. It was therefore decided that while the company could take no active or prominent part in approaching the Government, the Directors were willing and prepared to assist by providing funds for the purchase of arms and ammunition to be obtained in a constitutional manner, and stored in Kimberley for the sole purpose of defence. The previous order was consequently increased to 1,000 Lee-Metford rifles, 6 Maxim guns and 750,000 rounds of ammunition."

Harris also provided the authorities with a military survey of the town and its surroundings.

"My next suggestion was that Kimberley, Beaconsfield and the five mines should be fortified. With that end in view, I commissioned Sedgwick Woolley, a Government surveyor, and a retired officer of the Royal Artillery, to make a military survey of Kimberley and surroundings. With the aid of an assistant, he completed the work within six weeks, dividing the territory to be defended into five military districts having a perimeter of eleven and a quarter miles. The debris heaps were selected as forts and redoubts. Mines were marked out where the Boers could occupy positions to bring rifle fire to bear on the defenders. Careful measurements were made of all the surrounding rising ground which the enemy might occupy. So well and accurately was the survey made, that it was adopted in its entirety when war appeared imminent."

The pressure to do something about Kimberley was growing. At the request of the outgoing Premier, Sir J Gordon Sprigg, Colonel J K Trotter made a visit to Kimberley in June 1898. His objective was to prepare a plan[2] for the defence of the town and, as a result of the Bloemfontein Conference in June 1899 with the implied threat of war, the plan was now viewed as high priority.

The lack of activity meanwhile took its toll on the Volunteers whose strength in 1899 had dwindled. The Kimberley Rifles could muster no more than two companies and the Diamond Fields Horse almost ceased to exist and was totally without any horses. An inspection of the Diamond Fields Horse by Colonel Taylor RA in that year reported that it was armed with only four 7-pounders, there were no horses for the guns and the parade consisted of only 22 officers and men. The established strength should have been 132.

The military authorities were not the only ones who were aware of the dangers to Kimberley. Growing anxiety within the town itself brought a flurry of activity and meetings. On 12th June 1898, the Mayor sent a telegram to the Government at Cape Town seeking to heighten awareness of the predicament of Kimberley and asking that the Diamond Fields Artillery be re-equipped with new 7-pounder guns and that the store at King Williamstown be conveyed to Kimberley. The message ended in a plea that echoed the pioneer spirit that had built Kimberley, "If you cannot or will not protect us, give us arms and we will protect ourselves."

The situation in Cape Town lacked any of the nervousness and anticipation that so excited and enlivened the residents of Kimberley. The mood there was one of conciliation and the need to search for a political resolution to the brewing disharmony between Boer and Briton. A new Cape Premier, Mr Schreiner, replaced Sir J Gordon Sprigg and new thinking dominated the Assembly. The last thing Schreiner wanted was to send fresh military supplies so close to the border with the Free State and thereby inflame the passion of the Boers by demonstrating so openly a show of military preparation. The response from Cape Town characterised their new way of thinking:

> "There is no reason whatever for apprehending that Kimberley is, or in any contemplated event will be, in danger of attack; and Mr Schreiner is of opinion that your fears are groundless and your anticipation without foundation."

Harris believed Schreiner's views were not entirely objective:

> "Advocate Schreiner, KC, who was then Prime Minister … received an assurance from his brother-in-law, Reitz (formerly President of the Orange Free State), that if hostilities broke out the forces of the Republics would not invade the Cape Colony. Schreiner was a very honourable man, and unfortunately he placed too much reliance on the promise of his relatives. So poor Kimberley was left in the lurch! Schreiner was undoubtedly deceived, as the first movement of the Republican forces was an advance towards the Diamond Fields, and the occupation of Magersfontein, some sixteen miles from Kimberley. We were, therefore, cut off by rail from Colonial ports. With his legal mind Schreiner probably thought that he could apply to the High Court for an injunction to restrain the Boers from advancing into Colonial territory. Alas, his theory was rudely shattered."

By 24th August 1898, the Mayor of Kimberley, Mr Henderson, was being hounded by citizens who thought not enough was being done to protect them, their families and their livelihoods. What was needed, they demanded, was a defence plan for Kimberley. The request was sent to Cape Town. But the most that Cape Town could muster was that it was "fully alive to the importance of the defence of Kimberley in case need should arrive." Help did come to Kimberley but it was not through the offices of the Cape Government.

In comparison to Mr Schreiner, the Governor of the Cape and High Commissioner for South Africa, Sir Arthur Milner, was far more sympathetic to the plight that faced Kimberley. Assurances were given to the Mayor that Kimberley would feature in the plans being developed by the Imperial forces. The reality however, was not so reassuring. The distance of Kimberley from Imperial forces to the south and its close proximity to the Free State meant that a large military presence was unlikely to be sent and instead the town would have to fend for itself. Small initiatives were undertaken though and, following a request from Milner to Sir William Butler, Commander in Chief, on 4th July 1899, Colonel Trotter was sent back to Kimberley the same month to revise and enhance his earlier report[3] about Kimberley's defences. He was accompanied and assisted by

---

[2] See page 384 for the contents of his report.
[3] See page 385 for the contents of this report.

Preparations for a siege

Lieutenant D S MacInnes. When Colonel Trotter returned to Cape Town, he left a delicate situation behind. Milner would have liked to have had control over the Volunteers but this was not yet possible and the Cape Government's relaxed stance on Kimberley had not changed. Milner therefore decided it would be prudent to station two staff officers in Kimberley with the dual objectives of keeping an eye on events and making clandestine preparations with the leading inhabitants. The ideal choice was Trotter himself but his recent reappointment meant he could not be spared from Cape Town. His place was taken by Major H Scott-Turner, Royal Highlanders, an officer who had for some years been in special employment in Southern Rhodesia, was well known to the colonists and was, fortuitously, already in Kimberley. Major Scott-Turner went to work immediately and was soon joined by two other special service officers, Captain O'Meara and Lieutenant MacInnes, both from the Royal Engineers. O'Meara's task was intelligence and surveying while MacInnes was given the responsibility of designing defensive works and structures based on the plans he had already devised with Trotter.

Police Commissioner M B Robinson of the Cape Police was appointed by the Cape Government to command all the colonial troops and Police in Griqualand West, Bechuanaland and in Kimberley.

Arrival of Colonel Kekewich

Early in September 1899, Milner persuaded his Ministers to send two thousand Lee-Metford rifles and a small quantity of ammunition to Kimberley, and to order detachments of Cape Police to guard the more important points to the north and south of the town. Milner also made the further suggestion that a senior Imperial officer should be sent to Kimberley to report confidentially on what was happening. For this task, Lieutenant General Sir F Forestier-Walker, the new Commander in Chief of the British troops in South Africa, selected Lieutenant Colonel Robert George Kekewich, LNLR, and on 11th September Kekewich received his instructions personally from Milner. His brief was to investigate the arrangements being made for the protection of Kimberley and to check on the state of communications to Mafeking in the north and to Orange River station in the south. Kekewich was also told to keep his mission a closely guarded secret.

On 13th September, Kekewich arrived in Kimberley and he was immediately briefed by Scott-Turner and O'Meara. In their view, the Boers were clearly mobilising across the border and Kimberley was sure to be a target. Additionally, there were no regular troops available and fortifying the town had yet to begin. Further, the Volunteers were well below their authorised strength and their equipment was poor. Kekewich immediately reported back to Milner and Forestier-Walker on the lamentable situation and the report finally convinced the Prime Minister of the need for action. By 18th September, Kekewich had gained agreement for the despatch of some of his own men, the LNLR, some more artillery and ancillary troops and these arrived on 20th September:

Unit	Officers	Men
23rd Company RGA (with six 2.5-in RML guns on mountain carriages)	3	90
7th Company RE	1	50
Headquarters and 4 companies 1st LNLR	9	413
Detachment Army Service Corps	1	5
Detachment Royal Army Medical Corps	1	5
	15	563

The arrival of the LNLR in Kimberley. The band is in the front of the picture

Kimberley Siege Account and Medal Roll

This small force of regular troops, the first to be stationed in Kimberley for nearly a decade, was augmented by a mounted section of the LNLR on 26th September, consisting of one officer and 21 men.

The administrative conflict between the Colonial and Imperial troops could not exist for long and led to Kekewich succeeding Commissioner Robinson in command of all Colonial troops in Griqualand West and Bechuanaland on 21st September and Kekewich was gazetted Lieutenant Colonel in the Colonial Forces.

On 13th October the Cape Police were also placed under his orders thus giving him total control of all troops in the area.

Kekewich with his staff
Kekewich seated on the left. Scott-Turner seated on the right
MacInnes standing on the left. O'Meara on the right

Preparations for a siege

The Cape Police force consisted of 20 officers and 426 men distributed along the railway line between Kimberley and Mafeking, a distance of 217 miles (350 km) and stationed at 11 key points which ranged in size from 134 officers and men in the largest post to 16 in the smallest. Kekewich reduced these key points from 11 to 4, the largest force of 175 officers and men with two 7-pound guns being at Fourteen Streams. The other posts were at Kraai Pan (70 officers and men), Taungs (89 officers and men) and Vryburg (112 officers and men). Once war was declared, the Police left their posts and retired to Kimberley where they arrived over a number of days.

This action displeased Kekewich and in his diary entry for 24th October 1899 he wrote :

> "It is sad to think of all these retirements of Cape Police from the Posts to North without as far as I know any of them firing a shot or seeing anything of the enemy. It appears to me that in ordinary times the Police have little or no opportunity of systematic drill or military training, being constantly employed on police duty, stationed in small dets scattered over an immense area of country – officers and men of one division seldom coming in touch with officers and men of other divisions of the district."

Kekewich's need for intelligence extended outside Kimberley and to this end on 19th September he arranged for the building of a conning tower and mounted police patrols were organised to monitor the border region. He was also eager to know what was going on in the Free State and on 27th September, he despatched Captain O'Meara to Boshof, 33 miles (53 km) from Kimberley. O'Meara reported on his visit:

> "Leaving Kimberley a little after 6.30 in the morning, I rode the thirty-six miles to the Boer dorp on a bicycle; the track was sandy and a blazing sun beat down on the treeless veldt. Parts of the way it was impossible to pedal and there was nothing for it but to wheel my machine. It had already struck four in the afternoon before I reached Boshof. About two hours later, an armed party of Boers, with Cape Carts carrying impedimenta, arrived in the dorp and drew up in front of my hotel—it was at once rumoured that the little commando had ridden in from Winburg. The whole place was soon in a great state of excitement and much commotion arose.
>
> The hotel proprietor, a British subject, upon seeing the commando, exclaimed: "This means war," and expressed his intention to leave Boshof with his family next day. For many reasons I decided to spend the night in the dorp; it was a restless one, for throughout the hours of darkness much noise prevailed in the streets, giving me the impression that other parties of mounted men were on the move and arriving in Boshof. I was naturally anxious to get back to Kimberley at the earliest moment in order to give the alarm, but it would not have been wise to make an attempt to leave Boshof while it was still dark. Accordingly, I postponed my departure until 6 a.m. on the 28th, and then quietly started on my return journey, and, in order to allay suspicion, took a road leading in a westward direction.
>
> Between ten and eleven o'clock, I found myself at Windsorton Road railway station (twenty-seven miles west of Boshof), and at once sent short telegrams to Kimberley and Cape Town reporting what I had observed on the previous evening. Later in the day I returned to Kimberley by a goods train."

The intelligence uncovered by O'Meara was important and it justified the start of work on the defences. By 7th October Kekewich considered the defences reasonably secure although strengthening and improving work continued throughout the siege.

Raising of the local troops

Kekewich made Cape Town aware of his views on 29th September in the following message:

> "Information from so many independent sources indicates very strongly that offensive movement of some magnitude against Kimberley is intended; in consequence, personally credit Boers to have formed such a plan, however unsound strategically such movement may be, on account of great political results expected to follow.
>
> Would further point out even now greatest difficulty experienced in obtaining confirmation of reports and information of any value. Consider it is not unreasonable to suppose early information Boer movements will not be obtainable in event of hostilities, therefore strongly urge that every measure proposed for defence of Kimberley should be forthwith sanctioned."

On the same day, Milner gave permission for the enrolment of the Town Guard.

Scott-Turner, now local Lieutenant Colonel, had earlier foreseen the need to raise a Town Guard in Kimberley and Beaconsfield and as early as 15th September Kekewich had recorded in his diary how "The Mayor is moving quietly in the matter of taking names of citizens to form a Town Guard, and many are most anxious to be given rifles and to commence drilling at once, but of course anything as to this is at present undesirable, and apart from this, rifles are not available at present."

On the evening that permission was received, Kekewich held a meeting to progress the formation and to issue notices asking for more volunteers.

Notices first appeared on 30th September and within a week 1,156 men had joined, officers had been appointed, and non-commissioned officers of the regular troops tasked to provide instruction in rifle use and basic drill.

The remit of the Town Guards was "solely for local defence in case of attack from without," and its radius of service was constrained to 8 miles (13 km) from the Market Square in Kimberley.

Credit for the success of the Town Guard recruitment was due to the endeavours and energy of Colonel Harris and he was fittingly appointed to command them, with Kekewich as Commandant and Major Peakman as the staff officer. The Town Guard included a civil division under the Mayor which undertook police and hospital duty.

In Harris's autobiography, he indicates the civil population needed some encouragement to join up to the Town Guard:

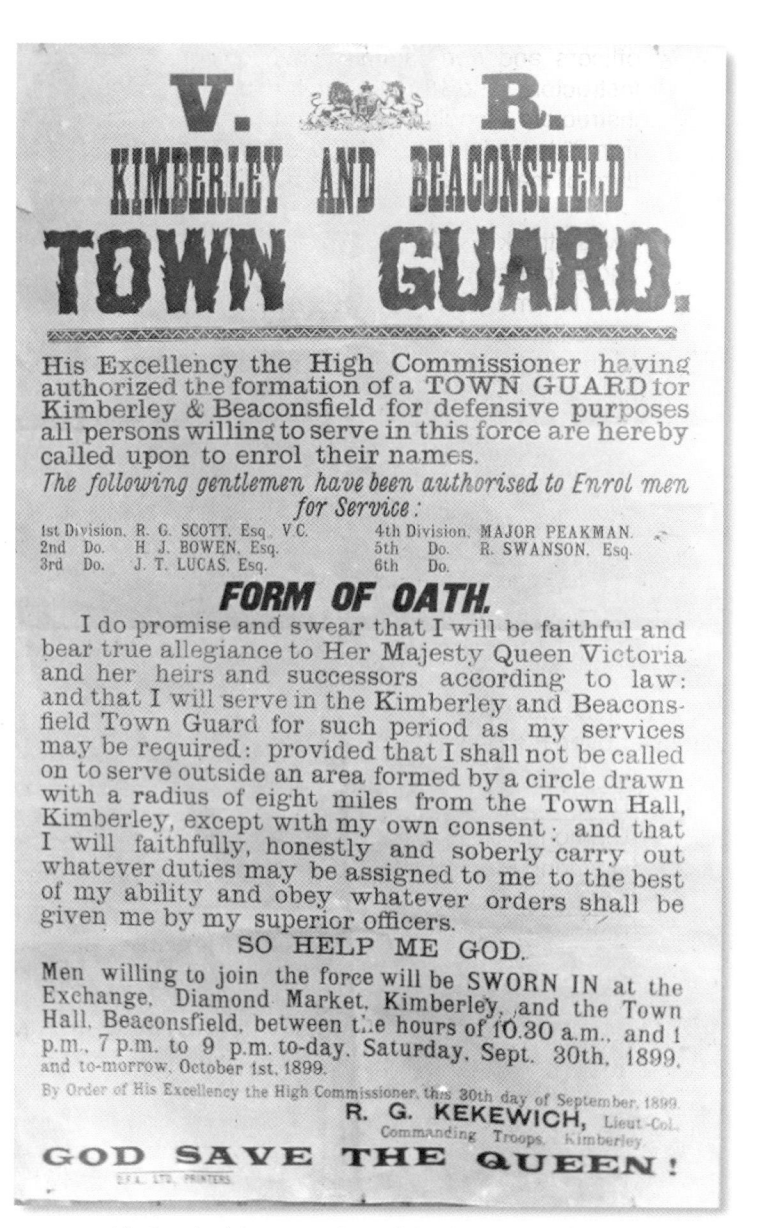

Notice inviting people to join the Town Guard

> "He [Kekewich] also pointed out that Colonel Scott Turner had endeavoured to raise a Town Guard, but there had been no real response from the citizens. Kekewich further mentioned that he intended advising Lord Milner to retire his force to the Orange River, for in the event of war his small column, if left in Kimberley, would be "in the air." He was perfectly right from a military point of view. I asked him to wait for a few days to see what could be done in the matter of raising a Town Guard.
>
> In the meantime I interviewed several of the large commercial employers of the town, and told them what Colonel Kekewich intended doing if there was not a ready response to his proclamation for the formation of a Town Guard, mentioning that De Beers Company would encourage their employees to join. This had an electrifying effect, and during the following week more recruits came forward than we could arm.
>
> We selected 3,000 men, a fair sprinkling of whom had seen service in previous campaigns either in the police or volunteers. I reported the result to Colonel Kekewich, who was obviously delighted at the outcome, and I promised to gladden his heart still more in the course of the following two or three weeks. He replied, "Harris, I wish you to take command," and I readily assented. Then came the herculean task of organising, officering, clothing and drilling this large body.
>
> We purchased all the .303 rifles obtainable in the Colony, bought up all the khaki suits locally and elsewhere, formed the men into companies of 100 strong, and appointed a small complement of

officers and non-commissioned officers. Some difficulty then arose concerning the need for drill instructors, and I brought this important matter to the notice of Kekewich. He asked me how many instructors I would require, and I said I would want at least sixty. "Where are you going to get them from?" he asked. "From the Loyal North Lancs," I answered. But he doubted if we could get even a third of that number from the half battalion then in Kimberley.

I was struck with a happy thought. It might be an inducement, I said, if I paid instructors two shillings and sixpence per drill of one and a half hours. "But, my dear boy, they don't exist!" said the Colonel, who left me with the promise that he would see what could be done in the matter. An order was immediately issued to the effect that the Officer Commanding the Town Guard was prepared to pay instructors at the rate of two shillings and sixpence per drill of one and a half hours, and that qualified men would be allowed to take two drills per day.

When this information passed through the ranks there was no dearth of instructors. Men tumbled over each other to get the jobs, and really good instructors they were. When I saw the Colonel some time later, he said to me with a smile, "Neither the Adjutant nor I ever realised we had anything approaching the number that has come forward from the North Lancs." Some of the soldiers drew as much as £7 a month, and remitted a large portion of this "bounty" to their relatives in Lancashire. It has never been disputed that money talks, and, as in peace so in war, one can get anything for it—even drill instructors!"

Along with the new Town Guards, recruitment was also active in the other volunteer corps and they were able to muster over 1,300 by the time Milner formally called them out on 2nd October:

Unit	Officers	Men
Diamond Fields Artillery (with six 7-pound field guns)	3	90
Diamond Fields Horse	6	142
Kimberley Regiment	14	285
Kimberley Town Guard (estimate)	60	800
	83	1,317

The volunteers called out

The *Diamond Fields Advertiser* played its part in encouraging the citizens to contribute to the defence and join the volunteers if they could. The citizens of Kimberley were probably not aware of the importance of the locally raised forces as, unbeknown to them, Kekewich's plan was to evacuate the town and leave it to its fate if a credible local defence force could not be raised.

A march past the Town Hall on 20th October 1899

The Volunteer and regular forces were further bolstered by the arrival of the withdrawing Cape Police but, even counting these, the force was still considered too small to defend Kimberley. The need for still more troops resulted in the raising of a second mounted corps, the Kimberley Light Horse, which started recruiting on 13th October. Rhodes was made the honorary Colonel and despite his antipathy towards all things military, he set about the task of raising the corps with his customary energy and resourcefulness. It was fortuitous that Rhodes found himself in Kimberley for the siege for, as Harris suggests, he was able to commit more of De Beers' resources than might otherwise have been the case:

> "Rhodes, Dr. Smartt and the Honourable Mr. Rochefort Maguire and Mrs. Rochefort Maguire arrived in Kimberley a few days before the siege[4]. They intended to proceed to Bulawayo, but soon after their arrival the Boers cut the line at Kraaipan, some miles from Mafeking, and on the main line to Rhodesia. The enemy in force also occupied Magersfontein, and with the cutting of the line there, Rhodes and party were perforce held up in Kimberley. This was indeed a fortunate happening for the town, as Rhodes, as Chairman of De Beers Company, shouldered much more responsibility than the entire Board would possibly have cared to exercise."

From Mr Fynn, who managed the De Beers farms, Rhodes purchased enough horses to give 400 to the Kimberley Light Horse, provide remounts for the Diamond Fields Horse and transport for Colonel Chamier's guns.

With war declared on 13th October, Kekewich could survey the situation with some degree of satisfaction having managed through a collaborative effort to create a tolerably credible force of some 900 mounted men, 3,000 soldiers, 12 muzzle-loading 7-pound guns and 12 Maxims. However, the task facing Kekewich was awesome. Most of the newly-enlisted troops under his command had no prior experience or training in warfare and only a few of the Volunteers had been to war before. Only 11% of the force were regular soldiers and Kekewich had only 19 professional Imperial officers through which to exercise command and control.

Shortage of arms and munitions

The size of the population in Kimberley meant that there was a plentiful supply of eligible recruits. The bottle-neck however was with arming them. To alleviate the problem a large number of rifles had been purchased from merchants in Cape Town, Port Elizabeth and Grahamstown during the first week in October. On 13th October, the De Beers' Board asked Milner for 1,000 rifles and their ammunition and even offered to pay for these themselves. Kekewich also requested more rifles but by now it was too late for rifles, ammunition and guns on their way to Kimberley would not reach the town in time. The store in the town was not sufficient to go around and obsolete Martini-Henrys were issued to the Town Guard and, when these ran out, Snider rifles were used. De Beers were able to supply 422 rifles.

---

[4] Rhodes and his party arrived on 10th October.

Preparations for a siege

The Diamond Fields Artillery had, only weeks previously, received 6 new 7-pounder guns. They had been fortuitous to take possession of these as Colonel Trotter had sent them from the Ordnance Store at King Williamstown in defiance of the wishes of Mr Schreiner. A section of the new 15-pounder Battery[5] of Prince Alfred's Own Cape Artillery tried to make it to Kimberley but was turned back at the Orange River and two 7-pounders passed through Kimberley on 12th October en route to Mafeking but these were captured by the Boers at Kraai Pan as O'Meara explains:

> "Baden-Powell had been promised two 7-pdr. guns by the military authorities at Cape Town, and he was naturally anxious to have them sent up to him before he was completely cut off from the south. When he had his talk with Kekewich on the 10th, these guns had not reached Kimberley, owing to some hitch with the Colonial authorities. In view of the concentration of Boers reported to have taken place near Maribogo, Kekewich was of opinion that the railway communications to the northward of Kimberley were already too seriously menaced to risk the attempt to rush guns, or indeed any military stores, from Kimberley to Mafeking; he accordingly explained his views to Baden-Powell, who, however, did not seem to take the same view as to the dangers and risks of a journey between the two places. Baden-Powell informed Kekewich that he had decided to send his armoured-train to Vryburg to meet the guns there and requested Kekewich to send them on as soon as they should arrive.
>
> The guns for Mafeking unfortunately did not reach Kimberley until the morning of 12th October; they were sent forward to Vryburg at once in the Kimberley armoured-train, the officer[6] in command of it being instructed to hand the guns over to the Mafeking armoured-train and to return south in daylight next day. The same evening, when it was already too late for Kekewich to take further action in the matter, reports were received in Kimberley from the railway officials at Maribogo stating that the telegraph communication between that place and Mafeking was interrupted and that a Boer commando had occupied Kraai Pan Siding. During the night, a further report was received to the effect that railway culverts at Kraai Pan had been destroyed by the enemy, and, at 4 a.m. on the 13th, definite information reached Kekewich that the Mafeking armoured-train had been derailed and its crew taken prisoners by the Boers. Kekewich had now become anxious as to the safety of the Kimberley armoured-train, and, as the day wore on, his anxiety was increased, owing to the receipt of a message reporting that 600 Boers, with guns, had moved up to the railway at Border Siding (about eleven miles north of the Vaal). Towards mid-day, Kekewich learnt with immense relief that our armoured-train had reached Fourteen Streams safely. As the route was still open, the railway authorities were instructed to remove into Kimberley all the railway-stock and as much as possible of the supplies in their custody at Vryburg; fortunately the Boers were not greatly daring, and a fair quantity of supplies was brought south in the trucks which were removed from Vryburg and reached Kimberley safely."

The only weaponry to reach Kimberley after 13th October were two of the 7-pounders and three Maxims belonging to the Cape Police which arrived from Vryburg on 17th October and 126 Martini-Henry rifles and 21,000 rounds that were obtained from the Resident Magistrate of Barkly West by G Heberden on 19th October.

Ammunition was another problem for Kekewich. The Lancashires had brought up with them 500,000 rounds and this was supplemented by a supply from Milner and 650,000 rounds held by De Beers to total 1.5 million Lee-Metford cartridges in Kimberley when the siege began. There were 58,500 rounds for the Martini-Henrys that were also supplied by De Beers. Shooting practice necessitated consumption of a portion of the reserve but there was no way to avoid this and there was also the problem that some of the ammunition was defective. There were only 2,600 rounds for the 7-pounders which equated to 185 rounds per piece[7]. Colonel Chamier was of the opinion that replying to the Boer artillery fire was a waste of ammunition, especially when the ranges involved meant that accuracy was very low. He did see the merit in firing a few rounds each day but this was justified on the grounds of morale rather than any military objective. To conserve the meagre stocks, Chamier elected to control all the firing from the Conning Tower, a practice he followed throughout the siege.

---

[5] A 15-pounder could fire a percussion shell 5,600 yards (5,120 m) compared to a 7-pounder which had a range of only 4,000 yards (3,600 m). For more information on the British artillery, see the appendix on Long Cecil (page 529).

[6] Webster's account of this journey can be seen on page 535.

[7] As a comparison, the number of shells expended by the Artillery at the battle of Elandslaagte was 497. The Lee-Metford cartridges fired at Elandslaagte totalled 61,212. At another one day battle, Talana, 1,237 shells and 82,000 cartridges were used.

The Cape Police Maxim

The need for ordnance focused Kekewich's and Chamier's attention on the few supplies available to him. As a consequence, De Beers' chief engineer, Mr George Labram was tasked with trying to make percussion fuses and shells and within a few days, on 16th November, he was able to produce some workable shells. Kekewich recorded on 21st November how "At a trial today they worked really well. Fuse shells and powder were in every way satisfactory." Production capacity was about 25 shells a day and each was stamped around the base with an abbreviation of 'Compliments of Cecil John Rhodes'

A De Beers' shell base

De Beers also contributed the 6 Maxims they owned. The problems of arms and munitions would have been much greater for Kekewich had not De Beers had the foresight to prepare themselves for the possibility of attack.

Kimberley and its environs

How best and what to defend in and around the town was a persistent problem for Kekewich. The town covered a wide area and it had grown up around the mines, to support them, with no particular thought given to town-planning. The mines consisted of:

1. Kimberley Mine
2. De Beers Mine
3. Du Toit's Pan Mine
4. Bultfontein Mines. Both Du Toit's Pan and Bultfontein Mines were supplied from the township of Beaconsfield, 1 mile (1.6 km) to the southeast of Kimberley. Beaconsfield was formerly known as Dutoitspan and was frequently refereed to as 'the Pan'. The Pan was the scene of the first dry diggings in the gold rush of 1870.
5. Premier Mine (later known as Wesselton Mine) was 2 miles (3.2 km) to the east of the village of Wesselton and 4 miles (6.4 km) from the centre of Kimberley. Wesselton was very close to the Free State border. The name was changed to Wesselton Mine in 1902 to avoid confusion with Premier Mine near Pretoria.
6. Otto's Kopje Mine

Preparations for a siege

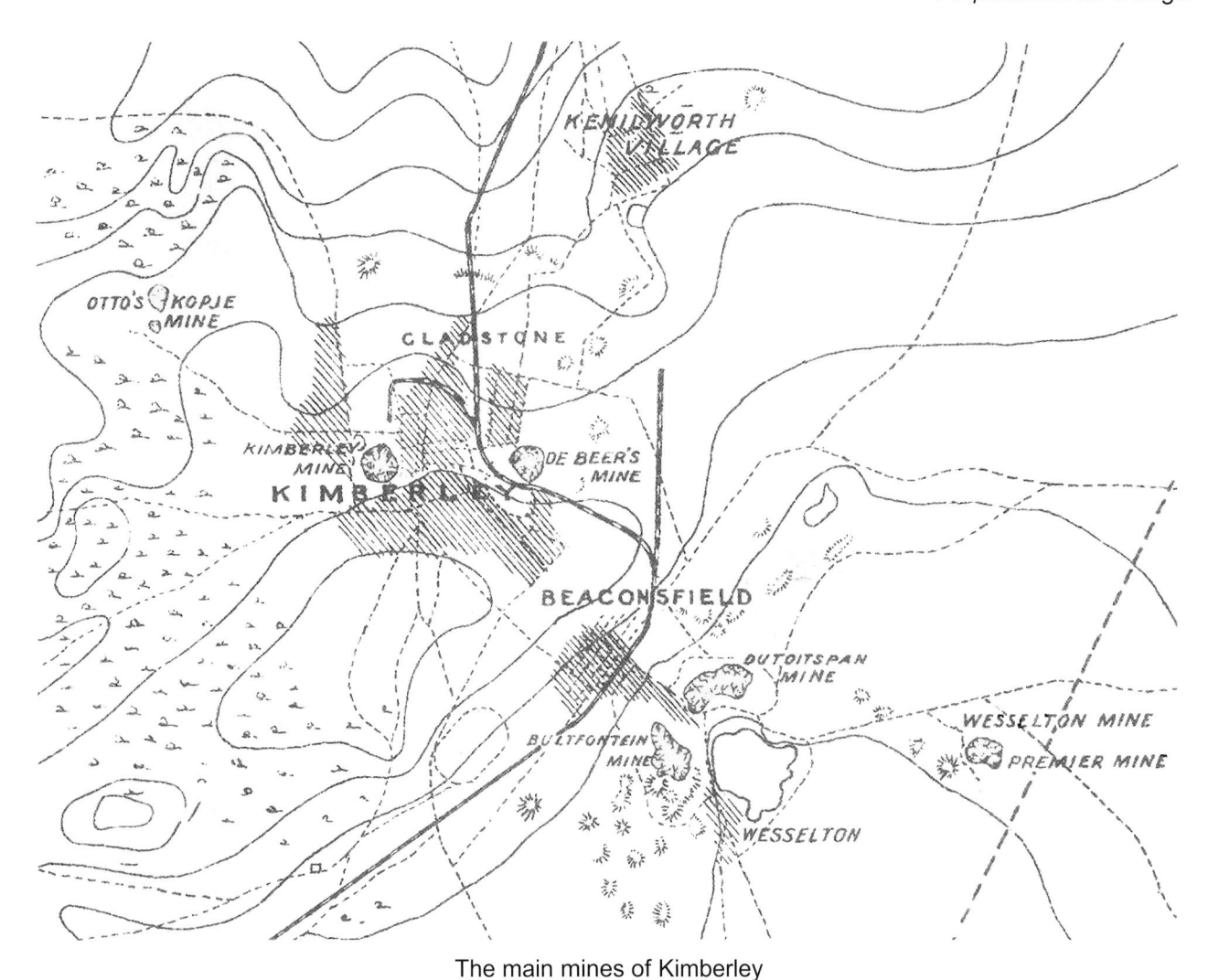

The main mines of Kimberley

At a distance of 3 miles (5 km) northeast of the city was Kenilworth which was created as a model village by Rhodes for the employees of De Beers. To the north the ground sloped slowly towards the valley of the Vaal River, the line broken by the Dronfield ridge (or Pringle's ridge) 6 miles (10 km) distant. To the east of Kimberley and Beaconsfield was a plain, stretching 10 miles (16 km) to a range of kopjes over the Free State border, strewn with heaps of debris[8]. To the south, the ground undulated gently until it reached the heights of Wimbledon, 6 miles (10 km) away. Carter's Ridge rose out of a shallow valley to the west and was to become important during the siege because it was the closest position to Kimberley that could be occupied that was out of the range of the town's artillery.

The open ground surrounding Kimberley[9] offered the Boers little in the way of cover for an attack and restricted them in the deployment of their favourite form of attack.

Area to be defended

Colonel Trotter's plan for the defence included only Kimberley and the Premier Mine. Premier Mine was included because of the spring water that could be used in Kimberley once the Boers cut the main supply at Riverton. Trotter's original plan was made without any reference to or knowledge of the people of Kimberley and when they learned of its limited scope and the fact that Kekewich was to base his defence strategy on this plan, there was an indignant protest, especially from those areas excluded from the design. Kekewich acceded to the demands to enlarge the areas covered by the defences, albeit that Beaconsfield would be defended independently of Kimberley. This also meant that two redoubts[10] to the north of Beaconsfield had to be maintained so that the water supply could be protected.

---

[8] The debris heaps were made from the spoil from the mines. They were composed of washed blue ground and kimberlite from which the diamonds had been extracted.
[9] See the pictures of Kimberley on page 284 to better appreciate the terrain.
[10] A redoubt is a small, outlying, temporary, entrenched stronghold or fortification, usually supplementary to the main defences.

Kimberley Siege Account and Medal Roll

The perimeter of the main defences was 9 miles (14 km). Taking into account the extensions to include Kenilworth, Wesselton and Otto's Kopje mine, the overall length of the perimeter was greater than 20 miles (32 km).

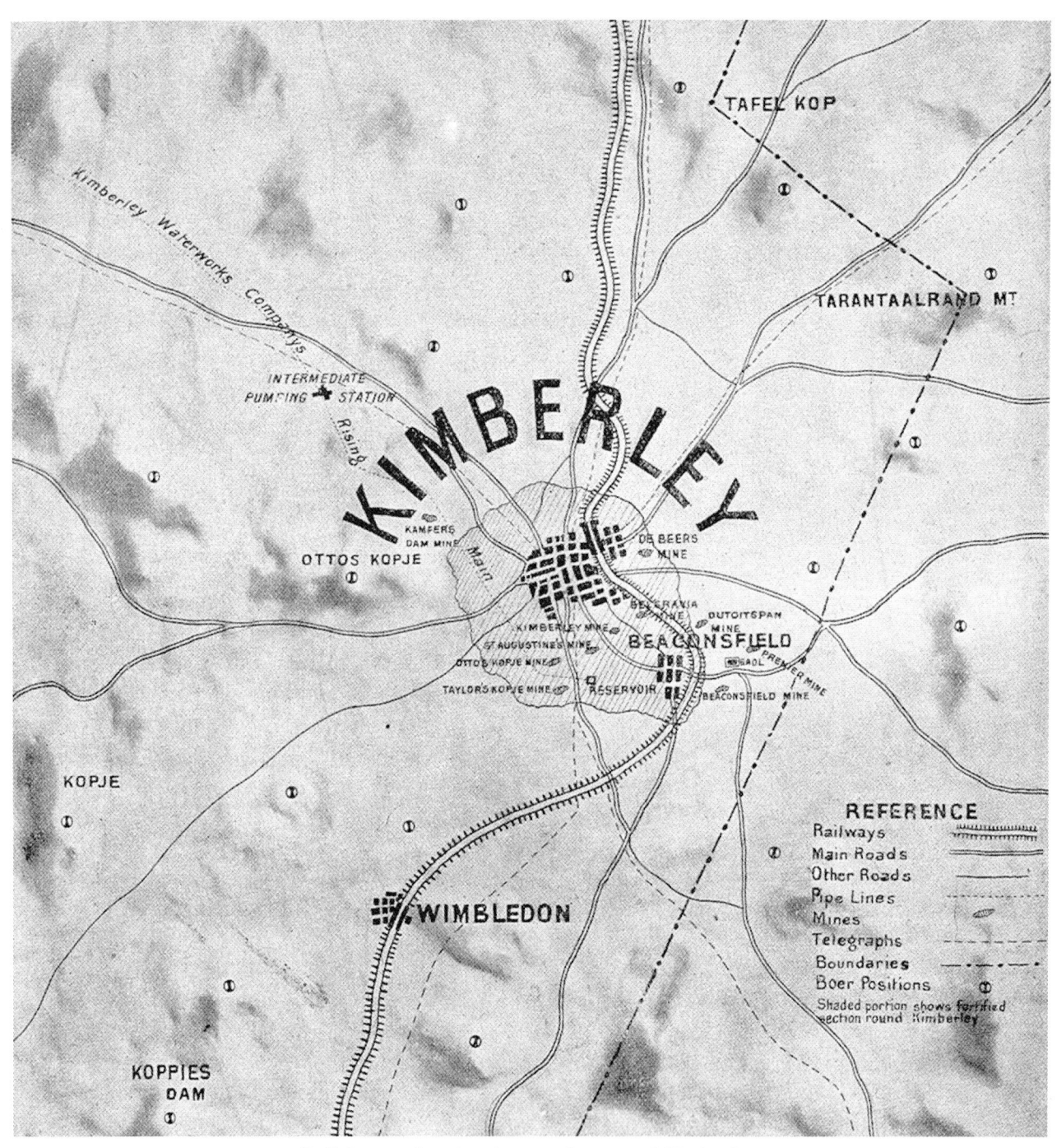

Relief map showing the terrain around Kimberley

The physical defences

Kimberley was divided into five sections:

Section A   From the Kimberley Mine in the west to the Transvaal Road, Section A encompassed the whole northwestern quadrant and included the tailing heaps surrounding the mine head, which were fortified and given names; Kimberley Breastworks[11], Old Kimberley Redoubt, New Kimberley Redoubt, Smith's Redoubt, No 1 and No 2 Searchlight Redoubts.

Section B   From the Transvaal Road to De Beers' Convict Station, including Kenilworth Redoubt, Kenilworth Dam, Stables Redoubt, Crusher Mill and Marosis Mount.

---

[11] A breastwork is a temporary defensive fortification, usually of chest height.

Preparations for a siege

Section C   From the De Beers Convict Station to the Lodge (just south of the railway), including Rinderpest Redoubt, De Beers Redoubt, Boshof Redan, and Belgravia Redoubt.

Section D   The Lodge to No 7 Redoubt, including Lodge Lunette, the Sanatorium and its breastworks, and Kumo House.

Section E   Completing the circle to the Kimberley Mine, including Camp Redoubt, Civil Service Redoubt, the Reservoir and Schmidt's Redoubts.

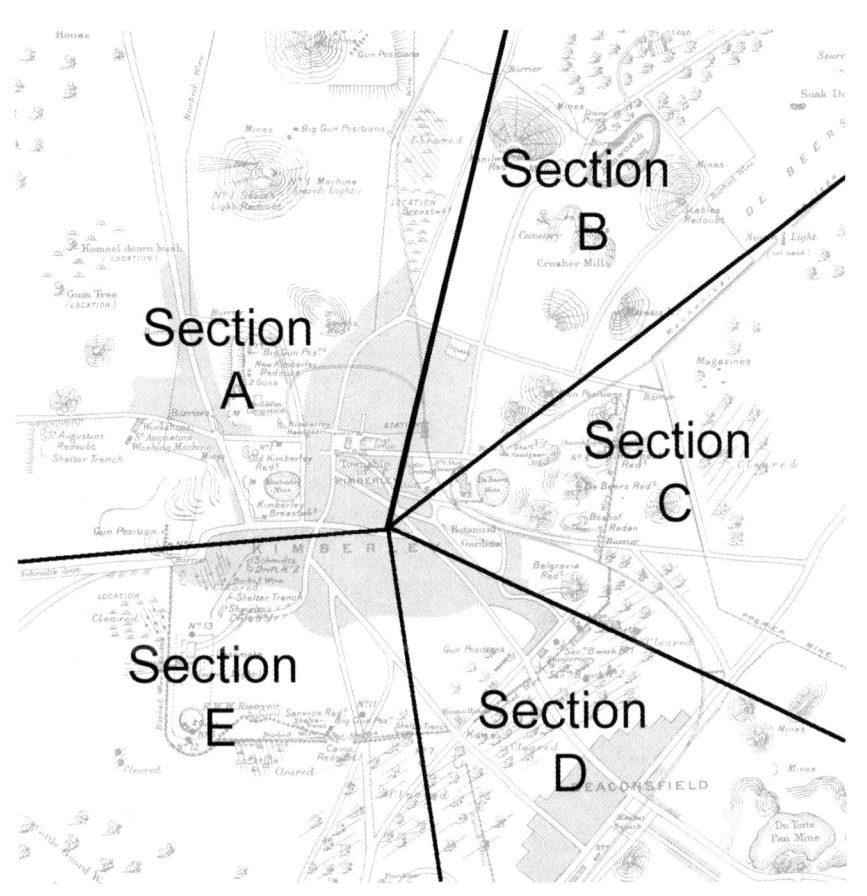

The five sections of the defences

The protection for Beaconsfield consisted of wire entanglements to the south which connected it to the main town's defences. There were also small redoubts and entanglements on the tailing heaps to the south of the Bultfontein Mine with the most advanced position being the redoubt on Davis's Heap, south of Wesselton.

Covering the water supply to the east of Du Toit's Pan were some light defences. Similarly, the water supply near Blankenberg's Vlei was protected by defences and a gun emplacement on New Gordon Heap.

The directors of De Beers placed the immense resources of the company at the disposal of Kekewich. They supplied labour for building the defences and, from 25th September, they supplied a large amount of labour as well as wood, iron, barbed wire, dynamite and batteries for the shelters, breastworks and entanglements. A barbed wire run was constructed stretching for 10 miles (16 km) and was reinforced by mimosa and thorn bushes that had been cut down to clear the line of sight. Defences were also constructed around Beaconsfield and Kenilworth and many of the observation platforms and lights were designed and built by De Beers employees.

The combined energy of the defenders, coupled with the prodigious resources of De Beers, meant that Kimberley had built credible defences by the time war was declared.

At the end of November, No 2 De Beers Redoubt (known as Fort Rhodes) was built on a tailing heap north of Kenilworth. To widen the defensive perimeter still further, small redoubts and shelters for the cattle guards were positioned outside the main defences.

Kimberley Siege Account and Medal Roll

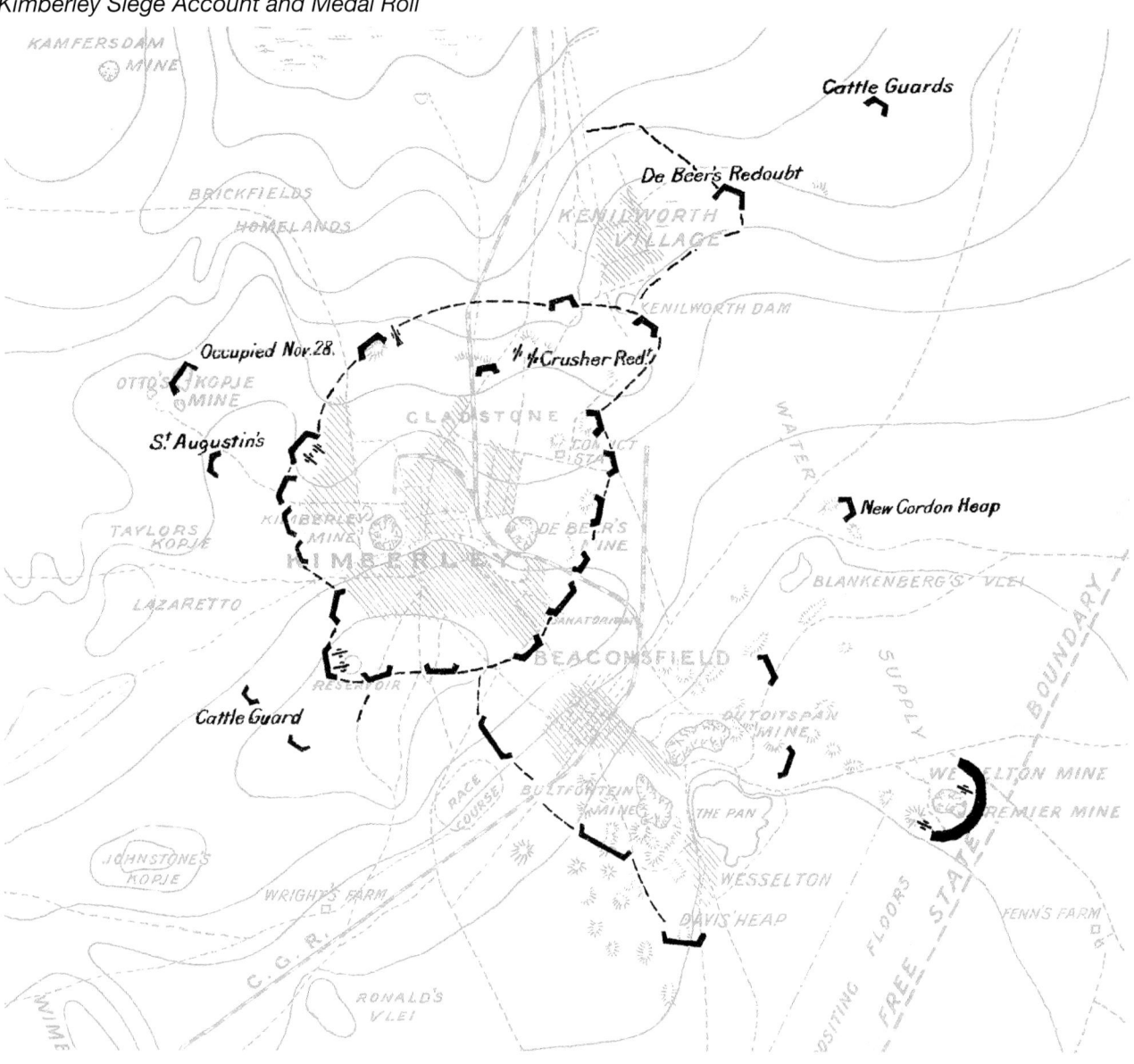

The defences around Kimberley

A vital component of the defence was the ability to maintain a watch for any attacking Boers both day and night. Once more, De Beers offered the solution. Five great searchlights that were ordinarily used to protect the depositing floors of the mines from trespassers were distributed around the perimeter. They were located at:

- Premier Mine
- Rinderpest Redoubt
- The Reservoir
- No 1 Searchlight Redoubt
- No 2 De Beers Redoubt (Fort Rhodes)

The searchlights had a power of between 12,000 and 25,000 candle power. The Boers nicknamed the searchlights 'Rhodes's Eyes'.

The Premier Mine searchlight

Preparations for a siege

Land mines were used on open ground beyond the perimeter. The plan was that these would be set off manually by remote detonation. Real mines were augmented by dummy mines and these were placed in open view to enhance their deterrence value. Ashe notes how "This little dodge was diligently talked about and very soon got over to the Boers, but as no one but the initiated few knew just where the dynamite was buried, it left the Boers with the pleasant feeling that wherever they chose to attack it was just as likely as not that their worthless insides would be blown out by dynamite, which I have no doubt did not much increase their ardour."

The co-ordination of the town's defences was greatly assisted by the telephones that connected much of the perimeter[12].

De Beers supplied the means by which the town was to be alerted to a possible attack by the Boers and the sign to man the defences – the mine hooter. This was a common sound in Kimberley to signal shift changes and its new use caused a degree of consternation amongst the public. Ashe explained what happened when it was first used: "Many people had been warned and expected the alarm, but in the lower quarters of the town it came as a surprise, and there was quite a panic there. In some of the better streets, too, where a few excitable women lived near each other, there was a lively state of things, for they ran around frightening each other.." An alternative was found for the hooter on 4th November. Ashe agreed with the decision: "… everybody was glad. It was a weird, ghastly sounding alarm, and scared nervous people out of their senses, so the Colonel stopped it and instituted a cone alarm, like a wind cone on a pier."

The headgear of the De Beers Mine was converted into a conning tower from where Kekewich controlled both the defences and the attacks during the siege. The tower had a height of 157 feet (47 m) and was the highest point in Kimberley. Chamier commanded his artillery units from here and an officer was continually on duty in the look-out post.

The Conning Tower

The following four pages consist of maps taken from contemporary publications. In both cases, the maps have been split into two so that they can be displayed at their maximum size. The first map comes from the *Times History* and the second from the MacInnes's account of the siege.

---

[12] See page 545 for information on the Postal Telegraph Department.

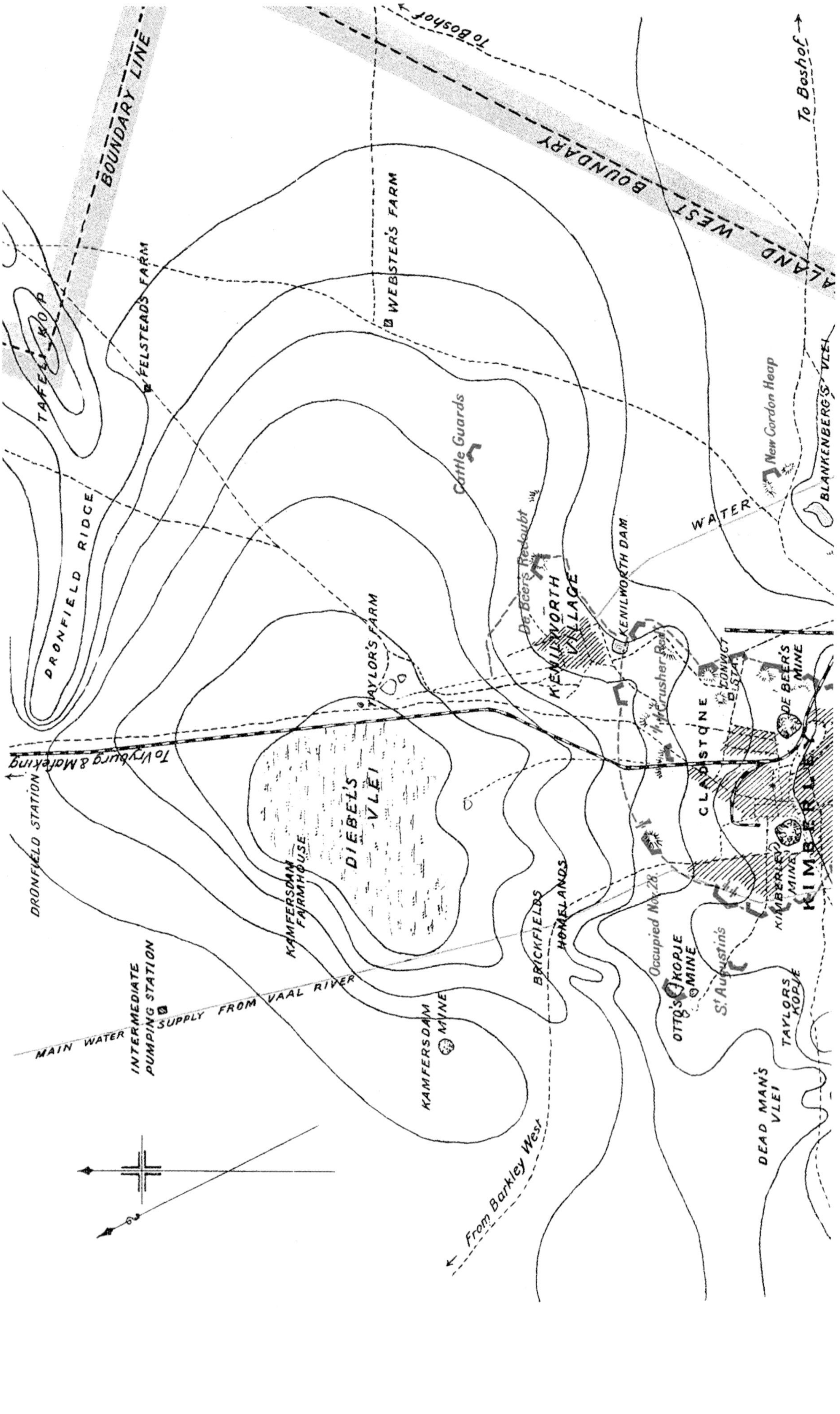

Preparations for a siege

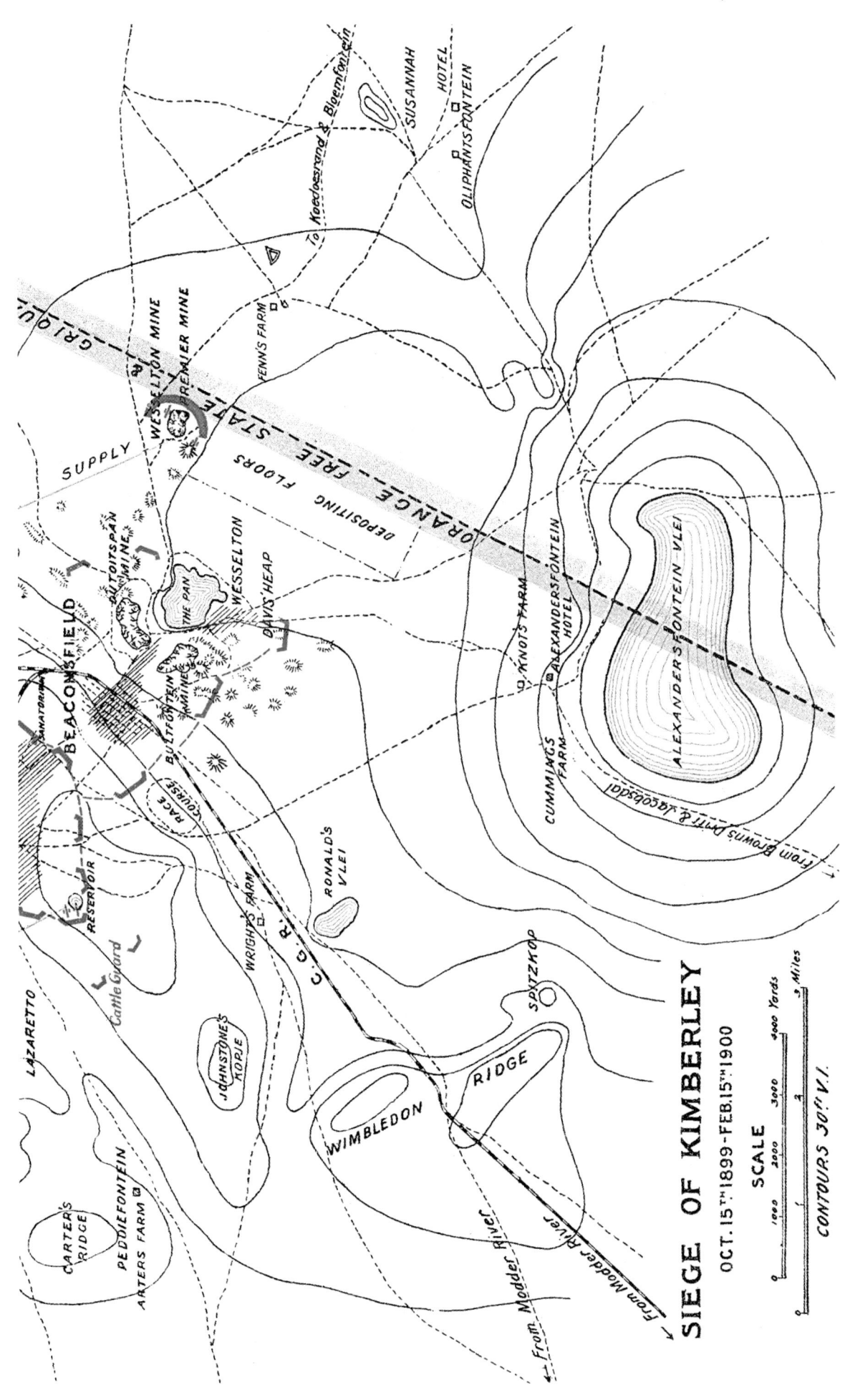

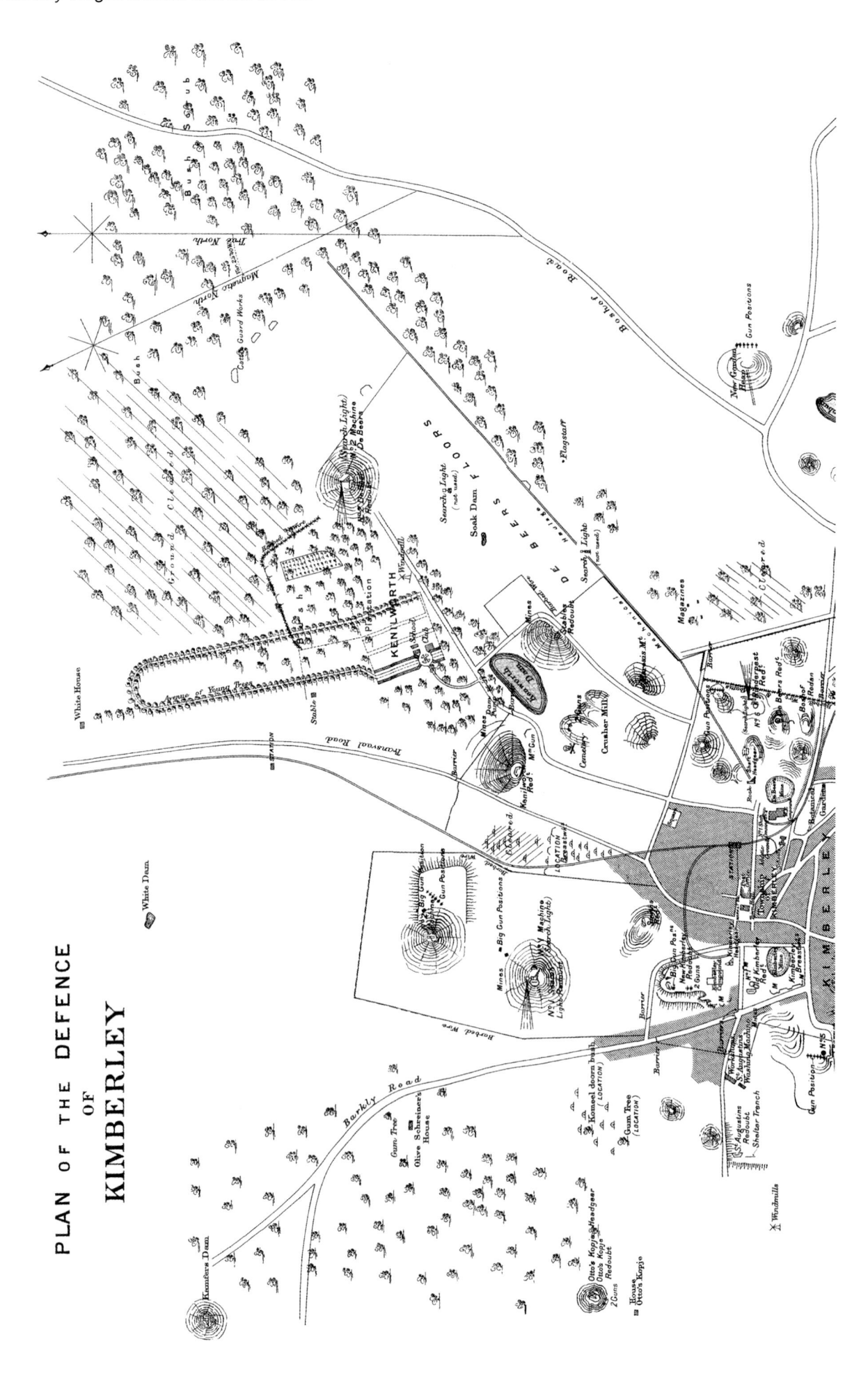

Kimberley Siege Account and Medal Roll

PLAN OF THE DEFENCE OF KIMBERLEY

Preparations for a siege

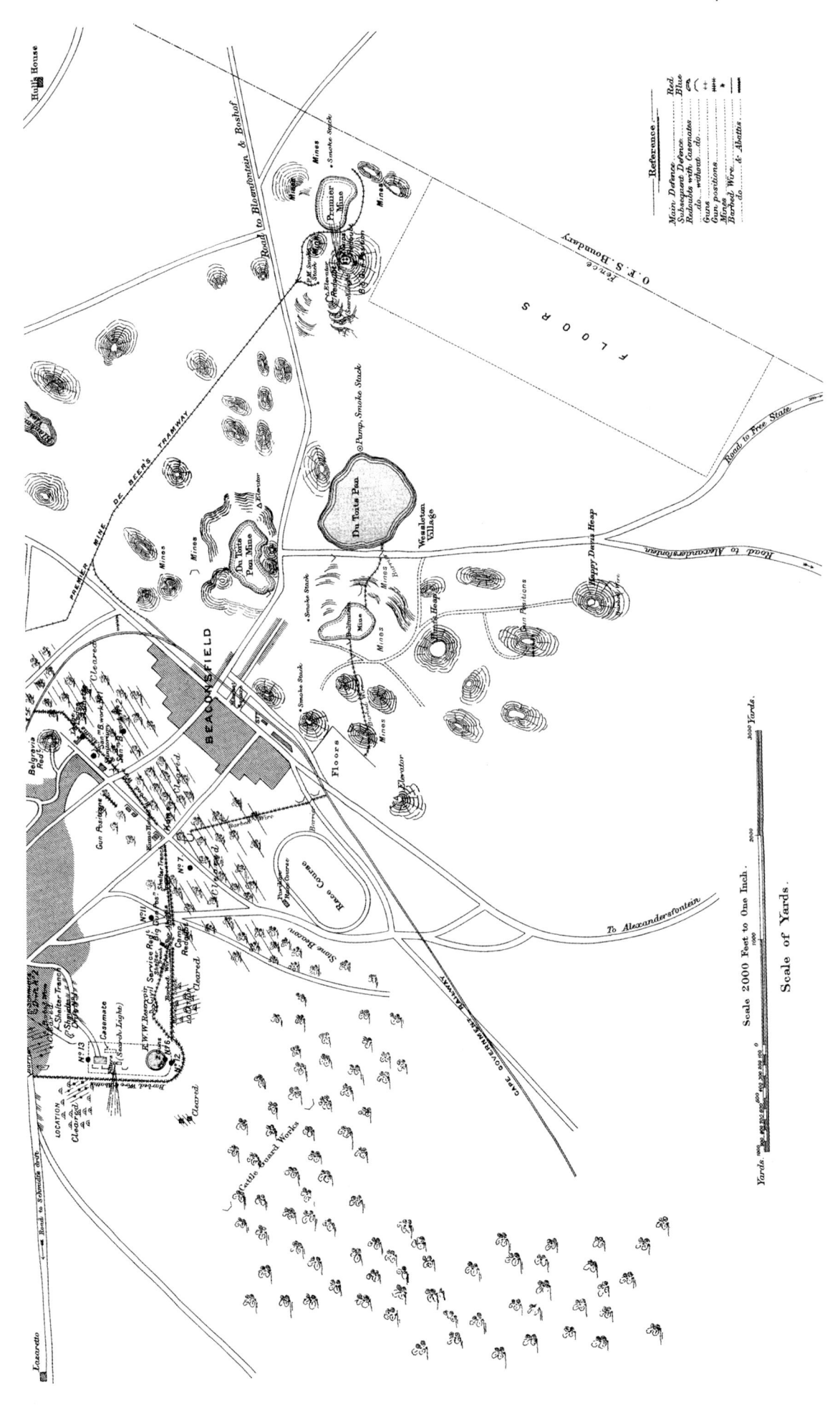

25

Kimberley Siege Account and Medal Roll

Troop locations

The perimeter defences were mainly manned by the Town Guard and, depending on the size of the defensive work, between 50 and 100 men would be stationed there. The importance of the Reservoir meant that it had to be strongly defended against attack with 200 men and two guns.

A company of the Loyal North Lancashire Regiment was posted at the isolated Premier Mine defence to bolster the local Town Guard of 300 men. Another company was posted at the Sanatorium.

The remainder of the Imperial troops, the mounted troops and the remaining artillery were stationed at the Botanical Gardens to the south of the De Beers Mine and probably the most central position that could be found. This force could quickly be despatched to any area on the perimeter that required supplementing should the need arise.

The command of the mounted troops was given to Colonel Scott-Turner.

Kekewich's staff was made up of Major O'Meara, the intelligence officer, Lieutenant MacInnes and Commissioner Robinson who was appointed as the Town Commandant. Captain H V Gorle, Army Service Corps, was in charge of supplies and also acted as the paymaster.

The Kimberley 'Buffs' engaged in their morning ablutions

The 12 Maxims available for the defence were distributed as follows:

23rd Company Western Division, Royal Garrison Artillery	- 1 at the Botanical Gardens - 1 at Premier Mine
Cape Police	- 1 at Schmidt's Drift road barrier - 1 at Circular Road - 1 at the Mounted Camp
De Beers Maxim	- 2 on the armoured train - 1 at Crusher Redoubt - 1 at the Reservoir - 1 at No 1 Searchlight - 1 at the Botanical Gardens
1st LNLR	- 1 at the Sanatorium

The 14 artillery pieces were distributed as follows:

23rd Company Western Division, Royal Garrison Artillery	• 2 guns at the Reservoir • 2 guns at Crusher Redoubt. They were moved later in the siege to Otto's kopje • 2 guns at the Premier Mine
Cape Police	• 2 guns in No 2 Redoubt north of Kimberley Mine
Diamond Fields Artillery	• 6 guns as a reserve in the Public Gardens, and employed with the mobile force as needed, usually a section at a time

Maxims and artillery pieces

Supplying the town

At the commencement of the siege, the population of Kimberley was estimated to be about 50,000:

- 13,000 whites and of these 6,000 worked for De Beers
- 16,000 coloureds and Asians
- 21,000 blacks and of these 12,000 worked for De Beers

However, migration to Kimberley just prior to the start of the war meant that the population was closer to 55,000. It is likely that the figure for blacks is understated.

As a major supply hub for the surrounding area, Kimberley was well provisioned at the start of the siege. As usually happens in times of tension, normal stock levels are boosted to take account of the uncertainty and De Beers had managed to lay in over 14,000 tonnes of wood, 7,000 tonnes of coal and sufficient provisions to feed 10,000 workers for 6 months. Some 1,500 to 2,000 oxen and horses were collected from outlying farms and concentrated at Kenilworth, just outside the town's defences. Some additional supplies destined for the Boer Republics and captured at Modder River were added to the town's stocks in a daring move on 14th October. O'Meara recounted the story:

> "The 14th was a day of restless activity in Kimberley; all sorts of rumours were flying about. However, a substantial report came in at six o'clock on that evening; at that hour the Stationmaster at Modder River telephoned to Kimberley stating that some Boer commandeering officers had arrived at his office and were demanding the foodstuffs in his possession consigned to merchants in Jacobsdal and Koffyfontein. He felt in a difficulty in the matter, owing to the proclamation issued by the High Commissioner forbidding the export of foodstuffs from Cape Colony into the enemy territory. The

Stationmaster was instructed to inform his unwelcome visitors that if they called next morning they could take away all they wanted; they seemed to have been satisfied with this answer. In the meanwhile, although night traffic was suspended on this section of the railway, instructions were given for an empty heavy goods train to be sent to Modder River at once; it started straightaway and with it went a strong gang of natives. The whole of the supplies in the Modder River Goods Depot were quickly loaded into the train, and about 11 p.m. the railway officials reported the safe return of the train at the Kimberley Depot. The boldness of this action apparently took the enemy by surprise."

Kekewich was able to report on 1st November that he had meat and bread to last 70 days and forage for 42 days.[13]

Kimberley Market Place

Under siege conditions, there was a rapid rise in commodity prices. As an example, paraffin increased from 15s to £4 per case and tinned goods also increased in price. The pages of the *Diamond Fields Advertiser* reflected the view of many disgruntled residents:

"I am one of the very many Kimberley men who responded to the call of duty and went out to the redoubts to defend our homes and the homes and stores and provisions of these very people who are now endeavouring to make life as hard as possible for us. Without us they would no doubt have had their stores looted and be absolutely ruined. Their return for our services is to try to ruin us. We are paying subscriptions to keep refugees from starving; we are defending our town; we are undergoing hardships in sleeping out in the trenches, &c, &c, while these worse than Shylocks are comfortably enjoying their beds and counting over their gains. It is contemptible… Everyone who has an ounce of manhood in him is helping in these times of stress and need. Let the storekeepers help too."

---

[13] This calculation of the stores remaining for bread and meat was made on a population estimate of 30,000 which was, as Kekewich found out later, a 60% under-estimate.

Preparations for a siege

In response to the escalation in prices, Kekewich issued a proclamation fixing the prices of most goods to their pre-war levels. The price of meat was allowed to rise but butchers could not sell more than one pound (450 g) per adult per day and one quarter pound (110 g) per day per child under 15, and steps were taken to ensure their compliance with the regulations.

Major Gorle bought as many of the biscuits and as much of the preserved meat as he was able to and all available forage was acquired. On 1st November, a Supply Committee was formed with the role of controlling the supply of bread and sugar and the committee would only issue a week's supply to dealers at a time. Proclamations were issued during the siege to set both prices and personal limits for supplies. There were no free issues of supplies to the public except in the case of the people who sheltered in the mines between 12th and 15th February.

The Riverton reservoir

Water, the other key resource in times of siege, was carefully managed. The town's main supply came from Riverton on the Vaal River, 18 miles (28 km) to the north. Using a series of pipes, the water was transported to Kimberley and held in the town's reservoir situated to the southwest of Kimberley. The local reservoir held only a few days' supply and so De Beers undertook to pump 8 to 10 million gallons per month or 300,000 gallons (1.3m lt) per day from the Premier Mine into the Waterworks reservoir[14] to mitigate the potential loss or interruption to the source at Riverton.

Concern about the water supply panicked many residents. As Ashe reports "My first move was to fill up my big rainwater tank, the big bath, and every available receptacle, so that we should have a reserve to fall back upon in case of need; and most of the people did the same thing." On 16th October a notice appeared informing residents that water was to be turned on for two hours each morning. A further notice that day warned that anyone found to be wasting water or using it on their garden would have their supply permanently cut off.

Ashe went on to say:

> "The first rumour about the waterworks had been that the Boers had blown up the pumping machinery on the first day of the siege, but this turned out to be incorrect. They took possession of it and of the enginemen, and were going to blow it up, but a wily engineman is reported to have said: "Why do you destroy your own property? When you have taken Kimberley, you will want a water supply just the same, and it will cost a good deal to replace the machinery." He went on to suggest that they could cut off the Kimberley water and do themselves a good turn at the same time by pulling up the pipes at a place six miles from the river where they ran through a pan which had water in it only after very heavy rains; then they could pump river-water into this pan, and thus have a watering place for their horses much nearer Kimberley. The Boers tumbled to this plan and carried it out. Of course the engineman's idea was to try and save the pumps if possible, but the Boers have laid dynamite ready to blow them up if they have to retreat, and they probably will do so unless the wily man manages to wet the dynamite.

The water restrictions continued throughout the siege.

---
[14] At the time, De Beers pumped an average of 5,201 gallons (23,600 lt) per hour from the De Beers Mine.

THE Kimberley Waterworks Co.

NOTICE.

The water supply will be turned on each day from 9 to 11 a.m. for strictly domestic purposes only until further notice.

R. FORD, Manager.

October 16, 1899.

The notice about water availability that appeared in the Diamond Fields Advertiser

PRICES OF PROVISIONS.

LARGE advances having taken place in local stores on some of the necessaries of life, and there being a likelihood of supplies running short if sold out in large quantities,

The following prices have been fixed with the local tradesmen until further notice, and no goods to be sold at higher prices than those mentioned under:—

Fresh Salmon, Kippered Herrings, &c., 1/3 per tin.
Sugar, all kinds, 4d per lb.
Rice, 3d per lb. Condensed Milk, 1/ per tin.
Candles, 1/ per 16oz. packet.
Corned Beef, 1lb. tins, 1/3; 2lb. tins, 2/.
Bacon, 1/6 per lb.
Boer Meal, Sifted, 3d per lb.
   Do.   Unsifted, 2½d per lb.
Tea and Coffee, no advance on original prices.
All other necessaries to be sold at same prices as before communication was cut off.

Any departure from the above will be dealt with by the Military Authorities.

Merchants and holders of Provision Stocks are hereby empowered to sell only in such quantities as they deem necessary according to number in family.

R. H. HENDERSON,
Mayor of Kimberley.

Approved.
   By order,
W. A. T. O'MEARA, Major.
Kimberley, 19th October, 1899.

The notice setting the price of provisions from the Diamond Fields Advertiser of 19th October 1899

The siege begins

President Kruger's ultimatum to the British Government expired at 17:00 on 11th October 1899, and next day the Boers crossed the border and occupied the Kraai Pan railway station. The Police contingent who had been stationed at Kraai Pan had already made the 35 mile (56 km) journey to Mafeking. The Boers continued their advance south forcing the police detachments that guarded the railway line from Vryburg to Kimberley to retreat before them. The Police had joined the garrison in Kimberley by 22nd October and the detachment arriving from Vryburg reported the suicide of Commissioner Scott which had happened en route to Kimberley.

The Boshof, Jacobsdal and Kroonstad commandos were the first to arrive in the Kimberley area. Their commander was Wessels. They formed a cordon which stretched from Olifantsfontein, through Benaudheidsfontein to Alexandersfontein. After Mafeking had been sealed off, Cronje despatched to Kimberley the Bloemhof, Lichtenburg and Wolmaransstad commandos, under General De La Rey. This force took the ground from the intermediate pumping station in the north, through Carter's Ridge and as far as Wimbledon ridge. The Boers prepared many emplacements for their artillery and moved their guns between positions during the siege. Other commandos were also involved, as were a group of Cape rebels formed into the Warrenton and Griqualand commando under Van Aswegen. The numbers of besieging Boers changed throughout the siege and not only did the number of men within a commando fluctuate, so did their assignments. While the commando was, for the most part, kept together, men could be detached to undertake other duties as happened when the Boers strengthened their force opposing Methuen's advance.

Boer commandos and their initial strength around Kimberley:

Transvaal:

Bloemhof	800
Lichtenburg	850
Wolmaransstad	400

OFS:

Bloemfontein	2,824
Boshof	1,030
Jacobsdal	250
Kroonstad	2,561

John Bosman and men of the Bloemhof Commando

The isolation of Kimberley started at 21:45 on 14th October when Kekewich's conversation with the High Commissioner was severed by the cutting of the wires by the Boers at Spytfontein. Less dramatic reports of the start of the siege say that Milner was delayed in starting the planned conversation with Kekewich and that the wires were cut before the discussion had even begun.

Kimberley Siege Account and Medal Roll

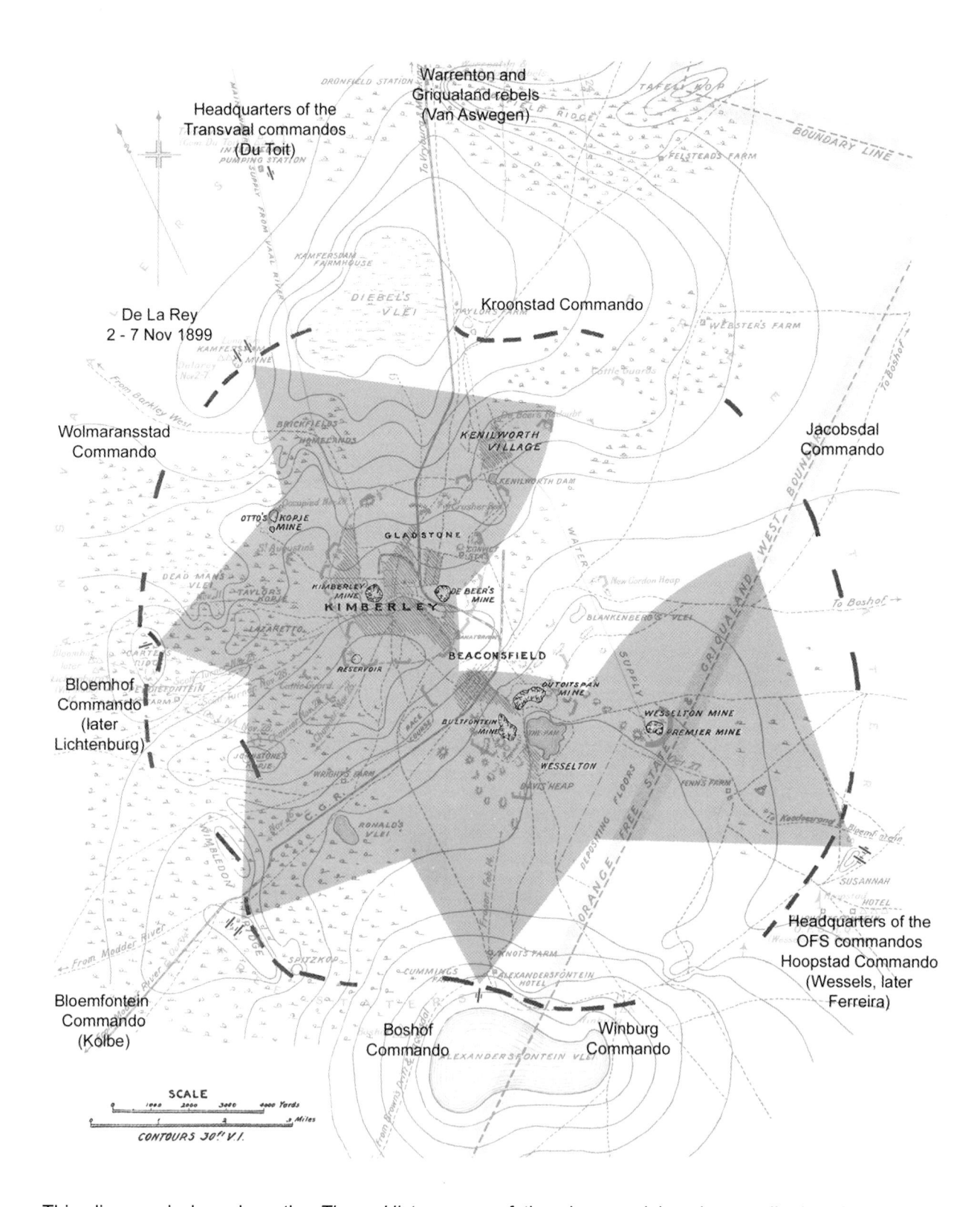

This diagram is based on the *Times History* map of the siege and has been edited to highlight the positions taken up by the Boers and to overlay the areas covered by their artillery. It can be seen that the artillery could penetrate all the areas of the town. The Boers took up positions on raised ground where they were able and were organised so that the commandos were kept together.

The siege begins

News of the start of the siege did not take long to reach the outside world. At midnight on 14th October, Trooper Brown[15], Cape Police, left Kimberley with despatches and covered the 50 miles (80 km) to the Orange River in thirteen hours.

A reconnaissance to the south on 15th October by the armoured train under Lieutenant Webster verified that the Boers with three guns and about 800 men were in command of the railway line between Spytfontein and Magersfontein. To the north, the Boers were also active. They attacked the small police post at the pumping station belonging to the Kimberley Waterworks Company at Riverton. Despite its importance to the town's supply, it would have been impossible to hold for any length of time and, accordingly, a party of mounted Cape Police was despatched to cover the retirement of the men.

During this operation, two men of the Cape Police, Sergeant Cullinan and Private Montleo were captured but later released. In Barkly West, the Resident Magistrate asked for troops to be sent from Kimberley to oppose the Boer threats to his town. Kekewich refused to help and instead made arrangements for the inhabitants to seek refuge in Kimberley.

The Riverton Pumping Station

Prompted by developments and President Steyn's proclamation of 14th October that Griqualand West was now part of Free State territory, Kekewich proclaimed the state of siege on the next day. The text of the proclamation can be seen in the appendices (page 418). Kekewich also assumed control of the civil population and appointed a court of Summary Jurisdiction under the presidency of Mr Justice Lange. Many Boer sympathisers were known to be inside Kimberley so Kekewich took steps to prevent them from providing any help to the besiegers:

V R PROCLAMATION

WHEREAS It has been brought to my knowledge that Her Majesty's enemies have issued Proclamations declaring that the territories of Griqualand West and Bechuanaland now form portions of the Orange Free State and the South African Republic, NOW THEREFORE,

I, ROBERT GEORGE KEKEWICH, Lieut Col Commanding Griqualand West and Bechuanaland, make it known that if any such Proclamations have been issued they are of no effect whatsoever, and do not in any way alter the status of British subjects in the aforesaid British territories of Griqualand West and Bechuanaland, and if any British subject is found to be assisting Her Majesty's enemies by word, deed, or in any other manner whatsoever, such person will be dealt with as a base rebel, and will be summarily punished as such.

Given under my hand at Army Headquarters, Kimberley, this 20th day of October, in the year of our Lord, 1899.

GOD SAVE THE QUEEN.

Ashe said there was widespread unhappiness with the functioning of the court of Summary Jurisdiction. It was partly staffed by military officers who were often too busy to attend and the civilians members were much more accustomed to hearing purely civil cases. Ashe wanted the court to put the interests of the town over those of legal procedure. As he put it "What was wanted was a court of men who knew no law, but understood common sense. A court like this would have decided that if there was the shadow of suspicion against a man, it would be safer to gaol him out of harm's way until the siege was over." He had a point. The number of incarcerates was low as most people who came up before the judges were given a caution.

The towns and villages around Kimberley were subjected to Boer attacks and small scale sieges. For example John Bosman sieged and captured Warrenton on 16th and 17th October as he was travelling to Kimberley with the Bloemhof Commando.

An indication of the ferocity of the spring heat in Kimberley was the death from sun stroke on 18th October of 2nd Lt Walter Fletcher of the LNLR. Fletcher was the first officer to die in the Boer War.

---

[15] See page 548 for a photograph of Trooper Brown.

Kekewich watched the Boers and was soon able to take to the field. With the mounted troops he was able to implement his plan to attack the Boers at times and in places that they least expected. On 18th October, a small force consisting of 200 Mounted Police and four guns of the Diamond Fields Artillery under Colonel Chamier was sent against the Boers at the Intermediate Pumping Station but the Boers had already retired by the time the force arrived. The next day Colonel Scott-Turner was appointed to command all mounted troops and his first exploit was on 20th October when he made an attempt to destroy the Boer's water supply at Riverton. This was not successful and resulted in the death of Sergeant A Blake.

The first encounter, 24th October 1899

The 24th October was the date of the first encounter between defenders and Boers and it took place at Macfarlane's Siding and on the ridges east of Dronfield.

The area around Macfarlane's Farm

Kekewich's objective had been to ascertain the strength of the Boers at Riverton Pumping Station but the troops from Kimberley did not manage to achieve this. A force of around 300 made up of the Cape Police, Kimberley Light Horse and Diamond Fields Horse left Kimberley at around 04:00. Lieutenant McClintock, accompanied the party in the armoured train and carried with him gelatine and detonators to put the pumping machinery at Riverton out of action and thus prevent its use by the Boers. The force reached Macfarlane's Farm at 07:15 and, not sighting any Boers, paused there for an hour for breakfast. An hour later, Scott-Turner left nearly half the troops in control of the knoll and farm buildings and pushed on towards Riverton. Within 15 minutes the Boers were seen to the east of Macfarlane's Farm. Scott-Turner returned to the farm and sent some Cape Police to monitor the Boer movements. Major Eliott, Cape Police, talked with the Boers under a flag of truce around 09:00 but this was later thought a ruse to gain the Boers time to reinforce. The Boers were seen to retreat but this did not lure Scott-Turner's men into the trap that it surely was. Growing in numbers as reinforcements arrived, the Boers now threatened to cut off the armoured train so Scott-Turner ordered its withdrawal to Kimberley. He heliographed to Kekewich for reinforcements at 10:15. Kekewich despatched two companies of the Lancashires under Major Murray by train and two guns of the Diamond Fields Artillery, two Maxims and 70 men of the Cape Police were sent by road to Mostert's and, from there, towards Dronfield.

Maurice takes up the story: "Meanwhile the enemy had received constant reinforcements from the eastward, and, thus strengthened, pushed through the bush to Dronfield ridge. Murray's train left Kimberley at 11.50 a.m. and reached the siding unmolested. It was now ordered back to Dronfield. The guns were approaching the ridge from the south, their escort having already passed it without observing the enemy. But, as the battery drew near, a sharp fire was opened on it from the summit of the ridge. Captain (local Major) S May, Diamond Fields Artillery, who was in command, immediately came into action at a range of 1,500 yards. The enemy continued to creep forward, and was within 1,000 yards of the battery when Murray's train came steaming back, and a short distance south of Dronfield, halted under the enemy's musketry. The infantry from the train quickly formed for attack under cover of the railway embankment, and advanced against the ridge.

The siege begins

They were received with a hot fusillade, but forced the burghers back into the valley to the north-east. Turner had, meanwhile, left the Macfarlane knoll, and was moving across the railway in Echelon of troops. Dismounting his men he completed the enemy's discomfiture. The Boer commando, whose strength was estimated at 800, fell back towards Boshof, leaving their leader, Petrus Botha, dead on the field. The British troops, reinforced at 2 p.m. by a company of the Kimberley Regiment, then returned to camp with a loss of three men killed and three officers and eighteen men wounded."

Casualties for 24th October 1899.
Killed (3): Private H J L Elliott, CP; Private R MacKenzie, CP; Trooper P Leipoldt, DFH.
Wounded (20): Lieutenant Lowndes, LNL, thigh, severe; Lieutenant Bingham, LNL, thigh, severe; Lieutenant McClintock, RE, side, slight; 4188 Private A Milner, LNL, thigh, severe; 3983 Private H Lee, LNL, arm, slight; Private C Hoskins, CP, arm, slight; Private F Simpson, CP, thigh, slight; Private Brady, KLH, hand, slight; Gunner M Hartigan, DFA, leg, slight; Corporal Harris, KLH, thigh, slight; Gunner F W Payne, DFA, foot, slight; Private W T Dye, CP, thigh, slight; Private J Gow, CP, side, slight; Private G Chapman, KLH, neck, slight; Private R McCaskill, KLH, head, slight; J B Petersen, CP, arm, slight; Bugler A F Dickinson, DFA, wrist, slight; Gunner A A Bankier, DFA, arm, severe; Private J C Dodds, KLH, leg, slight; L Cpl G Gradwell, CP.
Boers: Killed (2). Wounded (7).

Some of the wounded from the engagement

Just as it was the first military experience for many of the locally raised troops, the doctors too had little familiarity with modern warfare. A doctor's perspective was given by Ashe:

"We had a pretty busy time at the hospital when the wounded came in. I got five of them under my hands, but only two were more than trifles—an officer shot through the chest and a sergeant shot through the arm, splintering up the bone. We doctors had all of us seen a few bullet wounds with revolvers and such like, but had no experience of the modern rifle bullet, and it was a revelation to us. The bullet, especially of the Mauser rifle which the Dutch use, is so small and travels with such velocity that it drills clean through everything, and unless it strikes a vital part, or hits a bone or big artery, the injury it inflicts is ridiculous. The officer shot through the chest left the hospital on the eighth day, and returned to duty on the ninth, and his duty consisted of at least twelve miles' riding every day. Wounds through the fleshy parts heal in a couple of days, and give no trouble after a week."

Despite the abandonment of the original objective, the result of this engagement proved a considerable boost to the garrison. The British view was that the Boers, in losing their commandant and incurring what they thought was a greater number of casualties, had come off worse. Kekewich's detailed account can be seen on page 414.

35

Kimberley Siege Account and Medal Roll

Captain Lorimer, Cape Police, rode to the scene of the fighting and there identified the body of Commandant Botha. He also found a letter from Mr Justice Hertzog of the Free State Bench suggesting that Botha seize as many cattle in the area as possible.

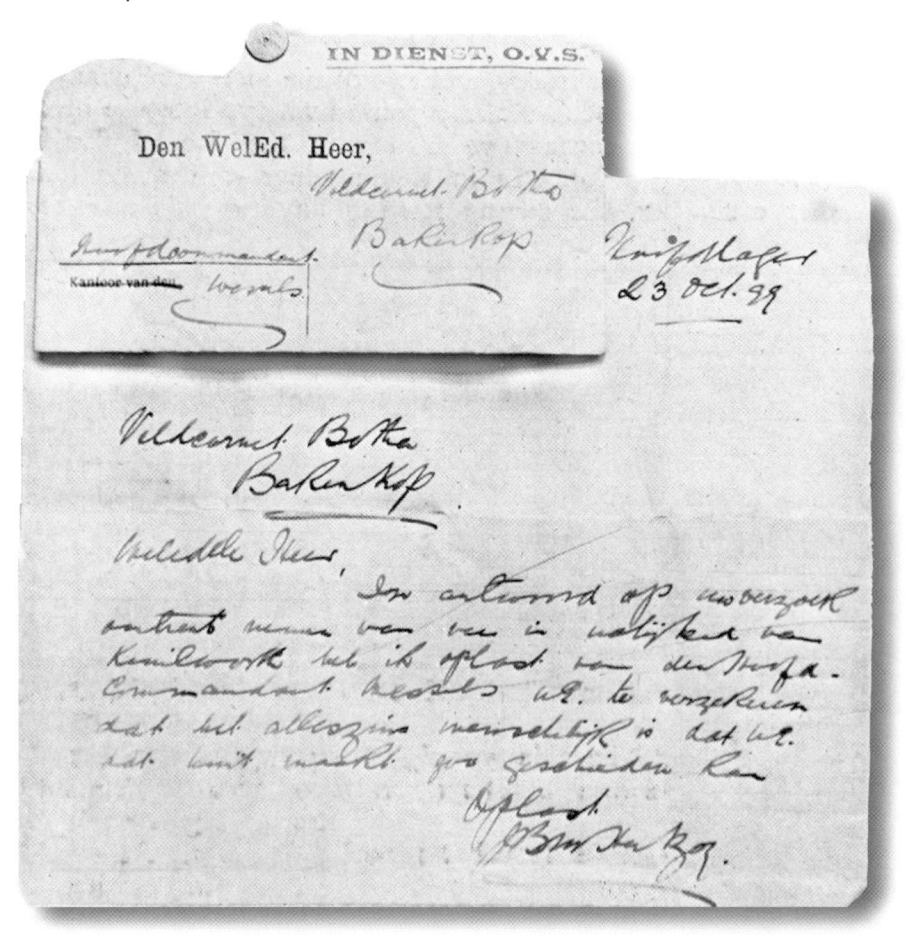

> Hoofd Laager, 23 Oct 99
> Sir,—In reply to your inquiry about the taking of cattle in the neighbourhood of Kenilworth, I am ordered by the Head Commandant Wessels to assure you that he considers it highly desirable that the same should be captured as soon as possible.
> I am &c, J B M Hertzog

This remained an enduring objective for the Boers and on 3rd November they succeeded in leading away 100 dairy cows, 200 oxen and the animals[16] used for the sanitary service of Dold and Childs. This was important as Ashe explained:

> "The sanitary system here is a pail system. All the closets have pails, and these are taken away, and fresh ones put in, every other night. The full pails are carted away in big covered vans ... There are a good many of these vans, and they take a lot of oxen to draw them. The work is done by short-sentence native prisoners, under proper guards, and vans, oxen, and natives—in fact, the whole plant—are kept at a big compound, a mile from town."

The sanitary service could not initially continue and residents were instructed to dig holes and bury their waste in their gardens. It was not long before De Beers provided mules to enable the service to restart.

In an article on the engagement, the *Diamond Fields Advertiser* noted that it was almost the first time since the battle of Bull Run that reinforcements had been conveyed by rail to the very scene of fighting and that it was probably the first time the wounded had been carried from the field of battle in comfortable saloon carriages. The quality of communication offered by the heliograph was augmented by the telephone which

---

[16] Estimates vary of the number of animals taken by the Boers. The 'Pottery Man' in his Journal puts it at 700 oxen, horses, cows and donkeys.

The siege begins

enabled Colonel Kekewich to keep in direct touch with the armoured train despite being stationed nearly 7 miles (11 km) away.

From a copy of the *Bloemfontein Express* which was found on a Boer prisoner some weeks later, the Boer view of the engagement was described. The author was the Landdrost[17] of Boshof.

> "October 25 — It is officially reported from the laager that Field Cornet Botha was killed; also H Zypel. G van Wijk was seriously wounded. Slightly wounded: L Hurley, W Lombaard, J Jacobs, Johannes du Plessis, G Wessels, and J du Toit. The report says that a patrol of our burghers met and confronted the armoured train. Small squadrons of burghers joined until there were about 600 men in the fight. The enemy had, besides the armoured train, cannon on trucks, and a mounted troop of about 400 men. Our burghers held Macfarlane's Siding, where they drove the enemy back, but further on they were not so successful. The burghers estimate that several of the enemy have been killed. Three were seen lying dead. One account says that the troops went in the direction of Warrenton. Another states that they were last seen in the direction of Kimberley. Dr Viljoen has just returned from the laager, where he made every provision for the wounded who are coming hither. Field Cornet Botha fell while trying to take a kopje with a small number of burghers. We lose a brave and exemplary officer and burgher in him "

This loss shook the Boers and it was a week before they felt confident enough to complete the encirclement of Kimberley. On 25th October, the Boers cut the final telegraph link with the outside world by knocking down some of the telegraph poles between Kimberley and Barkly West. Meanwhile Kekewich continued his tactic of probing the Boers constantly trying to determine their strengths or identifiable weaknesses. On 27th October, he sent out 339 men towards Spytfontein and later the same day Scott-Turner and 10 picked scouts reconnoitred the Boer position south of Premier Mine.

---

[17] The chief magistrate of a district.

November 1899

At 06:00 on 1st November, the Boers made a demonstration in force to the east of Premier Mine but stayed out of gun range. On the same day they occupied Macfarlane's farm and also blew up a large supply of dynamite at Dronfield Siding[18]. Their growing numbers also emboldened them a little and they resumed cattle-raiding sometimes with success. On 3rd November, some Boers approached Kenilworth from Dronfield and rustled some of the stock which was owned by De Beers and others. Major Peakman engaged the Boers with mounted troops and a Maxim and it was during this engagement that Major Ayliff, Cape Police, received a wound to his neck, his black horse making him a prominent target. Later that day Carter's Farm witnessed a second engagement. The Cape Police recorded two casualties. Private J Lubbe was killed and Sergeant F Watermeyer was wounded.

The losses of cattle had an immediate effect on the garrison. The meat ration was reduced to half a pound (225 g) per day for an adult and the number of oxen that could be slaughtered was reduced to 15 per day.

The hostile activities of the Boers led to the evacuation of the miners at Otto's Kopje Mine. On the night of 3rd November, Mr Chapman and 200 workers returned to Kimberley.

The Diamond Fields Horse outside Kenilworth

By early November, the combined Boer forces numbered approximately 3,000. The numbers of the besiegers was not constant but fluctuated over time and, for example, during November and December, some Transvaalers travelled south to fight the advance of Methuen. Later, the Boers to the south of Kimberley were reinforced by Cronje's men as they moved north after the battle of Magersfontein. The Kimberley garrison also received a few reinforcements at this time as O'Meara recounts:

> "Kimberley now received an unexpected reinforcement. Inspector Berrange, who was stationed at Upington (215 miles west of Kimberley) on the outbreak of war, decided, on his own initiative, to make an attempt to reach Kimberley with the men under his command. Leaving Upington on 21st October, with his Sub-Inspector, 2 N.C.O.'s and 18 men, he managed to evade the Boers and reached the Diamond Fields on 2nd November; he arrived only just in time, for, on the following day, it was noticed that the Boers had come in nearer to our defences, their numbers had also increased and they also showed more boldness — during the day they managed to drive off some of our cattle from the Commonage. It now seemed as if the enemy really intended to make things hum a bit at Kimberley. Berrange and those who were with him deserve great praise for having undertaken their plucky ride into Kimberley in the face of unknown dangers."

Other than cattle raiding, the Boers displayed little inclination to use their men to make a determined attack on Kimberley. When the attack did come, it was conveyed on paper.

---

[18] De Beers used the dynamite in their mining operations. The dynamite had been stored in Kimberley but the Town Council was very concerned that the Boers may shell Kimberley and blow up the supplies. As a result, the dynamite was moved to Dronfield Siding, 6 miles (10 km) from Kimberley, with journeys being made there for supplies as necessitated by demand. The loss of the supplies precipitated the closures of the mines.

November 1899

Wessels's ultimatum

On the morning of 4th November from his headquarters at Olifantsfontein, Chief Commandant Cornelius J Wessels sent a summons to Kekewich demanding the surrender of Kimberley.

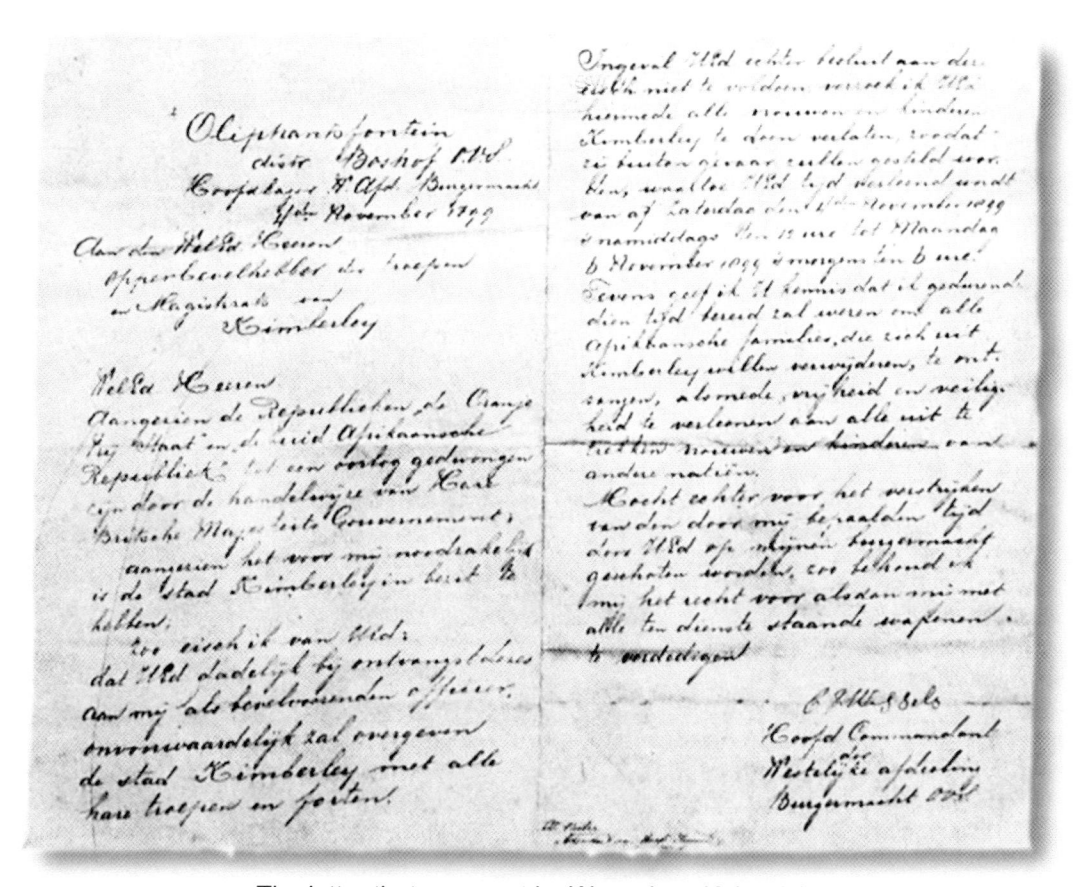

The letter that was sent by Wessels to Kekewich

> Oliphantsfontein, District Boshof, Head Laager, Western Division Burgher Forces. November 4th, 1899.
>
> To the Right Honourable the Officer Commanding the Troops and Magistrate, Kimberley.
>
> Right Honourable Sir,
>
> Whereas the Republics, the Orange Free State and the South African Republic, have been driven to war by the policy of Her Majesty's Government,
>
> And whereas it is necessary for me to take possession of the town of Kimberley,
>
> Therefore I demand of your honour :-
>
> That upon receipt of this you, as commanding officer, shall forthwith hand over to me the town of Kimberley with all its troops and forts. In case your honour should determine not to comply with this demand, I hereby request your Honour to allow all women and children to leave Kimberley, so that they may be placed out of danger, and for this purpose your honour is granted time from noon on Saturday 4th November, 1899, to 6 a.m. on Monday, 6th November, 1899.
>
> I further give notice that during that time I shall be ready to receive all Afrikander families who wish to remove from Kimberley, and also to offer liberty to depart in safety to all women and children of other nations desirous of leaving. If, however, my burgher forces are fired upon by your Honour before the expiration of the appointed time, I reserve to myself the right to defend myself with all the forces at my command.
>
> (signed) C.J. Wessels, Head Commandant, Western Division, Orange Free State Burgher Forces.

In consultation with Rhodes, Kekewich and his staff discussed the translation from Dutch. There appears to have been some confusion about the intent of the summons but Kekewich was quite clear when he made his response:

> Army Headquarters, Kimberley, 4th November, 1899.
> From: Lieut. Col. R G Kekewich, Officer Commanding Griqualand West and Bechuanaland.
> To: Head Commandant, The Western Division of the Burgher Force, Orange Free State, Bloemfontein.
>
> Sir,
>
> 1. I have the honour to acknowledge the receipt of your letter, dated Olifantsfontein 4th November, 1899.
> 2. Your desire being to obtain possession of Kimberley, you are hereby invited to effect the occupation of this town as an operation of war by the employment of the military forces under your command.
> 3. I hereby give you notice that since the forces of the two Republics, now at war with Her Britannic Majesty, have in the present war made frequent use of the flag of truce (white flag) in a manner not recognised by the usages and customs of war as practised by civilised nations, I have in consequence instructed the officers of the forces under my command that from this date persons bearing white flags and approaching them are to be fired upon.
>
> I have the honour to be, Sir, Your obedient servant,
> (signed) R. G. KEKEWICH, Lt. Col., Commanding Griqualand West and Bechuanaland.

The content of the response was simple and quick to write. At more leisure the meaning of Wessels' letter was debated. The sentence on the non-military personnel was construed to mean that the women and children could set up their own camp outside Kimberley. However, transport limitations and the logistics of maintaining a separate camp meant this was impossible.

The decision was taken not to publicise the letter except for the offer to Afrikaner families and this was not made public until the final day of the armistice. On the 8th November, an advertisement appeared in the *Diamond Fields Advertiser*:

> **V R NOTICE**
>
> Head Commandant Wessels, of the Western Division Burgher Force, OFS, having made known to the Commandant, Kimberley, that he is willing to receive into his camp any Afrikanders who are desirous of leaving Kimberley, the Commandant hereby gives notice that persons wishing to accept the invitation of Commandant Wessels are hereby given permission to do so, on the strict understanding that any persons accepting this invitation will not be allowed to enter Kimberley on any pretext whatsoever as long as a state of siege lasts.
>
> Persons who intend to accept Commandant Wessels' invitation are hereby directed to apply either to the Staff Officer, Army Headquarters, Lennox Street, or to the Commissioner of Police, Transvaal Road, for the necessary passes and instructions.
>
> By Order, D. S. MacInnes, Captain, Staff Officer. Kimberley, November 7, 1899.

Despite the size of the Afrikaner element in Kimberley, less than 5 families took up the opportunity. It was believed that some families concealed their desire to leave Kimberley in fear of being seen as Boer sympathisers. The wider scope of Wessels' offer became known to the people of Kimberley at the end of the month through a captured Pretoria newspaper which contained the full text of the offer and response. This led to some resentment towards the authorities because more inhabitants may have availed themselves of the offer for any family to pass through the Boer lines had they been aware of it at the time.

While Kekewich was reluctant to allow the white occupants to leave, he did not hold the same view about the black population. On the contrary and perhaps prompted by Wessels' suggestion, the decision was taken to try to release some of the black population in batches. Rhodes released approximately 3,000 blacks on the night of 5th November without Kekewich's knowledge. But the Boers, aware that the deadline for people crossing their lines was about to expire and perhaps piqued that so few families had left Kimberley, turned them back from their lines. This first release nearly ended in disaster as O'Meara recounted:

> "... as day broke, the situation to the north-east of Kimberley appeared to be serious. The officer on watch in the Conning Tower called Kekewich's attention to a large mass of men scattered to the north-eastward of Kenilworth — one of the weak points in our defence line; they appeared to be advancing

against our positions in that locality, and were already within some 1,500 yards of our works. As soon as the R.A. officer in command of the guns at the "Crusher Redoubt" observed the living mass which was approaching the Kimberley defences, he brought his guns into action and opened fire. Fortunately, it was soon discovered that our shells were being fired not at Boers but at unarmed natives; Kekewich quickly ascertained that this was so, and immediately ordered the "cease fire" to be sounded. It was afterwards learnt that 3,000 natives had been released from the De Beers compounds during the night under Rhodes' orders, but no notification of the fact had been sent to the military authorities, and accordingly the troops had not been warned."

Similar releases were attempted later in the siege and these met with much more success. Coached in what to say to the Boers by Mr Fynn and aware that the Boers wanted to stay on good terms with the tribes in the area, especially the Basutos and other northern tribes, as many as 8,000 blacks left Kimberley during the course of the siege. As work in the mines declined[19], the workforce had increasing amounts of time on their hands. Rhodes took advantage of this capacity to commence the relief works. Using some 4,000 blacks, roads were made, avenues planted and other work was undertaken to the long term benefit of Kimberley.

Kimberley under siege

The passing of the ultimatum at 06:00 on 6th November brought the commencement of the bombardment of Kimberley. The Boers' guns placed at Susannah fired a few shots[20] towards the Premier Mine about an hour after the expiry to convey their annoyance. The bombardment continued on 7th November when about 50 shells were fired from some 12 guns placed around the town. The damage reports extended to one cooking pot. The early shelling by the Boers focused on the defences but on 11th November the Boers advanced their guns with the result that the first shell fell into the town itself and claimed the first civilian casualty, a black woman who was in Dutoitspan Road. Of some 200 shells fired into Kimberley that day, mostly from 9-pounders to the west of the lazaretto[21], one hit the Greasham Bar. This damaged the ceiling but the landlady, who was standing behind the counter at the time, was unhurt. De La Rey's report on the bombardment said, "Our purpose was more particularly to throw our shells into the centre of the town, so as to cause the more damage to the enemy." On average, 1 in 20 of the shells caused any damage. There were many stories of close shaves. Part of the reason why so little damage was done is due to the fact that many shells failed to explode and this was attributed by some to their poor quality. Another reason was that the guns were being used at the extreme of their range and the shell, when it did explode, had far less velocity and thus caused much less damage than would have been the case had the guns been placed closer to their assigned target. For the most part, the shelling was desultory, intermittent and, thankfully, harmless. It was to become a feature of daily life in Kimberley – except on Sundays when the Boers did not fire any guns.

After the initial trepidation about the landing of shells, many people became more accustomed to the bombardment and, said one report "looked upon the Boer shelling much as they would have done an exhibition of fireworks." Talking about the shelling in the second week in November, Ashe said "During the seven days of active bombardment they fired at least seven hundred shells into the town, and the amount of damage done both to life and property was so small that it would hardly be believed." Shell fragments were gathered with eager interest and fascination. The price of a complete exploded shell was £5, a shell base sold for £1 to £2, and smaller pieces fetched varying amounts depending on their size but typically 3 to 15 Shillings. The people involved in this trade became very knowledgeable on the subject and could differentiate and discuss shrapnel, ring shell and different types of fuses.

The military authorities warned about the danger of such activities and, because they knew the Boers would read the notice, took the opportunity to reinforce the information that Kimberley was additionally protected by dynamite mines. They said:

> "The military authorities have observed that many persons who scramble for fragments of the Boer shells go in dangerous proximity to the mines which have been laid down for the defence of Kimberley; and by so doing incur a great risk. These mines are at all times 'live' ie the fuses and firing arrangements are so arranged that the mines can be fired either automatically or by observation, and they might under certain circumstances be ignited by the enemy's shells."

---

[19] Nearly a quarter of a million loads were hoisted out of the mines in the opening weeks of the siege, but the shortage of coal and the loss of the dynamite eventually necessitated a suspension of all mining operations.

[20] This was the first shell to land inside Kimberley's defences. The Boers had been firing at the reconnaissance parties outside the limits of the defences for some time, the first recorded shell being fired 31st October 1899.

[21] A building used to house people with contagious or infectious diseases. Kimberley's lazaretto was on the west of the town and extended over 22 acres.

Kimberley Siege Account and Medal Roll

A collection of projectiles and missiles that were used against Kimberley

Examples of keepsakes and mementos fashioned from shell fragments

The damage caused to the house of Mr A Webster by a 9-pounder shell

November 1899

In many ways and despite the shelling, life continued unchanged for the residents and new activities were arranged to provide a distraction for the besieged inhabitants. Concerts were held by the units that contained musicians amongst their ranks but their invitations contained an unusual caveat "Weather and Boers permitting":

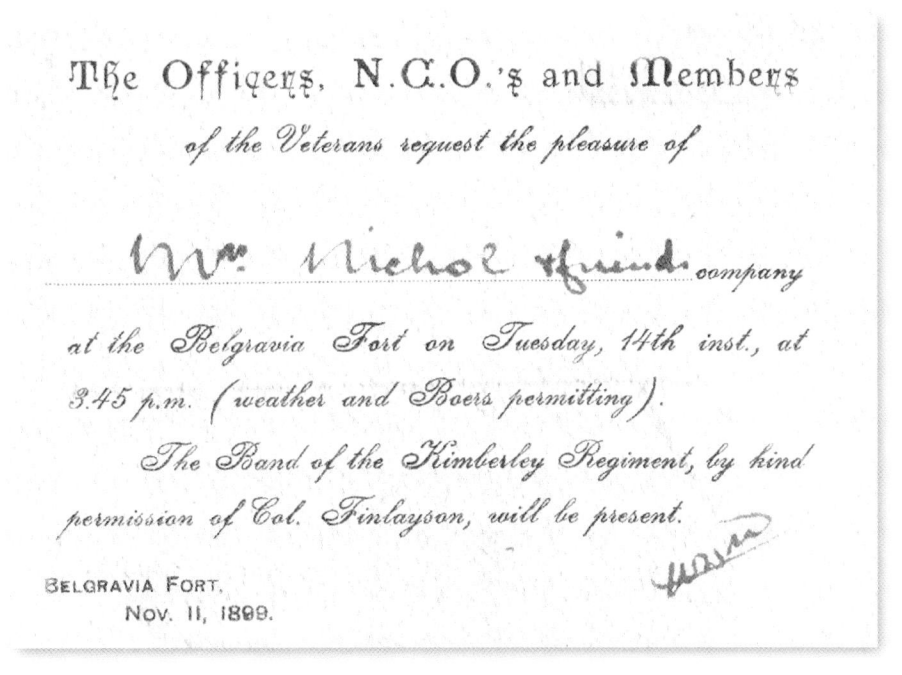

> The Officers, N.C.O.'s and Members of the Veterans request the pleasure of Mr. Nichol *friends* company at the Belgravia Fort on Tuesday, 14th inst., at 3.45 p.m. (weather and Boers permitting). The Band of the Kimberley Regiment, by kind permission of Col. Finlayson, will be present.
>
> BELGRAVIA FORT.
> Nov. 11, 1899.

An invitation to visit Belgravia Fort

A band playing at the Mounted Camp

Kimberley Siege Account and Medal Roll

A proactive approach

Refusing to wait out the siege and despite the paucity of his forces, Kekewich's strategy was to maintain an active and, at times, offensive stance. Reconnaissances were sent out on most days. About the engagement on 11th November, one report said "..our mounted troops, about 350 strong, were engaged in a brisk little encounter with the enemy near Otto's Kopje. A party of Boers advanced to attack our men, who at 800 yards poured in a hot fire at the enemy. Six Boers were distinctly seen to fall from their saddles, four of them being shot in quick succession by a well-known marksman of the Cape Police, a Colonial Dutchman to boot, Van der Merwe, of Graaff-Reinet. Several horses were also seen to be hit, and there is little doubt that other losses were sustained on the enemy's side. One of the men of the Cape Police, named Parker, was mortally wounded, and Sergeant Stumke, Kimberley Light Horse, was slightly injured. Another man had a narrow shave. He was standing by the side of his horse, with his arm leaning on the saddle, talking to a sergeant on the other side of the animal. A bullet struck the saddle, directly underneath his hand, and got embedded in the padding."

At the same time as the engagement near Otto's Kopje, Major Peakman with a squadron of Kimberley Light Horse engaged the Boers at Carter's Farm. Carter's Ridge was targeted again on 16th November by a force of 400 men and two guns. Major Peakman's squadron approached under the cover of a mist but this lifted to find the men some 400 yards (365 m) from the Boers. A rifle and artillery fight ensued and the Kimberley force withdrew when the Boers were seen to be reinforced. The garrison suffered 1 killed and 11 wounded in this engagement while the Boers reported losses of one man killed and none wounded. Major Peakman was amongst the wounded. From their position on the debris heaps, the Beaconsfield Town Guard helped delay the Boer reinforcements. An incident during the engagement shows how the search for shell fragments was not limited to the civilian population. The story goes that "a Boer gun opened from Carter's, and one of the shells passed through a group of half a dozen mounted men, one of whom fell from his horse; the next instant the whole six were seen to drop from their saddles, and Colonel Scott-Turner inferred that they were hastening to the assistance of their comrade supposing him to be wounded. He was much amused to find the whole six, including the wounded man, burrowing in the ground to collect fragments of the shell."

> **Casualties for 16th November 1899**
> **Killed (1):** Trooper T Goodall, KLH.
> **Wounded (11):** Trooper J Campbell, KLH; Sergeant Major J Churcher, KLH; Trooper E Clarke, KLH; Private H L Johnson, DFH; Private C Lester, DFH; Trooper W Mitchell, KLH; Trooper J Orr, KLH; Trooper D Parsons, KLH; Major T Peakman, KLH; Private W Rossiter, DFH; Lieutenant H Smith, DFH.
> **Boers:** Killed (1). Wounded (0).

On 17th November, the objective was Alexandersfontein by a force composed of the Diamond Fields Horse, Kimberley Light Horse and Cape Police under Scott-Turner and armed with a field gun and two Maxims. The intention was to find out the strength of the Boers in the area. The Boers shelled the small force and succeeded in hitting Captain Bodley in the leg. Five horses were also hit. On 22nd November, the cattle guard formed by the Diamond Fields Horse was augmented by the Cape Police and the small force moved towards the Boer lines. Despite being out for over three hours, not a single Boer was spotted. On the retirement of the force onto Kimberley the Boers began to shoot. Lieutenant Hawker and Trooper Armstrong, both Kimberley Light Horse, received chest wounds in the retirement. Lieutenant Hawker fell from his horse and was carried for some 2 miles (3.2 km) on an improvised stretcher made of rifles and bandoliers.

Rhodes' attitude

Rhodes expected the energies and resources he directed towards the defence of Kimberley to be matched and even bettered by the much greater resources available to the Imperial authorities to effect the relief of the town. Believing the civilian authorities would hasten to the relief of Kimberley, Rhodes was eager to be closely involved in the relief and, considering the military as lumbering and slow to respond, wanted the same level of involvement in the relief as he enjoyed in the De Beers Company. While he may have naturally expected to be involved to this extent, the contrary views of Colonel Kekewich were always going to provide the catalyst for the major confrontation and disagreement that was to occur.

Psychologically, you can understand how Rhodes must have felt. Now isolated in Kimberley with a meagre defence force and under military rule, Rhodes must have felt a keen sense of impotence and powerlessness. With his particular character and temperament, these were two adjectives that would not sit well with him and would not be endured silently for long. As soon as the isolation of Kimberley was effected by the Boers, Rhodes voiced his first call for relief. On 16th October he sent a telegram to Sir A Milner exhorting the armed forces to "strain a point" to relieve Kimberley, because, he argued "if Kimberley falls everything goes". Knowledgeable of the military situation in the area and of the available troops he suggested that "Surely you

November 1899

can put relief through, and then we can relieve Mafeking. I cannot understand delay." The conciliatory response sought to try to assure Rhodes that the authorities understood the importance of Kimberley but cautioned against commencing a relief with too weak a force. These delaying tactics were never going to pacify Rhodes. On 17th October, Rhodes tried a different approach. He sent a message to the Chartered Company asking them to contact Lord Rothschild in London and request that he militate for relief within the Cabinet and a day later the same approach was taken with Sir A Milner. Growing in frustration, Rhodes succeeded in persuading the Board of De Beers to send a combined message that expressed the hope that relief would be commenced now that General Buller had assumed command of the forces in South Africa and explained the potential problems of controlling its large workforce. The telegram of 31st October started "We hope with the arrival of General Buller measures will be taken for the immediate relief of this place. Our information, which is reliable, gives no more than 2,000 to 3,000 Boers between this place and Orange River, and in our opinion we could have been relieved without risk by the present force in Cape Colony." The message ended with the ominous line, "so as to enable us to take our own steps in case relief is refused." What did this mean? Buller construed it to portend the surrender of the town. He immediately telegraphed Kekewich to seek clarification. Kekewich tried to reassure Buller that this was not the underlying intention and even joked that surrender would only come if the Town Guard could not stand the strain of trench work.

Even though the war had only just commenced and the three sieges, Mafeking 13th October, Kimberley 15th October and Ladysmith 3rd November 1899, were in their early days, Milner wanted to subdue Rhodes' many attempts to gain support for the relief and made the prophetic statement that Kimberley would be safe for weeks. Rhodes could sense that relief would not come soon to the town. Buller had enquired for how many weeks the town's supplies could be eked out and meanwhile the ring of Boer forces had finally been joined to complete the isolation of Kimberley. Between 1st and 10th November, Rhodes despatched more telegrams and these were characterised by an increasing need for action and a growing concern of the possible effects if Kimberley was not relieved. Just as he had with the De Beers directors, Rhodes generated support from the Mayor, from the members of the Legislative Assembly in Kimberley and from Justice Lange. The language used was chosen carefully; "hordes of the enemy", "preservation of the lives of the inhabitants", and a "terrible disaster". Milner was powerless himself to do any more than offer the reassurance that Kimberley would not be forgotten and urged Rhodes to bolster the defence and use his considerable influence to build confidence and spirit within the besieged citizens. It is clear that the town's folk did not share Rhodes' more extreme views about what might happen to them and that Rhodes exaggerated both the reality and future possibilities as a tool to raise the priority for the relief.

A German postcard vividly depicting the perilous state of Kimberley

Kekewich too was concerned about the tone of Rhodes' messages that were being sent by his signallers and thus with his tacit agreement to their contents. In his diary of 10th November, he resolved to take a stronger line:

"Code messages have been allowed hitherto from De Beers etc to the High Commissioner and to the Military authorities but I must stop this, as I find that all kinds of alarmist reports are being sent. I have always tried to give all details as to the military situation, and have kept back nothing. I only hope all my messages have got through. I have represented in my telegrams the dangers and difficulties, as they affect the Military situation, with so many rich people here who can employ special despatch and pay them very highly, it is most difficult to control telegrams, letters, and newspapers etc coming into, or leaving town, but I shall now take stronger action in order that the military situation may not be misrepresented."

Ten days after Kekewich made this entry in his diary, there was an unexpected arrival of two men in Kimberley. T Richards and W Williams had made their way back to Kimberley after hearing of the siege whilst on leave in England. Harris reported the story:

"When war was declared, three sergeants of the Kimberley Regiment were in England on leave. They immediately sailed for Cape Town. One of them, Sergeant Devonshire, became attached to his old battalion, the Middlesex Regiment, and arrived with the Relief Column. The other two, both Scotsmen, reported themselves to the military authorities at Cape Town, and requested permits to rejoin their respective regiments in Kimberley. They were told that the town was closely invested; that mounted Boers were patrolling the district; and that they stood a better chance of being captured than joining their regiments. "We will take the risk," they answered. "We know every inch of the road. If you will kindly give us a permit that will pass us to the Orange River (seventy-five miles from Kimberley) where there is a British force, we will get into the town all right." Admiring their pluck, the officer gave them the necessary pass. They left that night by train for their destination, and they eventually arrived at the Drill Hall, Kimberley, and reported for duty, after experiencing many narrow escapes from being captured. It appeared that they had rested in some secluded spots during the day, and had marched through the night."

Initial plans for the relief

The demands for relief emanating from Kimberley and Buller's own views about the results of the fall of Kimberley[22] were an influence in persuading him to despatch Lord Methuen to undertake the relief of Kimberley. From within Kimberley, Boers were seen moving southwards on 21st November. Unbeknown to the town, these forces were being sent to oppose the relief force. On 23rd November a message was received via a runner from Major Reade, Shropshire Light Infantry and Deputy Assistant Adjutant General for the relief column, saying:

"Reade, Orange River, to O'Meara, 18th November. General leaves here with strong force on 21st November, and will arrive at Kimberley on 26th, unless delayed at Modder River. Look for signals by searchlight from us. They will be in cipher."

Only three days to wait! Eager to assist with the relief and command the attention of the besieging Boers, Kekewich decided to mount a large sortie that was to go out two days later on 25th November to Carter's Ridge. On the 24th November, the armoured train observed the Boers destroying railway culverts to the south of Kimberley. This gave more weight to the view that the relief column must be near at hand. O'Meara explains:

"Kekewich now felt that the time had arrived for him to do something with a view to relieving the pressure on the Relief Column, and, therefore, decided to make a sortie the next day on a scale larger than usual. In view of the information sent south as to the character of the country between the Modder River and Kimberley, Kekewich was of opinion that the Relief Column, in advancing from the Modder River, would probably keep well to the eastward of the railway. In these circumstances, he considered that it would be undesirable for the Kimberley troops to sortie in a south-easterly direction, as this might indicate to the enemy the line of advance of the Relief Column from the Modder River. He consequently arranged for a demonstration to be made in a south-westerly direction against Wimbledon Ridge; at the same time, an attack was to be made at daybreak against the Carter's Ridge position. The whole scheme was explained to the principal officers who were to take part in the sortie at a conference held on the afternoon of the 24th."

Attack on Carter's Ridge (25th November 1899)

Kekewich instructed Colonel Scott-Turner to attack the gun positions being constructed by the Boers at Carter's Ridge. The mounted force comprising A, B, C, and D Squadrons Kimberley Light Horse, B and C Squadrons Cape Police, and a detachment of the LNLR Mounted Infantry was to depart on the morning of the 25th November. The attack was to come from the side, with the troops first going to Otto's Kopje and then turning southwest for the 2.5 mile (4 km) advance to Carter's Ridge. As a diversion, Colonel Chamier was to take 900 men in the direction of Wimbledon and 50 Royal Engineers were sent to occupy Otto's Kopje. The two columns totalled 1,124 men or nearly 21% of the whole garrison. It was to be a bold strike.

The misty morning gave good cover to both columns as they left Kimberley at 04:30. En route, Lieutenant Clifford's scouts came upon a Boer outpost at the Lazaretto and captured the 6 Boers they found asleep there. Before reaching Wimbledon at around 04:45, Chamier's guns from the Diamond Fields Artillery under Major May, came into action against the Boers they discovered occupying Johnstone's (Ironstone) Kopje and, their presence disclosed, engaged in an artillery duel with the Boer guns on Wimbledon Ridge.

---

[22] In his evidence to the Royal Commission General Buller said "I feared the effect of its fall upon the native mind in general and upon the Basutos in particular. Moreover, though I felt the fullest confidence in Colonel Kekewich, I did not trust the other powers within the city."

November 1899

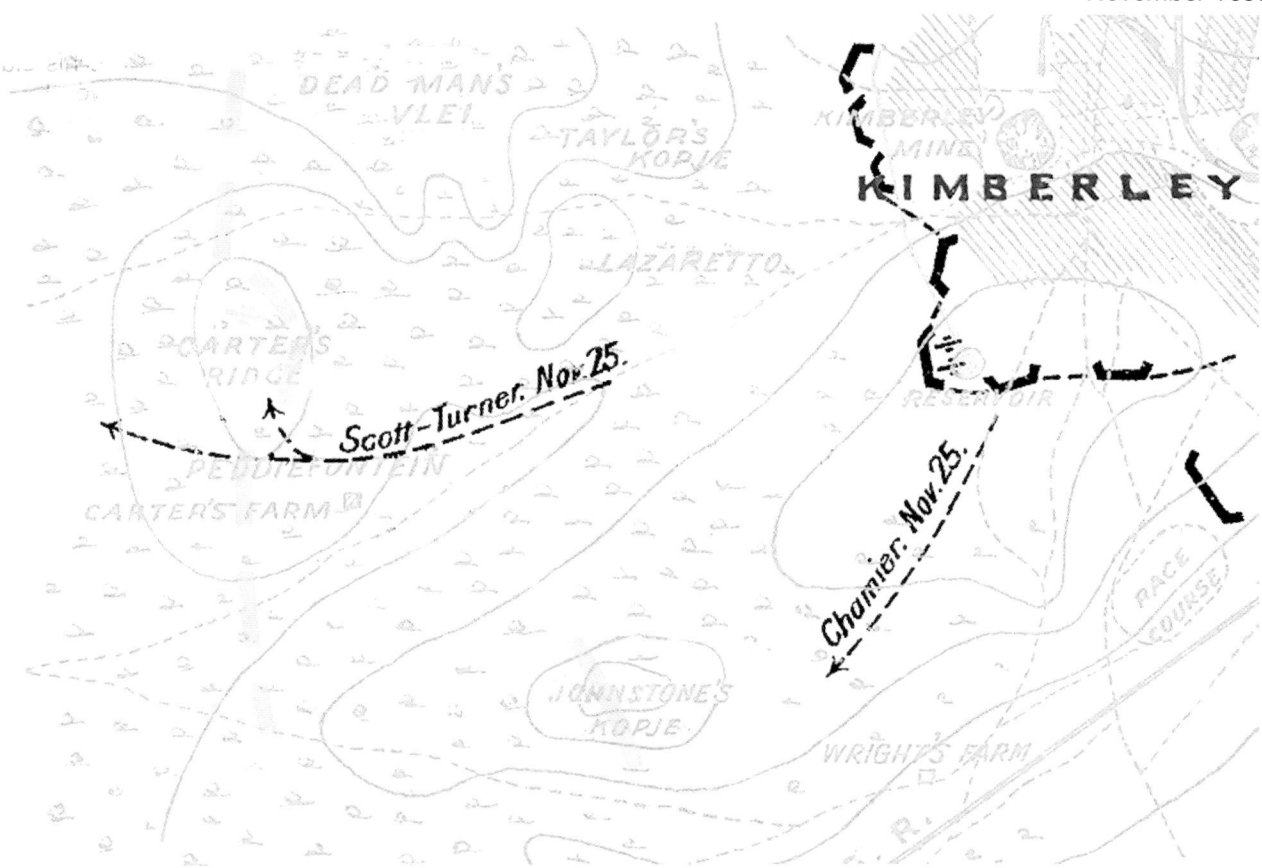

A map showing the route taken by the columns on 25th November

By this time at the base of Carter's Ridge, Scott-Turner dismounted his two squadrons of Cape Police and ordered them to extend and advance. Awakened by the firing and on their guard, men of the Bloemhof commando who were stationed on Carter's Ridge opened fire on the Cape Police. Involved in their first action and unaccustomed to war, the Boers disclosed their numbers to Scott-Turner. He guessed they numbered about 50 and decided they should be charged. He ordered a section of the Kimberley Light Horse to dismount and follow him up the ridge in the charge. There are accounts that his men were unaccustomed to using bayonets and made the charge with rifle in one hand and bayonet in the other! As one author said "Greater intrepidity could not have been displayed by trained infantry than was shown by these raw Kimberley lads when they hastened into the imminent deadly breach." The Bloemhof commando quickly disintegrated and surrendered after putting up meagre resistance.

A depiction by the artist F J Waugh of what he thought the attack by the Kimberley Light Horse and Cape Police might have been like but this is not supported by the surviving accounts

47

Kimberley Siege Account and Medal Roll

Scott-Turner quickly counted 9 wounded and 24 unwounded Boers in his possession. Meanwhile, Major R G Scott led his mounted troops into the Bloemhof laager which was located 800 yards (728 m) to the west of the ridge.

The armoured train under 2nd Lieutenant Webster was reconnoitring north and south along the railway line. The train was supported by three half companies of the Beaconsfield Town Guard under Major J R Fraser. The train's presence prevented the Boers from reinforcing Carter's Ridge from Wimbledon.

From his Kamfersdam laager to the north of the action, General Du Toit despatched 100 men of the Wolmaransstad commando to provide support to their countrymen on Carter's Ridge. These men arrived on the scene and opened fire at approximately the same time as Scott-Turner joined Major Scott on the ridge. The opportunity for further advance was slipping away so Scott-Turner took the correct decision to fall back on Kimberley. The time was 07:00. As soon as Kekewich could see what Scott-Turner was doing, he called back Chamier's force. The retirement was effectively completed. In the skirmish, 112 rounds were fired by the artillery and 40,000 cartridges by the infantry.

According to the official list, 6 men were killed and 30 wounded. One man, Trooper J Peiser Kimberley Light Horse died later in hospital having been operated on by Dr Ashe. He said "One poor youngster of eighteen was shot in the abdomen, and his bowel was cut open about ten times. I had to cut one piece about ten inches long clean out, and to stitch up a lot of other places; but I felt that he had no chance, and sent for his people and told them so at once. He died about six hours after. His father and mother had cleared out when the war scare began, but he would not go; he stayed and joined the Light Horse."

The Boers reported 10 killed and 20 wounded. The Boer prisoners were lodged in Kimberley jail where they spent the rest of the siege. Rhodes sent tobacco, pipes and new clothing to them. Valuable information was obtained from the prisoners and sent to Lord Methuen. This suggested there were 6,000 Boers to the south of Kimberley and that Cronje, reinforced from Mafeking, was making his way south as quickly as the trains would allow him to oppose the relieving force.

Casualties for 25th November 1899
Killed (6): Sergeant T Jones, CP; Corporal J Corrie, CP; Private A Hasenjäger, CP; Sergeant H Collier, KLH; Sergeant C Freislich, KLH; Trooper A Willmore, KLH.
Wounded (30): Lieutenant Colonel H Scott-Turner, RH, slight; Private J Walcroft, LNLR, severe; Private A Cooper, LNLR, slight; Sergeant H Bailey, CP, slight; Captain Rush, CP, slight; Private G Tarr, CP, slight; Private R Deere, CP, slight; Private J Stoltz, CP, slight; Private T Carlyle, CP, slight; Private G Mathieson, slight; Private W Clark, CP, slight; Private R Skinner, CP, slight; Private D O'Dell, CP, slight; Captain H Bowen, KLH, severe; Captain Hickson-Mahoney, KLH, severe; Trooper D Lanigan, KLH, slight; Trooper R Barron, KLH, slight; Trooper A Williams, KLH, severe; Sergeant W Mayston, KLH, slight; Trooper B Cawood, KLH, severe; Trooper J P Geoghegan, KLH, severe; Trooper E Gregory, KLH, severe; Corporal. M Pritchard, KLH, slight; Trooper C Legward, KLH, severe; Trooper N Skill, KLH, severe; Trooper L Farr, KLH, slight; Trooper J Peiser, KLH, mortally; Trooper G Ring, KLH, slight; Sergeant Major W H Oatley, KLH, severe; Private G Billing, KLH, slight.
Boers: Killed (10). Wounded (20). Prisoner (28).

The troops returning to Kimberley and passing the Town Hall

November 1899

After the engagement, Kekewich issued an order:

> "The Officer Commanding desires to thank all ranks who took part in today's engagement for their excellent behaviour. The garrison of Kimberley have this day shown that they can not only defend their positions, but can sally out and drive the enemy from their entrenched positions. He deplores the loss of the brave comrades who have so honourably fallen in the performance of their duty."

That night, two despatch riders brought fresh news about Methuen's success in pushing the Boers back at Belmont. Communication was established with Methuen on 27th November by searchlight. No indication was given as to Methuen's position but Kekewich decided to engage as many Boers as possible to stop them leaving the Kimberley area to oppose Methuen's advance.

Soldiers and wounded Boers at the hospital

Boer prisoners being brought into Kimberley.

Ashe met some of the Boers being marched into Kimberley and noted rather unkindly "We got a little way beyond the barrier when I met some of our men coming in with about a score of Dutch prisoners, and a dirty, low-class-looking lot they were."

Kimberley Siege Account and Medal Roll

Plans for another operation on 28th November 1899

The plan was for a stronger sortie outside the defensive lines that hoped to emulate the success of Carter's Ridge. The action was planned for the afternoon of 28th November and, contrary to Kekewich's usual strategy for innovation and variety, there was to be no element of surprise with this attack. Kekewich's intention was to arouse as much interest as he could in the Boers and to maintain this for as long as he could. The plan was to engage the Boers until nightfall and then bivouac in front of them so that they would remain engaged and thus not be able to oppose Lord Methuen's advance. The concept was well-founded.

The force was separated into three columns:

- Centre column. Under Colonel Chamier, consisting of the LNLR, two companies of the Kimberley Volunteer Regiment, a squadron of Kimberley Light Horse, a section of the 7th Company Royal Engineers, four Maxims, 6 guns of the Diamond Fields Artillery, approximately 900 men, was to move out on Johnstone's Kopje in order to threaten Wimbledon Ridge.

- Left column. Major Fraser, with 300 men of the Kimberley and Beaconsfield Town Guards, was to advance on the left. The armoured train under Lieutenant Webster was to support this column.

- Right column. Colonel Scott-Turner, with 640 mounted men drawn from the Kimberley Light Horse, Diamond Fields Horse, Cape Police and mounted infantry detachment of the LNLR was to move out in the direction of Carter's Ridge on the right. The men stationed at Otto's Kopje garrison were to join in on the right.

The three columns accounted for 1,871 men or over one third of the strength of the garrison.

To maintain a good view of the forces and to retain overall command, Kekewich stationed himself in the look-out tower at the Reservoir. He instructed Scott-Turner to take his commands from Chamier.

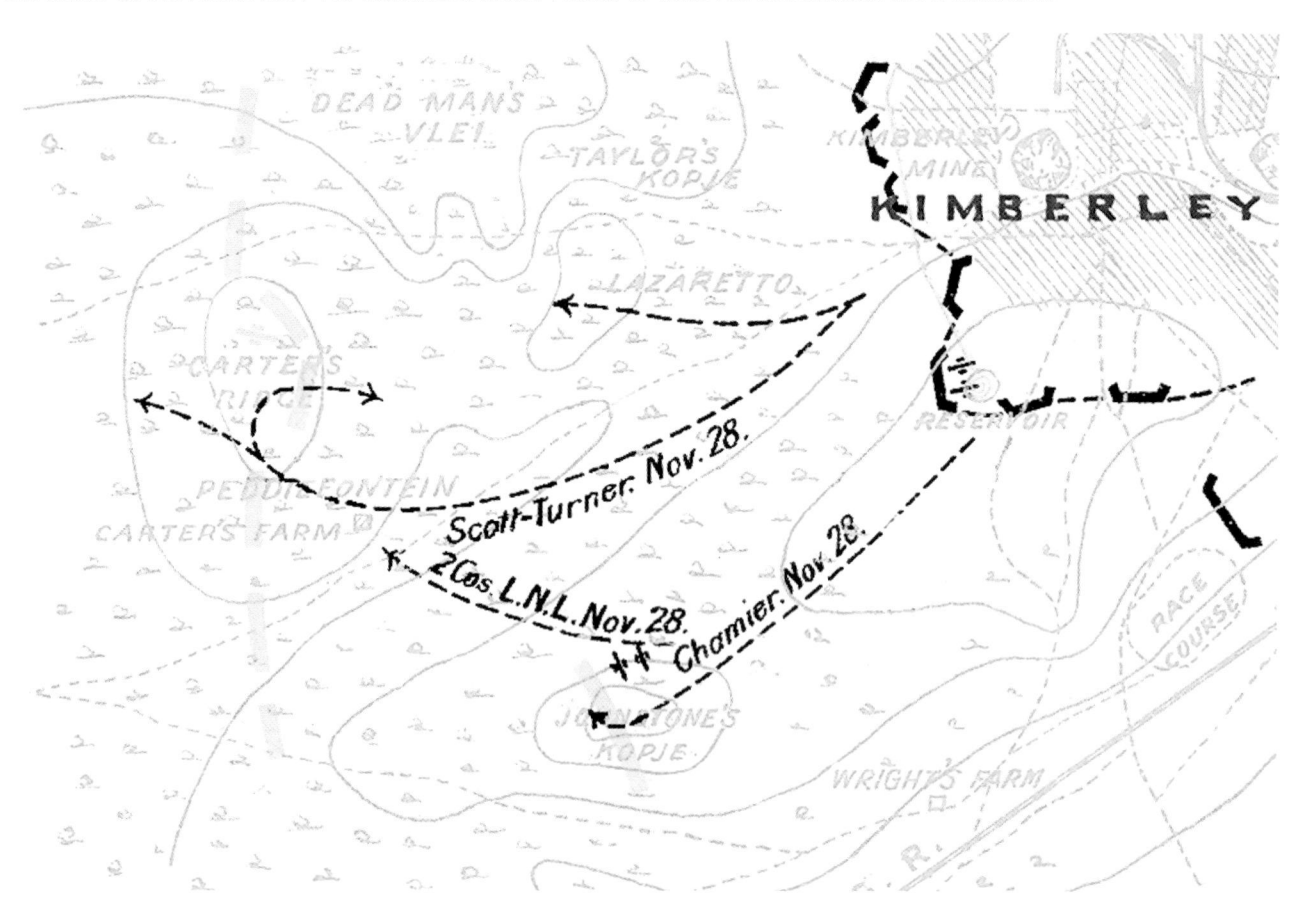

A map showing the route taken by the centre and right columns on 28th November

The trenches taken by Turner on the 25th November were known to have been re-occupied by the Boers, and, it was believed, strengthened. Kekewich cautioned Scott-Turner against turning the sortie into an attack. Kekewich's words were: "My dear chap, remember I do not want you to make an assault on Carter's Ridge or to capture it, unless it is unoccupied by the Boers, or so slightly occupied that there is every prospect of an attempt against it succeeding."

November 1899

The operation begins

The first movement was by the train which steamed north in an attempt to confuse the Boers and then returned to Kimberley. At about 14:50, the columns moved out. Chamier was able to seize Johnstone's Kopje easily as there was little opposition from the Boers. A section of his troops were then separated to occupy Wright's Farm, about 1 mile (1.6 km) east of Johnstone's Kopje.

> "I do not want you to make an assault on Carter's Ridge"
> Kekewich to Scott-Turner

Chamier reported his position by heliograph to Kekewich and added: "Propose taking up position overlooking Wimbledon and shelling Spitz Kop and Wimbledon ridge. Colonel Turner advances to Carter's." To this message Kekewich replied "Do as you think best, but the enemy's four redoubts west of Lazaretto appear to be strongly held, and you will doubtless require artillery to shell them out. Inform Colonel Turner." Lieutenant Webster in the armoured train passed Wright's Farm and began to engage the Boer guns on Spitzkop.

Scott-Turner occupied Carter's Farm which lay just over 1 mile (1.6 km) to the northwest.

Two photographs of Carter's Farm

The proximity of Carter's Farm to Chamier's position meant that he could offer support to Scott-Turner with his guns. In addition to artillery cover, Chamier sent to Scott-Turner two companies of the LNLR and some Engineers. These reached him by 16:45. A little later he sent two guns of the Diamond Fields Artillery and the mounted squadron commanded by Major Peakman.

At 16:45, Chamier was able to report to Kekewich that his position was strong and that he planned to stay put for the evening. At 18:00 Chamier rode back to see Kekewich.

Kimberley Siege Account and Medal Roll

Scott-Turner attacks Carter's Ridge

The plan was now to hold the position overnight. However, Scott-Turner was emboldened by his capture of Carter's Farm and strongly influenced by his success on the 25th November and, exceeding his orders, decided to try and capture Carter's Ridge. The Boers had improved their defences in the three days available to them. Along the inner edge of the ridge, the series of trenches and sangars had been reinforced. In about the centre of the ridge, the gun emplacement was well defended by sand bags and loop-holed defences. Scott-Turner therefore faced a very different scenario to the one on 25th November. Not only were the Boers better prepared, there would be no element of surprise. In spite of this, Scott-Turner prepared for the attack. His left flank was protected by Chamier's force and so he sent out a squadron of the Kimberley Light Horse towards the Lazaretto to protect him on the right. With the mounted forces available to him, Scott-Turner could have advanced them through the gap in the cordon created by the capture of Carter's Farm so as to attack the defences from the rear. Instead, he decided to employ the same tactics as he had on the 25th and to rush the defences, one at a time, from the flank, using dismounted troops. His attack force was small, consisting of men of the Cape Police, Kimberley Light Horse and LNLR mounted force.

From his base at Carter's Farm, Scott-Turner commenced his move against the ridge at approximately 17:00. Leaving the infantry and one squadron to hold the farm and giving orders that Major Peakman was to provide support for him, he set off against the ridge leading his men. The closest Boer position was 1,500 yards (1,365 m) away and the small force advanced towards it in skirmishing order. Covered by the Maxim gun, they moved forward in rushes and occupied the first redoubt as the Boers retreated. The attackers paused to catch their breath. As they did so, the guns of the Diamond Fields Artillery began to shell the main emplacement on the ridge and the attackers were further strengthened by another Maxim brought out from Carter's Farm.

The laager of the Bloemhof Boers, which had been visited by Major Scott only three days before was again subjected to an attack. This time Captain Shackleton and men of the Diamond Fields Horse, later reinforced by a section of the LNLR, were able to capture the laager. A large quantity of equipment was secured, including 149 x 9-pounder shells, 8 boxes of percussion caps, 6 kegs of gunpowder, a wagon and a span of oxen, a cape cart, and a gun limber. One horse was captured and this was ridden by Corporal Spalding who set off in search of reinforcements. Captain Shackleton was joined by a Sergeant and 20 men of the Lancashires and together they destroyed what could not be carried away.

The death of Scott-Turner

The time was now around 18:00. Scott-Turner roused his men to press ahead once again. The men rushed the second and third redoubts and forced the retreat of the Boers again. These successes meant the attackers were now within 60 yards (55 m) of the main redoubt at the centre of the ridge. The retreating Boers were concentrated in the relative safety of the main redoubt and, for the first time, were able to put up a credible defence. The Boers fired on the troops who were unable to find good cover. As he raised himself to fire his own weapon, Scott-Turner was killed by a bullet through the brain. Lieutenant Clifford saw what had happened and called on the men to charge the redoubt. He fell to the ground wounded on the scalp. The men who responded to his call were not able to advance against the fire from the Boers and the attack came to a halt. Major Peakman struggled to reach the firing line and lost 13 of the 40 men he had with him on his way. With casualties mounting, Peakman sent word to via Sergeant Nicholetts to Major Eliott, who was in command at Carter's Farm and also protecting the horses of the dismounted troops, to reinforce him. Elliot decided that he could spare no men and ordered Peakman to retire from the ridge.

A personal account

Lieutenant Braine, of the Diamond Fields Horse, provided a personal account of the battle:

> "We had now advanced so rapidly, almost unconsciously, that the distance between us and the huge sand bagged fort of the enemy was only 700 yards. From that fort a veritable tornado of rifle fire was issuing forth. The Police Maxim was following us, and seemed to be under the special control of Col Scott-Turner, for occasionally he turned from his men to regulate its fire by a movement of his head. During the Maxim fire our men made sudden rushes, and in this manner we gained another 200 yards upon the enemy. The formation remained the same—the Colonel on my left with his men taking cover behind small sand heaps, made by the enemy at regular intervals. The enemy had that distance measured to a yard; no one dared move from behind the heaps, so terrible was the storm of bullets. Major MacGregor, Cape Police, on my right, was now joined by Capt Gerrard, and everybody took cover behind stone or mound. How the men got out of such a position was a marvel. A slight lull in the volleying and off we went ahead; not far, however, before the storm was renewed, compelling us to take cover. Three of the Cape Police were shot dead in that rush. Here, too, Howell, of the Diamond Fields Horse, was shot, as also was McDonald who went to his aid. Powell, of the Light

Horse, was shortly afterwards shot above the heart, and remained there for three hours before the arrival of the ambulance. (He is himself again now.) It was here, too, that an unfortunate accident took place. While huddling behind the scant cover available, facing the enemy, a cross fire from our right rear made us start. It came from a squadron of Light Horse who, not having seen us rush forward, mistook us for the enemy. This made us feel very sick, but fortunately the fire did not last. Sergt King, Diamond Fields Horse, got a Lee-Metford bullet in the shoulder, and, as he was being moved, a Mauser in the body. (He is fit as ever now.) This contretemps only made us redouble our exertions to gain the fort. On we went through a withering fire. I saw fifteen men go down dead or wounded within the 100 yards run. Down we went again, every man prone. I kept an eye on Col Scott-Turner, and ere long saw him spring up and rush forward. We were now about 200 yards from the redoubt. I and the men about me immediately followed. The sight of the Colonel ahead of us, fearlessly breasting that stream of lead, was magnificent. He ran straight to the enemy's position, and, being a good runner, soon outstripped the best of us. He was now alone, and we could see the dust spitting all round him. Wonderful as it seems, he gained what we had thought was the front of the fort, and was soon joined by Cape Police, Diamond Fields Horse, and Kimberley Light Horse,. We were astonished to find only a shallow redoubt. The fort was still some sixty yards ahead. One of the first officers to join the Colonel was Lieut Clifford, 1st Loyal North Lancashire Regiment. There were also Maj McGregor and Capt Gerrard, Cape Police, and Lieut Wright, Kimberley Light Horse, whilst Capt Robertson-Cumming, Cape Police, was hard by, stimulating and encouraging poor King. McGregor had a narrow squeak, a bullet passing through the brim of his hat.

We remained quiet—almost breathless—for a few minutes, then came the misfortune of the day. I noticed the Colonel seize a rifle from a man near him and deliberately take aim and fire several shots, then he sank down, as I thought from fatigue. But it was not so, as we soon knew. A bullet had passed through his head, cutting his hat to pieces. We were staggered at this, but I cannot describe the feeling more particularly. Laying him down we next thought of the foe. The sand-bagged fort, thoroughly loop-holed, was plainly visible. From it the hail of bullets was incessant, and to show a head meant additional volleys. I ventured a couple of shots from my revolver, and quick as lightning a bullet cut the sand beside my hand. Lieut Clifford now moved round, and, seizing a rifle, leant over the bank and fired three shots. After the last he exclaimed, 'I've hit one' and down the brave little chap fell, as if struck by lightning, a stream of blood flowing from his head. Sorrow deepened in us, for all thought him dead. I got hold of him and held him in a sitting position. He remained quiet a few moments, then gasped, rubbed his fingers into the wound, and exclaiming 'It's only a scalp wound', gave the order 'Fix bayonets! Charge!' We promptly countermanded that order, for it meant certain death to all. Lieut Wright met his doom in a similar manner. Taking a rifle he looked up, took steady aim, and fired; at the same time a bullet entered his head. We counted another brave messmate gone. I think one of the most marvellous escapes on that eventful day was that of Lieut Col Peakman, Kimberley Light Horse. He came rushing to our assistance from the right, but found he had lost ten out of fourteen men who started with him, ere he joined us. We felt cornered. To move, far less advance or retreat, meant certain death. The gallant Colonel (Peakman) ordered three cheers with the intention of drawing supports, but our advance had been so rapid that I fancy our men again mistook us for the enemy, for three British cheers had no effect. Our situation was awful, and we knew not how to better it. Here we were huddled within a sandbank sixty yards from the enemy's stronghold, with open ground between—an enemy, too, who could make his mark every time at that distance when safely kneeling to a loophole. All this time we were witnesses of horrible work. Every now and again a man would rush towards us believing we had taken the fort. Our entreaties to such to 'keep down' and 'take cover' had no effect, and all were shot dead or wounded. The sight of dead and wounded was as much as some of us could bear.

One instance impressed itself on my memory very vividly. Two brave fellows—one of the Lancashires and one of the Light Horse—rushed out of their slight cover towards us. The Lancashire came dauntlessly forward, whilst the other came along zig-zag fashion. The soldier was shot—the volunteer escaped, but bandolier and water-bottle were shot off him. We made up our minds to wait for reinforcements or darkness, though our comparative safety was somewhat shaken when the enemy's 9-pounder grazed our sand bank. Sergt Nicholetts, Diamond Fields Horse, now volunteered to take the sad news to Col Kekewich, and this he did successfully. Next a trooper of the Cape Police volunteered to carry the body of our late leader, and with assistance, this too was done. Gradually, under cover of darkness, all retired to Carter's, where the wounded were cared for, some of our dead collected and placed in the ambulance wagons, and we marched back to camp between midnight and morning. I cannot close without stating that explosive bullets were mainly used by our enemy on that day, and that our ambulance (as also men carrying wounded to the wagon) was deliberately fired upon whenever the searchlight showed it up."

Kimberley Siege Account and Medal Roll

Return to Kimberley

Neither Kekewich nor Chamier could determine what was happening on the ridge although they were aware that a fight was going on and the outcome did not become apparent until nightfall. Kekewich sent orders to Peakman to fall back on Chamier and that the whole force should return to Kimberley the next morning. Major Eliott ordered the mounted troops to return directly to Kimberley and this movement was started before Kekewich's orders had arrived. As planned, Chamier returned to Kimberley the next morning.

The cost in terms of casualties of this engagement was high.

Casualties for 28th November 1899
Killed (22): Lieutenant Colonel H Scott-Turner, RH; Colour Sergeant A Heald, LNL; Private T Lutner, LNL; Sergeant Major G Brady, CP; Private C Dennison, CP; Private J Williams, CP; Corporal R Howell, DFH; Private H Cornwall, DFH; Private A Dare, DFH; Lieutenant S Wright, KLH; Lance Corporal H Hiscock, KLH; Private W Baker, KLH; Private J Hastings, KLH; Private H Harper, KLH; Private W McDonald, KLH; Private J Marshall, KLH; Private B Nicholas, KLH; Private C Screech, KLH; Private F Sharpe, KLH; Private C Stearns, KLH; Private J Thompson, KLH; Private H Taylor, KLH.
Wounded (33): Captain S Waldek, DFH, slight; Lieutenant H Watson, KLH, slight; Lieutenant W Clifford, LNL; Sergeant C King, DFH, severe; Trooper J Keller, KLH, dangerous (died 29th November); Trooper A Wood, KLH, slight; Trooper H Richardson, KLH, slight; Trooper H Stacpole, KLH, slight; Trooper F Day, KLH, severe; Trooper F Powell, KLH, severe; Private J Kenton, LNL, severe; Private T Tyldesley, LNL, severe; Private G Edkins, LNL, severe; Trooper F Arundale, CP, severe; Trooper P Salkeld, CP, severe (died later); Trooper W Spilsbury, CP, severe; Trooper J Howell, CP, severe; Trooper F Pool, CP, slight; Trooper J Grindrod, CP, slight; Trooper N Edy, CP, slight; Trooper C McNay, CP, slight; Trooper H Hillier, CP, slight; Trooper J Taylor, CP, slight; Trooper F Ferguson, DFH, severe; Trooper H Gordon, DFH, slight; Trooper C Glyn, DFH, slight; Trooper D Shepherd, DFH, slight; Trooper F Knight, DFH, slight; Trooper H Adler, DFH, slight; Private H Lee, LNL, slight; Sergeant Major J McDonald, KRV, slight; Private J Metrovitch, CP, slight; Private J Neville, LNL.
Boers: Killed (3). Wounded (11).

Kekewich issued a special order on the day after the engagement. It read:

> "The Officer Commanding has again to congratulate the troops of the garrison who engaged the enemy yesterday on their excellent behaviour and on the capture of the enemy's laager, with his supplies, ammunition, &c. It was in every respect a most creditable performance. He has also again to deplore the loss of many brave men who have fallen at the call of duty. It was with profound sorrow he learnt that Lieutenant Colonel Scott-Turner was killed while gallantly leading his men against the last stronghold of the enemy's defences. In Lieutenant Colonel Scott-Turner the garrison of Kimberley loses a brave and most distinguished comrade, and the Officer Commanding feels sure the whole population of Kimberley will join with them in mourning the loss of this true British officer, to whose skill and activity in the field is so largely due the complete success of our efforts to keep the enemy at a safe distance from this town."

The funeral of the killed took place on the afternoon of 29th November. Six volleys were fired over the graves and six blasts of the bugle were made before the large group of mourners that included Rhodes and the Mayor dispersed. The *Diamond Fields Advertiser* reported the solemn proceedings of the funerals which took place on the afternoon of 29th November (see page 538 for the full text).

> "Kimberley mourns the loss of some of her bravest sons, and her sorrow is intensified by the fact that Lieut.-Col. Scott-Turner, who has so gallantly led the mounted troops against the besiegers during the past month, is amongst the fallen. That such a career, with its almost certain promise of the highest distinction in a noble profession, should have been thus cut short is sad almost beyond expression, and we know of no event within recent recollection which has caused so widespread and profound a feeling of emotion … during the past few weeks Scott-Turner's name has been on everybody's lips. On every occasion that our troops have been seriously engaged he was their trusty leader. For long he bore a charmed life, and rode about unharmed amid the storm of bullets, seemingly indifferent to the terrible dangers which confronted him, and setting a bright example to his men at all times by his fearlessness and courage. On Saturday last he received a wound in the shoulder. He treated the injury lightly as a mere matter of sticking plaster, and not only did he remain at his post in the fight, but on his return to Kimberley he continued to perform his ordinary duties. … Nothing, alas, can minimise the cruel and irreparable loss which they have sustained, but it may perhaps be some slight consolation for them to know that the name of Scott-Turner will ever be cherished as that of the noblest of the band of heroes who died in the defence of Kimberley in the siege of 1899."

November 1899

The funeral of Scott-Turner

Scott-Turner's original grave

On the evening of 29th November, a despatch rider arrived from Methuen's force with a message expressing concern about the safety of Kimberley and to which Kekewich merely replied "Situation here not critical". Kekewich also provided Methuen with as much information as he knew about the forces that lay between them:

> "Enemy north and west of us are Transvaalers and number probably 1,200 men. On our east, Boers have withdrawn to the hills eight to ten miles from here—strength unknown. Boer prisoners captured in engagement of 25th November give number between here and Modder River as anything from 3,000 to 15,000 men; believe actual numbers to be about 6,000 men, partly Transvaalers and partly Free Staters."

It was not until the next day, 30th November, that Kekewich learnt of Methuen's position. A searchlight message was received and addressed 'To Clack, Cape Police Kimberley. Port Klokfontein delighted.'[23] From the message and a search of several maps it was determined that Klokfontein[24] was a farm near Modder River and thus Methuen was still south of the Modder. On the next evening, a despatch rider arrived with more news and for the first time, Kekewich learnt of the composition of Methuen's force.

---

[23] The message was continued the next morning and finished 'Delighted to receive wire all well. Orange River, Clack Cape Police'. Kekewich wasn't sure what the message meant nor if it was intended for him but it did provide him with vital information.

[24] See page 562 for a map showing the position of Klokfontein.

December 1899

Methuen's concept of relief

After the losses suffered by the garrison in the last week of November, the relief of the town was an increasingly important topic. However, rather than Methuen's advance having the intention of relieving Kimberley, the view within the besieged town was that Methuen would do no more than bring fresh supplies and more troops. On the 3rd December, Methuen communicated to Kekewich that a further half battalion of the Lancashires, Naval guns and a Naval Brigade would be stationed in Kimberley. The strengthened garrison would then be able to hold out until the actual relief was effected by Buller's force after it had taken Bloemfontein. Buller was of the opinion that the town could last longer if those people not connected with its defence or involved in the mines were removed from Kimberley.

This latest situation brought about the complete rift between Rhodes and Kekewich. O'Meara says:

> "Rhodes called later at the military Headquarters to learn the latest official news; he was informed that Methuen's message dealt with plans connected with the relief of Kimberley. Further, Kekewich emphasized the importance of the strictest secrecy being maintained on the subject. Rhodes was then told that, only on condition of his promising not to divulge any of the information concerning the relief arrangements, could Kekewich communicate to him the nature of the instructions that had been received. Rhodes gave the promise asked for and the full text of Methuen's message was then read to him; he was very displeased with the proposed arrangements. Late in the evening, it came to Kekewich's knowledge that Rhodes had communicated the information given to him, in the strictest confidence, to some of the De Beers' directors and also to some of the Company's officials; this leakage caused Kekewich much anxiety. Next day, a further message on the same subject was received at military Headquarters; it furnished a few more particulars as to the additional garrison to be provided for Kimberley. After this message had been decoded, Rhodes called at the office to inquire whether there were any further developments; he was told that another message had come in, but, said Kekewich: "I can only communicate the further information if you will give me a solemn assurance that you will keep whatever I may communicate to you strictly to yourself and not repeat it either to De Beers' directors or to the Company's officials."
>
> The storm which had been gathering at the Sanatorium Hotel since the earliest days of the siege now broke. Rhodes completely lost his temper and shouted: "That is exactly what you told me yesterday and I am not going to be told that by you again." Kekewich remained unruffled and quietly explained that he had learnt that Rhodes had communicated to others the information given to him in confidence on the previous day, and he had to consider the matter not alone from the point of view of a breach of the undertaking expressly given by Rhodes, but also from the point of view of the jeopardy in which military arrangements were placed by the possibility of the Boers obtaining full knowledge of the plans which the military authorities were intending to carry out. Rhodes' answer was that he intended to make whatever use he might think necessary of the information already given to him and refused to be bound in any way as to communications made to him by Kekewich; he left the office in high dudgeon, vowing all kinds of vengeance against Buller and Kekewich and his Staff. The rupture between the Commandant of Kimberley and the leading civilian in the town was now complete."

The plans to remove citizens

Kekewich was further directed by Methuen in a message received late on 4th December to make plans to remove the surplus population when the town was reached and railway communication opened. The message read:

> "Arrangements being made send as soon as possible large quantities of supplies. As communication may be interrupted again in view of consequent situation it is desirable reduce as far as possible total numbers. All should be sent straight away North[25] exception of troops persons required for management and working of town and working in mines, for purchasing cattle specifically required ends.
>
> Colonial Government desires all civil authorities should cooperate cordially with you in removing superfluous population expeditiously. This coincides with orders GOC has received; he will expect these orders to be carried [out] the day he reaches Kimberley and he will have a train ready to send persons away."

---

[25] This is an error and should have said 'south'.

December 1899

On the next morning, 5th December, Kekewich called together the Mayor and other citizens to form a committee to co-ordinate the removal of the surplus inhabitants. News spread quickly about this second aspect of Methuen's 'relief' and this was not well received. Not only were the inhabitants disappointed about the prospect of a prolonged siege if they stayed and the thought of a refugee life elsewhere in the Colony, Rhodes and the De Beers directors found out that they were unlikely to receive the supplies, coal and dynamite they needed to feed the black workers and enable the resumption of mining operations. On 5th December, Rhodes began his opposition to the plan. He sent a message to Methuen:

> "Kindly inform the High Commissioner De Beers will require for 3 months 1000 tons of English coal, and 120 tons dynamite. Also six weeks provisions for 10000 natives. Present De Beers with provisions will last six weeks. Ask High Commissioner if he approves to tell Fuller Dreyfus to place orders and forward by rail at once. Essential to continue work as loss to Colony is £14000 per diem. Have seen message removal civil population."

On 6th December, Kekewich reported back to Methuen with his projections. Kekewich hoped to remove about 45% of the entire population[26]:

> "Civil population numbers to leave Kimberley whites 8000, natives 120000. To remain if present garrison 3500 men and 1400 horses, whites employed in town and mines 5000, natives if mines are worked 16000, if mines are not worked 13000 additional natives must be removed from Kimberley. Natives should be taken such distance by rail from Kimberley that they cannot walk back. Natives cannot be sent to homes by road as they would be driven back into Kimberley by Boers and would become great danger in town. Best solution is to send as possible of coal and dynamite as Rhodes requires. Rhodes says working only two mines 500 tons coal would suffice."

On 7th December, a response was received to Rhodes' message and he did not receive the reassurance he wanted to hear:

> "As regards coal and dynamite these must wait guns troops and supplies for troops and necessary civil population have been got in and military operations connected with relief completed. Important to get away as many people as possible to economise supplies if communication interrupted."

That same evening, a long message from Rhodes to Milner began to be transmitted by searchlight. Rhodes threatened to close down De Beers and therefore hand over the responsibility for 13,000 blacks to the military authorities. Rhodes also believed the meagre increase in the strength of the troops added by Methuen would be inadequate for the task of defending the town and asked Milner for permission to raise a corps of 2,000 volunteers for the defence of Kimberley, undertaking that De Beers would pay all the costs that this incurred.

On 8th December Rhodes spoke to the De Beers Board, informed them of Methuen's plans. He explained the consequences of sending out of the town a minimum of 20,000 people and maximum of 35,000 if De Beers was forced to cease as a company. Rhodes called on the military authorities to protect the town and keep open the rail line to and from Kimberley. As a consequence of his protestations, the De Beers Board send two letters of protest to Kekewich, the first on the 8th December and a second on the 13th December. They argued that it would be easier to bring in supplies rather than expel people and that the first duty of the Government was to protect its citizens. Not content with this, Rhodes sought to intervene directly between Kekewich and Methuen. Rhodes asked Kekewich to send a message to Methuen:

> "Dear Methuen: If Spytfontein is in your opinion too big a job why not push an advance to Bisset's (Magersfontein), throw up a fort and leave infantry? This would leave you eleven miles from Beaconsfield. The Boers, as you know, never attack a fort. The men here could easily occupy Alexandersfontein and a joint movement could then occupy Scholtz's Water. The result would be that you would then hold the waters on which their Spytfontein position depends and complete connection from Modder River here without having risked the difficulties of the Spytfontein hilly country. In my opinion the Boers will then bolt from Spytfontein, as they must have very little water there and must supply their horses from Scholtz's and Bisset's."

Kekewich did not agree with either the content or the tone of the letter so declined to transmit it. Next, Rhodes asked Kekewich to send the letter and to inform Methuen that he had refused to endorse the content. This was a direct attack on Kekewich's authority and was also declined. Undeterred, Rhodes defied Kekewich and sent the communication by private runner.

---

[26] Kekewich had calculated the total population to number 43,000.

Kekewich had, through his chain of command, to obey the policy determined by Buller and this must not have been an easy task. The military authorities both inside and outside Kimberley were increasingly unhappy with the intervention of Rhodes. As a result, Methuen sent a message to Kekewich on 8th December telling him not to let Rhodes interfere:

> "Please understand that I can give you one and a half battalions and Naval Brigade, and you must cut your coat according to your cloth. I am arranging military defence with you, and Rhodes must understand that he has no voice in the matter. In fact he will have to leave with civilians on relief."

In spite of the protests of the citizens, preparations for the evacuation continued. Even Rhodes played a part in the preparation by making tentative arrangements to house and feed some of the refugees on his estate at Groote Schuur near Cape Town. On 11th December Kekewich received a written despatch containing instructions that not a single civilian or native was to remain in Kimberley after the relief "unless he satisfies you and myself that his services are essential for the protection of Kimberley, or some other good purpose." The plan was to send 15 trains to Kimberley containing food and supplies and double this number of trains would be employed for the conveyance of the surplus population away from Kimberley. The Mayor issued a notice informing people that free rail passes were to be offered to all citizens who wanted to leave the town when the railway links were restored and asking that names and destinations be received as soon as possible. Presumably not all the destinations could be honoured and the actual final destination of the trains was more likely to be the coastal towns of the Cape, as far away from the fighting as possible. The expected date for the arrival of supplies was 15th December and a week later for the departure of the citizens.

By 11th December the provisional number of evacuees had risen to 33,000. At the meeting to decide these figures, the Mayor and Town Council represented their protestation so strongly that Kekewich relented and agreed to send a message from them to Milner that evening:

> "From the Mayor, Kimberley. To the High Commissioner, Cape Town. With reference proposed removal white population from Kimberley would respectfully represent great suffering and hardship will be caused to women and children – which will far exceed any privations which could possibly result from continuance siege. Earnestly beg removal of white population may not be compulsory."

With the passage of another day, the Town Council's opinion had hardened still further to the extent that they refused to assist Kekewich in the removal of any citizens. Kekewich, sympathetic but equally bound by his orders, refused to accept the resolution and continued to press ahead with the planning.

The *Diamond Fields Advertiser* remonstrated as strongly as it could against the policy in an article entitled 'An impossible rumour' on 13th December[27]:

> "To speak plainly, it would mean not merely the banishment of the people from their homes for an indefinite period, but bankruptcy for many a struggling shopkeeper and professional man—abject penury and ruin for thousands of humble wage earners and their families who, away from Kimberley, would be quite unable to earn a livelihood. The terrible journey to the coast in densely overcrowded trains and over congested lines of railway—and most of us appreciate what that would mean for delicate women and children, with recollections of Glencoe and the more recent harrowing stories of the hegira from the Transvaal fresh in our memories—would perhaps be the least among the hardships to be faced. The coast towns, where our unhappy refugees would presumably be dumped down and left to shift for themselves, are overcrowded already, and hundreds, if not thousands, find it hard to procure shelter and food to eat. The distress among these people is notoriously great, far greater than the exertions of philanthropy can hope to cope with; and no sensible person can desire to see that misery added to or intensified by an enforced exodus from Kimberley. In deliberately asserting our opinion that this hideous and disturbing rumour must be and is wholly and absurdly untrue, we take, however, higher ground. Kimberley, as the most important inland town of the Colony, and as a great industrial centre where thirty millions of British capital are invested, occupies a position of wholly exceptional importance, and its claim for adequate protection in time of war cannot be disregarded without grievous loss of prestige in the eyes of the world. Admitting that the question of keeping open the communications is a difficult one, we would point out, that there are always difficulties of this kind to be accepted and faced in planning out a modern campaign, and they may be quite successfully surmounted without resorting - to any such an anomalous expedient as rumour talks about, viz, that a friendly and victorious army should proceed upon its arrival as a 'relieving' column to paralyse and impoverish the entire community, and metamorphose a busy industrial city— which has escaped, largely through its own exertions, unscathed from the worst an enemy could do

---

[27] The full text of the article appears in the Diamond Fields Advertiser appendix, page 539.

after a protracted siege—into the semblance of one of the dead cities of the Zuyder Zee. Such an unprecedented proceeding, following upon successful military operations, would cause doubt to be cast upon our victories, and, as we have said, be ruinous to British prestige in the eyes of the whole world; and, therefore, guided rather by pure reason and common sense than by any knowledge of what is passing in the official mind in Capetown, we have no hesitation in reiterating our entire disbelief in a rumour which we regard as mischievous and preposterous in an equal degree."

Persuasive as this argument was, it was not the *Diamond Fields Advertiser* that changed the mind of the military authorities.

Magersfontein and its effects

On 2nd December, Methuen flashed the message to Kekewich that he had "… gained passage Modder River after successful fight. Every one fit and keen." On 5th December, Methuen informed Kekewich that he was waiting for the arrival of fresh troops "on the supposition that Kimberley was in no immediate danger". Kekewich replied in the affirmative. The expectations of relief now rose exponentially but so too did the tension of waiting for news. Methuen's next encounter with the Boers was at Magersfontein on 11th December. Kekewich and his officers in the conning tower could see British shells bursting in the distance and the British war balloon was also clearly visible. Expectation was so high that school children asked for a holiday so that they could welcome in the relieving force in the belief that Methuen was fighting his way into Kimberley and that the hoped-for relief would soon be a reality. This great wave of hope was soon dashed when a message was flashed to Kekewich on the evening of 11th December saying simply, "I am checked". It was however another agonising four days before Kekewich learnt of the British defeat at Magersfontein. After so much anticipation this news came as a crushing blow to the populace. The only positive outcome for the town was that it finally put a stop to the issue of deportations and all the bad feeling this policy had engendered.

> "I am checked"
> Methuen

Kekewich had meanwhile planned another sortie against the Boers to coincide with Methuen's next engagement. When he did finally receive a copy of the plan, it arrived too late for him to act in co-ordination with the attack on Magersfontein. Methuen had said:

> "Now regarding my movements. I have been delayed two days by railway being destroyed near Enslin. First train crossed Modder river by seventh, and my additional men were crossed this morning. I bombard the enemy at Magersfontein this afternoon, assault to-morrow, and march to Abon's Farm, Hardings, Tuesday; attack Scholtz Nek, Wednesday, at daybreak. Of course, my plan may have to be altered, but I hope to keep you daily informed as to my movements; besides, I believe I can signal to Kimberley from Abon's Farm. Naturally I set great store on your valuable co-operation. After the fight I hope to see you, and may return to Kimberley with you."

After the losses suffered on 28th November, Kekewich had been holding back on any diversionary forays unless he could guarantee to be of assistance to Methuen. This was required to save both men and horses. He had in mind a movement towards Alexandersfontein and had refrained from any action that might have caused the Boers to strengthen their defences in this area as had been the case at Carter's Ridge. These plans came to nothing and there was to be no movement against Alexandersfontein for a further two months.

Eking out the supplies

Kekewich calculated his supplies on 1st December for the whole population of Kimberley:

Meat	25 days
Preserved	10 days
Breadstuffs	40 days
Forage	30 days

With his supplies dwindling and the possibility of an early relief receding quickly, the supply situation became Kekewich's overwhelming problem. To add to these woes he received a bewildering series of progressively worsening tidings. He was told on 16th December that he should "economise rations till 15th January", then on 18th December that he should "commence economising food to last till 30th January" and then on 20th December to "arrange your supplies to last till 15th February." Worse news still was to follow and on 26th December when Kekewich received news that the relief of Kimberley had been postponed indefinitely. On 1st January 1900, Kekewich was asked to husband his resources until the end of February.

Kimberley Siege Account and Medal Roll

The immediate impact of these messages meant that the control of supplies assumed paramount importance. On 20th December all the remaining stocks of tea, coffee and meal were purchased by the military authorities at a cost of £37,000, their control was taken over by the Supply Committee and the fixed rations were further lowered. Europeans and coloured colonials were entitled to 14 ounces (400 g) of bread or 10 ounces (280 g) of Boer meal and flour, 2 ounces (60 g) of either mealie or Kaffir corn, 2 ounces (60 g) of rice, 2 ounces (60 g) of sugar, ¼ ounce (7 g) of tea, and ½ ounce (15 g) of coffee. The meat ration was unchanged at ½ lb (230 g) per day, but it mostly consisted of bone and gristle and was of limited nutritional value. Asians were allowed 2 ounces (60 g) of mealie meal, 8 ounces (230 g) of rice, and the same allowance of tea, sugar and coffee as Europeans. The diet for black people consisted of 6 ounces (170 g) of mealie meal, 4 ounces (110 g) of Kaffir corn, 2 ounces (60 g) of samp (dried corn kernels), tea, coffee, and sugar the same as Asians and Europeans. Supplies were issued from various stores upon production of permits issued by the Food Supply Committee. Each storekeeper drew his supplies weekly, and there were special depots where food was supplied to Asians and black people.

In addition to husbanding his existing supplies, Kekewich made great efforts to capture cattle from the Boers. He employed blacks to do this and remunerated them for every animal they managed to bring in. The reward for each animal rose from 20 Shillings to £2 and several hundred cattle were obtained in this way. The slaughter of any cattle except on a military order was strictly prohibited. On 6th December, Kekewich ordered the building of a cold store by Mr Labram and approximately 100 cattle were slaughtered and the meat stored away.

On 27th December, groceries were included with the Supply Committee's remit. From this date shop keepers were only allowed to sell to individuals who presented permits for food issued to them by clerks from the ward of the town in which they lived and the shop keepers could only gain fresh supplies themselves by presenting a complete statement of their sales in the past week accompanied by the permits.

Coal, another important resource, was restricted to four uses; powering the searchlights, pumping out water from the mines, moving drinking water to the reservoir and powering the cold store. This equated to a usage of 300 tons per week. Coal was forecast to run out by the end of February.

Offensive operations scaled back

The necessity of conservation did not just extend to the supplies. The need to safeguard his fighting force meant that no operation on the same scale as that against Carter's Ridge on 28th November was undertaken during the remainder of the siege. However, this did not mean that Kekewich curtailed all his activities. His policy was to continually probe at the Boers surrounding him and to act on the offensive in small military manoeuvres.

Colonel Peakman continued to lead reconnaissances outside the town's defences. On 9th December, a small force of men, four Maxims and 6 guns of the Diamond Fields Artillery made a reconnaissance towards Kamfersdam to assess the Boer strengths in the area. Four guns of the Diamond Fields Artillery, under Major May, took up a position near the Homestead in the morning and fired towards Kamfersdam from around 3,000 yards (2,750 m). There was firing throughout the day and also from the two Royal Artillery guns at the searchlight. Three Boer guns responded and caused the death of Sergeant Major Moss, Diamond Fields Artillery, and the wounding of 6 men including Lieutenant J White, Cape Police. The mounted infantry of the LNLR and two guns were posted on Otto's Kopje while the Cape Police protected the dam wall. The Kimberley Light Horse created some rifle positions from prospectors' huts to cover the retreat of the force.

> **Casualties for 9th December 1899**
> **Killed (1):** Sergeant Major A Moss, DFA.
> **Wounded (6):** Lieutenant J White, CP; Trumpeter E Anderson, DFA; Sergeant R Canut,, DFA; Sergeant W Kidd, DFA; Gunner, C Lafevre, DFA; Driver A Stewart, DFA.
> **Boers:** Killed (0). Wounded (2).

On 20th December, a mounted force under Colonel Peakman accompanied by Maxims and 7-pounders under Major May set off at 02:00, going northwest this time through Kenilworth, past Webster's farm towards Tollpan in the Orange Free State. The guns shelled Tollpan from a distance of about 2,500 yards (2,300 m) and were themselves on the receiving end of return fire by the Boer guns on Klippiespan Ridge. While the shelling continued, the location of the Boers was investigated and they were found to be at Coetgie, Scholtz and Alexandersfontein with each area being a source of water.

On 22nd December, a combined mounted, infantry and artillery force set out at daybreak to reconnoitre in the direction of Carter's Ridge. On the right, the Diamond Fields Horse was commanded by Major Rodger and supported by a company of the LNLR under Lieutenant de Putron. An artillery duel commenced between the

December 1899

Boer's guns on Kamferdam and the guns of the Diamond Fields Artillery on Otto's Kopje. In the centre, Colonel Peakman with the Cape Police and Kimberley Light Horse made their way along the Lazaretto ridge. Peakman discovered that the ridge was only occupied by a Boer patrol which promptly retired and his men filled in the local wells to restrict the Boer's access to water. The left wing of the force was commanded by Colonel Chamier with the Royal Garrison Artillery guns and an escort under Major Snow. Chamier came under fire from the Boers on Wimbledon Ridge and, while fire was returned, the approach of a much larger Boer force necessitated the withdrawal of the expedition.

In addition to the reconnaissances, new outposts were established at Otto's Kopje and at Fort Gibraltar on Davis' Heap to the south of Wesselton, the first to prevent the Boers from occupying it and the second to protect the workers in the vegetable gardens between the fort and Wesselton.

Otto's Kopje defences

Christmas under siege

For the most part, the month of December and the Christmas period in particular passed without great excitement. There was sporadic artillery fire but little interest was shown by either side and minimal damage was caused. Unusually for the Boers, there was artillery fire on Christmas Day and there were 35 shells fired into the town which elicited 19 in return. Interestingly, the Boer gunners never concentrated their capability against any target with the intention of weakening or destroying it and appeared to be content with desultory and wide ranging-shelling.

The siege did not remove all the joy of Christmas as this account from Fort Armstrong demonstrates:

> "The redoubt was stormed by the wives and children of the men, the juveniles numbering but three short of a hundred. Their presence was accounted for by the provision of a gigantic Christmas tree; Father Christmas, impersonated by Private Strugnell, and an attendant imp with burnt cork complexion (Private Seaward) and banjo, provided some amusement until the last of the contingents arrived.
>
> The captain then welcomed his guests, and the representative of St. Nicholas explained that, owing to the action of the naughty Boers, his usual stock of presents had been stopped on the road, and it was owing to the generosity of Capt. Armstrong that Father Christmas was able to show himself without blushing. Then, assisted by Corpls. Townsend and Livingstone, the distribution commenced, and the half-hour following will not soon be forgotten by any of those present.

Kimberley Siege Account and Medal Roll

> The gifts were carefully selected to meet the size and age of the recipients, the baby in arms getting its rattle; budding maidens, silver bangles and companions, and the young man of fifteen a walking stick or some other useful article. In response to the call for cheers for the donor, Father Christmas and the rest of those concerned in the organization, the lusty voices of the youngsters made music that will last. 'God Save the Queen' and 'Auld Lang Syne' followed, and the merriest party in the beleaguered city of Kimberley on Christmas Day, 1899, dispersed."

On 24th December, a festive message was flashed from the Military Secretary at Cape Town. It said:

> "Convey to Colonel Kekewich and all the garrison and inhabitants of Kimberley His Excellency's best wishes for their good luck on Christmas Day and in the coming New Year."

Colonel Kekewich replied:

> "Kindly inform the Military Secretary that I and the garrison and inhabitants of Kimberley thank His Excellency for his kind message. We also wish respectfully to offer our very best wishes for Christmas and New Year."

Queen Victoria sent a message to the garrison:

> "I wish you and all my brave soldiers a happy Christmas; God protect and bless you all,"

On 1st January 1900, the inhabitants of Kimberley sent a very patriotic message back to the Queen:

> "The inhabitants of Kimberley humbly beg to send Your Majesty New Year's greetings. The troubles they have passed through, and are still enduring, only tend to intensify their love and loyalty towards Your Majesty's Throne and Person."

The Queen replied saying:

> "Am deeply touched by your kind New Year's greetings. I watch with admiration your determined and gallant defence, though I regret the unavoidable loss of life incurred."

The weather at the time was very hot with temperatures in the shade reaching 41°C (105°F). The *Diamond Fields Advertiser* expressed the sentiment felt by many in Kimberley when it wrote:

> "Excepting two or three of our inhabitants who shared the terrible privations of the siege of Paris[28], few of us have ever spent such a Christmas before, and few will ever care to spend such a Christmas again. The scarcity of turkeys and plum-pudding at this time of traditional plenty need only distress the gourmand. The majority of the people of Kimberley are happily made of sterner stuff, and do not look for luxuries in a time of siege."

With characteristic concern, Rhodes had collected together the ingredients to make 40 Christmas puddings and distributed them to the camps. The good cheer at this time found expression in the messages that were interchanged between camps. From the Mounted Camp to the Royal Artillery came the message: "Best wishes and longer range to your guns." From the artillery came the response: "May our range be always long enough for us to be guardian-angels to the Mounted Corps."

In December a committee was formed at the suggestion of Rhodes and presided over by the Mayor with the objective of providing relief to the dependents of those killed and wounded during the siege. De Beers donated £10,000 to the public fund that was established. A separate fund was also started to provide a monument[29] and lasting tribute to those who had died.

---

[28] Siege of Paris took place 1870-71.
[29] See page 377 for information on the Honoured Dead Memorial.

January 1900

Communication improvements

Signalling at this time was only possible by searchlight at night. The process was slow because the shutters on the searchlight at Premier Mine redoubt were difficult to operate and this was not helped by the short summer nights. Kekewich suggested to Methuen that they should try signalling by heliograph. Methuen agreed and so a station was set up in the conning tower. It took a while for communication to be established but on the morning of 12th January, contact was established with Methuen's men at Enslin (42 miles, 67 km away). The Boers themselves were able to read the messages except when they were encoded and to counter the process, they lit fires in the hope that the smoke they released would disrupt the communication. They even sent their own messages into Kimberley and many of these threatened, teased or amused the inhabitants such as, "How are you off for whisky?" and "We are coming into Kimberley tomorrow, which is the best hotel for us to stay at?"

Heliograph communication with Kimberley

The look-out station at Premier Mine, the garrison's most southerly point. The searchlight was added on 9th October 1899

The Premier Mine searchlight

Boers and their tactics

The number of Boers estimated to have remained at Kimberley is between 4,000 and 5,000 following the departure of De la Rey who went south to oppose Methuen's advance taking 1,500 men with him and the sending of more Boers to bolster the defences of Magersfontein. The remaining besieging commandos were further spaced out around the town. The area clockwise from Dronfield to Wimbledon was held by Free Staters from the Boshof, Hoopstad, Winburg, Jacobsdal, and Bloemfontein commandos. The Transvaal commandos came from Lichtenburg and Wolmarandsstad and were commanded by Commandant Du Toit. There was a small detachment of Griqualand rebels under Van Aswegen on Dronfield Ridge. The main Boer laager was located at Olifantsfontein. In accordance with Free State custom there was a vote at the end of the year to elect the position of Head Commandant. At this vote, Wessels was succeeded by Ferreira (who later was to meet his death at Paardeberg).

In January, the Boers strengthened their defences on Dronfield Ridge and moved against Webster's Farm to the northeast of the town and on 9th January they reoccupied Carter's Ridge which had been abandoned since the attack on 28th November. On 10th January, the Boers increased their rate of shelling and this signalled a more active approach from them. Unbeknown to the defenders, plans were being made for a much larger gun to be sent to Kimberley. The besiegers, having made a request to Pretoria, were to be sent the 155 mm Long Tom[30] that had been blown up by the British at Gun Hill near Ladysmith and since repaired in Pretoria.

---

[30] See the appendix on Long Tom on page 533.

January 1900

Two photographs that typify those taken of the Boers

Long Tom would arrive on site in February and Colonel de Villebois-Mareuil records the preparations as these excerpts from his *War Diary* show:

> "January 25.—We left early for Kimberley, after saluting the general. Our business was to make a tour of the besieged town, and find a position sufficiently near to mount a Long Tom and utilise its startling effects against a town we knew was at its last extremity. The Kaffirs, whom the English drive away under pain of being shot, state that the women and children are sometimes trampled under foot during the distribution of rations. They still have flour and Indian-corn; but everything else is lacking, or about to give out.
>
> January 27.—Yesterday and the previous day we visited the environs of Kimberley and the inconceivably extensive Boer positions. Arriving by way of Alexandersfontein, where there is a mountain-piece at an illusory distance, we reached Olifantsfontein, where at a farm belonging to the De Beers Company, outside the circle of investment, General Ferreira has his headquarters. The next day we crossed the Plain of Kimberley, in full view of the town, and noticed with interest only one height, south-east of Dronfield Station, whence could be obtained a very fine view, but which was at too great a distance (9800 yards) from the town.
>
> It was only when we reached the Kampfersdam Mine, where one of our guns, in view of its size, was useless, that we found the ideal position. It is a question of making a platform there, all the easier consolidated as the ground is artificial. Opposite, at 1900 yards, is a rideau supporting an English fort, which could be captured after a few shots. From that place we could rake the town from end to end, and particularly the rich quarter; where every shot would tell. The Boers, of course, would have to support the forward movement by occupying the positions as they were captured. But their work would really be greatly facilitated by the 155 at Kampfersdam which would commence to silence the nearest of the English works, that of Ottoskopje Mine."

De Villebois-Mareuil's plan to attack Kimberley was never carried through.

The Boers firing into Kimberley

Delay to the relief

The arrival of Roberts in Cape Town on 10th January as supreme commander led to a reassessment of the importance of relieving Kimberley. In a telegram to Methuen of 11th January, Roberts acknowledged the increasing difficulty in effecting the relief and expressed his opposition to him incurring even more losses. He said:

> "I agree with what you urge as to the undesirability of your retiring, and I much wish that it was in your power to relieve Kimberley. This has evidently become a far more difficult task than was anticipated, and even if it were possible to send you further reinforcements, I doubt if the enemy's extraordinary strong position (as explained to me by General Marshall) could be forced without a lamentable loss of life.
>
> Under these circumstances, I have come to the conclusion that I must ask you to act strictly on the defensive, and as it may be even necessary for me to withdraw a portion of your force, you should consider how your line of entrenchments could be sufficiently reduced to enable you to hold the

January 1900

position with two instead of three brigades, and possibly with one or two batteries and one regiment of Cavalry less than you have at present. Your request for four of the siege 4.7-inch guns will be complied with, and when these reach you, you will doubtless be able to make your position practically impregnable.

That the relief of Kimberley cannot be immediately effected, I am as sorry for, as I am sure you must be, but I trust that it will still be possible for you to give the brave garrison of that place a helping hand before they run short of supplies and ammunition. Please treat the subject of this letter as strictly confidential, and let me know what arrangements you propose to make in order to carry out these instructions."

To Kekewich, Roberts still talked about the impending relief as this telegram from 31st January shows:

"I fully appreciate the very natural feeling of apprehension felt by leading merchants of Kimberley as represented by you. The resolution shown by all classes under very trying circumstances in bearing so long and so patiently the privations of the siege has evoked the admiration and respect of all Her Majesty's subjects. You can assure the inhabitants of Kimberley from me that they are not being forgotten, and that with God's help all will be well ere long."

Long Cecil

The garrison's 7-pounder guns were no match for the larger ordnance that was ranged against Kimberley. While the garrison's guns were used in the early offensive actions, they were ineffectual against the guns that daily shelled the town. Towards the end of December, Mr Labram suggested that he should attempt to make a gun in the De Beers workshops. His suggestion was eagerly accepted and work started immediately. By 19th January, the workmen had completed their task and produced, by ingenuity and solely with available materials, a 28-pound breach-loading gun. They named it 'Long Cecil' in honour of Mr Rhodes. The manufacture of Long Cecil[31] was a remarkable achievement. It was designed and manufactured by a group of engineers who had no previous knowledge of ordnance, built with only the tools and machinery that was available to them in the De Beers workshops and was based on a design they enhanced from some basic plans discovered in the journal, *The Engineer*. From initiation to firing its first shell took just 24 days. It was handed over to the Diamond Fields Artillery and on the 21st January it fired its first shot against the Boers. Long Cecil was based near No 2 searchlight redoubt on a specially designed platform. It was in service throughout the siege and fired a total of 225 shells which were also produced in the De Beers workshop.

Long Cecil compared to a
7-pounder

Cecil Rhodes watching the
firing of Long Cecil

The lethargy which had characterised the Boer's approach to the siege was shaken off on 24th January perhaps because of the potential offered by Long Cecil or because of the rumour circulating that Lord Roberts was intent on relieving the town. Ashe reported how "On the morning of Wednesday (the 24th) the Boers began to shell us again quite early in the morning, and we soon found that it was quite different from the shelling we had had before. The shells came from all sides, and, as we found out later, at least 8 guns were at work. None of them were bigger than they used before, but they were either better guns or better worked and had better ammunition, for they reached every part of the town, except one small area near the De Beers mine." Some 300 shells were fired into Kimberley during the day. The casualties were thankfully few but they did include Maggie Maddocks, a young girl who was killed in Scholtz Street. The bombardment continued on the next day but the intensity was much reduced and for a few days afterwards there was a lull.

---

[31] See page 529 for more information on Long Cecil.

Supplies

The military authorities took increasing control over food supplies as it became evident that they would have to make stocks last longer.

The arrangements for milk were made by a special civil committee that consisted of Mr Oliver, the new Mayor, Mr Judge and four surgeons from the Kimberley Hospital, Doctors Ashe, Watkins, Mackenzie and Stoney.

In black areas, the Supply Committee established its own stores and sold supplies directly.

On 2nd January, the meat ration for adults was reduced to ¼ lb (115 g) for adults and 2 oz (60 g) for children under twelve. On 3rd January, the Supply Committee further extended its remit by incorporating the slaughter and retail of meat to prevent profiteering. Meat was henceforth distributed from the Market Hall.

On 8th January, horse flesh was included in the ration for the first time. In the remaining 7 weeks of the siege, some 600 horses were slaughtered for food. There is a story that Colonel Peakman was tasked with introducing horse flesh to the officers' mess of the Kimberley Light Horse. At the dinner he said "Gentlemen, as I was unable to get the whole of our ration in beef, a part of it had to be taken in horseflesh. Here is the beef," He carved the joint before him. "At the other end of the table is the horse. Any one who prefers it may help himself." There were no takers for the other joint. After a short pause, Peakman said "By Jove, I'm mistaken, of course *this* joint is the horse, the other is the beef!"

In addition to horse, donkey also became part of the menu from around 4th February. Ashe reported a feline addition to the menu "A few days ago my driver told me that a Chinaman had been offering Mackenzie's driver a good price for cats, which he wanted to eat— five shillings and sixpence for small ones and twelve-and-six for large ones. We have not come to that yet, but the Chinese are fond of cats at all times."

A soup kitchen was also established on the initiative of Captain Tyson with soup being issued in lieu of the meat ration. Even Rhodes contributed to this by donating vegetables from his gardens. Tyson was aided in his work by Mr Henderson and Dr Smartt. The soup kitchen was very successful with reports estimating as many as 16,000 pints (9,120 litres) were issued in a day.

Cecil Rhodes and Tim Tyson at the soup kitchen at the De Beers' Convict Station

January 1900

Creswicke reports how the Boers taunted the hungry inhabitants:

> "The Dutchmen were exceedingly ingenious in the invention of tricks and traps. One of these was to move a waggon with sixteen fat oxen in charge of but two men into the open Vlei (pond or small lake) below Taran-taal Ridge, and there to leave it, apparently unguarded, for two hours. They thought that this bait would lure forth the cattle-guard, but they were disappointed, for the authorities were too acute to allow them to get 'a bite.' They knew that in rear of the Vlei was a deep sand-drift, behind which a large body of men might be comfortably concealed and consequently left wagon and cattle severely alone."

The Boers continued their cattle-rustling tactics and tried continually to drive off what cattle they could to worsen the food situation. On 29th January, about 100 Boers rushed a man called Sheppey and a dozen mounted blacks who were tending a herd of around 1,000 cattle belonging to De Beers. The cattle drivers opened fire and were able to make their escape. The cattle minders required a guard of some 150 mounted men on a daily basis and this proved a continual drain on the available manpower.

Vegetables became increasingly scarce as the siege dragged on. To alleviate the problem, Kekewich suggested that the runners should be asked to bring in seeds when they returned to Kimberley. Using these and the other seeds available, a limited gardening programme was started but it had no impact on supplies and vegetables remained a siege luxury.

The figure for the Kimberley population drawing rations on 24th January gave the total as 56,764[32], the highest estimate of the siege population. Kekewich noted this figure with some scepticism when he wrote "some of these are doubtless drawing in two places and I hope to be able to stop this."

By 29th January, the rations were as follows[33]:

Food type	European & Coloured	Asian	Blacks
Boer meal & Flour or Bread	6 oz & 2 oz, 10½ oz	6 oz & 2 oz, 10½ oz	
Mealie meal	2 oz	-	5 oz
Kaffir corn	-	-	4 oz
Rice	-	1 oz	-
Samp	1 oz		1 oz
Sugar	2 oz	2 oz	2 oz
Coffee or tea	½ oz, ½ oz	½ oz, ¼ oz	½ oz, ¼ oz

Based on these rations, Kekewich sent a message to Methuen on 30th January giving the end of February as the date "to which food and forage will last." A few days later the supply of coal and wood was estimated to run out.

Sickness within Kimberley

The conditions of the siege and the reducing rations had an effect on the siege population and the incidence of sickness rose sharply at the end of January. Enteric and dysentery were particular problems. The worst problems were caused by scurvy which was a direct result of the poor diet. Milk was also in short supply and this led to many infant deaths. The mortality rate amongst white children was 671 per 1000 and 912 per 1000 for native children. At the suggestion of Mr E A Judge, the Civil Commissioner, and a committee of doctors, all the available milk was collected and issued to children and invalids upon production of a medical certificate.

---

[32] Defence force 4,500, Europeans and Coloured 28,468, Asians 1,520, Blacks 22,276. A later survey (3rd February 1900) revised this figure down to 46,371.

[33] Units are given as Imperial weights. For conversion, 1 oz = 28 g.

February 1900

Boers intensify the siege

The Boer Long Tom arrived on 6th February and was accompanied by M Leon, Creusot's representative, who had already visited the potential sites for the gun around Kimberley with De Villebois-Mareuil. The gun was mounted on an emplacement on top of a tailing heap at Kamfersdam.

A view of Kamfersdam

The Long Tom outranged Long Cecil and marked a dramatic escalation in the conflict. It fired its first shell into Kimberley around 11:00 on 7th February. Its targets were already well known, as O'Meara says:

> "When Bloemfontein was occupied some weeks later, a large-scale map of Kimberley was found at the Raadzaal; thereon were prominently marked all the buildings of importance, such as the military Headquarters in Lennox Street, the Kimberley Club, the Town Hall, the Hospital and several other premises of similar importance. A note on the map indicated that it was used at Kamfersdam for the purpose of laying "Long Tom" indirectly on the various targets fired at on the Diamond Fields."

Colonel de Villebois-Mareuil's outline plan of the storming of Kimberley was hatched at the end of January. As a prelude to this proposed attack by the Boers, Long Tom did begin shelling Otto's Kopje. It was de Villebois-Mareuil's plan to seize Otto's Kopje and to use this as a spring board into Kimberley. On the first day, he found the gunners had stopped firing due to the unevenness of the firing platform. The gunners also liked a sleep in the afternoon. On the basis of this and a number of other excuses, the attack was delayed and the potential offered to the Boers by Long Tom did not materialise.

Kekewich's response was that he was not going to allow the bombardment of Kimberley to go unanswered. Long Cecil was directed against Long Tom and was able to send the Boer gunners from the platform on a few occasions and once wounded 7 men. Trenches were advanced towards Kamfersdam so that the gun layers could be attacked with rifle fire from a distance of 1,800 yards (1,650 m). These picked marksmen were drawn from the various units and were exposed occasionally to shell fire from the very gun they targeted. They returned to their duty each day until the siege ended and enjoyed a degree of success. On 12th February, Leon was hit by a bullet fired from the trenches. The bullet passed through his eye and brain but

February 1900

miraculously he survived. The snipers would take their positions before day break and remain in their trenches until they could return safely to Kimberley under the cover of darkness.

The position from which Long Tom fired on Kimberley

A view of Long Tom's firing position when Kamfersdam had been vacated by the Boers

Kimberley Siege Account and Medal Roll

The bombardment of Kimberley cause considerable disruption to life in the town and this continued until the relief. Ashe expressed the feeling of concern felt by all residents at the size of this new gun and its shells, "This infernal shell was eighteen and a half inches long and six inches in diameter at the base, and weighed eighty-seven pounds. We found later that the shells were not very accurately made, many of them being twenty inches long and weighing over one hundred pounds. As you can imagine, the sight of this shell did not encourage us, for we knew that a gun big enough to carry this shell could reach any part of Kimberley or Beaconsfield, so that there was no possibility of getting out of its range, and we also saw that there was no building in Kimberley, except perhaps the strong-rooms at the banks, that could not be penetrated easily by it."

The destruction caused by a 100 lb shell on the workshop of John Orr & Co

Just as in Ladysmith, precautions were taken to warn the inhabitants of in-coming ordnance and the scheme in Kimberley was established on 8th February. A look-out was posted and a whistle blown whenever the smoke was seen from the muzzle of the Boer guns. A correspondent in the *Daily Telegraph* described the effect produced by the firing of Long Tom:

> "The shock caused by the firing of this gun was distinctly perceptible five feet under-ground at a distance of five miles, and the miniature earthquake thus created was clearly registered by the new seismograph at Kenilworth, the pendulum of which remained perfectly stationary during the firing of the smaller guns, or the passage of the most heavily laden trains or vehicles at very close quarters."

Each time the Boers fired the 100 pound shells, a bugle was sounded from the conning tower and everyone who was in hearing distance ran for cover. There was usually 15 seconds between bugle and impact. The size of Kimberley and the fact that Long Tom could hit any part of the city meant that a variety of warning signals were improvised. Ashe said "At the Sanatorium there was a look-out station on the roof, from which the puff of smoke could be seen, and the look-out there banged on the dinner-gong for all he was worth directly he saw it. I thought Rhodes was having plenty of meals when I heard the gong going so often, until I found out that it was a shell signal. At another place the look-out hammered one iron bar on another which was hung up by the end. This is a cheap sort of bell which is common in this country, and can be heard a long way. From many places people could see the red flag wave, though they did not hear the alarms. In front of the Town Hall a policeman was stationed in an auctioneer's pulpit to blow his whistle when he saw it."

February 1900

There was often a 7 minute interval between shells but this was not a predictable gap and a bombardment typically lasted for about two hours. The 9th February was one of the worst days for shelling which started about 06:00 and continued until dusk.

The death of George Labram

One of the last victims of Long Tom was George Labram himself who was killed by the last shot of the day on the 9th February while changing for dinner in the Grand Hotel, at the corner of the Market Square. His genius and creativity in producing Long Cecil was one reason why the Long Tom had been introduced.

Labram's bedroom at the Grand Hotel

His funeral was forced to take place at night as one attendee recounts:

> "As it was unsafe to hold a funeral by day, Mr Labram's remains were interred at 8 o'clock in the evening with the full military honours due to the man who had, in so many ways, rendered services which will be imperishably associated with the defence of Kimberley. A vast crowd assembled outside the hospital gates to watch the sad procession leave on its melancholy errand. The night was black and still, in keeping, as it seemed, with the solemnity of the occasion. Punctually on the stroke of eight the dead hero's remains were borne along through the hospital grounds into the street, the Union Jack wrapped around them. No one who witnessed it will ever forget the weird, impressive scene, unparalleled under the Southern Cross, and in some respects unlike anything that one has read of in the annals of war. The soldiers in two lines saluting the gun carriage as it passed out, the compact mass of regulars, volunteers, and citizen soldiers with arms reversed waiting to follow it, the immense concourse of private citizens, on horseback, in carriages, and on foot, stretching behind, the darkness of the night and the genuine look of seriousness imprinted on every face—these things made up a picture tinged with a melancholy which no mere words can express. Then followed a strange, uncanny thing. The clock struck the hour. As the last sound died away the warning note of the bugle rang out from the Conning Tower, then, after a few seconds of anxious suspense, came the boom of the Boer big gun, and a screeching sound in the air telling that one of the enemy's mammoth projectiles had been launched on its errand of destruction. All were taken by surprise. Here and there men threw themselves down on their faces and lay trembling on the ground. The whole

procession wavered. But they were Englishmen and not a sound or exclamation escaped their lips, save a sigh of relief as the shell passed over the heads of the mourners and exploded harmlessly in some adjoining thoroughfare. Then, as though nothing had happened, the bandmaster gave the signal, the band began the opening bars of Beethoven's "Funeral March," and with slow and measured steps the cortege moved onwards on its hazardous mission. Slow and seemingly interminable was that journey to the cemetery. It may have been pure accident, but treason seemed lurking in the very air. Shell after shell rained in upon the town. Even as the mourners gathered round the graveside and listened with bowed heads to the last words of splendid consolation the unnerving tumult went on."

Friction and opposition

The dissatisfaction felt by de Villebois-Mareuil over the ineffectiveness of Long Tom was not shared by the people on the receiving end of its attention. The loss of life caused within the town was not great but the effect of morale was most marked and a large measure of panic was generated. On 8th February Kekewich reported the situation as serious, "having regard to the population and the class of troops defending the town". Roberts responded with instructions to "reassure the inhabitants, many days cannot now elapse before your long-looked-for relief will be effected."

On 9th February, Rhodes informed Kekewich that he would call a public meeting in two day's time to discuss the situation if he was not given the full details of the plans for relief. Rhodes also pressured the Mayor to summon the meeting. Kekewich expressed to Roberts his fears that it would be "very difficult to resist the pressure of a large section of the public many more days, and said he feared he would be unable to stop Rhodes and his planned public meeting.

On 10th February, the *Diamond Fields Advertiser* published an article entitled 'Why Kimberley cannot wait'[34] in which the military authorities were denounced for undervaluing the town and its importance. The article was neither incorrect nor threatening to Kimberley but it was not acceptable to the military authorities.

On the same day, Rhodes, the Mayor and other citizens waited on Kekewich at 14:30 to deliver to him a message that was addressed to Lord Roberts. The message read:

> "Kimberley, February 10th. On behalf of the inhabitants of this town, we respectfully desire to be informed whether there is an intention on your part to make an immediate effort for our relief. Your troops have been for more than two months within a distance of little over twenty miles from Kimberley, and if the Spytfontein hills are too strong for them, there is an easy approach over a level flat. This town, with a population of over 45,000 people, has been besieged for 120 days, and a large portion of the inhabitants has been enduring great hardships; Scurvy is rampant among the natives; children, owing to lack of proper food, are dying in great numbers, and dysentery and typhoid are very prevalent. The chief food of the whites have been bread and horse-flesh for a long time past, and of the blacks meal and malt only. These hardships, we think you will agree, have been borne patiently and without complaint by the people. During the last few days the enemy have brought into action from a position within three miles of us a 6-inch gun throwing a 100-lb. shell, which is setting fire to our buildings and is daily causing death among the population. As you are aware, the military guns here are totally inadequate to cope with this new gun. The only weapon which gives any help is one of local manufacture. Under these circumstances, as representing this community, we feel that we are justified in asking whether you have any immediate intention of instructing your troops to advance to our relief. We understand large reinforcements have recently arrived in Cape Town, and we feel sure that your men at Modder River have at the outside 10,000 Boers opposed to them. You must be the judge as to what number of British troops would be required to deal with this body of men, but it is absolutely necessary that relief should be afforded to this place."

Kekewich told Rhodes that he would need to encode the message to stop the Boers from reading it. The length of the full message would take some time to code and send so he undertook to send a précis to Lord Roberts as soon as he could. Rhodes took this to mean the message would not be sent and flew into a rage. He ranted at Kekewich ""I know what damned rot your signallers are wasting their time in signalling. You low, damned, mean cur, Kekewich, you deny me at your peril" before storming out of the office. In spite of this threatening behaviour towards Kekewich, a précis was flashed to Roberts:

> "FM's of 9th Feb. and C85 this date communicated three leading citizens and I trust will have excellent effect. Mayor, Rhodes and nine other leading citizens held private meeting to-day before F. M.'s two messages received. Rhodes and Mayor called at my office this afternoon presenting lengthy

---

[34] The full text of this article can be seen on page 540.

document for communication by flash to you. Summary as follows: first, answer required whether immediate effort being made to relieve Kimberley; second, duration siege, shortness proper food, hardship endured, disease prevalent strongly represented; third, consternation destruction life and property caused by enemy's siege gun pointed out; fourth, their views military situation stated."

Rhodes' objective in sending the message was to raise awareness of the plight of the town and to agitate for its relief. Roberts held a contrary view and believed that Rhodes meant to oppose military rule in Kimberley by calling the public meeting. Roberts sensed a tone or an implied threat of impending surrender. He sent a forceful reply to Kekewich:

"I beg you will represent to the Mayor and Mr. Rhodes, as strongly as you possibly can, the disastrous and humiliating effect of surrendering after so prolonged and glorious a defence. Many days cannot possibly pass before Kimberley will be relieved, as we commence active operations to-morrow. Our future military operations depend in a large degree on your maintaining your position a very short time longer, and our prestige would suffer severely if Kimberley were to fall into the hands of the enemy; those, therefore, who counsel surrender should carefully consider the very serious responsibility they incur from a national point of view."

Kekewich passed on this information to Rhodes and informed Roberts that he expected it to have an "excellent effect". Indeed it did. News of the relief was just the information Rhodes wanted to hear. He wanted to send another reply to Roberts but Kekewich again refused. It is not difficult to understand why. The message read:

"There is no fear of our surrendering, but we are getting very anxious about the state of the British Army. It is high time you did something."

Rhodes amended the text and the following message was then transmitted:

"Thanks for your message. We have never thought or spoken of surrendering, but the endless delay of your predecessor led us to believe that no efforts were being made for our relief and by force of circumstances this community would have been crushed. I thought it right to send you the situation from the principal citizens."

In a separate message from Roberts to Kekewich, Roberts encouraged Kekewich to use the full extent of his powers to stop the meeting and even arrest Rhodes if necessary. He said:

"As I understand Kimberley is under martial law you have full power to prohibit, by force if necessary, any public meeting you consider undesirable under present circumstances, and also to arrest any individual, no matter what his position may be, who may act in a manner prejudicial to national interests. I desire you to exercise to the full, if necessary, your powers as defined above; you will have my fullest support in so doing. You can assure all who are now apprehensive that we shall strain every nerve to relieve you, which will, I hope, be in a few days' time."

Kekewich and his staff used their powers to prohibit the *Diamond Fields Advertiser* from publishing any more articles along the lines of 'Why Kimberley cannot wait.". The letter was signed by the Press Censor, O'Meara:

"Army Headquarters, Kimberley, February 10, 1900.
Sir,

Since the *Diamond Fields Advertiser* has now on two occasions printed leading articles on the military situation which are extremely injurious to the interests of the army and the defence of this town, without previously submitting the same to the military censor, I am directed to inform you that from this date the proof of the *Diamond Fields Advertiser* must be submitted to me before the copies of any daily number, leaflet, or other form of publication is issued to the public.

I am further requested to inform you, in your own interests, that on the two occasions referred to you have committed the most serious offences dealt with by the Army Act, under which Act you are liable to be tried.

Yours faithfully, W. A. O'Meara, Major, Military Censor"

Kimberley Siege Account and Medal Roll

The editor was unwilling to abide by the new process of editorial censorship and he had no plans to limit or curtail the content of his newspaper. As a result, the *Diamond Fields Advertiser* went into voluntary and temporarily suspension until it reappeared on 16th February.

The 10th February had been an extremely difficult day for Kekewich. He felt the need to put his side of the story before Roberts and explain again the position in which he found himself. In his telegram he said:

> "Rhodes during siege has done excellent work; and also, when his views on military questions have coincided with mine, he has readily assisted me, but he desires to control the military situation. I have refused to be dictated to by him. On such occasions, he has been grossly insulting to me, and in his remarks on the British Army. More can be explained when we meet. I have put up with insults so as not to risk the safety of the defence: the key to the military situation here in one sense is Rhodes, for a large majority of the Town Guardsmen, Kimberley Light Horse, and Volunteers are De Beers' employes.
>
> I fully realize the powers conferred on me by the existence of Martial Law, but have not sufficient military force to compel obedience. Conflict between the few Imperial troops here and the local levies has been, and must continue to be, avoided at all costs."

It was a thoughtful message and expressed this unenviable position. The continuing confrontations with Rhodes were only part of his problems. Kekewich also had the effects of Long Tom to deal with.

The need for shelter

The activity of Long Tom was having such an effect that something had to be done to assuage the panic generated by the shelling. Some citizens were able to create barricades in their own homes but, for the majority, there was no readily available shelter.

Some citizens thought Beaconsfield a safer place to be and moved there. Others went to the debris heaps on Boshof Road and some found safety under De Beers Bridge.

There was great activity to build new shelters as Ashe related:

> "All this day, besides the work on private shelters, big public shelters were being made wherever there were convenient places. These were made by the De Beers Company's boys and the natives who were working on the roads for the Relief Committee, about which I will tell you later on. Most of the shelters were made in the sides of the debris heaps, which are almost all over the town. A deep trench was cut in the sloping side of the heaps, and then this was lined and roofed with timber and galvanized iron, and a thick layer of earth was thrown on to the top and banked up against the front face of the shelter. Several of these shelters were many yards long and had several openings, so that people could get in and out easily. In Beaconsfield, on one side of the main road, there was a big heap with an almost perpendicular face, and here they just drove tunnels straight into the heap. It looked very funny from the road to see these catacombs. The big bridge which carried the road over the railway near the station was made into a shelter by leaning timbers against the sides of it, putting steel plates next them, and then banking up with sandbags and loose earth. Many people who lived near the station took refuge under trenches in the big station building, and in the engine-sheds, in the ashpits, and under the engines, of which we had a dozen or more in Kimberley.
>
> … everywhere you went, forts were being built, and the clang of sheet steel, railway rails, old iron railway sleepers, etc., etc., was heard all over the place. The streets were full of carts and handcarts and wheelbarrows, and even natives carrying materials for forts. Many people could not get boys, as the demand was so great for labour, and so they had to do the work themselves.
>
> Several of the merchants had large stocks of the coarse Boer salt, which is got by crystallisation from the salt pans, and they made forts of this. It is packed in large sacks, and answered splendidly. In the first bombardment, I had seen at a baker's a fort made entirely of sacks of flour. It was very good, but all the same, I was just as pleased I did not deal with that particular baker. But the gem of the collection in the way of forts was one I saw in the Malay camp. It belonged to a coolie, and he had a large dog in a kennel. He evicted the dog and banked up the kennel with old zinc baths and paraffin tins filled with earth, and I have no doubt was a little king in that yard, as nobody else had a fort at all there."

February 1900

'Shrapnel Hotel'

A shelter built in Kenilworth

Kimberley Siege Account and Medal Roll

A barricaded home

The so-called 'dug-outs' in which people sought shelter on Tyburn Street

February 1900

'Dug-outs' in Beaconsfield

A shelter built by De Beers

Kimberley Siege Account and Medal Roll

On Sunday, 11th February, there was the usual break in the shelling for 24 hours. Rhodes made a request to the general manager of De Beers, Mr Gardner Williams, to prepare the mines for any civilians who wished to shelter within them. Rhodes did not discuss this plan with Kekewich and many citizens, thinking Rhodes had private information on what was going to happen on the Monday, took great alarm at the appearance of the notices which read:

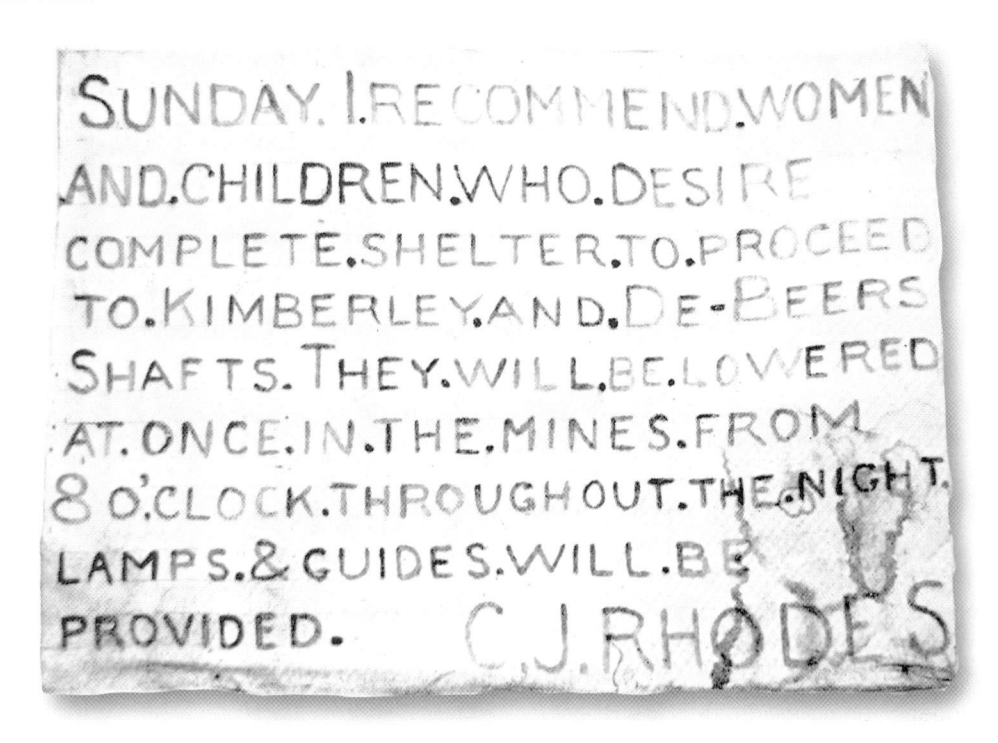

> Sunday, I recommend women and children who desire complete shelter to proceed to Kimberley and De Beers shafts, they will be lowered at once into the mines from 8 o'clock throughout the night. Lamps & guides will be provided — C J Rhodes

It was one of the few places that did offer complete shelter. Some 2,500 to 3,000 women and children (and a few men) took advantage of the offer. They were lowered to varying depths below the surface and some remained there in safety until Kimberley was relieved[35]. It was a slow process as the cage capacity was 6 people at a time but also because the urgency of the situation meant that the people were loaded first and then their belongings were sent after them. How people and belongings were re-united underground is not recorded.

One person who ventured down into the mine recorded her impressions:

> "We went down the mine, but only stayed one day. Of course, one felt safe, but it was so miserable; still, it was another siege experience, the crowds of people down there. On the 1000-feet level were 500 persons alone, and the buzz of tongues, and the children crying, and the noises altogether, besides the damp, were horrible; although Mr. Rhodes and those working under him did all in their power to make things as comfortable as possible. Hot coffee, soup, bread, milk for the children, everything obtainable was sent down; and some thousands of people were fed free of charge from the Saturday night till the following Friday morning."

---

[35] Creswicke's account of the opening of the mines to the public makes for interesting reading: "By the kindness of Mr. Rhodes the mines now became harbours of refuge for thousands of women and children, who, huddled together in the 1200-feet level, were thus protected from the shells which were launched in the midst of the town. Those days in dark diamondiferous caverns were full of strange experiences. There, over a thousand shrinking beings found asylum, bedding, food, and such comfort as could be secured for them. There, babes were born into the world—human diamonds brought into the daylight from the grottoes of the millionaires—babes which surely should take some strange part in the drama of the century. It was an underground village swarming with the weak and the distressed, a feminine populace, kept from panic and despair by the man who, large enough to make empires, yet proved himself capable of sympathy with the small sorrows and quakings of the sick and the fearful."

February 1900

People queuing to be lowered down De Beers Mine

Those lodged underground were spared the Boer bombardment that resumed on Monday, 12th February but, for no apparent reason, the shelling was lighter and stopped before nightfall. The damage was light and mostly to property as was the case on the 13th February. According to the *Siege of Kimberley*:

> "One of the liveliest spots was the Conning Tower, where Col. Kekewich, Col. Chamier, Capt. MacInnes and Maj. O'Meara remained on duty, although the enemy made constant and persistent efforts to hit the structure. The shooting at times was remarkably close—much too close to be pleasant. Quite a number of shells fell in the mine just behind the tower, one in the engine house in front, and several within a very slight radius round. One of the gallant officers afterwards remarked that being potted at in this fashion with a 100-pounder gun was a curious sensation; he felt like a crow in a tree."

Shelling by the Long Tom and some of the 9-pounders continued on 14th February. While the shelling continued, careful note was being taken of the Boer positions. Observations of movements within the Boer camps suggested that Lord Roberts's planned advance had begun because the indications were the Boers were on the move. On 13th February, some wagons and mounted Boers had been seen heading eastward from Spytfontein.

The taking of Alexandersfontein

Alexandersfontein, the village situated some 3 miles (4.8 km) south of Beaconsfield, was an ideal location for the Boers. It was a strong position with stone houses, rocky kopjes and high ground around it. A relieving force coming from the south would have to pass it and thus the fact that it was held by the Boers posed a potential problem. Its importance had led to special instructions being given to Lieutenant Jones of the Beaconsfield Town Guard, who was in command at Davis's Heap, to count the number of Boers at Alexandersfontein on a daily basis.

At 05:00 on 14th February, Lieutenant Jones reported surprisingly that no Boers were visible. This fact was corroborated by some blacks who had passed into Kimberley that day. Major Fraser immediately ordered Alexandersfontein to be seized by the detachment of 25 men from Davis's Heap. Fraser reported his intentions and went to join the troops. The absence of Boers from some areas was no trap and enabled part of the village to be taken. However, while the Boers were indeed leaving, they had not left. Private J Adamson, Beaconsfield Town Guard, an Englishman who was fluent in Dutch delayed the Boers from realising what was happening and also managed to capture a number of prisoners. Fraser, seizing the opportunity presented to him, called for reinforcements and took four officers and 100 men from the Beaconsfield Town Guard. These extra men, along with five Cape Police, captured five Boer wagons.

Alexandersfontein

A little later, around 10:00, the force at Alexandersfontein was augmented by some mounted troops, two guns of the Diamond Fields Artillery and two companies of Lancashires under Captain O'Brien and Lieutenant Hewett respectively[36].

A fire fight ensued. The Boers took up their positions on two sides of the small force and tried to eject them from Alexandersfontein. Boer artillery fire was also directed onto them from guns located at Wimbledon Ridge and Susannah. The fight lasted that day and continued into the next and was only ended when the advancing relief column made the Boer position no longer tenable. Amongst the wounded was Major Rodger who was hit in the left forearm breaking one of his bones but he refused to seek medical attention for the injury. It was said of him that "he went on and finished his day's work, ... Mackenzie saw him and wanted to order him off duty, but Rodger flatly declined, and I don't expect he will appear on the sick list at all. The Regulars call our Kimberley forces 'tin soldiers', and are a little inclined to be superior with them, but if this is a sample, the tin breed is the one for us."

Casualties for 14th February 1900
Wounded (6): Major T Rodger, KRV; Colour Sergeant Major L Fyvie, KRV; Private H Henderson, KRV; Sergeant H Whale, KRV; Private A Winter, KRV, Trumpeter A Dickenson, DFA.
Boers: Killed (2). Wounded (1).

In leaving at such short notice, the Boers abandoned a large amount of stores. These included vegetables, butter, fowl, geese, pigs, horses, cattle, rifles and ammunition. It was a while since the besieged had seen sights like these! Ashe reported the view: "I met the procession as I was coming in to lunch. It was first-rate, and the people turned out delighted, hoping that this was the beginning of better things. First came about twenty horses, then about the same number of cattle, and then a big waggon with a water tank on it, and drawn by sixteen lovely bullocks, so fat that our mouths watered just from looking at them."

---

[36] The force consisted of 3 officers, 145 men and 1 Maxim of the LNLR, 2 officers and 50 men of the mounted troops, 1 section of the DFA with 2 guns, 2 officers and 25 men of the KVR and 4 officers and 100 men of the Beaconsfield Town Guard.

The relief

15th February – the day Kimberley was relieved

Long Tom fired a few shots into Kimberley between 10:30 and 11:00 and then abruptly stopped. The reason for the cessation was not immediately clear. Around 14:30, a large group of mounted men was seen to be advancing towards Dutoitspan from the southeast and it was confirmed by heliograph that these were in fact British troops. The news spread quickly and soon the streets, so recently deserted because of the fearful Long Tom, were filled with people and troops trying to catch a glimpse of the relieving force. From Alexandersfontein at about 15:00 Fraser reported seeing a heliograph 15 miles (24 km) southeast of Kimberley. By 16:00, Kekewich was in heliographic communication with French's column. French said that he was advancing on the town. Soon afterwards, a patrol of Australian Horse rode into Kimberley.

To Colonel Paterson, a retired Australian, went the honour of being the first man to enter Kimberley. He was soon followed by Mr Beresford, correspondent of the London *Daily Telegraph*, who went to the Sanatorium to brief Rhodes. Captain Gale, Royal Engineers, attached to Rimington's Guides, was next.

It would have been easy to focus on the relief but Kekewich was also mindful of the Boers who were making their exit to the north. He gathered all the men he could spare and sent them northwards under Murray in an attempt to prevent the departure of the Boer artillery. Long Tom was removed by the Boers on 15th February and, slow though its progress was, it escaped capture. Unable to carry them away, the Boers left behind about 200 shells for Long Tom and a large quantity of rifle ammunition.

At around 17:00, Kekewich rode out to meet General French but mis-calculated his route and missed him. Instead, French was met by the Mayor, Councillor Oliver, and Mr J Denoon Duncan. Oliver greeted French and said he planned a more formal welcome. French reached the town around 19:00, visited the Kimberley Club and then went to the Sanatorium to see Rhodes.

O'Meara was present when Kekewich caught up with French:

"As we approached the building we heard sounds of merriment and many voices in the hall, and a few minutes later we entered the hotel. Tables were laid in the hall, laden with all manner of luxuries, champagne was flowing freely, and to us, who had seen nothing but the meagre rations served daily at the Kimberley Club for many weeks past, this display of dainties came as a great surprise. Rhodes, was now entertaining French and his staff, who, we learnt, had been invited to stay at the hotel as his guests during their halt in Kimberley. Rhodes was in the hall when Kekewich arrived; the two men had not met since the stormy interview of the afternoon of 10th February, and Kekewich naturally wished to avoid any altercation, so he remained by the door by which he had entered. Fortunately, a staff officer came along and Kekewich went forward and told him that he wished to see General French. Rhodes observed this and, rushing forward, attempted to block the stairway, shouting; "You shan't see French; this is my house, get out of it." Kekewich took no notice of Rhodes' ill-mannered conduct, but accompanied the staff officer upstairs. It may here be stated that the Sanatorium Hotel was in no way a private house, nor was it Rhodes' personal property; it belonged to the De Beers Company, like most things in Kimberley.

French meeting Rhodes at the Sanatorium

Kimberley Siege Account and Medal Roll

Kekewich went into the room occupied by French and saw him alone; the interview was extremely short, and the former at once returned to the Kimberley Club. The conclusions, if any, the Cavalry Commander had then come to as to the conduct of Kekewich during the siege must have been founded alone on information derived from ex parte statements made by Rhodes. On the ride back to the Club Kekewich said little, but from that little it was not difficult to draw the inference that he had met with an icy reception."

Creswicke reported how "A man, hearing that General French had arrived, approached a trooper who was holding a horse outside the Club, and asked if the good news was true. 'Yes,' was the reply; 'I'm 'is orderly; this is 'is 'at, and over there is 'is 'orse!' And the Kimberly man stared at the three objects before him as though he could never take his fill of satisfaction."

The fight at Dronfield on 16th February

Kekewich knew that French meant to pursue the Boers on the next morning and he had been invited to join them. One of the De Beers directors had offered £1,000 to anyone who could capture Long Tom. Kekewich and French departed at 06:00 the next morning. French's force joined up with Murray's troops and attacked the Boers at Dronfield and inflicted many casualties through shrapnel fire. He also captured a 9-pounder field gun and this was taken as a souvenir by the Cape Police.

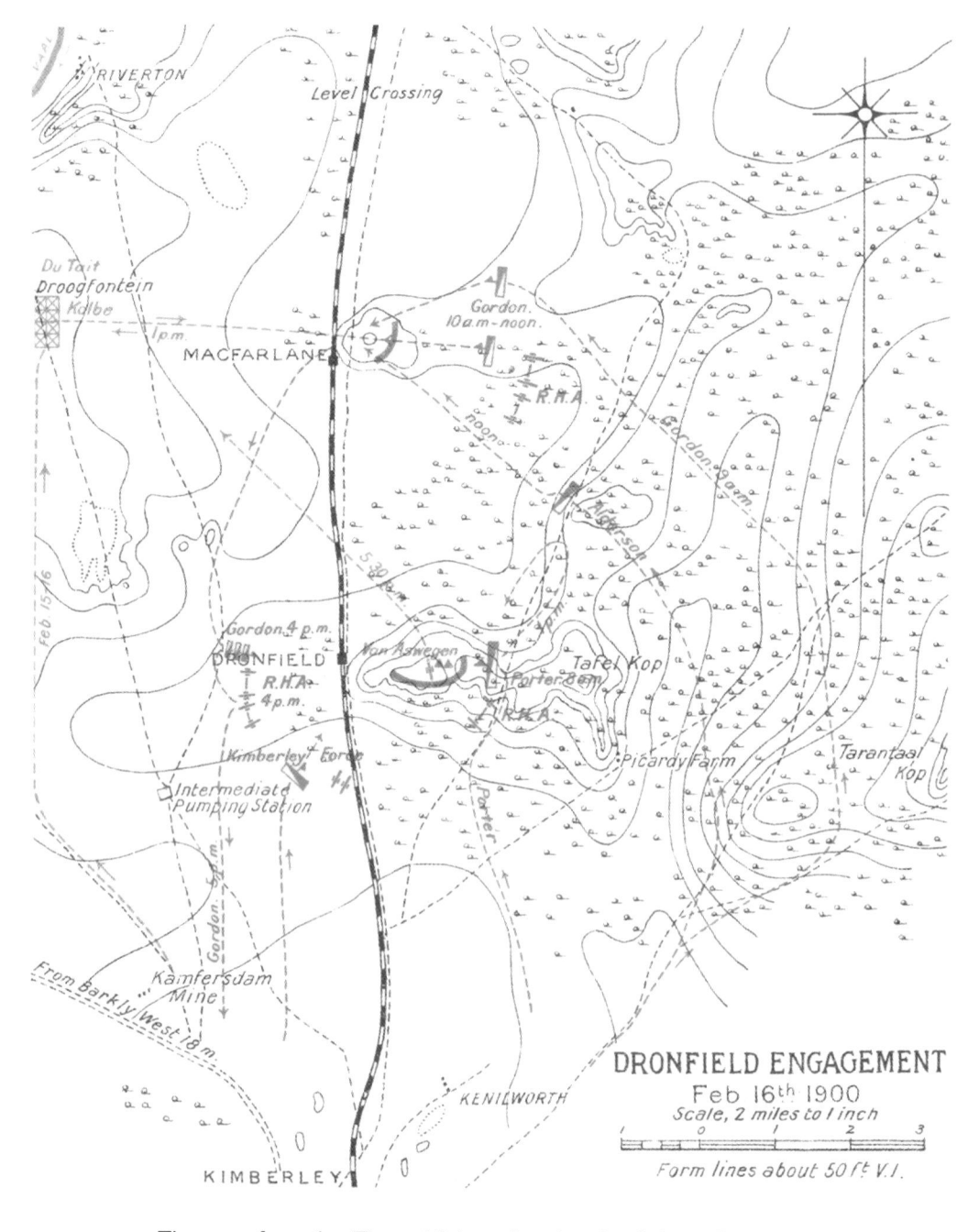

The map from the *Times History* showing the fight at Dronfield

O'Meara reported on the day:

> "When French's cavalry had joined in the fray, the battlefield extended from Dronfield to MacFarlane's Farm (some five miles apart). French now took up a position on the eastern edge of Dronfield Ridge and surveyed the field; we could see the Boers at MacFarlane's Farm retiring northward. An attack was now launched from the south and the east against the enemy at MacFarlane's; the Boers were driven out and were soon in full retreat. French rode on and when we reached a position some twelve miles north of Kimberley, we could distinctly see to the southward and westward of us a large scattered army of Boers making a desperate attempt to escape from the lance and the sword that had so unexpectedly made their appearance on the Diamond Fields. To the north of us, there lay an immense laager crowded with wagons; prisoners captured by the Australians stated that "Long Tom" was in that laager. But the efforts of the Cavalry Division to carry off this prize proved fruitless. A scorching sun was beating down on the veldt and no water was available for either man or beast. The horses were getting exhausted, and many lay down and died at once. French called off his troops late in the afternoon, and we started back on our return journey to Kimberley, the last four or five miles of which was a most distressing experience; we rode literally along a lane formed by the carcasses of mounts that had left Blankenberg Vlei in the early morning of this day. So far as the Cavalry Division was concerned, from the strategical point of view, the 16th was a wasted day."

Away from the fighting, the remaining elements of the besieging Boers slipped away that night. On the next day, Saturday 17th February, French left Kimberley for Paardeberg.

Kekewich is replaced

Kekewich was not aware of French's departure but this was not his only surprise that morning. When he arrived at his headquarters in Lennox Street he found Colonel Porter had been given command of Kimberley. The only explanation for this sudden change is that Rhodes must have talked French into replacing Kekewich. It reflects very badly on French that Kekewich's service in the defence should have ended in this way. Kekewich returned to command his regiment and it was not until 26th July 1901 that he was again given a position of responsibility with his appointment to command a mobile column and Kekewich believed that Rhodes continued to exert his influence to block his promotion until Rhodes died.

Appreciation for the relief

There was no opportunity to formally present the town's thanks to French. Instead, an address was sent by the Mayor. It read:

> "Sir—In the name of the inhabitants of Kimberley I extend to you, your staff, and the forces under you, a loyal and hearty welcome.
>
> As loyal subjects of the Queen we have, under the difficult and exceptional circumstances which have existed during the one hundred and twenty-four days of the siege, endeavoured at all times to faithfully carry out the orders of the Officer Commanding, and we are proud that with the assistance of a small military force of about five hundred men, we have, with our own citizen soldiers, been able to defend this town against the large force of the enemy and the superior artillery brought to bear against us, and thus assisted in maintaining British supremacy in South Africa.
>
> When it is remembered that we have a population of about 50,000 people, that our town is situated about 650 miles inland from Capetown, and that we have successfully held out for 18 weeks against the whole strength of the western portion of the Orange Free State forces and a large contingent from the Transvaal, it speaks well not only for the inhabitants, but also for the efficient defensive measures and the excellent organisation for regulating food supplies, &c, carried out under Col. Kekewich and his staff, of which we cannot speak too highly.
>
> A number of valuable lives have been lost, and our town has suffered severely from the heavy bombardment, but I think I gauge the courage and determination of the people of the Diamond Fields correctly when I say that they were prepared to suffer still greater privations and sacrifices, if necessary, in the fight for liberty, justice, and equal rights now being waged in this country; and that they would scorn the idea of surrender as long as foodstuffs lasted.
>
> Allow me, as representing the people of this town, again to express our deep sense of gratitude to you for the relief you brought us, and to congratulate you and your brave troops, among whom we are delighted to find brother-colonists from New South Wales, Queensland, and New Zealand, on your magnificent march to our relief—a march which we are sure will always be regarded as a brilliant military achievement.
>
> Signed on behalf of the inhabitants, H A Oliver, Mayor, Kimberley, February 15th, 1900."

Kimberley Siege Account and Medal Roll

A gathering of distinguished men

A celebration took place at the Town Hall on 1st March 1900. The attendees included Lord Roberts, Colonel Kekewich, the Mayor of Kimberley, Lord Kitchener, Lord Methuen, Cecil Rhodes, Sir Ellis Ashmead-Bartlett, Lord Loch and the Foreign Attaches of Lord Roberts' staff.

The reception for Lord Roberts

Roberts replied to the address by the Mayor by saying:

"I appreciate very highly the honour you have done me to-day, in inviting me to your Town Hall, to present me with the very complimentary address which has just been read by the Town Clerk. I can assure you that I feel very deeply the kind terms in which you have alluded to my services, but I can also assure you that any successes that may have been attained during the past 3 weeks in this portion of the theatre of war are due to the resolution, the endurance, and the courage of the magnificent body of troops which it is my pride and privilege to command.

I rejoice that I have found it possible to come here to-day to witness the scene of a defence which will ever be a memorable one, and to meet personally those whose heroism has preserved intact the honour of our flag in this distant land. In your speech, Sir, you alluded to the untiring efforts of the Right Hon. C. J. Rhodes during the siege, and the value of the services rendered by him to the inhabitants of this town. Watching, as we did, with anxious eyes the vicissitudes of the siege, it was a consolation to feel that Mr. Rhodes was in your midst, for we know that his untiring energy and remarkable personality would go far towards animating his fellow citizens in the arduous task before them. I also was glad to notice the high complimentary and appreciative terms in which you spoke of Lieut.-Colonel Kekewich, the gallant and distinguished Officer on whom has rested the responsibility of devising and carrying out the measures necessary for the defence of your town. This morning as I rode through the suburbs and saw the great length of the perimeter which had to be rendered secure against attack, it seemed to me almost impossible that the defence could have been maintained successfully or so long as has been the case. That you should have been able to do so is as creditable to Lieut.-Colonel Kekewich and to those who were immediately associated with him in carrying on the defence, as it is to the brave soldiers of the Imperial and Colonial Services and the many Volunteers who have so heroically borne the perils of the siege. I desire also to refer to the

The relief

patience and courage with which the women of this town have endured the horrors of the siege. Their heroism has won the respect and admiration of us all. I regret that my stay in Kimberley must necessarily, on this occasion, be a short one. Much remains to be done before the war is brought to a satisfactory conclusion, and peace, prosperity and freedom are restored throughout South Africa, but my visit here will ever be a memorable one to me, from the fact that shortly after I arrived here this morning, a telegram was put into my hands bearing the joyful news that Ladysmith had been relieved. I am confident that all whom I am addressing share my admiration for the glorious defence made by General Sir George White and his gallant force, and that you recognize as fully as I do the momentous results which have been achieved by the valour of the relieving force under General Sir Redvers Buller.

I will only add that I shall take the earliest opportunity of bringing to the notice of the Queen the loyal sentiments which you have expressed on behalf of your fellow citizens at the conclusion of your address. I will not detain you longer, but will only assure you, once more, how deeply I feel the kindness you have shown to me to-day."

The defence of Kimberley was certainly an event worthy of celebration and this mood was shared by many in the city.

Meyer recalled how, by Saturday 17th February, Kimberley was still in celebratory mood: "How different Kimberley looks since yesterday! On many houses British flags; De Beers rock shaft is decorated with flags from top to bottom; women and children, over 3,000, return to their homes, emerging from the mine shafts and, in their thousands, from the burrows and holes and shelters, from under the bridges and other places of safety, from West End and from Beaconsfield."

The aftermath

The privations of the siege were quickly removed. On 19th February, 60 cattle, 300 sheep and bags of flour arrived in Kimberley. The railway lines to Modder River were repaired and this allowed the first train for a while to steam into Kimberley station. Lord Methuen finally arrived in the city on 20th February and was able to report on 22nd February:

"Supply of food and forage are being pushed on as fast as possible, and that there will be coal enough, to start De Beers mines in 10 days. By this means great misery will be alleviated. Hospital arrangements reported perfect. There are 45 nurses, and wounded doing well."

By the end of the month, life had returned to normal. Meyer said "Kimberley's everyday life is as back to normal as before, people being, if anything, more arrogant than before. Railway, telegraph, telephone and postal services, shops, carts, wagons, auctions on the market and in front of private houses, even concerts, meetings etc." Martial Law continued to operate until early March.

The citizens of Kimberley did very well to keep the Boers at arm's length and to survive the siege, deprivation and bombardment. Part of the reason for this was because the mining industry in Kimberley had been built by people of exceptional character whose resolve and attitude was of great importance in sustaining the defence. The citizens, on whose shoulders the burden of protecting the town fell, did admirably well.

The town would not have survived if it had relied solely on the imperial troops sent there to protect it. The willingness of the local citizens to man the defences or to join a unit, the immense resources of De Beers that were so willingly given to support the defence (see page 553 for more details), the creation of Long Cecil and the talents of George Labram plus the all-encompassing energy of Rhodes were the most decisive factors in preventing the fall of Kimberley.

From the Boer perspective, it is remarkable that they did attempt a single assault on the town. They seemed content to wait out the siege and only towards the end did they intensify their activities. It is not likely that the defences could have withstood a determined, co-ordinated or concerted Boer attack and, given time, the bombardment by Long Tom would have produced a consequence; either the civilians would have forced a settlement or Kekewich would have been forced to destroy the gun.

The number of days of shelling by the Boers was:

November	December	January	February	Total
12	3	12	13	40

Kimberley Siege Account and Medal Roll

Estimates and reports vary about the number of shells fired over the 40 days. An approximate figure is 8,000. The number of injuries from artillery fire, including women and children, totalled 9 killed and 22 wounded. On more than 50% of the days when there was shelling (21 days), not a single person was hit. It was not the shelling that caused most damage but the effects of confinement. For the first month of the siege, the health of the town remained normal. From the middle of November onwards, sickness rapidly increased amongst the women and children and the blacks. The troops were proportionately less affected because of their outdoor lifestyle. The deaths from all causes, per month, were:

November	December	January	February	Total
133	302	585	607	1,627

This death rate was greater than the normal by a factor of three. The European death rate was 55 per 1000 in December and 45 per 1000 in January and the figures for blacks were 141 and 282 per 1000 for the same period. The mortality of children was as high as 671 per 1000 for Europeans, and 912 per 1000 for coloureds. There were 217 deaths from scurvy in January, principally among blacks with 850 cases being treated in early February. By the end of the siege, there had been 483 fatal cases from about 1,500 incidents of scurvy. Typhoid and dysentery were also very potent diseases that affected the town.

To conclude, it is fitting to leave the last word to one of the people who lived through the siege:

".. the proudest of the many proud traditions which will ever be associated with this memorable siege is the splendid self-control, the uncomplaining patience, the unconquerable determination shown by all ranks of the population through four weary months of privation and danger during which in the darkest hours the word 'surrender' was never even breathed."

A framed picture commemorating the siege and containing in the centre one of Queen Victoria's chocolate boxes

A cartoon entitled 'To be sold – Owner having no further use for it' showing the cage prepared for Rhodes by the Boers which the relief made redundant.

Note also the biscuit box from Germany containing shells, the Red Cross box containing arms and the boxes of expanding bullets.

Medal rolls

Analysis of the medal roll

Analysis

The total number of medals issued with the clasp for the Defence of Kimberley was, according to this roll of recipients, 5,458. The breakdown of this total for officers and men by unit, sorted by medals issued is as follows:

5,458
DoK QSAs

Unit	Officers	Men	Total	% of total
Kimberley Town Guard	179	2,512	2,691	49.30%
Kimberley Regiment of Volunteers	34	785	819	15.01%
Loyal North Lancashire Regiment	14	422	436	7.99%
Kimberley Light Horse	29	372	401	7.35%
Cape Police, District 2	25	372	397	7.27%
Diamond Fields Artillery	7	119	126	2.31%
Cape Police, District 1	11	101	112	2.05%
Royal Garrison Artillery	4	94	98	1.80%
Post Office Corps		75	75	1.37%
Nursing Staff		60	60	1.10%
Royal Engineers	3	51	54	0.99%
Damant's Horse	3	39	42	0.77%
De Beers' Maxim Battery		32	32	0.59%
Army Service Corps	2	17	19	0.35%
Commander in Chief's Body Guard		19	19	0.35%
Scottish Horse	1	13	14	0.26%
Scott's Railway Guards	6	6	12	0.22%
South African Constabulary	2	9	11	0.20%
Imperial Military Railways		6	6	0.11%
Royal Army Medical Corps	1	5	6	0.11%
Army Chaplains' Department	3		3	0.05%
Army Veterinary Corps	1	2	3	0.05%
Field Intelligence Department		3	3	0.05%
Imperial Light Horse		3	3	0.05%
Cape Police, Special Contingent	1	1	2	0.04%
Kitchener's Fighting Scouts		2	2	0.04%
14th Hussars		1	1	0.02%
2nd Dragoons		1	1	0.02%
Army Pay Corps		1	1	0.02%
Cape Colonial Ordnance Department	1		1	0.02%
Cape Mounted Rifles		1	1	0.02%
Dennison's Scouts		1	1	0.02%
Driscoll's Scouts		1	1	0.02%
Frontier Light Horse		1	1	0.02%
Geoghegan's Scouts	1		1	0.02%
Kitchener's Horse	1		1	0.02%
South African Mounted Irregular Forces	1		1	0.02%
Warwick's Scouts		1	1	0.02%
Total	330	5,128	5,458	

21 units were active during the siege but 38 are listed in the table above. Why are there so many more? The conclusion of the siege in February 1900 and the fact that the war lasted a further two years gave some of the

Kimberley Siege Account and Medal Roll

participants ample opportunity to see further military service. While some stayed in their original units, the disbandment of the KTG and the creation of many new units meant that the colonial men could serve for short periods in a wide number of them. Where someone served in a different unit, the rules for how their medal would be named are not clear. The medal could be named to any of the units in which they served, hence the proliferation of units in the above list.

Before the QSA was issued, clasps would be added to represent battles the recipient participated in, periods of service or states where he served. The maximum number of clasps seen on a medal containing the DoK clasp is 8. By far the most common number of clasps on a QSA is one. The following table lists the number of clasps by unit, sorted by the total number of QSAs issued to that unit:

Unit	0	1	2	3	4	5	6	7	8	Total
Kimberley Town Guard	75	2,316	97	110	62	20	7	4		2,691
Kimberley Regiment of Vols		307	169	189	115	35	4			819
Loyal North Lancashire Regt		36	37	320	40	3				436
Kimberley Light Horse		9	219	95	57	16	5			401
Cape Police, District 2		186	67	44	89	11				397
Diamond Fields Artillery		44	35	42	3	2				126
Cape Police, District 1		11	50	33	15	3				112
Royal Garrison Artillery		44	30	22	2					98
Post Office Corps		75								75
Nursing Staff	60									60
Royal Engineers		2	5	41	3	2	1			54
Damant's Horse		1	2	5	9	4	13	7	1	42
De Beers' Maxim Battery		24	3	2	2	1				32
Army Service Corps		7	5	3	4					19
Commander in Chief's BG				2	13	4				19
Scottish Horse				4	4	6				14
Scott's Railway Guards			2	4	2	3	1			12
South African Constabulary			2	3	5	1				11
Imperial Military Railways		4	1	1						6
Royal Army Medical Corps		3	1	2						6
Army Chaplains' Department		3								3
Army Veterinary Corps		1		1	1					3
Field Intelligence Department				2	1					3
Imperial Light Horse			1	1			1			3
Cape Police, Special Cont		1	1							2
Kitchener's Fighting Scouts					2					2
14th Hussars					1					1
2nd Dragoons			1							1
Army Pay Corps		1								1
Cape Colonial Ord Dept		1								1
Cape Mounted Rifles				1						1
Dennison's Scouts						1				1
Driscoll's Scouts						1				1
Frontier Light Horse			1							1
Geoghegan's Scouts			1							1
Kitchener's Horse					1					1
SA Mounted Irregular Forces			1							1
Warwick's Scouts					1					1
Total	135	3,076	731	927	432	113	32	11	1	5,458

Analysis of the medal roll

Nurses in the Boer War were not issued with any clasps and this is represented in the table. The 75 men of the KTG who were not enrolled are also listed. See page 508 for more information on these men and the reason why they received medals with no clasp.

In addition to the DoK clasp, the medal rolls contain 4,566 other clasps that appear on the recipient's QSA. The table below shows how many of the clasps have been recorded by unit. Note that the units named have been abbreviated and that the table is sorted by number of clasps awarded.

Unit	OFS	Tr	SA01	RoM	Paar[37]	SA02	Drie	Joh	DH	Witt	Belf	Belm	Natal	Rhod	MR	LN	Total
14H		1		1		1											3
2D				1													1
ASC	9	7	2		1	1				1		2					23
AVC	1	1	2	1													5
CinCBG	17	19	17	3	2	1											59
CMR			1			1											2
CP1	95	31	11	30	3	1	1							1			173
CP2	185	146	24	95	9	2						2		1	2		466
CPS		1															1
DBMB	7	4	3	1		2											17
DFA	70	49	10	2	1	1	1	1	1								136
DH	20	19	16	6	21	10	19	19	19	17	2	1					169
DrS	1	1	1			1											4
DS	1	1	1			1											4
FID	3							2	1		1						7
FLH	1																1
GeS	1																1
ILH	2	3	1	1		1											8
IMR	1	2															3
KFS	2	2	2														6
KitH		1			1					1							3
KLH	314	115	53	81	75	21	3	3		2	1	1					669
KRV	430	264	157	149	12	33	2			2		1	1		1		1,052
KTG	209	151	103	66	17	47	9	12	12	10	2		1	2		1	642
LNLR	373	352	36		20	3		15	9			1					809
RAMC	2	2	1														5
RE		39	2		4		51	2	2	8	1						109
RGA	22	40	16	2													80
SAC	9	7	2	5	1	1	1	1									27
SAMIF		1															1
ScH	10	14	13	2		5											44
SRG	9	9	3	4	2	3	1	1	1								33
WS	1	1	1														3
Total	1,795	1,282	477	449	172	135	89	56	45	41	7	6	4	4	3	1	4,566

The two most frequently occurring clasps are OFS and Transvaal. This is understandable given the proximity of the Boer republics to Kimberley and that much of the subsequent fighting took place in these areas. The

---

[37] The story behind the Paardeberg clasp combination is explained on page 512.

Kimberley Siege Account and Medal Roll

other clasps show where and when the recipient subsequently served. The two date clasps, South Africa 1901 and South Africa 1902, were issued for service in South Africa during these two years.

Army Order 94 established the rules for the clasps and how they could be issued. The Order stated that anyone who was issued with a clasp for an engagement within a state was not thereafter eligible for the clasp for that state. Thus, for example, no one could gain eligibility to the clasps for both OFS and Paardeberg. The following table shows in which states the engagements took place.

State clasp[38]	Clasps issued for actions within the state
Cape Colony[39]	Kimberley – Defence and Relief, Mafeking – Defence and Relief, Belmont and Modder River
Natal	Talana, Elandslaagte, Ladysmith – Defence and Relief, Tugela Heights and Laing's Nek
Orange Free State[40]	Paardeberg, Driefontein, Witterbergen and Wepener
Transvaal	Johannesburg, Diamond Hill and Belfast
Rhodesia	(no clasps issued)

One of the reasons why there is such a variety of clasps is that the recipients saw service, and gained entitlement, while serving either in their own or as part of a different unit. A total of 1,221 men (22%) have been recorded as serving in more than one unit.

Excluding the Kimberley siege units this is the list of other units in which the men served. The figure after the unit name represents the number of men recorded as serving for a period of time in that unit. The information is sorted alphabetically by unit.

A Albany DMT: 1; Army Service Corps: 46; Ashburner's Light Horse: 17; **B** Barkly West TG: 1; Bechuanaland Border Police: 1; Bechuanaland Rifles: 26; Border Horse: 5; Border Mounted Infantry: 1; Border Scouts: 1; Brabant's Horse: 13; British South Africa Police: 2; Bushveldt Carbineers: 1; **C** Canadian Scouts: 5; Cape Colony Cyclist Corps: 9; Cape Colonial Forces: 3; Cape Government Railways: 4; Cape Infantry: 2; Cape Medical Staff Corps: 2; Cape Mounted Rifles: 3; Cape Police, Special Contingent: 106; Cape Railway Sharpshooters: 59; Cattle Guards: 1; Christiana DMT: 2; Christiana Scouts: 1; Colonial Defence Force: 2; Colonial Light Horse: 3; Commander in Chief's Body Guard: 54; Corps of Guides: 1; Cullinan's Horse: 3; **D** Damant's Horse: 91; Daniel's Kuil TG: 1; Dennison's Scouts: 15; Dordrecht District Volunteer Guard: 1; Driscoll's Scouts: 5; Duke of Edinburgh's Own Volunteer Rifles: 4; **E** Edenburg TG: 2; **F** Field Intelligence Department: 46; Frontier Light Horse: 2; Frontier Mounted Rifles: 1; **G** Geoghegan's Scouts: 2; Gorringe's Flying Column: 2; Griqualand West Light Horse: 7; **H** Herschel Native Police: 1; **I** Imperial Hospital Corps: 3; Imperial Light Horse: 31; Imperial Military Railways: 13; Imperial Transport Service: 3; Imperial Yeomanry Scouts: 33; **J** Jagersfontein TG: 3; Johannesburg Mounted Rifles: 23; **K** Kaffrarian Rifles: 2; Kimberley Horse: 32; Kimberley Light Horse: 643; King Williamstown TG: 1; Kitchener's Fighting Scouts: 24; Kitchener's Horse: 4; Klerksdorp TG: 1; Klipdam TG: 4; Koffiefontein Defence Force: 4; **L** Ladismith TG: 2; Life Guards: 1; Loch's Horse: 2; Lumsden's Horse: 1; **M** Marshall's Horse: 8; Midland Mounted Rifles: 3; Mosita Squadron DMT: 1; Mossel Bay DMT: 1; **N** National Scouts: 2; Native Labour Corps: 3; Nesbitt's Horse: 9; New South Wales Imperial Bushmen: 1; **O** Orange River Colony Police (Provincial Mounted Police): 31; Orange River Colony Scouts: 4; **P** Pietersburg Light Horse: 3; Prince Alfred's Guard MI: 1; Prince Alfred's Volunteer Guard: 2; Prince Of Wales' Light Horse: 3; Provisional Transvaal Constabulary: 1; **R** Railway Pioneer Regiment: 10; Rand Rifles: 12; Rhodesia Regiment: 1; Road Steam Transport: 1; Roberts' Horse: 5; **S** Scottish Horse: 24; Scott's Railway Guards: 210; Somerset East TG: 1; South African Constabulary: 44; South African Light Horse: 4; South African Mounted Irregular Forces: 5; South Wales Borderers: 1; Steinaecker's Horse: 6; Stellenbosch DMT: 1; **U** Uitenhage TG: 1; Uitenhage Volunteer Rifles: 6; Upington TG: 2; **V** Vryburg Scouts: 1; Vryburg Special Police: 1; Vryburg TG: 10; **W** Warren's Mounted Infantry: 3; Warren's Scouts: 1; Warrenton DMT: 6; Warrenton TG: 7; Warwick's Scouts: 28; Western Light Horse: 25; Western Province Mounted Rifles: 5; Willowmore TG: 1; Windsorton and Wedberg DMT: 1; Windsorton and Wedberg TG: 2; Worcester DMT: 1.

---

[38] While not legally states, Transvaal, OFS, Cape Colony etc are generally referred to by this term.
[39] For more information on the Cape Colony clasp and Kimberley QSAs, see page 512.
[40] There are two examples in the medal rolls of QSAs that have the clasps OFS and Paardeberg.

Analysis of the medal roll

The final table contains a variety of information gleaned from analysis of the medal rolls. The table shows the number of QSAs awarded; the total number of clasps and the average number of clasps per QSA; the number of KSAs recorded; the number and percentage of men who served in other units (including the Kimberley siege units); the number and percentage of QSAs that have been recorded as being extant. The table is sorted alphabetically by abbreviated unit title.

Unit	QSAs awarded	Total number of clasps	Average clasps per QSA	KSAs[41] recorded	Served in different unit	Percentage served in different unit	Medal(s) extant	Percentage medals extant
14H	1	4	4.00	1		0%	1	100%
2D	1	2	2.00			0%		0%
ACD	3	3	1.00			0%	1	33%
APC	1	1	1.00	1		0%		0%
ASC	19	42	2.21	6	4	21%	4	21%
AVC	3	8	2.67	1	1	33%		0%
CCOD	1	1	1.00			0%		0%
CMR	1	3	3.00		1	100%	1	100%
CPD1	112	285	2.54	56	9	8%	22	20%
CPD2	397	863	2.17	177	37	9%	78	20%
CPS	2	3	1.50		1	50%	1	50%
CinCBG	19	78	4.11	1	19	100%		0%
DH	42	211	5.02	17	38	90%	12	29%
DBMB	32	49	1.53	1	8	25%	3	9%
DS	1	5	5.00		1	100%		0%
DFA	126	262	2.08	59	30	24%	24	19%
DrS	1	5	5.00	1	1	100%	1	100%
FID	3	10	3.33		1	33%	1	33%
FLH	1	2	2.00	1	1	100%	1	100%
GeS	1	2	2.99	1	1	100%	1	100%
ILH	3	11	3.67	2	3	100%	1	33%
IMR	6	9	1.50			0%	2	33%
KLH	401	1,070	2.67	58	228	57%	59	15%
KRV	819	1,871	2.28	302	352	43%	136	17%
KTG	2,691	3,258	1.21	49	438	16%	422	16%
KFS	2	8	4.00		1	50%	1	50%
KitH	1	4	4.00			0%		0%
LNLR	436	1,245	2.86	332	5	1%	145	33%
NS	60	0	-	2	2	3%	9	15%
POC	75	75	1.00			0%	14	19%
RAMC	6	11	1.83	4	1	17%	3	50%
RE	54	163	3.02	44		0%	19	35%
RGA	98	178	1.82	60	3	3%	28	29%
SRG	12	45	3.75	3	9	75%	3	25%
ScH	14	58	4.14	1	14	100%	1	7%
SAC	11	38	3.45	5	10	91%	4	36%
SAMIF	1	2	2.00		1	100%	1	100%
WS	1	4	4.00		1	100%		0%
	5,458	9,889	1.81	1,185	1,221	22%	999	18%

---

[41] Note that the KSA may be named to a different unit to the one the recipient served in to gain the QSA. A good example of this is the KTG. No KSAs were named to the KTG.

Format of the medal roll

The medal roll consists of three columns of information.

Column	Explanation
1	This column contains the recipient's name. The format used is: Surname, regimental number (if any), rank (if any), forename(s) or initial(s), unit.
2	The number and name of the clasps awarded to the QSA.
3	This section includes notes on where the recipient served during the siege, biographical details and information of any extant medals. 95% of all entries have notes. Missing medals are listed in square brackets. Where medals have been identified, the details usually show the location or dealer's name, date and cost (where known).

The abbreviations used in the medal roll are listed on page viii.

Caveats

The information in the medal roll needs to be read in the context of the following caveats:

1. Accuracy

   Producing a medal roll from the original documents can be a frustrating task to undertake. The process from viewing the original rolls to presenting them on these pages has the potential for errors to creep in. Part of the problem is the quality of the original documents and other issues include pages containing physical damage, feint ink and poor handwriting.

   The issue of unit naming has already been covered. As a result of this uncertainty, it is definite that there will be men who appear in the medal rolls with the wrong unit listed as their issuing unit. In these cases, the notes should contain the name of the unit to which the medal is named.

2. Consistency

   Where a man appears on more than one roll, there is always the chance that there will be inconsistency between some of the information, for example, surname, number, initials, dates of service etc. There is also the problem of double-barrelled names. For example is it Lieutenant R J S Raper or Lieutenant R J Stone-Raper? Where these occur, best endeavours have been used to determine the correct information.

3. Completeness

   From the evidence of the medal rolls, the colonial men changed units on a regular basis. The issue here is trying to ensure that all the entitlements have been gathered. When the rolls were compiled, there was a great effort to reconcile these problems by the addition of notes on the medal rolls listing where else the man served. These do provide useful pointers for further research and inquiry and while most of these have been followed up, it is certain that the task is incomplete and there will be examples on the medal rolls where a man is entitled to more clasps than are listed against his name.

   Eligibility for the clasps South Africa 1901 and South Africa 1902 was gained by service during these two years. There are many men who are recorded as having served between 1 January 1901 and the end of the war and should have been entitled to one or both of these clasps. However, despite many attempts to locate these clasps on the medal roll, no confirmation could be found. This is a particular problem for some colonial men.

4. Omission

   There can be a number of reasons why a man cannot be located on the medal rolls. First, the man may have forfeited his medal. All such forfeits have been removed (but see the note on page 515). Second, the spelling of the surname on the rolls is slightly different to the actual spelling. As the rolls have been compiled there have been many surname homonyms and also some transcription errors have eg Davison instead of Davidson, Frieslich for Freislich etc. If you cannot locate an entry, please check alternative spellings for the person whose name you are searching for.

   If none of these reasons explain or resolve the issue, please email as much information as possible to kimberley@angloboerwar.com.

Medal roll

A

Aaronson, Pte M J, KTG	QSA (1) DoK	G Company
Aaronson, Pte M M, KTG	QSA (1) DoK	No I Section, Belgravia Fort
Abbot, G B, KTG	QSA (0)	Roll states "Ambulance work in connection with scurvy outbreak"
Abbot, Col Sgt H J, KTG	QSA (1) DoK	Kimberley Mine Ambulance Company with mounted forces
Abrahams, Pte J, KTG	QSA (1) DoK	No IV Section, F Company, Mostert's Redoubt
Abrahamse, Pte A J, KTG	QSA (1) DoK	No IV Section, M Company, No 2 Redoubt
Abrahamse, Pte C J, KTG	QSA (1) DoK	No III Section, F Company, No 3 Redoubt
Abram, 876 Pte John, KRV	QSA (3) DoK OFS Tr	Also served KTG (H Company), CP2 (709) until discharged for misconduct and DH (41259) 20 Feb 02 to 30 Jun 02. KSA (2)
Absalom, 1061 Pte George Edward, KRV	QSA (2) DoK OFS	Also served KTG and KLH (310) 24 Oct 99 until DMU 24 Mar 00. KSA (2)
Acker, Pte J, KTG	QSA (1) DoK	Premier Mine. 50th Anniversary attendee. QSA (1), KStar. Glendining Feb 80 £105. Spink Mar 92. DNW Sep 05 £380. QSA (1). City Coins Dec 88. Chelsea Feb 06 £225. Morris Jan 07 £200
Adams, Sgt A W, KTG	QSA (1) DoK	No II Section, Mandy Fort
Adams, Capt H J Goold-, KTG	QSA (1) DoK	See his biography (page 337)
Adams, Pte J, KTG	QSA (1) DoK	No III Section, F Company, No 3 Redoubt and No III Section, Belgravia Fort. QSA (3). McGregor Museum
Adams, Pte P, KTG	QSA (1) DoK	
Adams, 25883 L Cpl R, RE	QSA (5) DoK Paar Drie Joh DH	KSA (2). From 6th Company
Adams, 272 Pte R C, KRV	QSA (1) DoK	DMU 31 Mar 00
Adams, Dvr W T, DBMB	QSA (2) DoK OFS	Botanical Gardens and Otto's Kopje
Adamson, Pte G D, KTG	QSA (1) DoK	Civil Service Redoubt
Adamson, Pte J, KTG	QSA (1) DoK	No I Section, A Company, Beaconsfield Town Guard and Gibraltar Fort, Davis's Heap. 50th Anniversary attendee
Adamson, 295 Pte R H, KRV	QSA (1) DoK	KSA (2)
Adamson, 287 Pte T W, KRV	QSA (2) DoK 01	Non effective 7 Mar 01
Adcock, Gnr H W A, DBMB	QSA (1) DoK	Armoured train section
Addicks, Pte A N, KTG	QSA (1) DoK	No II Section, K Company
Addison, Pte A, KTG	QSA (1) DoK	Premier Mine
Addison, Pte H, KTG	QSA (1) DoK	Cycle Corps, A Company
Adendorff, 831 Pte W L E, KRV	QSA (3) DoK OFS Tr	Discharged 11 Oct 00. Also served KTG (No I Section, A Company, Beaconsfield Town Guard) and Mossel Bay DMT
Adlam, 205 Band L, KRV	QSA (1) DoK	DMU. QSA (1), KStar
Adler, 522 Pte Henry Mark, KRV	QSA (4) RoM DoK OFS Tr	Wounded 28 Nov 99. Non effective 25 Jun 00. Discharged 15 Apr 01. Also served KLH (1114), ILH (2371) 21 Jun 01 to 21 Dec 01 and Pietersburg Light Horse (429). QSA (4), KSA (2) (Pietersburg LH). Spink Jan 76 £145
Adrianzen, 149 Gnr Jacobus Andrie, DFA	QSA (1) DoK	Enrolled DFA 13 Jun 99. Served Kimberley Rifles 4 Apr 88 to 16 Sep 91. DMU 16 Jul 00. Occupation carpenter

Kimberley Siege Account and Medal Roll

Ainsley, Pte G, KTG	QSA (1) DoK	No II Section, F Company, Mostert's Redoubt. 50th Anniversary attendee
Ainsworth, 5305 Pte J, LNLR	QSA (5) DoK OFS Tr 01 02	3rd Battalion
Airth, Pte J, KTG	QSA (1) DoK	H Company
Airth, W, KTG	QSA (0)	Roll states "Guarding Natives on construction work and trenches"
Akenhead, QMS A, DBMB	QSA (1) DoK	Botanical Gardens
Albrice, Pte J, KTG	QSA (1) DoK	No I Section, C Company, Beaconsfield Town Guard
Alderson, Pte A W, KTG	QSA (1) DoK	No II Section, No 2 Redoubt
Alexander, 38 Sgt Donald, CP2	QSA (1) DoK	CP dismounted branch (barrier & redoubt duties). KSA (2)
Alexander, Pte F, KTG	QSA (1) DoK	No 6 Redoubt. QSA (1), KStar. City Coins May 02
Alexander, Pte H M, KTG	QSA (1) DoK	No I Section, No 2 Redoubt
Alexander, 297 Cpl J, KRV	QSA (1) DoK	Non effective 1 Dec 00
Alexander, Pte J, KTG	QSA (1) DoK	No II Section, B Company, No 4 Redoubt
Alexander, Pte J, KTG	QSA (1) DoK	Premier Mine
Alexander, Pte J, KTG	QSA (1) DoK	H Company
Alexander, Pte J, KTG	QSA (1) DoK	No IV Section, L Company
Alexander, Pte R, KTG	QSA (1) DoK	No IV Section, L Company
Alexander, Pte S, KTG	QSA (1) DoK	No I Section, No 2 Redoubt
Alexander, Pte T, KTG	QSA (1) DoK	No 1 Redoubt
Alexander, 4364 Pte W, LNLR	QSA (3) DoK OFS Tr	KSA (2)
Alexander, Lt W W, KTG	QSA (1) DoK	No I Company, B Section, Reservoir
Alexander, Cpl William C, KTG	QSA (1) DoK	No 6 Redoubt. Also served SRG (21) 11 Feb 01 to 17 May 01
Alford, Pte C, KTG	QSA (1) DoK	
Algar, Mr E H, POC	QSA (1) DoK	
Allcock, 565 Pte Norman George, CP1	QSA (2) DoK OFS	A Squadron. Served 15 Sep 99 to 30 Nov 02. Also served MH (104), GFC and WLH (41316) 1 May 02 to 30 Jun 02. Served in the Bechuanaland Rebellion 1897 earning CGHGSM (1) Bech
Alldis, 463 Pte C, KRV	QSA (1) DoK	Non effective 1 Mar 00
Allen, 327 Pte F, KRV	QSA (1) DoK	DMU 20 Dec 99
Allen, Pte H, KTG	QSA (1) DoK	No II Section, L Company
Allen, 30 L Cpl Philip Henry, KLH	QSA (4) DoK Paar Drie Joh	Served 19 Oct 99 to 30 Apr 00. Also served NH from 23 Jan 01. KSA (2). Occupation speculator
Allen, 1234 Sapr S G, RE	QSA (3) DoK Drie Tr	Deserted 24 Jun 03. Medal and 3 clasps returned to Woolwich 8 May 14. KSA (2)
Allen, 306 Tpr T J, KLH	QSA (2) DoK OFS	Served 24 Oct 99 to 30 Apr 00
Allen, 5187 L Cpl W, LNLR	QSA (3) DoK OFS Tr	QSA (3), KSA (2), BWM, VM, Silver Wound Badge (426416). DNW Sep 06 £310
Allen, Pte W, KTG	QSA (1) DoK	No I Company, B Section, Reservoir
Allende, Pte J R, KTG	QSA (1) DoK	No IV Section, B Company, Beaconsfield Town Guard
Allinson, 4372 Pte J, LNLR	QSA (4) DoK OFS Tr 01	Wounded 1 Aug 01 at Schietfontein
Allison, Cpl H A, KTG	QSA (1) DoK	No II Section, F Company, Mostert's Redoubt
Allison, 366 Tpr Henry Palmer, KLH	QSA (3) DoK OFS Tr	Discharged 30 Apr 00. Nominal roll says served 18 Dec 99 to 14 Jun 00. Also served CPS (18) 7 Nov 00 to 30 Apr 02, IYS 23 Jul 00 to 17 Sep 00 and WLH (80) 30 Apr 02 to 30 Jun 02. QSA (2) excl Tr, [KSA (2)], KStar. Spink Dec 83

Allison, Mr J, POC	QSA (1) DoK	
Allisse, Pte J, KTG	QSA (1) DoK	No 6 Redoubt
Allnutt, 444 Cpl Alfred, CP1	QSA (2) DoK OFS	A Squadron. Born Liverpool 10 May 1870. To Natal 1890. Chief Statistician, Kleinfontein Group of Mines, Benoni, Transvaal 1911. [CGHGSM (1) Bech], QSA (2), [KSA (2)]. City Coins Jul 01. City Coins Aug 08
Ally, 217 Tpr J, KLH	QSA (2) DoK OFS	Served 19 Oct 99 to 30 Apr 00. Surname Atty on the nominal roll
Almond, 3816 Pte W, LNLR	QSA (4) DoK OFS Tr 01	QSA (4). Sotheby Jun 85. Liverpool May 88 £90
Amiel, Guard E, IMR	QSA (2) DoK Tr	
Amm, Pte R D, KTG	QSA (2) RoM DoK	No I Section, No 2 Redoubt. Richard Amm served as an Assistant in the Food Supply Staff but could be next man
Amm, Pte R G, KTG	QSA (2) RoM DoK	No II Section, Belgravia Fort
Amos, 1558 Pte E J, CP1	QSA (2) DoK OFS	B Squadron
Amunsen, Pte A, KTG	QSA (1) DoK	D Company (Veterans), Beaconsfield Town Guard
Anders, Pte P C, KTG	QSA (1) DoK	No II Section, No 2 Redoubt
Anderson, 81 Gnr Edward, DFA	QSA (1) DoK	Enrolled DFA 30 Jan 97. Wounded 9 Dec 99 by shrapnel. Resigned 7 Jul 03. Occupation overseer at De Beers
Anderson, Pte G, KTG	QSA (1) DoK	No II Section, C Company, Pickering's Redoubt No 2
Anderson, 200 Sgt Maj Tailor George, DFA	QSA (3) DoK OFS Tr	Enrolled DFA 3 Oct 99. Served DFH 1894 to 1897. Resigned 22 Oct 02. KSA (2). Served in the Bechuanaland Rebellion 1897 earning CGHGSM (1) Bech. Occupation pattern maker
Anderson, Pte H J, KTG	QSA (1) DoK	Ambulance Corps, Beaconsfield Town Guard
Anderson, Pte J E, KTG	QSA (1) DoK	No I Section, F Company, Mostert's Redoubt
Anderson, 4769 Pte J M, LNLR	QSA (1) DoK	Mounted Infantry. Died of disease 4 Jan 00
Anderson, Lt James Milne, KLH	QSA (2) DoK Paar	Served 30 Oct 99 to 6 Mar 00. Also served KTG
Anderson, Pte N, KTG	QSA (1) DoK	
Anderson, 319 Tpr Robert Buchanan, KLH	QSA (2) DoK OFS	Served 24 Oct 99 to 30 Apr 00. QSA (2). City Coins Sep 03. City Coins Nov 06
Anderson, Pte W, KTG	QSA (1) DoK	
Anderson, Pte W, KTG	QSA (1) DoK	
Anderton, 4723 Pte J, LNLR	QSA (1) DoK	Invalided to England 21 Aug 00
Andrews, Pte C, KTG	QSA (1) DoK	No I Section, K Company. KStar (Pvt C J Andrews M Coy TG). City Coins Jul 01
Andrews, 251 Band E, KRV	QSA (1) DoK	KSA (2)
Andrews, 523 Pte E, KRV	QSA (1) DoK	DMU 10 Mar 00. Also served WWDMT (231). OFS crossed through on the WWDMT QSA roll
Andrews, 739 Pte Frederick Henry, KRV	QSA (3) DoK OFS Tr	Served 8 Feb 00 to 14 May 01. Also served KTG (No I Section, C Company, Beaconsfield Town Guard), KLH (364) to 30 Apr 00, CPS (627) 6 Jul 01 to 6 Nov 01 and GWLH (28 & 41842) 15 Mar 02 to 30 Jun 02. KSA (2). Occupation miner
Andrews, Pte G, KTG	QSA (1) DoK	
Andrews, 880 Pte H, KRV	QSA (3) DoK OFS Tr	Also served KTG. Discharged 1 Jul 02. [QSA (3), KSA (2)], KStar. City Coins Mar 03
Andrews, Pte H R, KTG	QSA (1) DoK	Premier Mine and Gibraltar Fort, Davis's Heap
Andrews, 1042 Pte J, KRV	QSA (1) DoK	Also served KTG (No I Section, K Company). Discharged 1 Jul 02. QSA (1), [KSA (2)], KStar. DNW Sep 01 £190. Dixon Apr 02 £285

Name	Medals	Notes
Andries, 35559 Tpr Charles, DH	QSA (5) DoK OFS Tr 01 02	Served 15 Aug 01 to 30 Jun 02. Also served KTG (No I Section, No 2 Redoubt) and KRV (1037). KSA (2) on DH crossed through and clasps issued to QSA. Occupation carpenter
Angel, Capt T L, KTG	QSA (1) DoK	See his biography (page 337)
Angwin, Pte A, KTG	QSA (1) DoK	No 6 Redoubt
Annan, 613 Pte J, KRV	QSA (2) DoK OFS	Discharged 1 Jul 02. KSA (2)
Annetts, E, KTG	QSA (0)	Roll states "Construction of barricades and trenches"
Ansell, 3290 Col Sgt A, LNLR	QSA (3) DoK OFS Tr	KSA (2)
Anthony, 901 Pte D, KRV	QSA (3) RoM DoK OFS	Served 17 Mar 00 to 1 Jul 00. Also served KTG (No II Company, A Section, Reservoir) as Anthoney
Antill, Pte H, KTG	QSA (1) DoK	No IV Section, C Company, Beaconsfield Town Guard
Aplin, Pte Herbert Henry, KTG	QSA (2) DoK Tr	No I Section, F Company, Mostert's Redoubt. Also served BR (220 and 26183) from 6 Feb 01, joining in Kimberley. Occupation miner
Appleford, 78670 Gnr Henry, RGA	QSA (1) DoK	KSA (2)
Archer, 2186 Sapr Percy, RE	QSA (3) DoK Drie Tr	QSA (3), KSA (2), BWM, VM, LS&GC, KStar. RHQ
Archibald, Pte A, KTG	QSA (1) DoK	Construction of barricades and trenches. QSA (1). Liverpool Mar 88 £78
Arlt, Pte A E, KTG	QSA (1) DoK	Premier Mine
Armstrong, 54 Tpr Arthur Homer, KLH	QSA (2) DoK OFS	Wounded 22 Nov 99. Served 19 Oct 99 until DMU 24 Mar 00. MID. QSA (2). Liverpool Apr 94 £195
Armstrong, 53 Sgt E H B, KRV	QSA (3) DoK OFS Tr	CGHGSM (1) Bech (PAVG), QSA (1) DoK, KSA (2), Colonial Auxiliary Forces LS Medal, KStar
Armstrong, Cpl H G, KTG	QSA (1) DoK	Kimberley Mine Ambulance Company, A Section. QSA (1), KStar, BWM, VM (Spr SAEC). eBay Aug 07
Armstrong, Gnr J, DBMB	QSA (1) DoK	Armoured train section
Armstrong, Capt J, KTG	QSA (1) DoK	Kamfersdam Company
Armstrong, Sgt J, KTG	QSA (1) DoK	No II Section, B2 Company, No 3 Redoubt. QSA (1)
Armstrong, Pte J W, KTG	QSA (1) DoK	No I Section, L Company. QSA (1), KStar
Armstrong, 308 Sgt Maj John William, KLH	QSA (2) DoK OFS	Joined 26 Oct 99. Died of disease Boshof 22 Apr 00
Armstrong, Pte William Charles, KTG	QSA (3) DoK OFS Tr	No II Section, C Company, Pickering's Redoubt No 2. Also served SRG (1266) from 12 Feb 01, KLH (263) and DH (37981) 19 Sep 01 to 25 Mar 02. Occupation carpenter and painter
Arnold, Tpr Arthur Dickson, DH	QSA (7) DoK Paar Drie Joh DH Witt 01	Served 28 Feb 00 to 20 Jan 01. Also served KTG (Otto's Kopje Scouts). Middle name also given as Dixon. Occupation engineer
Arnot, Nurse D E, NS	QSA (0)	Kimberley Civil Hospital
Arthur, 4278 Gnr James, RGA	QSA (3) DoK Tr 01	Premier Mine. QSA (2) excl 01. Sotheby Jun 84
Artman, Pte Lennox, KTG	QSA (5) RoM DoK OFS 01 02	Kenilworth Defence Force. Also served KLH (480) 1 May 00 to 5 Jun 00, BR (207) 28 Jan 01 to 30 Jan 02, Warrenton Telegraph and Police Guard. Occupation carpenter
Artz, Tpr Michael, DH	QSA (7) DoK Paar Drie Joh DH Witt 01	Served 18 Feb 00 to 25 Jan 01. Also served KTG and NH (32970) from 13 Apr 01. Entry crossed through on NH Supplementary roll. Occupation engine driver. There is an M Artz on the CGHGSM medal roll serving with PAVG and earning Bas - same man?
Arundale, 665 Pte Francis R, CP2	QSA (1) DoK	C Squadron. Severely wounded 28 Nov 99. DMU 24 Aug 00

Medal roll

Arundel, Pte H, KTG	QSA (1) DoK	No I Section, A Company, Beaconsfield Town Guard
Ascott, 4958 Cpl H, LNLR	QSA (3) DoK OFS Tr	KSA (2)
Ash, Pte Frederick Charles, KTG	QSA (4) RoM DoK OFS Tr	No IV Section, K Company. Also served KLH (327 & 389) 6 Mar 00 to 24 Nov 00, ILH (1702) 26 Nov 00 to 25 May 01, SRG (599) from 1 Jun 01, BSAP (180) (no trace on roll) and BR (403) from 6 Dec 01. Occupation miner and/or saddler
Ashcroft, 4550 Pte J, LNLR	QSA (3) DoK OFS Tr	QSA (3) (initial A), KSA (2), KStar. Friar Oct 09 £700
Ashcroft, 4657 Pte T, LNLR	QSA (3) DoK OFS Tr	QSA (3), KSA (2), KStar. Christies Nov 92 £143. March Medals Aug 93 £200
Ashe, Med Off Evelyn Oliver, KTG	QSA (1) DoK	See his biography (page 337)
Ashford, Pte A J, KTG	QSA (1) DoK	H Company
Ashton, 126 Pte J S, KRV	QSA (1) DoK	Discharged 24 Dec 00. Roll says "Since dead". No trace on the casualty roll
Ashton, S, KTG	QSA (0)	Roll states "Construction of shelters for women and children"
Ashton, Pte W, KTG	QSA (1) DoK	H Company. QSA (1). Ackley 91 £175
Asquith, 683 Pte Herbert, CP2	QSA (1) DoK	CP dismounted branch (barrier & redoubt duties). QSA (1). Spink Jun 87
Assor, Pte D, KTG	QSA (1) DoK	No I Section, C Company, Beaconsfield Town Guard. QSA (1). DNW Apr 94 £60. Spink Dec 95 £95. Spink Oct 97 £110
Aston, 1071 Pte J S, KRV	QSA (4) DoK OFS Tr 01	Also served KTG and Cape Infantry. Severely wounded near Jacobsdal 3 Jun 01. Surname Ashton on casualty roll. QSA issued 31 Aug 04
Atherton, 3935 Pte J, LNLR	QSA (4) DoK OFS Tr 01	
Atkins, 407 Pte Andrew, CP2	QSA (4) RoM DoK OFS Tr	C Squadron. KSA (2). KSA reissued Apr 09 to Vancouver, BC. Severely wounded Lillyfontein 19 Oct 01. Slightly wounded Klip Drift 7 Mar 02. Served in the Bechuanaland Rebellion 1897 earning CGHGSM (1) Bech
Atkins, 27010 Cpl Frederick, RE	QSA (3) DoK Drie Witt	KSA (2) issued 30 Apr 04
Atkinson, 159 Pte G, KRV	QSA (3) RoM DoK OFS	Non effective 20 Jun 00. Possibly served in the Bechuanaland Rebellion 1897 with the DFH earning CGHGSM (1) Bech
Atkinson, 2488 Sgt J, LNLR	QSA (3) DoK OFS Tr	Transferred to 3rd Btn 3 Jun 01 and on roll for 3rd Btn. QSA (3), KSA (2), 14-15 Star (Pte ASC), BWM, VM (A Cpl ASC), KStar. Spink Mar 97 £270. City Coins Dec 05
Atkinson, 4859 Pte J, LNLR	QSA (3) DoK OFS Tr	KSA (2)
Atkinson, Pte James, KTG	QSA (1) DoK	No I Section, D Company. Also served KLH. KStar. City Coins Feb 95
Atkinson, Pte John Robert, KTG	QSA (1) DoK	Also served SRG (909)
Atkinson, Pte W, KTG	QSA (1) DoK	No 1 Redoubt
Atkinson, Pte W J, KTG	QSA (1) DoK	No III Section, Belgravia Fort
Attwell, Pte R A H, KTG	QSA (1) DoK	G Company
Attwood, Lt Arthur J, CP1	QSA (2) DoK OFS	See his biography (page 337)
Augury, Pte B, KTG	QSA (1) DoK	D Company (Veterans), Beaconsfield Town Guard
Austin, 372 Tpr Albert, KLH	QSA (4) DoK OFS Tr 01	Joined 26 Jan 00. DMU 24 Mar 00. Also served KTG (No I Section, C Company, Beaconsfield Town Guard), BR (331), CCCC and GWLH (26) 15 Mar 02 to 30 Jun 02. Occupation miner

Name	Medals	Notes
Austin, Pte C H, KTG	QSA (1) DoK	No III Section, A Company, Beaconsfield Town Guard. QSA (3) incl Tr & 02, KStar. Seaby Nov 80 £210. Spink Apr 93
Austin, 347 Tpr Charles H, KLH	QSA (4) RoM DoK OFS Tr	Served 24 Nov 99 to 6 Jun 00. Also served BR (238 and 30150) 4 Mar 01 to 28 Jan 02 and GWLH 15 Apr 02 to 30 Jun 02. KSA (2). Occupation machine man
Austin, 346 Tpr Henry Robert, KLH	QSA (4) RoM DoK OFS Tr	Served 3 Jan 00 until DMU 24 Mar 00. Also served KTG (No IV Section, B Company, Beaconsfield Town Guard), BR (236 and 30148) from 4 Mar 01 and GWLH 4 Apr 02 to 30 Jun 02. Occupation sorter
Austin, 329 Tpr Paddy, KLH	QSA (2) DoK OFS	Served KLH 24 Nov 99 to 30 Apr 00. Also served IYS (30) 14 May 00 to 6 Sep 00 with initial H
Avent, 264 Pte C, KRV	QSA (1) DoK	Non effective 1 Oct 00
Ayliff, Capt William Edward, CP2	QSA (2) DoK OFS	See his biography (page 337)
Ayrton, Pte George Henry, KTG	QSA (1) DoK	Premier Mine. Also served SRG (917) from 22 May 01. 50th Anniversary attendee. KStar. SAMMH

B

Name	Medals	Notes
Baatjes, 315 Tpr Henry, KLH	QSA (5) RoM DoK Paar Tr 01	Served 23 Jan 00 to 5 Jun 00 and (22825) Jan 01 to 31 Dec 01. 50th Anniversary attendee. Occupation baker
Babb, Pte C, KTG	QSA (1) DoK	Premier Mine
Backhouse, 1022 Pte J E, KRV	QSA (1) DoK	DMU 15 Feb 02. Also served KTG (No I Company, B Section, Reservoir) and Native Labour Corps (245). QSA reissued 2 Jul 09. KSA (2)
Backhouse, Pte T, KTG	QSA (2) Nat DoK	Also served ASC (245) and Native Labour Corps (51). Director of Railways Labour Department
Backman, Sgt J, KTG	QSA (1) DoK	G Company as Backmann
Backman, Mr W A, POC	QSA (1) DoK	Telegraph signaller. Initials A E E on the nominal roll. QSA (1). Glendining Jun 88 states is renamed. Toad Hall Dec 91 £95
Bacon, 867 Pte J, KRV	QSA (3) DoK OFS 01	Also served KTG (G Company). Discharged 30 Apr 01
Bacon, 5141 Pte W, LNLR	QSA (3) DoK OFS Tr	KSA (2)
Badrian, 219 Tpr Arthur, KLH	QSA (1) DoK	Served 20 Oct 99 and DMU 19 Feb or 23 Mar 00
Baggs, Pte C, KTG	QSA (1) DoK	No IV Section, C Company, Beaconsfield Town Guard
Bagley, 679 Pte John Charles, CP2	QSA (1) DoK	A Squadron. KSA (2)
Bailey, Pte E, KTG	QSA (1) DoK	Reserve Section, D Company. Water supply laying and fitting pipes
Bailey, 157 Cpl H, CP1	QSA (2) DoK OFS	A Squadron. Served 19 Dec 91 to 15 May 01. Wounded 25 Nov 99. Also served L Sqn CCF (179) and Lt Herschel Native Police. CGHGSM (1) Bech (Cpl CP), QSA (2), [KSA (2)]. Dixon Apr 98 £235
Bailey, 154 Dvr Harry George, DFA	QSA (2) DoK Tr	Enrolled DFA 22 Jun 99. Discharged at own request 1 Jul 02. KSA (2). Occupation painter
Bailey, Pte J, KTG	QSA (1) DoK	No III Company, A Section, Reservoir
Bailey, 1337 Pte P, CP1	QSA (3) RoM DoK OFS	QSA (4) inc CC. eBay Jul 07 £240
Bailey, 51 CSM R, KRV	QSA (3) DoK OFS Tr	Discharged 1 Jul 02. KSA (2)
Bailey, 4061 Pte R, LNLR	QSA (3) DoK OFS Tr	KSA (2)
Baillie, Pte J, KTG	QSA (1) DoK	No I Company, B Section, Reservoir
Bain, Pte H, KTG	QSA (1) DoK	No IV Section, K Company

Bain, Pte H D, KTG	QSA (1) DoK	
Bainbridge, Sister C, NS	QSA (0)	Kimberley Civil Hospital. MID 10 Sep 01
Baines, Lt H, KRV	QSA (3) DoK OFS Tr	KSA (2)
Baines, 3709 Pte J, LNLR	QSA (2) DoK OFS	Died 28 Aug 00 at Kroonstad
Baird, 361 Tpr Jacob, KLH	QSA (4) DoK OFS Tr 01	Joined KLH 23 Nov 99. Also served IYS (41) 23 May 00 to 6 Sep 00, and KR (460) 16 May 99 until DMU 11 Mar 01 with forename James
Baker, Pte G H, KTG	QSA (1) DoK	H Company
Baker, Pte J, KTG	QSA (1) DoK	No I Section, K Company. QSA (1). DNW Jun 98 £95. Dixon Sep 98 £110
Baker, 1245 Pte L, KRV	QSA (2) DoK OFS	Discharged 1 Jul 02. Also served KTG (No IV Section, B Company, No 4 Redoubt). Issued 1 Feb 06. QSA (2), KSA (2). Sotheby Mar 86. Burman Dec 94 £115
Baker, 5495 L Cpl R, LNLR	QSA (2) DoK OFS	Invalided to England 20 Oct 00
Baker, 343 Tpr Robert, KLH	QSA (3) DoK OFS Tr	Served KLH 6 Nov 99 to 6 Jun 00. Also served KRV (655) (Discharged for misconduct 11 Oct 99 for drunkenness and being continually filthy) and WS (40)
Baker, 266 Tpr William John, KLH	QSA (1) DoK	Joined 26 Oct 99. Killed in action 28 Nov 99
Ball, 32 RSM James, CP2	QSA (4) RoM DoK OFS Tr	C Squadron. Prisoner at Hoopstad 23 Oct 00. SAGS (1) (Pte 99th Foot), CGHGSM (1) Bech (Sgt CP), QSA (4), KSA (2), BWM, VM (Maj), 1902 Coronation, KStar
Ball, 1470 Pte T, CP1	QSA (2) DoK OFS	
Bamber, 4305 Pte Albert, LNLR	QSA (4) DoK Paar Joh DH	Mounted Infantry. Born in Preston in 1875, occupation piercer. Enlisted 2 Dec 93. Transferred to Army Reserve Dec 02 and discharged 7 Jan 1910. QSA (4), KSA (2), KStar. Sotheby Jan 77. DNW Dec 91 £170
Bamford, 78 Tpr Jack, KLH	QSA (2) DoK OFS	Served 1 Nov 99 to 30 Apr 00. Also served IYS (17) 11 May 00 to 6 Sep 00, CPS and CRSS (1131) from 12 Mar 01
Bands, Pte E, KTG	QSA (1) DoK	G Company
Bands, Pte H, KTG	QSA (1) DoK	No III Company, A Section, Reservoir
Banham, Lt W C, KRV	QSA (2) DoK OFS	KSA (2). Served in the Bechuanaland Rebellion 1897 earning CGHGSM (1) Bech. Awarded the Colonial Auxiliary Forces LS Medal (20 years of service) (25 Feb 1910)
Bankier, 202 Bombdr A A, DFA	QSA (1) DoK	Severely wounded 24 Oct 99. Also served JMR (1559). KSA (2)
Banks, Pte H, KTG	QSA (1) DoK	No 2 Schmidt's Breastwork
Bann, Pte J, KTG	QSA (1) DoK	No III Section, C Company, Beaconsfield Town Guard
Bannister, 3572 Pte J, LNLR	QSA (2) DoK OFS	QSA (2), [KSA (2)]. DNW Apr 95 £80. Liverpool Apr 97 £130
Barber, 925 Pte C M, KRV	QSA (4) RoM DoK OFS Tr	Discharged 31 Jan 02. Also served KTG (Otto's Kopje Scouts). KSA (2)
Barber, 1756 Pte H S, CP1	QSA (2) DoK OFS	A Squadron. KSA (2)
Bardin, 27658 Cpl J L, RE	QSA (3) DoK Drie Tr	QSA (3), KSA (2), 14-15 Star, BWM, VM (MID), LS&GC, MSM, KStar. RHQ
Barker, Pte C M, KTG	QSA (1) DoK	Also served KR
Barker, Pte H E, KTG	QSA (1) DoK	Ambulance Corps, Beaconsfield Town Guard
Barker, Pte H J, KTG	QSA (1) DoK	Premier Mine
Barker, 5148 Pte J, LNLR	QSA (4) DoK Paar Joh DH	Mounted Infantry. QSA (4), KSA (2). RHQ

Kimberley Siege Account and Medal Roll

Barlow, Col Sgt William James, KTG	QSA (3) DoK OFS Tr	No 2 Schmidt's Breastwork. Also served WS (2) from 19 Mar 00, BR (215 and 26176) 5 Feb 01 to 4 Aug 01 and CPS (810). Occupation platelayer. QSA (3). City Coins Sep 03. Dixon Dec 03 £300
Barnes, Pte G D, KTG	QSA (1) DoK	Premier Mine
Barnes, Pte G R, KTG	QSA (1) DoK	No IV Section, No 2 Redoubt
Barnes, Cpl G W, KTG	QSA (2) DoK OFS	Kimberley Mine Ambulance Company, A Section
Barnes, H, KTG	QSA (0)	Roll states "In charge of native guards"
Barnes, Pte H, KTG	QSA (1) DoK	No II Section, C Company, Pickering's Redoubt No 2
Barnes, Mr H, POC	QSA (1) DoK	Not on main roll but shown as medal issued
Barnes, Cpl J B, KTG	QSA (1) DoK	No 1 Redoubt
Barnes, Pte N, KTG	QSA (1) DoK	No 6 Redoubt. QSA (1). Glendining Nov 38. Listed as Pte M Barnes - this man?
Barnes, 516 Band T, KRV	QSA (1) DoK	DMU 5 Mar 00
Barnes, Pte W, KTG	QSA (1) DoK	No 6 Redoubt
Barrand, Pte M, KTG	QSA (1) DoK	No I Section, B Company, Beaconsfield Town Guard. Also served CGR
Barrass, Pte C, KTG	QSA (1) DoK	No IV Section, D Company. Also served IYS 9 Apr 00 to 2 Oct 00
Barrass, Pte J, KTG	QSA (1) DoK	No 6 Redoubt
Barrass, Pte James, KTG	QSA (1) DoK	No 6 Redoubt
Barrass, Pte W, KTG	QSA (1) DoK	No IV Section, D Company. QSA (1). Sotheby Oct 71 £34. Christies Jul 78 £60
Barrett, 106 Sgt Anthony, KLH	QSA (3) RoM DoK OFS	Served 19 Oct 99 to 5 Jun 00. Also served Lt KTG. CGHGSM (1) Bech (Cpl DFH), QSA (3), 14-15 Star (Pte SAVR), BWM, VM (Sgt SAVR), KStar. Glendining Oct 84
Barrett, 1017 Tpr William Charles, KLH	QSA (2) DoK OFS	Joined 19 Mar 00. Died of enteric at Kimberley 1 Jun 00
Barrie, Pte G, KTG	QSA (1) DoK	Kenilworth Defence Force
Barron, 195 Pte A, KRV	QSA (1) DoK	DMU 30 Mar 00
Barron, C, KTG	QSA (0)	Roll states "Searchlight maintenance"
Barron, 83 Tpr Robert B, KLH	QSA (5) DoK Belm Paar Drie Joh	See his biography (page 337)
Barry, Pte J, KTG	QSA (2) DoK OFS	Dismissed for drunkenness, 4th offence. Also served KLH (320) 1 Nov 99 until DMU 6 Nov 99, KRV (851) until dismissed for misconduct 30 May 00 and KDF (42)
Bartenbach, Pte H, KTG	QSA (1) DoK	G Company
Barter, 63 Tpr Edwin, KLH	QSA (5) RoM DoK Paar Tr 01	Served KLH 20 Oct 99 until discharged 5 Jun 00. Also served KH (23592) 17 Jul 00 to 1 Mar 01 and CinCBG (34725) 15 May 01 to 29 Jul 01
Bartho, Pte James P, KTG	QSA (3) DoK OFS Tr	No 3 Redoubt. Also served KLH (1018) 5 Apr 00 to 9 Nov 00 and CPS
Bartholomew, Pte H, KTG	QSA (2) DoK OFS	Kimberley Mine Ambulance Company, A Section. Also served KLH (413) 1 Oct 99 to 23 Mar 00. QSA (1) excl OFS, 14-15 Star (Pte 4th Dis Mtd Rfls), BWM, VM (Pte 9th SAH). Dixon Jun 98 £150
Bartholomew, 23 Sgt William, CP2	QSA (1) DoK	CP dismounted branch (barrier & redoubt duties)
Barton, 263 Cpl David, CP2	QSA (4) RoM DoK OFS Tr	A Squadron. KSA (2). Served in the Bechuanaland Rebellion 1897 earning CGHGSM (1) Bech
Barton, Pte H, KTG	QSA (1) DoK	No III Section, B Company, Beaconsfield Town Guard. QSA (1). Sotheby Jun 1906. Spink Mar 93 £140. Ursual Mar 04 £197

Barton, 52 Sapr W E, RE	QSA (3) DoK Drie Tr	See his medals on page 502
Bassom, 328 Tpr L, KLH	QSA (3) DoK OFS Tr	Served 25 Oct 99 to 4 Jun 01. Also served CPS (377, 1024 & 22783) to 25 Oct 01 and CRSS (1492) from 30 Dec 01. KSA (2). Occupation engineer. Surname also Bassan. Forename appears to be 'Le'
Bateman, 622 Pte Charles Julius, CP2	QSA (1) DoK	CP dismounted branch (barrier & redoubt duties)
Batten, C F S, KTG	QSA (0)	Roll states "Electrical work in connection with searchlight"
Batten, Pte G, KTG	QSA (1) DoK	No 6 Redoubt
Batting, Pte Frank Challice, KTG	QSA (5) RoM DoK OFS Tr 02	No 2 Schmidt's Breastwork. Also served KLH (371) 9 Mar 00 to 5 Jun 00 and CPS. 02 (but not 01) from CP roll as served 11 Feb 02 to 31 Mar 02
Battiss, 210 Pte J, KRV	QSA (3) RoM DoK OFS	Discharged 9 Jul 01
Bawden, Pte C, KTG	QSA (1) DoK	No I Section, K Company
Bawden, Pte F W, KTG	QSA (1) DoK	No II Section, D Company and No I Section, K Company
Bawden, Pte G, KTG	QSA (1) DoK	No II Section, D Company
Bawden, Pte N, KTG	QSA (1) DoK	Kamfersdam Company
Bawden, Pte W J, KTG	QSA (1) DoK	No III Section, C Company, Beaconsfield Town Guard. Also served SRG (110)
Baxter, Mr B J, POC	QSA (1) DoK	
Baxter, 25851 Sgt Charles Douglas, ScH	QSA (5) DoK OFS Tr 01 02	Served 3 Jan 01 until invalided 1 May 02. Also served KTG (No I Company, A Section, Reservoir)
Baxter, 690 Pte Fred, CP2	QSA (4) RoM DoK OFS Tr	CP No 2 Maxim gun detachment
Baxter, 75 Tpr G E, KLH	QSA (2) DoK Paar	Served 26 Oct 99 to 23 Mar 00. Also served FID. KSA (2)
Baxter, 715 Pte Walter C F, CP2	QSA (1) DoK	CP intelligence and detective staff
Bayly, Pte J B, KTG	QSA (1) DoK	No I Section, K Company
Bayman, Lt William, KTG	QSA (1) DoK	G Company. Also served Lt CRSS (1072) from 12 Mar 01, SRG and VTG (no trace on roll)
Bayne, Pte H P, KTG	QSA (1) DoK	Otto's Kopje Scouts and Premier Mine
Beadle, Pte C, KTG	QSA (1) DoK	No I Section, Mandy Fort
Beale, 674 Pte Richard James Ward, CP2	QSA (4) DoK OFS Tr 01	CP 7-pounder detachment. Discharged for misconduct 28 Feb 00. Also served BR (416) from 13 Dec 01 and KRV (1074). Severely wounded Roodewal 11 Apr 02. Occupation clerk. [QSA (4)], KStar
Beale, 97797 Gnr Thomas, RGA	QSA (1) DoK	Otto's Kopje
Beardwood, 4039 Pte J, LNLR	QSA (3) DoK OFS Tr	KSA (2)
Beart, 60 Sgt P A, KLH	QSA (2) DoK OFS	Served KLH 20 Oct 99 to 30 Apr 00. Also served IYS (2) 11 May 00 to 11 Oct 00
Beasley, Pte C V, KTG	QSA (1) DoK	Conducting works (redoubts, trenches etc)
Beasley, 167 Dvr George William, DFA	QSA (1) DoK	Enrolled DFA 6 Jul 99. Resigned 23 Mar 03. Also served SRG (26) 12 Feb 01 to 17 May 02. KSA (2). Occupation guard at De Beers Convict Station
Beasley, 211 Tpr Norman, KLH	QSA (2) DoK OFS	Served 1 Nov 99 until discharged 30 Apr 00
Beattie, 260 Dvr Samuel, DFA	QSA (1) DoK	Enrolled DFA 10 Sep 00 in DFA. Also served KLH 17 Mar 00 to 10 Jun 00. Deserted 3 Aug 01
Beatty, 155 Pte Alexander, CP2	QSA (1) DoK	CP intelligence and detective staff. KSA (2). Served in the Bechuanaland Rebellion 1897 earning GCHGSM (1) Bech. QSA (1)

Beatty, 40 Sgt James, CP2	QSA (1) DoK	C Squadron. DMU 30 Jun 01. Served in the Bechuanaland Rebellion 1897 earning CGHGSM (1) Bech
Beavis, Pte Eugene, KTG	QSA (4) DoK Tr 01 02	No 3 supply depot. Also served SRG (304) from 18 Feb 01 and CPS (809)
Bebb, 4781 Pte C, LNLR	QSA (3) DoK OFS Tr	QSA (3), [KSA (2)]. Sotheby Apr 81. LSE Jun 85 £88. DNW Nov 96 £110. Spink Mar 97 £165
Beck, Pte F, KTG	QSA (1) DoK	Ambulance Corps, Beaconsfield Town Guard. Frank Beck also served VTG (194) but could be next man
Beck, Pte F, KTG	QSA (1) DoK	
Beck, 5467 Pte J, LNLR	QSA (3) DoK OFS Tr	QSA (2) excl OFS, KSA (2), KStar. RHQ
Beck, 29 QMS John, CP2	QSA (1) DoK	CP dismounted branch (barrier & redoubt duties). QSA (1), KSA (2). Liverpool Nov 93 £98. Historik Orders Nov 03 £300. eBay Jun 05 £320
Beckett, 312 Pte Donald McP, CP2	QSA (4) RoM DoK OFS Tr	C Squadron. KSA (2). Served in the Bechuanaland Rebellion 1897 earning CGHGSM (1) Bech
Beckett, 630 Pte Ernest George, CP2	QSA (2) DoK Tr	CP dismounted branch (barrier & redoubt duties). Also served KLH (259 and 41964) 7 Apr 02 to 30 Jun 02. KSA (2). Prisoner near Vryburg 19 Jan 01. Sgt SAI during Great War. Occupation blacksmith. BSACM rev Mashonaland 1897 (413 Sgt BSAP), QSA (2), KStar, BWM, VM (12th SAI). City Coins Jan 94
Beckhelling, 807 Pte Charles, CP2	QSA (1) DoK	CP dismounted branch (barrier & redoubt duties). Also served KLH
Becman, Pte T J, KTG	QSA (1) DoK	
Beddome, Lt Edward Ingledew, KTG	QSA (1) DoK	No II Company, A Section, Reservoir. Died Dec 17. SAGS (1) 1878 (Tpr DFH), QSA (1), KStar. Glendining Dec 84 £310. Noble Numismatics, Jul 03 Au$ 2,300
Bedford, 84 Tmptr Alfred F, KLH	QSA (3) DoK OFS Tr	Served 27 Oct 99 to 30 Apr 00. Also served RoH (9197) 29 May 00 to 11 Mar 01 and Canadian Scouts (38171) to 26 Mar 02. KSA (2)
Bedggood, 185 Bombdr Arthur Fredrick, DFA	QSA (3) DoK OFS Tr	His group is being slowly pieced back together. QSA only Chelsea Mar 04 £195. QSA only Historik Orders May 04 £270. CGHGSM (1) Bech. Bonhams Apr 07. See his medals page 507
Beech, 218 Cpl E, KRV	QSA (1) DoK	QSA (1), KSA (2), 14-15 Star, (7th Infy), BWM, VM (SAVR), Colonial Auxiliary Forces LS Medal (SAVR), KStar. Kaplan Nov 03
Beeman, Pte T J, KTG	QSA (1) DoK	Kimberley Mine Ambulance Company with mounted forces. Served in the Bechuanaland Rebellion 1897 earning CGHGSM (1) Bech
Beer, 2567 Sgt F, LNLR	QSA (3) DoK OFS Tr	KSA (2)
Beer, Gnr H, DBMB	QSA (1) DoK	HQ and searchlight
Beet, Mr A J, POC	QSA (1) DoK	QSA (1). McGregor Museum. 50th Anniversary attendee
Beet, Pte George, KTG	QSA (1) DoK	See his biography (page 338)
Behrens, Mr J, POC	QSA (1) DoK	
Belcher, 758 Pte William Alan, KRV	QSA (5) DoK OFS Tr 01 02	Dismissed for misconduct. Also served KTG (No II Section, A Company, Beaconsfield Town Guard) and ScH (342) from 10 Jan 01 and (26054) 24 Jul 01 to 27 Mar 02
Belding, 254 Pte G T, KRV	QSA (1) DoK	DMU 19 Mar 00
Belk, Sgt Samuel Waterhouse, KTG	QSA (4) RoM DoK Paar Tr	See his biography (page 338)
Bell, Nurse B A, NS	QSA (0)	Kimberley Civil Hospital. Served 1 Oct 99 to 28 Feb 00. QSA (0), KStar. Dixon Sep 91 £500
Bell, Pte D, KTG	QSA (1) DoK	No I Section, Mandy Fort

Medal roll

Bell, 4565 Pte J, LNLR	QSA (3) DoK OFS Tr	KSA (2). Nr 4567 on KSA roll
Bell, Pte J T, KTG	QSA (1) DoK	No I Section, D Company. QSA (1). Spink Apr 72 £26. Spink Jun 78 £70. Romsey Medals 86 £125
Bell, 584 Pte James, CP2	QSA (4) RoM DoK OFS Tr	B Squadron. Dismissed time expired 5 May 01
Bell, 4259 Pte T, LNLR	QSA (3) DoK OFS Tr	KSA (2). Initial F on KSA roll
Bell, Pte T, KTG	QSA (1) DoK	No III Section, Belgravia Fort
Bell, 540 Pte William Francis, KRV	QSA (3) DoK OFS Tr	Served 4 Oct 99 to 23 Nov 00. Also served KLH, KFS (40 and 1567), CPS and WLH (538) 17 May 02 to 30 Jun 02. Served 1st KFS 14 Jan 01 to 29 Apr 01 and 2nd KFS 30 Apr 01 to 28 Aug 01. Discharged time expired KFS 27 Feb 02. KSA (2). Occupation miner
Bellas, Pte E, KTG	QSA (1) DoK	No 6 Redoubt
Bellas, Pte J, KTG	QSA (1) DoK	No IV Section, D Company
Bellas, Pte W, KTG	QSA (1) DoK	No IV Section, D Company
Bellfield, 5029 Pte W, LNLR	QSA (3) DoK OFS Tr	KSA (2). Surname Belfield on KSA roll
Bellingham, 26066 Tpr O'Brien Cairnes, ScH	QSA (5) DoK OFS Tr 01 02	Served 10 Jan 01 to 31 Jul 01. Also served KTG (No II Section, C Company, Pickering's Redoubt No 1), CPS, and KRV (786) until DMU 4 Apr 00
Bellows, Pte N, KTG	QSA (1) DoK	No II Section, No 2 Redoubt
Benadie, 475 Pte Gideon F, CP2	QSA (4) RoM DoK OFS Tr	C Squadron. Killed at Klip Drift 7 Mar 02
Bench, Pte D J, KTG	QSA (1) DoK	
Bendixon, Cpl H A, KTG	QSA (1) DoK	No I Section, C Company, Beaconsfield Town Guard
Benjamin, Pte Lionel Harry, KTG	QSA (1) DoK	See his biography (page 338)
Bennett, Lt G, KRV	QSA (3) DoK OFS Tr	KSA (2)
Bennett, 3717 Pte J, LNLR	QSA (3) DoK OFS Tr	KSA (2)
Bennett, Pte John Dawson, KTG	QSA (1) DoK	No IV Section, C Company, Pickering's Redoubt No 2. Also served SRG (134) from 11 Feb 01
Bennett, Pte R, KTG	QSA (1) DoK	No II Section, L Company. QSA (1), KStar. DNW Dec 05 £220
Bennett, Pte T, KTG	QSA (1) DoK	F Company
Bennett, 8926 Gnr Walter, RGA	QSA (2) DoK 01	Premier Mine. QSA (2), KStar. Spink Nov 05. Spink Apr 09
Bennette, Pte A, KTG	QSA (1) DoK	No II Section, A Company, Beaconsfield Town Guard
Bennetto, Pte F, KTG	QSA (1) DoK	Repairing gun carriages and transport wagons
Bennie, Lt A, KTG	QSA (1) DoK	No II Section, Belgravia Fort and depot supply paymaster
Benson, Pte J, KTG	QSA (1) DoK	No III Section, L Company
Benson, 4156 Sgt M, RAMC	QSA (2) DoK 01	Later served in No 11 General Hospital. To England 11 Jul 01
Benson, Sgt O P, KTG	QSA (1) DoK	No 2 Schmidt's Breastwork
Bentley, 3696 Cpl A, LNLR	QSA (3) DoK OFS Tr	KSA (2)
Bentley, 1096 Pte Miles W M, KRV	QSA (3) DoK OFS Tr	Discharged 1 Jul 02. Also served KTG (H Company) and KLH (26169). KSA (2). Occupation digger
Bentley, 4675 Cpl N, LNLR	QSA (3) DoK OFS Tr	QSA (1), DoK, KSA (2), 1914-15 Star (Cpl 7th Infy), BWM, VM (Cpl MTC). City Coins Jan 86
Benwell, 7611 Sgt F, ASC	QSA (3) DoK Tr Witt	MID. DCM LG 31 Oct 02

Berg, 583 Pte C G, KRV	QSA (3) DoK OFS Tr	Prisoner at Carter's Ridge 4 Nov 99. Discharged 1 Jul 02. KSA (2)
Bergmann, Mr F W, POC	QSA (1) DoK	
Bergmann, Pte V, KTG	QSA (1) DoK	No II Company, A Section, Reservoir
Bergmann, 225 Gnr Valdemar, DFA	QSA (2) DoK Tr	Enrolled DFA 10 Jan 00. Resigned 4 Mar 03. KSA (2). Occupation chemist
Bernhard, Pte C P, KTG	QSA (1) DoK	No I Company, B Section, Reservoir
Bernhard, Mr H, POC	QSA (1) DoK	
Bernhardi, Pte J, KTG	QSA (1) DoK	Kamfersdam Company
Berrange, Capt Christian A L, CP2	QSA (4) RoM DoK OFS Tr	See his biography (page 338)
Berrier, 543 Pte T J F, KRV	QSA (3) DoK OFS Tr	Discharged 14 Aug 02. Also served KLH (91) 4 Nov 99 until dismissed 30 Nov 99 and KTG (No 2 Schmidt's Breastwork). KSA (2)
Berry, 4250 Pte C, LNLR	QSA (3) DoK OFS Tr	KSA (2)
Berry, 657 Pte C W, KRV	QSA (2) DoK 01	Discharged 15 Jul 02
Berry, Pte James, KTG	QSA (2) DoK Tr	No I Section, B Company, No 4 Redoubt. Also served SRG (27 or 1032) from 11 Feb 01
Berry, William, KTG	QSA (0)	Roll states "Gun construction, repairs to Maxims and rifles". Occupation De Beers workshop foreman
Berryman, Pte J, KTG	QSA (1) DoK	No II Section, B2 Company, No 3 Redoubt
Beste, 614 Pte H F, KRV	QSA (2) DoK OFS	Discharged 3 Jul 02. QSA (2), [KSA (2)]. Warwick & Warwick Jun 09
Bestley, 318 Tpr W, KLH	QSA (3) DoK OFS 01	Served 20 Dec 99 until DMU 3 Aug 01. Medal issued 17 Oct 03. Occupation barman
Bethell, 381 Pte J, KRV	QSA (3) DoK OFS Tr	Discharged 29 Oct 01. Also served CPS (820) and rejoined KRV 12 Apr 02 until 1 Jul 02. KSA (2)
Betteridge, Sgt C, KTG	QSA (1) DoK	No I Company, A Section, Reservoir. QSA (1)
Bevan, 103 Sgt Ernest Henry, KLH	QSA (3) RoM DoK Paar	See his biography (page 338)
Bevan, 6 Tpr James, KLH	QSA (2) DoK Paar	Served 16 Oct 99 to 30 Apr 00. Served in the Bechuanaland Rebellion 1897 earning CGHGSM (1) Bech. QSA (2). Kaplan Aug 81 £345. Liverpool Aug 88 £90
Bevan, Mr W, POC	QSA (1) DoK	Telegraph signaller
Bewsher, 354 Pte John, CP2	QSA (3) DoK OFS 01	CP 7-pounder detachment. Died of wounds at Onderstedoorns 2 Feb 01
Beynon, Pte G, KTG	QSA (1) DoK	No III Section, L Company
Bezuidenhout, 1364 Pte G P, CP1	QSA (2) DoK OFS	C Squadron. QSA (2). Seaby Jan 75 £48
Bicker-Caarten, 22 Cpl Arnold Gerrard, KLH	QSA (2) DoK Paar	Served 18 Oct 99 to 30 Apr 01. Also served KTG (G Company) and CRSS (1055) 21 Feb 01 to 20 Aug 01. On QSA roll with initials O J, on nominal roll with initials A J and on KLH nominal roll with initials A E. SAGS (1) 1877-8-9 (Pte CMR), CGHGSM (1) Bas (Tpr CMR), QSA (2), KStar. Spink Jun 84
Biddles, 3451 L Cpl C, LNLR	QSA (3) DoK OFS Tr	KSA (2)
Billett, Pte E G, KTG	QSA (1) DoK	Premier Mine
Billing, 615 Sgt G, KRV	QSA (3) DoK OFS Tr	Wounded 25 Nov 99. KSA (2)
Billington, 658 Cpl C, KRV	QSA (3) DoK OFS Tr	Discharged 16 Aug 02. KSA (2)
Billington, 4368 Pte E, LNLR	QSA (3) DoK OFS Tr	QSA (3), KSA (2), BWM, VM, TFWM, DM, KStar. RHQ
Bilton, 2578 Sapr L H, RE	QSA (3) DoK Drie Tr	KSA (2)

Name	Medals	Notes
Bingham, Lt C H M, LNLR	QSA (4) DoK OFS Tr 01	See his biography (page 338)
Binyon, 137 Tpr Eldred Hickman, KLH	QSA (2) DoK OFS	Served 1 Nov 99 until discharged 30 Apr 00. Also served SRG (37) from 11 Feb 01
Birch, 1127 Sgt Thomas Newberry, KLH	QSA (3) DoK OFS Tr	Served 19 Oct 99 to 10 Nov 00. Prisoner Klerksdorp 25 Jul 00. QSA (3), KStar. Spink Feb 70 £70. QSA (3). City Coins Nov 07
Bircham, 8 Tpr Henry Robert, KLH	QSA (2) DoK Paar	Served 2 Nov 99 to 30 Apr 00. Also served CPS, DMT Mafeking and National Scouts
Bird, Lt I, KTG	QSA (1) DoK	No III Company, A Section, Reservoir. QSA (1), KSA (2) (renamed?), KStar. Glendining Feb 33. QSA (1), KStar. Sotheby May 82 £160
Bird, Pte J, KTG	QSA (1) DoK	No I Section, B2 Company, No 3 Redoubt
Bird, Sgt T, KTG	QSA (1) DoK	No IV Section, B Company, Beaconsfield Town Guard
Birkley, Pte R G, KTG	QSA (1) DoK	No 4 supply depot. Also served Warrenton DMT (8). OFS & Tr crossed through on Warrenton DMT QSA roll. QSA (1). Liverpool Nov 87 £85
Birks, 139 Sgt Robert, CP2	QSA (2) DoK OFS	B Squadron. Dismissed for misconduct 9 Jul 00
Birt, Lt A G, KTG	QSA (1) DoK	Food Supply Staff and Kamfersdam Company
Birtley, 759 Pte William H, KRV	QSA (2) DoK 01	Dismissed for misconduct 17 Nov 00. Also served KTG (Premier Mine) and 1st BrH (22760) 6 Dec 00 to 10 Jun 01. BrH QSA roll states QSA (2) CC 01 issued 3 Apr 29
Bishop, 258 Tpr Frederick John, KLH	QSA (2) DoK OFS	Served 19 Oct 99 to 6 Nov 00
Bishop, Pte H T, KTG	QSA (1) DoK	No IV Section, B Company, Beaconsfield Town Guard. QSA (1), KStar. City Coins May 02. Morris Nov 03 £350. Spink Apr 06 £310. Warwick & Warwick Sep 06
Bishop, Pte R, KTG	QSA (2) DoK Paar	H Company. Paar clasp issued 7 May 06
Bishop, 612 Pte R T, KRV	QSA (3) RoM DoK OFS	Discharged 1 Jul 00
Bishop, 576 L Cpl Reginald, KRV	QSA (4) RoM DoK OFS Tr	Also served DH (40282) 2 Feb 02 to 30 Jun 02. Dangerously wounded near Kimberley 27 Feb 01. KSA (2)
Bisset, Nurse H, NS	QSA (0)	Kimberley Civil Hospital
Bissett, 584 Pte A, KRV	QSA (2) DoK OFS	DMU 5 May 00
Bissett, 107 Cpl Stewart Finlay, KLH	QSA (2) DoK OFS	Served 20 Oct 99 to 6 Mar 00. Also served KTG
Bissett, Gnr W, DBMB	QSA (1) DoK	Crusher Redoubt and Otto's Kopje
Black, Maj Andrew Orman, KRV	QSA (2) DoK OFS	See his biography (page 338)
Black, Pte D, KTG	QSA (1) DoK	QSA (1). Ursual Mar 98. Liverpool Feb 00 £120
Black, Cpl J, KTG	QSA (1) DoK	Gibraltar Fort, Davis's Heap
Black, Mr R, POC	QSA (1) DoK	
Black, 216 Cpl W, KRV	QSA (3) RoM DoK OFS	Non effective 6 Jul 00
Black, Cpl W O, KTG	QSA (1) DoK	No II Company, A Section, Reservoir. QSA (1), KStar. Glendining Mar 75 £75
Blackbeard, Capt Charles Alexander, KTG	QSA (1) DoK	See his biography (page 338)
Blackbeard, 139 Tpr Dudley Donald, KLH	QSA (2) DoK OFS	Served 30 Oct 99 to 6 Mar 00
Blackbeard, Pte Lesley, KTG	QSA (1) DoK	No I Section, A Company, Beaconsfield Town Guard. Son of C A Blackbeard. QSA (1), KStar. City Coins Mar 03. Warwick & Warwick Sep 06
Blacking, Lt E, KTG	QSA (1) DoK	No I Section, A Company, Beaconsfield Town Guard

Blacking, Capt F, KTG	QSA (1) DoK	See his biography (page 339)
Blacklock, 814 Pte John, KRV	QSA (3) RoM DoK OFS	Discharged 1 Jul 00. Also served KTG (No IV Company, A Section, Reservoir) and CRSS (1327) from 28 Jun 01. Severely wounded Taungs Station 2 Sep 01 in an accident to the armoured train. Occupation engine driver
Blackmore, 415 Tpr A, KLH	QSA (2) DoK OFS	Discharged 23 Mar 00
Blaiberg, Pte B, KTG	QSA (1) DoK	No III Section, No 2 Redoubt
Blaine, 233 Pte Henry Robert, CP2	QSA (1) DoK	CP dismounted branch (barrier & redoubt duties). QSA (1), KStar. Kaplan Aug 07
Blair, 359 Pte James Cameron, CP2	QSA (4) RoM DoK OFS Tr	CP No 3 Maxim gun detachment. Severely wounded Hoopstad 23 Oct 00. Died of disease Kimberley 18 Aug 01. Served in the Bechuanaland Rebellion 1897 earning CGHGSM (1) Bech
Blake, 490 L Sgt Alfred, KRV	QSA (1) DoK	Killed in action 20 Oct 99 at Riverton Pumping station
Blake, Cpl J, KTG	QSA (1) DoK	No I Section, K Company
Blakeley, 4013 Pte J, LNLR	QSA (1) DoK	Invalided to England 28 Apr 00
Blakemore, Cpl A, KTG	QSA (1) DoK	Kimberley Mine Ambulance Company, E Section. Possibly identical with 415 A Blackmore, KLH
Blakemore, Pte D, KTG	QSA (1) DoK	No 1 Redoubt
Blakemore, Pte J M, KTG	QSA (3) RoM DoK OFS	Kimberley Mine Ambulance Company with mounted forces. Also served KLH (409) as Blackmore to 5 Jun 00
Blakemore, Pte W, KTG	QSA (1) DoK	No 1 Redoubt
Blassoples, 362 Pte Alexander, CP2	QSA (4) RoM DoK OFS Tr	CP 7-pounder detachment. CGHGSM (1) Bech, QSA (4), KSA (2), 14-15 Star (Sgt SAMR), BWM, VM (SAMR), Permanent Forces LS&GC, KStar. Kaplan Nov 08
Bligh, 1074 Pte Percy James, CP2	QSA (3) DoK OFS Tr	Also served KRV (510) until DMU 12 Jun 00 and DFH. KSA (2) not issued as struck off but further note says reissued 23 Apr 09. Duplicate QSA issued
Blount, 2870 Pte A, LNLR	QSA (1) DoK	Invalided to England 29 Jun 00
Blue, Pte Colin, KTG	QSA (4) DoK OFS Tr 01	No II Section, C Company, Pickering's Redoubt No 1. Also served DrS (20860) 7 Jan 01 to 7 Apr 01
Blue, 542 Pte H, KRV	QSA (2) DoK Tr	Transferred to DFA 12 Nov 99. KSA (2) as 212 Gunner. Possibly issued off DFA roll
Blum, Capt A, KTG	QSA (1) DoK	See his biography (page 339)
Blumenthal, Pte H, KTG	QSA (1) DoK	No I Company, B Section, Reservoir
Blumenthal, Pte M, KTG	QSA (1) DoK	No I Company, B Section, Reservoir
Blundell, Tpr Thomas Craven, DH	QSA (6) DoK Paar Drie Joh DH Witt	Served Feb 00 to 9 Aug 00. Also served KTG (Premier Mine). DoK incorrectly recorded as RoK on the DH QSA roll. QSA (6), 14-15 Star (Pte 2nd Infy), BWM, VM (2nd Cl WO SANLC), KStar. Glendining Dec 89 £170. See his medals (page 513)
Blunden, Pte Charles, KTG	QSA (3) DoK OFS Tr	Gibraltar Fort, Davis's Heap. Also served KLH (1022) and KH (133). Appears on the KLH nominal roll with four different periods of service and five regimental numbers! KSA (2). Occupation cab owner
Blur, 212 Gnr H, DFA	QSA (2) DoK Tr	Discharged 1 Jul 02. Also served Kimb Regt. KSA (2)
Bobbins, 66 CSM J, KRV	QSA (1) DoK	Previously Driver, Prince Alfred's Own Cape Volunteer Artillery, Basuto War including the operations in the Transkei 1880-81 and Bechuanaland Rebellion 1897. [CGHGSM (3)], QSA (1), [KSA (2)], Colonial Auxiliary Forces LS Medal (25 Aug 03), KStar. City Coins Mar 03
Bobroff, Pte E, KTG	QSA (1) DoK	QSA (1). Sotheby Jun 90
Bock, 953 Pte R C, KRV	QSA (3) RoM DoK OFS	Also served KTG (No 2 Schmidt's Breastwork). Discharged 1 Jul 00

Medal roll

Bodington, 267 Pte C R, KRV	QSA (1) DoK	DMU 6 Apr 00
Bodley, Cpl A, KTG	QSA (1) DoK	G Company
Bodley, Cpl C, KTG	QSA (1) DoK	No I Section, No 2 Redoubt
Bodley, Pte G, KTG	QSA (1) DoK	No I Company, B Section, Reservoir
Bodley, Capt Joseph Horatio, KRV	QSA (3) RoM DoK OFS	See his biography (page 339)
Bodley, Pte Percy Graham, KTG	QSA (3) DoK OFS Tr	Kimberley Mine Ambulance Company, B Section. Also served WS (27) 23 Mar 00 to 4 Sep 00 and GDC 29 Dec 00 to 20 Nov 02
Boffey, Pte G, KTG	QSA (1) DoK	No II Section, A Company, Beaconsfield Town Guard. QSA (1). Dixon Jun 03 £135. eBay Feb 04
Bolitho, 770 Pte J, KRV	QSA (4) RoM DoK OFS Tr	Served 20 Nov 99 to 24 Nov 99. Also served KTG (No I Section, B Company, Beaconsfield Town Guard) from 24 Nov 99 and KLH (358) 7 Mar 00 to 10 Nov 00. Killed 31 Dec 01 at Platberg. QSA (4), [KSA (2)]. City Coins No 18
Bolling, 4844 Pte A, LNLR	QSA (3) DoK OFS Tr	QSA (3), KSA (2). Historik Orders Aug 03 £245. eBay Dec 05 £525. Possibly entitled to BWM & VM
Bolton, 203 Sgt E, DFA	QSA (3) DoK OFS Tr	Enrolled DFA 14 Oct 99. Discharged 1 Jul 02. Served CMR 14 Sep 98 to 31 May 99. KSA (2). KSA issued to OC Royal Australian Artillery, Sydney. KSA reissued 7 May 09
Bolton, 3869 Pte J, LNLR	QSA (2) DoK OFS	Invalided to England 5 May 00. QSA (2), [KSA (2)], KStar. DNW Dec 03 £270
Bone, 659 Pte W H, KRV	QSA (3) DoK OFS Tr	Discharged 1 Jul 02. KSA (2)
Bonner, 425 Pte A G, KRV	QSA (3) RoM DoK OFS	Discharged 1 Dec 00. Previously Private, Griqualand West Rifle Brigade and served Bechuanaland Rebellion 1897 earning CGHGSM (1) Bech. QSA (0) (Officially reimpressed). Liverpool Jun 93 £28. QSA (3) (Officially reimpressed). Liverpool Jul 97 £160
Bonner, 3999 Pte H, LNLR	QSA (3) DoK OFS Tr	KSA (2)
Bonsor, 590 Pte Morris William, CP2	QSA (1) DoK	CP dismounted branch (barrier & redoubt duties). Discharged at own request 15 Oct 00
Boon, Sister E, NS	QSA (0)	Kimberley Civil Hospital
Booth, Lt J R, KTG	QSA (1) DoK	H Company. QSA (1). Kaplan Nov 08
Booth, Capt R D, KTG	QSA (1) DoK	SMO at Premier Mine and Ambulance Corps, Beaconsfield Town Guard. Also on roll for civil surgeons which was signed by O'Gorman 30 Dec 05 at the Military Hospital, Brighton
Booth, Sgt T, KTG	QSA (1) DoK	No IV Section, A Company, Beaconsfield Town Guard
Borcher, 763 Pte A, KRV	QSA (3) RoM DoK OFS	Discharged 15 Feb 01. Also served KTG (No II Section, A Company, Beaconsfield Town Guard). QSA (3). Glendining Mar 89. Liverpool Aug 91 £195
Borcher, Pte Harry, KTG	QSA (1) DoK	No I Section, No 2 Redoubt. Also served CPS (632) and KLH 8 May 02 to 30 Jun 02. Occupation blacksmith
Borgstrom, 144 Pte H S, KRV	QSA (1) DoK	DMU 4 Apr 00. 50th Anniversary attendee
Borgstrom, 216 Tpr H W P, KLH	QSA (3) DoK OFS Tr	Served 26 Oct 99 to 30 Apr 00. Also served CPS (768)
Borgstrom, 616 Pte Henry, KRV	QSA (4) DoK Tr 01 02	DMU 17 Oct 99. Also served KTG, KLH, KH (360), CPS (769) and CCCC (32649). Surname Bergstrom on KH KSA roll. Occupation debris washer. Two of the Borgstroms attended the 50th Anniversary reunion
Borner, 91597 Bombdr Henry R, RGA	QSA (1) DoK	Premier Mine. KSA (2). Surname Boner on KSA roll
Borrill, Cpl T, KTG	QSA (1) DoK	No II Section, L Company

Boscombe, 541 Pte George, KRV	QSA (5) DoK OFS Tr 01 02	DMU 28 Dec 99. Also served KTG, KR, WLH, DS (26196) 27 Dec 00 to 24 Mar 02 and GWLH 27 Mar 02 to 30 Jun 02
Boscombe, 289 Pte M, KRV	QSA (1) DoK	DMU 3 Jan 00. Also served KTG (Cycle Corps, A Company)
Boscombe, Pte W, KTG	QSA (1) DoK	No I Section, B Company, Beaconsfield Town Guard
Botha, Pte C C, KTG	QSA (1) DoK	Kimberley Mine Ambulance Company, A Section
Botha, Pte J A, KTG	QSA (1) DoK	No I Company, B Section, Reservoir
Botha, 332 Tpr Z Johannes, KLH	QSA (3) RoM DoK OFS	Served 3 Dec 99 to 5 Jun 00
Bott, 172 Gnr Joseph, DFA	QSA (2) DoK OFS	Enrolled DFA 3 Aug 99. Served Bulawayo Field Force. Resigned 26 Nov 02
Bottom, Pte W, KTG	QSA (1) DoK	G Company
Bottomley, Pte R H, KTG	QSA (1) DoK	No I Section, No 2 Redoubt
Bould, Pte J, KTG	QSA (1) DoK	Premier Mine
Boult, 593 Pte Gerard Cecil, CP2	QSA (1) DoK	Discharged time expired 24 May 01
Boult, Pte S E, KTG	QSA (1) DoK	No I Section, B2 Company, No 3 Redoubt
Bourhill, Pte H, KTG	QSA (1) DoK	No II Section, Belgravia Fort
Bourhill, Pte R, KTG	QSA (1) DoK	Cycle Corps, A Company
Bourke, 768 Pte William Patrick, CP2	QSA (3) DoK OFS Tr	C Squadron
Bourne, Tpr Stanley, DH	QSA (6) DoK Paar Drie Joh DH Witt	Served 18 Feb 00 to 28 Jan 01. Also served KTG. Occupation fitter. Wounded in the right knee 23 Feb 00
Bovey, Lt E, CP1	QSA (2) DoK OFS	A Squadron. KSA (2). Served in the Bechuanaland Rebellion 1897 earning CGHGSM (1) Bech
Bovey, 719 Cpl H, CP1	QSA (2) DoK OFS	Served 11 Oct 99 to 31 May 02. C Squadron. Served in the Bechuanaland Rebellion 1897 earning CGHGSM (1) Bech
Bowden, Lt Sidney Vincent, CP2	QSA (2) DoK OFS	See his biography (page 339)
Bowden, Pte William John, KTG	QSA (4) RoM DoK OFS Tr	Premier Mine. Also served KLH (172) 8 Mar 00 to 5 Jun 00, SRG (110) from 12 Feb 01 and CPS (140) 7 Nov 00 to 30 Apr 02. KSA (2)
Bowen, Capt Harry James Ap Owen, KLH	QSA (2) DoK OFS	See his biography (page 339)
Bowen, 366 Pte J, KRV	QSA (1) DoK	DMU 8 Jan 00
Bowen, 338 Tpr John Leo(lin), KLH	QSA (4) RoM DoK OFS Tr	Served 6 Dec 99 to 8 Jun 00. Also served SRG (24) from 11 Feb 01 and CPS (859)
Bower, 1011 Cpl John Henry, KLH	QSA (3) DoK OFS Tr	Served 19 Oct 99 to 6 Nov 00. SAGS (1) 1879 (Tpr FLH), CGHGSM (2) Transkei Bas (Nesbitt's LH), QSA (3), KStar. Christies Jul 85. Liverpool Jul 86 £580
Bower, 24 Tpr L, SAC	QSA (4) RoM DoK OFS Tr	Also served KLH (412) 10 Dec 00 to 8 Apr 03. KSA (2)
Bower, 67 Tpr Thomas, KLH	QSA (4) DoK Tr Witt 01	Served 20 Oct 99 to 30 Apr 00. Also served 1st BrH 12 Jul 00 to 15 Dec 01 and NSWIB
Bower, Dvr W, DBMB	QSA (1) DoK	Botanical Gardens
Bowers, 4508 Pte W, LNLR	QSA (2) DoK OFS	To England 2 Jul 00. KSA (2)
Bowes, Pte T, KTG	QSA (1) DoK	No 6 Redoubt
Bowler, 4163 Band A, LNLR	QSA (1) DoK	KSA (2)
Bowles, 1117 L Cpl A O, CP1	QSA (2) DoK OFS	B Squadron. Discharged time expired 11 Jun 02. KSA (2). Served in the Bechuanaland Rebellion 1897 earning CGHGSM (1) Bech
Bowman, Pte A, KTG	QSA (1) DoK	No I Section, D Company

Bowman, 617 Pte P B, KRV	QSA (3) DoK OFS Tr	Discharged 1 Jul 02. KSA (2)
Bown, 242 Pte Sidney Herbert, CP2	QSA (4) RoM DoK OFS Tr	B Squadron. KSA (2)
Bowness, 35530 Tpr George, DH	QSA (3) DoK OFS Tr	Served 1 Aug 01 to 30 Jan 02. Also served KTG (G Company), CinCBG (22147) 12 Nov 00 to 15 May 01, ALH (40280) 8 Feb 02 to 23 Mar 02 and WLH (42333) 8 May 02 to 30 Jun 02. OFS and Tr issued 2 May 05. Occupation miner
Bowness, 1239 Pte James, KRV	QSA (5) RoM DoK OFS Tr 01	Discharged KRV 24 May 01. Also served KTG (No 2 Schmidt's Breastwork) and KLH (388) as Bonas 7 Mar 00 to 5 Jun 00
Boxall, Cpl G, KTG	QSA (1) DoK	No I Company, B Section, Reservoir
Boyd, Pte F, KTG	QSA (1) DoK	No II Section, L Company. QSA (1). Kaplan Aug 08
Boyd, Pte J H, KTG	QSA (1) DoK	No IV Section, No 4 Redoubt
Boyd, Sgt R, KTG	QSA (1) DoK	No IV Section, C Company, Pickering's Redoubt No 2
Boyd, Pte R W, KTG	QSA (1) DoK	No II Section, L Company. Also served KRV (1012)
Boyes, 3845 Pte W, LNLR	QSA (3) DoK OFS Tr	KSA (2)
Braden, 1021 Pte F, KRV	QSA (2) DoK OFS	Discharged 1 Jul 02. Also served KTG (G Company). KSA (2)
Bradford, Pte J, KTG	QSA (1) DoK	No 1 Redoubt
Bradford, Pte W K, KTG	QSA (1) DoK	No II Section, Belgravia Fort
Bradley, Sgt F J, KTG	QSA (1) DoK	Mounted Section, B Company, Beaconsfield Town Guard
Bradshaw, Pte Thomas, KTG	QSA (1) DoK	Premier Mine. Also served KLH (189) 7 Mar 00 to 5 Jun 00. 50th Anniversary attendee
Brady, 15 Cpl Claude, KLH	QSA (2) DoK OFS	Wounded 24 Oct 99. Served 16 Oct 99 until DMU 24 Mar 00. Also served KTG
Brady, 391 Sgt Maj George Clifford, CP2	QSA (1) DoK	C Squadron. Killed in action 28 Nov 99. Medal issued 29 Sep 10. Born Ireland 27 Feb 58. Served in the Bechuanaland Rebellion 1897 earning CGHGSM (1) Bech. Occupation tallyman at De Beers from 1892
Brady, 778 Pte Herbert, CP2	QSA (1) DoK	CP dismounted branch (barrier & redoubt duties)
Brady, 618 Pte Thomas, KRV	QSA (2) DoK OFS	DMU 16 Dec 99. Also served KLH (397 & 220) 7 Mar 00 to 4 May 00. Dismissed KLH after 30 days IHL. KLH rolls says deserted KOYLI
Brain, 1160 Pte Francis Sturge, FLH	QSA (2) DoK OFS	Served 31 Mar 02 to 31 Jul 02. Also served CP1 (1474) (A Squadron) 11 Oct 99 to 20 May 01 and G Sqn CCF. CC clasp issued by FLH and recovered 25 Feb 1910. KSA (2) issued 16 Dec 10 by CPD1. Occupation saddler. QSA (2). Kaplan May 04. See his QSA on page 514
Braine, Lt W, KRV	QSA (2) DoK Paar	Previously served as Sgt DFH in the Bechuanaland Rebellion of 1897. CGHGSM (1) Bech (Sgt DFH), QSA (2), KStar
Brampton, Pte H H, KTG	QSA (1) DoK	Kenilworth Defence Force. Food supply
Brand, Sub Insp E C J, CPS	QSA (1) DoK	CGHGSM (1) Bech, QSA (1), BWM, VM, KStar. Spink Nov 95 £300. DNW Sep 01 £500. See his medals on page 503
Brand, J G, KTG	QSA (0)	Roll states "Construction of forts, trenches, barricades etc"
Brand, Capt Reginald, KLH	QSA (5) DoK Paar Tr 01 02	Resigned KLH 8 Mar 00. Also served KTG & SRG. MID 23 Jun 02
Brandham, Pte T, KTG	QSA (1) DoK	D Company (Veterans), Beaconsfield Town Guard
Brandt, Pte Frederick James, KTG	QSA (1) DoK	H Company. Also served CRSS (1446 & 4046) from 12 Nov 01. Occupation cab proprietor
Braske, Pte A, KTG	QSA (1) DoK	Premier Mine
Braske, Pte W, KTG	QSA (1) DoK	Ambulance Corps, Beaconsfield Town Guard as Braski

Brauns, 320 Cpl Herman Wilhelm, CP2	QSA (2) DoK OFS	CP HQ and depot mounted branch. KSA (2). Served in the Bechuanaland Rebellion 1897 earning CGHGSM (1) Bech
Bray, 996 Band Sgt G, LNLR	QSA (3) DoK OFS Tr	KSA (2)
Bray, Mr J K, POC	QSA (1) DoK	
Bray, Lt William John, SRG	QSA (4) RoM DoK OFS Tr	QSA (4), KSA (2) (Lt WLH), KStar. See his medals on page 514
Breda, Pte H, KTG	QSA (1) DoK	Gibraltar Fort, Davis's Heap
Breda, 815 Pte H A, KRV	QSA (3) RoM DoK OFS	Discharged 1 Jul 00. Also served KTG (No I Company, B Section, Reservoir and H Company)
Bredenkamp, Sp Const D C, CP2	QSA (1) DoK	
Bredenkamp, 357 Tpr John, KLH	QSA (3) DoK OFS Tr	Served 22 Jan 00 until dismissed 30 Mar 00. Also served KRV (409) 5 Oct 99 to 18 Jan 00, DH (34923) 12 Jun 01 to 19 Dec 01 and ALH (40212) from 18 Jan 02. Note suggests 'drunkeness and misconduct' in KRV. Killed 7 Mar 02 at Klip Drift. Occupation clerk
Bredenkamp, Pte M, KTG	QSA (1) DoK	No 6 Redoubt
Bredenkamp, 331 Tpr William, KLH	QSA (6) RoM DoK OFS Tr 01 02	Served 6 Dec 99 to 5 Jun 00. Also served FID 1 Sep 00 to 23 Nov 00 and ALH (34911) 30 Apr 01 to 31 Oct 01 & (40192) 17 Jan 02 to 24 Mar 02. Slightly wounded Widpoort 19 Sep 01. Occupation carpenter
Brennan, 86 Sgt Alexander, CP2	QSA (1) DoK	CP intelligence and detective staff. DMU 31 Dec 00
Brennan, Lt F H, KTG	QSA (1) DoK	No IV Company, A Section, Reservoir
Brennan, 2145 Dvr M, RE	QSA (3) DoK Drie Witt	KSA (2)
Brett, 197 Dvr Francis John, DFA	QSA (3) DoK OFS Tr	Enrolled DFA 25 Sep 99. Resigned 13 Jan 03. Occupation electrician at Kimberley Mine. QSA (3), KSA (2), KStar. Kaplan Feb 04. Dixon Sep 04 £475. Lockdales Nov 08
Brice, Pte A E, KTG	QSA (1) DoK	No III Section, Belgravia Fort
Brick, 1563 Pte T, CP1	QSA (1) DoK	C Squadron. Died of disease 17 Jan 00
Bridge, Capt J M, KRV	QSA (2) DoK OFS	See his biography (page 339)
Bridger, 26161 Tpr Henry William, ScH	QSA (4) DoK OFS Tr 01	Served 30 Jan 01 to 12 Jul 01. Also served KTG (No IV Section, B Company, Beaconsfield Town Guard)
Bridger, Pte W, KTG	QSA (3) DoK OFS Tr	No I Section, C Company, Beaconsfield Town Guard
Bridges, 805 Pte Alfred, CP2	QSA (1) DoK	CP dismounted branch (barrier & redoubt duties). KSA (2)
Bridle, 102 Band A, KRV	QSA (1) DoK	QSA (1), [KSA (2)]. Spink Apr 93. Spink Dec 95 £90. Morton & Eden Jul 08
Briggs, Pte M, KTG	QSA (1) DoK	No I Section, D Company
Briggs, 449 Pte R, KRV	QSA (1) DoK	Discharged 5 Aug 02. KSA (2)
Bright, 5587 Pte A, LNLR	QSA (3) DoK OFS Tr	KSA (2)
Brill, 760 Pte Frederick George, KRV	QSA (2) DoK 01	Dismissed 14 Aug 00, absence and drunkenness, 7th offence. Also served KTG (No 2 Schmidt's Breastwork) and FLH (1148). Occupation clerk. Had served CMR for 3 years
Brindle, 3952 Pte J, LNLR	QSA (1) DoK	Invalided to England 1 May 00
Brindle, 4093 Pte W, LNLR	QSA (3) DoK OFS Tr	QSA (3), KSA (2), KStar. Spink Sep 92
Brink, Pte A, KTG	QSA (1) DoK	No I Section, Belgravia Fort
Brink, Sub Insp S J H, CP2	QSA (1) DoK	Acting Sub Inspector attached to CP2. Served CPD2 HQ Staff

Medal roll

Briscoe, Pte R, KTG	QSA (1) DoK	No I Section, D Company. QSA (1), KStar. eBay Dec 05. Kaplan Nov 08
Bristow, Pte S A, KTG	QSA (1) DoK	No 2 supply depot. Served in the Bechuanaland Rebellion 1897 earning CGHGSM (1) Bech
Britton, 4345 Pte W, LNLR	QSA (3) DoK OFS Tr	KSA (2)
Britton, Lt W D, KTG	QSA (1) DoK	No III Section, A Company, Beaconsfield Town Guard
Broderick, Pte M, KTG	QSA (1) DoK	No II Section, C Company, Pickering's Redoubt No 2. CGHGSM (1) Bas (Tpr KLH), QSA (1), 14-15 Star (Pte Kimberley CDO), BWM, VM (Pte SAVR), KStar
Brodrick, 52 Gnr W J, DFA	QSA (1) DoK	Served in the Bechuanaland Rebellion 1897 earning CGHGSM (1) Bech
Broe, 1680 Sapr P, RE	QSA (3) DoK Drie Tr	QSA (3), KSA (2), 14-15 Star, BWM, VM (MID), LS&GC, KStar. RHQ
Brogan, 4765 Pte J, LNLR	QSA (3) DoK OFS Tr	QSA (3), [KSA (2)]. Bonhams Oct 03. Liverpool Jan 10 £330
Brooker, 414 Pte W M, KRV	QSA (1) DoK	DMU 14 Apr 00
Brooklyn, 175 Gnr John, DFA	QSA (1) DoK	Enrolled DFA 1 Jul 91. Served DFH 1 Jul 91 to 1 Jul 99. Discharged 17 Jul 06. During the Great War served as Sapper SAEC and Private South African Veteran Regiment. CGHGSM (1) Bech (Tpr DFH), BSACM rev Rhod 96 (0) (Tpr MRF), QSA (1), 14-15 Star (Spr SAEC), BWM, VM (Spr SAEC), KStar. Spink Oct 99 £550
Brooks, Pte C, KTG	QSA (1) DoK	In charge of natives on sanitary works
Brooks, 449 Clerk E J, ASC	QSA (1) DoK	
Brooks, Pte Herbert Hentram, KTG	QSA (2) DoK OFS	No IV Section, No 2 Redoubt. Also served SRG (167 or 166) from 12 Feb 01. Possibly served in the Bechuanaland Rebellion 1897 with Vryburg Volunteers earning CGHGSM (1) Bech
Brooks, Pte J, KTG	QSA (1) DoK	No III Section, A Company, Beaconsfield Town Guard
Brooks, 88 Tpr J L, KLH	QSA (1) DoK	Joined 28 Oct 99 and died of disease 15 Feb 00
Brooks, R H, KTG	QSA (0)	Roll states "Chief Electrical Department in charge of all searchlights, telephones and dynamite mines"
Brooks, 4462 Pte S, LNLR	QSA (4) DoK OFS Tr 01	Invalided to England 13 Feb 01
Brooks, Pte W, KTG	QSA (1) DoK	Kamfersdam Company
Brooks, Pte W, KTG	QSA (1) DoK	
Brooks, Pte William Thomas, KTG	QSA (4) DoK OFS Tr 01	Kamfersdam Company. Also served CinCBG (22409) 31 Oct 00 and discharged 24 Feb 01
Broom, Pte A, KTG	QSA (1) DoK	
Brophy, Pte Francis Michael, KTG	QSA (1) DoK	No III Section, L Company. Also served SRG (147) from 11 Feb 01
Brophy, Pte M T, KTG	QSA (1) DoK	Gibraltar Fort, Davis's Heap
Brophy, Pte R, KTG	QSA (1) DoK	Cycle Corps, A Company
Broughton, 4993 Pte C, LNLR	QSA (3) DoK OFS Tr	QSA (3), [KSA (2)]. Seaby Feb 75 £45
Brown, Pte A F, KTG	QSA (1) DoK	No IV Section, A Company, Beaconsfield Town Guard. Added to the roll in 1925
Brown, Pte A S, KTG	QSA (1) DoK	No III Section, L Company
Brown, 1017 Pte C, KRV	QSA (2) DoK OFS	DMU 13 May 02. Also served KTG (No 2 Schmidt's Breastwork). KSA (2)
Brown, Pte C A, KTG	QSA (1) DoK	
Brown, 53 Pte Charles, CP2	QSA (4) RoM DoK OFS Tr	C Squadron. KSA reissued 5 Mar 09. CGHGSM (1) Bech (Pte CP), QSA (4), KSA (2), BWM, VM (2nd SAI), KStar. Glendining Nov 92 £300

Brown, Sgt Charles Henry, KTG	QSA (1) DoK	No 2 Schmidt's Breastwork and No IV Section, No 2 Redoubt. Found guilty during the siege of discharging a rifle while drunk that resulted in a death. He was sentenced to 18 months imprisonment with labour. Possibly served in the Bechuanaland Rebellion 1897 with DFH earning CGHGSM (1) Bech
Brown, 211 Pte D, KRV	QSA (2) DoK OFS	Non effective 5 May 00
Brown, Pte H A, KTG	QSA (1) DoK	No 3 supply depot. SAGS (1) 1879 (Tpr 3rd Cape Yeo), CGHGSM (1) Bas (Tpr C M Yeo), QSA (1), KStar. Bonhams Apr 08 £1,410
Brown, 39 Pte Henry Philip, CP2	QSA (4) RoM DoK OFS Tr	C Squadron. Prisoner 4 Nov 00. Surname Browne on CPD2 QSA roll. Served 11 Oct 99 to 31 May 02. Also served Capt DS 21 Dec 00 to 4 Mar 02 and Capt KH from 5 Mar 02. KSA (2). Served in the Bechuanaland Rebellion 1897 earning CGHGSM (1) Bech
Brown, Nurse I, NS	QSA (0)	Kimberley Civil Hospital
Brown, 3968 Pte J, LNLR	QSA (3) DoK OFS Tr	QSA (3), [KSA (2)], KStar. RHQ
Brown, Cpl J, KTG	QSA (1) DoK	
Brown, J, KTG	QSA (0)	Roll states "In charge of natives on sanitary works"
Brown, Mr J H, POC	QSA (1) DoK	
Brown, Lt James Hendry, SRG	QSA (2) DoK OFS	Served 13 Feb 01 to 31 Mar 01. Also served KLH (105) 19 Oct 99 until discharged 7 Mar 00. CGHGSM (1) Bech (Pte DFH), QSA (2), 14-15 Star (Pte Kimberley Cdo), BWM, VM (Pte SAVR), KStar. Spink Jan 88 £400. Spink May 93 £300. QSA (2). Liverpool Feb 97 £150. DNW Sep 01 £220
Brown, Pte M, KTG	QSA (1) DoK	Medical Corps, No 1 Company, C Section
Brown, Pte N S, KTG	QSA (1) DoK	Food supply
Brown, Pte N S E, KTG	QSA (1) DoK	Food supply
Brown, 258 Pte P, KRV	QSA (1) DoK	DMU 9 Apr 00
Brown, 179 Bombdr Pelham Maitland, DFA	QSA (1) DoK	Served 11 Oct 99 to 26 Jul 00. Also served Capt SRG (56) 12 Feb 01 to 31 May 02. KSA (2)
Brown, 224 Cpl Peter, CP2	QSA (4) RoM DoK OFS Tr	A Squadron. KSA (2). Prisoner Manthe 25 Jun 01. Served in the Bechuanaland Rebellion 1897 earning CGHGSM (1) Bech
Brown, 5540 Pte R, LNLR	QSA (3) DoK OFS Tr	KSA (2)
Brown, 4688 Pte S, LNLR	QSA (2) DoK OFS	KSA (2)
Brown, Pte S A, KTG	QSA (1) DoK	No I Section, Mandy Fort
Brown, 128 Pte Samuel, CP2	QSA (2) DoK OFS	CP intelligence and detective staff. MID. Transferred to ORCP 31 Oct 00. CGHGSM (1) Bech, QSA (4) inc RoM, KSA (2), BWM, VM (Cpl ASC MT), KStar. Seaby Jan 47. See his photograph (page 548)
Brown, 3842 Pte T, LNLR	QSA (3) DoK OFS Tr	KSA (2)
Brown, Pte T A, KTG	QSA (1) DoK	No I Section, Mandy Fort
Brown, Pte T W, KTG	QSA (1) DoK	
Brown, Sgt W A, KTG	QSA (2) DoK OFS	Kenilworth Defence Force. Also served KLH (104) 19 Oct 99 to 12 Nov 99 when transferred to KTG
Brown, 206 Tpr William, KLH	QSA (2) DoK OFS	Served 19 Oct 99 to 30 Apr 00. Also served KRV (1182)
Browning, Sgt James, KTG	QSA (2) DoK 01	H Company. Served KTG Oct 99 to May 00. Also served DS (26095) 15 Jan 01 to 15 Mar 01 and SRG (598) 31 May 01 to 26 Nov 01

Name	Medals	Notes
Browning, Lt Robert Bently, KTG	QSA (2) DoK OFS	H Company. Also served Lt KRV. During Great War was Major & QM, 1st Btn Kimberley Regiment and served in GSWA. QSA (3), KSA (2), KStar, 14-15 Star (Maj 7th Infy), BWM, VM, Colonial Auxiliary Forces Decoration. Sotheby Feb 75 £150. Sotheby Mar 82. Glendining Sep 90 £430
Bruce, 539 Pte A, KRV	QSA (1) DoK	Also served KTG (Kenilworth Defence Force). Dismissed 7 Nov 99 for being absent from parade for patrol
Brun, Pte A, KTG	QSA (1) DoK	No II Section, No 2 Redoubt
Brunton, Pte R J, KTG	QSA (1) DoK	No I Section, L Company
Brunton, 697 Pte Walter George, KRV	QSA (4) RoM DoK OFS Tr	See his biography (page 339)
Bryant, Pte F, KTG	QSA (1) DoK	
Bryant, Pte G J, KTG	QSA (1) DoK	
Bryant, Pte J, KTG	QSA (1) DoK	No I Section, B2 Company, No 3 Redoubt and A Company, Cycle Corps
Bryce, Pte W G, KTG	QSA (1) DoK	H Company
Bryson, 660 Pte W J, KRV	QSA (1) DoK	DMU 8 Mar 00
Buchannan, Gnr T, DBMB	QSA (1) DoK	Armoured train section
Buckingham, Pte J, KTG	QSA (1) DoK	D Company (Veterans), Beaconsfield Town Guard
Buckley, 30144 Tpr Alfred, KLH	QSA (5) DoK OFS Tr 01 02	Served KLH 20 Oct 99 to 30 Apr 00 and 27 Feb 01 to 14 Sep 01. Also served KH (301) 1 May 02 to 30 Jun 02 and ALH (41232) 14 Feb 02 to 23 Mar 02. Occupation butcher
Buckley, 228 Pte James Daniel, KLH	QSA (4) RoM DoK OFS Tr	Served 16 Mar 00 to 5 Jun 00. Also served KTG (No 6 Redoubt) and FID. On KTG roll with incorrect initials J W. QSA (4). Spink Oct 99 £350. Burman Jun 00 £310
Budde, Pte J, KTG	QSA (1) DoK	G Company
Buddell, 220 Band J, KRV	QSA (1) DoK	DMU 9 Mar 00
Bugler, Pte Charles Francis, KTG	QSA (4) DoK Tr 01 02	Premier Mine. Medal and clasp returned to ADOS for retention 19 Mar 07. QSA (4) CC Tr 01 & 02 issued 11 Apr 07 by CPS. Also served KLH (193) 8 Mar 00 to 5 Jun 00, SRG (928) from 27 May 01 and CPS (718) 8 Oct 01 to 11 Apr 02
Bugler, Pte J, KTG	QSA (1) DoK	Medical Corps, No 1 Company, D Section
Bull, 7091 Gnr Charles, RGA	QSA (1) DoK	KSA (2)
Bullen, Pte H, KTG	QSA (1) DoK	No III Section, C Company, Pickering's Redoubt No 1
Bullock, 337 Tpr Henry, KLH	QSA (5) RoM DoK OFS Tr 01	Served KLH 3 Jan 00 to 30 Apr 01
Bullock, 74703 Gnr William, RGA	QSA (1) DoK	KSA (2)
Bumford, Cpl W, KTG	QSA (1) DoK	No I Company, B Section, Reservoir
Bunn, Gnr D, DBMB	QSA (1) DoK	HQ and searchlight. CGHGSM (1) Bech (Pte DEOVR), QSA (1), KStar
Bunyard, Pte A B, KTG	QSA (1) DoK	G Company. QSA (1), KStar. DNW Sep 03 £290. Warwick & Warwick Mar 04
Burden, Pte W, KTG	QSA (1) DoK	No 1 Redoubt
Burge, Pte F, KTG	QSA (1) DoK	H Company. QSA (1), KStar. Toad Hall Mar 81 £172
Burge, Pte J M, KTG	QSA (1) DoK	G Company
Burger, 729 Pte Andries Petrus, CP2	QSA (4) RoM DoK OFS Tr	C Squadron. KSA (2)
Burger, 730 Pte Gert Pieter, CP2	QSA (4) RoM DoK OFS Tr	C Squadron. KSA (2). Served in the Bechuanaland Rebellion 1897 earning CGHGSM (1) Bech
Burgess, 249 Sgt William Robert, KLH	QSA (2) DoK OFS	Served 19 Oct 99 to 30 Apr 00

Kimberley Siege Account and Medal Roll

Burnard, Cpl John Arthur, KTG	QSA (1) DoK	No II Section, C Company, Pickering's Redoubt No 1. Also served CRSS (1239) from 20 Apr 01. QSA (1) CC named to Sgt CRSS. Spink Nov 77 £22
Burney, Pte A, KTG	QSA (1) DoK	QSA (2) inc SA01. Neate Feb 96 £80
Burns, 184 Dvr G, DFA	QSA (3) DoK OFS Tr	QSA (3), KSA (2). City Coins No 18
Burns, Pte J, KTG	QSA (3) DoK OFS Tr	No I Section, Mandy Fort. Also served KLH (1137) to 6 Nov 00
Burt, Pte A T, KTG	QSA (1) DoK	
Burt, 340 Pte Francis Stevens, CP2	QSA (4) RoM DoK Paar Tr	C Squadron. Medal issued 4 Dec 06. KSA (2) issued to Lt. Served in the Bechuanaland Rebellion 1897 earning CGHGSM (1) Bech. Sub Inspector 1904. Resigned 16 Jul 1907
Burton, Sgt C L, KTG	QSA (1) DoK	No I Company, A Section, Reservoir. Served in the Bechuanaland Rebellion 1897 earning CGHGSM (1) Bech
Burton, Pte F H, KTG	QSA (1) DoK	No IV Section, C Company, Pickering's Redoubt No 2
Burton, 619 Pte G C, KRV	QSA (1) DoK	Dismissed 5 Jan 00 for breaking out of camp, third offence
Busby, Pte H, KTG	QSA (1) DoK	Otto's Kopje Scouts
Busby, Pte M C, KTG	QSA (1) DoK	
Bush, 302 RQMS Frederick Evangel, KLH	QSA (6) RoM DoK OFS Tr 01 02	Served 22 Oct 99 to 31 May 01. Also served KTG (Cycle Corps, A Company) 3 Oct 99 to 10 Mar 00, 1st ScH 6 Jan 01 to 30 Jul 01, CPS (784) 5 Nov 01 to 30 Apr 02 with forename Frank and JMR 21 May 02 to 31 May 02. Wounded Lichtenburg 3 Mar 01. Occupation mining engineer
Bush, Pte J, KTG	QSA (1) DoK	Kenilworth Defence Force
Bush, 837 Pte R J, KRV	QSA (3) RoM DoK OFS	Discharged 1 Jul 00. Also served KTG (Cycle Corps, A Company). Medal reissued 17 Aug 09
Bushell, 877 Pte B E, KRV	QSA (3) DoK OFS Tr	DMU 3 Feb 02. Also served KTG (No 3 Redoubt). KSA (2)
Bushney, Pte George, KTG	QSA (4) DoK OFS Tr 01	No III Section, A Company, Beaconsfield Town Guard. Also served KH (22526) 7 Jan 01 to 10 Dec 01
Busschan, Pte John James, KTG	QSA (7) DoK Paar Drie Joh DH Witt 01	Mounted Section, B Company, Beaconsfield Town Guard. Also served DH 18 Feb 00 to 21 May 01. Medal and clasp returned 05. Surname also Busschair. Slightly wounded Sanna's Post 31 Mar 00
Bussell, E H, KTG	QSA (0)	Roll states "Maintenance of telephones in redoubts"
Bussinne, Pte W, KTG	QSA (1) DoK	No I Section, C Company, Beaconsfield Town Guard
Busst, Cpl A, KTG	QSA (1) DoK	No IV Section, F Company, Mostert's Redoubt
Butcher, 281 Sapr M J, RE	QSA (3) DoK Drie Tr	KSA (2)
Butcher, Sgt W, KTG	QSA (1) DoK	No I Company, B Section, Reservoir. Roll notes 'deceased'. Not on the casualty roll
Butler, 4348 Pte A J, LNLR	QSA (2) DoK OFS	Died of disease 5 Jul 00 at Heilbron
Butler, 3140 Sgt J, LNLR	QSA (3) DoK OFS Tr	KSA (2)
Butler, 7293 Gnr James, RGA	QSA (1) DoK	Premier Mine. KSA (2)
Butler, 509 Pte Robert, KRV	QSA (3) DoK OFS Tr	DMU 6 Feb 02. Also served DH (303) 22 Feb 02 to 30 Jun 02. KSA (2)
Butler, Pte T, KTG	QSA (1) DoK	No I Section, L Company. Died of disease 2 Feb 00
Butler, Pte T W, KTG	QSA (1) DoK	H Company
Butterfield, 6674 Gnr Ernest, RGA	QSA (1) DoK	Otto's Kopje. KSA (2)
Button, QMS A, KTG	QSA (1) DoK	No 2 Schmidt's Breastwork

Button, Pte H, KTG	QSA (1) DoK	Premier Mine
Buxton, 234 Cpl John, CP2	QSA (5) DoK Belm MR OFS 01	IGS (1) Samana 1891 (L Cpl Manc Regt), QSA (5), 14-15 Star, BWM, VM (Pte Royal Fus), KStar. McGregor Museum
Buxton, Pte W A, KTG	QSA (1) DoK	L Company
Byrne, Pte D, KTG	QSA (1) DoK	No 1 Redoubt
Byrne, 294 Tpr John F, KLH	QSA (3) DoK OFS Tr	Served 6 Nov 99 to 30 Apr 00. Also served KTG (Otto's Kopje Scouts and No I Section, Belgravia Fort), IYS (5) to 11 Oct 00 and KRV (1190). Severely wounded Webster's Farm near Kimberley 27 Aug 01 and died the same day
Byrne, Lt R S, DFA	QSA (1) DoK	Resigned 7 Nov 99
Byrne, Pte Robert Starkey, KTG	QSA (5) DoK Paar Joh DH Witt	Also served DH 20 Feb 00 to 9 Aug 00. Occupation engineer
Byrnes, Pte J, KTG	QSA (1) DoK	
Byrnes, J H, KTG	QSA (0)	Roll states "Guarding natives on construction works"
Byrnes, Pte J H, KTG	QSA (1) DoK	QSA (1), KStar, 14-15 Star (Kimb Cmdo), BWM (SAVR), VM (Kimb Cmdo). Great War medals named to Byrne. City Coins Mar 93

C

Cadle, Sp Const J, CP2	QSA (1) DoK	
Cadle, 544 Pte W, KRV	QSA (4) RoM DoK OFS Tr	Discharged 15 Oct 02. KSA (2)
Cahill, 267 Dvr F D, DFA	QSA (4) RoM DoK OFS Tr	Discharged 1 Jul 02. Also served DFH (378) 10 Oct 99 to 8 Jan 01, CP and KRV (378) to 26 Jun 00. KSA (2)
Cahill, Pte T, KTG	QSA (1) DoK	Premier Mine. QSA (1). Spink Jul 80 £140. Spink Feb 84 £125. QSA (1), KStar. Walland Jun 95 £155. Liverpool Apr 07 £210
Cairns, Pte C, KTG	QSA (1) DoK	
Cairns, 95635 Gnr Herbert, RGA	QSA (2) DoK OFS	KSA (2)
Calder, Pte G W, KTG	QSA (1) DoK	No 2 supply depot. QSA (1). Sotheby Nov 81. Spink Nov 83 £110. Spink Jul 88. Burman Mar 98 £100
Caley, 204 Tpr A, KLH	QSA (2) DoK OFS	Discharged 5 Jun 00
Callaghan, 4589 Pte J, LNLR	QSA (3) DoK OFS Tr	KSA (2)
Callen, Lt Thomas, KTG	QSA (1) DoK	See his biography (page 339)
Callister, Pte J S, KTG	QSA (1) DoK	No I Company, A Section, Reservoir
Calmeyer, J, KTG	QSA (0)	Roll states "Construction of forts, barricades etc." Possibly served in the Basuto Wars with DEOVR earning CGHGSM (1) Bas
Calnan, 481 Pte W, KRV	QSA (1) DoK	Non effective 1 Dec 00
Calvert, 145 Sgt C E, DFA	QSA (3) DoK OFS Tr	QSA (3), KSA (2), 14-15 Star, BWM, VM (Maj 7th Infy), Colonial Auxiliary Forces Decoration (Maj), Colonial Auxiliary Forces LS Medal (Major). McGregor Museum
Came, Pte R, KTG	QSA (1) DoK	No I Section, B Company, Beaconsfield Town Guard
Cameron, 524 Pte Alan J, KRV	QSA (2) DoK Paar	Died of disease 9 Mar 00. KStar. Seaby Aug 57
Cameron, 21 Sgt Archibald, CP2	QSA (1) DoK	CP dismounted branch (barrier & redoubt duties)
Cameron, 163 Bombdr F, DFA	QSA (2) DoK OFS	Possibly served in the Bechuanaland Rebellion 1897 with DFH earning CGHGSM (1) Bech
Cameron, Col Sgt Frank, KTG	QSA (4) DoK OFS Tr 01	N Company. Also served CinCBG (22679) 17 Nov 00 to 13 May 01

Kimberley Siege Account and Medal Roll

Cameron, 525 Pte H, KRV	QSA (2) DoK OFS	DMU 13 Apr 00
Cameron, Pte T, KTG	QSA (1) DoK	No 1 Redoubt
Camp, 344 Tpr Robert William, KLH	QSA (3) RoM DoK OFS	Served 6 Nov 99 to 5 Jun 00. Also served CPD2 (861)
Camp, 3827 Pte W A, LNLR	QSA (1) DoK	Invalided to England 8 Apr 00. QSA (1), [KSA (2)]. Glendining Sep 91 £110. Glendining Jun 93 £80. Dixon Mar 94 £110
Campbell, Pte A, KTG	QSA (1) DoK	No II Section, B2 Company, No 3 Redoubt
Campbell, 159 Gnr C, DFA	QSA (1) DoK	DMU 16 May 00
Campbell, Sgt Daniel, KTG	QSA (2) DoK OFS	Also served KLH (407) 18 Nov 99 to 3 Mar 00. CGHGSM (1) Bas [Transkei] (Pte CMR), QSA (1), KStar. Glendining Mar 68 £58. Glendining Mar 96 £250. Dixon Dec 96 £290
Campbell, 545 Pte F H, KRV	QSA (1) DoK	DMU 20 Jan 00
Campbell, Pte G, KTG	QSA (1) DoK	No 2 Schmidt's Breastwork
Campbell, 565 Pte Hugh, CP2	QSA (4) RoM DoK OFS Tr	CP 7-pounder detachment and Otto's Kopje. Served in the Bechuanaland Rebellion 1897 earning CGHGSM (1) Bech
Campbell, 109 Tpr Innes Albert, KLH	QSA (2) DoK OFS	Served 20 Oct 99 and discharged 7 Mar 00. Nominal roll has DMU 27 Nov 99
Campbell, Pte J, KTG	QSA (1) DoK	H Company
Campbell, Pte J, KTG	QSA (1) DoK	Construction of shells and ammunition
Campbell, 108 Tpr James Nicol, KLH	QSA (2) DoK Paar	Served 10 Oct 99 to 22 Mar 00. Wounded 16 Nov 99
Campbell, 78260 Gnr John, RGA	QSA (3) DoK OFS Tr	14th Co RGA. Also served CP2. QSA (1) excl OFS & Tr. City Coins Dec 97. DNW Dec 03 £100
Campbell, 647 Sgt Lindsay, CP2	QSA (4) RoM DoK OFS Tr	CP HQ and depot mounted branch. Previously served Bechuanaland Rebellion 1897 with CMR earning CGHGSM (1) Bech
Campbell, Pte W J, KTG	QSA (1) DoK	H Company
Campion, 1478 Bombdr William, RGA	QSA (2) DoK Tr	Otto's Kopje. KSA (2)
Cane, Mr G F, POC	QSA (1) DoK	KStar. Lawrences Auctioneers Nov 05
Cann, 1118 Cpl J, KRV	QSA (3) RoM DoK OFS	DMU 18 Dec 00. Also served KTG (G Company)
Cannon, 5142 Pte C, LNLR	QSA (2) DoK OFS	QSA (2), KSA (2). Sotheby Jun 1906. QSA (3). RHQ
Cannon, 869 L Cpl T, KRV	QSA (4) RoM DoK OFS Tr	Discharged 1 Jul 02. Also served KTG (Mounted Section, Kenilworth Defence Force). KSA (2)
Cannon, 765 Pte Theodore, CP2	QSA (1) DoK	Discharged for misconduct
Cant, 495 Pte J, KRV	QSA (3) DoK OFS Tr	Discharged 1 Jul 02. KSA (2)
Canut, 110 Sgt R C, DFA	QSA (3) DoK OFS Tr	Wounded 9 Dec 99. KSA (2). Surname also spelt Caunt
Capern, 1310 Cpl Charles Henry, KLH	QSA (3) DoK OFS Tr	Served 22 Oct 99 to 19 Sep 00 and (30624 & 33633) 20 Feb 01 to 31 Aug 01. Also served KTG
Capes, Pte C, KTG	QSA (1) DoK	Kenilworth Defence Force. QSA (1). Dixon Apr 02 £185
Capper, 661 Pte A J, KRV	QSA (1) DoK	Served 11 Oct 99 to 25 Oct 01. Also served CPS (835) 19 Nov 01 to 30 Apr 02. KSA (2)
Cara, 416 L Cpl A, KRV	QSA (4) RoM DoK OFS Tr	Discharged 1 Jul 02. KSA (2)
Carey, Pte C, KTG	QSA (1) DoK	No II Section, B2 Company, No 3 Redoubt
Cargill, Pte J H, KTG	QSA (1) DoK	H Company
Cargill, 414 Tpr James Henry, KLH	QSA (2) DoK OFS	Discharged 30 Apr 00. Medal issued and returned

Medal roll

Carlos, Pte J F, KTG	QSA (1) DoK	Premier Mine. Also served CPS (57) 7 Nov 00 to 30 Apr 02. KSA (2). Served in the Bechuanaland Rebellion 1897 earning CGHGSM (1) Bech
Carlyle, 702 Pte Thomas, CP2	QSA (4) RoM DoK OFS Tr	See his biography (page 339)
Carlyon, Pte C, KTG	QSA (1) DoK	Medical Corps, No 1 Company, D Section
Carlyon, Pte E J, KTG	QSA (1) DoK	No III Section, Belgravia Fort
Carmichael, Pte P, KTG	QSA (1) DoK	No IV Section, A Company, Beaconsfield Town Guard
Carmichael, Pte W, KTG	QSA (1) DoK	Civil Service Redoubt
Carnegy, Pte P, KTG	QSA (1) DoK	No I Section, B2 Company, No 3 Redoubt. QSA (1), KStar. Sotheby Nov 81. Spink Jul 82 £175. Spink Jan 85 £120
Carnegy, Capt R B, KTG	QSA (1) DoK	QSA issued 2 Dec 02
Carnell, Pte A J, KTG	QSA (1) DoK	Driving searchlight engine
Carnell, Pte C, KTG	QSA (1) DoK	No 1 Redoubt. QSA (1). Spink Feb 80 £125. eBay Apr 07
Carnell, 230 Pte F, KRV	QSA (3) DoK OFS Tr	Non effective 29 Dec 00. QSA (3), 14-15 Star, BWM, VM. McGregor Museum
Carnell, 112 Tpr Samuel, KLH	QSA (2) DoK Paar	Served 19 Oct 99 until DMU 6 Mar 00. Also served KTG. QSA (2), 14-15 Star (Pte 7th Infy), BWM (A/Sgt SAMC), VM (Pte 7th Infy), KStar. City Coins Nov 07
Carney, 90 Tpr Ernest Robert, KLH	QSA (2) DoK Paar	Served 29 Oct 99 to 23 Mar 00. Also served KTG, WPMR (232) from 9 Jan 01, Cape Provincial Regiment and RR. Occupation moulder
Carolin, 787 Pte T, KRV	QSA (3) RoM DoK OFS	Discharged 1 Jul 00. Also served KTG
Carpenter, 1089 Pte A V, KRV	QSA (2) DoK 01	Also served KTG (No III Section, No 2 Redoubt)
Carpenter, 4605 Pte T, LNLR	QSA (3) DoK OFS Tr	KSA (2). Also served CP
Carr, 27551 Sapr A, RE	QSA (3) DoK Drie Tr	KSA (2)
Carr, 981 Pte Albert, CP2	QSA (2) DoK OFS	C Squadron. Served in the Bechuanaland Rebellion 1897 earning CGHGSM (1) Bech
Carr, 209 Dvr F D, DFA	QSA (3) DoK OFS Tr	KSA (2)
Carr, 120 Pte H J, KRV	QSA (3) DoK OFS Tr	Discharged 1 Jul 02. [CGHGSM (1) Bech], QSA (3), [KSA (2)]. City Coins Dec 05
Carr, 1034 Pte I L, KRV	QSA (4) DoK OFS Tr 01	Also served KTG
Carr, 1852 Tpr J A, SAC	QSA (4) DoK OFS Tr 01	Served 1 May 01 to 18 May 02. Also served KRV (662) to 1 May 01. KSA (2). KStar 'Pte D Coy KR'. Glendining Mar 98. Walland Mar 98 £85
Carr, 921 L Cpl J M, KRV	QSA (1) DoK	Discharged 7 May 02. Also served KTG (No IV Company, A Section, Reservoir). KSA (2)
Carr, 510 L Cpl J P, KRV	QSA (5) RoM DoK OFS Tr 01	Non effective 22 May 01. CGHGSM (1) Bech (Pte DFH), QSA (5). City Coins Jun 04. CGHGSM (1) Bech, QSA (4) excl 01. Liverpool Nov 04 £695
Carr, Lt John R, KTG	QSA (1) DoK	Kenilworth Defence Force
Carroll, Pte C, KTG	QSA (1) DoK	No IV Section, B Company, No 4 Redoubt. QSA (1). Glendining Jul 85, surname given as Carrell
Carroll, 4940 Cpl G, LNLR	QSA (2) DoK Tr	QSA (2), KSA (2), KStar. RHQ. KStar ('Presented to Cpl G Carroll'). Spink Apr 09
Carroll, Pte J, KTG	QSA (1) DoK	Kamfersdam Company. Possibly served with PAVG earning CGHGSM (2) Bas Bech
Carroll, Pte M, KTG	QSA (1) DoK	Kamfersdam Company
Carroll, Pte W, KTG	QSA (1) DoK	
Carruthers, Pte James Thomas, KTG	QSA (4) RoM DoK OFS Tr	No IV Section, F Company, Mostert's Redoubt. Also served KLH (115) 7 Mar 00 to 6 Nov 00

Kimberley Siege Account and Medal Roll

Carson, 101 Sgt Francis Richard, CP2	QSA (5) RoM DoK Paar Tr 01	B Squadron. Served 28 Nov 91 to 5 Dec 01. Severely wounded Luckhoff 27 Nov 00. MID 23 Jun 02. Served in the Bechuanaland Rebellion 1897 earning CGHGSM (1) Bech
Carson, Sgt James, DH	QSA (7) DoK Belm Paar Drie Joh DH Witt	Severely wounded at Tafel Kop on 20 Dec 01. MID 8 Mar 02 for gallantry at Tafel Kop 20 Dec 01. Served DH 19 Oct 99 to 30 Jun 02. His starting date with DH has been double checked. QSA (7), [KSA (2)]. Kaplan May 03. QSA has initial T rather than J
Carstairs Rogers, Lt Fergus, KTG	QSA (1) DoK	See his biography (page 340)
Carstens, Pte H, KTG	QSA (1) DoK	No I Section, L Company
Carswell, 330 Pte J B, KRV	QSA (1) DoK	Non effective 5 Mar 00. QSA (1), KStar. Glendining Sep 87 £100
Carswell, 858 Pte James Cook, CP1	QSA (3) DoK OFS Tr	C Squadron. DMU 31 Jul 01. Discharged 31 May 02. KSA (2). Served in the Bechuanaland Rebellion 1897 earning CGHGSM (1) Bech
Carter, Pte R, KTG	QSA (1) DoK	Kenilworth Defence Force
Carter, 637 Pte Thomas Robert, CP2	QSA (1) DoK	CP dismounted branch (barrier & redoubt duties). Discharged for misconduct 19 Apr 00
Carter, Sgt W, KTG	QSA (1) DoK	No IV Section, A Company, Beaconsfield Town Guard
Carter, Pte W C, KTG	QSA (1) DoK	No II Section, A Company, Beaconsfield Town Guard
Carter, 696 Pte W J, KRV	QSA (1) DoK	DMU 30 Apr 00
Cartmale, Pte J C, KTG	QSA (1) DoK	Kenilworth Defence Force
Cartwright, Pte C T, KTG	QSA (1) DoK	No I Company, B Section, Reservoir
Casley, 520 Pte W, KRV	QSA (5) RoM DoK OFS Tr 01	Non effective 26 Oct 01
Cass, Pte H, KTG	QSA (1) DoK	No IV Section, B Company, No 4 Redoubt. QSA (1), KStar, 14-15 Star (Pte Vet Regt). DNW Jun 02 £240
Castle, Pte G, KTG	QSA (1) DoK	
Castles, 47 Pte Thomas, CP2	QSA (2) DoK OFS	CP HQ and depot mounted branch. KSA (2). KSA reissued 5 Mar 09
Cathey, Sgt T, KTG	QSA (1) DoK	No I Section, C Company, Beaconsfield Town Guard
Cato, Pte J, KTG	QSA (1) DoK	Cycle Corps, A Company
Cato, 168 Tpr Thomas, KLH	QSA (2) DoK OFS	Served 1 Nov 99 to 6 Mar 00. Also served KTG
Caton, 3751 Pte T, LNLR	QSA (3) DoK OFS Tr	Initial W on KSA roll. QSA (3), KSA (2), KStar. RHQ
Cator, Pte A, KTG	QSA (1) DoK	G Company
Cator, Nurse K, NS	QSA (0)	Joined 1 Mar 00
Cawood, 114 Tpr Barrett Nelson, KLH	QSA (4) RoM DoK Paar Tr	Served 19 Oct 99 to 5 Jun 00. Severely wounded 25 Nov 99. Also served KTG and CPS (783) 5 Nov 01 to 30 Apr 02
Cawood, 12 Sgt J E, KRV	QSA (2) DoK 01	Non effective 5 Mar 01. Served in the Bechuanaland Rebellion 1897 earning CGHGSM (1) Bech. During the Great War served as CSM 1st Battalion Kimberley Regiment and in GSWA
Cawood, 191 Gnr R, DFA	QSA (1) DoK	
Cawood, Pte R H, KTG	QSA (1) DoK	Cycle Corps, A Company
Cayford, Pte F, KTG	QSA (1) DoK	No III Section, F Company, No 3 Redoubt
Cayler, Nurse E, NS	QSA (0)	St Michael's Home
Chadborn, 517 Pte John Arthur, CP2	QSA (4) RoM DoK OFS Tr	See his biography (page 340)
Chalmers, Pte H, KTG	QSA (1) DoK	
Chalmers, 898 Pte J, KRV	QSA (4) RoM DoK OFS Tr	Also served KTG (No IV Company, A Section, Reservoir). Severely wounded Maritzani 13 May 00. Discharged 1 Jul 02. KSA (2)

Chamberlain, 93525 Gnr Joseph, RGA	QSA (2) DoK Tr	KSA (2)
Chambers, 788 Pte A J, KRV	QSA (4) RoM DoK OFS Tr	Also served KTG (Gibraltar Fort, Davis's Heap). Discharged 18 Jul 02. KSA (2). Served in the Bechuanaland Rebellion 1897 earning CGHGSM (1) Bech
Chambers, 3965 Pte J, LNLR	QSA (1) DoK	Fell 70 feet from the conning tower during the night of 3 Jan 00 and died instantly
Chambers, 4056 Pte T, LNLR	QSA (3) DoK OFS Tr	QSA (3), [KSA (2)]. Warwick & Warwick May 88
Chamier, Lt Col George Daniel, RGA	QSA (3) DoK OFS Tr	See his biography (page 340)
Champion, Pte H B, KTG	QSA (1) DoK	No II Section, B Company, Beaconsfield Town Guard
Chandler, Pte L J, KTG	QSA (1) DoK	
Channer, Pte E W, KTG	QSA (1) DoK	Cycle Corps, A Company
Channer, Lt R W, KTG	QSA (1) DoK	No 6 Redoubt. Previously served as trooper in the Matebeleland Relief Force in the 1896 Rebellion. Worked for De Beers. QSA (1), KStar. City Coins Feb 95
Chapin, Tpr Charles Howard, DH	QSA (7) DoK Paar Drie Joh DH Witt 01	Served 18 Feb 00 to 18 Jun 00. Also served KTG (Otto's Kopje Scouts and No 2 Schmidt's Breastwork). Occupation miner. Nationality American
Chaplin, Tpr George S, DH	QSA (7) DoK Paar Drie Joh DH Witt 01	Served 20 Feb 00 to 28 Jan 01. Also served KTG (Otto's Kopje Scouts). Occupation farmer
Chapman, Pte Charles Richard, KTG	QSA (3) DoK OFS Tr	No II Section, B Company, Beaconsfield Town Guard. Also served DH (41237) from 15 Feb 00. Occupation farmer. QSA (1) DoK
Chapman, 247 Sgt Edwin, SAC	QSA (4) RoM DoK OFS Tr	Served 19 Oct 99 to 22 Apr 00 and 10 May 00 until pay stopped on 31 Jul 01. Meanwhile, transferred to SAC 12 Feb 01. Also served KTG, KLH (111) and National Scouts. CGHGSM (1) Bech (Tpr DFH) (renamed), QSA (5) inc CC, KSA (2) (Lt National Scouts), KStar. Morton and Eden May 03 £800
Chapman, 110 Tpr George E, KLH	QSA (2) DoK Paar	Served 20 Oct 99 until DMU 3 Jan 00. Wounded 24 Oct 99. Transferred to KTG (Cycle Corps, A Company)
Chapman, Capt W E, KTG	QSA (1) DoK	Otto's Kopje Company. QSA (1). Glendining Dec 35. QSA (1), KStar. DNW Dec 91 £160. Sotheby Nov 95
Chappell, Pte A, KTG	QSA (1) DoK	No I Section, Mandy Fort
Charles, Pte J, KTG	QSA (1) DoK	No 4 Redoubt. QSA (1). Burman Apr 94 £95 - could be next man. Pte J Charles served in the Bechuanaland Rebellion 1897 with Kimb Rifles earning CGHGSM (1) Bech
Charles, Pte J, KTG	QSA (1) DoK	No I Section, D Company
Charles, Pte W, KTG	QSA (1) DoK	Cycle Corps, A Company
Charlton, 830 Pte E, KRV	QSA (2) DoK OFS	Discharged 1 Jul 02. Also served KTG (No 2 Schmidt's Breastwork). KSA (2)
Chatfield, Nurse M G, NS	QSA (0)	Kimberley Civil Hospital
Chatfield, Lt Robert, KLH	QSA (2) DoK Paar	Served 1 Nov 99 and resigned 7 Apr 00. Also served KTG and IYS
Chauncey, 119 Tpr Percy, KLH	QSA (3) DoK OFS Tr	Served 20 Oct 99 to 19 Nov 00. Also served KTG (G Company) and CPS (73)
Chavasse, Pte S, KTG	QSA (1) DoK	Premier Mine. QSA (1), KStar. Spink Nov 05 £320
Cheen, Pte G, KTG	QSA (5) DoK OFS Tr 01 02	Kenilworth Defence Force. Also served 3rd RPR (2038) 8 Jan 01 to 7 Mar 02
Cheetham, Lt F G, KTG	QSA (3) DoK 01 02	Beaconsfield Town Guard. Also served ASC (25) Sep 00 to 31 May 02
Cheffins, F W, KTG	QSA (0)	Roll states "Clearing brushwood, making entanglements etc." SAGS (1) 1879, QSA (0), KStar
Cherry, 6 Sgt C, KRV	QSA (1) DoK	Non effective 28 Aug 00. CGHGSM (1) Bech, QSA (3) inc RoM & OFS, Colonial Auxiliary LS Medal, KStar

Kimberley Siege Account and Medal Roll

Cherry, 4351 Pte S, LNLR	QSA (3) DoK OFS Tr	Nr 4357 on KSA roll. QSA (3), KSA (2), BWM, VM, LS&GC, KStar. RHQ
Chester, Lt F, KTG	QSA (3) RoM DoK Paar	No II Section, B2 Company, No 3 Redoubt
Chew, 5121 L Cpl R, LNLR	QSA (3) DoK OFS Tr	QSA (3), [KSA (2)]. Spink Mar 74 £35. Glendining Oct 82. Liverpool Jun 83 £125
Child, Sister Jane C, NS	QSA (0)	Was in charge of the large surgical ward in the Kimberley Hospital from Oct 99 to Mar 01. MID 10 Sep 01. ARRC GV, Order of St John of Jerusalem, Serving Sister's breast badge, (Jane Child, 1901), QSA (0) (Nursing Sister), 14-15 Star (Matron, SAMNS), BWM, VM & MID (Matron, SAMNS), KStar, Greece Medal of the Red Cross. DNW Apr 04 £3,000
Chilman, Lt H R, KTG	QSA (1) DoK	No III Section, C Company, Beaconsfield Town Guard. Had enlisted in the FLH (380) on 14 Dec 78 and served during the Zulu Wars. Served as Lt in Landrey's Horse in the Basuto Was 1880-81
Chinner, Pte A, KTG	QSA (1) DoK	H Company
Christie, Pte C R, KTG	QSA (1) DoK	Ambulance Corps, Beaconsfield Town Guard
Christie, Pte J R, KTG	QSA (1) DoK	No I Section, A Company, Beaconsfield Town Guard
Christie, Pte John, KTG	QSA (4) RoM DoK OFS Tr	Gibraltar Fort, Davis's Heap. Also served KLH (339) 6 Mar 00 to 18 Apr 02 and GWLH (42256) 18 Apr 02 to 30 Jun 02. Occupation blacksmith
Church, Capt George, KRV	QSA (1) DoK	Resigned 27 Mar 00. Went to South Africa in 1879 with the Royal Engineers. Took part in operations in 1879 and during the First Boer War. He died in 1934
Churcher, 259 Sgt Maj Joseph Herbert, KLH	QSA (3) DoK OFS 01	Served 14 Oct 99 to 30 Apr 01. Slightly wounded 16 Nov 99
Cilliers, Pte J, KTG	QSA (1) DoK	Kimberley Mine Ambulance Company, E Section
Claassen, 318 Pte C, KRV	QSA (1) DoK	Non effective 20 Jul 00
Clack, Cpl A M, KTG	QSA (1) DoK	Premier Mine
Clack, 931 L Cpl G F, CP1	QSA (3) DoK OFS Tr	C Squadron. Served CP1 from 1 Aug 95 to 2 Dec 03. KSA (2). Served in the Bechuanaland Rebellion 1897 earning CGHGSM (1) Bech. 50th Anniversary attendee
Clack, Pte Thomas, KTG	QSA (1) DoK	Premier Mine. Also served SRG (30) from Feb 01
Clague, 766 Pte Ernest, CP2	QSA (3) DoK OFS Tr	A Squadron
Clancy, 710 Pte James William, CP2	QSA (1) DoK	A Squadron. Discharged for misconduct 2 Jul 00
Clare, 4464 Pte P, LNLR	QSA (1) DoK	Invalided to England 1 May 00. KSA (1) 02
Clarence, 383 Pte Hamilton Jeffery, KRV	QSA (4) DoK OFS Tr 01	Non effective 26 Mar 01. Also served KLH (32541) with forenames Herbert Jeffery 11 Apr 01 to 24 Oct 01. QSA (1) DoK. Neate Sep 93 £65. Occupation clerk
Clarence, Cpl Herbert Jeffery, DBMB	QSA (2) DoK OFS	Also served WS (25) from 21 Mar 00 and SRG from 18 Feb 01
Clarence, Pte W J, KTG	QSA (1) DoK	Premier Mine. Also served SRG
Clark, Pte A C, KTG	QSA (1) DoK	No II Section, A Company, Beaconsfield Town Guard
Clark, 35586 Tpr Arthur Dibbin, DH	QSA (1) DoK	Served 5 Aug 01 to 31 Jan 02 and (41287) 27 Feb 02 to 30 Jun 02. Also served KTG (No III Section, A Company, Beaconsfield Town Guard) with initials A M. Occupation fireman
Clark, Pte D, KTG	QSA (1) DoK	
Clark, Pte F, KTG	QSA (1) DoK	No I Company, B Section, Reservoir. QSA (1). City Coins Jul 01. City Coins May 02. Dixon Sep 02 £340
Clark, Pte F R, KTG	QSA (1) DoK	Premier Mine. Also served 34 Co ASC (487). Possibly served in the Bechuanaland Rebellion 1897 with KH earning CGHGSM (1) Bech

Clark, Pte G W, KTG	QSA (1) DoK	No I Company, B Section, Reservoir
Clark, Pte G W, KTG	QSA (1) DoK	
Clark, 20559 Sgt George, RE	QSA (3) DoK Drie Witt	DCM (26 Jun 02) for the erection of blockhouses and defences. Attested Nov 85 aged 14. Twice MID. Conduct 'exemplary'. DCM Ed VII, QSA (3), KSA (2), LS&GC (Ed VII, 1904), KStar. March Medals Sep 87 £535. Spink Aug 00
Clark, Col Sgt H E, KTG	QSA (1) DoK	No II Section, Belgravia Fort. QSA (1). Dixon Apr 98 £110
Clark, Pte H J, KTG	QSA (1) DoK	No II Section, A Company, Beaconsfield Town Guard
Clark, Cpl James, KTG	QSA (3) DoK 01 02	No I Section, F Company, Mostert's Redoubt. Also served KLH (33612) 3 Jul 01 to 14 Jan 02
Clark, Pte O G, KTG	QSA (1) DoK	Premier Mine
Clark, Pte R, KTG	QSA (1) DoK	No 3 Redoubt
Clark, Pte T G, KTG	QSA (2) DoK OFS	G Company. Also served ORCP (292)
Clark, Pte W, KTG	QSA (1) DoK	Kamfersdam Company
Clark, Pte W R, KTG	QSA (1) DoK	No IV Section, B Company, Beaconsfield Town Guard
Clark, 217 Pte William, CP2	QSA (1) DoK	B Squadron. Wounded 25 Nov 99. KSA (2). Served in the Bechuanaland Rebellion 1897 earning CGHGSM (1) Bech
Clark, Pte William Ralph, KTG	QSA (2) DoK OFS	Also served KLH (421) 16 Mar 00 to 30 Apr 00 and IYS (33) 16 May 00 to 6 Sep 00
Clarke, Pte A, KTG	QSA (1) DoK	Premier Mine
Clarke, Pte A J, KTG	QSA (1) DoK	G Company. QSA (1). Spink May 80 £140
Clarke, 732 Pte C, KRV	QSA (1) DoK	Dismissed for misconduct 4 Dec 00 for being drunk on duty, 11th offence
Clarke, Pte C, KTG	QSA (2) DoK Tr	No 2 Schmidt's Breastwork. Also served CPS (10) 14 Nov 00 to 30 Apr 02. KSA (2)
Clarke, 214 Tpr E P, KLH	QSA (2) DoK OFS	Served 20 Oct 99 to 3 Apr 00. Wounded 16 Nov 99
Clarke, 5564 Pte G, LNLR	QSA (3) DoK OFS Tr	Deserted 9 Dec 02. Medal not recovered. KSA (2)
Clarke, 381 Tpr H, KLH	QSA (2) DoK OFS	Served 1 Dec 99 to 30 Apr 00
Clarke, 4512 Pte J, LNLR	QSA (3) DoK OFS Tr	Clark on KSA roll. QSA (3), [KSA (2)], KStar, Kimberley Medal. Seaby May 51
Clarke, 4962 Pte J, LNLR	QSA (3) DoK OFS Tr	Wounded 5 May 01 at Brakpan. QSA (3), [KSA (2)]. Sotheby Nov 80
Clarke, Sgt J, KTG	QSA (1) DoK	No II Section, C Company, Pickering's Redoubt No 2. Also served CPS (45) 7 Nov 00 to 30 Apr 02. KSA (2). Possibly prisoner Manthe 25 Jun 01
Clarke, 526 Pte J P, KRV	QSA (1) DoK	Dismissed for misconduct 24 Aug 00 for being drunk on duty
Clarke, Pte N E, KTG	QSA (1) DoK	No II Section, D Company. QSA (1). Kaplan Feb 06
Clarke, Pte R J E, KTG	QSA (1) DoK	No III Section, F Company, No 3 Redoubt. Also served ASC
Clarke, 252 Cpl S R, KRV	QSA (2) DoK 01	Discharged 8 Aug 01. Nr 352 on Supplementary roll
Clarke, 789 Pte Thomas Henry, CP2	QSA (3) DoK OFS Tr	Killed Klip Drift 7 Mar 02
Clarkson, Pte W J, KTG	QSA (1) DoK	No III Section, B Company, Beaconsfield Town Guard and Kimberley Buffs. QSA (1), KStar. DNW Sep 04 £280
Claude, Pte A J, KTG	QSA (1) DoK	D Company (Veterans), Beaconsfield Town Guard. Served in the Bechuanaland Rebellion 1897 earning CGHGSM (1) Bech
Clay, 620 Pte J H, KRV	QSA (2) DoK OFS	Discharged 1 Jul 02. QSA (2), [KSA (2)]. Dixon Jul 93 £95. Spink Oct 99 £110. Dixon Dec 99 £155
Clay, Pte W, KTG	QSA (1) DoK	Mounted Section, Kenilworth Defence Force

Clayton, 118 Cpl John William, KLH	QSA (3) RoM DoK OFS	Served 20 Oct 99 to 5 Jun 00
Clayton, Pte W, KTG	QSA (1) DoK	No I Section, C Company, Beaconsfield Town Guard
Clear, 1247 Pte D D, KRV	QSA (5) DoK OFS Tr 01 02	Discharged 30 Jun 02. KSA issued in error and clasps added to QSA. Also served KTG (No I Company, B Section, Reservoir)
Cleator, Pte R J, KTG	QSA (1) DoK	No I Section, B2 Company, No 3 Redoubt. QSA (1). Liverpool Jul 88 £75
Cleaver, 408 Bearer Charles E, KLH	QSA (2) RoM DoK	Served 1 Oct 99 to 5 Jun 00. Also served Lt KTG (No 1 Redoubt)
Clements, 89023 Cpl Henry, RGA	QSA (3) DoK OFS Tr	Premier Mine. KSA (2)
Clements, Pte J, KTG	QSA (1) DoK	Premier Mine
Clifford, Pte H, KTG	QSA (1) DoK	No II Section, B Company, Beaconsfield Town Guard
Clifford, Lt Wigram, LNLR	QSA (4) DoK Paar Joh DH	See his biography (page 340)
Climpson, Pte C, KTG	QSA (1) DoK	No 6 supply depot
Climpson, Pte C C, KTG	QSA (1) DoK	
Clinkenberry, 65 Pte Peter, CP2	QSA (1) DoK	A Squadron. KSA (2). Served in the Bechuanaland Rebellion 1897 earning CGHGSM (1) Bech
Cloete, 858 Pte F P, KRV	QSA (3) RoM DoK OFS	Discharged 1 Jul 00. Also served KTG (No I Company, B Section, Reservoir)
Cloete, 574 Pte Henry, CP2	QSA (3) DoK OFS 01	B Squadron. Served 11 Oct 99 to 10 Aug 01
Cloete, 817 Pte J H, KRV	QSA (2) DoK OFS	DMU 18 Apr 00. Also served KTG (No III Company, A Section, Reservoir)
Close, Lt Hugh Marston, RGA	QSA (3) DoK Tr 01	See his biography (page 340)
Close, Pte R, KTG	QSA (1) DoK	Premier Mine
Close, Pte W H, KTG	QSA (1) DoK	No I Company, B Section, Reservoir
Clucas, Pte A B, KTG	QSA (1) DoK	No 4 supply depot
Coates, Pte H, KTG	QSA (1) DoK	No I Section, B Company, Beaconsfield Town Guard. QSA (1), BWM (Lt). Spink Dec 81 £150. Spink Feb 83 £100. Glendining Sep 88
Cock, Pte H, KTG	QSA (1) DoK	Premier Mine. Food supply to natives
Cocking, 4743 Pte T, LNLR	QSA (3) DoK OFS Tr	
Codrington, 621 Pte George, KRV	QSA (4) DoK OFS Tr 01	Discharged 31 Dec 00. Also served KTG and 2nd ILH (59) 4 Dec 00 to 26 Jun 01
Coetzee, 1923 Pte Abraham Carel, CP1	QSA (2) DoK OFS	Served 11 Oct 99 to 31 May 02. KSA (2) authorised 6 Dec 09
Coetzee, 1760 Pte Cornelius Jacobus, CP1	QSA (2) DoK OFS	A Squadron. KSA (2). Served in the Bechuanaland Rebellion 1897 earning CGHGSM (1) Bech
Coetzee, Sp Const D J, CP2	QSA (1) DoK	
Coghlan, Capt Charles Patrick John, KTG	QSA (1) DoK	See his biography (page 340)
Coghlan, Lt J J, KTG	QSA (1) DoK	No I Section, Belgravia Fort. QSA (1). Spink Dec 01 £240
Cogle, Pte C J, KTG	QSA (1) DoK	No II Section, A Company, Beaconsfield Town Guard
Cohen, QMS A A, KTG	QSA (1) DoK	H Company
Coker, Nurse M, NS	QSA (0)	Kimberley Civil Hospital
Colbeck, 581 Pte Tom Martin, CP2	QSA (1) DoK	B Squadron. KSA (2)
Colchester, Pte E J, KTG	QSA (1) DoK	No II Company, A Section, Reservoir

Medal roll

Cole, 724 Pte A, KRV	QSA (1) DoK	DMU 13 Oct 00. Also served KTG (No 2 Schmidt's Breastwork)
Cole, 65 Drum R, KRV	QSA (1) DoK	Non effective 18 Jul 00. Served in the Bechuanaland Rebellion 1897 with Kimb Rifles earning CGHGSM (1) Bech
Cole, W C, KTG	QSA (0)	Roll states "Guarding natives on construction work"
Coleman, Pte J H, KTG	QSA (1) DoK	
Coleman, 372 Pte M, KRV	QSA (3) DoK OFS Tr	Discharged 5 Aug 02. KSA (2)
Coleman, Pte P J, KTG	QSA (1) DoK	No II Section, K Company
Coleman, Pte W J, KTG	QSA (1) DoK	The QSA roll contains a question whether this is the same man as 1251 Ernest Gripper Coleman of the KRV. If so, he gained RoM, OFS & Tr with the KLH
Coleman, 456 Pte Walter Robert, CP2	QSA (5) RoM DoK OFS Tr 01	B Squadron. Died of disease 4 Jul 01. Served in the Bechuanaland Rebellion 1897 earning CGHGSM (1) Bech. QSA (5). Walland Feb 97 £280. Neate Dec 98 £250
Coles, Pte C A, KTG	QSA (1) DoK	Premier Mine. On nominal roll as Cole. QSA (1), KStar. Christies Jul 85 £97
Coles, Pte E, KTG	QSA (1) DoK	No IV Sections, L Company
Coles, 426 Pte Harry, KRV	QSA (5) RoM DoK OFS Tr 01	Non effective 6 Feb 01. Discharged 9 Jul 02. Also served SRG (183) from 12 Feb 01. QSA (4) excl 01. City Coins Dec 05
Colin, Pte P, KTG	QSA (1) DoK	No III Section, K Company. Wounded between 10 and 13 Jan 00
Colister, Pte J, KTG	QSA (1) DoK	No III Section, L Company. On nominal roll as Collister
Collard, Pte T J, KTG	QSA (1) DoK	No I Section, C Company, Pickering's Redoubt No 1. QSA (1). Spink Feb 86 £100. Glendining Jun 94. Bonhams Oct 04 £150. Dixon Sep 06 £250
Coller, Pte F W, KTG	QSA (1) DoK	Civil Service Redoubt
Collier, 393 Sgt Herbert Inglis, KLH	QSA (1) DoK	Joined 19 Oct 99. Killed in action 25 Nov 99. From Surrey, he went to South Africa in 1880 and moved to the Diamond Fields in 1889 when he joined De Beers and the DFH
Collins, Pte Thomas, KTG	QSA (1) DoK	Otto's Kopje Scouts. Also served BR (201 & 26134) 23 Jan 01 to 24 Jul 01. Slightly wounded near Litchenburg 14 May 01
Collins, 5439 L Cpl W, LNLR	QSA (3) DoK OFS Tr	KSA (2). Invalided to England 28 Apr 00
Colvin, Lt James William, CP2	QSA (1) DoK	B Squadron. QSA (1). Spink Sep 82 £150. Sotheby Mar 95. Spink Oct 95 £175
Committee, 143 Bugler Charles Richard, KRV	QSA (4) DoK OFS Tr 01	Non effective 26 Jun 00. Also served KLH (22820) 5 Jan 01 to 11 Jul 01. Occupation electrician
Committee, 8 Band Cpl J, KRV	QSA (1) DoK	DMU 19 Mar 00
Committee, 521 Pte J, KRV	QSA (1) DoK	Died of disease 3 Feb 00
Commons, 915 Pte J, KRV	QSA (2) DoK OFS	Dismissed for misconduct 4 Dec 00. Also served KTG
Compton, Pte G W, KTG	QSA (1) DoK	No II Section, Belgravia Fort
Compton, 1105 Pte R, KRV	QSA (4) RoM DoK OFS Tr	Discharged 1 Jul 02. Also served KTG (No I Company, A Section, Reservoir). KSA (2). Surname sometimes Compston
Condell, Pte R, KTG	QSA (1) DoK	No II Section, B2 Company, No 3 Redoubt. Also served Barkly West TG (91)
Condon, 339 Tpr M, KLH	QSA (2) DoK OFS	Joined 27 Oct 99 and dismissed for misconduct 14 Nov 99. Initial PH on KLH nominal roll
Condon, Pte Patrick Fay, KTG	QSA (1) DoK	No 2 Schmidt's Breastwork. Also served 1st ScH (24355) 28 Dec 00 until DMU 25 Jan 01
Conley, Cpl M, KTG	QSA (1) DoK	Premier Mine

Name	Medals	Notes
Conn, Pte Robert James, KTG	QSA (2) DoK 01	No I Section, A Company, Beaconsfield Town Guard. Served 24 Oct 99 to 10 Mar 00. Also served SRG (31) 12 Feb 01 to 10 May 01 and 30 May 01 to 29 Jun 01
Connell, Pte G, KTG	QSA (1) DoK	No I Section, No 2 Redoubt. QSA (1), KStar
Connolly, 153 Sgt J, KRV	QSA (4) DoK OFS Tr 01	Prisoner at Carter's Ridge 4 Nov 99. Non effective 14 May 01. Served in the Bechuanaland Rebellion 1897 with DFH earning CGHGSM (1) Bech
Connolly, 2000 Band T, LNLR	QSA (3) DoK OFS Tr	KSA (2)
Conradie, Pte D, KTG	QSA (1) DoK	No I Company, B Section, Reservoir
Conradie, Sp Const James Louis, CP2	QSA (1) DoK	Kimberley Regiment Long Range Trophy Medal for participation in the winning team in 1912, sold by City Coins, Dec 88
Conway, 395 Pte R, KRV	QSA (4) DoK OFS Tr 01	DMU 28 Dec 01. Severely wounded Swaitput 2 Aug 01. Possibly prisoner Klerksdorp 25 Jun 00
Cook, Col Sgt A G, KTG	QSA (1) DoK	G Company
Cook, Pte Horace, KTG	QSA (4) DoK OFS Tr 01	H Company. Also served KH (1029) 15 Dec 00 to 30 Jun 01
Cook, Pte L, KTG	QSA (1) DoK	No 6 Redoubt. QSA (1). eBay Jul 06. QSA (1), KStar. Historik Orders Sep 07 £430
Cook, 905 Pte S, KRV	QSA (3) DoK OFS Tr	Discharged 1 Jul 02. Also served KTG (No III Section, No 2 Redoubt). KSA (2)
Cook, 1389 Pte W G, CP1	QSA (4) RoM DoK OFS Tr	C Squadron. Discharged time expired 28 Oct 00
Cooke, Pte E, KTG	QSA (1) DoK	Premier Mine
Cooke, Pte E, KTG	QSA (1) DoK	No I Section, L Company
Coomber, 4548 Pte G, LNLR	QSA (1) DoK	Invalided to England 14 Mar 00
Coombes, 108 Pte H, KRV	QSA (2) DoK OFS	Discharged 25 Apr 00. Medal re-issued 2 Dec 55
Coomer, 748 Pte Frederick A, CP2	QSA (4) RoM DoK OFS Tr	C Squadron. KSA (2)
Cooney, 4797 Pte J, LNLR	QSA (3) DoK OFS Tr	QSA (3), [KSA (2)]. Glendining Jun 88. Spink Jul 07 £260. Liverpool Oct 07 £325. DNW Dec 09 £240
Cooper, 4045 L Cpl A J, LNLR	QSA (3) DoK Paar Joh	Wounded 25 Nov 99. KSA (2). Mounted Infantry
Cooper, 5339 L Cpl J, LNLR	QSA (4) DoK Paar Joh DH	KSA (2). Mounted Infantry. MID 23 Jun 02
Cooper, Pte J, KTG	QSA (1) DoK	
Cooper, Pte J A A, KTG	QSA (1) DoK	
Cooper, 4745 Sgt Maj W, RAMC	QSA (3) DoK OFS Tr	QSA (3), KSA (2), BWM (QM Lt), LS&GC (S Sgt RAMC). Kaplan Nov 04. For his medals see page 501
Copley, 3904 Pte R, LNLR	QSA (3) DoK OFS Tr	KSA (2). Bandsman on KSA roll
Corbett, Pte F, KTG	QSA (4) DoK OFS Tr 01	No 1 Redoubt. Also served CinCBG (22676) 17 Nov 00 to 13 May 01
Corbett, 46 Pte George, CP2	QSA (1) DoK	CP HQ and depot mounted branch. Served in the Bechuanaland Rebellion 1897 earning CGHGSM (1) Bech
Corbett, 1255 Tpr W E, KLH	QSA (4) RoM DoK OFS Tr	Discharged 10 Nov 00
Corbisher, Nurse M, NS	QSA (0)	St Michael's Home
Corfield, 41781 Tpr George H L, DH	QSA (4) RoM DoK OFS Tr	Served 25 Feb 02 until discharged on disbandment 15 Oct 02. Also served KLH (457) 9 May 99 (DFH) until DMU 9 Nov 99 and 4 Jan 01 to 8 Feb 02, KRV (821) 19 Nov 99 to 2 Jul 00, ORCP and RPR. Part of the Coronation Contingent. Middle names gives as Henry/Harry and Lester/Leslie. Occupation cook, engineer and stoker. QSA (4), [KSA (2)]. Sotheby Nov 78

Corless, 1195 Pte T H, KRV	QSA (5) DoK OFS Tr 01 02	Also served KTG (Kenilworth Defence Force). Discharged 1 Jul 02. KSA (2) issued and recalled due to insufficient service. Clasps added to QSA 5 Mar 1911
Cornwall, 513 Pte Henry, KRV	QSA (1) DoK	Killed in action 28 Nov 99
Cornwall, Pte J, KTG	QSA (1) DoK	Cycle Corps, A Company
Cornwall, Pte Moses, KTG	QSA (1) DoK	See his biography (page 340)
Corrie, 76 Pte James, CP2	QSA (1) DoK	C Squadron. Killed in action 25 Nov 99
Corrigan, Pte W J, KTG	QSA (1) DoK	No III Section, B Company, No 4 Redoubt. Removing bushes, making trenches etc
Cosgrove, 4254 Pte T, LNLR	QSA (3) DoK OFS Tr	KSA (2)
Costello, 64 Tpr T F, KLH	QSA (3) DoK Paar Tr	Served 20 Oct 99 to 16 Dec 00. Also served KTG
Cotterall, 5364 Pte W, LNLR	QSA (3) DoK OFS Tr	Slight wound 7 Jan 01 at Zeerust. QSA (3) (Cottrill), KSA (2), KStar. DNW Sep 03 £520
Cottle, 150 Pte Frank Waverley, CP2	QSA (2) DoK 01	
Cotton, 245 Sgt Harold S L, CP2	QSA (1) DoK	B Squadron. CP intelligence and detective staff
Cotton, Pte J L, KTG	QSA (1) DoK	Premier Mine
Cotty, Pte A F, KTG	QSA (1) DoK	Manager of black and Asian food supply stores
Cotty, Pte C T A, KTG	QSA (1) DoK	Premier Mine. 50th Anniversary attendee
Cotty, 116 Tpr William Alf Henry, KLH	QSA (3) RoM DoK Paar	Served 19 Oct 99 to 5 Jun 00. Also served KTG. On nominal roll twice with numbers 116 and 204
Cotzee, Pte M H, KTG	QSA (1) DoK	
Couch, Sister C, NS	QSA (0)	Kimberley Civil Hospital. MID 10 Sep 01
Coughlan, Pte J, KTG	QSA (1) DoK	No II Section, L Company. Possibly served KH (182) and gained 02 clasp. QSA (1). eBay Jan 06 £78
Coughlan, 138 Gnr M V, DFA	QSA (3) DoK OFS 01	Committed suicide 14 Feb 01. Supplementary roll gives date of death as 15 May 01 and casualty roll as 14 Mar 01. Possibly served in the Basuto Wars with DEOVR Volunteers earning CGHGSM (1) Bech
Coughlan, Pte W, KTG	QSA (1) DoK	Kenilworth Defence Force. Possibly served in the Basuto Wars with DEOVR earning CGHGSM (1) Bas
Coulter, 27395 Sapr R, RE	QSA (3) DoK Drie Tr	KSA (2)
Courtney, 4468 Pte R, LNLR	QSA (3) DoK OFS Tr	KSA (2)
Cousins, 573 Pte Henry, CP2	QSA (5) DoK OFS Tr 01 02	C Squadron. Dismissed for misconduct CP2 23 Jul 00. Also served 1st KFS (2029) 4 Jan 01 to 5 Jul 01, 2nd KFS (1019) 5 Jul 01 to 23 Dec 01, Canadian Scouts 30 Dec 01 to 28 Feb 02 and 1st KFS 1 Mar 02 to 31 Mar 02
Coutts, Pte J, KTG	QSA (1) DoK	No III Section, C Company, Beaconsfield Town Guard
Cowan, 39594 Pte Frederick Thomas, DS	QSA (5) DoK OFS Tr 01 02	Served 15 Nov 01 to 24 Mar 02. Two entries in the nominal roll. Also served CP2 (B Squadron) where he was discharged for misconduct (drunk on duty) 24 Sep 00
Coward, Cpl J W, KTG	QSA (1) DoK	No II and IV Sections, L Company. QSA (1), KSA (2) (6871 Pte RAMC), KStar
Cowell, Pte J W, KTG	QSA (1) DoK	QSA (1), KStar. Seaby Aug 77 £125. Christies Nov 85
Cowen, Pte M, KTG	QSA (1) DoK	Belgravia Fort. Possibly served in the Bechuanaland Rebellion 1897 with DFH earning CGHGSM (1) Bech
Cowieson, Lt David, CP2	QSA (1) DoK	CP dismounted branch (barrier & redoubt duties)
Cox, 161 Gnr G, DFA	QSA (1) DoK	

Cox, Lt J, KLH	QSA (3) DoK Paar Tr	Joined 21 Oct 99 and resigned 30 Jun 00. Also served Lt KTG
Cox, Pte J, KTG	QSA (1) DoK	No 6 Redoubt
Cox, Pte R, KTG	QSA (1) DoK	Food supply to natives and refugees. QSA (1). Walland Feb 97 £75
Cox, 1903 Gnr Robert, RGA	QSA (1) DoK	KSA (2)
Cox, 1168 Pte W E, KRV	QSA (3) DoK Paar Tr	Discharged 1 Jul 02. Also served KLH (28) 18 Oct 99 to 30 Apr 00. KSA (2). Served in the Bechuanaland Rebellion 1897 earning CGHGSM (1) Bech
Cox, Sgt W S, KTG	QSA (1) DoK	H Company
Coxen, Pte E H, KTG	QSA (1) DoK	No IV Section, B Company, Beaconsfield Town Guard
Coxen, Pte H, KTG	QSA (1) DoK	No I Section, B Company, Beaconsfield Town Guard
Coxen, Pte W C, KTG	QSA (1) DoK	No III Section, B Company, No 4 Redoubt
Coxwell, Cpl P D, KTG	QSA (1) DoK	Kimberley Mine Ambulance Company, B Section. 50th Anniversary attendee. QSA (1), KStar. City Coins Oct 93. DNW Dec 07 £360
Crabtree, Pte S, KTG	QSA (1) DoK	Cycle Corps, A Company. QSA (1). Clark Aug 89 £115
Craig, 5531 Pte J, LNLR	QSA (3) DoK OFS Tr	QSA (3), KSA (2). Glendining Nov 1909
Craig, Pte R M, KTG	QSA (1) DoK	No III Section, L Company
Craigie, Mr N, POC	QSA (1) DoK	
Cramond, Pte A, KTG	QSA (1) DoK	No II Section, C Company, Pickering's Redoubt No 2. QSA (1)
Cramp, 151 BQMS Harry Thomas, DFA	QSA (2) DoK OFS	Enrolled DFA 22 Jun 99. Occupation clerk. Served Matabeleland Relief Force 1896. Paymaster 27 Sep 99. QM 26 Sep 99. Deceased 31 Dec 02. BSACM rev Rhod 96 (OR SM MRF), QSA (2), [KSA (2)], KStar. Glendining Mar 76. Dixon Apr 98 £340
Cramp, Lt Robert Stead, DFA	QSA (1) DoK	He was born in 1858 and worked as a mine overseer at De Beers between 1899 and 1923. He died in 1940. CGHGSM (1) Bech (Lt DFH), QSA (1), KStar. Glendining Mar 76. DNW Apr 94 £500
Crampton, 702 Sgt G, KRV	QSA (3) DoK OFS Tr	On Supplementary roll as Lt. KSA (2)
Cranswick, Pte W F, KTG	QSA (1) DoK	No I Section, Mandy Fort
Cranswick, Pte W F, KTG	QSA (1) DoK	G Company
Crator, Pte G C, KTG	QSA (1) DoK	
Craven, Lt Archibald Kelson, KLH	QSA (2) DoK OFS	Joined 19 Oct 99 and resigned 6 Mar 00. Also served KTG. KStar. Christies Mar 90. QSA (1) DoK
Craven, Pte L S, KTG	QSA (1) DoK	Cycle Corps, A Company. QSA (1). Christies Jul 84 £80. Liverpool Sep 94 £75. DNW Sep 99 £120. Dixon May 08 £250
Crawford, Pte G H, KTG	QSA (1) DoK	No III Section, B Company, Beaconsfield Town Guard
Crawford, Pte G W, KTG	QSA (1) DoK	D Company (Veterans), Beaconsfield Town Guard
Crawford, Pte Harry, KTG	QSA (4) RoM DoK OFS Tr	No II Section, B Company, Beaconsfield Town Guard. Also served KLH (396) 7 Mar 00 to 24 Nov 00
Crawford, Pte R, KTG	QSA (1) DoK	Cycle Corps, A Company and L Company despatch rider
Crawford, Capt Robert Montgomery, CP2	QSA (2) DoK OFS	See his biography (page 341)
Crawford, Pte T, KTG	QSA (1) DoK	No IV Section, B Company, Beaconsfield Town Guard
Crayston, 5580 Pte R, LNLR	QSA (3) DoK OFS Tr	KSA (2)

Medal roll

Creed, Lt Harold, DH	QSA (6) DoK Paar Drie Joh DH Belf	Served 18 Mar 02 to Oct 02. Also served KTG (Otto's Kopje Scouts). Slightly wounded Boschbult 31 Mar 02. Part of the Coronation contingent. Occupation bookkeeper. KIA 15 Jul 16. QSA (6), KSA (2), 14-15 Star (Botha's Natal Horse), BWM, VM, KStar
Creen, Pte G B, KTG	QSA (1) DoK	G Company
Crellin, Sgt John Thomas, KTG	QSA (4) RoM DoK OFS Tr	No 1 Redoubt. Also served KLH (225) 16 Mar 00 to 5 Jun 00 and SRG (164) from 11 Feb 01. QSA (3) excl RoM & OFS inc CC, KStar. Spink Oct 99 £170. Dixon Dec 99 £250
Crick, 1214 Sapr H, RE	QSA (3) DoK Drie Tr	KSA (2)
Crittell, Pte Alfred, KTG	QSA (4) RoM DoK Paar Tr	No I Company, A Section, Reservoir. Also served KLH (379, 400 & 1253) 6 Mar 00 to 25 Jan 01
Croal, Pte G T, KTG	QSA (1) DoK	No I Company, B Section, Reservoir
Croft, 345 Pte A D, KRV	QSA (1) DoK	QSA (1). Glendining Sep 90. QSA (1), KSA (2). Liverpool Aug 91 £95
Croft, 1320 Pte Archer James, KRV	QSA (3) DoK OFS Tr	Also served KRV 9 Oct 99 to 7 Nov 99, KTG, KLH (415) with initials H A 12 Mar 00 to 17 May 00, IYS (32) 17 May 00 to 6 Sep 00 and ILH (1072 & 1213) 3 Nov 00 to 15 Jun 01. KSA (2)
Croft, Pte C T, KTG	QSA (1) DoK	No I Section, C Company, Pickering's Redoubt No 1
Croft, Pte J H, KTG	QSA (1) DoK	No IV Section, B Company, No 4 Redoubt
Crofts, 3987 Pte T, LNLR	QSA (3) DoK OFS Tr	QSA (3), KSA (2), KStar. RHQ
Cron, Pte M, KTG	QSA (1) DoK	No III Section, L Company. QSA (1). March Medals Jul 87 £98. Christies Apr 91
Cronin, 816 Pte A M, KRV	QSA (3) RoM DoK OFS	Discharged 1 Jul 00. Also served KTG (Medical Corps, No 1 Company, F Section)
Crook, 360 Pte F, KRV	QSA (2) DoK OFS	KSA (2)
Crook, 669 Pte Ignatius, CP2	QSA (1) DoK	CP dismounted branch (barrier & redoubt duties)
Crook, Pte R, KTG	QSA (1) DoK	H Company
Crookall, 4101 Pte M, LNLR	QSA (3) DoK OFS Tr	
Crookes, 66 Tpr F de E, KLH	QSA (2) DoK OFS	Joined 20 Oct 99 and dismissed 14 Nov 99. Nominal roll crossed out 'dismissed' and inserts transferred to KTG 29 Nov 99
Crooks, 183 Pte A, KRV	QSA (2) DoK 01	Non effective 8 Aug 01
Crooks, 94 Pte H J S, KRV	QSA (1) DoK	DMU 26 May 00
Crosbie, 892 Pte A E, KRV	QSA (4) RoM DoK OFS Tr	Discharged 1 Jul 02. KSA (2)
Crosbie, 1031 Tpr M P, KLH	QSA (5) DoK Paar Tr 01 02	Served 28 Oct 99 to 6 Nov 00. Also served CinCBG (22683) 19 Nov 00 to 13 May 01 and DOEVR (1097)
Crosbie, Lt Michael Joseph, KLH	QSA (2) DoK OFS	Joined 20 Oct 99 and resigned 6 Mar 00. Also served KTG and SRG. QSA (2), KStar. City Coins Dec 04
Crosbie, 41 Sgt Maj Pierce, CP2	QSA (1) DoK	A Squadron. CGHGSM (1) Bech, QSA (1), KSA (2), KStar. Hall Sep 86 £350
Crosby, Lt N, KTG	QSA (1) DoK	Transferred to KLH
Cross, Cpl J J, KTG	QSA (1) DoK	No 1 Redoubt. Also served 37th B Co ASC (3474) as Wheeler
Cross, Pte Walter, KTG	QSA (2) DoK Tr	No 6 Redoubt. Also served SRG (112) from 11 Feb 01
Crosslands, Pte J, KTG	QSA (1) DoK	No III Company, A Section, Reservoir
Crossley, 3152 Pte O, LNLR	QSA (1) DoK	Transferred to AR in South Africa 21 Feb 00. Also served CGR

Kimberley Siege Account and Medal Roll

Crossthwaite, Cpl W, KTG	QSA (1) DoK	No I Company, A Section, Reservoir. QSA (1). March Medals Aug 93 £125
Crouch, Pte T G, KTG	QSA (1) DoK	H Company
Crowther, Pte A, KTG	QSA (1) DoK	No I Section, F Company, Mostert's Redoubt. 21 Tpr Charles Foster Crowther on WS roll with OFS says served in the siege. Same man? There is also a C F Crowther on the KTG nominal roll but only a single Crowther on the QSA roll
Croxford, Lt P G, KTG	QSA (1) DoK	H Company
Crozier, 4256 Pte J, LNLR	QSA (3) DoK OFS Tr	KSA (2)
Crozier, Lt M K, CP1	QSA (1) DoK	See his biography (page 341)
Cruickshank, Capt Alex, KTG	QSA (1) DoK	Kimberley Mine Ambulance Company
Cruickshank, Mr D, POC	QSA (1) DoK	Travelled in the armoured train on 15 Oct 99 to ascertain if the newly cut telegraph wires could be repaired
Crumplin, 294 3rd Tpr Adolphus F, SAC	QSA (5) DoK OFS Tr 01 02	Also served KTG (No I Company, B Section, Reservoir). Served in the Bechuanaland Rebellion 1897 with DFH earning CGHGSM (1) Bech
Crumplin, 1471 Pte E J, CP1	QSA (3) DoK OFS 01	Served 11 Oct 99 to 5 Jan 01
Cudlipp, Pte J R, KTG	QSA (2) DoK 01	No 1 Redoubt. Also served SRG (1187) 1 Apr 01 to 12 Jun 01
Cuerdon, 3678 Pte W, LNLR	QSA (3) DoK OFS Tr	KSA (2). Initial J on KSA roll
Cullen, 612 Pte George, CP2	QSA (4) RoM DoK OFS Tr	CP dismounted branch (barrier & redoubt duties)
Cullinan, 93 Sgt John Carr, KLH	QSA (5) DoK Paar Tr 01 02	See his biography (page 341)
Cullum, 27209 Sapr H R, RE	QSA (3) DoK Drie Tr	KSA (2)
Cumming, Agent A W, FID	QSA (3) DoK Belm OFS	See his biography (page 341) and the appendix on the despatch riders (page 547)
Cumming, Pte C, KTG	QSA (3) DoK OFS Tr	Kamfersdam Company
Cumming, 1032 Tpr H V, KLH	QSA (3) DoK OFS Tr	Served 22 Oct 99 to 29 Aug 00. Surname sometimes Cummings
Cumming, Lt J R, CP1	QSA (3) DoK OFS Tr	A Squadron. Served in the Bechuanaland Rebellion 1897 earning CGHGSM (1) Bech
Cumming, 266 Pte John Alexander, KRV	QSA (1) DoK	Also served KTG, KLH (27841) 29 Jan 01 to 18 Nov 01 and WPMR (1070). Surname on KLH nominal roll is Cummings. CGHGSM (1) Bech (Pte Kimb Rfls), QSA (1), KSA (2), KStar. DNW Jun 02 £340
Cummings, Cpl J, KTG	QSA (1) DoK	No I Section, F Company, Mostert's Redoubt
Cundill, Pte A E, KTG	QSA (1) DoK	No II Section, B Company, No 4 Redoubt. QSA (1), KStar. City Coins Dec 88
Cundill, Pte J W, KTG	QSA (1) DoK	No III Section, C Company, Pickering's Redoubt No 1
Cundill, Pte T J, KTG	QSA (1) DoK	No II Section, Belgravia Fort and Controller black and Asian food supply stores
Cunningham, Pte G, KTG	QSA (1) DoK	G Company
Curgenven, Pte B, KTG	QSA (1) DoK	Cycle Corps, A Company
Curgenven, QMS F, KTG	QSA (1) DoK	Premier Mine. QSA (1), KStar. Glendining Mar 93 £130. Neate Feb 07 £475
Currey, Lt C C, SAMIF	QSA (2) DoK 01	Food Supply Staff and No I Section, Mandy Fort. QSA (1), KStar
Curry, Lt A W, KTG	QSA (1) DoK	Premier Mine. QSA (1), KStar (Lt A Wolf Curry). Kaplan Jul 05

Medal roll

Curtis, 4796 L Sgt C E, LNLR	QSA (3) DoK OFS Tr	QSA (3), KSA (2), KStar. Initial E on the KSA and KStar. Sotheby Mar 82 £160. Spink Nov 05. Spink Apr 09. Liverpool Jul 09 £675
Curtis, 4238 Pte W, LNLR	QSA (3) DoK OFS Tr	KSA (2). Surname Curtiss on KSA roll
Curtis, Pte W, KTG	QSA (1) DoK	Premier Mine
Cuthbert, S Sgt W Glynn, KTG	QSA (3) DoK OFS Tr	H Company. Also served Lt WS from 18 Mar 00 and SAMIF from 14 May 01
Cuthbertson, Sgt W M, KTG	QSA (1) DoK	Beaconsfield Town Guard. QSA (1). Spink Oct 80 £155
Cutting, 818 Pte H, KRV	QSA (2) DoK OFS	Discharged 13 Aug 00. Also served KTG (No III Company, A Section, Reservoir) and CPS (34)
Cutting, Pte John Henry, KTG	QSA (3) DoK OFS 02	No I Company, B Section, Reservoir. Also served KLH (332) 4 Nov 99 to 2 Dec 99, discharged 30 Apr 00 and DH (41230) 14 Feb 02 to 30 Jun 02. Imprisoned for theft. DH nominal roll has forename Henry. Occupation saddler
Cutting, Pte R, KTG	QSA (1) DoK	Premier Mine and No I Company, B Section, Reservoir

D

D'Arcy, Nurse E, NS	QSA (0)	Kimberley Civil Hospital
D'Arcy, Mr F, POC	QSA (1) DoK	
D'Eath, Nurse A, NS	QSA (0)	Kimberley Civil Hospital
D'Ewes, 275 Sgt J A, CP1	QSA (2) DoK OFS	KSA (2). Served in the Bechuanaland Rebellion 1897 earning CGHGSM (1) Bech
Da Fonseca, G T, KTG	QSA (0)	Roll states "Construction works, trenches, barricades etc"
Dacres, Pte T M, KTG	QSA (2) DoK OFS	Kimberley Mine Ambulance Company, B Section. Also served KLH (427) to 30 Apr 00
Daisley, 764 Pte W, KRV	QSA (4) RoM DoK OFS 02	Discharged 1 Jul 00. Also served KTG (No 2 Schmidt's Breastwork), KLH and Agent FID
Dakers, Pte W, KTG	QSA (1) DoK	Kamfersdam Company
Dale, Pte G H, KTG	QSA (1) DoK	No I Section, B Company, Beaconsfield Town Guard
Dale, Cpl J W, KTG	QSA (1) DoK	No I Section, B Company, Beaconsfield Town Guard
Dalgleish, Pte J, KTG	QSA (1) DoK	H Company
Dallas, Capt Seymour, KTG	QSA (1) DoK	Officer commanding No 3 Redoubt
Dally, 24289 Tpr William, ScH	QSA (5) DoK OFS Tr 01 02	Served 3 Dec 00 to 10 Jul 01 but QSA roll says discharged 7 Mar 02. Also served KTG and CP (839)
Dalton, Pte M C, KTG	QSA (1) DoK	
Daly, 8 Gnr A, DFA	QSA (1) DoK	
Daly, 31 Dvr Arthur William, DFA	QSA (3) DoK OFS Tr	Occupation fireman. QSA (3), [KSA (2)], 14-15 Star, BWM, VM (Pte 7th Infy), KStar. Spink Feb 80 £175
Daly, Pte J E, KTG	QSA (1) DoK	No III Section, L Company
Daly, Mr W, POC	QSA (1) DoK	
Daly, Pte William Robert, KTG	QSA (4) DoK OFS Tr 01	No I Section, L Company. Also served Imperial Transport and CinCBG (22686) 19 Nov 00 to 18 May 01
Dalziel, 2262 Sapr R, RE	QSA (2) DoK Drie	KSA (2)
Damant, 58 Pte E H, KRV	QSA (1) DoK	Non effective 11 Mar 00. Also served IMR
Damant, Lt Col Frederick Hugh, DH	QSA (6) DoK Paar Drie Joh DH Witt	See his biography (page 341)
Damon, Pte D, KTG	QSA (1) DoK	Ambulance Corps, Beaconsfield Town Guard
Daniel, F A, KTG	QSA (0)	Roll states "Guarding natives on construction works"
Daniel, Pte J N, KTG	QSA (1) DoK	Premier Mine

Kimberley Siege Account and Medal Roll

Dann, 4994 Pte G, LNLR	QSA (3) DoK OFS Tr	QSA (3), KSA (2), KStar. Sotheby Mar 79 £110
Darcey, 3914 Pte G, LNLR	QSA (3) DoK OFS Tr	KSA (2)
Dare, 379 Pte Arthur Spedding, KRV	QSA (1) DoK	Killed in action 28 Nov 99
Dare, Pte E M, KTG	QSA (1) DoK	
Dare, 120 Cpl Edward Richard Spedding, KLH	QSA (4) RoM DoK Paar Tr	Served 19 Oct 99 to 6 Nov 00. Also served KTS as S Dare and SRG (19) from 12 Feb 01. KSA (2)
Darvall, Pte H, KTG	QSA (1) DoK	No I Company, B Section, Reservoir
Dashwood, Pte Frank, KTG	QSA (3) DoK 01 02	Served G Company 15 Oct 99 to 10 Mar 00. Also served CRSS (1247) 19 Apr 01 to 23 Jan 02
Daulby, 4581 Pte G, LNLR	QSA (1) DoK	Died of disease 25 May 00
Davenport, 5348 Pte J, LNLR	QSA (3) DoK OFS Tr	KSA (2). Nr 5438 on KSA roll
Davey, Pte E G, KTG	QSA (1) DoK	No IV Section, K Company
David, Pte T J, KTG	QSA (3) DoK 01 02	Premier Mine
Davidson, Cpl A, KTG	QSA (1) DoK	Kenilworth Defence Force
Davidson, Pte A, KTG	QSA (1) DoK	No I Section, B Company, Beaconsfield Town Guard. QSA (1). Noble Numismatics Jul 97
Davidson, 106 Sgt Alexander, DFA	QSA (3) DoK OFS Tr	Enrolled DFA 1 Apr 98. Sgt 26 Aug 98. BQMS 31 Dec 02. Medically unfit 1 Dec 04. QSA (3) (renamed), KSA (2) (renamed), Volunteer LS Medal (Sgt DFA). Glendining Sep 73. Sotheby Nov 78
Davidson, Pte C R, KTG	QSA (1) DoK	
Davidson, Pte D, KTG	QSA (1) DoK	No 1 Section, F Company, Mostert's Redoubt
Davidson, Pte E, KTG	QSA (1) DoK	No 6 Redoubt
Davidson, Pte Hugh W, KTG	QSA (4) DoK OFS Tr 01	G Company. Also served 1st ILH (2226) 29 May 01 to 12 Aug 01 when transferred to 2nd ILH (834) serving to 4 Nov 01
Davidson, Cpl J, KTG	QSA (1) DoK	No IV Section, C Company, Pickering's Redoubt No 2
Davidson, Pte J, KTG	QSA (1) DoK	No III Section, K Company
Davidson, Pte John Forrester, KTG	QSA (6) DoK Paar Drie Joh DH Witt	Otto's Kopje Scouts. Also served DH 20 Feb 00 to 31 Jul 01 and FID. KSA (2). 50th Anniversary attendee
Davidson, Lt Thomas M, CP2	QSA (4) RoM DoK OFS Tr	A Squadron. MID 23 Jun 02. KSA (2). Served in the Bechuanaland Rebellion 1897 earning CGHGSM (1) Bech. Captain, 5th SAMR, 1 Apr 1913
Davidson, Pte W, KTG	QSA (1) DoK	Mandy Fort
Davie, 4 Band F W, KRV	QSA (2) DoK OFS	KSA (2)
Davie, 36 Sgt Sig Robert Thomas, KRV	QSA (3) RoM DoK OFS	Non effective 20 Jun 00. Also served SRG (14) from 12 Feb 01. Served in the Bechuanaland Rebellion 1897 earning CGHGSM (1) Bech
Davies, 884 Pte D, KRV	QSA (1) DoK	Dismissed for misconduct, drunk on parade, 8th offence. Also served KTG (No IV Company, A Section, Reservoir)
Davies, Sgt H, KTG	QSA (1) DoK	Premier Mine
Davies, 358 Cpl J E, KRV	QSA (3) DoK OFS Tr	Discharged 12 Feb 03. KSA (2)
Davies, Pte J E M, KTG	QSA (1) DoK	No II Section, Belgravia Fort
Davies, 719 Pte John D, CP2	QSA (4) RoM DoK OFS Tr	B Squadron. KSA (2). Surname given as Davis on QSA roll
Davis, Pte A, KTG	QSA (1) DoK	Kimberley Mine Ambulance Company, B Section

Davis, 24579 Dvr A A, RE	QSA (3) DoK Drie Witt	KSA (2)
Davis, Checker C R, ASC	QSA (1) DoK	Assistant for black and Asian food supply stores. On nominal roll with initials C W
Davis, 2774 Pion Sgt F, LNLR	QSA (3) DoK OFS Tr	MID 23 Jun 02. DCM Ed VII, QSA (3), KSA (2), LS&GC Ed VII, MSM GVI, KStar. RHQ
Davis, Pte G, KTG	QSA (1) DoK	Premier Mine
Davis, Pte Henry Francis, KTG	QSA (2) DoK OFS	No II Section, K Company. Also served ORCP (304) and SRG (373 or 927) from 27 May 01
Davis, Nurse I, NS	QSA (0)	Kimberley Civil Hospital
Davis, 30127 Sgt James, KLH	QSA (3) DoK OFS Tr	Joined 16 Oct 99. Also served KTG, SRG (1609) 23 Sep 01 to 23 Mar 02 and KH (226). Deserted post 10 to 16 Nov 00. KSA (2). Occupation painter
Davis, 939 Pte Lorenzo Louis, KRV	QSA (1) DoK	Non effective 17 Aug 00. Also served KTG (Premier Mine) and SRG (40) from 12 Feb 01
Davis, 663 Cpl S, KRV	QSA (3) DoK OFS Tr	Non effective 6 Jul 01. Discharged 30 Jun 02. KSA (2)
Davis, Rwy emp Valfrid Emanuel, IMR	QSA (1) DoK	See his biography (page 341)
Davis, Pte W H, KTG	QSA (1) DoK	No I Company, B Section, Reservoir. QSA (1). Spink Jan 93 £90
Davis, Lt William Henry, CP2	QSA (2) DoK OFS	B Squadron. KSA (2). Subsequently served as Captain, 5th SAMR and as Major in the GSWA operations from 20 Aug 1914 to 15 Nov 1916
Davison, 1122 Pte H R, KRV	QSA (2) DoK OFS	Discharged 1 Jul 02. KSA (2)
Dawe, 2326 Sapr S, RE	QSA (3) DoK Drie Tr	QSA (3), KSA (2). RHQ
Dawes, 623 Pte C H, KRV	QSA (1) DoK	DMU 6 Mar 00. Also served KTG
Dawkins, Pte T J, KTG	QSA (1) DoK	No I Section, Mandy Fort
Dawson, Pte F, KTG	QSA (1) DoK	
Dawson, 4669 L Cpl J, LNLR	QSA (3) DoK OFS Tr	QSA (3), KSA (2)
Dawson, 273 Tpr J W, KLH	QSA (2) DoK OFS	Served 23 Oct 99 to 4 Mar 00
Dawson, Cpl Joseph W, DH	QSA (3) DoK OFS Tr	Served 19 Nov 00 to 12 Feb 02. On roll of KLH (214) 23 Oct 99 to 6 Jun 00 as deserter. Also served KTG and ORCP. KSA (2)
Day, Pte B W, KTG	QSA (1) DoK	No I Section, Mandy Fort
Day, Pte E, KTG	QSA (1) DoK	Civil Service Redoubt
Day, 233 Gnr Frederick Herbert, DFA	QSA (2) DoK OFS	Severely wounded 28 Nov 99. Enrolled DFA 26 Jul 00. Also served KLH (210) 20 Oct 99 to 3 Apr 00. Resigned DFA 6 Jan 03. 84 days heavy labour for desertion 4 Feb 02. Discharged 6 Jan 03. KSA (2)
Day, Pte W D, KTG	QSA (1) DoK	No I Section, Mandy Fort
De Kock, 66 Tpr Ernest Plewman, KLH	QSA (2) DoK OFS	Served 1 Nov 99 until DMU 24 Mar 00. Also served KTG, worked as a press censor and with the FID. Born 1877. Served during the Great War as a Field Cornet in the Union Defence Force. MBE (2nd Type, civil, 1 Jan 1960), QSA (2), KSA (2), KStar. Spink 04 £360
De Lacy, Tpr James Michael, DH	QSA (6) DoK Paar Drie Joh DH Witt	Served 20 Feb 00 to 5 Feb 01. Also served KTG (No 2 Schmidt's Breastwork) where name is De Lacey. Occupation mason
De Lorme, 32509 Tpr Horace Donald, KLH	QSA (4) DoK OFS Tr 01	Served 27 Mar 01 to 30 Sep 01. Also served WWTG (253). Occupation engineer
De Melker, Pte A, KTG	QSA (1) DoK	No I Company, B Section, Reservoir. Possibly served in the Bechuanaland Rebellion 1897 with Kimb Rifles earning CGHGSM (1) Bech

Name	Medals	Notes
De Melker, Pte H G, KTG	QSA (1) DoK	No IV Section, K Company
De Melker, Pte J R, KTG	QSA (1) DoK	No 6 Redoubt
De Melker, Pte S, KTG	QSA (1) DoK	No I Section, K Company
De Putron, Lt Cyril, LNLR	QSA (3) DoK OFS Tr	See his biography (page 342)
De Reuck, 716 Pte Samuel Peter, CP2	QSA (1) DoK	B Squadron. KSA (2)
De Sconde, 890 Pte P C, KRV	QSA (3) RoM DoK OFS	Also served KTG (G Company) as Desconde on the KTG nominal roll. Killed in action 17 Jun 00 at Mafeking. Issued to widow 13 Nov 13. QSA (3)
De Smidt, 401 Pte A, CP2	QSA (4) DoK OFS Tr 01	CP 7-pounder detachment. Served 11 Oct 99 to 12 Jul 01
De Smidt, 152 Bombdr George Alfred, DFA	QSA (3) DoK OFS Tr	Enrolled DFA 22 Jun 99. Served Kimb Scottish 17 Nov 97 to 15 May 98. Taken prisoner & released Klip Drift 7 Mar 02. Resigned 1 Jul 03. KSA (2). Occupation storeman. 50th Anniversary attendee
De Smidt, 466 Pte M, KRV	QSA (2) DoK 01	Non effective 19 May 01. 50th Anniversary attendee
De Villiers, Pte H, KTG	QSA (1) DoK	Kimberley Mine Ambulance Company with mounted forces
De Villiers, Pte W, KTG	QSA (1) DoK	No II Section, D Company
De Witt, 251 Dvr John George, DFA	QSA (3) DoK OFS Tr	Served 16 Aug 00 to 1 Jul 02. Also served LNLR (34) and KTG (No II Section, K Company) 4 Dec 99 to 25 Mar 00. KSA (2). Occupation storeman. 50th Anniversary attendee
De Wyers, Pte J, KTG	QSA (1) DoK	No III Section, A Company, Beaconsfield Town Guard. QSA (0). DNW Sep 02. Liverpool Jul 04 £45 (says officially renamed)
Deacon, 1890 Pte E E, CP1	QSA (2) DoK OFS	A Squadron. KSA (2)
Dean, 4878 Pte C, LNLR	QSA (3) DoK OFS Tr	KSA (2). Initial E on KSA roll
Deane, 1718 Sgt Charles Wingfield, DH	QSA (5) DoK OFS Tr 01 02	Served 9 May 01 to 30 Jun 02. Also served CPD2 (176) (A Squadron) until discharged for misconduct Apr 01. Prisoner at Daniel's Kuil 11 Jan 01. Occupation clerk. CGHGSM (1) Bech (Tpr CP), QSA (6) inc CC, KStar. Courier Jul 87 £350
Deane, 68 Tpr James, KLH	QSA (2) DoK OFS	Served 20 Oct 99 to 4 Mar 00. Also served KTG as Dean
Deary, Pte J E, KTG	QSA (1) DoK	H Company
Deary, 223 Dvr J N, DFA	QSA (3) DoK OFS 01	Served in the Bechuanaland Rebellion 1897 earning CGHGSM (1) Bech
Deary, Pte P, KTG	QSA (1) DoK	No II Section, Belgravia Fort
Dedusey, Sgt G, KTG	QSA (1) DoK	B Company
Deere, 1013 L Cpl R H, CP1	QSA (3) RoM DoK OFS	C Squadron. Slightly wounded 25 Nov 99. QSA roll has Deare. CGHGSM (1) Bech, QSA (3), [KSA (2)]. City Coins Dec 04. Liverpool Jun 05 £685
Deith, Pte George, KTG	QSA (1) DoK	Served 3 Oct 99 to 10 Mar 00 (No II Section, F Company, Mostert's Redoubt). Also served CPS (24) as Deeth 7 Nov 00 to 30 Apr 02. KSA (2)
Delamere, Pte E, KTG	QSA (1) DoK	No 2 Schmidt's Breastwork
Delamere, Pte T H, KTG	QSA (1) DoK	No I Company, B Section, Reservoir
Delaney, 1248 Pte W P, KRV	QSA (3) DoK OFS Tr	Discharged 1 Jul 02. Also served KTG (No II Company, A Section, Reservoir) 7 Oct 99 to 10 Mar 00. KSA (2)
Delport, 848 Pte B, CP1	QSA (2) DoK OFS	A Squadron. KSA (2). Served in the Bechuanaland Rebellion 1897 earning CGHGSM (1) Bech
Delport, Pte H, KTG	QSA (1) DoK	
Demas, Pte J, KTG	QSA (1) DoK	Gibraltar Fort, Davis's Heap. QSA (1), KStar. Spink Mar 96

Medal roll

Dempster, Pte J, KTG	QSA (1) DoK	No III Section, No 2 Redoubt. QSA (1). DNW Jun 02 £120. Dixon Sep 02 £165. QSA (1), KStar. Hamilton Oct 83 £175. Burman Dec 05 £385
Dempster, Pte W, KTG	QSA (1) DoK	No I Section, L Company. Possibly William Dempster who died of typhoid fever 11 Feb 00
Denbigh, 207 Gnr Thomas Sharp, DFA	QSA (1) DoK	Enrolled DFA 26 Oct 99. DMU 19 Jul 00. Served Natal Naval Volunteers 1893 to 1895. Occupation clerk
Dennis, Pte J, KTG	QSA (2) DoK Tr	No III Section, C Company, Beaconsfield Town Guard. Also served BR (214)
Dennison, 656 Pte Clifford D, CP2	QSA (1) DoK	A Squadron. Killed in action 28 Nov 99. Son of Major C G Dennison DSO
Dennison, Mr Frederick Weatherley, POC	QSA (1) DoK	Born Rustenberg in 1879. Captured by the Boers at Kuruman but escaped to Kimberley. Joined the Rhodesian Postal Service in 1902. Retired 1939. Died 1957. QSA (1), KStar
Denvers, 747 Pte H J, KRV	QSA (2) DoK Tr	Discharged 1 Jul 02. Also served KTG (No 2 Schmidt's Breastwork) with initial J. KSA (2)
Denyer, J, KTG	QSA (0)	Roll states "Guarding natives on construction works"
Derringer, 92 Tpr D, KLH	QSA (2) DoK OFS	Served 24 Oct 99 to 30 Apr 00
Desler, 28374 2nd Cpl V, RE	QSA (3) DoK Drie Tr	KSA (2)
Devenish, Pte Albert Ernest, KTG	QSA (3) DoK OFS 01	Mounted Section, Kenilworth Defence Force. Also served KLH (45) 19 Oct 99 until transferred to KTG 30 Nov 99, IYS (6066) 27 Mar 00 to 4 Sep 00 and NH (1302) 20 Dec 00 to 8 Dec 01. Captured by the Boers at Roodewal 7 Jun 00 (released). Died 1951
Devenish, Nurse C F, NS	QSA (0)	Kimberley Civil Hospital. QSA (0). Kaplan Auction Aug 04
Devenish, Lt Ferdinand Augustus Keuler, KTG	QSA (3) DoK OFS Tr	No III Section, B Company, Beaconsfield Town Guard. Also served KH (34927) 14 Jun 01 to 20 Dec 01 and DH (41238) 15 Feb 02 to 30 Jun 02. Served in the Bechuanaland Rebellion 1897 earning CGHGSM (1) Bech. Subsequently served with the 1st Kimberley Regiment in GSWA. Occupation farmer
Devenish, Pte L I, KTG	QSA (2) DoK OFS	Ambulance Corps, Beaconsfield Town Guard. Also served SAC (372)
Devenish, Nurse V, NS	QSA (0)	Kimberley Civil Hospital
Dever, Pte M, KTG	QSA (1) DoK	B Company
Devlin, Pte T, KTG	QSA (1) DoK	No IV Section, L Company
Dexter, Pte A E, KTG	QSA (1) DoK	Premier Mine
Dexter, Pte F C E, KTG	QSA (1) DoK	No 1 Redoubt
Dexter, Pte H C, KTG	QSA (1) DoK	No I Section, L Company. QSA (1)
Dickason, 1832 Pte A E, CP1	QSA (3) RoM DoK OFS	Served 11 Oct 99 to 31 May 02. KSA (2). Possibly B Squadron
Dickason, 393 L Cpl J H, CP1	QSA (1) DoK	A Squadron. Died of disease 1 Apr 00
Dickens, 336 L Cpl E D, KRV	QSA (1) DoK	DMU 11 Nov 00. CGHGSM (1) Bech (DFH), QSA (1), 14-15 Star (S Sgt SASC Mt), BWM, VM (SANLC), KStar. Walland Jul 87 £375
Dickens, Pte J, KTG	QSA (1) DoK	Cycle Corps, A Company
Dickens, Pte W, KTG	QSA (1) DoK	No 2 Redoubt. QSA (1), 14-15 Star (Pte Kimberley Cdo), BWM (Lt), VM (Sgt SAVR), KStar. Dixon Apr 98 £230. Could be next man. One of these two men attended the 50th Anniversary reunion
Dickens, Pte W, KTG	QSA (1) DoK	No III Section, K Company
Dickenson, 3909 Pte W, LNLR	QSA (1) DoK	Invalided to England 15 Mar 01

Kimberley Siege Account and Medal Roll

Dickenson, 509 Pte William, CP2	QSA (2) DoK OFS	B Squadron. KSA (2). Served in the Bechuanaland Rebellion 1897 earning CGHGSM (1) Bech
Dicker, Pte William Rundle, KTG	QSA (3) RoM DoK OFS	Premier Mine. Also served KLH (192) 5 Mar 00 to 5 Jun 00
Dickinson, 136 Tmptr Arthur F, DFA	QSA (1) DoK	Enrolled DFA 7 Mar 99. Served Kimb Rifles 15 May 93 to 15 Apr 98. DFA 7 Mar 99 to 1 Apr 01. Wounded 24 Oct 99. "Another hero by common consent was Bugler Dickinson, who was struck in the hand just as he had raised the bugle to his lips, and who immediately transferred the instrument to his unhurt hand and blew the notes which he had begun when he received his wound." Also wounded 15 Feb 00. DMU 1 Apr 01. Occupation printer. KSA (2). Served in the Bechuanaland Rebellion 1897 earning CGHGSM (1) Bech
Dickinson, Pte G R, KTG	QSA (1) DoK	Kenilworth Defence Force
Dickson, Pte G, KTG	QSA (1) DoK	Wood cutting
Dickson, Pte J, KTG	QSA (1) DoK	No 2 Schmidt's Breastwork
Dickson, Pte J W, KTG	QSA (1) DoK	No I Section, No 2 Redoubt
Didbury, 4516 Pte T, LNLR	QSA (3) DoK Paar Tr	Mounted Infantry. Wounded 5 Feb 01 at Bothwell. Invalided home 1 Apr 01. QSA (2) excl Tr, KSA (2), 14-15 Star, BWM, VM, KStar. RHQ
Diederich, Pte H W, KTG	QSA (1) DoK	No II Section, Belgravia Fort
Dietrich, Pte M, KTG	QSA (1) DoK	No I Section, Mandy Fort
Dillon, 5278 Pte E, LNLR	QSA (3) DoK OFS Tr	QSA (3), [KSA (2)]. Sotheby Jun 1906. Spink Apr 78 £75. Christies Oct 91
Dillon, 759 Pte Walter Cecil, CP2	QSA (2) DoK OFS	CP No 3 Maxim gun detachment. KSA (2)
Dinwoodie, 31 Sgt Samuel, CP2	QSA (1) DoK	CP dismounted branch (barrier & redoubt duties)
Ditchfield, 4718 Pte S, LNLR	QSA (3) DoK OFS Tr	KSA (2). Discharged for felony
Dixon, Pte F, KTG	QSA (1) DoK	No 6 Redoubt
Dixon, Pte H, KTG	QSA (1) DoK	Cycle Corps, A Company
Dixon, Pte P, KTG	QSA (1) DoK	No 1 supply depot
Dixon, Pte R, KTG	QSA (1) DoK	Kimberley Mine Ambulance Company, B Section. Occupation miner
Dixon, Pte W, KTG	QSA (1) DoK	No II Section, L Company
Dlugadz, Pte D, KTG	QSA (1) DoK	No II Section, No 2 Redoubt
Dobbin, Pte F J, KTG	QSA (1) DoK	No 2 supply depot
Dobie, 703 Pte G W, KRV	QSA (1) DoK	Discharged 29 Apr 02. KSA (2)
Dobson, 32637 Cpl Joseph Edwin, DH	QSA (2) DoK 01	Served 15 May 01 to 26 Nov 01. Also served KTG (No 6 Redoubt). Occupation miner
Dodd, 4515 Pte C, LNLR	QSA (3) DoK OFS Tr	KSA (2)
Dodd, 1968 Pte G H, CP1	QSA (5) RoM DoK OFS Tr 01	A Squadron. Served 11 Oct 99 to 12 Dec 01. 50th Anniversary attendee
Dodd, Pte H, KTG	QSA (1) DoK	Mounted Section, B Company, Beaconsfield Town Guard
Dodd, Pte J, KTG	QSA (1) DoK	Mounted Section, B Company, Beaconsfield Town Guard. QSA (1), KStar. Frontier Medals Apr 02
Dodd, Pte W, KTG	QSA (1) DoK	Cycle Corps, A Company
Dodds, Pte J C, KTG	QSA (2) DoK OFS	No 3 Redoubt. Wounded 24 Oct 99. Also served KLH (61) 20 Oct 99 to 30 Apr 00 and Warrenton TG (12)
Dodds, Pte W W, KTG	QSA (1) DoK	No IV Section, B Company, Beaconsfield Town Guard
Doe, 3626 Band G, LNLR	QSA (3) DoK OFS Tr	KSA (2)

Doherty, Pte M, KTG	QSA (1) DoK	No 2 supply depot. 50th Anniversary attendee. 1141 M J Doherty served KRV and gained RoM, OFS & Tr. Same man?
Doherty, Pte T, KTG	QSA (1) DoK	No III Section, L Company
Dohse, Pte C, KTG	QSA (1) DoK	No I Section, B Company, Beaconsfield Town Guard
Doig, Pte D, KTG	QSA (1) DoK	No I Company, B Section, Reservoir
Doig, Pte James Anderson, KTG	QSA (2) DoK 01	H Company as Dvig on the nominal roll. Also served SRG (155) 12 Feb 01 to 18 Nov 01. QSA (1) excl 01. Spink Oct 76 £70
Dold, Pte C, KTG	QSA (1) DoK	Cycle Corps, A Company. Also served SRG
Dold, Pte Henry Clifford, KTG	QSA (2) DoK OFS	Also served KLH (121) 19 Oct 99 to 6 Mar 00 and SRG (200) from 20 Feb 01
Dold, Pte W S, KTG	QSA (1) DoK	In charge of forage store for mounted troops
Dolman, QMS F C, KTG	QSA (1) DoK	G Company. QSA (1). Liverpool May 91 £85. KStar (ZMS F C Dolman TG). Lusted Oct 73 £18. Spink Mar 79 £35. FJP Auctions Feb 08
Domper, Dvr Charles, DBMB	QSA (1) DoK	Botanical Gardens. Also served CRSS (1176) from 4 Apr 01 and SRG (788) from 26 Aug 01. Surname also Dumper. Occupation sailor
Donaldson, 160 Sgt A Mc D, KRV	QSA (2) DoK Paar	Non effective 4 May 00. Served in the Bechuanaland Rebellion 1897 earning CGHGSM (1) Bech. Served in the Great War with the South African Rifles. Died 1941
Donaldson, Pte J, KTG	QSA (1) DoK	No 3 Redoubt. Also served VTG (199) as Walter J. QSA (1), KStar. Sewell Sep 08 £495
Donelly, Pte R D, KTG	QSA (1) DoK	No IV Section, A Company, Beaconsfield Town Guard
Donelly, Pte Samuel John, KTG	QSA (5) DoK OFS Tr 01 02	No I Section, C Company, Beaconsfield Town Guard. Also served KLH (1108) 29 Dec 00 to 30 Jun 02 and CuH (13) 12 Oct 01 to 16 Mar 02
Donnelly, Pte W T, KTG	QSA (1) DoK	No I Section, Mandy Fort
Donoghue, Mr J, POC	QSA (1) DoK	
Donohoe, 22962 Sapr F, RE	QSA (4) DoK Drie Tr 01	
Donohoe, 20 Sgt William Joseph, CP2	QSA (1) DoK	CP dismounted branch (barrier & redoubt duties)
Donovan, 108 Cpl Charles F, CP2	QSA (4) RoM DoK OFS Tr	C Squadron. KSA (2). Served in the Bechuanaland Rebellion 1897 earning CGHGSM (1) Bech
Donovan, 119 Pte D, KRV	QSA (1) DoK	DMU 9 Apr 00. Also served DFA
Donovan, 269 Gnr Daniel, DFA	QSA (1) DoK	Enrolled DFA 16 Jan 01. Also served KRV (119) 4 Oct 99 to 9 Apr 00. DMU 3 May 02. KSA (2). Occupation barman
Dorey, 2133 Col Sgt J, LNLR	QSA (4) DoK OFS Tr 01	Killed in action 18 Feb 01 at Hartbeestfontein
Dorward, Pte A G, KTG	QSA (1) DoK	No I Section, Mandy Fort
Dott, 160 Sgt Richard Fraser, KLH	QSA (4) RoM DoK Paar Tr	Served 19 Oct 99 to 5 Jun 00. Also served KMC. Missing and released, Potchefstroom, 19 Jul 00. QSA (4). DNW Jul 93 £260
Dotter, 547 Pte A, KRV	QSA (3) RoM DoK OFS	Discharged 22 Jul 01
Dougherty, Pte J, KTG	QSA (1) DoK	No I Company, B Section, Reservoir
Douglas, 1932 Pte J, CP1	QSA (3) DoK OFS 01	C Squadron
Douglas, Pte W, KTG	QSA (1) DoK	Kenilworth Defence Force. QSA (1), KStar. Ursual list 72. Could be next man
Douglas, Pte W, KTG	QSA (1) DoK	Kamfersdam Company
Douglass, 546 Pte P, KRV	QSA (2) DoK OFS	Discharged 26 Feb 00. Also served Albany DMT
Downes, 273 Pte Frank Thomas, CP2	QSA (4) RoM DoK OFS Tr	C Squadron. QSA (4), [KSA (2)]. SpeedBid Mar 04

Kimberley Siege Account and Medal Roll

Downing, 696 Pte Harry Kaiser, CP2	QSA (4) RoM DoK OFS Tr	CP No 2 Maxim gun detachment. Served 11 Oct 99 to 31 May 02. KSA (2). Served in the Bechuanaland Rebellion 1897 earning CGHGSM (1) Bech
Dowrick, Pte Alfred, KTG	QSA (3) RoM DoK OFS	No III Section, C Company, Pickering's Redoubt No 1. Also served KLH (146) 8 Mar 00 to 5 Jun 00
Dowrick, 250 Sgt W, KRV	QSA (1) DoK	DMU 16 May 00
Doyle, Pte B, KTG	QSA (1) DoK	No I Company, B Section, Reservoir
Doyle, 854 Pte D, KRV	QSA (3) DoK OFS Tr	Discharged 1 Jul 02. Also served KTG (No 2 Schmidt's Breastwork). KSA (2)
Doyle, 115 Gnr Patrick, DFA	QSA (3) DoK OFS Tr	Enrolled DFA 11 Aug 98. Resigned 23 Jan 03. KSA (2). Occupation railway clerk
Doyle, 210 Gnr W, DFA	QSA (1) DoK	
Doyle, 70 Cpl W K, KRV	QSA (1) DoK	Non effective 25 Jul 00. Possibly served in the Bechuanaland Rebellion 1897 with Cape Mtd Yeo earning CGHGSM (1) Bech
Drake, 1011 Pte P E, KRV	QSA (1) DoK	Discharged 5 Sep 00. Also served KTG (No 3 Redoubt)
Draper, 585 Pte E J, KRV	QSA (2) DoK OFS	Served 11 Oct 99 until DMU 1 Jun 00. Also served DFH, ASC, BBP. Died 1912. Medal re-issued 4 Jul 10. QSA (2), [KSA (2)], KStar. Spink Mar 86 £165. QSA (2), [KSA (2), KStar]. Liverpool May 06 £210
Dremer, Pte E A, KTG	QSA (1) DoK	G Company
Drew, Capt G B, KTG	QSA (1) DoK	Medical Corps, No 1 Company, C Section
Drew, Lt Percy James Vaughan, KLH	QSA (3) DoK OFS Tr	Also served KTG (Premier Mine). Died of gun shot wound at Potchestroom 28 Jul 00. Medal issued 9 Jun 02. Previously served in the Bechuanaland Border Police in the Matebele War of 1893. Joined De Beers 1894
Dreyer, Pte P, KTG	QSA (3) DoK OFS Tr	Also served KLH (1035) 16 Oct 99 to 4 Jun 01
Drinkhill, 98126 Gnr John, RGA	QSA (1) DoK	Premier Mine. KSA (2)
Driscoll, 4086 Pte G, LNLR	QSA (3) DoK OFS Tr	KSA (2)
Driver, 22 Bombdr Thomas, DFA	QSA (2) DoK OFS	Enrolled DFA 22 May 94. Cpl 1902. Resigned 1 Dec 04. Occupation blaster
Droste, 773 Pte T, KRV	QSA (4) RoM DoK OFS Tr	Discharged 1 Jul 02. Also served KTG (No IV Company, A Section, Reservoir). KSA (2)
Druce, Lt James Charles, KTG	QSA (1) DoK	No 1 Redoubt. Served in the Bechuanaland Rebellion 1897 earning CGHGSM (1) Bech
Druce, Pte W G, KTG	QSA (1) DoK	No I Section, L Company. 50th Anniversary attendee
Drummond, 664 Pte R, KRV	QSA (3) DoK OFS Tr	Discharged 1 Jul 02. BSACM rev Rhodesia 1896 (Tpr Rhod Horse Vols), QSA (3), KSA (2), KStar. Duplicate QSA issued 23 Oct 12
Drummond, 904 Pte W, KRV	QSA (1) DoK	Discharged 10 Sep 00. Also served KTG (No I Company, A Section, Reservoir)
Drury, Pte D J, KTG	QSA (1) DoK	Otto's Kopje Company. On QSA roll as Duery
Drysdale, Cpl G, KTG	QSA (1) DoK	Cycle Corps, A Company. QSA (1). Seaby Feb 81 £140. LSE Apr 84 £95. Spink May 03 £130
Du Bois, 22685 Tpr Frederick Edmond William, CinCBG	QSA (4) DoK OFS Tr 01	Served 17 Nov 00 to 13 May 01 with firename Fritz. Also served KTG (Premier Mine) and CRSS (1453 & 9643) from 20 Nov 01. Surname also Dubois. Note says 'deceased' but no trace on the casualty roll. Occupation architect and surveyor
Du Pratt, 97 S Smith George Benjamin, DFA	QSA (3) DoK OFS Tr	Enrolled in DFA 18 Jan 98. Served Kimb Rifles 9 Mar 96 to 31 Dec 97. Served in the Bechuanaland Rebellion 1897 earning CGHGSM (1) Bech. Resigned 11 Mar 05. KSA (2). Occupation blacksmith. Surname seen as Duprat

140

Du Toit, Pte D, KTG	QSA (1) DoK	No III Company, A Section, Reservoir. QSA (1). McGregor Museum. Surname also spelled Dutoit
Du Toit, G J, KTG	QSA (0)	Roll states "Construction of trenches, removing bushes etc"
Du Toit, 1036 Pte Stephen Francis, KRV	QSA (1) DoK	Non effective 18 Aug 00. Also served KTG (No I Section, No 2 Redoubt) and SRG (118) from 11 Feb 01. Medal re-issued 22 Jul 22. 50th Anniversary attendee. Surname sometimes Dutoit
Duck, 848 Pte J, KRV	QSA (3) DoK OFS Tr	Discharged 1 Jul 02. Also served KTG (No 3 Redoubt). KSA (2)
Duckworth, 5105 Pte R, LNLR	QSA (3) DoK OFS Tr	KSA (2)
Duerden, 3665 Pte R, LNLR	QSA (3) DoK OFS Tr	KSA (2). Deserted 7 Oct 03. Medal not recovered
Duff, 665 Pte F, KRV	QSA (3) DoK OFS Tr	Discharged 1 Jul 02. QSA (3), KSA (2), KStar. Sotheby Jul 34
Duff, 2173 Sapr L, RE	QSA (3) DoK Drie Tr	KSA (2)
Duff, Pte R, KTG	QSA (2) DoK 01	No 2 Schmidt's Breastwork. Also served UVR (1154)
Duffin, 1080 Pte G J, KRV	QSA (4) RoM DoK OFS Tr	Discharged 3 Jul 02. KSA (2)
Duffus, 624 Pte S, KRV	QSA (1) DoK	Discharged 7 Mar 00
Duffy, 3643 Pte P, LNLR	QSA (4) DoK OFS Tr 01	Wounded 18 Feb 01. Invalided to England 7 Apr 01. QSA (3) excl 01. Glendining Dec 65
Duggan, QMS C, KTG	QSA (1) DoK	Kamfersdam Company. QSA (1). Christies Jul 85. Collett Dec 89 £110. KStar. SAMMH
Duggan, Pte G H, KTG	QSA (1) DoK	Kamfersdam Company
Duggan, Pte Gordon Valentine, KTG	QSA (4) DoK OFS Tr 01	Kamfersdam Company. Also served ORCP 5 Aug 00 to 5 Nov 00 and Sgt DH 19 Nov 00 to 14 Nov 01
Duggan, 203 Sgt H, KRV	QSA (4) DoK OFS Tr 01	Discharged 29 Nov 01
Duggan, Pte R H, KTG	QSA (1) DoK	No IV Section, A Company, Beaconsfield Town Guard
Duggan, Mr T, POC	QSA (1) DoK	
Dugmore, Pte J F, KTG	QSA (1) DoK	No 1 supply depot
Duirs, Capt M, KRV	QSA (2) DoK OFS	KSA (2). Served in the Bechuanaland Rebellion 1897 earning CGHGSM (1) Bech
Duke, 190 Gnr Edward Ernest, DFA	QSA (1) DoK	Enrolled DFA 23 Sep 00. Accidentally drowned near Barkly West 23 Sep 00. Medal roll has number as 119. Occupation turner
Duke, Gnr Herbert, DBMB	QSA (4) DoK OFS Tr 01	Armoured train section. Also served KFS (203) 31 Dec 00 to 30 Jun 01
Duke, Pte Hugh Penfold, KTG	QSA (7) DoK Paar Drie Joh DH Witt 01	Otto's Kopje Scouts. Also served DH 18 Feb 00 to 21 May 01. Occupation farmer. BSACM (1) Rhod (Tpr BSAP), QSA (1) DoK. City Coins Sep 03. Liverpool Jan 04 £420
Dunbar, 429 Band A, KRV	QSA (2) DoK 01	Non effective 27 Apr 01
Dunbar, Lt J Brander, KTG	QSA (1) DoK	See his biography (page 342)
Dunbar, Pte M, KTG	QSA (1) DoK	No 1 Redoubt
Duncan, Pte Alex, KTG	QSA (5) RoM DoK OFS Tr 01	Also served KH (381, 405, 1257 & 26205) 6 Mar 00 to 29 Jan 01 and 9 Feb 01 to 14 Sep 01 and SRG (853) from 16 Sep 01
Duncan, 213 Gnr Alexander, DFA	QSA (3) DoK OFS Tr	Enrolled DFA 17 Nov 99. Discharged 1 Jul 02. KSA (2). Occupation draftsman
Duncan, Pte C, KTG	QSA (3) DoK 01 02	No I Section, A Company, Beaconsfield Town Guard. Also served 1st DEOVR (3128). QSA (1) DoK. Sotheby Dec 80
Duncan, 315 Pte J H, KRV	QSA (4) DoK OFS Tr 01	Discharged 29 Sep 01. QSA (2) excl Tr & 01, KStar. Dixon Sep 98 £190. Burman Sep 04 £385

Kimberley Siege Account and Medal Roll

Duncan, 511 Pte Robert D, KRV	QSA (4) DoK OFS Tr 01	Discharged KRV 12 Nov 00. Also served CinCBG (22688) 17 Nov 00 to 2 Sep 01 and CPS (707)
Duncan, 61 Pipe Maj W G, KRV	QSA (1) DoK	Pipe Major, Kimberley Regiment Pipe Band when it was re-raised in 1929. Retired 1936. Died at Springs 1943 aged 96. SAGS (1) 1879 (916 Piper 91st Foot), CGHGSM (1) Bech (Pipe Major KR), QSA (1), KSA (2), 14-15 Star (Pte Vet Regt), BWM, VM (Pte SA Vet Regt), Col Aux LS Medal, ASM, KStar
Duncan, 865 Pte W G, KRV	QSA (1) DoK	Discharged 1 Jul 02. Also served KTG (No IV Section, K Company). KSA (2) issued 16 Jun 1911
Dunk, 453 Cpl Charles Henry, CP2	QSA (4) RoM DoK OFS Tr	CP 7-pounder detachment and Otto's Kopje. KSA (2). Served in the Bechuanaland Rebellion 1897 earning CGHGSM (1) Bech
Dunkerley, 5236 Pte A, LNLR	QSA (3) DoK OFS Tr	KSA (2)
Dunstan, Pte W, KTG	QSA (1) DoK	No 6 Redoubt
Duprat, 151 Pte F, KRV	QSA (2) DoK 01	Non effective 22 Feb 01
Durrell, Pte J H, KTG	QSA (1) DoK	No 2 supply depot
Durrheim, T, AVC	QSA (1) DoK	Civilian employee
Dyason, 667 Pte D'U C, KRV	QSA (2) DoK OFS	Discharged 27 Feb 00
Dyason, Pte H R, KTG	QSA (1) DoK	QSAs (1) to H R & J Dyason. eBay Jun 06
Dyason, Pte J, KTG	QSA (1) DoK	No I Section, B Company, No 4 Redoubt
Dye, 902 Cpl J B, CP1	QSA (4) RoM DoK OFS Tr	B Squadron. KSA (2). Previously served Bechuanaland Rebellion 1897. CGHGSM (1) Bech (Pte CP), QSA (4), KSA (2), WM, ASM, South African Police Medal (1st Cl Sgt), KStar
Dye, 1087 Pte Walter Thomas, CP1	QSA (3) RoM DoK OFS	C Squadron. Slightly wounded 24 Oct 99. DMU. Also served CRSS (1449) 16 Nov 01 to 30 Apr 02. KSA (2). Served in the Bechuanaland Rebellion 1897 earning CGHGSM (1) Bech
Dyer, 3981 Pte A, LNLR	QSA (3) DoK OFS Tr	KSA (2)
Dyer, Pte C, KTG	QSA (1) DoK	No 3 Redoubt
Dyer, 1120 Pte J, KRV	QSA (2) DoK 01	Discharged to pension 22 Apr 01. Supplementary roll says DMU 22 Apr 01. Also served KTG (No I Company, B Section, Reservoir). Served in the Bechuanaland Rebellion 1897 earning CGHGSM (1) Bech
Dyson, 666 Sgt H L, KRV	QSA (3) DoK OFS Tr	DMU 15 Jan 02. KSA (2)

E

Eadie, Sgt David, KTG	QSA (1) DoK	Civil Service Redoubt. Also served Capt UpTG. The QSA medal roll for the UpTG is signed by Eadie where he gives his unit as KTG
Eales, Pte A, KTG	QSA (1) DoK	No 1 Redoubt. 50th Anniversary attendee
Eales, Cpl R, KTG	QSA (1) DoK	No II Company, A Section, Reservoir
Eales, Pte William Joseph, KTG	QSA (2) DoK Tr	No IV Section, C Company, Pickering's Redoubt No 2. Also served WS (38) 4 Sep 00 to 1 May 01, CPS (70) 28 May 01 to 30 Apr 02 and WLH (530) 9 May 02 to 23 May 02. KSA (2)
Early, Pte A, KTG	QSA (1) DoK	No I Section, B Company, Beaconsfield Town Guard
Early, Pte T K, KTG	QSA (1) DoK	Premier Mine. QSA (1). Collett May 89 £95. Spink Dec 94 £96
Early, Pte W, KTG	QSA (1) DoK	Medical Corps, No 1 Company, D Section
Easton, Pte A J, KTG	QSA (1) DoK	H Company. QSA (1), KStar. City Coins Jul 01

Medal roll

Easton, 37 Tpr S J, KLH	QSA (2) DoK OFS	Served 19 Oct 99 until transferred to KTG 3 Jan 00. Also served MH (21494). Medal recovered from SA and reissued 12 Jan 05 to an address in Paris
Easton, 30 QMS William Herbert, DH	QSA (3) DoK OFS Tr	Served 25 May 01 to 30 Jun 02. Also served IYS (30) 27 Jul 00 to 6 Nov 00, KRV (548) to 12 Nov 00, CinCBG (22289) 10 Nov 00 to 9 May 01 and CuH (not on nominal roll). KSA (2). Accidentally wounded 24 May 02. Severely wounded Klerksdorp 24 May 02. QSA disc only
Eastwood, Pte William Ambrose, KTG	QSA (3) DoK OFS Tr	No I Section, Mandy Fort with initial J. Also served KLH (1037) 15 Nov 00 to 30 Nov 01 and 10 Feb 02 to 30 Jun 02. KSA (2). Occupation tobacconist
Eatock, 5550 Pte W, LNLR	QSA (3) DoK OFS Tr	KSA (2)
Eaton, 1364 Pte G W, KRV	QSA (5) DoK OFS Tr 01 02	DMU 25 Jun 02. Also served KTG (No IV Section, K Company)
Eaton, 83 Tpr Jack, KLH	QSA (2) DoK OFS	Served 2 Nov 99 to 4 Jun 00. Also served ASC
Eatonlowe, Pte D A, KTG	QSA (1) DoK	
Ebden, Pte H, KTG	QSA (1) DoK	
Ebdon, Pte Albert, KTG	QSA (1) DoK	No I Section, B2 Company, No 3 Redoubt. Also served SRG (136) from 11 Feb 01. 50th Anniversary attendee
Ebdon, W, KTG	QSA (0)	Roll states "Driving pumping engine for the town water supply"
Eddy, Pte J, KTG	QSA (1) DoK	No I Section, L Company. QSA (1). McGregor Museum
Eddy, Pte W, KTG	QSA (1) DoK	Cycle Corps, A Company. QSA (1), KStar. Glendining Nov 33. QSA (1). Spink Nov 98
Eden, Pte A, KTG	QSA (1) DoK	No 1 Redoubt
Eden, Pte D R, KTG	QSA (1) DoK	No III Section, K Company
Eden, 128 Band F W J, KRV	QSA (1) DoK	Non effective 12 Jun 00. QSA (1), KSA (2), KStar
Eden, 194 Band George Alexander, KRV	QSA (1) DoK	DMU 19 Apr 00. Also served SRG (169) from 13 Feb 01
Eden, Cpl J C, KTG	QSA (1) DoK	
Eden, Pte T A, KTG	QSA (1) DoK	No 1 Redoubt
Eden, 1012 Tpr Thomas Edward, KLH	QSA (3) DoK OFS Tr	Served 16 Oct 99 to 6 Nov 00. Also served CinCBG (22691) until 15 May 01 and ALH (39582) 8 Nov 01 to 24 Mar 02. KSA (2). Occupation moulder
Eden, 587 Pte W E, KRV	QSA (3) DoK OFS Tr	Taken Prisoner at Carter's Ridge 4 Nov 99. Discharged 23 Oct 02. KSA (2)
Edgar, Pte G, KTG	QSA (1) DoK	No IV Section, D Company
Edgecombe, Pte H, KTG	QSA (1) DoK	Premier Mine
Edgill, 137 Tpr Harry, KLH	QSA (2) DoK OFS	Served 19 Oct 99 to 22 Apr 00. Also served KTG (Premier Mine). Surname also Edghill and Edgell
Edgington, Pte T D, KTG	QSA (1) DoK	No I Section, Mandy Fort
Edkins, 4046 Pte George, LNLR	QSA (3) DoK OFS Tr	Severely wounded 28 Nov 99. Invalided to England 1 May 00. Also served SAC C Division. QSA (3), KSA (2) (Tpr SAC). Sotheby Nov 81. Dixon Jun 83 £90. QSA (3), KSA (2), KStar. Walland Sep 87 £220
Edmonds, 12950 L Cpl J J, ASC	QSA (2) DoK OFS	Sudan (Cpl), QSA (2), KSA (2), 1914 Star & Bar (SQMS), BWM, VM (WO), LS&GC, Khedive Sudan (0), KStar. Glendining 1989. DNW Dec 07 £1,800. See his medals on page 501
Edmonds, 715 Pte J R, KRV	QSA (4) RoM DoK OFS Tr	Non effective 10 Jul 01. Also served KTG, KLH (1258) and FID. KSA (2)
Edwards, 26040 Tpr Arthur George, ScH	QSA (3) DoK Tr 01	Served 8 Jan 01 to 20 Sep 01. Dismissed for misconduct. Also served KTG (Premier Mine)
Edwards, Pte B, KTG	QSA (1) DoK	No 6 Redoubt

Kimberley Siege Account and Medal Roll

Name	Medals	Notes
Edwards, Pte Charles H, KTG	QSA (3) DoK OFS Tr	D Company (Veterans), Beaconsfield Town Guard. Also served VTG (188). Sent out by General French to collect horses in the OFS. Taken prisoner to Waterval, Transvaal. Took up arms there with the column that released him about 6 Jun 00
Edwards, 449 Pte Edward H S, CP2	QSA (1) DoK	CP HQ and depot mounted branch
Edwards, Pte H, KTG	QSA (1) DoK	No I Section, K Company. Also served KRV (886) until 12 Apr 02. QSA (1) named to '886 Pte', [KSA (2)]. eBay Apr 06 £195
Edwards, Pte H C, KTG	QSA (1) DoK	
Edwards, 64847 Gnr James, RGA	QSA (3) DoK OFS Tr	Premier Mine
Edy, 672 Pte Norman Herbert, CP2	QSA (2) DoK OFS	A Squadron. Slightly wounded 28 Nov 99. KSA (2). Name also spelled Eddy. Previously served Bechuanaland Rebellion 1897
Egan, Pte M W, KTG	QSA (1) DoK	No II Section, C Company, Pickering's Redoubt No 1
Egan, Pte T D, KTG	QSA (1) DoK	No II Section, No 2 Redoubt
Egley, 589 Pte John, CP2	QSA (1) DoK	CP dismounted branch (barrier & redoubt duties)
Ehlers, 583 Pte Jacobus F M S, CP2	QSA (1) DoK	C Squadron. Discharged time expired 17 Apr 01. Also served Scout FID. KSA (2) issued off FID roll 3 Nov 08
Eilbeck, 1240 Pte William, KRV	QSA (5) RoM DoK OFS Tr 01	Non effective 28 May 01. Also served KTG (No 2 Schmidt's Breastwork), KLH (378, 408 & 1259) 6 Mar 00 to 6 Nov 00 and SRG (593) from 29 May 01
Eland, 205 Sgt Bert, KLH	QSA (2) DoK OFS	Served 21 Oct 99 to 31 May 00. Also served KTG. BSACM rev Rhodesia 96 (Tpr MRF), QSA (2), 14-15 Star, BWM, VM (2nd Cl WO SAEC), KStar. Initials also AEJ. Sotheby Nov 81. Dixon Oct 86 £230
Eland, Mr V A, POC	QSA (1) DoK	
Eliot, Lt Algernon Ernest Albert, KTG	QSA (1) DoK	See his biography (page 342)
Eliott, Maj Francis Augustus Heathfield, CP2	QSA (2) DoK OFS	See his biography (page 342)
Eliott, Pte G A, KTG	QSA (1) DoK	No II Section, C Company, Pickering's Redoubt No 2
Eliott, 1810 Pte H G, CP1	QSA (4) RoM DoK OFS Tr	C Squadron. Issued 8 Nov 05. KSA (2) as Elliott
Elkin, Capt W S, KTG	QSA (1) DoK	D Company
Elkington, Pte F, KTG	QSA (1) DoK	Kamfersdam Company
Elland, Pte A, KTG	QSA (1) DoK	No II Section, Mandy Fort
Elliot, Lt K C, KTG	QSA (1) DoK	No III Section, No 2 Redoubt. QSA (1), KStar, Kimberley Medal (unnamed). DNW Dec 91 £700. See his medals on page 506
Elliott, 586 Pte G, KRV	QSA (3) DoK OFS Tr	Prisoner at Carter's Ridge 4 Nov 99. Discharged 10 Oct 00
Elliott, Pte G C, KTG	QSA (1) DoK	No I Section, B Company, No 4 Redoubt
Elliott, 285 Pte Hugh Jardine Lewin, CP2	QSA (1) DoK	A Squadron. Killed in action 24 Oct 99
Elliott, 3731 Pte J, LNLR	QSA (3) DoK OFS Tr	KSA (2)
Elliott, 3974 Pte J, LNLR	QSA (3) DoK OFS Tr	KSA (2)
Elliott, Pte J, KTG	QSA (1) DoK	Medical Corps, No 1 Company, C Section
Ellis, 90622 Gnr Albert Edward, RGA	QSA (2) DoK 01	
Ellis, Pte C, KTG	QSA (1) DoK	No IV Section, C Company, Pickering's Redoubt No 2
Ellis, Pte C, KTG	QSA (1) DoK	Premier Mine

Ellis, 5572 Pte G, LNLR	QSA (3) DoK OFS Tr	KSA (2)
Ellis, Capt G K, KTG	QSA (3) DoK 01 02	No 2 Schmidt's Breastwork. Also served Agent FID
Ellis, 4880 Pte W, LNLR	QSA (3) DoK OFS Tr	KSA (2)
Ellis, Pte W, KTG	QSA (1) DoK	No IV Section, D Company
Ellis, Pte W J, KTG	QSA (1) DoK	No 6 Redoubt
Elphinstone, 654 L Cpl Frederick Stephen, KRV	QSA (2) DoK 01	See his biography (page 343)
Else, 1394 Pte H O J, CP1	QSA (2) DoK OFS	B Squadron. Discharged 21 Jan 01. KSA (2)
Else, Pte Harry, KTG	QSA (3) RoM DoK OFS	Premier Mine. Also served KLH (186) 8 Mar 00 to 5 Jun 00
Else, 117 Cpl S, KRV	QSA (3) DoK OFS Tr	KSA (2)
Emanuel, Pte Harry Jacob, KTG	QSA (1) DoK	No 3 Redoubt. Also served KLH (1117 & 1316) 17 Mar 00 to 9 Nov 00
England, Cpl J, KTG	QSA (1) DoK	No I Company, B Section, Reservoir
England, Pte R, KTG	QSA (1) DoK	No III Section, C Company, Beaconsfield Town Guard
Engledoe, Pte R G, KTG	QSA (1) DoK	Ambulance Corps, Beaconsfield Town Guard
Engledoe, Pte R J H, KTG	QSA (1) DoK	G Company
English, 431 Sgt J T, KLH	QSA (3) RoM DoK OFS	Served 1 Dec 99 to 5 Jun 00. Also served KTG (Kimberley Mine Ambulance Company with mounted forces)
English, Pte T R, KTG	QSA (1) DoK	No I Section, Mandy Fort
Ennor, Pte T, KTG	QSA (1) DoK	
Enright, 625 Pte A E, KRV	QSA (1) DoK	Discharged 1 Jul 02. KSA (2)
Enright, 731 Pte Gerald David, KRV	QSA (3) DoK OFS Tr	Served 11 Jan 00 until DMU 7 Mar 00. Also served KLH (277 & 472) 17 Mar 00 to 11 Jun 00 and CP (850) 21 Jun 00 to 31 Mar 03. RofM issued on CP roll but later returned as not entitled. KSA (2). Previously Trooper, British South Africa Company Police, Mashonaland Expedition (Pioneer column) 1890 and Trooper, Bechuanaland Border Police, Matabele War, 1893
Entwistle, 5386 L Cpl J, LNLR	QSA (4) DoK OFS Tr 01	Killed in action Schietfontein on 1 Aug 01
Erasmus, Pte A, KTG	QSA (1) DoK	
Erasmus, 435 Pte Jacobus C, CP2	QSA (4) RoM DoK OFS Tr	A Squadron. QSA (4), KSA (2), Permanent Forces LS&GC (1884 Const 5th SAMR). Glendining Feb 85 £270. DNW May 92 £380. Glendining Mar 93 £310. City Coins Sep 03
Erasmus, Pte Lourens, KTG	QSA (4) RoM DoK OFS 02	No III Section, C Company, Beaconsfield Town Guard. Also served KLH (389) 7 Mar 00 to 5 Jun 00, CDF, CCCC (no trace on roll), FID and M Sqn CCF (55). Forename sometimes Lawrence
Ericksen, 72 Pte John, CP2	QSA (1) DoK	CP dismounted branch (barrier & redoubt duties)
Erskine, 954 Pte Charles Alex W, KRV	QSA (4) RoM DoK OFS 01	Also served KTG (No 1 Redoubt), DFH, CRSS and BoH (21302) 29 Nov 00 to 15 May 01
Estment, Pte E W, KTG	QSA (1) DoK	Cycle Corps, A Company
Estment, 21 Tpr Harry, KLH	QSA (2) DoK OFS	Served 18 Oct 99 to 30 Apr 00. Also served NH (1768). KSA (2)
Ethell, 504 Pte Samuel, KRV	QSA (4) RoM DoK OFS Tr	Served 4 Oct 99 to 20 Jun 00. Also served DFH, CRSS (1297) 30 May 01 to 20 May 02, CinCBG (22689) 19 Nov 00 to 13 May 01. Occupation butcher. QSA (3) excl Tr, [KSA (2)]

Etheridge, 332 Pte J H, KRV	QSA (1) DoK	DMU 5 Dec 99. Also served CRSS
Etherington, Pte E, KTG	QSA (1) DoK	N Company, No 1 Redoubt
Etherington, Pte Essington Ward Hartley, KTG	QSA (1) DoK	Cycle Corps, A Company. Also served CRSS (1401) from 28 Sep 01. Occupation miner
Etherington, Cpl T, KTG	QSA (1) DoK	No 1 Redoubt. QSA (1). Glendining Mar 89. Liverpool Jan 90 £75
Ettling, Pte Max Henry Charles, KTG	QSA (1) DoK	G Company. Also served SRG (167) from 11 Feb 01
Ettwein, Pte G, KTG	QSA (1) DoK	No III Section, K Company
Eva, 926 Pte H M, KRV	QSA (2) DoK OFS	Discharged 2 Jan 01. Also served KTG (No I Company, A Section, Reservoir)
Evan, Pte E J, KTG	QSA (1) DoK	Premier Mine. QSA (1). McGregor Museum
Evans, 5233 Pte J, LNLR	QSA (3) DoK OFS Tr	KSA (2)
Evans, 1111 Pte J J, KRV	QSA (4) RoM DoK OFS Tr	Discharged 15 Oct 02. DCM LG 11 Oct 01 for gallantry on 12 Feb 01. Citation LG 3 Dec 01. Also served KTG (No II Company, A Section, Reservoir). KSA (2)
Evans, 116 Pte R, KRV	QSA (2) DoK OFS	Died 25 May 01. Served in the Bechuanaland Rebellion 1897 earning CGHGSM (1) Bech
Everill, 122 Tpr Sydney F H, KLH	QSA (2) DoK OFS	Discharged 4 Jun 00. Also served KTG (No I Section, C Company, Pickering's Redoubt No 1) and KR. QSA (2). Dixon Apr 98 £110. Romsey Medals 04 £180
Everington, Pte A, KTG	QSA (1) DoK	No 6 Redoubt
Everington, Pte H, KTG	QSA (1) DoK	No II Section, D Company
Everington, Pte J, KTG	QSA (1) DoK	B line of defence, No 3 Redoubt. QSA (1) Liverpool Jul 07 £210
Everleigh, Pte T, KTG	QSA (3) DoK OFS Tr	No I Company, B Section, Reservoir. Also served KLH (1151) 10 May 00 to 12 Nov 00
Evert, Pte G, KTG	QSA (1) DoK	Cycle Corps, A Company
Evert, Pte J B, KTG	QSA (1) DoK	H Company
Evert, Pte W J, KTG	QSA (1) DoK	No IV Section, C Company, Pickering's Redoubt No 2. QSA (1). Liverpool Aug 91 £85
Ewing, Pte Peter, KTG	QSA (1) DoK	No 6 Redoubt. Also served SRG (42) from 11 Feb 01
Ewing, 384 Pte W A, KRV	QSA (1) DoK	DMU 15 Mar 00
Exner, Pte F, KTG	QSA (1) DoK	No I Section, B Company, Beaconsfield Town Guard
Exter, Pte H G, KTG	QSA (1) DoK	Premier Mine
Exter, Pte J J, KTG	QSA (1) DoK	No III Section, A Company, Beaconsfield Town Guard
Eyre, 3698 Pte A, LNLR	QSA (1) DoK	Invalided to England 5 Mar 00. QSA (1). Langridge Feb 76 £58
Eyre, 1035 Pte E, KRV	QSA (1) DoK	Also served KTG (No 1 Redoubt) and ILH. KSA (2)
Eyre, 68853 Sgt Ins Edwin, RGA	QSA (3) DoK OFS Tr	See his biography (page 343)

F

Fabling, 228 Cpl Launcelot Matthew, CP2	QSA (4) RoM DoK OFS Tr	See his biography (page 343)
Fagan, 3773 Pte J, LNLR	QSA (3) DoK OFS Tr	QSA (3), KSA (2), KStar. Glendining Dec 1909. KStar. Sotheby Dec 80
Fagan, 77 Pte William, CP2	QSA (1) DoK	B Squadron
Fairbrass, 668 Pte William Mockett, KRV	QSA (6) DoK Belm MR Paar Tr 01	Served from 10 Oct 99 until DMU 4 Apr 00. Also served DH 19 Nov 00 to 28 Jan 01

Medal roll

Fairgrieve, Pte R, KTG	QSA (1) DoK	Kimberley Mine Ambulance Company, E Section
Fairley, Pte H W, KTG	QSA (1) DoK	No III Section, K Company
Fairweather, Pte C, KTG	QSA (1) DoK	No 1 Redoubt
Fairweather, Pte W, KTG	QSA (1) DoK	No 1 Redoubt. QSA (1). McGregor Museum
Falcon, 200 Pte George, CP2	QSA (1) DoK	CP dismounted branch (barrier & redoubt duties). Dismissed for misconduct 17 Oct 00
Farnham, 1152 Sgt Gilbert, KLH	QSA (3) DoK Paar Tr	Joined 16 Oct 99. Reattested 31 Dec 01. Also served KH (227) from 29 Mar 02. Occupation telegraphist. QSA (3), [KSA (2)], KStar. Lusted 74 £68
Farnworth, 4741 L Cpl H, LNLR	QSA (4) DoK Paar Joh DH	KSA (2)
Farquhar, Pte Charles John, KTG	QSA (1) DoK	No IV Section, No 2 Redoubt. Also served SRG (162) from 11 Feb 01
Farquhar, Cpl J, KTG	QSA (1) DoK	No I Section, Belgravia Fort
Farquhar, Pte W, KTG	QSA (1) DoK	Cycle Corps, A Company
Farquharson, Pte Percival Henry, KTG	QSA (5) RoM DoK Paar Tr 01	No III Section, A Company, Beaconsfield Town Guard. Also served KLH (41) 19 Oct 99 to 15 Feb 01 and CPS (662)
Farr, 1211 Cpl Leo George, KLH	QSA (3) DoK OFS Tr	Served 23 Nov 99 to 10 Nov 00. Also served KTG, ScH (26122) 20 Jan 01 to 24 Jan 02 and DH (41260) 20 Feb 02 to 30 Jun 02. Slightly wounded 25 Nov 99. KSA (2). Duplicate KSA (2) deleted off 1st ScH roll
Farrell, Sp Const J W, CP2	QSA (1) DoK	Possibly identical with 650 Cpl J P Farrell CP1 who served 11 Oct 99 to 31 Dec 01 and gained 01
Farrell, 389 Pte John Henry, CP2	QSA (4) RoM DoK OFS Tr	C Squadron. Served 11 Oct 99 to 17 Oct 01. Also served SRG (1707) 21 Oct 01 to 21 Apr 02. KSA (2). Served in the Bechuanaland Rebellion 1897 earning CGHGSM (1) Bech. Occupation clerk
Farrell, 210 Tpr Robert, KLH	QSA (4) DoK OFS 01 02	Served 1 Nov 99 to 30 Apr 00. Also served KTG and SRG (43) from 11 Feb 01
Farrelly, 62457 Gnr Peter John, RGA	QSA (3) DoK OFS 01	Premier Mine
Farren, 829 Pte J, KRV	QSA (1) DoK	DMU. Also served KTG (No 2 Schmidt's Breastwork and No II Section, K Company)
Faulds, Pte Alf, KTG	QSA (1) DoK	No III Section, A Company, Beaconsfield Town Guard. A different man of the same name (KR 1025) had his medal forfeited
Faulkner, 4518 Pte G, LNLR	QSA (3) DoK OFS Tr	KSA (2)
Faulkner, Capt T J, DFA	QSA (3) DoK OFS Tr	Operations in OFS & Tr. Resigned 31 Mar 03. KSA (2). Previously served as a gunner in Prince Alfred's Own Cape Volunteer Artillery and in the operations in Transkei and Basutoland, CGHGSM (2)
Faulkner, Capt W H, KTG	QSA (1) DoK	L Company. IGS (1) Perak (1643 Sgt 80th Foot), Abyssinia Medal (Boy 756 33rd Regt) (re-engraved), SAGS (1) 1879 (1643 Cpl 80th Foot), QSA (1), KStar. City Coins Sep 03
Faull, Pte W, KTG	QSA (1) DoK	No III Section, L Company
Fawcett, 259 Pte Alfred, CP2	QSA (4) RoM DoK OFS Tr	B Squadron. CGHGSM (1) Bech (Pte CP), QSA (4), KSA (2)
Fawkes, Pte I, KTG	QSA (1) DoK	Wood cutting. QSA (1). Liverpool Apr 89 £75. KStar. Spink Jul 08
Feather, 254 Tpr John, KLH	QSA (2) DoK OFS	Served 19 Oct 99 to 30 Apr 00. Also served IYS (30) 11 May 00 to 6 Sep 00. Possibly served in the Basuto Wars with PAVG earning CGHGSM (1) Bas
Feeney, Cpl E, KTG	QSA (1) DoK	No I Section, L Company. Also served JTG and IMR
Fenn, Capt Dudley Burgess, KLH	QSA (3) DoK OFS Tr	Served 10 Oct 99 to 30 Jun 02. Also served KH as Captain. KSA (2)

Kimberley Siege Account and Medal Roll

Fennelly, 18476 Gnr Michael, RGA	QSA (1) DoK	Premier Mine. KSA (2)
Ferguson, 549 Pte Fergus, KRV	QSA (4) RoM DoK OFS Tr	Severely wounded 28 Nov 99. Discharged 1 Jul 02. KSA (2)
Ferguson, Guard J, IMR	QSA (1) DoK	
Ferguson, 1039 Tpr James Arnold, KLH	QSA (5) DoK OFS Tr 01 02	Discharged 6 Nov 00. Also served KRV (986), 2nd BrH (20691) 23 Nov 00 until DMU 9 Jan 01, POWLH (25741) 17 Dec 00 to 1 Jul 01 and SRG (815)
Ferguson, 227 Tpr W A, KLH	QSA (2) DoK OFS	Served 20 Oct 99 to 14 Mar 00. Also served KTG with initials T W
Ferns, Lt H C, KTG	QSA (1) DoK	Beaconsfield Town Guard
Ferraro, 527 Sgt Ins E T, KRV	QSA (3) DoK OFS Tr	Discharged 1 Jul 02. KSA (2)
Ferris, 4875 Pte W, ASC	QSA (4) DoK OFS Tr 01	Died on service 16 Jan 01. Issued to brother 21 Oct 03. See page 501 for his medal
Ferro, 84 Cpl F W, KRV	QSA (1) DoK	Discharged 1 May 00 and since deceased (not on casualty roll). CGHGSM (1) Bech, QSA (1), KStar. Seaby Aug 72 £94. Christies May 88 £200. Dixon Jun 89 £245. eBay Oct 08 £522
Ferro, 123 Tpr Henry Vincent, KLH	QSA (3) RoM DoK OFS	Served 19 Oct 99 to 5 Jun 00. Also served KTG and SRG (45) from 11 Feb 01. Served in the Bechuanaland Rebellion 1897 earning CGHGSM (1) Bech
Ferry, Pte P, KTG	QSA (1) DoK	Reserve Section, D Company
Fewster, 4181 Pte G, LNLR	QSA (2) DoK OFS	Wounded Boshof 21 Apr 00. Invalided home 15 May 00. Enlisted 29 Jul 93 and served in India and Ceylon. Papers have forename Christopher. Discharged 28 Jul 05. QSA (2). Wellington Auctions May 07
Field, 28228 2nd Cpl G E, RE	QSA (3) DoK Drie Tr	Wounded at Frederickstad 30 Jul 00. QSA (3), KSA (2), BWM, VM (MID), LS&GC, 1935 Jubilee. RHQ
Field, Pte George W, KTG	QSA (1) DoK	No II Section, B Company, Beaconsfield Town Guard. Also served VTG (203)
Field, Lt Horatio George, KTG	QSA (1) DoK	See his biography (page 343)
Fielding, 84 Cpl Wilfred C D, CP2	QSA (1) DoK	CP HQ and depot mounted branch. KSA (2). Served in the Bechuanaland Rebellion 1897 earning CGHGSM (1) Bech
File, Pte A C, KTG	QSA (1) DoK	No 1 supply depot
Fillis, Pte H, KTG	QSA (1) DoK	No 2 supply depot
Filshie, 242 Gnr P, DFA	QSA (3) DoK OFS Tr	Enrolled DFA 11 Aug 00. Served DBMB 3 Oct 99 to 18 Feb 00. Resigned 13 Jan 03. KSA (2). Occupation clerk. Surname also spelled Filchie
Finch, Col Sgt G, KTG	QSA (1) DoK	No 3 Redoubt
Finlayson, Lt Col Robert Alexander, KRV	QSA (3) DoK OFS Tr	See his biography (page 343)
Finn, 1592 Pte W B, CP1	QSA (3) RoM DoK OFS	A Squadron. Discharged time expired 12 Apr 01
Finnerty, Pte R, KTG	QSA (1) DoK	No 1 Redoubt
Firth, 5474 L Cpl W, LNLR	QSA (2) DoK Tr	Accidentally wounded Klip Drift 7 Mar 02. QSA (2), [KSA (2)]. Spink Nov 05 £300
Fisher, 290 Pte Arthur Honor, CP2	QSA (2) DoK OFS	CP dismounted branch (barrier & redoubt duties). Also served Lt E Div SAC. Served in the Bechuanaland Rebellion 1897 earning CGHGSM (1) Bech
Fisher, 5004 Pte Christopher, LNLR	QSA (3) DoK Paar Joh	Mounted Infantry. See page 500 for his biography and medals
Fisher, Lt Edward Montague, CP2	QSA (4) RoM DoK OFS Tr	See his biography (page 343)
Fisher, 3571 Pte F, LNLR	QSA (3) DoK OFS Tr	Wounded Weltevreden 20 Oct 00. QSA (3), [KSA (2)]. DNW Jul 01 £210. Liverpool Aug 01 £290

Medal roll

Fisher, Pte Julius Alexander, KTG	QSA (5) RoM DoK OFS Tr 01	Otto's Kopje and A Section, Kimberley Mine Ambulance Company. Also served KRV (745) to 12 Apr 01. Served in the Bechuanaland Rebellion 1897 earning CGHGSM (1) Bech
Fisher, Pte T B, KTG	QSA (1) DoK	Kenilworth Defence Force
Fisher, 5301 Pte W, LNLR	QSA (3) DoK OFS Tr	QSA (3), KSA (2), KStar. eBay Mar 05
Fisher, Pte W A, KTG	QSA (1) DoK	No III Section, Belgravia Fort
Fishpool, Pte J, KTG	QSA (1) DoK	No I Section, C Company, Pickering's Redoubt No 1. QSA (1), KStar. Sotheby Jul 74 £65. Glendining Feb 79 £95. Spink Dec 85
Fitchett, 143 Dvr William Joseph, DFA	QSA (1) DoK	Enrolled DFA 23 May 99. Resigned 23 Jan 03. Occupation baker and farrier
Fitzgerald, 432 Pte Edward David, CP2	QSA (2) DoK OFS	A Squadron. KSA (2). Served in the Bechuanaland Rebellion 1897 earning CGHGSM (1) Bech
Fitzgerald, 314 Tpr Frederick, KLH	QSA (3) DoK Witt Belf	Served 24 Oct 99 to 24 Mar 00. Also served 2nd BrH (7041), StH (1245) and SAC (1956). KSA (2)
Fitzgerald, Lt P F, KTG	QSA (3) DoK OFS 01	G Company. Also served 3rd SWB and Remount Dept
Fitzpatrick, 3897 Pte E, LNLR	QSA (3) DoK OFS Tr	QSA (3), KSA (2), KStar. Sotheby Mar 82 £120
Fitzpatrick, 548 Sgt E W, CP1	QSA (2) DoK OFS	A Squadron. DMU 31 Aug 01. Served in the Bechuanaland Rebellion 1897 earning CGHGSM (1) Bech
Fitzpatrick, Pte J, KTG	QSA (1) DoK	No 1 Redoubt
Fitzpatrick, Pte J, KTG	QSA (1) DoK	No IV Section, C Company, Beaconsfield Town Guard
Fitzpatrick, Pte P D, KTG	QSA (1) DoK	Premier Mine
Fitzpatrick, 76 Pte Sidney Albert, KLH	QSA (6) RoM DoK OFS Tr 01 02	Also served KRV (1389) 31 Oct 99 until DMU 3 Jan 00, KLH (76) with initials P G 31 Dec 99 to 3 Jan 00, 2nd BrH (4330) with initials P G 15 Mar 00 to 8 May 00 and CinCBG (22693) 17 Nov 00 to 12 May 01
Fitzsimmons, 4357 Pte W, LNLR	QSA (3) DoK OFS Tr	KSA (2)
Fivay, Pte F J, KTG	QSA (1) DoK	No IV Section, A Company, Beaconsfield Town Guard
Fivaz, 731 Pte Charles Frederick, CP2	QSA (2) DoK Tr	B Squadron. KSA (2). KSA reissued 5 Mar 09
Flack, Pte E, KTG	QSA (1) DoK	No III Section, F Company, No 3 Redoubt
Flannery, 4200 Pte J, LNLR	QSA (3) DoK OFS Tr	KSA (2)
Fleischer, 781 Pte Spencer W, CP2	QSA (1) DoK	A Squadron. CGHGSM (1) Bech, QSA (1), KSA (2), 14-15 Star, BWM, VM, Permanent Forces LS&GC, KStar
Fleming, Pte J, KTG	QSA (1) DoK	No IV Section, B Company, No 4 Redoubt. QSA (1). McGregor Museum
Flesch, J A, KTG	QSA (0)	Roll states "Removing and burying dead horses"
Flesch, Pte P, KTG	QSA (1) DoK	
Fletcher, Pte A C, KTG	QSA (1) DoK	No II Section, C Company, Pickering's Redoubt No 2
Fletcher, Pte F C, KTG	QSA (1) DoK	
Fletcher, Nurse L, NS	QSA (0)	Kimberley Civil Hospital
Fletcher, 4707 Pte W, LNLR	QSA (3) DoK OFS Tr	KSA (2)
Fletcher, W, KTG	QSA (0)	Roll states "Electrical work, searchlights and telephones"
Fletcher, 2nd Lt Walter John Cumberlege, LNLR	QSA (1) DoK	See his biography (page 344)
Fleury, 126 Tpr Arthur, KLH	QSA (2) DoK OFS	Served 20 Oct 99 to 14 Mar 00. Also served KTG
Flood, Pte F, KTG	QSA (1) DoK	H Company

Kimberley Siege Account and Medal Roll

Flook, Pte W, KTG	QSA (1) DoK	Also served KLH (88) and CPS (125) as Flooks 27 Nov 00 to 30 Apr 02. Prisoner Manthe 25 Jun 01. KSA (2)
Floyd, 22692 Tpr Ernest Charles George, CinCBG	QSA (4) DoK OFS Tr 01	Served 23 Nov 00 to 22 May 01. Also served KTG (B line of defence, No 3 Redoubt)
Floyd, J, KTG	QSA (0)	Roll states "Construction of shelters for women and children"
Floyd, 196 Gnr William John, DFA	QSA (1) DoK	Enrolled DFA 25 Sep 99. DMU 7 Apr 02. KSA (2). Occupation electrician at Kimberley Mine
Fluke, 214 Dvr Sidney James, DFA	QSA (2) DoK OFS	Enrolled DFA 20 Nov 99. Resigned 20 Mar 03. Occupation boiler smith at De Beers. QSA (2). Liverpool Jan 98 £105. QSA (2), KStar. Dixon Sep 04 £425. Dixon Jun 06 £575
Flynn, 485 Pte H M, KRV	QSA (2) DoK OFS	Telegraphist ordered to return to Post Office duty 12 Apr 00
Flynn, Lt J F, KTG	QSA (1) DoK	Kenilworth Defence Force
Flynn, 124 Tpr Stephen, KLH	QSA (2) DoK OFS	Served 19 Oct 99 to 7 Mar 00. Also served KTG
Foley, Pte F W, KTG	QSA (1) DoK	G Company
Foley, 572 Pte William Patrick, CP2	QSA (2) DoK Tr	CP dismounted branch (barrier & redoubt duties). Discharged for misconduct 11 Sep 00. Also served DS (58) 18 Dec 00 to 4 Feb 01 and BR (218 and 26197) from 7 Feb 01. Occupation labourer
Foot, 450 L Cpl Chas H, KRV	QSA (2) DoK 01	Discharged 8 Jan 01. Also served CCCC (26032)
Foot, Mr F G, POC	QSA (1) DoK	
Forbes, 41314 Tpr James McLaren, DH	QSA (4) RoM DoK OFS Tr	Served 25 Feb 02 to 20 Sep 02. Also served KTG (No 3 Redoubt) and KLH (1040 and 22823) 13 Aug 00 to 12 Feb 02. KSA (2). Occupation miner
Forbes, 4989 Pte W, LNLR	QSA (4) DoK OFS Tr 01	QSA (4). Sotheby Oct 71. Seaby Mar 72 £6
Ford, 11809 Pte E, ASC	QSA (2) DoK OFS	QSA (2), [KSA (2)]. Glendining Jun 90 £95. Now RHQ
Ford, Pte F, KTG	QSA (1) DoK	Construction of redoubts, splinterproofs etc
Ford, Pte H F, KTG	QSA (1) DoK	No I Section, Belgravia Fort
Ford, Pte J E, KTG	QSA (1) DoK	No II Section, Belgravia Fort
Ford, 1118 Pte J J, KRV	QSA (4) RoM DoK OFS Tr	Discharged 1 Jul 02. Nr 1188 on Supplementary and KSA rolls. Also served KTG (No II Section, A Company, Beaconsfield Town Guard) 10 Oct 99 to 7 Mar 00. QSA (3) excl Tr, KSA (2), KStar. Sotheby Mar 83 £380. Sotheby Jul 87. DNW Dec 06 £650
Ford, Lt Thurston James, KRV	QSA (1) DoK	KSA (2). Served in the Bechuanaland Rebellion 1897 earning CGHGSM (1) Bech. Promoted Captain 5 Jan 03. During the Great War served in East Africa and GSWA operations
Ford, 48 Tpr William Peter, KLH	QSA (2) DoK Paar	Served 19 Oct 99 to 30 Apr 00. Also served IYS (14) 11 May 00 to 6 Sep 00, BoH, CPS (107), FID and ScH. KSA (2)
Forrester, Pte Q, KTG	QSA (1) DoK	Premier Mine
Forshaw, 708 Pte Robert, CP2	QSA (1) DoK	CP dismounted branch (barrier & redoubt duties). KSA (2)
Forsyth, 804 Pte D, KRV	QSA (1) DoK	Discharged 4 Jul 02. Also served KTG (No 2 Schmidt's Breastwork). KSA (2)
Forsyth, 23 CSM G, KRV	QSA (1) DoK	DMU 23 Apr 00. Served in the Bechuanaland Rebellion 1897 earning CGHGSM (1) Bech
Foster, Pte A W, KTG	QSA (1) DoK	No 5 supply depot
Foster, Mr C H, POC	QSA (1) DoK	Telegraph signaller
Foster, 791 Pte Ernest Laurimer, CP2	QSA (1) DoK	A Squadron. Wounded during the siege (date unknown). Served 11 Oct 99 to 31 May 02. KSA (2)

Medal roll

Foster, H, KTG	QSA (0)	Roll states "Gun construction, repairing rifles and Maxims"
Foster, 5480 Pte J, LNLR	QSA (3) DoK OFS Tr	KSA (2). Invalided to England 30 Apr 01
Foster, Pte J, KTG	QSA (1) DoK	Medical Corps, No 1 Company, D Section
Foster, 1306 Sapr J T, RE	QSA (3) DoK Drie Tr	QSA (3), KSA (2), 14-15 Star (Sgt RE), BWM, VM (Capt). Glendining Nov 77 £125
Foster, Pte W B, KTG	QSA (1) DoK	No 6 Redoubt and No 2 Schmidt's Breastwork
Foster, Pte William, KTG	QSA (3) DoK OFS 02	Served KTG (Fitting and laying pipes for the town water supply) as Forster. Also served ORS (173) 16 Apr 02 to 30 Jun 02. Occupation fitter and plumber
Foules, Sgt C, DBMB	QSA (1) DoK	HQ and searchlight. QSA (1). Seaby Mar 80 £130. Morton and Eden Oct 03 £440. City Coins Aug 08 £850
Fowler, 3662 Pte J, LNLR	QSA (3) DoK OFS Tr	KSA (2)
Foxcroft, 587 Pte R J, CP2	QSA (1) DoK	Appears on the QSA roll with a no clasp medal and note saying discharged for misconduct 24 Mar 01. His name appears on the nominal roll as serving in the HQ staff and depot mounted branch
Foy, 5454 Pte J, LNLR	QSA (4) DoK OFS Tr 01	Invalided to England 9 Jan 01
Foy, Capt Louis Arnold, CP1	QSA (1) DoK	See his biography (page 344)
Frames, Pte L G, KTG	QSA (1) DoK	No II Section, Belgravia Fort
Frampton, Pte W T, KTG	QSA (1) DoK	
Franceys, Lt A L, KTG	QSA (1) DoK	No II Section, No 2 Redoubt
Francis, Pte A, KTG	QSA (1) DoK	No 1 Redoubt
Francis, Sgt H, KTG	QSA (1) DoK	Kamfersdam Company
Francis, 75 L Cpl R, KRV	QSA (4) DoK OFS Tr 01	Killed in action 2 Aug 01 at Swaitputs
Franke, Pte A K R, KTG	QSA (1) DoK	Premier Mine. Also served KRV (54) until DMU 5 Dec 99
Franklin, Cpl A O, KTG	QSA (1) DoK	H Company. 50th Anniversary attendee
Franklin, 1041 Tpr C D, KLH	QSA (4) DoK Paar Tr 01	Served 22 Oct 99 to 30 May 01. 50th Anniversary attendee with initials C de M
Franklin, Pte John James, KTG	QSA (4) RoM DoK OFS Tr	Also served KLH (357 & 409) 15 Mar 00 to 5 Jun 00, KR (1092) 23 Jul 00 to 6 Aug 00, CPS (135) 23 Nov 00 to 30 Apr 02 and WWTG (356) 5 May 02 to 30 Jun 02. KSA (2)
Franklin, Pte M W, KTG	QSA (1) DoK	Kimberley Mine searchlight and telephone section and No II Section, L Company
Franklin, 277 Pte Sidney, CP2	QSA (1) DoK	CP dismounted branch (barrier & redoubt duties)
Fraser, Cpl A M, KTG	QSA (1) DoK	No III Section, K Company
Fraser, Pte D, KTG	QSA (1) DoK	No II Company, A Section, Reservoir
Fraser, Pte D, KTG	QSA (1) DoK	No III Section, C Company, Beaconsfield Town Guard
Fraser, Pte G, KTG	QSA (1) DoK	
Fraser, 696 L Cpl H B, CP1	QSA (2) DoK OFS	DMU 30 Jan 01. Served in the Bechuanaland Rebellion 1897 earning CGHGSM (1) Bech
Fraser, 1015 Pte J, KRV	QSA (1) DoK	Also served KTG (No I Section, Belgravia Fort) and KLH. Discharged 1 Jul 02. KSA (2)
Fraser, 300 Tpr James, KLH	QSA (2) DoK OFS	Served 20 Oct 99 to 30 Apr 00. Also served Warren's Scouts (9), DEOVR (1477) and Daniel's Kuil TG
Fraser, Maj John Randal, LNLR	QSA (3) DoK OFS Tr	See his biography (page 344)
Frederick, 530 Pte Wybert, CP2	QSA (3) DoK OFS Tr	A Squadron. QSA reissued 10 Mar 14. QSA (3). DNW May 92 £85. Dixon Dec 92 £150
Fredericks, Mr F, POC	QSA (1) DoK	
Freel, Pte J, KTG	QSA (1) DoK	No 6 Redoubt

Name	Medals	Notes
Freeman, Pte H, KTG	QSA (2) DoK OFS	No III Section, C Company, Beaconsfield Town Guard. Also served KRV (1093)
Freeman, Pte J, KTG	QSA (1) DoK	Premier Mine
Freeman, 158 Sgt Ins J T, KRV	QSA (4) RoM DoK OFS Tr	Served as drill instructor in DFH. Discharged 13 Mar 03. KSA (2). Served in the Bechuanaland Rebellion 1897 earning CGHGSM (1) Bech
Freeman, Pte W F, KTG	QSA (1) DoK	Premier Mine
Freeman, 244 Sgt Sdlr W L, KRV	QSA (4) DoK OFS Tr 01	
Freestone, 1375 Pte G W, KRV	QSA (3) DoK 01 02	Also served KTG (Premier Mine). Duplicate medal issued
Freislich, 317 Sgt Charles Edmund, KLH	QSA (2) DoK OFS	Joined 1 Oct 99. Killed in action 25 Nov 99
Freislich, Pte Herbert William, KTG	QSA (1) DoK	No I Section, C Company, Pickering's Redoubt No 1. CGHGSM (1) Bech, QSA (1), KStar. See his medals on page 506
Friedrichs, Pte C J E, KTG	QSA (1) DoK	Also served KWTTG. QSA (1), KStar. Collett Dec 89 £180
Friend, Sgt Francis W, KTG	QSA (3) DoK OFS Tr	No 2 Schmidt's Breastwork. Also served WS (22) 20 Mar 00 to 31 Aug 00
Frond, Pte D, KTG	QSA (1) DoK	No IV Section, C Company, Pickering's Redoubt No 2
Frost, Capt Fred Joseph Guy, KLH	QSA (4) RoM DoK Paar Tr	Served 8 Mar 00 to 30 Jun 02. Also served KTG. MID 1 Mar 02
Fry, Pte H W, KTG	QSA (3) DoK 01 02	No II Section, B Company, No 4 Redoubt. Also served SRG (44). Served in the Bechuanaland Rebellion 1897 earning CGHGSM (1) Bech
Fry, Nurse I, NS	QSA (0)	Kimberley Civil Hospital
Fry, Pte Ivan, KTG	QSA (3) DoK OFS 01	Premier Mine. Also served WS (30) from 31 Mar 00 and FID from 28 Apr 01
Fryar, Pte J, KTG	QSA (1) DoK	No IV Section, C Company, Pickering's Redoubt No 2
Fuche, 95 Pte L, KRV	QSA (1) DoK	Non effective 5 Jul 00
Fullaway, 496 Pte H R, KRV	QSA (3) RoM DoK OFS	Non effective 20 Jun 00. CGHGSM (1) Bech (Kimb Rfls), BSACM rev Rhod 96 (Tpr MRF), QSA (3), KStar. Christies Oct 91 £400
Fuller, Pte F, KTG	QSA (1) DoK	
Fuller, Nurse M, NS	QSA (0)	Kimberley Civil Hospital
Furmidge, Pte E R, KTG	QSA (1) DoK	G Company. Also served CRSS (1182). QSA (1), 14-15 Star (7th Infy), BWM, VM (11th SAI), KStar. Spink Aug 00 £218. Surname sometimes Furnidge
Furmidge, Pte S, KTG	QSA (1) DoK	No I Section, Mandy Fort
Furness, Pte J, KTG	QSA (1) DoK	Kamfersdam Company
Furness, Pte John Benjamin, KTG	QSA (4) RoM DoK OFS 01	Kamfersdam Company. Also served KLH (338) 15 Mar 00 to 5 Jun 00 and 1st BrH (22755) 5 Dec 00 to 10 Jun 01
Fyfe, 855 Pte David, KRV	QSA (4) DoK OFS Tr 01	Non effective 22 Jul 00. Also served KTG (No I Section, K Company) and ScH (361 & 26028) 7 Jan 01 to 24 Jul 01. QSA (4), KStar. Christies Nov 83. LSE Apr 84 £125. Glendining Jun 91. QSA (5) inc CC. City Coins Dec 00
Fynn, Lt W D, KTG	QSA (1) DoK	Superintendent of De Beers Farms for over 33 years. 50th Anniversary attendee
Fyvie, 19 CSM L C, KRV	QSA (1) DoK	Wounded 14 Feb 00. Discharged 22 Mar 00. Served in the Bechuanaland Rebellion 1897 earning CGHGSM (1) Bech

G

Gaddies, 330 Tpr Andrew, KLH	QSA (2) DoK Paar	Served 1 Nov 99 to 1 Feb 02. Three periods of service with KLH. Also served IYS (11) 11 May 00 to 6 Sep 00, 2nd ILH (476) 7 Jan 01 to 4 Jul 01 and ALH (40299) 9 Feb 02 to 24 Mar 02. Slightly wounded Klip Drift 7 Mar 02. KSA (2). Occupation painter. Surname sometimes Geddies
Gain, Mr A, POC	QSA (1) DoK	
Gainsford, Pte E R, KTG	QSA (2) DoK Tr	Premier Mine. Also served CPS (868) with DoM but this is believed to be a mistake for DoK. QSA (2), KStar
Gainsford, Pte Robert Francis, KTG	QSA (4) RoM DoK OFS Tr	Premier Mine. Also served KLH (179) 8 Mar 00 to 5 Jun 00 and CPS (864). Wounded Klip Drift 7 Feb 02. QSA (4)
Gallow, Pte A H, KTG	QSA (1) DoK	No I Section, C Company, Pickering's Redoubt No 1. Served in the Bechuanaland Rebellion 1897 earning CGHGSM (1) Bech
Gallow, E, KTG	QSA (0)	Roll states "Guarding natives on construction works"
Gallow, Pte J, KTG	QSA (1) DoK	Cycle Corps, A Company
Gallow, Pte W F, KTG	QSA (1) DoK	H Company
Gammie, 588 Pte J, KRV	QSA (1) DoK	DMU 8 Mar 00. QSA (1), KStar. Dixon Jun 98 £200
Ganghillo, Pte J, KTG	QSA (1) DoK	
Gard, 980 Gnr Albert Frank, RGA	QSA (2) DoK Tr	KSA (2)
Garde, 172 Sgt Thomas William, CP2	QSA (4) RoM DoK OFS Tr	A Squadron. KSA (2). Dismissed 1904
Garden, Sgt F, KTG	QSA (1) DoK	No IV Section, K Company. QSA (1). City Coins Aug 96
Gardiner, 620 Pte Charles, CP2	QSA (1) DoK	CP dismounted branch (barrier & redoubt duties). KSA (2) not issued as struck off
Gardiner, Pte F J, KTG	QSA (1) DoK	No II Section, Belgravia Fort
Gardiner, Pte T J G, KTG	QSA (1) DoK	Civil Service Redoubt
Gardiner, Mr W J, POC	QSA (1) DoK	QSA (1). City Coins Dec 05. See his medal on page 507
Gardner, Pte G, KTG	QSA (1) DoK	Cycle Corps, A Company
Gardner, Pte W, KTG	QSA (1) DoK	D Company
Garner, 844 Pte F, KRV	QSA (2) DoK 01	Non effective 29 May 01. Also served KTG (No 3 Redoubt)
Garner, 3458 Band H, LNLR	QSA (3) DoK OFS Tr	Invalided to England 28 Apr 00
Garrard, 3609 Tmptr Frank Yule, 14H	QSA (4) DoK Paar Drie Tr	QSA (4), KSA (2), KStar. DNW Dec 2004 £380. See his medals and biography on page 511
Garrett, 369 Pte Geoffrey Herbert, CP2	QSA (3) RoM DoK OFS	B Squadron. CGHGSM (1) Bech (Pte CP), QSA (3), KSA (2), 14-15 Star (Cpl 5th SAMR), BWM, VM (Cpl 5th SAMR), Permanent Forces LS Medal (Cpl 5th SAMR). Sotheby Nov 78. Glendining Feb 85 £440. Spink Dec 88. Liverpool Jan 98 £580
Gartrell, Pte H, KTG	QSA (1) DoK	No II Company, A Section, Reservoir
Gartrell, Pte H, KTG	QSA (1) DoK	No I Section, D Company
Gartrell, Pte J, KTG	QSA (1) DoK	No 6 Redoubt. QSA (1). Spink Nov 99
Gartrell, Pte R, KTG	QSA (1) DoK	No III Section, D Company
Gasson, Pte W, KTG	QSA (1) DoK	No II Section, Belgravia Fort
Gates, Pte A A, KTG	QSA (1) DoK	Construction of shelters for women and children
Gates, Pte H C, KTG	QSA (1) DoK	No IV Section, K Company
Gatland, Mr F, POC	QSA (1) DoK	QSA (1), KStar. Sotheby Nov 78. Gibbons Mar 80 £340
Gaven, 3743 Pte M, LNLR	QSA (3) DoK OFS Tr	KSA (2). Gavon on KSA roll
Gavera, Pte J, KTG	QSA (1) DoK	No III Section, C Company, Beaconsfield Town Guard

Medal roll

153

Kimberley Siege Account and Medal Roll

Geary, 5065 Pte W, LNLR	QSA (3) DoK OFS Tr	QSA (3), [KSA (2)]. Gibbons Sep 90 £110. Spink Nov 05 £240. Dixon Apr 06 £350
Geddes, Clerk W, ASC	QSA (1) DoK	Also served KTG
Geduld, Pte D, KTG	QSA (1) DoK	No III Section, C Company, Beaconsfield Town Guard
Gee, Pte J B, KTG	QSA (1) DoK	Repairing saddlery
Geldard, 3729 Pte W, LNLR	QSA (3) DoK OFS Tr	KSA (2)
Geldenhuis, 770 Pte Dirk, CP2	QSA (1) DoK	CP dismounted branch (barrier & redoubt duties). QSA (1), KStar. Dixon Sep 98 £185
Geldenhuis, 767 Pte John, CP2	QSA (2) DoK OFS	A Squadron. Duplicate medal issued on payment 26 Feb 09. KSA (2)
Gelston, 2867 Cpl J, LNLR	QSA (3) DoK OFS Tr	KSA (2)
Genis, Nurse S, NS	QSA (0)	Kimberley Civil Hospital. KStar. City Coins Dec 88
Gentleman, Lt J W, KTG	QSA (1) DoK	H Company. QSA (1), KStar. Kaplan Jul 05
Geoghegan, 329 Pte James J, KRV	QSA (1) DoK	DMU 30 Apr 00. Note says QSA (2) inc OFS issued as Captain. Also served Geoghegan's Scouts as Capt 15 Nov 00 to 13 Jan 02. Possibly issued off Geoghegan's Scouts roll
Geoghegan, 129 Lt John Patrick, Geoghegan's Scouts	QSA (2) DoK OFS	Severely wounded 25 Nov 99. Also served KTG, KLH (129) 19 Nov 99 until DMU 24 Mar 00, and SRG (46). BSACM rev Rhodesia 96 (Tpr Gaghegan BSAP), QSA (4) inc 01 & 02, KSA (2) (Capt Geoghogan's Scouts). City Coins Dec 82
George, 4246 Pte D, LNLR	QSA (4) DoK Paar Joh DH	KSA (2). Mounted Infantry. Also served with SAC (103)
George, 402 Pte J L, KRV	QSA (1) DoK	Also served CP. DMU 2 Apr 00. Possibly also served KTG (Reserve Section, D Company) with initials L J
George, 669 Pte L F, KRV	QSA (1) DoK	DMU 23 Aug 00. Also served DFA (240). KSA (2) from DFA roll. Served in the Bechuanaland Rebellion 1897 earning CGHGSM (1) Bech
George, Tpr Philip Henry, KTG	QSA (4) DoK OFS Tr 01	No III Section, No 2 Redoubt. Also served CinCBG (22694) 17 Nov 00 to 29 Apr 01 and 20th Co ASC from 19 Apr 01. QSA (1) DoK, 14-15 Star (Pte 7th Infy), BWM (Pte SAVR), VM (Pte 7th Infy), KStar. City Coins Aug 08
George, Pte W, KTG	QSA (1) DoK	No IV Section, C Company, Beaconsfield Town Guard
Geraghty, Dvr John, IMR	QSA (1) DoK	QSA (1), KStar. Sotheby Nov 78. Sotheby Mar 82 £360
Gerans, Pte J, KTG	QSA (1) DoK	Reserve Section, D Company
Gerrard, Lt John Henry, CP2	QSA (1) DoK	B Squadron. QSA clasps unclear as roll damaged but probably just DoK. KSA (2). KSA roll notes 'deceased'. Not recorded in the casualty roll. Served in the Bechuanaland Rebellion 1897 earning CGHGSM (1) Bech
Gething, 1317 Sgt W B, KFS	QSA (4) DoK OFS Tr 01	Served 19 Mar 01 until DMU 16 Jul 01 in Pretoria. Also served KRV (412) to 9 Jul 00. QSA (4). Liverpool Mar 86 £115
Geyer, Pte J H, KTG	QSA (1) DoK	No I Section, B Company, Beaconsfield Town Guard
Geyer, Pte W, KTG	QSA (1) DoK	Kimberley Mine Ambulance Company, B Section
Giani, 409 Pte Alfred Eward, CP2	QSA (3) DoK OFS Tr	Served in the Bechuanaland Rebellion 1897 earning CGHGSM (1) Bech. QSA (3). City Coins Mar 03. Warwick & Warwick Sep 06
Gibbon, Pte R, KTG	QSA (3) DoK OFS Tr	Premier Mine. Also served KRV (1194). Discharged 1 Jul 02. KStar named to 'R. GIBBONS JUNR. K.T.G. – P.M.D' South African Militaria, Jan 04 £142. QSA (3), KSA (2). Bonhams Apr 03. QSA (2) OFS & Tr (Pte KTG), KSA (2) (1194 Cpl KRV) plus QSA (1) DoK. Dixon Jul 04 £260 & £200 respectively
Gibbon, Pte R, KTG	QSA (1) DoK	Premier Mine. QSA (1). Bonhams Apr 03. This QSA was stolen in Autumn 2004

Gibbs, 559 Pte Egbert Alfred Homsley, CP2	QSA (4) RoM DoK OFS Tr	CP No 2 Maxim gun detachment. [QSA (4)], KSA (2). Lockdales Jul 08
Gibbs, Pte H, KTG	QSA (1) DoK	
Gibbs, 815 Pte Harry Mordaunt, CP2	QSA (2) DoK OFS	KSA (2)
Gibbs, Pte J, KTG	QSA (1) DoK	No II Section, C Company, Pickering's Redoubt No 2. 50th Anniversary attendee
Gibbs, 137 Bombdr Jack, DFA	QSA (3) DoK OFS Tr	Enrolled DFA 16 Mar 99. Resigned 29 Jan 03. Occupation engine man at De Beers. KSA (2)
Gibson, 29 Sgt J, KRV	QSA (1) DoK	DMU 15 Mar 00
Gibson, Pte P, KTG	QSA (1) DoK	No I Company, B Section, Reservoir
Gibson, 5103 Pte R, LNLR	QSA (3) DoK OFS Tr	QSA (3), [KSA (2)]. Sotheby Jun 1906. Spink Mar 93 £70. Liverpool Jun 93 £125
Gibson, 40348 Cpl Robert Turriff, DH	QSA (6) RoM DoK OFS Tr 01 02	Served 1 Feb 02 to 15 Oct 02. Also served KTG (No I Section, No 4 Redoubt), KLH (410, 423, 1260), SRG (633) from 10 Jun 01 and CPS (7). Occupation engine driver and diamond driller
Gibson, 197 Sgt Maj William Mitchell, KLH	QSA (4) RoM DoK OFS Tr	See his biography (page 344)
Giddy, B H, KTG	QSA (0)	Roll states "In charge of alarm signals"
Gie, 241 Pte John Conrad, KRV	QSA (1) DoK	DMU 23 May 00. Also served SRG (592) from 28 May 01
Gietzmann, Pte C, KTG	QSA (1) DoK	No I Company, B Section, Reservoir
Gietzmann, Pte W F, KTG	QSA (1) DoK	Guarding natives on construction works
Gifford, Nurse Lady Sophie, NS	QSA (0)	See her biography (page 344)
Gilbert, 257 Tpr A, KLH	QSA (2) DoK OFS	Discharged 4 Mar 00
Gilbert, 215 Tpr Arthur, KLH	QSA (3) RoM DoK OFS	Served 21 Oct 99 to 5 Jun 00
Gilbert, Pte F, KTG	QSA (1) DoK	No III Section, No 2 Redoubt
Gilbert, Mr H, POC	QSA (1) DoK	
Gilbert, 10650 Gnr Henry, RGA	QSA (2) DoK Tr	KSA (2)
Gilbert, Sp Const J, CP2	QSA (1) DoK	
Gilbert, Mr J, POC	QSA (1) DoK	
Gilbert, 228 Gnr John, DFA	QSA (3) DoK OFS Tr	Enrolled DFA 12 Mar 00. Also served KTG (H Company) 4 Oct 99 to 28 Feb 00. Wounded Klip Drift 7 Mar 02 while serving in the Pom Pom section. KSA (2)
Gilbert, 90431 Sgt John, RGA	QSA (2) DoK OFS	KSA (2)
Gilbert, 49 Pte Thomas, CP2	QSA (1) DoK	Discharged on gratuity
Gilburt, Sp Const T, CP2	QSA (1) DoK	
Gilby, 168 Cpl Henry John, DFA	QSA (3) DoK OFS Tr	Enrolled DFA 18 Jul 99. Served Channel Islands Artillery 1891 to 1894. Resigned 23 Jan 03. KSA (2). Occupation barman
Gilchrist, W, KTG	QSA (0)	Roll states "Signaller at alarm post" QSA (0). Glendining Jun 91 where says is officially renamed
Giles, Pte H M, KTG	QSA (1) DoK	
Giles, Pte J G, KTG	QSA (1) DoK	No III Section, F Company, No 3 Redoubt
Gill, Capt H J, LNLR	QSA (3) DoK OFS Tr	Captain Quartermaster. MID 4 Sep 01. KSA (2)
Gill, Pte Lionel Walter John, KTG	QSA (1) DoK	Civil Service Redoubt. See his biography (page 344)
Gill, Nurse M, NS	QSA (0)	Kimberley Civil Hospital

Gillard, 374 Cpl A E, KRV	QSA (2) DoK OFS	Discharged 4 Nov 02. KSA (2)
Gillbee, Pte G F, KTG	QSA (1) DoK	Premier Mine
Gillespie, 4 Sgt John Maitland, KLH	QSA (3) DoK Paar Tr	Discharged 30 Apr 00. Also served KTG, BR (412) with initial M from 11 Dec 01, NH, BoH, SRG 12 Feb 01 to 30 Apr 02 and Maj WLH 1 May 02 to 30 Jun 02. KSA (2). Address Blenheim, New Zealand
Gillett, Pte John Lionel, KTG	QSA (1) DoK	Civil Service Redoubt. See his biography (page 344)
Gilling, 803 Pte G W, KRV	QSA (1) DoK	Also served KTG (No 3 Redoubt). Died in hospital at Barkly West 20 Apr 00. Medal re-issued 9 Apr 13
Gillward, Capt F W H, CP1	QSA (2) DoK OFS	C Squadron. KSA (2). Earned CGHGSM (3) Trans Bas Bech
Gilmore, Gnr G, DBMB	QSA (1) DoK	Crusher Redoubt
Gilmore, 67858 Gnr Robert, RGA	QSA (1) DoK	
Gilmore, Pte T, KTG	QSA (1) DoK	
Gilvary, 10631 Gnr Dennis, RGA	QSA (1) DoK	KSA (2)
Glanville, Dvr G, DBMB	QSA (3) RoM DoK OFS	Botanical Gardens. Also served KLH (203) 12 Mar 00 to 8 Jun 00 with forenames William George
Glass, W B, KTG	QSA (0)	Roll states "In charge of natives (scurvy patients)"
Gleave, Gnr John, DBMB	QSA (5) DoK OFS Tr 01 02	Botanical Gardens. Also served KTG 11 Oct 99 to 5 Mar 00, KLH (26101) 15 Jan 01 to 18 Aug 01 and SRG (778) 17 Aug 01 to 17 Feb 02. Occupation fireman. [QSA (5)], KStar (J Gleave Maxim Baty). Liverpool Mar 81 £75. QSA (5) CC OFS Tr 01 02 named to KLH also known
Glen, Sgt G H, KTG	QSA (1) DoK	No III Section, B Company, Beaconsfield Town Guard
Glen, 735 Pte J W, KRV	QSA (3) RoM DoK OFS	Non effective 20 Jun 00. Also served KTG (No III Section, B Company, Beaconsfield Town Guard). QSA (3), 14-15 Star, BWM, VM (Pte). Sold with QSA (1) CC to Mr J Glen IMR. Double issue perhaps or family group? City Coins Nov 06. QSA (3) group of four. Liverpool Apr 07 £595
Glen, Pte James, KTG	QSA (1) DoK	No I Section, A Company, Beaconsfield Town Guard
Glennie, Sgt J T, DBMB	QSA (1) DoK	Reservoir Redoubt. Possibly served in the Bechuanaland Rebellion 1897 with DFA earning CGHGSM (1) Bech
Glover, Gnr E, DBMB	QSA (1) DoK	Botanical Gardens. Severely wounded 11 Feb 00. Roll says dead (but no death recorded on the casualty roll)
Glover, QMS E, KTG	QSA (1) DoK	Otto's Kopje Scouts. QSA (1). DNW May 93 £85. Spink Jul 00 £130
Glover, 38 Band Sgt F W, KRV	QSA (1) DoK	KSA (2)
Glover, Lt Louis Samuel, SRG	QSA (3) DoK Paar Tr	See his biography (page 344)
Glover, 671 Pte R, KRV	QSA (1) DoK	QSA (1), KSA (2), KStar. City Coins May 02. Warwick & Warwick Sep 06. eBay Mar 07
Glover, 28 Tpr Thomas Percival, KLH	QSA (2) DoK Paar	Served 18 Oct 99 to 30 Apr 00
Glover, Pte W, KTG	QSA (1) DoK	No III Section, F Company, No 3 Redoubt
Glover, 626 Pte W A, KRV	QSA (3) RoM DoK OFS	Non effective 26 Jun 00. QSA (3), KStar
Gluyas, Pte J, KTG	QSA (1) DoK	Kimberley Mine Ambulance Company with mounted forces
Glyn, 670 Pte Charles, KRV	QSA (1) DoK	Wounded 28 Nov 99. Discharged on grounds of wounds 19 Feb 00. Also served KTG
Goate, Lt E W C, KTG	QSA (1) DoK	Kamfersdam Company

Medal roll

Gobey, 470 Tpr John, KLH	QSA (4) RoM DoK OFS Tr	Discharged KLH 12 Nov 00. Also served KTG (Gibraltar Fort, Davis's Heap) 4 Oct 99 to 2 Mar 00 and KRV (1228) until discharged 1 Jul 02. KSA (2)
Goddard, Mr H E, POC	QSA (1) DoK	
Goddard, Mr S, POC	QSA (1) DoK	QSA (1). Dixon Apr 07 £485
Godfrey, 5586 Pte H, LNLR	QSA (3) DoK OFS Tr	QSA (3), [KSA (2)]. Burman Mar 02 £110
Godwin, 334 Farr Sgt A G, KRV	QSA (3) DoK Tr 02	Non effective 20 Jun 00. Also served CP and JMR (2602)
Goldie, 849 Pte Robert, KRV	QSA (2) DoK OFS	Discharged 13 Mar 02. Also served KLH (32515) and KTG (No 2 Schmidt's Breastwork) as Gouldie. KSA (2). Occupation saddler
Goldstucker, Cpl W, KTG	QSA (1) DoK	H Company
Goldswain, 388 Sgt C, CP1	QSA (2) DoK OFS	C Squadron. DMU 31 Dec 01. Prisoner Koopmansfontein 5 Jan 01. Served in the Bechuanaland Rebellion 1897 earning CGHGSM (1) Bech
Goldwyer, 1062 Pte W, KRV	QSA (3) DoK OFS Tr	Discharged 1 Jul 02. Served in the Bechuanaland Rebellion 1897 earning CGHGSM (1) Bech. QSA (3), [KSA (2)]. City Coins Dec 04
Good, 22696 Tpr William Alfred, CinCBG	QSA (4) DoK OFS Tr 01	Joined 17 Nov 00 and transferred to KFS 14 Feb 01. Also served KTG (Cycle Corps, A Company and No III Section, D Company), 4th RPR (2159) and 2nd KFS (288) 27 Jul 01 to 28 Sep 01
Goodall, 278 Tpr Thomas J, KLH	QSA (2) DoK OFS	Joined 23 Oct 99. Killed in action 16 Nov 99. He arrived in Kimberley in 1891 and joined the Kimberley Scots. Occupation carpenter at De Beers. QSA (2). Corbitt Jun 81 £225
Goodchild, 468 L Cpl W J, KRV	QSA (1) DoK	Discharged 1 Jul 02. KSA (2)
Goodman, Pte H L, KTG	QSA (1) DoK	
Goodrick, Nurse D, NS	QSA (0)	Kimberley Civil Hospital
Goose, Pte A, KTG	QSA (1) DoK	G Company
Gordon, 788 Pte Frederick, CP2	QSA (1) DoK	CP dismounted branch (barrier & redoubt duties). KSA (2)
Gordon, 22695 Sgt Harry John, CinCBG	QSA (4) DoK OFS Tr 01	Served 12 Nov 00 and discharged 7 Feb 01. Wounded 28 Nov 99. Also served DFH and KRV (551) until discharged 14 May 00
Gordon, Matron J, NS	QSA (0)	Kimberley Civil Hospital. MID 10 Sep 01
Gordon, QMS J E, KTG	QSA (1) DoK	Otto's Kopje Scouts
Gordon, Pte Thomas, KTG	QSA (3) DoK 01 02	No 1 Redoubt. Also served DH 2 Sep 01 to 12 Mar 02. Occupation labourer. QSA (1) DoK. Burman Jul 99 £110
Gordon, W, KTG	QSA (0)	Roll states "Chief carpenter. In charge of all woodwork erected at the suggestions of the RE Officer"
Gordon, Pte W, KTG	QSA (1) DoK	No 3 Redoubt
Gore, Pte R, KTG	QSA (1) DoK	Cycle Corps, A Company
Gore, 268 Cpl William, CP2	QSA (4) RoM DoK OFS Tr	CP No 2 Maxim gun detachment. KSA (2). Served in the Bechuanaland Rebellion 1897 earning CGHGSM (1) Bech
Gorham, 94797 Gnr Edward, RGA	QSA (2) DoK Tr	Premier Mine. KSA (2)
Gorle, Maj H V, ASC	QSA (2) DoK OFS	See his biography (page 344)
Gorman, 672 Pte A, KRV	QSA (1) DoK	Discharged 1 Jul 02. QSA re-issued. KSA (2)
Gormley, 4314 Pte J, LNLR	QSA (4) DoK OFS Tr 01	QSA (3) excl 01. Sotheby Mar 80. Liverpool Aug 95 £125. Neate Apr 00 £135. A F Brock Oct 06. Lockdales Jul 08
Gould, 742 Pte Bertram Parker, CP2	QSA (1) DoK	B Squadron. Discharged by purchase. 50th Anniversary attendee. QSA (1), KStar, BWM (Sgt SAMC). Dixon Mar 04 £350. eBay Feb 06

Name	Medals	Notes
Gould, Pte F, KTG	QSA (1) DoK	No II Section, Mandy Fort
Gouldie, Pte H, KTG	QSA (1) DoK	Premier Mine and Kenilworth Defence Force. QSA (1), KStar. Christies Apr 92 £230. Lockdales Nov 08
Gouldie, Pte J, KTG	QSA (1) DoK	No 6 Redoubt
Gouldie, Pte J, KTG	QSA (1) DoK	No III Section, L Company
Gouldie, Pte J, KTG	QSA (4) DoK OFS Tr 01	Also served 2nd RPR (1119) as Goldie
Gouldie, Pte William Henry, KTG	QSA (1) DoK	No 6 Redoubt. Also served SRG (910) from 21 May 01
Gouws, Pte A E S, KTG	QSA (1) DoK	Kenilworth Defence Force
Gove, 1125 Pte W E, KRV	QSA (1) DoK	H Company. Dismissed for misconduct 6 Nov 00. Also served KTG
Gow, 247 Pte James, CP2	QSA (4) RoM DoK OFS Tr	C Squadron. Wounded 24 Oct 99. Died of disease at Kimberley 28 Jun 01. Served in the Bechuanaland Rebellion 1897 earning CGHGSM (1) Bech. QSA (4). eBay Apr 05 £455
Gower, 514 Pte H C, KRV	QSA (3) RoM DoK OFS	Non effective 20 Jun 00
Gowie, Pte T S, KTG	QSA (1) DoK	No II Section, K Company
Grace, 70 Tpr J H, KLH	QSA (2) DoK OFS	Served 20 Oct 99 to 29 Oct 00
Grace, 718 Pte John James, CP2	QSA (1) DoK	B Squadron. DMU. Served in the Bechuanaland Rebellion 1897 earning CGHGSM (1) Bech
Gradwell, Pte A, KTG	QSA (1) DoK	
Gradwell, 469 L Cpl G W, CP2	QSA (2) DoK 01	A Squadron. Served 11 Oct 99 to 31 Mar 01. Wounded 24 Oct 99. Served in the Bechuanaland Rebellion 1897 earning CGHGSM (1) Bech
Grafton, 2979 Cook Sgt D, LNLR	QSA (3) DoK OFS 01	Invalided to England 18 Apr 01
Graham, Pte E, KTG	QSA (1) DoK	No IV Section, F Company, Mostert's Redoubt
Graham, Pte G, KTG	QSA (1) DoK	QSA (1), KStar. Glendining Sep 74. Elite Nov 09 £475
Graham, Col Sgt T, KTG	QSA (1) DoK	No 6 Redoubt
Graham, Sgt W, KTG	QSA (1) DoK	No I Section, L Company
Graham, Pte W, KTG	QSA (2) DoK OFS	No IV Company, A Section, Reservoir. Also served Pte JTG and Capt Edenburg TG
Grahan, 44 Sgt Herbert William, CP2	QSA (1) DoK	CP dismounted branch (barrier & redoubt duties). Transferred to WD Dept
Grainger, 132 Tpr Edward Paddon, KLH	QSA (3) RoM DoK OFS	Served 19 Oct 99 to 5 Jun 00
Grainger, Nurse F, NS	QSA (0)	Kimberley Civil Hospital
Grainger, Pte W, KTG	QSA (1) DoK	No I Company, B Section, Reservoir
Granger, Pte R, KTG	QSA (1) DoK	No 3 Redoubt
Grant, Pte C, KTG	QSA (1) DoK	No I Section, D Company. QSA (1). Dixon Sep 99 £110. Dixon Jul 07 £250
Grant, Lt Douglas, KTG	QSA (4) RoM DoK OFS Tr	Kenilworth Defence Force. Also served Lt KLH 1 Apr 00 to 2 Dec 00 and SAC from 3 Dec 00
Grant, 673 Cpl Henry McKay, KRV	QSA (1) DoK	Non effective 22 Nov 00. Also served KTG and SRG (111) from 12 Feb 01
Grant, J, KTG	QSA (0)	Roll states "In charge of pump for the town water supply"
Grant, Pte J, KTG	QSA (1) DoK	Kamfersdam Company. QSA (1), 1914-15 Star, BWM, VM (Pte Veteran Regt), KStar. Corbitt Jun 05. Lockdales Jan 09. Could be next man
Grant, Pte James, KTG	QSA (1) DoK	No I Section, D Company. Occupation engineer
Grant, Pte T, KTG	QSA (1) DoK	

Medal roll

Grant, Lt William Gordon, KTG	QSA (1) DoK	Kenilworth Defence Force. Member of the South African Railway Ambulance Division and of the Railways and Harbour Brigade. He died in 1927
Grassie, Pte P, KTG	QSA (1) DoK	No I Section, Belgravia Fort. QSA (1). Spink Jun 83 £100
Grattan, 22238 Tpr Richard Joseph, CinCBG	QSA (4) DoK OFS Tr 01	Served 19 Nov 00 to 1 Jun 01. Also served CP2 (740) (A Squadron) until DMU
Grattan, 160 Sgt Ins W, DFA	QSA (1) DoK	Also awarded a silver medal engraved on the obverse to Sgt Grattan and on the reverse with 'Dismtg Ordnance / Artly Sports / Kby Siege / 1900'
Graugh, Pte E J, KTG	QSA (1) DoK	
Graves, Lt Algernon Sydney, CP2	QSA (3) DoK OFS Tr	C Squadron. KSA (2). Served in the Bechuanaland Rebellion 1897 earning CGHGSM (1) Bech
Gray, 589 Pte A, KRV	QSA (1) DoK	Discharged 20 Aug 02. KSA (2)
Gray, Pte A, KTG	QSA (1) DoK	No IV Section, D Company
Gray, Pte C W, KTG	QSA (1) DoK	G Company
Gray, 11 Tpr H G, KLH	QSA (2) DoK Paar	Served 16 Oct 99 to 30 Apr 00. Also served IYS (37) 22 May 00 to 6 Sep 00 and CPS (56)
Gray, 5340 Pte J, LNLR	QSA (2) DoK OFS	Died of disease at Heilbron on 30 Jul 00
Gray, Pte R, KTG	QSA (1) DoK	No IV Company, A Section, Reservoir
Gray, 552 Pte W, KRV	QSA (1) DoK	Dismissed for misconduct, drunkenness, 6th offence 12 Mar 00
Gray, 181 Pte William, CP2	QSA (1) DoK	CP dismounted branch (barrier & redoubt duties). Dismissed
Greatbatch, Pte D W, KTG	QSA (1) DoK	No II Section, Belgravia Fort
Greatbatch, Pte R, KTG	QSA (1) DoK	No I Section, Mandy Fort
Green, Capt Arthur James, KRV	QSA (2) DoK 01	See his biography (page 345)
Green, Pte Ben, KTG	QSA (1) DoK	No 6 supply depot
Green, Mr C, POC	QSA (1) DoK	
Green, 627 Pte Ernest Robert Angell, CP2	QSA (2) DoK OFS	B Squadron. Also served Mosita Squad DMT (73)
Green, Pte G, KTG	QSA (1) DoK	No I Section, A Company, Beaconsfield Town Guard
Green, Pte G H, KTG	QSA (1) DoK	No 2 supply depot
Green, 333 Tpr George W, KLH	QSA (2) DoK OFS	Served 2 Nov 99 to 30 Apr 00
Green, 4539 L Cpl J, LNLR	QSA (3) DoK OFS Tr	QSA (3), [KSA (2)]. Dixon Apr 95 £110. Neate Dec 98 £140. Holditch Nov 07 £575
Green, 5431 Pte J, LNLR	QSA (3) DoK OFS Tr	Invalided to England 14 Nov 00. QSA (1), KStar, BWM, VM (Pnr RE). Toad Hall May 87 £140
Green, Pte J J, KTG	QSA (1) DoK	No I Section, A Company, Beaconsfield Town Guard
Green, Pte William Henry, KTG	QSA (3) RoM DoK OFS	No II Section, K Company. Also served KLH (208) 13 Mar 00 to 8 Jun 00
Greenhalgh, 4988 Pte R, LNLR	QSA (3) DoK OFS Tr	KSA (2)
Greenspan, Pte S, KTG	QSA (1) DoK	No IV Section, B Company, Beaconsfield Town Guard
Greenway, Pte J, KTG	QSA (1) DoK	Cycle Corps, A Company. QSA (1), KStar. City Coins Jul 01. City Coins May 02. Dixon Sep 02 £340
Greenwood, 90145 Cpl John, RGA	QSA (1) DoK	QSA (1), KSA (2), LS&GC. Liverpool Feb 85 £145
Greer, Pte V, KTG	QSA (1) DoK	No I Company, B Section, Reservoir

Name	Medals	Notes
Greetham, 129 Pay Sgt Clarence George, KLH	QSA (4) RoM DoK Paar Tr	Served 19 Oct 99 to 30 Jan 01. Also served KTG, Lt JMR (surname Greetam) and Lt FID. MID 1 Mar 02. KSA (2). In the Great War served as Private, C Squadron, East African Mounted Rifles and was discharged 9 Nov 1914
Gregory, 130 Tpr Edward Patrick, KLH	QSA (4) RoM DoK Paar Tr	Served 19 Oct 99 to 5 Jun 00. Wounded 25 Nov 99. Also served KTG (No I Section, A Company, Beaconsfield Town Guard) and SRG (190) from 12 Feb 01
Gregson, 4628 Pte R, LNLR	QSA (3) DoK OFS Tr	QSA (3), KSA (2). RHQ
Greig, 80 Tpr William, KLH	QSA (2) DoK OFS	Discharged 23 Mar 00. Also served SRG (775) from 17 Aug 01 and DH (41791) 28 Feb 02 to 30 Jun 02. KSA (2). Occupation tin smith and plumber
Grey, Mr G H, POC	QSA (1) DoK	
Greyling, 675 Pte Johannes C, CP2	QSA (2) DoK OFS	B Squadron. KSA (2)
Grierson, 700 Pte Bernard Grant, KRV	QSA (4) RoM DoK Paar Tr	Discharged 12 Nov 00. Also served RR (29522) 25 Jan 01 to 27 Aug 01. Occupation amalgamator. Address Lerwick, Shetland Islands
Grierson, Pte D, KTG	QSA (1) DoK	G Company. QSA (1), KStar. eBay Sep 09
Grieve, 62 Cpl P, KRV	QSA (1) DoK	DMU 23 Mar 00. Served in the Bechuanaland Rebellion 1897 earning CGHGSM (1) Bech
Grieve, 833 Pte R, KRV	QSA (3) RoM DoK OFS	Discharged 1 Jul 00. Also served KTG (F Company, Mostert's Redoubt)
Grieves, 847 Pte W, KRV	QSA (3) DoK OFS Tr	Also served KTG (No 2 Schmidt's Breastwork). Roll says died (not on casualty roll). Issued to father. KSA roll says discharged 12 May 02 and issued KSA (2)
Griffin, 211 Pte Frederick Thomas, CP2	QSA (1) DoK	CP dismounted branch (barrier & redoubt duties)
Griffin, 42 CSM M, KRV	QSA (4) RoM DoK OFS Tr	Also served KLH (1158). KSA (2) issued to Lt KRV. Served in the Bechuanaland Rebellion 1897 earning CGHGSM (1) Bech
Griffin, 787 Pte Michael, CP2	QSA (4) RoM DoK OFS Tr	A Squadron. Prisoner Hoopstad 23 Oct 00
Griffin, Pte P, KTG	QSA (1) DoK	G Company
Griffin, Sgt William, KTG	QSA (1) DoK	No IV Section, D Company. Also served SRG (931) from 28 May 01
Griffiths, 342 Pte A, KRV	QSA (1) DoK	Non effective 24 Sep 00
Griffiths, Pte D, KTG	QSA (1) DoK	Kenilworth Defence Force
Griffiths, Pte E, KTG	QSA (1) DoK	Cycle Corps, A Company
Grimme, 3697 Band J, LNLR	QSA (3) DoK OFS Tr	KSA (2)
Grimmer, Pte G, KTG	QSA (1) DoK	
Grimmer, Capt Irvine, KTG	QSA (1) DoK	No 1 Redoubt. MID 4 Sep 01
Grindlay, Pte D, KTG	QSA (1) DoK	Premier Mine
Grindley, 298 Pte S D, KRV	QSA (1) DoK	DMU 21 Apr 00. QSA (1), KStar
Grindrod, 462 Pte John Henry, CP2	QSA (2) DoK Tr	A Squadron. Wounded 28 Nov 99. DMU. Also served Bushveldt Carbineers (18), QMI and Morley's Scouts. 01 and entry crossed through on Pietersburg Light Horse Supplementary roll. Surname sometimes Grinrod. QSA (2)
Grinyer, 720 Pte I, KRV	QSA (1) DoK	DMU 28 Feb 00
Grinyer, 196 Sgt J J, KRV	QSA (3) DoK OFS Tr	DMU 9 Jun 02. KSA (2)
Grobler, 1769 Pte J, CP1	QSA (3) DoK OFS 01	B Squadron. Served 11 Oct 99 to 31 Dec 01. Also served UTG (1059)
Grose, Pte T, KTG	QSA (1) DoK	Kenilworth Defence Force. 50th Anniversary attendee

Grotique, Pte S, KTG	QSA (1) DoK	
Growden, 1934 Pte J, CP1	QSA (3) DoK Paar Tr	B Squadron. Discharged time expired 26 Apr 02. MID for Blood River Poort, 17 Sep 01, "galloped 600 yards across open, under heavy fire, to warn an officer he was mistaking enemy for our own men"
Grunig, Pte F C J H, KTG	QSA (1) DoK	Premier Mine
Guild, Pte F R, KTG	QSA (1) DoK	No IV Section, C Company, Pickering's Redoubt No 2
Guiney, 627 Pte C R, KRV	QSA (3) DoK OFS Tr	DMU 3 Jun 02. KSA (2)
Gunders, Pte Frederick C, KTG	QSA (2) DoK OFS	H Company. Also served WS (18) 20 Mar 00 to 11 May 00
Gundlock, 550 Pte Ernest, KRV	QSA (2) DoK 01	Dismissed for misconduct 11 May 01. Also served CRSS (1506) from 6 Jan 02. Occupation cook
Gunn, 628 Pte George, KRV	QSA (2) DoK 01	DMU 18 Jun 01. Also served SRG (694) from 28 Jun 01. Occupation miner. QSA (2). Sotheby Dec 75 £45
Gunning, Pte E R, KTG	QSA (1) DoK	No IV Section, F Company, Mostert's Redoubt
Gunning, 5240 Pte J, LNLR	QSA (3) DoK OFS Tr	KSA (2)
Guthrie, 328 Piper T W, KRV	QSA (1) DoK	Non effective 1 Mar 00. QSA (1), KStar. City Coins Oct 89

H

Hackett, 29893 Sapr J, RE	QSA (3) DoK Drie Tr	QSA (3), KSA (2), KStar. Glendining Jul 85. Sold with BWM, VM and IGS (1) Afghan NWF 1919 (24544 Gnr J Hackett RA) but not as one group
Hackett, 28224 Cpl K, RE	QSA (3) DoK Drie Tr	KSA (2). MID 23 Jun 02
Haddock, Lt R S, KTG	QSA (1) DoK	G Company. 50th Anniversary attendee
Haddock, Cpl W L, KTG	QSA (1) DoK	G Company. Served in the Bechuanaland Rebellion 1897 earning CGHGSM (1) Bech
Hadlow, 186 Dvr Henry Osmund, DFA	QSA (2) DoK Tr	Enrolled DFA 20 Sep 99. DMU 21 Jan 02. KSA (2). Occupation machineman
Hadlow, Pte James Handby, KTG	QSA (2) DoK 01	No II Section, No 2 Redoubt. Also served SRG (128) from 12 Feb 01
Hagerman, 1527 Pte C, CP1	QSA (3) DoK OFS 01	Served 11 Oct 99 to 6 Feb 01
Hagger, 4625 Pte W, LNLR	QSA (4) DoK Paar Joh DH	KSA (2). Mounted Infantry
Haidler, Capt F, KTG	QSA (1) DoK	H Company
Haile, Pte T, KTG	QSA (1) DoK	No I Section, Mandy Fort
Hale, Pte R C, KTG	QSA (1) DoK	No III Section, A Company, Beaconsfield Town Guard
Hale, Sgt S W R, KTG	QSA (1) DoK	Mounted Section, B Company, Beaconsfield Town Guard. KStar (Sgt S W R Hale B M T G). Spink Aug 95 £130. Spink Apr 98 £130. Bloomsbury Sep 05
Hales, Lt F C, KTG	QSA (1) DoK	Kenilworth Defence Force
Haley, 5309 Pte T, LNLR	QSA (1) DoK	Wounded 16 Feb 00. Invalided to England 29 Jun 00
Halkett, 1113 Sgt James Frank, KLH	QSA (3) DoK OFS Tr	Served 19 Oct 99 to 30 Jun 02. Also served KTG and KH (81). MID 23 Jun 02. QSA (3), KSA (2). Spink Oct 99 (no sale). Spink Dec 00 £320. Spink May 02. KStar. Gordon Feb 93 £85. QSA (3), KSA (2), KStar. Dixon Nov 08 £530
Hall, Nurse A, NS	QSA (0)	Kimberley Civil Hospital
Hall, Pte A N, KTG	QSA (1) DoK	Clerical assistant to Paymaster. N Company
Hall, 26783 Sapr C G, RE	QSA (3) DoK Drie Tr	KSA (2)
Hall, 623 Pte Charles, CP2	QSA (1) DoK	CP dismounted branch (barrier & redoubt duties). Died of disease Kimberley 7 Jun 00

Hall, 4720 L Cpl F, LNLR	QSA (3) DoK OFS Tr	KSA (2)
Hall, Pte G, KTG	QSA (1) DoK	
Hall, Cpl H, KTG	QSA (1) DoK	No IV Section, A Company, Beaconsfield Town Guard. Also served KDF (24). OFS clasp crossed out on KDF roll. QSA (1), KStar. Spink Oct 99 £180
Hall, 1203 Sapr J, RE	QSA (3) DoK Drie Tr	KSA (2). Died after the war. Medals issued to father
Hall, 498 Pte J W, KRV	QSA (1) DoK	DMU. Roll says no medal
Hall, 5234 Pte S, LNLR	QSA (1) DoK	Died of disease on 11 Feb 00
Hall, 3738 Pte W, LNLR	QSA (1) DoK	
Hall, Pte W S, KTG	QSA (1) DoK	No 1 Redoubt
Hallett, 5208 Pte C, LNLR	QSA (3) DoK OFS Tr	KSA (2)
Halley, 180 Pte A, KRV	QSA (3) DoK OFS Tr	Discharged 1 Jul 02. KSA (2). Served in the Bechuanaland Rebellion 1897 earning CGHGSM (1) Bech
Halling, 201 Pte Augustus Charles, CP2	QSA (1) DoK	CP dismounted in Beaconsfield. Dismissed. Also served ORCP (441). GCHGSM (1) Bech, QSA (1), KStar. City Coins May 02. Dixon Apr 03 £435. Warwick & Warwick Nov 03
Halloran, Pte J J, KTG	QSA (1) DoK	No II Section, C Company, Pickering's Redoubt No 2
Halse, Lt G B, CP1	QSA (3) DoK OFS Tr	A Squadron. KSA (2). Served in the Bechuanaland Rebellion 1897 earning CGHGSM (1) Bech
Halstead, Pte S, KTG	QSA (1) DoK	Otto's Kopje Company. Appears on the nominal roll as Smith Halstead
Halverston, Pte Charles Oscar, KTG	QSA (2) DoK OFS	No 2 Schmidt's Breastwork. Also served KLH (71) 17 Oct 99 until dismissed 18 Dec 99
Hambly, 392 L Cpl R, CP2	QSA (2) DoK OFS	B Squadron. Killed 21 Dec 99. Not on medal roll
Hambly, 522 Pte William John, CP2	QSA (3) DoK OFS Tr	See his biography (page 345)
Hamer, 790 Pte H A, KRV	QSA (3) RoM DoK OFS	Discharged 1 Jul 00. Also served KTG (Premier Mine). Served in the Bechuanaland Rebellion 1897 earning CGHGSM (1) Bech
Hamilton, 42 Tpr Dacre Brinsley, KLH	QSA (4) RoM DoK Paar Tr	Served 19 Oct 99 to 6 Nov 00. Also served SRG (391) from 4 Mar 01, DS (37961) 4 Sep 01 to 3 Feb 02, Vryburg Scouts (27 & 42461) 1 Mar 02 to 30 Apr 02 and WLH (80) 1 May 02 to 3 Jun 02. KSA (2)
Hamilton, Pte G, KTG	QSA (1) DoK	No I Company, B Section, Reservoir
Hamilton, 375 Sgt James, KLH	QSA (4) DoK OFS Tr 01	Also served KRV (1143) to 28 Nov 00, BR (235 and 26126) 21 Jan 01 to 20 Jul 01, CuH (29) 5 Aug 01 to 23 Oct 01 and VMR. Occupation farmer. SAGS (1) 1879 (Tp Sgt 2nd Cape Yeo), QSA (5) inc CC
Hamilton, Pte T, KTG	QSA (1) DoK	H Company
Hammond, 1938 L Cpl E, CP1	QSA (3) DoK OFS Tr	A Squadron. Served 11 Oct 99 to 12 Apr 02. KSA (2)
Hammond, Pte G, KTG	QSA (1) DoK	Cycle Corps, A Company
Hammond, Pte J B, KTG	QSA (1) DoK	Premier Mine
Hammond, Pte J E, KTG	QSA (1) DoK	H Company
Hampson, Pte B, KTG	QSA (1) DoK	No II Section, Belgravia Fort
Hampton, 4203 Pte W, LNLR	QSA (3) DoK OFS Tr	QSA (3), [KSA (2)]. Liverpool Jun 03 £240
Hancock, Pte C, KTG	QSA (1) DoK	No II Section, L Company
Hanekom, 725 Pte Dick Jacobus Theron, CP2	QSA (2) DoK OFS	C Squadron. Also served KH (281)

Medal roll

Hanlon, 1445 Pte Robert, CP2	QSA (3) DoK 01 02	CP dismounted branch (barrier & redoubt duties). Also served SRG (1455) 25 Nov 01 to 6 Mar 02. Occupation labourer
Hannam, Pte W H, KTG	QSA (1) DoK	H Company and Otto's Kopje Company. SAGS (1) 1877-8-9 the unofficial 1880-81 clasp (Sgt FAM Police), CGHGSM (2) Bas Bech (Sgt CMR), QSA (1), KStar. Christies Nov 86. Spink Apr 07 £850. See his medals on page 507
Hannan, Pte Charles, KTG	QSA (3) DoK OFS Tr	No 1 Redoubt. Also served KLH (1045) 1 Apr 00 to 6 Dec 00, DFA (264) 10 Dec 00 to 1 Jul 02. KSA (2)
Hannan, 1007 Pte Dominick, KRV	QSA (2) DoK 01	DMU. Also served KTG (No III Section, K Company), WS (46) 4 Sep 00 to 31 Oct 00, KLH (38010) 7 Oct 01 to 12 Dec 01 and POWLH (26179) 5 Feb 01 until DMU 12 Jun 01. Occupation miner. Aged 48 in 1901
Hannell, 29805 L Cpl W T, RE	QSA (3) DoK Drie Witt	KSA (2)
Hannibal, 642 Cpl H, CP1	QSA (3) RoM DoK OFS	C Squadron. KSA (2). Served in the Bechuanaland Rebellion 1897 earning CGHGSM (1) Bech
Hansen, 513 Pte H, CP2	QSA (5) RoM DoK OFS Tr 01	A Squadron. Served 11 Oct 99 to 5 Feb 01
Hansen, Pte M P, KTG	QSA (1) DoK	Kimberley Mine Ambulance Company, E Section and Kimberley Mine searchlight and telephone section
Hardacre, Pte W, KTG	QSA (1) DoK	No IV Section, A Company, Beaconsfield Town Guard
Hardacre, Pte W, KTG	QSA (1) DoK	No II Section, A Company, Beaconsfield Town Guard
Harding, 469 Pte C, KRV	QSA (5) RoM DoK OFS Tr 01	Non effective 29 Jan 01
Harding, Pte C, KTG	QSA (1) DoK	
Harding, Pte C D, KTG	QSA (5) DoK OFS Tr 01 02	Also served KRV (1322)
Harding, 40 Tpr E J, KLH	QSA (2) DoK Paar	Served 19 Oct 99 to 30 Apr 00
Harding, 49 Tpr James, KLH	QSA (2) DoK Paar	Served 19 Oct 99 to 30 Apr 00. Also served KTG (No 2 Schmidt's Breastwork). Wounded Warrenton 13 Mar 00
Harding, 477 Pte John S, KLH	QSA (5) RoM DoK OFS Tr 01	Served from 6 Nov 00. Also served KTG (No 2 Schmidt's Breastwork), KRV (832) and Christiana Scouts (27). QSA (5), 14-15 Star (Pte Botha's MR), BWM (Pte 4th SAI), [VM]. eBay Apr 09 £367
Harding, 774 Pte Joseph Ernest, CP2	QSA (4) RoM DoK OFS Tr	CP No 3 Maxim gun detachment. 50th Anniversary attendee. QSA (4), KSA (2). City Coins Feb 87. DNW Jun 02 £270. Liverpool Feb 03 £475
Harding, 528 Pte W, KRV	QSA (4) RoM DoK OFS Tr	Discharged 12 Jul 02. Also served Christiana DMT. KSA (2)
Harding, 529 Cpl W G, KRV	QSA (4) RoM DoK OFS Tr	Discharged 21 Oct 02. KSA (2)
Hardisty, 2306 Pte C, LNLR	QSA (3) DoK OFS Tr	Time expired. To England 15 Oct 00
Hardman, Pte J W, KTG	QSA (1) DoK	No 6 Redoubt
Hardman, Gnr W, DBMB	QSA (1) DoK	HQ and searchlight. Roll says dead (not on casualty roll)
Hardware, Gnr W, DBMB	QSA (1) DoK	Reservoir Redoubt
Hardy, 437 Bearer George, KLH	QSA (3) RoM DoK OFS	Discharged 5 Jun 00. Also served KTG (Kimberley Mine Ambulance Company with mounted forces), SRG (121) 14 Feb 01 to 11 Nov 01. Initial also given as J
Hardy, 37928 Sgt James Robert, DH	QSA (4) RoM DoK Paar Tr	Served 20 Aug 01 to 15 Oct 02. Also served DS (53) 18 Dec 00 to 4 Feb 01 and KLH (26208) 9 Feb 01 to 20 Aug 01. Occupation painter. QSA (4) inc OFS excl Paar, [KSA (2), 1902 Coronation]. Kaplan Nov 08
Harford, Lt C J, KTG	QSA (1) DoK	No II Section, C Company, Pickering's Redoubt No 1. Also served SRG (48)

163

Kimberley Siege Account and Medal Roll

Hargreaves, 3871 Cpl T, LNLR	QSA (4) DoK OFS Tr 01	
Harmon, 577 Pte C H, KRV	QSA (2) DoK OFS	Non effective 25 Jun 00
Harper, 415 Pte G, KRV	QSA (1) DoK	Discharged 16 Feb 03. QSA (1), KSA (2), KStar. Neate Feb 92 £175
Harper, 228 Tpr Henwood George, KLH	QSA (2) DoK OFS	Joined 20 Oct 99. Killed in action 28 Nov 99
Harper, 52 Sgt J, KRV	QSA (1) DoK	Non effective 13 Sep 00. Discharged 16 Feb 02. KSA (2). Served in the Bechuanaland Rebellion 1897 earning CGHGSM (1) Bech
Harper, 1830 Tpr Lawrence John James, SRG	QSA (3) DoK OFS Tr	Discharged 21 May 00. Also served KTG (No II Section, K Company), KRV (1014), DrS (29975) 29 Jan 01 to 31 Jul 01, JMR (1865) to 26 Dec 01 and WLH (262) 15 Jan 02 to 30 Jun 02
Harper, Col Sgt T W, KTG	QSA (1) DoK	K Company
Harper, Pte W T, KTG	QSA (1) DoK	
Harries, 405 Cpl F J, KRV	QSA (1) DoK	Discharged 30 Jul 02. KSA (2)
Harries, 165 Cpl I C, KRV	QSA (1) DoK	Non effective 8 Jul 00. CGHGSM (1) Bech (Pte Kimb Rifs), QSA (1), 14-15 Star, [BWM], VM (Pte 9th F Amb SAMC). Glendining Feb 97. Spink Dec 97 £275. Bonhams Dec 98
Harrington, 230 Tpr J, KLH	QSA (3) DoK OFS Tr	Discharged 31 Aug 00
Harrington, Pte J L, KTG	QSA (1) DoK	H Company. Manufacturing shells and ammunition
Harrington, 302 Tpr John William, KFS	QSA (4) DoK OFS Tr 01	Enlisted as 4560 Private J Warwick in the LNLR and joined 2nd KFS under this name 17 Jan 01 gaining CC, OFS & Tr and SA01 from 1st KFS. Returned to LNLR 18 May 01. Medals forfeited by LNLR but issued by KFS 12 Dec 05
Harris, 147 Cpl Albert Edward, KRV	QSA (5) RoM DoK OFS Tr 01	Served 4 Oct 99 to 31 Jan 01. Also served Lt JMR. QSA (5), KStar. Glendining Jul 76 £180
Harris, Pte B, KTG	QSA (1) DoK	No I Section, Mandy Fort
Harris, Pte D, KTG	QSA (3) RoM DoK OFS	Also served KLH (394) 7 Mar 00 to 6 Apr 00
Harris, Lt Col David, KTG	QSA (1) DoK	See his biography (page 345)
Harris, Capt George H F, KLH	QSA (2) DoK OFS	Joined 19 Oct 99 as Tpr (133) and resigned KLH 14 Mar 00. Wounded during siege. 50th Anniversary attendee
Harris, 767 Pte H, KRV	QSA (4) RoM DoK OFS Tr	Also served KTG (No IV Section, C Company, Beaconsfield Town Guard). Discharged 6 Nov 00
Harris, Pte J, KTG	QSA (1) DoK	
Harris, Pte J J, KTG	QSA (2) DoK Tr	Premier Mine. Also served as Assistant Traffic Manager in the IMR
Harris, Sgt J R, KTG	QSA (1) DoK	Premier Mine
Harris, Lt L W H, KTG	QSA (1) DoK	No IV Section, B Company, No 4 Redoubt
Harris, Pte R, KTG	QSA (1) DoK	No II Section, L Company
Harris, 134 Cpl Roy Joseph Rose, KLH	QSA (3) DoK OFS Tr	Wounded 24 Oct 99. Served 19 Oct 99 to 6 Mar 00. Also served WS (32) 4 Sep 00 to 15 Mar 01, Lt SRG 27 Mar 01 to 30 Apr 02 and Lt WLH 1 May 02 to 30 Jun 02. KSA (2)
Harris, Sgt W, KTG	QSA (1) DoK	No III Section, No 4 Redoubt
Harris, Pte W J, KTG	QSA (1) DoK	Premier Mine
Harris, 810 Pte Walter, CP2	QSA (2) DoK OFS	CP dismounted branch (barrier & redoubt duties). QSA (2), KSA (2), 1914-15 Star, BWM, VM (Sgt 7th Infy), KStar. Kaplan Nov 09
Harris, Lt Wilfrid Solomon, KTG	QSA (1) DoK	No II Section, F Company, Mostert's Redoubt. Son of David Harris. Born 1878
Harris, 15 Tpr William Duckett, KLH	QSA (3) RoM DoK OFS	Served 17 Mar 00 to 5 Jun 00

Harrison, 203 Tpr A, KLH	QSA (2) DoK OFS	Served 21 Oct 99 to 30 Apr 00
Harrison, Pte A E, KTG	QSA (1) DoK	G Company
Harrison, Pte A J, KTG	QSA (1) DoK	No IV Section, F Company, Mostert's Redoubt
Harrison, Pte A T, KTG	QSA (1) DoK	No IV Section, F Company, Mostert's Redoubt
Harrison, 82 Tpr Alexander, KLH	QSA (2) DoK Paar	Discharged 30 Apr 00. Also served Klipdam TG
Harrison, Pte C, KTG	QSA (1) DoK	
Harrison, 4762 Pte E, LNLR	QSA (3) DoK OFS Tr	KSA (2)
Harrison, Capt Fred, KRV	QSA (3) DoK OFS Tr	See his biography (page 345)
Harrison, Sgt H, KTG	QSA (1) DoK	No II Section, No 2 Redoubt. Replacement medal issued 25 May 20
Harrison, Pte H S, KTG	QSA (1) DoK	H Company
Harrison, Pte J, KTG	QSA (1) DoK	No II Section, D Company
Harrison, Pte J H, KTG	QSA (1) DoK	Cycle Corps, A Company
Harrison, 1024 Pte T A, KRV	QSA (4) DoK OFS 01 02	Also served KTG. KSA issued in error and recovered
Harsant, Pte S W, KTG	QSA (1) DoK	No I Company, B Section, Reservoir
Hart, 419 Pte A D, KRV	QSA (3) RoM DoK OFS	Non effective 26 Jun 00
Hart, 135 Tpr Joseph Walter, KLH	QSA (2) DoK Paar	Served 20 Oct 99 to 30 Apr 00. QSA (2), KStar, Royal Red Cross Medal
Hart, 279 Tpr Oliver Charles, KLH	QSA (2) DoK OFS	Served 21 Oct 99 to 30 Apr 00. On KTG nominal roll for Otto's Kopje Company
Hartigan, 169 Gnr Marcus Michael, DFA	QSA (2) DoK OFS	See his biography (page 345)
Hartley, 230 Cpl A, KLH	QSA (2) DoK OFS	Served 20 Oct 99 to 14 Mar 00
Hartley, Pte C V, KTG	QSA (1) DoK	L Company
Hartley, Cpl D R, KTG	QSA (1) DoK	Otto's Kopje Scouts. BSACM rev Rhod (Tpr MMP), QSA (1). Liverpool Feb 86 £190
Hartley, Pte Edward, KTG	QSA (3) RoM DoK OFS	Premier Mine. Also served KLH (174) 8 Mar 00 to 5 Jun 00
Hartley, Pte F, KTG	QSA (1) DoK	No II Section, B Company, Beaconsfield Town Guard
Hartley, Cpl G, KTG	QSA (1) DoK	No 6 Redoubt and No 2 Schmidt's Breastwork and No II Section, B Company, Beaconsfield Town Guard
Hartley, Pte H, KTG	QSA (1) DoK	
Hartley, Pte H T, KTG	QSA (1) DoK	Premier Mine
Hartley, 1136 Pte J, KRV	QSA (2) DoK OFS	DMU 6 Jan 02. Also served KTG (No II Section, Belgravia Fort) 4 Oct 99 to 6 Mar 00. KSA (2)
Hartley, Sgt J W, KTG	QSA (1) DoK	Otto's Kopje Scouts. QSA (1), KStar - could be next man. Glendining Mar 81. Spink Sep 81 £140
Hartley, Sgt J W, KTG	QSA (1) DoK	
Hartley, Pte K, KTG	QSA (1) DoK	H Company
Hartley, 24 Cpl L, KRV	QSA (1) DoK	QSA (1), KSA (2), Colonial Auxiliary Forces LS Medal, KStar. Spink Jul 77 £128. Dixon Apr 95 £295. Spink Oct 99 £320. Kaplan Feb 07
Hartley, 4071 Pte L, LNLR	QSA (3) DoK OFS Tr	KSA (2)
Hartley, Lt S P, KRV	QSA (1) DoK	KSA (2)
Hartley, Pte W H, KTG	QSA (1) DoK	No 1 Redoubt
Hartog, Pte V, KTG	QSA (1) DoK	
Harty, Pte W, KTG	QSA (1) DoK	Premier Mine

Kimberley Siege Account and Medal Roll

Hartzenberg, Pte A, KTG	QSA (1) DoK	QSA (1). Seaby Dec 74 £45. Seaby Jun 75 £52. Liverpool May 91 £85. QSA (1), KStar. Warwick & Warwick Mar 04
Harvett, Pte A, KTG	QSA (1) DoK	Cycle Corps, A Company
Harvett, 133 L Cpl J, KRV	QSA (1) DoK	DMU
Harvey, 5172 Pte E, LNLR	QSA (3) DoK OFS Tr	MID 4 Sep 01. KSA (2)
Harvey, Pte G F, KTG	QSA (1) DoK	Late claim in 1907. QSA (1). Spink Jul 05 £140. Liverpool Sep 05 £210
Harvey, Pte J, KTG	QSA (1) DoK	No IV Section, Mostert's Redoubt
Harvey, 22697 Tpr William, CinCBG	QSA (3) DoK OFS Tr	Served 11 Nov 00 to 31 May 01. Also served KTG, KR (180) 11 Oct 99 to 6 Apr 00, KLH (395, 419 & 1046) 7 Mar 00 to 13 Nov 00, CRSS (1140) 6 Mar 01 to 5 Jun 01 and CPS (380) 10 Jun 01 to 30 Apr 02. KSA (2). Occupation clerk
Hasenjäger, 1570 Pte August Eimel, CP1	QSA (1) DoK	B Squadron. Killed in action 25 Nov 99
Hasler, Pte G, KTG	QSA (1) DoK	No III Section, B Company, No 4 Redoubt
Haslett, 386 Pte J M, KRV	QSA (3) DoK OFS Tr	Discharged 5 Feb 01. Also served CPS (65). Killed Klip Drift 7 Feb 02
Hassell, 29 Pte J, KTG	QSA (1) DoK	Also served KDF (29). OFS clasp crossed out on KDF roll
Hasset, Sgt J B, KTG	QSA (1) DoK	No I Section, A Company, Beaconsfield Town Guard
Hassett, Pte A A, KTG	QSA (2) DoK OFS	Also served ORCP (285)
Hassett, Pte Frederick Bartholomew, KTG	QSA (2) DoK OFS	No II Section, A Company, Beaconsfield Town Guard. Also served KLH (1044) 30 Apr 00 until DMU 24 May 00. Missing Fourteen Streams 13 May 00 and rejoined
Hassett, Pte Michael John, KTG	QSA (2) DoK OFS	No IV Section, B Company, Beaconsfield Town Guard. Also served KLH (407) 20 Apr 00 to 11 Jun 00 and ORCP from 14 Jun 00
Hassett, 136 Tpr Patrick, KLH	QSA (3) DoK OFS 01	Served 20 Oct 99 to 3 Apr 00. Also served KTG, KRV (1287), CP2 (64 & 159) (B Squadron) and 1st KFS (305) 18 Dec 00 to 23 Jun 01. QSA (1) DoK. Christies Apr 92 £180. Dixon Dec 92 £130. Neate Feb 96 £85
Hastie, 90 Pte James Archibald, CP2	QSA (4) RoM DoK OFS Tr	C Squadron. Prisoner at Hoopstad 23 Oct 00. Medal returned unclaimed 30 Jun 08 and reissued 28 Aug 15. Served in the Bechuanaland Rebellion 1897 earning CGHGSM (1) Bech
Hastings, 1077 Sgt George, CP2	QSA (4) RoM DoK OFS Tr	A Squadron. Transferred from CP1 (1330) 17 Jun 01. KSA (2)
Hastings, 274 Tpr John W, KLH	QSA (2) DoK OFS	Joined 20 Oct 99. Killed in action 28 Nov 99
Hatcher, Pte William, KTG	QSA (1) DoK	No 2 Schmidt's Breastwork. Also served VTG (88)
Hatton, Pte A J, KTG	QSA (1) DoK	No II Section, K Company
Hatwell, 4057 L Sgt H, LNLR	QSA (3) DoK OFS Tr	KSA (2)
Hauptfleisch, Pte G S, KTG	QSA (1) DoK	Kimberley Mine Ambulance Company, B Section
Hauptfleisch, Pte J, KTG	QSA (1) DoK	No II Section, F Company, Mostert's Redoubt. Died of disease during the siege
Hauptfleisch, Pte P, KTG	QSA (1) DoK	Kenilworth Defence Force
Hawes, 99 Sgt Herbert Henry, DFA	QSA (1) DoK	Enrolled DFA 15 Feb 98. Occupation railways clerk. Resigned 17 Feb 03
Hawker, Lt Charles H, KLH	QSA (4) RoM DoK OFS Tr	Served 16 Oct 99 to 24 Sep 00 ('services dispensed with'). Wounded 22 Nov 99. MID. Also served CMR, CPD2, Lt WMI 28 Feb 01 to 23 Aug 01 and Lt CLH. KSA (2). Initials sometimes CA. His WMI attestation papers give his trade/calling as gentleman

Medal roll

Hawkins, Pte Bertram Austin, KTG	QSA (1) DoK	No 1 Redoubt. Also served SRG (123) from 11 Feb 01
Hawkins, Pte F D, KTG	QSA (1) DoK	No II Section, C Company, Pickering's Redoubt No 1
Hawkins, Pte J H, KTG	QSA (1) DoK	No 1 Redoubt
Hawley, Pte C T, KTG	QSA (1) DoK	No 3 Redoubt. 50th Anniversary attendee
Hawley, 355 Tpr William Henry, KLH	QSA (2) DoK OFS	Served 15 Nov 99 to 8 Mar 00
Hay, 1005 Pte G, KRV	QSA (2) DoK 01	Non effective 7 May 01. Also served KTG (No III Company, A Section, Reservoir) and RR
Hay, Pte H W, KTG	QSA (1) DoK	Otto's Kopje Scouts and No III Company, A Section, Reservoir
Hayes, Pte C, KTG	QSA (1) DoK	Otto's Kopje Scouts. QSA (1). Spink Dec 88
Hayes, Lt H, CP1	QSA (2) DoK OFS	A Squadron. DMU. KSA (2). He had served in the Basuto War 1880-81 and in the Bechuanaland Rebellion of 1897 earning CGHGSM (2) Bas Bech
Hayes, 651 Pte Manus, CP2	QSA (3) DoK OFS Tr	B Squadron. QSA (3), [KSA (2)]. Kaplan Feb 03
Hayes, 1540 Pte P C, CP1	QSA (2) DoK OFS	B Squadron. DoK clasp added 15 Dec 05. KSA (2)
Hayes, 255 Pte R P, KRV	QSA (4) RoM DoK OFS Tr	Discharged 1 Jul 02. KSA (2). Served in the Bechuanaland Rebellion 1897 earning CGHGSM (1) Bech. 50th Anniversary attendee
Hayes, 43 Band Sgt W, KRV	QSA (2) DoK OFS	KSA (2). Possibly served in the Bechuanaland Rebellion 1897 with DEOVR earning CGHGSM (1) Bech
Haygarth, 117 Sgt Maj Tailor H, KRV	QSA (1) DoK	Discharged 31 Dec 00. Duplicate medal issued
Haylett, Pte Arthur Henry, KTG	QSA (1) DoK	Premier Mine. On nominal roll as Heylett. Also served SRG (51) from 11 May 01
Haynes, Pte E, KTG	QSA (1) DoK	No 6 Redoubt. Engine driver for searchlight dynamo
Hayston, Sgt John, KTG	QSA (1) DoK	Medical Corps, No 1 Company, C Section
Hayston, Sgt Jos, KTG	QSA (1) DoK	Medical Corps, No 1 Company, D Section
Hayston, Pte R B, KTG	QSA (1) DoK	No IV Section, No 2 Redoubt
Hayston, Lt W, KTG	QSA (1) DoK	No 6 Redoubt
Hayston, Pte W, KTG	QSA (1) DoK	Belgravia Fort
Hayward, 4320 Pte W, LNLR	QSA (2) DoK OFS	Invalided to England 23 May 00
Hazell, Pte A J, KTG	QSA (1) DoK	No III Section, Belgravia Fort
Heacock, 411 Cpl A, KRV	QSA (3) DoK OFS 01	DMU 17 Apr 01. QSA (3), KStar, 14-15 Star (Armr S Sgt), BWM, VM (S Sgt). Sotheby Dec 98
Head, Pte J, KTG	QSA (1) DoK	No 1 Redoubt
Head, Pte J, KTG	QSA (1) DoK	No II Section, L Company
Headon, 24 Pte Charles F, CP2	QSA (1) DoK	CP dismounted in Beaconsfield. QSA (1). McGregor Museum
Heads, Mr J, POC	QSA (1) DoK	
Heald, 2393 Col Sgt A, LNLR	QSA (1) DoK	Killed in action 28 Nov 99
Heale, Pte J, KTG	QSA (1) DoK	Kimberley Mine Ambulance Company, E Section
Healy, Pte Michael, KTG	QSA (3) DoK OFS Tr	Mounted Section, Kenilworth Defence Force. Also served WS (15) 20 Mar 00 to 31 Aug 00 and CDF (306)
Heaps, 3710 Pte G, LNLR	QSA (3) DoK OFS Tr	KSA (2). Invalided to England 1 Apr 01
Heaps, 3795 Pte J, LNLR	QSA (3) DoK OFS Tr	KSA (2)
Hearn, Lt D P, KTG	QSA (1) DoK	No I Section, No 2 Redoubt

Name	Medals	Notes
Hearn, 28 Sgt Herbert Arthur, CP2	QSA (1) DoK	CP dismounted branch (barrier & redoubt duties). QSA (1) (unit erased). Glendining Mar 98. Walland Sep 98 £85
Hearns, 773 L Cpl W R, CP1	QSA (2) DoK OFS	B Squadron. Discharged time expired 20 May 01. CGHGSM (1) Bech (Pte), QSA (2), KStar. City Coins Feb 87. Burman Mar 00 £425
Heath, Pte A, KTG	QSA (1) DoK	No 1 Redoubt
Heath, H H, KTG	QSA (0)	Roll states "Electrical work; dynamite mines and telephones"
Heathcote, 1579 L Cpl G F, CP1	QSA (3) DoK Paar Drie	
Heberden, Surg Capt George Alfred, KLH	QSA (2) DoK OFS	See his biography (page 345)
Hedger, 4787 Pte A, LNLR	QSA (3) DoK OFS Tr	QSA (3), [KSA (2)]. Glendining May 80
Heeney, Pte Edward, KTG	QSA (3) DoK OFS Tr	H Company. Also served KLH (204 & 147) 8 Mar 00 to 4 Dec 00 and MH (22964) 8 Dec 00 to 31 May 02. QSA (3), [KSA (2)], KStar. Glendining Feb 1909. Spink Oct 74 £55
Heffer, Pte Charles, KTG	QSA (2) DoK Tr	No 1 Redoubt. Also served SRG (180) from 11 Feb 01. Served in the Bechuanaland Rebellion 1897 earning CGHGSM (1) Bech
Hefferman, 5466 Pte W, LNLR	QSA (3) DoK OFS Tr	KSA (2)
Heldsinger, Pte F, KTG	QSA (1) DoK	No III Section, A Company, Beaconsfield Town Guard
Heldsinger, Pte P, KTG	QSA (1) DoK	No III Section, A Company, Beaconsfield Town Guard. QSA (1), 39-45 Star, WM, ASM. Dixon Apr 98 £120
Helfrich, 1913 Pte G, CP1	QSA (2) DoK OFS	C Squadron. Discharged time expired 5 May 02. KSA (2)
Hellard, 3892 Sgt E W, LNLR	QSA (3) DoK Paar Tr	Mounted Infantry. QSA (3), KSA (2), 14 Star & Bar, BWM, VM, LS&GC GV, KStar. RHQ
Hellard, 2814 Sgt H, LNLR	QSA (5) DoK OFS Tr 01 02	Wounded 16 Feb 00. Invalided to England 21 Aug 00
Hellegren, Pte A, KTG	QSA (1) DoK	No 1 Redoubt
Hellstrom, 135 Pte Ferdinand, CP2	QSA (4) RoM DoK OFS Tr	B Squadron. KSA (2)
Hellyer, Pte Harry, KTG	QSA (4) DoK Tr 01 02	No II Section, B Company, Beaconsfield Town Guard. Also served JMR (2219). Duplicate QSA returned. KStar. SAMMH
Hemming, Pte F Haydon, KTG	QSA (4) DoK OFS Tr 01	Gibraltar Fort, Davis's Heap. Also served KitH (23210) as Heeming and Hemming 20 Aug 00 to 15 Dec 00, 2nd BrH (22746) with initial H 5 Dec 00 until DMU 5 Jan 01 and NH (1420) from 12 Dec 01 with forename Haydon. Occupation painter
Hemsley, 590 L Cpl T W, KRV	QSA (1) DoK	DMU 14 Apr 01. IGS (2) Burma 85-87 Hazara, QSA (1), 14-15 Star, BWM, VM. Royal Welch Fusilier RHQ
Hemsworth, 938 Pte F, KRV	QSA (1) DoK	Also served KTG (Cycle Corps, A Company)
Hemsworth, Cpl H, KTG	QSA (1) DoK	Cycle Corps, A Company. Possibly served in the Bechuanaland Rebellion 1897 earning CGHGSM (1) Bech
Henderson, 1251 Pte A E, CP1	QSA (2) DoK OFS	B Squadron. Discharged time expired 25 Jul 00. CGHGSM (1) Bech, QSA (2)
Henderson, Sgt D H, KTG	QSA (1) DoK	No II Section, Belgravia Fort
Henderson, 170 Tpr E, SRG	QSA (3) RoM DoK Tr	Also served KTG and KR (902)
Henderson, 171 Pte E, KRV	QSA (3) RoM DoK Tr	
Henderson, 579 Pte E O, KRV	QSA (1) DoK	Non effective 1 Mar 00

Henderson, 902 Pte Edward Charles, KRV	QSA (4) RoM DoK OFS Tr	Also served KTG (H Company) and SRG (171) from 12 Feb 01
Henderson, 687 Pte Francis Scott, CP2	QSA (3) DoK OFS Tr	C Squadron. Slightly wounded Hoopstad 23 Oct 00. BSACM rev Mashonaland 97 (Sgt BSAP), QSA (3), KSA (2), KStar. DNW Jul 04 £550
Henderson, 497 Pte Hamilton Platt, KRV	QSA (3) DoK Tr 01	Wounded 14 Feb 00. DMU 12 May 00. Also served ScH (255) 14 Jan 01 to 1 Aug 01. Brother of the Mayor. Died in a shooting accident c 1904. QSA (3). McGregor Museum
Henderson, Gnr Hugh William Gordon, DBMB	QSA (1) DoK	Served DBMB 30 Oct 99 to 14 Mar 00. Also served KLH (233) 20 Mar 00 to 30 Apr 00 and Imperial Transport Service
Henderson, 873 Pte J A, KRV	QSA (1) DoK	Also served KLH and KTG (No 2 Schmidt's Breastwork). Discharged 1 Jul 02. KSA (2)
Henderson, Gnr R, DBMB	QSA (1) DoK	HQ and searchlight
Henderson, Capt R H, KTG	QSA (1) DoK	See his biography (page 345)
Hendricks, 1257 Pte W, KRV	QSA (4) DoK OFS Tr 01	Non effective 1 Feb 01. Served in the Bechuanaland Rebellion 1897 earning CGHGSM (1) Bech
Hendrikz, Sgt L, KTG	QSA (1) DoK	Kimberley Mine Ambulance Company, E Section
Hendry, Cpl D, KTG	QSA (1) DoK	No I Company, B Section, Reservoir
Hendry, G, KTG	QSA (0)	Roll states "Repairing gun limbers, wheels etc." QSA (0)
Hendry, Pte G S, KTG	QSA (1) DoK	No IV Section, B Company, No 4 Redoubt
Heneke, Pte P, KTG	QSA (1) DoK	No II Section, B2 Company, No 3 Redoubt. QSA (1). Spink Nov 98. KStar. City Coins Jul 01
Henley, 231 Cpl Francis Joseph, CP2	QSA (1) DoK	C Squadron. CGHGSM (1) Bech (Pte CP), QSA (2) inc OFS, KSA (2), South African Police Medal for Faithful Service Medal (525 Hd Const), KStar. City Coins Dec 04. Bill Friar Sep 08 £695. See his medals on page 505
Henman, 423 Pte E V, KRV	QSA (2) DoK OFS	DMU 3 Apr 00
Henman, Mr R A, POC	QSA (1) DoK	
Hennesey, Pte B, KTG	QSA (1) DoK	No III Section, No 2 Redoubt. Also served 34th Co ASC (119)
Hennessey, 629 Pte W P, KRV	QSA (3) DoK OFS Tr	KSA (2)
Hennessy, 1156 Pte J E, CP1	QSA (4) RoM DoK OFS Tr	A Squadron. Tr clasp added 11 Dec 05. KSA (2). Served in the Bechuanaland Rebellion 1897 earning CGHGSM (1) Bech
Hennessy, 9 Sgt Patrick, CP2	QSA (1) DoK	CP dismounted in Beaconsfield
Henning, Pte William Robert, KTG	QSA (2) DoK Tr	Premier Mine. Also served SRG (915) from 22 May 01
Henry, Mr A, POC	QSA (1) DoK	
Henry, Mr J, POC	QSA (1) DoK	
Henry, Pte James, KTG	QSA (1) DoK	No II Section, C Company, Pickering's Redoubt No 1. Also served SRG (665) from 6 Jun 01. Occupation labourer
Henry, 188 Dvr James John, DFA	QSA (2) DoK OFS	Enrolled DFA 22 Sep 99 and retired 1 Jan 03. Served Kimberley Cadets 96-98. Occupation overseer at De Beers. QSA (3) inc SA01
Henry, Pte S, KTG	QSA (1) DoK	A Company, Cycle Corps. QSA (1). Dixon Jul 83 £90. Liverpool Oct 84 £110. QSA (1), KStar. Burman Mar 00 £235
Herbert, 5039 L Cpl E, LNLR	QSA (3) DoK OFS Tr	KSA (2)
Herbert, 3993 Sgt H, LNLR	QSA (3) DoK OFS Tr	KSA (2)
Herbert, 298 Pte John James, CP2	QSA (2) DoK OFS	B Squadron. KSA (2)

Herboldt, 1146 Pte Lewis Leonard, KRV	QSA (4) RoM DoK OFS Tr	DMU Jan 02. Also served KTG, KLH (220) until dismissed 20 Dec 99 and WLH (35) 29 Apr 02 to 30 Jun 02. KSA (2)
Herd, Mr W H, POC	QSA (1) DoK	
Herridge, 916 Pte A J, KRV	QSA (1) DoK	Discharged 1 Jul 02. Also served KTG (H Company). KSA (2)
Hersee, 592 Pte Edwin, KRV	QSA (1) DoK	Died of disease 13 Jun 00 in Kimberley. QSA (1). Monarch Medals Sep 05 £280
Hertog, Capt Charles Edward, KTG	QSA (1) DoK	See his biography (page 345)
Hertzenstein, Pte S, KTG	QSA (1) DoK	
Hescroft, 630 Pte Robert, KRV	QSA (4) DoK OFS 01 02	Served 11 Oct 99 until dismissed for misconduct 7 Nov 99. Also served KTG (G Company) 20 Nov 99 to 10 Mar 00, ALH (37993) 26 Sep 01 to 24 Mar 02 and Lt WLH 9 Apr 02 to 30 Jun 02. Occupation book keeper
Heunes, 213 Pte Martinus C, CP2	QSA (1) DoK	A Squadron. KSA (2). Surname spelled Heunis on KSA roll
Hewett, Lt Arthur Wedderburn, LNLR	QSA (3) DoK OFS Tr	See his biography (page 346)
Hewitson, Pte Thomas, KTG	QSA (3) RoM DoK OFS	Premier Mine. Also served KLH (182) 8 Mar 00 to 5 Jun 00 and SRG (52) from 11 Feb 01
Hewitt, 171 Dvr Charles Farmer, DFA	QSA (4) DoK OFS Tr 01	Enrolled DFA 1 Aug 99. Also served 1st Royal Dragoons and DEOVR (not found on rolls). Slightly wounded, Boshof, 5 Jan 01. Died of enteric, Kimberley, 6 Dec 01
Hewitt, Pte J B, KTG	QSA (1) DoK	No I Company, B Section, Reservoir
Heydenrijk, 88 Cpl David, DFA	QSA (3) DoK OFS Tr	Enrolled DFA 3 Jun 97. Taken prisoner and released Klip Drift 7 Mar 02. Resigned 5 May 05. KSA (2). Occupation farmer
Heydenrych, 86 Pte Francis Abraham, KRV	QSA (3) DoK OFS Tr	Also served 1st ILH (40027 and 3019) 27 Dec 01 to 24 Jun 02. KSA (2)
Heynes, Pte J F, KTG	QSA (1) DoK	No 2 supply depot
Hickens, Pte J J, KTG	QSA (1) DoK	K Company
Hickman, Sgt W, KTG	QSA (1) DoK	No 6 Redoubt
Hickman, W, KTG	QSA (0)	Roll states "Fireman searchlight engine." QSA (0). City Coins May 02. City Coins Dec 04. See his medal on page 509
Hicks, 417 Pte Alfred Ernest, CP2	QSA (1) DoK	CP dismounted branch (barrier & redoubt duties). KSA (2)
Hicks, 65 Tpr Harold Bound, KLH	QSA (4) DoK OFS 01 02	Served 18 Oct 99 to 7 Mar 00 and 22 Mar 01 to 18 Apr 01. Also served CinCBG (25512) 12 Dec 00 to 24 Jan 01 (noted as 'undesirable') and SRG (1243) from 22 Apr 01. Occupation clerk
Hicks, 215 Pte Henry Harry, CP2	QSA (1) DoK	CP dismounted branch (barrier & redoubt duties)
Hickson-Mahoney, Capt J C, KLH	QSA (4) DoK OFS Tr 01	See his biography (page 346)
Hickson-Mahoney, Pte S, KTG	QSA (1) DoK	No III Section, B Company, Beaconsfield Town Guard
Higgins, 153 Tpr Francis Edmund, KLH	QSA (2) DoK OFS	Served 26 Nov 99 until DMU 24 Mar 00
Higgins, 4406 Pte J, LNLR	QSA (3) DoK OFS Tr	QSA (3), KSA (2), TFEM GV (Cpl 4/Loyal Regt), LS&GC (Cpl LNLR), KStar. DNW Sep 04 £460
Higgins, 3852 Pte T, LNLR	QSA (3) DoK OFS Tr	KSA (2). Initial F on KSA roll
Higson, 5750 Pte A, LNLR	QSA (2) DoK Tr	QSA (2), KSA (2), 14-15 Star (Hyson), BWM, VM (2714 S Lanc Regt). Glendining Sep 90 £180

Medal roll

Hiles, 73 Tpr Douglas Edward Stanley, KLH	QSA (3) DoK Paar 02	Served 3 Nov 99 until DMU 24 Mar 00. Also served ORS (18) 12 Mar 02 to 30 Jun 02. Occupation fireman. QSA (3), KStar
Hill, Pte A B, KTG	QSA (1) DoK	No I Company, B Section, Reservoir
Hill, Pte C, KTG	QSA (1) DoK	No IV Section, D Company
Hill, 295 Pte George, CP2	QSA (2) DoK OFS	CP intelligence and detective staff
Hill, Pte J, KTG	QSA (1) DoK	No IV Section, F Company, Mostert's Redoubt and No I Section, C Company, Beaconsfield Town Guard. QSA (1). Spink Nov 81 £140. Spink May 83 £125
Hill, 38 Dvr James Henry Jacobus, DFA	QSA (1) DoK	Enrolled 3 Dec 95. Occupation blacksmith at De Beers
Hill, Pte P J, KTG	QSA (1) DoK	No I Section, F Company, Mostert's Redoubt
Hill, Pte R, KTG	QSA (1) DoK	No 1 supply depot
Hill, Pte S W, KTG	QSA (1) DoK	No I Section, K Company
Hill, Pte Thomas Jerome, KTG	QSA (4) DoK OFS Tr 01	Also served CinCBG (22700) 17 Nov 00 to 13 May 01. QSA (1) DoK. Sotheby Jul 74 £48. Glendining Sep 73 £32. Spink Mar 94. Bonhams Dec 95. Gordons Apr 98 £95
Hill, Lt W, AVC	QSA (4) RoM DoK OFS Tr	Civil Veterinary Surgeon. Attached 36th Co ASC. Also on roll for ASC with same 4 clasps. KSA (2)
Hill, 1048 Tpr William Charles, KLH	QSA (3) DoK Paar Tr	See his medal on page **Error! Bookmark not defined.**
Hillditch, 3781 Pte T, LNLR	QSA (3) DoK OFS Tr	Possibly renamed to Hilditch in 1909. Died 1909. Initial E on KSA roll. QSA (3), [KSA (2)]. RHQ
Hillier, Pte F J, KTG	QSA (1) DoK	H Company
Hillies, Pte W, KTG	QSA (1) DoK	No IV Section, L Company
Hillman, Pte J, KTG	QSA (1) DoK	B line of defence, No 3 Redoubt
Hills, Mr J L, POC	QSA (1) DoK	QSA (1), KStar. City Coins May 02
Hills, 450 Pte William Harry, CP2	QSA (1) DoK	Entry crossed through on QSA roll but appears on the nominal roll as serving on the Intelligence and Detective Staff. Served in the Bechuanaland Rebellion 1897 earning CGHGSM (1) Bech
Hilton, 294 Pte A, KRV	QSA (5) RoM DoK OFS 01 02	Served 11 Oct 99 to 20 Jun 00. Also served CPS and CPD2 10 Jan 02 to 31 May 02
Hinchin, 4933 Cpl J, LNLR	QSA (3) DoK OFS Tr	KSA (2)
Hindle, 4728 Pte W, LNLR	QSA (3) DoK OFS Tr	KSA (2). Initial J on KSA roll
Hine, Pte T A, KTG	QSA (1) DoK	Ambulance Corps, Beaconsfield Town Guard
Hines, Dvr W, DBMB	QSA (3) DoK OFS Tr	Reservoir Redoubt. Also served SRG (189) as Hind, A L, WS (24) as Hind, Alexander Lemuel 21 Mar 00 to 21 Aug 00 and FID as Hind H L 12 Feb 01 to 23 Nov 01. KSA (2)
Hinks, Pte C G, KTG	QSA (1) DoK	No III Section, C Company, Pickering's Redoubt No 1
Hinks, Pte O W, KTG	QSA (1) DoK	Cycle Corps, A Company
Hinsch, Pte R, KTG	QSA (1) DoK	G Company
Hipwell, 271 Cpl William, CP2	QSA (2) DoK Tr	CP HQ and depot mounted branch. KSA (2). Severely wounded Klip Drift 7 Mar 02
Hiscock, 250 Tpr Herbert, KLH	QSA (2) DoK OFS	Joined 21 Oct 99. Killed in action 28 Nov 99. Possibly on KTG roll as Hiscock, C
Hitchcock, Pte G, KTG	QSA (1) DoK	
Hitchman, Pte George Thomas, KTG	QSA (1) DoK	H Company. Also served SRG (923) from 23 May 01. 50th Anniversary attendee
Hitchman, Pte W, KTG	QSA (1) DoK	H Company
Hoare, Pte A J, KTG	QSA (1) DoK	No IV Section, K Company

Hobbs, 17297 Sgt G, RE	QSA (3) DoK Drie Tr	KSA (2)
Hobbs, 5222 Pte J, LNLR	QSA (3) DoK OFS Tr	QSA (3), [KSA (2)]. DNW Sep 06 £300
Hobbs, Pte Philip, KTG	QSA (1) DoK	No III Section, A Company, Beaconsfield Town Guard and Gibraltar Fort, Davis's Heap. Also served VTG (45) and possibly CPS (207) and Warrenton TG (111)
Hobson, 856 Pte A W, KRV	QSA (1) DoK	DMU 31 May 00. Also served KTG and SAC. KSA (2)
Hobson, Lt Charles Henry, KLH	QSA (3) DoK OFS Tr	Joined 19 Oct 99 and DMU 13 Mar 00. On nominal roll as Tpr (139). Also served KTG. KSA (2)
Hobson, 836 Pte H L, KRV	QSA (3) RoM DoK OFS	Discharged 1 Jul 00. Also served KTG (No IV Company, A Section, Reservoir)
Hobson, 1059 Pte Herbert Errison, KRV	QSA (1) DoK	Non effective 10 Dec 00. Also served KTG (No IV Company, A Section, Reservoir) and SRG (124) from 11 Feb 01
Hobson, 1109 Pte J, KRV	QSA (4) RoM DoK OFS Tr	Discharged 1 Jul 02. Also served KTG (Cycle Corps, A Company) and CP. KSA (2)
Hobson, Pte J, KTG	QSA (1) DoK	No IV Section, C Company, Pickering's Redoubt No 2
Hobson, Pte J N, KTG	QSA (1) DoK	Cycle Corps, A Company
Hobson, Pte W, KTG	QSA (1) DoK	
Hobson, Pte William Stephen, KTG	QSA (4) RoM DoK OFS 01	No IV Section, B Company, No 4 Redoubt and Kenilworth Defence Force. Also served KLH (137) 20 Oct 99 to 23 Mar 00, KRV (741) to 20 Jun 00 and SRG (160) 14 Feb 01 to 15 May 01
Hockey, Pte C H, KTG	QSA (1) DoK	No III Section, B Company, No 4 Redoubt
Hockey, Pte J, KTG	QSA (1) DoK	
Hockey, Lt S, KTG	QSA (1) DoK	D Company (Veterans), Beaconsfield Town Guard. QSA (1). City Coins Dec 00
Hocking, 913 Pte J, KRV	QSA (3) DoK OFS Tr	Killed in action 21 Dec 00 at Christiana. Casualty roll has 31 Dec 01. Also served KTG (No IV Section, D Company and No 6 Redoubt and No IV Company, Municipal Guard)
Hocking, Pte J, KTG	QSA (1) DoK	No IV Section, D Company and No 6 Redoubt and No IV Company, A Section, Reservoir
Hocking, Pte N H, KTG	QSA (1) DoK	No 3 Redoubt. QSA disc only. McGregor Museum
Hocking, 941 Pte W, KRV	QSA (2) DoK OFS	Discharged 1 Jul 02. Also served KTG (No 2 Schmidt's Breastwork). KSA (2)
Hocking, Pte W J H, KTG	QSA (1) DoK	No IV Section, C Company, Pickering's Redoubt No 2
Hodges, Pte R W, KTG	QSA (3) DoK Tr Witt	Also served 4th Co ASC and FID with initial N W. KSA (2)
Hodgetts, 343 Cpl G W, KRV	QSA (3) DoK OFS Tr	Non effective 19 Feb 01. KSA (2)
Hodgkinson, 88 Sgt W J, KRV	QSA (2) DoK OFS	DMU 23 Apr 00. Served in the Bechuanaland Rebellion 1897 earning CGHGSM (1) Bech. 50th Anniversary attendee
Hodgson, 2566 Col Sgt C, LNLR	QSA (3) DoK OFS Tr	MID 4 Sep 01. DCM LG 27 Sep 01. KSA (2)
Hodgson, 632 Pte F H, KRV	QSA (1) DoK	Discharged 1 Jul 02. KSA (2)
Hodgson, Pte G, KTG	QSA (1) DoK	H Company. 50th Anniversary attendee
Hodgson, Pte H, KTG	QSA (1) DoK	No II Section, D Company and No IV Section, L Company
Hodgson, 367 Pte J, KRV	QSA (1) DoK	DMU 19 Mar 00
Hodgson, Pte J, KTG	QSA (1) DoK	No 2 Schmidt's Breastwork
Hodgson, Pte J, KTG	QSA (1) DoK	F Company
Hodgson, Pte T, KTG	QSA (1) DoK	No 6 Redoubt and No IV Section, L Company. QSA (1). Neate Nov 01 £135

Name	Clasps	Notes
Hoffmeyer, 140 Tpr Stephen John, KLH	QSA (2) DoK OFS	Served 20 Oct 99 to 6 Mar 00
Hogan, Sgt C, KTG	QSA (1) DoK	
Hogan, 7199 Gnr Michael, RGA	QSA (2) DoK Tr	KSA (2)
Hogg, 762 Pte J F, KRV	QSA (3) RoM DoK OFS	Discharged 1 Jul 00. Also served KTG (No III Section, C Company, Beaconsfield Town Guard and Gibraltar Fort, Davis's Heap). DoM on the KTG roll. RoM on the KRV roll. Possibly served in the Bechuanaland Rebellion 1897 with Kimb Rifles earning CGHGSM (1) Bech. See page 511
Hogg, 910 Pte J W, KRV	QSA (4) DoK OFS Tr 01	Also served KTG (No IV Company, A Section, Reservoir)
Hogg, Lt James Cuthbert, KTG	QSA (2) DoK 01	Pickering's Redoubt No 1 and No IV Section, C Company, No 2 Redoubt. Also served Lt SRG (11) from 10 Feb 01
Hoggitt, 4959 Cpl J, LNLR	QSA (3) DoK OFS Tr	KSA (2)
Holbeck, Capt William Arthur, KRV	QSA (1) DoK	Honorary Chaplain of the KRV. MID 10 Sep 01. He arrived in South Africa in 1876, was rector of Dutoitspan 77-81 and Archdeacon of Kimberley 95-02. Dean of Bloemfontein 02-05
Holder, Pte H J, KTG	QSA (1) DoK	Kenilworth Defence Force. QSA (1), KStar. Spink Jul 94
Holderness, 581 Pte C, KRV	QSA (1) DoK	DMU 2 May 00
Holding, 553 Cpl F J, KRV	QSA (5) RoM DoK OFS Tr 01	Non effective 28 May 01. CGHGSM (1) Bech (Pte Kimb Rifles), QSA (5), 14-15 Star, BWM, VM (Pte 1st F Amb SAMC), KStar. City Coins Dec 04
Holgate, 2307 Cpl A, LNLR	QSA (3) DoK OFS Tr	MID 4 Sep 01. KSA (2)
Holgate, 3926 Pte J, LNLR	QSA (4) DoK OFS Tr 01	Died of disease on 25 Feb 01
Holing, Pte S, KTG	QSA (1) DoK	No III Section, B Company, Beaconsfield Town Guard
Holing, Pte William, KTG	QSA (4) DoK OFS Tr 01	No III Section, B Company, Beaconsfield Town Guard. Also served KLH (22789) 29 Dec 00 to 10 Jun 01 and CRSS (1423) from 17 Oct 01. Severely wounded Lichtenburg 3 Mar 01. Occupation engine driver
Holland, 471 Cpl Joseph Robberds, CP2	QSA (3) DoK Paar Tr	C Squadron. KSA (2)
Holley, 434 Band E R, KRV	QSA (1) DoK	Discharged 13 Sep 02. KSA (2)
Holliday, Capt C, KTG	QSA (1) DoK	G Company
Holliday, 149 Cpl William, CP2	QSA (1) DoK	C Squadron. KSA (2). Served in the Bechuanaland Rebellion 1897 earning CGHGSM (1) Bech
Hollingworth, Capt R H, KRV	QSA (3) DoK OFS 01	Non effective 16 Mar 01. QSA (3), KStar. Spink Dec 83
Holloway, 397 Pte Edward Downing, CP2	QSA (1) DoK	He appears on the QSA roll with a no clasp medal and his entry crossed through but his name appears on the nominal roll as serving in C Squadron. Missing Damascus 2 May 01 and rejoined
Holloway, 153 Dvr William, DFA	QSA (3) DoK OFS Tr	Enrolled 22 Jun 99. Discharged 1 Jul 02. Occupation fireman. KSA (2)
Holman, Pte J, KTG	QSA (1) DoK	No 3 Redoubt and Kenilworth Defence Force. QSA (1), KStar. Seaby May 80 £150
Holman, Pte Samuel, KTG	QSA (1) DoK	Also served CRSS (1137) from 6 Mar 01. Occupation carpenter
Holman, Pte T C, KTG	QSA (1) DoK	No IV Section, C Company, Pickering's Redoubt No 2
Holmes, 138 Tpr Alfred, KLH	QSA (3) RoM DoK OFS	Served 19 Oct 99 to 5 Jun 00. Served in the Bechuanaland Rebellion 1897 earning CGHGSM (1) Bech

Holmes, 4568 Pte G, LNLR	QSA (3) DoK Paar Joh	KSA (2). Mounted Infantry
Holmes, 1 Sgt Maj John, KLH	QSA (2) DoK OFS	Served 16 Oct 99 to 30 Apr 00. Discharged as unsatisfactory. Also served ASC. QSA (2). DNW Feb 98 £130
Holmes, Pte L S, KTG	QSA (1) DoK	No III Section, C Company, Pickering's Redoubt No 1
Holroyd, 776 Pte Arthur James, KRV	QSA (2) DoK OFS	Discharged 5 Apr 00. Also served KTG (No IV Section, No 2 Redoubt) and CRSS (1238) from 19 Apr 01
Holt, 4236 Pte Matthew, LNLR	QSA (4) DoK OFS Tr 01	Invalided to England 28 Apr 01. QSA (3) excl SA01. Glendining Oct 78. DNW Dec 04 £230. Chelsea Feb 05 £330
Holt, 5433 Pte W, LNLR	QSA (3) DoK OFS Tr	QSA (3), [KSA (2)]. Dixon Sep 83 £90
Holton, Col Sgt H, KTG	QSA (1) DoK	Medical Corps, No 1 Company, D Section
Holtzhausen, Pte D S, KTG	QSA (2) DoK OFS	No III Section, B Company, Beaconsfield Town Guard. Also served KRV (822) until dismissed for misconduct 22 Apr 00. KStar. City Coins Dec 97. Spink Apr 98 £110
Homan, Pte J, KTG	QSA (1) DoK	
Homer-Mole, Nurse E L, NS	QSA (0)	Kimberley Civil Hospital
Hone, Gnr W, DBMB	QSA (4) DoK Tr 01 02	Crusher Redoubt. Roll notes 'Not known'. Possibly also served JMR (2161) as Pte R Hons with Tr
Honey, Sp Const G, CP2	QSA (1) DoK	
Honeyman, 633 Pte J, KRV	QSA (3) DoK OFS Tr	Discharged 1 Jul 02. KSA (2)
Hooper, 406 Sgt D T, KRV	QSA (2) DoK OFS	KSA (2)
Hooper, 55 Pte Frederick, CP2	QSA (1) DoK	CP dismounted branch (barrier & redoubt duties). QSA (1), KStar. Spink Oct 99 £150. City Coins May 02
Hooper, 79575 Cpl Thomas H, RGA	QSA (2) DoK 01	
Hooper, Pte W E, KTG	QSA (1) DoK	No II Section, B2 Company, No 3 Redoubt
Hope, 5104 Pte B, LNLR	QSA (4) DoK OFS Tr 01	Medal forfeited and returned 30 May 03. Slightly wounded Warrenton 31 Mar 01. QSA (3) excl 01, KStar. Glendining Sep 86 £160. Spink Apr 90 £200
Hopewell, 461 Pte Charles Henry, CP2	QSA (1) DoK	B Squadron. KSA (2)
Hopkins, 34324 Tpr Daniel William, DH	QSA (7) DoK Paar Drie Joh DH Witt 01	Served 18 Feb 00 to 28 Jan 01 and 21 May 01 until died of wounds 20 Dec 01 at Tafel Kop. Also served KTG (Otto's Kopje Scouts). Occupation carriage smith. A man of this name was a prisoner at Sanna's Post 31 Mar 00. Same man?
Hopkinson, 5563 Pte L, LNLR	QSA (3) DoK OFS Tr	KSA (2)
Hopkirk, Pte J R, KTG	QSA (1) DoK	Premier Mine. QSA (1). Liverpool Jul 89 £70
Hopley, Pte C E, KTG	QSA (1) DoK	No II Section, B Company, No 4 Redoubt. In charge of natives at sanitary pits
Hopley, 917 Pte Frederick William, CP2	QSA (1) DoK	Note suggests issued off 22nd Co IY
Hopper, Pte T, KTG	QSA (1) DoK	No I Section, Mandy Fort. QSA (1), KStar. Spink Dec 83. Liverpool Mar 85 £105
Hopwood, 3705 L Cpl J, LNLR	QSA (2) DoK Paar	Mounted Infantry. Invalided to England 11 Jun 00
Horn, 5 Arm Sgt F, KRV	QSA (2) DoK 01	Discharged 1 Sep 01. Served in the Bechuanaland Rebellion 1897 earning CGHGSM (1) Bech
Horn, Pte J, KTG	QSA (1) DoK	No 6 Redoubt
Hornby, Sgt J H, KTG	QSA (1) DoK	Kimberley Mine Ambulance Company. Occupation miner

Hornby, Capt W, KTG	QSA (1) DoK	Officer commanding No 6 Redoubt
Horne, 879 Pte G, KRV	QSA (1) DoK	Also served KTG (Gibraltar Fort, Davis's Heap). Dismissed for misconduct 30 Oct 00, 4 months IHL
Horne, 67 Pte J P, KRV	QSA (1) DoK	DMU 6 Mar 00
Horner, 486 Pte B J N, KRV	QSA (1) DoK	DMU 10 Mar 00
Horril, 265 Tpr William, KLH	QSA (2) DoK OFS	Served 19 Oct 99 to 30 Apr 00. Surname Horil on nominal roll. Also served Condr A L Dept
Hortop, Pte J, KTG	QSA (1) DoK	No II Section, L Company
Horwood, Nurse M, NS	QSA (0)	Joined 6 Mar 00
Hosking, Pte H J, KTG	QSA (1) DoK	No IV Section, No 2 Redoubt
Hosking, Pte Richard, KTG	QSA (3) DoK OFS Tr	Also served IYS (27) 13 May 00 to 6 Sep 00 and DH (40265) 9 Nov 00 to 30 Sep 01 and 6 Feb 02 to 30 Jun 02. Occupation mining engineer. QSA (1) DoK, [KSA (2)], KStar. City Coins Oct 89
Hoskins, 1105 L Cpl C H, CP1	QSA (3) DoK OFS Tr	A Squadron. Wounded 24 Oct 99. KSA (2). Served in the Bechuanaland Rebellion 1897 earning CGHGSM (1) Bech. In the Great War served in GSWA
Hough, 3563 Pte R, LNLR	QSA (3) DoK OFS Tr	Initial J on KSA roll. QSA (3), [KSA (2)]. Spink Feb 70 £4
Houghton, 3862 Pte J, LNLR	QSA (3) DoK OFS Tr	QSA (3), [KSA (2)]. Liverpool Oct 84 £125
Houston, 430 Pte A W, KRV	QSA (1) DoK	DMU 19 Apr 01
Houston, 154 Sgt William Andrew, CP2	QSA (1) DoK	CP dismounted in Beaconsfield
Howard, Pte A E, KTG	QSA (1) DoK	G Company
Howard, 278 Tpr C E, KLH	QSA (2) DoK OFS	Served 17 Nov 99 to 3 Apr 00
Howard, Sgt C H, KTG	QSA (1) DoK	No 1 Redoubt
Howard, Pte H W, KTG	QSA (1) DoK	No I Section, Belgravia Fort
Howard, 834 Pte Martin J, KRV	QSA (2) DoK OFS	Discharged 19 Mar 01. Also served KTG (No 2 Schmidt's Breastwork)
Howard, Pte William Henry, KTG	QSA (7) DoK Paar Drie Joh DH Witt 01	Also served DH 18 Feb 00 to 25 Jan 01. Occupation farmer
Howcroft, 3766 Pte J, LNLR	QSA (3) DoK OFS Tr	KSA (2). Wounded at Brakenlaagte 30 Oct 01
Howe, Pte H, KTG	QSA (1) DoK	No III Section, F Company, No 3 Redoubt
Howe, Sgt H W, KTG	QSA (1) DoK	Ambulance Corps, Beaconsfield Town Guard
Howell, Cpl E T, KTG	QSA (1) DoK	No I Section, B2 Company, No 3 Redoubt
Howell, 263 Tpr H W, KLH	QSA (2) DoK OFS	Served 21 Oct 99 to 30 Apr 00
Howell, Dvr J R, DBMB	QSA (1) DoK	Botanical Gardens
Howell, 1773 Pte James Henry, CP1	QSA (2) DoK OFS	A Squadron. Wounded 28 Nov 99. Enlisted Aug 98. Retired from the Police in Feb 1930 aged 50. Re-enlisted in the Essential Services Protection Corps in 1930 and died 4 Sep 1943. QSA (2), KSA (2), 14-15 Star (Cpl Hartigan's Horse), BWM, VM (Cpl Hartigan's Horse), WM, ASM, SA Police Good Service Medal, KStar. Burman Jun 02 £615. DNW Sep 07 £1,500
Howell, 960 Pte John Rowland, CP2	QSA (3) DoK OFS Tr	
Howell, 248 Cpl Richard, KRV	QSA (1) DoK	Killed in action 28 Nov 99
Howes, 719 Pte F E S, KRV	QSA (1) DoK	Discharged 1 Jul 02. KSA (2)

Kimberley Siege Account and Medal Roll

Howie, Capt C, KRV	QSA (1) DoK	See his biography (page 346)
Howie, Pte T S, KTG	QSA (1) DoK	No II Section, F Company, Mostert's Redoubt
Howieson, Pte J, KTG	QSA (1) DoK	Reserve Section, D Company
Hoyle, 487 Cpl R, KRV	QSA (3) DoK OFS Tr	Discharged 13 Oct 02. KSA (2)
Huband, 5081 Pte A, LNLR	QSA (1) DoK	QSA (3), KSA (2), 14-15 Star, BWM, VM, DM, KStar. RHQ
Huddlestone, 335 Pte F, KRV	QSA (1) DoK	DMU 7 Mar 00
Hudson, 34 QMS Edward Charles, KLH	QSA (4) DoK Paar Tr 01	Served 19 Oct 99 to 10 Nov 00. Also served KTG, POWLH (20464) 13 Dec 00 to 24 Jun 01 and remounts
Hudson, Pte Hougham H, KTG	QSA (1) DoK	Also served Lt UpTG
Hudson, Cpl P M, KTG	QSA (1) DoK	Kenilworth Defence Force
Hudson, Sgt W H, KTG	QSA (1) DoK	No II Section, No 2 Redoubt
Hudson, Pte W M, KTG	QSA (1) DoK	No III Section, Belgravia Fort
Hughes, 3771 Pte C, LNLR	QSA (3) DoK OFS Tr	KSA (2)
Hughes, 591 Pte D T, KRV	QSA (3) RoM DoK Tr	Prisoner 4 Nov 99. Discharged 1 Jul 00
Hughes, 791 Pte H, KRV	QSA (4) RoM DoK OFS Tr	Discharged 11 Aug 02. Also served KTG (No I Company, A Section, Reservoir) and KLH (128 & 1265). KSA (2)
Hughes, 10786 Pte J, RAMC	QSA (1) DoK	Later served in No 11 General Hospital. KSA (2)
Hughes, 2255 Sapr J H, RE	QSA (1) DoK	
Hughes, Pte P R, KTG	QSA (1) DoK	Also served KLH (213) 23 Oct 99 to 30 Apr 00 (Court marshalled 19 Nov 99). Possibly served in the Bechuanaland Rebellion 1897 with DEOVR earning CGHGSM (1) Bech
Hughes, 24410 Tpr Robert, DH	QSA (8) DoK Paar Drie Joh DH Witt 01 02	Served 18 Feb 00 to 31 Jan 01 and 10 Jun 01 to 24 Dec 01. Also served KTG (No IV Section, K Company) and JMR (2633). Occupation machinist
Hull, Pte G H, KTG	QSA (1) DoK	No III Section, Belgravia Fort
Hulley, Lt T H, KTG	QSA (1) DoK	No 1 Redoubt
Human, 232 Pte John Lewis, CP2	QSA (1) DoK	Taken prisoner during the siege. CGHGSM (1) Bech, QSA (1), KStar. Dixon Apr 03 £465. Warwick & Warwick Nov 03
Humberstone, 443 Pte C W, KRV	QSA (1) DoK	Discharged 15 May 00. QSA (1), BWM, VM (Cpl SA RODS), KStar. DNW Sep 07 £450. DNW Sep 09 £390
Humberstone, Pte W H, KTG	QSA (1) DoK	H Company
Humbly, 316 Pte Arthur, CP2	QSA (3) DoK OFS Tr	C Squadron. Also served Lt BoS 18 Apr 02 to 31 Jul 02. CGHGSM (1) Bech (Pte CP), BSACM rev Rhod 96 (Tpr Gifford's Horse), QSA (3), KSA (2) (Lt BoS). DNW Sep 03 £650
Humphreys, Pte T, KTG	QSA (1) DoK	No II Section, F Company, Mostert's Redoubt
Humphries, 288 Tpr Charles, KLH	QSA (3) DoK OFS Tr	Served 23 Oct 99 to 30 Apr 00. Also served RR, IYS (6) 11 May 00 to 6 Sep 00 and StH 7 Feb 02 to 15 Jul 02
Humphries, Pte W, KTG	QSA (1) DoK	No IV Section, C Company, Beaconsfield Town Guard
Humphries, W H, KTG	QSA (0)	Roll states "Relief man at pump for the town water supply"
Humphries, W J, KTG	QSA (0)	Roll states "Clerical assistant to Paymaster"
Humphrys, Capt Edward Thomas, KRV	QSA (2) DoK OFS	See his biography (page 346)
Hunt, 4011 Pte A, LNLR	QSA (3) DoK OFS Tr	KSA (2)
Hunt, Sgt A C, KTG	QSA (1) DoK	No IV Section, C Company, Beaconsfield Town Guard

Hunt, Pte G, KTG	QSA (1) DoK	Kimberley Mine Ambulance Company with mounted forces and Kamfersdam Company. QSA (1), BWM, VM (Pte 7th SAH), KStar. City Coins Jun 77
Hunt, Pte W G, KTG	QSA (1) DoK	
Hunt, Pte William H, KTG	QSA (4) DoK Tr 01 02	Kamfersdam Company. Also served 1st BrH (22757) 5 Dec 00 to 10 Jun 01 and CPS (711) 2 Oct 01 to 30 Apr 02
Hunter, Pte E, KTG	QSA (1) DoK	Kenilworth Defence Force
Hunter, G, KTG	QSA (0)	Roll states "Casting shells and repairing locomotives"
Hunter, Pte G M, KTG	QSA (1) DoK	No IV Section, No 2 Redoubt and No 6 supply depot. 50th Anniversary attendee
Hunter, 674 Pte T W, KRV	QSA (3) DoK OFS Tr	Discharged 1 Jul 02. Slightly wounded Klip Drift 7 Mar 02. KSA (2)
Hunter, Pte W, KTG	QSA (1) DoK	Premier Mine
Hunter, Pte W, KTG	QSA (1) DoK	No III Section, A Company, Beaconsfield Town Guard
Hunter, Pte W G, KTG	QSA (1) DoK	No III Section, C Company, Beaconsfield Town Guard
Hunter, 26328 Gnr William, RGA	QSA (2) DoK 01	QSA (2)
Huntington, Pte Thomas Walker, KTG	QSA (3) RoM DoK OFS	Premier Mine. Also served KLH (222) 14 Mar 00 to 5 Jun 00 and CPS (101) 12 Nov 00 to 30 Apr 02. KSA (2)
Hurdus, Mr T, POC	QSA (1) DoK	
Hurford, 68 Cpl T G, KRV	QSA (3) DoK OFS Tr	KSA (2)
Hurley, 675 Pte A E, KRV	QSA (2) DoK OFS	Discharged 27 Feb 00
Hurlston, 300 Pte Harold W, KRV	QSA (1) DoK	Dismissed for misconduct. Also served KLH (91 & 438) as Hurleston 16 Mar 00 to 6 May 00 and CRSS (1293) from 28 May 01
Hurst, Sp Const G, CP2	QSA (1) DoK	
Hurst, Pte J, KTG	QSA (1) DoK	No 6 Redoubt. QSA (1). Bonhams Dec 02
Hurst, 3870 Band W, LNLR	QSA (3) DoK OFS Tr	QSA (3), [KSA (2)]. Surname Herst on the QSA roll. Sotheby Feb 75 £40. Sotheby Jun 76. Glendining Jun 82. Dixon Sep 83 £110
Husband, Pte P L, KTG	QSA (1) DoK	H Company. QSA (1)
Hussey, Cpl Martin, KTG	QSA (1) DoK	Ambulance Corps, Beaconsfield Town Guard. QSA (1). Spink Dec 95 £90. Spink Sep 96 £90. KStar. Noble Numismatics Jul 97
Hutchings, Sgt F, KTG	QSA (1) DoK	No II Section, F Company, Mostert's Redoubt
Hutchinson, Pte A T, KTG	QSA (1) DoK	Otto's Kopje Company
Hutchinson, QMS Alexander, KTG	QSA (1) DoK	K Company
Hutchison, J, KTG	QSA (0)	Roll states "In charge of cattle kraals"
Hutt, 235 Farr Sgt John, KLH	QSA (2) DoK OFS	Served 24 Oct 99 to 30 Apr 00. Had served as Trooper, CMR, in the Basuto War 1880-81 and in the Matabeleland Relief Force 1896. BSACM rev Rhod 96 (Tpr MRF), QSA (2), KStar. Dixon Sep 01 £475
Hutton, 4339 Pte W, LNLR	QSA (3) DoK OFS Tr	QSA (3), [KSA (2)]. RHQ
Hyde, 303 Tpr A C, KLH	QSA (2) DoK OFS	Served 24 Oct 99 to 20 Apr 00. Also served ORCP (283)
Hyde, Pte A J, KTG	QSA (1) DoK	Premier Mine
Hyde, Sgt A W, KTG	QSA (1) DoK	Beaconsfield Town Guard
Hyland, Pte F, KTG	QSA (1) DoK	No III Section, K Company
Hyland, 2171 Sapr L A W, RE	QSA (3) DoK Drie Tr	QSA (3), [KSA (2)]. Courier Apr 87 £110. DNW Jun 00 £150
Hyles, 1593 Pte M, CP1	QSA (2) DoK OFS	

Hynes, 62 Pte William, CP2	QSA (1) DoK	CP dismounted branch (barrier & redoubt duties). KSA (2) not issued as struck off. Served in the Bechuanaland Rebellion 1897 earning CGHGSM (1) Bech

I

Ibbs, 273 Cpl L J, KRV	QSA (1) DoK	DMU 22 Nov 99
Idebski, Lt William Martin, KTG	QSA (1) DoK	See his biography (page 346)
Indge, Pte W J, KTG	QSA (1) DoK	Medical Corps, No 1 Company, F Section. QSA (1). Advance Guard Militaria Oct 09
Ingleton, Sgt H, KTG	QSA (3) RoM DoK OFS	No I Company, A Section, Reservoir. Also served KRV (792) to 1 Jul 00. DoM on the KTG roll. RoM on the KRV roll. QSA (1) DoK. See page 511
Ingram, 4192 Pte H, LNLR	QSA (3) DoK OFS Tr	Wounded 16 Feb 00. QSA (3), [KSA (2)]. Glendining Dec 65. Glendining Jun 82
Ingram, Pte Harold, KTG	QSA (1) DoK	No II Section, D Company. Also served SRG (145) from 11 Feb 01
Innes, Sgt J D, KTG	QSA (1) DoK	No II Section, C Company, Pickering's Redoubt No 1. Possibly served in the Bechuanaland Rebellion 1897 earning CGHGSM (1) Bech. QSA (1). Collett Feb 98 £95. DNW Sep 09 £210
Innes, 909 Pte W A, KRV	QSA (2) DoK OFS	Discharged 1 Jul 02. Also served KTG (No I Section, C Company, Pickering's Redoubt No 1). KSA (2)
Innes, 316 Pte William Stephen, KRV	QSA (2) DoK OFS	DMU 7 May 00. Also served SRG (53) from 11 Feb 01
Irvine, 580 Pte Henry Augustus, KRV	QSA (3) RoM DoK OFS	Joined 3 Oct 99. Non effective 20 Jun 00. Discharged 1 Apr 01. Also served Lt Irish Yeomanry. Served in the Bechuanaland Rebellion 1897 earning CGHGSM (1) Bech
Irving, Pte C, KTG	QSA (1) DoK	No I Company, B Section, Reservoir
Irving, 874 Pte C E J, KRV	QSA (1) DoK	Discharged 1 Jul 02. Also served KTG (No 2 Schmidt's Breastwork and No I Company, A Section, Reservoir). KSA (2)
Irving, Pte R, KTG	QSA (1) DoK	No II Section, B Company, No 4 Redoubt
Irving, Mr R G, POC	QSA (1) DoK	
Irving, 141 Tpr William Rook, KLH	QSA (2) DoK OFS	Served 19 Oct 99 until dismissed 16 Feb 00. Note says cancelled
Irwin, Lt G, KTG	QSA (1) DoK	No I Section, B Company, Beaconsfield Town Guard
Irwin, 369 Cpl James A, KLH	QSA (3) DoK OFS Joh	Served 16 Oct 99 to 23 Feb 00. Also served Lumsden's Horse (4), Condr ASC and 1st and 2nd ILH (3273 & 1713) 7 Dec 00 to 22 Feb 02 and 14 May 02 to 20 Jun 02. Part of the Coronation contingent. KSA (2). See the Diamond Fields Advertiser article on the siege pig
Iseley, E352 TSM J, SAC	QSA (2) DoK OFS	Also served KRV (505) and ORCP (137)
Ives, Pte John Arthur, KTG	QSA (3) DoK OFS Tr	No III Section, K Company. Also served KLH (1054) 31 Mar 00 to 12 Nov 00, CinCBG (22701) 19 Nov 00 to 19 Jun 01, CPS (363) and JMR (2638). MID 8 Dec 01
Ivey, Pte T, KTG	QSA (1) DoK	No 1 Redoubt
Ivison, Pte R, KTG	QSA (1) DoK	No 6 Redoubt

J

Jack, 368 Pte Charles Morrison, CP2	QSA (2) DoK OFS	A Squadron. KSA (2). Served in the Bechuanaland Rebellion 1897 earning CGHGSM (1) Bech
Jackson, Pte C, KTG	QSA (1) DoK	G Company. QSA (1). eBay Nov 03
Jackson, Pte C H, KTG	QSA (1) DoK	No II Section, C Company, Pickering's Redoubt No 2
Jackson, Pte Charles Lee, KTG	QSA (1) DoK	Premier Mine. Also served CRSS (1074) from 11 Mar 01

Medal roll

Jackson, Pte Charles Michael, KTG	QSA (1) DoK	Premier Mine. Also served SRG (924) from 23 May 01
Jackson, 748 Pte E, KRV	QSA (1) DoK	DMU 12 Dec 00. Also served CP. QSA (1). Seaby Jan 75 £55
Jackson, Pte F, KTG	QSA (1) DoK	Premier Mine
Jackson, Sgt G W, KTG	QSA (1) DoK	No I Section, C Company, Pickering's Redoubt No 1. CGHGSM (1) Bech (Sgt Maj DFH), QSA (1). City Coins Dec 04. Dixon Sep 05 £375
Jackson, Pte H, KTG	QSA (1) DoK	G Company
Jackson, Pte J, KTG	QSA (1) DoK	No 4 supply depot
Jackson, Cpl J W, KTG	QSA (1) DoK	
Jackson, Pte J W, KTG	QSA (1) DoK	No IV Section, F Company, Mostert's Redoubt
Jackson, Pte Richard, KTG	QSA (3) RoM DoK OFS	No III Section, No 2 Redoubt. Also served KLH (224) 16 Mar 00 to 3 Jun 00 and SRG (201) from 11 May 01
Jackson, Pte W, KTG	QSA (3) DoK Tr 01	No 2 Schmidt's Breastwork and Reserve, No 4 Redoubt. Also served JMR (2012 & 39560) to 26 Nov 01 but could be next man
Jackson, Pte W, KTG	QSA (1) DoK	No 2 Schmidt's Breastwork and Reserve, No 4 Redoubt
Jacobs, Pte C, KTG	QSA (1) DoK	Ambulance Corps, Beaconsfield Town Guard
Jacobs, Pte D, KTG	QSA (1) DoK	Ambulance Corps, Beaconsfield Town Guard. QSA (1), KStar. Clark Apr 93 £175
Jacobs, Pte H, KTG	QSA (1) DoK	No IV Section, K Company. Possibly served in the Bechuanaland Rebellion 1897 with DEOVR earning CGHGSM (1) Bech. QSA (1)
Jacobs, 197 Pte William Daniel, CP2	QSA (4) RoM DoK OFS Tr	C Squadron. KSA (2). Served in the Bechuanaland Rebellion 1897 earning CGHGSM (1) Bech
Jacobson, Pte A, KTG	QSA (1) DoK	Reserve Section, D Company
Jager, 233 Tpr F, KLH	QSA (2) DoK OFS	Served 21 Oct 99 to 30 Apr 00. Nominal roll says deserted 6 Nov 99
Jagger, Cpl T J, DBMB	QSA (1) DoK	Armoured train section
Jakins, 87 Sgt A J, KRV	QSA (1) DoK	Non effective 24 Oct 00. Served in the Bechuanaland Rebellion 1897 earning CGHGSM (1) Bech
Jakins, 143 Tpr Frederick Mills, KLH	QSA (3) RoM DoK OFS	Served 19 Oct 99 to 6 Mar 00. Occupation miner
James, Pte E H, KTG	QSA (2) DoK OFS	No II Company, A Section, Reservoir. Also served IMR as Railway Employee
James, 4820 Pte F, LNLR	QSA (4) DoK OFS Tr 01	Invalided to England
James, Tpr Henry, DH	QSA (5) DoK OFS Tr 01 02	Served 30 Aug 01 to 20 Mar 02. Also served KTG (No 2 Schmidt's Breastwork)
James, Pte J, KTG	QSA (1) DoK	B line of defence, No 3 Redoubt
James, Pte James Herbert, KTG	QSA (1) DoK	No 6 Redoubt. Also served CRSS (1025 or 1205) from 18 Feb 01
James, Pte P, KTG	QSA (1) DoK	G Company
James, Pte R C, KTG	QSA (1) DoK	Medical Corps, No 1 Company, F Section and No II Section, B Company, Beaconsfield Town Guard
James, 470 Band T, KRV	QSA (1) DoK	Discharged 1 Jul 02. KSA (2)
James, Pte V, KTG	QSA (1) DoK	No II Company, A Section, Reservoir. Also served IMR as Railway Employee
Jameson, Pte Henry, KTG	QSA (2) DoK OFS	No 3 Redoubt. Also served KLH (425) 15 Mar 00 to 29 Aug 00. Possibly served in the Bechuanaland Rebellion 1897 with Kimb Rifles earning CGHGSM (1) Bech. QSA (1), KStar. Kaplan Feb 08
Jameson, 863 Cpl T R, KRV	QSA (3) DoK OFS Tr	Discharged 1 Jul 02. Also served KTG (No 3 Redoubt). KSA (2)
Jamieson, 52 Pte Charles, CP2	QSA (4) RoM DoK OFS Tr	C Squadron. Served in the Bechuanaland Rebellion 1897 earning CGHGSM (1) Bech

Name	Medals	Notes
Jamieson, 442 Pte Crawford, KRV	QSA (1) DoK	Non effective 5 Oct 00. Also served SRG (181) from 13 Feb 01
Jamieson, 4156 Sgt G, LNLR	QSA (3) DoK OFS Tr	Prisoner Vaalkop 9 Sep 01. QSA (3), KSA (2), BWM, VM, LS&GC GV, KStar. RHQ
Jamieson, W, KTG	QSA (0)	Roll states "Electrical work; searchlights and dynamite mines"
Jamieson, Pte W, KTG	QSA (1) DoK	No 2 Schmidt's Breastwork. Also served CLH (39)
Jansen, Pte J, KTG	QSA (1) DoK	Ambulance Corps, Beaconsfield Town Guard
Jansen, 776 Pte Johann Thomas, CP2	QSA (1) DoK	C Squadron. Also served WMI from 24 Jan 01 and was killed near Plaat Drift 16 Jun 01. QSA (1), KStar. LSE Sep 84 £120. QSA (1). Walland Feb 95 £115. Spink Jul 97 £320
Jardine, 3488 Pte J, LNLR	QSA (1) DoK	Retransferred to AR in South Africa 21 Feb 00. Employed on CGR. 20 J Jardine served CPS and gained 01 & 02. Same man?
Jarrett, 4082 Pte H, LNLR	QSA (3) DoK OFS Tr	QSA (3), [KSA (2)]. Liverpool Nov 95 £125
Jarrett, 634 Pte William Richard, KRV	QSA (4) RoM DoK OFS Tr	Served 9 Oct 99 until DMU 3 Apr 00. Also served KLH (1059 & 35504) 17 Apr 00 to 11 Feb 01 and 13 Jul 01 to 4 Feb 02. KSA (2). Occupation fitter
Jarvis, 593 Pte C H, KRV	QSA (1) DoK	DMU 2 Apr 00. 50th Anniversary attendee
Jarvis, Pte R, KTG	QSA (1) DoK	Cycle Corps, A Company. QSA (1), KStar. Spink Sep 76 £70. Spink Sep 82 £185. DNW Sep 99 £180
Jebb, 812 Pte A C, KRV	QSA (2) DoK 01	Also served KTG (No 3 Redoubt). Invalided to England 1901
Jefferies, 11503 Pte G, RAMC	QSA (1) DoK	Also served at No 16 Stationery Hospital and Temporary Hospitals at Lichtenburg and Zeerust. QSA (1), KStar. DNW Dec 06 £330. Chester Militaria May 07 £495
Jeffery, 1082 Pte C, KRV	QSA (1) DoK	Discharged 28 May 02. Also served KTG. KSA (2)
Jeffrey, Pte A G, KTG	QSA (1) DoK	No III Section, K Company. QSA (1). Spink Mar 80 £125. Glendining Nov 92 £60
Jeffrey, Pte S, KTG	QSA (1) DoK	No II Section, Mandy Fort
Jeffrey, Sgt W, KTG	QSA (1) DoK	No II Section, A Company, Beaconsfield Town Guard
Jenkins, Pte A, KTG	QSA (1) DoK	Premier Mine
Jenkins, Pte A R, KTG	QSA (1) DoK	No III Section, B Company, Beaconsfield Town Guard. 50th Anniversary attendee
Jenkins, Pte E C, KTG	QSA (1) DoK	No IV Section, B Company, No 4 Redoubt. QSA (1), 14-15 Star, BWM, VM, KStar
Jenkins, 5323 Pte H, LNLR	QSA (3) DoK OFS Tr	KSA (2)
Jenkins, Cpl H J, KTG	QSA (1) DoK	No I Section, A Company, Beaconsfield Town Guard
Jenkins, Pte W J, KTG	QSA (1) DoK	No III Section, C Company, Beaconsfield Town Guard
Jenkins, Pte W P, KTG	QSA (1) DoK	No 6 Redoubt
Jenkins, 2 Sgt William Henry, CP2	QSA (1) DoK	A Squadron. KSA (2). Served in the Bechuanaland Rebellion 1897 earning CGHGSM (1) Bech
Jenkinson, Pte E D, KTG	QSA (1) DoK	No I Section, A Company, Beaconsfield Town Guard. Possibly served in the Bechuanaland Rebellion 1897 with Cape Mtd Yeo earning CGHGSM (1) Bech
Jenkinson, Pte R, KTG	QSA (1) DoK	No IV Section, A Company, Beaconsfield Town Guard. QSA (1). McGregor Museum
Jennings, 1049 Pte A, CP1	QSA (2) DoK OFS	B Squadron. Discharged time expired 26 Apr 01. Served in the Bechuanaland Rebellion 1897 earning CGHGSM (1) Bech
Jennings, Pte G H, KTG	QSA (1) DoK	Mounted Section, Kenilworth Defence Force
Jennings, 1416 Pte H, CP1	QSA (4) RoM DoK OFS Tr	CP No 1 Maxim gun detachment
Jennings, Pte J, KTG	QSA (1) DoK	No I Section, B2 Company, No 3 Redoubt

Medal roll

Jennings, Pte J, KTG	QSA (1) DoK	No 4 Redoubt
Jennings, 104 Sgt Samuel, CP2	QSA (1) DoK	B Squadron. KSA (2). Served in the Bechuanaland Rebellion 1897 earning CGHGSM (1) Bech
Jennings, 725 Pte William S, KRV	QSA (4) DoK OFS Tr 01	DMU 3 Oct 00. Also served KTG (No I Section, B Company, Beaconsfield Town Guard), KLH (26207) 9 Feb 01 to 20 Aug 01 and CPS. Occupation painter
Jensen, Cpl R P, KTG	QSA (1) DoK	No II Section, B Company, Beaconsfield Town Guard
Jensen, Pte W, KTG	QSA (1) DoK	Gibraltar Fort, Davis's Heap
Jensen, 368 Cpl William Edward, KLH	QSA (4) RoM DoK OFS Tr	Served 14 Dec 99 to 29 Aug 00. Also served KH (41888), CinCBG (22702) 10 Nov 00 to 11 Nov 01, 2nd KFS (22702) 11 Nov 01 to 28 Nov 01 and ALH (39989) 3 Dec 01 to 24 Mar 02. KSA (2). Surnames sometimes Jansen. Occupation miner
Jessett, 1200 Pte George Edmund, KRV	QSA (5) DoK OFS Tr 01 02	Served 4 Sep 00 until DMU 31 May 01. Also served KTG (No 3 Redoubt) 24 Oct 99 to 10 Mar 00, WS (3) 17 Mar 00 to 15 May 00 and CPS (715) 18 Oct 01 to 30 Apr 02
Jessiman, Pte W, KTG	QSA (1) DoK	No IV Section, C Company, Pickering's Redoubt No 2
Jessup, Pte A, KTG	QSA (1) DoK	No III Section, Belgravia Fort
Jewell, Sister S, NS	QSA (0)	Kimberley Civil Hospital. MID 10 Sep 01
Jeyes, Cpl C, KTG	QSA (1) DoK	No III Section, A Company, Beaconsfield Town Guard. Possibly also served Warrenton DMT (58). OFS & Tr crossed through on Warrenton DMT QSA roll
Jobson, Pte R C, KTG	QSA (1) DoK	Served in the Bechuanaland Rebellion 1897 with Kimb Rifles earning CGHGSM (1) Bech. 50th Anniversary attendee
John, Pte W O, KTG	QSA (1) DoK	Mounted Section, Kenilworth Defence Force. Possibly served in the Bechuanaland Rebellion 1897 with PAVG earning CGHGSM (1) Bech
Johns, Sgt H T, KTG	QSA (1) DoK	No I Section, B Company, No 4 Redoubt
Johns, Lt S, KTG	QSA (1) DoK	No II Section, K Company
Johns, Pte T, KTG	QSA (1) DoK	No 2 Schmidt's Breastwork
Johns, 96166 Gnr Thomas, RGA	QSA (1) DoK	Premier Mine. KSA (2)
Johnson, Pte A, KTG	QSA (1) DoK	Kimberley Mine Ambulance Company, E Section. QSA (1), 14-15 Star, BWM, VM (7th Infy), KStar (could be next man). Spink Feb 80 £150. Glendining Oct 81 £110. Christies Nov 84 £151. Chelsea Sep 05
Johnson, Pte A, KTG	QSA (1) DoK	No III Section, C Company, Beaconsfield Town Guard. QSA (1), BWM, VM (Pte 1st SAI), KStar (could be previous man). Spink Jan 78 £140. Spink Nov 98
Johnson, 226 Gnr Arthur, DFA	QSA (1) DoK	Enrolled 12 Feb 00. Served Royal Marines 86-98. Discharged 1 Jul 06. Occupation fireman
Johnson, Pte C W, KTG	QSA (1) DoK	No II Section, C Company, Pickering's Redoubt No 2. QSA (1), KStar. City Coins Dec 04
Johnson, 5031 Pte E, LNLR	QSA (3) DoK OFS Tr	KSA (2)
Johnson, 387 Sgt E E, CP1	QSA (5) Rhod RoM DoK OFS Tr	Rhod was issued 12 Dec 05. Served in the Bechuanaland Rebellion 1897 earning CGHGSM (1) Bech
Johnson, 5135 Pte E G, LNLR	QSA (3) DoK OFS Tr	Deserted. Medal not recovered. QSA (3), [KSA (2)]. Sotheby Jun 12
Johnson, Pte G, KTG	QSA (1) DoK	Kenilworth Defence Force
Johnson, Lt G H, KTG	QSA (1) DoK	No I Section, K Company. On nominal roll with surname Johnston
Johnson, Pte H, KTG	QSA (1) DoK	No 1 Redoubt
Johnson, 556 Pte H Luttman, KRV	QSA (2) DoK OFS	Wounded 16 Nov 99. Discharged 26 Mar 00

181

Johnson, Lt J, KTG	QSA (1) DoK	No III Section, L Company
Johnson, Pte J J, KTG	QSA (1) DoK	No IV Section, K Company. QSA (1)
Johnson, 7577 Gnr John, RGA	QSA (1) DoK	Premier Mine. QSA (1), [KSA (2)], KStar. Sotheby Jul 87
Johnson, Pte John George, KTG	QSA (2) DoK Tr	Also served BR (226 and 26184) from 6 Feb 01 and CRSS (1356) from 26 Aug 01. Occupation chef
Johnson, Pte M A, KTG	QSA (1) DoK	Also served KRV (862). Possibly also served KLH (197) gaining RoM and Tr
Johnson, 1197 Pte Walter, KRV	QSA (6) RoM DoK OFS Tr 01 02	Also served KTG (No II Section, C Company, Pickering's Redoubt No 1), KLH (197) to 5 Jun 00, CRSS (1260) from 29 Apr 01 and BSAP (1425). Surname also spelled Johnston. Slightly wounded Christiana 28 Feb 02. QSA (5) inc CC excl 01 & 02. DNW Sep 05 £410. Dixon Apr 06 £575. Lockdales Nov 08. eBay Jul 09 £720
Johnson, Sgt Walter Pierce, KTG	QSA (2) DoK 01	Otto's Kopje Scouts and No II Section, Mandy Fort. Also served KFS (365) 12 Dec 00 to 27 Jun 01
Johnston, 706 Pte George Milne, CP2	QSA (4) RoM DoK OFS Tr	Died of disease Kimberley 13 Aug 01
Johnston, Lt Hugh Bertie Henriques, RGA	QSA (3) DoK Tr 01	On roll for 23rd Company RGA. See his biography (page 346)
Johnston, 554 Pte J, KRV	QSA (2) DoK OFS	DMU 6 Aug 00
Johnston, Lt J W, KTG	QSA (1) DoK	No II Section, D Company. QSA (1). McGregor Museum
Johnston, 934 Pte T, KRV	QSA (2) DoK OFS	Discharged 1 Jul 02. Also served KTG (No I Company, A Section, Reservoir). QSA (2), KSA (2). LSE Jun 85 £98
Johnston, Pte W J, KTG	QSA (1) DoK	Premier Mine
Johnstone, Cpl George Hugh, KTG	QSA (6) DoK Paar Drie Joh DH Witt	Also served JMR (1560 & 35507), DH 20 Feb 00 to 26 Jan 01 and BS (491) 22 to 27 Mar 01 (Tried 27 Mar 01 for being AWOL, fined £2, reduced to ranks and discharged). KSA (2). Surname sometimes Johnston. QSA (1) DoK, [KSA (2)], KStar. Glendining Mar 73 £28
Johnstone, 792 Pte James, CP2	QSA (1) DoK	CP dismounted branch (barrier & redoubt duties). DMU
Johnstone, Pte W, KTG	QSA (1) DoK	Premier Mine
Jolly, Pte F, KTG	QSA (1) DoK	B line of defence, No 3 Redoubt
Jolly, 22 Sgt James Buchanan, CP2	QSA (4) DoK OFS Tr 01	CP HQ and depot mounted branch. QSA (4), KStar. Spink Sep 86 £180. CGHGSM (2) Bas Bech (Pte CMR), QSA (4), KStar. Spink Dec 83. DNW Mar 08 £880
Jones, Pte Alexander Evan, KTG	QSA (2) DoK OFS	Also served KLH (142) 20 Oct 99 to 6 Mar 00 and SRG (54) from 12 Feb 01
Jones, 22231 Gnr Arthur S F, RGA	QSA (1) DoK	Premier Mine. Died of enteric 7 Jan 00
Jones, 363 Tpr Charles Edward, KLH	QSA (4) RoM DoK OFS Tr	Served 27 Nov 99 to 12 Nov 00. Also served KRV (1244) to 9 Jun 01 and DH (41873) 19 May 02 to 31 May 02. Occupation barman. QSA (4), KSA (2), KStar. Spink May 77 £140. City Coins Dec 77
Jones, 17597 Sgt Charles Henry, RGA	QSA (3) DoK OFS Tr	Born Fulham 1862. Attested 31 Jan 82, aged 20. Served 21 yrs 3 days. Occupation weaver. QSA (3), KSA (2). LSE Sep 84 £98. Dixon Aug 98 £150. Romsey Sep 08 £400
Jones, Pte Charles Percy, KTG	QSA (3) DoK OFS Tr	Gibraltar Fort, Davis's Heap. Also served KLH (1058 & 22827) 17 Mar 00 to 24 Nov 00 and 9 Jan 01 to 28 Feb 02. KSA (2)
Jones, 5259 Pte D, LNLR	QSA (2) DoK OFS	Died at Krugersdorp on 28 Aug 00
Jones, Pte E, KTG	QSA (1) DoK	
Jones, Pte E, KTG	QSA (1) DoK	No IV Section, L Company
Jones, Pte E P, KTG	QSA (1) DoK	Premier Mine

Jones, Lt Ernest, KTG	QSA (1) DoK	Gibraltar Fort, Davis's Heap
Jones, 457 Pte Ernest Robert, CP2	QSA (1) DoK	A Squadron. KSA (2). Served in the Bechuanaland Rebellion 1897 earning CGHGSM (1) Bech
Jones, Pte F W, KTG	QSA (1) DoK	
Jones, Pte G G, KTG	QSA (1) DoK	QSA (1). McGregor Museum
Jones, Pte H W, KTG	QSA (1) DoK	No 1 supply depot. QSA (1). Dixon Jul 07 £250
Jones, 437 Pte J, KRV	QSA (1) DoK	DMU 5 Jun 00. Also served KLH. QSA (1). City Coins Oct 93. DNW Feb 98 £85. City Coins Jun 04
Jones, 4174 Pte J, LNLR	QSA (3) DoK OFS Tr	KSA (2)
Jones, Pte J C, KTG	QSA (1) DoK	Kenilworth Defence Force
Jones, Pte J E, KTG	QSA (1) DoK	
Jones, Pte J M, KTG	QSA (1) DoK	
Jones, 578 Pte Philip Luke, KRV	QSA (4) DoK Paar Drie Tr	DMU 2 Jan 00. Roll states, medal stamped 249 in error. Also served DH 18 Feb 00 to 25 Apr 00, 1st BrH (9422) to 13 May 01, 2nd KFS (431) 26 Sep 01 to 19 Nov 01, Pietersburg Light Horse (474) and 1st BoH. Wounded 7 Mar 00. KSA (2) issued 24 Jul 1930
Jones, Pte R H, KTG	QSA (1) DoK	Supply Depot
Jones, 101 Cpl Robert Price, DFA	QSA (1) DoK	Enrolled 22 Feb 95. Resigned 6 Mar 03. Occupation railway clerk
Jones, 47 Sgt S D, KLH	QSA (2) DoK OFS	Served 19 Oct 99 to 30 Apr 00
Jones, Pte T L, KTG	QSA (1) DoK	No II Section, Belgravia Fort
Jones, 68 Pte Thomas, CP2	QSA (1) DoK	B Squadron. Killed in action 25 Nov 99. Served in the Bechuanaland Rebellion 1897 earning CGHGSM (1) Bech
Jones, 5174 Pte Thomas, LNLR	QSA (1) DoK	Wounded 10 Feb 00. Invalided 25 Apr 00
Jones, 2547 Gnr Ulric W, RGA	QSA (2) DoK Tr	KSA (2). Note says deceased (not on casualty roll)
Jones, 3928 Band W, LNLR	QSA (3) DoK OFS Tr	KSA (2)
Jones, Pte W A, KTG	QSA (1) DoK	Kimberley Mine searchlight and telephone section and No II Section, L Company
Jones, Pte W H, KTG	QSA (1) DoK	Reserve Section, D Company
Jones, 7183 Gnr William George Barnes, RGA	QSA (2) DoK OFS	QSA (1) excl OFS, KSA (2), KStar. Payne collection. QSA (2), KSA (2), [KStar]. Sotheby Oct 71. DNW Jul 01 £200. Chelsea May 02 £285
Jordan, Pte George Henry, KTG	QSA (1) DoK	Kenilworth Defence Force. Also served CRSS (1063) from 9 Mar 01
Jordan, Sgt Orlando Richard, KTG	QSA (1) DoK	H Company. Also served CRSS (1065) from 9 Mar 01
Jordan, 93922 Bombdr William James, RGA	QSA (1) DoK	KSA (2)
Jose, 929 Pte W, KRV	QSA (1) DoK	Also served KTG (No I Section, A Company, Beaconsfield Town Guard). Discharged 1 Jul 02. KSA (2)
Joshua, Pte P, KTG	QSA (1) DoK	No I Section, A Company, Beaconsfield Town Guard
Joslin, Pte V, KTG	QSA (1) DoK	No 2 supply depot
Jourdan, 555 Pte C, KRV	QSA (1) DoK	DMU 12 Jan 00
Joyce, Lt Edward Walker, KLH	QSA (3) DoK OFS Tr	Joined 11 Dec 99 and resigned 30 Jun 00. Also served KTG. Later served as Captain BR in Mar 03. Captain 2nd Kimberley Regiment in GSWA 10 Oct 14 to 13 Aug 15
Joyce, Pte Henry, KTG	QSA (4) RoM DoK OFS Tr	Also served KTG (No 2 Schmidt's Breastwork), KLH (380 & 1057) 6 Mar 00 to 6 Nov 00, 1st ILH (1538) 19 Nov 00 to 16 Nov 01 and 1st RPR (1240) 28 Nov 01 to 30 Jun 02. Surname also spelled Joice. QSA (4). Glendining May 70. Glendining Sep 88. eBay Apr 05

Name	Medals	Notes
Jubber, Mr C D B, POC	QSA (1) DoK	Telegraph signaller
Jubber, Pte Q H, KTG	QSA (1) DoK	Beaconsfield Town Guard
Jubilees, 1316 Pte J, CP1	QSA (3) DoK OFS Tr	B Squadron. KSA (2)
Judd, 26217 Tpr Chas Henry, DH	QSA (4) RoM DoK OFS Tr	Served DH 9 Feb 01 to 13 Feb 02. Also served KR (730) 10 Jan 00 to 25 Jun 00, KTG and DS (62) 18 Dec 00 to 4 Feb 01. Note suggests a duplicate medal or clasp was issued by KRV. Wounded Tweefontein 5 Apr 00 and again near Edenburg 27 Apr 01. KSA (2). Occupation carpenter
Judd, Pte G M, KTG	QSA (1) DoK	No 3 Redoubt. Also served Agent FID
Judge, 412 Pte Edward, CP2	QSA (4) RoM DoK OFS Tr	C Squadron. KSA (2). Served in the Bechuanaland Rebellion 1897 earning CGHGSM (1) Bech
Judge, 826 Pte P, KRV	QSA (3) DoK OFS Tr	Discharged 1 Jul 02. Also served KTG (No I Section, K Company). QSA (3), [KSA (2)]. Spink Feb 75 £54
Jullien, Pte G, KTG	QSA (1) DoK	No II Section, No 2 Redoubt. 713 G R Julien served CPS and gained Tr. Same man?
Jurgenson, 530 Pte C, KRV	QSA (5) RoM DoK OFS Tr 01	Discharged 22 Apr 01

K

Name	Medals	Notes
Kalkschmidt, Pte H, KTG	QSA (1) DoK	Medical Corps, No 1 Company, F Section
Kallenborn, Pte John Bathurst, KTG	QSA (4) DoK OFS Tr 01	Kenilworth Defence Force and Otto's Kopje Scouts. Also served KRV (1164) 16 Aug 00 to 31 Oct 01, WS (11) 18 Mar 00 to 31 Aug 00, SRG (57) 12 Feb 01 to 11 Nov 01 and CPS 6 Jan 02 to 31 May 02. QSA with CC issued by SRG and QSA with DoK by KTG. KSA (2)
Kavanagh, 34928 Tpr Harry, KLH	QSA (4) DoK OFS 01 02	Served 15 Apr 02 to 30 Jun 02. Also served KH (109) from 15 Apr 02. Occupation carpenter. 81 Cpl H Kavanagh served KLH 29 Oct 99 until discharged for misconduct 7 Feb 00. Same man?
Kavanagh, 4009 Drum J, LNLR	QSA (3) DoK OFS Tr	KSA (2). Invalided to England 21 Jun 01
Kay, 4340 Pte J, LNLR	QSA (4) DoK OFS Tr 01	
Kay, Mr Ronald E, POC	QSA (1) DoK	KStar (initials R C). Glendining Jun 93
Kayser, Pte Arthur Frederick, KTG	QSA (1) DoK	Also served SRG (184) from 11 Feb 01
Keane, 32 Tpr William, KLH	QSA (2) DoK OFS	Served 19 Oct 99 to 30 Apr 00
Kearney, Pte R L, KTG	QSA (1) DoK	
Kearns, Sgt B C, KTG	QSA (1) DoK	Medical Corps, No 1 Company, F Section. SAGS (1) 1878 (Tpr One Star Diamond Contingent), QSA (1). City Coins Aug 08
Kearns, Pte C, KTG	QSA (1) DoK	Cycle Corps, A Company. QSA (1). City Coins Aug 08
Kearns, Lt F, KTG	QSA (1) DoK	B line of defence, No 3 Redoubt
Kearns, Pte J J, KTG	QSA (1) DoK	Mounted Section, Kenilworth Defence Force
Kearsley, 400 Pte H, KRV	QSA (1) DoK	Non effective 8 Jul 00
Keast, 3477 Gnr George, RGA	QSA (1) DoK	Premier Mine. Died of enteric 20 Feb 00. QSA (1), KStar. Spink May 03 £340. Chelsea Jun 04 £375
Keat, Pte H, KTG	QSA (1) DoK	No III Section, K Company. 50th Anniversary attendee
Keathley, QMS W, KTG	QSA (1) DoK	
Keating, Lt E W, KTG	QSA (1) DoK	No IV Section, B Company, Beaconsfield Town Guard. QSA (1), KStar. Walland Mar 98 £330. DNW Apr 03 £280. Elite Collections Feb 04 £480
Keating, Pte G C, KTG	QSA (1) DoK	Ambulance Corps, Beaconsfield Town Guard
Keating, Pte S, KTG	QSA (1) DoK	D Company (Veterans), Beaconsfield Town Guard

Medal roll

Keatley, 51 Tpr George, KLH	QSA (2) DoK Paar	Served 19 Oct 99 to 30 Apr 00. Also served Condr Transport Department
Keddie, Pte Adam Cubie, KTG	QSA (4) DoK OFS Tr 01	No 3 Redoubt. Also served 2nd RPR (1240) 2 Dec 00 to 6 Jun 01 and CRSS (1490) from 31 Dec 01. Occupation carpenter
Kedian, Pte James, KTG	QSA (4) DoK OFS 01 02	No 2 Schmidt's Breastwork. Also served KRV (1250) to 1 Jun 01, DH (34951) 24 Jun 01 to 28 Dec 01, BR and WS (9). KRV supplementary roll says discharged 3 Feb 02. Occupation painter
Kedian, Pte William Henry, KTG	QSA (3) DoK OFS Tr	Served 21 Aug 01 to 20 Mar 02. Also served KTG, WS (10) 18 Feb 00 to 31 Aug 00, DS (30) 14 Dec 00 to 4 Feb 01, BR (228 & 26185) 6 Feb 01 to 10 Aug 01 and KH (258) 7 Apr 02 to 30 Jun 02. Occupation shunter and painter. QSA (3), [KSA (2)]. City Coins No 18
Keegan, 676 Sgt J, KRV	QSA (3) DoK OFS Tr	Discharged 1 Jul 02. KSA (2)
Keen, 1323 Pte T H C, CP1	QSA (2) DoK 01	Served 11 Oct 99 to 31 Jul 01. Served in the Bechuanaland Rebellion 1897 earning CGHGSM (1) Bech
Keenan, 3456 Band A E, LNLR	QSA (3) DoK OFS Tr	[QSA (3), KSA (2)], KStar. Morris May 96 £50
Keers, 22704 Tpr Robert, CinCBG	QSA (4) DoK Paar Tr 01	Served 19 Nov 00 to 21 May 01. Also served KTG (Cycle Corps, A Company). May also be entitled to RoM. Occupation builder
Keet, 293 Pte M, KRV	QSA (1) DoK	DMU 4 Apr 00. 50th Anniversary attendee
Keevy, Pte J M, KTG	QSA (1) DoK	No IV Section, L Company
Kegel, 104 Sgt August Frederick W, KLH	QSA (4) RoM DoK OFS Tr	Discharged 5 Jun 00. Also served CPS and StH (1580) with forenames Arthur William Frederick 29 Nov 01 until transferred to SAC 9 Jan 03. KSA (2)
Keith, Pte Angus Cecil, KTG	QSA (2) DoK 02	Premier Mine. Also served SRG (939) from 4 Jan 02. Medal reissued 9 Sep 15. Employed at De Beers
Keith, Sgt C, KTG	QSA (1) DoK	
Kekewich, Col Robert George, LNLR	QSA (3) DoK OFS Tr	See his biography (page 346)
Keleher, 1274 Tpr David, KLH	QSA (4) RoM DoK Paar Tr	Served 19 Oct 99 to 6 Nov 00. Also served CinCBG (22705) from 17 Nov 00. Killed 3 Jan 01. Note on the CinCBG nominal roll says missing 3 Jan 01 and that the Court of Enquiry decision was that he had been killed.
Keller, 285 Tpr Henry George, KLH	QSA (4) DoK OFS 01 02	DMU 3 Jan 00. Also served CinCBG (34325) 21 May 01 until transferred to JMR on 16 Jul 01, JMR (34325) to 19 Nov 01 and WPMR (413)
Keller, 202 Tpr Joseph Andrew, KLH	QSA (2) DoK OFS	Joined 21 Oct 99. Died of wounds 29 Nov 99
Kellet, Pte W, KTG	QSA (1) DoK	No II Section, Belgravia Fort
Kellett, 160 Sgt Theodore Young, CP2	QSA (4) RoM DoK OFS Tr	C Squadron. KSA (2). Served in the Bechuanaland Rebellion 1897 earning CGHGSM (1) Bech
Kelley, 1016 Pte G, KRV	QSA (2) DoK OFS	Discharged 18 Feb 02. Also served KTG (No III Company, A Section, Reservoir) as Kelly. KSA (2)
Kellsey, Pte A, KTG	QSA (1) DoK	No I Company, B Section, Reservoir. Possibly served in the Bechuanaland Rebellion 1897 with DFH earning CGHGSM (1) Bech. QSA (1). DNW Jul 04 £110. Liverpool Nov 04 £185
Kelly, 293 Tpr Alfred Francis, KLH	QSA (2) DoK OFS	Joined 23 Oct 99. Transferred to KTG 8 Jan 00. On KTG roll with initials A E. Served in the Bechuanaland Rebellion 1897 earning CGHGSM (1) Bech
Kelly, 145 Tpr Arthur Clement, KLH	QSA (4) RoM DoK OFS 01	Served 20 Oct 99 to 5 Jun 00. Also served SRG (119) Feb 01 to Aug 01. QSA (3) excl 01, KStar. City Coins Aug 96
Kelly, Pte B, KTG	QSA (1) DoK	No 1 Redoubt
Kelly, 635 Pte E, KRV	QSA (3) DoK OFS Tr	Discharged 1 Jul 02. KSA (2)

Kelly, Cpl E W, KTG	QSA (1) DoK	Cycle Corps, A Company and Kimberley Mine searchlight and telephone section. QSA (1), 14-15 Star (CSM SAEC), BWM, VM (2nd Cl WO SAEC), ASM. City Coins Sep 03
Kelly, Pte F, KTG	QSA (1) DoK	Cycle Corps, A Company and No III Section, L Company
Kelly, Pte G, KTG	QSA (1) DoK	Premier Mine. 50th Anniversary attendee
Kelly, 242 Pte George, KRV	QSA (1) DoK	Found dead in Kimberley Mine 30 Dec 99. Occupation engine driver
Kelly, Pte H, KTG	QSA (1) DoK	
Kelly, 4272 Pte J, LNLR	QSA (3) DoK OFS Tr	QSA (3), [KSA (2)]. Sotheby Jun 73
Kelly, Pte J, KTG	QSA (1) DoK	Cycle Corps, A Company
Kelly, Pte J D, KTG	QSA (1) DoK	Kamfersdam Company
Kelly, Pte J J, KTG	QSA (1) DoK	No III Section, C Company, Pickering's Redoubt No 1
Kelly, Pte J P, KTG	QSA (1) DoK	No 1 Redoubt. QSA (1). Spink Sep 85 £100. Spink Mar 86 £90
Kelly, Pte John Joseph, KTG	QSA (1) DoK	D Company (Veterans), Beaconsfield Town Guard. Also served SRG (133) from 11 Feb 01
Kelly, Pte R, KTG	QSA (1) DoK	No III Section, L Company
Kelly, Cpl T, KTG	QSA (1) DoK	No IV Section, B Company, Beaconsfield Town Guard
Kelly, Pte W, KTG	QSA (1) DoK	
Kelly, Pte W J, KTG	QSA (1) DoK	N Company, No 1 Redoubt
Kelly, 761 Pte William Edward, KRV	QSA (3) RoM DoK OFS	Discharged 10 Nov 00. Also served KTG (No I Section, C Company, Beaconsfield Town Guard), KLH and DFH
Kemm, Pte H R, KTG	QSA (1) DoK	No II Section, A Company, Beaconsfield Town Guard
Kemp, 39 Tpr Cecil George Eric, KLH	QSA (2) DoK OFS	Served 19 Oct 99 to 23 Mar 00
Kemp, 903 Pte J, KRV	QSA (2) RoM DoK	Discharged 1 Jul 00. Also served KTG (No I Section, F Company, Mostert's Redoubt)
Kemp, 439 Pte T, KRV	QSA (1) DoK	DMU 15 Dec 99
Kempner, Pte L, KTG	QSA (1) DoK	No II Section, K Company
Kemsley, Pte G E, KTG	QSA (1) DoK	In charge of telephone exchange to redoubts
Kendall, Pte A, KTG	QSA (1) DoK	No IV Section, F Company, Mostert's Redoubt. QSA (1), KStar. Noble Numismatics Jul 98
Kendall, Pte J, KTG	QSA (1) DoK	No I Section, D Company
Kendall, 1281 Pte R, KRV	QSA (1) DoK	Discharged 1 Jul 02. Also served KTG (No I Section, D Company). KSA issued in error and recovered
Kennedy, 3667 Pte B, LNLR	QSA (3) DoK OFS Tr	Wounded Zeerust 7 Jan 01. QSA (3), [KSA (2)], KStar. Glendining Dec 93 £140. Spink Dec 95 £185
Kennedy, Pte P, KTG	QSA (4) DoK OFS Tr 01	No II Section, F Company, Mostert's Redoubt. Also served Irregular Co CMSC 27 Jul 00 to 15 Jul 01
Kennedy, 222 Pte S Mc M, KRV	QSA (3) DoK OFS Tr	DMU 19 Dec 00 (month very difficult to read). QSA (3)
Kennedy, 771 Pte Thomas, CP2	QSA (1) DoK	
Kennedy, Pte W, KTG	QSA (1) DoK	Premier Mine
Kennedy, 18 Sgt William, CP2	QSA (1) DoK	CP dismounted branch (barrier & redoubt duties). KSA (2). Note says discharged as unsuitable. Served in the Bechuanaland Rebellion 1897 earning CGHGSM (1) Bech
Kennedy, Pte William Matthew, KTG	QSA (2) DoK OFS	Also served KLH (1062) 15 Mar 00 to 29 Aug 00
Kennett, 28 Bugler G, KRV	QSA (1) DoK	KSA (2). Served in the Bechuanaland Rebellion 1897 earning CGHGSM (1) Bech
Kennett, Pte H J W, KTG	QSA (1) DoK	Premier Mine
Kennett, 1209 Pte W R, KRV	QSA (3) DoK OFS Tr	Also served KTG. KSA (2)

Name	Medals	Notes
Kenniford, Pte William John, KTG	QSA (1) DoK	No II Section, C Company, Pickering's Redoubt No 1. Also served SRG (150) from 11 Feb 01
Kenny, Col Sgt E, KTG	QSA (1) DoK	No II Section, C Company, Pickering's Redoubt No 1
Kenny, 1117 Pte M, KRV	QSA (3) DoK OFS Tr	Discharged 1 Jul 02. Also served KTG (No II Section, B2 Company, No 3 Redoubt). KSA (2)
Kenny, 3561 Pte P, LNLR	QSA (3) DoK OFS Tr	KSA (2)
Kensil, Pte A, KTG	QSA (1) DoK	No IV Section, A Company, Beaconsfield Town Guard
Kent, Pte C, KTG	QSA (1) DoK	No 2 Schmidt's Breastwork and No I Company, B Section, Reservoir
Kenton, 4857 Pte James, LNLR	QSA (1) DoK	Wounded 28 Nov 99. KSA (2)
Kenyon, Pte P H, KTG	QSA (1) DoK	H Company
Keogan, 16 CSM P, KRV	QSA (1) DoK	DMU 7 May 00
Keogh, Pte M, KTG	QSA (1) DoK	Premier Mine
Keown, Pte J, KTG	QSA (1) DoK	No III Section, C Company, Beaconsfield Town Guard
Kerby, Pte A S, KTG	QSA (1) DoK	No I Section, A Company, Beaconsfield Town Guard
Kermeen, Pte W J, KTG	QSA (1) DoK	Premier Mine
Kernick, Pte G S, KTG	QSA (1) DoK	Premier Mine. QSA (1)
Kerr, Cpl E, KTG	QSA (1) DoK	No 1 Redoubt. Possibly served in the Bechuanaland Rebellion 1897 with Kimb Rifles earning CGHGSM (1) Bech
Kerr, 37 Pte James Wyllie, ScH	QSA (3) DoK Tr 01	Served 18 Jan 01 to 7 Aug 01. Also served KRV (234) until 21 Jan 01
Kershaw, Pte C, KTG	QSA (1) DoK	No I Section, Belgravia Fort. QSA (1). Hall Jan 88 £70
Kershaw, Pte C, KTG	QSA (1) DoK	
Kershaw, Sgt J H, KTG	QSA (1) DoK	No II Section, K Company
Kessler, 208 Sgt P, KRV	QSA (4) DoK OFS Tr 01	Non effective 17 Feb 01. Possibly served in the Basuto Wars with Cape Mtd Yeo earning CGHGSM (1) Bas
Kewley, Pte Charles, KTG	QSA (1) DoK	No II Section, Mandy Fort. Headmaster of St Cyprian's College. QSA (1). Spink Oct 99 £80. City Coins May 02
Key, Pte C W, KTG	QSA (1) DoK	No I Section, K Company
Key, Pte J G, KTG	QSA (1) DoK	No 5 supply depot. On nominal roll as Keys
Key, 219 Band J H, KRV	QSA (1) DoK	Non effective 1 May 01. Discharged 23 Aug 02. KSA (2)
Keys, 5593 Pte H A, LNLR	QSA (3) DoK OFS Tr	QSA (3), [KSA (2)]. RHQ
Keytal, Pte H B, KTG	QSA (1) DoK	Civil Service Redoubt
Kidd, Lt A, DFA	QSA (3) DoK OFS Tr	Ops in OFS & Tr. MID 3 Dec 01 for excellent work 24 Aug 01. Resigned 31 Dec 03. KSA (2). Served in the Bechuanaland Rebellion 1897 earning CGHGSM (1) Bech
Kidd, 103 Sgt William Edward, DFA	QSA (2) DoK OFS	Wounded 9 Dec 99. Enrolled 1 Mar 98. Resigned 18 Jul 03. Occupation wire splicer
Kiddle, Pte William Richard, KTG	QSA (1) DoK	No I Section, L Company. Also served CRSS (1035) from 18 Feb 01
Kidwell, 147 Cpl Arthur Charles, KLH	QSA (2) DoK OFS	Served 20 Oct 99 to 14 Mar 00. Also served KTG
Kidwell, Capt Frederick William, SRG	QSA (4) RoM DoK OFS Tr	Served 12 Feb 01 to 31 May 02. Also served KLH (144) 20 Oct 99 to 5 Jun 00. KSA (2). 50th Anniversary attendee
Kidwell, 122 Tpr Lennie Julius, KLH	QSA (3) DoK OFS 01	Served 1 Nov 99 to 14 Mar 00. Also served NH 17 Oct 00 to 31 Dec 01 and Cond ASC. Medal forfeited and returned
Kieser, Pte D F, KTG	QSA (1) DoK	Premier Mine
Kieser, Pte W P, KTG	QSA (1) DoK	Premier Mine
Kilpin, 15893 Gnr G C, RGA	QSA (1) DoK	Died of enteric 4 Feb 00

Name	Medals	Notes
Kilroe, Tpr Geoffrey Richard, DH	QSA (6) DoK Paar Drie Joh DH Witt	Served 18 Feb 00 to 26 Jan 01. Also served KTG (No 2 Schmidt's Breastwork) and FID. DoK incorrectly recorded as RoK on the DH QSA roll. KSA (2). Occupation amalgamator
Kilroe, QMS R, KTG	QSA (1) DoK	No 3 Redoubt
Kilroe, Pte R, KTG	QSA (1) DoK	Otto's Kopje Scouts
Kilroe, Pte T, KTG	QSA (3) DoK OFS Tr	No 3 Redoubt. Also served MH with initials J T. QSA (1) DoK. Christies Nov 85
Kimble, Pte M, KTG	QSA (1) DoK	Cycle Corps, A Company
King, 339 Pte Albert E, KRV	QSA (1) DoK	DMU 19 Mar 00. Also served KLH (82 & 33631) 25 Jun 01 to 20 Mar 02
King, Pte C, KTG	QSA (1) DoK	Construction of forts and barricades etc
King, 594 Pte Charles William, KRV	QSA (4) RoM DoK OFS Tr	Served 11 Oct 99 to 20 Jun 00. Wounded 28 Nov 99. Also served KLH and Lt SAMIF. KSA (2)
King, 149 Tpr Dick Percy, KLH	QSA (2) DoK OFS	Served 20 Oct 99 to 6 Mar 00. Also served KTG
King, 151 Tpr Edward Thomas, KLH	QSA (2) DoK OFS	Served 20 Oct 99 to 7 Mar 00
King, Lt G C, KTG	QSA (1) DoK	Premier Mine
King, Pte G F, KTG	QSA (1) DoK	No I Section, B2 Company, No 3 Redoubt
King, 123 Gnr George Donald, DFA	QSA (1) DoK	Enrolled 13 Oct 98. Discharged 8 Mar 00. Occupation railway carpenter
King, 283 Pte J A, KRV	QSA (1) DoK	DMU 2 Jan 00. Served in the Bechuanaland Rebellion 1897 earning CGHGSM (1) Bech
King, Rev Percy John Feltham, ACD	QSA (1) DoK	Curate of Bethulie 1893-95, Curate of Windsorton 1895-97, Curate of St Cyprians 1899-1903. Rector of Vryburg 1903. He had served as Acting Chaplain to the Forces 1897-99. CGHGSM (1) Bech (Chapn Bech FF), QSA (1) (Rev C to F), KStar. Spink Feb 83 £575. Spink Sep 86 £480
King, 148 Cpl Percy Lloyd, KLH	QSA (2) DoK Paar	Served 19 Oct 99 to 23 Mar 00. Also served KTG, 2nd Life Guards (2389), Lt KDF and Kaffr Rifles
King, Cpl R A, KTG	QSA (1) DoK	No 2 Schmidt's Breastwork. Also served 34th Co ASC (83)
King, Pte W S, KTG	QSA (1) DoK	No I Section, C Company, Pickering's Redoubt No 1. QSA (1)
Kingsbury, 78 Pte Frederick, CP2	QSA (1) DoK	CP dismounted branch (barrier & redoubt duties). QSA (1). eBay Jun 09 £250
Kingston, 37 Pte Frank Henry, CP2	QSA (1) DoK	CP dismounted branch (barrier & redoubt duties). Applied for KSA medal but refused 1930
Kingston, 126 Pte George Gordon, CP2	QSA (1) DoK	CP dismounted branch (barrier & redoubt duties)
Kingston, Pte P A, KTG	QSA (1) DoK	No II Section, C Company, Pickering's Redoubt No 1
Kingswell, 908 Pte H J, KRV	QSA (3) DoK OFS Tr	Discharged 1 Jul 02. Also served KTG (No 3 Redoubt). KSA (2)
Kingwell, 173 Gnr Arthur, DFA	QSA (2) DoK OFS	Enrolled 7 Jan 97 and 18 Jul 99. Occupation draper
Kinley, Pte J, KTG	QSA (1) DoK	No III Section, C Company, Beaconsfield Town Guard
Kinnear, Pte G, KTG	QSA (1) DoK	No III Section, A Company, Beaconsfield Town Guard
Kinnear, 1131 Pte H, KRV	QSA (3) DoK OFS 01	DMU 7 Jan 01. Also served KTG (No III Section, A Company, Beaconsfield Town Guard)
Kinnear, 1133 Pte James William, KRV	QSA (4) DoK OFS Tr 01	Also served KTG (No III Section, A Company, Beaconsfield Town Guard) and ALH (40272) 6 Feb 02 to 24 Mar 02. Occupation blacksmith
Kipling, 34981 RQMS Herbert Samuel, DH	QSA (5) DoK OFS Tr 01 02	Served 18 Jul 01 to 15 Jan 02. Also served KTG (No III Section, No 2 Redoubt). Occupation upholdsterer
Kirby, 3984 Pte A, LNLR	QSA (3) DoK OFS Tr	Wounded 16 Feb 00. QSA (3), [KSA (2)]. Glendining Dec 65. Liverpool Nov 93 £75
Kirby, Pte W, KTG	QSA (1) DoK	Kamfersdam Company

Kirkhan, 197 Tpr W J, SRG	QSA (3) DoK OFS Tr	Also served KTG (No II Section, B Company, No 4 Redoubt) as Kirkman, W
Kirkness, 5549 Pte J, LNLR	QSA (3) DoK OFS Tr	QSA (3), KSA (2), 14 Star, BWM, VM (Sgt Liv Regt), Belgian Croix de Guerre, KStar. Glendining Oct 83
Kirsten, Pte Christian Joseph George, KTG	QSA (2) DoK 02	Pickering's Redoubt No 1. Also served KH (332) 15 May 02 to 30 Jun 02. Surname Kirston on KH roll. QSA (1) excl 02. Spink Dec 75 £60. LSE Sep 84 £85
Kirsten, F B A, KTG	QSA (0)	See his biography (page 347)
Kirton, 290 Pte H, CP1	QSA (2) DoK OFS	A Squadron. On QSA roll as Kurton. Served in the Bechuanaland Rebellion 1897 earning CGHGSM (1) Bech. QSA (2), KSA (2), KStar. Dixon Apr 98 £230
Kitchin, Pte D, KTG	QSA (1) DoK	No 1 Redoubt
Kitching, 1521 Pte J, CP1	QSA (4) RoM DoK OFS Tr	A Squadron. KSA (2)
Kitto, Sgt E J, KTG	QSA (1) DoK	No III Section, D Company
Kitto, Pte J H, KTG	QSA (1) DoK	No I Section, D Company
Klein, 41261 Tpr August, DH	QSA (4) DoK OFS Tr 02	Served 20 Feb 02 to 30 Jun 02. Also served KTG (No II Section, A Company, Beaconsfield Town Guard). QSA (4), KStar. Spink Oct 99 £210
Klein, Pte B, KTG	QSA (1) DoK	No I Section, C Company, Beaconsfield Town Guard
Klein, Pte J, KTG	QSA (1) DoK	No IV Section, A Company, Beaconsfield Town Guard and No III Section, C Company, Beaconsfield Town Guard
Klein, Pte W, KTG	QSA (1) DoK	No IV Section, A Company, Beaconsfield Town Guard
Knight, 194 Gnr Alfred, DFA	QSA (2) DoK 01	Enrolled 25 Aug 99. Served Bechuanaland Field Force 95 to 96. Civil employment from 30 Apr 01. Discharged 17 Feb 03. Occupation guard at De Beers
Knight, 231 Tpr Charles James, KLH	QSA (3) RoM DoK OFS	Served 19 Oct 99 to 5 Jun 00. Also served ORCP (294) 6 Aug 00 to 6 Nov 00, DH 19 Nov 00 to 14 Nov 01 and FID 29 Dec 01 to 31 May 02. KSA (2). Served in the Bechuanaland Rebellion 1897 earning CGHGSM (1) Bech
Knight, 4541 Pioneer F, LNLR	QSA (3) DoK OFS Tr	KSA (2)
Knight, 200 Pte Frank S, KRV	QSA (3) RoM DoK OFS	Wounded 28 Nov 99. Non effective 20 Jun 00
Knight, Cpl H J, KTG	QSA (1) DoK	Mounted Section, B Company, Beaconsfield Town Guard
Knight, Pte J, KTG	QSA (1) DoK	
Knight, 11410 Gnr John Henry, RGA	QSA (1) DoK	KSA (2)
Knight, Pte P, KTG	QSA (1) DoK	No I Section, C Company, Beaconsfield Town Guard
Knight, Pte W A, KTG	QSA (1) DoK	No I Section, C Company, Beaconsfield Town Guard
Knott, 94947 Gnr Leonard C, RGA	QSA (1) DoK	Premier Mine. Invalided and discharged 16 Jun 01
Knowles, 4858 Pte J, LNLR	QSA (3) DoK OFS Tr	KSA (2)
Knowles, Pte J, KTG	QSA (1) DoK	No III Section, D Company. In charge of water supply to cattle and horses
Knowles, 3973 Pte T, LNLR	QSA (3) DoK OFS Tr	KSA (2)
Knowles, Pte W, KTG	QSA (1) DoK	No I Section, F Company, Mostert's Redoubt. QSA (1). Langridge Feb 76 £50. Spink May 02. Could be next man
Knowles, Pte W, KTG	QSA (1) DoK	No III Company, A Section, Reservoir
Koen, 150 Tpr Herman, KLH	QSA (2) DoK OFS	Served 20 Oct 99 to 6 Mar 00
Koen, 1061 Tpr Jacob, KLH	QSA (2) DoK OFS	Served 26 Oct 99 to 10 Nov 00. Also served DH (35510 & 41823) 10 Jul 01 to 18 Feb 02 and 10 Mar 02 to 30 Jun 02. KSA (2)
Koen, Pte P, KTG	QSA (1) DoK	No I Section, K Company

Koningsberg, Pte A, KTG	QSA (1) DoK	No II Company, A Section, Reservoir and No II Section, K Company
Kromm, 349 Tpr Philip, KLH	QSA (2) DoK OFS	Served 10 Nov 99 to 7 Mar 00. Nominal roll says dismissed for misconduct
Kube, Pte C, KTG	QSA (1) DoK	Gibraltar Fort, Davis's Heap
Kukard, 1273 Pte F F G, CP1	QSA (2) DoK OFS	A Squadron. Served in the Bechuanaland Rebellion 1897 earning CGHGSM (1) Bech. QSA (2), [KSA (2)]
Kuppers, 239 Pte Walter, CP2	QSA (4) RoM DoK OFS Tr	Roll says died of disease (not on casualty roll)
Kurten, Pte H, KTG	QSA (1) DoK	No III Section, A Company, Beaconsfield Town Guard. QSA (1). Seaby Aug 80 £140. Spink Jan 84 £125
Kurten, 311 Tpr Walter Otto, KLH	QSA (3) RoM DoK OFS	Served 24 Oct 99 to 5 Jun 00

L

Lace, Pte E, KTG	QSA (1) DoK	Died 9 Dec 99
Ladyson, Pte W, KTG	QSA (1) DoK	No IV Section, B Company, No 4 Redoubt. Surname also seen as Ladych. SAGS (1) 1879 (KH), CGHGSM (1) Bas (KH), QSA (1), KStar. Kaplan Oct 05
Laing, 132 Gnr Charles T, RGA	QSA (1) DoK	Otto's Kopje. KSA (2)
Laing, Pte J, KTG	QSA (1) DoK	Premier Mine
Laing, Pte J, KTG	QSA (1) DoK	No IV Section, C Company, Beaconsfield Town Guard
Laing, 92 L Cpl L R, KRV	QSA (1) DoK	DMU 9 Feb 00
Laing, QMS R C H, KTG	QSA (1) DoK	No 1 Redoubt
Laird, W, KTG	QSA (0)	Roll states "Carpentering general work and repairing wagons"
Lambe, 74 Sgt Henry, CP2	QSA (4) RoM DoK OFS Tr	A Squadron. KSA (2)
Lambert, Mr A J, POC	QSA (1) DoK	
Lambert, Pte H R, KTG	QSA (1) DoK	
Lambert, 4338 Pte T, LNLR	QSA (3) DoK OFS Tr	KSA (2). Nr 4538 on KSA roll
Lambourne, Lt G, KTG	QSA (1) DoK	No I Section, D Company
Lamont, Pte A, KTG	QSA (1) DoK	H Company
Lancaster, Clerk H J, ASC	QSA (4) DoK OFS 01 02	Also served KTG (No I Section, No 2 Redoubt). Possibly also served Warrenton TG (102). 50th Anniversary attendee
Lancaster, 4749 Pte J, LNLR	QSA (4) DoK OFS Tr 01	
Land, 3770 Gnr Hubert, RGA	QSA (3) DoK OFS Tr	QSA (3), KSA (2), KStar. Lusted 73 £68
Lane, Pte C, KTG	QSA (1) DoK	No I Company, B Section, Reservoir
Lange, Pte W F, KTG	QSA (1) DoK	Premier Mine
Langford, 595 Pte A W T, KRV	QSA (2) DoK Paar	DMU 4 Apr 00
Langford, Sgt R E, KTG	QSA (1) DoK	No I Section, A Company, Beaconsfield Town Guard and Gibraltar Fort, Davis's Heap
Langley, Pte J H, KTG	QSA (3) DoK 01 02	No I Company, B Section, Reservoir. Also served UVR (685). QSA (1) excl 01 & 02, KStar. Spink Dec 85 £100. DNW Mar 08 £330. DNW Dec 09 £330
Langmaid, Pte C C, KTG	QSA (1) DoK	Premier Mine
Langman, 677 Pte W H A, KRV	QSA (3) DoK OFS Tr	Discharged 1 Jul 02. Also served CP. KSA (2)
Langsley, Pte Sheridan Alexander, KTG	QSA (7) DoK Paar Drie Joh DH Witt 01	Mounted Section, B Company, Beaconsfield Town Guard. Also served DH 20 Feb 00 to 26 Jan 01 with surname Lansley. Prisoner at Sanna's Post 31 Mar 00

Lanhoff, Pte S, KTG	QSA (1) DoK	
Lanigan, 25 Tpr D J, KLH	QSA (2) DoK OFS	Served 18 Oct 99 until DMU 24 Mar 00. Wounded 25 Nov 99
Lanz, Pte F, KTG	QSA (1) DoK	No IV Section, No 2 Redoubt
Lardner-Burke, Sgt C T, KTG	QSA (1) DoK	
Larney, E248 3rd Tpr J, SAC	QSA (2) DoK OFS	Also served KTG (No 2 Schmidt's Breastwork). QSA (2). Harwood Nov 80 £120. Dixon Sep 83 £215. Liverpool Oct 87 £60
Laskey, 86 Cpl John, KLH	QSA (4) RoM DoK OFS Tr	Served 19 Oct 99 to 30 Apr 01. Also served CinCBG (22708) 17 Nov 00 to 16 May 01, SRG (591) from 28 May 01 and CPS (726) as Lasky. QSA (4). Liverpool Mar 86 £245
Laverack, Rev G W, KTG	QSA (1) DoK	Reverend. Ambulance Corps, Beaconsfield Town Guard
Laversage, 240 Pte Ferdinand, CP2	QSA (1) DoK	Entry crossed through on QSA roll but appears on the nominal roll as serving with A Squadron
Lavin, 353 Tpr George Michael, KLH	QSA (2) DoK OFS	Joined 14 Nov 99. Deserted 2 May 00. Medal issued. Also served BS (487) with initials J W V and CPS (34). KSA (2)
Law, 401 Tpr A, KLH	QSA (5) RoM DoK OFS Tr 01	Discharged 15 Apr 01. QSA (4) excl 01. Walland Sep 87 £375
Law, Pte A, KTG	QSA (1) DoK	No 2 Schmidt's Breastwork
Law, Pte Charles, KTG	QSA (1) DoK	B line of defence, No 3 Redoubt. Also served CRSS (1465) from 5 Dec 01. Occupation seaman
Law, Pte E G, KTG	QSA (1) DoK	Kimberley Mine Ambulance Company, E Section
Law, Cpl J, KTG	QSA (1) DoK	No III Section, Belgravia Fort
Law, Pte W, KTG	QSA (1) DoK	In charge of dynamo room
Lawler, Pte M, KTG	QSA (1) DoK	No I Section, No 2 Redoubt. KStar. Spink Dec 85 £55
Lawn, Pte J G, KTG	QSA (1) DoK	No I Section, Belgravia Fort
Lawrence, 442 Sgt A E, CP1	QSA (4) RoM DoK OFS Tr	Initial possibly G. CGHGSM (1) Bech (L Cpl CP), QSA (3) excl RoM, [KSA (2)], KStar. Christies Apr 91 £154
Lawrence, Pte C G, KTG	QSA (1) DoK	Premier Mine. QSA (1). City Coins Jan 80. eMedals Aug 09
Lawrence, Pte D, KTG	QSA (1) DoK	No I Section, B Company, No 4 Redoubt
Lawrence, Sister H E A, NS	QSA (0)	Joined staff 7 Feb 00. Also on SAC roll with clasps DoK, OFS & Tr crossed through and with forename Charlotte
Lawrence, 1087 Pte H J, KRV	QSA (4) RoM DoK OFS Tr	Discharged 23 Jul 02. Also served KTG (No III Section, B2 Company, No 3 Redoubt) and KLH (911). Slightly wounded at Platberg 31 Dec 01. KSA (2)
Lawrence, Pte J R, KTG	QSA (1) DoK	No II Company, A Section, Reservoir
Lawrence, 25 CSM N, KRV	QSA (1) DoK	KSA (2). Served in the Bechuanaland Rebellion 1897 earning CGHGSM (1) Bech
Lawrence, 131 Tpr Robert Duthie, KLH	QSA (2) DoK OFS	Served 23 Oct 99 to 7 Mar 00. QSA (2), KStar. City Coins May 02
Lawrence, Pte W, KTG	QSA (1) DoK	No I Section, B Company, No 4 Redoubt
Lawrence, Pte W, KTG	QSA (1) DoK	No I Section, Belgravia Fort
Lawrence, Pte William, KTG	QSA (1) DoK	No 2 supply depot. QSA (1), KStar. Glendining Sep 90 £100
Lawrence, Lt William, KTG	QSA (1) DoK	No IV Section, No 2 Redoubt. Born Brechin, Scotland. Served in the Bechuanaland Rebellion 1897 earning CGHGSM (1) Bech
Lawrenson, Pte J, KTG	QSA (1) DoK	
Lawrie, Pte A J, KTG	QSA (1) DoK	Kenilworth Defence Force
Lawry, Pte E, KTG	QSA (2) DoK OFS	No I Section, L Company. Also served ETG as Lowry and JTG. Note says 'Returned Edenburg TG'

Lawson, 152 Tpr Charles Frederick, KLH	QSA (2) DoK Paar	See his biography (page 347)
Lawson, 1113 Pte E R, KRV	QSA (4) RoM DoK OFS Tr	Discharged 26 Jul 02. Also served KTG (No IV Section, C Company, Beaconsfield Town Guard) and KLH. KSA (2)
Lawson, Pte J, KTG	QSA (1) DoK	D Company (Veterans), Beaconsfield Town Guard
Lawson, Pte P, KTG	QSA (1) DoK	No IV Section, L Company
Lawson, 813 Pte T H, KRV	QSA (2) DoK OFS	Discharged 1 Jul 02. Also served KTG (No III Company, A Section, Reservoir). KSA (2)
Le Cordeur, Pte August Peter, KTG	QSA (3) DoK OFS Tr	No III Section, B Company, Beaconsfield Town Guard. Also served WS (5) 19 Mar 00 to 20 Jul 00. Wounded Oliphant's Nek 20 Jul 00 and died same day
Le Cordeur, Pte J, KTG	QSA (3) DoK OFS Tr	6 Tpr Martin Le Cordeur on WS roll with CC, OFS & Tr and on CPS (65) roll. Same man?
Lea, 337 Tpr St John, KLH	QSA (3) DoK OFS Tr	Served 3 Nov 99 to 5 Dec 00. QSA roll has 5 Dec 99. Also served KTG (H Company) with surname Lee. Possibly also served BR (242) to 3 Sep 01 with surname Lee. This man and the next look to be one and the same but there is nothing to connect them
Lea, 712 Pte St John Wildman, CP2	QSA (1) DoK	DMU. Note says 'issued from 21st Co IY'
Leach, 805 Pte B W, KRV	QSA (1) DoK	Also served KTG (No 2 Schmidt's Breastwork). Discharged 25 Mar 02. BSACM rev Rhodesia 1896 (Tpr Gwelo Vols), QSA (1), [KSA (2)], KStar. City Coins Feb 95
Leach, 222 Dvr Sidney, DFA	QSA (3) DoK OFS Tr	Enrolled 22 Dec 99. Resigned 1 Jul 02. Occupation overseer. KSA (2). KSA nr 226
Leach, Pte Sidney Oxford, KTG	QSA (1) DoK	Also served SRG (62) from 11 Feb 01 and DFH
Leach, 1278 Pay Sgt William Aylward, KLH	QSA (4) RoM DoK OFS Tr	Served from 20 Oct 99 and Mar 02 to 30 Jun 02. Also served SRG (591). KSA (2)
Lean, Pte J J, KTG	QSA (1) DoK	No I Section, F Company, Mostert's Redoubt. In charge of cattle kraal guards. QSA (1). Harwood Nov 80 £120. Liverpool Aug 82 £110. Dixon Sep 83 £100
Leck, Pte J, KTG	QSA (1) DoK	Medical Corps, No 1 Company, C Section. 50th Anniversary attendee
Leck, Pte W, KTG	QSA (1) DoK	Medical Corps, No 1 Company, C Section
Leckie, Cpl James Alexander, KTG	QSA (2) DoK OFS	No II Section, B2 Company, No 3 Redoubt. Also served KLH (153) and SRG (58) from 12 Feb 01
Leddy, Pte Henry William, KTG	QSA (1) DoK	No II Section, C Company, Pickering's Redoubt No 2. Also served SRG (912) from 20 May 01
Ledger, Mr B B, POC	QSA (1) DoK	50th Anniversary attendee
Lee, 370 Tpr Edward Joseph, KLH	QSA (4) RoM DoK OFS Tr	Served 15 Dec 99 to 5 Jun 00. Also served KTG (Food Supply Stores), KitH (9640) to 15 Jan 01, MMR (138), SRG (498) from 27 Mar 01 (dismissed misconduct) and Canadian Scouts (38081) 15 Jan 02 to 30 Jun 02. QSA with CC & OFS issued and recovered by MMR. KSA (2). Occupation cook. Possibly served in the Bechuanaland Rebellion 1897 earning CGHGSM (1) Bech
Lee, 4942 Pte G, LNLR	QSA (3) DoK Tr 01	QSA (1) DoK. Glendining Dec 65. Glendining Jun 90 £97. Spink Oct 90 £130
Lee, Pte G T, KTG	QSA (1) DoK	No III Section, B Company, No 4 Redoubt. Possibly served in the Bechuanaland Rebellion 1897 earning CGHGSM (1) Bech
Lee, 3983 Pte H, LNLR	QSA (2) DoK OFS	Wounded 24 Oct 99 and 28 Nov 99. KSA (2)
Lee, Pte J, KTG	QSA (1) DoK	No I Company, B Section, Reservoir
Lee, Pte J, KTG	QSA (1) DoK	No I Section, Mostert's Redoubt
Lee, 192 Tpr John Bunting, KLH	QSA (2) DoK OFS	Served 1 Nov 99 until DMU 23 Apr 00

Lee, 4463 Pte P, LNLR	QSA (3) DoK OFS Tr	KSA (2). Initial J on KSA roll
Lee, Pte R M, KTG	QSA (1) DoK	No II Section, F Company, Mostert's Redoubt. QSA (1). City Coins Dec 04. Dixon Dec 05 £200
Leeming, 4708 Pte J, LNLR	QSA (4) DoK OFS Tr 01	KSA (2). Invalided to England 8 Jan 01. RoM marked for issue and removed
Lees, Pte A, KTG	QSA (1) DoK	Working searchlight
Lees, Pte John, KTG	QSA (1) DoK	Reserve Section, D Company. Working searchlight. KStar. Hamilton Jan 85 £60
Leeson, 329 Tpr F J, KLH	QSA (2) DoK OFS	Discharged 3 Apr 00. Also served KTG (Premier Mine). Served in the Bechuanaland Rebellion 1897 earning CGHGSM (1) Bech
Leeson, Pte F S, KTG	QSA (1) DoK	Gibraltar Fort, Davis's Heap
Lefevre, 108 Cpl Charles, DFA	QSA (2) DoK OFS	Enrolled 21 Apr 98. Wounded 9 Dec 99. Transferred to Kimb Regt 1 Apr 07. Occupation ironmonger. KSA (2). 50th Anniversary attendee
Legg, Capt Archer Sidney, CP2	QSA (4) Rhod RoM DoK Tr	KSA (2)
Leggatt, 295 Tpr James, KLH	QSA (4) DoK OFS Tr 01	Served 23 Oct 99 until DMU 23 Mar 00 as Leggate. Also served RoH (9141) 15 May 00 to 22 Mar 01, SRG (269) as Legate from 27 Mar 01 and CPS (724) as Legate. Occupation fitter. QSA (2) excl Tr & 01, KStar. City Coins May 02. Dixon Sep 02 £340
Leggatt, Pte William H A, KTG	QSA (1) DoK	Premier Mine. Also served Somerset East TG (68) to 21 Aug 01 and MMR (no trace on QSA roll)
Legward, 1311 Tpr Charles, KLH	QSA (2) DoK OFS	Served 20 Oct 99 until DMU 24 Mar 00. Wounded 25 Nov 99. Number also 1309. Also served Lt SRG (7) from 12 Feb 01
Leigh, 187 Pte John, CP2	QSA (1) DoK	CP dismounted branch (barrier & redoubt duties). Dismissed for misconduct (breach of discipline). Also served CPS (224) and suggests medal issued from CPS. Served in the Bechuanaland Rebellion 1897 earning CGHGSM (1) Bech
Leimer, 309 Tpr O F, KLH	QSA (2) DoK OFS	Served 10 Nov 99 to 5 Dec 99. Also served KTG
Leipoldt, 557 Pte Peter, KRV	QSA (1) DoK	Killed in action 24 Oct 99
Leishman, 1476 Pte O S, CP1	QSA (4) RoM DoK OFS Tr	B Squadron. Served GSWA 22 Feb to 25 May 1915. Officer Commanding Kroonstad District in 1920. QSA (4), KSA (2), 14-15 Star (Lt Hartigan's Horse), BWM, VM (Lt). Sotheby Dec 98. Liverpool Feb 99 £395. Liverpool Jan 10 £850
Leithar, Pte F W, KTG	QSA (1) DoK	There is a Pte H Liether of G Company on the nominal roll. Same man? QSA (1). Burman Jul 03 £165. eBay Sep 05 £255. eBay Oct 05 £220
Leonard, Pte E, KTG	QSA (1) DoK	No III Section, B Company, No 4 Redoubt
Leonard, Pte G, KTG	QSA (1) DoK	
Leppan, 1784 Cpl V, CP1	QSA (2) DoK Tr	A Squadron
Leslie, J, KTG	QSA (0)	Roll states "Electrical work; dynamo room"
Leslie, 177 Cpl John Durant, CP2	QSA (3) DoK OFS Tr	C Squadron. KSA (2). Served in the Bechuanaland Rebellion 1897 earning CGHGSM (1) Bech
Lester, 506 Pte Charles Reginald, KRV	QSA (2) DoK OFS	See his biography (page 347)
Leversage, 41306 Tpr Frederick, DH	QSA (4) DoK OFS Tr 02	Served 24 Feb 02 to 27 May 02. Also served CP2 (240) 10 Oct 99 to 4 Dec 00. Served in the Bechuanaland Rebellion 1897 earning CGHGSM (1) Bech. QSA (4)
Levey, Pte G J, KTG	QSA (1) DoK	No I Company, B Section, Reservoir

Levi, 4529 Pte W, LNLR	QSA (3) DoK OFS Tr	KSA (2)
Levinshon, Pte S, KTG	QSA (1) DoK	
Levis, 442 Pte James George, CP2	QSA (1) DoK	A Squadron. A Jameson Raider. [BSACM Rev Rhod 96], QSA (1), [KSA (2)], KStar. City Coins Dec 04. Liverpool Jun 05 £210
Levy, Pte Thomas, KTG	QSA (2) DoK Tr	No III Section, C Company, Beaconsfield Town Guard. Also served KLH (1063) as Levey 24 Apr 00 to 6 Nov 00
Lewis, 70013 Gnr Antony, RGA	QSA (3) DoK OFS 01	
Lewis, Pte Arthur Desmond, KTG	QSA (1) DoK	Premier Mine. Also served SRG (60) from 11 Feb 01
Lewis, 5302 Cpl C, LNLR	QSA (3) DoK OFS Tr	KSA (2)
Lewis, Pte C, KTG	QSA (1) DoK	No 3 Redoubt
Lewis, Pte J, KTG	QSA (2) DoK Tr	G Company. Also served BR (198)
Lewis, Pte M, KTG	QSA (1) DoK	G Company. 50th Anniversary attendee
Lewis, 716 Pte R, KRV	QSA (1) DoK	DMU 18 May 00
Lewis, Pte Richard Ernest, KTG	QSA (2) DoK Tr	H Company. Also served KLH (1170) 20 Apr 00 to 9 Nov 00, 1st ILH (1532) 17 Nov 00 to 6 Dec 00 (dismissed with ignominy), DrS (22999) 15 Dec 00 to 2 Jul 01 and CLH (932) 16 Sep 01 to 17 Mar 02. KSA (2)
Lewis, 14115 Pte W, ASC	QSA (4) Nat DoK OFS Tr	
Lewis, Pte William, KTG	QSA (4) DoK OFS DH Belf	Also served KLH (90) 2 Nov 99 until dismissed 24 Dec 99, RoH (4573) 3 Mar 00 to 29 Dec 00 and MH (25981) 13 Jan 01 to 31 May 02. KSA (2)
Lewis-Roberts, Pte T A, KTG	QSA (1) DoK	
Leyland, 4349 Pte W, LNLR	QSA (3) DoK OFS Tr	Invalided to England 8 Feb 01. QSA (3), KSA (2), KStar. LSE Sep 83 £175
Lezard, Pte H, KTG	QSA (1) DoK	No IV Section, F Company, Mostert's Redoubt
Lezard, Pte Julien C, KTG	QSA (1) DoK	Otto's Kopje and Kimberley Mine Ambulance Company, A Section. Occupation jeweller
Lezard, Pte Louis F, KTG	QSA (1) DoK	No IV Section, F Company, Mostert's Redoubt. Served in the Bechuanaland Rebellion 1897 earning CGHGSM (1) Bech. 50th Anniversary attendee
Liddall, Cpl L B, KTG	QSA (1) DoK	No IV Section, B Company, Beaconsfield Town Guard. Also served Sgt FS (annotation difficult to read)
Liddell, Mr H G, POC	QSA (1) DoK	QSA (1), KStar. Sotheby Mar 79
Liddiard, 142 Bugler Eaben John, KRV	QSA (2) DoK OFS	See his biography (page 348)
Liebenberg, Pte C, KTG	QSA (1) DoK	Gibraltar Fort, Davis's Heap
Liesching, Pte C F, KTG	QSA (1) DoK	Premier Mine
Liesching, Pte Fred Thomas, KTG	QSA (2) DoK 01	Premier Mine. Also served DH 19 Nov 00 to 19 Dec 01
Liesching, Pte Philip, KTG	QSA (2) DoK Tr	Premier Mine. Also served SRG (922) from 23 May 01
Lill, 1347 Pte A E, CP1	QSA (2) DoK OFS	A Squadron. Discharged time expired 20 Feb 01. Also served FID and Lt ORS
Limberg, Pte C, KTG	QSA (1) DoK	
Lindsay, QMS J, KTG	QSA (1) DoK	L Company. Possibly served in the Bechuanaland Rebellion 1897 with Kimb Rifles as Vet Lt earning CGHGSM (1) Bech
Linehan, Pte T G, KTG	QSA (1) DoK	Belgravia Fort
Ling, Pte B, KTG	QSA (1) DoK	No II Company, A Section, Reservoir
Ling, Pte W J, KTG	QSA (1) DoK	No I Section, Mandy Fort

Medal roll

Lingard, 596 Pte W, KRV	QSA (3) RoM DoK OFS	Discharged 4 Jul 01. Also served KTG
Lippiatt, 3910 Pte G, LNLR	QSA (3) DoK OFS Tr	KSA (2)
Lithie, Pte C, KTG	QSA (1) DoK	Cycle Corps, A Company
Litkie, Capt E M, KRV	QSA (1) DoK	Paymaster. Died of disease 12 Dec 99. Not on roll
Litkie, 164 Bombdr Edward Maxmillan, DFA	QSA (1) DoK	Enrolled 3 Jul 99. Served Kimb Rifles Jan 91 to Jan 97 and Matabeleland Relief Force Apr to Dec 96. Struck off 19 Sep 03. Occupation electrician at De Beers
Little, Pte A, KTG	QSA (1) DoK	No I Company, A Section, Reservoir
Liver, Mr A, POC	QSA (1) DoK	QSA (1). Dixon May 88 £140
Livingstone, 878 Sgt J, KRV	QSA (2) DoK OFS	Discharged 21 Mar 02. Also served KTG (Kamfersdam Company). KSA (2)
Llewellyn, 165 Gnr Louie Gwilym, DFA	QSA (1) DoK	Enrolled 4 Jul 99. Served RN 94 to 97. Resigned 2 Apr 03. Occupation electrician at De Beers
Lloyd, Pte J P, KTG	QSA (1) DoK	No III Section, L Company
Lloyd, Mr W, POC	QSA (1) DoK	
Locke, 673 Pte Walter, CP2	QSA (1) DoK	CP dismounted branch (barrier & redoubt duties)
Locker, Pte H E, KTG	QSA (1) DoK	No I Section, A Company, Beaconsfield Town Guard
Lockhart, 1405 Pte A A, CP1	QSA (2) DoK OFS	Possibly served B Squadron. KSA (2)
Lockhart, 1068 Pte H T, KRV	QSA (4) DoK OFS 01 02	Also served KTG (Otto's Kopje Company) and CPS. Non effective 3 Jan 01. QSA (4), KStar. Spink Dec 88
Lodder, Pte J C, KTG	QSA (1) DoK	
Lodder, Pte James, KTG	QSA (1) DoK	Also served CRSS (1295) from 28 May 01. QSA (1). Neate Feb 93 £80. Glendining Jun 93
Lodder, 477 Pte W H, KRV	QSA (3) DoK OFS Tr	KSA (2)
Loder, 854 Pte J O, CP1	QSA (3) DoK OFS Tr	A Squadron. KSA (2). Served in the Bechuanaland Rebellion 1897 earning CGHGSM (1) Bech
Lodge, Pte Hubert, KTG	QSA (1) DoK	No I Section, K Company. KStar. SAMMH
Lodge, 1095 Pte J A, KRV	QSA (3) DoK OFS 01	DoM clasp shown on the roll and crossed out with a note says DoK issued. OFS and SA01 added and issued 7 Jul 14
Lodge, Pte W A, KTG	QSA (1) DoK	Food Supply Staff
Lofts, 7426 Bombdr George, RGA	QSA (2) DoK OFS	QSA (2), [KSA (2)]. Spink May 78 £85
Logan, Pte J R, KTG	QSA (1) DoK	Premier Mine
Logie, 232 Tpr D, KLH	QSA (2) DoK OFS	Served 19 Oct 99 to 30 Apr 00
Lomax, 4677 Sgt J, LNLR	QSA (3) DoK OFS Tr	QSA (3), KSA (2), KStar. LSE Sep 84 £135. Glendining Jun 91 £140
London, 22707 SQMS John, CinCBG	QSA (4) DoK OFS Tr 01	Served 20 Nov 00 to 19 May 01. Also served KTG and CP. Occupation engineer
Lonergan, 25965 Gnr Pat, RGA	QSA (1) DoK	Note says "To 16th Co RGA China"
Long, Pte Arthur Herbert, KTG	QSA (1) DoK	Premier Mine. Also served SRG (59) from 11 Feb 01
Long, 866 Pte C F, KRV	QSA (2) DoK 01	DMU 8 Nov 00. Also served KTG (No IV Section, F Company, Mostert's Redoubt)
Long, 728 Pte J S, KRV	QSA (4) DoK OFS Tr 02	Non effective 12 Sep 00. Discharged 14 May 02. Also served KTG (No II Section, B2 Company, No 3 Redoubt)
Long, 2302 Sapr M, RE	QSA (3) DoK Drie Tr	KSA (2)
Long, Pte W J, KTG	QSA (1) DoK	No I Section, C Company, Pickering's Redoubt No 1

195

Longcake, Pte N W, KTG	QSA (1) DoK	No III Section, F Company, No 3 Redoubt
Longhurst, Sgt A, KTG	QSA (1) DoK	No 1 Redoubt
Longmore, 154 Tpr Charles Croker, KLH	QSA (3) DoK Paar Tr	Served 20 Oct 99 to 14 Mar 00. QSA (1) issued by KTG. Also served Lt BS from 17 Nov 01. CGHGSM (1) Bech (Tpr Transport Corps), [QSA (3), KSA (2)]. Dixon Apr 03
Lonie, Pte John, KTG	QSA (1) DoK	Kamfersdam Company. Also served SRG (926) from 25 May 01
Lord, Pte Edward S, KTG	QSA (2) DoK Tr	Otto's Kopje Scouts. Also served KLH (1121) 16 Mar 00 to 16 Dec 00
Lord, 4535 Pte H, LNLR	QSA (3) DoK OFS Tr	KSA (2)
Lorimer, Pte G, KTG	QSA (1) DoK	Premier Mine
Lorimer, Capt Samuel, CP2	QSA (2) DoK OFS	CP dismounted branch (barrier & redoubt duties). Also served with Roberts' force after the siege and as Major ORCP. In Nov 01 he organised the Cape Criminal Investigation Dept. KSA (2). Occupation Inspector of Police
Loriston, A, KTG	QSA (0)	Roll states "Water pump. Engine driver"
Lotter, 693 Pte Martinus Johannes, CP2	QSA (1) DoK	CP dismounted in Beaconsfield. Served in the Bechuanaland Rebellion 1897 earning CGHGSM (1) Bech
Loudon, A H, KTG	QSA (0)	Roll states "Construction of forts, barricades etc"
Louw, Pte W J, KTG	QSA (1) DoK	No III Company, A Section, Reservoir
Lovegrove, Sgt F R, KTG	QSA (1) DoK	No I Section, No 2 Redoubt
Low, 1154 Pte Arthur John, KRV	QSA (3) DoK OFS Tr	Also served KLH (345) 6 Nov 99 to 24 May 00 and CPS (706) as Lowe. KSA (2)
Low, 339 Tpr Peter George, KLH	QSA (3) DoK OFS 01	Served 24 Apr 00 until DMU 30 Apr 00. Also served 2nd BoH 6 Nov 00 to 21 Jan 01, WMI (222) 24 Jan 01 to 19 Jul 01, Worcester DMT and DEOVR (3237) 27 Jan 02 to 21 Jun 02 as Louw. Occupation miner and plate layer
Lowden, Pte H, KTG	QSA (1) DoK	B line of defence, No 3 Redoubt
Lowden, Pte J W, KTG	QSA (1) DoK	No III Section, D Company. Water supply; inspecting mains
Lowdon, Pte J H, KTG	QSA (1) DoK	No 6 Redoubt
Lowdon, Pte T, KTG	QSA (1) DoK	No 6 Redoubt
Lowe, 1340 Band C W, KRV	QSA (4) DoK OFS 01 02	Discharged 21 Jul 00 and again 30 Jun 02
Lowenburg, 424 Pte L, KRV	QSA (2) DoK 01	DMU 8 Mar 01
Lown, Pte D E, KTG	QSA (1) DoK	No III Section, F Company, No 3 Redoubt
Lowndes, Capt John Gordon, LNLR	QSA (1) DoK	See his biography (page 348)
Lowrie, Pte J, KTG	QSA (1) DoK	Premier Mine
Lowther, Pte John, KTG	QSA (1) DoK	No 1 Redoubt. Also served CRSS (1085) from 11 Mar 01
Lowther, Pte R, KTG	QSA (1) DoK	
Lubbe, 745 Pte Johannes Jacobus, CP2	QSA (1) DoK	B Squadron. Killed in action 3 Nov 99
Lucas, Lt Claude Davis, KTG	QSA (1) DoK	See his biography (page 348)
Lucas, 226 Cpl H C, KRV	QSA (2) DoK 01	Non effective 10 Jan 01. QSA (2). Spink Oct 99 £150. QSA (2), KStar. Elite Collections Nov 01 £275
Lucas, Capt J T, KTG	QSA (1) DoK	Not on roll. Served in the Bechuanaland Rebellion 1897 earning CGHGSM (1) Bech
Lucas, 71 Sgt Joseph J, CP2	QSA (1) DoK	B Squadron
Lucey, 155 Tpr Timothy Michael, KLH	QSA (3) DoK Paar Tr	Served 19 Oct 99 to 6 Mar 00
Ludick, Pte R, KTG	QSA (1) DoK	Also served Cond Crosbie's Transport

Luman, Pte H M, KTG	QSA (1) DoK	No IV Section, K Company
Lunnon, Mr W C, POC	QSA (1) DoK	Telegraph signaller
Lunt, 208 Tpr George Walters, KLH	QSA (2) DoK OFS	Served 20 Oct 99 until DMU 16 Mar 00. Also served KTG
Lunt, Pte T W, KTG	QSA (1) DoK	Kamfersdam Company
Lunt, Pte W H, KTG	QSA (1) DoK	Kamfersdam Company
Luscombe, Pte J, KTG	QSA (1) DoK	D Company (Veterans), Beaconsfield Town Guard
Luscombe, Pte W, KTG	QSA (1) DoK	No 1 Redoubt
Lust, 178 Sgt John, DFA	QSA (3) DoK OFS Tr	Enrolled 8 Aug 99. Also served DFH. Resigned 7 Jul 03. KSA (2). Occupation guard at De Beers
Lutner, 3746 Pte T, LNLR	QSA (1) DoK	Killed in action 28 Nov 99
Luxon, Pte Thomas Henry, KTG	QSA (3) RoM DoK OFS	Kimberley Mine Ambulance Company, A Section. Also served KLH (438) to 5 Jun 00 and SRG (559) from 10 May 01. Served in the Bechuanaland Rebellion 1897 earning CGHGSM (1) Bech. QSA (1) DoK, KStar. Sotheby Mar 86
Lyall, Cpl A F, KTG	QSA (1) DoK	No II Section, No 2 Redoubt
Lyle, Pte James, KTG	QSA (5) DoK OFS Tr 01 02	No 2 Schmidt's Breastwork. Also served ScH (383 & 26051) 8 Jan 01 to 7 Aug 01, DH (37955) 31 Aug 01 to 19 Mar 02 and KH (252). Occupation painter
Lynch, Pte F, KTG	QSA (1) DoK	No I Section, Belgravia Fort
Lynch, Lt F S, KTG	QSA (1) DoK	Water Supply Officer. QSA (1). McGregor Museum
Lynn, 636 Pte J, KRV	QSA (1) DoK	Discharged 1 Jul 02. KSA (2)
Lyon, QMS D M, KTG	QSA (1) DoK	Pickering's Redoubt No 1 and No IV Section, C Company, No 2 Redoubt
Lyons, Pte L H, KTG	QSA (1) DoK	D Company (Veterans), Beaconsfield Town Guard

M

Mabbett, 2811 Sgt G, LNLR	QSA (3) DoK OFS Tr	KSA (2). MID 4 Sep 01
Macauley, Pte J H, KTG	QSA (1) DoK	No II Section, No 2 Redoubt
Macdonald, 827 Pte Andrew Fraser, KRV	QSA (2) DoK OFS	Served 13 Mar 00 to 18 Jun 01. Also served KTG and CRSS (1326) 26 Jul 01 to 31 May 02. KSA (2). Occupation clerk
MacDougall, Lt Ewan Alan, KLH	QSA (3) DoK Paar Tr	Also served Pte KTG. KSA (2)
MacGill, Pte D, KTG	QSA (1) DoK	No II Section, Belgravia Fort
Macher, 598 Pte Alexander Charles, KRV	QSA (2) DoK OFS	DMU 6 Jun 00. Also served 3rd RPR (3130 & 34971) 9 Jul 01 to 5 Mar 02
MacInnes, Lt Duncan Sayre, RE	QSA (3) DoK Tr Witt	See his biography (page 348)
Mackay, Pte C C, KTG	QSA (1) DoK	
Mackay, Pte G, KTG	QSA (1) DoK	
Mackay, Pte H C, KTG	QSA (1) DoK	Medical Corps, No 1 Company, F Section. QSA (1), 14-15 Star, BWM, VM (S/Sjt SAMC), St John Ambulance Brigade Silver LS&GC (538 C/Offr, Cape Prov Dist S. Africa SJABO 1926), KStar. Sotheby Nov 81. Frontier Nov 03 £445
Macken, 3713 L Cpl J, LNLR	QSA (3) DoK OFS Tr	QSA (3), [KSA (2)]. Spink Jan 76 £53. Glendining Oct 79 £70
MacKenzie, 304 Pte J A, KRV	QSA (2) RoM DoK	Non effective 26 Jun 00
MacKenzie, Sgt J R, KTG	QSA (1) DoK	No I Section, No 2 Redoubt and M Company
MacKenzie, Med Off John Eddie, KTG	QSA (1) DoK	See his biography (page 348)

MacKenzie, 311 Pte Roderick Stuart, CP2	QSA (1) DoK	B Squadron. Killed in action 24 Oct 99
Mackie, Pte H, KTG	QSA (1) DoK	No I Company, B Section, Reservoir
Mackintosh, Pte J, KTG	QSA (1) DoK	No III Section, F Company, No 3 Redoubt. Also served KRV (1060) until discharged 1 Jul 02. KSA (2)
Maclachlan, Sgt J, KTG	QSA (1) DoK	Cycle Corps, A Company
MacLachlan, 743 Pte William Malcolm, CP2	QSA (2) DoK OFS	CP HQ and depot mounted branch. KSA (2). Surname spelled McLachlan on KSA roll
Maclennan, Lt H V, KTG	QSA (1) DoK	Water Supply Officer. QSA (1). McGregor Museum
MacMahon, 478 Pte S J, KRV	QSA (1) DoK	DMU 3 Mar 00
MacNamara, Pte G, KTG	QSA (1) DoK	Premier Mine
Maconachie, Pte W R, KTG	QSA (1) DoK	No II Section, C Company, Pickering's Redoubt No 1. Worked on the production of a 1/12th scale model of Long Cecil for L Reyersbach and received a share of the £15 paid. QSA (1), KStar. City Coins Jul 01. City Coins May 02
Macpherson, 679 Pte A, KRV	QSA (1) DoK	Discharged 31 Dec 00
Macpherson, Lt A B, KTG	QSA (1) DoK	Premier Mine
Madden, 158 Tpr Patrick Edward, KLH	QSA (2) DoK Paar	Served 19 Oct 99 to 6 Mar 00. Also served KTG
Madoc, Maj Henry William, SAC	QSA (3) DoK OFS Tr	See his biography (page 349)
Maggs, 566 Cpl Charles Edward, CP2	QSA (2) DoK OFS	B Squadron. Promoted Lt 24 Oct 02. KSA (2) issued to Lt. Served as Lt 5th SAMR 20 Aug 14 to 15 Nov 15
Maguire, 34 Sgt George, CP2	QSA (1) DoK	CP dismounted branch (barrier & redoubt duties). QSA (1). City Coins Feb 87
Maguire, 5232 Pte T, LNLR	QSA (1) DoK	Invalided to England 31 Mar 00. QSA (1). Liverpool Sep 86 £95. Liverpool Feb 96 £160. Spink Jul 04 £300
Mahon, 105 Sgt Gilbert, CP2	QSA (3) DoK OFS Tr	A Squadron. KSA (2). Served in the Bechuanaland Rebellion 1897 earning CGHGSM (1) Bech
Mahoney, Pte M, KTG	QSA (1) DoK	No 6 Redoubt
Maile, Pte P R, KTG	QSA (1) DoK	No 3 Redoubt
Main, 1149 Pte E E, KRV	QSA (4) DoK OFS Tr 01	Also served KLH (292) 23 Oct 99 to 30 Apr 00
Main, Sgt W, KTG	QSA (1) DoK	No IV Section, F Company, Mostert's Redoubt. Possibly served in the Bechuanaland Rebellion 1897 with Kimb Rifles earning CGHGSM (1) Bech. 50th Anniversary attendee
Mair, Cpl G, KTG	QSA (2) DoK 01	Also served KRV (359) to 17 Feb 01. KStar. Neate Feb 92 £60. QSA (1) DoK. City Coins Feb 87. Liverpool Apr 97 £90
Mair, 809 Pte John, CP2	QSA (4) RoM DoK OFS Tr	CP No 3 Maxim gun detachment. Appointed Lt on Col de Lisle's staff
Makin, Pte G, KTG	QSA (1) DoK	Kenilworth Defence Force
Malamphy, 4686 Pte J, LNLR	QSA (3) DoK OFS Tr	KSA (2)
Malan, Sp Const J P, CP2	QSA (1) DoK	
Malarkey, 22711 QMS Patrick, CinCBG	QSA (4) DoK OFS Tr 01	Served 19 Nov 00 to 22 Sep 01 as Malarky. Also served CP2 (278). Discharged CP time expired. Irish engineer
Malarkey, 691 Pte Thomas Frederick, CP2	QSA (1) DoK	CP dismounted branch (barrier & redoubt duties)
Malcolm, 704 Pte Adam Neil, CP2	QSA (2) DoK OFS	A Squadron. KSA (2)

Medal roll

Maldicke, Sp Const G, CP2	QSA (1) DoK	
Mallett, Capt Percy W, KTG	QSA (1) DoK	See his biography (page 349)
Maloney, Pte C, KTG	QSA (1) DoK	No IV Section, B Company, No 4 Redoubt
Maloney, Pte John Henry, KTG	QSA (1) DoK	No 4 Redoubt. Also served SRG (63) from 12 Feb 01. Possibly served in the Bechuanaland Rebellion 1897 with Kimb Rifles earning CGHGSM (1) Bech
Maltmann, Pte W F, KTG	QSA (1) DoK	No I Section, Mandy Fort. Served in 1st and 7th South African Infantry during the Great War
Mandy, Capt Frank, KTG	QSA (1) DoK	See his biography (page 349)
Manning, Pte F S, KTG	QSA (1) DoK	No III Section, No 2 Redoubt. QSA (1) Bonhams Dec 07 £235
Manning, 22712 Tpr Frederick Richard, CinCBG	QSA (4) DoK Paar Tr 01	Served 11 Nov 00 to 19 May 01. Also served KTG (No III Section, No 2 Redoubt), KRV to 17 Aug 00 and CRSS (1287) from 25 May 01
Manning, 64748 Gnr Henry, RGA	QSA (1) DoK	Premier Mine. Born Devon 1869. Joined RA Nov 87. Imprisoned for desertion Oct 92. Discharged 1902. QSA (1), KSA (2), BWM (Gnr CGA). DNW Jun 98 £95. Spink Oct 99 £140
Mapp, Pte J, KTG	QSA (1) DoK	No III Section, No 2 Redoubt
Marillier, 935 Pte Francis Robert, KRV	QSA (3) DoK OFS Tr	Non effective 2 Aug 00. Also served KTG (Premier Mine) and SRG (70) from 11 Feb 01
Marillier, 149 Pte H E F, KRV	QSA (4) DoK OFS Tr 01	Non effective 28 Jan 01
Marillier, 150 Pte Philip Richard, KRV	QSA (1) DoK	Non effective 2 Aug 00. Also served KTG and SRG (69) 12 Feb 01 to 31 Mar 01
Maris, Pte L, KTG	QSA (1) DoK	G Company. QSA (1). City Coins Mar 03
Markgraaff, Pte A, KTG	QSA (1) DoK	No III Section, C Company, Pickering's Redoubt No 1
Markgraaff, Pte G, KTG	QSA (1) DoK	Cycle Corps, A Company
Markgraaff, 515 Pte J J, KRV	QSA (1) DoK	DMU 4 Apr 00
Marks, Pte J, KTG	QSA (1) DoK	D Company (Veterans), Beaconsfield Town Guard. QSA (1). Bostock Nov 04 £300
Marks, Pte S J, KTG	QSA (1) DoK	No II Section, No 2 Redoubt. Also served Klerksdorp TG. Medal issued to sister. QSA (1), KStar. Glendining Apr 77 £85
Marnitz, Pte G, KTG	QSA (1) DoK	No 6 Redoubt. 50th Anniversary attendee
Marnitz, Pte H J, KTG	QSA (1) DoK	No I Section, B2 Company, No 3 Redoubt
Marriott, Pte C E, KTG	QSA (1) DoK	Kimberley Mine Ambulance Company, B Section. QSA (1). DNW Jun 02 £95. QSA (1), KStar. eBay Feb 05
Marriott, Pte John Whitely, KTG	QSA (1) DoK	No 1 Redoubt. Also served SRG (114) from 11 Feb 01
Marriott, Pte W C, KTG	QSA (1) DoK	No 1 Redoubt. QSA (1), KStar. Kaplan Aug 81 £200
Marsburg, 431 Pte A, KRV	QSA (1) DoK	Discharged 6 Nov 02. KSA (2)
Marsden, 399 Cpl A E, CP1	QSA (1) DoK	B Squadron. Served in the Bechuanaland Rebellion 1897 earning CGHGSM (1) Bech
Marsden, 2960 Cpl J, LNLR	QSA (3) DoK OFS Tr	QSA (3), KSA (2). DNW Mar 08 £220
Marsh, Pte W G, KTG	QSA (1) DoK	No 3 Redoubt
Marshall, 246 Cpl A L, KRV	QSA (3) DoK OFS Tr	DMU 6 Jun 00. Also served Lt MH 9 Jun 00 to 18 Jan 01. KSA (2)
Marshall, 77147 Bombdr Frederick G J W, RGA	QSA (1) DoK	QSA (1), [KSA (2)]. Glendining Mar 89. City Coins Nov 06
Marshall, Lt H, KTG	QSA (1) DoK	No II Section, B Company, No 4 Redoubt and No IV Section, L Company

Marshall, Pte H, KRV	QSA (1) DoK	Also served KTG (No 4 Redoubt). Listed on the KTG roll but not found on the KRV roll. QSA (1). Victorian Medals Dec 04 £200. eBay Apr 06 £205
Marshall, 271 Tpr John Thomas, KLH	QSA (2) DoK OFS	Joined 20 Oct 99. Killed in action 28 Nov 99
Marshall, Pte Walker, KTG	QSA (1) DoK	Pickering's Redoubt No 1 and No IV Section, C Company, No 2 Redoubt. QSA (1). Spink Jun 82 £100. Spink Jul 94
Martheze, 224 Pte W, KRV	QSA (1) DoK	Non effective 13 Jul 00
Martin, Lt A H, KRV	QSA (4) RoM DoK OFS Tr	Also served Lt DH 1 Mar 02 to 30 Jun 02. KSA (2). Served in the Bechuanaland Rebellion of 1897
Martin, 1589 Pte Alfred Wright Henry, CP1	QSA (3) RoM DoK OFS	B Squadron. Discharged time expired 13 Dec 01. Occupation farmer. QSA (3), KStar. Glendining Mar 89 £180. Spink Oct 99 £320
Martin, Pte F, KTG	QSA (1) DoK	Kamfersdam Company. Repairing ironwork generally under RE Officer. Possibly served in the Bechuanaland Rebellion 1897 with DFH earning CGHGSM (1) Bech
Martin, Pte G, KTG	QSA (1) DoK	50th Anniversary attendee
Martin, 316 Tpr H, KLH	QSA (2) DoK OFS	DMU 24 Mar 00
Martin, Pte H, KTG	QSA (1) DoK	No IV Section, C Company, No 2 Redoubt
Martin, 222 Tpr Harry, KLH	QSA (2) DoK OFS	Served 19 Oct 99 to 3 Apr 00. Also served KTG
Martin, 930 Pte J, KRV	QSA (2) DoK OFS	Discharged 1 Jul 02. Also served KTG (Otto's Kopje Scouts). KSA (2)
Martin, Pte J, KTG	QSA (1) DoK	
Martin, 238 Tpr Montgomery, KLH	QSA (2) DoK OFS	Served 19 Oct 99 to 3 Apr 00
Martin, 2709 Sgt R, LNLR	QSA (4) DoK OFS Tr 01	
Martin, 1260 Pte R H, KRV	QSA (5) DoK OFS Tr 01 02	Also served KTG (G Company). KSA issued in error and recovered
Martin, 648 Pte Sidney Ernest, CP2	QSA (4) RoM DoK OFS Tr	CP HQ and depot mounted branch. Discharged by purchase. Also served Lt SRG. 165 L Cpl Sydney E Martin served VTG - same man?
Martindale, Pte A, KTG	QSA (1) DoK	No II Section, L Company
Martindale, 4267 Pte W, LNLR	QSA (2) DoK OFS	Invalided to England 21 Aug 00
Marvell, Pte Harry, KTG	QSA (3) DoK OFS Tr	Cycle Corps, A Company. Also served SRG (73) from 12 Feb 01
Marwick, Pte J, KTG	QSA (1) DoK	No III Section, F Company, No 3 Redoubt
Masencamp, Pte F, KTG	QSA (1) DoK	Premier Mine
Mashford, Pte F, KTG	QSA (1) DoK	No 1 Redoubt
Maskovitz, 625 Pte J, CP2	QSA (4) DoK OFS Tr 01	B Squadron. Served 11 Oct 99 to 31 May 02
Mason, Pte A, KTG	QSA (1) DoK	Premier Mine
Mason, 279 L Cpl G R, KRV	QSA (3) DoK OFS Tr	Discharged 15 Mar 02. KSA (2). MID 8 Mar 01 "In action at Koffyfontein, June 3, a man being wounded in an exposed position, Mason went to his help and remained with him under fire until an ambulance fetched him"
Mason, Pte H F, KTG	QSA (1) DoK	No III Section, No 2 Redoubt. QSA (1). McGregor Museum
Mason, 7766 Gnr James, RGA	QSA (1) DoK	QSA (1), KSA (2) (initial I), KStar. Spink Oct 99 £200. Bonhams Oct 08
Mason, Pte John F, KTG	QSA (3) DoK OFS Tr	No 2 Schmidt's Breastwork. Also served WS (29) 31 Mar 00 to 15 Dec 00
Massey, C E, KTG	QSA (0)	Roll states "Ambulance work in connection with scurvy outbreak"

Massey, Pte G, KTG	QSA (1) DoK	
Massey, Pte H, KTG	QSA (1) DoK	
Massey, Pte W, KTG	QSA (1) DoK	No 3 Redoubt
Masters, 113 Tmptr Robert Ernest, DFA	QSA (3) DoK OFS Tr	Enrolled 21 Jul 98 aged 14. Resigned 2 Oct 02. QSA (3) (officially renamed), KSA (2), KStar. Christies Jul 85
Masters, 41 Sgt Robert Henry, DFA	QSA (3) DoK OFS Tr	Enrolled 13 Mar 96. Resigned 2 Oct 02. Father of RE Masters. CGHGSM (1) Bech (Gnr), QSA (3), KSA (2). Christies Jul 85. Liverpool Apr 94 £250
Matham, 159 Tpr Henry Cornelius, KLH	QSA (2) DoK OFS	Served 19 Oct 99 to 14 Mar 00 with surname Mathar on QSA roll and Maytham on nominal roll. Also served KTG and Native Labour Corps 5 Jun 02 to 31 Aug 02
Mather, Pte Robert Alexander, KTG	QSA (2) DoK OFS	No I Section, B Company, Beaconsfield Town Guard from 24 Nov 99. Also served KLH (331) 1 Nov 99 to 24 Nov 99, KR (726) to 13 Dec 00, SRG (101 or 131) from 12 Feb 01 and FID with initial A. KSA (2)
Mathias, Med Off James, KTG	QSA (1) DoK	Stationed at the Rock Shaft, De Beers Mine
Mathieson, 713 Pte George Robert, CP2	QSA (2) DoK OFS	C Squadron. Wounded 25 Nov 99. KSA (2)
Matthews, Pte F, KTG	QSA (1) DoK	No IV Section, D Company
Matthews, 1076 Pte J L, KRV	QSA (4) RoM DoK OFS Tr	Also served KTG (No III Company, A Section, Reservoir). Died of disease Kimberley 10 Aug 01. QSA (5) inc 01. Sotheby Nov 78
Matthews, 923 Pte J T, KRV	QSA (1) DoK	Dismissed for misconduct 4 May 00. Also served KTG (A Company, Cycle Corps)
Matthews, 118 Sgt John, CP2	QSA (3) DoK OFS Tr	C Squadron. Slightly wounded Hoopstad 23 Oct 00. KSA (2). Served in the Bechuanaland Rebellion 1897 earning CGHGSM (1) Bech
Matthews, Lt T H, KRV	QSA (3) DoK OFS Tr	Wounded near Cradock 1 May 01. KSA (2). Served in the GSWA operations during the Great War as Captain 2nd Kimberley Regiment. CGHGSM (1) Bech (Sgt Kimb Rif), QSA (3), KSA (2) (Capt KRV), 14-15 Star (Capt 7th Infy), BWM, VM (Capt), KStar. Burman Jun 04 £1,065
Matthews, Pte T M, KTG	QSA (1) DoK	D Company (Veterans), Beaconsfield Town Guard
Maude, 13532 Gnr George, RGA	QSA (3) DoK OFS Tr	QSA (3), [KSA (2)]. Hamilton Dec 86 £75
Maude, Pte S, KTG	QSA (1) DoK	Premier Mine. 198 Cpl S Maude KMC died of disease Boshof 28 Apr 00. Same man?
Maxwell, Pte R F T, KTG	QSA (1) DoK	No I Section, No 2 Redoubt
May, Pte A J, KTG	QSA (1) DoK	No II Section, B2 Company, No 3 Redoubt. Died of disease during the siege (date unknown)
May, 164 Tpr Sydney James, KLH	QSA (3) DoK Paar 02	Served 20 Oct 99 to 6 Mar 00. Also served KTG as F May, SRG from 31 Mar 02 and WLH (200) 31 Mar 02 to 30 Jun 02. Occupation electrician
May, Pte T R, KTG	QSA (1) DoK	
May, Maj Thomas James, DFA	QSA (2) DoK OFS	See his biography (page 349)
May, Cpl W, KTG	QSA (1) DoK	No I Section, B Company, No 4 Redoubt
Mayers, 4036 Pte E, LNLR	QSA (3) DoK OFS Tr	KSA (2)
Mayman, 5589 Pte T, LNLR	QSA (3) DoK OFS Tr	QSA (3), [KSA (2)]. Spink Jan 79 £85
Maynard, 4482 Pte C, LNLR	QSA (3) DoK OFS Tr	KSA (2)
Mayo, 4387 Pte J, LNLR	QSA (3) DoK OFS Tr	Invalided to England 5 May 00
Mayston, 42 Sgt W H D, SAC	QSA (4) DoK Paar Drie Joh	Wounded 25 Nov 99. Also served KTG (Premier Mine) and KLH (335) 16 Oct 99 to 9 Jun 00. Killed 27 Sep 01

McAdam, Pte A, KTG	QSA (1) DoK	Premier Mine. QSA (1), KStar. City Coins Dec 05. Dixon Sep 06 £450
McAdam, Pte Alexander, KTG	QSA (2) DoK Tr	Premier Mine. Also served SRG (934) from 30 May 01
McAdam, Sgt J, KTG	QSA (1) DoK	No I Section, B Company, Beaconsfield Town Guard
McAdam, Pte W S, KTG	QSA (1) DoK	Ambulance Corps, Beaconsfield Town Guard. QSA (1), KStar, Beaconsfield Siege Medal. Hall Sep 86 £175
McAllister, Pte T, KTG	QSA (1) DoK	Kenilworth Defence Force
McArthur, J H, KTG	QSA (0)	Roll states "Telephone and searchlight construction"
McArthur, 15 Sgt Ins R, KRV	QSA (2) DoK OFS	KSA (2)
McArthur, 2 Tpr T H, KLH	QSA (2) DoK OFS	Served KLH (2) 16 Oct 99 to 30 Nov 99. Medal also issued by KRV. Medal forfeited
McBean, Sgt D M, KTG	QSA (1) DoK	No III Section, Belgravia Fort
McBean, Pte L, KTG	QSA (1) DoK	No III Section, Belgravia Fort
McCaffery, Pte Thomas Dennis, KTG	QSA (2) DoK OFS	No 2 Schmidt's Breastwork and No I Company, B Section, Reservoir. Also served KLH (35) 17 Mar 00 to 10 Nov 00, CPD2 (133) 23 Nov 00 to 28 Feb 01 and 21 Mar 01 to 31 Jul 01 and CRSS (1424) 17 Oct 01 to 15 Apr 02. KSA (2)
McCallum, Pte J, KTG	QSA (1) DoK	Kamfersdam Company
McCallum, Pte J D, KTG	QSA (1) DoK	Premier Mine
McCallum, Lt S H, KRV	QSA (3) DoK OFS Tr	DCM for the siege. KSA (2)
McCann, Sgt P, KTG	QSA (1) DoK	No II Company, A Section, Reservoir
McCarthy, Pte C, KTG	QSA (1) DoK	No I Section, A Company, Beaconsfield Town Guard. QSA (1). Liverpool Aug 91 £85. Glendining Nov 99
McCarthy, Pte D, KTG	QSA (1) DoK	Cycle Corps, A Company. One of the D McCarthys attended the 50th Anniversary reunion
McCarthy, Pte D, KTG	QSA (1) DoK	No 4 Redoubt
McCarthy, Pte G, KTG	QSA (1) DoK	Premier Mine
McCarthy, Pte J, KTG	QSA (1) DoK	Premier Mine
McCarthy, Pte J, KTG	QSA (1) DoK	No III Section, B Company, Beaconsfield Town Guard
McCarthy, 737 Pte James, CP2	QSA (1) DoK	CP dismounted in Beaconsfield. KSA (2) not issued as struck off
McCarthy, 221 Farr John Thompson, KLH	QSA (4) RoM DoK OFS 01	Served 26 Jan 00 to 5 Jun 00. Also served KTG and SRG (72) 12 Feb 01 to 11 Oct 01. 50th Anniversary attendee
McCarthy, 8 Tpr Justin, KLH	QSA (5) DoK Paar Drie Tr 01	Served 16 Oct 99 to 23 Mar 00. Also served KTG 28 Dec 99 to 21 Feb 00, DH 18 Feb 00 to 7 Apr 00, Corps of Guides (42 days) and CinCBG (22714) 11 Nov 00 to 2 Jan 01
McCartney, Cpl G, KTG	QSA (1) DoK	Medical Corps, No 1 Company, D Section
McCaskill, 151 Tpr Ronald, KLH	QSA (2) DoK OFS	Served 20 Oct 99 to 6 Mar 00. Wounded 24 Oct 99. 50th Anniversary attendee as MacAskill
McClintock, Lt Robert Lyle, RE	QSA (4) DoK Paar Drie Witt	See his biography (page 348)
McCloskey, Pte A, KTG	QSA (1) DoK	No II Section, B2 Company, No 3 Redoubt
McClusky, Cpl W, KTG	QSA (1) DoK	No IV Section, A Company, Beaconsfield Town Guard
McColgan, Pte J, KTG	QSA (1) DoK	
McColl, 1175 Tpr James Charles, KLH	QSA (4) DoK OFS Tr 01	Served 1 May 00 to 9 Nov 00. Also served KTG (No IV Section, K Company) and 2nd RPR (1381) 7 Oct 00 to 6 Dec 01
McCormick, 1077 Pte W, KRV	QSA (4) RoM DoK OFS Tr	Discharged 1 Jul 02. Also served KTG (H Company). QSA (4), KSA (2). Liverpool Jul 97 £310
McCracken, Pte S, KTG	QSA (1) DoK	No IV Section, No 2 Redoubt

McCreary, 3361 Pte J, LNLR	QSA (3) DoK OFS Tr	KSA (2)
McCreath, Pte James, KTG	QSA (1) DoK	No III Section, A Company, Beaconsfield Town Guard
McCullum, 872 Pte C M, KRV	QSA (2) DoK OFS	Discharged 1 Jul 02. Also served KTG. KSA (2). KSA roll has McCallum
McCurdy, Cpl J, KTG	QSA (1) DoK	H Company. QSA (1). Noble Numismatics Jul 98
McCurrie, Pte J, KTG	QSA (1) DoK	No 1 Redoubt
McCurrie, Pte J, KTG	QSA (1) DoK	No IV Section, L Company
McCurrie, Pte J, KTG	QSA (1) DoK	No IV Section, L Company
McDermid, 20 Sgt Archibald D, KRV	QSA (2) DoK OFS	DMU 27 Mar 00. Also served VTG (197)
McDermott, 3752 Pte A, LNLR	QSA (3) DoK OFS Tr	Wounded 13 Feb 00. MID 4 Sep 01. KSA (2)
McDermott, Pte E, KTG	QSA (3) DoK OFS Tr	No III Section, C Company, Beaconsfield Town Guard. Pte McDermot also served Kenilworth Defence Force - same man? Also served KR (1084) to 1 Jul 02 where surname is McDiarmid. QSA (1) DoK, [KSA (2)]. Glendining Jul 78
McDonagh, 3917 Pte J, LNLR	QSA (3) DoK OFS Tr	Wounded Nooitgedacht 17 Oct 00. KSA (2). Deserted 1 Dec 03
McDonald, Sgt A R, KTG	QSA (1) DoK	No 2 Schmidt's Breastwork and No III Section, No 2 Redoubt
McDonald, 41825 Tpr Charles A, DH	QSA (6) RoM DoK OFS Tr 01 02	Served 10 Mar 02 to 15 Oct 02. Also served KTG, KRV (1210) until discharged for misconduct 22 Sep 00, KLH (84 & 26143) 25 Jan 01 to 7 Jan 02, KFS (26145), SRG (310) from 28 Feb 01 and DFA. Part of the Coronation contingent. Served in the Bechuanaland Rebellion 1897 with Kimb Rifles earning CGHGSM (1) Bech
McDonald, 700 Sapr D, RE	QSA (2) DoK Drie	QSA (2), [KSA (2)]. Sotheby Mar 86. QSA (2), [KSA (2)]. QSA has OFS not Drie. Glendining Mar 89 £130. DNW Dec 00 £200. DNW Sep 01 £240
McDonald, Pte D, KTG	QSA (1) DoK	B line of defence, No 3 Redoubt
McDonald, Pte F, KTG	QSA (1) DoK	No I Section, B2 Company, No 3 Redoubt
McDonald, Pte G, KTG	QSA (1) DoK	No 6 Redoubt
McDonald, Lt H, KTG	QSA (1) DoK	Cycle Corps, A Company
McDonald, 270 Pte Hugh Christian, KRV	QSA (3) DoK 01 02	DMU 15 May 00. Also served CinCBG (22715) 7 Jan 01 to 27 Jul 01 and KH (333 & 42358) 13 May 02 to 30 Jun 02
McDonald, 221 Tpr James, KLH	QSA (3) DoK OFS 01	Discharged 30 Apr 00. Also served DH (32603) 4 Mar 01 to 5 Nov 01. Occupation digger
McDonald, 27 Sgt Ins John Robb, KRV	QSA (1) DoK	Wounded 28 Nov 99. Killed in action 16 Feb 00. The inscription on the Honoured Dead Memorial says he was wounded on the 16th and died on the 19th. CGHGSM (1) Bech (SM DFH), QSA (1). Dixon Jun 07 £680
McDonald, 223 Tpr M, KLH	QSA (2) DoK OFS	Served 20 Oct 99 until DMU 3 Jan 00
McDonald, Pte M, KTG	QSA (1) DoK	G Company. QSA (1), KStar. Dixon Jun 98 £190
McDonald, 103 Pte R, KRV	QSA (1) DoK	DMU 10 Jul 00
McDonald, 269 Tpr Walter, KLH	QSA (2) DoK OFS	Joined 20 Oct 99. Killed in action 28 Nov 99. QSA (2)
McDonald, Pte William Henry, KTG	QSA (4) DoK OFS Belf	No III Section, B Company, No 4 Redoubt. Also served SALH (1251 & 1547) and KLH (124) 6 Mar 02 to 30 Jun 02. KSA (2)
McDonough, 681 Pte Patrick, CP2	QSA (4) RoM DoK OFS Tr	A Squadron
McDougall, 2178 Sapr Peter, RE	QSA (3) DoK Drie Tr	QSA (3), KSA (2), BWM, VM (A Sgt 85 Can Infy), KStar, Memorial Plaque. Spink Jun 95 £350

McDougall, 460 Pte Peter Renny, CP2	QSA (2) DoK 01	B Squadron. Served 11 Oct 99 to 11 Sep 01
McEvoy, Pte B, KTG	QSA (1) DoK	No 5 supply depot
McEvoy, Pte Philip, KTG	QSA (3) RoM DoK OFS	Premier Mine. Also served KLH (176) 8 Mar 00 to 5 Jun 00 and CRSS (1434)
McEwan, 268 L Cpl Moses Thomas, KLH	QSA (2) DoK OFS	Served 22 Oct 99 to 3 Apr 00. Also served KTG with initial T
McEwen, Pte D, KTG	QSA (1) DoK	No III Section, C Company, Pickering's Redoubt No 1
McEwen, Pte J W, KTG	QSA (1) DoK	No II Section, B Company, No 4 Redoubt
McEwen, Pte John, KTG	QSA (1) DoK	No 4 Redoubt. Also served KR (868) until DMU 1 Aug 00 and SRG (68) as McEwan from 12 Feb 01
McFarlane, 206 Sgt Ins D K, KRV	QSA (2) DoK OFS	MID 23 Jun 02. KSA (2). Surname Macfarlane on KSA roll. Served in the Bechuanaland Rebellion 1897 earning CGHGSM (1) Bech
McFarlane, Pte P, KTG	QSA (1) DoK	Reserve Section, D Company
McGill, 2530 Band J, LNLR	QSA (4) DoK OFS Tr 01	
McGrath, 562 Pte J, KRV	QSA (1) DoK	Dismissed for misconduct 20 Nov 99
McGrath, Pte J, KTG	QSA (1) DoK	Kenilworth Defence Force
McGrath, 1538 Gnr John, RGA	QSA (1) DoK	KSA (2)
McGreavy, 5015 Pte J, LNLR	QSA (3) DoK OFS Tr	Died of wounds 12 Mar 02. KSA (2)
McGregor, Lt Charles Frederick Murray, CP2	QSA (2) DoK OFS	C Squadron. He had served in the Zulu War 1879 and in the Bechuanaland Rebellion 1897 earning CGHGSM (1) Bech
McGregor, 98 Pte Frank, CP2	QSA (1) DoK	CP dismounted branch (barrier & redoubt duties)
McGregor, Pte R W, KTG	QSA (1) DoK	No IV Section, No 2 Redoubt
McGuinness, Pte Charles Henry, KTG	QSA (5) DoK OFS Tr 01 02	No I Section, C Company, Beaconsfield Town Guard. Also served KLH (1067) 24 Apr 00 to 7 Nov 00, SRG (309) 26 Feb 01 to 27 Feb 01, CRSS (705) 9 Jul 01 to 9 Jan 02 and WLH (527) 8 May 02 to 30 Jun 02. Occupation draper
McGuinness, 889 Pte Christopher, CPS	QSA (2) DoK Tr	Also served KTG (No IV Section, C Company, Beaconsfield Town Guard) and KH (399) 30 May 02 to 30 Jun 02
McGuinness, Pte Christopher Alexander, KTG	QSA (3) DoK OFS Tr	Premier Mine. Also served KLH (1009) 12 Mar 00 to 7 Nov 00 and Sgt DH 19 Nov 00 to 30 Jun 02. KSA (2)
McGuinness, Pte F, KTG	QSA (1) DoK	No III Section, L Company
McGuinness, 740 Pte W J, KRV	QSA (3) DoK OFS Tr	Discharged 1 Jul 02. Also served KTG. KSA (2)
McHardy, Pte Donald, KTG	QSA (1) DoK	See his biography (page 348)
McHardy, Lt William, KTG	QSA (1) DoK	See his biography (page 348)
McIntosh, Pte D, KTG	QSA (1) DoK	No I Section, C Company, Beaconsfield Town Guard. QSA (1). Dixon Apr 98 £95
McIntosh, 100 Sgt Edward McKenzie, CP2	QSA (2) DoK OFS	C Squadron. Served 11 Oct 99 to 31 May 02. He had served in the Matabele War 1893. GCHGSH (1) Bech, QSA (2), KSA (2). City Coins Jan 80. QSA (2), KSA (2). Spink Dec 88
McIntosh, 2190 Sapr James, RE	QSA (3) DoK Drie Tr	From Elgin. Enlisted 1898 aged 22. Served until 1910. QSA (3), [KSA (2)], KStar. Collett Dec 89 £170. KSA (2) also known
McIntyre, Pte C, KTG	QSA (1) DoK	No II Section, A Company, Beaconsfield Town Guard
McIntyre, Cpl K G, KTG	QSA (1) DoK	Mounted Section, Kenilworth Defence Force
McIvor, Pte J, KTG	QSA (1) DoK	No II Section, B2 Company, No 3 Redoubt
McIvor, M, KTG	QSA (0)	Roll states "Electrical work; dynamo room and mines"

McKay, Pte C C, KTG	QSA (1) DoK	No 1 Redoubt
McKay, Agent C H, FID	QSA (3) DoK OFS Joh	Also served KTG (No I Section, A Company, Beaconsfield Town Guard), KLH and SAC
McKay, Pte D J, KTG	QSA (1) DoK	No 1 Redoubt
McKay, 238 CSM E, KRV	QSA (2) DoK OFS	Discharged 1 Jul 02. KSA (2)
McKay, 160 Tpr G, KLH	QSA (2) DoK OFS	Discharged 3 Apr 00. SAGS (1) 1877-8 was issued to Tpr G McKay, DFH. Same man?
McKay, Lt G G, KTG	QSA (1) DoK	Cycle Corps, A Company and Premier Mine. QSA (1). City Coins Feb 87
McKay, Pte R C, KTG	QSA (1) DoK	No 1 Redoubt
McKenna, 3736 Pte F, LNLR	QSA (3) DoK OFS Tr	KSA (2)
McKenna, 410 Pte J D, KRV	QSA (4) DoK OFS Tr 02	Non effective 20 Jun 00. Discharged 30 Jun 02. Also served KLH (410). Severely wounded Klip Drift 7 Mar 02. Served in the Bechuanaland Rebellion 1897 with DFH earning CGHGSM (1) Bech
McKenzie, Pte A, KTG	QSA (1) DoK	Kenilworth Defence Force
McKenzie, Pte E, KTG	QSA (1) DoK	No 1 supply depot
McKenzie, 140 L Cpl J, KRV	QSA (1) DoK	DMU 11 Apr 00
McKenzie, Pte J, KTG	QSA (1) DoK	G Company
McKenzie, Pte J M, KTG	QSA (1) DoK	No 1 supply depot. KStar. Sotheby Sep 70
McKenzie, 39 Sgt R J, KRV	QSA (1) DoK	Non effective 6 Jul 00. Served in the Bechuanaland Rebellion 1897 with Kimb Rifles earning CGHGSM (1) Bech
McKenzie, 125 Pte W, KRV	QSA (1) DoK	Non effective 20 Jul 00. CGHGSM (1) Bech (Pte Kimb Rifles), QSA (1), KStar. Spink Nov 79 £350. Spink Jan 81 £375. Armoury Nov 81 £460
McKenzie, 162 Band W, KRV	QSA (1) DoK	DMU 9 Apr 00. Served in Bechuanaland Rebellion 1897 with Griqualand West Brigade earning CGHGSM (1) Bech
McKernan, 4062 Pte E, LNLR	QSA (3) DoK OFS Tr	KSA (2)
McKerrow, A, KTG	QSA (0)	Roll states "Repairing gun carriages and carpentering." Served in the Bechuanaland Rebellion 1897 with DFH earning CGHGSM (1) Bech. QSA (1) (officially reimpressed). DNW Apr 06 £150. DNW Sep 06 £110. Chelsea Sep 07 £175
McKimmie, G, KTG	QSA (0)	Roll states "In charge of natives on construction works"
McKinley, 169 Cpl Frederick David, CP2	QSA (3) DoK Paar OFS	C Squadron. CGHGSM (1) Bech, QSA (3), KSA (2), 14-15 Star, BWM, VM, MSM, LS&GC, KStar. DNW Dec 91 £400. OFS & Paar should not appear on the same QSA
McKinnon, Pte David, KTG	QSA (1) DoK	No III Section, B Company, No 4 Redoubt
McKnight, Lt T J, KTG	QSA (1) DoK	Also served Sgt KRV (479) to 15 Feb 00. Served in the Bechuanaland Rebellion 1897 with Kimb Rifles earning CGHGSM (1) Bech
McLaren, Cpl G C, KTG	QSA (1) DoK	No II Section, B Company, No 4 Redoubt
McLaren, Pte J, KTG	QSA (1) DoK	No IV Section, A Company, Beaconsfield Town Guard
McLaughlin, Sgt W, KTG	QSA (1) DoK	Premier Mine. BSACM, QSA (1), KStar. City Coins Mar 03
McLaughton, 182 Drum W J, KRV	QSA (1) DoK	Non effective 1 Aug 00. Served in the Bechuanaland Rebellion 1897 with Kimb Rifles earning CGHGSM (1) Bech
McLean, Pte D, KTG	QSA (1) DoK	Cycle Corps, A Company
McLean, Pte G D, KTG	QSA (1) DoK	H Company. QSA (1), KStar. Burman Oct 05 £385
McLean, Civilian Dresser J, AVC	QSA (3) RoM DoK Paar	Civilian Dresser
McLean, 777 Pte L C, KRV	QSA (3) DoK OFS Tr	Discharged 13 Jul 01. Also served KTG (No IV Company, A Section, Reservoir) and KLH (1066) to 24 Nov 00

Name	Medals	Notes
McLeish, 559 Pte F R, KRV	QSA (3) RoM DoK OFS	Discharged 22 Jul 01. QSA (3), KStar. DNW May 92 £220. City Coins Nov 06
McLelland, 204 Gnr William, DFA	QSA (2) DoK OFS	Enrolled 16 Oct 99. Also served DFH 96 to 98. Resigned 24 Apr 03. Occupation fitter
McLennan, 328 Pte William John, CP2	QSA (4) RoM DoK OFS Tr	C Squadron. Served 11 Oct 99 to 30 Sep 00. Also served ALH 10 Apr 01 to 31 Oct 01. Lt 1 Nov 01. Transferred to KLH as Capt 5 Mar 02. KSA (2). Served in the Bechuanaland Rebellion 1897 earning CGHGSM (1) Bech
McLeod, Pte F W, KTG	QSA (1) DoK	No IV Section, A Company, Beaconsfield Town Guard. QSA (1), VM (Dvr SASC), ASM. DNW Sep 03 £150
McLeod, 26024 Scout George Douglas, ScH	QSA (5) RoM DoK Tr 01 02	Served 6 Jan 01 to 2 Jan 02. Also served KTG (No IV Company, A Section, Reservoir) 27 Oct 99 to 28 Feb 00, KR (753) 6 Mar 00 to 30 Jun 00 and RR (3699)
McLeod, Sgt H, KTG	QSA (1) DoK	No II Section, Mandy Fort
McLeod, 678 Pte J, KRV	QSA (3) DoK OFS 01	Discharged 31 Oct 02. QSA (2) excl 01 (renamed and copy DoK clasp). Sotheby Nov 78. Spink Dec 83
McLoughlin, 639 Pte C, KRV	QSA (2) DoK OFS	DMU 9 Mar 00
McLoughlin, Col Sgt M, KTG	QSA (1) DoK	No II Section, B Company, No 4 Redoubt
McLoughlin, W, KTG	QSA (0)	Roll states "In charge of natives acting as despatch carriers." 127 William Thomas McLoughlin SRG issued QSA (1) CC. Same man?
McLucas, 924 Pte D, KRV	QSA (1) DoK	Discharged 1 Jul 02. Also served KTG. KSA (2). Pte McClusas on the nominal roll served Kenilworth Defence Force. Same man?
McMahon, 29256 Sapr J, RE	QSA (3) DoK Drie Tr	KSA (2)
McMaster, 531 Pte C A, KRV	QSA (3) DoK Paar Drie	DMU 18 Apr 00. Also served FID
McMaster, 532 Pte K J, KRV	QSA (2) DoK OFS	DMU 5 Apr 00
McMasters, 209 Tpr David James Alexander, KLH	QSA (3) DoK Paar Tr	Served 2 Nov 99 to 2 Nov 00. Also served SRG (149). Possibly prisoner Klerksdorp 25 Jul 00. Served in the Bechuanaland Rebellion 1897 with Kimb Rifles earning CGHGSM (1) Bech
McMasters, Sgt J, KTG	QSA (3) DoK OFS Tr	Gibraltar Fort, Davis's Heap. Also served KR (743) until discharged 13 Jul 01. QSA (1) excl OFS & Tr. Spink Jul 07 £160. Dixon Feb 08 £235
McMillan, Pte D S, KTG	QSA (1) DoK	Reserve Section, D Company
McMinn, 749 Pte J, KRV	QSA (2) DoK OFS	Also served KTG (No III Section, C Company, Beaconsfield Town Guard and Gibraltar Fort, Davis's Heap). DMU 31 May 00
McMorrin, Sgt Thomas, KTG	QSA (4) RoM DoK Paar Tr	No I Company, A Section, Reservoir. Also served KH (434). QSA (4), [KSA (2)]. DNW Apr 01 £280. Liverpool May 01 £425
McMullen, Pte H, KTG	QSA (1) DoK	No III Section, L Company
McNally, 312 L Cpl P, KRV	QSA (1) DoK	Non effective 14 Aug 00. QSA (1). Collett Dec 89 £95
McNamara, 132 Cpl Thomas Joseph, DFA	QSA (3) DoK OFS Tr	Enrolled 3 Feb 99. Resigned 8 Jan 03. Also served DFH. KSA (2). Occupation saddler
McNaughton, Pte W, KTG	QSA (1) DoK	No 1 supply depot
McNay, 488 Pte Charles George, CP2	QSA (4) RoM DoK OFS Tr	A Squadron. Wounded 28 Nov 99
McNeil, Sgt C, KTG	QSA (1) DoK	No II Section, L Company
McNeil, Pte J, KTG	QSA (1) DoK	No II Section, B2 Company, No 3 Redoubt. QSA (1), KStar (Jos M'Neil). Sotheby Jul 86. Spink Dec 97 £170

Medal roll

McNeil, 5 Sgt Norman Stewart, KLH	QSA (2) DoK Paar	Served 16 Oct 99 to 30 Apr 00. Also served IYS (1) 10 May 00 to 10 Oct 00 and RR (29767) from 2 Apr 01. Occupation contractor
McNeill, 261 Pte E, KRV	QSA (1) DoK	DMU 6 Mar 00
McNish, Pte David Wheatley Wilson, KTG	QSA (1) DoK	No 1 Redoubt. Also served SRG (71) from 11 Feb 01
McNish, 212 Tpr Joseph, KLH	QSA (2) DoK Paar	Served 1 Nov 99 to 30 Apr 00. Also served KTG, CPS (60) as McNeish and Klipdam TG. Possibly prisoner Brussels Siding 10 Jan 01
McNish, Pte W, KTG	QSA (1) DoK	No 1 Redoubt
McNish, Pte William, KTG	QSA (1) DoK	No 1 Redoubt. Also served SRG (39) from 11 Feb 01. 430 William McNish served KLH 27 Mar 00 to 5 Jun 00 and gained RoM and Tr. Could also be previous man
McQueen, 722 Pte W, KRV	QSA (2) DoK 01	Also served KTG (No 2 Schmidt's Breastwork). Discharged to Road Steam Transport 8 Jun 01
McTavish, Cpl D, DBMB	QSA (2) DoK OFS	Reservoir Redoubt
McTavish, Pte D, KTG	QSA (1) DoK	Premier Mine. Also served SRG (75)
McVittie, Pte J, KTG	QSA (1) DoK	Reserve Section, D Company
Meade, 796 Pte Robert Joclyn, CP2	QSA (3) DoK OFS Tr	KSA (2). KSA issued in Mar 13 to a New Zealand address
Meade, 2137 Cpl W, LNLR	QSA (4) DoK OFS Tr 01	Killed in action at Hartbeestfontein on 18 Feb 01
Meadows, Pte John, KTG	QSA (2) DoK OFS	No 3 Redoubt. Also served KLH (18) 19 Mar 00 until died of disease 12 Jul 00 in Kimberley
Measure, 4621 Pte G, LNLR	QSA (3) DoK OFS Tr	QSA (3), [KSA (2)], KStar. RHQ
Meder, 9 Sgt John, DH	QSA (4) DoK Paar OFS Tr	Served 19 Nov 00 to 15 Oct 02. Also served KTG (Mounted Section, B Company, Beaconsfield Town Guard). Duplicate QSA issued. Occupation saddler. QSA (4), KSA (2), 1902 Coronation. DNW Dec 91 £340. OFS & Paar should not appear on the same QSA
Meeks, Pte William, KTG	QSA (1) DoK	No III Section, C Company, Pickering's Redoubt No 1. Also served SRG (67) from 11 Feb 01
Meere, 535 Pte Alexander Cormack, CP2	QSA (1) DoK	B Squadron
Megan, 292 Pte W, KRV	QSA (1) DoK	Died in hospital 30 May 00
Megaw, 74 Tpr T, SRG	QSA (5) DoK OFS Tr 01 02	Also served KTG (No II Section, B Company, No 4 Redoubt). On the KTG nominal roll as Magan. 50th Anniversary attendee
Meiklejohn, Pte William Cameron, KTG	QSA (1) DoK	Also served SRG (154) from 13 Feb 01
Meintjies, 447 Pte Andries Gideon, CP2	QSA (1) DoK	A Squadron
Meiring, 350 Tpr Gert Johannes, KLH	QSA (4) RoM DoK OFS Tr	Served 10 Nov 99 to 24 Nov 00. Also served ORCP (222) 16 Sep 00 to 26 Dec 00. A G Meiring is on the KTG nominal roll for Otto's Kopje Company. Prisoner near Potchefstroom 19 Jul 00 and released. QSA (4), [KSA (2)]. City Coins Jun 80
Meldrum, 641 Pte William, CP2	QSA (1) DoK	CP dismounted in Beaconsfield
Mellett, Pte C, KTG	QSA (1) DoK	G Company. QSA (1), KStar. Seaby Sep 72 £40. KStar. Chelsea Jun 98 £115. Aldershot Nov 09 £265
Mellett, Pte T B, KTG	QSA (1) DoK	Kimberley Mine Ambulance Company, B Section. Served in the Bechuanaland Rebellion 1897 with Kimb Rifles earning CGHGSM (1) Bech
Melville, 433 Pte H G, KRV	QSA (2) DoK OFS	DMU 12 May 00. Note says 'expunge name off roll' but not crossed out. Served in the Bechuanaland Rebellion 1897 with Kimb Rifles earning CGHGSM (1) Bech

Name	Medals	Notes
Menary, 337 Pte Thomas Henry, KRV	QSA (3) DoK Tr 02	Served 4 Oct 99 to 18 Jul 00. Also served CPS (304) 1 Feb 01 to 30 Apr 02 and WLH (103) 5 Mar 02 to 30 Jun 02
Mendelsohn, Pte I, KTG	QSA (1) DoK	No II Section, Belgravia Fort
Mendelssohn, Pte M, KTG	QSA (1) DoK	No 6 supply depot
Mends, Pte J G, KTG	QSA (1) DoK	No II Section, F Company, Mostert's Redoubt. QSA (1), KStar. Sotheby Mar 80
Mennie, Pte J G, KTG	QSA (1) DoK	Premier Mine
Mercer, Pte H T, KTG	QSA (3) RoM DoK OFS	Premier Mine. Also served KLH (301) with initial F 26 Mar 00 to 5 Jun 00
Mering, Cpl F, KTG	QSA (1) DoK	H Company. Also served KR (896) until DMU 12 Apr 01 and DFA (273). KSA (2) from DFA
Merry, 576 Pte Charles, CP2	QSA (1) DoK	CP dismounted branch (barrier & redoubt duties). KSA (2)
Merry, 164 Cpl Henry Charlton, CP2	QSA (1) DoK	A Squadron. Served in the Bechuanaland Rebellion 1897 earning CGHGSM (1) Bech. QSA (1). Cybermilitaria Jan 05 £134. eBay Jun 07
Merton, 3147 Tpr Arthur Henry, ILH	QSA (2) DoK Tr	Served 30 Dec 01 to 30 Jun 02 with surname Myrton. Also served SRG (690) and KR (558). KSA (2)
Mesmer, 322 Arm Sgt F, KLH	QSA (2) DoK OFS	Served 1 Nov 99 to 19 Mar 00
Metelerkamp, Pte F W, KTG	QSA (1) DoK	Civil Service Redoubt
Metelerkamp, Pte F W, KTG	QSA (1) DoK	No I Section, Mandy Fort. Initials P W on nominal roll
Metrovitch, 322 Pte Joseph George, CP2	QSA (4) RoM DoK OFS Tr	B Squadron. Wounded 28 Nov 99. Killed in action Taungs 25 Jun 01. QSA (4)
Mey, 1772 Pte C, CP1	QSA (3) RoM DoK OFS	C Squadron
Meyer, Pte C, KTG	QSA (1) DoK	Also served BR (313). 849 C Meyers served CPS and gained Tr. Same man?
Meyer, Eduard, KTG	QSA (1) DoK	Kimberley Mine Ambulance Company, E Section. Not on roll
Mickish, 4162 Pte H, LNLR	QSA (1) DoK	KSA (2)
Mickle, Sgt W, DBMB	QSA (1) DoK	Armoured train section
Micklethwaite, 402 SQMS Bertrand, ILH	QSA (3) DoK OFS Tr	Served 2nd ILH 8 Dec 00 to 7 Jul 02. Also served KRV (637) 11 Oct 99 to 8 Dec 00. Wounded Castrol Nek 20 Mar 01. Served in GSWA until DMU May 1915 and then in the ASC. QSA (3), KSA (2), 14-15 Star (Pte 12th Infy), BWM, VM (A Cpl ASC), KStar. Christies Jul 83. City Coins Mar 03
Middleton, Pte J R, KTG	QSA (1) DoK	Medical Corps, No 1 Company, C Section
Middleton, 236 Tpr R, KLH	QSA (2) DoK OFS	Served 21 Oct 99 to 3 Apr 00
Mierke, F, KTG	QSA (0)	Roll states "Construction of forts and barricades"
Milborrow, 420 Pte A, KRV	QSA (2) DoK OFS	DMU 2 Apr 00
Milborrow, Pte R H, KTG	QSA (1) DoK	No II Section, Mandy Fort
Mildred, 1470 Pte Charles, CP1	QSA (3) RoM DoK OFS	See his biography (page 349)
Mileham, Pte E, KTG	QSA (1) DoK	No III Section, K Company. QSA (1). Glendining Jun 87
Miles, Pte F E, KTG	QSA (1) DoK	Kimberley Mine Ambulance Company with mounted forces
Miles, Pte J W, KTG	QSA (1) DoK	No 3 Redoubt and B Company
Millar, Sgt E J, KTG	QSA (1) DoK	No 3 Redoubt. Also served ASC as Civil Clerk
Millar, Pte N J, KTG	QSA (2) DoK OFS	G Company

Millar, Pte W, KTG	QSA (1) DoK	No 5 supply depot
Miller, 918 Pte W D, KRV	QSA (1) DoK	Dismissed for misconduct 22 May 00. Also served KTG (No 2 Schmidt's Breastwork)
Mills, 73894 Gnr W H, RGA	QSA (2) DoK Tr	KSA (2)
Milne, 47 Gnr A, DFA	QSA (1) DoK	
Milne, 597 Pte C H, KRV	QSA (4) RoM DoK OFS Tr	KSA (2)
Milne, Rev P, KTG	QSA (1) DoK	Reverend. Ambulance Corps, Beaconsfield Town Guard. QSA (1), KStar. Bullock Sep 09 £750
Milne, 3763 Pte W, LNLR	QSA (3) DoK OFS Tr	KSA (2)
Milne, Lt W G, KRV	QSA (3) DoK OFS Tr	See his biography (page 349)
Milner, 4188 Pte A, LNLR	QSA (1) DoK	Wounded 24 Oct 99. Invalided 5 Mar 00
Minaar, 264 Tpr F, KLH	QSA (2) DoK OFS	Served 21 Oct 99 to 30 Apr 00
Minaar, Pte J, KTG	QSA (1) DoK	No II Section, K Company
Minch, Pte Percy Edward, KTG	QSA (3) DoK OFS Tr	H Company. Also served KLH (1070 & 22786) 16 Mar 00 to 30 Jun 01, PTC 14 Jun 00 to 23 Oct 00 (on release from KMC) and CPS (196) 6 Oct 01 to 30 Apr 02. KSA (2)
Misdall, 321 Pte Arthur Harrison, CP2	QSA (4) RoM DoK OFS Tr	A Squadron. KSA (2). Served in the Bechuanaland Rebellion 1897 earning CGHGSM (1) Bech
Misselbrook, Pte G, KTG	QSA (1) DoK	QSA (1). City Coins Dec 77 (initial P). Floyd Johnson & Pain Aug 03
Mitcham, Lt P H, SRG	QSA (2) DoK OFS	Resigned SRG 10 Feb 02. This entry and the next one may be one and the same man
Mitcham, 510 Pte Percival Henry, CP2	QSA (1) DoK	Entry crossed through on QSA roll but appears on the nominal roll as serving with C Squadron
Mitchell, Pte A, KTG	QSA (1) DoK	No 6 Redoubt and Kenilworth Defence Force
Mitchell, Sgt D, KTG	QSA (1) DoK	No 6 Redoubt. QSA (1). Christies Jul 85. Glendining Jun 90 £80
Mitchell, 852 Pte D, KRV	QSA (1) DoK	Discharged 1 Jul 02. Also served KTG. KSA (2)
Mitchell, Cpl J, KTG	QSA (1) DoK	No IV Section, No 2 Redoubt
Mitchell, Pte J, KTG	QSA (1) DoK	Kamfersdam Company. QSA (1). Dixon Jun 98 £95. Could be next man
Mitchell, Pte J, KTG	QSA (1) DoK	No I Company, B Section, Reservoir
Mitchell, Pte J S, KTG	QSA (1) DoK	H Company
Mitchell, Pte P, KTG	QSA (2) DoK 01	No 1 Redoubt. Also served KR (1083) and discharged 25 Sep 01
Mitchell, 94316 Gnr R J, RGA	QSA (3) DoK Tr 01	Invalided
Mitchell, Mr S F, POC	QSA (1) DoK	
Mitchell, Pte T, KTG	QSA (1) DoK	L Company. QSA (1), KStar. Lusted 74 £58
Mitchell, Pte Walter, KTG	QSA (4) DoK Paar Tr 01	No 1 Redoubt. Wounded 16 Nov 99. Also served KLH (161) 19 Oct 99 to 3 Apr 00 and CinCBG (22709) 19 Nov 00 to 20 Apr 01
Mitchell, 156 Pte William Chalmers, KRV	QSA (2) DoK OFS	Non effective 14 May 00. Born Scotland 1872 and enrolled 27 Mar 96. Occupation telegraphist and postmaster. CGHGSM (1) Bech (Pte Kimb Regt), QSA (2), 14-15 Star (Pte SAFT & PC), BWM, VM (2nd C/WO DSC), KStar. DNW Oct 95 £400. DNW Apr 03 £420
Mitchelson, 699 Pte Vivian E, KRV	QSA (1) DoK	DMU 30 Mar 00. Also served SRG (191) from 12 Feb 01
Moberley, Lt David Hugh, CP2	QSA (3) RoM DoK Tr	CP No 2 Maxim gun detachment. Slightly wounded Zoutlief 16 Sep 01. KSA (2). Served in the Bechuanaland Rebellion 1897 earning CGHGSM (1) Bech

Moffett, 162 Sgt William, KLH	QSA (2) DoK OFS	Served 19 Oct 99 to 6 Mar 00. Also served KTG
Moir, Sgt Jimmy, KTG	QSA (1) DoK	No I Section, Belgravia Fort
Moir, Pte R H, KTG	QSA (1) DoK	No III Section, Belgravia Fort
Moir, Pte W Mc G, KTG	QSA (1) DoK	No III Section, Belgravia Fort. QSA (1), KStar. Glendining Jul 85
Molloy, 17 Sgt Andrew, CP2	QSA (1) DoK	CP dismounted branch (barrier & redoubt duties)
Molloy, 1085 Pte Eugene, KRV	QSA (3) DoK OFS 01	DMU 13 Apr 01. Also served KTG (Ambulance Corps, Beaconsfield Town Guard) and CRSS (1241) from 22 Apr 01
Molloy, Pte M, KTG	QSA (1) DoK	
Molloy, 838 Pte Michael Bernard, CP2	QSA (2) DoK OFS	
Moloney, Mr R J, POC	QSA (1) DoK	
Molyneaux, Pte F, KTG	QSA (1) DoK	
Molyneaux, Pte John, KTG	QSA (5) DoK OFS Tr 01 02	No I Section, C Company, Beaconsfield Town Guard. Also served KLH (34585), PAGMI (1657) and ORS (320) 31 May 02 to 30 Jun 02. Occupation clerk
Monk, 2377 Cpl J E, LNLR	QSA (1) DoK	Retransferred to AR in South Africa 21 Feb 00. Employed on CGR
Monk, 2 Sgt Cook W A, KRV	QSA (2) DoK 01	Discharged 1 Nov 01
Monro, Lt David, CP2	QSA (3) DoK OFS Tr	KSA (2). Replacement QSA & KSA issued 28 May 20. Served in the Bechuanaland Rebellion 1897 earning CGHGSM (1) Bech
Montague, 307 Sgt Frederick, KLH	QSA (2) DoK OFS	Served 1 Nov 99 to 24 Mar 00. Also served KTG and FID
Montague, Pte H S, KTG	QSA (1) DoK	No II Section, Belgravia Fort
Montague, Pte J F V, KTG	QSA (1) DoK	No II Section, No 2 Redoubt
Montgomery, 806 Pte G, KRV	QSA (2) DoK 01	Non effective 16 Jan 01. Also served KTG (No 2 Schmidt's Breastwork)
Montgomery, Pte J, KTG	QSA (1) DoK	Medical Corps, No 1 Company, F Section
Montgomery, Pte J A, KTG	QSA (3) DoK OFS Tr	Served 1 Nov 99 to 10 Mar 00. Also served KRV (1178) 18 Aug 00 to 28 Jun 01 and CPS (623) 1 Jul 01 to 30 Apr 02. KSA (2)
Montleo, 57 Pte G L, CP2	QSA (3) DoK OFS Tr	CP HQ and depot mounted branch. Served 11 Oct 99 to 30 Sep 00. Prisoner 15 Oct 99
Moon, 462 Pte H, KRV	QSA (1) DoK	DMU 21 Apr 00
Moon, 711 Pte W J, KRV	QSA (2) DoK OFS	Discharged 1 Jul 02. QSA (2), [KSA (2)]. R J B Militaria Aug 07 £200
Moony, Lt J H O E, CP1	QSA (2) DoK OFS	C Squadron. Paar issued and later withdrawn as not entitled. Slightly wounded Heilkranz 13 Oct 01. KSA (2). Served in the Bechuanaland Rebellion 1897 earning CGHGSM (1) Bech
Moorcroft, 112 Pte George, CP2	QSA (1) DoK	C Squadron. Note says died but cannot locate on any casualty list
Moore, Cpl B, KTG	QSA (1) DoK	No 6 Redoubt
Moore, Sp Const D J, CP2	QSA (1) DoK	
Moore, 1202 L Cpl J, RE	QSA (3) DoK Drie Tr	Part of the 1902 Coronation contingent
Moore, Pte J P, KTG	QSA (1) DoK	No I Company, B Section, Reservoir
Moore, 3547 Pte W, LNLR	QSA (3) DoK OFS Tr	QSA (3), KSA (2), BWM, VM (Pte RWF), KStar. Chelsea Sep 05 £590. Historik Orders Dec 05 £760
Moore, Pte W, KTG	QSA (1) DoK	No I Company, B Section, Reservoir

Moorhead, Lt J, CP2	QSA (1) DoK	CP dismounted branch (barrier & redoubt duties). QSA clasps unclear as roll damaged but probably just DoK. Died of disease at Kimberley 24 Dec 01 (rank of Sub Insp on casualty roll). Served in the Bechuanaland Rebellion 1897 earning CGHGSM (1) Bech
Moran, 4763 Pte A, LNLR	QSA (3) DoK OFS Tr	KSA (2). Deserted 23 Feb 04
Morcom, Pte John, KTG	QSA (4) DoK OFS Tr 01	No III Section, L Company. Also served 2nd RPR (3038) 10 Jun 01 to 30 Dec 01
Morgan, Pte E, KTG	QSA (1) DoK	H Company
Morgan, Pte G A, KTG	QSA (1) DoK	No III Section, Belgravia Fort. Also served Warrenton TG and Warrenton DMT as Lt. OFS & Tr crossed through on Warrenton DMT QSA roll
Morgan, 1660 Sapr H, RE	QSA (3) DoK Drie Tr	KSA (2)
Morgan, Pte H, KTG	QSA (1) DoK	
Morgan, Pte Robert Spencer, KTG	QSA (1) DoK	No II Section, No 2 Redoubt. Also served CRSS (1349) from 6 Aug 01. Occupation grocer
Morgan, Pte S H, KTG	QSA (1) DoK	Premier Mine
Morkel, P L, KTG	QSA (0)	Roll states "Construction of forts and barricades"
Morley, 4074 Pte E, LNLR	QSA (5) DoK Paar Joh DH Belf	KSA (2). Deserted. Medal not recovered
Morley, Pte G H, KTG	QSA (1) DoK	Civil Service Redoubt. Prisoner during siege. Also served Scout FID
Morom, 483 Bugler Stanley Arthur, KRV	QSA (3) RoM DoK OFS	Non effective 20 Jun 00. Also served SRG (159) 11 Feb 01 to 15 May 01 and from 23 May 01
Morphy, Pte J, KTG	QSA (1) DoK	No III Section, C Company, No 2 Redoubt and No I Company, B Section, Reservoir
Morphy, 265 Gnr James Langford, DFA	QSA (5) DoK Paar Drie Joh DH	Enrolled 14 Dec 99. Also served DFA 94 to 98, KTG to 17 Feb 00 and DH 18 Feb 00 to 18 Jun 00. Discharged from DFA 1 Jul 02. Occupation overseer. KSA (2). Served in the Bechuanaland Rebellion 1897 with DFA earning CGHGSM (1) Bech
Morris, 698 Pte Charles John, CP2	QSA (1) DoK	CP dismounted branch (barrier & redoubt duties). Also served FID. BSACM rev Rhod 96 (Tpr MRF), QSA (1), KSA (2), Natal (0) (Sgt Durban Mil Res), 14-15 Star (Pte 1st Infy), BWM, VM (Sgt 6th SAI), KStar. Spink Oct 99 £500
Morris, Nurse F, NS	QSA (0)	Kimberley Civil Hospital
Morris, Rev J S, KTG	QSA (1) DoK	Reverend. Ambulance Corps, Beaconsfield Town Guard. MID 10 Sep 01
Morris, Pte L, KTG	QSA (1) DoK	
Morris, Pte P, KTG	QSA (1) DoK	No I Section, C Company, Beaconsfield Town Guard. QSA (1), KStar. Bonhams Dec 02
Morris, 240 Tpr Victor Ebenezer Robert, KLH	QSA (2) DoK OFS	Served 20 Oct 99 to 20 Apr 00. Also served KTG
Morrison, J, KTG	QSA (0)	Roll states "Carpentering work under direction of RE Officer." QSA (0). Spink Jul 88. Burman Dec 01 £210
Morrison, 110 Cpl R, KRV	QSA (1) DoK	Non effective 28 Aug 00
Morrison, 357 Tpr Stewart, KLH	QSA (2) DoK OFS	Discharged 23 Mar 00. Also served CP (489) (A Squadron) from 2 Jan 00 where note says dead (not on casualty roll)
Morse, Sgt A, KTG	QSA (1) DoK	No III Section, C Company, Pickering's Redoubt No 1
Mortimer, Mr J M, POC	QSA (1) DoK	
Morton, Pte B, KTG	QSA (1) DoK	
Morton, 316 Tpr Harry, KLH	QSA (2) DoK OFS	DMU 24 Apr 00. Also served KTG

Name	Medals	Notes
Morton, Capt J, KTG	QSA (1) DoK	Quartermaster for the KTG. MID. QSA (1). Victorian Medals Dec 04 £350. See his medal on page 506
Morton, Pte R, KTG	QSA (1) DoK	No II Section, B Company, No 4 Redoubt. In charge of natives on sanitary work
Morton, Pte W D, KTG	QSA (1) DoK	No II Section, Belgravia Fort. Possibly William Dunlop Morton, De Beers accountant, who was narrowly missed by a fragment of 100lb shell on 7 Feb 00
Mortonson, 680 L Cpl R, KRV	QSA (2) DoK OFS	Discharged 2 May 03. KSA (2)
Moseley, Pte A E, KTG	QSA (1) DoK	No I Company, B Section, Reservoir
Moseley, Capt E H, KTG	QSA (1) DoK	Officer commanding F Company, Mostert's Redoubt. Served in the Bechuanaland Rebellion 1897 with Kimb Rifles earning CGHGSM (1) Bech
Moseley, 681 Pte M J, KRV	QSA (1) DoK	DMU 2 Nov 99
Moss, 95 BSM Alfred, DFA	QSA (1) DoK	Enrolled 20 Oct 97. Occupation instructor. Killed in action 9 Dec 99
Moss, 95207 Gnr J J, RGA	QSA (1) DoK	KSA (2)
Mostert, 1135 Pte G M, CP1	QSA (1) DoK	C Squadron. DMU 30 Jun 00. Served in the Bechuanaland Rebellion 1897 earning CGHGSM (1) Bech
Mostert, Pte T, KTG	QSA (1) DoK	
Moston, Pte J, KTG	QSA (1) DoK	QSA (1). SAMMH
Motherwell, Sgt D, KTG	QSA (1) DoK	No I Section, F Company, Mostert's Redoubt
Moult, 83 Sgt A, KRV	QSA (2) DoK 01	Discharged 4 Nov 02. 50th Anniversary attendee. Possibly served in the Bechuanaland Rebellion 1897 with Kimb Rifles earning CGHGSM (1) Bech
Moult, 358 Tpr James B, KLH	QSA (3) RoM DoK OFS	Served 24 Nov 99 to 5 Jun 00
Moult, Pte T M, KTG	QSA (1) DoK	No II Section, B Company, No 4 Redoubt
Mourilyan, Nurse E, NS	QSA (0)	St Michael's Home
Moyes, 931 Pte J, KRV	QSA (1) DoK	Discharged 20 Sep 02. Also served KTG (No I Section, K Company). KSA (2)
Muckleston, 4520 Pte W, LNLR	QSA (3) DoK OFS Tr	QSA (3), [KSA (2), KStar]. Sotheby Mar 86. Courier Nov 86 £90. eBay Aug 07 £207. QSA (3), [KSA (2)], KStar. DNW Jul 03 £410
Mudge, Sgt Maj Ernest Cecil, LNLR	QSA (3) DoK OFS Tr	MID 4 Sep 01. DCM LG 27 Sep 01. KSA (2)
Muir, Sgt Albert John, KTG	QSA (1) DoK	Kenilworth Defence Force. Also served GFC from 4 Feb 01. Occupation policeman
Mulcaster, QMS W, KTG	QSA (1) DoK	No 6 Redoubt
Mulder, 927 Pte J L, KRV	QSA (4) RoM DoK OFS Tr	Discharged 1 Jul 00. Also served KTG (G Company), KLH, DFH, Agent FID and ORCP (291). KSA (2)
Mulder, Pte M, KTG	QSA (1) DoK	Cycle Corps, A Company
Mulholland, 58 Pte James, CP2	QSA (1) DoK	CP dismounted branch (barrier & redoubt duties). No KSA but number on KSA roll is 54
Mullally, 163 Tpr Michael, KLH	QSA (4) DoK OFS 01 02	Served 20 Oct 99 until DMU 24 Mar 00. Also served KTG, SRG (76) from 11 Feb 01 and DH (40211) from 19 Jan 02. Killed in action 25 Mar 02
Muller, Pte J H, KTG	QSA (2) DoK OFS	Also served ORCP (291)
Muller, 800 Pte J J, KRV	QSA (4) RoM DoK OFS Tr	Discharged 1 Jul 02. Also served KTG. KSA (2)
Muller, 158 Dvr James, DFA	QSA (3) DoK OFS Tr	Enrolled 1 Jul 99. Discharged 1 Jul 02. KSA (2). Occupation carpenter
Mulligan, 153 Pte John Henry, CP2	QSA (4) RoM DoK OFS Tr	A Squadron. KSA (2). MID for gallantry under fire in Maj Chamier's despatch from Schweizer Reneke. Served in the Bechuanaland Rebellion 1897 earning CGHGSM (1) Bech

Mullins, 28361 2nd Cpl G, RE	QSA (2) DoK Drie	QSA (2), KStar
Mundell, 561 Pte Robert A, KRV	QSA (3) RoM DoK OFS	Non effective 25 Jun 00. Served in the Bechuanaland Rebellion 1897 with DFH earning CGHGSM (1) Bech. Joined the Kimberley Regiment during the Great War and died in 1940
Munford, 268 Pte G, KRV	QSA (1) DoK	DMU 2 Dec 99. Also served KTG (No 1 Redoubt) as cyclist
Munks, Cpl A G, KTG	QSA (1) DoK	G Company. QSA (1). City Coins May 02
Munks, Pte H G, KTG	QSA (1) DoK	No I Section, L Company
Munn, Cpl G J, KTG	QSA (1) DoK	Premier Mine
Munnik, Pte F, KTG	QSA (1) DoK	
Munnik, Pte G, KTG	QSA (1) DoK	Ambulance Corps, Beaconsfield Town Guard
Munnik, Pte J A, KTG	QSA (2) DoK OFS	G Company. Also served KLH (359) as Munick 23 Oct 99 to 30 Nov 99 when transferred to KTG
Munro, 638 Pte A, KRV	QSA (1) DoK	Discharged 31 Dec 00
Munro, Pte D, KTG	QSA (1) DoK	No II Section, Belgravia Fort. QSA (1). Liverpool Feb 97 £85
Munro, J, KTG	QSA (0)	Roll states "Guarding natives on construction work"
Munro, Pte J, KTG	QSA (1) DoK	No II Section, Mandy Fort
Munro, Pte James Dryden, KTG	QSA (4) RoM DoK OFS Tr	Premier Mine. Also served SRG (925), KLH (435, 384, 1279) 6 Mar 00 to 13 Aug 00, WS (49) 4 Sep 00 to 1 May 01, SRG (925) from 25 May 01 and DH (41305) 24 Feb 02 to 30 Jun 02. Occupation farrier. QSA (1), [KSA (2)]. Kaplan Aug 04
Munro, 382 Pte S C, CP2	QSA (5) RoM DoK OFS Tr 01	C Squadron. Served CP2 11 Oct 99 to 30 Jun 01. Served in the Bechuanaland Rebellion 1897 earning CGHGSM (1) Bech. QSA (5), KStar. Christies Jul 85 £151. Spink May 02 £391
Munro, Mr W M, POC	QSA (1) DoK	
Munroe, 560 Pte John C R, KRV	QSA (4) DoK OFS Tr 02	Non effective 20 Jun 00. Also served KTG, KLH (1115) as Munro, CPS, ALH (41244) 18 Feb 02 to 24 Mar 02 and DH (41946) 30 Apr 02 to 30 Jun 02. Occupation barrister
Murch, Mr F W, POC	QSA (1) DoK	
Murdoch, 26140 Scout William, ScH	QSA (3) DoK OFS Tr	Served 24 Jan 01 to 31 Jan 02. Also served KTG (No II Section, B Company, No 4 Redoubt) 15 Oct 99 to 10 Mar 00, KLH (232) 17 Mar 00 to 5 Jun 00, SRG and WLH (180) 14 Feb 02 to 29 Jun 02. KSA (2)
Murphy, 201 Tpr Daniel Joseph, KLH	QSA (2) DoK OFS	See his biography (page 350)
Murphy, 4733 Pte J, LNLR	QSA (3) DoK OFS Tr	QSA (3), [KSA (2)]. March Medals Aug 93 £125
Murphy, Pte J, KTG	QSA (1) DoK	No II Section, Mandy Fort
Murphy, 49 Pte John, CP2	QSA (1) DoK	CP dismounted branch (barrier & redoubt duties)
Murphy, 9286 Gnr P, RGA	QSA (1) DoK	Premier Mine
Murphy, 1936 Pte T, CP1	QSA (3) DoK OFS Tr	B Squadron. KSA (2)
Murphy, 1019 Pte W, KRV	QSA (3) DoK OFS 01	Also served KTG (No IV Section, L Company). Non effective 20 Apr 01. Transferred to DFA 1 Jan 03
Murphy, Pte W, KTG	QSA (1) DoK	No IV Section, L Company
Murray, 4902 Pte D, LNLR	QSA (3) DoK OFS Tr	QSA (3), KSA (2), KStar
Murray, Pte D, KTG	QSA (1) DoK	H Company
Murray, Pte Frederick, KTG	QSA (1) DoK	No IV Section, B Company, Beaconsfield Town Guard. Also served SRG (560) from 3 Apr 01

Murray, Pte G, KTG	QSA (1) DoK	Medical Corps, No 1 Company, C Section
Murray, 1023 Pte H, KRV	QSA (2) DoK OFS	Discharged 1 Jul 02. Also served KTG. KSA (2)
Murray, Pte J, KTG	QSA (1) DoK	No III Section, F Company, No 3 Redoubt
Murray, Pte J, KTG	QSA (1) DoK	Premier Mine
Murray, 306 Pte J C, KRV	QSA (2) RoM DoK	Non effective 20 Jun 00. QSA (2). McGregor Museum
Murray, 4854 Pte J C, LNLR	QSA (3) DoK OFS Tr	QSA (3), KSA (2). City Coins No 18. Clark Feb 93 £275
Murray, 3481 Pte M, LNLR	QSA (3) DoK OFS Tr	KSA (2)
Murray, Pte P, KTG	QSA (1) DoK	H Company. QSA (1). Liverpool Jan 91 £80. Dixon Jul 94 £95. QSA (1), KStar. Dixon Aug 08 £480
Murray, 223 Pte R H, KRV	QSA (2) DoK OFS	Non effective 3 Jun 00
Murray, Pte W, KTG	QSA (1) DoK	No I Section, C Company, Beaconsfield Town Guard
Murray, Lt Col W H E, LNLR	QSA (3) DoK OFS Tr	See his biography (page 350)
Mutton, Pte T W, KTG	QSA (1) DoK	No III Section, Belgravia Fort
Myburgh, Pte C F, KTG	QSA (1) DoK	QSA (1). City Coins Dec 88
Myburgh, Pte I, KTG	QSA (1) DoK	
Myers, Pte A, KTG	QSA (3) DoK OFS 01	Also served UVR (680)
Myers, 819 Pte W G, KRV	QSA (4) RoM DoK OFS Tr	Discharged 1 Jul 02. Also served KTG (No II Company, A Section, Reservoir). KSA (2)
Mylrea, Lt Arthur G G, ASC	QSA (4) Nat DoK OFS Tr	Temporary Lt. Also on roll for FID as Agent. KSA (2)
Myrton, 558 Pte Arthur Henry, KRV	QSA (2) DoK OFS	DMU 18 Jun 01. Also served SRG (690) from 19 Jun 01 and 1st ILH (3147) 30 Dec 01 to 30 Jun 02. KSA (2). Occupation carpenter

N

Nagel, Pte F, KTG	QSA (1) DoK	Gibraltar Fort, Davis's Heap
Nagel, 751 Pte John A, KRV	QSA (5) RoM DoK OFS Tr 01	Discharged 22 Sep 00. Also served KTG (Gibraltar Fort, Davis's Heap) and KLH (282, 30136 & 42242) 9 Feb 01 to 7 Nov 01 and 15 Apr 02 to 30 Jun 02
Nanbarrow, Pte W, KTG	QSA (1) DoK	
Nankervis, 750 Pte Thomas, KRV	QSA (4) RoM DoK OFS Tr	Discharged 1 Jul 00. Also served KTG (Gibraltar Fort, Davis's Heap and No III Section, C Company, Beaconsfield Town Guard), CinCBG (22716) 17 Nov 00 to 15 May 01, 1st BrH 3 Jun 01 to 6 Jan 02 and 2nd ILH (1473 & 41519) 22 Feb 02 to 23 Jun 02. KSA (2)
Napier, Pte W, KTG	QSA (1) DoK	No 6 Redoubt
Napper, 564 Pte E W, KRV	QSA (2) DoK OFS	Discharged 1 Jul 02. KSA (2)
Narroway, 1780 Pte H G, CP1	QSA (2) DoK OFS	B Squadron. Discharged time expired 6 Sep 01
Nash, Pte A, KTG	QSA (1) DoK	QSA (1). Spink Nov 94
Naude, 267 Pte J A, CP1	QSA (2) DoK OFS	DMU 31 Nov 01. Served in the Bechuanaland Rebellion 1897 earning CGHGSM (1) Bech. QSA (2). City Coins Sep 03
Naude, 1304 Pte L P, CP1	QSA (3) DoK OFS 01	Served 11 Oct 99 to 2 Apr 01. On Supplementary roll with initials S P
Nava, 248 Tpr Harold Anthony, KLH	QSA (2) DoK OFS	Served 20 Oct 99 to 14 Mar 00

Nava, 1108 Pte Percy, KRV	QSA (4) DoK OFS Tr 01	Also served KTG and KLH (364) 28 Nov 99 to 5 Jun 00. Discharged KRV 19 Jul 02
Neal, Pte G H, KTG	QSA (1) DoK	Premier Mine
Neal, 1033 Pte R P, KRV	QSA (2) DoK OFS	Also served KTG (Gibraltar Fort, Davis's Heap). Discharged 1 Jul 02. KSA (2)
Neale, Pte G, KTG	QSA (1) DoK	No I Company, B Section, Reservoir
Neale-Shutte, Capt Richard Francis, CP2	QSA (4) RoM DoK OFS Tr	See his biography (page 350)
Neander, Pte J H, KTG	QSA (1) DoK	
Needham, 173 Farr Sgt George, DFA	QSA (2) DoK OFS	Enrolled 30 Sep 95. Transferred to Kimb Regt 1 Apr 07. Occupation farrier at De Beers. [CGHGSM (1) Bech, QSA (2)], Colonial Auxiliary Forces LS Medal (Far QM Kimb Regt), KStar. City Coins May 02
Neely, 2880 L Sgt H, LNLR	QSA (3) DoK OFS Tr	Invalided to England 22 Jan 01. Neeley on KSA roll. QSA (3), KSA (2), KStar. Glendining Jun 79
Neilmayer, 193 Pte Johannes Elisa, CP2	QSA (1) DoK	CP dismounted branch (barrier & redoubt duties). Note says services dispensed with
Neilson, Pte J C, KTG	QSA (1) DoK	No IV Section, C Company, Pickering's Redoubt No 2
Nel, 889 L Cpl J J D, CP1	QSA (4) RoM DoK OFS 01	Served 11 Oct 99 to 21 May 01. Served in the Bechuanaland Rebellion 1897 earning CGHGSM (1) Bech
Nell, 955 Pte L F, CP1	QSA (3) RoM DoK OFS	B Squadron. Discharged time expired 31 Dec 01. Served in the Bechuanaland Rebellion 1897 with initials S F earning CGHGSM (1) Bech
Nell, 1314 Pte P J, CP1	QSA (2) DoK OFS	DMU 31 Aug 00
Nelson, 165 Tpr Benjamin, KLH	QSA (3) RoM DoK OFS	Served 19 Oct 99 to 5 Jun 00. Also served KTG (Kenilworth Defence Force)
Nelson, 42 Sgt Davis, CP2	QSA (1) DoK	CP intelligence and detective staff
Nelson, Nurse E C, NS	QSA (0)	Joined 1 Apr 00
Nelson, 406 Sgt E J, KLH	QSA (2) DoK Paar	Served 23 Nov 99 to 30 Apr 00
Nelson, 9088 Gnr George, RGA	QSA (1) DoK	To 16th Co RGA, China. QSA (1), China (0) (No 91 Co, RGA), KStar. Glendining Sep 92 £270
Nelson, 1261 L Cpl J, LNLR	QSA (3) DoK Paar Tr	KSA (2)
Nelson, Tpr John Edward, DH	QSA (7) DoK Paar Drie Joh DH Belf 01	Served 20 Feb 00 to 26 Jan 01. Also served KTG (Mounted Section, B Company, Beaconsfield Town Guard). Possibly wounded Wegdraai 29 Dec 00
Nelson, 563 Pte P, KRV	QSA (1) DoK	Dismissed for misconduct 13 Oct 99. Note records he was dirty, refused to obey an order and was drunk in camp. His medal entitlement is dubious
Nelson, Pte R D, KTG	QSA (1) DoK	Kimberley Mine Ambulance Company, A Section and No 1 Redoubt
Nelson, Capt W, KTG	QSA (1) DoK	
Nelson, Cpl W, KTG	QSA (1) DoK	No 6 Redoubt
Nelson, Pte W, KTG	QSA (1) DoK	No III Section, B Company, Beaconsfield Town Guard. QSA (1). Spink Nov 05
Nelson, Pte W G, KTG	QSA (1) DoK	No 3 Redoubt. QSA (1), VM (Cdr SASC). City Coins No 18
Nesemann, 265 Pte H, KRV	QSA (1) DoK	DMU 28 Feb 00. CGHGSM (1) Bas (Tpr CMY), QSA (1), KStar. Spink Jun 85. DNW Sep 09 £550
Nettleton, Lt Thomas S, KTG	QSA (1) DoK	No 3 Redoubt. Also served Warrenton TG and Warrenton DMT as Capt. OFS & Tr crossed through on Warrenton DMT QSA roll
Neville, 4649 Pte J, LNLR	QSA (3) DoK Paar Joh	Wounded 28 Nov 99. KSA (2). Mounted Infantry
Newby, Pte W G, KTG	QSA (1) DoK	No II Section, Mandy Fort

Newdigate, Lt William, KLH	QSA (2) DoK OFS	Joined 20 Oct 99. Resigned 6 Mar 00. Also served Capt KTG. Occupation chief surveyor at De Beers
Newman, 498 Pte Alexander, CP2	QSA (1) DoK	CP dismounted branch (barrier & redoubt duties). Discharged misconduct. Also served CinCBG (22717) 22 Nov 00 to 29 Sep 01
Newton, Pte C R, KTG	QSA (1) DoK	Premier Mine. Medal reissued 7 Dec 09
Newton, Pte G E, KTG	QSA (1) DoK	
Newton, Pte J, KTG	QSA (1) DoK	No II Company, A Section, Reservoir
Newton, Pte J, KTG	QSA (1) DoK	
Newton, 171 Tpr William John, KLH	QSA (2) DoK OFS	Served 20 Oct 99 to 14 Mar 00
Nicholas, 215 Tpr Benjamin Leonard, KLH	QSA (1) DoK	Joined 20 Oct 99. Killed in action 28 Nov 99
Nicholas, Pte R, KTG	QSA (1) DoK	
Nicholetts, 519 Cpl Ashley Brontrees, KRV	QSA (3) RoM DoK OFS	Served 11 Oct 99 to 20 Nov 00. Also served KLH 19 Apr 00 to 29 Aug 00, Lt SRG 12 Feb 01 to 30 Apr 02 and Capt WLH 1 May 02 to 30 Jun 02. MID for carrying despatches during the siege. KSA (2)
Nicholls, Pte D J, KTG	QSA (1) DoK	Cycle Corps, A Company
Nicholls, Pte E F, KTG	QSA (1) DoK	No 4 supply depot
Nicholls, Pte J, KTG	QSA (1) DoK	B line of defence, No 3 Redoubt
Nicholls, Pte R J, KTG	QSA (1) DoK	No 6 Redoubt
Nicholls, Pte S, KTG	QSA (1) DoK	H Company
Nicholls, Pte T, KTG	QSA (1) DoK	No 6 Redoubt. QSA (1), KStar. Dixon Apr 98 £185
Nicholson, Pte A, KTG	QSA (1) DoK	Cycle Corps, A Company. QSA (1). City Coins Jun 04
Nicholson, Sister Christina Anne, NS	QSA (0)	Kimberley Civil Hospital. MID 10 Sep 01. Also on roll for SAC with clasps DoK, OFS & Tr crossed though. Order of St John, Serving Sister (1901), QSA (0), KSA (0), KStar. Sotheby Feb 90 £250
Nicholson, Lt J, KTG	QSA (1) DoK	
Nicholson, Pte Murdo Norman, KTG	QSA (4) RoM DoK OFS Tr	No II Section, F Company, Mostert's Redoubt. Also served Lt KH 7 Mar 00 to 30 Jun 00 as Nicolson. QSA (4), [KSA (2)]. Glendining Mar 89 £210
Nicholson, Lt N, KTG	QSA (1) DoK	No 6 Redoubt
Nicholson, 182 Cpl Peter, DFA	QSA (2) DoK Tr	Enrolled 31 Aug 99 until DMU 2 Jun 02. Previously served RA and DFA 96 to 98. Occupation miner. IGS, CGHGSM (1) Bech, QSA (2), KSA (2), KStar
Nicholson, 843 Pte R G, KRV	QSA (1) DoK	Discharged 1 Jul 02. Also served KTG (No 1 Redoubt). KSA (2)
Nicol, 204 Pte W, KRV	QSA (1) DoK	Non effective 1 Nov 00
Nicolson, Pte R G, KTG	QSA (1) DoK	No 6 Redoubt
Niekerk, 263 Pte Cornelius Johannes Hendrick, CP1	QSA (3) DoK OFS 01	Served 11 Oct 99 until DMU 31 Dec 01. Served in the Bechuanaland Rebellion 1897 earning CGHGSM (1) Bech
Nienaber, Pte W, KTG	QSA (1) DoK	
Nightingale, 4630 Drum B, LNLR	QSA (3) DoK OFS Tr	QSA (3), KSA (2), KStar. DNW Nov 96 £180
Nightingale, Nurse H, NS	QSA (0)	Kimberley Civil Hospital. QSA (0). McGregor Museum
Niven, Pte C K, KTG	QSA (1) DoK	No III Section, K Company
Nixon, 4661 Pte D, LNLR	QSA (3) DoK OFS Tr	QSA (5) inc 01 & 02, [KSA (2)]. Glendining May 85. QSA (3), [KSA (2)]. Dixon Sep 95 £85
Nixon, 169 Tpr Frank, KLH	QSA (3) RoM DoK Paar	Served 19 Oct 99 to 5 Jun 00. Surname also spelled Nickson. Also served KTG
Nixon, Pte J, KTG	QSA (1) DoK	No 6 Redoubt

Medal roll

Nixon, Pte J, KTG	QSA (1) DoK	No I Section, No 2 Redoubt
Noake, 167 Tpr Thomas, KLH	QSA (2) DoK Paar	Served 20 Oct 99 until DMU 24 Mar 00
Noble, 13293 L Cpl W H, ASC	QSA (3) DoK OFS Tr	41st Co
Noble, Pte W R, KTG	QSA (1) DoK	
Nolan, 4830 Drum A, LNLR	QSA (3) DoK OFS Tr	KSA (2)
Nolan, 346 Tpr B, KLH	QSA (2) DoK OFS	Served 27 Oct 99 until dismissed 14 Nov 99
Nomell, Pte E W, KTG	QSA (1) DoK	Construction of redoubts and entanglements etc
Noonan, Pte I J, KTG	QSA (1) DoK	No 6 Redoubt. QSA (1). Neate Feb 92 £85. Gordon Feb 93 £95
Noonan, Pte Joseph Daniel, KTG	QSA (1) DoK	See his biography (page 350)
Norden, 533 Pte J C, KRV	QSA (4) DoK OFS Tr 01	Discharged 5 Aug 02
Norris, Lt Charles, KLH	QSA (5) RoM DoK OFS Tr 01	Served 19 Oct 99 to 23 Dec 01. Also served KTG (No IV Section, L Company)
Norris, Pte G M, KTG	QSA (1) DoK	No 1 Redoubt
Norris, Pte W B, KTG	QSA (1) DoK	No IV Section, No 2 Redoubt
Northcote, Pte S J, KTG	QSA (1) DoK	G Company
Northey, Pte J, KTG	QSA (1) DoK	No 1 Redoubt
Norton, 1311 Tpr Bert, KLH	QSA (3) DoK OFS Tr	Served 29 Dec 99 to 19 Jul 00
Norvall, Pte F A, KTG	QSA (2) DoK OFS	Premier Mine. Also served Guide FID
Nosworthy, 1409 Pte F T, CP1	QSA (4) RoM DoK OFS Tr	A Squadron. CGHGSM (1) Bech (Tpr Fst C Vol), QSA (4), KSA (2). Glendining Sep 92 £210
Nothard, Pte H, KTG	QSA (1) DoK	No 3 supply depot
Nothard, Pte Tom, KTG	QSA (1) DoK	No 3 supply depot. CGHGSM (1) Bas (Pte PAVG), QSA (1), KStar. DNW Sep 02 £400. Monarch Medals Aug 03 £575
Nottman, 304 Sgt James Robert, KLH	QSA (2) DoK OFS	Served 26 Oct 99 to 5 Jun 00. Surname sometimes Notman. Nominal roll says appointed Captain 26 Oct 99. Also served DH and SRG. QSA (2). McGregor Museum
Nourse, 793 Pte Alan Gordon, KRV	QSA (5) RoM DoK OFS Tr 01	Discharged 1 Jul 00. Also served KTG, 1st KFS (553) and FID
Nowell, 4847 Pte J, LNLR	QSA (3) DoK OFS Tr	KSA (2)
Nurton, Pte W H, KTG	QSA (1) DoK	No IV Section, F Company, Mostert's Redoubt
Nutting, 4365 Pte F, LNLR	QSA (4) DoK OFS Tr 01	
Nutzhorn, Pte E C, KTG	QSA (1) DoK	Premier Mine and No II Section, A Company, Beaconsfield Town Guard

O

O'Brien, Pte B, KTG	QSA (1) DoK	Medical Corps, No 1 Company, F Section
O'Brien, 177 Tpr George William, SRG	QSA (6) RoM DoK OFS Tr 01 02	Served 12 Feb 01 to 15 May 01. Also served KLH (110) 27 Dec 99 to 14 Mar 00 and DH (41963) 21 Feb 02 to 30 Jun 02. 50th Anniversary attendee
O'Brien, J M, KTG	QSA (0)	Roll states "Manufacturing shells and loading cartridges"
O'Brien, Pte J W, KTG	QSA (1) DoK	Premier Mine
O'Brien, 680 Pte John, CP2	QSA (2) DoK OFS	CP dismounted branch (barrier & redoubt duties). KSA (2). Served in the Bechuanaland Rebellion 1897 earning CGHGSM (1) Bech

O'Brien, 391 Pte John Avionsmith, SAC	QSA (3) RoM DoK OFS	Served 13 Nov 00 to 11 Dec 01. Also served KTG (Premier Mine) and KLH (151, 354 and 40262) 22 Feb 00 to 5 Jun 00 and 4 Feb 02 to 30 Jun 02. QSA (3) inc Paar excl OFS, 14-15 Star (7th SAI), BWM (SAVR), VM (7th SAI)
O'Brien, Lt Philip William, CP1	QSA (2) DoK OFS	B Squadron. KSA (2). Served in the Bechuanaland Rebellion 1897 earning CGHGSM (1) Bech
O'Brien, Pte T, KTG	QSA (1) DoK	No 6 Redoubt
O'Brien, Capt Thomas Henry, LNLR	QSA (4) DoK OFS Tr 02	See his biography (page 350)
O'Callaghan, Pte Charles, KTG	QSA (3) RoM DoK OFS	No I Section, L Company. Also served KLH (441) 19 Mar 00 to 5 Jun 00
O'Connell, 121 Cpl Thomas, CP2	QSA (3) DoK OFS Tr	CP intelligence and detective staff. Killed in action at Hoopstad 23 Oct 00
O'Connor, Pte G, KTG	QSA (1) DoK	No I Section, L Company
O'Connor, 4968 Pte J, LNLR	QSA (3) DoK OFS Tr	QSA (3), [KSA (2)], KStar. Seaby Jun 74 £65
O'Connor, 188 Cpl John, CP2	QSA (4) RoM DoK OFS Tr	CP HQ and depot mounted branch. Served in the Bechuanaland Rebellion 1897 earning CGHGSM (1) Bech
O'Connor, Pte M, KTG	QSA (1) DoK	No I Company, B Section, Reservoir
O'Connor, 307 Pte Thomas, KRV	QSA (4) RoM DoK OFS Tr	Non effective 20 Jun 00. Also served SRG (81) from 11 Feb 01
O'Dell, 194 Pte David, CP2	QSA (1) DoK	C Squadron. Wounded 25 Nov 99. KSA reissued 28 Jan 10. Served Bechuanaland Border Police 10 Nov 94 to 15 Nov 95 and CP 16 Nov 95 to 30 Jun 04. CGHGSM (2) Bas Bech (Pte CP), [QSA (1), KSA (2)]. Dixon Dec 92 £260. Ursual Dec 02
O'Dowd, 223 Pte Michael, CP2	QSA (2) DoK OFS	Served 11 Oct 99 to 31 May 02. KSA (2). Served in the Bechuanaland Rebellion 1897 earning CGHGSM (1) Bech
O'Gorman, Capt C J, RAMC	QSA (3) DoK OFS Tr	See his biography (page 350)
O'Halloran, 141 Tpr Henry Fenwick Norman, KLH	QSA (3) RoM DoK OFS	Served 9 Mar 00 to 5 Jun 00. Also served KTG (Premier Mine) 3 Oct 99 to 10 Mar 00 and SRG (78) 11 Feb 01 to 14 Dec 01
O'Hara, 5257 Pte W, LNLR	QSA (3) DoK OFS Tr	QSA (3), [KSA (2)]. Glendining Dec 65
O'Leary, 30137 QMS George Daniel, KLH	QSA (4) DoK OFS Tr 01	Served 29 Oct 99 to 20 Apr 00 and 27 Feb 01 to 27 Aug 01
O'Malley, Pte W, KTG	QSA (1) DoK	No I Section, L Company
O'Mara, Pte J, KTG	QSA (1) DoK	Otto's Kopje Scouts
O'Meara, Capt B E A, KTG	QSA (1) DoK	See his biography (page 351)
O'Meara, Maj Walter Alfred John, RE	QSA (5) DoK Paar Drie Tr 01	See his biography (page 351)
O'Molony, Lt S, KTG	QSA (1) DoK	Reservoir
O'Neil, 3475 Pte A, LNLR	QSA (3) DoK OFS Tr	KSA (2)
O'Neill, 9337 Gnr Antony, RGA	QSA (2) DoK Tr	Premier Mine. KSA (2)
O'Neill, 1483 Pte Patrick Lawrence, CP1	QSA (3) DoK OFS Tr	CP (No 1 Maxim gun detachment). Discharged time expired 24 Feb 02. Also served 1st ILH (2128) 4 May 01 to 31 Aug 01
O'Regan, Pte Myles, KTG	QSA (3) DoK OFS Tr	No II Section, B Company, No 4 Redoubt. Also served SRG (80) from 11 Feb 01
O'Reilly, 454 Pte A, KRV	QSA (1) DoK	DMU 13 Nov 00. QSA (1). Clark Oct 89 £95
O'Sullivan, Sgt J P, KTG	QSA (1) DoK	D Company (Veterans), Beaconsfield Town Guard
O'Toole, 130 Gnr John William, DFA	QSA (2) DoK OFS	Enrolled 2 Feb 99. Also served DFH. Resigned 26 Sep 03. Occupation engine driver at De Beers. QSA (2). Dixon Sep 92 £140. Spink Oct 99 £110

Medal roll

O'Toole, 599 Pte Stephen John, KRV	QSA (1) DoK	Non effective 11 Dec 00. Also served SRG (302) 15 Feb 01 to 15 May 01
Oakes, 633 Pte Frank Harvey Aston, CP2	QSA (5) RoM DoK OFS Tr 01	C Squadron. Served 11 Oct 99 to 3 Jul 01. QSA (5). March Medals Jun 94 £250
Oates, Pte F, KTG	QSA (1) DoK	Also served KR (1041) to 1 Jul 02. KSA (2). Surname also Oats
Oatley, 301 Sgt Maj William Henry, KLH	QSA (2) DoK OFS	Served 1 Nov 99 until transferred to KTG 24 Jan 00. Wounded 25 Nov 99. Also served KTG (No 2 Redoubt). DCM, BSACM rev Rhodesia 96 (Lt MRF), QSA (1) excl OFS, KSA (0) (5 Hd Cond ASC), KStar. City Coins Sep 03
Oats, Lt Francis, KTG	QSA (1) DoK	See his biography (page 351)
Oats, Pte J, KTG	QSA (3) DoK 01 02	No 6 Redoubt and No 2 Schmidt's Breastwork. Also served KRV (1311) to 1 Jul 02. Surname also Oates. QSA (1) DoK. Glendining Oct 81 £95
Odendaal, Pte D C, KTG	QSA (1) DoK	Kimberley Mine Ambulance Company, E Section
Oehley, 56 Tpr John McGregor, KLH	QSA (2) DoK OFS	Served 21 Oct 99 to 30 Apr 00. Also served Kimberley Municipal Police 9 Mar 01 to 31 Dec 04. 50th Anniversary attendee. QSA (2)
Ogilvie, Nurse E A, NS	QSA (0)	Kimberley Civil Hospital
Oglethorpe, 3708 Pte J, LNLR	QSA (3) DoK OFS Tr	QSA (3), [KSA (2)]. Glendining Nov 99. eBay Jan 05. QSA (3), [KSA], KStar. Spink Sep 01 £220
Okes, 130 Pte Henry Thomas, CP2	QSA (3) DoK OFS Tr	B Squadron. KSA (2). Served in the Bechuanaland Rebellion 1897 earning CGHGSM (1) Bech
Olds, Pte H F, KTG	QSA (1) DoK	No I Section, Belgravia Fort
Olds, Pte J, KTG	QSA (1) DoK	
Oliphant, 85 Sgt T, KRV	QSA (1) DoK	Non effective 15 Jul 00. Possibly served in the Bechuanaland Rebellion 1897 as Olifant with Kimb Rifles earning CGHGSM (1) Bech
Olive, Pte W A, KTG	QSA (1) DoK	Premier Mine
Oliver, Capt H A, KTG	QSA (1) DoK	See his biography (page 351)
Oliver, 582 Pte R, KRV	QSA (4) DoK OFS Tr 02	Discharged 1 Jul 02. KSA (2)
Olivier, Pte C, KTG	QSA (1) DoK	No 1 Redoubt
Olsen, Pte J, KTG	QSA (1) DoK	Ambulance Corps, Beaconsfield Town Guard. Also served CPS (424)
Olver, Pte H, KTG	QSA (1) DoK	Ambulance Corps, Beaconsfield Town Guard
Olver, Pte R, KTG	QSA (1) DoK	Premier Mine
Olver, 2062 Sapr W J, RE	QSA (2) DoK Drie	
Oostermeyer, H G, KTG	QSA (0)	Roll states "Manufacturing shells and repairing Maxims"
Oostermeyer, Pte J J, KTG	QSA (1) DoK	No II Section, C Company, Pickering's Redoubt No 1
Oosthuizen, 142 Pte John, CP2	QSA (5) RoM DoK OFS Tr 01	B Squadron. Served in the Bechuanaland Rebellion 1897 earning CGHGSM (1) Bech
O'Pie, 227 Gnr William, DFA	QSA (1) DoK	Enrolled 8 May 00. Resigned 13 Jan 03. Occupation miner. Surname also spelled Opie. QSA (3) inc OFS Tr. Glendining Sep 88. QSA (1). Neate Sep 93 £95. Liverpool Feb 99 £115
Orborne, Pte A, KTG	QSA (1) DoK	
Orchard, 2866 L Cpl A, LNLR	QSA (3) DoK OFS Tr	KSA (2)
Orchard, 224 Cpl Horace Lancelot, KLH	QSA (2) DoK OFS	Served 20 Oct 99 to 30 Apr 00. Also served CPS (119) with initial N
Orpen, 399 Pte Charles, CP2	QSA (4) RoM DoK OFS Tr	C Squadron. KSA (2)
Orr, Pte J, KTG	QSA (1) DoK	No II Section, Mandy Fort

Orr, Lt John, KTG	QSA (1) DoK	See his biography (page 351)
Orr, 244 Cpl John, KLH	QSA (3) DoK OFS Tr	Served 23 Oct 99 to 30 Apr 00. Wounded 16 Nov 99. Also served 1st KFS (555) 2 Jan 01 to 7 Jul 01. QSA issued 10 May 05. KSA (2)
Orr, 132 Pte T H, KRV	QSA (1) DoK	DMU 13 Apr 00
Orrell, 3848 Pte W, LNLR	QSA (3) DoK OFS Tr	KSA (2). Wounded Nooitgedacht 17 Oct 00
Orren, 388 Pte F E, KRV	QSA (4) DoK OFS Tr 02	Discharged 26 Feb 02. KSA (2)
Ortell, Pte J, KTG	QSA (1) DoK	No IV Section, A Company, Beaconsfield Town Guard
Ortlepp, Surg Lt Albert James, DFA	QSA (5) DoK OFS Tr 01 02	See his biography (page 351)
Ortlepp, 281 Pte J, KRV	QSA (5) RoM DoK OFS Tr 01	Discharged 1 Sep 01
Osborne, Pte Alfred, KTG	QSA (1) DoK	No II Section, B Company, Beaconsfield Town Guard. Died of disease 16 Jan 00
Osborne, Lt C, KTG	QSA (1) DoK	No II Section, B Company, Beaconsfield Town Guard. QSA (1), KStar. City Coins May 02
Osborne, 166 Sgt Joseph Peter, DFA	QSA (3) DoK OFS Tr	Attached DBMB (Botanical Gardens). Enrolled 4 Jul 99. Also served RE 75 to 82, RA 82 to 98. Occupation seaman at De Beers. KSA (2). Served in the Bechuanaland Rebellion 1897 with DFA earning CGHGSM (1) Bech
Osman, Mr F, POC	QSA (1) DoK	Telegraph signaller. Initials C H on the nominal roll
Osner, Cpl W, KTG	QSA (1) DoK	No 2 Schmidt's Breastwork
Osselair, Pte F, KTG	QSA (1) DoK	No I Section, A Company, Beaconsfield Town Guard. Also served 34th Co ASC (28)
Ott, Pte C S, KTG	QSA (1) DoK	K Company
Otto, 284 Pte C, KRV	QSA (1) DoK	DMU 6 Jan 00. There is 115 C Otto on the Warrenton DMT roll with OFS & Tr crossed through. Same man?
Otto, Pte C, KTG	QSA (1) DoK	
Otto, 502 Sgt J H, CP1	QSA (2) DoK OFS	B Squadron. DMU 31 Mar 02. CGHGSM (1) Bech (Cpl CP), QSA (2), KSA (2), KStar. Dixon Apr 98 £325
Otto, 373 Tpr Peter, KLH	QSA (3) RoM DoK OFS	Served 2 Feb 00 to 5 Jun 00. QSA (3). Christies Jul 85
Outong, Pte C, KTG	QSA (1) DoK	
Outram, E H, KTG	QSA (0)	Roll states "Electrical work, searchlights etc"
Overall, 4480 Pte G, LNLR	QSA (4) DoK Paar Joh DH	KSA (2). Mounted Infantry
Overberg, Pte P, KTG	QSA (3) RoM DoK Tr	Also served KLH (324) and KH (149). KSA (2)
Owen, 172 Cpl Arthur Duncan, KLH	QSA (2) DoK Paar	Served 19 Oct 99 to 5 Jun 00. On QSA roll as Orren
Owen, 928 Pte Hugh, KRV	QSA (5) RoM DoK OFS Tr 01	Discharged 11 Jul 02. Also served KTG (No III Section, C Company, Beaconsfield Town Guard), KLH (1282) 5 Mar 00 to 24 Nov 00 and FID. QSA (4) excl 01. Glendining Mar 89
Owen, Pte L M, KTG	QSA (1) DoK	No 6 supply depot
Owen, 367 Sgt Lewis Llewellyn, KLH	QSA (4) DoK OFS Tr 01	Joined 12 Jan 00. Also served KRV (682) until DMU 5 Jan 01. Died of pneumonia at Wynberg 16 Feb 01
Owen, Pte R T, KTG	QSA (1) DoK	
Owen, 146 Gnr Randal Charles, DFA	QSA (2) DoK OFS	Enrolled 30 May 99. Resigned 4 Feb 03. Occupation railway clerk
Owen, 191 Tpr Richard Edward, KLH	QSA (3) RoM DoK Paar	Served 7 Mar 00 to 5 Jun 00. On QSA roll as Orren. Also served KTG (Premier Mine) and SRG (79) from 12 Feb 01
Owens, Pte W H, KTG	QSA (1) DoK	Kimberley Mine searchlight and telephone section. In charge of searchlight apparatus
Oxford, Pte S, KTG	QSA (1) DoK	N Company, No 1 Redoubt

Medal roll

Oxley, Sister E M, NS	QSA (0)	QSA (0), KSA (2). Spink Jul 09
Ozard, 698 Sgt R, KRV	QSA (3) DoK OFS Tr	DMU 20 Jan 03. Severely wounded Klip Drift 7 Mar 02. CGHGSM (1) Bech (Kimb Rifles), QSA (3), KSA (2). Christies Jul 85. QSA (3), KSA (2). Collett May 89 £165

P

Pack, 185 Sgt E, KRV	QSA (1) DoK	Non effective 6 Jul 00. KStar (named to Sgt KTG). Seaby Apr 82 £60
Packer, Cpl Fred William, DH	QSA (4) DoK OFS 01 02	Served 19 Nov 00 to 20 Dec 01. Also served KTG (No I Section, No 2 Redoubt and Premier Mine). Wounded Diepfontein 10 Apr 01. Occupation artist
Packet, 996 L Cpl William, CP1	QSA (2) DoK Tr	C Squadron. Born 11 Nov 1874 and joined the CP in 1895. Detective Probationer in 1916. Detective Sgt in 1919. Discharged Nov 1925. CGHGSM (1) Bech (Pte CP), QSA (2), KSA (2), SA Police Good Service Medal, KStar. DNW Dec 03 £620
Page, 842 Pte Charles, KRV	QSA (2) DoK Tr	DMU 6 Dec 01. Also served KTG (No I Company, A Section, Reservoir), CPS, BR (447) 8 Jan 02 to 16 Apr 02 and WLH (362) 5 May 02 to 30 Jun 02. KSA (2). Occupation butcher
Page, Pte Edward Cumming, KTG	QSA (1) DoK	No II Section, K Company. Also served SRG (82) 12 Feb 01 to 10 May 01
Page, 417 Cpl F C, KRV	QSA (4) RoM DoK OFS Tr	Served 11 Oct 99 to 22 May 01. Also served CPS (752) 28 Oct 01 to 27 Jan 02. KSA (2)
Page, 1307 Pte George E, KRV	QSA (5) DoK OFS Tr 01 02	Discharged KRV 16 Aug 02. Also served KTG (Premier Mine) and SRG (84) 12 Feb 01 to 15 May 01
Page, Pte Herbert Edward, KTG	QSA (6) DoK Paar Drie Joh DH Witt	Premier Mine. Also served DH 24 Feb 00 to 26 Jan 01
Page, Cpl J, KTG	QSA (1) DoK	
Page, 839 Pte J H, KRV	QSA (2) DoK OFS	Discharged 1 Jul 02. Also served KTG (No IV Section, K Company). KSA (2)
Page, 488 Pte J W, KRV	QSA (1) DoK	DMU 17 Mar 00
Page, Pte K B, KTG	QSA (1) DoK	No II Section, K Company
Page, 173 Tpr Reginald George, KLH	QSA (2) DoK OFS	Served 19 Oct 99 to 14 Mar 00. Also served KTG. QSA (2). Neate Nov 95 £95
Page, 33 Sgt Thomas Henry, KLH	QSA (4) RoM DoK Paar Tr	Served 18 Oct 99 to 17 Jun 02. KSA (2)
Pain, 1160 Pte Joseph James, KRV	QSA (3) DoK OFS Tr	Served 14 Aug 00 to 30 Jun 02. Also served KLH (211) 20 Oct 99 to 30 Apr 00. KSA (2)
Paley, Lt George, KTG	QSA (1) DoK	No III Section, D Company. Occupation mechanical engineer at De Beers
Palm, B, KTG	QSA (0)	Roll states "In charge of natives employed on forts"
Palm, Pte W, KTG	QSA (1) DoK	No III Section, A Company, Beaconsfield Town Guard. QSA (1), KStar
Palmer, Sgt G, KTG	QSA (1) DoK	No IV Section, B Company, No 4 Redoubt
Palmer, Pte J, KTG	QSA (3) Rhod DoK Tr	No IV Section, A Company, Beaconsfield Town Guard. Also served 37th Co ASC as Head Conductor
Palmer, Pte Kenneth George Livingstone, KTG	QSA (1) DoK	No IV Section, No 2 Redoubt. Also served SRG (152) from 11 Feb 01
Palmer, 768 Pte T, KRV	QSA (3) RoM DoK OFS	Discharged 1 Jul 00. Also served KTG (No II Section, A Company, Beaconsfield Town Guard). Wounded Fourteen Streams 16 Mar 00
Palvie, S C, KTG	QSA (0)	Roll states "Ambulance work in connection with scurvy outbreak"
Pappin, Sgt H, KTG	QSA (1) DoK	No I Section, B2 Company, No 3 Redoubt

Name	Medals	Notes
Park, Pte Edward, KTG	QSA (4) DoK OFS Tr 01	No 6 Redoubt. Also served CinCBG (22718) 17 Nov 00 to 16 May 01, Stellenbosch DMT (no trace on roll) and 1st BrH 3 Jun 01 to 4 Dec 01
Park, Pte J, KTG	QSA (1) DoK	B line of defence, No 3 Redoubt. QSA (1), KStar. Noble Numismatics Jul 97
Parker, Pte A, KTG	QSA (1) DoK	No I Section, C Company, Pickering's Redoubt No 1
Parker, 609 Pte Algernon, CP2	QSA (1) DoK	A Squadron. Killed in action 11 Nov 99. QSA (1). DNW Apr 06 £550
Parker, 4095 Pte E, LNLR	QSA (3) DoK OFS Tr	KSA (2)
Parker, Pte E, KTG	QSA (1) DoK	No II Section, C Company, Pickering's Redoubt No 2. 395 E Parker served CPS and gained Tr. Same man?
Parker, Pte H, KTG	QSA (1) DoK	No I Company, B Section, Reservoir
Parker, 853 Pte I, KRV	QSA (1) DoK	Discharged 4 Jul 02. Also served KTG. [QSA (1), KSA (2)], KStar. Spink Apr 07 £110
Parker, Pte J K, KTG	QSA (1) DoK	No II Section, No 2 Redoubt and H Company
Parker, Pte R, KTG	QSA (1) DoK	Cycle Corps, A Company
Parker, 327 Pte Robert Charles, CP2	QSA (4) RoM DoK OFS Tr	B Squadron. [QSA (4), KSA (2)], KStar. Toad Hall Dec 89 £65
Parker, Pte S A, KTG	QSA (1) DoK	No I Section, No 2 Redoubt
Parker, Pte T, KTG	QSA (1) DoK	No I Section, No 2 Redoubt
Parker, 1180 Pte T H, KRV	QSA (4) DoK OFS Tr 01	Non effective 10 Jul 01. Discharged 18 Sep 02. Also served KTG (No II Section, A Company, Beaconsfield Town Guard)
Parker, 95390 Gnr Thomas, RGA	QSA (3) DoK OFS Tr	KSA (2)
Parkin, Pte Durant Clifford, KTG	QSA (4) RoM DoK OFS Tr	No 2 Schmidt's Breastwork. Also served KLH (61 & 1287) as Parkins 19 Mar 00 to 10 Nov 00
Parkin, Pte E D, KTG	QSA (1) DoK	No 2 Section, Maundy Fort, Boshof Road, No 2 Schmidt's Breastwork and No II Section, Mandy Fort
Parkin, Cpl Julius Minet, KTG	QSA (3) Rhod DoK 01	See his biography (page 351)
Parkins, Pte T, KTG	QSA (1) DoK	No 2 Section, Maundy Fort, Boshof Road and No II Section, Mandy Fort
Parkins, 4189 L Cpl W, LNLR	QSA (3) DoK OFS Tr	QSA (3), [KSA (2)], KStar. RHQ
Parr, Pte J B G, KTG	QSA (1) DoK	Premier Mine
Parrington, 4310 Pte G, LNLR	QSA (3) DoK OFS Tr	QSA (3), [KSA (2)]. Sotheby Mar 83 £100
Parry, 5428 Pte J, LNLR	QSA (3) DoK OFS Tr	Invalided to England 10 Dec 00. QSA (3), KStar. RHQ
Parry, 9706 Gnr Joseph, RGA	QSA (2) DoK Tr	KSA (2)
Parsons, 246 Tpr David, KLH	QSA (2) DoK OFS	Served 22 Oct 99 to 29 Aug 00. Wounded 16 Nov 99. Also served Condr Imperial Transport and FID. QSA (2), KStar, 14-15 Star (Rfm 4th SAMR), BWM, VM (Rfm 4th SAMR). Spink Apr 93. DNW Apr 94 £190. Burman Aug 98 £285. Glendining Mar 01. Dixon Jun 02 £485
Parsons, 10 Tpr David George, KLH	QSA (3) DoK OFS 01	Served 16 Oct 99 until DMU 24 Mar 00. Also served RoH (9151) 16 May 00 to 22 Mar 01, SRG (525) from 22 Apr 01 and Cape Infantry. Occupation blacksmith
Parsons, 18 Tpr W G, KLH	QSA (2) DoK OFS	Served 16 Oct 99 to 4 Mar 00
Partington, 4038 Pte J, LNLR	QSA (3) DoK OFS Tr	QSA (3), [KSA (2)], 14-15 Star, BWM, VM, KStar. Sotheby Mar 84
Partridge, Pte G T, KTG	QSA (1) DoK	No 1 Redoubt
Partridge, Pte J F, KTG	QSA (1) DoK	No II Company, A Section, Reservoir

Name	Medals	Notes
Partridge, Cpl John Robert, KTG	QSA (3) RoM DoK OFS	No 3 Redoubt. Also served KLH (402) 15 Mar 00 to 5 Jun 00
Partridge, 895 Pte S W, KRV	QSA (4) RoM DoK OFS Tr	Discharged 25 Jul 02. Also served KTG (No IV Company, A Section, Reservoir). Severely wounded Christiana 28 Feb 02. KSA (2)
Pascual, Pte E, KTG	QSA (1) DoK	No I Section, B2 Company, No 3 Redoubt
Paskin, 49 Band G F, KRV	QSA (1) DoK	KSA (2)
Passmore, 708 Pte A C, KRV	QSA (3) DoK OFS Tr	Discharged 9 Jan 03. KSA (2)
Passmore, 4186 OR Sgt S, LNLR	QSA (2) DoK OFS	KSA (2). Wounded Serfontein 26 Jun 00
Pate, Pte A, KTG	QSA (1) DoK	No IV Section, C Company, Beaconsfield Town Guard
Paterson, Pte R C, KTG	QSA (1) DoK	Civil Service Redoubt. QSA (1). McGregor Museum
Paton, Nurse F, NS	QSA (0)	Kimberley Civil Hospital
Pattenden, Pte E, KTG	QSA (1) DoK	No IV Section, No 2 Redoubt
Pattenden, 216 Dvr George Charles, DFA	QSA (2) DoK OFS	Enrolled 27 Nov 99. Resigned 11 Feb 03
Patterson, 303 Pte D, KRV	QSA (1) DoK	Dismissed for misconduct 11 Dec 99
Patterson, Pte Frank Hay, KTG	QSA (1) DoK	Kenilworth Defence Force. Also served CRSS (1572) from 11 Jan 02. Occupation prospector. QSA (1). Spink Dec 79 £125. Spink Apr 81 £140. Spink Apr 83 £120
Patterson, Pte G, KTG	QSA (1) DoK	No 2 Schmidt's Breastwork. 871 G Patterson served CPS and gained Tr. Same man?
Pattrick, 174 Sgt Horace, KLH	QSA (3) DoK OFS Tr	Discharged 3 Apr 00. Also served KTG (No IV Section, B Company, No 4 Redoubt) and SRG (196) 12 Feb 01 to 28 May 02. KSA (2)
Paulie, Pte A, KTG	QSA (1) DoK	H Company
Payne, 170 Gnr Fred W, DFA	QSA (3) DoK OFS Tr	Enrolled 1 Aug 99. Wounded 24 Oct 99. DMU 6 Mar 00. Occupation carpenter. Also served Bechuanaland Field Force
Payne, Pte George, KTG	QSA (1) DoK	H Company. Also served SRG (140) from 11 Feb 01. QSA (1), KStar. City Coins Dec 97. Spink Apr 98 £240. Spink Jul 00 £230
Payne, 261 Sgt George Thomas, KLH	QSA (2) DoK OFS	Served 19 Oct 99 to 30 Apr 00. Also served Dordrecht Dist Vol Gd (349), KLH (261) and FMR (413)
Paynter, Sgt J L, KTG	QSA (3) DoK OFS Tr	H Company. Also served Lt SRG. QSA (1) DoK, KStar. Sotheby Jun 88 £132. Glendining Jun 94 £180
Peachey, Nurse N, NS	QSA (0)	St Michael's Home
Peachy, Sgt Shadrach, KTG	QSA (1) DoK	Kenilworth Defence Force. Also served SRG (83) from 12 Feb 01
Peacock, 138 Pte Clampitt Walter, CP2	QSA (2) DoK OFS	B Squadron. CGHGSM (1) Bech, QSA (2), [KSA (2)]. Kaplan Feb 04. Kaplan Mar 05
Peacock, 356 Pte G, KRV	QSA (2) DoK 01	Non effective 23 May 01
Peacock, 4995 Pte T, LNLR	QSA (3) DoK OFS Tr	QSA (3), KSA (2). Neate Jun 02 £245
Peake, Lt S, KTG	QSA (1) DoK	No IV Section, A Company, Beaconsfield Town Guard
Peakman, Lt Col Thomas Cox, KLH	QSA (4) RoM DoK OFS Tr	See his biography (page 352)
Pearce, Mr F A, POC	QSA (1) DoK	QSA (1), KStar. City Coins Jul 99
Pearson, Pte A, KTG	QSA (1) DoK	No II Section, C Company, Pickering's Redoubt No 1. Also served SRG (83)
Pearson, Pte C A, KTG	QSA (1) DoK	Premier Mine. QSA (1). City Coins May 02
Pearson, 823 Pte F T, KRV	QSA (3) RoM DoK OFS	Discharged 1 Jul 00. Also served KTG and 1st KFS (584). KSA (2)
Pearson, Pte G T, KTG	QSA (1) DoK	G Company

Name	Medals	Notes
Peasland, Pte Samuel Francis, KTG	QSA (4) RoM DoK OFS Tr	Mounted Section, Kenilworth Defence Force. Also served KLH (34583) 9 Mar 00 to 10 Nov 00, DS 14 Dec 00 to 23 Jan 01, CPS (660) and FID
Peat, 242 Tpr J, KLH	QSA (1) DoK	Joined 26 Oct 99. Died of disease 18 Feb 00
Peat, QMS R C, KTG	QSA (1) DoK	D Company
Peate, Pte W H, KTG	QSA (1) DoK	No 2 Schmidt's Breastwork
Peddle, Pte Edward J J, KTG	QSA (3) RoM DoK OFS	Premier Mine. Also served KLH (194) 8 Mar 00 to 5 Jun 00
Peebles, 436 Pte T, KRV	QSA (1) DoK	DMU 5 Dec 99
Peel, Pte W, KTG	QSA (1) DoK	No IV Section, C Company, Beaconsfield Town Guard
Peglar, 3680 Pioneer H, LNLR	QSA (3) DoK OFS Tr	QSA (3), KSA (2). Glendining Sep 88
Peglar, 5538 Pte R, LNLR	QSA (3) DoK OFS Tr	KSA (2)
Peiser, 318 Tpr John, KLH	QSA (2) DoK OFS	Joined 1 Nov 99. Died of wounds received 25 Nov 99
Pennett, Cpl A, KTG	QSA (1) DoK	Kenilworth Defence Force. QSA (1), KStar. Spink Jun 89
Penniall, Sgt Alfred, KTG	QSA (3) DoK OFS Tr	No III Section, B Company, Beaconsfield Town Guard. Also served KLH (1074) 23 Mar 00 to 6 Nov 00
Penniket, 4590 Band R, LNLR	QSA (4) DoK OFS Tr 01	Invalided to England 8 Jan 01. QSA (4), 14 Star, BWM, VM (Sgt LNLR), KStar. Glendining Mar 92 £160
Penning, 212 Pte Albert William, CP2	QSA (2) DoK OFS	CP HQ and depot mounted branch. KSA (2). KSA reissued 5 Mar 09. Served in the Bechuanaland Rebellion 1897 earning CGHGSM (1) Bech
Penny, Lt E A, KTG	QSA (1) DoK	No IV Section, F Company, Mostert's Redoubt
Penny, 187 Dvr Philip Henry, DFA	QSA (2) DoK OFS	Enrolled 20 Sep 99. Served DFA 96-97. Resigned 12 Jan 03. Occupation harness maker
Pepper, Cpl E, KTG	QSA (1) DoK	No IV Section, C Company, Beaconsfield Town Guard
Percy, Pte G, KTG	QSA (1) DoK	No III Section, Belgravia Fort. SAGS (1) 1878 (Inspr Griqualand W Constabulary), QSA (1). City Coins Jun 04
Percy, Lt R J, KTG	QSA (1) DoK	G Company. QSA (1), 14-15 Star, BWM, VM (Lt 7th Infy). Liverpool Feb 97 £225
Perdica, Pte C, KTG	QSA (1) DoK	No IV Section, C Company, Beaconsfield Town Guard
Perdue, 44 Band Cpl W J, KRV	QSA (2) DoK OFS	KSA (2). Served in Bechuanaland Rebellion 1897 with Griqualand West Brigade earning CGHGSM (1) Bech
Perkins, 249 Pay Sgt F J, KRV	QSA (1) DoK	Discharged 11 Mar 03. KSA (2)
Perry, 722 Pte John James, CP2	QSA (3) DoK OFS Tr	A Squadron. KSA (2)
Perry, 890 Pte William Henry, CP2	QSA (3) DoK Paar Tr	Also served IY. Note says CC issued off 21st Co IY
Persson, Pte J, KTG	QSA (1) DoK	
Persson, Pte Lars, KTG	QSA (3) RoM DoK OFS	No II Section, No 2 Redoubt. Also served KLH (403 & 447) 16 Mar 00 to 5 Jun 00, KR (1203) 6 Sep 00 to 23 May 02 and WLH (416 & 612) with forename Louis 29 May 02 to 30 Jun 02. KSA (2)
Peters, Pte C, KTG	QSA (1) DoK	Ambulance Corps, Beaconsfield Town Guard
Peters, Nurse M, NS	QSA (0)	Kimberley Civil Hospital
Peters, Pte T J, KTG	QSA (1) DoK	
Peters, 1018 Pte W F, KRV	QSA (1) DoK	Discharged 1 Jul 02. Also served KTG (Ambulance Corps, Beaconsfield Town Guard). KSA (2)
Peters, 135 L Cpl W J, KRV	QSA (2) DoK OFS	Discharged 7 Aug 00. CGHGSM (1) Bech (Pte DFH), QSA (2), BWM (2nd Cl WO SANLC). Bonhams Dec 05 £400
Petersen, Pte H, KTG	QSA (1) DoK	
Petersen, 794 Pte John Bernard, CP2	QSA (1) DoK	B Squadron. Wounded 24 Oct 99

Peterson, Sgt E, KTG	QSA (1) DoK	132 E Petersen served CPS. Same man?
Peterson, 69 Cpl John Daniel, KLH	QSA (2) DoK OFS	Served 20 Oct 99 to 3 Apr 00 and 15 May 02 to 30 Jun 02. Also served IYS (39) 22 May 00 to 6 Sep 00, CPS (668) as Petersen, SRG (77) and FID. KSA (2)
Petrazzas, Pte P, KTG	QSA (1) DoK	No I Section, B Company, Beaconsfield Town Guard
Petrie, 21 CSM J, KRV	QSA (1) DoK	DMU 8 Mar 00. Possibly served in the Bechuanaland Rebellion 1897 with DFH earning CGHGSM (1) Bech. KStar. Spink Apr 00 £85
Petrie, 277 Tpr J, KLH	QSA (2) DoK OFS	Served 19 Oct 99 to 30 Apr 00
Petrie, Pte R L, KTG	QSA (1) DoK	No II Section, F Company, Mostert's Redoubt
Petzer, 271 Cpl H C, KRV	QSA (1) DoK	KSA (2)
Peverelle, Sp Const L, CP2	QSA (4) DoK OFS Tr 01	Also served H Co CMSC 2 May 00 to 30 Apr 01
Phelan, Pte J, KTG	QSA (1) DoK	No I Company, B Section, Reservoir
Phieffer, Pte L, KTG	QSA (1) DoK	No IV Section, L Company
Philip, Pte G H, KTG	QSA (1) DoK	No I Section, Belgravia Fort
Philips, Pte A R, KTG	QSA (1) DoK	No III Section, K Company
Phillips, 4835 Pte A, LNLR	QSA (4) DoK OFS Tr 01	SA01 issued 14 Jun 07. QSA (4), KStar. Seaby Jan 74 £46
Phillips, Cpl B, KTG	QSA (1) DoK	No 2 Schmidt's Breastwork
Phillips, 463 Pte Frank, CP2	QSA (1) DoK	CP dismounted branch (barrier & redoubt duties). Discharged for misconduct. Also served IYS (43) 23 May 00 to 6 Sep 00
Phillips, 801 Cpl G, KRV	QSA (3) DoK OFS Tr	Discharged 1 Jul 02. Also served KTG (No I Company, B Section, Reservoir). KSA (2)
Phillips, 91515 Bombdr Harold Wilbert, RGA	QSA (4) RoM DoK OFS Tr	14th Co RGA. Also served CP2. Transferred to Johannesburg Mounted Railway Police 23 Oct 00
Phillips, Pte J, KTG	QSA (1) DoK	H Company
Phillips, Pte R, KTG	QSA (1) DoK	No II Section, K Company
Phillips, Pte W, KTG	QSA (1) DoK	No II Company, A Section, Reservoir
Phillipson, Pte J A, KTG	QSA (1) DoK	No 2 Schmidt's Breastwork
Philp, Pte S Y, KTG	QSA (1) DoK	No 3 supply depot
Pickering, Pte Frederick Edward, KTG	QSA (2) DoK OFS	No I Section, B2 Company, No 3 Redoubt. Also served SRG (165) from 13 Feb 01
Pickering, Capt W, KTG	QSA (1) DoK	See his biography (page 352)
Pickwell, 97526 Gnr Jonathan, RGA	QSA (2) DoK Tr	KSA (2)
Pienaar, Pte J W, KTG	QSA (1) DoK	No I Company, B Section, Reservoir
Pierce, 813 Pte Arthur George, CP2	QSA (1) DoK	DMU. QSA (1). Glendining Jun 92
Pierce, 2197 Sapr F W, RE	QSA (3) DoK Drie Tr	QSA (3), KSA (2), 14 Star and Bar, BWM, VM, KStar. RHQ
Pierce, 565 Pte William, KRV	QSA (5) RoM DoK OFS Tr 01	Dismissed for misconduct 14 Dec 99. Also served KTG (No III Company, A Section, Reservoir), KLH (377 & 446) 6 Mar 00 to 6 Nov 00, MH (no trace on QSA roll), Transport Stock Riders and 1st ILH (1534) from 17 Nov 00. Killed 5 Jan 01
Piercy, 85 Sgt Arthur, CP2	QSA (1) DoK	Served CPD2 HQ Staff. KSA (2)
Pigg, Guard C, IMR	QSA (3) DoK OFS Tr	QSA (2) excl OFS, KStar. Morris Jul 98. Glendining Nov 99. Sold with brother's (?) medal, QSA (2) Rhod & RoM who served with No 2 armoured train (engineers) as a guard and "was at all times careful and obliging and took his train through many dangers and difficulties without accident!"

Kimberley Siege Account and Medal Roll

Pike, Pte D, KTG	QSA (3) DoK OFS Tr	No III Company, A Section, Reservoir). Also served KRV (996) to Jul 02. KSA (2). QSA (1) excl OFS & Tr. Shirley Nov 04 £190. Wakefield Jan 08 £280
Pilcher, Pte M, KTG	QSA (1) DoK	Kamfersdam Company. On nominal roll as Pitcher
Pilkington, 5152 Pte J, LNLR	QSA (3) DoK OFS Tr	QSA (3). Glendining Apr 77 £60
Pilkington, 4315 Pte W, LNLR	QSA (3) DoK OFS Tr	Invalided to England 18 Apr 00. KSA (1) 02
Pim, Capt H, KTG	QSA (1) DoK	Officer commanding No 4 Redoubt. CBE, QSA (1)
Pine, J, KTG	QSA (0)	Roll states "Construction of forts and barricades"
Pinnock, 4937 Pte E, LNLR	QSA (3) DoK OFS Tr	KSA (2). 4939 on KSA roll
Pinnock, Pte E W, KTG	QSA (1) DoK	No II Section, Mandy Fort. QSA (1)
Pinnock, Sgt G, KTG	QSA (1) DoK	No I Section, C Company, Pickering's Redoubt No 1
Pinnock, 380 Pte Robert, CP2	QSA (4) RoM DoK OFS Tr	C Squadron. Prisoner at Hoopstad 23 Oct 00. Served in the Bechuanaland Rebellion 1897 earning CGHGSM (1) Bech
Piper, 660 Pte Percy, CP2	QSA (3) DoK OFS Tr	CP dismounted in Beaconsfield. DMU. Also served DS 12 Dec 00 to 4 Feb 01 and FID. KSA (2)
Pirzenthal, 499 Pte E B, KRV	QSA (3) DoK OFS 01	DMU 26 Feb 01
Pirzenthal, Pte H F, KTG	QSA (1) DoK	No I Company, B Section, Reservoir
Pirzenthal, 467 Pte O E, KRV	QSA (1) DoK	Discharged 1 Jul 02. KSA (2)
Pitchers, Pte J, KTG	QSA (1) DoK	No IV Section, A Company, Beaconsfield Town Guard
Pitchers, Pte V, KTG	QSA (1) DoK	Premier Mine
Pitt, 13477 Dvr S, ASC	QSA (3) DoK Paar Tr	KSA (2)
Plane, Lt F W, KTG	QSA (1) DoK	Mounted Section, B Company, Beaconsfield Town Guard
Plank, Pte G W, KTG	QSA (2) DoK 01	No I Section, B2 Company, No 3 Redoubt. Also served CCCC (26125) where surname is Planks
Platt, 276 Sgt R, KRV	QSA (1) DoK	Non effective 13 Aug 00. Medal re-issued 16 Apr 24
Pocock, Pte Frederick G E, KTG	QSA (1) DoK	There is a W Pocock on the KTG nominal roll serving in G company. Same man? QSA (1), BWM, Merc Marine (Frederick G E Pocock), KStar. City Coins Sep 03
Pole, Pte H, KTG	QSA (1) DoK	Premier Mine
Polsue, Pte Edwin Arthur Linnell, KTG	QSA (4) DoK OFS Tr 01	Also served KTG (No II Section, K Company), KLH (34968) 21 Jul 01 to 20 Sep 01 and 16 Apr 02 to 30 Jun 02, CPS (93), ORCP (356) and ALH (39630) 22 Nov 01 to 24 Mar 02. Occupation farrier
Polworth, Pte R, KTG	QSA (1) DoK	Medical Corps, No 1 Company, D Section
Polworth, Pte W, KTG	QSA (1) DoK	No 6 Redoubt. Wood cutting under RE Officer
Pomeroy, Pte T, KTG	QSA (1) DoK	No 2 Schmidt's Breastwork. Deceased (not on casualty roll). Issued to sister 27 May 09
Pomfret, 5011 Pte D, LNLR	QSA (3) DoK OFS Tr	QSA (3), KSA (2), BWM, VM, KStar. Sotheby Nov 78
Pool, 736 Pte Frank H, CP2	QSA (3) DoK OFS Tr	A Squadron. Wounded 28 Nov 99. KSA (2)
Poole, Cpl A W, DBMB	QSA (1) DoK	Armoured train section. Served in the Bechuanaland Rebellion 1897 with DFH earning CGHGSM (1) Bech
Poole, 407 Pte H, KRV	QSA (1) DoK	Dismissed for misconduct 30 May 00
Poole, 5562 Pte J, LNLR	QSA (3) DoK OFS Tr	KSA (2)
Poole, Lt W F, KTG	QSA (1) DoK	No 2 Schmidt's Breastwork. Note says Capt W F Poole is on the Black List
Pooley, Pte E, KTG	QSA (1) DoK	G Company

Pooley, Capt J, KTG	QSA (1) DoK	H Company
Pope, Pte A E, KTG	QSA (1) DoK	Kimberley Mine Ambulance Company, E Section
Pope, Nurse E, NS	QSA (0)	St Michael's Home
Pope, Pte W, KTG	QSA (1) DoK	No 1 supply depot
Popham, 871 Pte Henry Temple, KRV	QSA (5) RoM DoK OFS Tr 01	Discharged 1 Jul 00. Also served KTG (G Company) and CinCBG (22627) 9 Jan 01 to 10 Jul 01
Porter, 5157 Pte C, LNLR	QSA (1) DoK	Invalided to England 1 May 00
Porter, Pte C, KTG	QSA (3) DoK OFS Tr	No III Section, F Company, No 3 Redoubt. Also served KR (757)
Porter, 482 Pte Edward William, KRV	QSA (2) DoK OFS	Served 11 Oct 99 to 24 Dec 99. Also served CRSS (1218) 11 Apr 01 to 17 Jul 01 and (1341) 22 Jul 01 to 21 Apr 02. KSA (2)
Porter, 1212 Pte H J, KRV	QSA (1) DoK	Discharged 1 Jul 02. Also served KTG (No 2 Schmidt's Breastwork). KSA (2)
Porter, 5482 L Cpl J, LNLR	QSA (3) DoK OFS Tr	
Porter, 22 Sgt Mc L, KRV	QSA (1) DoK	Discharged 3 May 01. Served in the Bechuanaland Rebellion 1897 with Kimb Rifles earning CGHGSM (1) Bech
Porter, Pte W D, KTG	QSA (1) DoK	No IV Section, D Company. QSA (1). Christies Jul 86. QSA (1), KStar. Thomas Jul 87 £135
Porter, Pte William, KTG	QSA (2) DoK 01	G Company. Also served KLH (1189) 20 Apr 00 to 10 Nov 00 and CRSS (1076) 11 Mar 01 to 27 Sep 01
Poulton, Pte Charles, KTG	QSA (4) DoK OFS Tr 02	Mounted Section, Kenilworth Defence Force and No 6 Redoubt. Also served KH (206, 394 & 42424) 12 Mar 00 to 31 May 00 and 29 May 02 to 30 Jun 02 and CPS (711)
Poulton, Pte P, KTG	QSA (1) DoK	No 3 supply depot. 50th Anniversary attendee
Poulton, Sgt William Nicholas James, KTG	QSA (1) DoK	Premier Mine. Also served KLH (304) 9 Mar 00 to 11 Jun 00 and Paget's Horse (IY)
Powell, 260 L Cpl Frank, KLH	QSA (3) DoK OFS Tr	Served 20 Oct 99 to 30 Apr 00. Wounded 28 Nov 99. Also served KTG and WS (31) 8 May 00 to 31 Aug 00. QSA (2) excl Tr. Spink Oct 85 £100
Powell, QMS H, KTG	QSA (1) DoK	Cycle Corps, A Company
Powell, 172 Cpl J M, KRV	QSA (3) RoM DoK OFS	Non effective 20 Jun 00. Served in the Bechuanaland Rebellion 1897 with DFH earning CGHGSM (1) Bech. 50th Anniversary attendee
Powell, 331 Pte O P, KRV	QSA (2) DoK OFS	Discharged 25 Feb 00
Powell, 259 Cpl Richard Samuel Bressy, KRV	QSA (4) RoM DoK OFS 01	Discharged 28 Dec 00. Also served Lt 1st KFS from 24 Dec 00 to 28 Sep 01. He had served in the Matabeleland Relief Force, 1896. Died 1935
Power, Pte P T, KTG	QSA (1) DoK	No I Section, C Company, Pickering's Redoubt No 1. QSA (1). Glendining Jun 87. Liverpool Aug 98 £95
Powiss, 4049 Pte W, LNLR	QSA (4) DoK OFS Tr 01	Invalided to England 12 Jun 01. QSA (3) excl 01. DNW Dec 06 £200. Liverpool Apr 07 £340
Pownall, 3849 Pte J, LNLR	QSA (4) DoK OFS Tr 01	Wounded at Hartbeestfontein 18 Feb 01
Powrie, Col Sgt J E, KTG	QSA (1) DoK	No 1 Redoubt. 223 Tpr James Ebenezer Powrie served KLH 16 Mar 00 to 28 May 00 earning OFS. Same man? QSA (1). Spink Dec 00 £120
Poynton, 144 Cpl Henry James, CP2	QSA (3) DoK OFS Tr	CGHGSM (1) Bech, QSA (3), KSA (2). Sotheby Feb 12 £3. Hamilton Apr 79 £340. Miniatures inc KStar. Sotheby Jun 85
Pratley, Pte G, KTG	QSA (1) DoK	No 1 Redoubt
Pratley, Sgt J M, KTG	QSA (1) DoK	No III Section, A Company, Beaconsfield Town Guard. QSA (1). McGregor Museum
Pratt, 175 Tpr George, KLH	QSA (2) DoK OFS	Joined 19 Oct 99. Killed in action 13 Mar 00

Kimberley Siege Account and Medal Roll

Prentice, Pte J, KTG	QSA (1) DoK	No II Section, C Company, Pickering's Redoubt No 1
Presow, Pte G, KTG	QSA (1) DoK	No I Section, C Company, Beaconsfield Town Guard
Presow, Lt R, KTG	QSA (1) DoK	No III Section, C Company, Beaconsfield Town Guard
Preston, 7 Sgt G, KRV	QSA (2) DoK OFS	Non effective 6 Jul 00. Served in the Bechuanaland Rebellion 1897 with Kimb Rifles earning CGHGSM (1) Bech
Preston, 507 Pte John Alec Stanley, CP2	QSA (1) DoK	CP HQ and depot mounted branch. Discharged for misconduct
Price, Pte A E, KTG	QSA (1) DoK	
Price, Pte H, KTG	QSA (1) DoK	No I Company, B Section, Reservoir
Price, 43 Tpr P, KLH	QSA (2) DoK OFS	Served 19 Oct 99 to 30 Apr 00
Price, 224 Gnr William Tantum, DFA	QSA (2) DoK 01	Enrolled 2 Jan 00. DMU 8 Mar 01. Occupation grocer
Price, 127 Gnr William Thomas, DFA	QSA (1) DoK	Enrolled 26 Jan 99. DMU 31 Jul 00 or 8 Mar 01. Occupation grocer. QSA (1). Spink Jan 80 £125
Prince, 125 Cpl Arthur, DFA	QSA (3) DoK OFS 01	Enrolled 24 Jan 99. Served DFA 94-97. Resigned 4 Jan 04. Occupation saddler at De Beers
Prince, 156 Dvr Claude, DFA	QSA (3) DoK OFS Tr	Enrolled 1 Jul 99. Resigned 1 Jul 03. KSA (2). Occupation driver at De Beers
Prince, Pte E, KTG	QSA (1) DoK	No 6 Redoubt. Accidentally killed by own men when returning after a scouting mission (date unknown)
Prince, Pte F C, KTG	QSA (1) DoK	D Company (Veterans), Beaconsfield Town Guard
Prince, Pte J, KTG	QSA (1) DoK	No 6 Redoubt. Engine driver electrical department
Prince, 5051 Pte T, LNLR	QSA (3) DoK OFS Tr	KSA (2)
Pringle, Pte J, KTG	QSA (1) DoK	No III Section, B Company, No 4 Redoubt
Pringle, Nurse S L, NS	QSA (0)	Kimberley Civil Hospital
Prior, Lt C E, KTG	QSA (1) DoK	No I Section, C Company, Beaconsfield Town Guard
Pritchard, 534 Pte J, KRV	QSA (1) DoK	Discharged 21 Dec 00
Pritchard, 176 Cpl Matthew John, KLH	QSA (2) DoK Paar	Served 20 Oct 99 to 6 Mar 00. Wounded 25 Nov 99. Also served KTG. CGHGSM (1) Bech (Tpr DFH), QSA (2), 1914-15 Star (Spr SAEC). City Coins Feb 87
Pritchard, Clerk T H, ASC	QSA (2) DoK Tr	Also served KTG (No 4 supply depot) and BMI (no trace on nominal roll)
Procter, 192 Cpl Wilfred, CP2	QSA (2) DoK OFS	CP 7-pounder detachment. KSA (2). Served in the Bechuanaland Rebellion 1897 earning CGHGSM (1) Bech
Pruden, 198 Pte E L, KRV	QSA (1) DoK	Non effective 21 Jul 00
Pryra, Pte B, KTG	QSA (1) DoK	No II Section, B2 Company, No 3 Redoubt
Pryra, 317 Tpr Christian, KLH	QSA (4) RoM DoK OFS Tr	Served 28 Dec 99 to 8 Nov 01 and 2 May 02 to 30 Jun 02. KSA (2)
Pryra, Pte E, KTG	QSA (1) DoK	No I Section, A Company, Beaconsfield Town Guard
Puckers, Pte S G, KTG	QSA (1) DoK	H Company
Pugh, Pte W J, KTG	QSA (1) DoK	No III Section, No 2 Redoubt
Puller, 325 Tpr T, KLH	QSA (2) DoK OFS	Discharged 3 Apr 00. Also served KRV
Purcell, 74499 Gnr William, RGA	QSA (1) DoK	KSA (2)
Purchase, Pte A, KTG	QSA (1) DoK	D Company (Veterans), Beaconsfield Town Guard. Also on roll for Ladismith Town Guard
Putter, 1226 Pte George, KRV	QSA (5) Nat DoK Paar Tr Witt	Also served KLH (444) 1 Nov 99 to 30 Apr 00 and IYS (25) 10 May 00 to 6 Sep 00. KSA (2)
Pyall, Pte S P, KTG	QSA (1) DoK	Kimberley Mine Ambulance Company, A Section

Q

Quaile, Pte T, KTG	QSA (1) DoK	Kimberley Mine Ambulance Company, B Section
Quaile, Pte W, KTG	QSA (1) DoK	No 6 Redoubt
Quentrall, Pte T, KTG	QSA (1) DoK	No I Section, Belgravia Fort
Quincey, Pte E B, KTG	QSA (1) DoK	No I Section, F Company, Mostert's Redoubt
Quinlan, 215 Gnr Michael, DFA	QSA (2) DoK OFS	Enrolled 24 Nov 99 and resigned 6 Mar 02. Occupation guard at De Beers. Died Nov 10. QSA (2), KStar. DNW Jun 98 £90. DNW Sep 00 £190. A F Brock Oct 04
Quinn, Pte D, KTG	QSA (1) DoK	222 D Quinn served CPS. Same man?
Quinn, Pte P, KTG	QSA (1) DoK	No IV Section, C Company, Beaconsfield Town Guard

R

Raaff, Pte A, KTG	QSA (1) DoK	H Company
Raaff, Pte J, KTG	QSA (1) DoK	G Company. QSA (1)
Raaff, Pte J, KTG	QSA (1) DoK	No I Company, B Section, Reservoir
Raaff, 177 Tpr John William Edwin, KLH	QSA (2) DoK OFS	Served 19 Oct 99 to 23 Mar 00. Also served SRG (137) from 11 Feb 01
Raaff, Pte T, KTG	QSA (1) DoK	No I Company, B Section, Reservoir
Raaff, 802 L Cpl T H, KRV	QSA (4) RoM DoK OFS Tr	Also served KTG (No 2 Schmidt's Breastwork). Discharged KRV 8 Oct 02. Killed in a mining accident in 1905. CGHGSM (1) Bech, BSACM for Matabeleland 1896, QSA (4), KSA (2), 1902 Coronation, KStar
Raath, 165 Pte Christoffel, CP2	QSA (2) DoK Tr	CP dismounted branch (barrier & redoubt duties). Discharged for misconduct. Also served CPS (882)
Raath, 638 Pte David John Philip, CP2	QSA (2) DoK 01	C Squadron. Also served Warrenton DMT (74). Entry and OFS & Tr crossed through on Warrenton DMT QSA roll
Raath, 19 Cpl George Daniel, KLH	QSA (3) DoK OFS 01	Served 16 Oct 99 to 23 Mar 00
Rabe, Pte H, KTG	QSA (1) DoK	No III Section, D Company. QSA (1). City Coins Feb 84
Radcliffe, Pte L, KTG	QSA (1) DoK	Premier Mine. QSA (1), KStar. Neate May 94 £135
Radcliffe, 502 Pte Lewis, KRV	QSA (3) DoK OFS 01	Discharged 14 Oct 02. Also served KLH (195) 9 Mar 00 to 5 Jun 00. KSA (2)
Radloff, Pte J C, KTG	QSA (1) DoK	Civil Service Redoubt. 50th Anniversary attendee
Rae, 137 Cpl A, KRV	QSA (1) DoK	Non effective 5 Oct 00. CGHGSM (1) Bech (Pte Kimb Rfls), QSA (1), 14-15 Star (Pte Vet Regt), BWM, VM (Pte Vet Regt), KStar. DNW Dec 93 £260
Rae, Pte C, KTG	QSA (1) DoK	No I Company, B Section, Reservoir
Rafferty, 807 Pte James, KRV	QSA (3) DoK OFS 01	DMU 18 Apr 01. Also served KTG (No 2 Schmidt's Breastwork) and SRG (708) from 9 Jul 01
Rainford, 4350 Pte H, LNLR	QSA (3) DoK OFS Tr	KSA (2)
Rainsford, Pte A A, KTG	QSA (1) DoK	Premier Mine
Ralph, Pte E, KTG	QSA (1) DoK	Possibly served in the Bechuanaland Rebellion 1897 with DFH earning CGHGSM (1) Bech. QSA (1). Bonhams Mar 07 £210. Dixon Feb 08 £250
Ralph, Pte J, KTG	QSA (1) DoK	Kimberley Mine Ambulance Company, A Section and L Company
Ralph, 58 Sgt James, CP2	QSA (4) RoM DoK OFS Tr	C Squadron. CGHGSM (1) Bech, QSA (4), KSA (2), KStar. LSE Sep 84 £375
Ramsay, Pte A, KTG	QSA (1) DoK	No I Section, Belgravia Fort. QSA (1), KStar. City Coins Aug 08
Ramsay, 577 Pte Francis Watson, CP2	QSA (1) DoK	CP dismounted branch (barrier & redoubt duties). Discharged time expired

Kimberley Siege Account and Medal Roll

Rand, 25263 Tpr Ernest John, CinCBG	QSA (5) RoM DoK OFS Tr 01	Served 3 Dec 00 to 10 Jun 01. Also served KTG (No I Section, F Company, Mostert's Redoubt), KLH (398) 7 Mar 00 to 5 Jun 00 and ASC as Civil Clerk
Randall, 4587 Pte J, LNLR	QSA (3) DoK OFS Tr	KSA (2)
Rankin, Mr D, POC	QSA (1) DoK	Telegraph signaller
Rapeport, Pte L, KTG	QSA (1) DoK	
Raper, Pte D, KTG	QSA (1) DoK	No IV Company, A Section, Reservoir
Raper, 208 Gnr David Sydney, DFA	QSA (2) DoK 01	Enrolled 27 Oct 99. DMU 10 Jul 01. Occupation labourer. Possibly also served CPS (832) gaining Tr
Raper, 1303 Pte George Albert, KRV	QSA (6) RoM DoK OFS Tr 01 02	Also served KTG (No I Section, F Company, Mostert's Redoubt) and CPS. Note says was released from the KRV 13 Nov 01 and served CPS (837) while still a member of this corps. Killed in action 7 Mar 02
Raper, 907 Pte J A, KRV	QSA (3) DoK OFS Tr	Discharged 16 May 02. Also served KTG (No III Section, B2 Company, No 3 Redoubt). KSA (2)
Rask, Pte A W L, KTG	QSA (1) DoK	No II Section, K Company
Ratcliffe, 5197 Pte D, LNLR	QSA (3) DoK OFS Tr	KSA (2). Wounded Twyfelaar 27 Jan 01
Ratcliffe, 885 L Cpl J, KRV	QSA (1) DoK	Non effective 15 Sep 00. Also served KTG (No 2 Schmidt's Breastwork). QSA (1), KStar. Sotheby Mar 84
Rathbone, 466 Pte G H, CP1	QSA (4) RoM DoK OFS Tr	C Squadron. Also served FID. KSA (2). Served in the Bechuanaland Rebellion 1897 earning CGHGSM (1) Bech
Rattham, 100 Pte W, KRV	QSA (4) RoM DoK OFS Tr	Non effective 30 Jun 00 and discharged 1 Jul 02. Also served KTG (Cycle Corps, A Company) and SRG (22) with forename Henry from 11 Feb 01. Surname also Ratham. QSA (1) DoK, [KSA (2)]. Hamilton Mar 86 £100
Rawcliffe, 4304 Sgt E, LNLR	QSA (3) DoK OFS Tr	KSA (2)
Rawcliffe, 3804 Pte J, LNLR	QSA (3) DoK OFS Tr	KSA (2)
Rawlinson, 558 Pte William Jackson, CP2	QSA (1) DoK	CP dismounted branch (barrier & redoubt duties). Discharged by purchase
Rawson, Lt T G, KTG	QSA (1) DoK	No 2 Schmidt's Breastwork. QSA (1). City Coins Jan 80
Rayden, 342 Pay Sgt Charles James, KLH	QSA (3) RoM DoK OFS	Served 6 Nov 99 to 5 Jun 00. Served in the Bechuanaland Rebellion 1897 with DFH earning CGHGSM (1) Bech
Rayner, Pte A E, KTG	QSA (1) DoK	No IV Section, F Company, Mostert's Redoubt. Also served DH (40258) 27 Jan 02 until DMU 21 Jun 02 with surname Reiner and forenames Alors Emile Charles. Served in the Bechuanaland Rebellion 1897 with Kimb Rifles earning CGHGSM (1) Bech
Rayner, 79312 Sgt George H, RGA	QSA (3) DoK Tr 01	Premier Mine
Rayner, 59 Pte W A, KRV	QSA (1) DoK	DMU 5 May 00. Served in the Bechuanaland Rebellion 1897 with Kimb Rifles earning CGHGSM (1) Bech
Raynham, Lt E F, KTG	QSA (1) DoK	See his biography (page 352)
Reabow, 735 Pte Ferdinand, CP2	QSA (1) DoK	CP dismounted in Beaconsfield
Read, Pte W, KTG	QSA (1) DoK	No I Company, B Section, Reservoir
Reader, Pte J H, KTG	QSA (1) DoK	G Company
Reardon, 888 Pte B, KRV	QSA (1) DoK	Dismissed for misconduct 6 Jun 00. Also served KTG (No I Section, F Company, Mostert's Redoubt)
Red, 711 Pte William John, CP2	QSA (1) DoK	CP dismounted branch (barrier & redoubt duties)
Reddie, Pte A, KTG	QSA (1) DoK	No I Section, C Company, Beaconsfield Town Guard. QSA (1), KStar. Spink Dec 01 £230
Redfern, 4892 Pte O, LNLR	QSA (1) DoK	KSA (2)

Redman, 27770 Sapr J, RE	QSA (3) DoK Drie Tr	KSA (2)
Redpath, Pte W D, KTG	QSA (1) DoK	No III Section, Belgravia Fort
Reed, 4152 Pte A, LNLR	QSA (3) DoK Paar Joh	Mounted Infantry. KSA (2)
Reed, 808 Pte C, KRV	QSA (1) DoK	DMU 20 Sep 00. Also served KTG (H Company)
Reed, 27578 Sapr F C, RE	QSA (3) DoK Drie Tr	KSA (2)
Reed, 641 Pte J, KRV	QSA (3) DoK OFS Tr	Discharged 1 Jul 02. KSA (2)
Reed, 22722 Tpr Rowlands, CinCBG	QSA (4) DoK OFS Tr 01	Served 19 Nov 00 to 18 May 01. Also served KTG (No I Section, K Company)
Reed, 737 Cpl T E, CP1	QSA (2) DoK OFS	C Squadron. KSA (2). Served in the Bechuanaland Rebellion 1897 earning CGHGSM (1) Bech
Reeland, 367 Pte Charles John, CP2	QSA (4) RoM DoK OFS Tr	See his biography (page 352)
Reeler, Pte E G, KTG	QSA (1) DoK	No II Section, K Company
Rees, 5451 Pte F W, LNLR	QSA (3) DoK OFS Tr	QSA (3), KSA (2), KStar. RHQ
Rees, 225 Tpr G, KLH	QSA (2) DoK OFS	Served 19 Oct 99 to 30 Apr 00. Also served IYS (35) 14 May 00 to 6 Sep 00 as Reece on his discharge papers and Rees on his attestation papers
Rees, 97360 Gnr Thomas, RGA	QSA (3) DoK Tr 01	
Reeves, 5581 L Cpl G, LNLR	QSA (2) DoK OFS	Died of disease 11 May 00
Reid, Pte G J A, KTG	QSA (1) DoK	Civil Service Redoubt
Reid, Sgt J L, KTG	QSA (2) DoK OFS	Cycle Corps, A Company. Also served KLH (340) 4 Nov 99 and dismissed 14 Dec 99. Served as Trooper, Northern Districts Mounted Rifles in the Zulu Rebellion, 1906. QSA (1), Natal (1) 1906 (surname Reed), KStar. City Coins Dec 97
Reid, 27530 Sapr T, RE	QSA (1) DoK	QSA (1), KStar. RHQ
Reid, Pte W, KTG	QSA (1) DoK	No 4 Redoubt
Rendell, 178 Tpr Alfred Hugh, KLH	QSA (2) DoK OFS	Discharged 14 Mar 00. Also served KTG. Possibly served in the Bechuanaland Rebellion 1897 with DEOVR earning CGHGSM (1) Bech
Renfree, Pte H, KTG	QSA (1) DoK	Kamfersdam Company
Renney, Pte R J, KTG	QSA (1) DoK	Premier Mine
Rennie, Sgt G, KTG	QSA (1) DoK	Kamfersdam Company. Issued to 2 Neptune Terrace, Aberdeen
Reunert, QMS Theodore, KTG	QSA (1) DoK	See his biography (page 352)
Revell, 7171 Bombdr Charles, RGA	QSA (1) DoK	Otto's Kopje. Died of disease Bloemfontein 28 May 00
Revell, Pte D G, KTG	QSA (1) DoK	No 1 Redoubt
Reyersbach, Pte L, KTG	QSA (1) DoK	See his biography, page (352)
Reynhardt, Pte A, KTG	QSA (1) DoK	Otto's Kopje Scouts
Reynolds, 3366 Sgt A, LNLR	QSA (3) DoK OFS Tr	QSA (3), [KSA (2)]. Spink Nov 05 £180. Dixon Apr 06 £320. QSA (3), [KSA (2)], KStar. DNW Mar 07 £390
Reynolds, Pte A, KTG	QSA (1) DoK	No I Section, L Company
Reynolds, 937 Pte Norman H, KRV	QSA (3) DoK OFS 01	Also served KTG (Cycle Corps, A Company) and CCCC (20913). Discharged 23 Jul 01. 50th Anniversary attendee
Reynolds, 600 Pte Percy, KRV	QSA (4) RoM DoK OFS Tr	Discharged 1 Jul 02. KSA (2). Severely wounded Christiana 3 Sep 01. Prisoner and released Bessielaagte 22 Apr 02

Kimberley Siege Account and Medal Roll

Reynolds, Pte T, KTG	QSA (1) DoK	D Company (Veterans), Beaconsfield Town Guard
Reynolds, 340 Pte W H, KRV	QSA (1) DoK	DMU 6 Jul 00
Reynolds, 1282 Pte W R, KRV	QSA (1) DoK	Discharged 10 Jul 02. Also served KTG (No I Section, No 2 Redoubt). KSA (2)
Reynolds, 166 Pte William Henry, CP2	QSA (3) DoK OFS Tr	C Squadron. KSA (2). Prisoner at Hoopstad 23 Oct 00. Served in the Bechuanaland Rebellion 1897 earning CGHGSM (1) Bech
Rhodes, Hon Col Cecil John, KRV	QSA (1) DoK	See his biography (page 352)
Riach, Capt James Grant, ScH	QSA (3) DoK Tr 01	On black list for ScH. Served 20 Jan 01 to 10 May 01. Also served in the intelligence department in Kimberley
Rice, 683 Pte A, KRV	QSA (3) DoK OFS Tr	Discharged 1 Jul 02. KSA (2)
Rice, 491 Band W F, KRV	QSA (2) DoK 01	Discharged 6 Jun 01. QSA (1). Spink Jan 75 £70
Richards, Pte A, KTG	QSA (1) DoK	Construction of forts and barricades
Richards, Pte Daniel, KTG	QSA (2) DoK Tr	H Company. Also served KLH (1031) 16 Mar 00 to 29 Jul 00 and SRG (1724) from 14 Nov 01. Occupation stone mason
Richards, Lt H C, KLH	QSA (2) DoK OFS	Joined 16 Oct 99. Resigned 10 Nov 00. Born 27 Feb 67. Died 1919. QSA (2). Spink Oct 74 £65. Sotheby Nov 77. Dixon Mar 94 £145
Richards, Maj S, KTG	QSA (1) DoK	See his biography (page 353)
Richards, Nurse S, NS	QSA (0)	Kimberley Civil Hospital
Richards, 810 Pte T, KRV	QSA (1) DoK	Accidentally drowned 22 Oct 00. Also served KTG (K Company). QSA (1). GB Military Antiques Apr 03 £225
Richards, Pte T, KTG	QSA (1) DoK	K Company
Richards, 115 CSM T B, KRV	QSA (5) DoK OFS Tr 01 02	Arrived in Kimberley 20 Nov 99. Non effective 1 Mar 00. DMU KRV 6 Mar 02. Occupation miner. CGHGSM (1) Bech (Sgt), QSA (2) DoK OFS, KStar, Colonial Auxiliary Forces LS Medal (Sgt). Spink Mar 78 £275
Richardson, 262 Tpr Henry, KLH	QSA (2) DoK OFS	Served 21 Oct 99 to 30 Apr 00. Wounded 28 Nov 99. Also served ORCP (401)
Richardson, Cpl J, KTG	QSA (1) DoK	Cycle Corps, A Company. One of the J Richardsons also served KLH (315) earning OFS but also dying of disease 13 Jan 00
Richardson, Pte J, KTG	QSA (1) DoK	Medical Corps, No 1 Company, C Section
Richardson, Pte J, KTG	QSA (1) DoK	H Company
Richardson, 537 Cpl J G, KRV	QSA (3) RoM DoK OFS	Non effective 20 Jun 00
Richardson, 1230 Pte W, KRV	QSA (3) DoK OFS Tr	Discharged 1 Jul 02. Also served KTG (No IV Section, C Company, Beaconsfield Town Guard). KSA (2). Slightly wounded Klip Drift 7 Mar 02
Richardson, Pte W, KTG	QSA (1) DoK	No 1 Redoubt
Richardson, Mr W, POC	QSA (1) DoK	Not on main roll but shown as medal issued
Richardson, 6008 Bombdr Walter, RGA	QSA (1) DoK	Premier Mine. QSA (1), KSA (2). DNW Sep 99 £130. Spink Dec 99 £195
Riches, Pte F H, KTG	QSA (1) DoK	No I Company, A Section, Reservoir
Riches, Pte T, KTG	QSA (1) DoK	No I Company, B Section, Reservoir
Richmond, 44 Tpr Percy, KLH	QSA (2) DoK OFS	Served 19 Oct 99 until DMU 28 Feb 00. Roll says deleted off but entry not crossed through. Also served ILH (256 & 1999) 16 Nov 00 to 1 Feb 01 and 3 Aug 01 to 27 Jan 02. KSA (2)
Richter, Pte A, KTG	QSA (1) DoK	No III Section, B Company, Beaconsfield Town Guard
Ricketts, Pte A E, KTG	QSA (1) DoK	Kenilworth Defence Force
Ricketts, Pte A W, KTG	QSA (1) DoK	No I Section, Belgravia Fort

Medal roll

Ricketts, Capt C A Langworthy, CCOD	QSA (1) DoK	Assistant Commissioner of Ordnance. MID for the siege
Ricketts, Pte W A, KTG	QSA (1) DoK	No III Section, Belgravia Fort
Rickman, Capt William Edward, KLH	QSA (3) DoK OFS Tr	See his biography (page 353)
Riddell, 218 Tpr George, KLH	QSA (2) DoK OFS	Served 20 Oct 99 to 30 Apr 00. Also served KTG
Riddle, 198 Bombdr William James, DFA	QSA (3) DoK OFS Tr	Enrolled 25 Sep 99. Resigned 31 Jan 03. KSA (2). Occupation fireman at De Beers
Rigby, 3584 Pte J, LNLR	QSA (3) DoK OFS Tr	Wounded Pitsani 28 Nov 01. QSA (3), KSA (2), KStar. Dixon Dec 02 £275
Rigby, 4321 Pte J, LNLR	QSA (3) DoK OFS Tr	KSA (2)
Rigg, Cpl J, KTG	QSA (1) DoK	Medical Corps, No 1 Company, C Section and Reserve Section, D Company
Rigg, Pte W J, KTG	QSA (1) DoK	Kimberley Mine Ambulance Company, E Section
Riley, 4705 Pte T, LNLR	QSA (3) DoK OFS Tr	KSA (2)
Ring, 179 Tpr Dennis Thomas, KLH	QSA (3) DoK OFS 01	Served 19 Oct 99 to 24 Nov 00 and 29 Dec 00 to 10 Jul 01. Also served KTG and CPS
Ring, 324 Tpr George, KLH	QSA (5) DoK OFS Tr 01 02	Served 1 Nov 99 to 16 Mar 00. Wounded 25 Nov 99. Also served cyclist ScH (22828) 5 Jan 01 to 24 Feb 01, FID and DH 19 Jan 02 to 27 Mar 02. There is a G Ring on the KTG nominal roll who served at No 2 Schmidt's Breastwork. 50th Anniversary attendee. QSA (2) DoK OFS. Ursual Dec 03 £285
Ring, 149 Tpr R, KLH	QSA (2) DoK OFS	Discharged 14 Mar 00. Also served as Sub Conductor in ASC
Ringrove, Pte H, KTG	QSA (1) DoK	Kamfersdam Company. QSA (1), KStar. Seaby May 72 £45. QSA (1). Seaby Jan 73 £26
Rinkquest, Pte D, KTG	QSA (1) DoK	No IV Section, C Company, Pickering's Redoubt No 2
Rittmann, 536 L Cpl J E, KRV	QSA (5) RoM DoK OFS Tr 01	Non effective 1 Jun 01
Robb, Pte F W, KTG	QSA (1) DoK	No I Section, No 2 Redoubt
Robb, Pte George, KTG	QSA (1) DoK	No I Company, B Section, Reservoir. Also served CRSS (1541) from 11 Jan 02. Occupation fitter. QSA (1), KStar, BWM (Pte 1st SAI), VM (Pte 8th SAI). eBay Oct 03
Roberts, Pte E R, KTG	QSA (1) DoK	No III Section, Belgravia Fort
Roberts, 684 Pte H J G, KRV	QSA (3) DoK OFS Tr	DMU 17 Jul 02. Number 680 on KSA roll. Also served KTG (No I Section, Mandy Fort). KSA (2)
Roberts, Pte James Henry, KTG	QSA (3) DoK OFS Tr	No 2 Schmidt's Breastwork and Reserve Section, D Company. Also served SRG (594) from 29 May 01
Roberts, 365 Tpr John, KLH	QSA (4) RoM DoK OFS 01	Served 10 Nov 99 to 9 Nov 00. Also served Beaconsfield TG, CPS (148) and Vryburg Special Police
Roberts, Pte R, KTG	QSA (1) DoK	No 1 Redoubt. QSA (1), KStar. Seaby Nov 81 £140
Roberts, 80351 Gnr Samuel, RGA	QSA (1) DoK	Otto's Kopje. QSA (2), [KSA (2)]. DNW Dec 00 £110. City Coins May 02
Roberts, 32612 Tpr William, DH	QSA (6) DoK Paar Drie Joh DH Witt	For his medals, see page 514
Robertson, Pte A, KTG	QSA (1) DoK	Cycle Corps, A Company
Robertson, 75876 A Bombdr Charles George, RGA	QSA (4) RoM DoK OFS Tr	14th Co RGA. Also served CP. Invalided to England 25 Jun 00. QSA (4)
Robertson, 64 Dvr Charles Montague, DFA	QSA (2) DoK OFS	Enrolled 8 Dec 96. Resigned 8 Jan 03. Occupation fireman at De Beers

Name	Medals	Notes
Robertson, 640 Pte G H, KRV	QSA (3) DoK OFS Tr	Discharged 1 Jul 02. KSA (2)
Robertson, G M, KTG	QSA (0)	Roll states "Electrical work; dynamite mines." 50th Anniversary attendee
Robertson, 712 Pte H, KRV	QSA (1) DoK	Discharged 1 Jul 02. KSA (2)
Robertson, Pte J, KTG	QSA (1) DoK	Cycle Corps, A Company
Robertson, Pte J, KTG	QSA (1) DoK	No I Company, B Section, Reservoir
Robertson, 105 Pte J M, KRV	QSA (1) DoK	Non effective 4 Oct 00. Served in the Bechuanaland Rebellion 1897 with Kimb Rifles earning CGHGSM (1) Bech
Robertson, Capt James W, KLH	QSA (4) RoM DoK Paar Tr	See his biography (page 353)
Robertson, 195 Gnr John Samuel, DFA	QSA (3) DoK OFS Tr	Enrolled 25 Sep 99. Killed in action Klip Drift 7 Mar 02. Also served CMR 75-87 and Umtali Rifles 96-97. Occupation overseer at De Beers. CGHGSM (1) Bas (Cpl CMR), QSA (3), KStar. LSE Sep 83 £325. Christies Jul 88
Robertson, Pte S, KTG	QSA (1) DoK	Medal reissued 13 May 05 to Shetland Island's address
Robertson, Pte Thomas, KTG	QSA (1) DoK	No 2 Schmidt's Breastwork. Also served SRG (86) from 11 Feb 01
Robertson, 721 Pte Thomas, KRV	QSA (3) RoM DoK OFS	Also served KTG (Premier Mine) and KLH (175) 8 Mar 00 to 4 Jun 00. KSA (2) issued 3 Aug 06
Robertson, Pte W, KTG	QSA (1) DoK	No IV Section, K Company
Robins, Pte F, KTG	QSA (3) RoM DoK OFS	Kimberley Mine Ambulance Company with mounted forces (KLH 1 Oct 99 to 5 Jun 00). On KLH roll as Stretcher Bearer
Robinson, Pte C G, KTG	QSA (1) DoK	Premier Mine
Robinson, C H, KTG	QSA (0)	Roll states "Construction of shelters for women and children". QSA (0). City Coins Jan 94
Robinson, Pte E A, KTG	QSA (1) DoK	No I Section, No 2 Redoubt
Robinson, Pte G H, KTG	QSA (1) DoK	Premier Mine
Robinson, Pte G M, KTG	QSA (1) DoK	No I Section, No 2 Redoubt
Robinson, Lt Col McLeod Bartree, CP2	QSA (1) DoK	See his biography (page 354)
Robinson, 130 Pte W W, KRV	QSA (1) DoK	Non effective 5 Oct 00. CGHGSM (1) Bech (Pte Kimb Rifles), QSA (1). City Coins Jun 77
Robinson, 22719 Tpr William E, CinCBG	QSA (3) DoK OFS Tr	Joined 23 Nov 00 and note says 'did not return from furlough'. Also served DFH and KRV (371) until DMU 9 May 00. Occupation engine driver
Robson, Pte C E, KTG	QSA (1) DoK	No III Section, No 2 Redoubt
Robson, Cpl P, KTG	QSA (1) DoK	No II Section, B2 Company, No 3 Redoubt
Robson, 705 Pte R M M, KRV	QSA (2) DoK 01	Discharged 12 Jul 02
Robson, Pte T, KTG	QSA (1) DoK	No III Section, D Company. Repairing pumps and making tent pegs
Rodel, 141 Dvr Gottlief, DFA	QSA (2) DoK OFS	Enrolled 23 May 99. Also served Matabeleland Relief Force 96. Struck off 18 Jul 03. KSA (2). Occupation baker
Rodger, Maj Thomas Henderson, KRV	QSA (4) RoM DoK OFS Tr	See his biography (page 354)
Rodocanachi, Pte George, KTG	QSA (3) DoK OFS Tr	Medical Corps, No 1 Company, F Section. Also served SRG (85) from 11 Feb 01
Rodwell, 57 Sgt T, KRV	QSA (1) DoK	Non effective 19 Jul 00. CGHGSM (3) Trans Bas Bech, QSA (1), 14-15 Star, BWM, VM, KStar. McGregor Museum
Roe, 4804 Band J, LNLR	QSA (3) DoK OFS Tr	Surname Rowe on KSA roll. KSA (2)
Roffe, Pte H, KTG	QSA (1) DoK	No III Company, A Section, Reservoir
Roffey, Pte C, KTG	QSA (1) DoK	Premier Mine

Roger, Pte A, KTG	QSA (1) DoK	No IV Section, K Company
Rogers, 1057 Pte A D A, KRV	QSA (2) DoK 01	DMU 15 Apr 01. Also served KTG (Premier Mine)
Rogers, Pte A E, KTG	QSA (1) DoK	Premier Mine. QSA (1), 14-15 Star (Capt Vet Regt), BWM, VM (Capt). Glendining Mar 89
Rogers, 795 Pte George, CP2	QSA (1) DoK	CP dismounted branch (barrier & redoubt duties). KSA (2)
Rogers, Pte H W, KTG	QSA (1) DoK	Premier Mine
Rogers, Pte J, KTG	QSA (1) DoK	No III Section, C Company, Beaconsfield Town Guard and Gibraltar Fort, Davis's Heap. QSA (1). Christies Nov 84 £81. Spink Feb 85 £100
Rogers, 535 Pte J J, KRV	QSA (2) DoK OFS	Discharged 26 Feb 00. Possibly served in the Bechuanaland Rebellion 1897 with KH earning CGHGSM (1) Bech
Rogers, Pte T, KTG	QSA (1) DoK	No 6 Redoubt. QSA (1) (but could be next man). DNW Apr 04 £140. Ursual Sep 04 £190
Rogers, Pte T, KTG	QSA (1) DoK	No III Section, C Company, Beaconsfield Town Guard. QSA (1) (could be previous man). McGregor Museum
Rogers, Pte W C, KTG	QSA (1) DoK	
Rogers, 297 Cpl William, CP2	QSA (4) RoM DoK OFS Tr	CP 7-pounder detachment. Prisoner at Hoopstad 23 Oct 00. KSA (2)
Rolf, 4611 L Cpl W, LNLR	QSA (3) DoK OFS Tr	KSA (2)
Rome, Nurse E, NS	QSA (0)	Kimberley Civil Hospital
Ronaldson, Sgt George Scott, KTG	QSA (1) DoK	G Company. Issued to Outtison Mine, Victoria, Australia. Worked as a diamond merchant. QSA (1), KStar. City Coins May 02. QSA (1). Liverpool Oct 02 £220
Ronaldson, 346 Pte R Mc K, KRV	QSA (2) DoK OFS	DMU 4 Apr 00. QSA (2), KStar. City Coins May 02. QSA (2). Liverpool Oct 02 £175
Rook, 828 Pte W, KRV	QSA (3) DoK OFS Tr	DMU 12 Apr 02. Also served KTG (No 2 Schmidt's Breastwork). KSA (2)
Roper, 566 Pte C W, KRV	QSA (2) DoK 01	Dismissed for misconduct 8 May 01 – sleeping at post (13th offence)
Rose, Pte A, KTG	QSA (1) DoK	G Company
Rose, Sgt H, KTG	QSA (1) DoK	Cycle Corps, A Company. Possibly served in the Bechuanaland Rebellion 1897 with DEOVR earning CGHGSM (1) Bech
Rose, 180 Tpr James Esterhuizen, KLH	QSA (2) DoK OFS	Served 19 Oct 99 to 6 Mar 00. Also served SRG (936) from 1 Jul 01. Occupation overseer. 50th Anniversary attendee
Ross, Sgt C, KTG	QSA (1) DoK	Look-out at the Reservoir
Ross, 334 Tpr E, KLH	QSA (2) DoK OFS	Served 1 Nov 99 until DMU 24 Mar 00
Ross, Cpl G C, KTG	QSA (1) DoK	No II Section, C Company, Pickering's Redoubt No 2
Ross, 29829 Dvr G O, RE	QSA (4) DoK Drie Tr Witt	QSA (4), KSA (2), 14-15 Star, BWM, VM (16th Can Infy), KStar. Seaby Nov 76 £128. Sotheby Jun 85
Ross, 889 Pte H S, KRV	QSA (2) DoK 01	Discharged 24 Apr 01. Also served KTG (Premier Mine)
Ross, Cpl J T, KTG	QSA (1) DoK	Kenilworth Defence Force
Ross, 608 Pte John, CP2	QSA (1) DoK	CP dismounted branch (barrier & redoubt duties)
Ross, Pte L G, KTG	QSA (1) DoK	No IV Section, B Company, Beaconsfield Town Guard
Ross, Pte S E M, KTG	QSA (1) DoK	Premier Mine
Rossam, Pte G, KTG	QSA (1) DoK	No IV Section, No 2 Redoubt
Rossiter, 176 Band W, KRV	QSA (2) DoK OFS	Wounded 16 Nov 99. DMU 19 Apr 00. Served in the Bechuanaland Rebellion 1897 with Kimb Rifles earning CGHGSM (1) Bech
Rosslee, Pte W, KTG	QSA (1) DoK	No II Section, B2 Company, No 3 Redoubt

Kimberley Siege Account and Medal Roll

Rothman, 230 Gnr W, DFA	QSA (3) DoK OFS Tr	Enrolled 28 Jul 00. Also served Victorian Rifles and Kimb Cycle Corps. Resigned 1 Jul 02. KSA (2). Enrollment form has Rootman. Occupation printer
Roulston, 341 Pte G, KRV	QSA (1) DoK	DMU 19 Apr 00
Rourke, 3901 Drum T, LNLR	QSA (2) DoK OFS	Re-issued 2 May 13
Rouse, Pte Albert Edward, KTG	QSA (1) DoK	No 1 Redoubt. Also served SRG (87) from 11 Feb 01
Rouse, Pte J C, KTG	QSA (1) DoK	Premier Mine. QSA (1), 14-15 Star (Pte Vet Regt), BWM, VM (L Cpl Vet Regt), KStar. Spink Dec 83
Rouse, 181 Tpr Thomas, KLH	QSA (2) DoK OFS	Served 19 Oct 00 to 14 Mar 00. Also served KTG
Rouse, Pte W D, KTG	QSA (1) DoK	H Company
Rowbotham, 3943 Cpl S, LNLR	QSA (2) DoK 01	
Rowe, Pte A, KTG	QSA (1) DoK	No 6 Redoubt
Rowe, 727 Sdlr Sgt Edward, CP2	QSA (1) DoK	B Squadron. Also served FID. KSA (2)
Rowe, Pte H, KTG	QSA (1) DoK	No 6 Redoubt. QSA (1) (but could be next man)
Rowe, Pte H, KTG	QSA (1) DoK	No IV Section, D Company
Rowe, Pte J, KTG	QSA (1) DoK	B line of defence, No 3 Redoubt. QSA (1). Hayward's Gazette Jul 78 £65. Dixon Sep 01 £150. Could be next man. Either this J Rowe or the next served in KLH (183) 19 Oct 99 to 14 Mar 00 and 1st ILH, earning OFS
Rowe, Pte J, KTG	QSA (1) DoK	No 6 Redoubt
Rowe, Pte S, KTG	QSA (1) DoK	Reserve Section, D Company. KStar (G C S Rowe D Co 2 Div KTG). Presumed this man. Dixon Sep 99 £90
Rowe, Pte T, KTG	QSA (1) DoK	No I Section, D Company
Rowe, Pte Thomas, KTG	QSA (4) RoM DoK OFS Tr	G Company. Also served KLH (151 & 376) from 6 Mar 00, DH (32571) 23 Apr 01 to 5 Nov 01 and Canadian Scouts (39430) 21 Nov 01 to 5 Mar 02. KSA (2). Occupation miner
Rowe, Pte W, KTG	QSA (1) DoK	No 2 Schmidt's Breastwork and Reserve Section, D Company
Rowe, 186 Pte W, KRV	QSA (3) DoK OFS Tr	Discharged 14 Oct 02. KSA (2)
Rowe, 22720 Tpr William, CinCBG	QSA (4) DoK OFS Tr 01	Served 17 Nov 00 to 7 Jun 01. Also served KTG (No 2 Schmidt's Breastwork and Reserve Section, D Company) and IY Corps Depot. Occupation miner
Rowell, 795 Pte John, KRV	QSA (4) RoM DoK OFS Tr	Also served KTG (No III Company, A Section, Reservoir) and KLH (1290) 9 Mar 00 to 6 Nov 00
Rowland, Lt A C, KTG	QSA (2) DoK Tr	Cycle Corps, A Company. Also served BR (391) and SRV. Severely wounded Rooival 11 Apr 02. Served in the Bechuanaland Rebellion 1897 with Kimb Rifles earning CGHGSM (1) Bech. KStar. eBay Mar 08
Rowland, 37 Sgt H T, KRV	QSA (1) DoK	DMU 14 Apr 00. Note says 'since died' (not on casualty roll)
Rowland, 4732 Pte J, LNLR	QSA (3) DoK OFS Tr	KSA (2)
Rowlands, 22723 L Cpl David, CinCBG	QSA (5) RoM DoK OFS Tr 01	Served 17 Nov 00 to 15 May 01. Also served KTG (No IV Section, C Company, Beaconsfield Town Guard) and KR (824) to 1 Jul 00. Welsh miner
Rowlands, Pte Hugh, KTG	QSA (4) DoK OFS Tr 02	No II Section, C Company, Pickering's Redoubt No 2. Also served 1st ILH (3125) 15 Jan 02 to 30 Jun 02
Rowles, 118 Dvr Edward, DFA	QSA (3) DoK OFS Tr	Enrolled 1 Sep 98. Also served Kimb Cadet Corps. Resigned 5 Jan 03. Taken prisoner and released Klip Drift 7 Mar 02. KSA (2). Occupation machine man

Roylance, 1137 Pte W H, KRV	QSA (4) RoM DoK OFS Tr	Discharged 1 Jul 02. Also served KTG (No II Section, F Company, Mostert's Redoubt). KSA (2)
Rucastle, Pte J, KTG	QSA (1) DoK	No II Section, L Company
Rudd, 313 Pte C A, KRV	QSA (1) DoK	DMU 9 Jul 00. Also served CPS (40)
Rudkin, 15465 Gnr James A, RGA	QSA (1) DoK	KSA (2)
Rudlin, Pte F, KTG	QSA (1) DoK	D Company (Veterans), Beaconsfield Town Guard
Rudman, Pte Joseph James, KTG	QSA (1) DoK	No 1 Redoubt. Also served SRG (117) from 11 Feb 01
Ruffell, Pte Nelson Otto, KTG	QSA (1) DoK	No II Section, Mandy Fort. Occupation chemist in Kimberley
Rugen, Pte Alexander Anderson, KTG	QSA (1) DoK	No II Section, F Company, Mostert's Redoubt. Also served CRSS (1387) from 18 Sep 01. Occupation blacksmith
Rugg, Capt H, KTG	QSA (1) DoK	Reservoir
Rule, Pte G, KTG	QSA (1) DoK	Premier Mine
Rule, 685 Pte J, KRV	QSA (2) DoK OFS	DMU 3 May 00. Also served KTG (No I Section, L Company). QSA (2). Glendining Mar 89. Liverpool Aug 91 £95
Rule, Pte T H, KTG	QSA (1) DoK	Premier Mine
Rundle, Pte C, KTG	QSA (1) DoK	No 6 Redoubt and No I Section, D Company
Rush, Lt William Welsh, CP2	QSA (2) DoK Paar	See his biography (page 354)
Rusher, 981 Cpl C J, KRV	QSA (2) DoK 01	DMU 16 Jul 01. Also served KTG (No I Section, K Company)
Russell, 305 Tpr Albert, KLH	QSA (2) DoK Paar	Served 24 Oct 99 to 20 Apr 00. Also served SAMIF (26890)
Russell, 741 Pte Denis, CP2	QSA (1) DoK	CP dismounted branch (barrier & redoubt duties)
Russell, 182 Tpr George Benjamin, KLH	QSA (2) DoK Paar	Served 19 Oct 99 to 6 Mar 00. Also served KTG and SRG (172) from 11 Feb 01
Russell, Pte J, KTG	QSA (1) DoK	Otto's Kopje Scouts
Russell, Sgt Maj James Peers, KTG	QSA (1) DoK	Cycle Corps, A Company. DCM for the siege. See KTG section of Kekewich's despatch (page 334) for details. Died 23 Dec 22 and buried in Victoria, Australia. DCM, QSA (1), KStar
Russell, Med Off William, KTG	QSA (1) DoK	
Rutherford, Pte C G, KTG	QSA (1) DoK	No III Section, Belgravia Fort
Rutherford, 50 Sdlr Sgt G, CP2	QSA (1) DoK	CP HQ and depot mounted branch. KSA (2). Served in the Bechuanaland Rebellion 1897 earning CGHGSM (1) Bech
Rutherford, Pte L, KTG	QSA (1) DoK	G Company
Rutherford, Pte R, KTG	QSA (1) DoK	Kenilworth Defence Force
Ryan, Pte Edwin P, KTG	QSA (2) DoK OFS	Also served KLH (320) 20 Oct 99 until DMU 24 Mar 00
Ryan, 531 Cpl Francis Kearns, CP2	QSA (2) DoK OFS	See his biography (page 354)
Ryan, 3573 Pte J, LNLR	QSA (2) DoK OFS	Died of disease at Norval's Pont 26 Aug 00
Ryan, Pte J, KTG	QSA (1) DoK	No II Section, C Company, Pickering's Redoubt No 2. Possibly also served CPS (851) gaining Tr
Ryan, 217 Cpl John Thomas, DFA	QSA (2) DoK Tr	Enrolled 30 Nov 99. Medically unfit 8 Sep 00. Resigned 8 Aug 03. Occupation carpenter
Ryan, 4204 Pte M, LNLR	QSA (3) DoK OFS Tr	KSA (2)
Ryan, 532 Pte Michael, CP2	QSA (2) DoK OFS	A Squadron. KSA (2)

Rybnikar, 475 Band Mst G C, KRV	QSA (1) DoK	KSA (2)
Rynd, Lt F F, RGA	QSA (1) DoK	See his biography (page 354)

S

Sach, 94375 Gnr Henry, RGA	QSA (2) DoK Tr	KSA (2)
Saddler, 192 Gnr William Clifford, DFA	QSA (1) DoK	Enrolled 25 Sep 99. Also served Kimb Rifles. Resigned 16 Nov 03. Occupation overseer at De Beers
Sadler, 720 Pte Eric Clive, CP2	QSA (1) DoK	A Squadron. Discharged for misconduct
Sadler, Lt J M, KTG	QSA (1) DoK	H Company. Served in the Bechuanaland Rebellion 1897 with DFH earning CGHGSM (1) Bech. 50th Anniversary attendee
Sadler, 569 Pte Walter, CP2	QSA (1) DoK	CP dismounted branch (barrier & redoubt duties). Served 11 Oct 99 to 31 May 02. KSA (2). Possibly served in the Bechuanaland Rebellion 1897 with Kimb Rifles earning CGHGSM (1) Bech
Salaman, Lt Sam, KRV	QSA (4) RoM DoK OFS Tr	See his biography (page 354)
Salisbury, Pte Philip, KTG	QSA (1) DoK	See his biography (page 355)
Salkeld, 148 Pte Philip D'Oyley, CP2	QSA (1) DoK	A Squadron. Killed in action 28 Nov 99
Salmon, Pte G H, KTG	QSA (1) DoK	No I Section, Belgravia Fort
Salo, Pte M, KTG	QSA (1) DoK	QSA (1). Neate Mar 94 £55. Liverpool Aug 95 £75
Salo, Pte P, KTG	QSA (1) DoK	No IV Section, C Company, Beaconsfield Town Guard. QSA (1) (officially renamed), KStar. Glendining Jun 93
Salt, 778 Pte J, KRV	QSA (4) RoM DoK OFS 01	Discharged 1 Jul 00. Also served KTG (No IV Section, C Company, Beaconsfield Town Guard)
Sampson, Pte Alfred Weston, KTG	QSA (3) DoK OFS 01	Otto's Kopje Scouts and No II Section, No 2 Redoubt. Also served 34th Co ASC and NH from 5 Mar 00. Occupation farmer
Sampson, 861 Pte D, KRV	QSA (3) DoK OFS Tr	Also served KTG and KLH (1086) to 24 Nov 00
Samuel, Pte Evan, KTG	QSA (1) DoK	Also served CRSS (1173) as Samuels from 3 Apr 01
Samuel, Pte J, KTG	QSA (1) DoK	H Company
Samuel, Pte W, KTG	QSA (1) DoK	H Company
Samuels, 601 Pte P V, KRV	QSA (3) DoK OFS Tr	Discharged 1 Jul 02. KSA (2)
Sanders, Pte W A, KTG	QSA (1) DoK	No 6 Redoubt
Sandford, 900 Pte G, KRV	QSA (2) DoK OFS	Discharged 1 Jul 00. Also served KTG (No IV Company, A Section, Reservoir)
Sandham, Pte J, KRV	QSA (4) RoM DoK OFS Tr	Discharged 1 Jul 02. KSA (2)
Sandham, Lt J, KTG	QSA (1) DoK	No I Section, C Company, Beaconsfield Town Guard
Sandham, Pte J, KTG	QSA (1) DoK	No 2 Schmidt's Breastwork
Sandham, Cpl R, KTG	QSA (1) DoK	Medical Corps, No 1 Company, C Section. QSA (1). Bonhams Apr 06 £188
Sandilands, Pte J, KTG	QSA (1) DoK	Premier Mine
Sandison, Col Sgt C, KTG	QSA (1) DoK	
Sands, Nurse L, NS	QSA (0)	QSA (Nursing Sister L Sands) 1914-15 Star (Sister F L Sands, QAIMNSR), BWM, VM (Nursing Sister), KStar, QAIMNSR Medal. City Coins Feb 87. Spink 90 £200

Sangster, Pte David Kilgour, KTG	QSA (4) DoK OFS Tr 01	Served 14 Oct 99 to 14 Feb 00. Premier Mine. Also served DH. He had served in the Natal Mounted Police 1889-92 and CMR 1893-95. QSA (1) DoK, KStar. City Coins Jun 77
Sarif, Pte A, KTG	QSA (1) DoK	
Sarsons, 686 Pte F, KRV	QSA (3) DoK OFS Tr	Killed in action at Klip Drift 7 Mar 02. KSA (2)
Sathas, Pte N, KTG	QSA (1) DoK	No I Section, B Company, Beaconsfield Town Guard
Saunders, 434 S Sgt A W, APC	QSA (1) DoK	Attached to HQ Staff. KSA (2)
Saunders, 321 Tpr Ernest, KLH	QSA (3) DoK OFS Tr	Served 24 Oct 99 to 6 Nov 00. Also served KTG, CinCBG (22724) 19 Nov 00 to 18 May 01, CPS and StH (1579) 29 Nov 01 until transferred to IMR 12 Sep 02. KSA (2)
Saunders, Pte G, KTG	QSA (1) DoK	No II Section, F Company, Mostert's Redoubt
Saunders, Capt G A, KTG	QSA (1) DoK	D Company
Saunders, 112 Pte R, KRV	QSA (3) RoM DoK OFS	QSA (3). Burman Dec 94 £475. For his medal see page 505
Saunders, 492 Pte W, KRV	QSA (4) DoK OFS Tr 01	Served 11 Oct 99 to 14 Mar 00. Discharged from KRV to railway service 31 Dec 00. One W Saunders attended the 50th Anniversary reunion
Saunders, Pte W S, KTG	QSA (1) DoK	No IV Company, A Section, Reservoir
Saundry, Cpl J, KTG	QSA (1) DoK	Medical Corps, No 1 Company, D Section
Savage, 448 Pte Arthur Hugh, KRV	QSA (4) DoK OFS Tr 01	DMU 8 Dec 99. Also served KTG (H Company), WS (7) from 19 Mar 00, Rhod Regt (282), Geoghegan's Scouts 15 Nov 00 to 30 Jun 01 and JMR (2003 & 35519) to 25 Nov 01. Served in the Bechuanaland Rebellion 1897 with Kimb Rifles earning CGHGSM (1) Bech
Savage, Pte H, KTG	QSA (1) DoK	No IV Section, L Company
Savage, 256 Pte H A, KRV	QSA (2) DoK 01	DMU 19 Mar 00. 50th Anniversary attendee
Savage, Sgt W J, KTG	QSA (1) DoK	Clerk and issuer at the Reservoir
Saville, 570 Pte E W, KRV	QSA (1) DoK	Dismissed for misconduct 22 Feb 00 – Absence (5th offence)
Sayers, 4521 Pte H, LNLR	QSA (3) DoK OFS Tr	QSA (3), KSA (2), KStar. Glendining Dec 33. Sotheby Feb 70 £79
Scannell, 93 Pte Daniel, CP2	QSA (2) DoK OFS	CP HQ and depot mounted branch. KSA (2)
Scannell, 10835 Gnr Edward, RGA	QSA (3) DoK OFS Tr	Premier Mine. Invalided and discharged 26 Feb 01
Scard, 339 Tpr J, KLH	QSA (2) DoK OFS	DMU 4 Mar 00
Schaefer, 483 Pte Ferdinand Emil, CP2	QSA (4) RoM DoK OFS Tr	CP 7-pounder detachment and Otto's Kopje. KSA (2)
Scheibe, Pte J S, KTG	QSA (1) DoK	
Scheibe, Pte Jacobus, KTG	QSA (3) RoM DoK OFS	B line of defence, No 3 Redoubt and Reserve Section, D Company. Also served KLH (229) 16 Mar 00 and 5 Jun 00
Schenck, 31 Tpr H, KLH	QSA (2) DoK OFS	Discharged 3 Apr 00
Schlemmer, Pte J G, KTG	QSA (1) DoK	
Schley, 1368 L Cpl G T, CP1	QSA (2) DoK Paar	B Squadron
Schmidt, Lt H, KTG	QSA (1) DoK	No III Section, K Company. Occupation produce merchant and owner of Schmidt & Co. KStar. Neate Feb 92 £75. QSA (1). McGregor Museum
Schmidt, Sgt W A, KTG	QSA (1) DoK	No III Section, K Company
Schoeman, 202 Pte Hendrick, CP2	QSA (1) DoK	B Squadron. KSA (2)

Name	Medals	Notes
Schoemin, 109 Tpr Martinius J, KLH	QSA (6) RoM DoK OFS Tr 01 02	Served 24 Dec 99 until discharged for misconduct 31 Oct 00. Also served KR (1086), SAC (11 months), SALH (38795) (214 days) and 2nd KFS (879) 7 May 02 to 7 Jul 02
Schofield, 4506 Pte J, LNLR	QSA (2) DoK OFS	Died of disease at Bloemfontein 28 Jul 00
Schouw, Pte C, KTG	QSA (1) DoK	D Company (Veterans), Beaconsfield Town Guard
Schouw, Pte T, KTG	QSA (1) DoK	No II Section, A Company, Beaconsfield Town Guard
Schultz, Pte William Charles, KTG	QSA (4) RoM DoK OFS 01	Premier Mine. Also served KLH (235) 21 Mar 00 to 6 Jun 00 and SRG (174) from 11 Feb 01. Served in the Bechuanaland Rebellion 1897 with DFA earning CGHGSM (1) Bech
Schwabe, 221 Pte R, KRV	QSA (1) DoK	DMU 28 Feb 00
Scoble, Pte T, KTG	QSA (1) DoK	No III Section, D Company
Scott, Pte A, KTG	QSA (1) DoK	Kimberley Mine Ambulance Company, A Section and L Company. Occupation engine driver
Scott, Pte C J, KTG	QSA (1) DoK	No I Section, B2 Company, No 3 Redoubt
Scott, Pte Charles H, KTG	QSA (3) DoK OFS Tr	No IV Section, C Company, Beaconsfield Town Guard. Also served SRG (92) from 11 Feb 01
Scott, 263 Sgt D A, KRV	QSA (2) DoK 01	Non effective 21 Sep 00. QSA (1) excl 01, KStar. Glendining Jun 79 £130. QSA (1) excl 01. DNW Sep 05 £190. KStar. Liverpool May 90 £40. DNW Mar 07 £110
Scott, Pte H, KTG	QSA (2) DoK OFS	No II Section, A Company, Beaconsfield Town Guard. Also served ORCP (295)
Scott, 53 Tpr J, KLH	QSA (2) DoK OFS	Died 11 Apr 00
Scott, 567 Cpl J, KRV	QSA (5) RoM DoK OFS Tr 01	Discharged 18 Aug 02
Scott, Pte J C, KTG	QSA (1) DoK	G Company
Scott, 1294 Tpr Joseph, KLH	QSA (4) RoM DoK OFS Tr	Killed in action 23 Jul 00 at Potchefstroom
Scott, Pte R W, KTG	QSA (1) DoK	No IV Section, K Company. Possibly also served ORCP as Scott, R A, gaining OFS
Scott, Maj Robert George, KLH	QSA (2) DoK OFS	See his biography (page 355)
Scott, 568 Pte W, KRV	QSA (3) DoK OFS Tr	Discharged 1 Jul 02. KSA (2)
Scott, 5245 Pte W, LNLR	QSA (3) DoK OFS Tr	QSA (3), [KSA (2)]. Seaby Jun 77 £80. DNW Dec 04 £230
Scott, Pte W A, KTG	QSA (1) DoK	No IV Section, A Company, Beaconsfield Town Guard. QSA (1). Glendining Sep 73. Spink Jul 09
Scott, 1285 Pte W J, KRV	QSA (2) DoK 01	DMU 4 Jul 01. Also served KTG (No I Section, C Company, Beaconsfield Town Guard)
Scott, 389 Pte W R, KRV	QSA (1) DoK	Non effective 28 Jul 00
Scott, Mr W W, POC	QSA (1) DoK	
Scott, Capt William, DH	QSA (6) DoK Paar Drie Joh DH Witt	See his biography (page 355)
Scott, 35 Sgt William Henry, CP2	QSA (1) DoK	CP dismounted branch (barrier & redoubt duties)
Scott-Turner, Lt Col H S, KLH	QSA (1) DoK	See his biography (page 355)
Scrad, Pte J, KTG	QSA (1) DoK	No IV Section, B Company, Beaconsfield Town Guard
Screech, 287 Tpr Charles, KLH	QSA (2) DoK OFS	Killed in action 28 Nov 99. Also served KTG
Seaborne, 89 Band Cpl E, KRV	QSA (2) DoK 01	Discharged 10 Jan 01

Sealey, 846 Cpl T, KRV	QSA (1) DoK	Discharged 1 Jul 02. Also served KTG (No 1 Redoubt). KSA (2)
Sealey, Pte W J, KTG	QSA (1) DoK	No III Section, F Company, No 3 Redoubt
Searle, Cpl R, KTG	QSA (1) DoK	No IV Section, B Company, No 4 Redoubt
Seaton, 932 Pte C McA, KRV	QSA (4) DoK OFS Tr 01	DMU 5 Oct 01. Also served KTG (No IV Section, K Company)
Seaton, Pte J, KTG	QSA (1) DoK	No III Section, D Company. Supply department, issuing to natives
Seaward, Pte H, KTG	QSA (1) DoK	Kamfersdam Company. 50th Anniversary attendee
Seed, 1583 Pte F H, CP1	QSA (2) DoK OFS	C Squadron. DMU 31 Mar 01
Seeley, Pte W, KTG	QSA (1) DoK	Premier Mine
Sefton, Sgt T, KTG	QSA (1) DoK	No 6 Redoubt. Possibly served in the Bechuanaland Rebellion 1897 with DFH earning CGHGSM (1) Bech
Seidel, 1383 Pte W, CP1	QSA (1) DoK	A Squadron. Deceased 7 Jan 00
Selland, 86 Tpr A, SAC	QSA (3) RoM DoK Tr	Also served KLH (1083) and JMR (2321). KSA (2)
Selling, 47 Sgt Ins W G, KRV	QSA (1) DoK	CGHGSM (1) Bech, QSA (1), [KSA (2)], Colonial Auxiliary Forces LS Medal. McGregor Museum
Selzer, Pte Fred, KTG	QSA (2) DoK 01	No I Section, B Company, Beaconsfield Town Guard. Wounded and prisoner, 22 Feb 00 (not on casualty roll)
Selzer, Pte George William, KTG	QSA (1) DoK	No I Section, B Company, Beaconsfield Town Guard. Also served KLH (385) 6 Mar 00 and dismissed the same day and 9 Oct 01 to 30 Jun 02
Senier, Pte P, KTG	QSA (1) DoK	Ambulance Corps, Beaconsfield Town Guard. 50th Anniversary attendee
Sewell, 373 Pte E C, KRV	QSA (2) DoK OFS	Discharged 1 Jul 02. KSA (2)
Sewell, Mr W G, POC	QSA (1) DoK	
Shackblock, 603 Pte Edward Henry, KRV	QSA (1) DoK	Served 4 Oct 99 until DMU 8 Jun 01. Also served KTG as G Shacklock and CRSS 16 Jan 02 to 22 May 02. KSA (2). Occupation bookseller and stationer
Shackell, QMS J H, KTG	QSA (1) DoK	F Company
Shackleton, Capt C C, KRV	QSA (4) RoM DoK OFS Tr	See his biography (page 356)
Shackleton, Pte T F, KTG	QSA (1) DoK	No I Company, B Section, Reservoir
Shalders, Pte W A, KTG	QSA (1) DoK	G Company
Shand, Pte W B, KTG	QSA (1) DoK	Civil Service Redoubt. QSA (1). Dixon Sep 92 £120
Sharland, Sgt George, KTG	QSA (1) DoK	No III Section, C Company, Beaconsfield Town Guard. Also served CRSS (1470) from 6 Dec 01. Occupation engine driver
Sharp, 1147 Sapr W B, RE	QSA (3) DoK Drie Tr	KSA (2)
Sharpe, Pte E J, KTG	QSA (1) DoK	No II Section, C Company, Pickering's Redoubt No 2
Sharpe, 291 Tpr Frederick, KLH	QSA (2) DoK OFS	Joined 26 Oct 99. Killed in action 28 Nov 99
Sharpe, Sgt R, KTG	QSA (1) DoK	D Company
Sharples, 4973 Pte J, LNLR	QSA (3) DoK OFS Tr	KSA (2)
Sharrock, 186 Pte William, CP2	QSA (1) DoK	CP dismounted branch (barrier & redoubt duties). CGHGSM (1) Bech (Pte CP), QSA (1), KStar. Dixon Jun 98 £300. DNW Sep 02 £340
Shaw, Pte B, KTG	QSA (1) DoK	Civil Service Redoubt
Shaw, 3644 Pte D, LNLR	QSA (3) DoK OFS Tr	MID 4 Sep 01. KSA (2)

Shaw, 4146 Cpl G, LNLR	QSA (3) DoK OFS Tr	KSA (2)
Shaw, 5276 Pte J, LNLR	QSA (3) DoK OFS Tr	QSA (3), [KSA (2)]. Sotheby Feb 85. Liverpool Apr 85 £85
Shaw, Pte J, KTG	QSA (1) DoK	No IV Section, L Company. QSA (1). McGregor Museum
Shaw, 394 Cpl Thomas, CP2	QSA (1) DoK	C Squadron. KSA (2)
Shearer, 313 Tpr Alfred, KLH	QSA (2) DoK OFS	Discharged 30 Apr 00
Sheasby, Lt James Barnwell, KTG	QSA (1) DoK	No IV Section, No 2 Redoubt
Sheehan, 1056 Pte Thomas, KRV	QSA (5) DoK OFS Tr 01 02	Served 27 Jun 00 until DMU 16 Mar 01. Also served KTG (No I Company, A Section, Reservoir), DS (32503) 22 Mar 01 to 6 Jan 02 and WLH (45) 21 Apr 02 to 30 Jun 02. Occupation engine driver
Sheffield, 181 Gnr John Davidson, DFA	QSA (2) DoK OFS	Enrolled 15 Aug 99. Resigned 10 Sec 04. Occupation railway clerk
Shelley, Pte P, KTG	QSA (1) DoK	H Company
Shelton, 5579 Pte F, LNLR	QSA (3) DoK OFS Tr	QSA (3), [KSA (2)]. Sotheby Jun 88
Shepherd, Pte A S, KTG	QSA (5) DoK OFS Tr 01 02	Also served KLH, 1st KFS (964) 8 Jan 01 to 27 Jun 01, IHC and 2nd KFS (912) 9 May 02 to 7 Jul 02. Medal issued by 2nd KFS (912) and returned as duplicate 7 Jul 13
Shepherd, Pte B B, KTG	QSA (1) DoK	No II Section, Mandy Fort. QSA (1), KStar. City Coins Jul 01. Liverpool Nov 01 £130
Shepherd, 277 Pte Daniel D, KRV	QSA (2) DoK OFS	Wounded 28 Nov 99. Non effective 20 Jun 00. Born near Grahamstown in 1880 and attested with the DFH 1898. Discharged Dec 1912. Re-enlisted Sep 1914 for service in GSWA, also serving in Egypt and France. Recommended for the DCM Feb 1918. Discharged Feb 1918. 50th Anniversary attendee. QSA (2), 14-15 Star (Sgt 7th Infy), BWM, VM (CSM 7th SAI), MSM (CSM 1st SAI Infy), Colonial Auxiliary Forces LS Medal (CSM 7th Infy). City Coins Nov 06
Shepherd, 141 Sgt Maj Godfrey, CP2	QSA (4) RoM DoK OFS Tr	B Squadron. Served in the Bechuanaland Rebellion 1897 earning CGHGSM (1) Bech
Shepherd, Pte J, KTG	QSA (1) DoK	Cycle Corps, A Company
Shepherd, 250 Cpl John Henry, CP2	QSA (4) RoM DoK OFS Tr	C Squadron. KSA (2)
Shepherd, Pte R, KTG	QSA (1) DoK	No 6 Redoubt
Shepherd, Pte Robert Austin, KTG	QSA (3) DoK OFS Tr	No III Section, F Company, No 3 Redoubt. Also served KLH 17 Mar 00 to 24 Mar 00. Nominal roll records service in IHC & KFS but this is believed to be A S Shepherd
Shepherd, Pte W, KTG	QSA (1) DoK	No III Section, B Company, No 4 Redoubt
Shepherd, 278 Pte William F, KRV	QSA (2) DoK OFS	Non effective 1 Aug 00. Born 1876. Occupation plumber. 50th Anniversary attendee. CGHGSM (1) Bech (Pte DFH), QSA (2). Spink Dec 83. Liverpool Jan 84 £310
Sheppard, Clerk E, ASC	QSA (2) DoK OFS	Food Supply Staff
Sheppard, 4505 Pte G, LNLR	QSA (4) DoK OFS Tr 01	Died of disease Klerksdorp 17 Feb 01. SA01 issued to mother 6 Jan 11
Sheppy, Cattle Ranger E, ASC	QSA (1) DoK	Cattle Ranger. Possibly served in the Bechuanaland Rebellion 1897 with DFH earning CGHGSM (1) Bech. QSA (1), KStar
Sherbourne, 780 Pte G, KRV	QSA (3) RoM DoK OFS	Discharged 1 Jul 00. Also served KTG (No IV Section, C Company, Beaconsfield Town Guard and Gibraltar Fort, Davis's Heap)
Sheriff, Sgt E J, KTG	QSA (1) DoK	No III Company, A Section, Reservoir

Name	Medals	Notes
Sheriff, 83 Pte John James, CP2	QSA (1) DoK	CP dismounted branch (barrier & redoubt duties). QSA (1). March Medals Dec 87 £95. Christies Apr 91. QSA (1), KStar. eBay Jan 05. eBay Apr 05
Sherman, Pte S, KTG	QSA (4) DoK OFS 01 02	No II Section, No 2 Redoubt. Also served KRV (1349) until discharged 1 Jul 02
Shields, Pte J, KTG	QSA (1) DoK	
Shields, Med Off Thomas Leadbetter, KTG	QSA (1) DoK	
Shillaw, Pte C, KTG	QSA (1) DoK	Medical Corps, No 1 Company, C Section
Shingler, Pte W J, KTG	QSA (1) DoK	Premier Mine
Shoobert, Pte A, KTG	QSA (1) DoK	No I Section, No 2 Redoubt
Shorrock, 4626 Pte A, LNLR	QSA (3) DoK OFS Tr	KSA (2)
Short, 26194 Cyclist Alf George, ScH	QSA (4) DoK OFS Tr 01	Served 7 Feb 01 to 15 Aug 01. Also served KTG (Premier Mine)
Short, Pte J, KTG	QSA (1) DoK	No III Section, B Company, No 4 Redoubt
Shortt, 349 Cpl William Way, CP2	QSA (4) RoM DoK OFS Tr	CP 7-pounder detachment Otto's Kopje. KSA (2). Served in the Bechuanaland Rebellion 1897 earning CGHGSM (1) Bech
Siebert, 393 Pte C, KRV	QSA (1) DoK	DMU 1 Apr 00. Also served CPS (665)
Siebert, Pte James, KTG	QSA (1) DoK	No IV Section, C Company, Pickering's Redoubt No 2. Also served SRG (149) as John Martin Siebert from 18 May 01
Siebert, Pte John, KTG	QSA (1) DoK	No IV Section, C Company, Pickering's Redoubt No 2
Siebert, 320 Pte S, KRV	QSA (1) DoK	Non effective 22 Jul 00. QSA (1). Kaplan Aug 08
Siems, Pte G, KTG	QSA (1) DoK	QSA (1), KStar. City Coins Dec 97. Spink Sep 98 £240
Silbert, Pte P, KTG	QSA (1) DoK	H Company
Siljeur, Pte A, KTG	QSA (1) DoK	
Sillwood, 3625 Gnr Ernest J, RGA	QSA (3) DoK OFS 01	DCM VR, QSA (3). Initial as A and A J respectively. Spink Dec 97 £620. DNW Sep 02 £1,100. Liverpool Feb 03 £1,550
Silson, Pte R, KTG	QSA (1) DoK	G Company. QSA (1). eBay Oct 07 £185
Simkins, Pte P, KTG	QSA (1) DoK	
Simmons, Pte M, KTG	QSA (1) DoK	No I Company, B Section, Reservoir
Simon, Pte J, KTG	QSA (1) DoK	
Simpkiss, 234 Tpr Henry Stoner, KLH	QSA (2) DoK OFS	Served 20 Oct 99 to 30 Apr 00. Also served Lt Klipdam TG. QSA (2). Spink Dec 80 £145
Simpson, Mr C J, POC	QSA (1) DoK	Telegraph signaller. Initials W J on the nominal roll
Simpson, 1378 L Cpl F D, CP1	QSA (4) RoM DoK OFS Tr	C Squadron. Wounded 24 Oct 99. QSA (4), KSA (2), KStar, 1902 Coronation. City Coins Mar 93
Simpson, 1092 Tpr G, KLH	QSA (3) DoK OFS Tr	Discharged 10 Nov 00
Simpson, Pte H, KTG	QSA (1) DoK	No III Section, L Company
Simpson, Pte J, KTG	QSA (1) DoK	No II Company, A Section, Reservoir. QSA (1), KStar. Neate Feb 93 £160
Simpson, Mr T T, POC	QSA (1) DoK	QSA (1), KStar. City Coins Sep 03. Monarch Medals Feb 04 £520
Sinclair, Lt D K, KTG	QSA (1) DoK	No IV Section, C Company, Pickering's Redoubt No 2. Occupation senior boilermaker foreman. QSA (1). City Coins Feb 95. QSA (1), KStar. City Coins May 02
Sinclair, Pte H M L, KTG	QSA (1) DoK	No IV Section, C Company, Pickering's Redoubt No 2
Sinclair, Pte John, KTG	QSA (3) RoM DoK OFS	No I Section, B2 Company, No 3 Redoubt. Also served KLH (144) 15 Mar 00 to 5 Jun 00
Sivertson, 226 Tpr L, KLH	QSA (2) DoK OFS	Served 21 Oct 99 until DMU 24 Mar 00
Skelding, Pte R A, KTG	QSA (1) DoK	No II Section, Belgravia Fort

Skeldon, Pte J, KTG	QSA (1) DoK	No II Section, L Company
Skeldon, Pte P, KTG	QSA (1) DoK	No II Section, F Company, Mostert's Redoubt. QSA (1), KStar
Skelton, Pte Henry, KTG	QSA (1) DoK	Died of disease 18 Dec 99
Skelton, Pte T, KTG	QSA (1) DoK	No 1 Redoubt
Skill, 327 Tpr N Charles, KLH	QSA (1) DoK	Wounded 25 Nov 99. Discharged 26 Feb 00
Skinner, Col Sgt C, KTG	QSA (3) DoK OFS Tr	Mounted Section, Kenilworth Defence Force. Also served CPS (4) 7 Nov 00 to 30 Apr 02. Severely wounded Lilliefontein 19 Oct 01. KSA (2)
Skinner, 381 Cpl R L, CP2	QSA (3) DoK OFS Tr	C Squadron. Wounded 25 Nov 99. Served 11 Oct 99 to 31 May 02. KSA (2). Served in the Bechuanaland Rebellion 1897 earning CGHGSM (1) Bech
Skirving, QMS David, KTG	QSA (1) DoK	No I Section, Mandy Fort. Founded the Kimberley Golf Club in 1890. Born 1842 and died 1903
Skrine, Pte Tryon James, KTG	QSA (3) RoM DoK OFS	No 3 Redoubt. Also served KLH (386 & 456) 6 Mar 00 to 5 Jun 00
Skuse, 1296 Tpr Francis Augustus, KLH	QSA (4) RoM DoK Paar Tr	Discharged 8 Dec 00. Also served StH. KSA (2)
Skuse, Dvr W, DBMB	QSA (1) DoK	Botanical Gardens
Skutnas, Pte A, KTG	QSA (1) DoK	Premier Mine
Slattery, 3858 Pte R, LNLR	QSA (3) DoK OFS Tr	KSA (2)
Slicer, 4976 Pte W, LNLR	QSA (3) DoK OFS Tr	Wounded Witcom 16 May 01. KSA (2)
Smales, 4224 Cpl P, LNLR	QSA (3) DoK OFS Tr	KSA (2)
Small, Pte J J, KTG	QSA (1) DoK	No 6 Redoubt
Smart, Pte W, KTG	QSA (1) DoK	QSA (1). LSE Dec 81 £105. Spink Jul 94
Smartt, Int Off T W, KTG	QSA (1) DoK	See his biography (page 356)
Smedley, 14063 Gnr Alfred, RGA	QSA (3) DoK OFS Tr	Otto's Kopje. KSA (2)
Smith, Pte A, KTG	QSA (1) DoK	No IV Section, D Company
Smith, Pte A D, KTG	QSA (1) DoK	No III Section, C Company, No 2 Redoubt
Smith, 33 Drum Maj A F, KRV	QSA (3) DoK Tr 01	Died of disease at Christiana 2 Jan 01
Smith, Pte A F, KTG	QSA (1) DoK	No II Section, B Company, No 4 Redoubt. Also served KR (1305)
Smith, Nurse B, NS	QSA (0)	Kimberley Civil Hospital
Smith, 1305 Pte C, KRV	QSA (5) DoK OFS Tr 01 02	Discharged 1 Jul 02. Also served KTG
Smith, 4885 Pte Sdlr C, LNLR	QSA (2) DoK OFS	Invalided to England 5 Oct 00. On roll as Pte and on roll as Sadd. QSA (2), [KSA (2)]. DNW 15 Dec 00 £110. Liverpool Feb 01 £175
Smith, 5321 Pte C, LNLR	QSA (3) DoK OFS Tr	KSA (2)
Smith, 27547 2nd Cpl C, RE	QSA (2) DoK Drie	
Smith, Pte C, KTG	QSA (1) DoK	Kamfersdam Company. QSA (1). DNW May 93 £50 but could be next two men
Smith, Pte C, KTG	QSA (1) DoK	No I Company, B Section, Reservoir
Smith, Pte C, KTG	QSA (1) DoK	No III Section, B Company, Beaconsfield Town Guard
Smith, 185 Tpr Charles Benjamin, KLH	QSA (2) DoK OFS	Served 19 Oct 99 to 19 Jul 00. QSA (2) (initials C V), KStar. DNW Sep 07 £380

Smith, 448 Pte Charles Newbold, CP2	QSA (2) DoK 01	CP HQ and depot mounted branch. Served 11 Oct 99 to 19 Feb 01. Served in the Bechuanaland Rebellion 1897 earning CGHGSM (1) Bech
Smith, 338 Pte D, KRV	QSA (1) DoK	Non effective 15 Jul 00
Smith, Lt D W, KTG	QSA (1) DoK	Cycle Corps, A Company
Smith, 56 Cpl Daniel, WS	QSA (4) DoK OFS Tr 01	Served 4 Sep 00 to 20 Jun 01. Also served CPD2 31 Jul 01 to 31 Dec 01 (can't find on roll) and RR (33632). No DoK on the WS which is unusual and makes this a suspect entry
Smith, 181 Sgt E T F, KRV	QSA (3) DoK OFS Tr	Discharged 30 Jun 02. KSA (2). Served in the Bechuanaland Rebellion 1897 with Kimb Rifles earning CGHGSM (1) Bech
Smith, 359 Sgt Ernest Rupert, KLH	QSA (3) DoK OFS Tr	Joined 16 Oct 99. Medal roll says dismissed 18 Aug 00. Nominal roll says deserted 1 Mar 00. See the Diamond Fields Advertiser article on the siege pig
Smith, Pte F, KTG	QSA (1) DoK	No 6 Redoubt
Smith, 718 Pte F E, KRV	QSA (1) DoK	Discharged 1 Jul 02. KSA (2)
Smith, Pte F J, KTG	QSA (1) DoK	Premier Mine
Smith, Pte F R H, KTG	QSA (1) DoK	No II Section, Mandy Fort
Smith, Lt F W, KTG	QSA (1) DoK	QSA (1), KStar. Spink Sep 77 £125. Spink Dec 83. Glendining Oct 84
Smith, 24719 Tmptr Francis, RGA	QSA (1) DoK	KSA (2)
Smith, Sgt G, KTG	QSA (1) DoK	Kimberley Mine Ambulance Company, B Section
Smith, Pte G, KTG	QSA (1) DoK	No IV Section, B Company, Beaconsfield Town Guard. 781 Pte G Smith served KRV, gained OFS and dying 9 May 00. This or next man? QSA (1). Liverpool Feb 94 £75
Smith, Pte G, KTG	QSA (1) DoK	No IV Section, C Company, Beaconsfield Town Guard
Smith, 607 Pte G B, KRV	QSA (4) RoM DoK OFS Tr	Discharged 1 Jul 02. Also served KLH (1240) 4 Oct 99 to 31 Mar 00. KSA (2)
Smith, 99 Sgt George, CP2	QSA (1) DoK	C Squadron. Discharged by purchase
Smith, Pte H, KTG	QSA (1) DoK	No IV Section, L Company
Smith, Pte H, KTG	QSA (1) DoK	
Smith, Pte H J, KTG	QSA (1) DoK	Premier Mine
Smith, 228 Sgt H S, KRV	QSA (2) DoK 01	Non effective 1 Jun 01. QSA (1) DoK. Carter Jul 90 £78
Smith, Lt H W, KRV	QSA (5) RoM DoK OFS Tr 01	Wounded 16 Nov 99
Smith, Pte H W, KTG	QSA (1) DoK	G Company
Smith, 56 L Cpl J, KRV	QSA (2) DoK OFS	Wounded Fourteen Streams 23 Mar 00. Discharged (wounds) 3 Apr 00
Smith, 131 Pte J, KRV	QSA (2) DoK OFS	DMU 4 May 00
Smith, 187 Sgt J, KRV	QSA (1) DoK	KSA (2)
Smith, 3841 Pte J, LNLR	QSA (3) DoK OFS Tr	KSA (2)
Smith, 4285 Pte J, LNLR	QSA (3) DoK OFS Tr	KSA (2)
Smith, Pte J, KTG	QSA (1) DoK	Premier Mine. Also served KR (1158) and KLH (299)
Smith, 3679 Pte J, LNLR	QSA (3) DoK OFS Tr	Forfeited and restored. KSA (2)
Smith, Cpl J J, KTG	QSA (1) DoK	No II Section, Belgravia Fort and Ambulance Corps, Beaconsfield Town Guard
Smith, Pte J J, KTG	QSA (1) DoK	No I Company, B Section, Reservoir
Smith, Surg Maj James Alexander Jones, KRV	QSA (1) DoK	See his biography (page 356)

Kimberley Siege Account and Medal Roll

Smith, 299 Tpr John, KLH	QSA (3) DoK OFS Tr	Served 23 Oct 99 to 13 Apr 00. Also served KRV (1158) 14 Aug 00 to 30 Jun 02. Wounded Warrenton 22 Mar 00. KSA (2). Number also given as 322
Smith, 666 Pte John, CP2	QSA (1) DoK	CP dismounted branch (barrier & redoubt duties)
Smith, 209 Pte John Godfrey, CP2	QSA (1) DoK	B Squadron. Discharged on gratuity. Served in the Bechuanaland Rebellion 1897 earning CGHGSM (1) Bech
Smith, 189 Cpl John Macaulay, DFA	QSA (3) DoK OFS Tr	Enrolled 23 Sep 99. Served Highland Vol Art 96 to 98. Resigned 8 Jan 03. Occupation guard at De Beers Mine. KSA (2)
Smith, Nurse L, NS	QSA (0)	Kimberley Civil Hospital
Smith, 717 Cpl L C, CP1	QSA (1) DoK	B Squadron. Also served Willowmore TG (no trace on roll or for Willowmore DMT)
Smith, Cpl M C, KTG	QSA (1) DoK	No II Company, A Section, Reservoir
Smith, Cpl P R, KTG	QSA (1) DoK	Premier Mine
Smith, 1763 Gnr Richard, RGA	QSA (1) DoK	KSA (2)
Smith, Lt Robert Alfred Lange, KTG	QSA (1) DoK	See his biography (page 356)
Smith, Pte S J, KTG	QSA (1) DoK	G Company
Smith, Pte S W, KTG	QSA (1) DoK	No II Section, A Company, Beaconsfield Town Guard
Smith, 217 Tpr Samuel Hamilton, DH	QSA (4) DoK OFS Tr 01	Served 21 Sep 01 to 26 Mar 02. Prisoner 4 Nov 99. Also served KRV (608) to 9 Jun 00 and 1st KFS (698) 21 Dec 00 to 18 Jun 01
Smith, 4678 Pte T, LNLR	QSA (3) DoK OFS Tr	KSA (2)
Smith, Pte T, KTG	QSA (1) DoK	No 1 Redoubt. QSA (1), KStar. Glendining Jul 85 but could be next two men
Smith, Pte T, KTG	QSA (1) DoK	Kenilworth Defence Force
Smith, Pte T, KTG	QSA (1) DoK	No II Section, L Company
Smith, T F, KTG	QSA (0)	Medical Corps, No 1 Company, F Section. Roll states "Ambulance work in connection with scurvy outbreak"
Smith, Pte V, KTG	QSA (1) DoK	
Smith, 122 Cpl W, KRV	QSA (1) DoK	Non effective 10 Jul 00
Smith, 838 Band W, KRV	QSA (2) DoK OFS	Discharged 1 Aug 02. Also served KTG. KSA (2)
Smith, 2269 Pte W, LNLR	QSA (3) DoK OFS Tr	Time expired to England 3 Dec 00
Smith, 3828 Pte W, LNLR	QSA (3) DoK OFS Tr	KSA (2)
Smith, 4898 Pte W, LNLR	QSA (3) DoK OFS Tr	QSA (1) DoK, [KSA (2)]. DNW Mar 07 £160. Dixon Jul 07 £300
Smith, Pte W, KTG	QSA (1) DoK	H Company
Smith, 643 Pte W D, KRV	QSA (2) DoK OFS	DMU Apr 00
Smith, Pte W D, KTG	QSA (2) DoK 01	Also served JMR (1084 & 26234) and UVR
Smith, 98 Pay Sgt W H, KRV	QSA (1) DoK	Non effective 6 Jul 00
Smith, 642 Pte W H, KRV	QSA (1) DoK	DMU 17 Mar 00
Smith, Pte W H, KTG	QSA (1) DoK	Also served KRV as Lt
Smith, 186 Cpl W J, KLH	QSA (2) DoK OFS	Served 20 Oct 99 until DMU 24 Mar 00. Also served KTG
Smith, 203 Cpl William Barberow, CP2	QSA (2) DoK Tr	C Squadron. KSA (2)
Smith, 670 Pte William John, CP2	QSA (2) DoK Tr	CP dismounted branch (barrier & redoubt duties). Dismissed misconduct. Also served CPS (863)

Smithyes, 471 Band A G, KRV	QSA (1) DoK	KSA (2)
Smyth, Pte H W, KTG	QSA (1) DoK	No III Section, Belgravia Fort. Also served CPS (346)
Smyth, Sgt J J, KTG	QSA (1) DoK	No III Section, No 2 Redoubt and No 5 supply depot
Smyth, Nurse Z L, NS	QSA (0)	Kimberley Civil Hospital
Snaith, Pte H, KTG	QSA (1) DoK	No III Section, D Company. QSA (1). Sotheby Apr 81. Chelsea Dec 98 £105. QSA (1), KStar. Glendining Sep 88
Snape, Pte W, KTG	QSA (1) DoK	Kimberley Mine Ambulance Company, A Section
Snapper, 227 Pte E, KRV	QSA (5) RoM DoK OFS Tr 01	Non effective 26 Apr 01
Snedden, Pte D, KTG	QSA (1) DoK	Cycle Corps, A Company
Snedden, Pte W, KTG	QSA (1) DoK	No 1 supply depot
Snell, Pte T, KTG	QSA (1) DoK	No I Section, B2 Company, No 3 Redoubt
Snell, Pte W, KTG	QSA (1) DoK	No I Section, C Company, Pickering's Redoubt No 1
Snow, Capt Arthur Baring, CP2	QSA (3) DoK OFS Tr	See his biography (page 356)
Soderblom, Pte A, KTG	QSA (1) DoK	No I Section, A Company, Beaconsfield Town Guard
Soffe, 1242 Pte William C, KRV	QSA (4) DoK OFS Tr 01	Served 26 Nov 00 to 29 May 01. Also served KTG, CRSS (1302) 6 Jun 01 to 10 Dec 01, SRG and KLH (41807) 4 Mar 02 to 30 Jun 02. Occupation grocer
Sohami, 10530 Pte J, ASC	QSA (1) DoK	KSA (2)
Solomon, 887 Pte B W, KRV	QSA (3) DoK OFS Tr	Discharged 1 Jul 02. Also served KTG (Cycle Corps, A Company). KSA (2)
Solomon, Pte E, KTG	QSA (1) DoK	Cycle Corps, A Company
Solomon, Cpl H S, KTG	QSA (1) DoK	Premier Mine
Solomon, QMS J, KTG	QSA (1) DoK	G Company
Solomon, Pte P, KTG	QSA (1) DoK	Premier Mine
Solomon, Lt R, KTG	QSA (1) DoK	Cycle Corps, A Company
Solomon, Pte W H, KTG	QSA (1) DoK	No III Section, Belgravia Fort
Southern, Pte F, KTG	QSA (1) DoK	No I Section, C Company, Beaconsfield Town Guard
Southward, 845 Cpl B, KRV	QSA (3) DoK OFS 01	DMU 7 Jun 01. Also served KTG (No 1 Redoubt). QSA (3). Glendining Sep 87
Southward, 729 Pte Isaac Henry, KRV	QSA (4) DoK OFS Tr 01	DMU 21 Jun 00. Also served KTG (No 2 Schmidt's Breastwork) and 2nd RPR (1118) 5 Dec 00 to 4 Jun 01
Spalding, 606 Pte F W, KRV	QSA (3) DoK OFS 01	Dismissed for misconduct 11 Jan 01. Also served ORCP (163)
Spangenberg, 606 Pte David Frederick, CP2	QSA (1) DoK	B Squadron. Discharged time expired
Spangenberg, 216 Pte John Peter, CP2	QSA (1) DoK	B Squadron. KSA (2) nr given as 182. Served in the Bechuanaland Rebellion 1897 earning CGHGSM (1) Bech
Spargo, Pte J, KTG	QSA (1) DoK	No I Section, C Company, Beaconsfield Town Guard
Sparkes, Pte W, KTG	QSA (1) DoK	No 2 Schmidt's Breastwork
Sparkes, 569 Pte W S, KRV	QSA (4) RoM DoK OFS Tr	Discharged 1 Jul 02. KSA (2)
Sparks, 825 Pte A, KRV	QSA (1) DoK	Discharged 1 Jul 02. Also served KTG (No III Section, K Company). KSA (2)
Spence, Pte A, KTG	QSA (1) DoK	No 6 Redoubt
Spence, 811 Pte D J, KRV	QSA (2) DoK 01	Discharged 17 Feb 01. Also served KTG (Gibraltar Fort, Davis's Heap)
Spence, Pte H, KTG	QSA (1) DoK	D Company (Veterans), Beaconsfield Town Guard
Spence, Pte H, KTG	QSA (1) DoK	Premier Mine

Kimberley Siege Account and Medal Roll

Spence, Pte J E, KTG	QSA (1) DoK	Cycle Corps, A Company. QSA (1), KStar and Kimberley shooting medal (son's?). BMF Jan 08 £425. QSA (1). eBay Aug 09 £195
Spence, Cpl John William, DH	QSA (6) DoK Paar Drie Joh DH Witt	Served 18 Feb 00 to 1 Feb 01. Also served KTG (Premier Mine) and FID. KSA (2)
Spence, Pte N, KTG	QSA (1) DoK	No 6 Redoubt
Spence, 7 Gnr T, DFA	QSA (1) DoK	
Spence, 397 Pte W J, KRV	QSA (3) DoK Tr 01	Discharged 4 Jul 01. Also served CPS (239). Prisoner Zoutlief 16 Sep 01. 50th Anniversary attendee
Spencer, Lt Charles H W, CP2	QSA (4) RoM DoK OFS Tr	CP No 3 Maxim gun detachment. KSA (2). Served in the Bechuanaland Rebellion 1897 with initials C E W earning CGHGSM (1) Bech
Spencer, Mr G R, POC	QSA (1) DoK	
Spencer, 5473 Pte J, LNLR	QSA (3) DoK OFS Tr	KSA (2)
Sperling, 687 L Cpl H, KRV	QSA (3) DoK OFS Tr	Discharged 1 Jul 02. KSA (2)
Spilsbury, 1312 L Cpl W G, CP1	QSA (3) RoM DoK OFS	A Squadron. Wounded 28 Nov 99. QSA (3), [KSA (2)]. Liverpool May 91 £225
Spooner, 139 Gnr Edward, DFA	QSA (1) DoK	Served 6 Apr 02 to 1 Jul 02. Also served Loch's Horse and SRG. Occupation farmer
Spooner, Pte F, KTG	QSA (1) DoK	No IV Section, K Company
Spooner, Pte H, KTG	QSA (2) DoK OFS	Kimberley Mine Ambulance Company, B Section. Also served KLH and discharged 4 Mar 00
Spooner, 187 Tpr Percy, KLH	QSA (3) RoM DoK OFS	Served 19 Oct 99 to 5 Jun 00. Also served KTG
Spriddell, Pte W, KTG	QSA (1) DoK	No II Section, D Company. QSA (1). Sotheby Mar 80. Spink Feb 81 £140. Spink Nov 83 £100
Sprigg, Lt Albert Percy, KLH	QSA (4) RoM DoK OFS Tr	Joined 4 Dec 99. Transferred to SAC as Capt 1 Nov 00. KSA (2). Subsequently a farmer in Tembani. He died Nov 1908
Sprong, 467 Sgt J L, CP1	QSA (2) DoK OFS	B Squadron. KSA (2) as Sprang. Served in the Bechuanaland Rebellion 1897 as Sprang earning CGHGSM (1) Bech and later served in the 5th SAMR during the Great War
Sprong, Pte J R, KTG	QSA (1) DoK	No II Section, C Company, Pickering's Redoubt No 2
Sprong, Pte John Robert, KTG	QSA (1) DoK	No III Section, C Company, Pickering's Redoubt No 1. Also served SRG (116) 11 Feb 01 to 15 Jun 01. Note on the attestation says 'Won't sign'
Sprong, Pte P D, KTG	QSA (1) DoK	No III Section, C Company, Pickering's Redoubt No 1
Sprong, Pte P D S, KTG	QSA (1) DoK	
Spry, Pte J, KTG	QSA (1) DoK	No II Section, L Company. QSA (1), KStar. DNW Sep 00 £210. Ursual Nov 00 £280
Squire, 257 Sgt J L, CMR	QSA (3) DoK 01 02	Occupation store keeper. Also on roll for CCOD. QSA (1), KStar (Sgt Colonial Ordnance Cape Mtd R), Cape LS&GC (N 257 3rd Cl Sgt C M Riflemen). eBay May 09 £2,050
St Quinton, 582 Pte Allan, CP2	QSA (4) RoM DoK OFS Tr	CP 7-pounder detachment and Otto's Kopje. KSA (2)
Stables, Pte J, KTG	QSA (1) DoK	Premier Mine
Stack, Cpl G, KTG	QSA (1) DoK	Cycle Corps, A Company
Stacpole, 207 Tpr Henry Francis, KLH	QSA (2) DoK OFS	Served 19 Oct 99 until DMU 24 Mar 00. Wounded 28 Nov 99. Also served RoH (no trace on QSA roll) and KitH (9479). Surname sometimes Stacpoole and Stackpoole
Staddon, Pte C, KTG	QSA (1) DoK	
Staff, Pte George E, KTG	QSA (1) DoK	No 1 supply depot
Staff, Pte R F, KTG	QSA (1) DoK	No 1 supply depot

Stanford, 387 Pte Ernest Robert, CP2	QSA (4) RoM DoK OFS Tr	C Squadron. KSA (2)
Stanley, 22230 Sgt Bertram, CinCBG	QSA (4) DoK OFS Tr 01	Served 20 Nov 00 to 15 Mar 01. Also served KR, 2nd KFS (284 and 36031) 22 Jul 01 until DMU 26 Oct 01 and ASC
Stanley, 602 Pte G, KRV	QSA (1) DoK	
Stanley, 4786 Pte J, LNLR	QSA (2) DoK OFS	Died of disease Krugersdorp 24 Jul 00
Stanley, Gnr J, DBMB	QSA (1) DoK	Botanical Gardens. Also served KTG (No II Section, A Company, Beaconsfield Town Guard)
Stannard, Pte Frederick Thomas, KTG	QSA (3) RoM DoK OFS	Premier Mine. Also served KLH (184) 8 Mar 00 to 5 Jun 00
Stanner, Pte W G S, KTG	QSA (1) DoK	No III Section, F Company, No 3 Redoubt
Stanton, Pte B, KTG	QSA (1) DoK	No I Section, C Company, Beaconsfield Town Guard
Stark, Pte George Fred, KTG	QSA (1) DoK	Occupation piano tuner. QSA issued 27 Jul 56. QSA (1). DNW Jun 02 £110. QSA (1), KStar. Morris Sep 05 £375
Starkey, Pte R, KTG	QSA (1) DoK	No I Company, B Section, Reservoir
Starkie, 5150 Pte W, LNLR	QSA (2) DoK OFS	Died of disease Kimberley 6 Apr 00
Stassen, 372 Pte John Nicholas, CP2	QSA (4) RoM DoK OFS Tr	A Squadron. Wounded during the siege. Accidentally injured at Kimberley 27 Jun 01
Staton, Pte H J, KTG	QSA (1) DoK	No I Company, B Section, Reservoir
Statzkowski, Pte C, KTG	QSA (1) DoK	B line of defence, No 3 Redoubt
Stavers, Pte W A, KTG	QSA (1) DoK	No III Section, L Company. QSA (1). Seaby Feb 81 £130
Stead, Sgt A W C, KTG	QSA (1) DoK	No IV Section, L Company
Stead, Lt B, KTG	QSA (1) DoK	No II Section, Belgravia Fort. Served in the Bechuanaland Rebellion of 1896 with the Griqualand West Brigade earning CGHGSM (1) Bech
Stearns, 233 Tpr Charles Cullen, KLH	QSA (2) DoK OFS	Killed in action 28 Nov 99. QSA (2)
Steele, 22725 Tpr Henry, CinCBG	QSA (5) RoM DoK OFS Tr 01	Served 17 Nov 00 to 16 May 01. Also served KTG (Kenilworth Defence Force), KLH (193) 17 Mar 00 to 5 Jun 00, SRG (596), Cattle Ranger and ASC as cattle innoculator (94). Occupation miner
Steele, Pte J, KTG	QSA (1) DoK	No III Section, D Company. QSA (1), KStar. Glendining Nov 92 £140
Steins, Pte W O, KTG	QSA (1) DoK	D Company (Veterans), Beaconsfield Town Guard
Stenson, 93644 Gnr Edward Henry, RGA	QSA (1) DoK	QSA (1), KSA (2), KStar. City Coins Jul 01. Liverpool Nov 01 £240
Stenson, Pte W, KTG	QSA (1) DoK	No 3 Redoubt. Died of enteric 17 Jan 00
Stephens, Pte F, KTG	QSA (1) DoK	No I Section, D Company
Stephens, 5084 Pioneer G, LNLR	QSA (3) DoK OFS Tr	KSA (2)
Stephens, Pte J G, KTG	QSA (4) DoK OFS 01 02	No I Section, B2 Company, No 3 Redoubt. Also served CTH (1502)
Stephens, Pte P, KTG	QSA (1) DoK	Kimberley Mine Ambulance Company
Stephens, Mr W W, POC	QSA (1) DoK	Telegraph signaller
Stephenson, 243 Tpr Charles, KLH	QSA (2) DoK OFS	Served 20 Oct 99 to 30 Apr 00. Also served KTG as Stevenson. QSA (2). Argyll Etkin May 06. Dixon Sep 06 £265
Stephenson, Pte M, KTG	QSA (1) DoK	No II Section, L Company. QSA (1), KStar. Glendining Dec 85
Stephenson, 3733 Pte R, LNLR	QSA (3) DoK OFS Tr	QSA (5) inc 01 & 02, [KSA (2)], KStar. Sotheby Feb 75 £110. Dixon Apr 05 £350. Lockdales Jan 09

Name	Medals	Notes
Stephenson, Pte William James, KTG	QSA (4) DoK OFS Joh DH	Premier Mine. Also served Loch's Horse (Ross Machine Gun Battery) 1 Apr 00 to 4 May 00, DFA (287), SRG (685) 12 Jun 01 to 17 Dec 01 and ALH (40048) as Stevenson 6 Jan 02 to 24 Mar 02. KSA (2)
Sterley, Pte W, KTG	QSA (1) DoK	Cycle Corps, A Company
Stern, Pte L, KTG	QSA (1) DoK	Kenilworth Defence Force
Sternsdorf, 188 Tpr Herman, KLH	QSA (2) DoK OFS	Served 19 Oct 99 to 14 Mar 00. Also served KTG as Sterndorp
Stevens, 72 Tpr C W, KLH	QSA (2) DoK Paar	Discharged 30 Apr 00. QSA (2). City Coins Jul 01
Stevens, Pte J, KTG	QSA (1) DoK	No III Section, B Company, No 4 Redoubt
Stevens, Pte J, KTG	QSA (1) DoK	No III Section, C Company, Beaconsfield Town Guard
Stevenson, 100 Sgt George, DFA	QSA (1) DoK	Enrolled 12 Feb 98. Discharged 3 Dec 01. Occupation railway clerk
Stevenson, Capt J, KTG	QSA (1) DoK	No 1 Redoubt. Possibly served in the Bechuanaland Rebellion 1897 with Kimb Rifles as Sgt earning CGHGSM (1) Bech
Stevenson, Sp Const J R, CP2	QSA (1) DoK	
Stewart, 206 Dvr A W, DFA	QSA (3) DoK OFS Tr	Wounded 9 Dec 99. Wounded Klip Drift 7 Mar 02. Discharged 15 Sep 03. KSA (2)
Stewart, Sgt C W, KTG	QSA (1) DoK	No 1 Redoubt
Stewart, Pte D, KTG	QSA (2) DoK OFS	No II Section, B Company, No 4 Redoubt. Also served KR (855 Pte Stuart)
Stewart, Pte D C, KTG	QSA (1) DoK	No 2 supply depot. On nominal roll as Stuart. QSA (1). Christies Nov 84 £70
Stewart, 914 Pte G, KRV	QSA (1) DoK	Discharged 1 Jul 02. Also served KTG (H Company). KSA (2)
Stewart, 189 Tpr George Martin Patrick, KLH	QSA (2) DoK OFS	Served 19 Oct 99 to 14 Mar 00. Also served KTG
Stewart, Lt J, KTG	QSA (1) DoK	No II Section, C Company, Pickering's Redoubt No 1
Stewart, 32 Sgt J, KRV	QSA (1) DoK	CGHGSM (1) Bech (Kimb Rfls), QSA (1), VM, Col Aux Forces LS Medal. McGregor Museum
Stewart, Pte J K, KTG	QSA (1) DoK	No 3 Redoubt
Stewart, Pte J N, KTG	QSA (1) DoK	No 1 Redoubt
Stewart, 297 Tpr John, KLH	QSA (2) DoK OFS	Discharged 4 Mar 00. Possibly also served CPS (142). QSA (2). City Coins Dec 74
Stewart, Pte L C, KTG	QSA (1) DoK	QSA (1). Christies Jul 85. DNW Dec 01 £90. Liverpool Jun 02 £145
Stewart, Pte P J, KTG	QSA (1) DoK	
Stewart, Pte R, KTG	QSA (1) DoK	No III Section, F Company, No 3 Redoubt
Stewart, Pte S, KTG	QSA (1) DoK	No III Section, B Company, No 4 Redoubt
Stewart, Lt S A, KTG	QSA (1) DoK	
Stewart, 195 Tpr Sam Alex, KLH	QSA (3) RoM DoK OFS	Served 20 Nov 99 to 5 Jun 00. Number duplicated on roll
Stewart, Lt W M, KTG	QSA (2) DoK OFS	F Company
Stewart, 196 Tpr William Mason, KLH	QSA (3) RoM DoK OFS	Served 12 Oct 99 to 5 Jun 00. KSA (2). Also served FID and Lt SAC. Served in the Bechuanaland Rebellion 1897 with DFH earning CGHGSM (1) Bech
Steytler, 69 Pte N V, KRV	QSA (4) DoK Tr Witt 01	Non effective 5 Jan 01. Served in the Bechuanaland Rebellion 1897 with Kimb Rifles earning CGHGSM (1) Bech
Stibbs, Pte J B, KTG	QSA (1) DoK	
Still, 26070 Cyclist Edmund Stamford Lloyd, ScH	QSA (5) RoM DoK OFS Tr 01	Served 11 Jan 01 to 30 Jul 01. Also served KTG (Premier Mine) and KLH (190 & 1297) 7 Mar 00 to 5 Jun 00

Medal roll

Stinkfield, Pte R, KTG	QSA (1) DoK	
Stockenstroom, Pte F, KTG	QSA (1) DoK	No III Section, D Company
Stockhill, Pte F, KTG	QSA (1) DoK	G Company
Stockwell, 35 Sgt E H, KRV	QSA (1) DoK	DMU 21 Apr 00. Served in the Bechuanaland Rebellion 1897 with Kimb Rifles earning CGHGSM (1) Bech
Stokes, Pte S, KTG	QSA (1) DoK	No I Section, Belgravia Fort
Stokes, 517 Band W, KRV	QSA (2) DoK OFS	Discharged 31 Jul 02. KSA (2)
Stolz, 1161 Pte J J, CP1	QSA (2) DoK OFS	C Squadron. Wounded 25 Nov 99. KSA (2). Served in the Bechuanaland Rebellion 1897 earning CGHGSM (1) Bech
Stone, 5488 Pte C, LNLR	QSA (3) DoK OFS Tr	KSA (2)
Stone, 769 Pte Charles Arthur, CP2	QSA (1) DoK	B Squadron. Served 11 Oct 99 to 14 Feb 01. Discharged for drunkenness (with CP2) and neglect of duty. DoK clasp not issued even though shown on roll. Also served KLH (186), DS (30132) 20 Feb 01 to 4 Mar 02 and WLH (483) 13 May 02 to 30 Jun 02. KSA (2)
Stone, 286 Tpr George Campbell, KLH	QSA (2) DoK OFS	Served 20 Oct 99 to 30 Apr 00. Also served IYS (13) 10 May 00 to 6 Sep 00, JMR 4 Dec 00 to 30 Sep 01 and StH (324) 10 Feb 02 to 2 Jun 02
Stone, 244 Cpl James Ernest, DH	QSA (6) DoK Paar Drie Joh DH Witt	Served 18 Feb 00 to 15 Oct 02. Also served KTG. Coronation Contingent. Coronation Contingent. Occupation clerk. QSA (6), KSA (2), 1902 Coronation, KStar. City Coins Dec 82
Stone, Pte W A, KTG	QSA (2) DoK OFS	Otto's Kopje Scouts. Also served ORCP (347). QSA (1), KStar. Burman Dec 02 £325
Stonebanks, 605 Pte G, KRV	QSA (1) DoK	DMU 16 Mar 01
Stone-Raper, Lt Richard John, KLH	QSA (4) RoM DoK OFS Tr	Also served KTG (No 3 Redoubt), ORCP 16 Sep 00 to 5 May 01 and SAC. Slightly wounded Mark's Drift 21 May 02. KSA (2) to R J S Raper
Stoney, Pte G H, KTG	QSA (1) DoK	No I Section, Mandy Fort and possibly ASC according to the nominal roll
Stoney, Med Off William Walter, KTG	QSA (1) DoK	Stationed at the Reservoir. He moved to South Africa in 1897 and worked in the De Beers laboratory investigating the rinderpest outbreak. In 1898 he was appointed Medical Officer of Health and in 1902 district surgeon. He died in 1915
Stonnill, Pte R E, KTG	QSA (1) DoK	No II Section, Belgravia Fort
Stopforth, Pte P, KTG	QSA (1) DoK	No II Section, D Company
Store, Pte A, KTG	QSA (1) DoK	No II Section, Mandy Fort. QSA (1), KStar. Welz & Co May 00. QSA (1). Liverpool Feb 02 £130
Storer, 699 Pte Ernest, CP2	QSA (1) DoK	CP dismounted branch (barrier & redoubt duties). QSA (1), KStar. DNW Sep 00 £210. Ursual Nov 00 £280. eBay Jan 04. See his medals (page 504)
Storey, Pte J, KTG	QSA (1) DoK	No III Section, Belgravia Fort
Stouffer, 396 Pte William Hayes, CP2	QSA (1) DoK	C Squadron. Also served FID. MID for gallant conduct near Kenhardt, Cape Colony, 17 May 01. KSA (2). Served in the Bechuanaland Rebellion 1897 earning CGHGSM (1) Bech
Stouppe, J, KTG	QSA (0)	Roll states "Manufacturing shells and ammunition"
Stouppe, Pte R, KTG	QSA (1) DoK	No II Section, K Company
Strachen, Pte J, KTG	QSA (1) DoK	No II Section, B Company, No 4 Redoubt. Erecting shelters and splinterproofs
Strang, 688 Pte J, KRV	QSA (1) DoK	Discharged 1 Jul 02. KSA (2)
Stratford, Pte J A, KTG	QSA (1) DoK	No 3 Redoubt. QSA (1). Bonhams Mar 02

Stratten, Lt T, KTG	QSA (1) DoK	No I Section, L Company
Streak, Pte M A, KTG	QSA (1) DoK	No IV Section, A Company, Beaconsfield Town Guard
Street, 195 Cpl Francis Herman, KLH	QSA (3) RoM DoK Paar	Served 20 Oct 99 to 5 Jun 00. Number duplicated on roll
Street, Pte S C, KTG	QSA (1) DoK	Kimberley Mine Ambulance Company, A Section. Occupation miner
Strickland, Pte C, KTG	QSA (1) DoK	H Company. QSA (1). City Coins Mar 03
Strickland, Sister E, NS	QSA (0)	Kimberley Civil Hospital. MID 10 Sep 01
Striker, Pte H, KTG	QSA (1) DoK	Premier Mine
Stroach, Pte W O, KTG	QSA (1) DoK	
Strong, Pte O C H, KTG	QSA (1) DoK	
Strong, Sgt P, KTG	QSA (3) RoM DoK OFS	No 2 Schmidt's Breastwork. Also served KLH (309 & 374) 6 Mar 00 to 5 Jun 00 and ORCP
Strong, Pte William George Sydney, KTG	QSA (2) DoK Tr	Civil Service Redoubt and No IV Section, C Company, Beaconsfield Town Guard. Also served BR (249 & 32551) from 12 Apr 01. Occupation sorter
Stuart, 4519 Cpl A, LNLR	QSA (1) DoK	Invalided to England 25 Apr 00
Stuart, 883 Pte D, KRV	QSA (2) DoK OFS	Discharged 4 Jul 02. Also served KTG (No I Section, B2 Company, No 3 Redoubt). KSA (2). Duplicate QSA issued 14 Dec 08. Possibly served in the Bechuanaland Rebellion 1897 with DEOVR earning CGHGSM (1) Bech
Stuart, 644 Pte J K, KRV	QSA (1) DoK	Dismissed for misconduct 3 Jan 00. Also served KTG (No I Section, Belgravia Fort)
Stuart, 645 Pte W T, KRV	QSA (1) DoK	Discharged 1 Jul 02. KSA (2)
Stubbs, 211 Gnr James Neely, DFA	QSA (1) DoK	Enrolled 8 Nov 99. Served DFA 93-96. Resigned 29 Jan 03. Occupation engine driver
Stubbs, 2296 Sapr W G, RE	QSA (3) DoK Drie Tr	KSA (2)
Stumke, 30146 QMS John Charles Augustus, KLH	QSA (3) DoK OFS Tr	Served 16 Oct 99 to 30 Mar 00. Wounded 11 Nov 99. Also served Lt KH. Kekewich spelled his name Stumkie. KSA (2). He had served Cpl PAOCA in the Bechuanaland Rebellion 1897 earning CGHGSM (1) Bech and was 2nd Lt VMR 1 Nov 98. Later served as Lt South African Intelligence Corps during the Great War
Suggett, 476 Band A, KRV	QSA (1) DoK	DMU 3 Nov 99
Sullivan, 145 Pte J, KRV	QSA (1) DoK	Non effective 15 Jul 00. Possibly served in the Bechuanaland Rebellion 1897 with Kimb Rifles earning CGHGSM (1) Bech
Sullivan, Sgt J, KTG	QSA (1) DoK	B line of defence, No 3 Redoubt
Sullivan, 190 Tpr Joseph Francis, KLH	QSA (2) DoK OFS	Served 19 Oct 99 to 6 Mar 00. Also served KTG. QSA (2) (initials J H). LSE Apr 82 £95
Summers, Cpl Alexander, KTG	QSA (1) DoK	No 3 Redoubt. Also served RR (28636) from 23 Jan 01. Occupation machinist
Sumner, Pte F, KTG	QSA (1) DoK	No 1 Redoubt. QSA (1), KStar. DNW Sep 01 £210
Sumner, Pte J, KTG	QSA (1) DoK	No 1 Redoubt. QSA (1), KStar. Spink Apr 99 £180. Romsey Medals Sep 05 £395. Bullock Militaria Mar 06 £395
Sumner, Pte R, KTG	QSA (1) DoK	No 1 Redoubt. KStar. Neate Dec 00
Sumner, 3186 Pte T, LNLR	QSA (3) DoK OFS Tr	KSA (2)
Sumpton, J, KTG	QSA (0)	Roll states "Electrical work; searchlights and telephones"
Sunde, Pte K, KTG	QSA (1) DoK	No I Section, Belgravia Fort
Sundien, Pte Joseph, KTG	QSA (1) DoK	No II Section, No 2 Redoubt. Also served CRSS (1411) from 9 Oct 01. Occupation painter

Sutch, 701 Pte J H, KRV	QSA (4) RoM DoK OFS Tr	Discharged 1 Jul 02. KSA (2)
Sutcliffe, 3760 Pte W, LNLR	QSA (3) DoK OFS Tr	QSA (3), [KSA (2)]. Walland Sep 87 £120
Suter, 646 Pte C, KRV	QSA (3) DoK OFS 01	Non effective 1 Feb 01. Discharged 5 Jan 03
Sutherland, 1099 Pte A, KRV	QSA (4) RoM DoK OFS Tr	Died of wounds 7 Nov 00 near Christiana. Also served KTG
Sutherland, Pte Arthur Forbes, KTG	QSA (5) DoK OFS Tr 01 02	No I Company, B Section, Reservoir. Also served KLH (32554) 13 Apr 01 to 20 Jun 01, JMR (1626 & 35538) and RR
Sutherland, Pte G W, KTG	QSA (1) DoK	No II Section, Belgravia Fort
Sutherland, 547 Pte George William, CP2	QSA (5) RoM DoK OFS Tr 01	CP 7-pounder detachment. Served 11 Oct 99 to 23 Oct 01
Sutherland, Pte J, KTG	QSA (1) DoK	Otto's Kopje Scouts
Sutherland, S, KTG	QSA (0)	Roll states "Wood work generally under the RE Officer"
Sutherland, Pte William, KTG	QSA (1) DoK	No II Section, C Company, Pickering's Redoubt No 2. Also served CRSS (1199) from 1 Jun 01
Suttie, Pte D, KTG	QSA (1) DoK	No IV Company, A Section, Reservoir. QSA (1). Glendining Nov 76 £75. Glendining Oct 82
Sutton, 193 Tpr A C, KLH	QSA (2) DoK OFS	Served 19 Oct 99 to 3 Apr 00
Sutton, Pte Edward Cecil, KTG	QSA (3) DoK OFS Tr	No II Section, B Company, No 4 Redoubt. Also served SRG (93) from Feb 01
Sutton, Col Sgt Henry, KTG	QSA (4) DoK Paar Drie Joh	Cycle Corps, A Company. Also served DH 18 Feb 00 until DMU 9 Jun 00 with forename Harry
Sutton, 191 Tpr Jeremiah, KLH	QSA (2) DoK OFS	Joined 19 Oct 99. Died of wounds 16 Feb 00. Also served KTG
Swain, 809 Pte W W, KRV	QSA (3) DoK OFS Tr	Discharged KRV 1 Jul 02. Also served KTG (H Company). KSA (2)
Swan, Pte C M, KTG	QSA (1) DoK	No II Section, A Company, Beaconsfield Town Guard
Swan, Pte J A, KTG	QSA (1) DoK	No II Section, B Company, No 4 Redoubt. 50th Anniversary attendee. QSA (1). McGregor Museum
Swan, Pte R, KTG	QSA (1) DoK	Civil Service Redoubt
Swanepoel, 1129 Pte Daniel, KRV	QSA (6) RoM DoK OFS Tr 01 02	DMU 9 Jan 01. Also served KTG, KLH (362, 91 & 40056) and BR (248 & 32546) from 10 Apr 01. 84 days IHL in KLH. Occupation miner
Swanson, Capt J, KTG	QSA (1) DoK	Premier Mine. Later served in the Kimberley Central Commando and SAVR during the GSWA campaign. VM (Lt). City Coins Nov 06
Swanvelder, Pte C J, KTG	QSA (1) DoK	No III Section, B Company, Beaconsfield Town Guard. Also served SRG (1067) from 9 Mar 01
Swartz, 568 Pte M D B, CP1	QSA (4) RoM DoK OFS Tr	B Squadron. KSA (2). Served in the Bechuanaland Rebellion 1897 with initials M D O earning CGHGSM (1) Bech
Sweeney, 301 Pte Arthur, CP2	QSA (4) RoM DoK OFS Tr	C Squadron. Served in the Bechuanaland Rebellion 1897 earning CGHGSM (1) Bech
Sweeney, Pte W, KTG	QSA (1) DoK	No I Section, F Company, Mostert's Redoubt. Also served CRSS (1129) with forename Tom
Sweet, 41 Pte A J, KRV	QSA (1) DoK	Non effective 26 Jul 00. Served in the Bechuanaland Rebellion 1897 with Kimb Rifles earning CGHGSM (1) Bech
Swift, 97887 Gnr Christopher, RGA	QSA (3) DoK OFS Tr	KSA (2)
Swift, 899 Pte Daniel, KRV	QSA (4) DoK OFS Tr 02	Discharged 4 Sep 00. Also served KTG, CPS (308) and SALH (40990) 15 Feb 02 to 31 May 02. SALH supplementary roll has a '?' against SA01. Wounded Zwartkoppiefontein 20 Apr 00

Name	Medals	Notes
Swift, Pte H, KTG	QSA (1) DoK	No IV Section, Mostert's Redoubt
Switzer, Pte H A, KTG	QSA (1) DoK	No II Section, B2 Company, No 3 Redoubt
Switzer, Pte Robert Edwin, KTG	QSA (3) RoM DoK OFS	No III Section, C Company, Pickering's Redoubt No 1. Also served KLH (157) 2 Apr 00 to 5 Jun 00 and SRG (88) 11 Feb 01 to 10 May 01. QSA (1) DoK. Spink Apr 09
Sydney, Pte E J, KTG	QSA (1) DoK	No 2 Redoubt
Sydney, 326 Tpr Frederick, KLH	QSA (2) DoK OFS	Served 26 Oct 99 to 4 Mar 00
Symington, 1326 Pte J, CP1	QSA (1) DoK	A Squadron. DMU 30 Jun 00
Symonds, Med Off Henry, KTG	QSA (1) DoK	No I Section, D Company. He first married Freida Tyrrell, matron of the Kimberley Hospital, the union producing 7 children. He later remarried and died in 1933. QSA (1), BWM (Capt). Kaplan Nov 04
Symons, Sgt H, KTG	QSA (1) DoK	
Symons, Mr J E, POC	QSA (1) DoK	Telegraph signaller

T

Name	Medals	Notes
Tabuteau, Capt Charles, KTG	QSA (3) DoK 01 02	No 4 Redoubt. Also served Lt BS 27 Jan 01 and Capt BS 1 Mar 01. Wounded 8 Jul 01. Previously served in Egypt
Tabuteau, Lt Harry, KTG	QSA (3) DoK 01 02	B line of defence, No 3 Redoubt. MID for the siege. Also served Capt BS 8 Jan 01. Egypt (1) Gemaizeh (Sgt 2/KOSB), QSA (3) (Lt). Spink Apr 93. Egypt (1) Gemaizeh (Sgt 2/KOSB), QSA (3) (Lt), Khedive Star, KStar. Liverpool Nov 98 £495. Lockdales Jan 09
Tabuteau, 609 Pte J, KRV	QSA (2) DoK OFS	Died of disease 13 Mar 00. QSA (2). Spink Apr 93. Liverpool Nov 98 £100. Bostock Mar 07 £395
Tait, Lt S, KTG	QSA (1) DoK	No IV Section, K Company. 50th Anniversary attendee
Tait, Pte T A, KTG	QSA (1) DoK	D Company (Veterans), Beaconsfield Town Guard
Tangney, Pte M, KTG	QSA (1) DoK	G Company
Tanner, Pte Albert, KTG	QSA (5) DoK OFS Tr 01 02	No 3 Redoubt. Also served KLH (338) 4 Nov 99 to 3 Jan 00 as Turner and DMU 3 Jan 00, IYS (12) 11 May 00 to 6 Sep 00, ORCP (555), 1st KFS (743) 4 Jan 01 to 4 Jun 01, SAMIF (4194) and DH (41981) 15 Apr 02 to 29 Jun 02. He had served in the Bechuanaland Rebellion 1897 with the Transport Corps earning CGHGSM (1) Bech. When he attested for DH he gave his occupation as soldier!
Tanser, 10904 Gnr Frank, RGA	QSA (2) DoK Tr	Premier Mine. KSA (2)
Tarpey, 4306 Pte J, LNLR	QSA (3) DoK OFS Tr	KSA (2)
Tarr, Pte Mortimer George, KTG	QSA (3) RoM DoK OFS	No III Section, A Company, Beaconsfield Town Guard. Also served KLH (382) 6 Mar 00 to 5 Jun 00
Tarr, Pte Walter Claud, KTG	QSA (3) RoM DoK OFS	No III Section, A Company, Beaconsfield Town Guard. Also served KLH (349) 6 Mar 00 to 5 Jun 00
Tarrant, Pte J, KTG	QSA (1) DoK	G Company
Tarrant, 380 Pte Thomas, DH	QSA (6) DoK Paar Drie Joh DH Witt	Served 18 Feb 00 to 30 Jun 02. Attestation papers say DMU 1 Dec 01. Also served KTG. KSA (2). Occupation farrier
Tatters, Pte J, KTG	QSA (1) DoK	No 1 Redoubt
Tattersall, 4276 Sgt A, LNLR	QSA (3) DoK OFS Tr	KSA (2)
Taylor, Pte A, KTG	QSA (1) DoK	No I Section, B Company, No 4 Redoubt
Taylor, Pte C, KTG	QSA (2) DoK Tr	No 6 Redoubt. Also served KLH (1120) 19 Apr 00 to 10 Nov 00
Taylor, Cpl David C, KTG	QSA (1) DoK	Kimberley Mine Ambulance Company. Occupation storeman

Taylor, 494 Sgt F, KRV	QSA (1) DoK	Discharged 10 Jul 02. KSA (2)
Taylor, 3791 Pte G, LNLR	QSA (2) DoK Tr	KSA (2)
Taylor, 10899 Pte G, RAMC	QSA (1) DoK	KSA (2)
Taylor, 180 Gnr Harry Marshall, DFA	QSA (1) DoK	Enrolled 10 Aug 99. Medically unfit 1 Jan 00. Occupation storekeeper at De Beers
Taylor, 225 Tpr Herbert, KLH	QSA (2) DoK OFS	Joined 20 Oct 99. Killed in action 28 Nov 99
Taylor, 5225 Pte J, LNLR	QSA (3) DoK OFS Tr	Wounded Klip Drift 7 Mar 02. MID 4 Sep 01. DCM, [QSA (3), KSA (2)]. City Coins Aug 98. Liverpool Jun 99 £575. QSA (3), KStar. Spink Jan 66 £6. Glendining Jul 75. QSA (3). Liverpool Feb 96 £230
Taylor, Pte J, KTG	QSA (1) DoK	Premier Mine. A man of this name served DS (32567) 22 Apr 01 to 13 Mar 02 gaining OFS, Tr, 01 & 02 but which J Taylor?
Taylor, J, KTG	QSA (0)	Roll states "Guarding natives on construction works"
Taylor, Pte J, KTG	QSA (1) DoK	No II Section, K Company
Taylor, Sgt James, KTG	QSA (4) DoK OFS Tr 01	G Company. Also served CinCBG (22730) 11 Nov 00 to May 01. Occupation moulder. QSA (1), Kimberley Medal (Sgt J Taylor KTG), K Star. Glendining May 43. Christies Jul 90 £462. DNW Jul 93 £620. Dixon Mar 94 £795
Taylor, 81 Cpl John, CP2	QSA (1) DoK	Note says pensioned
Taylor, 1455 Pte John Ford, CP1	QSA (4) RoM DoK OFS Tr	A Squadron. Wounded 28 Nov 99. Discharged time expired. Also served 1st ILH (3120) 13 Jan 02 to 30 Jun 02
Taylor, Nurse M, NS	QSA (0)	Joined 1 Apr 00
Taylor, 5012 Drum R, LNLR	QSA (3) DoK OFS Tr	QSA (3), KSA (2)
Taylor, Pte R, KTG	QSA (1) DoK	No I Company, B Section, Reservoir
Taylor, 317 Pte R J, KRV	QSA (1) DoK	
Taylor, Pte R L, KTG	QSA (1) DoK	H Company
Taylor, Cpl S, KTG	QSA (1) DoK	No I Section, B Company, Beaconsfield Town Guard. QSA (1). DNW Apr 01 £80. Chelsea Jun 04 £195. Historik Orders Dec 04 £180
Taylor, Pte T N, KTG	QSA (1) DoK	No I Section, B Company, No 4 Redoubt and Reserve Section, D Company
Taylor, Pte Thomas H, KTG	QSA (5) DoK OFS Tr 01 02	Also served KLH (504), CPS (367), ILH, CinCBG (22729) 17 Nov 00 to 16 May 01, ALH (39581) 7 Nov 01 to 12 Mar 02 and WLH (504) 8 May 02 to 30 Jun 02. Occupation overseer
Taylor, 3586 Pte W, LNLR	QSA (3) DoK OFS Tr	KSA (2)
Taylor, 4496 Pte W, LNLR	QSA (4) DoK OFS Tr 01	Died of disease Zeerust 7 Mar 02
Taylor, Cpl W, KTG	QSA (1) DoK	No I Section, D Company
Taylor, Pte W, KTG	QSA (1) DoK	No II Section, F Company, Mostert's Redoubt
Taylor, Pte W H, KTG	QSA (1) DoK	Premier Mine. QSA (1), KStar. Glendining Jul 99. QSA (1). Dixon Jul 07 £250
Taylor, 1590 Pte W H C, CP1	QSA (3) RoM DoK OFS	C Squadron. KSA (2). Later served as Lt South African Police. During the Great War he served as Lt Hartigan's Horse and in the GSWA operations. Later Lt Col
Taylor, Pte W J, KTG	QSA (1) DoK	No 2 Schmidt's Breastwork
Teale, 4893 Pte J, LNLR	QSA (4) DoK OFS Tr 01	QSA (3) excl 01, KStar. Spink Nov 75 £62. Christies Oct 81 £140
Teare, 997 Bugler T, KRV	QSA (2) DoK OFS	Also served KTG (No III Company, A Section, Reservoir). Died of disease at Kimberley 4 Jan 02. KSA (2). Medals issued to widow

Name	Medals	Notes
Tedder, 5468 Pte G, LNLR	QSA (3) DoK OFS Tr	Killed in action Klip Drift 7 Mar 02. QSA (3), [KSA (2)]. Glendining Nov 76 £60. Liverpool Aug 82 £150
Tee, 1898 Pte Albert Edward, CP1	QSA (2) DoK OFS	C Squadron. KSA (2) authorised 30 Sep 13
Tee, 501 Pte Richard, CP2	QSA (2) DoK OFS	B Squadron. KSA (2)
Temlett, 1606 Pte J R, CP1	QSA (3) DoK OFS 01	QSA reissued 28 Jan 10
Tennant, Pte J, KTG	QSA (1) DoK	Civil Service Redoubt. QSA (1). Glendining Mar 90. Spink Dec 90 £95
Tennant, Pte R D, KTG	QSA (1) DoK	No III Section, B Company, Beaconsfield Town Guard
Terras, Pte John, KTG	QSA (3) DoK OFS Tr	Premier Mine. Also served KLH (180 & 1122) 8 Mar 00 to 9 Apr 00 sometimes as Terriss and SRG (96) from 11 Feb 01 as Terris. Wounded Warrenton 8 May 00
Terras, Pte William Green, KTG	QSA (2) DoK OFS	Premier Mine. Also served KLH (181 & 1299) 8 Mar 00 to 7 Jan 01
Tetley, 1408 L Cpl F J, CP1	QSA (5) RoM DoK OFS 01 02	B Squadron. Slightly wounded Daniel's Kuil 8 Jan 01. KSA (2)
Thane, 161 L Cpl S, KRV	QSA (1) DoK	DMU 23 Apr 00
Theaker, 24401 Tmptr George, RGA	QSA (2) DoK Tr	KSA (2)
Theys, Pte F, KTG	QSA (1) DoK	No I Section, B Company, Beaconsfield Town Guard
Thirer, Pte C, KTG	QSA (1) DoK	No III Company, A Section, Reservoir
Thomas, Pte B, KTG	QSA (1) DoK	No IV Section, D Company
Thomas, Pte C B, KTG	QSA (1) DoK	Premier Mine
Thomas, Pte D, KTG	QSA (1) DoK	
Thomas, 977 Gnr Eli, RGA	QSA (2) DoK Tr	QSA (3) inc OFS, KSA (2), 14 Star & Bar, BWM, VM, LS&GC, KStar. Glendining Jun 32
Thomas, Pte G, KTG	QSA (1) DoK	No III Section, C Company, Beaconsfield Town Guard
Thomas, Pte G J, KTG	QSA (1) DoK	
Thomas, 4985 Cpl H, LNLR	QSA (3) DoK OFS Tr	QSA (3), KSA (2), KStar. Glendining Jul 77 £90
Thomas, Pte J A, KTG	QSA (1) DoK	Kimberley Mine Ambulance Company with mounted forces
Thomas, Pte K R, KTG	QSA (1) DoK	See his biography (page 356)
Thomas, Pte R B, KTG	QSA (1) DoK	No II Section, L Company
Thomas, Pte T, KTG	QSA (1) DoK	G Company
Thomas, 723 Cpl W, KRV	QSA (3) DoK OFS Tr	Discharged 1 Jul 02. Also served KTG. KSA (2)
Thomas, Pte W H, KTG	QSA (1) DoK	No III Section, D Company. Gun construction and shell making
Thompson, 247 Tpr A, KLH	QSA (3) DoK OFS 01	Served 26 Oct 99 to 30 Apr 00. Also served KTG (Gibraltar Fort, Davis's Heap), CCCC (31207) and Kaffr Rifles (1112) to 26 Nov 00. Medal and clasps reissued 28 Oct 15
Thompson, Pte A W, KTG	QSA (1) DoK	No 2 Schmidt's Breastwork. QSA (1). DNW Dec 06 £160. Dixon Jul 07 £250
Thompson, Pte C, KTG	QSA (1) DoK	Kenilworth Defence Force
Thompson, Pte C M, KTG	QSA (1) DoK	No II Section, No 2 Redoubt
Thompson, 3558 Pte D, LNLR	QSA (1) DoK	Invalided to England 16 Mar 00. QSA (1), KStar. RHQ
Thompson, Pte G, KTG	QSA (1) DoK	No II Section, A Company, Beaconsfield Town Guard
Thompson, Pte H B, KTG	QSA (1) DoK	Kenilworth Defence Force
Thompson, Pte H J, KTG	QSA (1) DoK	G Company
Thompson, 325 Pte H S, KRV	QSA (1) DoK	DMU 12 Jan 00

Medal roll

Thompson, 1839 Pte J, LNLR	QSA (3) DoK OFS Tr	QSA (3), KSA (2). Glendining Mar 98
Thompson, Pte J, KTG	QSA (1) DoK	Medical Corps, No 1 Company, D Section
Thompson, 276 Tpr Joseph, KLH	QSA (2) DoK OFS	Joined 19 Oct 99. Killed in action 28 Nov 99
Thompson, Nurse M, NS	QSA (0)	Kimberley Civil Hospital
Thompson, 1205 Pte Peter, KRV	QSA (4) RoM DoK OFS Tr	Served 10 Sep 00 until DMU 17 Mar 02. Also served KTG (No III Company, A Section, Reservoir) and KLH (241) 22 Oct 99 to 11 Jun 00. KSA (2)
Thompson, 782 Cpl R, KRV	QSA (4) RoM DoK OFS Tr	Discharged 6 Aug 02. Also served KTG (No IV Section, No 2 Redoubt). QSA (1) DoK, [KSA (2)]. Sotheby Jan 74 £48. Spink Nov 79 £100
Thompson, 3595 Pte R, LNLR	QSA (3) DoK OFS Tr	Wounded Twyfelaar 27 Jan 01. Discharged for misconduct (8626 Liverpool Regt) 27 Feb 05. Medals restored 5 Aug 36. QSA (3). Sotheby Mar 80
Thompson, Pte R, KTG	QSA (1) DoK	No IV Company, A Section, Reservoir. QSA (1). Sotheby Mar 86. QSA (1), KStar. DNW Apr 94 £100. Spink Dec 95 £160
Thompson, 812 Pte Robert Alfred, CP2	QSA (3) DoK OFS Tr	B Squadron. QSA (3), KSA (2), BWM, VM, KStar. Dixon Jun 86 £130
Thompson, 26 CSM W J, KRV	QSA (2) DoK 01	Discharged 8 Aug 01
Thompson, Pte William, KTG	QSA (3) DoK OFS Tr	No III Section, C Company, Pickering's Redoubt No 1. Also served KLH (1204) to 5 Jun 00 and SRG (95) from 11 Feb 01 as Thomson
Thompson, 22071 Gnr William, RGA	QSA (1) DoK	Otto's Kopje. Invalided
Thomson, Pte A, KTG	QSA (1) DoK	
Thomson, 703 Pte Arthur Edward, CP2	QSA (2) DoK OFS	Served 11 Oct 99 to 15 May 02. Discharged for misconduct. Also served NH (1867) with first name Charles 27 May 02 to 31 May 02. Severely wounded Hoopstad 23 Oct 00. KSA (2). Duplicate QSA issued by NH and recovered 20 May 08. Occupation barman
Thomson, Pte J, KTG	QSA (1) DoK	No III Company, A Section, Reservoir
Thomson, 998 Pte J, KRV	QSA (1) DoK	Discharged 1 Jul 02. Also served KTG. KSA (2)
Thomson, 1234 Pte John, KRV	QSA (4) DoK OFS Tr 01	DMU 7 Oct 01. Also served KTG and DFA (221) 18 Dec 99 to 31 Aug 00. Occupation telegraphist. Surname also spelled Thompson on DFA QSA roll
Thomson, 26203 Tpr Robert, ScH	QSA (4) DoK OFS Tr 01	Served 8 Feb 01 to 14 Aug 01. Also served KRV (647) until DMU 20 Jan 00
Thomson, Pte W, KTG	QSA (1) DoK	Premier Mine
Thorn, Pte D T, KTG	QSA (1) DoK	No II Section, Belgravia Fort. Served in the Bechuanaland Rebellion 1897 with DFH earning CGHGSM (1) Bech
Thorne, 690 Pte E H V, KRV	QSA (2) DoK Paar	Discharged 25 Feb 00. Also served Lt UVR. QSA (2), KSA (2) (Lt UVR), 14-15 Star (Lt Brands F S Rfls), BWM, VM (Lt), KStar, ASM
Thornhill, 3960 Pte S, LNLR	QSA (3) DoK OFS Tr	QSA (3), [KSA (2)]. Spink Jun 84
Thornley, 310 Pte George, CP2	QSA (4) RoM DoK OFS Tr	CP 7-pounder detachment. Severely wounded Hoopstad 23 Oct 00. CGHGSM (1) Bech (Pte CP2), QSA (4), KSA (2). Spink Oct 99 £320. Liverpool Nov 99 £495
Thornton, 235 Pte E E, KRV	QSA (2) DoK OFS	DMU 5 Apr 00
Thornton, 1301 L Cpl H H, KLH	QSA (2) DoK OFS	Served 1 Nov 99 to 6 Nov 00
Thorp, Pte A T, KTG	QSA (1) DoK	
Thorpe, Lt J H, KTG	QSA (1) DoK	Beaconsfield Town Guard

Name	Medals	Notes
Thwaites, 79 Bugle Maj A H, KRV	QSA (2) DoK OFS	Non effective 20 Jun 00. CGHGSM (1) Bech (Tpr Maj DFH), QSA (2), 14-15 Star (Sgt Vet Regt), BWM, VM (Sgt SAVR), Col Aux Forces LS Medal, KStar. City Coins Jun 04
Tidd-Pratt, Lt Arthur W B, DFA	QSA (1) DoK	Enrolled 16 Apr 00. Left 10 Feb 02. Also on roll for KTG. Operations in CC 30 Nov 00 to 31 May 02. Resigned 30 Apr 03. [QSA (1), KSA (2)], KStar. Spink Jan 54 £1. Sotheby Nov 88. Lockdales Jul 08 £270
Tidd-Pratt, Capt S, KTG	QSA (1) DoK	Pickering's Redoubt No 1
Tideswell, 841 Pte J, KRV	QSA (1) DoK	Discharged 1 Jul 02. Also served KTG (No III Company, A Section, Reservoir). KSA (2)
Tidmarsh, Pte J F, KTG	QSA (1) DoK	Civil Service Redoubt
Tiernay, Pte J M, KTG	QSA (1) DoK	Premier Mine
Tillard, 689 Pte Max Ogilvie, KRV	QSA (2) DoK OFS	See his biography (page 356)
Tillemans, Lt A A, KRV	QSA (2) DoK OFS	KSA (2) on the KSA roll for the Kimberley Cadet Corps (attached to Kimb Regt)
Tillemans, 40025 Tpr Herbert Peter, DH	QSA (3) DoK OFS Tr	Served 24 Dec 01 to 15 Oct 02 as Tillemen. Also served KTG (No I Section, K Company) and SRG (1162) from 9 Mar 01. Occupation plumber
Tillemans, 1298 Tpr Laurence Joseph, KLH	QSA (4) RoM DoK OFS Tr	Joined 16 Oct 99. Also served FID from 31 Mar 01. KSA (2)
Timbrell, 175 Band R M, KRV	QSA (1) DoK	Discharged 14 Jul 02. KSA (2). Served in the Bechuanaland Rebellion 1897 with Kimb Rifles earning CGHGSM (1) Bech
Timby, Pte W, KTG	QSA (1) DoK	No I Section, L Company
Timm, Pte R, KTG	QSA (1) DoK	No I Section, B2 Company, No 3 Redoubt. 50th Anniversary attendee. QSA (1), KStar. Gordon Mar 94 £175
Timm, 82 Pte W M A, KRV	QSA (1) DoK	DMU 13 Aug 00
Timmann, Pte W, KTG	QSA (1) DoK	No I Section, B Company, No 4 Redoubt
Timms, 610 Pte E L, KRV	QSA (3) DoK OFS 01	Served 11 Oct 99 until DMU 4 Apr 00. Also served MMR (167) 1 Apr 01 to 19 Dec 01
Timms, E M, KTG	QSA (0)	Roll states "Electrical work; dynamos for mines"
Timperley, 4777 L Cpl C, LNLR	QSA (4) DoK OFS Tr 01	Invalided to England 22 Jan 01
Tinley, Cpl E, KTG	QSA (1) DoK	Civil Service Redoubt
Tinson, Sgt J B, KTG	QSA (1) DoK	No III Section, F Company, No 3 Redoubt
Tippett, Pte H, KTG	QSA (1) DoK	Medical Corps, No 1 Company, D Section
Tippett, Pte W H, KTG	QSA (1) DoK	No 6 Redoubt
Tirbutt, 755 Pte Spencer Arden, KRV	QSA (5) RoM DoK OFS Tr 01	Discharged 1 Jul 00. Also served KTG (G Company), 1st KFS 11 Feb 01 to 29 Apr 01 and 2nd KFS (772) 30 Apr 01 to 4 Aug 01
Tobin, Pte E J, KTG	QSA (1) DoK	No III Section, No 2 Redoubt
Todd, Lt C W, KTG	QSA (1) DoK	No I Section, B2 Company, No 3 Redoubt
Todd, Pte Henry, KTG	QSA (1) DoK	No 1 Redoubt. Also served CRSS (1357) from 30 Aug 01. Occupation miner
Togwell, 2235 Sapr A E, RE	QSA (3) DoK Drie Tr	KSA (2)
Toke, 274 Pte Gilbert Willoughby, CP2	QSA (1) DoK	C Squadron. KSA (2). Served in the Bechuanaland Rebellion 1897 earning CGHGSM (1) Bech
Tomlin, Pte H, KTG	QSA (1) DoK	No I Section, C Company, Pickering's Redoubt No 1
Tomlinson, 4617 Pte C, LNLR	QSA (3) DoK OFS Tr	KSA (2)
Tomlinson, Pte J, KTG	QSA (1) DoK	No I Section, A Company, Beaconsfield Town Guard

Tomlinson, 4673 Pte W, LNLR	QSA (2) DoK OFS	KSA (2)
Tonkin, 1983 Sgt Thomas, SRG	QSA (5) DoK Paar Drie Joh DH	Discharged 24 Feb 02. Also served Canadian Scouts (34432), 2nd BrH (20040) 2 Nov 00 to 15 May 01 and WLH (394) 24 Feb 02 to 30 Jun 02. Occupation miner
Toovey, 512 Pte G D, KRV	QSA (5) RoM DoK OFS Tr 01	Killed in action 3 Jun 01 near Jacobsdal
Topp, Pte A B, KTG	QSA (1) DoK	Mounted Section, B Company, Beaconsfield Town Guard
Topp, Pte J B, KTG	QSA (1) DoK	No II Section, C Company, Pickering's Redoubt No 2
Topp, Pte R C, KTG	QSA (1) DoK	No III Section, B Company, Beaconsfield Town Guard
Topper, Pte H P, KTG	QSA (1) DoK	No III Section, F Company, No 3 Redoubt. QSA (1). DNW Dec 00 £95
Torrington, 94004 Bombdr Albert, RGA	QSA (2) DoK Tr	QSA (2), KSA (2), KStar. City Coins Jun 04
Towell, Pte F, KTG	QSA (1) DoK	No III Section, Belgravia Fort
Townsend, Cpl G, KTG	QSA (1) DoK	Kamfersdam Company. QSA (1). Seaby Aug 80 £150
Townsend, Cpl T, KTG	QSA (1) DoK	QSA (1)
Townsend, Pte W, KTG	QSA (1) DoK	No I Company, B Section, Reservoir
Townsend, Cpl W, KTG	QSA (1) DoK	
Townshend, Lt George Armstrong, SRG	QSA (5) DoK OFS Tr 01 02	Served as Tpr SRG from 13 Feb 01 and Lt SRG 3 Oct 01 to 30 Apr 02. Also served KTG (No I Section, C Company, Pickering's Redoubt No 1 and No II Section, No 4 Redoubt) 15 Oct 99 to 7 Mar 00 with initial G H, Lt KLH and Lt WLH 1 May 02 to 30 Jun 02
Tozer, 46 RSM E E M, KRV	QSA (2) DoK 01	DMU 13 Mar 01. Served in the Bechuanaland Rebellion 1897 with Kimb Rifles earning CGHGSM (1) Bech
Tozer, 704 Cpl P D, KRV	QSA (1) DoK	Non effective 10 Jul 00. QSA (2)
Tracy, 280 Tpr Thomas, KLH	QSA (3) DoK OFS 02	Served 21 Oct 00 to 30 Apr 00 and 21 May 02 to 30 Jun 02. A man of this name served in the Klipdam TG and was captured at Wittefontein 24 May 01. Same man?
Trainer, 50 Tpr A H, KLH	QSA (2) DoK OFS	Served 19 Dec 99 until DMU 24 Mar 00. Also served ORCP (562)
Treadwell, 4596 Pte F, LNLR	QSA (3) DoK OFS Tr	QSA (3), KSA (2), KStar. Sotheby Jun 12
Treadwell, Pte W, KTG	QSA (1) DoK	No 2 Schmidt's Breastwork
Tredrea, Pte T B, KTG	QSA (1) DoK	No II Section, Mandy Fort. 50th Anniversary attendee
Tredrea, Pte W H, KTG	QSA (1) DoK	50th Anniversary attendee
Tredrea, Cpl W J, KTG	QSA (1) DoK	H Company. QSA (1). Spink Dec 83
Tregonning, Pte F, KTG	QSA (1) DoK	No III Section, C Company, Beaconsfield Town Guard
Tregonning, Pte H, KTG	QSA (1) DoK	No 6 Redoubt. QSA (1), 14-15 Star, BWM, VM (Pte SAVR), KStar. Dixon Jun 98 £230
Trembath, Pte John, KTG	QSA (6) RoM DoK OFS Tr 01 02	Otto's Kopje Scouts. Also served KLH (387, 461 & 1300) 7 Mar 00 to 6 Oct 00. Also served 1st BrH (22735) as Trembarth 21 Nov 00 until dismissed 7 Jul 01 and WPMR (1259) from 23 Dec 01. Occupation miner
Trembath, Pte R, KTG	QSA (1) DoK	B line of defence, No 3 Redoubt. QSA (1). Glendining Sep 85
Trenery, 30 Cpl W, KRV	QSA (1) DoK	Discharged 30 Mar 01
Trengrove, Pte E, KTG	QSA (1) DoK	Reserve Section, D Company. QSA (1). Bonhams Oct 06 £200. Dixon Jul 07 £250
Trenwick, Pte J S, KTG	QSA (1) DoK	Mounted Section, Kenilworth Defence Force
Tretheway, Pte J, KTG	QSA (1) DoK	No 2 Schmidt's Breastwork
Trevithick, Pte A, KTG	QSA (1) DoK	Cycle Corps, A Company
Trevor-Smith, Pte C W, KTG	QSA (1) DoK	Food Supply Staff and No I Section, Belgravia Fort

Trigg, 97344 Gnr John Henry, RGA	QSA (1) DoK	KSA (2)
Trobridge, G, KTG	QSA (0)	Roll states "Carpentering for RE before Guard formed"
Trodd, 59807 CQMS Henry, RGA	QSA (1) DoK	DCM LG 27 Sep 01. KSA (2)
Troup, Lt J, KTG	QSA (1) DoK	No II Section, A Company, Beaconsfield Town Guard
Trudgian, 59 Tpr Thomas, KLH	QSA (2) DoK Paar	Served 21 Oct 99 to 3 Apr 00. Also served IYS (4) 12 May 00 to 6 Sep 00 with surname Tondgian
Trueman, 804 Pte Thomas John, CP2	QSA (1) DoK	CP dismounted branch (barrier & redoubt duties)
Truran, Pte J H, KTG	QSA (1) DoK	Premier Mine
Truter, Pte D, KTG	QSA (1) DoK	Food Supply Staff
Truter, Pte G, KTG	QSA (1) DoK	No III Section, C Company, Pickering's Redoubt No 1
Truter, 404 Pte Peter John, KRV	QSA (1) DoK	Discharged 30 Mar 01. Also served WPMR (436) from 16 Jan 01. Occupation carpenter
Tuck, Pte F L, KTG	QSA (1) DoK	Civil Service Redoubt
Tucker, 482 Pte Arthur, CP2	QSA (2) DoK Paar	B Squadron. Paar added 11 Dec 05. KSA (2). Served in the Bechuanaland Rebellion 1897 earning CGHGSM (1) Bech
Tucker, 85120 Gnr William, RGA	QSA (2) DoK 01	KSA (2)
Tulby, 201 Pte J H, KRV	QSA (1) DoK	DMU 1 Mar 00
Tull, Pte W, KTG	QSA (1) DoK	Kamfersdam Company
Tullis, 209 Tpr John Joseph, KLH	QSA (2) DoK OFS	Served 21 Oct 99 to 3 Apr 00
Tunney, 4757 Pte J, LNLR	QSA (3) DoK Paar Tr	Mounted Infantry. Served 1895 to 1904. MID 4 Sep 01. QSA (3), [KSA (2)]. Spink Mar 83 £110. Clark Oct 89 £135
Turnbull, Cond A M, ASC	QSA (1) DoK	QSA (1). Glendining Nov 76. QSA (1) copy clasp, KStar. DNW Jun 97 £170. DNW Sep 01 (no sale). DNW Sep 02 £150
Turnbull, 3911 Band S, LNLR	QSA (3) DoK OFS Tr	KSA (2)
Turner, 74 Tpr A G, KLH	QSA (2) DoK Paar	Served 24 Oct 99 to 29 Nov 00. Also served IYS (38) 22 May 00 to 6 Sep 00
Turner, 919 Pte Alfred Ernest, KRV	QSA (1) DoK	See his biography (page 357)
Turner, Pte C, KTG	QSA (1) DoK	Kimberley Mine Ambulance Company, E Section
Turner, 811 Pte Daniel, CP2	QSA (1) DoK	C Squadron. DMU
Turner, 864 Pte H R, KRV	QSA (3) DoK OFS Tr	DMU 30 Aug 02. Also served KTG (No 3 Redoubt). KSA (2). Slightly wounded Klip Drift 7 Mar 02
Turner, 119 Tpr Herbert William, KLH	QSA (5) DoK OFS Tr 01 02	Wounded Warrenton 13 Mar 00. DMU 3 Nov 00. Also served KTG and 1st ILH (3146) 31 Dec 01 to 30 Jun 02
Turner, Pte J, KTG	QSA (1) DoK	No I Section, No 2 Redoubt
Turner, Pte J, KTG	QSA (1) DoK	N Company, No 1 Redoubt
Turner, 571 Pte J, KRV	QSA (1) DoK	DMU 16 Aug 00
Turner, Pte J B, KTG	QSA (1) DoK	
Turner, Pte J C, KTG	QSA (1) DoK	No II Section, Mandy Fort
Turner, 205 Bombdr Richard, DFA	QSA (2) DoK 01	Enrolled 17 Oct 99. Medically unfit 5 Aug 01. Occupation bricklayer
Turner, Pte William, KTG	QSA (2) DoK Tr	No I Company, B Section, Reservoir. Also served KLH (1134) 19 Apr 00 to 24 Nov 00, 1st ILH (1697) 24 Nov 00 to 28 May 01 and 1st KFS (1499 & 2031) 31 Jul 01 until disbandment on 15 Oct 02. KSA (2). Part of the KFS Coronation Contingent

Name	Medals	Notes
Tute, 706 Cpl H A, KRV	QSA (2) DoK 01	Discharged 18 Mar 01. Medal handed to Mr Tute by DDOS 15 Jul 09
Tutelmann, Pte J, KTG	QSA (1) DoK	
Tutt, 648 Pte C J, KRV	QSA (1) DoK	DMU 25 Jul 00
Tutt, 166 Sgt Maj Tailor W B, KRV	QSA (1) DoK	Non effective 20 Jun 00. Served in the Basuto Wars with DEOVR earning CGHGSM (1) Bas. 50th Anniversary attendee
Twigg, Cpl J, KTG	QSA (1) DoK	No III Section, L Company
Twigg, Pte J, KTG	QSA (1) DoK	No II Section, L Company. QSA (1). March Medals (date unknown) £95. Christies Jul 85
Twigg, Pte Thomas, KTG	QSA (1) DoK	No 1 Redoubt. Also served SRG (920) from 22 May 01. Dangerously wounded Devondale 10 Dec 01 and died the next day
Twigg, Pte William John, KTG	QSA (1) DoK	No II Section, L Company. Also served SRG (901) from 17 May 01
Twiss, 196 Pte Charles William, CP2	QSA (2) DoK 01	Served 11 Oct 99 to 15 Aug 01. Also served Sub Inspector ORCP
Tyldesley, 4261 Pte T, LNLR	QSA (2) DoK OFS	Wounded 28 Nov 99. KSA (2). Surname Tydlesbury on KSA roll
Tyler, 4566 Pioneer G, LNLR	QSA (3) DoK OFS Tr	KSA (2)
Tyler, 4563 Pte J, LNLR	QSA (3) DoK OFS Tr	KSA (2)
Tyson, Lt John Daughtrey, KTG	QSA (1) DoK	See his biography (page 357)
Tyson, Capt Thomas Gilbee, KTG	QSA (1) DoK	See his biography (page 357)

U

Name	Medals	Notes
Ubsdell, Pte G, KTG	QSA (1) DoK	No I Company, A Section, Reservoir. QSA (1), KStar. Dixon Apr 02 £325
Ubsdell, 391 Bugler T C, KRV	QSA (2) DoK OFS	DMU 16 May 00
Ueberle, Pte M, KTG	QSA (1) DoK	
Ulrichsen, 875 Pte O A, KRV	QSA (1) DoK	Also served KTG (H Company). KSA (2). Surname Ulricksen on KSA roll
Unsted, 649 Pte F, KRV	QSA (3) DoK OFS Tr	Discharged 1 Jul 02. KSA (2)
Upfold, Mr J, POC	QSA (1) DoK	Telegraph signaller
Upstill, Pte P, KTG	QSA (1) DoK	No I Section, F Company, Mostert's Redoubt
Uren, 370 Pte J, KRV	QSA (3) RoM DoK OFS	Non effective 19 Jul 00. QSA (3) named to Kimberley DFH, BWM (Pte J Uren 4th SAI). City Coins Jul 01. QSA (3). Liverpool Nov 01 £250. Burman Mar 02 £325
Uren, Pte L, KTG	QSA (1) DoK	N Company, No 1 Redoubt
Uren, Pte W M, KTG	QSA (1) DoK	No II Section, C Company, Pickering's Redoubt No 2
Urquhart, Pte D, KTG	QSA (1) DoK	Premier Mine
Urquhart, 371 Tpr E, KLH	QSA (2) DoK OFS	Served 23 Jan 00 to 3 Apr 00. Also served KRV (489) and dismissed for drunkeness (5th offence)
Usendorff, 174 Pte F, KRV	QSA (3) RoM DoK OFS	Non effective 21 Jun 00

V

Name	Medals	Notes
Vallaney, 663 Pte William Bertram, CP2	QSA (2) DoK Paar	A Squadron. KSA (2)
Van Blerk, 291 Pte A C, KRV	QSA (3) RoM DoK OFS	Non effective 20 Jun 00. QSA (3). Glendining Feb 80 £150

Kimberley Siege Account and Medal Roll

Van Blerk, C H, KTG	QSA (0)	Roll states "Engine driver for dynamos"
Van Blerk, Pte C H, KTG	QSA (1) DoK	No 6 Redoubt. QSA (1), 14-15 Star (Pte Victoria Regt), BWM, VM (SAVR). Glendining Jun 79 £110. Australian dealer Jul 08 £325
Van Blerk, C J, KTG	QSA (0)	Roll states "Telephone exchange for redoubts"
Van Blerk, Pte H, KTG	QSA (1) DoK	No IV Section, D Company
Van Blerk, 299 Pte P B, KRV	QSA (1) DoK	Non effective 17 Aug 00. Later served in the Great War as Private, 10th Field Ambulance, SAMC. QSA (1), [BWM], VM. City Coins Dec 04. Liverpool Jun 05 £210
Van Breda, G H, KTG	QSA (0)	Roll states "Clerical work; Paymaster's office"
Van Breda, 786 Pte Kurt, CP2	QSA (1) DoK	B Squadron. Discharged on gratuity
Van Copenhagen, Pte R, KTG	QSA (1) DoK	
Van Der Gryp, 713 Pte A, KRV	QSA (2) DoK 01	Also served KTG (No IV Company, A Section, Reservoir). Non effective 14 Mar 01. Surname also spelled Vandergryp
Van Der Gryp, 74 Sgt Frank, KRV	QSA (3) DoK OFS Tr	Discharged 15 Jul 02. Slightly wounded Klip Drift 7 Mar 02. Surname also spelled Vandergryp. Born Mossel Bay in 1877 and enlisted Jun 97. He served in the Matabele Rebellion 1896 and in GSWA in the Great War. CGHGSM (1) Bech (Pte Spl Pce), QSA (3), KSA (2), [14-15 Star], BWM, VM (Pte 7th Infy), KStar. City Coins Nov 06
Van Der Gryp, 361 Pte Frederick, CP2	QSA (2) DoK OFS	B Squadron. KSA (2). Served in the Bechuanaland Rebellion 1897 earning CGHGSM (1) Bech. During the Great War served as Private, 1st SAI and in GSWA until DMU Sep 15
Van Der Hayden, Pte C, KTG	QSA (1) DoK	No II Section, B2 Company, No 3 Redoubt. 50th Anniversary attendee
Van Der Linde, Pte B, KTG	QSA (1) DoK	No III Section, A Company, Beaconsfield Town Guard
Van Der Merwe, Pte Ardrian, KTG	QSA (6) RoM DoK OFS Tr 01 02	No 2 supply depot. Also served KLH (340) 3 Jan 00 to 5 Jun 00, DH (32604) 4 May 01 to 5 Nov 01 and 1st ILH (3018) 27 Dec 01 to 20 Jun 02. Occupation farmer
Van Der Merwe, 133 Pte Jacob J, CP2	QSA (4) RoM DoK OFS Tr	A Squadron. KSA (2). KSA reissued 8 Feb 09. Served in the Bechuanaland Rebellion 1897 earning CGHGSM (1) Bech
Van Der Merwe, Pte W, KTG	QSA (1) DoK	Ambulance Corps, Beaconsfield Town Guard
Van Der Schyff, 468 Pte Lucas Hendrick, CP2	QSA (1) DoK	A Squadron. Discharged time expired
Van Dujker, 57 Tpr Peter William, KLH	QSA (2) DoK OFS	Served 21 Oct 99 to 3 Apr 00
Van Eyssen, Pte F, KTG	QSA (1) DoK	Cycle Corps, A Company
Van Eyssen, 197 Tpr H, KLH	QSA (2) DoK OFS	Served 20 Oct 99 and transferred to KTG 30 Oct 99 (No IV Section, B Company, No 4 Redoubt). Discharged 4 Mar 00
Van Niekerk, Sp Const B, CP2	QSA (1) DoK	
Van Niekerk, Pte Christian A, KTG	QSA (3) DoK OFS Tr	No IV Section, C Company, Beaconsfield Town Guard. Also served KLH (93, 1102 & 40237) 15 Apr 00 to 30 Nov 01 and 9 Jan 02 to 17 Jun 02. QSA (1), KSA (2) (Tpr KH). Burman Mar 05 £325
Van Niekerk, Pte Henry, KTG	QSA (3) DoK 01 02	No III Section, No 2 Redoubt. Also served KRV (1341) and SRG (1273) from 13 May 01
Van Reenan, 198 Tpr Isaac William, KLH	QSA (2) DoK OFS	Served 20 Oct 99 to 4 Mar 00
Van Reenen, Pte W D, KTG	QSA (1) DoK	Beaconsfield Town Guard

Van Wyk, 739 Pte Abram Johannes, CP2	QSA (1) DoK	KSA roll has surname as Van Wijk. Served in the Bechuanaland Rebellion 1897 earning CGHGSM (1) Bech. QSA (1), [KSA (2)]. Kaplan Oct 05. QSA (1), [KSA (2)], KStar. City Coins Aug 08
Van Wyk, 296 Tpr Richard, KLH	QSA (2) DoK OFS	Served 23 Oct 99 until dismissed 21 Dec 00. Also served with Cattle Guards
Vandam, Pte W, KTG	QSA (1) DoK	There is a W Voaden on the KTG nominal roll serving in G Company. Same man?
Vandergryp, Pte S W, KTG	QSA (1) DoK	No III Section, L Company. Surname also spelled Van Der Gryp. QSA (1). DNW Sep 00 £120. Ursual Nov 00 £160
Varrie, Pte A S, KTG	QSA (1) DoK	No I Section, L Company
Varrie, 508 Pte J, KRV	QSA (4) DoK OFS Tr 01	Discharged 7 Jul 02
Vass, Pte H, KTG	QSA (1) DoK	No III Section, L Company and Otto's Kopje Company
Vaughan, 347 Tpr E J, KLH	QSA (2) DoK OFS	Served 7 Nov 99 and transferred to KTG 30 Nov 99. Served in the Bechuanaland Rebellion 1897 with Kimb Rifles earning CGHGSM (1) Bech
Vaughan, Capt W, KitH	QSA (4) DoK Paar Tr Witt	Medal recovered from SA and reissued 12 Jan 05 to an address in Paris
Veale, Pte C H, KTG	QSA (1) DoK	No III Section, B Company, No 4 Redoubt
Veale, Pte P H, KTG	QSA (1) DoK	No 6 Redoubt
Venables, 659 Pte Alexander Edward, CP2	QSA (1) DoK	CP dismounted branch (barrier & redoubt duties). Served CP 24 Sep 99 to 26 Apr 01. Discharged for unsuitability. Also served CRSS (1340) 23 Jul 01 to 2 Oct 01, KLH (38022) 10 Oct 01 to 10 Apr 02 and KH (102) 11 Apr 02 to 30 Jun 02. KSA (2). Occupation butcher
Venables, Pte William Ennis, KTG	QSA (5) DoK OFS Tr 01 02	No III Section, F Company, No 3 Redoubt. Also served KLH from 7 Mar 00, WS (16) 20 Mar 00 to 18 Dec 00, BR (212 & 26158) 29 Jan 01 to 28 Sep 01, JMR (1550) and CRSS (1549) from 25 Mar 02. Occupation wheelwright
Venner, 354 Tpr John, KLH	QSA (2) DoK OFS	Dismissed 6 Feb 00. Forfeited on KTG roll
Venter, Pte G R M, KTG	QSA (1) DoK	Ambulance Corps, Beaconsfield Town Guard
Venter, Pte J M, KTG	QSA (1) DoK	Ambulance Corps, Beaconsfield Town Guard
Venter, 157 Pte Johannes Phillipus, CP2	QSA (1) DoK	C Squadron. KSA (2). Served in the Bechuanaland Rebellion 1897 earning CGHGSM (1) Bech
Venter, 317 Pte Petrus Johannes, CP2	QSA (1) DoK	C Squadron. KSA (2)
Verceuil, Pte S H, KTG	QSA (1) DoK	No I Company, B Section, Reservoir. Surname also spelled Vercenil
Verge, 5224 Pte G, LNLR	QSA (3) DoK OFS Tr	KSA (2). Initial W on KSA roll
Verheyen, Cpl G, KTG	QSA (1) DoK	No III Section, No 2 Redoubt
Verheyen, Pte Jos, KTG	QSA (1) DoK	No III Section, No 2 Redoubt. QSA (1), KStar. Toad Hall Jul 89 £115. 50th Anniversary attendee
Vermaak, Nurse M, NS	QSA (0)	Kimberley Civil Hospital
Vernal, Chaplain A, ACD	QSA (1) DoK	4th Class Chaplain
Veroghan, Pte L, KTG	QSA (1) DoK	Premier Mine
Vialoux, Pte Alf, KTG	QSA (1) DoK	No 2 Schmidt's Breastwork. Also served KRV (650) until DMU 9 Jan 00
Vicary, Pte A, KTG	QSA (1) DoK	No I Section, B Company, No 4 Redoubt
Vicary, Pte J, KTG	QSA (1) DoK	Mounted Section, Kenilworth Defence Force. QSA (1). Warwick & Warwick Nov 03
Vicary, J, KTG	QSA (0)	Roll states "Construction works before the Guard was formed"
Vicary, Pte W A, KTG	QSA (1) DoK	No III Section, B Company, No 4 Redoubt

Kimberley Siege Account and Medal Roll

Vickers, 10135 Gnr Stephen, RGA	QSA (2) DoK 01	Premier Mine
Viggers, Col Sgt W, KTG	QSA (1) DoK	No II Company, A Section, Reservoir
Vigne, Cpl J T, KTG	QSA (1) DoK	No III Section, Belgravia Fort
Vihroy, 365 Pte O, KRV	QSA (1) DoK	DMU 24 Feb 00
Viljoen, 1193 Pte C, KRV	QSA (3) DoK OFS Tr	Discharged 1 Jul 02. Also served KTG (No II Section, No 2 Redoubt). KSA (2)
Viljoen, 1227 Pte J S, KRV	QSA (3) DoK OFS Tr	Discharged 1 Jul 02. Also served KTG (No II Section, B Company, Beaconsfield Town Guard) and IYS (19) 10 May 00 to 6 Sep 00. KSA (2)
Villet, Pte G, KTG	QSA (1) DoK	No 6 supply depot
Vincent, Cpl E, KTG	QSA (1) DoK	No III Section, B Company, No 4 Redoubt
Vincent, Pte E, KTG	QSA (1) DoK	No II Section, Mandy Fort
Vines, Pte C Granville, KTG	QSA (1) DoK	No III Section, Belgravia Fort. Worked one of the searchlights. Manager of black and Asian food supply stores
Vipond, Pte J, KTG	QSA (1) DoK	No IV Section, D Company. QSA (1). Liverpool Oct 83 £110. Could be next man
Vipond, Pte J, KTG	QSA (1) DoK	There are two men of this name on the QSA roll but only one on the nominal roll
Voegt, Pte H D, KTG	QSA (1) DoK	G Company
Voekings, 513 Cpl H J, CP1	QSA (2) DoK OFS	C Squadron. DMU 31 Jun 02
Voges, Pte P J, KTG	QSA (1) DoK	No 4 supply depot
Volkebron, 51 Pte Charles Henry, CP2	QSA (3) DoK OFS Tr	A Squadron. KSA (2). Served in the Bechuanaland Rebellion 1897 earning CGHGSM (1) Bech
Von Brandis, Pte J, KTG	QSA (1) DoK	No I Company, B Section, Reservoir
Von Buddenbock, 1575 L Cpl W, CP1	QSA (4) RoM DoK OFS Tr	C Squadron. KSA (2) as Buddenbrock, W D
Von Moltke, 55 Tpr W F, KLH	QSA (2) DoK OFS	Served 19 Oct 99 to 3 Apr 00
Von Musits, Pte Stephen, KTG	QSA (6) DoK Paar Drie Joh DH Witt	Otto's Kopje Scouts. Also served DH as 18 Feb 00 to 16 Dec 00. Surname sometimes Van Nusitts and Van Musik. Nationality American
Von Plaster, Pte E H, KTG	QSA (1) DoK	QSA (1), KStar. City Coins Dec 04
Von Witt, 542 Pte William Stephen, CP2	QSA (5) DoK Belm MR OFS Tr	A Squadron. Belm & MR issued 18 Feb 08. BSACM rev Matabeleland 1893 (BB Police) (renamed), CGHGSM (1) Bech (CPD2) (renamed), QSA (5) (renamed), KSA (2), 1914-15 Star (Lt SASC-T&R), BWM, VM (Lt). City Coins Jun 80
Voules, 508 Cpl Tom Arthur, CP2	QSA (4) RoM DoK OFS Tr	CP No 3 Maxim gun detachment. Promoted Lt 16 Jun 02. KSA (2) issued to Lt. Served in the Bechuanaland Rebellion 1897 earning CGHGSM (1) Bech
Vyall, Pte G H, KTG	QSA (1) DoK	No I Section, Belgravia Fort

W

Waddington, Rwy emp F A, IMR	QSA (1) DoK	
Waddington, Sgt J, KTG	QSA (1) DoK	No 6 Redoubt
Waddington, 4266 Pte T, LNLR	QSA (3) DoK OFS Tr	Invalided to England 16 Jul 00. Also served SAC (1272). KSA (2)
Wade, Pte Albert Weston, KTG	QSA (3) DoK OFS Tr	No III Section, B Company, Beaconsfield Town Guard. Also served KLH (1093) 22 Mar 00 to 10 Nov 00, CRSS (1425) from 17 Oct 01 and CPS (345). Occupation miner. Possibly prisoner Potchefstroom 22 Jul 00

Name	Clasps	Notes
Waggoner, 717 Pte C, KRV	QSA (2) DoK 01	Discharged 16 Jul 02
Wakeford, 1161 Pte Ernest Victor, KRV	QSA (4) RoM DoK OFS Tr	Also served KTG (No II Section, B Company, Beaconsfield Town Guard), CPS (786), SRG (933) from 28 May 01 and KH (374 & 42410) 22 May 02 to 30 Jun 02. QSA (4). eBay Jul 09 £396
Walcroft, 4525 Pte J, LNLR	QSA (1) DoK	Wounded 25 Nov 99. Invalided 26 Jun 00. QSA (1). Glendining Jul 75. Seaby Oct 78 £80
Waldek, Pte I, KTG	QSA (1) DoK	Kenilworth Defence Force
Waldek, Lt P, KTG	QSA (1) DoK	No 6 Redoubt. 50th Anniversary attendee. QSA (1), KStar. Dixon Apr 98 £220
Waldek, Capt S P, KRV	QSA (3) DoK OFS 01	Wounded 28 Nov 99. Transport Officer. Resigned 1 Feb 01. QSA (3). Neate May 93 £200
Walick, Pte E, KTG	QSA (1) DoK	QSA (1). Liverpool Nov 00 £120. DNW Apr 04 £130. DNW Dec 08
Walker, 1107 Pte C C, KRV	QSA (4) RoM DoK OFS Tr	Discharged 1 Jul 02. Also served KTG. KSA (2)
Walker, Pte E, KTG	QSA (1) DoK	Fireman searchlight engine
Walker, Pte Edward, KTG	QSA (1) DoK	Reserve Section, D Company. Also served SRG (99) 11 Feb 01 to 10 May 01
Walker, 5303 Pte G, LNLR	QSA (2) DoK OFS	Invalided to England 12 May 00
Walker, 4472 Pte H, LNLR	QSA (3) DoK OFS Tr	KSA (2)
Walker, 202 Sgt H J, KRV	QSA (1) DoK	KSA (2) issued to Lt KRV. Resigned commission 21 Dec 02. QSA (1), [KSA (2)], KStar. Aberdeen Medals Mar 08 £385
Walker, Pte H P, KTG	QSA (3) DoK 01 02	Cycle Corps, A Company. Also served CCCC (38816) with RoK instead of DoK
Walker, 115 Sgt Herbert Cauderm, CP2	QSA (1) DoK	CP dismounted branch (barrier & redoubt duties). No KSA but number on KSA roll given as 155
Walker, Pte J, KTG	QSA (1) DoK	No III Section, L Company. QSA (1). Neate Feb 95 £70
Walker, J, KTG	QSA (1) DoK	Manufacturing ammunition etc
Walker, 66 Pte Robert, CP2	QSA (2) DoK OFS	CP HQ and depot mounted branch. Served 11 Oct 99 to 31 May 02. OFS clasp issued 17 Dec 09. KSA (2). Served in the Bechuanaland Rebellion 1897 earning CGHGSM (1) Bech
Walker, Cpl T, KTG	QSA (1) DoK	No I Section, C Company, Beaconsfield Town Guard
Walker, Pte T W, KTG	QSA (1) DoK	No 6 Redoubt
Walker, Pte W, KTG	QSA (1) DoK	Gibraltar Fort, Davis's Heap
Walker, 1 Band W C, KRV	QSA (1) DoK	Joined DFH 1887. Griqualand West Brigade Band 1896. QSA (1), KSA (2), Colonial Auxiliary Forces LS Medal (1907), KStar. City Coins Nov 07
Walkerley, 574 Pte W A, KRV	QSA (1) DoK	Discharged 9 Jul 00
Wall, 229 Pte Thomas Walter Jackson, CP2	QSA (1) DoK	B Squadron. Discharged on gratuity. QSA (1). Spink Jul 04 £160
Wallace, Sister A, NS	QSA (0)	Kimberley Civil Hospital. MID 10 Sep 01
Wallace, Lt Augustus Robert, LNLR	QSA (3) DoK OFS Tr	See his biography (page 357)
Wallace, Pte C, KTG	QSA (1) DoK	No IV Section, F Company, Mostert's Redoubt
Wallace, 226 Tpr Charles Owen, KLH	QSA (4) RoM DoK OFS Tr	Served 17 Mar 00 to 5 Jun 00. Enrolled DFA 1 Oct 99 as Gnr (199). Also served Lt 50th Co IY. Occupation clerk
Wallace, 455 Pte D, KRV	QSA (2) DoK Tr	DMU 3 Aug 00. Also served MH (902). KSA (2). Possibly entitled to OFS on MH roll
Wallace, Pte E, KTG	QSA (2) DoK 01	Also served CCCC (32635). QSA (1). Chelsea Nov 05 £225 - could be next man

Wallace, Pte E, KTG	QSA (1) DoK	No III Section, B Company, Beaconsfield Town Guard
Wallace, Pte H, KTG	QSA (1) DoK	No II Section, D Company
Wallace, Pte William Frank, KTG	QSA (1) DoK	No II Section, L Company. Also served KLH (34591) 20 May 01 to 14 Sep 01, SRG (179) from 11 Feb 01 and KRV (1079)
Waller, Nurse E, NS	QSA (0)	Kimberley Civil Hospital
Wallis, 201 Dvr Edwin George, DFA	QSA (2) DoK OFS	Served 4 Oct 99 to 30 Apr 03. KSA (2). Served in the Bechuanaland Rebellion 1897 with Kimb Rifles earning CGHGSM (1) Bech. Occupation blacksmith at De Beers
Walsh, 3556 Pte J, LNLR	QSA (3) DoK OFS Tr	KSA (2)
Walsh, Pte J, KTG	QSA (1) DoK	No IV Section, M Company, No 2 Redoubt
Walsh, Pte T, KTG	QSA (1) DoK	No II Section, C Company, Pickering's Redoubt No 1
Walsh, Pte T, KTG	QSA (1) DoK	No I Company, B Section, Reservoir
Walshe, 26076 Tpr Albert William, ScH	QSA (5) DoK OFS Tr 01 02	Served 12 Jan 01 to 30 May 02. Also served KTG as Arm Sgt and RR (34493). QSA (5). Sotheby Nov 78
Walshe, Pte George Patrick, KTG	QSA (3) RoM DoK OFS	Also served KLH (472) 27 Mar 00 to 21 Jul 00
Walshe, Pte Maurice Richard, KTG	QSA (1) DoK	Premier Mine. Also served KLH (177) 8 Mar 00 to 5 Jun 00
Walter, 370 Pte Percy Glover, CP2	QSA (3) DoK OFS Tr	A Squadron. KSA (2)
Walters, 783 Pte C J, KRV	QSA (2) DoK OFS	Also served KTG. Discharged 31 May 00
Walters, 572 Pte Francis, KRV	QSA (4) RoM DoK OFS Tr	Non effective 15 Feb 01. Also served 1st ILH (2584) 25 Jun 01 to 30 Dec 01 and JMR (2339) to 7 Jul 02. KSA (2)
Walters, Pte G, KTG	QSA (1) DoK	Kenilworth Defence Force
Walters, 113 Sgt J J, KRV	QSA (1) DoK	Non effective 15 Aug 01. E&W Africa (1) Benin River 1894 (Sto HMS Widgeon), CGHGSM (1) Bech (Pte Kimb Rfls), QSA (1), KStar, 14-15 Star (Pte SA Vet Regt), BWM, VM (Sgt). Glendining Mar 99
Walton, Pte Robert William, KTG	QSA (1) DoK	Premier Mine, No IV Section, C Company, Beaconsfield Town Guard and Gibraltar Fort, Davis's Heap. Also served SRG (919) from 22 May 01 and ORCP (467)
Ward, Pte C, KTG	QSA (1) DoK	No II Section, Mandy Fort
Ward, Pte F, KTG	QSA (1) DoK	No II Section, B Company, Beaconsfield Town Guard
Ward, 691 Pte F R, KRV	QSA (1) DoK	Non effective 27 Jul 00. CGHGSM (1) Bech (Pte Kimb Rifles), QSA (1). Dixon Jun 98 £260
Ward, 261 Pte Frank Edward, CP2	QSA (4) RoM DoK OFS Tr	CP No 3 Maxim gun detachment. KSA (2). KSA reissued 7 Apr 09. Dangerously wounded Klip Drift 7 Mar 02. Served in the Bechuanaland Rebellion 1897 earning CGHGSM (1) Bech
Ward, Pte H, KTG	QSA (1) DoK	No II Section, C Company, Pickering's Redoubt No 2
Ward, Mr J, POC	QSA (1) DoK	
Ward, Pte J W, KTG	QSA (1) DoK	No 1 Redoubt. Possibly served in the Bechuanaland Rebellion 1897 with Kimb Rifles earning CGHGSM (1) Bech
Ward, Rev Joseph, ACD	QSA (1) DoK	Clasp entitlement crossed through on the roll
Ward, Pte P R, KTG	QSA (1) DoK	No 3 Redoubt
Ward, 115 Tpr Patrick, KLH	QSA (6) RoM DoK OFS Tr 01 02	Discharged 6 Mar 00. Also served DH (35532) 2 Aug 01 to 29 Jan 02. Occupation miner
Ward, Pte R A, KTG	QSA (1) DoK	Belgravia Fort. QSA (1). Liverpool Nov 93 £75
Ward, 5068 Pte T, LNLR	QSA (2) DoK OFS	Died of disease Kroonstad 17 Jul 00
Ward, 4853 Pte W, LNLR	QSA (3) DoK OFS Tr	QSA (3), [KSA (2)]. Glendining Dec 65

Medal roll

Ward, Pte W G, KTG	QSA (1) DoK	No III Section, A Company, Beaconsfield Town Guard
Warder, Cpl R, KTG	QSA (1) DoK	No III Section, F Company, No 3 Redoubt
Wardle, 613 Pte William George James, CP2	QSA (1) DoK	CP dismounted branch (barrier & redoubt duties). Discharged time expired. Served in the Bechuanaland Rebellion 1897 earning CGHGSM (1) Bech. QSA (1). Liverpool Aug 88 £60
Wardley, 4711 Pte J, LNLR	QSA (3) DoK OFS Tr	QSA (3), KSA (2), 14-15 Star, BWM, VM, KStar. RHQ
Ware, Pte F, KTG	QSA (1) DoK	No I Company, B Section, Reservoir
Waring, 4740 Pte P, LNLR	QSA (3) DoK Paar Joh	KSA (2). Mounted Infantry. No 4700 on KSA roll
Warne, Pte T, KTG	QSA (1) DoK	
Warner, Pte E A, KTG	QSA (1) DoK	Cycle Corps, A Company
Warr, 330 Cpl Henri, CP2	QSA (3) DoK OFS Tr	C Squadron. KSA (2). Served in the Bechuanaland Rebellion 1897 earning CGHGSM (1) Bech
Warren, 199 Tpr C, KLH	QSA (3) RoM DoK OFS	Served 20 Oct 99 to 5 Jun 00. Also served KTG
Warren, Cpl E M, KTG	QSA (1) DoK	Ambulance Corps, Beaconsfield Town Guard
Warren, Pte J W, KTG	QSA (1) DoK	No II Section, C Company, Pickering's Redoubt No 2
Warren, Pte R, KTG	QSA (1) DoK	Premier Mine
Warren, 692 Pte W, KRV	QSA (1) DoK	DMU 8 Mar 00
Warren, Pte W H, KTG	QSA (1) DoK	Also served UVR (888)
Watcham, Col Sgt James Henry, KTG	QSA (3) RoM DoK OFS	L Company. Also served KLH (234) 17 Mar 00 to 5 Jun 00. During the Great War served in GSWA 1914-16 and France 1916-18. Severeky wounded 15 Jul 1917. CGHGSM (1) Bech (Tpr DFH), QSA (3), 14-15 Star (Pte SASC MB train), BWM, VM (Gnr SAHA), KStar. Christies Mar 88 £250. Bullock Mar 07 £1,450. Liverpool Oct 09 £1,100 (no KStar)
Watchurst, 109 Band E A, KRV	QSA (1) DoK	Discharged 3 Nov 02. KSA (2)
Waterhouse, 4929 Cpl W, LNLR	QSA (3) DoK OFS Tr	KSA (2). Wounded Kaalfontein 23 May 01
Watermeyer, 94 Sgt Maj Frederick Edward, CP2	QSA (2) DoK OFS	C Squadron. Wounded 3 Nov 99. Promoted Lt 4 Dec 01. OFS clasp issued 20 Dec 05. KSA (2) issued to Lt. Served in the Bechuanaland Rebellion 1897 earning CGHGSM (1) Bech
Waterston, Pte A A, KTG	QSA (1) DoK	Premier Mine
Waterworth, Pte Charles, KTG	QSA (2) DoK OFS	H Company. Also served WS (19) 20 Mar 00 to 30 Oct 00, CinCBG (22731) from 19 Dec 00, imprisoned 5 Feb 01 (9 months HL), KFS and IHC
Watkins, Med Off Arnold Hirst, KTG	QSA (1) DoK	See his biography (page 357)
Watkins, 413 CSM George Edward, KRV	QSA (3) DoK OFS 01	Served 11 Oct 99 to 24 Jun 00. Also Lt SRG 11 Feb 01 to 12 Dec 01. CGHGSM (1) (Sgt DFH), QSA (3), KSA (2) (renamed), BWM, VM (Sgt SAMC), KStar. Glendining Jul 01
Watridge, Pte C, KTG	QSA (1) DoK	No 1 Redoubt. 50th Anniversary attendee where initials are W J
Watson, Nurse C L, NS	QSA (0)	Kimberley Civil Hospital
Watson, 808 Pte Ernest, CP2	QSA (1) DoK	CP dismounted branch (barrier & redoubt duties). Discharged for misconduct
Watson, Pte George, KTG	QSA (3) DoK OFS Tr	No 2 Schmidt's Breastwork. Also served KLH (392) 8 Mar 00 to 6 Nov 00 and 1st ILH (1540) 19 Nov 00 to 24 Apr 02. KSA (2)
Watson, Lt H G, KLH	QSA (4) RoM DoK OFS Tr	Joined 16 Oct 99. Wounded 28 Nov 99. On black list. Service dispensed with 10 Sep 00. Also served KRV (72) with initials J H

Watson, 538 Pte J, KRV	QSA (2) DoK OFS	Non effective 25 Jun 00. Also served FID. QSA (2), KSA (2), KStar. Spink Dec 83. Dixon Sep 85 £148
Watson, Pte J, KTG	QSA (1) DoK	K Company
Watson, Lt J W, KTG	QSA (1) DoK	No I Section, B Company, No 4 Redoubt
Watson, 922 Pte R, KRV	QSA (2) DoK OFS	DMU 7 Jul 02. Also served KTG (No IV Section, No 2 Redoubt). KSA (2)
Watson, 112 Dvr Samuel, DFA	QSA (1) DoK	Enrolled 19 Jul 98. Served Kimb Rifle Vols for 6 yrs. Resigned 8 Feb 05. Occupation railway painter
Watt, Mr G J, POC	QSA (1) DoK	
Watters, Lt C J, KTG	QSA (3) DoK OFS 01	Served 3 Oct 99 to 7 Mar 00 (No 4 Redoubt). Also served KR (783) 8 Mar 00 to 31 May 00 and Lt SRG 2 Mar 01 to 18 Nov 01
Watterson, Pte R, KTG	QSA (1) DoK	No III Section, D Company. On nominal roll as Waterson
Watts, Pte G, KTG	QSA (1) DoK	Kimberley Mine Ambulance Company with mounted forces
Watts, Pte George, KTG	QSA (1) DoK	F Company, Mostert's Redoubt
Watts, Pte J L, KTG	QSA (1) DoK	No III Section, F Company, No 3 Redoubt
Weall, 3886 Sgt H, LNLR	QSA (3) DoK OFS Tr	KSA (2)
Wearne, Pte J, KTG	QSA (1) DoK	No I Company, B Section, Reservoir
Wearne, Pte J, KTG	QSA (1) DoK	
Wearne, Pte S F, KTG	QSA (1) DoK	G Company
Weatherdon, 245 Pte R S, KRV	QSA (3) RoM DoK OFS	Non effective 20 Jun 00
Weaver, 4613 Pte F, LNLR	QSA (3) DoK OFS Tr	Initial J on KSA roll. QSA (3), [KSA (2)]. RHQ
Webb, Pte H J, KTG	QSA (1) DoK	No II Section, B Company, No 4 Redoubt
Webber, Pte George Walter, KTG	QSA (4) DoK Tr 01 02	No II Section, B Company, Beaconsfield Town Guard. Also served SRG (932) 28 May 01 to 3 Dec 01 and BR (451) from 8 Jan 02 to 31 May 02. Occupation overseer
Webber, Checker I, ASC	QSA (1) DoK	
Webber, 1014 Cpl John Henry, KLH	QSA (3) DoK OFS Tr	Served 6 Nov 99 to 30 Jun 02 (three periods of service). Also served CPS (147) and CinCBG (22733) 11 Nov 00 to 20 Sep 01. KSA (2). Occupation boiler maker
Webber, Pte W, KTG	QSA (1) DoK	No I Section, B Company, No 4 Redoubt
Webber, Pte W J, KTG	QSA (1) DoK	No I Section, B Company, No 4 Redoubt
Webbstock, Lt Horace James, KTG	QSA (3) DoK OFS 01	No I Section, C Company, Pickering's Redoubt No 1. Also served Lt SRG 12 Feb 01 to 17 Aug 01. Served in the Bechuanaland Rebellion 1897 with the First Grahamstown Volunteers earning CGHGSM (1) Bech and subsequently in the GSWA operations 1 Oct 14 to 13 Aug 15
Webster, Lt Alexander McC, LNLR	QSA (3) DoK OFS Tr	See his biography (page 357)
Webster, 111 Sgt Alexander Thompson, KRV	QSA (3) DoK OFS Tr	Non effective 20 Jun 00. QSA (3), KSA (2), KStar. Seaby Aug 78 £130. DNW Jun 09 £620
Webster, Pte C, KTG	QSA (1) DoK	Kamfersdam Company
Webster, 148 L Sgt J, KRV	QSA (3) RoM DoK OFS	
Webster, 651 Pte J, KRV	QSA (1) DoK	DMU 10 Mar 00
Webster, Pte J G, KTG	QSA (1) DoK	
Webster, Sgt J R H, KTG	QSA (1) DoK	No I Section, K Company

Webster, 1095 Tpr John William, KLH	QSA (5) DoK OFS Tr 01 02	Served 17 Mar 00 to 6 Nov 00, 22 Mar 01 to 30 Sep 01 and 28 Apr 02 to 30 Jun 02. Also served KTG (No I Company, B Section, Reservoir). QSA disc only. Glendining Nov 77. QSA (3) DoK OFS Tr. Glendining Mar 85. QSA (6) inc CC. Spink May 02 £195. QSA (4) inc CC excl 01 & 02. H Dukes Auctions Aug 03 £220
Webster, Lt R, KTG	QSA (1) DoK	Pickering's Redoubt No 1
Webster, Pte Sydney Everard, KTG	QSA (1) DoK	No III Section, B Company, Beaconsfield Town Guard. Also served SRG (101) 11 Feb 01 to 10 May 01
Wedderburn, Sgt G R, KTG	QSA (1) DoK	No III Section, No 2 Redoubt. QSA (1). Spink Dec 90 £95
Wedderburn, 693 Pte W H, KRV	QSA (1) DoK	DMU 17 Aug 00
Wedgbury, 39857 Sgt Harry F, RGA	QSA (2) DoK Tr	DCM (Sgt No 1 Co RGA), QSA (2), KSA (2) (Sgt RGA), 1911 Royal Parks issue Coronation Medal, LS&GC Ed VII (CSM RGA), MSM GVI (CSM), KStar. Spink Jul 96
Weetman, Pte F, KTG	QSA (1) DoK	No IV Section, C Company, Beaconsfield Town Guard. QSA (1). Spink Dec 84 £75
Wehmeyer, Pte W, KTG	QSA (1) DoK	No III Section, No 2 Redoubt
Weideman, 352 Tpr John, KLH	QSA (2) DoK OFS	Served 13 Nov 99 until DMU 24 Mar 00
Weir, 89 Tpr A, KLH	QSA (2) DoK OFS	Discharged 30 Apr 00
Weir, Pte Alexander, KTG	QSA (1) DoK	Premier Mine. Also served SRG (199) from 11 Feb 01
Weir, 398 Pte D, KRV	QSA (1) DoK	
Weir, Pte G, KTG	QSA (2) DoK 01	No I Section, B Company, No 4 Redoubt. Discharged 1 Sep 01
Weir, 399 Pte W, KRV	QSA (1) DoK	QSA (1), KSA (2). Wright Auction Apr 05. Burman Feb 08 £385
Welch, CQMS A T, KTG	QSA (1) DoK	Reservoir
Welch, Pte F H, KTG	QSA (1) DoK	QSA (1). Kaplan Jul 05
Welch, 3050 Pte J, LNLR	QSA (2) DoK Tr	KSA (2). Invalided to England 5 May 00
Wellen, Sp Const H, CP2	QSA (1) DoK	Possibly also served CPS (715) as Wellin gaining Tr
Wells, Pte A, KTG	QSA (1) DoK	No IV Section, L Company
Wells, Lt E R, KTG	QSA (1) DoK	Reservoir
Wells, Pte E T, KTG	QSA (1) DoK	No II Section, F Company, Mostert's Redoubt
Wells, Pte F G S, KTG	QSA (1) DoK	Premier Mine
Wells, Lt William Harrison, KTG	QSA (1) DoK	See his biography (page 357)
Welsh, 85 Tpr G P, KLH	QSA (2) DoK OFS	Dismissed 13 Dec 00
Welsh, 293 Pte George Burgess, CP2	QSA (4) RoM DoK OFS Tr	A Squadron. Discharged by purchase. Served in the Bechuanaland Rebellion 1897 earning CGHGSM (1) Bech
Welsh, 8661 Gnr James, RGA	QSA (2) DoK OFS	To 16th Co RGA China
Welshman, 28726 L Cpl F, RE	QSA (6) DoK Paar Drie Joh DH Belf	KSA (2). From 6th Company. QSA (6) inc RoK excl DoK. eBay Dec 08 £210. It is believed that Welshmen should have received the RoK clasp as did other men of the 6th Co. The error must have been spotted when the medal was made up.
Wentzel, Mr J, POC	QSA (1) DoK	
West, Pte E, KTG	QSA (1) DoK	No II Section, C Company, Pickering's Redoubt No 1
West, Pte F, KTG	QSA (1) DoK	No II Section, B Company, Beaconsfield Town Guard
West, 769 Pte F J, KRV	QSA (3) RoM DoK OFS	Discharged 1 Jul 00. Also served KTG

Name	Medals	Notes
West, 220 Dvr Frederick, DFA	QSA (1) DoK	Enrolled 16 Dec 99. Also served DFH. Resigned 23 Jan 03. KSA (2)
West, 219 Dvr Samual Shaftoe, DFA	QSA (3) DoK OFS Tr	Enrolled 16 Dec 99. Resigned 20 Mar 03. KSA (2)
Westbrook, Pte E J, KTG	QSA (1) DoK	No I Company, A Section, Reservoir. QSA (1). Spink Jun 92 £80
Westerfield, Med Off Charles Joseph, KTG	QSA (1) DoK	Stationed at the Sanatorium
Westerman, Pte H, KTG	QSA (1) DoK	
Westley, Pte A, KTG	QSA (2) DoK Tr	G Company. Also served CPS (790). QSA (1), KStar. Burman Nov 98 £200
Westley, 38 Tpr George William, KLH	QSA (3) DoK OFS 01	Served 22 Oct 99 to 4 Mar 00. Surname Wesley. Also served CinCBG (25540) 24 Dec 00 to 10 Jul 01 and RR (30277). Occupation bricklayer. QSA (4) inc Tr (surname Wesley). City Coins Oct 93
Westley, Pte H J, KTG	QSA (1) DoK	Premier Mine
Westley, 76 Sgt H J C, KRV	QSA (1) DoK	Non effective 1 Dec 00
Westley, Pte P, KTG	QSA (1) DoK	G Company
Weston, Pte E E, KTG	QSA (1) DoK	No IV Section, No 2 Redoubt
Weston, Pte E W, KTG	QSA (1) DoK	No IV Section, No 2 Redoubt. QSA (1), KStar (Pvt M Coy). DNW Jun 98 £160. Dixon Sep 98 £210
Weston, 20 Tpr Frank, KLH	QSA (4) DoK OFS Tr 01	Also served CinCBG (22734) 11 Nov 00 to 13 May 01, ASC, CPS (366) and IYS (31) 11 May 00 to 6 Sep 00. Occupation sailor. QSA (3) CC DoK 01. Neate Feb 93 £110. Glendining Jun 93 £80
Whale, 139 Sgt Henry, KRV	QSA (3) DoK OFS Tr	Wounded 14 Feb 00. Non effective 20 Jun 00. Also served ORCP (467) 9 Sep 00 to 3 Jan 01 and SRG (903) 18 May 01 to 18 May 02. CGHGSM (1) Bech (Sgt DFH), BSACM rev Rhodesia 1896 (Sgt Med St Corps), QSA (3), KSA (2) (RSM SRG), KStar. Sotheby Jul 75 £310. Spink Sep 75 £355. City Coins Jun 77
Whalley, 3866 Pte J, LNLR	QSA (3) DoK OFS Tr	KSA (2)
Whammond, Pte A E, KTG	QSA (1) DoK	No I Section, C Company, Beaconsfield Town Guard
Wheatley, 98076 Gnr Benjamin, RGA	QSA (2) DoK Tr	KSA (2)
Wheatley, 6961 Gnr Elijah, RGA	QSA (1) DoK	Died of disease 11 May 00. Initial given as B
Wheatman, Pte William, KTG	QSA (3) DoK OFS Tr	No 2 Schmidt's Breastwork. Also served WS (20) 20 Mar 00 to 31 Aug 00, VMR and Christiana DMT
Wheaton, 157 Sgt James, DFA	QSA (1) DoK	Enrolled 1 Jul 99. Served RN 76-90. Resigned 6 Jan 03. Occupation electrician at De Beers
Wheeler, 333 Pte F, KRV	QSA (1) DoK	DMU 13 Feb 00
Whelan, Sp Const E, CP2	QSA (1) DoK	
Whibley, 22732 Tpr Percy George, CinCBG	QSA (4) DoK OFS Tr 01	Served 17 Nov 00 to 25 May 01. Also served KLH (237) to 30 Apr 00
Whiley, Lt G E, KTG	QSA (1) DoK	Assistant Paymaster. On nominal roll with initials G H
Whitaker, Lt J H, KRV	QSA (4) RoM DoK OFS Tr	KSA (2)
Whitaker, 397 Cpl P J, CP1	QSA (2) DoK OFS	B Squadron. KSA (2). Served in the Bechuanaland Rebellion 1897 earning CGHGSM (1) Bech
Whitburn, Pte W, KTG	QSA (1) DoK	No 6 Redoubt
White, Pte A, KTG	QSA (1) DoK	No I Section, C Company, Beaconsfield Town Guard
White, Pte Charles William J, KTG	QSA (2) DoK OFS	Otto's Kopje Scouts. Also served KLH (283) until dismissed 3 Jan 00 and 1st ILH (1149) 6 Nov 00 to 9 Jun 02. KSA (2)

Name	Medals	Notes
White, 364 Pte E, KRV	QSA (1) DoK	DMU 4 Apr 00. QSA (1). Carter Jul 90 £46. Morris Dec 97 £60
White, 917 Pte E H, KRV	QSA (3) DoK OFS Tr	Discharged 1 Jul 02. Also served KTG (H Company). KSA (2)
White, Pte E J, KTG	QSA (1) DoK	
White, 695 Pte Everard, CP2	QSA (2) DoK Paar	CP intelligence and detective staff. KSA (2)
White, Lt F, KTG	QSA (1) DoK	No II Section, L Company. QSA (1), KStar. DNW Sep 04 £290. Arctic Medals Nov 06. eBay Jul 07
White, 326 Pte F G, KRV	QSA (1) DoK	DMU 15 Mar 00
White, 543 Cpl Francis Edward William, CP2	QSA (4) RoM DoK OFS Tr	CP 7-pounder detachment. Served 11 Oct 99 to 15 Jan 02. Also served SALH (41467) 24 Feb 02 to 31 May 02. QSA (4), [KSA (2)], KStar. Sotheby Jun 19. Sotheby Nov 78. March Medals Dec 90 £225. Spink Oct 99 £270
White, Pte Fred, KTG	QSA (1) DoK	No III Section, Belgravia Fort. QSA (1), KStar. DNW Apr 03 £230. Dixon Dec 03 £350. Liverpool Oct 09 £495
White, Capt Greenwood, KTG	QSA (1) DoK	See his biography (page 357)
White, Mr J, POC	QSA (1) DoK	Telegraph signaller
White, Lt James Thomas, CP2	QSA (3) DoK OFS Tr	See his biography (page 357)
White, 16 Sgt John, CP2	QSA (1) DoK	CP dismounted in Beaconsfield. Promoted Lt 27 Jun 02. KSA (2) not issued as struck off. Served in the Bechuanaland Rebellion 1897 earning CGHGSM (1) Bech
White, Pte John Henry Martin, KTG	QSA (1) DoK	Premier Mine. Also served KLH (173) 8 Mar 00 to 5 Jun 00
White, Pte Peter, KTG	QSA (1) DoK	Premier Mine. Also served SRG (107) from 12 Feb 01 but could be the next man
White, Pte Peter, KTG	QSA (1) DoK	No I Section, B2 Company, No 3 Redoubt
White, 611 Pte S, KRV	QSA (2) DoK Paar	Non effective 20 Jun 00
White, Pte S, KTG	QSA (1) DoK	H Company
White, Sgt W, KTG	QSA (1) DoK	No III Section, F Company, No 3 Redoubt
White, Pte W J, KTG	QSA (1) DoK	No IV Section, C Company, Pickering's Redoubt No 2. Also served CPS (214). He had served as Sgt Kaffrarian Volunteer Artillery and as Captain in the Basuto War 1880-81. SAGS (1) 1877-78 (Sgt Kaffm Vol Arty), CGHGSM (1) Bas (Lt Kaffn Vol Arty), QSA (1), KStar. City Coins Dec 04
Whitebeard, Pte T A, KTG	QSA (4) DoK OFS Joh DH	Premier Mine and No II Section, A Company, Beaconsfield Town Guard. Also served FID
Whitehead, Cpl A R, KTG	QSA (1) DoK	Medical Corps, No 1 Company, F Section
Whitehead, 4028 Pte E, LNLR	QSA (2) DoK OFS	Invalided to England 16 Jul 00. QSA (2). Spink Mar 69 £8
Whitehead, Pte J G, KTG	QSA (2) DoK OFS	No 3 Redoubt. Also served KLH (213) to 30 Apr 00
Whitehead, Guide T, FID	QSA (4) DoK OFS Joh DH	
Whitehead, Pte W B, KTG	QSA (1) DoK	No II Section, Mandy Fort. Also served VTG (151)
Whitehorn, 1277 Pte J A, KRV	QSA (4) DoK OFS 01 02	Non effective 25 Jul 01. Discharged KRV 1 Jul 02. Also served KTG (No 2 Schmidt's Breastwork)
Whiteing, 5067 Cpl J, LNLR	QSA (3) DoK OFS Tr	KSA (2). Surname Whiting on KSA roll
Whitfield, Pte D, KTG	QSA (1) DoK	No II Section, B Company, Beaconsfield Town Guard
Whitham, Mr L, POC	QSA (1) DoK	QSA (1), KStar. Spink Oct 99 (no sale). Spink Jul 00 £340. Spink Jul 07 £400
Whittaker, 5005 Pte T, LNLR	QSA (3) DoK OFS Tr	QSA (3), [KSA (2)]

Name	Medals	Notes
Whittaker, 5062 Pte W, LNLR	QSA (3) DoK OFS Tr	QSA (1), [KSA (2)]. Spink Mar 58 15s. QSA (3), [KSA (2)]. Spink Nov 05 £240
Whitter, Pte T R, KTG	QSA (1) DoK	No IV Section, C Company, Pickering's Redoubt No 2
Whitter, Pte W, KTG	QSA (1) DoK	No II Section, C Company, Pickering's Redoubt No 1. QSA (1)
Whittingham, 5139 Pte F W, LNLR	QSA (3) DoK OFS Tr	KSA (2)
Whittle, 5442 Pte A, LNLR	QSA (3) DoK OFS Tr	KSA (2)
Whittle, 4166 OR Sgt J, LNLR	QSA (3) DoK OFS Tr	Wounded Nooitgedacht 17 Oct 00. QSA (3), [KSA (2)]. Bosleys Dec 08
Whittock, 296 Pte G H, KRV	QSA (1) DoK	DMU 27 Jul 00
Whitton, Pte R, KTG	QSA (1) DoK	N Company
Whitton, 240 Pte R A, KRV	QSA (4) RoM DoK OFS Tr	Discharged 1 Jul 02. KSA (2)
Whitworth, 323 Tpr Albert, KLH	QSA (2) DoK OFS	Served 15 Mar 00 to 30 Apr 00. Also served KTG (No II Section, B2 Company, No 3 Redoubt), IYS (8) to 6 Sep 00 and CPS (9). QSA (2), KStar. DNW Dec 01 £230. Dixon Apr 02 £325. A F Brock Jun 03
Whitworth, 4092 Pte Samuel, LNLR	QSA (3) DoK OFS Tr	KSA (2)
Whyte, Pte Tom, KTG	QSA (1) DoK	No II Section, Mandy Fort
Wickham, Pte F, KTG	QSA (1) DoK	No III Section, K Company. QSA (1)
Wienaud, 52 Tpr H, KLH	QSA (2) DoK OFS	Discharged 4 Mar 00
Wightman, Pte F, KTG	QSA (1) DoK	No I Section, F Company, Mostert's Redoubt
Wightman, Pte J S, KTG	QSA (1) DoK	H Company. Also served SRG (102)
Wilcock, 91 Cpl A G H, KRV	QSA (3) DoK OFS Tr	Discharged 23 Mar 03. KSA (2). Served in the Bechuanaland Rebellion 1897 with Kimb Rifles earning CGHGSM (1) Bech
Wilcock, 60 Cpl J, KRV	QSA (1) DoK	Non effective 8 Jul 00. Possibly served in the Bechuanaland Rebellion 1897 with Kimb Rifles earning CGHGSM (1) Bech
Wilcock, 4689 Pte S, LNLR	QSA (3) DoK OFS Tr	KSA (2)
Wilcock, Pte W, KTG	QSA (1) DoK	No III Section, D Company. QSA (1). Neate Dec 98 £95. eBay Jan 09
Wilcox, Lt W J, KRV	QSA (1) DoK	
Wild, 5107 L Cpl F, LNLR	QSA (1) DoK	Died of disease 15 Jan 00
Wild, Pte George, KTG	QSA (1) DoK	Also served Warrenton TG (2)
Wilder, Pte W, KTG	QSA (1) DoK	Premier Mine
Wildie, 5085 Pte B, LNLR	QSA (3) DoK OFS Tr	KSA (2)
Wilding, Pte John, KTG	QSA (1) DoK	No II Section, B2 Company, No 3 Redoubt. Also served CRSS (1543) from 17 Mar 02. Occupation carver. QSA (1), KStar. Glendining Sep 89 £320
Wilding, Pte T, KTG	QSA (1) DoK	G Company. Possibly also served CPS (377). QSA (1). Glendining Sep 85
Wiley, Pte T S, KTG	QSA (1) DoK	No IV Section, No 2 Redoubt. QSA (1). McGregor Museum
Wilkie, 1553 Pte H M, CP1	QSA (3) DoK OFS Tr	B Squadron
Wilkins, Lt A, KTG	QSA (1) DoK	Medical Corps, No 1 Company, C Section. Occupation chemist
Wilkins, Pte Alfred Henry, KTG	QSA (5) RoM DoK OFS Tr 01	No 3 Redoubt. Also served KLH (465, 390 & 1304) 7 Mar 00 to 9 Nov 00 and CPS (71)

Medal roll

Wilkins, Pte F E, KTG	QSA (1) DoK	B line of defence, No 3 Redoubt and Kimberley Mine Ambulance Company, B Section
Wilkins, 148 Gnr H, DFA	QSA (1) DoK	Enrolled 16 Feb 99. DMU 31 Dec 99. Also served DFA in 1897 and Kimb Regt. Occupation accountant
Wilkins, 207 Tpr Henry Joseph, KLH	QSA (3) RoM DoK OFS	Discharged 5 Jun 00. Also served DBMB (Botanical Gardens)
Wilkins, 1302 Tpr John Saw, KLH	QSA (4) RoM DoK OFS Tr	Served 10 Nov 99 to 25 Mar 02 and GWLH (158 & 41893) 26 Mar 02 to 30 Jun 02. KSA (2)
Wilkinson, 2677 Col Sgt E, LNLR	QSA (3) DoK OFS Tr	MID 4 Sep 01. DCM LG 27 Sep 01. KSA (2)
Wilkinson, 90568 Gnr H, RGA	QSA (3) DoK Tr 01	Slightly wounded Schweizer Reneke 29 Nov 00
Wilkinson, 90568 Gnr Herbert, RGA	QSA (2) DoK Tr	23rd Co. Invalided
Wilkinson, Pte J, KTG	QSA (1) DoK	No I Section, B Company, No 4 Redoubt
Wilkinson, Pte W, KTG	QSA (1) DoK	No II Section, D Company
Willcock, Pte E, KRV	QSA (1) DoK	50th Anniversary attendee
Willcox, 88 Sgt George Arthur, CP2	QSA (1) DoK	CP dismounted in Beaconsfield
Willey, Pte E E, KTG	QSA (1) DoK	G Company
Williams, 194 Tpr A E, KLH	QSA (3) RoM DoK OFS	Wounded 25 Nov 99. Discharged 5 Jun 00
Williams, Capt Albert S, SAC	QSA (4) RoM DoK OFS Tr	Served from 30 Oct 00. Also served Lt KLH. KSA (2)
Williams, Pte C, KTG	QSA (1) DoK	No I Section, D Company
Williams, Pte Charles, KTG	QSA (4) DoK Tr 01 02	Also served JMR (1577) to 28 Feb 02 and CRSS (1547) from 24 Mar 02. Occupation barman
Williams, 12 Sgt Maj Charles Francis, CP2	QSA (3) DoK OFS Tr	KSA (2). Served in the Bechuanaland Rebellion 1897 earning CGHGSM (1) Bech
Williams, Pte D, KTG	QSA (1) DoK	Ambulance Corps, Beaconsfield Town Guard. QSA (1), KStar. Argyll Etkin May 06. Could be next man
Williams, Pte D, KTG	QSA (1) DoK	H Company
Williams, Pte D H, KTG	QSA (2) DoK 01	
Williams, Pte Dan Augustus, KTG	QSA (5) RoM DoK OFS Tr 01	Also served KLH (391 and 466) 7 Mar 00 to 5 Jun 00 and SRG (104) 12 Feb 01 to 10 May 01. QSA (1). Spink Feb 76 £65. LSE Sep 84 £85. QSA (1), KStar. Glendining Mar 97. Monarch Medals Mar 04 £380
Williams, Pte E, KTG	QSA (1) DoK	Premier Mine
Williams, Pte E J, KTG	QSA (1) DoK	Premier Mine
Williams, 1010 Pte G W, KRV	QSA (4) DoK OFS Tr 01	Discharged 17 Oct 02. Also served KTG (H Company) and JMR (1897)
Williams, 850 Pte H, KRV	QSA (3) DoK OFS Tr	Discharged 7 Jul 02. Also served KTG (No 2 Schmidt's Breastwork). KSA (2)
Williams, Mr H, POC	QSA (1) DoK	
Williams, 652 L Cpl H A, KRV	QSA (2) DoK 01	Discharged 6 Jun 02
Williams, 784 Pte J, KRV	QSA (5) RoM DoK OFS Tr 01	DMU 17 Apr 01. Also served KTG
Williams, Bearer J, KLH	QSA (3) RoM DoK OFS	Discharged 5 Jun 00
Williams, Pte J, KTG	QSA (1) DoK	Kamfersdam Company
Williams, J G, KTG	QSA (0)	Roll states "Repairing tents and making tent pegs"
Williams, 9147 Gnr J J, RGA	QSA (1) DoK	23rd Co. Invalided. QSA (1). Hayward's Gazette Jul 78 £85. Spink Jul 07 £240
Williams, 1928 Pte James Ernest, CP1	QSA (1) DoK	A Squadron. Killed in action 28 Nov 99

Name	Medals	Notes
Williams, Pte L J, KTG	QSA (1) DoK	No I Company, B Section, Reservoir
Williams, 881 Pte T, KRV	QSA (3) DoK OFS Tr	Also served KTG (No 2 Schmidt's Breastwork). Died of disease near Kuruman 22 Jan 02. KSA (2)
Williams, 464 Sgt W, KRV	QSA (1) DoK	Arrived Kimberley 20 Nov 99. Discharged 31 Dec 00. Occupation miner
Williams, 694 Pte W, KRV	QSA (4) DoK OFS Tr 01	Discharged 1 Jul 00 and 1 Jul 02. Also served KTG and DFA
Williams, W C, KTG	QSA (1) DoK	Occupation farrier
Williams, 79 Pte William, CP2	QSA (3) DoK OFS Tr	CP HQ and depot mounted branch. QSA (3), KSA (2), KStar. Glendining Jun 90 £200
Williamson, 22731 Tpr George, CinCBG	QSA (5) DoK OFS Tr 01 02	Served 17 Nov 00 to 28 Jul 01. Also served KTG (No 4 Redoubt), KLH (183) 8 Mar 00 to 5 Jun 00, ALH (39972) 28 Nov 01 until killed in action, Klip Drift, 7 Mar 02. Occupation mine secretary. His son also served in ALH and was captured 3 Jan 02. Possibly served in the Bechuanaland Rebellion 1897 with PAVG earning CGHGSM (1) Bech
Willis, 5123 Pte E, LNLR	QSA (2) DoK OFS	KSA (1) SA02
Willis, 312 Tpr F J, KLH	QSA (2) DoK OFS	Served 24 Oct 99 to 4 Mar 00. Possibly also served CinCBG (not on nominal roll)
Willis, 356 Tpr George Noel, KLH	QSA (3) DoK Paar Tr	Served 18 Nov 99 until DMU 24 Mar 00. Also served DFA (235) 1 Aug 00 to 1 Jul 02. KSA (2). Occupation clerk
Willis, 5312 L Cpl H, LNLR	QSA (3) DoK OFS Tr	KSA (2)
Willis, Pte J, KTG	QSA (1) DoK	No I Company, A Section, Reservoir
Willis, Pte J, KTG	QSA (1) DoK	No IV Section, B Company, Beaconsfield Town Guard
Willis, 616 Pte Philip, CP2	QSA (2) DoK Tr	B Squadron. KSA (2)
Willmore, 53 Tpr Albert Edwin, KLH	QSA (2) DoK OFS	Killed in action 25 Nov 99
Willmore, 23 Tpr Edward Fletcher, KLH	QSA (2) DoK Paar	DMU 24 Mar 00. QSA (2). Neate Nov 94 £125. QSA (2), KStar. Spink Oct 99 £130. Kaplan Feb 03
Willmore, 24 Tpr F H, KLH	QSA (2) DoK Paar	Discharged 24 Mar 00. Also served CPS (62)
Willock, 1214 Tpr J, KLH	QSA (3) DoK OFS Tr	Also served KTG (B line of defence, No 3 Redoubt). Also served KRV (785), SAC and ORCP 16 Sep 00 to 21 Jan 02. Surname Willcock on KLH nominal roll
Willoughby, 4849 L Cpl J, LNLR	QSA (3) DoK OFS Tr	QSA (3), KSA (2), KStar. RHQ
Willoughby, 4598 Pte W, LNLR	QSA (2) DoK OFS	KSA (2)
Wills, Pte G L, KTG	QSA (1) DoK	No 1 Redoubt. QSA (1), 14-15 Star (Pte 7th Infy), BWM, VM (Pte 7th Infy). Dixon Apr 98 £130
Wills, Cpl J, KTG	QSA (1) DoK	H Company
Wills, Pte John, KTG	QSA (3) DoK 01 02	No IV Section, D Company. Also served KH (18), CRSS (1414) from 11 Oct 01 and ALH (41797) from 1 Mar 02. Occupation miner/engine driver
Wills, Pte W, KTG	QSA (1) DoK	No I Section, L Company
Wilson, Pte A, KTG	QSA (1) DoK	G Company and H Company. QSA (1). Spink Apr 94 £90
Wilson, Mr A, POC	QSA (1) DoK	Telegraph signaller
Wilson, Pte A C, KTG	QSA (1) DoK	No I Section, B2 Company, No 3 Redoubt and No I Company, B Section, Reservoir
Wilson, Pte A J, KTG	QSA (1) DoK	No IV Section, B Company, Beaconsfield Town Guard
Wilson, Pte A T, KTG	QSA (1) DoK	Also served Ladismith TG
Wilson, 697 Pte Alexander, CP2	QSA (1) DoK	CP dismounted branch (barrier & redoubt duties). Discharged unsuitability. Clasp issued 8 Feb 07

Medal roll

Wilson, 132 Sgt Charles Digby, CP2	QSA (3) RoM DoK OFS	B Squadron. KSA (2). Killed at Klip Drift 7 Mar 02. Served in the Bechuanaland Rebellion 1897 earning CGHGSM (1) Bech
Wilson, Pte D E, KTG	QSA (1) DoK	Premier Mine. QSA (1)
Wilson, Cpl G, KTG	QSA (1) DoK	No III Section, C Company, Pickering's Redoubt No 1
Wilson, Pte G, KTG	QSA (1) DoK	No II Section, B Company, Beaconsfield Town Guard
Wilson, 568 Pte George, CP2	QSA (4) RoM DoK OFS Tr	CP 7-pounder detachment. CGHGSM (1) Bech, QSA (4), KSA (2), KStar. Glendining Jun 32
Wilson, Pte H, KTG	QSA (1) DoK	No I Company, B Section, Reservoir
Wilson, 310 L Cpl H E, KRV	QSA (1) DoK	Discharged 14 Jul 02. QSA (1), [KSA (2)], KStar. Sotheby Jan 72. DNW May 92 £140. Glendining Jul 95 £110. Dixon Jun 96 £175
Wilson, J C, KTG	QSA (1) DoK	Construction of forts and redoubts etc. QSA (1). Laidacker Dec 81. Spink Jul 07 £170. Dixon Feb 08 £250
Wilson, Lt J F, KTG	QSA (1) DoK	No IV Section, D Company
Wilson, Mr J I, POC	QSA (1) DoK	
Wilson, 26 Tpr James D, KLH	QSA (2) DoK OFS	Discharged 30 Apr 00. Also served IYS from 10 May 00. Died Lindley 15 Sep 00
Wilson, Pte John, KTG	QSA (2) DoK Tr	Also served BR (206 and 26153) 28 Jan 01 to 22 Jul 01. Occupation mason
Wilson, 3693 Pte R, LNLR	QSA (3) DoK OFS Tr	KSA (2). Wounded Klip Drift 7 Mar 02
Wilson, Pte R, KTG	QSA (1) DoK	Kamfersdam Company
Wilson, 413 Pte Robert, CP2	QSA (4) RoM DoK OFS Tr	C Squadron. KSA (2). Slightly wounded Witputs 14 Nov 00
Wilson, 806 Pte Rodney, CP2	QSA (3) DoK OFS Tr	C Squadron. KSA (2)
Wilson, Pte S J, KTG	QSA (1) DoK	No IV Section, B Company, Beaconsfield Town Guard
Wilson, 4057 Pte T, 2D	QSA (2) DoK Paar	See his biography (page 511)
Wilson, Sgt T A, KTG	QSA (1) DoK	No II Section, B Company, Beaconsfield Town Guard. QSA (1), KStar. Neate Feb 92 £150
Wilson, Cpl W, KTG	QSA (1) DoK	No II Section, B Company, Beaconsfield Town Guard
Wilson, Pte W, KTG	QSA (1) DoK	Premier Mine
Wilson, 29429 Sapr W J, RE	QSA (3) DoK Drie Tr	KSA (2)
Windsor, Pte D, KTG	QSA (1) DoK	Cycle Corps, A Company
Windsor, 234 Gnr Frances E James, DFA	QSA (4) RoM DoK OFS Tr	Served 23 Jul 00 until DMU 15 Jan 03. Also served KTG, KRV (897) 17 Mar 00 to 12 Jun 00. Occupation painter. QSA (4), [KSA (2)]. Payne Collection. Spink Sep 58 £1. Seaby Oct 78 £165. City Coins Aug 08
Windsor, 200 Tpr John Victor, KLH	QSA (2) DoK Paar	Discharged 6 Mar 00. Also served KTG
Windsor, Pte Peter Ford, KTG	QSA (1) DoK	Previously served Galeka War 1878 and CMR. Founder of Windsorton. Laid the foundation stone for Windsorton Town Hall in 1928, the year of his death
Wingrove, Pte H, KTG	QSA (1) DoK	Mounted Section, Kenilworth Defence Force
Wingrove, Pte W B, KTG	QSA (1) DoK	Mounted Section, Kenilworth Defence Force
Winrow, 5494 Pte J, LNLR	QSA (1) DoK	Invalided to England 10 Apr 00
Winter, 734 Pte Alexander, KRV	QSA (3) DoK 01 02	Wounded 14 Feb 00. Discharged from KRV (wounded) 19 Apr 00. Court martialled. Also served KTG (Gibraltar Fort, Davis's Heap) and DH (34909) 10 Jun 01 to 20 Mar 02. Occupation wire splicer
Winteridge, Dvr J, DBMB	QSA (1) DoK	Botanical Gardens
Wiseman, Pte H, KTG	QSA (1) DoK	No 3 Redoubt

Wittig, 472 Band L, KRV	QSA (1) DoK	Discharged 8 Nov 99
Woleck, Pte E, KTG	QSA (1) DoK	No II Section, No 2 Redoubt. Private E Wolveck served No III Section, A Company, Beaconsfield Town Guard. Same man?
Wolstenholme, Pte H, KTG	QSA (1) DoK	No III Section, B Company, No 4 Redoubt, Cycle Corps, A Company and L Company
Womack, 10 Sgt Robert, DFA	QSA (2) DoK 01	Enrolled 25 Nov 91. Resigned 31 Mar 03. Occupation engine driver. Enrollment forms have Wormack. QSA (1) excl 01, KStar. City Coins Dec 00
Wood, 671 Pte Alfred, CP2	QSA (1) DoK	Dismissed for misconduct
Wood, 22824 Tpr Alfred, KLH	QSA (3) DoK OFS Tr	Wounded 28 Nov 99. Also served KTG, KRV (575), ORCP (440) 1 Sep 00 to 31 Dec 00, PAVG (1869), BS (808 & 40008), DrS (20890 & 609) 10 Jan 01 to 31 Mar 02 and ALH (37944) 26 Sep 01 to 26 Nov 01. KSA (2). Occupation bookmaker
Wood, 653 Pte E G, KRV	QSA (3) DoK OFS Tr	Discharged 1 Jul 02. KSA (2)
Wood, 555 Pte Frederick, CP2	QSA (1) DoK	CP HQ and depot mounted branch. DMU
Wood, 109 Pay Sgt Ralph, DFA	QSA (2) DoK OFS	Enrolled 25 Apr 98. Occupation miner at De Beers. Lt on KSA roll. KSA (2). Embezzled DFA funds and left DFA 28 Mar 03
Wood, 472 Pte William Fordyce, CP2	QSA (1) DoK	A Squadron. Discharged for unsuitability
Woodbourne, Pte Edward Turner, KTG	QSA (2) DoK Tr	Also served SRG (900) as Woodburn from 16 May 01
Woodbourne, Lt T J, KTG	QSA (1) DoK	No 1 Redoubt
Woodhouse, 4363 Cpl H, LNLR	QSA (3) DoK OFS Tr	KSA (2)
Wooding, 32562 Sgt Maj George, DH	QSA (2) DoK OFS	Served 19 Apr 01 to 2 Nov 01. Also served KRV (127) until discharged 21 Dec 00, CPS (223) and 1st ILH (3020 & 40028) 17 Dec 01 to 23 Jun 02. KSA (2). Possibly served in the Bechuanaland Rebellion 1897 with Kimb Rifles earning CGHGSM (1) Bech. Occupation miner
Wooding, 61 Pte Henry, CP2	QSA (2) DoK OFS	CP HQ and depot mounted branch. [QSA (2), KSA (2)], KStar. Glendining Nov 92. QSA (1) DoK. City Coins Feb 95
Woodlands, Pte H J, KTG	QSA (1) DoK	Medical Corps, No 1 Company, C Section
Woodman, Lt Thomas, KTG	QSA (1) DoK	Reverend Canon. Ambulance Corps, Beaconsfield Town Guard. MID 10 Sep 01. Minister of the All Saint's Parish Church, Beaconsfield
Woodruff, Cpl Cranmer, KTG	QSA (5) RoM DoK OFS Tr 01	Kimberley Mine Ambulance Company with mounted forces. Also served KLH to 5 Jun 00 and SRG (176) from 11 Feb 01. Slightly wounded Hartebeestpan 15 Jun 01. Served in the Bechuanaland Rebellion 1897 with DFH earning CGHGSM (1) Bech
Woods, 737 L Cpl C, KRV	QSA (3) DoK OFS 01	Discharged 1 Jul 02. Surname Wood on Supplementary roll. QSA (2), KStar. Glendining Jun 79 £110. Spink Nov 80 £150
Woods, 4355 Pte S, LNLR	QSA (3) DoK OFS Tr	KSA (2)
Woods, 5489 L Cpl W, LNLR	QSA (3) DoK OFS Tr	KSA (2)
Woodward, Pte F J, KTG	QSA (1) DoK	No IV Section, K Company
Woodward, Lt F W, LNLR	QSA (3) DoK OFS Tr	See his biography (page 358)

Woodward, Pte William A, KTG	QSA (6) RoM DoK OFS Tr 01 02	No I Company, B Section, Reservoir. Also served KLH (1096) from 26 Feb 00, ILH, RR and JMR (2160)
Wookey, Nurse F, NS	QSA (0)	Kimberley Civil Hospital
Woolenschlager, Pte H, KTG	QSA (1) DoK	H Company
Woolgar, Pte Henry, KTG	QSA (3) DoK OFS Tr	No III Section, C Company, Beaconsfield Town Guard. Also served KLH (1099) 27 Apr 00 to 7 Nov 00 and CPS (45) 28 Dec 00 to 30 Apr 02. QSA (1) DoK. Seaby Mar 72
Woolley, 3027 Pte J, LNLR	QSA (2) DoK OFS	Died of disease Boshof 24 May 00
Woolmer, Pte Theophilus, KTG	QSA (2) DoK OFS	Premier Mine. Also served KLH (142) to 3 Mar 00
Woon, Lt E W, CP1	QSA (3) DoK OFS Tr	See his biography (page 358)
Worrall, 7 Tpr Alf Barrett, KLH	QSA (3) DoK Paar 01	Served 15 Oct 99 to 31 Dec 00. Also served SRG (17) 12 Feb 01 to 15 Nov 01. MID 23 Jun 02. Severely wounded Gannaputs 26 Jun 01
Worrall, Sgt W, KTG	QSA (1) DoK	No I Section, B Company, No 4 Redoubt
Wren, Pte W M, KTG	QSA (1) DoK	
Wright, 707 Bugler A J, KRV	QSA (1) DoK	DMU 30 Sep 00. Also served Warrenton TG (19)
Wright, 1116 Pte A J, KRV	QSA (1) DoK	Discharged 17 Aug 00. Also served KTG (Cycle Corps, A Company and No 1 Redoubt)
Wright, Capt A J, KRV	QSA (2) DoK OFS	See his biography (page 358)
Wright, 733 Pte C, KRV	QSA (2) DoK 01	Discharged 24 Jan 01. Also served KTG
Wright, Pte E H, KTG	QSA (1) DoK	Cycle Corps, A Company
Wright, 1214 Pte E O, KRV	QSA (2) DoK 01	Non effective 6 Apr 01. Also served KTG (Mounted Section, B Company, Beaconsfield Town Guard)
Wright, Pte G C, KTG	QSA (1) DoK	Otto's Kopje Scouts
Wright, 96 Sgt G F, KRV	QSA (1) DoK	Served in the Bechuanaland Rebellion 1897 with Kimb Rifles earning CGHGSM (1) Bech
Wright, 321 Pte H O, KRV	QSA (2) DoK 01	Discharged 20 Sep 01. QSA issued 24 Oct 12
Wright, 507 Pte H W, KRV	QSA (1) DoK	Non effective 27 Jul 00. QSA (1). Kaplan Oct 05
Wright, Pte J, KTG	QSA (1) DoK	No 1 Redoubt
Wright, 63 Sgt J L, KRV	QSA (3) DoK OFS 01	Died of disease at Kimberley 22 Dec 01. Possibly served in the Bechuanaland Rebellion 1897 with Kimb Rifles as drummer earning CGHGSM (1) Bech
Wright, Pte L O, KTG	QSA (1) DoK	No 2 Redoubt
Wright, Pte L S, KTG	QSA (1) DoK	No IV Section, K Company
Wright, Pte O D, KTG	QSA (1) DoK	No I Section, Belgravia Fort. QSA (1). DNW Apr 01 £130
Wright, Lt Stephen Osborne, KLH	QSA (1) DoK	See his biography (page 358)
Wright, 5044 Pte T, LNLR	QSA (3) DoK OFS Tr	Wounded at Hartbeestfontein 12 Feb 01. Invalided to England (date unknown). QSA (3), [KSA (2)]. Spink Jul 60 £1
Wright, Pte T, KTG	QSA (1) DoK	No 2 Schmidt's Breastwork
Wright, Pte T W, KTG	QSA (1) DoK	No III Section, F Company, No 3 Redoubt
Wright, 3585 Pte W, LNLR	QSA (3) DoK OFS Tr	Replacement QSA issued. KSA (2)
Wright, Lt W G, KTG	QSA (1) DoK	Civil Service Redoubt
Wright, Pte W J, KTG	QSA (1) DoK	No I Section, D Company and G Company
Wright, W O, KTG	QSA (0)	Roll states "In charge of guard over scurvy patients"

Wright, 26023 Sgt Maj W R C, ScH	QSA (4) DoK OFS Tr 01	Served 6 Jan 01 to 28 Oct 01. Also served KTG
Wrightson, 695 Cpl P, KRV	QSA (2) DoK OFS	Discharged 1 Jul 02. KSA (2)
Wustmann, Col Sgt F R, KTG	QSA (1) DoK	D Company. Served in the Bechuanaland Rebellion 1897 with DFH earning CGHGSM (1) Bech. 50th Anniversary attendee as Wustman
Wyatt, 4481 Pte G, LNLR	QSA (3) DoK OFS Tr	KSA (2)
Wylam, Pte J, KTG	QSA (1) DoK	Premier Mine
Wylie, 237 Tpr A, KLH	QSA (2) DoK OFS	DMU 24 Mar 00
Wylie, Nurse A J, NS	QSA (0)	Kimberley Civil Hospital. QSA (0), KSA (0) renamed. DNW Apr 04 £380
Wyngaard, Pte J J, KTG	QSA (1) DoK	No III Section, C Company, Pickering's Redoubt No 1
Wyngard, 840 Pte A, KRV	QSA (3) DoK OFS Tr	Discharged 1 Jul 02. Also served KTG (No III Section, K Company). KSA (2)
Wyngard, Pte J, KTG	QSA (1) DoK	H Company. QSA (1). City Coins Jul 99. Spink Jul 07 £240. Could be next man
Wyngard, Pte J, KTG	QSA (1) DoK	H Company

Y

Yates, Lt F G, KTG	QSA (1) DoK	No IV Section, C Company, Beaconsfield Town Guard. QSA (1)
Yates, 793 Pte Thomas Joseph, CP2	QSA (5) RoM DoK OFS Tr 01	B Squadron. Died of disease Bloemfontein 29 Jan 01
Yeadon, 690 Sgt A W, DrS	QSA (5) DoK OFS Tr 01 02	Also served KRV (575) until dismissed for drunkenness 12 Jan 01 and PAVG. QSA (5), KSA (0), KStar
Yelland, Pte Francis Puckey, KTG	QSA (4) DoK OFS Tr 01	Premier Mine. Also served 1st ScH (26181) 6 Feb 01 to 15 Aug 01. Born 1875 in Cumberland and died in South Africa iaround 1937. QSA (1). eBay Dec 08
Yeowart, 362 Pte W, KRV	QSA (1) DoK	Non effective 21 Jul 00. 50th Anniversary attendee
Young, 289 Cpl Anthony Rogers, CP2	QSA (2) DoK OFS	See his biography (page 358)
Young, Lt D R, KTG	QSA (1) DoK	No III Section, Belgravia Fort. QSA (1), KStar. City Coins Sep 03. Monarch Medals Mar 04 £540. Lockdales Jul 08
Young, Pte George, KTG	QSA (1) DoK	Also served SRG (153) from 12 Feb 01. QSA (1), KStar. Seaby Nov 72 £40
Young, Pte J T, KTG	QSA (1) DoK	No 6 Redoubt. QSA (1). Dixon Dec 96 £90
Young, Pte J W, KTG	QSA (1) DoK	No 1 Redoubt
Young, 4379 Pte P, LNLR	QSA (3) DoK OFS Tr	KSA (2)
Young, Cpl S, KTG	QSA (1) DoK	D Company (Veterans), Beaconsfield Town Guard

Z

Zederick, Pte R, KTG	QSA (1) DoK	No I Section, A Company, Beaconsfield Town Guard
Zeederberg, Pte W, KTG	QSA (1) DoK	Otto's Kopje Scouts and No 2 Schmidt's Breastwork. QSA (1), KStar. Glendining Nov 96. Glendining Mar 97. DNW Sep 01 £200
Zeiss, 99 Pte T, KRV	QSA (1) DoK	
Ziegenbein, 681 Pte August Henry, ILH	QSA (6) RoM DoK OFS Tr 01 02	Served 25 Jul 01 to 17 Feb 02. Also served KTG (No III Section, F Company, No 3 Redoubt) and KRV (738) to 9 Nov 00
Ziegenbein, Lt H A, KTG	QSA (1) DoK	No III Section, F Company, No 3 Redoubt
Zondagh, Nurse H E, NS	QSA (0)	Kimberley Civil Hospital

Appendices

Appendix 01 – Chronology of the siege

	October 1899							November 1899							December 1899							January 1900							February 1900					
M	T	W	T	F	S	S	M	T	W	T	F	S	S	M	T	W	T	F	S	S	M	T	W	T	F	S	S	M	T	W	T	F	S	S
						1			1	2	3	4	5					1	2	3	1	2	3	4	5	6	7				1	2	3	4
2	3	4	5	6	7	8	6	7	8	9	10	11	12	4	5	6	7	8	8	10	8	9	10	11	12	13	14	5	6	7	8	9	10	11
9	10	11	12	13	14	15	13	14	15	16	17	18	19	11	12	13	14	15	16	17	15	16	17	18	19	20	21	12	13	14	15	16	17	18
16	17	18	19	20	21	22	20	21	22	23	24	25	26	18	19	20	21	22	23	24	22	23	24	25	26	27	28	19	20	21	22	23	24	25
23	24	25	26	27	28	29	27	28	29	30				25	26	27	28	29	30	31	29	30	31					26	27	28				
30	31																																	

The siege lasted 124 days from 15th October 1899 to 15th February 1900.

1899

14th October	Communication by telegraph was cut off to the south at 21:15 and to the north at 21:45. Official and Press messages were sent at midnight by despatch rider to Modder River. Steyn proclaimed Griqualand West part of Free State territory.
15th October	Martial law proclaimed within the territories of Griqualand West and Bechuanaland. Court of Summary Jurisdiction appointed. The water supply from the Vaal River cut off by the Boers. An armoured train left Kimberley and found men in position at Spytfontein. At 11:00 the alarm sounded, and defences were manned in anticipation of an attack. No morning services at most churches.
16th October	Armoured train with mounted troops in support made a reconnaissance and reported the Boers at Spytfontein. Water rationing began.
17th October	Platelayers arrived from Modder River and reported partial destruction of the railway bridge. The Boers lifted rails to north and south. 170 Cape Police with two 7-pounders and three Maxims arrived safely from Fourteen Streams. Commodity prices rose.
18th October	Boers occupied the Intermediate Pumping Station. Strong reconnoitring party sent out but the Boers had already left.
19th October	Price of provisions further increased. Major Scott-Turner appointed to command mounted troops, and superintend raising of the Kimberley Light Horse.
20th October	Colonel Kekewich issued proclamation and fixed the prices of some commodities. Reconnaissance made in direction of Intermediate Pumping Station. Losses: 1 killed. Kekewich issued counter-claim to Steyn's proclamation that Griqualand West is Free State territory. Traffic along Schmidt's Drift Road stopped by the Boers.
22nd October	Vryburg detachment of the Cape Police arrived. They confirmed news of the evacuation of Vryburg. Death of Assistant Commissioner H T Scott reported.
24th October	First serious engagement with the Boers at Dronfield and Macfarlane's farm. Boers repulsed. Commandant Botha killed. Losses: 3 killed, 20 wounded.
25th October	Boers closed in around Kimberley. Their closest position was 6,000 yards (5,500 m) from Wesselton Mine. Telegraph line to Barkly West cut. Kimberley totally isolated.
27th October	Kimberley Light Horse recruitment continued. Reconnaissances sent out to Spytfontein and Premier Mine.
30th October	Blacks who escaped from Spytfontein stated the Boers were commandeering blacks.
31st October	Boers fired first shell at reconnoitring party from position near Olifantsfontein police station; also made a show of force, but well out of the range of local guns. Colonel Kekewich issued further proclamation regulating food supply. Not more than 15 oxen to be slaughtered daily; beef not to be supplied in larger quantities than ½ pound (225 g) per day for each member of household; flour and meal only to be sold at rate of 1 pound (450 g) per week for each member of household.
1st November	Inspection of Royal Artillery and Diamond Fields Artillery at Newton. Boers occupied Macfarlane's farm and raided cattle. About 14:00, large explosion heard. Patrol reported dynamite supply at Dronfield Siding blown up. Supply Committee formed.
2nd November	Proclamation issued saying that bread was to be made of 25% flour and 75% meal. Inspector Berrange and the police contingent arrived from Upington.

Appendices

3rd November	Hooters sounded at 10:00. Boers intent on capturing cattle moved towards Kenilworth at noon. They were engaged by Major Peakman and immediately withdrew. Later in afternoon mounted men had small engagement with the Boers near Carter's Ridge. Losses: 1 killed, 2 wounded. Production ceased at Kimberley Mine. Otto's Kopje mine evacuated. Sanitary and other cattle captured by the Boers.
4th November	Commandant C J Wessels, demanded the immediate surrender of Kimberley. He also offered to receive any Afrikaner families who wanted to leave Kimberley and offered safe conduct to women and children of any nationality. Colonel replied inviting the Boer Commandant to undertake the occupation of Kimberley as 'an operation of war'. Captain Brown and 6 men on patrol duty taken prisoner.
5th November	Residents in the West End advised to leave their homes. 3,000 blacks left Kimberley but were turned back by the Boers.
6th November	At 06:00 the Boer ultimatum expired. First Boer shells fired at the defences.
7th November	Wesselton and Newton bombarded by Boer artillery. 50 shells from 12 guns fired at the defences. Reported losses – one cooking pot.
8th November	Wessels's offer printed in the *Diamond Fields Advertiser*.
9th November	Boers blew up more culverts on the railway north of Kimberley. The armoured train reconnoitred in that direction and was fired upon but there was no damage.
10th November	No bombardment. Armoured train fired upon.
11th November	Bombardment of the town commenced. Firing from 05.20 to 07:00. About 06:00 shell hit the pavement in front of the Catholic Church in Dutoitspan Road, and killed a black woman, the first civilian fatality. Mounted troops, under Colonel Scott-Turner, engaged the enemy near Otto's Kopje about 16:00. Losses: 1 killed, 1 wounded.
13th November	Boers seen strengthening their artillery position at Carter's Ridge with earthworks. Royal Artillery returned fire from the Reservoir. At 17.20 shelling of Premier Mine and Beaconsfield began. At 22:00 Boers fired at Kimberley. About 90 shells fired.
14th November	Further bombardment of Kimberley with a heavy spell between 12:00 and 14:00. St. Cyprian's Church hit. Total shells fired about 60. Royal Artillery fire from the Reservoir ended the Boer shelling. The 'Buffs' were 'At Home' to their friends at Belgravia Redoubt with tea and music. Cecil Rhodes and several ladies attended.
15th November	Bombardment resumed. After 46 rounds, heavy thunderstorm and downpour of rain brought the shelling to an end.
16th November	De Beers started to make shells. Sortie and engagement at Carter's Ridge. Losses: 1 killed, 16 wounded. First use of shrapnel by the Boers. Shelling of the Town Guard at the Reservoir.
17th November	Intermittent bombardment. Sortie beyond the defence works at Beaconsfield to assess defences around Alexandersfontein. Losses: 1 wounded.
19th November	General De La Rey sent in flag of truce, asking that families be sent out to his camp. His request is refused. Colonel Kekewich, on receipt of Head Commandant Wessels's offer to receive Afrikaner families into his camp, gave all such people the opportunity of leaving.
20th November	Boer sniping at Kenilworth repulsed by Maxim fire. Military authorities warned of the dangers of collecting pieces of Boer shells. Two De Beers miners arrive from Orange River. The absence of news from outside emphasised the isolation.
21st November	Skirmish beyond Kenilworth. Boer directed their shells towards the cattle guards. Relief column began march north.
22nd November	More sniping outside Kenilworth. Losses: 2 wounded. Boer gun at Spitskop fired 12 shells at the racecourse.
23rd November	Battle of Belmont.
24th November	Boer snipers at Kenilworth shelled. *Diamond Fields Advertiser* made first definite announcement that a Relief Column had set off for Kimberley. Boer destroyed railway culverts.
25th November	Mounted troops under Colonel Scott-Turner attacked the redoubts at Carter's Ridge. 28 Boers taken prisoner. Capture of Mauser rifles and ammunition. Losses: 6 killed, 30 wounded. Colonel Scott-Turner slightly wounded. Battle of Rooilaagte (Graspan/Enslin).

Kimberley Siege Account and Medal Roll

26th November	Heavy hailstorm.
27th November	Short artillery duel between the Boer gun at Carter's Ridge and the Reservoir. The armoured train made several trips to the north to draw the Boers. Shells fired into the town resulted in little damage. Communication by searchlight was established with Methuen's column.
28th November	Largest sortie of the siege. Mounted troops occupied Carter's Farm and then attacked the Boer redoubts on the Schmidt's Drift Road. Some shells and camp equipment captured. Attack then continued against the redoubts cleared on the attack of the 25th November. Three redoubts taken but failed at the fourth. After dark, the troops retired on Carter's Ridge. Colonel Scott-Turner was killed. Losses: 22 killed, 33 wounded. Battle of Modder River.
29th November	Funeral of Colonel Scott-Turner and the other fallen, with full military honours. More night signalling with the Relief Column. Major Peakman gazetted as officer commanding mounted troops.
1st December	Methuen at Klokfontein.
2nd December	Message from Methuen: "Gained passage Modder River after successful fight".
3rd December	Excursion by mounted troops. New outlying redoubt built. Methuen explained his plans for the relief. Rift between Kekewich and Rhodes complete.
4th December	Production ceased at De Beers Mine due to shortages of fuel and dynamite. Plans to remove citizens began.
5th December	Demonstration by the British troops towards the west. The Boers shell Premier Mine.
7th December	Reconnaissance by Colonel Chamier near Otto's Kopje.
9th December	Artillery duel between the field artillery posted near Otto's Kopje and Kamfersdam. Losses: 1 killed, 6 wounded.
10th December	Heavy firing heard from Spytfontein.
11th December	Battle of Magersfontein. British shells seen bursting over the kopjes.
15th December	Artillery duel between Wesselton Mine and the Boers at Susannah.
20th December	Military Authorities took control of tea, coffee and meal. Reconnaissance towards Tollpan, no casualties.
22nd December	Reconnaissance to Carter's Ridge by mounted troops with Diamond Fields Artillery and a detachment of North Lancashire Regiment. One horse the only casualty.
23rd December	Temperatures measured at over 41° C (105° F) in the shade.
25th December	Christmas message received from the Queen via the Relief Column; "I wish you and all my brave soldiers a happy Christmas. God protect and bless you all". A message was also received from the High Commissioner to the garrison and inhabitants of Kimberley conveying "Best wishes for their good luck on Christmas Day and in the coming New Year".
26th December	Boers shelled the Wesselton Mine. Heavy artillery fire heard from Spytfontein. Work commenced on Long Cecil.
28th December	Further proclamation issued regulating the sale of food.
30th December	Loyal New Year message sent to Her Majesty the Queen. Private Kelly, KRV, found dead in Kimberley Mine.
31st December	Edict said all lights have to be extinguished at 21:30. Boers fired a shell at Premier Mine at midnight. Ferreira replaced Wessels.
1900	
1st January	Reconnaissance made towards Carter's Farm. 13 private cattle captured by the Boers.
2nd January	Meat ration reduced to a ¼ pound (115 g) per adult and 2 ounces (60 g) per child per day.
3rd January	Meat only to be issued from the Market Hall. Colonel Kekewich issued a Proclamation prohibiting lights after 21:00.
5th January	Sale of intoxicating liquors outside barriers prohibited. Lieutenant Colonel Peakman made reconnaissance near Tollpan.

Appendices

7th January	Boers made unsuccessful attempts to rustle cattle near Kenilworth.
8th January	Artillery duel between No 1 Redoubt and the Boer guns at Kamfersdam. Horse meat served for the first time.
9th January	Boers re-occupied Carter's Ridge.
10th January	Shelling renewed by Boers from several positions and at an increased level. Roberts arrives in Cape Town.
11th January	Boer shells targeted the Premier Mine.
12th January	Heliographic communication established with Methuen.
13th January	Price of meat raised. Beef is 12 Pence per lb (450 g) and horseflesh 9 Pence per lb.
16th January	Soup kitchen opened. 3,000 pints (1,710 lt) of soup were distributed on the first day and this rose to 16,000 pints (9,120 lt) by the end of the siege.
17th January	Lieutenant Colonel Peakman and Lieutenant Cramp made a successful reconnaissance near Olifantsfontein.
19th January	Long Cecil is fired for the first time.
20th January	The following notice appeared outside meat supply building; "The full ration of half-pound of meat for two days can be allowed to-day".
23rd January	Long Cecil fired shells at the Intermediate Station and Kamfersdam.
24th January	Kimberley shelled by nine 9-pounder guns on all sides from 03.30 until after dark. Most parts of Kimberley affected. Miss Maggie Maddocks, 16 Scholtz Street, killed in her room. Several shells fell near Nazareth House and the Hospital. Much damage to property resulted. Approximately 300 shells fired into the town. Long Cecil fired 60 shells and then went out of action.
25th January	Intermittent night-time shelling followed by day-time bombardment. High level of property damage.
26th January	Level of shelling much reduced.
3rd February	Boers at Kamfersdam fired at Kimberley Mine searchlight.
7th February	Long Tom, the 100-pounder, mounted at Kamfersdam, began to shell the town at 11:00.
8th February	Long Tom fired 29 shells into Kimberley during the afternoon. Damage considerable. One shell struck Middlebrook's Studio. A splinter from it parted the Cross from its mounting at St Mary's Catholic Cathedral.
9th February	About 04:00, the 100 pound shells begin to rain onto Kimberley. Shelling intermittent until 18:00. Death of George Labram in the Grand Hotel.
10th February	Bombardment continued with great damage to property. Funeral of Labram at 20:00. Boers shelled the vicinity from 20:00 until midnight. One person wounded and considerable damage to property. The Mayor appealed to Roberts for relief. *Diamond Fields Advertiser* published "Why Kimberley cannot wait" and was banned.
11th February	No shelling as it was a Sunday. Over 2,500 people, mostly women and children, descended 1,200 feet into Kimberley and De Beers Mines at the invitation of Cecil Rhodes. The bomb-proof shelters in Pniel Road, Boshof Road and Transvaal Road, and under De Beers Road railway bridge were crowded. Many shelters erected.
12th February	Houses burnt down at Kenilworth by shelling. Solid and shrapnel shells burst near the Sanatorium and Hospital. Men ordered up from the mines.
13th February	The theatre was again struck by shrapnel, and the Presbyterian Church and organ were damaged. All parts of the town were damaged by shelling.
14th February	More 100-pounder shells fired into the city. Seizure of Alexandersfontein with 6 men wounded.
15th February	The final day of shelling by the Boers. Only six 100-pounder and a few smaller shells fell in town. The relieving troops were seen from Kimberley around 14.30 and they rode into town about 17:00. General French arrived around 19:00. The end of the siege.
16th February	Battle of Dronfield. The Boers escaped with Long Tom. The *Diamond Fields Advertiser* restarted publication.

Appendix 02 – Photographs of Kimberley

De Beers Compound from the Conning Tower, looking west

De Beers Compound with the Botanical Gardens behind, looking south

Appendices

The view from the Conning Tower, looking north

The view from the Conning Tower, looking north

A contemporary publication gave the town this rather unflattering description: "The town itself is very unattractive. The streets are not laid out in regular lengths, wide and straight, with crossings at right angles at equal distances, as in most other South African towns, but are irregular and unequal, a formation traceable to its 'mushroom' origin. Only those in search of wealth would willingly live in Kimberley. It is in an

Kimberley Siege Account and Medal Roll

unpicturesque region, flat and monotonous, without any foliage or hills of any height to relieve the dulness. Sometimes months elapse without rainfall, and as a consequence the streets are often swept by choking dust-storms. There are several public buildings, such as the handsome Court House, in Market Square, the Masonic Temple, the new Town Hall, and the Kimberley Club; but the majority of the houses are by no means elegantly constructed, and are rendered even more ugly by corrugated iron roofing."

A view of Kimberley looking north west

A view of to Wimbledon Ridge and Spitzkop

Appendix 03 – Garrison strength

In Kekewich's despatch, weekly returns are included for the period from 4th October 1899 to 22nd November 1899. It is not clear why the records stopped so early.

4th October 1899

Unit	Officers	Men	Total
Staff	3		3
RGA	3	90	93
RE	1	50	51
LNLR	11	420	431
RAMC	1	5	6
ASC	1	4	5
DFA			
Maxim			
KRV			
DFH			
KLH			
CP			
KTG			
Total	20	569	589

11th October 1899

Unit	Officers	Men	Total
Staff	3	0	3
RGA	4	90	94
RE	1	50	51
LNLR	11	424	435
RAMC	1	5	6
ASC	1	4	5
DFA	4	93	97
Maxim	0	32	32
KRV	16	386	352
DFH	6	172	178
KLH	0	0	0
CP	1	25	26
KTG	80	1,223	1,303
Total	128	2,504	2,582

18th October 1899

Unit	Officers	Men	Total
Staff	3	0	3
RGA	4	90	94
RE	1	50	51
LNLR	12	424	436
RAMC	1	5	6
ASC	1	8	9
DFA	5	103	108
Maxim	0	32	32
KRV	15	365	380
DFH	6	162	168
KLH	0	0	0
CP	10	240	250
KTG	81	1,760	1,841
Total	139	3,239	3,378

25th October 1899

Unit	Officers	Men	Total
Staff	2	0	2
RGA	4	90	94
RE	1	50	51
LNLR	11	424	435
RAMC	1	5	6
ASC	1	8	9
DFA	5	103	108
Maxim	0	32	32
KRV	15	326	341
DFH	6	162	168
KLH	2	210	212
CP	10	227	237
KTG	85	1,823	1,908
Total	143	3,460	3,603

1st November 1899

Unit	Officers	Men	Total
Staff	2	0	2
RGA	4	90	94
RE	1	50	51
LNLR	11	423	434
RAMC	1	5	6
ASC	1	8	9
DFA	5	98	103
Maxim	0	32	32
KRV	16	383	399
DFH	7	160	167
KLH	17	298	315
CP	15	320	335
KTG	105	2,167	2,272
Total	185	4,034	4,219

8th November 1899

Unit	Officers	Men	Total
Staff	2	0	2
RGA	4	90	94
RE	1	50	51
LNLR	11	423	434
RAMC	1	5	6
ASC	1	8	9
DFA	5	99	104
Maxim	0	32	32
KRV	15	383	398
DFH	8	159	167
KLH	17	332	349
CP	17	336	353
KTG	116	2,280	2,396
Total	198	4,197	4,395

15th November 1899

Unit	Officers	Men	Total
Staff	2	0	2
RGA	4	90	94
RE	1	50	51
LNLR	11	423	434
RAMC	1	5	6
ASC	1	8	9
DFA	4	102	106
Maxim	0	32	32
KRV	15	385	400
DFH	8	157	165
KLH	17	334	351
CP	19	334	353
KTG	117	2,296	2,413
Total	200	4,216	4,416

22nd November 1899

Unit	Officers	Men	Total
Staff	2	0	2
RGA	4	90	94
RE	1	50	51
LNLR	11	423	434
RAMC	1	5	6
ASC	1	8	9
DFA	4	104	108
Maxim	0	32	32
KRV	15	386	401
DFH	8	157	165
KLH	18	343	361
CP	18	327	345
KTG	130	2,520	2,650
Total	213	4,445	4,658

Kimberley Siege Account and Medal Roll

The overall strength of the garrison has never been definitively agreed. One reason for this is that the number of people under arms varied from time to time. The table that follows takes the various estimates that have been produced and tries to estimate what the total strength of the garrison would have been.

5,750 Garrison strength

Unit	Times History[42]	19 Nov 1899[43]	25 Nov 1899	10 Dec 1899	Medal roll[44]	Nominal roll[45]	Estimated total[46]
Staff[47]		10				124	25
RGA	93	94	94	578	98	94	98
RE	51	51	52		54	51	54
LNLR	444	455	434		436	435	434
RAMC		6	6		6		6
ASC		9	9		19	9	19
DFA	113	106	108		126	113	126
Maxim	44	32	34		32	38	32
KRV	495	565	401	1,376	819	584	819
DFH[48]	232	165	165				0
KLH	427	353	361		401	437	401
CP	478	352	386		511	574	511
KTG	2,353	2,573	2,649	2,636	2,616	3,117	3,117
Other		-165	15		265		108
Total	4,730	4,606	4,711	4,590	5,383	4,128	5,750

Based on this analysis, it is estimated the military garrison had a strength of 5,750 men and women. The difference of 367 between the garrison total and the medal roll total is accounted for by the facts that, first, the medals with no clasps to the KTG have been omitted and, second, there are many mens' names on the nominal roll who are not reflected in the published medal roll. The reasons for their omission are not clear. Perhaps they served for only a short time, they were not enrolled (like the 75 already identified as such) or they may have moved away from Kimberley after the siege and could not be traced by the military authorities when it came to compile the rolls. On the positive side, the authorities do seem to have recognised the participation of the majority of the garrison and the evidence is that the debates about who served in the siege continued long after the Boer War had ended.

42 Summarised figures based on the table in the Times History, Volume IV, page 538. Note that some units have been omitted from this summary eg ASC.
43 The figures for these 3 columns are taken from Kekewich's diary entries on 19th November 1899, 25th November 1899 and 10th December 1899.
44 The medal roll figures will under-estimate the total because, in those instances where a man forfeited his QSA, the man's name is omitted from the roll. The 75 no clasp QSAs to the KTG have been omitted but to the total has been added the 75 medals awarded to the POC resulting in no net change for the KTG.
45 The nominal rolls require careful counting as there are several instances of the same man being listed for two different locations eg DDMB as a whole unit and the detachment at Otto's Kopje.
46 The 60 nurses' QSAs have also been omitted from all the sets of figures but they have been included in the 'Other' row for the estimated total.
47 There was no separate staff during the siege. Instead, the officers who composed Kekewich's staff were drawn from the other units. In the nominal roll, 124 men were listed as comprising the HQ staff and this figure included the supply depot staff and some of the telegraph signallers. The 25 men in the Estimated Total column mainly come from the black and Asian supply depots plus 9 other men who do not appear on the medal rolls.
48 The Diamond Fields Horse was included with the KRV in the medal roll.

Appendix 04 – Officers involved in the siege

Kimberley Siege Account and Medal Roll

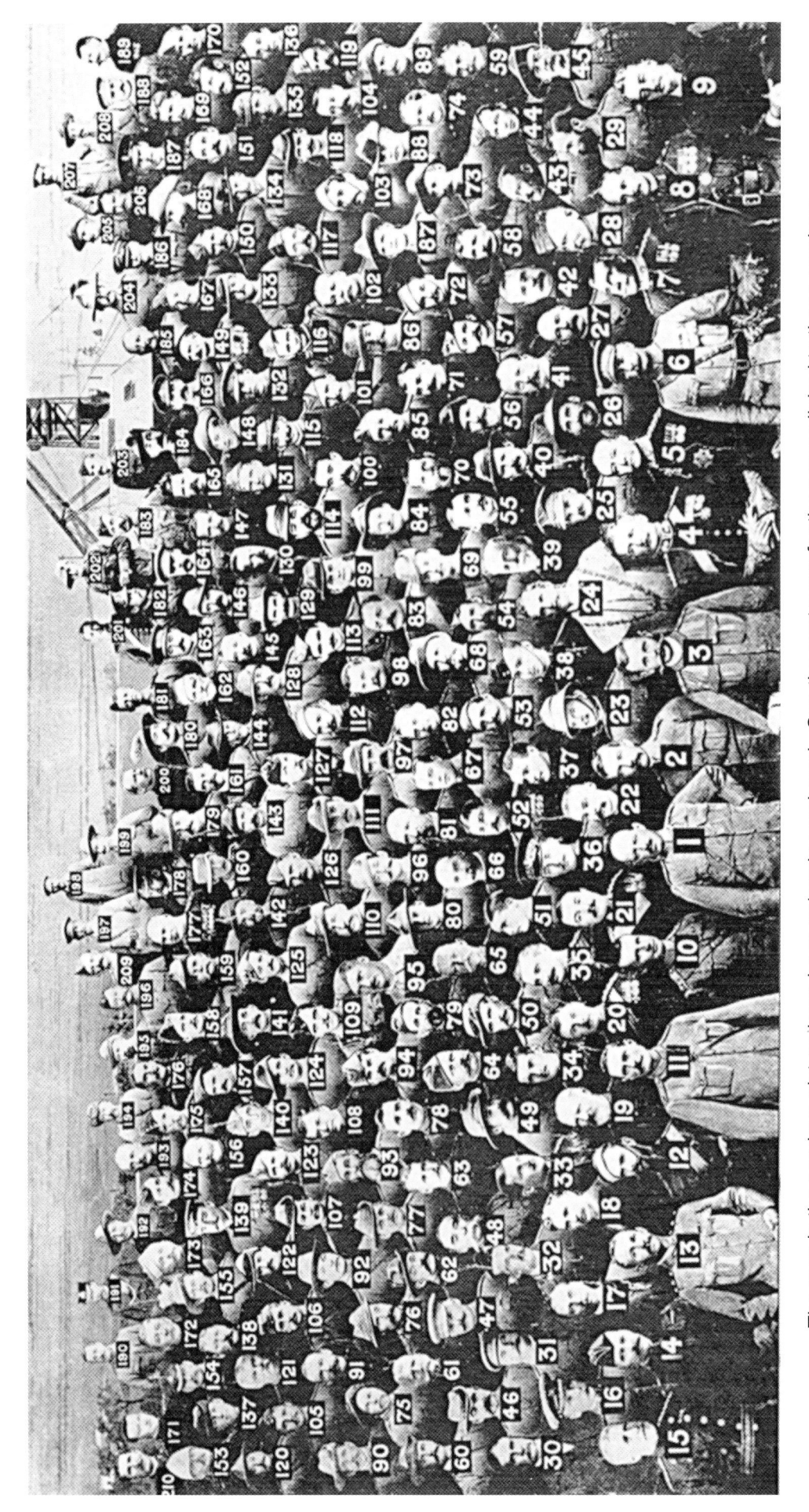

290

The men in the previous picture have been uniquely numbered. See the next page for the names linked to these numbers.

Appendices

#	Name
68	Adams, Capt H Goold, KTG
69	Angel, Capt T L, KTG
62	Armstrong, Capt J, KTG
42	Ashe, Dr E O, KTG.
207	Attwood, Lt A J, CP
28	Ayliff, Maj W E, CP
163	Banham, Lt W C, KRV
119	Bayman, Lt W, KTG
81	Beddome, Capt E I, KTG
197	Belk, Lt S W, KLH
167	Bennett, Lt G, KRV
156	Bennie, Lt A, KTG
186	Berrange, Capt C A L, CP
38	Bingham, Lt C H M, LNLR
153	Bird, Lt I, KTG
84	Birt, Lt A G, KTG
132	Bishop, Lt R *
177	Black, Maj A O, KRV
70	Blackbeard, Capt C A, KTG
89	Blacking, Lt E, KTG
64	Blum, Capt A, KTG
154	Bodley, Capt J H, KRV
44	Booth, Capt R D, KTG
123	Booth, Lt J R, KTG
80	Bowen, Capt H J Ap O, KLH
180	Braine, Lt W, KRV
198	Brand, Capt R, KLH
164	Bridge, Capt J M, KRV
92	Britton, Lt W D, KTG
152	Callen, Lt T, KTG
104	Carstairs Rogers, Lt F, KTG
4	Chamier, Lt Col G D, RGA
95	Channer, Capt A J, KRV
193	Chatfield, Lt R, KLH
160	Chilman, Lt H R, KTG
165	Church, Capt G, KRV
33	Clifford, Lt W R, LNLR
202	Close, Lt H M, RGA
194	Coghlan, Capt C P J, KTG
195	Coghlan, Lt J J, KTG
191	Colvin, Capt J W, CP
208	Cowieson, Capt D, CP
127	Croxford, Lt P G, KTG
82	Cruickshank, Capt A, KTG
150	Curry, Lt A W, KTG
61	Dallas, Capt S, KTG
139	Damant, Lt F H, KTG
187	Davis, Capt W H, CP
32	De Putron, Lt C, LNLR
128	Devenish, Lt F A R, KTG
57	Drew, Lt P J V, KLH
93	Druce, Lt J C, KTG
21	Dunbar, Capt J B, KTG
137	Eliot, Lt A E A, KTG
23	Eliott, Maj F A H, CP
54	Elkin, Capt W S, KTG
88	Elliot, Lt K C, KTG
79	Ellis, Capt G K, KTG
58	Faulkner, Capt W H, KTG
183	Faulkner, Lt T J, DFA
106	Field, Lt H G, KTG
6	Finlayson, Lt Col R A, KRV
205	Fisher, Capt E M, CP
34	Fletcher, Lt W J C, LNLR.
157	Flynn, Lt J F, KTG
175	Ford, Capt T J, KRV
111	Franceys, Lt A L, KTG
11	Fraser, Maj J R, LNLR
141	Fynn, Lt W D, KTG
130	Gentleman, Lt J W, KTG
31	Gill, Lt H J, LNLR
155	Goate, Lt E W C, KTG
41	Goffe, E
16	Gorle, Maj H V, ASC
184	Green, Capt A J, KRV
140	Haddock, Capt R S, KTG
67	Haidler, Capt F, KTG
5	Harris, Lt Col D, KTG
151	Harris, Lt L W H, KTG
122	Harris, Lt A H, KRV
158	Harrison, Lt F, KRV
185	Hayes, Capt H, CP
209	Hayston, Lt W, KTG
99	Hearn, Lt D P, KTG
181	Heberden, Capt G A, KLH
18	Henderson, Capt R H, KTG
55	Hertog, Capt C E, KTG
196	Hickson-Mahony, Maj J, KLH
199	Hobson, Lt C H, KLH
149	Hogg, Lt J C, KTG
179	Hollingworth, Lt R H, KRV
27	Holton, Lt H, KTG
53	Hornby, Capt W, KTG
138	Hulley, Lt T H, KTG
25	Humphrys, Capt E T, KRV
121	Idebski, Lt W M.
146	Irwin, Lt G, KTG
114	Johns, Lt S, KTG
107	Johnson, Lt G H, KTG
201	Johnston, Lt H B H, RGA
143	Johnston, Lt J W, KTG
131	Jones, Lt E, KTG
129	Jones, Lt T J M *
171	Joyce, Lt E W, KLH
39	Judge, E A
135	Kearns, Lt F, KTG
142	Keating, Lt E W, KTG
1	Kekewich, Lt Col R G, LNLR
115	King, Lt G C, KTG
22	Labram, G
126	Lambourne, Lt G, KTG
94	Lawrence, Lt W, KTG
189	Lorimer, Maj S, CP
37	Lowndes, Lt J G, LNLR
176	MacDougall, Lt E A, KLH
10	MacInnes, Lt D S, RE
113	Macpherson, Lt A B, KTG
178	Madoc, Lt H W, SAC
40	Mallett, Capt P W, KTG
56	Mandy, Capt F, KTG
77	Marshall, Lt H, KTG
173	Martin, Lt A H, KRV
161	Matthews, Lt T H, KRV
12	May, Maj T J, DFA
43	McClintock, Lt R L, RE
116	McKay, Lt G G, KTG
169	Milne, Lt W G, KRV
73	Moseley, Capt E H, KTG
15	Murray, Lt Col W H E, LNLR
188	Neale-Shutte, Capt R F, CP
49	Nelson, Capt W, KTG
105	Nicholson, Lt N, KTG
35	O'Brien, Capt T H, KTG
20	O'Gorman, Lt C J, RAMC
29	O'Meara, Capt B E A, KTG
2	O'Meara, Maj W A J, RE
148	O'Molony, Lt S, KTG
75	Oats, Lt F, KTG
24	Oliver, Capt H A, KTG
203	Ortlepp, Surg A J, DFA
144	Osborne, Lt C, KTG
117	Paley, Lt G, KTG
87	Peake, Lt S, KTG
13	Peakman, Lt Col T C, KLH
100	Penny, Lt E A, KTG
85	Percy, Lt R J, KTG
74	Pickering, Capt W, KTG
66	Pim, Capt H, KTG
120	Plane, Lt F W, KTG
172	Pooley, Capt J, KTG
103	Presow, Lt R, KTG
9	Rhodes, Col C J, KRV
200	Rickman, Capt W E, KLH.
109	Rind, Lt *
8	Robinson, Lt Col M B, CP
7	Rodger, Maj T H, KRV
63	Rugg, Capt H, KTG
190	Rush, Capt W W, CP
182	Rynd, Lt F F, RGA
125	Sadler, Lt J M, KTG
166	Salaman, Lt S, KRV
72	Sandham, Capt J, KTG
65	Saunders, Capt G A, KTG
108	Schmidt, Lt H, KTG
48	Scott, Capt W, DH
192	Scott, Maj R G, KLH
3	Scott-Turner, Lt Col H, KLH
174	Shackleton, Capt C C, KRV
147	Sheasby, Lt J B, KTG
17	Smartt, Dr Hon T W, KTG
134	Smith, Lt D W, KTG
102	Smith, Lt F W, KTG
112	Smith, Lt R A L, KTG
14	Smith, Surg Maj J A J, KRV
133	Solomon, Lt R, KTG
204	Sprigg, Capt A P, KLH
83	Stead, Lt B, KTG
59	Stevenson, Capt J, KTG
145	Stewart, Lt J, KTG
50	Swanson, Capt J, KTG
60	Tabuteau, Capt C, KTG
47	Tabuteau, Capt H, KTG
124	Tait, Lt S, KTG
96	Thorpe, Lt J H, KTG
45	Tidd-Pratt, Capt S, KTG
170	Tillemans, Lt A A, KRV
118	Troup, Lt J, KTG
71	Tyson, Capt T D, KTG
110	Tyson, Lt J D, KTG
162	Waldek, Capt S P, KRV
51	Wallace, Lt A R, LNLR
136	Wallace, Lt C O
19	Watkins, Dr A H, KTG
78	Watson, Lt J W, KTG
76	Webbstock, Lt H J, KTG
36	Webster, Lt A McC, LNLR
91	Wells, Lt E R, KTG
86	Wells, Lt W H, KTG
98	Whiley, Lt G E, KTG
46	White, Capt G, KTG
210	White, Lt J T, CP
168	Wilcox, Lt W J, KRV
90	Wilkins, Lt A, KTG
206	Williams, Capt A S, KLH
30	Williams, Gardner F
97	Woodbourne, Lt T J, KTG
26	Woodman, Lt Rev T, KTG
52	Woodward, Lt F W, LNLR
159	Wright, Capt A J, KRV
101	Yates, Lt F G, KTG

* Military officers that cannot be find on the medal roll. Lt Rind is possibly a duplicate of Lt Rynd? Note that some men (eg Belk & Holton) appear on the medal rolls as NCOs.

Appendix 05 – 50th Anniversary reunion (15th February 1950)

Extreme back row (pillar to pillar, left to right): H Norman Reynolds, R Timm, Donald McHardy, A J Beet, H van der Heyden, Jos Verheyen, G Hitchman, *Colonel H F Lardner DSO MC VD*, B B Ledger, Louis F Lezard, W G Druce, W J Watridge, ----, "Wallie" Dickens, H J Savage, G M Hunter, *N Cameron*.

Third and fourth rows (left to right): S Tait, "Shamus" O'Brien, ----, G M Robertson, P J (Piet) Waldek, A R Jenkins, ----, J Adamson, J Swan, T Megaw, ----, ----, ----, J F Davidson, ----, J C W Radloff, ----, G Clack, *P Laing*, J Leck, *A E Nieuwenhuis*, T B Tredrea, T I Bradshaw, H Keat, D D Shepherd, W F Shepherd, C Lefevre, ----, H Borgstrom, ----, ----, P Poulton, P D Coxwell, ----, W H Tredrea, M E Doherty, T J Grose, M Keet, ----, J C Acker, W Yeowart, R S Haddock, D McCarthy, ----, J T McCarthy, M J de Smidt, G A de Smidt, ----, J Gibbs, P Senier, W Saunders.

Second row (left to right): W J Hodgkinson, E Willcock, G H Marnitz, F A Wustman, G Ainsley, A E Eales, H S J Borgstrom, G H F Harris, J E Rose, ----, ----, ----, J E Harding, C de M Franklin, G Ring, ----, W Martin, A H Ebdon, A M Moult, E Bevan, G Hodgson, W J Spence, W Main, J M Bridge, J Oehley, B P Gould.

Seated in front row (left to right): J M Sadler, G W O'Brien, C T A Cotty, *J Blunden*, ----, C H Jarvis, F W Kidwell, G H Ayrton, S F (Fanie) du Toit, R C Jobson, A O Franklin, "Gabbie" Smith, W D Fynn, Hon R H Henderson CMG, H J Lancaster, L J Edmeades (Mayor, 1950), J M Powell, W B Tutt, R MacAskill, E Pilkington, J Sharp, H J C Seaward, H D Baatjes, J G de Witt, C E Hertog.

Seated on ground (left to right): Markie Lewis, R P Hayes, G H Dodd.

Standing at front left front (left to right): G Kelly, C T Hawley.

Standing at right front (left to right): Felix du Prat, J McCurdy.

(Names in grey, italic text have not been traced on the medal roll)

292

Appendix 06 – Plans of the defences

In his report to the RE Institute, Lt MacInnes included a number of plans of the defensive works. These are reproduced here.

The map on the right provides a key to the fifteen plans that follow:

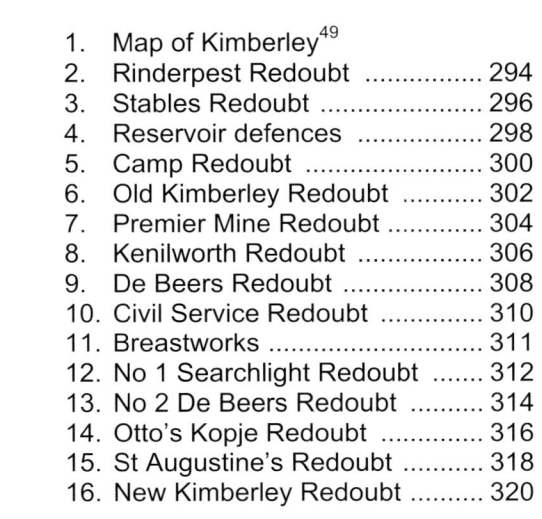

Index of the plans:

1. Map of Kimberley[49]
2. Rinderpest Redoubt 294
3. Stables Redoubt 296
4. Reservoir defences 298
5. Camp Redoubt 300
6. Old Kimberley Redoubt 302
7. Premier Mine Redoubt 304
8. Kenilworth Redoubt 306
9. De Beers Redoubt 308
10. Civil Service Redoubt 310
11. Breastworks 311
12. No 1 Searchlight Redoubt 312
13. No 2 De Beers Redoubt 314
14. Otto's Kopje Redoubt 316
15. St Augustine's Redoubt 318
16. New Kimberley Redoubt 320

The text that accompanied these plans can be seen on page 384.

See page 493 for photographs of the defences.

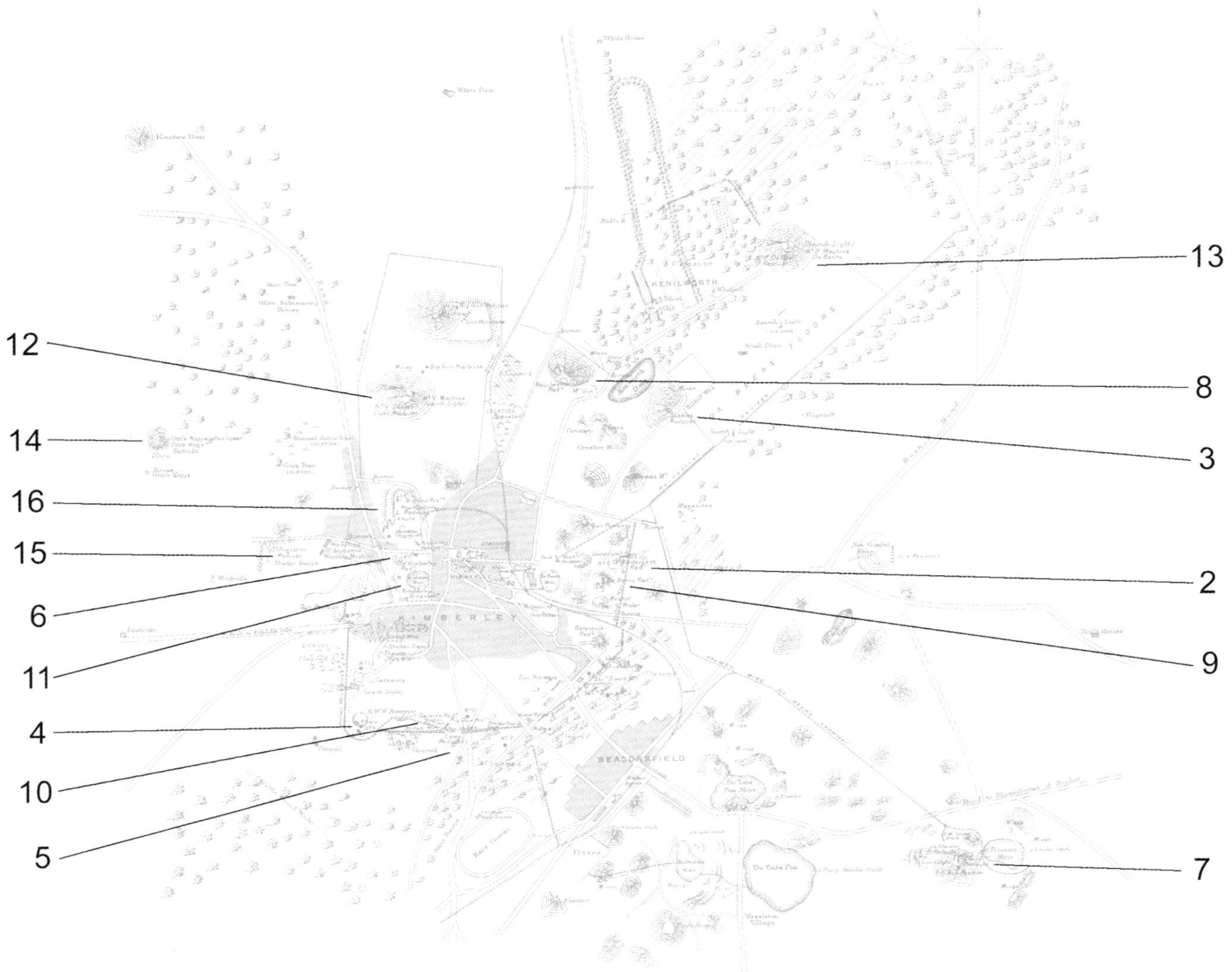

---

[49] This map is reproduced on page 24

293

Kimberley Siege Account and Medal Roll

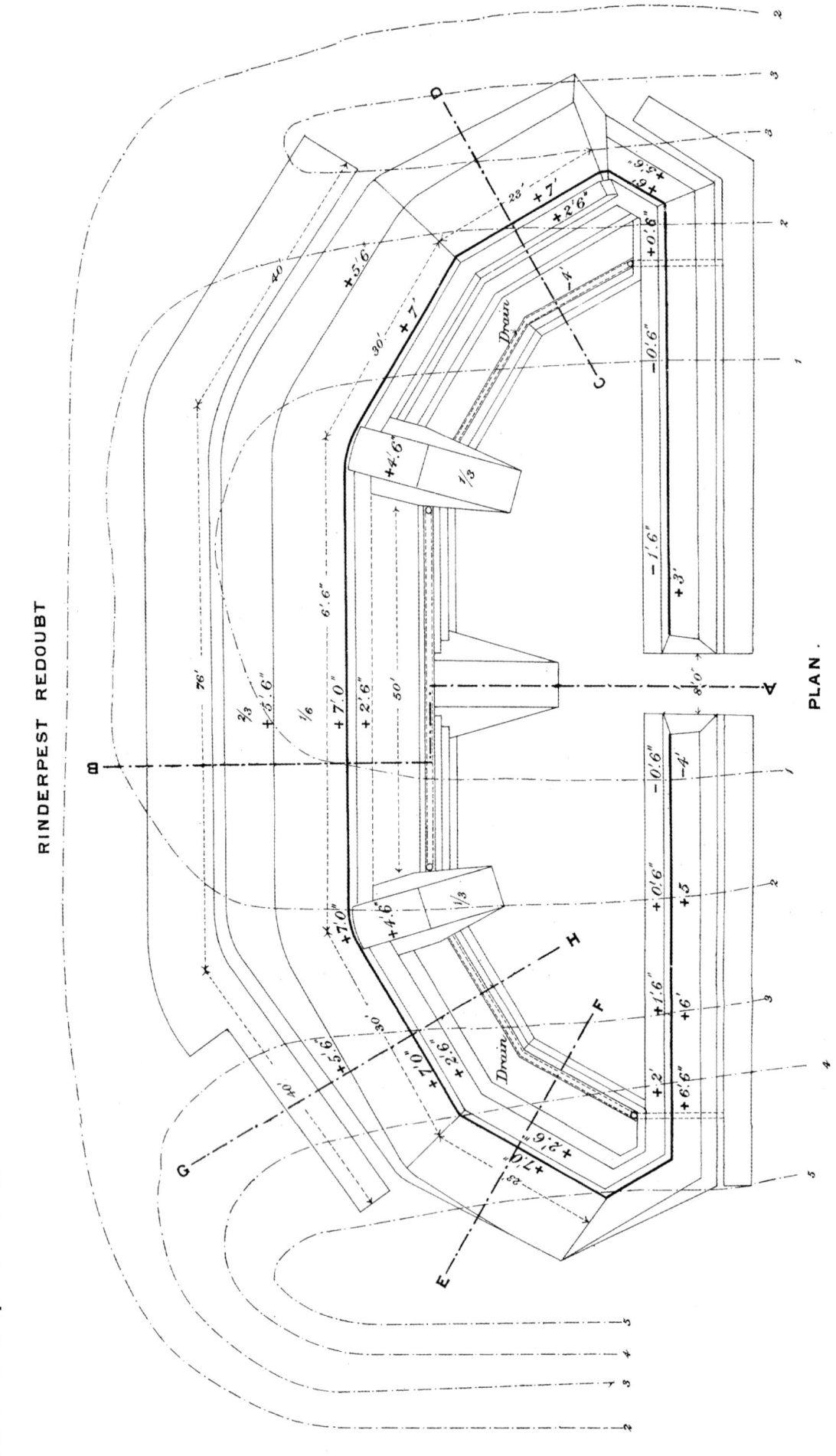

Plan 2: Rinderpest Redoubt

Appendices

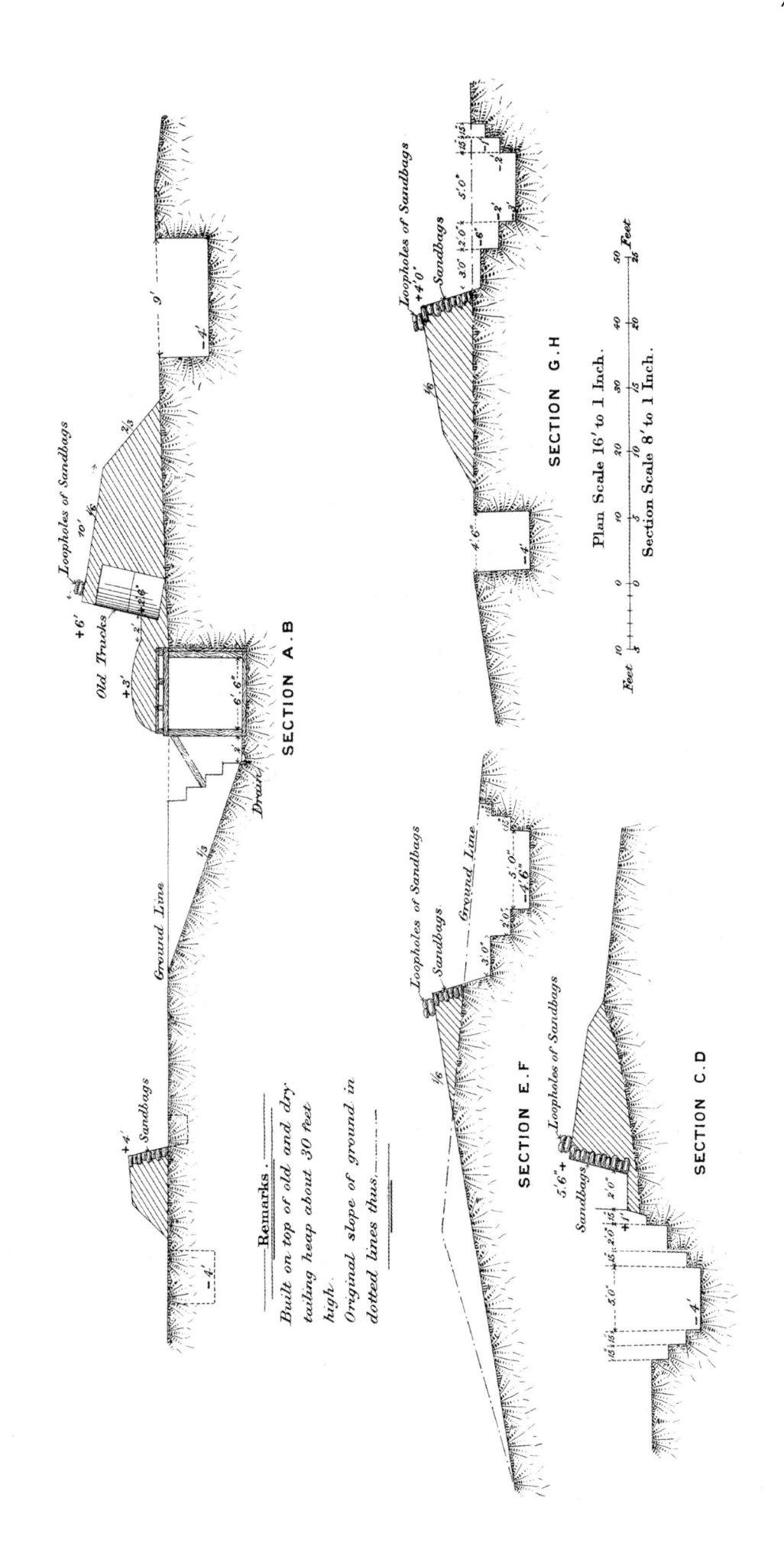

Plan 3: Stables redoubt

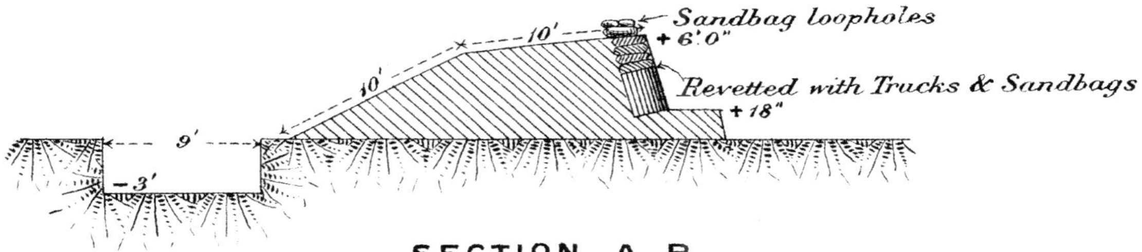

SECTION A.B.

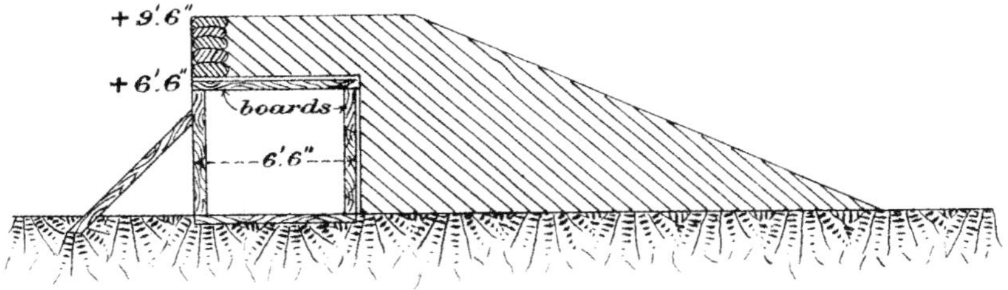

Sandbag loopholes
+ 6'.0"
Revetted with Trucks & Sandbags
+ 18"
10'
10'
9'
- 3'

SECTION C.D.

+ 9'.6"
+ 6'.6"
boards
6'.6"

Remarks.

Built on top of tailing heap about 60 feet high. Heap very wet indeed and much trouble was experienced with revetments &c. sinking in the mud, consequently the blindage could not be placed under the parapet.

Plan Scale 24' to 1 inch. 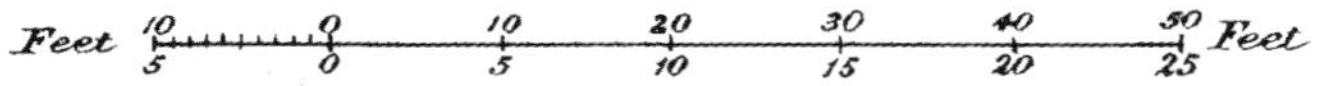
Section Scale 12' to 1 inch.

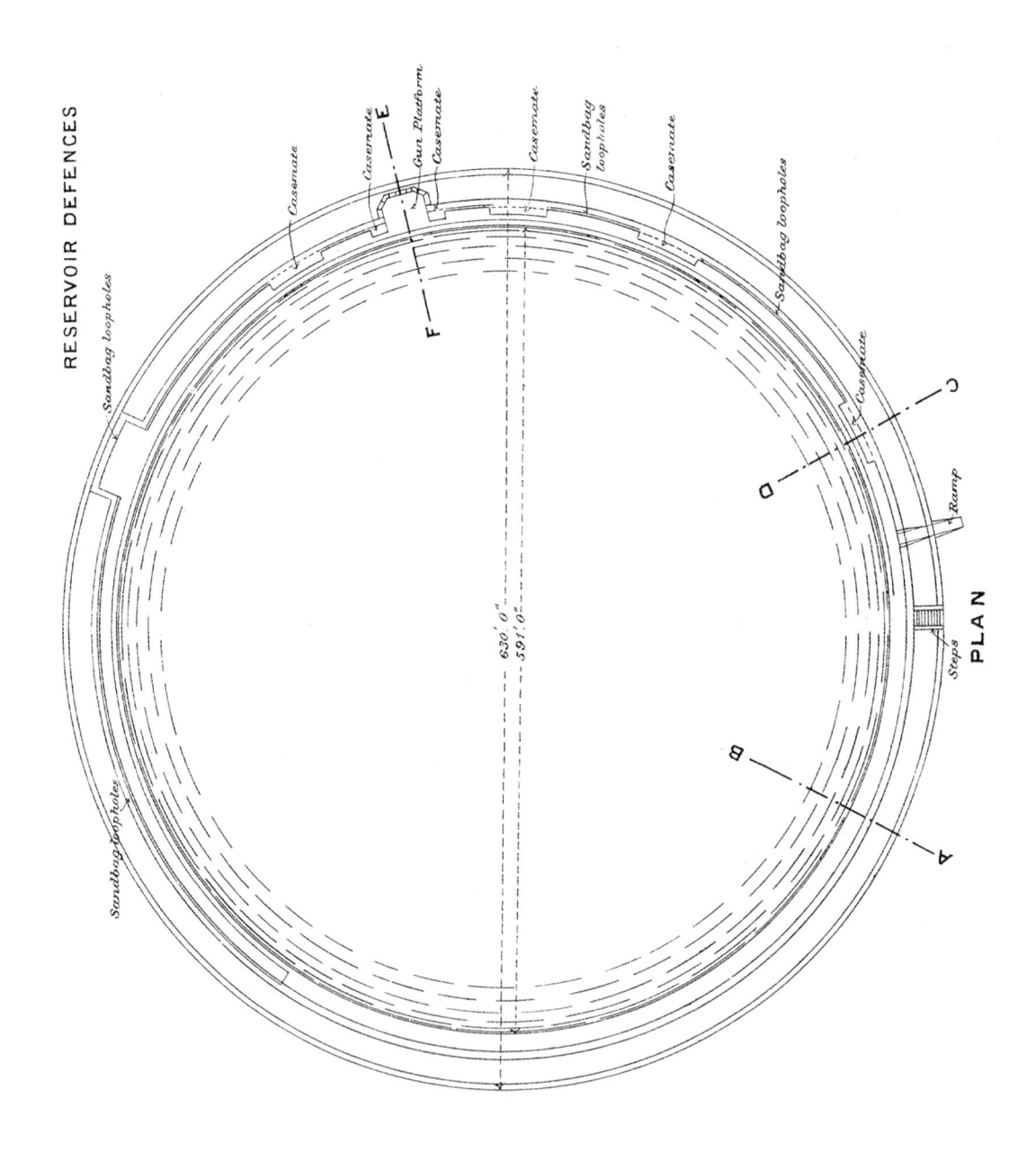

Kimberley Siege Account and Medal Roll

Plan 4: Reservoir defences

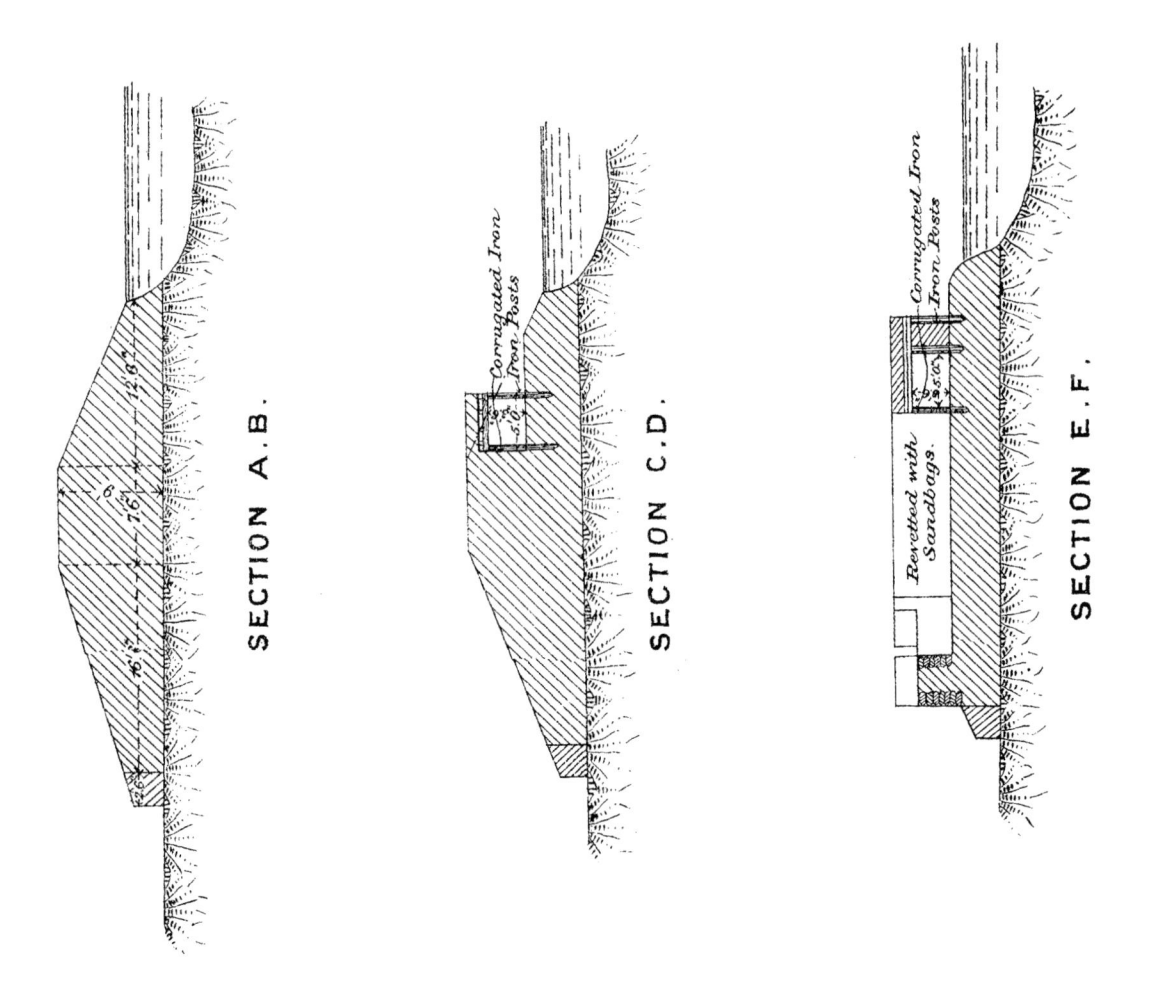

SECTION A.B.

SECTION C.D.
Corrugated Iron
Iron Posts

SECTION E.F.
Corrugated Iron
Iron Posts
Revetted with Sandbags.

Kimberley Siege Account and Medal Roll

Plan 5: Camp Redoubt

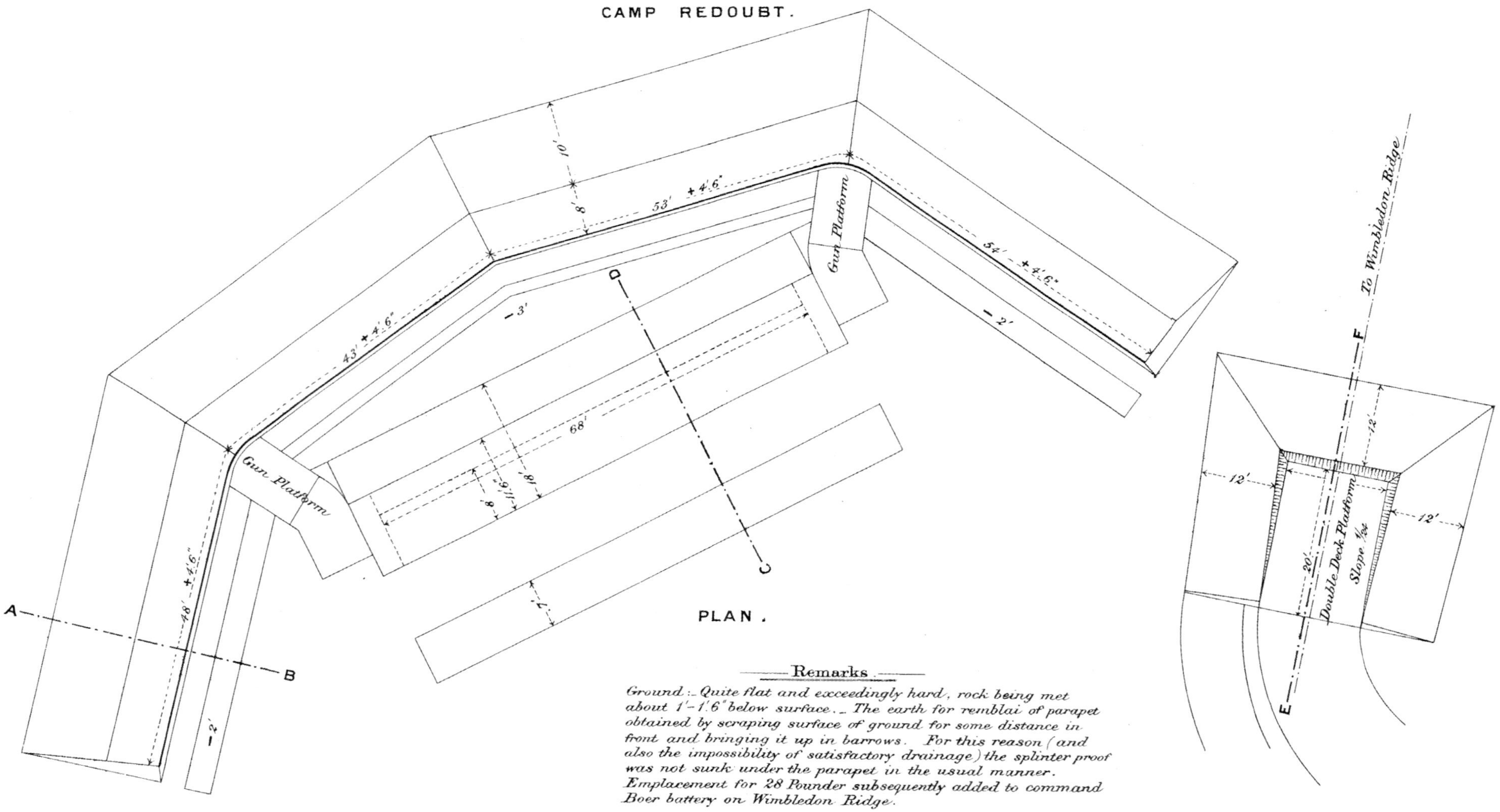

CAMP REDOUBT.

PLAN.

To Wimbledon Ridge

Double Deck Platform
Slope ¾

Gun Platform

Gun Platform

Remarks

Ground:- Quite flat and exceedingly hard, rock being met about 1'-1'6" below surface. - The earth for remblai of parapet obtained by scraping surface of ground for some distance in front and bringing it up in barrows. For this reason (and also the impossibility of satisfactory drainage) the splinter proof was not sunk under the parapet in the usual manner. Emplacement for 28 Pounder subsequently added to command Boer battery on Wimbledon Ridge.

Appendices

SECTION E.F.

Revetted with Sandbags.
Double Deck Platform
Slope 1/24
+3'
-3'

SECTION C.D.

Sandbags
11'
Iron Corrugated Iron Frame
11.6
18'
+7.6"
5'
10'
7'
-2'

SECTION A.B.

Sandbag loopholes
Sandbags
+4'6"
8'
10'
4'
-2'

Plan Scale, 16' to 1 inch.
Section Scale, 8' to 1 inch.

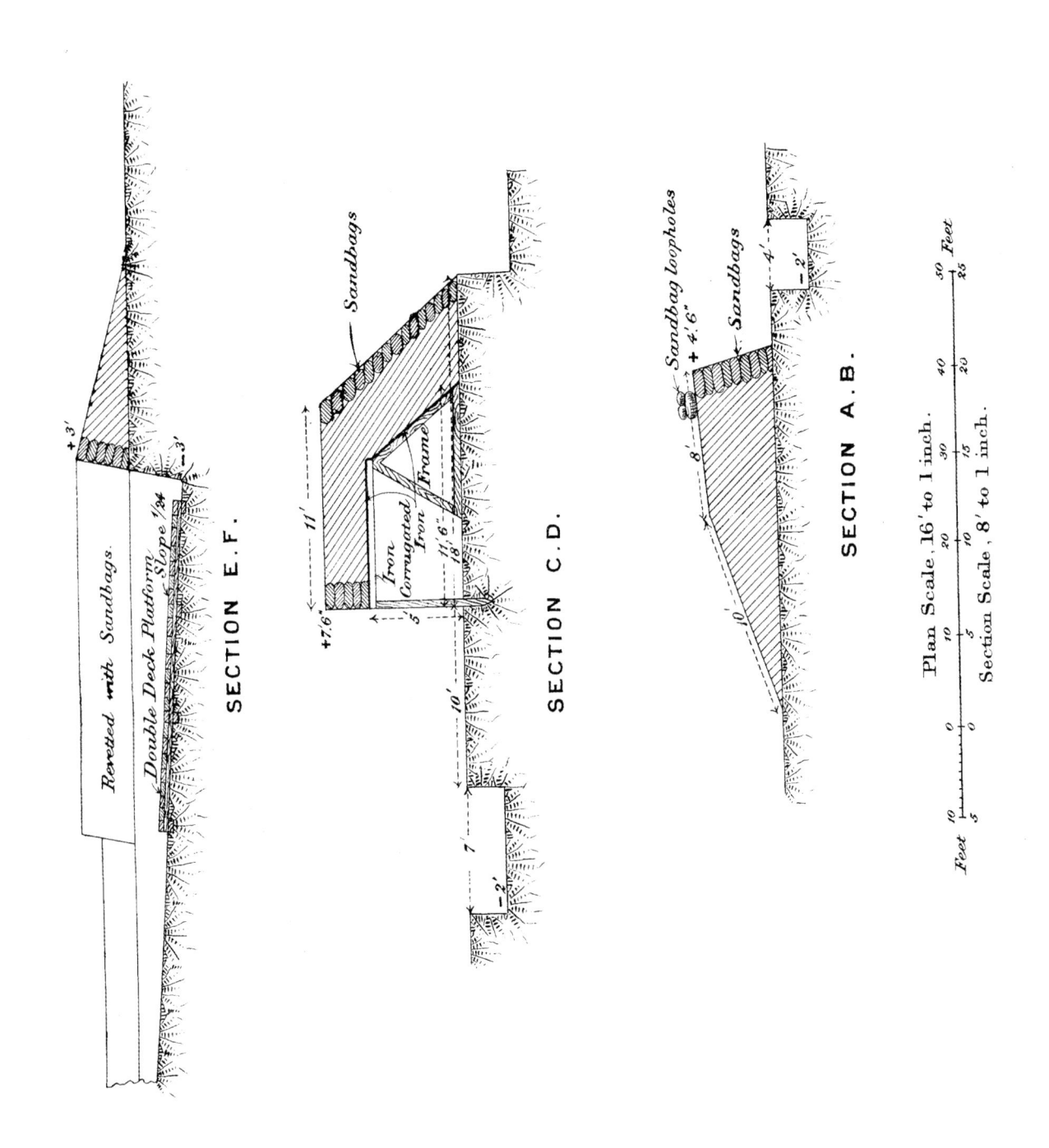

Feet

Kimberley Siege Account and Medal Roll

Plan 6: Old Kimberley Redoubt

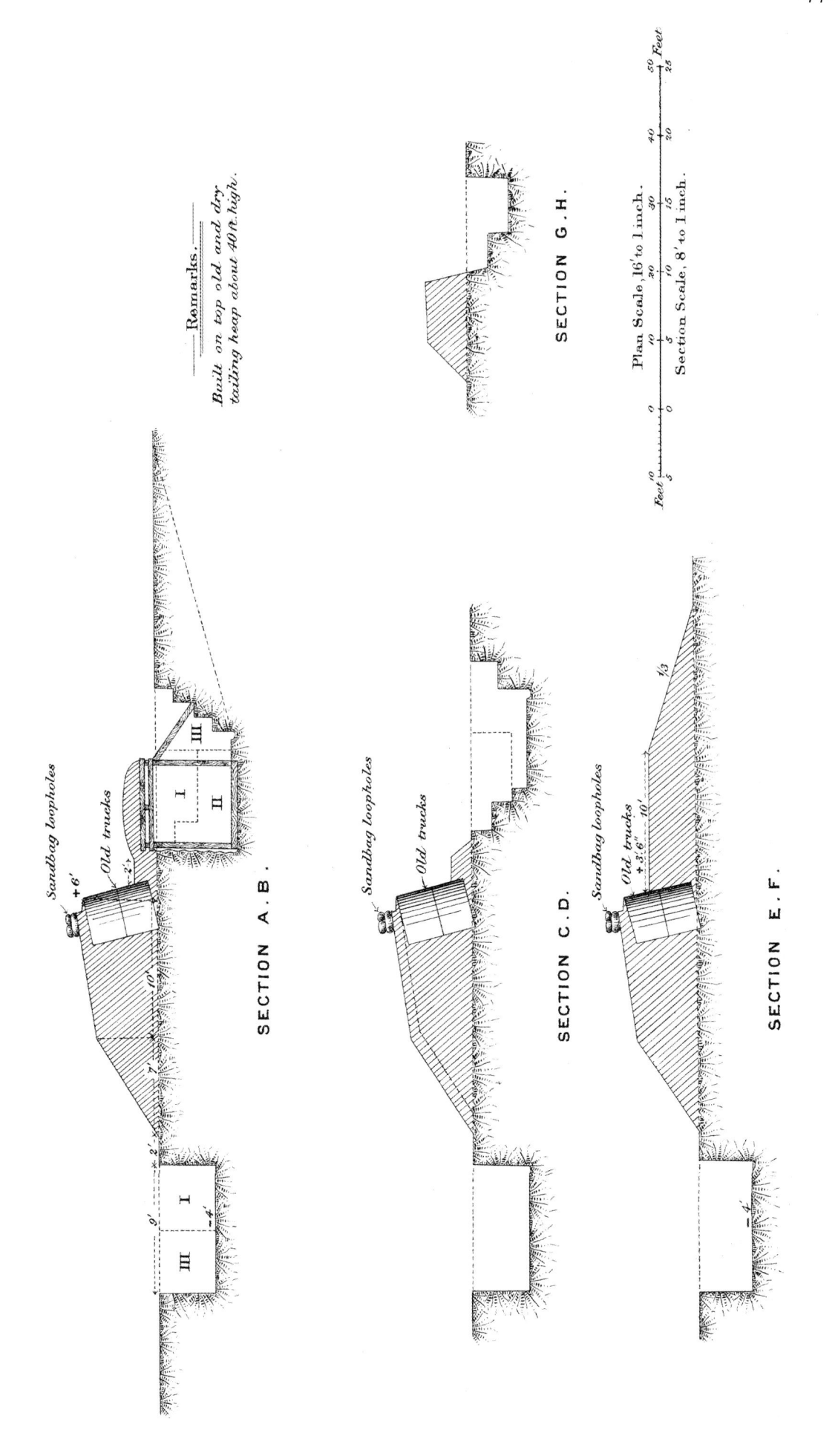

Appendices

Remarks.

Built on top old and dry tailing heap about 40 ft. high.

SECTION G.H.

Plan Scale, 16' to 1 inch.
Section Scale, 8' to 1 inch.

SECTION A.B.

SECTION C.D.

SECTION E.F.

303

Plan 7: Premier Mine Redoubt

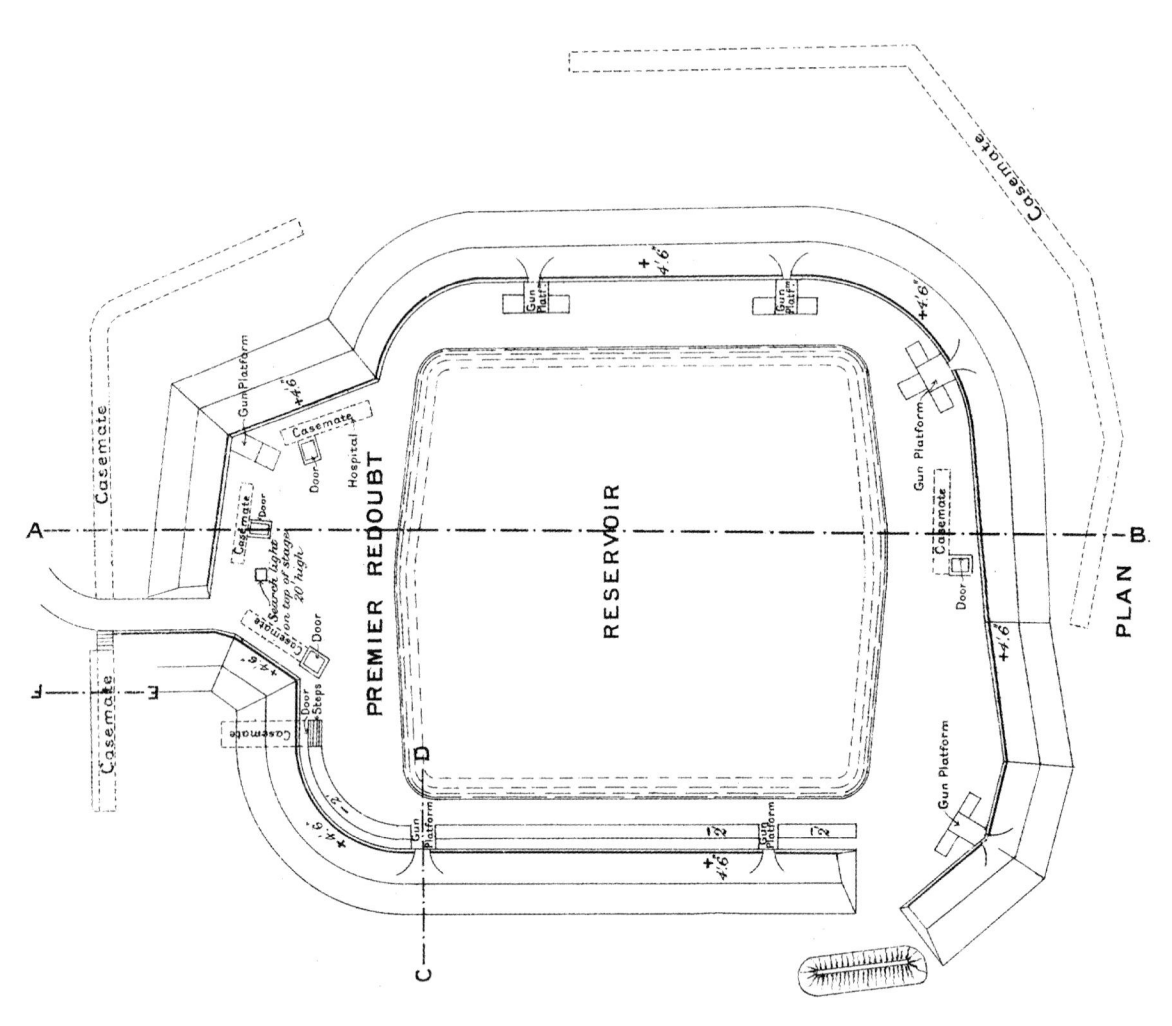

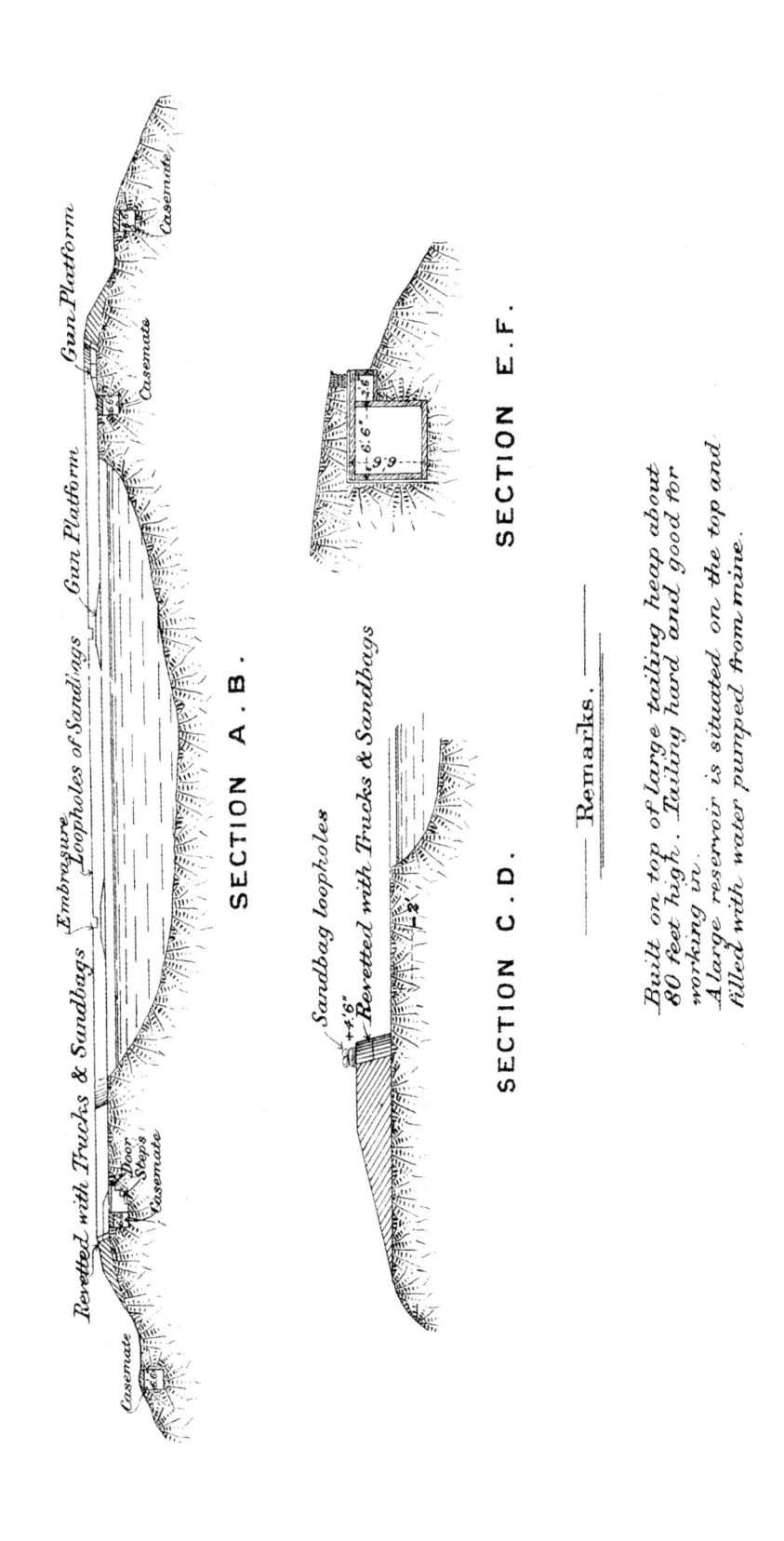

Appendices

SECTION A.B.

Revetted with Trucks & Sandbags
Casemate
Poor Steps Casemate
Embrasure
Loopholes of Sandbags
Gun Platform
Gun Platform
Casemate
Casemate

SECTION C.D.

Sandbag loopholes
4'6"
Revetted with Trucks & Sandbags

SECTION E.F.

7'6"
6'6"
9'9"

Remarks.

Built on top of large tailing heap about 80 feet high. Tailing hard and good for working in.
A large reservoir is situated on the top and filled with water pumped from mine.

305

Kimberley Siege Account and Medal Roll

Plan 8: Kenilworth Redoubt

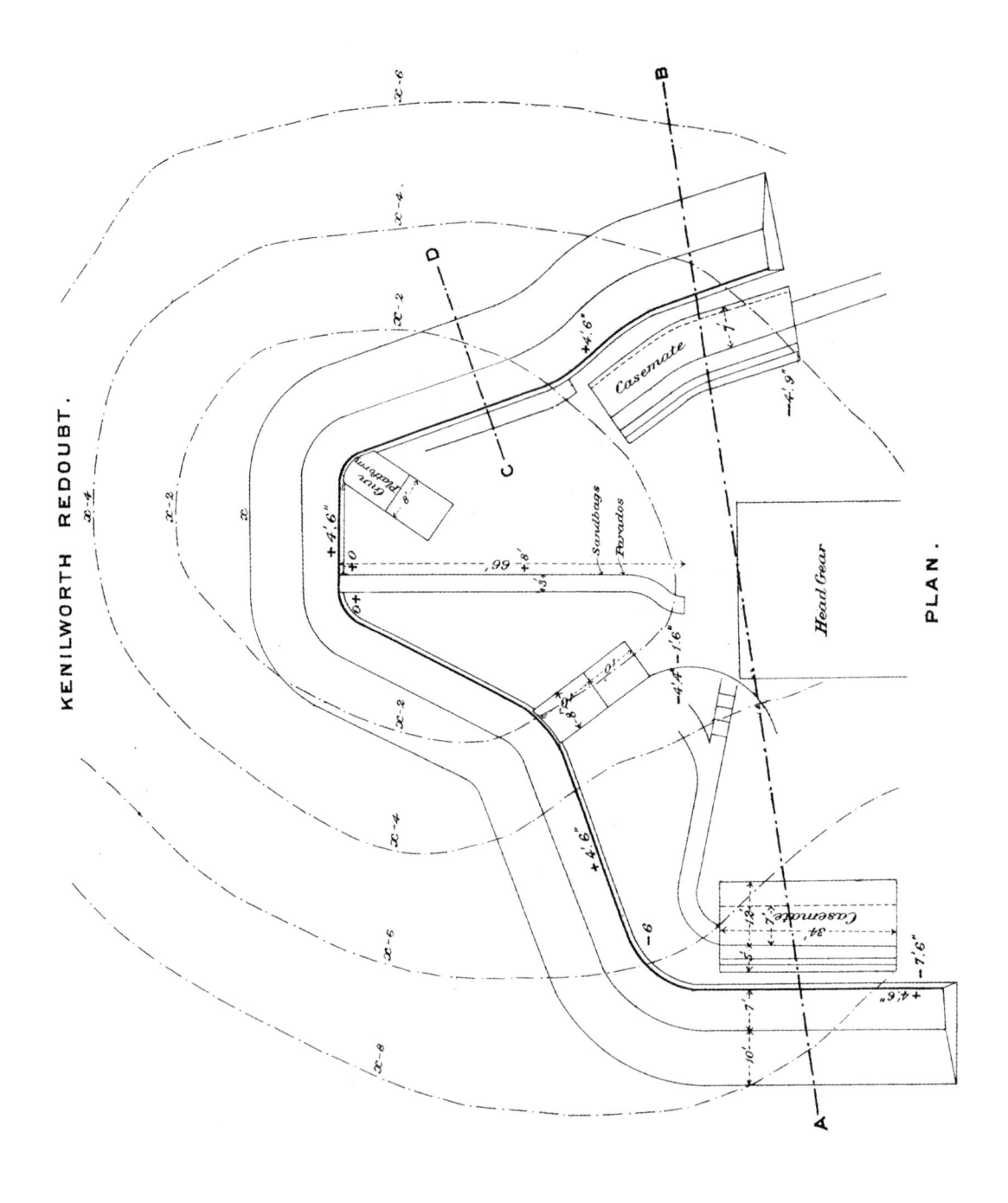

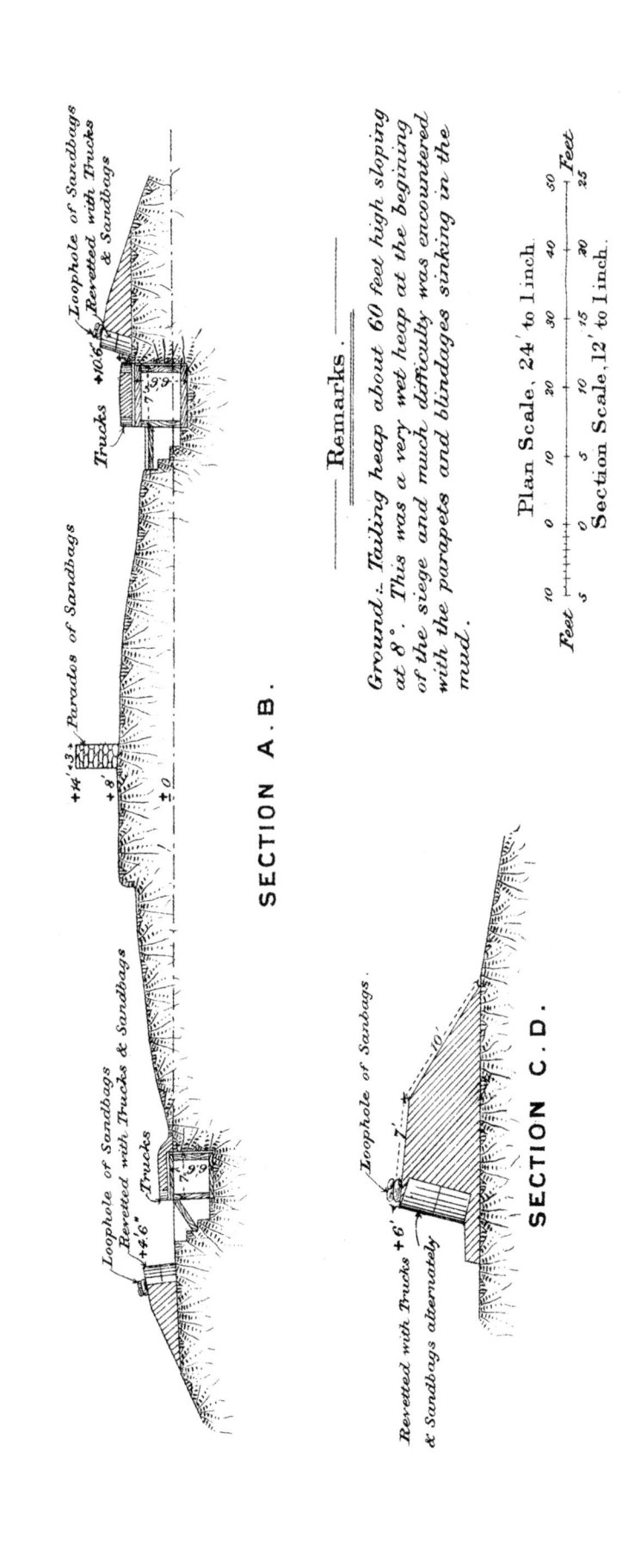

SECTION A.B.

Loophole of Sandbags Revetted with Trucks & Sandbags
Trucks +10'6"
Parados of Sandbags
+4'3"
+8"
±0
Loophole of Sandbags Revetted with Trucks & Sandbags
+4'6"
Trucks

SECTION C.D.

Loophole of Sandbags
Revetted with Trucks +6' & Sandbags alternately

Remarks.

Ground:- Tailing heap about 60 feet high sloping at 8°. This was a very wet heap at the beginning of the siege and much difficulty was encountered with the parapets and blindages sinking in the mud.

Plan Scale, 24' to 1 inch.
Section Scale, 12' to 1 inch.

Kimberley Siege Account and Medal Roll

Plan 9: De Beers Redoubt

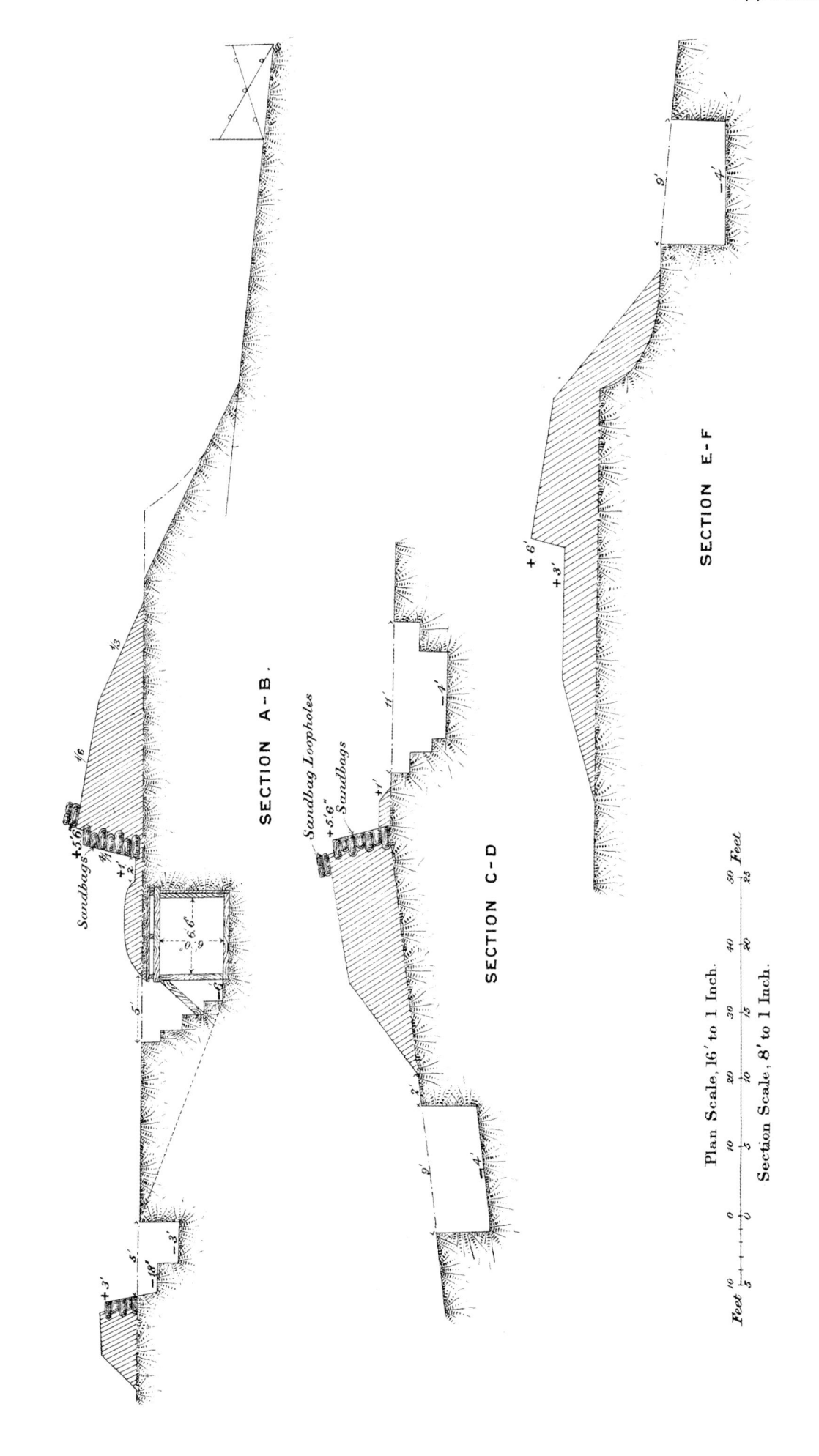

Appendices

SECTION A–B

SECTION C–D

SECTION E–F

Sandbag Loopholes
Sandbags

Plan Scale, 16′ to 1 Inch.
Section Scale, 8′ to 1 Inch.

Plan 10: Civil Service Redoubt

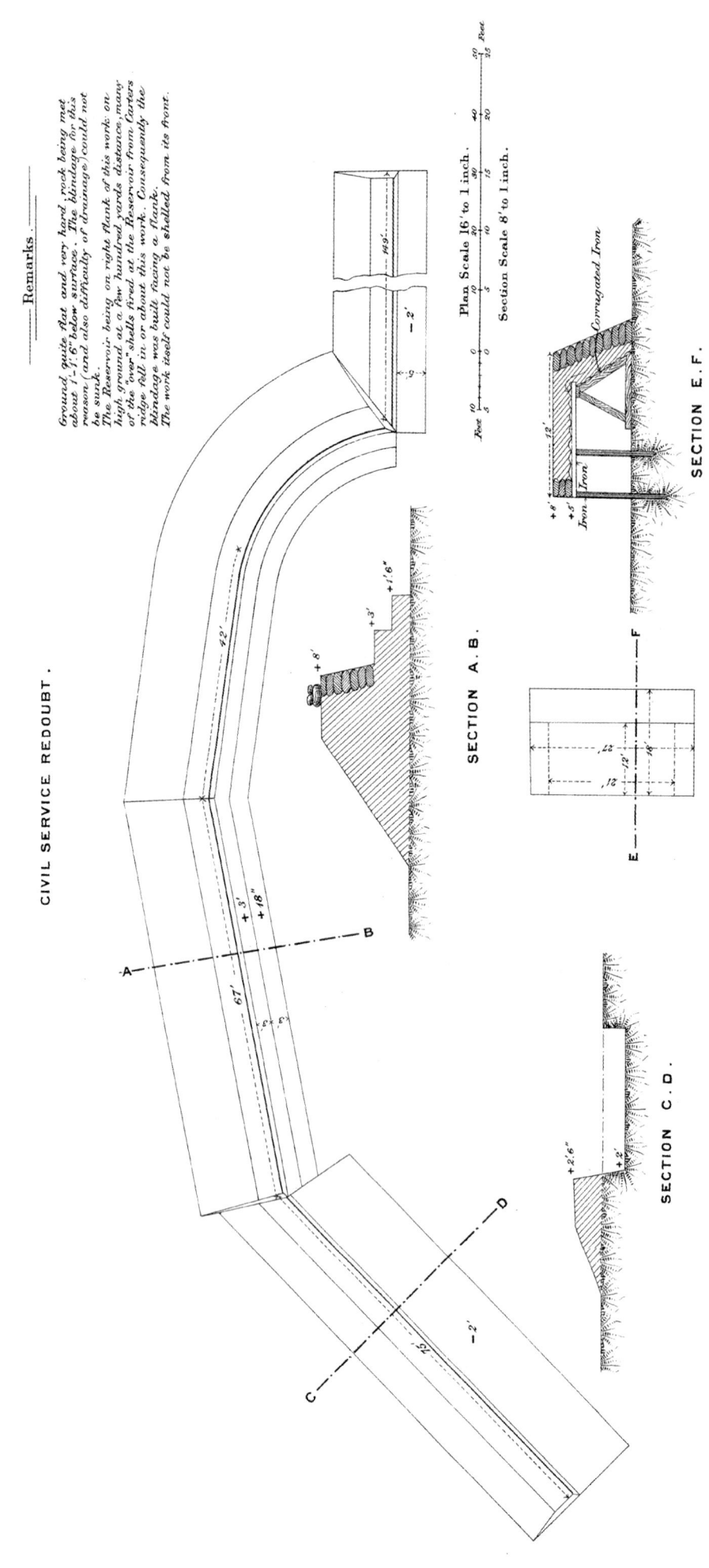

Appendices

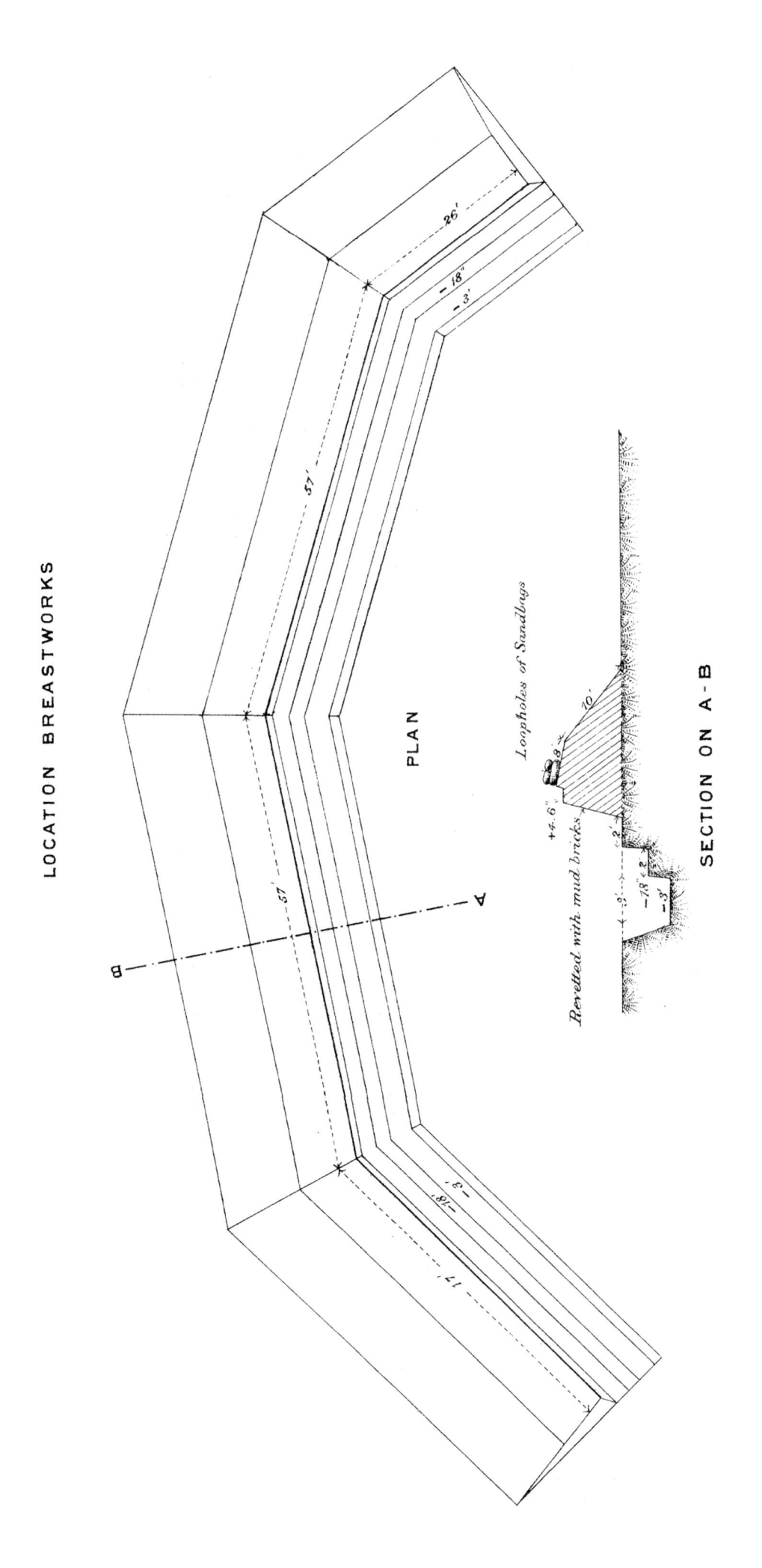

Plan 11: Breastworks

Plan 12: No 1 Searchlight Redoubt

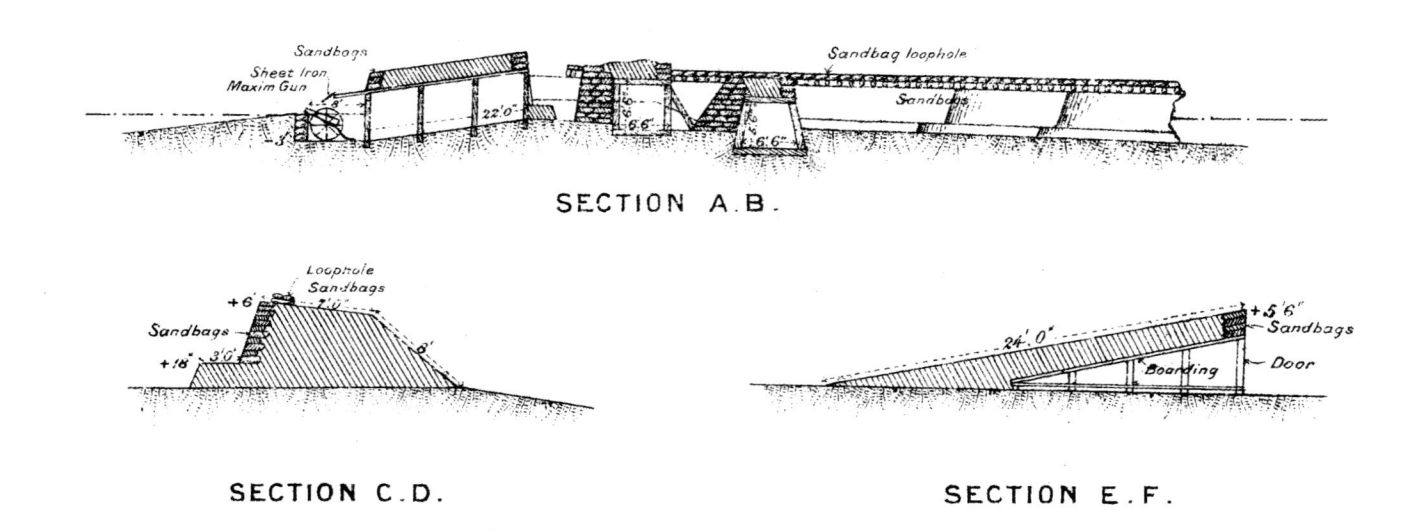

SECTION A.B.

Sheet Iron
Maxim Gun
Sandbags
Sandbag loophole
Sandbags

SECTION C.D.

Loophole
Sandbags
Sandbags

SECTION E.F.

Sandbags
Door
Boarding
24' 0"

Remarks.

Built on top of tailing heap about 130 feet high.
Original slope of ground shewn by dotted lines thus ------.
This was a new and very wet heap and much trouble was
experienced at first as the parapets tended to sink bodily.
For this reason, also, it was impossible to place the blindages
under the parapet.

Plan Scale; 24' to 1 inch.
Section Scale; 12' to 1 inch.

Kimberley Siege Account and Medal Roll

Plan 13: No 2 De Beers Redoubt

Appendices

SECTION C.D.

Sandbag loopholes
Revetted with boards
+ 4'6"

SECTION A.B.

Sandbag loopholes
Revetted with Sandbags
Sandbag loopholes
Revetted with Boards
Steps
Water Tank
Parados
Sandbags
Sandbag loophole
Revetted with
Gun Platform

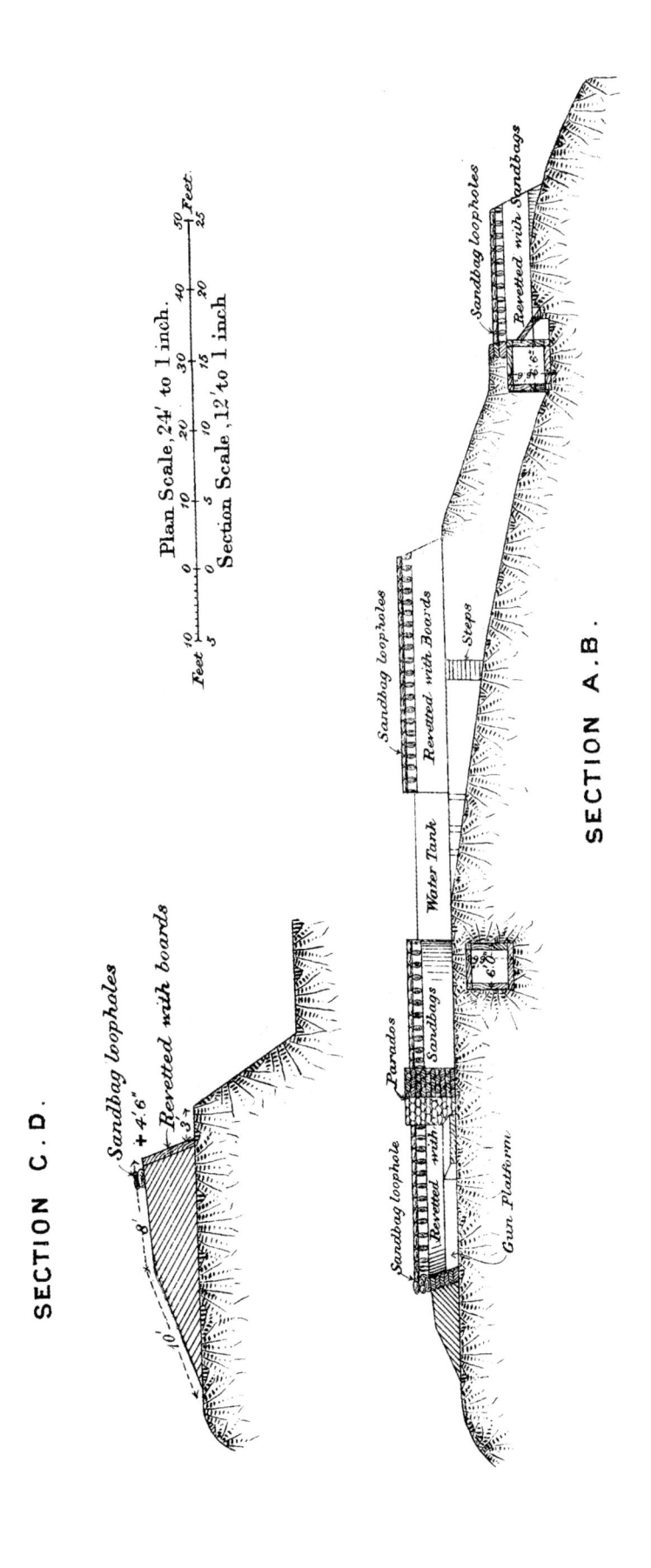

Plan Scale, 24' to 1 inch.
Section Scale, 12' to 1 inch.

Plan 14: Otto's Kopje Redoubt

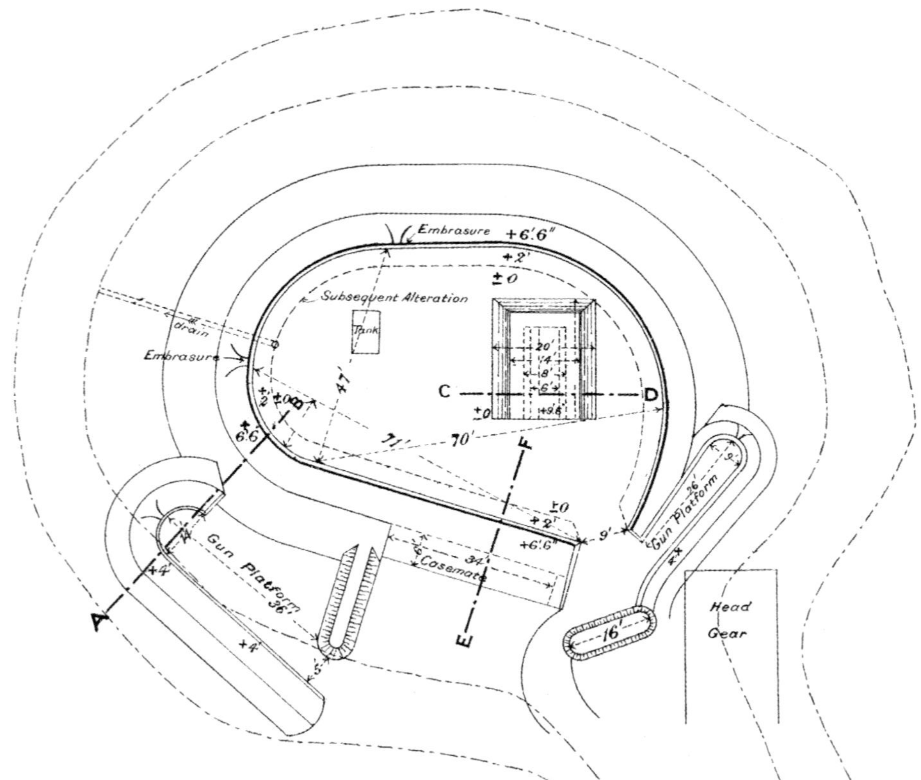

Appendices

SECTION A.B.

Sandbag Loopholes
+6'6"
+2'
±0
Subsequent alteration
+4'
Embrasure
14'
+4'

SECTION C.D

+9'6" Sandbags
+6'6"
14'
8"
6'
9"×3" Boarding
8'
20'
±0

SECTION E.F

Sandbag loopholes
+6'6"
+2'
±0
Subsequent alteration
12'
Corrugated Iron
6'0"
+6'6"

Plan Scale 32' to 1 Inch.
Section Scale 8' to 1 Inch.

317

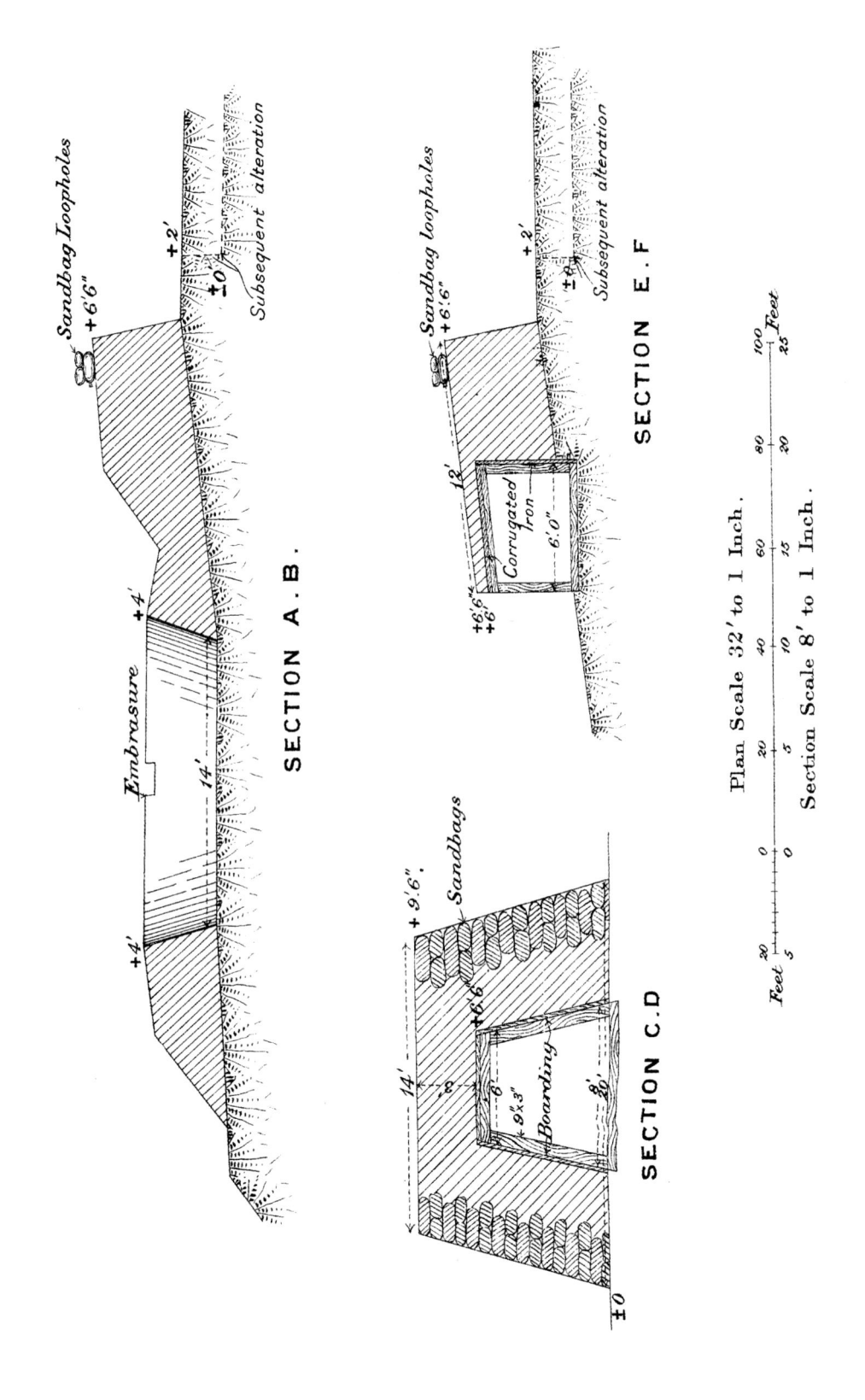

Plan 15: St Augustine's Redoubt

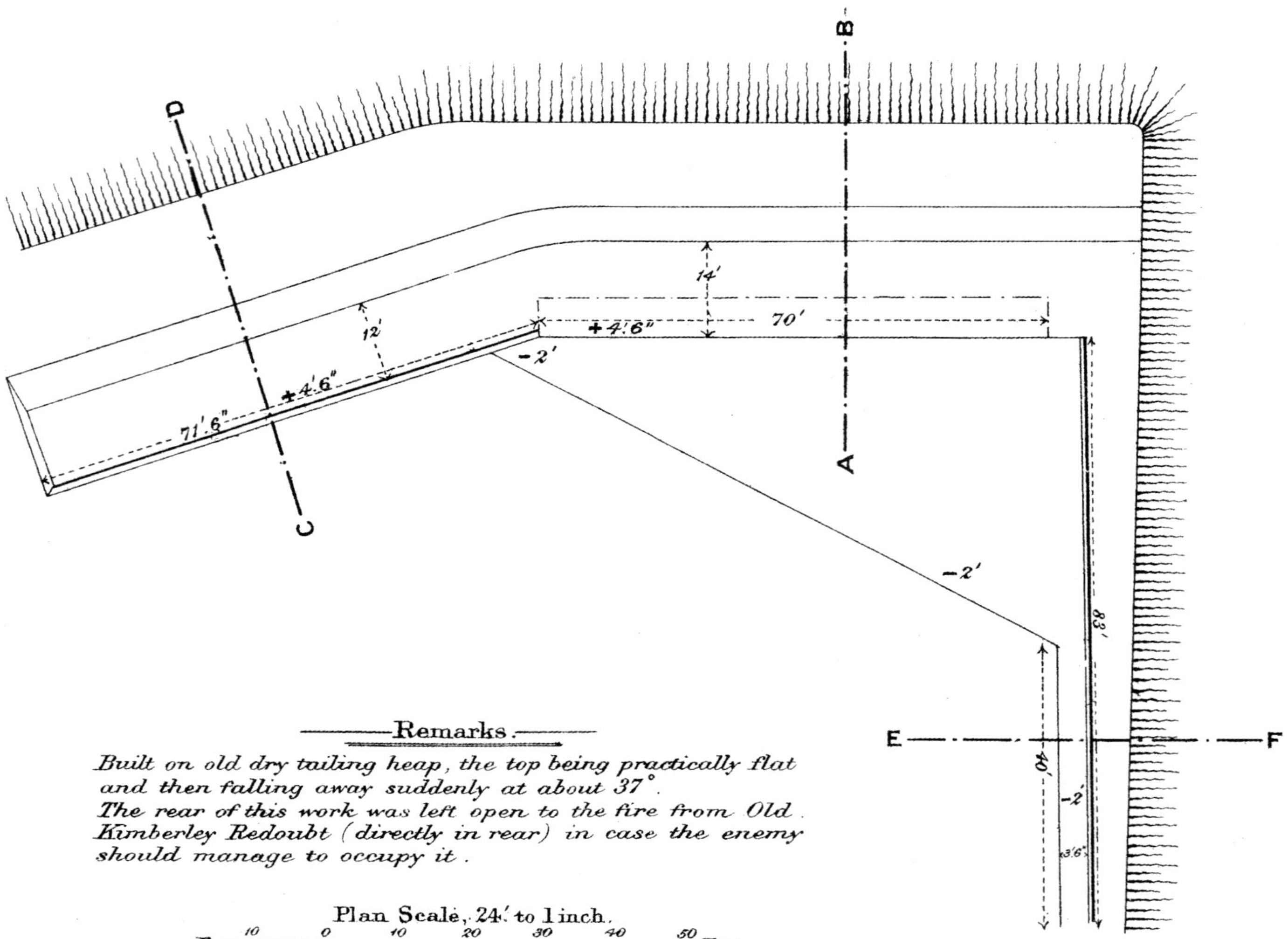

Remarks.—
Built on old dry tailing heap, the top being practically flat and then falling away suddenly at about 37°. The rear of this work was left open to the fire from Old Kimberley Redoubt (directly in rear) in case the enemy should manage to occupy it.

Plan Scale, 24' to 1 inch.
Section Scale, 12' to 1 inch.

Appendices

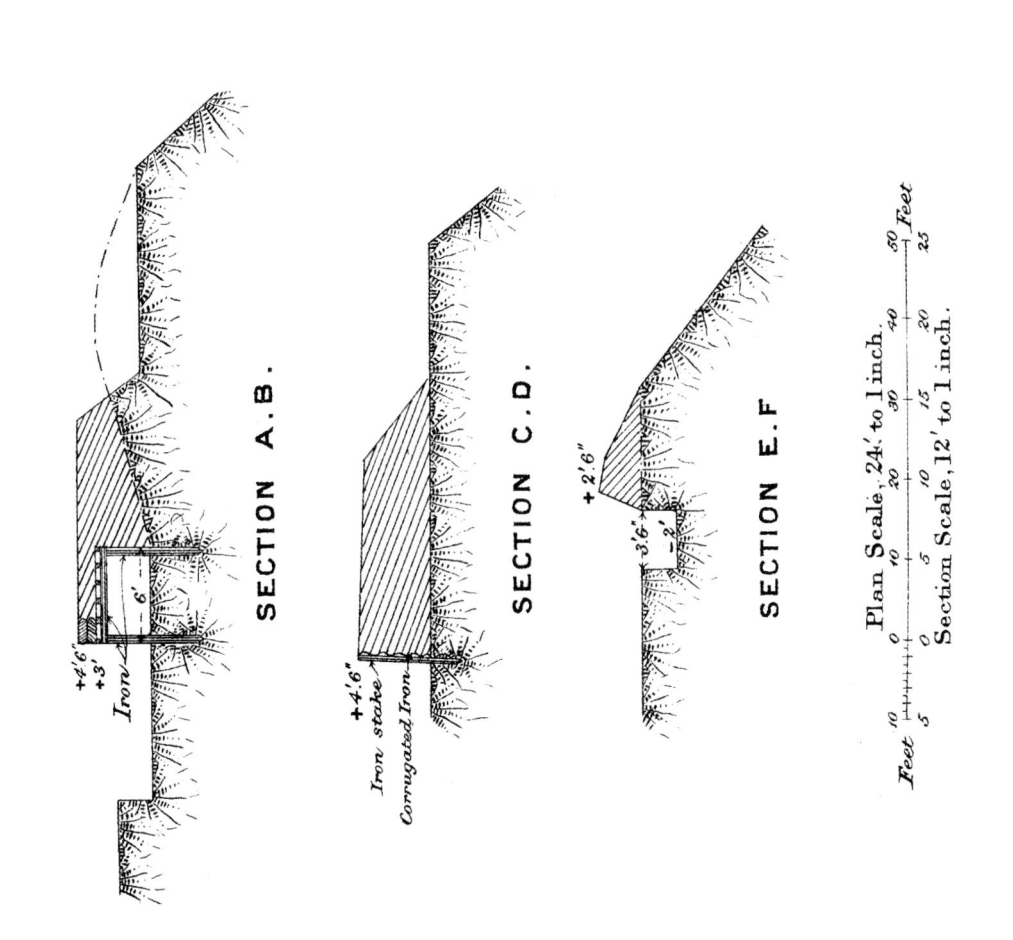

319

Plan 16: New Kimberley Redoubt

Appendices

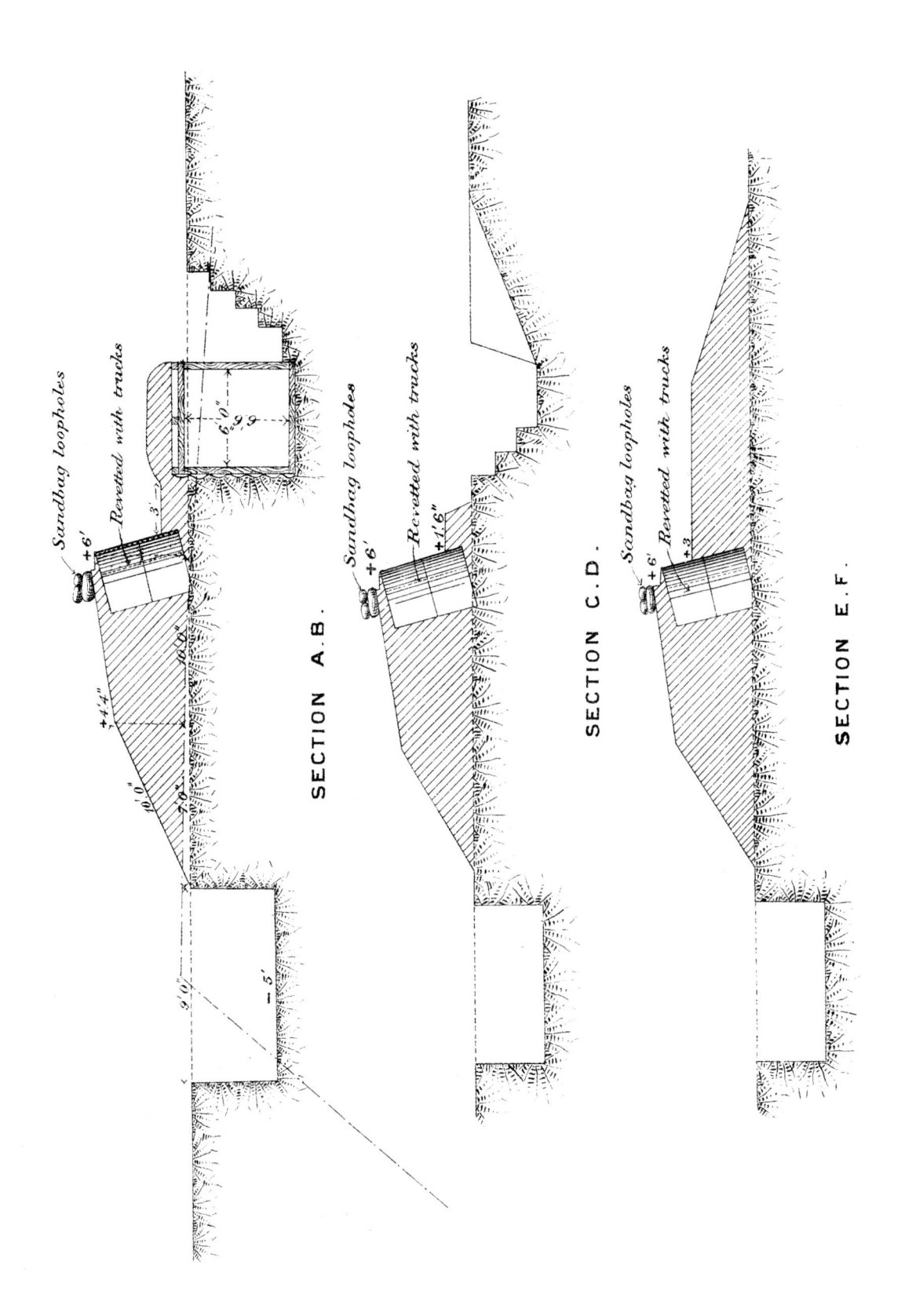

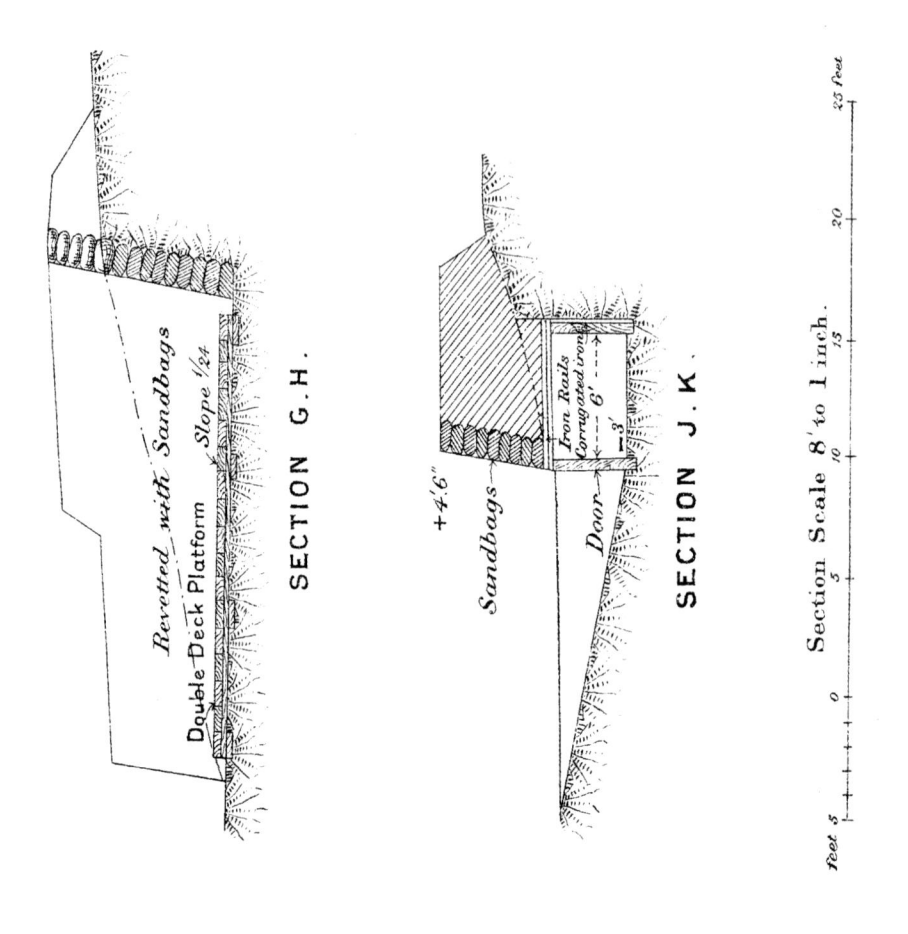

SECTION G.H.

Revetted with Sandbags
Slope 1/24
Double Deck Platform

SECTION J.K.

+4'6"
Sandbags
Iron Rails
Corrugated iron
6'
3'
Door

Section Scale 8' to 1 inch.

Feet 5 0 5 10 15 20 25 Feet

Appendix 07 – Troops involved in engagements

The information in this appendix is taken from Kekewich's despatch. For each of the major engagements, a detailed return of the men and equipment that took part was completed. Where names of casualties are given, these have been cross-referenced with the casualty list and some corrections have been made. Note that there are names of known casualties who are not listed on these returns.

Information on the following engagements is listed here:

```
24th October 1899  ................................................. 323
11th November 1899 ............................................ 325
16th November 1899 ............................................ 326
17th November 1899 ............................................ 327
25th November 1899 ............................................ 328
28th November 1899 ............................................ 330
9th December 1899 .............................................. 332
```

24th October 1899

Unit	Strength Officers	WOs	Sgts	Trump/Drum	ORs	Total all ranks	Horses/mules	Guns Field	Guns Machine	Ammunition Artillery	Ammunition Small arms	Casualties Killed Officers	Killed WOs	Killed NCOs & men	Killed Horses	Wounded Officers	Wounded WOs	Wounded NCOs & men	Wounded Horses
1/LNLR	7	1	10	3	157	196					2400								
Armoured train	1		1		16				2							2		2	
RAMC	1		1		1	3										1			
Mounted Corps – staff	6					6	6												
Cape Mounted Police	9				259	268	268				2900			2	1			6	5
Diamond Fields Horse	4				46	50	50				1861			1					12
Kimberley Light Horse	3				63	66	66				863				4			5	4
Diamond Fields Artillery	3		2		20	25	18	2		80					4			4	4
Maxim Battery			3		8	11	5		2		1240				1			1	2
Kimberley Regiment	3	2	10	2	57	74													
Total	37	3	27	5	627	699	413	2	4	80	9264			3	6	3		18	27

Unit	Equipment lost or damaged	Names of killed	Names of wounded	Nature of wound
1/LNLR Armoured train	2 scabbards, 1 bayonet, 1 centre buckle of belt, 1 knife, 1 field dressing, 1 pull-through, 1 water bottle		Lt J G Lowndes Lt C H M Bingham 3983 Pte H Lee 4188 Pte A Milner	Thigh (severely) Thigh (severely) Right arm Thigh (severely)
RAMC	1 stretcher complete, 1 stretcher sling			
Mounted Corps – staff			Lt R L M McClintock RE	Side
Cape Mounted Police	Lost – 6 saddles complete, 1 rifle, 1 revolver, 2 horses (including 1 wounded)	Pte H J L Elliott, Pte R S MacKenzie	Pte James Gow Pte J B Petersen Pte F Simpson Pte C H Hoskins Pte W T Dye L Cpl G W Gradwell	Chest and hip Arm Posterior Wrist Thigh Leg
Diamond Fields Horse	Lost – 2 water bottles, oil can, 1 stirrup iron and leather, 1 bandolier, 1 bayonet, 150 rounds of ammunition, 1 wounded horse	Pte P A Leipoldt		
Kimberley Light Horse	Lost – 7 saddles complete, 4 rifles, 3 pairs stirrup irons and leathers, 1 overcoat, 1 bridle, 8 horses		Cpl R J R Harris Tpr R M McCaskill Tpr G E Chapman Tpr J C Dodds Tpr C Brady	Thigh Forehead Neck Leg Hand
Diamond Fields Artillery			Gnr M Hartigan Gnr A Bankier Tptr A Dickinson Gnr F W Payne	Leg (severely) Right arm and left hand (sev) Hand (slight) Foot (severely)
Maxim Battery	1 shaft broken, 3 wheels splintered, 1 trail bent			

11th November 1899

Unit	Officers	WOs	Sgts	Trump/Drum	ORs	Total all ranks	Horses/mules	Field	Machine	Artillery	Small arms	Officers	WOs	NCOs & men	Horses	Officers	WOs	NCOs & men	Horses
1/LNLR MI	1		1		14	16	16												
Armoured train	1		2		24	27			2										
Staff of Mounted Corps	4					4	4												
Cape Mounted Police	7				109	116	116				3740							1	
Diamond Fields Horse	6				57	63	63				168								3
Kimberley Light Horse	11				177	188	188				476				1			1	2
Maxim detachment, CP					7	7	8		1		110								
Total	30		3		388	421	395		3		4494				1			2	5

Unit	Equipment lost or damaged	Names of killed	Names of wounded	Nature of wound
Cape Mounted Police	Lost – 1 field service cap, 1 smasher hat, 1 nosebag, 1 horse brush, 1 currycomb, 1 gun bucket and shield		Sgt A Parker	Mortally (since dead)
Kimberley Light Horse	Lost – 2 smasher hats, 6 pairs putties, 2 saddlebags, 1 haversack, 100 rounds LM ammunition		Tpr J C A Stumke	Forehead

16th November 1899

Unit	Strength					Horses/mules	Total all ranks	Guns		Ammunition expended		Casualties						
	Officers	WOs	Sgts	Trump/Drum	ORs			Field	Machine	Artillery	Small arms	Killed			Wounded		
												Officers	WOs	NCOs & men	Horses	Officers	WOs	NCOs & men	Horses
1/LNLR MI	1		3		16	20	20				150								
Staff of Mounted Corps	4					4	4												
Cape Mounted Police	5		9		26	40	40				979								2
Diamond Fields Horse	7		14		95	116	116				1522				1	1		3	1
Kimberley Light Horse	12		24		117	223	223				4436			1	2	1		6	9
Maxim detachment, CP			1		5	6	7		1		1120								1
Diamond Fields Artillery	1		3	1	26	31	23	2		27					1				3
Total	30		54	1	355	440	433	2	1	27	8207			1	4	2		9	16

Unit	Equipment lost or damaged	Names of killed
Cape Police	Lost – 2 saddles, 2 bridles, 2 nosebags, 1 pair spur	
Diamond Fields Horse	Lost – 1 sight protector, 1 rifle, 1 cape, 3 water bottles	Tpr T J Goodall
Kimberley Light Horse	Lost – 1 saddle, 1 bridle, 5 nosebags, 6 spurs, 6 sight protectors, 5 rifles, 4 capes, 1 water bottle, 3 saddlebags, 3 haversacks, 6 hats, 24 pairs putties, 1 rifle bolt	

Names of wounded	Nature of wound
Lt H W Smith	Bruised by ricochet bullet
Tpr W Rossiter	Abdomen (dangerous)
Tpr C R Lester	Leg
Tpr H L Johnson	Scalp (slight)
Maj T C Peakman	Thigh (slight)
Sgt J H Churcher	Foot
Tpr J N Campbell	Leg
Tpr W Mitchell	Leg (slight)
Tpr J Orr	Thigh (slight)
Tpr D Parsons	Leg
Tpr E P Clarke	Abdomen (dangerous)

17th November 1899

Unit	Strength						Guns		Ammunition expended		Casualties					
											Killed			Wounded		
	Officers	WOs	Sgts	Trump/Drum	ORs	Total all ranks	Horses/mules	Field	Machine	Artillery	Small arms	Officers	WOs	NCOs & men	Horses	Officers	WOs	NCOs & men	Horses
1/LNLR MI	1				19	20	20				700								3
Staff of Mounted Corps	4					4	4												
Cape Mounted Police	11		31		169	211	211				379								1
Diamond Fields Horse	6				105	111	111								1				
Kimberley Light Horse	10		26		167	203	203				1123								3
Diamond Fields Artillery	1		3	1	26	31	24	2	1	44									
Beaconsfield Town Guard	14		9		210	233	4				600								
Total	47		69	1	696	813	577	2	1	44	2802				1				7

Unit	Equipment lost or damaged	Names of killed	Names of wounded	Nature of wound
Diamond Fields Horse	Lost – 1 water bottle, 6 pairs putties		Capt J H Bodley	Calf of leg
Diamond Fields Artillery	Lost – 1 billhook, 1 felling axe, 1 shovel, 1 blanket. Damaged – 1 bridle			

25th November 1899

Unit	Strength Officers	WOs	Sgts	Trump/Drum	ORs	Total all ranks	Horses/mules	Guns Field	Guns Machine	Ammunition Artillery	Ammunition Small arms	Casualties Killed Officers	WOs	NCOs & men	Horses	Casualties Wounded Officers	WOs	NCOs & men	Horses
Staff	1				5	6	2												
7th Field Co, RE	1	1	1		44	46	4				204								
1/LNLR	3		10	2	164	180					1159							2	
1/LNLR MI	1		1		17	19					1600								
Armoured train detachment	1		2		22	25			2		55								
Staff, Mounted Corps	4					4	4												
Cape Mounted Police	6		13		106	125	125				19375			3	2	1		9	12
Kimberley Light Horse	12		18		175	205	205				15249			4	2	2		13	4
Diamond Fields Artillery	2		5	1	49	57	35	4		112									
Cape Police (dismounted)	3				79	82					600								
Kimberley Regiment	5		16	2	109	132	2											1	
Maxim detachments			4		19	23	9		2		1690								
Kimberley Town Guard	6		8		71	85	2												
Beaconsfield Town Guard	6		6		106	118	12												
Post Office Signallers					2	2													
Ambulance detachment			1		14	15	12												
Total	51	1	85	5	982	1124	431	4	4	112	39932			7	4	3		25	16

Unit	Equipment lost or damaged	Names of killed
7th Field Co, RE	Lost – 1 pair wire cutters	
1/LNLR	Damaged – 1 waist belt and braces	Sgt T Jones Pte J Corrie Pte A Hasenjäger
Cape Police	Lost – 2 hats, 12 haversacks, 3 pairs putties, 5 water bottles, 2 bags, 4 saddles, 2 wallets, 1 cleaning rod, 3 bridles, 4 pairs spurs, 6 nosebags, 2 field	

Names of wounded	Nature of wound
4525 Pte J Walcroft	Chest (severe)
4045 Pte A Cooper	Thigh
Capt W Rush	Arm
Sgt H Bailey	Leg
Pte R Skinner	Thigh
Pte D O'Dell	Thigh
Pte R Deere	Thigh

Appendices

Unit	Equipment lost or damaged	Names of killed	Names of wounded	Nature of wound
	service caps, 2 reserve pouches, 3 straps, 1 patrol tin, 3 bandoliers, 3 gun buckets, 1 mess tin, 3 revolvers, 6 rifles. Damaged – 1 rifle		Pte G Mathieson	Leg
			Pte J Stolz	Leg
			Pte T Carlyle	Thigh
			Pte G Tarr	Scalp
			Pte W Clark	Thumb
Kimberley Light Horse	Lost – 1 greatcoat, 2 pairs putties, 1 hat, 1 saddle, 4 rifles, 1 bayonet, 3 water bottles, 1 pouch, 1 bridle, 1 wallet, 1 stirrup iron, 1 bandolier Damaged – 2 rifles	Sgt H I Collier	Capt H J Bowen	Fracture, lower maxillary
		Sgt C Freislich	Capt J Hickson-Mahoney	Shoulder
		Pte A E Willmore	Sgt Maj W Oatley	Eye and head
		Pte J Peiser	Sgt W Mayston	Hip
			Cpl M J Pritchard	Hip
			Tpr D Lanigan	Left wrist
			Tpr R Barron	Foot
			Tpr B Cawood	Arm
			Tpr J P Geoghegan	Chest
			Tpr E P Gregory	Hand
			Tpr A Williams	Arm
			Tpr C Legward	Wrist and arm
			Tpr L Farr	Stomach
			Tpr G Ring	Forearm
			Tpr N Skill	Hand
Kimberley Regiment			Pte G Billing	Right hip (slight)

28th November 1899

Unit	Strength Officers	WOs	Sgts	Trump/Drum	ORs	Total all ranks	Horses/mules	Guns Field	Machine	Ammunition Artillery	Small arms	Casualties Killed Officers	WOs	NCOs & men	Horses	Wounded Officers	WOs	NCOs & men	Horses
Staff	2		1	1	6	6	5												
7th Field Co, RE	1		1		46	48	14												
1/LNLR	5	1	14	5	222	247	25				1400			2		1		5	
1/LNLR MI	1		1		18	20	20				600								
Armoured train detachment	1		2		24	27			2		55								
Staff, Mounted Corps	4					4	5					1							
Cape Mounted Police	8		18		219	245	262				8360			3				10	
Diamond Fields Horse	6		15		84	105	105				2760			3	2	1		8	2
Kimberley Light Horse	13		30		219	262	262				3570	1		13		1		5	
Diamond Fields Artillery	4		11	1	62	78	57	6		98									
Cape Police (dismounted)	2		4		46	52													
Kimberley Regiment	12		35	3	292	342													
Maxim detachments			2		10	12	13		2										
Kimberley Town Guard	13	2	13	2	160	190	2				510								
Beaconsfield Town Guard	15		12		193	220	12												
Ambulance detachment			1		12	13													
Total	87	3	160	12	1609	1871	782	6	4	98	17255	2		21	2	3		28	2

Unit	Equipment lost or damaged	Names of killed
1/LNLR	Lost – 1 cap, 1 canteen, 2 canteen covers, 5 field dressings, 1 emergency ration, 4 greatcoats, 4 rifles, 2 bayonets, 1 bayonet bolt spring, 1 bandolier, 2 waist belts, 4 pouches, 2 pairs braces, 2 canteen straps, 11	2393 C Sgt A Heald 3746 Pte T Lutner

Names of wounded	Nature of wound
Lt W R Clifford	Head
4857 Pte J Kenton	Right shoulder (severe)
4046 Pte G Edkins	Left thigh (severe)
4261 Pte T Tyldesley	Right thigh (severe)
3983 Pte H Lee	Right hand (slight)
4649 Pte J Neville	Head

Appendices

Unit	Equipment lost or damaged	Names of killed	Names of wounded	Nature of wound
Staff, Mounted Corps	water bottles, 6 water bottle straps, 5 oil bottles, 4 pull throughs, 6 slings, 2 scabbards, 1 wire cutter, 1 haversack, 1 revolver pouch, 11 rounds revolver ammunition, 2 helmets	Brevet Maj H S Turner		
Cape Police	Lost – 4 saddles, 4 bridles, 3 head stalls, 1 blanket, 5 rifles, 5 water bottles, 3 revolvers, 1 revolver pouch, 3 patrol tins, 1 haversack, 1 pair spurs	Sgt Maj G C Brady Pte C Dennison Pte J E Williams	Pte C McNay Pte J Howell Pte N H Edy Pte W G Spilsbury Pte J Grindrod Pte H Hillier Pte F Pool Pte P D'O Salkeld (since dead) Pte J G Metrovitch Pte F R Arundale	Thigh Chest Shoulder Thigh Head Leg Leg Leg Slight Stomach and chest
Diamond Fields Horse	Lost – 5 rifles, 7 bandoliers, 8 water bottles, 4 bayonets, 1 boot, 2 capes, 1 handguard (rifle)	Cpl R Howell Pte H Cornwall Pte A S Dare	Capt S P Waldek Sgt Maj J R McDonald Sgt C W King Pte H M Adler Pte D D Shepherd Pte F Ferguson Pte F S Knight Pte H J Gordon Pte C Glyn	Slight Arm (slight) Arm (slight) Arm (slight) Arm (slight) Severe Slight Slight Slight
Kimberley Light Horse	Lost – 2 saddles, 2 bridles, 2 kneebands, 2 saddlebags, 6 haversacks, 6 pairs putties, 6 Kaffir sheets, 25 rifles, 6 pairs spurs, 10 bayonets, 1 nummah, 1 hat	Lt S O Wright L Cpl H Hiscock Tpr W J Baker Tpr J W Hastings Tpr G H Harper Tpr W McDonald Tpr J T Marshall Tpr J Keller (died in hospital) Tpr B L Nicholas Tpr C Screech Tpr F Sharpe Tpr C C Stearns Tpr J Thompson Tpr H Taylor	Lt H G Watson L Cpl F Powell Pte F H Day Pte H Richardson Pre H F Stacpole Pte A Wood	Neck Abdomen Head Shoulder Arm Arm

Kimberley Siege Account and Medal Roll

Unit	Equipment lost or damaged	Names of killed	Names of wounded	Nature of wound
Diamond Fields Artillery	Lost – 1 hook bill, 1 axe (felling), 1 shovel, 1 blanket			
Supply branch, mounted troops	Lost – 750 lbs oats, 200 lbs mealies			

9th December 1899

Unit	Strength Officers	WOs	Sgts	Trump/Drum	ORs	Total all ranks	Horses/mules	Guns Field	Machine	Ammunition Artillery	Small arms	Casualties Killed Officers	WOs	NCOs & men	Horses	Wounded Officers	WOs	NCOs & men	Horses
Staff	1			1		2	2												
RGA maxim detachment			1		2	3	3		1										
7th Co RE	1		1		45	47	8												
1/LNLR	4	1	13	4	235	237													
Mounted Infantry	1				19	20	20												
Staff, Mounted Corps	3					3	3												
Cape (Mounted) Police	5		2		123	130	130				130					1			
Kimberley Light Horse	5				97	102	102												
Diamond Fields Artillery	3		11	2	72	88	54	6		156								5	1
Maxim detachment			2		8	10	11		2										
Kimberley Town Guard	4		6		47	57								1					
Total	27	1	36	7	628	699	333	6	3	156	130			1		1		5	1

Unit	Equipment lost or damaged	Names of killed	Names of wounded	Nature of wound
RGA	Lost – 1 mule (missing), 1 head collar, 1 rein		Capt J White	Foot
Cape Police		BSM A Moss	Cpl Canut	Bruised heel (slight)
			Cpl Kidd	Bruised kneecap (severe)
			Gnr Anderson	Bruised hip (severe)
Diamond Fields Artillery	Lost – 1 water bucket, 1 billhook, 3 water bottles, 2 bridles		Gnr C Lefevre	Bruised kneecap (slight)
			Dr Stewart	Bruise on left eye (slight)

Appendix 08 – Honours and awards

Mentions in Despatches

Kekewich's despatch of the siege dated 15th February 1900 (LG 8th May 1900) ended with a list of those people he though rendered special service during the siege:

Staff — I wish to place on record the brilliant services of the late Brevet Major (local Lieutenant Colonel) H S Turner; in him the Army has lost a most valuable officer; he was a great organiser, full of energy, and possessed of real ability and courage; he was the principal organiser of the Town Guards, and acted as my staff officer, carrying out his duties with marked success under great difficulties; ... he commanded the mounted troops in numerous reconnaissances and sorties, and I cannot speak too highly of the manner in which he conducted them and loyally carried out my orders. Captain (local Major) W A J O'Meara, RE, my intelligence officer, carried out his many duties to my entire satisfaction, ... and is, I consider, a most hardworking and capable staff officer; ... he also successfully carried out the duties of Director of Army Telegraphs; I cannot praise his good work too highly. Lieutenant (local Captain) D S MacInnes, RE, worked out most carefully and constructed with marked ability and success the engineer operations for the defence; on Major Turner taking over command of mounted troops, Captain MacInnes relieved him as my staff officer, and I cannot speak too highly of the manner in which he carried out his heavy and very responsible duties.

Royal Garrison Artillery — Major (local Lieutenant Colonel) G D Chamier commanded the artillery in the siege operations; he has carried out his very responsible duties [to] my satisfaction, and the efficient and mobile condition of the artillery is greatly due to his energy; his advice has always been of the greatest assistance to me.

Royal Engineers — Lieutenant R L McClintock has done good work, both in the field and in the fortress.

Loyal North Lancashire Regiment — Major (local Lieutenant Colonel) W H E Murray was in command of half the battalion and the Infantry Reserve during siege, and performed his duties with success; also rendered valuable service in connection with supplies. Captain T H O'Brien was in command of a very important section of the defences; he performed his responsible duties to my entire satisfaction. Lieutenant F W Woodward did excellent work as signalling officer, and after Lieutenant and Adjutant Lowndes was wounded he also took over duties of acting adjutant. Lieutenant C du Putron did excellent work as assistant signalling officer; also performed duties of brigade transport officer to my entire satisfaction. Lieutenant (local Captain) W Clifford commanded mounted infantry detachment, and had much hard work in connection with patrolling duties in early days of siege; has subsequently performed duties of acting adjutant Kimberley Light Horse with marked success; his conduct in action on many occasions has been most distinguished (wounded November 28th). 2nd Lieutenant A McC Webster commanded armoured train in reconnaissances and sorties in neighbourhood, and displayed excellent judgment on all occasions. Sergeant Major E C Mudge, Sergeants H Herbert, H Helland, Corporal J Hopwood are deserving of mention for good work.

Army Service Corps — Captain (local Major) H V Gorle had an exceedingly onerous task to fulfil in arranging for victualling and supply of garrison and 50,000 people in the town; I cannot speak too highly of his zeal and resource. Corporal F Benwell has done excellent work, and is worthy of special promotion.

Royal Army Medical Corps — Lieutenant C J O'Gorman was the only officer of his Corps here, and in consequence had much hard work and responsibility; I consider him a very valuable officer.

Cape Police — Commissioner (local Lieutenant Colonel) M B Robinson assisted me in every way in his power; his duties have been many and various, and he has carried them out to my entire satisfaction. Inspector (local Major) F H Elliot [sic] performed the heavy duties of staff officer to the mounted troops with much tact and zeal; has shown much gallantry in action on numerous occasions. Inspector (local Major) W E Ayliff is a brave and efficient officer (wounded November 3rd). Inspector (local Major) S Lorimer rendered most valuable services, and has been of the greatest assistance in connection with intelligence and other duties.

Sub Inspector (local Captain) J W Colvin most successfully performed duties of quartermaster under most difficult circumstances. Sub Inspector (local Captain) M K Crozier performed excellent service as adjutant to the mounted police. Sub Inspector (local Captain) S [sic should be J T] White commanded artillery section with great success (wounded December 9th). Sub Inspector (local Captain) Cummings is a most deserving officer, and has shown conspicuous gallantry on several occasions. Corporal F R Carson, Privates J Maloney, A Carr, G R Mathieson, S Brown are deserving of mention for good work.

Colonial Ordnance Department — Captain C L Ricketts has proved himself a most valuable officer; I much appreciate the zealous and careful manner in which he has carried out his very responsible duties; also rendered valuable services in connection with supplies.

Diamond Fields Artillery — Captain (local Major) S May invariably handled his guns with much coolness under fire; is a most deserving and efficient officer. Surgeon Lieutenant A J Ortlepp (attached) rendered considerable assistance to wounded in the field.

Diamond Fields Horse — Major T H Rodger is a resourceful and excellent officer, always ready and cool under fire. Sergeant A B Nicholetts on several occasions undertook duties which involved great personal risk; he carried despatches to our troops engaged on November 28th.

Kimberley Regiment — Lieutenant Colonel R A Finlayson commanded his regiment and a section of defence with marked success. Major A O Black commanded a section of defence, and rendered good service. Captain and Adjutant E T Humphrys performed his duties with great zeal and tact. Surgeon Major J A J Smith (attached) rendered most valuable assistance to wounded in the field. Sergeant S H McCallum is deserving of mention for good work.

Kimberley Light Horse — Major (local Lieutenant Colonel) T C Peakman was associated in early days of siege with organisation of Town Guard; his experience and local knowledge were of great assistance to me; subsequently he commanded a squadron of Light Horse, and on death of Lieutenant Colonel Turner was selected by me for command of all mounted corps; he has shown much courage under fire, and is a most deserving and excellent officer (wounded November 18th). Major R G Scott, VC, is an officer of tried experience and gallantry; has on all occasions exhibited the best qualities of an officer. Captain H T Ap-Bowen commanded a squadron with much success, and has on several occasions shown great gallantry in action (very severely wounded November 25th). Captain H [sic] Mahoney performed distinguished service (wounded November 25th).

Captain J A Smith as quartermaster performed much hard work in connection with equipping irregular forces under great difficulties. Captain J W Robertson performed the duties of paymaster, and has also acted as galloper to the late Lieutenant Colonel Turner in a most efficient manner. Captain W E Rickman handled his men with great coolness; his conduct on many occasions has been most distinguished. Captain G E Heberden, Medical Officer, frequently accompanied mounted troops in several sorties and reconnaissances, and rendered most valuable services in attending to wounded. Lieutenant C A Hawker performed excellent service (wounded November 22nd).

Lieutenant W Newdigate did much good work with his squadron; has also executed valuable survey work in connection with defence works. Lieutenant D B Fenn proved himself an invaluable officer; he supplied much valuable information before the outbreak of the war, and has done real good work with mounted troops from the first day Imperial troops arrived. Lieutenant G Harris has done good service and shown conspicuous gallantry. Lieutenant R Chatfield is an excellent officer; he has shown conspicuous gallantry. Sergeant Major W H Oatley, Corporal H Harris, Trooper A H Armstrong are deserving of mention for good work.

Beaconsfield Town Guard — Major J R Fraser, late Loyal North Lancashire Regiment (retired list), at first as staff officer, and later as commanding officer, did excellent work, and has shown great energy and resource. Captain C A Blackbeard did much good work in connection with interior economy of Town Guard and keeping order in township of Beaconsfield. Captain W Nelson performed valuable services in connection with collection of information, and also in procuring enemy's cattle for food supply of garrison.

Kimberley Town Guard — Lieutenant Colonel D Harris, VD, arrived when Town Guard was in course of being raised; he threw himself most heartily into the work, and was of the greatest assistance; much praise is due to him for his good work in looking after the comforts and interests of Town Guard in different works and redoubts, which entailed much hard work and fatigue. Captain S Richards did good work as staff officer. Captain B E A O'Meara performed duties of garrison adjutant and quartermaster with much zeal and energy; has rendered valuable services. Captain T Tyson performed duties of assistant military censor to my complete satisfaction. Captain W Pickering rendered much valuable assistance from date of my arrival, and during a portion of siege commanded a section of defence with success. Captain T L Angel did good work in command of Cyclist Corps. Lieutenant E F Raynham, assistant to the intelligence officer, rendered me very great assistance in dealing with correspondence of a confidential nature.

The following officers also did good work —Captains F Mandy, L R [sic] Grimmer, W S Elkin, H Pim, J Adams, C E Hertog, J Morton, C Tabuteau, E H Moseley, G White, W H Faulkner, A Blum, H Rugg, J Armstrong; Lieutenants C D Lucas, H Tabuteau, J J Coghlan, T Callen, W G Wright, J R Carr, J B Dunbar, S O'Molony. Sergeant Major J P Russell, late RE, as warrant officer, did much valuable work in connection with superintendence of native labour employed on construction of defence works. Sergeant J Russell, Cyclist Corps, is deserving of mention for good work.

Civilians — Right Honourable C J Rhodes (Honorary Colonel, Kimberley Light Horse), took a special interest in the raising of Kimberley Light Horse, and worked most zealously in providing horses for all mounted troops; to him, therefore, is, in a large measure, due the credit for rapidity with which mobility of my mounted corps was obtained.

The Mayor, Mr H A Oliver, rendered excellent services, of which I cannot speak too highly; he has shown real courage, and to him is due much credit for keeping up the spirits of inhabitants during the most trying period of siege. The ex-Mayor, Mr R H Henderson, was indefatigable, and rendered most valuable services in connection with formation of committees dealing with questions of internal order, supplies, etc; to him was also due the efficiency of Fire Brigade and Municipal Police.

Mr J Denoon Duncan performed excellent work as Prosecutor before the Court of Summary Jurisdiction; also rendered most valuable assistance in connection with the regulating of supplies; his advice on legal matters has been invaluable. Mr E A Judge, Civil Commissioner, has done excellent work as a member of the Court of Summary Jurisdiction, and rendered me considerable assistance in other matters. Mr G C Bayne, Resident Magistrate, did valuable work as a member of Court of Summary Jurisdiction. Mr C K O'Molony, Town Clerk, did good work in connection with records of numerous committees which assembled from time to time. Mr L H Cochrane, District Engineer, Cape Government Railways, rendered valuable assistance in connection with railway work. Mr J Gilbert, Superintending Engineer, Cape Government Telegraphs, did good work in connection with telephone service to various forts. Mr W D Fynn rendered valuable assistance in procuring intelligence of enemy's movements, etc. Mr W J Gardiner, Acting Postmaster, did much good work in connection with duties of postal department. Mr J E Symons did excellent work in connection with signalling duties of fortress.

Kimberley Hospital — Dr W Russell, MD, Resident Surgeon, rendered services in connection with reception and treatment of sick and wounded, of which I cannot speak too highly. Dr T L Shiels, MD, Assistant Resident Surgeon, did a considerable amount of hard work in attending to wounded. I cannot speak too highly of the energy and zeal displayed by the following visiting surgeons: Drs E O Ashe, A H Watkins, J E Mackenzie, J Mathias, W J Westerfield, W W Stoney.

Lord Roberts' Despatch of 4th September 1901 (LG 10th September 1901) contained a section on civilians who had rendered good service. The section entitled 'Civil Staff, Kimberley', included the names:

Reverend Archdeacon Holbech, Canon Woodman, J Gifford, H Isaacs, J S Morris, W Pescod, J Scott, W H Richards, Father Morice; Mr Mark Henderson; Captain T Tyson; Dr Smart (sic); Miss Gordon, Matron, Kimberley Hospital; Misses Bainbridge, Child, Couch, Jewell, Nicholson, Strickland, Wallace Sisters; Sister Henrietta, St Michael's Nursing Home; Nurse Watkins; Miss F Brice, Mrs Ashe, Mrs Cornwall, Mrs Watkins[50].

In Lord Kitchener's Final Despatch dated 23rd June 1902 (LG 29th July 1902), there was a mention for Kekewich himself:

Brevet Col. R G Kekewich, CB, has throughout this long campaign maintained his high reputation as a fine soldier of character, loyalty and discretion; he is well qualified to hold high command.

---

[50] Mrs Watkins was the president, Mrs Ashe the Secretary and Mrs Cornwall the Treasurer of the Kimberley Benevolent Society.

Military honours

There were no honours and awards specially given for the defence of Kimberley. Instead, a mention in despatches may result in the gazetting of a military honour some time later. For example the DSO for Captain Angel appeared in the London Gazette on 19th April 1901 while that for Captain Pickering appeared on 27th September 1901. This list is therefore a best estimate of the honours and awards that were issued.

Award	Recipient	Rank	Unit	Notes
CB	Kekewich, R G	Lt Colonel	LNLR	See his biography (page 346)
CMG	Berrange, C A L.	Captain	CP	See his biography (page 338)
	Chamier, G D	Lt Colonel	RGA	See his biography (page 340)
	Finlayson, R A	Lt Colonel	KRV	See his biography (page 343)
	Fraser, J R	Major	LNLR	See his biography (page 344)
	Harris, D	Lt Colonel	KTG	See his biography (page 345)
	Henderson, R H	Mr	Mayor	See his biography (page 345)
	May, T J	Major	DFA	See his biography (page 349)
	Oliver, H A	Mr	Mayor	See his biography (page 351)
	O'Meara, W A J	Major	RE	See his biography (page 351)
	Peakman, T C	Lt Colonel	KLH	See his biography (page 352)
	Robinson, McC B	Lt Colonel	CP	See his biography (page 354)
DSO	Angel, T L	Captain	KTG	See his biography (page 337)
	Bowen, H J Ap O	Captain	KLH	See his biography (page 339)
	Clifford, W R	Lieutenant	LNLR	See his biography (page 340)
	Gorle, H V	Captain	ASC	See his biography (page 344)
	Heberden, G A	Surg Capt	KLH	See his biography (page 345)
	MacInnes D S	Lieutenant	RE	See his biography (page 348)
	McClintock, R L	Lieutenant	RE	See his biography (page 348)
	O'Gorman, C J	Lieutenant	RAMC	See his biography (page 350)
	O'Meara, B E A	Captain	KTG	See his biography (page 351)
	Pickering, W	Captain	KTG	See his biography (page 352)
	Raynham, E F	Lieutenant	KTG	See his biography (page 352)
	Richards, S	Captain	KTG	See his biography (page 353)
	Rickman, W E	Captain	KLH	See his biography (page 353)
	Rodger, T H	Major	DFH/KRV	See his biography (page 354)
	Scott, R G	Major	KLH	See his biography (page 355)
	Smith, J A J	Surg Major	KRV	See his biography (page 356)
DCM	McCallum, S H	Sgt	KRV	LG 27 September 1901
	Mudge, E C	Sgt Maj	LNLR	LG 27 September 1901
	Oatley, W H	Sgt Maj	KLH	LG 27 September 1901
	Russell, J P	Sgt Maj	KTG	LG 27 September 1901

Campaign medal

Almost all of the military personnel received the campaign medal, the Queen's South Africa Medal, with the single clasp 'Defence of Kimberley'. For most[51] this was the only clasp they received as they saw no further military service. However, for many, it was just one of the clasps they received. The medal rolls show the clasps earned by the recipients.

There is an appendix dealing with exceptions to the general rule that the besieged soldiers received the Defence of Kimberley clasp in all cases. This can be seen on page 508.

The unofficial commemorative medals are discussed on page 516.

---

[51] 56% of all recipients received the single clasp. This excludes the 135 people who received the no clasp QSA.

Appendix 09 – Biographies

Abrams, Louis. He was born 18 Oct 1854 near Swindon. He was educated at Highfield Grammar School and married Charlotte Jane Bellow. He was in Kimberley during the siege but not under Military pay so therefore did not receive a medal. He supplied a large number of horses and mules to the British Government during the Boer War. During the Basuto War of 1881-2, he had supplied most of the horses. He used to hold claims in De Beers in the early years of Kimberley and supplied the town with most of its water.

Adams, Sir (Hamilton) John Goold-. He was born in County Cork, Ireland, on 27 Jun 1858. He was educated privately and on the training ship Conway. He joined the Army in Jan 1878, receiving his Captaincy seven years later, and his Majority in the Royal Scots in 1895. He served in Sir Charles Warren's Bechuanaland Expedition in 1884-5 and later commanded the BBP in the Matabele War of 1893. During the Boer War he served during 1899 and 1900, first as Resident Commissioner in Bechuanaland, afterwards having command of the Kimberley Town Guard during the latter half of the siege (twice MID). He retired from his regiment, the Royal Scots, in Mar 1901, when he was appointed Lieutenant-Governor of the ORC. He served as High Commissioner, Cyprus, 1911-14 and then Governor of Queensland. He died in Cape Town, 12 Apr 1920. He received the KCMG and CB (Civil).

Altham, Sir Edward Altham. He was born 13 Apr 1856, at Wilton. He was educated at Winchester, and Christ Church, Oxford. He joined the Royal Scots in 1876, and was employed with the MI Company of that regiment through Warren's Bechuanaland Expedition in 1884-5. He was District Adjutant in Cape Town, 1885-7. psc 1889. He was employed in the Intelligence division of the War Office from 1896 to 1899, except from Jul 1896 to Mar 1897, when he was Military Secretary to the GOC in South Africa, Sir W Goodenough. During the Boer War Colonel Altham served as AAG for Intelligence on White's staff up to the relief of Ladysmith, and subsequently on Lord Methuen's staff in the OFS. He retired on half-pay in 1904. Colonel Altham married in 1880 Emily Georgina, daughter of W Macpherson Nicol, of Inverness. CMG (1901). CB (1904). He served in the Great War and was made KCB 1916 and KCIE 1919. He died 27 Sep 1943.

Angel, Thomas Lombard. He was born 10 Jan 1867, son of John Angel, of Torquay, Devon. He was educated at St Luke's, Torquay, and became a Mechanical Engineer. He served with the Kimberley Regiment in Bechuanaland and again served in the Boer War. During the siege, he was Captain in the Kimberley Cycle Corps. He was MID and created a DSO 19 Apr 1901. He served in the Great War, between 1914-15, as Captain in the Imperial Army, and was later invalided home, became Assistant to the Colonel in Charge of Records, No 6 District, Lichfield, and No 10 District, Hounslow. He first married Mabel, daughter of Charles Abbey, Sculptor, of Richmond, Surrey, and second, Agnes Dunlop, daughter of J Carbery. His medal entitlement was: DSO, CGHGSM (1) Bech (Lt Kimb Regt), QSA (1), KStar. DNW Sep 03 £2,400. CGHGSM (1) Bech, QSA (1). Sotheby Feb 27. QSA (1), KStar. BDW May 93 £600.

Ashe, Dr Evelyn Oliver. He served during the siege as a doctor attached to the Kimberley Hospital and served in the KTG. His account is called '*Besieged by the Boers*'. QSA (1) (officially reimpressed). City Coins Aug 08 £785.

Attwood, Arthur J. He enlisted 22 Sep 1890 and served in the Bechuanaland Rebellion 1897 with the rank of Corporal. During the siege he served with C Squadron, Cape Police and earned QSA (2) and KSA (2). Sub Inspector 1 Nov 1901. Lieutenant, 1st South African Mounted Rifles 1 Apr 1913. Took part in the 1914 Rebellion 1 Sep to 23 Oct 1914. Operations in German South West Africa 18 May to 9 Jul 1915. Acting Magistrate, Otkiwarongo, South West Africa 1915 and Major, Union Defence Force, in WWII. He died in Pietermaritzburg Hospital 1973, aged 102.

Ayliff, William Edward. He first saw action in the Basuto War of 1880-1. He was promoted Sub Inspector 15 Oct 1885 and Lieutenant during the Bechuanaland Rebellion of 1897. Promoted Inspector 7 Jul 1897. He served in the Cape Police during the siege and was wounded 3 Nov 1899. He was MID and received KSA (2). A duplicate QSA was issued to him in 1910.

Barron, Robert B. He served KLH 2 Nov 1899 until DMU 24 Mar 1900 being wounded 25 Nov 1899. His name appears as Barson and Baron. He also served in the FID. The medal roll says he "Came out of Kimberley with despatches and correspondence at Belmont". Appointed Lt 21 Mar 1901. QSA (2) DoK OFS. [KSA (2)]. Sotheby Jan 72. See the appendix on the despatch riders.

Bayne, George Clipperton. He was Resident Magistrate of Kimberley 1895-1900. During the siege, he was a member of the Court of Summary Jurisdiction and was MID by Kekewich. He died in 1907 in Monte Carlo.

Beet, George. He was born 30 Apr 1853 in Canterbury and arrived in South Africa in 1856. By the age of 11 he started work as a copyist. After several jobs he moved to the diamond fields in the early days and began work with the paper, the *Diamond News*, as sub-manager. When he retired from journalism, he became a Law Agent. He took part in the Diggers' Rebellion of 12 Apr 1875 on the Government side. During the siege he served as a Private in the Kimberley Buffs and served in the defences for two months. He took part in the sortie of 28 Nov 1899 and was later appointed Issuer of Permits in the Town Hall.

Belk, Samuel Waterhouse. He was born Sheffield in 1867 and enlisted 18 Jun 1886 in the York and Lancaster Regiment. He served in Halifax, Nova Scotia, West Indies, South Africa and St Helena. He was imprisoned for desertion 20 Sep 1888 to 30 Mar 1889. He transferred to the British Army Reserve at Cape Town 10 Oct 1895. He served in D Troop, Mashonaland Mounted Police, during the Jameson Raid, was captured and repatriated to England. He next served as a Trooper, Matebeleland Relief Force, 1896. During the siege he served KLH from 19 Oct 1899 (Lieutenant 8 Mar 1900) and later as Captain KH. He earned the QSA (4) and KSA (2).

Benjamin, Lionel Harry. He was born in Graaff Reinet, 1 Jun 1858. He arrived in Kimberley in 1894 as Finance Manager of St Augustine Diamond Mine. He served during the siege in KTG. QSA (1). Liverpool Mar 86 £90.

Berrange, Christian Anthony Lawson. Was born 28 Oct 1864 in Graaff Reinet. After leaving school, he joined the Stockenstroom Volunteer Rifles. He saw action in the Galeka War in 1877-8, then the Basuto War in 1881 and joined the Cape Mounted Police in 1883. He was commissioned in 1892, gained his Captaincy in 1897 and majority in 1899. He served in the Bechuanaland Expedition in 1896-7, and the Boer War in 1899-1902. He entered Kimberley after the siege started and later took part in the relief of Mafeking. He was involved in the capture of the 15lb Boer gun that now resides under the Cape Police Monument. Second in command of Colonel Scobell's column 1900. He was captured by the Boers at Schweizer-Reneke in June 1900 and again at Tweebosch on 7 Mar 1902. He commanded a detachment of Cape Police at the Coronation of King Edward in 1902. He earned the QSA (4), KSA (2), CMG 1902 and was MID 2 Apr 1901. Second District Inspector District No 2 May 1903 to March 1904. Acting Commissioner March 1904. Lieutenant-Colonel and Commanding Officer, 5th South African Mounted Rifles 1 Apr 1913. Served in German South West Africa operations 5 Mar to 9 Jul 1915. Inspector-General, South African Forces. Brigadier-General and Brigade Commander 2nd South African Infantry Brigade 15 Dec 1915. East Africa operations February 1916 to March 1917. He retired in 1921 and died in Pretoria 3 Aug 1922. His medal entitlement was: CMG, DSO, SAGS, CGHGSM, QSA, KSA, 14-15 Star, BWM, VM, 1902 Coronation.

Bevan, Ernest Henry. Born in Pietermaritzburg 18 Oct 1870. Enlisted 9 Jan 1891 as Trooper, British South Africa Police (No 683). Joined E Troop at Fort Tuli and Main Drift and was discharged 31 Dec 91. Constable, Mashonaland Civil Police. Served as Trooper, A Troop, Salisbury Horse, Matabele War 1893. Received the Freedom of the City of Bulawayo 4 Nov 1893. Served during the siege in KLH 19 Oct 1899 to 5 Jun 1900. Served in the Kimberley Regiment during the Great War including German South West Africa operations. Also served South African Native Labour Corps. In December 1933 he attended the Rhodesian Pioneers reunion to mark the 40th Anniversary of the occupation of Matebeleland and attended the 50th Anniversary reunion for the siege. During WWII served in 1st Reserve Brigade, Union Defence Force.

Bingham, Charles Henry Marion. He served during the siege with the LNLR. He was severely wounded during the siege (24 Oct 1899) and also on 7 Jan 1901 when he was accidentally shot by a sentry. After the siege he served in ORC in Jul 1900, Transvaal Jul 1900 to May 1901. MID 10 Sep 1901.

Black, Andrew Orman. He was born 1855 and worked as a tailor. He served in the Zulu War and was Staff Sgt Kimberley Scots 1890. Lt Kimberley Rifles 1895. Received the QSA (2), KSA (2) and was awarded the Colonial Auxiliary Forces LS Medal (14 Sep 1909). He was MID 23 Jun 1902. He married Elizabeth Ann and had three sons. He died in 1937.

Blackbeard, Charles Alexander. He was born in Grahamstown 19 Dec 1848. He had a long association with Kimberley and was several times elected Mayor. He served as a trooper in the DFH in the Kaffir War of 1877-8, became Captain in the DFH in 1889. He served as Adjutant in the Beaconsfield Town Guard during the siege, being MID 8 May 1900. At the same time was the Mayor of Beaconsfield. He served as a JP and was a prominent Freemason. He was Chairman of the local Public School, the local branch of the South African League, of the Kroonstad Coal and Estate Company and director of the Griqualand West Diamond Company. He married Miss Annie Robinson McKay on 8 Dec 1875. SAGS (1) 1878 (Tpr DFH), QSA (1) (Capt & Adj KTG), KStar. City Coins Aug 08.

Appendices

Blacking, Fred. Mayor of Beaconsfield and officer commanding D Company of Beaconsfield TG. He died during the siege and was buried on 17 Dec 1899.

Blum, A. He served in the Northern Border Police (No 8 Troop, Frontier Armed and Mounted Police), in the Gaika and Galeka War of 1878 and in the Moirosi's stronghold operations of 1879. During the siege he served as Captain, Kimberley Town Guard (No 3 Redoubt).

Bodley, Joseph Horatio. He had arrived in the Diamond Fields in 1873 and his occupation was cycle agent and cigar importer. He joined the DFH in 1887 and served in the Bechuanaland Rebellion in 1897 earning CGHGSM (1) Bech. During the siege, he served in the KRV and DFH. He was wounded 17 Nov 1899 while serving with the DFH. He left the KRV 20 Jun 1900. He received the Colonial Auxiliary Forces Long Service Medal (10 Jul 1908), served as a recruiting officer 1914-18 and as Adjutant in the Active Defence Rifle Association. He took part in the 1914 Rebellion and died in Johannesburg in 1948.

Botha, Petrus Johannes. He was a Commandant in the Boer forces and was killed in the fight on 24 Oct 1899. He was well known in Kimberley and was identified on the battlefield by someone who knew him.

Bowden, Sidney Vincent. He was born in Troqueer, Scotland in 1871. He enlisted 1889 as a Trooper, Cape Mounted Rifles and was discharged 1894. He served as a Trooper, Bechuanaland Border Police in 1895 and with K Troop, British South Africa Company Police, in the Jameson Raid. He was captured by the Boers at Doornkop, 2 Jan 1896. Repatriated to England from Durban aboard the *Harlech Castle* 24 Jan 1896. Served as Private, Cape Police, in the Bechuanaland Rebellion 1897. He was Lieutenant, District No 1, during the Boer War and served CP 7-pounder detachment during the siege. Sub Inspector, King Williamstown 1904. Chief Constable of Kenhardt 1908. He was dismissed from the Cape Mounted Police in 1911. Served as Second Lieutenant, 4th West Riding (Howitzer) Brigade 26 Mar 1915. Operations in France. Temporary Captain, Transport Section, Royal Field Artillery. Captain, Territorial Force Reserve 18 Dec 1919. His medal entitlement was: CGHGSM (1) Bech (Lt CP), QSA (2), KSA (2), BWM, VM (Capt), DM. Spink 1999.

Bowen, Harry James Ap-Owen. He was born 9 Feb 1867 and worked as a solicitor and was a steward of the Jockey Club of South Africa. He served in the Boer War 1899-1901 in the KLH, was severely wounded 25 Nov 1899, MID LG 10 Sep 1901 and was made a DSO LG 27 Sep 1901. He married, in 1904, Amy Langford Pote.

Bridge, J M. He joined the Kimberley Rifles in 1893 and served as Lt until 31 Jan 1899. He saw service in the Bechuanaland Rebellion in 1897. Served as Captain and Signals Officer, 1st Kimberley Regiment 1 Oct 1914 and later served in the GSWA operations. He attended the 50th Anniversary reunion. His medal entitlement was: CGHGSM (1) Bech (Lt Kimb Rifles), QSA (2) (Capt KVR), KSA (2) (Capt KVR), 14-15 Star (Capt 7th Infy), BWM, VM (Capt), Col Aux Forces Decoration (Capt 7th Infy), KStar. City Coins Sep 03

Brunton, Walter George. Born in Sep 1871, he went to Kimberley in 1872 and joined the DFH in 1890. According to the medal rolls, he served in the KRV, 11 Oct 1899 to 11 Dec 1900, DS as Lt 19 Dec 1900 to 4 Mar 1902 and KH as Captain 5 Mar 1902 to 31 May 1902, gaining the QSA (4) and KSA (2). His biography in *South African Who's Who* suggests he gained entitlement to the clasps for RoK and DoK but this is not possible. In 1903 he was manager of the sorting department at Premier Mine. He was president of the Philharmonic Society and of Sorters Football and Cricket Club.

Butler, Sir William. He was born 31 Oct 1838 in County Tipperary, Ireland. He was commissioned in 1858 and served in India, Canada and Ashanti. He went to Natal in 1875 on Sir Garnet Wolseley's staff. In 1877 he married the artiste Elizabeth Thompson. He saw limited service in the Zulu War but much fighting in Egypt and Sudan. By now a Major General, he returned to South Africa in 1898 as Commander in Chief, succeeding General Goodenough, and High Commissioner during the absence of Milner between Dec 1898 and Feb 1899. He reported that Britain was ill-prepared for a war with the Boers and was much criticised for his openness. In Sep 1899 he resigned and returned to England. He saw no service during the Boer War. He wrote several books based on his experiences and died 7 Jun 1910.

Callen, Thomas. Born in 1857 in Scotland, he worked in the Town Surveyor's Office in Kimberley from 1880, rising to City Engineer by 1887 and retiring in 1920. He was stationed at the Kimberley Reservoir Waterworks during the siege and was involved in the construction of shelters for non-combatants. He died in 1938.

Carlyle, Thomas. Born in 1877 he served as a Trooper in the Mashonaland Mounted Police during the Jameson Raid where he was captured. Repatriated to England from Durban aboard the *Harlech Castle,* he next served as a Trooper, Matebeleland Relief Force, Matabele Rebellion 1896 and in the Bechuanaland Rebellion 1897 gaining GCHGSM (1) Bech. During the siege he served with B Squadron, Cape Police, and was slightly wounded 25 Nov 1899. Afterwards he served in the FID. In the Zulu Rebellion of 1906 he served as a Trooper, Zululand Mounted Rifles. He was Sergeant, Rand Light Infantry during the Great War and served in German South West Africa 16 Sep 1914.

Carstairs Rogers, Fergus. He was born in 1864 and was educated at Dollar Academy and George Watson's School. In London he articled to John MacVicar Anderson. After moving to South Africa, he started his own architect's practice in Kimberley in 1892. He designed the Kimberley Town Hall and other local buildings. He served as Lieutenant in the KTG during the siege and was wounded. He died in 1927.

Chadborn, John Arthur. He was born around 1870 and joined as 2nd Lieutenant, 2nd Volunteer Battalion, Gloucestershire Regiment 11 Jul 1894 before resigning his commission 24 Apr 1895. He next served as Trooper, Artillery Troop, Mashonaland Mounted Police in the Jameson Raid where he was captured. Repatriated to England 24 Jan 1896 he was soon back in South Africa as Paymaster Sergeant Major, Matebeleland Relief Force, taking part in the Matabele Rebellion 1896. During the siege he served in A Squadron of the Cape Police. He was killed at Hoopstad 23 Oct 1900. QSA (4). Lusted May 78 £185.

Chamier, George Daniel. He was born in the East Indies, 24 Sep 1860, the son of Lt General S H E Chamier, CB. He was educated at Cheltenham College and the RMA, Woolwich, where he was gymnastic champion in 1879. He served in the Royal Horse and Field Artillery in India between Mar 1880 and Dec 1885, at Gibraltar in the Royal Garrison Artillery between May 1888 and Jan 1890 and 1891 to 1897, and from 1891 and 1896 as Adjutant in the Lancs Artillery. He took part in the Boer War, and commanded the Artillery in the defence of Kimberley, with the local rank of Lt Colonel, was commandant of Kimberley (graded as DAAG), 1900-01, defended Schweizer-Reneke, in the Transvaal, and commanded a mobile column in the attack on Petrusburg, ORC, in 1901, when the town was captured. He was appointed Commandant and Special Commissioner in the Bloemhof District, Transvaal, in 1901-2. He was created a CMG. He served in Hong Kong Jun 1908 to Dec 1911 when he retired. He was OIC RGA records in Mar 1913. During the Great War he was Inspector of the RGA and Coast Defences in India. He married, in 1903, Amy St Leger, widow of James Buchanan, and daughter of H J Bertram, of Queenstown, South Africa. He died 3 May 1920. His medal entitlement was: CMG, QSA (3), KSA (2), BWM (Brig Gen), KStar. Spink Oct 99 no sale. Spink Aug 00 £2,185.

Clifford, Wigram R. He was born 20 Feb 1876 and was educated at US College, Westward Ho! and the Royal Military College, Sandhurst. He joined the LNLR as 2nd Lieutenant on the 25 Mar 1891 and became Lieutenant, 16 Apr 1899. He served in the Boer War 1899-1901, was present in the siege where he commanded the Mounted Infantry detachment. He was slightly wounded 28 Nov 1899 and was awarded the DSO LG 19 Apr 1901. The Insignia were sent to the Commander-in-Chief in South Africa, and Lord Kitchener was asked to return it. It was presented by the King 25 Jul 1901. He was promoted Captain, Northumberland Fusiliers,12 Oct 1901. He next served on the North-West Frontier of India, 1908, taking part in the Mohmand Expedition. He served as Adjutant, Indian Volunteers, 17 Aug 1912 to 1915. He served in the Great War 1914 to 1917, and was promoted Major, Northumberland Fusiliers, 1 Sep 1915. He married Eva Miles in 1903. He died 20 May 1917. His medal entitlement was: DSO, QSA (4), IGS 1908 (1), 14-15 Star, BWM, VM.

Close, Hugh Marston. He was born 24 Sep 1877. He served in South Africa between Apr 1897 and Dec 1897, Mauritius between Dec 1897 and Sep 1899 and again in South Africa from Sep 1899 to Jan 1902. Promoted to Captain 22 Jan 1902, he was placed on half pay 11 Jun 1904 and entered the reserve on 28 Sep 1907.

Coghlan, Charles Patrick John. Goghlan was born 24 Jun 1863 in King Williamstown. He was educated in Grahamstown and Cape Town. During the siege, he served as a Captain in the KTG. He was elected Member of the Legislative Council for Western Division, Rhodesia, 1908. He was selected as the Rhodesian Delegate to the National Convention of Sep 1908. He served as the first Premier of Southern Rhodesia from 1 Oct 1923 until is death on 28 Aug 1927. He was knighted and buried near Rhodes in the Matopo Hills near Bulawayo.

Cornwall, Moses. Born in Dublin on 6 Jul 1841, he emigrated to South Africa in 1859 and was one of the early settlers in the Diamond Fields in 1870. He was Mayor of Kimberley in 1881, 1882, and 1893 and represented the district of Kimberley in the Cape House of Assembly from 1884 to 1888. For many years he was a member of the Borough Council and Divisional Council. He was Chairman of the Kimberley Hospital Board, the Public Library, and the Rhodes Memorial Committee. He served in the Griqualand West War of 1878 as a Volunteer and during the Boer War in the KTG. He married, 29 Feb 1864, Margaret Lundie, and died in 1906. His medal entitlement was: Order of St John, Officer's badge, SAGS (0) (G W Vol Arty) (medal renamed), QSA (1), KStar. City Coins Dec 04.

Appendices

Crawford, Robert Montgomery. He was born in Ireland in 1863 and went to Cape Town in 1880. He initially worked as a clerk in Kimberley and joined the Cape Police aged 22 on 19 Aug 1885. His starting rate of pay was 9 shillings per day. He worked in Kimberley in the Diamond Detective Department. He reached the rank of Sub Inspector and with it an annual salary of £300. He served throughout the siege and afterwards became Commissioner in Cape Town in 1905. For the opening of the South African parliament in Nov 1910, Crawford was responsible for the protection of the Duke of Connaught and received the MVO. He retired in 1914 after 29 years in the Cape Police. His medal entitlement was: MVO, CGHGSM (1) Bech, QSA (2), KSA (2), Union of SA Medal. Spink Dec 88 £1,200. His medals are shown on page 504.

Cronje, Pietrus Arnoldus. Born in Colesberg in 1836, he was present at the Battle of Boomplaats in 1848 at the age of 12. He distinguished himself by his fighting abilities and was Commandant of Potchefstroom in the First Anglo Boer War. He served on the Executive Council of the Transvaal Volksraad. He was the Commandant of the Boer Army to whom the Jameson Raiders surrendered at Doornkop in 1896. When the Boer War broke out, he was in command of the Western Transvaal, and took park in the siege of Mafeking and then the siege at Kimberley. He participated in the Battles of Modder River, Magersfontein and Paardeberg. Creswicke says of him "in spite of his tricks and tyrannies, he has shown himself a first-class fighter, and a remarkable leader of men. He profoundly detests the British, but the British, while returning the compliment, have a generous appreciation of his abilities." At Paardeberg he was forced to surrender to Lord Roberts with over 4,000 men on 27 Feb 1900. He was sent to St Helena as a prisoner of war. He died in 1911.

Crozier, M K. He served as Captain in the Cape Police during the siege and was MID. He died of disease at Daniel's Kuil on 15 Nov 1900. CGHGSM (1) Bech (Sgt Cape Police), QSA (1) DofK (Lt Cape PD1). Spink Nov 05. Liverpool Feb 06 £670.

Cullinan, John Carr. He served in KLH during the siege being discharged 23 Mar 1900. Afterwards he served in DH (37927) 20 Aug 1901 to 24 May 1902, BSAP, DS 13 Dec 1900 to 4 Feb 1901 and CP2. He joined Cullinan's Horse 1 Mar 1901 and was discharged 27 Jul 1901. He was taken prisoner 15 Oct 1899 near Riverton Waterworks and was MID 1 Jun 1902

Cumming, Arthur William. He was born in 1859 in Chester. He went to the Diamond Fields in 1875 and soon after saw service in the Sekukuni War. He served in the First Boer War of 1881, was captured, but escaped to Delagoa Bay through Swaziland, and went to Durban. During the siege, he made five journeys through the lines, both for the military authorities and Cecil Rhodes. He was present at the battles of Belmont and Magersfontein. At the request of Colonel Henderson, Lord Roberts' Chief Intelligence Officer, he joined the Headquarter Staff after the siege. At the conclusion of hostilities he was made a Captain of the Colonial Forces. He entered Parliament as Member for Barkly West. He married in 1884, Olivia Frances. His medal entitlement was OBE, SAGS (1) 1877-8-9, QSA (6) DoK Belmont OFS RoK Paar Drief, 14-15 Star, BWM, VM with MID, KStar. QSA possibly named to the Klipdam Town Guard. See his medals on page 513.

Damant, Frederick Hugh. He was born in the district of King Williamstown in 1864. He served during the siege in command of a mounted section of the Town Guard Station at Otto's Kopje and afterwards in command of a column from 6 May 1901. After the Relief of Kimberley he served with Rimington's Guides, and in 1901 was appointed to command them. In the same year the name of the Guides was changed to Damant's Horse. Shortly afterwards Major Damant commanded a column in the Orange Free State, and was promoted to Lieutenant Colonel. In a desperate struggle with 800 Boers he received five bullet wounds, but succeeded in saving the guns entrusted to his charge. Later, he took part in operations in the Western Transvaal until the cessation of hostilities. He was MID 31 Mar 1900, 4 May 1900, 4 Aug 1900 and 8 Feb 1901. In addition to the brevet of Colonel, he was created a CB 1902 and DSO 1901. He later became Resident Magistrate for the District of Lydenberg, Transvaal. He died 13 Oct 1926.

Davis, Valfrid Emanuel. He was born 4 Apr 1874 in Sweden. After an education in Sweden he went to South Africa in Oct 1893 and joined the CGR in Mar 1894. He served as shunter, guard, trains foreman, station foreman, acting station master, relief foreman and station inspector. He transferred to the IMR, 1 Oct 1900 and held many positions. He was captured nine times by the Boers during the Boer War. He was fluent in English, French, German and three Scandinavian languages.

De La Rey, Jacobus Hercules (Koos). He was born near Winburg in 1847, the son of a Voortrekker. He lived near Lichtenburg and first worked as a transport rider in the diamond fields and saw military service in the third Basuto war of 1865 and against Sekhukhune in 1876. He entered politics in 1893 and represented Lichtenburg in the Volksraad. Although opposed to the Boer War, he joined the commandos and, being promoted to General, successfully operated in the west, taking part in the battles of Graspan and Modder River. At the battle of Modder River he was wounded and his son was killed. While not fit enough to fight at

Kimberley Siege Account and Medal Roll

Magersfontein it was he who suggested the line of entrenchment should be at the base of the hills rather than the top as the British expected. He was known as the 'The Lion of the West'. He attacked the British camp at Nooitgedacht and was able to capture Lord Methuen at Tweebosch in March 1902. He participated in the peace negotiations. He became a Senator in the Union Parliament and later commanded government troops during the 1914 Johannesburg strike. He met an unfortunate death. While driving through Fordsburg with General Beyers, the car he was travelling in failed to stop at a road block in Johannesburg that was set up to catch the Foster gang. The car was fired on. He was killed by the shot but General Beyers was totally uninjured in the incident.

De Villebois-Mareuil, Georges. He was born in Nantes, France, in 1847. He passed out from St Cyr Military Academy in 1868 and was commissioned into the Infanterie de Marine, being sent to French Indo-China. In 1870 he returned to France and participated in the Franco-Prussian war. He also served in the Tunisian Campaign of 1881 in the Foreign Legion. He offered his services as a military adviser to the Boers at the start of the Boer War. He was present at Colenso and Caesar's Camp/Wagon Hill on 6 January 1900. In the Western Theatre he was for a time involved in the siege of Kimberley and later escaped capture from the surrender at Paardeberg. He formed an international brigade with the rank of General and located himself back in the area to the east of Kimberley. He met his end at Tweefontein near Boshof in April 1900. Lord Methuen buried him with full military honours. His body was exhumed in 1971 and reinterred in the Burgher Memorial at Magersfontein.

De Putron, Cyril. He was born in 1874. Commissioned 2nd Lieutenant (from Militia), 1st LNLR in 1895 and Lieutenant in 1897. He was Assistant Signalling Officer and Brigade Transport Officer during the siege and was MID. Captain 2nd Lancashire Fusiliers 15 Jun 1901. He was Instructor, School of Musketry (Hythe), 1 Apr 1909 to 31 Mar 1913. He was attached to the General Staff (graded Brigade-Major), Northern Command, 1 Dec 1913 to 16 Mar 1915. He served during the Great War in Gallipoli, Mar 1915 to Oct 1915, the Balkans Oct 1915 to April 1916 and Nov 1916 to Jun 1917. He served on the Western Front May 1916 to Nov 1916; with the Egyptian Expeditionary Force, Jun 1917 to May 1918. Commandant, School of Musketry Southern Command, 19 Aug 1918 to 11 Mar 1919. Lieutenant Colonel 22 Mar 1920. Colonel 22 Mar 1924. Officer in Command Record and Pay Office Royal Tank Corps 12 Mar 1927. His medal entitlement was: QSA (3), KSA (2) (Capt C de Putron. Lanc Fus), KStar, 1914-15 Star (Capt Lan Fus), BWM, VM & MID (Col), France, Legion of Honour, Knight's Badge, France, Croix de Guerre 1914-18, avec palmes. Spink Jul 06 £1,800.

Dunbar, J Brander. During the siege he was the officer commanding at Otto's Kopje as a Lieutenant in the KLH. He had previously served in the Cameron Highlanders. There were around 40-50 men stationed at Otto's Kopje, hence their nickname as the 'Forty Thieves'. Heberden said the 'roughest men in Kimberley' were stationed there.

Duncan, James Denoon. He was born 30 Sep 1861 and arrived in Kimberley in 1881. Admitted Conveyancer of the High Court of Griqualand in 1887, he became Attorney-at-Law and Notary Public at the Supreme Court, Cape Colony, in 1888. He was a member of Kimberley School Board and Library Committee, and Chairman of the Kimberley Branch of the South African Imperial Union. On the outbreak of the Boer War, he volunteered his services and was appointed their legal adviser, subsequently being appointed Military Crown Prosecutor during the siege where he rendered services in connection with the regulating of supplies and a scheme for the removal of the inhabitants. For information about his medal claim, see page 510.

Eliot, Algernon Ernest Albert. He was born in Cape Town on 19 Apr 1867. He enlisted on 1 Apr 1890 as a trooper in the British South Africa Police, transferring to the Pioneer Corps six months later. He served in the Mashonaland Expedition of 1890. During the siege, he served as a Lieutenant in the KTG in the Cycle Corps, A Company.

Eliott, Francis Augustus Heathfield. He was born 3 Jul 1867 and was educated at the Oxford Military College, Cowley. He joined the Bechuanaland Border Police in 1892. On the annexation of the Crown Colony to the Cape Colony, he was appointed Sub Inspector in the CMP. He served during the Bechuanaland Campaign of 1896-97 gaining GCHGSM (1) Bech and in the Boer War 1899-1902, taking part in the siege and in operations in the OFS. He was MID 8 May 1900 and 10 Apr 1901. He was created DSO LG 9 Nov 1907 for services on the North-West Frontier of South Africa and was twice MID for conduct on the German Frontier (South-West Africa) in 1907, when he was operating in conjunction with the Imperial German Troops against Morenga. Besides the DSO, he received the 2nd Class Order of the Royal Crown of Prussia with Swords, and the German South West Africa Commemorative Medal with clasp 'Kalahari 1907'. He became Major in the Cape Colonial Forces, and District Inspector in the CMP. He served in the Great War 1914-18, seeing service in the campaign in South-West Africa, under General Botha, as Lieutenant Colonel in command of the 3rd South African Mounted Riflemen. He also served under General Smuts in East Africa, with the 6th Mounted Brigade, in command of the 4th South African Horse, and with the 1st Mounted Brigade, and was mentioned in Despatches twice. He was subsequently in France on the Staff of the 5th Army until invalided with malaria. He married, in 1890, Evelyn Georgina, and died 29 Jul 1937.

Elphinstone, Frederick Stephen. Born in Aberdeen 24 Jun 1875, he was educated at Gordon's College and Aberdeen University. He arrived in South Africa in 1898 and worked as a maths and science teacher 1898-9 and 1902. He served during the siege in the KRV. He started a career in surveying in 1903 and was admitted to the practice in 1906.

Eyre, Edwin. He was born in Mar 1866 at King Williamstown, Cork, and enlisted at Londonderry in Sep 1888. He lost his left eye in Oct 1895. Despite this injury he became Sergeant in 1896, and was promoted to Sergeant Instructor of Gunnery in Apr 1898, posted to the Depot Establishment, Western Division, Cape District. After service during the siege he re-engaged at Cape Town, to complete his 21 years service. He returned from South Africa in May 1906 and was posted as Quartermaster Sergeant Instructor of Gunnery to the School of Gunnery at Sheerness. He was discharged in Jan 1909 and, in the following July, joined the Corps of Commissionaires with whom he served until October 1935. He died at New Barnet on 28 Jul 1945. His medal entitlement was: QSA (3), KSA (2), KStar, Corps of Commissionaires Order of Merit. DNW Jun 99 £280.

Fabling, Launcelot Matthew. He was born around 1877 and before the age of 20 had been captured by the Boers during the Jameson Raid (A Troop, Mashonaland Mounted Police). Repatriated to England from Durban, he next served as a Private, Cape Police, in the Bechuanaland Rebellion 1897. During the siege he served with the CP 7-pounder detachment. Corporal, Cape Mounted Police in 1904. He applied to be a Chief Constable and was recommended to be a Sergeant in 1905. He died in the Cape Province around 1924. His medal entitlement was: CGHGSM (1) Bech (Pte CP), QSA (4), [KSA (2)], KStar. City Coins Oct 89. City Coins Nov 07.

Ferreira, Ignatius S. He was born in Pretoria and spent some of his life in Kimberley. He was one of the first pioneers of the Johannesburg gold fields in 1886. A Colonel in 1886 he was Boer general at the start of the Boer War. He succeeded C J Wessels on 1 Jan 1900. He was accidentally killed at Paardeberg. De Wet said of him "It was while I was engaged in my efforts to relieve Cronje, that a gun accident occurred in which General Ferreira was fatally wounded. Not only his own family, but the whole nation, lost in him a man whom they can never forget. I received the sad news the day after his death, and, although the place of his burial was not more than two hours' ride from my camp, I was too much occupied with my own affairs to be able to attend his funeral."

Field, Horatio George. He served as a despatch rider in KTG during the early part of the siege. He was captured 22 Nov 1899 and escaped from Bloemfontein 19 Dec 1899, returning to Kimberley 9 Jan 1900. Heberden said in her diary "Jan 9th, Mr Field, a Despatch Rider from here who was captured some weeks ago and sent to Bloemfontein, escaped, and arrived back this morning. Jack says his complexion is marvellously pale and clear, almost like that of a person who is dead. He had had most exciting adventures and been practically 9 days without food." He later served with the Scottish Horse 20 Dec 1900 to 24 Apr 1902 and earned KSA (2). Prior to the Boer War, he probably served with the Griqualand West Brigade in the Bechuanaland Rebellion of 1897 earning GCHGSM (1) Bech.

Finlayson, Robert Alexander. Born 11 Oct 1857, he was educated at John Watson's, Edinburgh. He went to South Africa in 1875. In 1882 he was working in the Railway Department. He joined the Kimberley Regiment as Lieutenant in 1889 and was promoted Captain in 1891 and Major in 1895. He commanded the Infantry at Phokwani in the Bechuanaland Rebellion of1896-97 being promoted Lieutenant Colonel in the year the Boer War commenced. He commanded the Kimberley Regiment and a section of the defences during the siege. Afterwards, he served on columns operating in OFS and Transvaal, 1900-1902. He was awarded the CMG and retired in 1904. During the Great War, he raised and commanded 3/6 Battalion Royal Sussex Regiment, 1915-19. He married, in 1887, Miss Emily Bees, of Kimberley. His death was recorded on 28 Nov 1940. His medal entitlement was: CMG, CGHGSM (1) Bech (Maj, Kimb Rfs), QSA (3) (Lt Col, CMG, Kim. Rgt), KSA (2) (Lt Col, CMG Kimberley Vol Regt), Colonial Auxiliary Forces Decoration GV (Lt.-Col, Ex. Kim. R). Glendining Sep 89 £1,200. His medals can be seen on page 505.

Fisher, Edward Montague. He enlisted 13 May 1887 in the 10th Hussars and was commissioned into the 2nd Volunteer Battalion of the Suffolk Regiment. He enlisted again, in the Cape Police, 6 Feb 1892 with the rank of sergeant. Served in the Bechuanaland Rebellion of 1897, he was promoted Sub Inspector 12 Apr 1899. During the siege he served with C Squadron of the Cape Police and earned KSA (2). Inspector 18 Aug 1902. Captain, 5th South African Mounted Rifles 1 Apr 1913 and served during the Great War with the rank of Major.

Kimberley Siege Account and Medal Roll

Fletcher, Walter John Cumberlege. He was born 26 Nov 1879, educated at Tonbridge School, and entered the LNLR from the Militia in May 1899. He then joined the 1st Battalion in Cape Town, and proceeded to Kimberley in October. He died of sunstroke at Kimberley, 18 Oct 1899 aged 19. He was the first officer to die during the war.

Foy, Louis Arnold. He enlisted as a Trooper in the Frontier Armed and Mounted Police and took part in the Gaika and Galeka War 1877-78. He joined the CMR and was discharged in 1878. He saw service as Lieutenant, Baker's Horse, in the Zulu War 1879 and as Lieutenant, Baca Contingent, in the Transkei Rebellion of 1881. He worked in the Imperial Telegraph's Department, Natal and as Temporary Clerk to the Resident Magistrate, Mr Ayliff. Promoted Sub Inspector, Cape Police 15 Jan 1888 and Inspector 1 Jan 1890. During the siege he served as Captain, Cape Police (A Squadron) and later joined the FLH as Captain. He earned the QSA (1) and KSA (2).

Fraser, John Randal. He was first commissioned 1 May 1878 in the LNLR. During the siege, he commanded the Beaconsfield Town Guard. He was promoted Honorary Lieutenant Colonel 12 Apr 1917 and died Jan 1924. He was awarded the CMG for his Boer War service. [CMG], QSA (3). Seaby Dec 58 £7.

Gibson, William Mitchell. He was a Trooper, Bechuanaland Border Police in the Matabele War, 1893 including action at Shangani. He was present during the Jameson Raid in K Troop, British South Africa Company Police and was captured. He resided in Mafeking in 1896. He next served as a Trooper, Mashonaland Mounted Police, in the Matabele Rebellion 1896. During the siege he served as Sergeant Major, KLH. He was discharged 17 Jul 1900.

Gifford, Sophie Catherine. She joined the Kimberley nursing service on 1 Mar 1900 and appears on the medal roll. She was an Honorary Serving Sister of the Order of St John of Jerusalem in England. She married, in 1880, Lord Gifford.

Gill, Lionel Walter John. He was born 21 May 1874 in Cape Town. He was educated in the Diocesan College, Cape Town and married in 1901, Daisy Heywood. He had joined the Cape Civil Service in Jan 1894 and rose to Chief Magistrate in Johannesburg in Feb 1907. During the siege he served in the KTG.

Gillett, John Lionel. He was born 1878 in Bordeaux, France and educated privately. He arrived in South Africa in 1892 and joined the Postal Telegraph Department at Montagu. He was appointed to the Postmaster General's Office in 1895 and transferred to the Law Department in 1897. He served during the siege and was Press Censor and Intelligence Officer at Uniondale in 1901.

Glover, Louis Samuel. He was born in London 10 May 1875. Having been shipwrecked en route to New Zealand he worked there for four years before returning home to gain some experience of tin mining before heading for the gold fields. Unable to find mining work he joined the Rhodesian Police for 5 shillings per day. He took part in the Mashonaland Rebellion of 1886-7. He contracted malaria and was discharged medically unfit. He joining De Beers in 1898 and served as galloper for Colonel Scott in the KLH during the siege. He followed Scott to the SRG and was commissioned. After the Boer War he took up farming in Bechuanaland. During the Great War he volunteered for the SANLSC and served in France. His medal entitlement was: CBE (Civil), BSACM (1) Mashonaland 1897 (70 BSAP), QSA (3), KSA (2), BWM, VM (Lt SANLSC), 1953 Coronation Medal, KStar.

Goodenough, William Howley. He was born in 1833. In 1896 he was serving as General Officer Commanding the troops in South Africa. Wolseley, then Commander in Chief of the Army, had encouraged Goodenough to draw up plans for the defence of South Africa. For a short period in 1898, he was Acting Governor of Cape Colony. He died in 1898.

Gordon Sprigg, Sir John. Born 1830, he began work as a shorthand writer at the Houses of Parliament. He visited South Africa in 1858 as a form of recuperation but settled and took up farming. He was elected to the House of Assembly in 1869 and was called on nine years later to form a Cabinet, being Prime Minister until 1881. He was Premier again Nov 1886 to Oct 1890, Jan 1896 to Oct 1898 and for the fourth time Jun 1900 to Feb 1904. KCMG 1886. Privy Councillor 1897. He died in 1913.

Gorle, Harry Vaughan. He was born at Poughill, Cornwall, 3 Sep 1868 and educated privately. He joined the Royal Berkshire Regiment from the Militia on 28 Jun 1890, becoming Lieutenant, Lincoln Regiment, 29 Sep 1893. He joined the ASC and was promoted Captain 1 Apr 1898. During the siege, he served as supply officer. See his account (page 555). He participated in operations in ORC, May to 29 Nov 1900, operations in Cape Colony, north of Orange River; operations in ORC, Mar to 31 May 1902, operations in Cape Colony 30 Nov 1900 to Mar 1902. He was MID 6 May 1900, and 19 Sep 1901. He was awarded the DSO LG 27 Sep

Appendices

1901. He was promoted to Major 3 Feb 1905 and retired 6 Jun 1908. He served in the Great War 1914-18 and in Salonika 1916-18. He married in 1895, Ethel Katherine (who died in 1904). Their son was Temporary Lieutenant Robert Vaughan Gorle, VC. He married again in 1914, Edith Mary. He died 9 Jan 1937.

Green, Arthur James. Born in 1856 in Grahamstown, he moved to Kimberley in 1883 and worked for Holt & Holt. He saw service in the Frontier Wars of 1877-8, Bechuanaland Rebellion 1896-7 and during the siege as Captain and Paymaster of KRV. He was manager of Cuthbert's Ltd for 30 years. He was twice married and had 9 children.

Green, George Alfred Lawrence. Born in Portsmouth in 1868, he arrived in South Africa in 1894, joining the staff of the *Cape Times*. He was editor of the *Diamond Fields Advertiser* from 1898 and throughout the siege. He married Katherine Bell in 1899.

Hambly, William John. During the siege Hambly was employed in the Field Intelligence Detective Branch. During his police career he was commended twice. His medal entitlement was: BSACM (1) Rhod 96 (Cpl BB Police), QSA (3), KSA (2), 14-15 Star (Sgt 5th SAMR), BWM, VM (Sgt), KStar, 1902 Coronation. GB Military Antiques Jul 03 £1,800. GB Military Antiques Feb 2004 £1,400.

Harris, David. He was born in London, 12 Jul 1852 and educated at Coxford's College, London. He arrived in Cape Colony in 1871, served in the Diamond Fields Horse through the Gaika-Galeka War, 1877-8 (MID), took part in the Griqua War of 1878 and commanded the Field Force in the Bechuanaland Rebellion in 1896 for which he received the thanks of the Government. During the siege he commanded the KTG. He was MID and awarded the CMG. He also received the Volunteer Decoration, and won medals, cups, and team trophies for rifle shooting. He entered the Cape Parliament as a Progressive member for Kimberley in 1897. He was a director of De Beers. He married, 12 Nov 1873, Rosa Gabriel, of Pomerania, Prussia. He died 23 Sep 1942.

Harrison, Fred. He was born 23 Feb 1873 and migrated to South Africa in 1895. He served as a sergeant in the Kimberley Regiment in 1896 and was involved in the Bechuanaland Rebellion of 1897 earning CGHGSM (1) Bech. Promoted Lieutenant in 1899 he served throughout the siege and gained the KSA (2). He retired in 1902 but again served as a Captain in the 2nd Kimberley Regiment in German South West Africa. He was killed in action at Trekkopies 26 Apr 1915.

Hartigan, Marcus Michael. Born in 1878, he was educated at Portora School, Enniskillen. He served in the Boer War and was wounded during the siege while serving with the DFA. He also served in PMP and SAC as Lieutenant. In the Great War, he raised and commanded Hartigan's Horse serving in South West Africa and then with the 9th South African Horse he served in East Africa. Later he served with the 10th battalion Royal Dublin Fusiliers and 2nd battalion Royal Munster Fusiliers in France. With the Munster Fusiliers he was wounded and captured (31 Mar 1918). His medal entitlement was: CMG, DSO and bar, QSA (2), KSA (2), 14-15 Trio with MID, KStar. Miniatures only DNW Apr 03 £260.

Heberden, George Alfred. He was born 27 Apr 1860, son of Reverend George Heberden. He was educated at Malvern College, at Jesus College, Cambridge and at St George's Hospital, London (MRCS, England; LRCP, London, 1888). He was District Commissioner of Predasdorp, 1888-89, Surgeon, Cape Government Railway, 1890-92, District Surgeon, Kenhardt, 1893-94, Barkly West, 1895. He was in Barkly West in Sep 1899 and moved to Kimberley with his wife, son of three, Reggie, and cousin, leaving everything they had behind them. He served in the Boer War as Medical Officer to the Mounted Forces during the Siege of Kimberley, was MID and created a DSO LG 19 Apr 1901. He also served as civil surgeon attached Royal Army Medical Corps. Captain Heberden married, in 1895, Winifred, daughter of Reverend Henry Cottam. Winifred Heberden's siege diary has been published in the Military History Journal, volume 3.

Henderson, Robert Hugh. He was born in Armagh in 1862 and arrived in South Africa in 1884. Shortly afterwards, he opened a business in Kimberley. He married Mattie in 1892. He was Mayor of Kimberley when the siege commenced and also afterwards in 1903. He was awarded the CMG for his services. His CMG was presented by Sir Walter Hely-Hutchinson. Henderson said "I felt specially honoured when the Governor, Sir Walter Hely-Hutchinson, came to Kimberley to pin the decoration on me, which he did on the Kimberley station. Sir Walter was a member of a well-known North of Ireland family, whose estate was adjacent to my own home. He assured me it was a great honour to be able to decorate a fellow countryman." He attended the 50th Anniversary reunion. His Kimberley Star was sold at Spink, Dec 1995, £80. His QSA is held by the McGregor Museum.

Hertog, Charles Edward. Born 3 Sep 1872 in Port Elizabeth, he was educated in Holland. During the siege he served as Paymaster of the KTG and was MID. He attended the 50th Anniversary reunion. He married Elise Gabriella, daughter of David Harris, in 1898.

Hewett, Arthur Wedderburn. He was born Dec 1875, educated at Sutton Valence School, and entered the LNLR from the Royal Military College Sep 1896, being promoted Lieutenant Sep 1899. He served with the 1st Battalion in South Africa, and took part in the siege. He was also present at the action at Carter's Ridge and the subsequent operations in the ORC. Lieutenant Hewett saw much service in connection with convoys, and was invalided home Aug 1900. On recovering, he returned to South Africa in the following Nov and joined Lieutenant General Lord Methuen's column. He was killed in action at Hartebeestfontein 16 Feb 1901. He fell while leading his men under a very severe fire from the Boer position.

Hickson-Mahoney, J C. He worked as the assistant registrar of the Native Department, Kimberley and had charge of the Beaconsfield office. He served as Captain in Ross and Hickson's Horse in the Basuto War 1880-81. He served as Lieutenant in the Cape Infantry Regiment in Feb 1882 and in the Cape Mounted Rifles in 1889. During the siege he commanded D Squadron, KLH and was wounded 25 Nov 1899. After resigning from the KLH, he served in SRG 16 Mar 1901 to 31 May 1901.

Holbech, William Arthur. He was born in 1850 and emigrated to South Africa in 1876. He was Rector of Dutoitspan 1877-81 and Archdeacon of Kimberley 1895-1902. He served during the siege as Honorary Chaplain of the KRV. He became Dean of Bloemfontein in 1902 and served until 1905.

Howie, C. He served in the Kimberley Rifles and took part in the Bechuanaland Rebellion 1897 earning CGHGSM (1) Bech. He was in charge of a company of the regiment during the siege. Afterwards he served as APM in Kimberley and RSO in Vryburg and Kimberley and was awarded the QSA and KSA (2).

Humphrys, Edward Thomas. He served in the Bechuanaland Rebellion 1897 as Lieutenant, Kimberley Rifles earning CGHGSM (1) Bech. During the siege, he was Captain and Adjutant, Kimberley Regiment. MID twice and awarded the QSA and KSA (2). He was Captain and Adjutant, 7th Infantry (Kimberley Regiment) 1 Jan 1913 and Brevet Major 1 Jul 1913. He served in the German South West Africa operations 24 Aug 1914 to 30 Apr 1915. He died in Scotland 3 May 1916 and was buried Kirkee, Scotland. His QSA is held by the McGregor Museum.

Idebski, William Martin. He was born in 1850 in Glasgow, the son of a Polish nobleman. He was educated privately in Devon, and arrived in South Africa in 1873. He went to Kimberley as a digger, but joined the Griqualand West Constabulary the following year. He had charge of the mounted police in Kimberley and was also attached to the Diamond detective department, of which he eventually became chief. He received the appointment of Chief Detective Inspector of Johannesburg with the rank of Deputy Commissioner of Police for the Transvaal. He was a JP. Stories of his exploits in catching illicit diamond buyers can be found in Douglas Blackburn's *Secret Service in South Africa* and Sir Lionel Phillips' *Some Reminiscences*. QSA (1). Carter Feb 95 £155. Spink Oct 99 £480.

Johnston, Hugh Bertie Henriques. Born 10 Nov 1874 he joined the RGA and was promoted Captain 4 Jan 1902. He served in South Africa Apr 1897 to Apr 1901, Bermuda between Oct 1907 to Apr 1908 and Canada from Apr 1908 to Dec 1909. He was killed in action in France in 1916. He was buried in Flatiron Copse Cemetery, Mametz, Somme and is commemorated in Cheltenham Cemetery.

Judge, Edward Arthur. He was born in Cape Town in 1835. He entered the Colonial Civil Service in 1856 and was appointed in 1882 to be Civil Commissioner and Registrar of Deeds in Kimberley. During the siege, he was a member of the Court of Summary Jurisdiction and was MID by Kekewich.

Kekewich, Robert George. He was the second son of Trehawke Kekewich of Peamore in Devon and was born 17 Jun 1854. He was educated at King Edward's School, Birmingham and Marlborough College afterwards entering the army through the militia in 1874. His first campaign service was with the Perak expedition of 1875-6 where he was awarded the medal and clasp. His second war service was with the Soudan expedition of 1888 as DAAG and QMG of British troops. He took part in the action at Gemaizeh was MID LG 11 Jan 1889, awarded the medal and two clasps and the 4th class of the Medjidie. By 1890 he was a Major in the Royal Inniskilling Fusiliers. He was posted to South Africa before hostilities commenced and arrived in Kimberley to take command of the troops in the town. He served in command of the 1st Loyal North Lancashire Regiment to Dec 1900 and as commander Griqualand West and Bechuanaland. After Kimberley, he served in command of a mobile column from Dec 1900 to Jan 1901 and from Jul 1901 to Jan 1902 and afterwards in command of a group of mobile columns from Feb 1902 to the end of hostilities. He was severely wounded at Moedwil on 30 Sep 1901. He was MID thrice LG 8 May 1900, 3 Dec 1901 and 29 Jul 1902. Granted Brevet of Colonel, he was promoted Major General for distinguished service, LG 31 Oct 1902 and made a CB. He was found dead on 5 Nov 1914 at his residence at Whimple, near Exeter, with a gunshot in the head. He had committed suicide. The Major, Councillors and Citizens of Kimberley passed a resolution recalling 'with deepest gratitude their immense obligations to Major General Kekewich and sincerely deplored his death'. At the inquest it was stated that he suffered from suppressed gout, insomnia and an unsatisfactory state of the heart. He worried over being unable to serve his country and depression overcame him. The verdict 'suicide whilst temporarily insane' was returned. The funeral took place in Exminster. His medal entitlement was: CB, IGS 54 (1) Perak (Lt 3rd Foot), Egypt (2) The Nile 1884-5 Gemaizah 1888 (Capt E Kent Regt), QSA (3) (Col L N Lancs), KSA (2) (Col CB Staff), Turkey Order of Medjidie 4th, Khedive's Star 1884-6, Denmark Order of the Dannebrog FVIII Commander. See page 500 for his medals.

Kirsten, Frederick Benjamin Adolphe. He was born in 1872 in Bethulie, ORC. He was educated in Kimberley and married Mabel Hitchman in Jun 1898. He was employed by De Beers for 21 years. He was part inventor of the diamond recovery process with George Labram. During the siege he was involved with the "construction of forts and barricades etc" but, as he was not under Military pay, he was not entitled to the DoK clasp to his QSA.

Kolbe, Willem J. Born near Philippolis, OFS, in 1847. He grew up in Bloemfontein and saw active service in 1865 in the Basuto War. He led the Bloemfontein Commando during the Boer War. He was present during the siege of Kimberley and later at Paardeberg, Driefontein and the Brandwater Basin. He also accompanied De Wet during his incursion into Cape Colony in February 1901.

Lange, Johannes Henricus. He was born in 1852 and educated at Trinity College, Cambridge and called to the Bar of the Inner Temple 1876. He was Parliamentary Draughtsman and Clerk of the Legislative Council of Griqualand West from Dec 1878, until its annexation to the Cape Colony in Oct 1880. He was practising at the Bar of the High Court of Griqualand West. He was a Member of the House of Assembly for Kimberley from 1888 until his appointment as Crown Prosecutor of Griqualand West in Nov 1892. He was appointed Judge, Supreme Court, 1896. During the siege, he was President of the Court of Summary Jurisdiction. He died in 1923.

Labram, George F. He was born in Detroit, Michigan in 1859. His father was an engineer and influenced George to follow in his footsteps. His family had little means and his schooling was often intermittent. However his enquiring mind and access to engineering literature helped him to develop a good understanding of engineering principles. By the time he was 5, his father was working at the Quincy Mine in Hancock, Michigan. In his youth, he was employed by S F Hodge and Co working in machine manufacture. He held a number of jobs in manufacturing working for companies including M C Bullock, the Silver King Mining Company, the Boston and Montana Consolidated Copper and Silver Mining Company and the Butte and Boston Mining Company. His work saw him living in Arizona, Montana and then Dakota. He became involved with De Beers in 1893, aged 33, when he was asked to go to London to work on plans for a concentrating plant for Kimberley. He moved to South Africa and rose to become Chief Engineer of De Beers in 1896. His record of achievements is astounding. Chief amongst these was the discovery, with F B A Kirsten, of a method for recovering diamonds which is still in use. Labram wanted to return to America and resigned from De Beers on 30 Sep 1899. The imminence of war made him stay on in Kimberley and employ his knowledge and experience for the city's benefit during the siege. The privations of the siege brought out the best in him and he developed many solutions to problems that were of immense help to the town. The zenith of his achievements was the production of Long Cecil (for more details see page 529). He also fitted out four armoured siege trains, build the conning tower for Kekewich, created a telephone network, build retractable searchlight platforms, built a water supply system for the town when the pumping station was destroyed, built the cold storage facility to provide meat and made ordnance both for Long Cecil and the other artillery pieces. His engineering genius was matched by his character and he was much admired and liked in the town. He was one of the few people during the siege who could call Kekewich and Rhodes friends. His lodgings were in the Grand Hotel and it was there he returned on the evening of 9 Feb 1900. He was tragically killed by a shell from the Boer Long Tom. He left a wife and son.

Lawson, Charles Frederick. Born around 1864, he was a Jameson Raider (A Troop, Mashonaland Mounted Police) and was captured in 1896. Repatriated to England he was in South Africa the same year to participate as a Sergeant in the Matabele Relief Force, Matabele Rebellion 1896. He served with the KLH 19 Oct 1899 to 14 Mar 1900 and after the siege as Lieutenant Border Scouts 27 Apr 1901 to 31 May 1902. BSACM reverse Rhodesia 1896 (Sgt MRF), QSA (2). Spink Feb 80 £375. DNW Dec 91 £240.

Lester, Charles Reginald. He was Sergeant, A Troop, Mashonaland Mounted Police, and took part in the Jameson Raid. After his capture and repatriation he served as Squadron Sergeant Major, Mashonaland Mounted Police, in the Matabele Rebellion of 1896. He was a Locomotive Department employee, Kimberley, in 1897. During the siege he served with KRV, wounded 16 Nov 1899 and discharged 10 May 1900.

Liddiard, Eaben John. He was born in Kimberley 26 Oct 1880. During the siege he was Staff Trumpeter in the KRV, being discharged medically unfit 12 Apr 1900. Afterwards he was Director of the Dickie Power Generator Syndicate and was electrical contractor to the Kimberley Council.

Lowndes, John Gordon. He served in the Loyal North Lancashire Regiment, being promoted 2nd Lieutenant 30 Jul 1890 and Lieutenant 24 Aug 1892. He was promoted to Captain 12 Mar 1900, served in the Boer War 1899-1900 and was severely wounded 24 Oct 1899. MID 10 Sep 1901.

Luard, G M C. He was a war correspondent working with Reuters news agency.

Lucas, Claude Davis. He was born in 1875 in Queenstown. He was educated at St Andrew's College, Grahamstown and went on to marry in 1899 Mabel Vaughan Smith. During the siege, he served as Intelligence Officer in the KTG and was MID. He used his surveying knowledge to help with the sighting and ranging of Long Cecil. He went to Johannesburg in 1903 and joined the Land Department as Surveyor. Subsequently he opened a practice in Ermelo. His *Notes on the siege of Kimberley* were published in the St Andrew's College Magazine, May 1900.

MacInnes, Duncan Sayre. Born in Hamilton, Ontario, 19 Jul 1870, he was the son of Honourable Donald MacInnes. He was educated for the Navy but entered the Royal Military College, Kingston, Canada, from which, he passed out at the head of his year with Sword of Honour and Gold Medal. He obtained a commission as 2nd Lieutenant in the Royal Engineers on 16 Jul 1891. He saw service in Ashanti and was MID. Afterwards, he was employed on the design and building of the fort at Coomassie. The fort was besieged by fifteen thousand Ashantis in 1900, and held out until relieved by Colonel Sir James Willcocks, who described it as the best defensive post he saw in West Africa. He acted as Resident at Coomassie. Posted to South Africa he served in the siege as Staff Officer to Kekewich. He was again MID. He then served in the ORC and awarded the DSO LG 19 Apr 1901. He was promoted Captain on 1 Apr 1902. He married Millicent Wolfeston Thomas on 22 Oct 1902 in Montreal. He was employed with the SAC between Nov 1902 and Dec 1904. From 1905 to 1908 he was employed on the Staff in Canada, first as DAQMG and later as DAAG. MacInnes then returned to England and later attended the Staff College. He was GSO3 between Apr 1910 and Oct 1912 and was then employed as Secretary to the Royal Flying Corps Committee which led to the formation of the RFC. He served in the Great War and took part in the retreat from Mons. Wounded in Nov 1914, he held a number of posts including Director of Aeronautical Equipment, with the rank of Brigadier General. He returned to France in Mar 1917 as RE Commander of the 42nd Division and later appointed Inspector of Mines at Headquarters. On 23 May 1918, he was killed and was buried in the Military Cemetery at Etaples. His medal entitlement was: CMG, DSO, Ashanti Star, QSA (3), KSA (2), 14 Star, BWM, VM, Russia Order of St Stanislaus, France Legion d'Honneur.

McClintock, Robert Lyle. Born 26 Mar 1874, the son of Colonel W McClintock, RA, of Dunmore, County Donegal. He was educated at Wellington College and entered the Army, as 2nd Lieutenant, Royal Engineers, 25 Jul 1893. He served with the Niger Expeditionary Force, 1897-98, including the Illah Expedition and was MID. He served in the Boer War on the Staff, and was present during the siege being slightly wounded 24 Oct 1899). He took part in the operations in the OFS, Feb to May 1900, including actions at Poplar Grove and Driefontein. Operations in ORC May to Nov 1900, including action at Wittebergen and operations in ORC and Cape Colony, 1900-02. He was MID and awarded the DSO LG 19 Apr 1901. He was promoted Captain 1 Apr 1904 and given the Brevet of Major 2 Apr 1904. He served in the Great War in East Africa, 1914-18, Brevet of Lieutenant Colonel 1 Jan 1917 and CMG 1919. He died 11 Jul 1943. His medal entitlement was: CMG, DSO, E&W Africa (1), QSA (4), KSA (2), 14-15 Star, BWM, VM.

McHardy, Donald. He was born in Kimberley in 1882, son on William McHardy. He was educated at St Cyprian's Grammar School and the School of Mines. He married in Sep 1905 and worked at the Premier Mine in Transvaal from Mar 1903. He attended the 50th Anniversary reunion.

McHardy, William. He was born in 1846 in Ballater, Aberdeen and educated in Aberdeen. He married in 1880, Evelina McCormick, and they had 7 children. He arrived in Cape Colony in 1860 and went to Kimberley in 1874. He was employed on the Mining Board for 2 years and subsequently had the management of Premier Mine. He had already been manager of the Kimberley Mine, until its amalgamation with De Beers in 1889. He served during the siege in the KTG.

MacKenzie, John Eddie. Son of a missionary, he was born in Bechuanaland in 1860. Having qualified as a surgeon he returned to South Africa and served in the Bechuanaland Border Police. He started a private practice in Kimberley in 1885. During the siege he was stationed at the Kimberley Mine Compound. He was a member of the School Board, founding member of the YMCA and member of the Kimberley Club.

Appendices

Madoc, Henry William. He was educated at Highgate. He served in South Africa in the CMR and SAC and in the Boer War 1899-1902. He joined the KLH and resigned 30 Oct 1900 to join the SAC. He was Commandant of a prisoner camp during the Great War (CBE & MVO). He held the King's Police Medal and the Order of St John. He was Chief Constable of the Isle of Man. In 1906 he married Isabel Messer and died 9 Jan 1937.

Maguire, Julia Beatrice. Daughter of the first Viscount Peel and wife of James Rochfort Maguire. She acted as War Correspondent for *The Times* and her article *'Life in Kimberley during the siege'* was published on 19 Mar 1900.

Maguire, James Rochfort. He was born 4 Oct 1855 and educated at Cheltenham and Oxford. It was at Oxford that he met Rhodes. In 1888, Rhodes sent him with Charles Rudd and Frank Thompson to negotiate a concession of land and mineral rights in Matebeleland from Chief Lobengula at Bulawayo. The British South Africa Company was formed a year later and he would always be associated with it. He was Chairman 1923-5, director of the Consolidated Gold Fields of South Africa and Chairman of the Rhodesian railway system. He married Julia Beatrice in 1895 and died 18 Apr 1925.

Mair, George. An assistant mechanical engineer who worked on the construction of Long Cecil during the siege. He was born in 1875 and worked for De Beers.

Mallett, Percy W. He was born in the 1850s in Grahamstown and by 1889 was working for the law firm Edward Vigne in Kimberley. He served in the Gaika-Galeka War and was a Lieutenant in the Kimberley Rifles between 1891 and 1893. During the siege he served as a Captain in the KTG and was stationed at No 2 Redoubt. He died in 1935.

Mandy, Frank. He was born in Grahamstown around 1838 and spent many years as a trader and hunter. Hume Expedition to Damaraland, Mashonaland and Matebeleland 1870 and 1872. Ostrich Farmer of Port Elizabeth 1881. Lieutenant, Pioneer Corps 26 May 1890. Officer in-charge of Rear Party, Tuli 11 Jul 1890. Prospector of Maquadzi and Umvukwes area of Rhodesia. Manager for De Beers, Kimberley 1892-1903. During the siege, he commanded the fort on the Boshof Road which was known as Mandy Fort. He had also served with the Papal Zouaves. His son Frank Raymond Mandy died while serving with Rimington's Guides in Jul 1900. Frank Mandy died 28 Jun 1903. QSA (1), KStar. Sotheby Nov 1977, Spink Dec 1983 and Spink Sep 1989 £450.

May, Thomas James. He was born in 1864 and served in the Bechuanaland Field Force 1884–85, the DFH 1889-94, the Matebeleland Relief Force 1896 and in the DEOVR in 1897. He enrolled in the DFA 1 Apr 1899 and was made Captain the same day and Major on 16 Oct 1899. After the siege, he was saw service in the OFS and CC. He was MID 8 May 1900 and 16 Apr 1901. He served in the Royal Artillery in the Great War and with the Royal Navy during the Second World War. His medal entitlement was: CMG, BSACM rev Rhodesia 1896 (0) (Lt MRF), CGHGSM (1) Bech (Lt DEOVR), QSA (2) (Major, DFA), KSA (2) (Major DFA), 1914 Star (Major CMG, RFA), BWM, VM (Major), 1939-45 Star, F&G Star, DM, WM, KStar. Sotheby Jun 84. See page 507 for his medals.

Meyer, Carl. He was born 15 Nov 1850 in Germany, his family moving to South Africa when he was 7. Carl followed his father into missionary work and worked at the Pniel Mission Station. The first church in Kimberley, the Lutheran Church, was supervised by him. He married in 1878 and moved to Kimberley a year later. His diary of life during the siege was published in 1999 under the title *'Days of Horror'*. Carl died in Jun 1902. His son, Eduard, served in the ambulance section of the KTG during the siege.

Mildred, Charles Ashwell. Born in Bedford in 1878, he went to South Africa in 1890. He joined the CMR in 1893, serving for 4 years and then served with the CMP until 1901. He served during the Bechuanaland Rebellion of 1897, in the siege and relief of Mafeking and was discharged from the Cape Police 12 Feb 1901. He also served with the Indwe DMT (nr 12). After the War he managed a hotel in Indwe. His medal entitlement was: CGHGSM (1) Bech, QSA (3), KStar. Dixon Dec 84 £380.

Milne, W G. By the time of the siege, he had 14 years service and was serving in the Kimberley Regiment as Acting Adjutant. After the siege he was involved in operations in ORC and Transvaal. He received the QSA and KSA (2) for his Boer War service.

Milner, Sir Alfred. He was educated in Germany, London and Oxford and was called to the Bar in 1881. He worked in journalism and moved into politics in 1885. He was Private Secretary to Mr Goschen 1887-9, Undersecretary for Finance 1889-92 and Chairman, Board of Inland Revenue 1892-7. He was Governor of the Cape of Good Hope 1897-1901 and Governor of Transvaal and ORC 1901-5. He served as High Commissioner for South Africa 1897-1905. Privy Councillor 1901, GCB (c) 1901, GCMG 1897.

Mungeam, William. He was born in 1857 in Brussels. He moved to South Africa in 1880 and joined the Civil Service as a Clerk in 1881. The next year, he was working in the Crown Prosecutor's Office in Kimberley. In 1899 he was appointed Assistant Resident Magistrate in Beaconsfield and carried out the same role in Kimberley in 1900. During the siege, he was a member of the Court of Summary Jurisdiction.

Murphy, Daniel Joseph. He was born in Balranald, New South Wales, in 1873 and worked as a labourer and fisherman. He served with A Troop, Mashonaland Mounted Police, in the Jameson Raid and was captured. He next saw service as a Trooper, Matebeleland Relief Force, Matabele Rebellion 1896. During the siege he served in the KLH 22 Oct 1899 to 3 Apr 1900 and also in the KTG and IYS (3) 11 May to 11 Oct 1900. He was captured by the Boers at Johannesburg on 30 Jun 1900 and was released soon after. Back in Australia he volunteered for the 1st Battalion, Australia Commonwealth Horse, but his application was refused. He died 30 May 1919.

Murray, William Hugh Eric. He was born 3 Oct 1858 and he served in the Zhob Valley Expedition of 1884 and during the Boer War 1899–1902 with the LNLR. He was Commandant at Vryburg. He was involved in operations in OFS, Feb to May 1900, Transvaal Jul to Nov 1900, ORC May to Nov 1900 including the actions at Lindley and Rhenoster River. He commanded the 1st Battalion Royal Scots 5 Jan to 19 May 1902. Operations in the Transvaal 30 Nov 1900 to Jul 1901 and Jan to 31 May 1902. Operations in ORC Apr 1902, Cape Colony Jul to Dec 1901. He was MID 8 May 1900. He received the brevet Lieutenant Colonel, QSA (3) and KSA (2). He commanded the 2nd Battalion Royal Scots 1904-08 and the Notts and Derby Territorial Brigade 1909-11. CB 1913. He died 2 Feb 1915.

Neale-Shutte, Richard Francis. He was born in England and enlisted 1 Nov 1888. He served as Trooper, Cape Police in 1891 and was promoted Sergeant in 1895. He saw action in the Bechuanaland Rebellion of 1897 and promoted Sub Inspector in the same year. He was Acting Chief Constable, Richmond, in 1898. During the siege he served with the Cape Police and afterwards took part in the relief of Mafeking. He earned the KSA (2). His surname on the QSA roll is Shutte. He was Acting Inspector, April 1900 and Inspector, 10 Jun 1900. Seconded as Inspector to B Division, Cape Police 1 Nov 1901 to 18 May 1902. Acting Commissioner of Police, District No 3, Cape Town, March 1901. Acting Inspector, District 2, Nov 1903 to Mar 1904. Inspector, CMP in 1904. He transferred from Vryburg to Command U Division (Beaufort West) 1 Jan 1905. He died in 1951.

Noonan, Joseph Daniel. He was born in 1880 in Kimberley and served during the siege. Afterwards he worked as an Attorney and Notary of the Supreme Court of Cape Colony.

Notcutt, Henry Clement. He was born in Cheltenham in 1865, educated at the London University, went out to Cape Colony in 1895 and was appointed Assistant Professor at the South African College, Cape Town, which appointment he held for four and a half years, subsequently becoming Headmaster of the Boys' High School, Kimberley. During the siege he served in the Cycle Corps of the Town Guard (but does not appear on the medal rolls) and published an account entitled '*How Kimberley was held for England*'. He was elected President of the South African Teachers' Association in 1902, became a member of the Council of the University of the Cape of Good Hope in 1903, and was appointed Professor of English Language and Literature in the same year. He married, in 1904, Lilian, daughter of George Healey, of Kimberley.

O'Brien, Thomas Henry. He was 2nd Lieutenant, 5 Sep 1888, Lieutenant, 1 Oct 1891 and Captain, 7 Apr 1897. He served in the Boer War 1899-1900. Operations in ORC, Transvaal and Cape Colony and was MID. During the siege he commanded the troops at Premier Mine. He is on the LNLR and KTG medal rolls.

O'Gorman, Charles John. He was born 24 Jul 1872 and educated at Clongowes before entering the RAMC on 28 Jan 1898. He served in the Boer War, and after the siege saw service in the OFS Apr to May 1900, the Transvaal Jul to Nov 1900 and in the ORC May to Jul 1900, including actions at Lindley and Rhenoster River. He was MID 8 May 1900 and 16 Apr 1901 and awarded the DSO LG 27 Sep 1901. He became Captain, 28 Jan 1901 and was employed with the SAC from 31 Dec 1904. He was made Major, 28 Jan 1910 and Lieutenant Colonel, 1 Aug 1915. He served as Assistant Director of Medical Services, 2nd East African Division, East African Force, 23 Feb to 31 Mar 1916, Assistant Director of Medical Services, East African Force, 10 Dec 1916 to 22 Feb 1918, Assistant Director of Medical Services, 23 Feb to 31 May 1918 and as Assistant Director of Medical Services, 18th Division, British Armies in France, 18 Feb 1919. He died 11 May 1930. Having lost his Boer War medals, duplicates were issued on 14 Apr 1919. His medal entitlement was: DSO, QSA (3) (Capt DSO, RAMC) (late issue), KSA (2) (Capt DSO, RAMC) (late issue), 1914-15 Star (Maj

DSO, RAMC), BWM, Victory Medal with MID (Lt Col). Glendining 1991 £920. DNW Dec 06 £2,200. Dixon Mar 07 £2,895. See page 501 for his medals.

O'Meara, Bulkeley Ernest Adolphus. Born at Umballa, India on 1 Feb 1867, he was the son of Alfred O'Meara, of St Mark's, Simla, India. He was educated at Dulwich College, and at King's College School, Somerset House, London. He served as a trooper in the original Pioneer Force which annexed Rhodesia to the British Empire, 1889-91 and later worked as Surveyor in the De Beers Consolidated Mines, Kimberley. He served in the siege. He was transferred to the Intelligence Department in 1900, and was Intelligence Officer for Griqualand West, as far as Mafeking. He was SO1 to the Vryburg and Carnarvon Columns, Press Censor, Interpreter and Intelligence Officer at Oudtshoorn. He was four times MID and was awarded the DSO LG 19 Apr 1901. He was subsequently appointed Government Surveyor for the Cape and Transvaal Colonies, practising at Johannesburg. He was a keen sportsman and died 31 Aug 1916. DSO, QSA (1) (Capt DSO, KTG) (renamed), 1914-15 Star (Lt, EAMR). Spink Dec 1983 £1,200.

O'Meara, Walter Alfred John. He was born in 1863. He was severely wounded in the Burma War of 1885-86. He served in South Africa during the Jameson Raid and was in Kimberley as Chief Staff Officer during the siege. In 1900 he was Mayor, councillor and town clerk in Johannesburg and was Commander of the Orange River Colony Police. When he left the military, he became Chief Engineer of the Post Office. After Kekewich's death he wrote a strong rebuttal of Kekewich's time as Commandant of Kimberley. He died in 1939. His medal entitlement was: CMG, IGS (1) Burma 85-87 (Lt), QSA (5), 1902 Coronation, KStar. Glendining Nov 65. Spink Dec 83. Medals now in the MacGregor Museum, Kimberley. His medals can be seen on page 502.

O'Molony, Chidley Kearnan. He was born at Cawnpore, Jan 1845, while the first Sikh War was raging, his father being present at the battles of Moodkee, Ferozeshah, Aliwal, and Sobraon. His early years were spent in the Royal Navy from where he retired with the rank of Paymaster. He served in Australia and in New Zealand at the end Maori War in the 1860s. He also served in the South Sea Islands, including the Samoa and Fiji and on the West Coast of Africa. During the siege, he was MID for services in his civil capacity. Later he was Town Clerk and Treasurer in Kimberley. JP. He married, in 1872, Emma, daughter of Selwyn Schofield Sugden, formerly Deputy Governor of HM Prison at Gibraltar.

Oats, Francis. Born in 1848, he emigrated to South Africa in 1875 to work as a mining engineer in Griqualand West. He served as a member of the Legislative Assembly and was also on the Board of De Beers. He was manager of the Diamond Mining Company in 1887. During the siege, he served as a Lieutenant in Mandy's 'Buffs'. He was Chairman of the Kimberley Club 1912-14 and during the Great War was on the Kimberley Recruiting Committee.

Oliver, Henry Alfred. He was born in Nottingham in 1854 and moved to South Africa when he was 11. After an education in Cape Town he sought his fortune in Kimberley. Returning to Cape Town for a short while, the lure of Kimberley brought him back once more. He started a business. He succeeded R H Henderson as Mayor on 1 Jan 1900 in mid-siege. One biography notes that "the town had a unique experience of a Mayor presiding one hour over a Council meeting, and at another shouldering his rifle in the trenches." During a visit to England after the siege, he presented King Edward VII with a model of Long Cecil that was constructed from the shells fired into Kimberley by the Boers. On the visit by the Duke of York, he was presented with the CMG LG 23 Aug 1901. He was instrumental in the creation of the Kimberley Medal and the issue of the Mayor's Siege Medal, the Kimberley Star. His medal entitlement was CMG, QSA (1), 1937 Coronation Medal. See page 506 for a picture of his miniature medals.

Orr, John. He was born in 1858 and arrived in South Africa in 1883. He started as a shopkeeper in Stellenbosch before opening a store in Kimberley and, later, in other parts of the country. He served as a Lieutenant in the KTG during the siege. He was elected to the Kimberley Town Council in 1905 and served until 1931. He was Mayor 1910-11, 1916-8 and died in 1932.

Ortlepp, Albert James. He enrolled in the DFA on 1 Aug 1899 and served until 21 Jan 1901. He served in the OFS and Tr and was MID 8 May 1900 and 16 Apr 1902. His occupation was surgeon. Resigned from the DFA 31 Mar 03. Served as Civil surgeon to the troops in Transvaal 22 Jul 1901 to 19 Jul 1902.

Parkin, Julius Minet. He served as a Trooper, Artillery Troop, Mashonaland Mounted Police, in the Jameson Raid when he was captured. In the same year he served as Trooper, Matebeleland Relief Force, Matabele Rebellion 1896. During the siege he served with the KTG (No I Section, B Company, Beaconsfield Town Guard) and later with WLH and BSAP (654 & 1092).

Peakman, Tom C. Tom Peakman had commanded the Griqualand West Volunteer Brigade. He joined the KLH as second in command and was wounded 16 Nov 1899. He recovered quickly and was engaged in the fighting on 28 Nov 1899. He took over command of the KLH upon Scott-Turner's death. After the siege he took part in the relief of Mafeking and was awarded the CMG. He died on 23 Nov 1909 aged 49 and was buried in Kimberley.

Penfold, Hugh Marchant. He served in the Royal Naval Reserve and worked as a Captain for the shipping company Donald Currie & Co. He served as port Captain and Shipping Master at Table Bay in 1879 and was Marshal of the Vice Admiralty Court in 1881. He was Dock Captain at Table Bay in 1890 and retired in 1896. He was an admirer of Rhodes and tried to make his way into Kimberley during the siege. He was a director of De Beers and died in 1902. The fourth trial message on the night of 27 Nov 1899 from Methuen was about Penfold's attempt to reach Kimberley. It read 'To Rhodes. The Commodore is coming up in uniform'.

Pickering, William. He was born 25 Feb 1856, son of Reverend E Pickering. He started work at the age of 15 at Standard Bank. He served with Prince Alfred's Guard on the operations against the native chief, Kreli. During the Zulu War, he joined Baker's Horse and served for 6 months. He was at the final battle of Ulundi. For his services during the Boer War he was awarded the DSO LG 27 Sep 1901. The DSO was presented at Port Elizabeth, by the Governor of Cape Colony, 5 Apr 1905. He was Secretary to the De Beers Consolidated Mines, Limited, 1897 to 1917, and was a Director 9 Oct 1917. He married, in 1890, Ethel Annie, daughter of George Wright, of Grahamstown and died 24 Feb 1933.

Raynham, Eustace Frederick. He served in the Boer War and for his services received the DSO LG 19 Apr 1901. During the siege he served with the Kimberley Mine Ambulance Company. He was Secretary of De Beers Consolidated Mines in 1917-29 and died 28 Mar 1939.

Reeland, Charles John Headingham. He was born in 1865 and served as a Trooper, Bechuanaland Border Police in the Matabele War 1893 and as Sergeant, K Troop, BSAP in the Jameson Raid where he was captured. In the same year he served as Trooper, Matebeleland Relief Force, Matabele Rebellion 1896 and as Private (Special Police), Cape Police District No 1 (Vryburg detachment), Bechuanaland Rebellion 1897. During the siege he served in the Cape Police (C Squadron) and was subsequently severely wounded at Hoopstad 23 Oct 1900. In 1904 he applied for a pension due to injuries he sustained during the Boer War.

Reunert, Theodore. He was born in 1856 in Leeds and was educated in Leeds and Germany. He arrived in Kimberley in 1879 and moved to Johannesburg in 1889. He was Chairman of the Johannesburg Public Library and President of the Association of Engineers.

Reyersbach, Louis J. He was born in Hanover, Germany, in 1869. He worked for Wernher, Beit and Company and shuttled between Kimberley and London in charge of the diamond business. He joined Eckstein & Co at the end of 1901. He was in Kimberley during the siege in the KTG. He married, in 1897, Miss Martha Wallach, of Aix-la-Chapelle. QSA (1). LSE Sep 84 £85.

Rhodes, Cecil J. A visionary giant of the Victorian age; a self-made man who amassed a colossal fortune within his lifetime, a man pivotal in the history of Southern Africa, who wielded enormous political and business influence on the world's stage and who evoked equal passions of amity and enmity amongst his contemporaries. He was born, the son of a vicar at Bishop Stortford, in England on 5 Jul 1853. He attended the local grammar school and although a sickly child he excelled in academic studies. He left school in 1869, where he had shown prowess and dogged determination, characteristics which he would later need, after developing a lung infection which required a long convalescence and he travelled to South Africa and there joined his brother Herbert in Natal and took up cotton planting. In 1871, with Cecil's health restored the brothers gave up farming and went diamond prospecting in Kimberley. Between 1873 and 1881 Cecil was extremely successful and despite Herbert's death in 1874, he continued alone and laid the foundation of his vast wealth. He also continued his studies and during this time he received both his BA and MA degrees from Oriel College, Oxford. Apart from diamonds, Rhodes had an equally passionate belief in the good an expanded British Empire could bring in terms of improvements and enlightenment for the African continent and he nurtured deep resentment to the Boers whom he saw as backward-thinking and hindering this expansion. His first foray into empire-building was in forcing the Boers from Bechuanaland and he envisaged an ultimate grand plan of a United South Africa under the British flag. In 1884 he joined the cabinet as Treasurer of Cape Colony and in 1890 he became Premier of the Cape. He retained this position until the disastrous results of the Jameson Raid in 1896 made his resignation inevitable and exposed the underlying friction between Briton and Boer which would ultimately result in the Boer War. Ever practical in outlook Rhodes fervently believed in expanding the empire northwards and the establishment of a Cape to Cairo railway while containing the two Boer Republics. Now unfettered by political office, he next turned his attention to Matebeleland and Mashonaland, where mineral resources were known to be abundant. Rhodes extracted a lucrative concession from King Lobengula in Bulawayo, covered an area of 750,000 square miles, and brought about the creation of the British South Africa Company. The subsequent influx of foreigners into these lands led in turn to the Matabele War of 1893 and the bloody rebellion of 1896. Rhodes bravely went unarmed to parlay with the indunas in the Matopo Hills and brought the war to a conclusion and led to the creation of Rhodesia. In October 1899, Rhodes travelled to Kimberley where he exerted all his efforts in helping with the defence of the town throughout the siege and through the infinite resources of his company De Beers Consolidated Mines. This brought him at times into direct and open conflict with Colonel Kekewich. Rhodes harboured deep antipathy towards military authority and although created Colonel of the Kimberley Light Horse and the Kimberley Regiment he was never photographed in uniform. His health began to seriously decline in 1901 and he died on 26 Mar 1902 of an aneurism of the heart. Among his last words were, 'So little done, so much to do' and he was buried in the Matopo Hills after a state funeral in Cape Town. So passed a towering figure of the age, unmarried and on whom a grateful country had bestowed no honours. Rhodes was a resolute man of absolute conviction of purpose, practical, irascible and with a gift for inculcating his great vision to others. Cecil Rhodes was a highly complex visionary driven by an unerring mission to bring the perceived benefits of the British Empire to the African continent, but in a paternalistic and benevolent manner. His enormous wealth provided him with unparalleled opportunities of the time and in death he bequeathed large provisions for agricultural development and international scholarships. His medal entitlement was: BSACM Rhod 96 (Col the Rt Hon C J Rhodes RHV), QSA (1) (Col Rt Hon C J Rhodes Kim Vol Rgt), KStar (Hon C J Rhodes PC MLA). National Museum, Zimbabwe.

Richards, Sidney. He was educated at Cheltenham College. He joined the Victoria Rifles, late Duke of Edinburgh's Own Volunteer Rifles. He served throughout the siege in the KTG and was rewarded with the DSO LG 19 Apr 1901. He was also promoted to Major.

Rickman, William Edward. He was born in 1855. He served as Lieutenant, Border Horse, 5 Mar 1879, in the Zulu War in 1879 and the Basuto War of 1880-81. He served in the Boer War, 1900-02 and in the siege in the KLH. He was MID and created a DSO LG 19 Apr 1901. The DSO was presented by the King 29 Oct 1901. He also earned the QSA and KSA (2). Captain Rickman married, in 1895, Margaret Menzies Haliburton and he died 1 Jun 1927.

Roberts, Lord Frederick Sleigh. Born in India, 30 Sep 1832, he was educated at Eton, Sandhurst, and Addiscombe, and received his first commission as 2nd Lieutenant in the Bengal Artillery at the age of nineteen. He saw his first active service in the Indian Mutiny in 1857-8, taking part in the siege and capture of Delhi, where he was wounded. It was then that Lieutenant Roberts (as he then was) won his VC. While following up the retreating enemy he saw a couple of Sepoys escaping with a standard. Galloping after them Roberts overtook them, when the men turned and faced him. Lieutenant Roberts seized the standard, cutting down the man from whom he took it. While this struggle was going on the other Sepoy levelled his musket point blank at him and pulled the trigger. Fortunately it miss-fired, and the standard and the future Field Marshal were saved. The same day Lord Roberts rode up to the rescue of a Sowar, who was being attacked by a rebel, armed with a bayonet. A few years later Lord Roberts was again actively employed in India in the North-West Frontier Expedition of 1863. He then served through the Abyssinian Expedition in 1868 and the Looshai Expedition of 1871-2. The Afghan War of 1878-80 next brought Lord Roberts into prominence, on which occasion he commanded the Kuram Valley Field Force at the capture of Pelwar Kotal. He then had command of the Kabul Field Force and commanded the whole force in the historic march from Kabul to Kandahar, after a series of brilliant victories inflicting a crushing defeat on Ayoob Khan. On his return to England at the age of 49, he received the thanks of Parliament, and was created a Baronet, KCB, and GCB. In 1883 he was appointed Commander in Chief in India. In Dec 1899 Lord Roberts was asked to take command in South Africa. His operations in the OFS included the capture of General Cronje's forces at Paardeberg, and the actions at Poplar Grove, Driefontein, Vet River, and Zand River. Leaving Bloemfontein, Lord Roberts followed in the wake of the President of the South African Republic. He entered the Transvaal, and engaged the Boer forces about Johannesburg, Pretoria, and Diamond Hill on 11 - 12 Jun 1900. From July to November of that year Lord Roberts was occupied in the Transvaal and his last action was at Belfast on 26 Aug 1900. By this time the Boer States were apparently subjugated, and Lord Roberts returned home to be created an Earl and a Knight of the Garter, receiving also the QSA with six clasps. He was made an OM in 1902. He died in France in Nov 1914 while visiting Indian troops fighting in the Great War.

Robertson, James W. He acted as Clerk in the Customs Department, Bechuanaland, in 1890, and as Clerk to the Civil Commissioners at Bulawayo, Salisbury, and Umtali from 1895-99. He took part in the Mashonaland Rebellion in 1896 and joined the KLH as Lieutenant 16 Oct 1899 to 1 Jun 1900. After the siege, he commanded the garrison at Koffyfontein from 1900-1901. He appears on the medal roll for the KDF. He was appointed Assistant Resident Magistrate at Koffyfontein in 1900. Resident Magistrate at Hoopstad in 1901, and at Thaba Nchu in 1904.

Robinson, Macleod Bartree. He was born at Grahamstown on 12 Jan 1858. He joined the Cape Civil Service in 1875 and held various appointments. He served with the Queenstown Volunteer Rifles in the Gaika and Galeka War, 1877-8 and was Captain of Nesbitt's Light Horse in the Transkei Rebellion in 1880-1. In 1894 he became commissioner of the Cape Police, District 2. He commanded a force of Mounted Police and Volunteers at Phokwani, in the Bechuanaland Rebellion of 1896-7. In 1899 he was appointed Commandant of Colonial Forces in 1899 in Griqualand West and Bechuanaland, with the local rank of Lieutenant Colonel. He served during the siege and later commanded the 2nd Division of the Cape Colonial Forces from Jul to Sep 1902. In May 1904, he was appointed Chief of the Detective Department in Kimberley, and Commissioner of the Cape Police, District No 2. He married, first, in 1887, Annie, daughter of James Ayliff, and, secondly, in 1896, Theodora, daughter of Laurence Dahl. He died in 1935. His medal entitlement was: CMG, SAGS (1) 1877-8 (Pte Queenstown R Vols), CGHCSM (2) Trans Bech (Capt Nesbitt's Horse) QSA(1) (Lt Col Cape Police), KSA (2) (Lt Col CP Distr2), BWM (Lt Col), KStar. Sotheby Jun 73 £450. City Coins Nov 2009. His medals can be seen on page 503.

Rodger, Thomas Henderson. Born at Wynberg, near Cape Town, 10 Mar 1860. He served in the DEOVR in the Gaika-Galeka War of 1877-78, and in the Diamond Fields Horse in the Langberg Rebellion, Bechuanaland, 1896-97. He was promoted Captain, 1894 and Major, 1899. He served during the Boer War 1899-1902. He took part in operations in the OFS Feb to May 1900 and in the Relief of Mafeking. Also in operations in the Transvaal, May and Jun 1900, operations in ORC, May to 29 Nov 1900, operations in Cape Colony, north of Orange River, operations in the Transvaal, ORC and Cape Colony 30 Nov 1900 to 31 May 1902. He was MID LG 8 May 1900 and 16 Apr 1901. Awarded the DSO LG 19 Apr 1901. In 1902 he became Officer Commanding the Kimberley Horse, with the rank of Lieutenant Colonel. Served in the German South West Africa operation 30 Sep 1914 to 10 Sep 1915 as Lieutenant Colonel in the 2nd Kimberley Regiment. He married, in 1885, Elizabeth Johanna, daughter of W J Merrington, of Claremont, Cape Colony. His medal entitlement was: DSO, CGHGSM (1) Bech, QSA (4), KSA (2), 14-15 Star, BWM, VM (MID), Colonial Auxiliary Forces Decoration, Colonial Auxiliary Forces LS Medal, 1910 Union of South Africa Medal, French Croix de Guerre with palme.

Rush, William Welsh. He was born in 1870 at Great Marlow, Buckinghamshire and was the third son of Sgt Maj David Rush VC. He went to South Africa in 1887 and joined the Cape Mounted Police. During his 33 years of service he took part in the Langberg Rebellion, siege of Kimberley (Wounded 25 Nov 1899) and in South West Africa during the Great War. He accompanied General Berrange across the Kalahari Desert in 1915 and subsequently commanded the 1st and 5th Regiments of the SAMR. He was mentioned in despatched thrice and awarded the DSO (22 Aug 1918 for distinguished service in German South West Africa 1914-15). He died 19 Feb 1941. His medal entitlement was: DSO, CGHGSM (1) Bech (Sub Insp CP), QSA (2), (Lt CP), KSA (2) (Capt CP2), 14-15 Star (Lt Col 5th SAMR), BWM, VM & MID (Lt Col), 1911 Coronation. DNW Dec 91 £1,000. Spink Oct 99 £1,400. Dixon Dec 99 £1,895. Miniatures Sotheby Nov 81. His medals can be seen on page 504.

Ryan, Francis Kearns. He was born in Dublin 8 Mar 1869. He served as a Trooper, 3rd Dragoon Guards and as Trooper, Bechuanaland Border Police in 1895. He was a Jameson Raider, being a Trooper of G Troop, BSAP. After his capture and repatriation he resided in Mafeking. He served as Trooper, Diamond Fields Horse and later as a Private, Special Cape Police. He took part in the Bechuanaland Rebellion 1897. During the siege he served in the Cape Police (HQ and depot mounted branch) and gained the KSA (2). He was Squadron Sergeant Major, 5th South African Mounted Rifles during the Great War and Warrant Officer, Natal Division, South African Police. His medal entitlement was: CGHGSM (1) Bech (Pte Sp Pol), QSA (3) inc Tr, KSA (2), 14-15 Star (SSM 5th SAMR), BWM, VM (2nd Cl WO 5th SAMR), MSM (SSM SAMR), Permanent Forces LS&GC (SSM 3rd SAMR), KStar. DNW Jul 04 £2,200.

Rynd, Francis Fleetwood. He was born 19 Aug 1877, son of the Reverend J W Rynd, Rector of Brasted, Kent. He had his first commission as a Second Lieutenant in the Royal Artillery 22 Dec 1898, in which he was promoted Lieutenant 16 Feb 1901. He saw active service in the Boer War 1899-1902, taking part in the siege and in the operations in Cape Colony, north of Orange River. For his services he received the DSO LG 27 Sep 1901. He was invested by the King 18 Dec 1902. He was, from Oct 1904 to Oct 1907, employed as a Volunteer Adjutant, receiving his Captaincy 30 Jun 1904, and was Garrison Adjutant, Cape Colony District, from Aug 1909 to Aug 1913; was promoted Major 30 Oct 1913. He was Acting Lieutenant Colonel for short periods in 1916 and 1917; was appointed Camp Commandant, Mesopotamian Expeditionary Force, 8 May 1918. His medal entitlement was: DSO, QSA (1) DoK (Lt, DSO RGA), KSA (2) (Lt, DSO RGA), Kimberley Star. Glendining 1989. Dixon 1989 £620. Spink 1999 £1,700. Vimy Militaria Jan 05 £3,500. eMedals Sep 05 £3,500. His medals can be seen on page 502.

Salaman, Sam. Born in Manchester 6 Feb 1862, he moved to South Africa in 1879. Before emigration, he had served in the 6th Lancashire Rifle Volunteers. In South Africa, he saw action in Willoughby's Horse in the

Pondoland and Basutoland Rebellions. He joined the DFH on its formation in 1877. He also served in the first Boer War. During the siege he earned QSA (4) and KSA (2). He was promoted Captain 1 Aug 1901 and was Commanding Officer of the Kimberley Regiment in 1911. He retired 19 Jun 1924. He also worked as a journalist for the *Diamond Fields Advertiser* 1887 – 93.

Salisbury, Philip. He was born in London and educated privately. He arrived in Cape Colony in 1892 and settled in Kimberley in 1894. He was a Fellow of the Society of Accountants in Cape Colony. During the siege, he was stationed at No I Section, Belgravia Fort.

Schreiner, William Philip. He was born in Cape Colony in 1857, the son of a German missionary and brother of the novelist, Olive Schreiner. He attended the Universities of Cape Town, Cambridge, and London. He took a Senior in Law Tripos and the Chancellor's Legal Medal in 1881 and was called to the Bar of the Inner Temple in 1882. He was admitted an Advocate of the Supreme Court of the Cape Colony. Between 1885-93 he was Legal Adviser to the High Commissioner. In 1893, when he joined Cecil Rhodes' second Ministry as Attorney General, having in that year been elected as member for Kimberley in the Cape House of Assembly. He resigned the Attorney Generalship later in 1893 and was elected member for Barkly West. He again became Attorney General in Sep 1893. His good relations with Rhodes were broken off by the Jameson Raid, and he left the Cabinet, declining to accept the same portfolio in the new Ministry under Sir Gordon Sprigg. He became Premier in Oct 1898, retaining that position until Jun 1900. During his Premiership he neither prevented nor promoted the Boer War. One biography said "He is said to have resisted British measures of coercion, and to have given no encouragement to anti-British aims. He neither stopped arms going into the Transvaal through Cape Colony, nor permitted an early organised defence of Kimberley and the Cape Colonial frontier, nor did he, by a display of resolution, appear to aim at convincing President Kruger that the Colony would tolerate no disloyal actions on the part of British subjects in the event of his issuing an ultimatum. In short, his halting methods of conciliation in the pre-war period stood a very good chance of being misinterpreted by a large section of the British." He died in 1919.

Scott, Herbert Thring. He was born and educated in England. He was a member of the Cape Mounted Rifles and Assistant Commissioner in the Cape Police. He had seen service in the Gaika Galeka campaign of 1877-8 and in Basutoland in 1880-1. He also took part in the Phokwani Rebellion and the Langberg campaign of 1896-7. He was in charge of the Cape Police in Vryburg at the start of the Boer War. The largely Dutch population advised him to retire to Kimberley with his small force of 60 men to avoid being attacked by the Boers. During the retirement, he took his own life. His death was reported on 21 Sep 1899.

Scott VC, Robert George. He was born in Peterborough 22 Apr 1857 the son of a naval surgeon. He served in the Zulu Wars of 1877-79; in the Gaika and Galeka Campaigns. He received the Victoria Cross for conspicuous gallantry and devotion during an attack on Moirosi's Mountain. He volunteered to throw time-fuse shells as hand-grenades, over a line of stone barricades from behind which the enemy were bringing a heavy fire to bear on the Colonial troops, which it was impossible effectually to return. After causing all the men of his party to seek cover in case the shell should burst prematurely, Sergeant Scott advanced under heavy fire, and reaching the wall, made two attempts to throw shells across to the other side. In consequence of some defect in the fuse, which had been ignited before casting, the shell exploded prematurely. His right hand was blown to pieces and he was severely wounded in the left leg, but suffered only minor wounds on the body and limbs. In the Boer War he served in the operations in Cape Colony, the Transvaal and the Orange Free State with the KLH, SRG and CRSS. He was rewarded with the DSO LG 27 Sep 1901. During the Great War he was Lieutenant Colonel and Commandant of the Kimberley Commando. He died 3 Oct 1918 in Wynberg.

Scott, William. He was born 5 Jul 1858 in Scotland and moved to South Africa in 1881. He worked for the Swaziland Government 1 Oct 1890 to Sep 1899 and was JP for Swaziland 1889-99. After the siege he joined Damant's Horse as Captain and Officer Commanding, B Squadron. He was awarded the DSO LG 31 Oct 1902, MID 8 Mar 1902, QSA (6) and KSA (2). Served in the Provisional Swaziland Administration in 1903 and rejoined as Farrier Sergeant, Natal Mounted Rifles for the Zulu Rebellion of 1906. He was Captain, Natal Mounted Rifles 1 Jul 1910 and died in Swaziland 23 Jan 1923.

Scott-Turner, Henry. He entered the Black Watch at the age of twenty in 1887. Alter taking part in the operations in Matebeleland in 1893-94, he was, in 1894 placed on the 'Special Extra Regimental Employment List'. In 1896, he served with the Matebeleland Relief Force as adjutant and paymaster. For this service he was mentioned in despatches and received a brevet majority. After serving with the British South African Police and as magistrate of Umtali in Rhodesia, Major Scott-Turner was reappointed as a 'Special Service Officer'. He was killed at Carter's Ridge on 28 Nov 1899. He was the son-in-law of Sir Lewis Mitchell, General Manager of the Standard Bank South Africa and a personal friend of Cecil Rhodes.

Shackleton, C C. He served in Warren's Bechuanaland Expedition 1884-85. He enlisted again in 1895 and was promoted Lieutenant, Diamond Fields Horse, 1 Jan 1896, serving the next year in the Bechuanaland Rebellion. Captain 14 Jan 1897. During the siege he was Captain KRV. Afterwards, he was involved in the relief of Mafeking, Orange Free State and Transvaal operations. He was MID 23 Jun 1902. Captain and Commanding Officer, Diamond Fields Artillery 1 Jun 1903. He was Major 1 Jun 1903 and resigned 15 Sep 1903. QSA (4), [KSA(2)], KStar. City Coins Aug 08

Smartt, Sir Thomas William. An Irishman by birth and trained for the medical profession, qualifying as a doctor. He served as Colonial Secretary in the Sprigg Ministry, May to Oct 1898, Commissioner for Public Works 1900 and Commissioner of Crown Lands and Public Works in the Jameson Ministry of 1904. He was Secretary for Agriculture 1921-24. KCMG 1911. PC 1921. He died 17 Apr 1929

Smith, James Alexander Jones. He was born in 1853 in Scotland, one of 12 children. He trained in medicine at Edinburgh University, qualifying in 1877 and 1881. He received his license to practice in the Cape of Good Hope on 4 Feb 1878. He joined the CMR and served in the Basuto War 1880-1. He also served in the Boer War 1899-1901, as Surgeon Major in the KRV and for his services was MID and awarded the DSO LG 19 Apr 1901. He also served as Captain Quartermaster in the KLH until 28 Oct 1900. He died of pneumonia 2 Aug 1901.

Smith, Robert Alfred Lange. He enlisted 2 Dec 1889 and was Lance Corporal, B Troop, British South African Police. He served in the Mashonaland Expedition, 1890. He was a despatch rider between Fort Salisbury and Umtali. He was in C Troop in Oct 1891 and was discharged (Tuli depot) 14 Nov 91. He was Sergeant Major, Intelligence Department during the Bechuanaland Rebellion, 1897. During the siege he served as Lieutenant, KTG at the Premier Mine.

Snow, Arthur Baring. He enlisted 7 Sep 1889 as a Trooper in the CMR being promoted Sub Lieutenant in the Bechuanaland Border Police Jun 1890 and Lieutenant a year later. He served in the Matabele War of 1893 and the Bechuanaland Rebellion 1897 earning CGHGSM (1) Bech. Before the siege started, he commanded the post at Fourteen Streams. He and his detachment arrived in Kimberley on 17 Oct 1899. After the siege, he also served in the FID between 15 Dec 1901 and 28 Feb 1902 and during May 1902. The KSA roll comments "Service with CP2 dispensed with as it was considered that this officer was unsuited for his position. Decided to award medal as he was subsequently employed with the FID."

Steyn, Martinus T. He was born near Winburg in 1857. He was educated in Bloemfontein, Holland and London. His legal expertise led to his appointment as State Attorney for the Free State, 1889-1893. He was later appointed to be First Puisne Judge, 1893-1896. In 1896, he became State President of the Orange Free State, aged 39. He played a prominent part in the Conference at Bloemfontein in 1899 and acted as mediator between President Kruger and Sir Alfred Milner. When war was inevitable, he joined his commando in the field. When Bloemfontein fell to the British in March 1900, he joined General de Wet's commandos and took part in all three De Wet hunts; the first into the Transvaal, where he encouraged the Transvaal forces in the Eastern Transvaal, and the second and third hunts to invade the Cape Colony. He was nearly captured near Bothaville in November 1900 and in Reitz in July 1901. Towards the end of the war he became very ill. The illness prevented him from signing the peace treaty. He died in 1916.

Thomas, Kenneth Robert. Born in Wynberg in 1880 he was educated at the Diocesan College, Rondebosch. Joined the Cape Civil Service in August 1897 in the Attorney General's Office. One biography said he was captured by the Boers on 16 Oct 1899 and that he was awarded the DCM. While there is no doubt that he served in the siege, neither of these other facts have been verified.

Tillard, Max Ogilvie. He was born 7 Jan 1880 in Grahamstown and educated in Cape Town. He served with the DFH and KRV and later with the ASC and Nesbitt's Horse. He was discharged from KRV 25 Feb 1900. After the War, he worked in a variety of mining jobs and moved to the Transvaal in 1901.

Trotter, Sir James Keith. He was born 24 Jul 1849 and joined the RA in 1870. psc 1882. He was on Special Service in Bechuanaland Expedition of 1884-5. He then served as Brigade Major RA in Cork Oct 1886 to May 1887 and in Malta May 1887 to Jan 1890. He was DAAG Sep 1892 to Sep 1895 and AAG for South Africa in 1899. CMG 1897. He was DAG, Lines of Communication during the Boer War 1899-1901. CB 1900. AQMG HQ 1901-03. Commanded the troops in West Africa 1905-06. Commanded Southern Coast Defences 1908-11. Retired in 1911 and KCB 1912. He commanded the 62nd Division in 1915. Colonel Commandant of the RA 1921-32. He died 30 Sep 1940.

Appendices

Turner, Alfred Ernest. He was born in Nov 1866 in Cardiff and joined the Imperial Postal Service in July 1886. He transferred to the Cape Service in Jan 1889 and to Kimberley in 1891. He served during the siege in the KTG. In 1904 he was Superintendent of the Cape Colony Travelling Post Offices.

Tyson, John Daughtrey. Born in 1864 in Sheffield and educated in Grahamstown and King Williamstown. He joined the Bank of Africa in 1881 and started his own business as an accountant in Kimberley in 1898. In Dec 1904 he was elected Mayor and again in 1905. During the siege he was appointed Controller of Food Supplies Staff with the rank of Lieutenant in the KTG (H Company).

Tyson, Thomas Gilbee. He was born in 1848 and arrived in South Africa in 1872. He served in the Gaika-Galeka War with the DFH under Colonel Warren. In 1884 he joined the Bechuanaland Field Force as Captain. He served a Secretary of the Kimberley Club 1887-1902. During the siege he was assistant military sensor and served in No I Section, Belgravia Fort. He is credited with the idea of the soup kitchen during the siege but in a letter to the *Diamond Fields Advertiser* of 24 Jan 1900 he said the chemist Mr J W McBeath deserved the credit. He was appointed to the De Beers Board on 21 Nov 1902 and served until his death on 19 Nov 1912.

Wallace, Augustus Robert. He was born Jan 1872 and educated at Marlborough. He entered the LNLR in January 1893, being promoted Lieutenant May 1895. Lieutenant Wallace was with his battalion in South Africa when war was declared, and served throughout the campaign in 1899-1900. He was accidentally killed by the explosion of a mine, at Zeerust, 13 Jan 1901. His name was inscribed on a tablet placed in Marlborough College Chapel in memory of all Marlburians who fell in the war.

Watkins, Arnold Hirst. He was born in England in 1851 and educated in Scotland. He arrived in South Africa in 1875 working as a doctor in Boshof between 1878 and 1885 at which time he went to Kimberley. He served as a member of Parliament 1910 to 1921 and died in 1927.

Webster, Alexander McCallum. Born 8 May 1878, he joined the LNLR as 2nd Lt 16 Feb 1898. He was made Lieutenant 18 May 1900. He served in South Africa between 1899 and 1902. After the siege of Kimberley where he commanded the armoured train (see page 535), he went to the OFS Apr to May 1900 and the Transvaal Jul to 29 Nov 1900. He took part in operations in ORC between May and Jul 1900 and saw action at Lindley (26 Jun 1900). He also served in Cape Colony, was MID 8 May 1900 and received the QSA (3) and KSA (2). At the end of the Great War, he was serving in the Reserve of Officers in the Assistant Provost Marshal's office.

Wells, William Harrison. Born around 1842, he first saw service in the Crimean War and Indian Mutiny. He emigrated to South Africa and took up journalism, becoming the first editor of the *Penny Mail* in Grahamstown. He commanded the Grahamstown Volunteer Horse Artillery in 1877. He served as gaoler in Beaconsfield for 18 years and also worked for De Beers. During the siege he served in Mandy's 'Buffs' as Lieutenant. He died in 1913. QSA (1). Spink Dec 83.

Wessels, Cornelius J. From Hoopstad, OFS and a member of the OFS Volksraad. He was Chief Commandant until his retirement on 31 Dec 1899 at which time he was replaced by General Ignatius Ferreira.

White, Greenwood. He was born in 1849 in Bradford and arrived in Cape Town in 1881, moving to Kimberley in 1891. During the siege he served as Captain of the KTG. He was a JP and Senior Partner of White and Sons, merchants in Port Elizabeth and Kimberley.

White, James Thomas. He served as Corporal, Bechuanaland Border Police in the Matabele War, 1893 and as Lance Sergeant from 1895. He transferred to the Cape Police 2 Jan 1895 and was Trooper, District No 2. He refused to join the Jameson Raiders and was later tasked to carry despatches to Raleigh Grey ordering him, Jameson and Willoughby to stop and move as quickly as possible out of the Transvaal. He gave evidence at Dr Jameson's trial at Bow Street Court, London on 25 Mar 1896. He was Sergeant, Cape Police, during the Bechuanaland Rebellion of 1897 gaining GCHGSM (1) Bech. Sub Inspector 1 Apr 1899. During the siege he served with the Cape Police 7-pounder detachment. He was wounded 9 Dec 1899 and awarded the QSA and KSA (2). Inspector, 1 Jun 1902.

Williams, Alpheus Fuller. He was the son of G F Williams and was born in Oakland, California, on 21 Jun 1874. He was educated in the USA and went to South Africa in Jan 1899. He deputised for his father and worked as Assistant General Manager.

Williams, Gardner Fred. During the siege, he was a General Manager of the De Beers Consolidated Mines. He was born in Saginaw, Michigan in 1842 and graduated from the University of California. Worked around the USA in Utah, Colorado and Montana before moving to South Africa. He was an authority on mining and wrote *The Diamond Mines of South Africa — an account of their rise and development* (1902).

Woodward, Francis Willoughby. He was born 5 Dec 1872, son of Willoughby Woodward and educated at Shrewsbury School and at the RMC, Sandhurst; was gazetted to the LNLR 21 Oct 1893 and became Lieutenant, 14 Mar 1896. He served in the Boer War 1899-1902. During the siege, he was Signalling Officer. Afterwards, he took part in the operations in the OFS Apr to May 1900, operations in the Transvaal, west of Pretoria, Jul to 29 Nov 1900, operations in the ORC, May to Jul 1900, including actions at Lindley (1 Jun) and Rhenoster River; operations in Cape Colony, north and south of Orange River, 1899 to 1900. He served as Adjutant, 1st LNLR, 5 Jun 1901 to 31 May 1902 (and after the Boer War to 4 Jun 1904), and was promoted to Captain, 24 Dec 1901. Captain Woodward was present at operations in the Transvaal 30 Nov 1900 to Jun 1901, operations in Cape Colony, Jul 1901 to May 1902. MID LG 8 May 1900 and 10 Sep 1901 and awarded the DSO LG 27 Sep 1901 and invested by the King 24 Oct 1902. From 23 Mar 1906 to 22 Mar 1916, he was employed with the Egyptian Army (3rd Class Medjidie and 3rd Class Order of the Nile). Promoted to Major 12 Sept 1914, was acting Lieutenant Colonel, commanding a service battalion Manchester Regiment, 19 Feb to 20 Mar 1917, and 6 May to 20 Dec 1917. He was Temporary Colonel 21 Dec 1917, promoted to Lieutenant Colonel 13 Sep 1918. Commanded the 1st LNLR. He died 27 Dec 1927. His medal entitlement was: DSO, QSA (3) (Lt 1/LNL), KSA (2) (Capt & Adj, DSO, LNL), BWM, VM with MID (Col), Kimberley Star, Khedive's Sudan Zeraf 1913-14, Croix de Guerre (France), Italy Order of St Maurice & St Lazarus 4th Class, Italy Croce di Guerra, Egypt Order of the Nile 3rd Class, Turkey Order of the Medjidie 3rd Class. Spink Mar 81 £975. DNW Dec 91 £1,500. Spink 92 £2,250. Liverpool Dec 93 £2,100. Dixon Apr 02 £4,600. His medals can be seen on page 500.

Woon, E W. He served in the Bechuanaland Rebellion of 1897 and during the siege with CP No 3 Maxim gun detachment and at Otto's Kopje. Slightly wounded Ruiter's Kraal 13 Aug 1901 and later served as Captain, GFC. He was MID 8 Dec 1901 for conspicuous gallantry under fire with Colonel Gorringe's column in Cape Colony. He gained the QSA (3) and KSA (2). Became Inspector, South African Police. In the Great War he was Temporary Major, South African Irish 1 Nov 1914 and was awarded the MC (LG 22 Aug 18) for gallantry during operations in German South West Africa. Inspector, No 12 District (Grahamstown), South African Police. Seconded to the East African Expeditionary Force 16 Nov 1915. Major and Second in command, 5th Battalion, South African Infantry. Operations in East Africa. Awarded the DSO for gallantry at Kangata 20 Jun 1916. Rejoined South African Police 14 Feb 17. Lieutenant Colonel, South African Police, in 1924.

Wright, A J. He served as a Private, Cradock Burghers, in the Basuto War 1880-81 and in the operations in Transkei. He was Sergeant, Duke of Edinburgh's Own Volunteer Rifles, in the Bechuanaland Rebellion, 1897. During the Boer War he was Honorary Captain, KRV and served after the siege in the OFS. He was awarded the QSA and KSA (2). QSA (2). Spink Oct 99 £220.

Wright, Stephen Osborne. He was born in 1869 and arrived in Kimberley in the early years and shortly after the death of his father. He worked for De Beers Mine and was very interested in football. Served during the siege as Lieutenant in the KLH until he was killed 28 Nov 1899.

Young, Antony Rogers. He served as a Trooper, K Troop, BSAP during the Jameson Raid and was captured. He next saw service as Trooper, Matebeleland Relief Force, Matabele Rebellion 1896. During the siege he served with the Cape Police (HQ and depot mounted branch) and gained the QSA and KSA (2).

Appendix 10 – Portraits

Angel,
Thomas Lombard

Ashe,
Dr Evelyn Oliver

Beet,
George

Benjamin,
Lionel Harry

Berrange,
Christian Anthony Lawson

Black,
Andrew Orman

Blacking,
Fred

Brunton,
Walter George

Chamier,
George Daniel

359

Kimberley Siege Account and Medal Roll

Church,
George

Coghlan,
Charles Patrick John

Cumming,
Arthur William

Dallas,
Seymour

Damant,
Frederick Hugh

Davis,
Valfrid Emanuel

De Villebois-Mareuil,
Georges

Eliott,
Francis Augustus Heathfield

Elphinstone,
Frederick Stephen

Appendices

Ferreira,
Ignatius S

Finlayson,
Robert Alexander

Gillett,
John Lionel

Goffe,
Edward

Gordon Sprigg,
John

Gorle,
Harry Vaughan

Green,
George Alfred Lawrence

Harris,
David

Henderson,
Robert Hugh

Hertog, Charles Edward

Howie, C

Idebski, William Martin

Kekewich, Robert George

Kirsten, Frederick Benjamin Adolphe

Labram, George F

Liddiard, Eaben John

Lowndes, John Gordon

Lucas, Claude Davis

Appendices

MacInnes, Duncan Sayre	Maguire, James Rochfort	Mair, George
Matthews, T H	May, Thomas James	Mildred, Charles Ashwell
Milne, W G	Moir, Jimmy	Murray, W H E

Nelson,
W

Noonan,
Joseph Daniel

Notcutt,
Henry Clement

O'Meara,
Walter Alfred John

Oliver,
Henry Alfred

Ortlepp,
Albert James

Peakman,
Tom C

Pickering,
William

Reyersbach,
Louis J

Appendices

Rhodes,
Cecil J

Roberts,
Lord Frederick Sleigh

Robinson,
Macleod Bartree

Rodger,
Thomas Henderson

Rush,
William Welsh

Salaman,
Sam

Schreiner,
William Philip

Scott,
Robert George

Smartt,
Sir Thomas William

Smith,
James Alexander Jones

Steyn,
Martinus T

Thomas,
Kenneth Robert

Turner,
Alfred Ernest

Tyson,
Thomas Gilbee

Wessels,
Cornelius J

White,
Greenwood

Williams,
Alpheus Fuller

Williams,
Gardner Fred

Appendix 11 – Military casualties

Military casualties were incurred on both sided of the siege, particularly in the early part to the end of November 1899. The lists for both sides that follow record only these casualties sustained during the siege. Some of the casualties are pictured here.

Commandant Petrus Botha
Killed 24th October 1899

Sergeant H Collier, KLH
Killed 25th November 1899

Trooper Hugh J L Elliott, CP
Killed 24th October 1899

2nd Lieutenant W Fletcher, LNLR
Died 18th October 1899

Sergeant C E Freislich, KLH
Killed 25th November 1899

Trooper J W Hastings, KLH
Killed 28th November 1899

Corporal R Howell, KRV
Killed 28th November 1899

Private T Jones, CP
Killed 25th November 1899

Lt Colonel Henry Scott-Turner, RH
Killed 28th November 1899

Kimberley Siege Account and Medal Roll

British and Colonial casualties

The casualty figures given below are derived from Regimental histories, the medal rolls and publications such as *Last Post, Summer of 1899, Siege of Kimberley, Black and White, The Times* and *Diamond Fields Advertiser*. According to this list, there were a total of 191 casualties of all types during the siege. Where a man was injured more than once, each injury is counted towards the total. Four men were injured more than once, each a total of twice. Of the casualties, 12% were sustained by officers and 88% by NCOs and men.

Casualty summary:

39	Killed/DOW
116	Wounded
36	Other
191	**Total**

This is a summary of casualties by unit:

Unit	Officers Killed	Officers Wounded	Officers Other	NCOs and men Killed	NCOs and men Wounded	NCOs and men Other	Total
CP		3	1	11	28	6	49
DFA				1	10		11
DFH[52]		2		1	3		6
DBMB					1		1
KLH	2	7		18	31	2	60
KRV		2	1	4	13	8	28
KTG			1		1	10	12
LNLR		3	1	2	11	4	21
RE		1					1
RGA						2	2
	2	18	4	37	98	31	191

The following table lists the casualties of all types in alphabetical order:

Name	Rank	Nr	Regt	Date	KIA	Wounded	Other	Details
Adler, Henry Mark	Pte	522	KRV	28 Nov 99		✓		Slight wound to the arm
Anderson, Edward	Trptr	81	DFA	9 Dec 99		✓		Slightly wounded in the hip
Anderson, J M	Pte	4769	LNLR	4 Jan 00			✓	Died of disease
Armstrong, Arthur H	Tpr	54	KLH	22 Nov 99		✓		Severely wounded in chest
Arundale[53], Francis R	Pte	665	CP2	28 Nov 99		✓		Severely wounded stomach and chest
Ayliff, William Edward	Maj		CP2	3 Nov 99		✓		Slightly wounded in the neck
Bailey, H	Sgt	157	CP1	25 Nov 99		✓		Slightly wounded in the leg
Baker, William John	Tpr	266	KLH	28 Nov 99	✓			Killed
Bankier, A A	Bombdr	202	DFA	24 Oct 99		✓		Severely wounded in the right arm (compound fracture) and left hand
Barron, Robert B	Tpr	83	KLH	25 Nov 99		✓		Slightly wounded in the foot
Berg, C G	Pte	583	KRV	4 Nov 99			✓	Prisoner at Carter's Ridge
Billing, G	Pte	615	KRV	25 Nov 99		✓		Slight wound to right hip
Bingham, Charles H	Lt		LNLR	24 Oct 99		✓		Compound fracture to thigh
Blake, Alfred	L Sgt	490	KRV	20 Oct 99	✓			Killed
Bodley, Joseph H	Capt		DFH	17 Nov 99		✓		Wounded in the leg
Bowen, Henry J Ap O	Capt		KLH	25 Nov 99		✓		Severely wounded in the jaw
Brady, Claude	Tpr	15	KLH	24 Oct 99		✓		Slight wound to the hand
Brady, George C	Sgt	391	CP2	28 Nov 99	✓			Killed
Brick, T	Pte	1563	CP1	17 Jan 00			✓	Died of disease
Brooks, J L	Tpr	88	KLH	15 Feb 00			✓	Died of disease
Brown, Henry Philip	Capt		CP2	4 Nov 99			✓	Imprisoned in Bloemfontein

---

[52] No medals were issued to the DFH. Instead, the DFH men were listed on the KRV medal rolls.
[53] Heberden reports how "As Jack was putting a very badly wounded trooper, named Arundale, into the Ambulance, the trooper said quietly: 'Dulce et decorum est pro patria mori.' (It is a sweet and blessed thing to die for one's country.) 'You can leave out the last word, old chap,' said Jack. 'Do you think so, Doctor?' was his cheerful answer, as the Ambulance moved away with him."

Appendices

Name	Rank	Nr	Regt	Date	KIA	Wounded	Other	Details
Butler, T	Pte		KTG	2 Feb 00			✓	Died of disease
Campbell, James N	Tpr	108	KLH	16 Nov 99		✓		Slight wound
Canut, R C	Sgt	110	DFA	9 Dec 99		✓		Wounded by a bruise to the heel
Carlyle, Thomas	Pte	702	CP2	25 Nov 99		✓		Slightly wounded in the thigh
Cawood, Barrett N	Tpr	114	KLH	25 Nov 99		✓		Severely wounded in the arm
Chambers, J	Pte	3965	LNLR	3 Jan 00			✓	Fell 70 feet from the conning tower and died instantly
Chapman, George E	Tpr	110	KLH	24 Oct 99		✓		Slightly wounded in the neck
Churcher, Joseph H	Sgt Maj	259	KLH	16 Nov 99		✓		Slight wound to the foot
Clark, William	Pte	217	CP2	25 Nov 99		✓		Slightly wounded in the thumb
Clarke, E P	Tpr	214	KLH	16 Nov 99		✓		Severe wound to the abdomen
Clifford, Wigram R	Lt		LNLR	28 Nov 99		✓		Slightly wounded in the scalp
Collier, Herbert Inglis	Sgt	393	KLH	25 Nov 99	✓			Killed
Colin, P	Pte		KTG	Unknown		✓		Wounded between 10 - 13 Jan 00
Committee, J	Pte	521	KRV	3 Feb 00			✓	Died of disease
Connolly, J	Cpl	153	KRV	4 Nov 99			✓	Prisoner at Carter's Ridge
Cooper, A J	Pte	4045	LNLR	25 Nov 99		✓		Slightly wounded in the thigh
Cornwall, Henry	Pte	513	KRV	28 Nov 99	✓			Killed
Corrie, James	Pte	76	CP2	25 Nov 99	✓			Killed
Cullinan, John Carr	Sgt	6	CP	15 Oct 99			✓	Prisoner at Riverton Waterworks
Dare, Arthur S	Pte	379	KRV	28 Nov 99	✓			Killed
Davies, R T	Pte		KTG	28 Oct 99			✓	Died of a haemorrhage. Not on the medal, nominal or casualty rolls
Day, Frederick H	Tpr	210	KLH	28 Nov 99		✓		Severely wounded in the head
Deere, R H	Pte	1013	CP1	25 Nov 99		✓		Slightly wounded in the thigh
Dennison, Clifford D	Pte	656	CP2	28 Nov 99	✓			Killed
Dickinson, Arthur F	Trptr	136	DFA	24 Oct 99 / 15 Feb 00		✓ / ✓		Slight wound to the hand / Slight wound to the arm
Dodds, J C	Tpr	61	KLH	24 Oct 99		✓		Slightly wounded in the leg
Dye, W T	Pte	1087	CP1	24 Oct 99		✓		Slight wound to the thigh
Edy, Norman H	Pte	672	CP2	28 Nov 99		✓		Slightly wounded in the shoulder
Eden, W E	Pte	587	KRV	4 Nov 99			✓	Prisoner at Carter's Ridge
Edkins, George	Pte	4046	LNLR	28 Nov 99		✓		Severely wounded in the left thigh
Elliott, G	Pte	586	KRV	4 Nov 99			✓	Prisoner at Carter's Ridge
Elliott, Hugh Jardine L	Pte	285	CP2	24 Oct 99	✓			Killed
Farr, Leo George	Tpr	1211	KLH	25 Nov 99		✓		Slightly wounded in the stomach
Ferguson, Fergus	Pte	549	KRV	28 Nov 99		✓		Severely wounded
Field, H G	Lt		KTG	22 Nov 99			✓	Prisoner. Returned 9 Jan 00
Fletcher, Walter J C	2nd Lt		LNLR	18 Oct 99			✓	Died of sunstroke
Foster, Ernest L	Pte	791	CP2	Unknown		✓		Wounded
Freislich, C E	Sgt	317	KLH	25 Nov 99	✓			Killed rescuing a wounded comrade
Fyvie, L C	C S M	19	KRV	14 Feb 00		✓		Severely wounded
Geoghegan, John P	Tpr	129	KLH	25 Nov 99		✓		Severely wounded
Glover, E	Dvr		DMB	11 Feb 00		✓		Wounded by shell fragments
Glyn, Charles	Pte	670	KRV	28 Nov 99		✓		Slightly wounded in the chest
Goodall, Thomas J	Tpr	278	KLH	16 Nov 99	✓			Killed
Gordon, Harry John	Pte	551	KRV	28 Nov 99		✓		Slightly wounded
Gow, James	Pte	247	CP2	24 Oct 99		✓		Slight wound to the chest and hip
Gradwell, G W	L Cpl	469	CP	24 Oct 99		✓		Slight wound to the leg
Gregory, Edward P	Tpr	130	KLH	25 Nov 99		✓		Severely wounded in the hand
Grindrod, John Henry	Pte	462	CP2	28 Nov 99		✓		Slight wound to the head
Hall, S	Pte	5234	LNLR	11 Feb 00			✓	Died of disease

Kimberley Siege Account and Medal Roll

Name	Rank	Nr	Regt	Date	KIA	Wounded	Other	Details
Hambly[54], R	L Cpl	392	CP	21 Dec 99			✓	Killed by accident
Harper, Henwood G	Tpr	228	KLH	28 Nov 99	✓			Killed
Harris, G H F	Capt		KLH	Unknown		✓		No details known
Harris, Roy J R	Cpl	134	KLH	24 Oct 99		✓		Severe wound to the leg
Hartigan, Marcus M	Gnr	169	DFA	24 Oct 99		✓		Slight wound to the leg
Hasenjäger, August E	Pte	1570	CP1	25 Nov 99	✓			Killed
Hastings, John W	Tpr	274	KLH	28 Nov 99	✓			Killed
Hauptfleisch, J	Pte		KTG	Unknown			✓	Died of disease
Hawker, Charles H	Lt		KLH	22 Nov 99		✓		Severely wounded in chest
Heald, A	Col Sgt	2393	LNLR	28 Nov 99	✓			Killed
Henderson, H P	Pte	497	KRV	14 Feb 00		✓		Severely wounded in the head
Hickson-Mahoney, J	Capt		KLH	25 Nov 99		✓		Severely wounded in the shoulder
Hillier, H W	Pte	1927	CP	28 Nov 99		✓		Slight wounded to the leg Not on the medal rolls
Hiscock, Herbert	L Cpl	250	KLH	28 Nov 99	✓			Killed
Hoskins, C H	Pte	1105	CP1	24 Oct 99		✓		Slight wound to the wrist
Howell, James H	Pte	1773	CP1	28 Nov 99		✓		Severely wounded in the chest
Howell, Richard	Cpl	248	KRV	28 Nov 99	✓			Killed
Hughes, D T	Pte	591	KRV	4 Nov 99			✓	Prisoner at Carter's Ridge
Human, John Lewis	Pte	232	CP2	Unknown			✓	Prisoner
Johnson, H Luttman	Pte	556	DFH	16 Nov 99		✓		Slight wound to the scalp
Jones, Arthur S F	Gnr	22231	RGA	7 Jan 00			✓	Died of enteric
Jones, Thomas	Pte	5174	LNLR	10 Feb 00		✓		Severe wound from Long Tom
Jones, Thomas	Pte	68	CP2	25 Nov 99	✓			Killed
Keller, Joseph A	Tpr	202	KLH	28 Nov 99	✓			Mortally wounded. Died 29 Nov 99
Kelly, George	Pte	242	KRV	30 Dec 99			✓	Found dead in Kimberley Mine
Kenton, James	Pte	4857	LNLR	28 Nov 99		✓		Severely wounded right shoulder
Kidd, William E	Sgt	103	DFA	9 Dec 99		✓		Wounded with a bruised kneecap
Kilpin, G C	Gnr	15893	RGA	4 Feb 00			✓	Died of enteric
King, Charles W	Pte	594	KRV	28 Nov 99		✓		Slight wound to the arm
Knight, Frank S	Pte	200	KRV	28 Nov 99		✓		Slight wound
Lace, E	Pte		KTG	9 Dec 99			✓	Died
Lanigan, D J	Tpr	25	KLH	25 Nov 99		✓		Slight wound to left wrist
Lee, H	Pte	3983	LNLR	24 Oct 99 / 28 Nov 99		✓ / ✓		Slight wound in the arm / Slight wound to the right hand
Lefevre, Charles	Gnr	108	DFA	9 Dec 99		✓		Slight wound to the kneecap
Legward, Charles	Tpr	1311	KLH	25 Nov 99		✓		Severely wounded wrist and arm
Leipoldt, Peter	Pte	557	DFH	24 Oct 99	✓			Killed
Lester, C R	Pte	506	DFH	16 Nov 99		✓		Slight wound to the leg
Litkie, E M	Capt		KRV	12 Dec 99			✓	Died of disease
Lowndes, John G	Lt		LNLR	24 Oct 99		✓		Compound fracture to the thigh
Lubbe, Johannes J	Pte	745	CP2	3 Nov 99	✓			Killed by a wound to the head
Lutner, T	Pte	3746	LNLR	28 Nov 99	✓			Killed
MacKenzie, Roderick	Pte	311	CP2	24 Oct 99	✓			Killed
Marshall, John T	Tpr	271	KLH	28 Nov 99	✓			Killed
Mathieson, George R	Pte	713	CP2	25 Nov 99		✓		Slight wound to the leg
May, A J	Sgt		KTG	Unknown			✓	Died of disease
Mayston, W H D	Sgt	335	KLH	25 Nov 99		✓		Slight wound to the hip
McCaskill, Ronald	Tpr	151	KLH	24 Oct 99		✓		Slight wound to the forehead
McClintock, Robert L	Lt		RE	24 Oct 99		✓		Slight wound to the side

---

[54] Ashe states "On the 21st we had another sad mishap. A corporal in the Mounted Police, after going round and inspecting his outlying pickets, went off towards the Boer lines without saying anything to his men. They did not see him go, and consequently when they saw a man some four or five hundred yards away spying and scouting about, they fired at and killed him. It was just getting dark, and he had not said a word to any one about going, so no blame could possibly be attached to the men. It was absolutely his own fault, but it is very sad to kill one's own men all the same."

Appendices

Name	Rank	Nr	Regt	Date	KIA	Wounded	Other	Details
McDermott, A	Pte	3752	LNLR	13 Feb 00		✓		Wounded
McDonald, John R	Sgt Maj	27	KRV	28 Nov 99		✓		Slight wound to the arm
McDonald, Walter	Tpr	269	KLH	28 Nov 99	✓			Killed
McNay, Charles G	Pte	488	CP2	28 Nov 99		✓		Slight wound to the thigh
Metrovitch, Joseph G	Pte	322	CP2	28 Nov 99		✓		Slight wound
Milner, A	Pte	4188	LNLR	24 Oct 99		✓		Severe wound to the thigh
Mitchell, Walter	Tpr	161	KLH	16 Nov 99		✓		Slight wound to the leg
Montleo, G L	Pte	57	CP2	15 Oct 99			✓	Prisoner at Riverton Waterworks
Morley, G H	Pte		KTG	Unknown			✓	Prisoner during siege
Moss, Alfred	Sgt Maj	95	DFA	9 Dec 99	✓			Killed
Neville, J	Pte	4649	LNLR	28 Nov 99		✓		Wounded in the head
Nicholas, Benjamin L	Tpr	215	KLH	28 Nov 99	✓			Killed
O'Dell, David	Pte	194	CP2	25 Nov 99		✓		Slight wound to the thigh
Oatley, William H	Sgt Maj	301	KLH	25 Nov 99		✓		Severely wounded eye and head
Orr, John	Tpr	244	KLH	16 Nov 99		✓		Slight wound to the thigh
Osborne, Alfred	Pte		KTG	16 Jan 00			✓	Died of enteric
Parker, Algernon	Pte	609	CP2	11 Nov 99	✓			Killed
Parsons, D	Tpr	246	KLH	16 Nov 99		✓		Slight wound to the leg
Payne, Fred W	Gnr	170	DFA	24 Oct 99		✓		Severe wound to the foot
Peakman, Thomas C	Maj		KLH	16 Nov 99		✓		Slight wound to the thigh
Peiser, John	L Cpl	318	KLH	25 Nov 99	✓			Died of wounds
Petersen, John B	Pte	794	CP2	24 Oct 99		✓		Slight wound to the arm
Pool, Frank Harvy	Pte	736	CP2	28 Nov 99		✓		Wounded in the leg
Powell, Frank	L Cpl	260	KLH	28 Nov 99		✓		Severely wounded in the abdomen
Prince, E	Pte		KTG	Unknown			✓	Accidentally killed by own men
Pritchard, Matthew J	Tpr	176	KLH	25 Nov 99		✓		Slight wound to the hip
Richardson, Henry	Tpr	262	KLH	28 Nov 99		✓		Slight wound
Richardson, J	Tpr	315	KLH	13 Jan 00			✓	Died of disease
Ring, George	Tpr	324	KLH	25 Nov 99		✓		Slight wound to the forearm
Rodger, Thomas H	Maj		KRV	14 Feb 00		✓		Wounded in the arm
Rossiter, W	Pte	176	DFH	16 Nov 99		✓		Dangerous wound to the abdomen
Rush, William W	Lt		CP2	25 Nov 99		✓		Slight wound to the arm and chest
Salkeld, Phillip D'O	Pte	148	CP2	28 Nov 99	✓			Mortally wounded in the leg
Scott-Turner, H S	Lt Col		KLH	25 Nov 99 28 Nov 99	✓	✓		Slight wound to the shoulder Killed
Screech, Charles	Tpr	287	KLH	28 Nov 99	✓			Killed
Sharpe, Frederick	Tpr	291	KLH	28 Nov 99	✓			Killed
Shepherd, Daniel D	Pte	277	KRV	28 Nov 99		✓		Slight wound to the arm
Simpson, F D	Pte	1378	CP1	24 Oct 99		✓		Slight wound to thigh/posterior
Skelton, Henry	Pte		KTG	18 Dec 99			✓	Died of disease
Skill, N Charles	Tpr	327	KLH	25 Nov 99		✓		Severely wounded in the hand
Skinner, R L	Pte	381	CP2	25 Nov 99		✓		Slight wound to the thigh
Smith, H W	Lt		DFH	16 Nov 99		✓		Slight wound. Bruised by ricochet
Smith, Samuel H	Pte	608	KRV	4 Nov 99			✓	Prisoner at Carter's Ridge
Spilsbury, W G	L Cpl	1312	CP1	28 Nov 99		✓		Severely wounded in the thigh
Stacpole, Henry F	Tpr	207	KLH	28 Nov 99		✓		Slight wound to the arm
Stassen, John N	Pte	372	CP2	Unknown		✓		Wounded
Stearns, Charles C	Tpr	233	KLH	28 Nov 99	✓			Killed
Stenson, W	Pte		KTG	17 Jan 00			✓	Died of enteric
Stewart, A W	Dvr	206	DFA	9 Dec 99		✓		Wounded in the left eye
Stolz, J J	Pte	1161	CP1	25 Nov 99		✓		Slight wound to the leg
Stumke, John C A	Tpr	30146	KLH	11 Nov 99		✓		Slight wound to the forehead
Tarr, G	Pte	1548	CP	25 Nov 99 17 Jan 00		✓	✓	Slight wound to the scalp Died of disease Not on the medal rolls
Taylor, Herbert	Tpr	225	KLH	28 Nov 99	✓			Killed
Taylor, John F	Pte	1455	CP1	28 Nov 99		✓		Slight wound

371

Kimberley Siege Account and Medal Roll

Name	Rank	Nr	Regt	Date	KIA	Wounded	Other	Details
Thompson, Joseph	Tpr	276	KLH	28 Nov 99	✓			Killed
Tyldesley, T	Pte	4261	LNLR	28 Nov 99		✓		Severely wounded in the right thigh
Walcroft, J	Pte	4525	LNLR	25 Nov 99		✓		Severely wounded in the chest
Waldek, S P	Capt		KRV	28 Nov 99		✓		Slight wound
Watermeyer, F E	Sgt	94	CP2	3 Nov 99		✓		Severely wounded in the lung
Watson, H G	Lt		KLH	28 Nov 99		✓		Slight wound to the neck
Whale, Harry	Sgt	139	KRV	14 Feb 00		✓		Slight wound
White, James T	Lt		CP2	9 Dec 99		✓		Slightly wound to foot from shrapnel
Wild, F	Pte	5107	LNLR	15 Jan 00			✓	Died of disease
Williams, A E	Tpr	194	KLH	25 Nov 99		✓		Severely wounded in the arm
Williams, James E	Pte	1928	CP1	28 Nov 99	✓			Killed
Willmore, A E	Tpr	53	KLH	25 Nov 99	✓			Killed
Winter, Alexander	Pte	734	KRV	14 Feb 00		✓		Wounded
Wood, Alfred	Tpr	22824	KLH	28 Nov 99		✓		Slight wound to the arm
Wright, Stephen O	Lt		KLH	28 Nov 99	✓			Killed

This table shows the casualties of all type sustained by month. Note that for 9 men, the date of injury is not known and these men have therefore been excluded from this table:

Month	Oct 99	Nov 99	Dec 99	Jan 00	Feb 00
Casualties	28	119	12	9	14

The casualties by date:

Date	Killed	Wounded	Other	Description
15 Oct 99			2	
18 Oct 99			1	
20 Oct 99	1			Attempt to destroy the water supply at Riverton.
24 Oct 99	3	20		Macfarlane's farm.
28 Oct 99			1	
3 Nov 99	1	2		Carter's Farm and Kenilworth.
4 Nov 99			7	A patrol of 6 men was captured by the Boers. In Kekewich's diary of 5 Nov 99 he said "I am very sorry to say that 6 men of the Diamonds Field Horse are missing. They went out on patrol in Carter's Farm direction. Of course the Mounted Troops do not understand patrolling work well at present, and in addition they are inclined to be careless." Other sources suggest the capture of the men took place at Alexandersfontein. At about the same time Capt H P Brown was also captured by the Boers but this may have been in a separate incident.
11 Nov 99	1	1		Otto's Kopje.
16 Nov 99	1	11		Carter's Farm.
17 Nov 99		1		Alexandersfontein.
22 Nov 99		2	1	Kenilworth.
25 Nov 99	7	29		The first attack on Carter's Ridge.
28 Nov 99	24	31		The second attack on Carter's Ridge.
9 Dec 99	1	6	1	Artillery duel near Kamfersdam.
12 Dec 99			1	

Date	Killed	Wounded	Other	Description
18 Dec 99			1	
21 Dec 99			1	
30 Dec 99			1	
3 Jan 00			1	
4 Jan 00			1	
7 Jan 00			1	
13 Jan 00			1	
15 Jan 00			1	
16 Jan 00			1	
17 Jan 00			3	
2 Feb 00			1	
3 Feb 00			1	
4 Feb 00			1	
10 Feb 00		1		Boer shelling of the Gardens Camp.
11 Feb 00		1	1	Sustained through artillery fire.
13 Feb 00		1		Sustained through artillery fire.
14 Feb 00		5		The taking of Alexandersfontein.
15 Feb 00		1	1	
Unknown		4	5	
Total	39	116	36	

Boer casualties

The casualty figures for the Boers are taken from *Summer of 1899*. As is to be expected, the casualty information is less complete than the British and Colonial data. There is uncertainty about some of the names, units (Commandos), types and dates of the injuries sustained. That said, this is the most comprehensive list of the Kimberley siege casualties for the Boer side. Note that only a few ranks have been recorded so no distinction is make between officers and men. This is a unit summary of casualties:

Commando	Killed	Wounded	Other	Total
Bloemfontein	1			1
Bloemhof	14	21	33	68
Boshof	1		1	2
Brandfort			1	1
Gordonia			1	1
Griqualand West	1			1
Hoopstad		1		1
Jacobsdal	1	2		3
Kroonstad	1			1
Ladybrand	1			1
Lichtenburg		2		2
Potchefstroom	1			1
Schweizer-Reneke		1		1
Winburg	1			1
Wesselton			1	1
OFS Artillery		1	1	2
Creusot agent		1		1
Unknown	8	27	3	38
	30	56	41	127

Casualty summary:

30 Killed/DOW
56 Wounded
41 Other

127 Total

Kimberley Siege Account and Medal Roll

The next table shows the casualties of all type sustained by month. The 13 men for whom no casualty date is known have been excluded.

Month	Oct 99	Nov 99	Dec 99	Jan 00	Feb 00
Casualties	9	90	3	2	10

The following table lists the casualties of all types in alphabetical order:

Name	Commando	Date	KIA	Wounded	Other	Details
Alberts, J J P	Bloemhof	25 Nov 99		✓		Severely wounded
Barnard, M	Bloemhof	25 Nov 99			✓	Prisoner
Beale, H	Unknown	25 Nov 99	✓			Killed in action
Benade, H	Bloemhof				✓	Prisoner
Benade, J	Bloemhof	25 Nov 99			✓	Prisoner
Bester, J	Griqualand West	15 Feb 00	✓			Killed in action
Bester, W	Bloemhof	25 Nov 99			✓	Prisoner
Bezuidenhout, C J	Bloemhof	25 Nov 99		✓		Slightly wounded
Bezuidenhout, G	Schweizer-Reneke	11 Nov 99		✓		Slightly wounded
Blackaller	Unknown	02 Jan 00		✓		Severely wounded
Bolton, P W J	Unknown	29 Nov 99	✓			Killed in action
Botes, A L	Kroonstad	23 Jan 00	✓			Killed in action
Botha, J H	Unknown	24 Oct 99	✓			Killed in action
Botha, N J	Unknown	03 Nov 99	✓			Killed in action
Brand, F R	Unknown	28 Nov 99		✓		Severely wounded
Bredinand, P	Bloemhof	25 Nov 99		✓		Slightly wounded
Brits, T	Bloemhof	25 Nov 99			✓	Prisoner
Britz, Dolf	Unknown	03 Nov 99		✓		Wounded
Broese, J H	Bloemhof	25 Nov 99			✓	Prisoner
Burger, A	Jacobsdal	17 Nov 99		✓		Wounded, leg
Burger, J	Bloemhof	25 Nov 99		✓		Wounded, leg & shoulder
Burger, J	Bloemhof	25 Nov 99			✓	Prisoner
Coetser, J	Bloemhof	25 Nov 99			✓	Prisoner
Coetzer, J	Wesselton				✓	Prisoner
De Beer, J	Bloemhof	25 Nov 99			✓	Prisoner
De Klerk, A P J	Hoopstad	14 Feb 00		✓		Wounded
De Lange, G	Unknown	02 Nov 99		✓		Wounded
De Wet, J	Gordonia	25 Nov 99			✓	Prisoner
Deile, H T	Bloemhof	25 Nov 99		✓		Severely wounded
Du Plessis, J	Unknown	24 Oct 99		✓		Slightly wounded
Du Plessis, S I	Unknown	29 Nov 99	✓			Mortally wounded
Du Plooy, A	Bloemhof	25 Nov 99		✓		Severely wounded, neck & chest
Du Toit, Herklaas	Unknown	03 Nov 99		✓		Wounded
Du Toit, J	Unknown	24 Oct 99		✓		Slightly wounded
Fourie	Bloemhof	25 Nov 99	✓			Mortally wounded
Fourie	Unknown	25 Nov 99		✓		Severely wounded, neck & chest
Fourie, L	Unknown	25 Nov 99			✓	Prisoner
Fourie, L C G	Unknown	14 Feb 00	✓			Killed in action
Fourie, N D	Bloemhof	25 Nov 99			✓	Prisoner
Gagiano, J J	Unknown	11 Nov 99		✓		Slightly wounded, thigh
Gouws, M G	Lichtenburg	09 Dec 99		✓		Slightly wounded, arm
Greeff, G P	Bloemhof	25 Nov 99			✓	Prisoner
Hallett, W A	Bloemhof	25 Nov 99			✓	Prisoner
Harmse, C J H	Bloemhof	28 Nov 99		✓		Severely wounded
Henning, F H	Bloemhof	25 Nov 99	✓			Killed in action
Hurley, L	Unknown	24 Oct 99		✓		Slightly wounded
Ibberson	Unknown				✓	Unknown

374

Name	Commando	Date	KIA	Wounded	Other	Details
Jacobs, D	Unknown	28 Nov 99		✓		Slightly wounded
Jacobs, J	Unknown	24 Oct 99		✓		Slightly wounded
Jacobs, L M B	Bloemhof	28 Nov 99	✓			Killed in action
Jacobs, L M D	Unknown	28 Nov 99		✓		Slightly wounded
Joubert, C J	Unknown	28 Nov 99		✓		Slightly wounded
Joubert, F J	Ladybrand	18 Nov 99	✓			Killed in action
Kleinhans, T	Bloemhof	25 Nov 99		✓		Severely wounded, neck & chest
Klopper	OFS Artillery	02 Nov 99			✓	Injured
Kok, W J	Bloemhof	25 Nov 99			✓	Prisoner
Kok, W L	Bloemhof				✓	Prisoner
Kotzee, H G	Lichtenburg	09 Dec 99		✓		Slightly wounded
Krieg, C J	Unknown	28 Nov 99		✓		Slightly wounded
Leon, S	Creusot agent	12 Feb 00		✓		Wounded
Liebenberg, C	Bloemhof	25 Nov 99			✓	Prisoner
Liebenberg, C	Bloemhof	25 Nov 99	✓			Killed in action
Liebenberg, G P	Bloemhof				✓	Unknown
Lock, H	Bloemhof	25 Nov 99			✓	Prisoner
Lombaard, W	Unknown	24 Oct 99		✓		Slightly wounded
Lubbe, J P S	Bloemhof	25 Nov 99	✓			Killed in action
Marais, E J	Bloemhof	25 Nov 99		✓		Severely wounded
Mare, J	Unknown				✓	Severely wounded
Maree, J J	Bloemfontein	16 Nov 99	✓			Killed in action
Meijer, G H	Bloemhof	25 Nov 99		✓		Slightly wounded
Meijer, J	Bloemhof	25 Nov 99			✓	Prisoner
Meijer, W	Bloemhof	25 Nov 99		✓		Slightly wounded
Meyer, J G	Bloemhof				✓	Prisoner
Meyer, J P	Bloemhof	25 Nov 99	✓			Killed in action
Meyer, S	Bloemhof	25 Nov 99			✓	Prisoner
Meyer, S F	Bloemhof	00 Dec 99	✓			Killed in action
Nel, H J	Winburg	14 Feb 00	✓			Killed in action
Nieuwoudt, J H	Bloemhof	25 Nov 99			✓	Prisoner
Nieuwoudt, S F	Bloemhof	28 Nov 99	✓			Killed in action
Opperman, H J P	Bloemhof	25 Nov 99	✓			Killed in action
Pienaar, W	Bloemhof	25 Nov 99			✓	Prisoner
Pieterse	OFS Artillery	11 Nov 99		✓		Wounded, eye
Pretorius, J L J	Bloemhof	28 Nov 99	✓			Killed in action
Pretorius, M	Bloemhof	25 Nov 99			✓	Prisoner
Pretorius, S J	Bloemhof	25 Nov 99		✓		Slightly wounded
Prinsloo	Unknown	15 Feb 00		✓		Wounded
Putter, D	Bloemhof	25 Nov 99			✓	Prisoner
Putter, J C	Unknown	28 Nov 99		✓		Slightly wounded
Putter, J D J	Unknown	28 Nov 99		✓		Slightly wounded
Putter, N J	Bloemhof				✓	Prisoner
Ras, M	Bloemhof	25 Nov 99			✓	Prisoner
Ras, P	Bloemhof	25 Nov 99		✓		Slightly wounded
Reinecke, D J	Bloemhof	25 Nov 99			✓	Prisoner
Reinecke, J G	Bloemhof				✓	Prisoner
Schultz, W	Brandfort	05 Feb 00			✓	Died of disease
Smit, B G	Unknown	28 Nov 99		✓		Slightly wounded
Snyman, C R P	Unknown	23 Nov 99	✓			Mortally wounded
Sonnekus, W F	Bloemhof	25 Nov 99	✓			Killed in action
Sonnekus, R H	Bloemhof	25 Nov 99		✓		Slightly wounded
Steenkamp, G A	Bloemhof	25 Nov 99		✓		Slightly wounded
Steyn, C J	Bloemhof		✓			Killed in action
Steyn, J J	Bloemhof	25 Nov 99	✓			Killed in action

Kimberley Siege Account and Medal Roll

Name	Commando	Date	KIA	Wounded	Other	Details
Steyn, P J	Boshof	15 Feb 00			✓	Prisoner
Swanepoel, C J	Bloemhof	25 Nov 99	✓			Killed in action
Swanepoel, D J	Bloemhof			✓		Slightly wounded
Theron, A H L	Bloemhof	25 Nov 99		✓		Severely wounded
Van der Merwe	Unknown	15 Feb 00		✓		Wounded
Van der Merwe, J F	Bloemhof	25 Nov 99		✓		Severely wounded
Van der Merwe, N J S	Bloemhof	25 Nov 99		✓		Slightly wounded
Van der Westhuizen, H	Bloemhof	25 Nov 99			✓	Prisoner
Van Heerden, A	Unknown				✓	Unknown
Van Niekerk, A A	Unknown	21 Nov 99	✓			Killed in action
Van Niekerk, C	Bloemhof	25 Nov 99			✓	Prisoner
Van Niekerk, C	Jacobsdal	17 Nov 99	✓			Mortally wounded
Van Niekerk, J A	Bloemhof	25 Nov 99			✓	Prisoner
Van Niekerk, S R	Unknown	28 Nov 99		✓		Slightly wounded
Van Rensburg, A	Jacobsdal	17 Nov 99		✓		Slightly wounded, arm
Van Rensburg, J J D P	Bloemhof	25 Nov 99		✓		Slightly wounded
Van Vrede, P	Bloemhof	25 Nov 99			✓	Prisoner
Van Wyk, G	Unknown	24 Oct 99		✓		Severely wounded
Varivis	Potchefstroom	02 Feb 00	✓			Mortally wounded
Venter, W	Unknown	11 Nov 99		✓		Slightly wounded
Viljoen, A J J	Unknown	28 Nov 99		✓		Slightly wounded
Vosloo, J P	Bloemhof	25 Nov 99		✓		Slightly wounded
Wahldat, W	Bloemhof				✓	Prisoner
Wessels, G	Unknown	24 Oct 99		✓		Slightly wounded
Zybel, C J	Boshof	24 Oct 99	✓			Killed in action

Appendix 12 – Memorials

This appendix is about the memorials and graves of those who died during the siege.

Honoured Dead Memorial

The Honoured Dead Memorial stands in Kimberley at the highest point in the city on Memorial Hill. It was erected to perpetuate the memory of the men who lost their lives in the defence. Its design was based on a Nereid monument, discovered at Xanthos, Asia Minor, in 1840, and was chosen by a committee led by Cecil Rhodes. It is 52 feet (16 m) high, uses stone taken from the Matopo Mountains in Rhodesia, weighs in excess of 2,000 tons and cost more than £10,000 to build, funded partly by public donations.

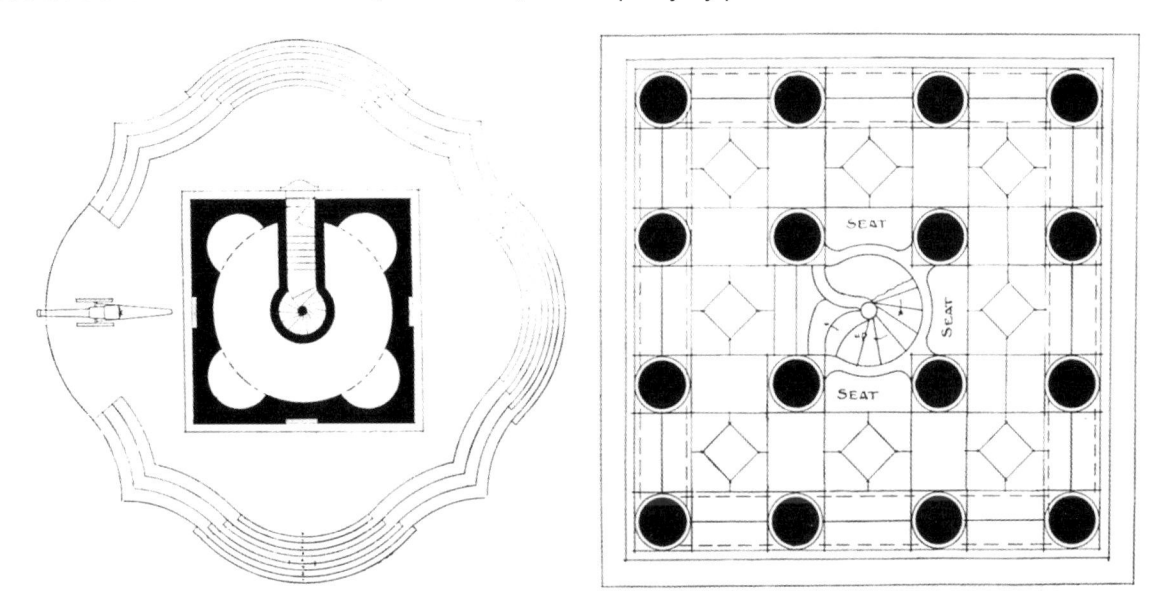

Above, two plan views of the Monument. Below, a recent photograph of the Monument.

Kimberley Siege Account and Medal Roll

On the west wall is an inscription by Rudyard Kipling. It says:

> This for a charge in our children, in sign of the price we paid,
> The price that we paid for freedom, that comes unsoiled in your hand;
> Head, revere, and uncover: here are the victors laid:
> They who died for the City, being sons of the land.

Two tablets in bronze, designed by Lockwood Kipling, are set into the walls of the Memorial. The first carries the names of the 42 men who were killed during the siege (to 16th February 1900), and the second depicts 'Long Cecil' and George Labram. The images below show the detail from the first of these two tablets.

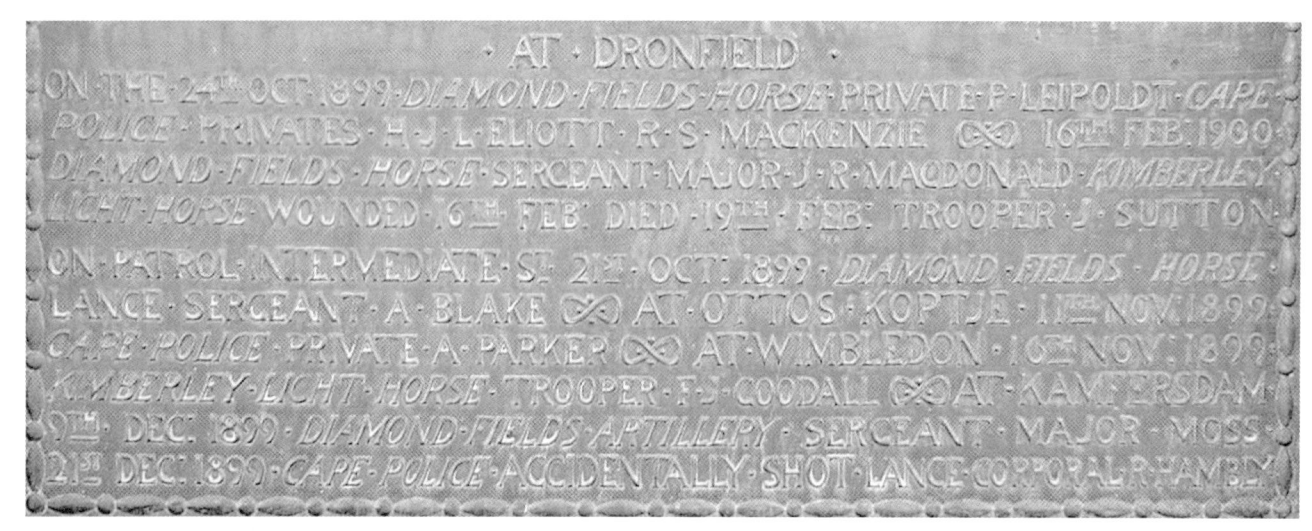

The remains of 27 men lie within a vault inside the Memorial. The Memorial was dedicated on 28th November 1904, a poignant fifth anniversary of the siege's largest engagement. It is fitting too that Long Cecil stands on the stylobate of the Memorial.

Appendices

Cape Police Monument

The Cape Police and their role in the siege is remembered at a separate monument that is also located in Kimberley. The Monument commemorates the men of the Cape Police Districts 1 and 2, and the Special Contingent who lost their lives during the Boer War. At the base of the monument is the gun that was captured in a fight at Dronfield, near Kimberley, on 16th February 1900.

On the left, a contemporary postcard of the monument and on the right a recent picture of the figure on top of the Monument. There was a period of 99 years between the two images.

The inscription from the base of the Cape Police Memorial

379

Kimberley Siege Account and Medal Roll

Carter's Ridge Monument

This cairn is located on the top of Carter's Ridge, to the west of Kimberley. Although the skyline of Kimberley has changed over the years, it is still possible to look across to Kimberley as the Boers used to do.

A contemporary view of the Carter's Ridge monument showing the newly-erected cairn and one of the Boer gun pits

THIS CAIRN MARKS THE PLACE WHERE LIEUT COLONEL HENRY SCOTT TURNER ROYAL HIGHLANDERS, AND THE FOLLOWING OFFICER, N.C.OFFICERS AND MEN FELL IN THE DEFENCE OF KIMBERLEY ON THE 28TH NOVEMBER 1899.

LIEUT STEPHEN OSMOND WRIGHT	KIMBERLEY LIGHT HORSE	
COLOUR SERGT HEALD	1ST L.N.L.REGT	
PRIVATE LUTNER	DO	
SERGT MAJOR GEORGE CLIFFORD BRADY	CAPE POLICE	
PRIVATE CLIFFORD DENNISON	DO	
" JAMES ERNEST WILLIAMS	DO	
CORPORAL RICHARD HOWELL	DIAMOND FIELDS HORSE	
PRIVATE HENRY CORNWALL	DO	
" ARTHUR SPEDDON DARE	DO	
LC CORPL HERBERT HISCOCK	KIMBERLEY LIGHT HORSE	
PRIVATE WILLIAM JOHN BAKER	DO	
" JOHN W. HASTINGS	DO	
" GEORGE HENWOOD HARPER	DO	
" WALTER McDONALD	DO	
" JOHN W. MARSHALL	DO	
" BENJAMIN LEONARD NICHOLAS	DO	
" CHARLES SCREECH	DO	
" FREDERICK SHARPE	DO	
" CHARLES CULLEN STEARNS	DO	
" JOSEPH THOMPSON	DO	
" HERBERT TAYLOR	DO	

THIS TABLET IS ERECTED TO THE MEMORY OF
SERGT THOMAS JONES CAPE POLICE
CORPL JAMES CORRIE " "
PTE AUGUST EMEL HASENJAGER " "
SERGT HERBERT INGLIS COLLIER KIMBERLEY LIGHT HORSE
" CHARLES EDMUND FREISLICH " " "
TROOPER ALBERT EDW N WILLMORE " "
" JOHN PEISER " " "
WHO FELL IN THE DEFENCE OF THEIR COUNTRY IN THE VICINITY OF THIS SPOT ON THE 25TH NOVEMBER 1899.

The two tablets that are displayed on the cairn. The image on the left commorates the battle on the 28th. The image above commemorates the engagement on the 25th.

Age has caused some of the letters to fall out of the tablets but the two are still very legible.

380

Appendices

Loyal North Lancashire Regiment Monument

This memorial now stands in Avenham Park, close to the centre of Preston, Lancashire and commemorates the fallen for all battalions of the LNLR. The memorial was dedicated on 6th October 1904 and used to stand in Preston town centre.

Fittingly, Kekewich was present at the dedication (he is visible in the picture on the left).

The dedication ceremony in 1904

The Monument in its present-day location

The regimental inscription from one of the four tablets at the base of the Monument

381

Kimberley Siege Account and Medal Roll

OFFICERS
LIEUTENANTS A.R. WALLACE. K.Z.R. MACAULAY. A.W. HEWETT. W.H. CREAK. G.C. WOOD.
SECOND LIEUTENANTS R.C. WILTSHIRE. W.J.C. FLETCHER.
NON-COMMISSIONED OFFICERS AND MEN OF THE 1ST BATTALION
COLOUR SERGEANTS A. HEALD. J. DOREY.
SERGEANTS F. WILSON. R. RICHARDSON. C. BOWMAN.
LANCE SERGEANTS J. HARRISON. J. MORLEY.
CORPORALS W. MEADE. C. MULCOCK. E. SCOTT.
LANCE CORPORALS J. HALL. C. REEVES. W. OUSLEY. J. GERRARD.
W. HAWKINS. J. ENTWISTLE.
PRIVATES A. KEELEY. J. COLE. H. BELL. J. COLBOURNE. F. OWENS.
T. JOHNSON. T. PLATT. T. ALMOND. H. SOUTH. A. DODD.

The inscription for the officers and 1st Battalion NCOs

1ST BATTALION.
PRIVATES H. CHANTLER. R. STANLEY. J. BLACOW. J. NIXON. H. DINN.
" H. COOPER. E. BEARD. R. WILCOCK. A. GARVEY. C. ELLIS.
" P. MOORE. F. HUGHES. J. STARKIE. J. CHAMBERS. T. LUTNER.
" J. ANDERSON. S. HALL. F. WILDE. J. BLACKHOUSE. D. CALVERT.
" C. DAULBY. J. ROUSE. E. WARD. W. STANLEY. P. LUCEY.
" W. THOMPSON. J. RYAN. D. JONES. J. BAINES. P. QUINN. A. BUTLER.
" J. CHARNOCK. J. GRAHAM. A. WHITE. J. MAGUIRE. J. HICKEY. M. CAINE.
" W. JENKS. W. DAVIS. M. GALLAGHER. A. THOMPSON. F. PERRY. C. MOSS.
" C. HALL. A. MADDELL. R. RIGBY. C. SHEPPARD. J. WILLIAMS. J. JOHNSTON.
" C. TEDDER. J. McCREAVY. J. LOMAS. W. TAYLOR. J. GRAY. J. WOOLEY.
" F. BRANDON. A. LEE. F. SCHOFIELD. H. HOLGATE. J. BUTLER.

The inscription for the 1st Battalion men

Graves

The graveyards around Kimberley contain the last resting place of many of the people who died during the siege and also many of the casualties from the relieving force and subsequent engagements.

IN LOVING MEMORY OF
MAJOR HENRY SCOTT TURNER
OF THE 42ND ROYAL HIGHLANDERS (BLACK WATCH)
WHO FELL WHILST GALLANTLY LEADING A SORTIE
FROM KIMBERLEY ON NOVEMBER 28TH 1899,
AGED 32 YEARS.
PRO CHRISTO, ET REGINA, ET PATRIA.

The grave of Henry Scott-Turner

Appendices

The grave of George Labram

The grave of Petrus Botha
(at Magersfontein)

The grave of Walter Fletcher

The grave of Henry Skelton

Appendix 13 – Organisation of the defence

This appendix is comprised of three reports compiled by Lt MacInnes of the Royal Engineers.

First report on the proposed defence of Kimberley (1898) 384
Second report on the proposed defences of Kimberley (June 1899) 385
Report of Royal Engineers' Siege of Kimberley 388

First report on the proposed defence of Kimberley (1898)

The general scheme of defence compiled by Colonel Trotter CMG, is to surround Kimberley with a girdle or small redoubts garrisoned with 50 to 100 men on a radius of about 1½ miles from the centre of the town and at an average distance of ¾ mile apart. Retrenchments are formed at De Beers and Kimberley Mine enclosures.

It is proposed to divide the defence into five sections. To carry out the necessary works, labour would be obtained from the De Beers Company, but as it would be difficult to employ large parties of Natives with any prospect of attack while work was in progress, it is proposed that the redoubts should be constructed at once. I attach a tabular statement showing the work to be carried out in each section - first beforehand, second when an attack is expected. It will be seen from this that small parties are only required on the outside work. After the redoubts have been completed there will probably be no lack of volunteers from the Engineer Department to superintend the gang of labourers required. The larger parties required in the retrenchments would not be subject to sudden attack and are close to their compounds. The De Beers Company has materials for carrying out the proposed defences.

- Revetting[55] materials (Old trucks, corrugated iron, sand bags, timber, steel plates), material for obstacles, barbed wire 3,000 yards, plain wire (unlimited supply) and some small trees for abatis[56] will be available for section D of defence.

- Explosives: Dynamite (with electric detonators) – the large stock of dynamite is now in sheds to the NW of the town, it is under consideration whether this could not be buried in debris heaps outside the town.

- Communications: The roads are good throughout. Telephonic communication already exists to most of the provision of the proposed defences and can be quickly completed to other points. Ramps will have to be constructed to the various debris heaps selected for artillery positions.

- Defences: I attach a detail drawing of No 4 redoubt, which is fairly typical of the works, the permanent garrison is 50 men, but in accordance with instructions, I have designed the redoubts for a garrison of about 75 to 100 men to allow of their being re-enforced if attacked. Machine gun positions are placed in each redoubt though the guns would probably be kept in a central position in the first place. Parapets have been designed so that if necessary the third relief can be omitted.

I have arranged with the head of the Survey Department of the De Beers Company to take and mark the ranges round each position.

The demolitions required would be chiefly the removal of corrugated iron fences and native huts round the two retrenchments.

The sections[57] of the defence are as follows:

- Section A – Kimberley Mine to Transvaal Road. The redoubts form part of the retrenchments. It is proposed also to place shelter trenches at the most commanding points as well epaulments for field or machine guns, a sand bag parapet on top of the rock shaft gear frame will allow of a few rifles bringing in effect fire on the various roads, the barricades across the roads can be quickly made by haulage trucks filled with earth placed two or three deep across the road, they are at the right height for firing over.

---

[55] To revet means to retain or reinforce a structure with supporting material.
[56] A defensive construction made from trees, branches and bushes.
[57] A map showing these sections appears on page 19.

It was intended to place a redoubt on Kimberley No 1 debris heap, but this heap is too wet to allow of anything more than a low parapet being built. The Chief Engineer, Mr Labram, states that he can arrange to run up a sufficient supply of dry earth to form a parapet and a platform can be made of old planks and sand bags. This can therefore be used as an advanced position.

The positions best suitable for artillery are marked on the plan. I consider that a fence placed across the open ground from Mostert's to the railway essential to prevent a rush by mounted men.

- Section B – Transvaal Road to Convict station No 3 redoubt will have to be constructed with earth taken from the ditch in front of the parapet as the heap is still too wet to allow of an interior trench. This however will not interfere with the strength of the work. The field of fire is good except that trees along the Kenilworth Road require clearing.

- Section C – Convict Station to the Lodge. The field of fire of the redoubts is good, but there is some unseen ground close to them due to the steep slopes of the heaps. It will, therefore, be necessary to surround with wire entanglement. The slaughter kraal in front requires demolition. It is intended to defend Be Beers enclosure similarly to Kimberley enclosure.

- Section D – the Lodge to No 7 Redoubt. It is necessary here to defend the Lodge and Sanatorium on the left of the Beaconsfield Road, and one house on the right of it. As artillery fire from the Bultfontein heaps may be expected, the first step would be to construct shelter trenches with light splinter-proof cover along the edge of the enclosure. Afterwards if time permits it will be necessary to put the houses in a state of defence. A reserve line of defence is also required along the Hospital enclosure and Hemming Street.

- Section E – No 7 Redoubt to Kimberley Mine. The redoubt is pushed forward so as to support section D. The reservoir enclosure is too large for a small garrison to defend effectively. I therefore propose to build a redoubt with the reservoir closing the gorge. To take full advantage of the reservoir embankment a path would be made round it, and parapets placed on it at intervals. A parapet will also be constructed on the filter beds to command the Radloff Road, Premier Mine.

This is intended as an isolated post. It is strong on the north, south and east, but a deep cutting on the west side will require to be carefully blocked to prevent an enemy forming a lodgement. An artillery position will be made on the debris heap on the other side of the cutting. I am giving Major Turner a full statement of the labour, tools, and material required from the De Beers Company, so that the necessary arrangements for them can be made.

I hope to be able to arrange with Mr Labram for the careful organisation of the parties required under heading 2. It will be necessary to have a section of Royal Engineers to generally assist under a Senior Commissioner Officer.

Second report on the proposed defences of Kimberley (June 1899)

General scheme of defence. It is proposed to defend Kimberley by a reserve force kept in a central position ready to move in any direction. This force is to be supported by a girdle of small redoubts with a minimum garrison of 50 men. These redoubts are placed on a radius of about 1½ miles from the centre of the town and about ¾ apart. The two mine enclosures – Kimberley and De Beers – are to act as retrenchments to the NW and SE sides of the town respectively. It is intended to hold the Premier Mine in an advanced position. I attach a detailed statement of the defence works to be executed, and show the working parties, materials etc required. If all this work were to be left to the last moment, considering that the majority of the troops would have to be armed and equipped at the same time, confusion would result. It, therefore, seems to me absolutely essential if hostilities are expected that the steps should be taken to carry out all the work possible before hand. I have, therefore, detailed the work under the two heads:

(1) Work which can be carried out at once,
(2) Work to be done on warning of attack.

The construction of each redoubt requires on average a gang of 150 men for two shifts and 100 men for a third shift, giving a total of 3,200 men for one shift or, if the Premier Mine is included, 4,000 men,

The materials required are chiefly old material and corrugated iron, which, as bolting down is not necessary, would not be greatly damaged, there would also be some expense in connection with a temporary trolley line at the Reservoir, the putting up of wire fencing and mining. I can furnish tracing of the plans of the redoubts when required. The working parties are worked out on a liberal scale, which would be necessary if they were to be constructed in a hurry, but, if done before hand, the Chief Engineer would no doubt make his own arrangements to carry out the work, and a saving in men would be effected.

Kimberley Siege Account and Medal Roll

With regard to the second class of work, its success will entirely depend on organisation before hand.

The following appears to me to be the necessary steps. First, appointment of two members of the Engineering staff of the company, or other suitable volunteers to the charge of each section of defence. Second, detailing of gangs of workmen, including artisans, to form the working party of each section.

The Engineer in charge of each section will arrange for, first, tools and material required. Second, organisation of his gang into sections suitable for the work required. Third, make himself thoroughly acquainted with the details of the work in his section.

If the materials and tools are not available from the company's stores, arrangements could no doubt be made to obtain them locally. The materials and tools should as far as possible be collected at a central spot in each section. If the whole of the works are to be left to the last, a much larger staff of skilled labour will be required, and careful plans before hand still more necessary. The general work to be done in the defence is: first, ranges taken and marked for every point, and a plan and list made ready for the commander of each work. Second, armoured trains got ready. There ought to be no difficulty in carrying this out in the shops if arrangements are made beforehand. Third, sign posts put up to show the directions of the various points in the defence.

The distribution of the dynamite was mentioned by Colonel Trotter to Mr Labram, but no definite conclusion was come to. Action at any rate would be taken to stop further supplies coming in if hostilities become imminent.

The following is the work necessary in each section of the defence.

Section A – Kimberley Mine to Transvaal Road.

    1a. Two redoubts Nos 1 & 2. No difficulty in construction in these redoubts

    1b. Communications to artillery positions. There are four probable artillery positions to which ramps are required, and communications to them generally improved:

- At Kimberley No 2.
- At Kimberley No 1.
- Near the compound to the North of Kimberley enclosure.
- On debris heaps to south west of enclosure.

    1c. Wire fence from Mostert's farm to railway. This is most necessary to check a rush on the town between the redoubts.

    2a. Kimberley Mine enclosure. To put the new and old mine enclosures into a state of defence, I propose to put epaulments for guns and shelter trenches at suitable points, the total length being about 500 yards, the gear frame would have a sandbag parapet placed on it. The corrugated fencing would have to be removed in some places and at other points defended. There is a great deal of demolition which ought to be carried out – such as small houses on the road to the west of the enclosure, which would afford cover to the attack. I have detailed 100 men as the party to do this, but if circumstances permitted the party would be increased.

    2b. Barricades: The main barricades are required in this section on the Barkly Road, but in addition to this the road would be blocked with wire etc, in other places, the trucks held in readiness to block the mechanical haulage line and road alongside it. Two other rows of trucks will make an effective barricade.

    2c. Advanced positions: These are shown on the map. Mr Labram has visited No 1 Kimberley with me, and knows what is required there.

    2d. Demolitions: Vide A above

    2e. Mines: These are intended to be placed in the debris heaps to the south west of the enclosure. They would require to be laid down by the mining staff.

Section B

    1a. Two redoubts Nos 3 & 4. These redoubts are at De Beers No 7 & 8 and No 1. There are no particular difficulties, but in the event of attack it will be necessary to remove the gearing frame. No 1 heap is too soft for an interior trench to be dug in the redoubt.

    1b. A wire fence under the fire of the redoubts is necessary round the engine house at No 4.

Appendices

1c. The artillery positions are at the Pulsator and on a debris heap near the Convict Station. At the former, some work is necessary to form the ramps to the top of the heap.

2a. The clearing of the trees along Kenilworth Road is of great importance. The trees would be used to form an abatis.

2b. The barricades are: First, across the Transvaal Road at Mostert's farm. The buildings here would be put in a state of defence as a picquet guard room. Second, across the Kenilworth Road at the bend at the Reservoir.

2c. Shelter trenches are required on the debris heap marked A on the map for a section of men.

2d. Removal of the gear frame. Specially detailed men would be required for this.

2e. In the second relief the above work would be completed and the field of fire of the redoubts improved. The stables would form good cover to an enemy if he got inside, but they might easily be held by a part of the reserve force.

Section C

1a. The two redoubts are on heaps which require some improvement. The sluits cut by the rainwater will require filling in, and in the case of No 5 the heap on its left will require to be levelled off on top.

1b. Artillery communications. The positions for the guns are between No 5 and 6 redoubts and in rear of No 6. Telephone lines to the redoubts are required.

2a. De Beers Mine Enclosure. This requires the same treatment as the Kimberley enclosure. The fence will require to be taken down. The Savoy Hotel, new engine house, and Compound put in a state of defence.

2b. Barricades. These are on the Boshof Road and the Railway and Hull Street. Wire and trucks are required.

2c. Demolitions. These consist of: first, removal of cow stables opposite No 6 redoubt. Second, general demolitions round De Beers enclosure. Any spare men would be employed on this in the second relief.

2d. The debris heaps to the north of the enclosures would be mined to deny them to the enemy's artillery.

2e. The view from No 5 and No 6 redoubts is restricted by other smaller heaps. It is necessary to make entanglement to prevent the enemy occupying the dead places.

Section D

None of the work in this section can be done before hand.

2. The great difficulty here is the rocky nature of the ground, however, there ought to be enough earth in the gardens of the houses to make breastworks. If necessary it can be added to from a debris heap in rear of the Lodge. The work required is:

2a. Put the Lodge in a state of defence.

2b. Put the Sanatorium in a state of defence.

2c. Put a house on the west side of the road in a state of defence. The order of the work in each of these cases would be: first, make machine guns emplacement and shelter trenches along the fences of the houses facing towards Beaconsfield. Secondly, defend the houses by preparing loop holes, barricading doors, arranging for water and earth to put out fires, putting a sand bag parapet on the verandah of the Sanatorium and demolition of obstruction to the defenders' fire.

2d. The barricade would be placed near the tram shed to allow of it being flanked by the Sanatorium. The spare rails stacked there would be used for the barricade.

2e. General work such as cutting down trees in front making abatis and rough entanglement in the interval. If time permitted, a second line of defence would be made at Nazareth House along the Hospital fence and Hemming Road. The main road would be again barricaded at that point.

Section E

The same difficulty is met with here in rock being close to the surface. It will be necessary to run the greater part of the earth by truck or wagons from the debris heaps in rear. Special arrangements are therefore necessary. I do not know on whose property the proposed site of the redoubt is situated, but as this is the weakest point of the defence, the redoubt and work at the reservoir should certainly be built before hand.

Kimberley Siege Account and Medal Roll

    2a. Parapet on the filter bed to cover Radloff Road. This will be made on the embankment of the bed.
    2b. Parapet in Reservoir Embankment. These will be made at intervals in the Embankment so as to allow the small garrison to direct its fire wherever required.
    2c. Barricades on Radloff Road. In addition to the barricade a trench is required for the reserve force to occupy if necessary.
    2d. Obstacles. The redoubt and intervals between it and the works on either side require well wiring to prevent a rush. There will probably not be time for more than a rough entanglement or trip wires.
    2e. In the second relief the native camp would be demolished.

Premier Mine

    The work here would be placed on top of the debris heap used for the water supply. It will consist of a heavy breast work placed along the edge with splinter proof cover on the east face. A platform for guns and shelter trenches for the escort will be placed on top of the debris heap now in use, and good communications made to it from the work.

    2a. The road between the two heaps must be completely blocked to the enemy.

    2b. Demolition. The Compound should be opened up to the fire from the trenches.

    2c. Mines. There are many small heaps about the main work which can well be mined.

Report of Royal Engineers' Siege of Kimberley

(1) In the main these original proposals for the defence were adhered to, though additional works were built and by the inclusion of Beaconsfield and subsequently Kenilworth the line was much extended. Retrenchments were not employed except on the sides most threatened by the enemy. The De Beers Consolidated Mines Limited, gave every assistance in the Company's power. Labour and materials were throughout the siege put at the disposal of the RE officers. This assistance was most valuable as on account of the large area the works covered it was impossible for the small party of Engineers available to carry out the work alone.

(2) The order to begin work was given on September 25th, one section of 7th Field Company RE under Lieutenant McClintock having arrived on September 21st. The more important parts of the defence were put in hand at once. The execution of the work was as follows:

Commenced	Work	Completed
25 September 99	Rinderpest Redoubt	3 Oct 99
	Stables Redoubt	7 Oct 99
	Reservoir Defences	13 Oct 99
	Camp Redoubt	10 Oct 99
	Sanatorium House & Breastworks	7 Oct 99
26 September 99	Old & New Kimberley Redoubt	7 Oct 99
27 September 99	Kenilworth Redoubt	17 Oct 99
	Smith's Redoubt	10 Oct 99
	Schmidt's Drift Redoubt	13 Oct 99
	De Beers Redoubt	30 Oct 99
28 October 99	Civil Service Redoubt	10 Oct 99
4 October 99	Belgravia Redoubt	10 Oct 99
10 October 99	Transvaal Road Breastworks	17 Oct 99
18 October 99	No 1 Searchlight	6 Nov 99
28 November 99	No 2 De Beers[58]	
4 January 00	Otto's Kopje	10 Jan 00
15 January 00	St Augustine's	27 Jan 00

---

[58] No date was given in the report for the completion of the No 2 De Beers.

Appendices

The other minor works of the defence including obstacles were carried out as opportunity offered, either concurrently or subsequently. Mines were also laid. A large quantity of Mimosa bush was cut down outside the line of defences with the double object of clearing the front and supplying material for abatis. Some demolitions had also to be carried out. These included half of No 1 Location, the whole of No 4 Location, three private houses near Schmidt's Drift Road, and some fences in the Went End and in No 3 Location. Owing to frequent alarmist rumours as to a projected attack by the enemy, the work was pushed on as fast as possible. This entailed additional expense as the small staff of the Royal Engineers were unable to superintend all of the work going on. The main works were all in a defensible state by 8th October 1899.

(3) Labour available: The work was carried out under the superintendence of the 45 NCO's and Sappers of No 1 Section 7th Field Company RE, which arrived 21st September.

The working parties were at different times:-

    (a) Infantry working parties of 1st LNLR.
    (b) Compound natives supplied by De Beers.
    (c) Native labour supplied by Contractors.
    (d) Convict labour - natives.
    (e) Relief work boys.

(a) Infantry working parties were used to build, only one work – i.e. camp redoubt and to clear the ground in front and form an abatis round this work. It was not practicable to supply this form of labour more extensively, as, owing to the small number of regular Infantry (½ Battalion) available and the very extended nature of the defence, it was not considered advisable to take then away from their posts. In the early part of the siege they were fully employed at night on patrol duties.

(b) The De Beers Company was able in the earlier part of the siege to supply large numbers of natives from the mines under their own overseers. This, though the best available, was not an entirely satisfactory type of labour on account of the innate indolence and stupidity of the black and the difficulty the sappers had in getting them or their overseers to understand what was wanted. Consequently, although accustomed to the use of pick and shovel, the maximum of work was never got out of them. Further, being Compound boys, when taken out of De Beers enclosure they were found difficult of discipline. Later in the siege, owing to scarcity of food, De Beers turned the greater part of their natives out to go to their homes, so this kind of labour then ceased to be available, and (c) (d) and (e) were resorted to.

(c) Contract. Certain portions of the work were executed by natives under contractors. This form of labour was perhaps the most satisfactory as, the contractor having a very much greater hold over his men, and also the native being of a better class, a very much higher percentage of work was done in the same time.

(d) Convict. Small portions of work - chiefly on the Mounted Camp - were executed by native convicts. This was a most unsatisfactory form of labour as the convicts did as little as they could and had to work under armed escort.

(e) Relief work natives. Late in the siege, January 1900, De Beers natives being no longer obtainable - relief work natives were employed on works partly to assist in employing these natives. This labour was not very good as the natives were underfed at the time and unable to perform a fair day's work. However, it was the best labour obtainable at the time and fulfilled one of its objects in giving employment to the natives.

(4) Material available: The chief materials required in the defence were:

    (a) For Revetting.
    (b) For Blindages[59].
    (c) For Head cover.
    (d) For Mines.
    (e) For Obstacles.
    (f) For Shelters and latrines.
    (g) For Tools.

---

[59] A cover or protection for a trench formed from earth supported by a framework.

(a) Revetting. For this purpose were used:

(i) Old mine trucks: This made a very good and permanent revetment when carefully placed, however, a good deal of time and trouble was necessary to place them.

(ii) Mud bricks: A large quantity of these became available, notably for the Transvaal Road works, by pulling down the Native location there. This made a very good and permanent revetment, especially when the crevices were subsequently stopped with mud.

(iii) Tramway sleepers (wood): For revetting the Sanatorium breastworks. A quantity of these were borrowed from the depot of the tram line, which was close at hand. An excellent revetment in every way.

(iv) Sacks: A very large quantity of sacks were consumed for this purpose, especially in the case of the works on the softer tailing-heaps, and where works had to be quickly made defensible under fire and subsequently improved. This was not a very satisfactory form of revetment as the sacks rapidly rotted and had to be replaced.

(v) Galvanised iron: Certain breastworks were revetted with corrugated iron sheets held back by iron stakes and anchorages. A good form of revettment where the ground is not rocky.

(b) Blindages: Constructed out of squared timber and galvanized iron supplied by De Beers. This expensive form was necessary as there is no native rough wood available.

(c) Head cover: Sacks supplied by De Beers and local dealers, also one thousand tarred bags brought up by RE for defence of Modder River.

(d) Mines: The dynamite, loads and batteries ware supplied by De Beers. Dynamite was alone used; the small quantity of powder available being required for shells, etc.

(e) Obstacles: It was necessary to surround the defence with an efficient obstacle to compensate for the paucity of the garrison and to prevent a rush at night between the works. Accordingly a barbed wire fence was run around almost the whole of the eleven and a half miles of the main defence. Where practicable this was strengthened by a stiff abatis of mimosa bush cut down to clear the front. Large amounts of wire fence and abatis were also constructed round Beaconsfield and Kenilworth. Where there were no bushes the fence was increased in height and strength. Iron poles were necessary on account or the rocky nature of the ground. These were made at De Beers forge by pointing the end of old pieces of iron pipe and rail. The wire (with the exception of a small quantity in charge of RE for defence of Modder River) was obtained from De Beers. A very large quantity was used.

(f) Shelters and latrines: As very few tents were available for the Garrisons of the numerous redoubts, breastworks and barrier posts in the very extended defence, shelters had to be built at each point. These were constructed out of wood with canvass sides and galvanized iron roofs. Had the eventual duration of the siege been in the least anticipated they would have been more solidly constructed; as it was, after a couple of months' use, they required constant repairs. Latrines were constructed at each post out of galvanized iron or canvas and wood.

(g) Tools: The De Beers Company were able to lend us as many picks and shovels as were necessary, also axes and wheelbarrows. The RE Section had a certain supply also.

(5) Searchlights: At the commencement of the siege, De Beers was in possession of several searchlights and complete plant, these being used to prevent thefts at night from the 'floors'. The projectors and reflectors were of the usual service pattern - ie Schuckert projectors with automatic lamp and parabolic reflectors. At the beginning of the siege 3 of these were put in use, one being mounted at Premier 9th October, one at Rinderpest redoubt (same date) and one at No 1 Search Light (already in position). These ran at 60 Volts and 60 Amperes. Subsequently two Mangin projectors with hand lamps were mounted, one at No 8 De Beers and the other at the Reservoir, on 8th November. These were not very satisfactory.

Later in the siege, the Schuckert and Mangin at the Rinderpest Redoubt and Reservoir were exchanged as the latter place became of more importance in the defence. The operators were RE and De Beers men - the latter being accustomed to run these lights in peace time, proved very useful.

Appendices

(6) Mines: Land mines were very extensively employed in the defence, especially where there was any dead ground which could not be searched by fire from our works. These were entirely 'Observation Mines', the electro-contact or mechanical systems being too dangerous for employment on account of the number of natives who were always about. These mines varied in size from 5 lbs in ordinary cases to mines of about 30 lbs in the case of buildings which it was undesirable to pull down, but which might afford the attackers cover close to our works. Dynamite was used in all cases. Both firing batteries of Leclanche cells and dynamo exploders of Toflin and Rand pattern were used; also the current from the electric arc light circuit. The leads were insulated in most cases, lead of size of C7 supplied by De Boers and laid in pipes. However when this ran out, air line of copper or iron wire was employed, buried loads being used for the last 100 yards or so. The air line was run a few inches above the ground and concealed as far as possible. The IR and CR were tested periodically. In some cases dummy mines ware laid with some publicity in places where 'live' mines would have been undesirable. The presence of those mines – live and dummy - is admitted by the Boors to have exercised a restraining moral effect on them.

(7) Water Supply: The original water supply of Kimberley was pumped from Riverton (Vaal River) to an Intermediate Station about 10,000 yards from Kimberley, and thence to the Kimberley Reservoir. On the 16th October the enemy cut the main close to the Intermediate and the supply ceased. Arrangements were at once made with De Beers to pump the water from the Wesselton Mine direct into the Waterworks Reservoir. However, as only a limited supply could be pumped from Wesselton, the consumption was limited to 2 hours per diem and even then demand (and consumption) exceeded supply. The mains from Wesselton to the Waterworks were already in position, but as the line of main ran a short distance outside our defence, and as a shell might at any moment stop the supply by damaging the pumping engine, a committee was appointed to enquire into well supply. This would have been adequate in case of emergency, but was never required. Early in the investment it was seen that the possession of Riverton would give the Boers adequate water supply at the Intermediate for a force of any size, two attempts were made to cut it at Riverton, but in neither case was the force of Mounted Infantry and RE sent out, able to reach the objective.

(8) Cattle Guard Works: In addition to main defence of Kimberley and the two subsidiary defences of (1) Beaconsfield and (2) Kenilworth, it was found necessary to throw out small breastworks about 1500 yards to the front in different directions. These are shown in blue on the defence plan and were intended to give cover to the guard of Mounted Infantry which daily escorted the cattle to the grazing grounds outside the main line of defence, in case of attack. The ground in front of these was cleared of bush and other cover as far as possible. The work was done by natives under RE superintendence - the working party at the time being covered by an escort of Mounted Infantry. The work had very often to be carried out under artillery and long range Infantry fire. On the Reservoir side, those works had to be chiefly built out of sacks of earth as the ground is practically all rock.

(9) Telephones: Every redoubt and post was connected with a central exchange, so any post could call up and talk to any other. The Conning Tower had also 3 wires running to the Exchange to allow the OC to communicate his orders without delay. There being two systems of telephones in Kimberley, the PO and De Beers these had to be connected with three wires. In this way any inconvenience due to having two exchanges was overcome.

(10) The garrison of Kimberley consisted at first of:

Imperial Forces	RA, 23rd Co RGA with 6 x 2.5" guns.
	RE,1 section of 7th Field Company RE.
	1st LNLR, half battalion and one section MI Co.
Colonial Forces	DF Artillery,1 battery, six x 2.5" guns.
	Kimberley Regiment, Unmounted 350 men, Mounted 150 men.
	Maxim Battalion (De Beers) 6 maxims.
	Town Guard, 2,500 men.

The original idea of the defence was that the works should be occupied by the Local Corps consisting of the Town Guard and Kimberley Regiment while the ½ battalion Lancashire Regiment was to be kept as a central reserve. The guns and maxims were also to be kept in reserve, positions having been made for them at various points of the defence to be occupied in case of attack. This idea was in the main kept to, but it was soon found that the DFH and one company of cyclists were quite insufficient to do the patrolling and scouting.

A local irregular mounted corps 350 strong called the Kimberley Light Horse, was therefore raised, and in addition to this corps, the various garrisons of Cape Police along the Frontier early evacuated their posts and found their way to Kimberley. These increased the garrison of Kimberley by 350 men, 3 Maxims, and two 7-

pounder guns. The whole mounted force in Kimberley was thus raised to 800 men with 3 galloping Maxims and by its mobility formed a valuable offensive force. By its bold use in the early part of the siege the enemy obtained an exaggerated idea of the fighting strength of the garrison and in all probability therefore gave up all idea of being able to attack Kimberley with success. The distribution of the Town Guard in the defence works is shown in diagram attached to the report. The redoubts were designed for a minimum garrison of 50 men and the diagram will show that the garrison was distributed accordingly. The main defence was divided into six sections with the Beaconsfield and subsequently the Kenilworth forces distinct. In this way the men and officers who had practically no military training obtained a thorough knowledge of their sections and were able to organise a more effective system of sentries and patrols. Each man was told off to his own position in the work to which he belonged and was drilled to use his rifle at that position. In addition to this the men were instructed by NCOs of the Lancashire Regiment and Kimberley Regiment in simple drill movements and very soon became efficient in these. On occasions when called upon to act against the enemy beyond the line of defences the men showed great keenness and acquitted themselves most creditably.

(11) General aspect of Siege from RE point of view.

1. The siege of Kimberley presented several unusual characteristics in that one of the chief objects of the defence was the protection of the various mines and their valuable machinery. So, as these mines were extended over a very wide area round the town, the line of defence was necessarily extended out of all proportion to the available garrison. Further, as each mining area contained one or more large debris heaps - varying from 40' - 120' high - and as these were all commanding points within close artillery range of the town, and were practically the only high ground in the vicinity, it became necessary to occupy them all even at the risk of too great extension.

2. The defence was still further handicapped, as, owing to the pacific policy of the Cape Government nothing of the nature of defence works was allowed to be undertaken till the actual outbreak of Hostilities beyond drawing up the plans and arranging as far as possible for the distribution of materials.

3. However, by dint of grave exertions the majority of the more important works were in a defensible state by date of first alarm, 11th October, and after this date were permanently occupied by their garrisons and completed as rapidly as possible.

4. While the main defence of Kimberley was in progress, the defences of the suburb of Beaconsfield were being organised by Major Fraser (late 1st LNLR) these being originally only intended to hold the enemy in check in case of an attack on this side long enough to enable the inhabitants to retreat into Kimberley.

5. About the middle of November it became apparent that the enemy did not intend pushing the attack home; at the same time it became necessary to find grazing ground for the herds of cattle forming the food supply of the town. Accordingly, the already too extended line was further advanced to include Kenilworth and cover the grazing ground between Kenilworth and Felsted.

6. The two sides of the enceinte threatened by the enemy were the North (Kenilworth) and the West (Reservoir to Kimberley Redoubts). During November the enemy had taken cover and entrenched himself in a dense clump of bush several hundred yards long about 2,000 yards in front of No 2 De Beers. Kenilworth was then occupied (see paragraph 5) and after numerous skirmishes we succeeded in gaining possession of this advanced post of theirs, cutting down the bush and filling up the trenches. A search light was mounted on No 2 De Beers. A few advanced earthworks were constructed about 1500 yards in front of No 2 De Beers for the cattle guard and the enemy then temporarily transferred their attention to the Western side.

7. The Western side (Boer positions - Carter's Ridge) was the scene of the most severe engagements between ourselves and the Boers; on 25th November we carried their entrenched positions and but for the arrival of reinforcements would have captured their laager. On 27th, while attempting to act in conjunction with the relieving column, we again attacked the same position but met with such severe resistance that the attack had to be abandoned with considerable loss. The effect of these two attacks was to cause the enemy to evacuate Carter's Ridge and keep at a respectful distance, but on January 7th after the battles of Magersfontein and Tugela they again occupied the ridge in much greater force than before. They also showed far greater activity at night both in patrolling and in further entrenching themselves. They also commenced sniping at our patrols and cattle guards daily. Owing to these new entrenchments

and to the information received that the nine 15-pounders captured at Tugela were to be brought against us, the OC ordered all works on Western side to be strengthened. This was accordingly done, extra blindages were added to existing works and additional works and shelter trenches thrown up in the Intervals. A more advanced position was also taken up among broken ground in front of No 1 Kimberley in order to offer several successive lines of entrenchments to a possible assault. Otto's Kopje was also occupied to act as an advanced post of observation and to strike a blow if possible at their communications and to bring flanking fire to bear in case of an attack.

8. As regards the Boer artillery fire, during the earlier part or the siege (6th November 1899 – 6th February 1900) only nine field guns up to 12-pounders were in use. Employed as it was mainly by single guns and at excessive ranges, it had no effect at all on the works. Hits were seldom obtained (most of the fire being directed on the town area) even direct hits did practically no damage, the maximum penetration being about 3 foot in case of common shell. Owing to the large amount of splinter proof cover provided in each liable to artillery fire, and also to the sharp look-out kept by the garrisons, no damage was done by their shrapnel fire in the few cases where they ventured close enough to use it. Their percussion fuzes appeared to be very quick acting as occasional blind shells penetrated considerably further into earth than those which burst. However, on 7th February 1900 the enemy unmasked a 6" BL gun, throwing 100 lb shell, at Kamfersdam. Practically no shells were fired at the works and no hits were reported. The fire of this gun was almost entirely directed on the town and did a great deal of damage, several houses being set on fire and others considerably damaged. Both common and shrapnel (usually percussion) were employed and several people were killed and wounded. The houses in Kimberley being chiefly constructed of galvanised iron and wood offered no or at any rate little protection from this bombardment; on the contrary they were admirably adapted to burst any shell that might hit them and give the splinters full effect. None of these houses having cellars (the sub-soil being rock) most of the inhabitants built themselves bomb-proofs out of sacks of earth etc. Besides these, large casements were constructed for the women and children behind the various debris heaps, and a considerable number of the inhabitants took refuge in the mines.

9. Shortly before the relief the enemy, owing to a false alarm, evacuated Alexandersfontein and we occupied it. Being an important point on one of their lines of communication and one of their best sources of water supply the Officer Commanding, knowing that important movements or the part of the relief force were pending, determined to hold the place. The enemy brought two guns against the holding force and a warm cross rifle fire. The Section RE with some infantry had to throw up shelter trenches under this fire throughout the 14th and 15th February.

With reference to the value of the defences against attack, it is stated by the enemy themselves that the mines and searchlights restrained them from attempting an assault, so no idea can be gained of the value of the defence works and obstacles to an infantry attack. It cannot, however, be doubted that these works, standing as the great majority do on tailing heaps forty to eighty feet above the surrounding country and interconnected by barbed wire and thorn abatis, would have proved a very serious obstacle to assaulting infantry; at least if we can judge from our own experiences in attacking much less formidable works hold by the Boers round Kimberley.

10. Practical value of the Searchlights: It cannot be doubted that the numerous searchlights around Kimberley were a great protection, even if they did not (as is very probable) prevent an assault by night, as they prevented the enemy's patrols coming close enough in to examine our obstacles and other defences. The general situation of Kimberley is especially favourable to the fullest employment of searchlights, as the surrounding country is flat and open, while the lights themselves were mounted on headgears of tailing heaps from forty feet to two hundred feet above the surrounding plain. At the same time, even under these most favourable circumstances, experience shows that an observer behind the light cannot see even large bodies further than two thousand yards, except in the case of mounted troops, which are easily seen by the reflecting of the light from the horses eyes. The moral effect of a searchlight on a man unused to it is very considerable, as, when in the light of the beam, he is quite convinced that his every movement is watched, while as a matter of fact he is most probably quite invisible to the enemy or operator. It may be remarked that out of the three towns besieged Kimberley was the only one on which no assault was delivered. This was probably due in part to the searchlights, as Mafeking and Ladysmith both had employed mines and had not the handicap of the enormous extension of the Kimberley defences combined with a totally inadequate garrison. In support of this view it may be mentioned that the enemy came down very close to Kenilworth at night until a light was mounted on No 2 De Beers, after which they cleared off.

Kimberley Siege Account and Medal Roll

(12) The original camp for the troops who arrived on 21st September 1899 (23rd Co RGA, No 1 Section 7th Field Company RE, 4 Companies 1st LNLR) was inside the reservoir enclosure. However, owing to the representations of the Medical Officer of Health, it was shifted on the 23rd to the veldt near Newton Home. Latrines were built and water laid on from the Kimberley Water Works main which passed close at hand. On 4th October the Diamond Fields Artillery and the Kimberley Regiment were called out and joined the camp. Latrines and water supply were similarly arranged. On 11th October the various works were occupied by the units of regulars, volunteers and town guard told off to them. Shelters, latrines and water supply were arranged at each work. On 12th October the reserve of Regulars and Volunteers was moved to a central position at the Botanical Gardens. The latrines were shifted and water supply again arranged. On 17th October a camp was formed close to De Beers Workshops for the Mounted troops; mangers and troughs were provided for the horses and latrines and water supply for the men. On 26th December the Royal Artillery and Diamond Fields Artillery was moved to a different site. Owing to the fact that on the 16th October the enemy cut the main of the Vaal River water supply it became necessary to economise water. It was accordingly turned on for two hours per diem. Consequently, to provide the troops with water for the rest of the twenty four hours tanks had to be built at each camp and filled each morning. De Beers were able to supply a number of 400 gallon oil drums which were extensively used for this purpose. By order of the Medical Officer all water for drinking purposes had to be boiled. Utensils for doing this were made by cleansing out and putting handles on old 10 gallon oil drums. Tanks were in some cases supplied for storage of drinking water. Shelters of wood and canvas were provided to supply deficiency of tents (see F) at most of the redoubts.

(13) Armoured trains: In all there were three engines and four trucks armoured. This was done at the De Beers Workshops. Of these, two engines and two trucks were built for Mafeking and sent there, but were destroyed by the enemy near Kraaipan while escorting some guns at the commencement of the war. The other engine and two trucks were built by order of the Officer Commanding in December. In addition to this an engine and two trucks were sent up from Salt River and were used throughput the siege, and though several times under both rifle and shell fire were never damaged and were found most useful in drawing off the enemy while sorties were made by leading them in other directions.

(14) Station enlarged: Early in December when the relief of Kimberley was expected and there was a prospect of a large body of troops having to be entrained and detrained, extra sidings were constructed and the entrance to the station from the South improved by the points being altered from meeting to trailing points. When the relief actually did take place those additions and alterations proved of the greatest value. Immediately Kimberley was relieved, working parties were organised for the repair of the railway to the south and in this way over half of the distance between Kimberley and Modder River was overhauled and repaired from Kimberley. Telegraph parties also took the telegraph lines in hand.

(15) Cold Storage: Towards the end of December the veldt having been practically eaten off, it became a problem how to keep meat for the inhabitants. In order to allow of as many cattle as possible being killed off the Officer Commanding ordered the De Beers Company to put in hand a Cold Storage house for three hundred head. This was put in hand at once and completed within a fortnight. It worked most satisfactory, though ashes had to be used for packing in place of sawdust.

(16) The 28lb Gun and Shells: Another item of interest from an engineering point of view was the construction of a 4.1" gun firing a 28-pound shell. This was made under the superintendence of Mr Labram, Chief Engineer to the De Beers Company. This took only a fortnight to make, though the machinery for rifling had to be made in addition, and the gun proved a most effective and accurate weapon, though some difficulty was experienced with the obturator bolt, for which there was no steel sufficiently tough.

It is deeply to be regretted that Mr Labram was killed by one of the enemy's shells on February 9th. Both the Royal Engineer officers in the siege were deeply indebted to him for his ever-ready help and kindly suggestions. He was always ready to do anything to assist us in the siege, was often under fire, and was only killed in his own room after having been present throughout the day with the 4 inch gun in its duel with the enemy's 100 pounder.

[Signed] D MacInnes,
Lieutenant RE and local Captain.

Appendix 14 – Kekewich's despatch of 15th February 1900

From   Lt. Col. R. G. Kekewich, Commanding Griqualand West and Bechuanaland.

To   The Chief of the Staff, South Africa.

Sir,

I have the honour to submit the following report concerning the military operations which have recently taken place in Griqualand West and Bechuanaland.

2[60]. On my arrival in Kimberley on the morning of 13th September, 1899, I met the following Imperial Officers who had been detailed for special services on the western frontier of the Orange Free State, viz :-

> Capt & Brevet Major H S Turner, Royal Highlanders, Staff Officer, Kimberley.
>
> Capt W A J O'Meara, Royal Engineers, Intelligence Officer, Kimberley.
>
> Lieut D S MacInnes, Royal Engineers, detailed for special duties in connection with Royal Engineer services.

3. These officers had been employed for several weeks in Kimberley and the adjacent country; in consequence many questions relating to the defence of Kimberley and the eastern frontiers of Bechuanaland and Griqualand West had been already investigated by them and were submitted for my consideration. For political and other reasons no immediate steps could be taken by me in connection with the preparations for the defence of Kimberley.

   Capt. H.V. Gorle, Army Service Corps, arrived in Kimberley on 20th September, 1899, and at once took up all questions relating to supplies and transport.

4. At this time the defence of the Cape Government Railway from the Orange River Railway Bridge northwards was in the hands of the Cape Government, and a certain number of important points on the railway and also the larger railway bridges north of Kimberley were being guarded by small detachments of the Cape Police.

5. On the date of my arrival in Kimberley, portions of the Burgher Forces of the South African Republic were already out on 'commando' along the Bechuanaland border. Many reports having been received that not only disloyalists in Cape Colony, but also certain Burghers of the Orange Free State had expressed a determination to destroy the Orange River and Modder River railway bridges, I arranged on the 15th September with Commissioner M B Robinson, Cape Police, for small Police guards at the two bridges referred to.

6. On the 20th September, the following Imperial Troops arrived in Kimberley:

   > 23rd Co Royal Garrison Artillery (Western Div.) with six 7 pounder RML guns (3 officers and 90 NCOs and men).
   >
   > 1 Section 7th Field Co Royal Engineers (1 Officer and 50 NCOs and men).
   >
   > HQ and 4 Co 1st Bn Loyal North Lancashire Regt (9 Officers and 413 NCOs and men).
   >
   > Detachment Army Service Corps (5 NCOs and men).
   >
   > Detachment Royal Army Medical Corps (1 Officer and 5 NCOs and men).

   On the 26th September, a detachment of Mounted Infantry, 1st Bn. Loyal North Lancashire Regiment (1 Officer and 21 NCOs and men), also arrived in Kimberley.

7. The Volunteer Force in Vryburg (5 Officers and 56 NCOs and men) was called out on the 24th September and was subsequently placed under the command of the late Asst Commissioner H T Scott, Cape Police, who was in military command at that town.

   The Volunteer Force in Kimberley (composed as under) was called out on the 4 October:

   > 1 Battery Diamond Fields Artillery with 6-7 pr. Field guns (8 Officers and 90 NCOs and men).
   >
   > Diamond Fields Horse (6 Officers and 142 NCOs and men).
   >
   > Kimberley Regiment (14 Officers and 285 NCOs and men).

---

[60] The report starts with point 2.

Kimberley Siege Account and Medal Roll

Every effort was made to increase the numbers of this Volunteer Force and to provide horses for the mounted portion thereof. 84 recruits and nearly all the horses required were obtained in the seven days following the mobilisation of this Force.

8. As the movements of the Burgher Forces of the Orange Free State reported to be taking place opposite the Griqualand West frontier of the Cape Colony indicated that an attack on Kimberley might be made without any warning at an early date, the construction of certain important portions of the defence works of Kimberley was commenced on the 18th September.

9. It was on the 27th September that the earliest reliable information was obtained that the Burghers of the Orange Free State had been ordered out on 'commando'. On this date Captain W A J O'Meara, Royal Engineers, had proceeded to Boshof, Orange Free State, on duty. As soon as he reached that village detachments of the burgher Force of the Orange Free State also commenced to arrive there. As detachments of armed Burghers continued to arrive in the village throughout the night of 27th-28th September and immediately returned to Kimberley and reported what he had observed.

10. There being now little doubt as to the intentions of the Government of the Orange Free State, the construction of the defence works required for the protection of Kimberley and Beaconsfield was pushed on with the utmost rapidity under the direction of Lieutenant D S MacInnes, Royal Engineers.

11. HE The High Commissioner had authorised the formation of the Kimberley and Beaconsfield Town Guards, and on the 30th September the scheme which had been prepared in Kimberley for these organizations was brought into operation, and by the 7th October 1,156 combatant members had been enrolled. NCOs of the 1st Bn Loyal North Lancashire Regiment were detailed to afford the necessary instruction in the use of the arms issued and to teach a few simple drill movements to the members of these Town Guards.

12. Since the 28th September, the burgher Forces of the Orange Free State and the South African Republic had been gradually approaching our borders, and on the 4 October advance bodies of the enemy were within 12 miles of Kimberley.

13. The Cape Police Force guarding the railway had been augmented to 446 officers and men, and by the 1st October a concentration of this Force at the most important points along the railway between the Vaal River and Mafeking had been effected as follows:

Kraaipan	(70 officers and men).
Vryburg	(112 officers and men).
Taungs	(89 officers and men).
Fourteen Streams	(175 officers and men with 2 x 7 lb field guns).

It was not till the 13th October that the Cape Police Force (District No. 2) was placed under my orders for employment in the defence of the Colony.

14. By the 7th October the arrangements for the defence of Kimberley were so advanced that the town was practically safe against any attempt on the part of the enemy to suddenly rush it.

15. On the 10th October, I sanctioned the movement of the Police at Kraaipan to Mafeking. This detachment arrived at the latter place on the morning of Wednesday, the 11th October.

16. The first act of overt hostility on the part of the enemy occurred at Kraaipan, the railway siding at this point was occupied by the enemy on the 12th October, and at 3 pm on that day the Boers interrupted all telegraphic communication north of Kraaipan. During the same evening an armoured train (under the command of Lieutenant Nesbitt) conveying 2 guns and artillery ammunition from Vryburg to Mafeking was brought to a standstill south of Kraaipan Siding, owing to the destruction of the railway at the point. Lieutenant Nesbitt engaged the enemy with the small force at his disposal during the night of 12th October and the following morning. The armoured train was, however, completely wrecked by the enemy's artillery fire. The engine driver of the pilot engine which preceded the armoured train escaped, but of the men composing the British Force some fell into the hands of the enemy and others were killed. I have not received any official report (giving details) of what occurred on this occasion.

17. Several attempts were made to communicate with Mafeking by despatch riders from Kimberley. The Europeans employed were, however, captured by the enemy, and the Natives similarly employed returned to Kimberley at different times, having failed in their efforts to reach Mafeking.

18. On the evening of the 14th October, the enemy crossed the frontier into Griqualand West, and commenced the destruction of the Cape Government railway and telegraph. Telegraphic communication north of Kimberley ceased at 9 pm 14th October, and at 10.45 pm on the same evening

Appendices

all the telegraph wires south of Kimberley were entirely interrupted. A despatch service was at once inaugurated, and the first messenger left for Orange River railway bridge the same evening.

19. At 3 am, 15th October, an armoured train (under the command of 2nd Lieutenant A Mc Webster, 1st Bn Loyal North Lancashire Regiment) was directed to proceed southwards and locate the spot where our telegraph lines had been destroyed. On reaching Spytfontein Railway Station the train was fired upon by the enemy's guns posted in the rocky hills (kopjes) south east of the station. The enemy's fire was returned by our machine guns, but as the enemy had 3 guns in position, 2nd Lieutenant Webster took the Station Master of Spytfontein, his family, and also some railway gangers on board the armoured train and returned to Kimberley without having sustained any damage or loss.

20. Since direct telegraphic communication with head-quarters, Cape Town, was completely interrupted and could not be restored for some time to come, I proclaimed martial law in Kimberley at noon on the 15th October.

21. On the 16th October, I learnt that Fourteen Streams railway-bridge had been abandoned on the previous evening by the Police Detachment detailed for its defence, and that this force was retiring on Kimberley. The Police Detachment at Taungs had been ordered to fall back on Fourteen Streams on the 14th October, and was doing so at this time. On the 17th October, it was reported that the Police Detachment detailed for the defence of Vryburg had also abandoned that place at 4.30 pm on the 15th October, and was also retiring on Kimberley. The members of the Volunteer Force at Vryburg dispersed to their homes on the evening of the 15th October. In fact, on the evening of the 15th October, the Police Detachments, which had been placed along the railway from Vryburg southwards, were all retiring, and by 5 pm on the 22nd October they had arrived safely in Kimberley.

22. The want of mounted troops to operate against the enemy investing Kimberley was greatly felt during the first few days of the investment. HE The High Commissioner had given me authority (in a conversation held on the telegraph wire on the 13th October) to raise an irregular mounted corps; in consequence, steps were taken to increase the numbers of the mounted men and also to increase the mobility of the artillery in Kimberley. The Rt Hon C J Rhodes, and also the De Beers Consolidated Mines Ltd, came most generously to my assistance in the matter of providing horses and mules.

23. On the 19th October, Captain and Brevet Major H S Turner was appointed by me to the command of all the Mounted Corps in Kimberley, and the raising of the Kimberley Light Horse, was also entrusted to him. On this date Lieutenant D S MacInnes, Royal Engineers, took over the duties of Staff Officer, Kimberley.

24. The rapid increase in the numbers and the mobility of the mounted troops in Kimberley which now took place made it possible for me to send out reconnoitring parties at frequent intervals in every direction in this neighbourhood. The armoured train was sent out in support of the mounted troops whenever possible. The enemy's fire was drawn on almost every occasion that our troops sallied out beyond the line of our defences.

25. During the period referred to in the last paragraph small bodies (numbering from 100 to 250 men) of the enemy were busily engaged marching into and demanding the surrender of undefended towns and villages in Griqualand West. In some instances the Government officials, the members of the Police Force, and even unoffending traders in towns, villages, etc, occupied by the Boers were made prisoners; on these occasions all Government property and much private property of British subjects was 'commandeered' (i.e. forcibly seized) by the Boers. It was further reported to me that proclamations had been issued by Her Majesty's enemies, declaring Bechuanaland a province of the South African Republic, and Griqualand West, similar, a province of the Orange Free State. On receipt of this information, I issued a counter-proclamation, in order, if possible, to check the spread of a rebellion in the above named territories[61].

26. On the 24th October, a strong reconnoitring party was sent northwards from Kimberley, with the armoured train in support, and came into collision with a force of the enemy (estimated at 800 men) near Macfarlane Siding; and it became necessary to reinforce the mounted men with guns and infantry. The enemy was repulsed, and the Boer Commander himself killed. This engagement has been made the subject of a separate despatch. No authentic information has been obtained of the loss the enemy's forces suffered in this engagement, but natives report that many Boer's were killed and wounded.

27. On the 25th October, the enemy began to tighten his line of investment; his position nearest to our defences was on this date about 6,000 yards south of the Premier Mine. This position of the enemy being an isolated one, it was carefully reconnoitred on several occasions, and the fact ascertained that 2 guns were posted behind some entrenchments thrown up in a naturally strong position. On the 31st

---

[61] A copy of the proclamation is shown on page 418.

October, the enemy opened fire with these guns as well as with rifles on a mounted reconnoitring party sent eastward from the Premier Mine by me; no one was hit.

28. On the first November, a body of the enemy which was known to be at Riverton Road Station drew nearer to Kimberley and occupied Macfarlane Farm. At 2.5 pm on this date an explosion was heard and a column of smoke was seen ascending near Dronfield Siding (about 7 miles north of Kimberley). It was believed at the time that the enemy had destroyed the whole of the dynamite store in the magazines in that neighbourhood.

29. Early on the morning of the 3rd November, the enemy made a determined attempt to drive off our live stock grazing north of Kenilworth, and opened fire on our mounted troops guarding same both with artillery and rifle. During this engagement Major W E Ayliff, Cape Police, was wounded in the neck with a rifle bullet. Again, on the afternoon of the same day, another body made a second advance on Kimberley from Peddiefontein, a farm three and a half miles west of Kimberley. Both these attacks were driven back by the mounted troops under Brevet Major (local Lieutenant Colonel) H S Turner, assisted by the guns of the Royal Garrison Artillery and the Diamonds Fields Artillery. During the afternoon's engagement Private J Lubbe, Kimberley Light Horse, was killed, and Sergeant F E Watermeyer, Cape Police, was wounded. The enemy did not succeed in driving away any cattle from Kenilworth in the morning, but during the afternoon the Boers were more successful, and captured several head of cattle which their owners had allowed to stray too far from our defences on the north west of Kimberley. The enemy's losses on this day were not ascertained.

30. About noon on the 4th November, Head Commandant C J Wessels, of the Burgher Forces, Orange Free State, sent in a 'arlementaire' demanding the surrender of Kimberley. (His letter is marked A and attached). I replied in terms of the attached letter marked B.

31. At 7 pm November 8th, the enemy fired two shells at our defences at the Premier Mine; the first regular bombardment of Kimberley, however, did not commence until 5.30 am 7th November. On the latter date, the enemy commenced shelling the section of our defences between the Kimberley Waterworks Reservoir and the Sanatorium (the majority of the shells being apparently intended for the latter building). The enemy appeared to have 3 guns in position along the ridge south west of Wimbledon rifle ranges. On the 7th November, the enemy also shelled our position at the Premier Mine from their position south of the same. Although the enemy's shells fell in close proximity to our defence works south of Kimberley and at the Premier Mine, no one was injured and practically no damage was done. On this date the enemy fired at the extreme limit of range of his artillery.

32. On November 8th, I issued a proclamation withdrawing all arms and ammunition in the possession of the civil population. In this manner the possibility of active hostile acts being committed against the enemy by irresponsible non-combatants was prevented, and at the same time many disloyal British subjects in Kimberley, who were reported to be in communication with the enemy, were disarmed.

33. After the bombardment of November 7th, it became evident that the enemy was not satisfied with his artillery positions on the ridge west of the Wimbledon rifle range.

    During the three following days the enemy's artillery did not fire a single shell against our defences, but there were many indications that new positions were being prepared by the enemy for his guns.

    Subsequent dates on which the bombardment of Kimberley and our defences was continued are recorded in Appendix 2[62].

34. My general plan for the defence of Kimberley was based on the principle of always keeping the enemy on the move and constantly in fear of attack from an unexpected quarter.

    Later, when the advance of the Relief Column from the Orange River commenced and I was put in possession of information concerning the probable date of its arrival at Kimberley, I adopted such measures as I hoped would cause the retention of a large force of the enemy in my immediate neighbourhood, and thus enable the Relief Column to deal with the Boer force in detail. It was with these objects that the numerous sorties and demonstrations in force were made by portions of the garrison of Kimberley. Particulars of the more important engagements which ensued on these occasions are recorded in Appendix 3[63].

    It will be observed that portions of the mounted corps were employed on every occasion. The work which fell on the detachment 1st Bn. Loyal North Lancashire Regiment, Cape Police, Diamond Fields Horse and Kimberley Light Horse, and the Diamond Fields Artillery was in consequence very arduous; not only did the corps mentioned respond cheerfully, but nothing can exceed the bravery and dash with which these troops attacked the enemy on several occasions in his entrenched positions.

---

[62] See page 404.
[63] See page 400.

Appendices

35. It will be realised that, under the peculiar circumstances in which the defence of a scattered town, containing over 40,000 inhabitants and much valuable machinery, was entrusted in the first instance to a force consisting of about 570 Imperial Troops and 680 Colonial Troops, my efforts would have been of no avail had it not been for the valuable assistance and advice which many citizens afforded me in a military as well as a civil capacity. Where so many are concerned, I find it impossible to bring to notice by name every individual who has thus assisted me.

36. On the outbreak of war, with an enemy in numbers superior to those under my command and also possessing great mobility, it was unfortunately an unavoidable situation that a large portion of British Territory should have been overrun by the enemy. I felt great sympathy for those British subjects who were compelled to suffer many indignities at the hands of the enemy in consequence of the undefended state of the neighbourhood in which they were residing. But in the matter of affording protection to these British subjects, as well as in that concerning the defence of the Modder River Railway Bridge, I was most anxious that no disposition of troops made by me should give the enemy a chance of scoring a first success, even where the smallest body of British troops might be concerned. Taking into consideration that the enemy would probably not regulate his movements in accordance with the dictates of sound strategy, that he was in possession of mobile artillery in my immediate neighbourhood (and of this I had reliable information), I felt convinced that if I had detached a small body of troops (necessarily without artillery) which it was not in my power to support from Kimberley, the enemy would in all probability concentrate very superior numbers, with artillery, against the small British post, and endeavour to destroy the troops composing the same. It was principally for this reason that I determined to concentrate all my available forces, including the Cape Police, who had retired from their defence posts along the railway, at the point of greatest importance in my command, viz Kimberley. In the case of the Cape Police, I was further influenced by my opinion that only under the leadership of Imperial Officers could this body be utilized as a useful defensive force, since the officers of the Cape Police, from the very nature of their ordinary duties in times of peace, could not possess sufficient military experience to be entrusted with independent commands in outlying districts.

37. I wish to record my high appreciation of the conduct and behaviour of the regular and Colonial forces employed in the defence of Kimberley, but I would more particularly call attention to the great patriotism displayed by the citizens of Kimberley and Beaconsfield, who so willingly and spontaneously undertook obligations of a military nature at a time of great emergency by enrolling themselves in the Kimberley Light Horse and the Town Guards of Kimberley and Beaconsfield. The cheerful spirit in which the members of these forces obeyed all military orders was most commendable.

38. I further wish to place on record the brilliant services of the late Brevet-Major (local Lt. Col.) H.S. Turner. In him the Army has lost a most valuable officer; he was a great organiser, full of energy, and possessed of real ability and courage. A better all round officer I have never met. He was the principal organiser of the Town Guards, and acted as my Staff Officer, carrying out his duties with marked success under great difficulties, until he took over the organisation and command of the Kimberley Light Horse and the Mounted Troops. He commanded the Mounted Troops in numerous reconnaissances and sorties in the neighbourhood of Kimberley, and I cannot speak too highly of the manner in which he conducted them and loyally carried out my orders. His horse was shot under him on the 25th November and he himself wounded, but continued to perform his duties until killed in action on the 28th November.

39. I beg to bring the officers of my Staff most especially to notice, and I trust that their valuable services will be rewarded[64].

---

[64] The mentions in despatches are shown on page 333.

Kimberley Siege Account and Medal Roll

Bombardments of the town[65]

1. 11th November[66] - Enemy commenced bombardment of the northern portion of Kimberley at 6.30 am with three guns from a position west of the Lazaretto, and with one gun at Kamfersdam; one gun also fired from the enemy's position south of Premier Mine at our defences in that neighbourhood, and a fifth gun opened fire from the ridge north of Kenilworth at our northern defences. Our guns directed a slow fire on the enemy's artillery positions, but the range was too great, and little damage could have been done to the enemy. The enemy's shells fell in the northern portions of Kimberley (many fortunately into Kimberley Mine itself), several buildings were struck, and unfortunately a Kaffir woman was killed in the street opposite the Roman Catholic Church. The enemy fired nearly 400 shells this day.

2. 13th November - The enemy commenced bombardment of Premier Mine and Beaconsfield at 9.20 am from his position south of Premier Mine, and the shelling of Kimberley was commenced at 10 am from the enemy's artillery position west of Lazaretto. Our artillery replied at long intervals to the enemy's fire. It was noticed that only two of the enemy's guns were fired from the position near the Schmidt's Drift road. Several buildings were again struck, and one of the shells falling into a street in the northern portion of the town injured the driver of a cab, and killed one of his horses; a second civilian was also hit during this day. The enemy fired about 90 shells this day.

3. 14th November - The enemy commenced the bombardment of Kimberley, Beaconsfield and the Premier Mine at 1 pm from his positions west of the Lazaretto and south of the Premier Mine. Several of the shells fell in the streets in the northern portion of Kimberley and into the Kimberley Mine. Some buildings, including St. Cyprian a Church and the Queen's Hotel, were struck, but fortunately no human beings were hit. The enemy fired about 60 shells this day.

4. 15th November - The enemy commenced the bombardment of Kimberley at 5.15 am from his position west of the Lazaretto, and fired 46 shells; our artillery replied at long intervals. A few buildings were struck by the enemy's shells and one civilian wounded. At 9.30 am, the enemy commenced the bombardment of Kenilworth; our artillery replied, and the enemy ceased fire after his 12th round.

5. 16th November - The enemy commenced the bombardment at Beaconsfield at 6.55 am from his position south of the Premier Mine; our artillery at the latter place replied, and silenced the enemy's guns after the seventh round. There was no bombardment of Kimberley on this date, as the enemy's attention was diverted by the sortie reported in Appendix 3 (c).

6. 17th November - Enemy commenced bombardment of Kimberley at 11.35 am with one gun from his position west of the Lazaretto; our artillery replied, and the enemy ceased fire after his ninth round. At 4.15 pm, the enemy again attempted the bombardment of Kimberley from his position west of the Lazaretto, and was brought to silence by our guns after his 10th round.

7. 18th November - The enemy attempted the bombardment of Kimberley at 11.5 am and 4.15 pm this date from his position west of the Lazaretto. He was brought to silence in the morning after his third round, and in the afternoon after his fifth round. No damage whatever was done by the enemy.

8. 22nd November - The enemy had moved his guns into the neighbourhood of the position near Spitzkop, from which he opened fire on Kimberley on 7th November. At 6.15 am, the bombardment of Kimberley was commenced, but the enemy's shells fell into the racecourse. The enemy ceased fire after his 15th round.

9. 25th November - At 3.30 pm the enemy commenced bombarding our redoubt at the Premier Mine and the guns of the Royal Garrison Artillery replied. The enemy's fire ceased after his 12th round.

10. 27th November - The enemy commenced the bombardment of the south-western portion of our defences at 5.15 am and again at 2.40 pm from his position west of the Schmidt's Drift road. On each occasion the guns of the Royal Garrison Artillery at the Reservoir replied to the enemy's fire. The enemy's guns did not continue the bombardment after our guns had opened fire. The enemy only fired nine rounds in all this day.

---

[65] Details of the bombardment suffered by Kimberley were presented by Kekewich as part of his despatch. Lord Roberts omitted them but they are presented here as they provide an interesting and factual account.

[66] This is the first mention of a bombardment by Kekewich but the first shells fell on 6th November, the day the ultimatum expired.

Appendices

11. 28th November - The enemy commenced to bombard the town of Kimberley at 3.30 am from his position west of the Lazaretto. The guns of the Royal Garrison Artillery at the Reservoir replied to the enemy's fire, and the Boer artillery ceased fire after the 10th round.

12. 5th December - The enemy commenced bombarding our position at the Premier Mine at 3.30 pm; the guns of the Royal Garrison Artillery replied to the enemy's fire; the Boer artillery ceased fire after firing 10 rounds.

13. 15th December - At 11.30 am the enemy commenced bombarding the Premier Mine Redoubt, and continued his fire for 40 minutes; the guns of the Royal Garrison Artillery stationed there replied; no damage was done and there were no casualties on our side; the enemy fired in all about 20 shells.

14. 26th December - At 9 am the enemy commenced the shelling of Premier Mine redoubt, and continued his bombarding for 2 hours; the guns of the Royal Garrison Artillery made a reply; no damage was done, and there were no casualties on our side; the enemy fired in all about 80 shells.

15. 8th January - At 1.30 pm the enemy's guns on Wimbledon ridge opened fire on our south-western defences, and at 4.15 pm his gun at Olifantsfontein opened on Premier Mine redoubt, and during the day occasional shots were fired at the searchlight from Kamfersdam. The guns of the Royal Garrison Artillery made reply. No damage was done, and there were no casualties on our side. The enemy fired in all about 20 shells.

16. 9th January - At various times during the day, the enemy fired an occasional shot at No. 1 searchlight. The guns of the Royal Garrison Artillery stationed there replied. No damage was done, and there were no casualties on our side. The enemy fired in all nine shells.

17. 10th January - At 3.30 am the enemy commenced the bombardment of our defences from Kamfersdam; his guns at Wimbledon ridge, Alexandersfontein and Oliphantsfontein kopje took up the shelling about 2 hours later. The guns of the Royal Garrison Artillery made reply. No damage was done, and there were no casualties on our side. The enemy fired in all about 35 shells.

18. 12th January - At 4 pm the enemy's guns at Alexandersfontein, Oliphantsfontein kopje and Kamfersdam commenced shelling Premier Mine redoubt, Beaconsfield and the northern defences of Kimberley. The guns of the Royal Garrison Artillery made reply. No damage was done, and there were no casualties on our side. The enemy fired in all about 35 shells.

19. 15th January - At 9 am the enemy's gun on the Wimbledon ridge fired a few shells at our south-western defences, and at 6 pm the guns on Carter's ridge opened fire on our western defences. The guns of the Royal Garrison Artillery made reply. No damage was done, and there were no casualties on our side. The enemy fired in all 11 shells.

20. 16th January - At 10 am the enemy's guns on Carter's ridge and Kamfersdam commenced the bombardment of our northern defences; about an hour later, his guns on the Wimbledon ridge commenced the bombardment of our south-western defences and Beaconsfield. The guns of the Royal Garrison Artillery and the Diamond Fields Artillery made reply. No damage was done, and there were no casualties on our side. The enemy fired about 40 shells in all.

21. 17th January - At 6.25 am the enemy's guns at Kamfersdam and Smith's farm opened fire on the northern defences; about on hour later his guns at Alexandersfontein and Wimbledon ridge opened on the defences of Beaconsfield. The guns of the Royal Garrison Artillery and the Diamond Fields Artillery replied. No damage was done, and there were no casualties on our side. The enemy fired in all about 32 shells.

22. 23rd January - At 6 am the enemy's guns on Wimbledon ridge, Smith's farm, Kamfersdam Mine and Carter's ridge commenced the bombardment of our northern defences and Beaconsfield. The guns of the Royal Garrison Artillery fired an occasional round in reply. No damage was done, and there were no casualties on our side. The enemy fired in all about 22 shells.

23. 24th January - At 4 am the enemy's guns on Carter's ridge, Wimbledon ridge, Oliphantsfontein kopje, Kamfersdam, Alexandersfontein and Smith's farm commenced the bombardment of the towns of Kimberley and Beaconsfield and our defences at the Premier Mine redoubt. The bombardment continued throughout the day and even after dark. The guns of the Royal Garrison Artillery and the Diamond Fields Artillery replied. Miss Maddocks was killed by the fragment of a shell, and a native

sustained a flesh wound; several buildings in the towns were struck and slightly damaged. The enemy fired about 300 shells during the day.

24. 25th January - At 12.53 am the enemy opened fire with his guns at Carter's ridge, Wimbledon ridge, Smith's farm, Kamfersdam, Oliphantsfontein Kopje and Alexandersfontein, and commenced the bombardment on the town of Kimberley and Beaconsfield and also our defences; the guns of the Royal Garrison Artillery and the Diamond Fields Artillery made reply. Mrs Webster and her two children were struck with fragments of a shell and very severely injured, the elder child succumbing to her injuries; Mr J W Pope, Superintendent of the Fire Brigade, was struck by a shell and injured in the hand and leg; several buildings were also struck, but the damage done was slight; the enemy fired over 300 shell in all during the day.

25. 26th January - At 6.10 am the enemy's gun at Oliphantsfontein kopje opened fire on the Premier Mine redoubt. At 6.20 am the enemy's gun at Kamfersdam commenced to bombard our northern defences. The Boer guns on Carter's and Wimbledon ridges joined in the bombardment later in the day. A few shells were also fired into Beaconsfield during the day. Our gunners replied to the enemy's artillery fire. The enemy fired about 30 shells in all this day. No damage was done and no one was injured.

26. 30th January - At daybreak the enemy opened fire with a 3 pounder Nordenfeldt from Alexandersfontein on the Beaconsfield defences; our sharpshooters replied to this fire. The enemy fired about 70 rounds, but no damage was done and no one was injured. The enemy also fired an occasional shell from his guns at Kamfersdam and on Wimbledon ridge, at the town and our defences.

27. 1st February - At 7.45 am the enemy's gun at Kamfersdam opened fire on our defences; and at different hours of the day the Boer guns on Carter's and Wimbledon ridges fired an occasional shot at our defences, the town, and Kenilworth village. Our guns replied to the enemy's artillery fire. The enemy fired about 50 shells during the day. No damage was done and no one was injured.

28. 2nd February - At 4.45 pm the enemy commenced shelling the Premier Mine redoubt, firing some dozen rounds. At 11.30 am the enemy's gun at Smith's farm opened fire on Kenilworth village, firing about another dozen rounds. No damage was done and we suffered no casualties.

29. 3rd February - At 6.40 am the enemy's gun at Smith's farm opened fire on our northern defences. Later in the day the enemy's guns at Kamfersdam and at Carter's ridge also fired an occasional shell at the northern defences and into the town. Our guns replied to the enemy's artillery fire. The enemy fired about 40 shells this day. No damage was done and no one was injured.

30. 5th February - At 6.45 am the enemy's guns at Kamfersdam and on Carter's ridge also fired an occasional shell at our northern defences and into the town. Our guns replied to the enemy's artillery fire. The enemy's gun at Oliphantsfontein kopje also fired a few shells at the Premier Mine redoubt. During the afternoon the shelling became more continuous, the Boer guns at Smith's farm and on Wimbledon ridge lending their aid. Our guns replied to the enemy's artillery fire. The enemy fired 60 shells in all this day. No damage was done and no one was injured.

31. 6th February - At 6.35 am the enemy's gun at Oliphantsfontein kopje opened fire at the Premier Mine redoubt, and about the same time the enemy's guns on Wimbledon ridge, Carter's ridge and at Kamfersdam also commenced to bombard our northern and western defences. About dusk the Boer gun at Smith's also fired a few shells. Our guns replied to the enemy's artillery fire. The enemy fired about 40 shells this day. No damage was done and no one was injured.

32. 7th February - At 6.30 am the enemy's gun on Wimbledon ridge opened fire on our western defences, and a few minutes later the Boer gun on Carter's ridge joined in this bombardment, At 10.45 am the enemy's gun at Oliphantsfontein kopje commenced to shell the Premier Mine redoubt. Soon after 11 am the enemy commenced to bombard the town with a 6-inch siege gun from Kamfersdam. During the evening the Boer gun at Smith's farm also fired a few shells at our defences. Our guns replied to the enemy's artillery fire. The enemy fired 55 shells in all this day (22 of which were fired by the Boer siege gun). Considerable damage was done to property, and a civilian (W Nash) and a coloured child were unfortunately injured, the latter succumbing to his wounds.

33. 8th February - At 5.55 am the enemy's gun on Carter's ridge opened fire on our western defences, and at 9.10 am the Boer gun at Oliphantsfontein kopje commenced to bombard the Premier Mine redoubt. At 3.30 pm the Boers commenced the bombardment of the town with the 6-inch siege gun at Kamfersdam, the smaller guns being principally directed against our defences. Our guns replied to the

Appendices

enemy's artillery fire, and sharpshooters were pushed to within 2,000 yards of the siege gun at Kamfersdam to annoy the gun layers. The guns and garrison at Premier Mine redoubt had also to deal with the enemy who had occupied a position at Ostelow's house. The enemy fired in all about 80 shell this day (30 of which were fired from the 6-inch siege gun). Considerable damage was done to property, Cuthbert's boot store in Dutoitspan Road being set on fire. A civilian was unfortunately killed, and four persons and one child injured by fragments of 6-inch shell. It has since been reported that five Boers were wounded at Kamfersdam this day by our sharpshooters.

34. 9th February - At 5.45 am the enemy's gun at Oliphantsfontein kopje opened fire on Premier Mine redoubt, and at 6.15 am the enemy's guns at Smith's farm and on Carter's ridge opened fire on our northern and western defences. At the last-mentioned hour the enemy's siege gun at Kamfersdam commenced the bombardment of Kenilworth village; later in the day the fire of this gun was directed on the town. Our guns replied to the enemy's artillery fire, and sharpshooters were pushed forward to annoy the enemy's gun layers at Kamfersdam. Two guns, Diamond Fields Artillery, and a Maxim were also sent down to reinforce the garrison of Premier Mine redoubt, in order to drive back the enemy from his entrenchments at Osterlow's (within 4,000 yards of our works at the Premier Mine). The enemy fired about 170 shells in all this day (74 of which were fired from the 6-inch siege gun). Considerable damage was done to property. Mr George Labram, Chief Engineer of De Beers Consolidated Mines, Limited, who had rendered invaluable assistance in the defence of Kimberley, was unfortunately killed by a 6-inch shell at the Grand Hotel; one woman was killed by the fall of debris in the Diamond Market, and a shell falling into a house near the railway station, injured Mr R Solomon, his wife and child, the two latter succumbing to their injuries. It was subsequently learned that M Leon (Creusot's agent), who was a gun layer, was this day shot through the head by our sharpshooters; the enemy also had further casualties during the day.

35. 10th February - At 5.30 am the enemy commenced the bombardment of the town and our defences with his 6-inch siege gun at Kamfersdam. During the day the Boer guns on Wimbledon and Carter's ridges and at Smith's farm joined in the bombardment of the town and our defences. Fire ceased about dusk, but soon after the hour fixed for the funeral of the late Mr George Labram the enemy recommenced the bombardment of the town, the first 6-inch shell falling at the cross roads, Dutoitspan Road (opposite Dr. Fuller's), a point which the funeral cortege was likely to pass, and the second 6-inch shell falling in the vicinity of the hospital. The enemy continued to shell the town until 11.40 pm, our guns replied to the enemy's artillery fire during daylight, and sharpshooters were again pushed to within 2,000 yards of the siege gun to annoy the gun layers. The enemy fired about 120 shells in all this day (62 of which were fired from the siege gun). Considerable damage was done to property. No. 5174 Private T Jones, 1st Battalion Loyal North Lancashire Regiment, and Driver Glover, Maxim Battery, were severely wounded by fragments of 6-inch shell in the Gardens Camp; a native was also wounded.

36. 12th February - At 7 am the enemy commenced the bombardment of Kenilworth village with his siege gun at Kamfersdam; at the same hour a Boer field piece came into action against our cattle guards and defences north east of Kenilworth. The enemy's guns at Carter's ridge, Wimbledon ridge and Smith's farm also fired a few rounds during the day at the town and out defences. Our guns replied to the enemy's artillery fire, and sharpshooters were pushed to within 2,000 yards of the siege gun to annoy the gun layers. The enemy's guns fired about 100 shells this day (46 of which were fired by the siege gun). Four houses at Kenilworth were set on fire, but no one was hurt during the day.

37. 13th February - At 6.50 am the enemy's siege gun at Kamfersdam commenced the bombardment of the town and our defences. The enemy's field guns at Felstead's, and on Wimbledon and Carter's ridges also fired occasional shell at our defences and at Kenilworth village. Our artillery replied to the enemy's fire, and our sharpshooters were pushed out to within 2,000 yards of the siege gun. The enemy fired about 30 shells in all this day (19 of which were fired from the siege gun). Some damage was done to property, and one woman, one child and three civilians were injured by the fall of a chimney, which was struck by a 6-inch shell.

38. 14th February - At 6.30 am the enemy's field piece commenced shelling our northern defences, and about 7 am the enemy's siege gun at Kamfersdam commenced the bombardment of our defences and the town. Alexandersfontein was seized by us this day, and in consequence the enemy's guns at Wimbledon ridge and Oliphantsfontein kopje devoted their attention almost exclusively to our troops holding that position. The Boer guns took up positions south-east and south-west of the Alexandersfontein Hotel (about 4,500 yards range), and brought a cross fire to bear on our defences being constructed at Alexandersfontein. Our artillery replied to the enemy's guns. The Boer guns fired about 200 shells in all this day (35 of which were fired by the siege gun). Some damage was done in

the town. Our casualties this day occurred in connection with the occupation of Alexandersfontein (vide operations 14th, 15th and 16th February).

39. 15th February - At 7 am the enemy commenced the bombardment of the town and our defences round Kimberley and at Alexandersfontein. Our guns replied to the enemy's artillery fire. At about 3 pm the advance of General French's Cavalry Division was observed, but the enemy's artillery continued in action until the advance of the Cavalry Division reached Alexandersfontein. The enemy fired about 150 rounds in all this day (five of which were fired by the Boer siege gun). Some damage was done to property in town. All our casualties occurred in connection with operations beyond our defences (vide operations 14th, 15th and 16th February).

NB - On several other occasions the enemy fired a few shell at the town and our defences, but such events are too unimportant to record in detail

Details of actions[67]

1. 24th October - An engagement took place this day in the neighbourhood of Macfarlane farm, and has been made the subject of a separate despatch[68].

2. 11th November - Lieutenant Colonel H S Turner advanced beyond our defence barrier at 3.45 am with 25 Officers and 312 non-commissioned officers and men of the mounted corps, and occupied the Otto's Kopje Mine, where he took up a defensive position. The enemy was driven back in confusion, but during the fight Sergeant A Parker, Cape Police, was mortally wounded (since dead), and Private J C A Stumkie, Kimberley Light Horse, was wounded. At 5.50 am on the same morning, the armoured train was sent out northwards to a distance of about 2 miles from the Kimberley Railway Station, in order to create a diversion. The Boer artillery opened fire on the armoured train, but could not hit it. Our troops returned to camp at 9.45 am Natives have reported that during this day the enemy suffered heavily; one native states that he himself saw 7 killed and 19 wounded Boers.

3. 16th November - Lieutenant Colonel Turner issued out beyond our defence barriers in the neighbourhood of the Kimberley Reservoir at 3.45 am with 25 Officers and 380 non-commissioned officers and men of the mounted corps; two guns of the Diamond Fields Artillery and one Maxim were sent out soon after 4 am to support the mounted men. The enemy was met south-east of Peddiefontein (Carter's Farm), and a hot engagement ensued. The Boers moved two of their guns from their bombardment position west of the Lazaretto to Peddiefontein, and opened fire on our artillery and mounted troops. The two guns of the Royal Garrison Artillery, mounted at the Kimberley Reservoir, came into action against the enemy's guns, and assisted to silence them. Our troops commenced a retirement into Kimberley at 6.30 am. Major T C Peakman and Lieutenant H W Smith, Kimberley Light Horse, also 9 non-commissioned officers and men, were wounded during the fight. The enemy's loss was not ascertained; natives, however, report that several of the enemy were killed and wounded.

4. 17th November - Lieutenant Colonel H S Turner proceeded beyond the line of our defences south of Beaconsfield about 3 pm with 28 Officers and 517 non-commissioned officers and men; he was supported by two guns Diamond Fields Artillery, one Maxim and a detachment of the Beaconsfield Town Guard. The enemy appeared from the direction of Alexandersfontein, and opened a heavy rifle fire on our troops. The Boers brought a field gun into action near the farm Uitzecht, Orange Free State, but this piece was silenced by our artillery after it had fired seven rounds. The guns of the Royal Garrison Artillery mounted in the Premier Mine Fort assisted our mobile troops. After engaging the enemy for over an hour, our troops retired within our line of defences. Our only casualty was Captain J H Bodley, Diamond Fields Horse, slightly wounded. Several of the enemy were seen to fall, but the Boer loss could not be ascertained.

5. 25th November - I had received an official despatch on the morning of the 23rd November, informing me that the Relief Column would arrive in Kimberley on 26th November, unless delayed at the Modder River; at the same time it was announced that an attempt would be made to communicate with me by searchlight signals. I was of opinion that the advance of the Relief Column could be best assisted from here by a demonstration on a large scale towards the enemy's main position west and south-west of Kimberley; consequently, I issued instructions for the following operations to be carried out at daybreak on the 25th November: - Four guns, Diamond Fields Artillery, and two Maxims, with an escort of Cape Mounted Police (82 all ranks), two companies, Loyal North Lancashire Regiment (180 all ranks), one

---

[67] Originally, this part of the despatch would have been accompanied by a sketch map but this is no longer available. The map references have however been retained in the text.
[68] See page 414.

Appendices

company, Kimberley Regiment (132 all ranks), and an ambulance detachment, formed a column under Major (local Lieutenant Colonel) G D Chamier, Royal Garrison Artillery, and was ordered to advance from a position south-west of Kimberley. The left of this column was to be eventually protected by the armoured train under the command of 2nd Lieutenant A McWebster, 1st Battalion Loyal North Lancashire Regiment (25 all ranks). A detachment of the Beaconsfield Town Guard (112 all ranks), under Major J R Fraser, was also to advance along the railway towards Wright's farm in order to prevent the enemy destroying the railway track in rear of the armoured train. A second column, under Brevet Major (local Lieutenant Colonel) H S Turner, composed of portions of the mounted corps (352 all ranks), was ordered to leave Kimberley at the same hour as the first column, and to first occupy Otto's Kopje Mine. A detachment, consisting of one section, 7th Company, Royal Engineers (46 all ranks), one Maxim, signallers and ambulance detachments, under Lieutenant R H McClintock, Royal Engineers, was ordered to follow the column under Lieutenant Colonel Turner, and hold Otto's Kopje Mine, in order to prevent the enemy's reinforcements from Kamfersdam Mine and the Intermediate Pumping Station getting in rear of Lieutenant Colonel Turner's right flank when he finally advanced to carry out the main object of this day's operations, viz, to advance as far westward as possible along the ridge west of Peddiefontein in order to look into the enemy's position near Spytfontein Railway Station and Wimbledon Siding, and, if possible, to locate his laagers west and south-west of Kimberley. Lieutenant Colonel Turner was directed to drive away the enemy from his artillery position west of the Lazaretto, if he found the force under his command to be sufficiently strong for this purpose. The armoured train had also been directed to proceed first in a northward direction, in order to draw the enemy from Kamfersdam Mine and the Intermediate Pumping Station towards the railway, and thus delay the arrival of Boer reinforcements at the enemy's artillery position west of the Lazaretto. Detachments of the Kimberley Town Guard were ordered to hold points in advance of our defence works on the Kimberley - Barkly West road and the railway north of Kimberley, in order to facilitate the retirement of the detachment from Otto's Kopje Mine, and to prevent the destruction of the railway in rear of the armoured train.

At daybreak on this day, the enemy were occupying the ridge from Spitzkop to the railway cottage south-west of the rifle ranges in force, and held the ironstone kopje 4,000 yards west of the Kimberley Reservoir as on advanced post. Peddiefontein and the ridge extending thence towards the Kamfersdam Mine were also held by the enemy. The troops taking part in this day's operations commenced to leave their camp ground at 3 am, and at 3.30 am were issuing beyond our defence barriers. The Infantry formed for attack on passing the line of our defences, and at 4 am the armoured train proceeded northwards from Kimberley Station to the White Dam. The movement of the train northwards drew out detachments of the enemy from the Intermediate Pumping Station, but the number so drawn was not so large as usual. At 4.43 am, the guns of the Diamond Fields Artillery came into action in a position about 2,000 yards west of the Reservoir against the enemy holding the ironstone kopje already referred to. This was done to divert the enemy's attention from the movement about to be carried out by Lieutenant Colonel Turner, and it was at the same time the prearranged signal for the advance of the mounted troops from Otto's Kopje Mine. At 5 am the armoured train commenced its return journey south towards the rifle ranges. The mounted troops had remained hidden from the enemy's view at Otto's Kopje Mine, but at 5.10 am Lieutenant Colonel Turner was observed to be advancing rapidly with his command on to the enemy's artillery position west of the Lazaretto, whence a few Boers immediately opened a heavy rifle fire on the mounted troops. The enemy's main body, however, was completely surprised, and at 5.26 am the force under Lieutenant Colonel Turner had rushed and occupied the enemy's redoubts, capturing 24 unwounded and 9 wounded prisoners, and also a quantity of arms and ammunition. At 5.50 am, two of the enemy's guns opened from a position near the railway cottage west of the rifle ranges on our troops, and an exchange of artillery and rifle fire at long ranges between our troops and the enemy commenced on the west of the Kimberley Reservoir. Our Infantry continued to advance, and took up a position commanding the valley in which the rifle ranges are situated. At 6.41 am the armoured train was seen to arrive abreast of Wright's farm, having been met at the level crossing on the Kimberley - Alexandersfontein road by a detachment of the Beaconsfield Town Guard. The advance of the train and the Beaconsfield Town Guard soon attracted the fire of the enemy's gun near Spitzkop. By this hour the enemy had already commenced to send forward from the Intermediate Pumping Station and the Kamfersdam Mine reinforcements to the Boer artillery position west of the Lazaretto. Lieutenant R H McClintock, RE, had observed this movement, and had reported the same to me at the Observatory, Kimberley Reservoir. The section, 7th Field Company, Royal Engineers, and the Maxim stationed at Otto's Kopje Mine opened fire on these Boer reinforcements at a range of 1,000 yards, and in consequence the enemy made a wider detour to reach his artillery position west of the Lazaretto. By 7 am the reinforcements which had reached the enemy caused the force under Lieutenant Colonel Turner to be considerably outnumbered; and, thereupon, this Officer decided to fall back with his right on the Lazaretto, and his left and centre towards Peddiefontein, preparatory to the retirement on Kimberley. I ordered the two guns of the Diamond

Fields Artillery remaining in camp to proceed to the Lazaretto, escorted by a detachment of the Kimberley Town Guard. At 8.10 am the left and centre of the mounted troops had fallen back well in rear of the column under Lieutenant Colonel Chamier, and I therefore sent a message to the latter Officer directing him to retire his force on Kimberley. At 8.22 am the Boers were once more in possession of their redoubts west of the Lazaretto, and the guns of the Royal Garrison Artillery at the Reservoir opened fire on bodies of the enemy occupying the ridge west of the Lazaretto, where the Boer guns had been mounted. At this time the Boers were firing wildly at our mounted troops at the Lazaretto, the Boer prisoners had been safely conducted into Kimberley, and our troops continued their retirement to their camp grounds. By 10 am all our troops had arrived safely within our line of defences.

Our troops engaged this day behaved very steadily both under Artillery and Infantry fire.

Our casualties during the engagement were as follows:

Seven non-commissioned officers and men killed. Lieutenant Colonel H S Turner; Captain W W Rush, Cape Police; Captains H J Bowen and H Mahoney, Kimberley Light Horse, and 25 non-commissioned officers and men wounded.

It was subsequently learnt that the enemy's loss during this day was, exclusive of the prisoners, 11 killed, and about 50 wounded.

6. 28th November - About 8.35 pm on the 27th November, searchlight signals were observed well south of Kimberley, and a message was read stating that a cypher communication from Lieutenant General Lord Methuen would be signalled to me in an hour's time. A sharp lookout was kept, but the signals were not again observed during the night 27th - 28th November. From the position of the signals referred to, I concluded that the Relief Column had reached Modder River. Further, I had observed that a considerable movement in a southward direction of the enemy had been taking place in this neighbourhood; natives had also reported that the enemy had vacated his laagers at Spitzkop and Spytfontein, and that the Boers had gone towards the Orange River. In view of the military situation which thus presented itself to me, I was of opinion that the advance of the Relief Column on Kimberley could be best assisted from here by a demonstration in force against the enemy's main position (south-west of Kimberley). I hoped, by this means, to divide the enemy's forces by causing the retention of a large body of Boers in my immediate neighbourhood. In consequence, I issued instructions on the morning of 28th November for the movement of a portion of the garrison of Kimberley under Major (local Lieutenant Colonel) G D Chamier, Royal Garrison Artillery, towards the enemy's main position (south-west of Kimberley). The troops placed under Lieutenant Colonel Chamier's command were to issue beyond our line of defence at three points, viz., the Right Column, composed of the detachment Mounted Infantry, 1st Battalion Loyal North Lancashire Regiment, and portion of Cape Mounted Police, Diamond Fields Horse, and Kimberley Light Horse, (total 633 all ranks), under Brevet-Major (local Lieutenant Colonel) H S Turner, by the barrier on the Schmidt's Drift road; the Centre Column, composed of portions of the Cape Mounted Police and Kimberley Light Horse, (total 105 all ranks), under Major Peakman, the battery Diamond Fields Artillery (six guns), four Maxims, one section 7th Field Company, Royal Engineers (48 all ranks), three companies 1st Battalion Loyal North Lancashire Regiment (247 all ranks), detachment Cape Police (32 all ranks), two companies Kimberley Regiment (342 all ranks), and an ambulance detachment by the barrier south of the Kimberley Reservoir; the Left Column, under Major J R Fraser, was composed of detachments of the Kimberley and Beaconsfield Town Guards (total 803 all ranks), advanced along the railway from Beaconsfield Railway Station; the armoured train (27 all ranks), under Second Lieutenant A McWebster, 1st Battalion Loyal North Lancashire Regiment, was directed to first proceed northwards and then to proceed southwards to Wright's farm. In order to prevent the enemy from seizing Otto's Kopje Mine, and also to compel his reinforcements on the north to make a wide detour on the journey to Peddiefontein, a detachment of the Kimberley Town Guard (54 all ranks) was directed to hold Otto's Kopje Mine, and a second detachment Kimberley Town Guard (55 all ranks) took up a position on the Kimberley - Barkley West road in advance of our defences. On the morning of 28th November the enemy was holding the ridge from Spitzkop to the railway cottage south-west of the rifle ranges, and had also garrisons in the redoubts on the ridge west of the Lazaretto. Peddiefontein (Carter's Farm) was occupied by a few Boers.

My general intention was that Lieutenant Colonel Chamier should occupy the ridge from Wright's farm to the ironstone kopje (4,000 yards west of the Reservoir), and occupy the attention of the enemy. He was directed to detach, a portion of the mounted troops under his command to Peddiefontein;. Engineers were to accompany this detached force to assist in strengthening, the position occupied by the mounted troops, and guns were also to be sent to the high ground near Peddiefontein, should it be necessary to shell the enemy out of his redoubts west of the Lazaretto. The advance of our troops was to take place in broad daylight in order that it might be fully observed by the enemy.

The armoured train proceeded northwards at 1.30 pm in order to draw the enemy at Kamfersdam Mine and the Intermediate Pumping Station towards the railway and also to prevent the enemy's cordite gun being moved from its position at the intermediate pumping station to the ridge west of the Lazaretto. At 2.25 pm I took up my position at the Observatory, Kimberley Reservoir. Our troops commenced to pass the defence barriers at 2.50 pm and at 3.10 pm the enemy's gun on the ridge west of the Lazaretto opened fire on the mounted troops as they were advancing towards Peddiefontein from the barrier on the Schmidt's Drift road. The enemy's shell passed well over our mounted troops and commenced to fall in front of the redoubt, Kimberley Reservoir; the guns of the Royal Garrison Artillery in this work were directed by me to return the enemy's fire. At 3.15 pm Wright's farm and the kopje north of the same were occupied by the Kimberley and Beaconsfield Town Guards. On passing our defence barriers south of the Reservoir, the Infantry formed for attack, the three companies 1st Battalion Loyal North Lancashire Regiment, with one Maxim, in the first line, and the Kimberley Regiment in the second line, and at 3.18 pm the whole force, under Lieutenant Colonel Chamier, had been deployed, the guns of Diamond Fields Artillery, with their mounted escort and one Maxim, being echeloned on the right of and in the rear of the Infantry, whilst the mounted troops under Lieutenant Colonel Turner covered the right of our advance. The Boers holding the ironstone kopje (4,000 yards from the Reservoir) commenced to retire, before our troops, and at 3.21 pm this kopje and the ridge commanding the valley in which the rifle ranges are situated were occupied practically without opposition by the mounted escort to the guns; at the same hour the guns of the Diamond Fields Artillery came into action about 2,000 yards west of the Reservoir, the first target being bodies of the enemy at Peddiefontein. At 3.39 pm rifle shots were exchanged between our troops at the ironstone kopje and a body of Boers near the railway cottage south-west of the rifle range. Our Infantry continued their advance, and the Boers fell back to a distance of about 3,000 yards from our troops and continued to keep up rifle fire at this range; our Infantry made no reply to the Boer fire, but advanced as far as the ironstone kopje, occupied it (relieving the escort; to the guns at this point and commenced preparations for the defence of the position occupied. At 3.57 pm the guns of the Diamond Fields Artillery changed their target and directed their fire on the enemy's two guns near Spitzkop and the railway cottage. At 4.10 pm I received the following message by heliograph at the Kimberley Reservoir from Lieutenant Colonel Chamier:

> "Have taken Johnson's kopje without opposition. Propose taking up position overlooking Wimbledon and shelling Spitzkop and Wimbledon ridge. Colonel Turner advances on Carter's."

I noticed that Lieutenant Colonel Chamier had the six guns of the Diamond Fields Artillery still with the Centre Column, and in consequence I replied by heliograph to him as follows: -

> "Do as you think best, but enemy's four redoubts west of Lazaretto appear to be strongly held, and you will doubtless require artillery to shell them out. Inform Colonel Turner."

At 4.15 pm, Lieutenant Colonel Chamier, in confirmation of his heliograph message, had sent the following written despatch by mounted orderly from Johnson's kopje: -

> "Have occupied a position with Wright's farm on the left, Johnson's kopje our centre, mounted troops on right flank up to Carter's Farm. Appears to me a better position than Wimbledon, as we there might be cut off by enemy occupying this ridge on our rear; enemy on Wimbledon ridge in small numbers."

Lieutenant Colonel Chamier had ordered one company 1st Battalion Loyal North Lancashire Regiment to proceed to Peddiefontein, and in consequence Second Lieutenant A W Hewett had marched off in the direction with "A" Company, 1st Battalion Loyal North Lancashire Regiment (66 rank and file), at 4.15 pm, and was accompanied by a detachment 7th Field Company, Royal Engineers, with pack mules (15 non-commissioned officers and men). At this hour, the guns of the Diamond Fields Artillery were still engaging the enemy's guns near Spitzkop and the railway cottage south-west of the rifle ranges, whilst the guns of the Royal Garrison Artillery at the Reservoir were firing on the enemy's guns west of the Lazaretto. The enemy's guns paid no attention to the fire of our guns at the Kimberley Reservoir, but continued to fire on the troops under Lieutenant Colonel Chamier along the whole front occupied from Wright's farm to the Ironstone kopje (4,000 yards west of the Reservoir). At 4.45 pm, Lieutenant Hewett reached Peddiefontein with his company, 1st Battalion Loyal North Lancashire Regiment; the mounted troops, under Lieutenant Colonel Turner, had already occupied the farm buildings after driving the enemy from the same, and was at the same time also holding a position on the ridge 1/2 mile north of Peddiefontein, with portions of the mounted troops who had been sent forward on foot from the farm buildings. The horses had been left under cover at Peddiefontein, one squadron Cape Mounted Police, under Major A Snow, was also at this spot in support. One squadron, Kimberley Light Horse, under Major R G Scott, VC, was at this time moving forward to the Lazaretto. Lieutenant Colonel Turner now directed Lieutenant Hewett to post one section of his company to the position already occupied by the mounted troops 1/2 mile north of Peddiefontein. Lieutenant Hewett posted a section of his company in the farm buildings and advanced the remaining two sections of his company as ordered. At 4.31 pm the enemy directed the fire from his gun in the redoubt west of the Lazaretto on to our troops at Peddiefontein and advancing northwards from there. The guns of the Diamond Fields Artillery and those of the Royal Garrison Artillery mounted on the Reservoir had made no change in their targets. At 4.55 pm the rifle fire between our troops and the enemy in the neighbourhood of Peddiefontein was very heavy. At 5 pm, Lieutenant Colonel Chamier directed Major T C Peakman to move his squadron, Kimberley light Horse, to Lieutenant Colonel Turner's support; this squadron had up to this time been employed as escort to the guns, Diamond Fields Artillery. At the last-named hour, two guns Diamond Fields Artillery were sent forward to Peddiefontein, and at 5.5 pm the Commander of the section, "A" Company, 1st Battalion Loyal North Lancashire Regiment, left at this farm received an order to reinforce the remainder of his company, under Lieutenant Hewett, with his section. At 5.40 pm portions of the Cape Mounted Police and Kimberley Light Horse, and 1st Battalion Loyal North Lancashire Regiment, were advancing on the southernmost of the enemy's earthworks west of the Lazaretto under a very heavy rifle fire, and I ordered the guns of the Royal Garrison Artillery at the Reservoir to discontinue their fire in order to avoid danger to our own troops. At this hour the squadron, Kimberley Light Horse, under Major Scott, VC, had taken up a position near the Lazaretto in order to prevent the Boers moving between our defence works and Lieutenant Colonel Turner's right flank. At 5.18 pm our men had rushed and occupied the enemy's work nearest to Peddiefontein and were continuing their advance. At the same hour a section of the Diamond Fields Horse had inclined to the westward and seized the enemy's laager, and were later joined by a detachment of the 1st Battalion Loyal North Lancashire Regiment; this party proceeded to destroy the enemy's tents, stores of clothing, supplies, and everything they would be unable to remove, and made arrangements to remove an ox wagon carrying artillery ammunition, gun limber and a Cape cart together with several other articles. At 5.23 pm Major Peakman's squadron, Kimberley Light Horse, was observed to be advancing at a very rapid pace towards the enemy's redoubts west of the Lazaretto. At 5.25 pm the following heliograph message was being sent from Peddiefontein, and was read at the Reservoir, viz:- "Send guns at once, can clear ridge." It was not clear whether the message had been read by any of the signallers with Lieutenant Colonel Chamier. In consequence, I caused the message to be repeated to him from the Reservoir. At this hour the remainder of the section 7th Field Company, Royal Engineers, was also sent to Peddiefontein. At 5.30 pm two guns of the Diamond Fields Artillery were observed to be in action about 1/2 mile north of Peddiefontein; they were firing shrapnel at about 1,000 yards range at the enemy's main redoubt west of the Lazaretto.

At this hour a body of Boers were advancing from the west towards Peddiefontein, probably in order to get on to the flank and rear of the guns in action near that farm; two Maxims which had been sent to Peddiefontein were in consequence advanced on to the left of these guns and opened fire on the enemy who gave up his attempt to reach our position. About this time some of the enemy's horses were observed to be loose north-west of Peddiefontein; Major Snow, whose squadron Cape Mounted Police had been left at Peddiefontein, was directed if possible to drive in these animals within our lines: he detached a party for this purpose, but soon discovered that a large body of the enemy was hiding in the bush who prevented the capture of these horses, a heavy fire was opened on our men, and as the numbers of the enemy could not be calculated, the attempt to capture these horses was abandoned. During this time our troops north of Peddiefontein continued their advance, and captured three of the Boer redoubts in succession. The last work captured was within 60 yards of the enemy's main work in which the Boer gun was mounted. A very heavy rifle fire was now poured on our troops holding the enemy's redoubts by the Boers holding the main redoubt which was provided with ample head cover. Lieutenant Colonel Turner was in the captured redoubt nearest to the enemy, he raised his head above the parapet to fire his revolver, and whilst in the act of doing so was shot dead. Lieutenant Clifford, who was also in this redoubt, a few minutes later was struck on the head by a bullet and made to lie down. At 6.11 pm a determined rush was made by a few of our men towards the enemy's main redoubt, the commanding position of the same and the excellent cover it afforded to the Boers alone prevented our troops from capturing this redoubt. At 6.17 pm the rifle fire between our troops and the enemy engaged west of the reservoir increased in volume for a short time, but no advance took place on either side. At 6.22 pm the enemy's rifle fire from the main redoubt west of the Lazaretto began to slacken. During the afternoon the enemy's two guns near Spitzkop and above the railway cottage south-west of the rifle ranges kept up a steady fire on our troops, the guns of the Diamond Fields Artillery remaining west of the Reservoir replied to the same at intervals. At 6.43 pm the enemy's guns fired their last shot, and the fire of our artillery also ceased for the day; but rifle fire continued until 6.57 pm, after which hour only an occasional shot was fired on the ridge west of the Lazaretto. It was now dusk, and as it had been arranged by me in the morning that the force employed this day was to spend the night in bivouacs along the position, Wright's farm to Peddiefontein, in order to act in accordance with the new situation which I expected would be made known to me during the night by flash signals by the Officer Commanding the Relief Column, I issued orders confirming my instructions regarding the position to be held. About 9.45 pm a mounted orderly arrived with a verbal message for me from Major Peakman, who had assumed command of the troops engaged west of the Lazaretto. Major Peakman informed me that Lieutenant Colonel Turner had been killed, and also that if reinforced he could capture the remaining Boer redoubt. I did not consider that the advantages to be gained by the capture of this redoubt were sufficient to risk the loss of life involved. Consequently, to save time, I sent instructions at 10 pm to Major Peakman direct appointing him to the command of all mounted corps in Kimberley, and directing him to retire to Peddiefontein, as it was imperative that the right of the forces under Lieutenant Colonel Chamier should be secure. He was also informed to communicate with the latter Officer for further orders. At the same hour I sent a second messenger to Major Scott, VC, informing him of the situation, and directing him to hold on to his position at the Lazaretto. Lieutenant Colonel Chamier was informed of the new situation in the following terms:

> Kimberley, 10.03 pm, 28th November 1899. The following verbal message has been delivered to me by Sergeant Nicholas, sent in by Major Peakman: - "Major Peakman sends me to say he wants at least 100 men to reinforce him, he is within 60 yards of the Boer fort, nobody of ours can show himself. Colonel Turner was shot dead and several others. The men cannot charge the position with bayonets because we would lose every man. All the horses are at Carter's Farm, and a big Boer commando are coining up on other side. If he stays where he is, he is perfectly safe; if he retires, he will lose every man."

I have replied to Major Peakman as follows: -

> "You are placed in command of all mounted corps. I regret I am unable to reinforce you; seize your opportunity, therefore, to retire on Carter's Farm under cover of darkness. Lieutenant Colonel Chamier is holding the line from Wright's farm to Carter's Farm; it is imperative that you should secure his right at Carter's till daylight to-morrow. Lieutenant Colonel Chamier will send you further instructions to Carter's Farm. Major Scott is at Lazaretto, and is directed to hold on to his position till daylight. Please act according to situation tomorrow morning. By order, W A J O'MEARA, Major. "NB - it is reported that Major Peakman has successfully retired on Carter's Farm."

A mounted orderly left the Kimberley Club with this message at 10.03 pm. At 2 am, I learnt that the mounted orderly had failed to deliver the message I had sent to Major Peakman, and about the same time I further learnt that owing to the enemy opening fire every time a light was struck in the neighbourhood of the Lazaretto, Major Scott had not been able to read the orders I had sent him, and in consequence portions of the mounted troops and two guns, Diamond Fields Artillery, had returned to Kimberley. A mounted orderly was therefore sent with the following message to Lieutenant Colonel Chamier, at 2.25 am, 29th November 1899:

> Kimberley, 2.25 am, 29th November 1899. "Major Peakman did not receive his orders, and Major Scott was not able to read his orders, and consequently both have returned to Kimberley with their men. Two guns, Diamond Fields Artillery, have also returned to Kimberley. I understand from Major Peakman that you must have portions of the Kimberley Light Horse, Diamond Fields Horse, and Cape Police with you. Utilize this mounted force to cover your right flank, and retire your whole force (including Major Fraser's command at Wright's) at daybreak tomorrow. Should the mounted force at your disposal be insufficient, kindly inform me at once by bearer of this despatch. I am informed by Majors Peakman and Scott that Carter's, Lazaretto, and Taylor's kopje are, to the best of their belief, completely evacuated by our troops. The armoured train proceeds to Wright's at 4 am to assist the retirement on your left. Kindly give 2nd Lieutenant Webster instructions as to the part you wish him to play. Officer Commanding will be at the Reservoir at 6 am. By order, W A J O'MEARA, Major"

In order to ensure that Lieutenant Colonel Chamier had received his instructions and fully understood them, I directed Major O'Meara to ride out to the Ironstone kopje, west of the Reservoir at 2.30 am and report to me when the return movement of the troops commenced. Our casualties during the engagement were - Brevet Major H S Turner, Lieutenant S O Wright, Kimberley Light Horse, and 22 non-commissioned officers and men killed; Lieutenant W E Clifford, Captain S P Waldek, Diamond Fields Horse, Lieutenant H G Watson, Kimberley Light Horse, and 29 non-commissioned officers and men wounded. The enemy's loss was not ascertained, but two days after the fight it was found that he had moved his camp 2 miles further from Kimberley, and the carcases of 20 horses and three oxen which had been shot were lying near the main redoubt. The gun limber, ox wagon with team, a quantity of artillery ammunition, lifting jack, Cape cart, and several other articles were brought safely into Kimberley by the mounted troops when they retired from the enemy's laager.

7. 9th December - Since 28th November the enemy had added considerably to his defences at Kamfersdam Mine. In order to cause the enemy to disclose his disposition and numbers in that portion of his line of investment; also, if possible, to induce him to detach larger numbers to hold the same. I decided to make a demonstration with a portion of the garrison towards the Kamfersdam Mine position. On the 7th December, Major (local Lieutenant Colonel) G D Chamier, Royal Garrison Artillery, made a personal reconnaissance of the ground over which it was necessary for the troops to operate. On 9th December, one section 7th Field Company, Royal Engineers (47 all ranks), three companies 1st Battalion Loyal North Lancashire Regiment, portions of the Cape (Mounted) Police, Diamond Fields Horse and Kimberley Light Horse, (a total of 237 all ranks from mounted corps), the battery Diamond Fields Artillery (six guns), a Maxim detachment (two machine guns), and a detachment Kimberley Town Guard (57 all ranks), were placed under the command of Lieutenant Colonel Chamier, who was directed to effect the object of the demonstration as he might think best. The troops mentioned commenced to pass the military defence barriers on the north-west of Kimberley at 4 am, the advance of the guns and Infantry was covered by a screen formed by a portion of the mounted troops (150 men). By 5 am four guns, Diamond Fields Artillery, with an escort of 50 mounted men, had taken up a position at the Homestead and the remaining two guns, Diamond Fields Artillery, with an escort of 25 mounted men, together with the section 7th Field Company, Royal Engineers had occupied Otto's Kopje Mine. About the same hour, the three companies 1st Battalion Loyal North Lancashire Regiment, with the detachment Kimberley Town Guard in support, reached a position between the Otto's Kopje Mine and the Homestead, at a distance of 2,500 to 3,000 yards from the enemy's works at Kamfersdam Mine. During this advance, no opposition was offered by the enemy. The mounted troops remained in observation of the front occupied by the remainder of the force. At 5.05 am, the guns, Diamond Fields Artillery, commenced ranging on the enemy's artillery position at Kamfersdam Mine, but the Boer artillery made no reply to this fire. At 5.38 am our mounted men made a small forward movement towards Kamfersdam Mine, and at 5.39 am, the enemy's two guns, situated north-east of the "tailing heap" of that mine, opened fire on our guns at the Homestead. An artillery duel now ensued, which lasted till 6.50 am. At 5.53 am, 200 mounted Boers left the Intermediate Pumping Station to reinforce the enemy holding the Kamfersdam Mine position. At 6.40 am, the enemy opened fire with one gun (firing cordite) from a position south-west of the Kamfersdam Mine "tailing heap" at our guns at Otto's Kopje Mine. The fire of our two guns in this position was, however, so effective that the enemy's guns "ceased fire" at 7.15 am At 7.30 am, a gun limber was seen to leave the enemy's position at Kamfersdam Mine and proceed to the Intermediate Pumping Station. Throughout the day the guns of the Diamond Fields Artillery and the two guns of the Royal Garrison Artillery at No 2 Searchlight continued to fire occasional shots at the Boer defences at Kamfersdam Mine; to this fire the Boer artillery made no reply. At 3.55 pm, small detachments of mounted Boers were seen to leave the Intermediate Pumping Station for the Kamfersdam Mine position. At 4.25 pm, a further detachment of mounted Boers arrived at the last-mentioned place, a number of them dismounted, and proceeded to climb up to the top of the "tailing heap". At the same time the enemy commenced to drag the gun which had been in position south-west of the "tailing heap" on to the top of the same. This operation was successfully accomplished, and at 5.17 pm, the Boers opened with shrapnel from this gun at our artillery at the Homestead. The return fire from our guns at the Homestead, and also at Otto's Kopje Mine, disconcerted the Boer artillerymen sufficiently to make their practice at our guns very erratic, but they continued to discharge their pieces with great rapidity. A fragment of a shrapnel bursting in proximity to our guns at the Homestead unfortunately struck Battery Sergeant Major A Moss, Diamond Fields Artillery, killing him instantly. Captain S [sic should be J T] White (attached to the Royal Garrison Artillery) was also struck on the foot by the splinter of a shell and injured by the same. The enemy's artillery "ceased fire" for the day at 6.10 pm, but the guns of the Diamond Fields Artillery continued to shell the enemy's position till 7.30 pm. Throughout this day, the enemy made no attempt to advance against our troops, and in consequence our infantry were not engaged. A small party of Boers opened fire upon our mounted troops during the early part of the day, but the few rounds fired in reply caused the enemy to retire out of range. The operations conducted by Lieutenant Colonel Chamier on this day resulted in two short artillery duels, and also caused the enemy to move three guns and some 500 men into his defences at Kamfersdam Mine for the day. A miner who escaped from the Intermediate Pumping Station two or three days later stated that the fire of our artillery on this date had killed two Boers and wounded seven others; and further, that in the case of one gun, a wheel had been badly broken, and the elevating gear damaged. Soon after 7.30 pm, our troops commenced the return journey to their camp grounds, which were reached by 9 pm.

Appendices

8. 17th January - Having received a message from the General Officer Commanding 1st Division, South African Field Force, on 16th January, that the troops at Modder River would that day make a strong demonstration against the enemy's position south of Scholtz's Nek, it appeared probable that a portion of the enemy's forces investing Kimberley would be drawn off towards Modder River on that day; in consequence arrangements were made to drive cattle into Kimberley from the Orange Free State. Natives were, therefore, sent out at dusk on the 16th January into the Orange Free State towards Koodoes Dam in order to drive the enemy's live stock reported to he in that neighbourhood into Kimberley, and Lieutenant Colonel T C Peakman was directed to proceed towards Koodoes Dam before daybreak on the morning of 17th January, in order to engage the enemy at Oliphantsfontein Police Station, and thus assist the natives to return to Kimberley. In accordance with the above instructions, Lieutenant Colonel Peakman left the Mounted Camp at 2.30 am, 17th January, with portion of the Cope Mounted Police, Diamond Fields Horse, Kimberley Light Horse, (one Maxim and 375 men of all ranks), and two guns, Diamond Fields Artillery, and advanced towards the Orange Free State, via the New Gordon heap. On passing the debris heaps near Amsterdam, the two squadrons Cape Mounted Police (134 all ranks) with a Maxim, under Major A Snow, Cape Police, were detached to the south towards Fenn's farm, with instructions to occupy the farm buildings there. The main body of the force under Lieutenant Colonel Peakman's command advanced in extended order towards the Laundry, and a detachment was pushed forward as far as the Police Station on the Kimberley - Koodoes Dam road. The stone kraal near the Police Station was occupied by our troops, and preparations put in hand for placing the Police Station itself in a state of defence. In the meantime the detachment under Major Snow's command successfully occupied Fenn's farm. As day broke the enemy's gun at Oliphantsfontein kopie opened fire on our guns (then near the Laundry) and at the same time about 70 Boers advanced from Oliphantsfontein kopje through the bush towards Fenn's farm. The Maxim at Fenn's was brought into action against the advancing enemy who at once displayed a white flag, but as the enemy continued to receive reinforcements, the Maxim remained in action, whereupon the enemy retired to his trenches at the kopje. A sharp look-out was kept, but up to 10.30 am there were no signs of the cattle which it was hoped the natives would procure, and in consequence, instructions were sent to Lieutenant Colonel Peakman to retire, which he did without loss. The enemy's losses were not ascertained.

Operations of 14th, 15th and 16th February 1900.

9. 14th February - At daybreak on the morning of 14th February, intelligence was received from natives that the enemy had during the night evacuated Alexandersfontein on receipt of information concerning a Boer reverse near Jacobsdal. Major J R Fraser (Officer Commanding Beaconsfield Town Guard), on being informed that the enemy had left Alexandersfontein, at once sent out scouts to ascertain the truth of this report. Our scouts returned and reported that the Boer trenches, etc, at Alexandersfontein were unoccupied, and Major Fraser at once advanced with 25 men of the Beaconsfield Town Guard, seized the enemy's trenches, and reported his action to Headquarters. The importance of holding Alexandersfontein in connection, with the advance of the Relief Column had long been fully realized, and since despatches had been received announcing that operations for the relief of Kimberley were in progress, it was decided to at once reinforce the Beaconsfield Town Guard in occupation of the enemy's works at Alexandersfontein. Major Fraser had ordered an additional 100 men of the Beaconsfield Town Guard to support him. The enemy now advanced from Wimbledon ridge and Benaauwheidsfontein, but were held in check by Major Fraser. In the meantime, the Officer Commanding Mounted Troops, Kimberley, had been ordered to reinforce Major Fraser at Alexandersfontein, and Lieutenant Colonel Peakman moved out from Kimberley with 100 mounted men and reached Alexandersfontein soon after 10 am. Just prior to the arrival of the mounted men at Alexandersfontein the enemy had opened fire (at a range of 4,500 yards) on the positions occupied by the Beaconsfield Town Guard with one gun from the eastern extremity of Wimbledon ridge. Orders were issued at 8 am to Captain T H O'Brien, 1st Battalion Loyal North Lancashire Regiment, to proceed to Alexandersfontein and take over the command of the post there, and at the same time, two guns, Diamond Fields Artillery, and further reinforcements were also ordered to proceed to Alexandersfontein. About noon, the enemy's gun at Oliphantsfontein Police Station was moved to Benaauwheidsfontein and also came into action against our now post. At 1.30 pm, the troops holding Alexandersfontein consisted of:

> Detachment, 7th Field Company, Royal Engineers (25 all ranks). 1 Company, 1st Battalion Loyal North Lancashire Regiment, with Maxim (100 all ranks). Mounted troops (100 all ranks). 2 guns, Diamond Fields Artillery. Detachment, Kimberley Regiment (25 all ranks). Beaconsfield Town Guard (114 all ranks). Ambulance party (20 all ranks).

On arrival at Alexandersfontein, the detachment Royal Engineers, under Lieutenant R L McClintock, assisted by a working party of the 1st Bn Loyal North Lancaster Regiment, commenced to entrench the position under the fire of the enemy's gun on Wimbledon ridge and his sharpshooters; the latter had advanced to within 1,400 yards firm Spitzkop and to within a similar distance south-east of the Alexandersfontein Hotel. The guns, Diamonds Field Artillery, were posted to the west of the position occupied by our troops in order to keep down the fire of the enemy's gun on Wimbledon ridge, the major part of the mounted troops being posted, in advance of the guns to keep down the fire of the Boer sharpshooters south-west of Alexandersfontein. The extent of front occupied by the small force detailed above was 3 miles, yet the enemy made no determined attempt to drive back our troops, but kept up a cross fire of guns and rifles against the position occupied, until after nightfall. During darkness, the work of strengthening our position was continued and mounted patrols were pushed well forward to both flanks to give timely warning should the enemy advance under cover of darkness.

15th February - It was not till 7.45 am that the enemy's guns on Wimbledon ridge and Benaauwheids-fontein came into action against our position at Alexandersfontein. The detachment Royal Engineers having completed the defences required for the firing line during the night, commenced soon after daybreak to prepare cover for the reserves, the enemy's guns and sharpshooters paid considerable attention to the working party during the progress of this work. About 1 pm, the vigour of the enemy's artillery and rifle fire continued to increase, so much so that it became necessary to send reinforcements to our right flank. At 3.30 pm both flanks were so hotly engaged that Captain O'Brien sent in a request to Headquarters for reinforcements. However, before any action could be taken in this matter, a large body of mounted troops was seen to be advancing on Kimberley across the open plain between the Scholtz's Nek and the kopjes near Wild's farm on the Kimberley - Petrusberg road. The signallers with the troops now announced that it was the advance of General French's Cavalry Division that our troops were witnessing; the enemy had realized this fact even earlier, for before the heliograph message from the Column had been completely received, the Boers had already taken to flight, both from Benaauwheidsfontein and Wimbledon ridge. A new problem now presented itself. The enemy's 6-inch gun and some smaller pieces in the works west, north-west, north and north-east of Kimberley had been in action during the day against the town and our defences, and it was known that considerable forces were still to the north and west of Kimberley. It was felt that an advance northwards, threatening the retreat of the guns, might have the effect of retaining a large Boer force in the immediate neighbourhood of Kimberley, and thus give General French's Cavalry Division an opportunity the following day of cutting off the retreat of a considerable portion of the enemy. In consequence all the Imperial troops and Volunteers who had manned the southern portions of the defences of Kimberley were immediately withdrawn from their posts, and together with all other available troops in Kimberley, were placed under the command of Major (local Lieutenant Colonel) W H E Murray, 1st Battalion Loyal North Lancaster Regiment. Lieutenant Colonel Murray was directed to proceed northward across the open veldt on the west of the Cape Government Railways, and endeavour, if possible, to cut off the retreat of the enemy's siege gun. At 5.30 pm, Lieutenant Colonel Murray marched off with the following troops: -

    2 companies, 1st Battalion Loyal North Lancaster Regiment (150 all ranks). Mounted troops (300 all ranks). 4 guns, Diamond Fields Artillery. Kimberley Regiment (200 all ranks). 3 Maxims.

As soon as the line of our defences was passed, our mounted troops formed a screen to cover the advance of the remainder of Lieutenant Colonel Murray's command. By the time Deibel's Vlei was reached it was already dusk. The scouts thrown out by the Diamond Fields Horse reported that the enemy's works near Deibel's Vlei were still occupied by Boers, the gun redoubt being especially strongly held. However, our advance did not draw the enemy's fire, and Lieutenant Colonel Murray decided to threaten the left flank of the enemy's works, and with this object inclined to the eastward. As soon as the movement was commenced the Boers fell back from their works. The scouts of the Diamond Fields Horse reported the retirement of the enemy and pushed forward. The two companies, 1st Battalion Loyal North Lancaster Regiment, were then pushed forward and occupied the enemy's redoubt, whilst a portion of the mounted troops, the four guns, Diamond Fields Artillery, and the Kimberley Regiment were detached under Major R G Scott VC and occupied the second Boer redoubt. At the same time the reconnoitring party of the Diamond Fields Horse advanced towards the Intermediate Pumping Station, the enemy allowed the scouts to approach within 200 yards of the Pumping Station and then opened a sharp fusillade on them, causing them to fall back, the only loss on our side being one horse killed. Lieutenant Colonel Murray made preparations to attack the enemy holding the Intermediate Pumping Station with Artillery and Infantry. It was, however, so late that a message was sent him from Headquarters directing him to simply hold the line he had already gained. The two Boer redoubts were therefore held during the night, outposts were posted to the north, and 120 men drawn from the mounted troops together with one Maxim were pushed northward along the railway towards Dronfield.

16th February - General French's Cavalry Division advanced on this date at daybreak from the east of Kimberley northwards, and engaged the enemy from Dronfield to Riverton Road Station, the portion of the Kimberley garrison engaged north of Kimberley during the previous evening being employed this day in co-operating with the larger movement of the Cavalry Division. The arrival of the Cavalry Division released the Kimberley Garrison from many duties beyond our line of defences, the men so released were collected and sent forward to join the troops already under Lieutenant Colonel Murray about daybreak. At daybreak a small patrol was sent by Lieutenant Colonel Murray towards the Intermediate Pumping Station, and reported the same evacuated by the Boers. One company Kimberley Regiment was, in consequence, sent forward to occupy the Pumping Station, Lieutenant Colonel R A Finlayson being placed in command of the post. It having been ascertained that Boers were still in the occupation of the western extremity of Dronfield ridge and that their cattle were still grazing north of the position held, Lieutenant Colonel Murray sent forward the four guns, Diamond Fields Artillery, and all available men of the Kimberley mounted troops to cut off the cattle. As soon as our men had approached within long-range rifle fire, the Boers opened on them with a 12-pounder gun and small arms from their position near Dronfield Siding: in consequence our troops withdrew out of range of the enemy's rifle fire, but continued to hold the Boers from a position west of the railway. At 7.30 am the guns of Diamond Fields Artillery came into action (at a range of 2,700 yards) against the enemy's laager from a position southwest of Dronfield Siding and about 8 am the Artillery of the 1st Cavalry Brigade also came into action against the same laager from a position eastward of Dronfield Siding. Towards 9 am all firing having ceased from the eastward of the enemy's laager, Lieutenant Colonel Murray moved the remainder of his mounted men (200 all ranks) towards the east of Macfarlane farm. A second Maxim was also sent to the Kimberley mounted troops already on the railway south of Dronfield, and half of the mounted troops there were withdrawn.

The Kimberley mounted troops advancing on Macfarlane farm now came in contact with a body of the enemy occupying a kopje about 1 mile north-west of Dronfield Siding. A detachment of the Kimberley Light Horse, was gallantly led forward by Major R G Scott, VC, and cleared the Boers out of their position in this kopje. The Kimberley troops at the same time came in touch with the New Zealand Mounted Infantry (also advancing on Macfarlane farm). The Kimberley mounted troops and the New Zealanders, acting in co-operation, now drove the enemy steadily forward towards the north over the open veldt as far as the Vaal River near Riverton. The Kimberley mounted troops had however been fighting for three days continuously, during which period the men and horses had had very little food and water, and in consequence showed signs of exhaustion. Lieutenant Colonel Murray having ascertained that the troops of the Cavalry Division were more than able to cope with the body of Boers in front of them, withdrew the Kimberley mounted troops to the Intermediate Pumping Station, which was reached at 2 pm Lieutenant Colonel Murray had accompanied the mounted portion of his command to the Vaal River, and on his return journey, when in the neighbourhood of Dronfield Siding, he heard a heavy fusillade in progress from the position where he had left his Maxims with the Kimberley mounted troops. He, therefore, sent orders for the company, 1st Battalion Loyal North Lancashire Regiment, under Lieutenant C de Putron, and a company of the Kimberley Regiment which had been in occupation of the enemy's redoubts at Deibel's Vlei since the previous evening to advance on the enemy's position at Dronfield Siding. The batteries of the 1st Cavalry Brigade were at this time vigorously shelling the enemy's laager at Dronfield Siding, but as soon as the Infantry under Lieutenant de Putron reached the railway south of the enemy's laager, the guns of the 1st Cavalry Brigade ceased firing. The Infantry under Lieutenant de Putron were advancing northwards firing volleys preparatory to delivering an assault on the enemy's position, at this moment (about 5 pm) Major-General French with his Staff passed the Kimberley troops engaged at Dronfield Siding, and an order was issued to Lieutenant Colonel Murray on no account to press his attack. The Kimberley troops therefore remained throughout the night in the positions they were occupying. On the morning of 17th February it was discovered that the enemy had fled from his laager at Dronfield. Lieutenant Colonel Murray advanced to the laager at 6 am and took possession of a 12-pounder ML gun and a large quantity of ammunition, stores, etc, abandoned by the enemy. Guards were left at the enemy's laagers north of Kimberley, and the remainder of the Kimberley troops returned to their camps. Our casualties in connection with the operations at Alexandersfontein and north of Kimberley amounted to 1 non-commissioned officer killed, 2 non-commissioned officers and 6 men wounded. The enemy's casualties are unknown.

10. Shots were frequently exchanged by our mounted troops guarding the cattle and bodies of the enemy, who attempted to drive off the same, and it even became necessary at times to send forward guns to assist our mounted troops, as the enemy had a gun posted on the ridge north of Kenilworth from which they frequently fired shell at our cattle and the mounted troops.

Kimberley Siege Account and Medal Roll

Engagement at Macfarlane – Dronfield

From Lieutenant Colonel R G Kekewich, Commanding Griqualand West and Bechuanaland, to the Chief of the Staff, South Africa.

Army Headquarters, Kimberley, 27th October 1899.
Sir,

I have the honour to report that a portion of the troops' under my command (vide return attached) engaged the enemy north of Kimberley under the following circumstances on the 24th October 1899:

2. Brevet-Major (local Lieutenant Colonel) H S Turner, Royal Highlanders, was directed to carry out a reconnaissance towards Riverton with portions of the Cape Mounted Police and of the mounted troops recently raised in Kimberley. The object of the reconnaissance was to locate, if possible, a body of the enemy reported to be in that neighbourhood, and also to ascertain their numbers &c.

3. Lieutenant Colonel Turner's command left the camp of the mounted corps, Kimberley, at 4 am, and advanced on Dronfield Siding. This point, as well as the country on the flanks of Lieutenant Colonel Turner's line of march, was found to be unoccupied by the enemy. At 6.45 am the armoured train (under 2nd Lieutenant A McWebster, 1st Battalion Loyal North Lancashire Regiment), which had been sent out from Kimberley, reached the position occupied by Lieutenant Colonel Turner, who continued his advance towards Macfarlane's ridge. At 7.15 am the Macfarlane farm was reached by the mounted troops, and the farm buildings were at once occupied. No enemy being in sight, a halt was made at this point.

4. At 8.30 am Lieutenant Colonel Turner advanced with a portion of his command (175 mounted men) on Riverton Road Station and Riverton Waterworks, the remainder of the force being left to hold the farm buildings already referred to. At 8.45 am the enemy was sighted by the look-outs at Macfarlane's farm, and Lieutenant Colonel Turner notified. The enemy was at this time in the valley, K, G, B, E (vide sketch map attached), east of Macfarlane's farm. On receipt of this information, Lieutenant Colonel Turner at once halted his force, and occupied the ridge, C, with a party of Cape Mounted Police. The enemy now began to appear in considerable numbers from the bush and in the adjoining valley K, L, east of the position taken up by Lieutenant Colonel Turner.

5. At 9 am a small party of the enemy advanced with a flag of truce; being aware of the unscrupulous use which the Boers have made of the flag of truce, Lieutenant Colonel Turner sent forward Major F J Eliott, Cape Police, in order to bring back the bearer of the flag of truce to him. It was soon ascertained that the Boers were only endeavouring to gain time, and, in consequence, Major Eliott returned at once. The enemy now maintained a watching attitude, and, in consequence, the armoured train was sent northwards by Lieutenant Colonel Turner to reconnoitre Riverton Road Station, and, if possible, to secure and bring back the enemy's supplies and stores reported to be on the railway line 2 miles north of Macfarlane's Station. During this time the numbers of the enemy continued to increase, and at 9.50 am the armoured train was signalled to and directed to return southwards.

6. At 9.55 am the enemy began to move across Lieutenant Colonel Turner's front at a range of 1,800 yards, evidently with the intention of turning his right flank, and also of intercepting the armoured train at Dronfield Siding. Lieutenant Colonel Turner, in consequence, reinforced his advanced line and endeavoured to draw the enemy on to Dronfield Siding. Fire was first opened on a small party of the enemy, who fled in confusion into the gully, G; our fire soon became general, and the greater part of the enemy also moved into the gully, G. The few Boers left in the sand heap, K, were next driven out thence, and retired into the bush, D.

7. At 10.15 am, Lieutenant Colonel Turner despatched the following message to me by heliograph (received at 10.50 am): "I think they are trying to draw me on. I intend to withdraw to Dronfield and await events. You might send two guns and two Maxims to Mostert's in case of need".

8. In view of a possible hidden danger, I at once decided to reinforce Lieutenant Colonel Turner's force and issued orders to Major (local Lieutenant Colonel) W H E Murray, 1st Battalion Loyal North Lancashire Regiment, to proceed immediately with two companies 1st Battalion Loyal North Lancashire Regiment, to Macfarlane's Station by rail. I may add, such a contingency had been foreseen, and a train had been held in readiness for the conveyance of reinforcements northwards.

Appendices

9. Lieutenant Colonel Turner was informed by heliograph as follows: "11.5 am Murray with 150 men proceeds at once by train to your position. Two guns, two Maxims, and 70 (mounted) police proceed to Mostert's as requested."

10. Even before the despatch of the above message (paragraph 9) the heliograph flashed the intelligence that shots had already been fired. Before Lieutenant Colonel Turner's message (paragraph 6) had reached me, his force was already hotly engaged. At 10.20 am the whole rising ground at L became covered with Boers riding from the direction of Leeuwfontein (a farm about 6 miles south of Boshof), while other parties appeared at the point M. At this time the armoured train was at Macfarlane's Station.

11. Lieutenant Colonel Turner noticed an inclination on the part of the enemy to again envelop his right, and, in consequence, gradually moved his force to the ridges south of the farm buildings, and made preparations to retire over the open ground at O.

12. At 11.30 am I received the following message by heliograph from Lieutenant Colonel Turner: "Can guns come to Macfarlane's? Grand chance, at least 500 here now; awful funks [sic]." The above request was almost at once modified, and Dronfield suggested as a destination for the guns.

13. The message referred to in paragraph 12 was despatched by Lieutenant Colonel Turner about 11 am, at which time he also ordered back Captain Bodley with 125 mounted men to the south of Dronfield with instructions to meet the guns and act as escort to them.

14. At 11.30 am two guns, Diamond Fields Artillery, and two Maxims with an escort of 75 Cape Mounted Police, which had been ordered out to support Lieutenant Colonel Turner on receipt of his message (paragraph 6), were seen by me to be arriving at Mostert's (about 2 miles north of Kimberley Railway Station), and Lieutenant Colonel Murray, with two Companies 1st Battalion Loyal North Lancashire Regiment, was also marching off from his camp ground for the railway station.

15. At 11.45 am a copy of Lieutenant-Colonel Turner's message (paragraph 12) was forwarded by bicycle orderly to the Officer Commanding Diamond Fields Artillery (then at Mostert's), who was further directed to proceed to Macfarlane's farm with the guns.

16. At 11.56 am Lieutenant Colonel Murray's command had been entrained, and preceded by a pilot engine, was leaving Kimberley Station for Macfarlane's Station. At 12.05 pm the guns with their escort were also seen to be moving from Mostert's northwards.

17. At 12.30 pm Lieutenant Colonel Turner noticed that the enemy in great numbers was coming out of the gulley, G, and entering the bush, D; keeping well inside the bush the Boers rode off at a rapid rate towards a rocky ridge (Pringle's). Lieutenant Colonel Turner concluded that the intention of the Boers was to tear up the rails at Dronfield Siding, and perhaps even to attempt the destruction of the armoured train by exploding the 100 tons of dynamite stored at that point.

18. At 1 pm it came up thick and rainy from the south-west, and simultaneously the train conveying the Infantry (under Lieutenant Colonel Murray) reached the neighbourhood of the position occupied by Lieutenant Colonel Turner. A fold in the ground hid the train from my view.

19. Lieutenant Colonel Murray had passed a mounted orderly (sent back by Lieutenant Colonel Turner) near Dronfield Siding, and had communicated with him and thus learnt that his force of infantry would be required at Macfarlane's farm. On reaching the position occupied by Lieutenant Colonel Turner, Lieutenant Colonel Murray was informed that the enemy had moved southwards towards Dronfield Siding. Since the enemy's movement threatened the line of retreat by rail, Lieutenant Colonel Murray decided to return to Dronfield Siding immediately. Lieutenant Colonel Turner was at the same time withdrawing his men from the position, C, F, towards the point Q (south of Macfarlane's farm).

20. At 1.10 pm, from my position in the "lookout," I noticed our Artillery suddenly come into action in what was undoubtedly an unfavourable position some 5 miles north of Kimberley Station (marked S on accompanying sketch map). It appears that the scouts thrown out by the escort to the guns were some 600 yards in advance of the latter, and continued to move forward on Dronfield Siding without discovering the presence of the enemy in the bush on Pringle's ridge. The Boers, moreover, cleverly allowed the escort to proceed unmolested with the intention, no doubt, of "wiping out" our gunners before the gun could come into action. Captain S May, Diamond Fields Artillery, in command of the guns had, however, noticed the Boers, but thinking that they were some of our own men, had continued to advance for a distance of about 300 yards after sighting the enemy. The guns were suddenly fired

upon, and Captain May instantly unlimbered and came into action to his right in the position, S, already referred to (first range 1,500 yards).

21. Captain May next noticed that the enemy was approaching close up to his guns, and was at the same time moving nearer to the railway (the nearest body of the enemy being 1,000 yards from his position).

22. Having heard the fire of our guns, Lieutenant Colonel Murray halted his train about 300 yards south of Dronfield Siding, but before the detrainment of the Infantry could be completed the enemy fired into the train. The two companies, 1st Battalion Loyal North Lancashire Regiment, were rapidly got into attack formation under cover of the railway embankment, and an advance was at once made against the enemy engaging our guns.

23. When the two companies, 1st Battalion Loyal North Lancashire Regiment, had proceeded some 500 yards east of the railway the enemy poured in a very heavy fire on them. It was at this period of the engagement that Lieutenant C H M Bingham was wounded in front of his company, which he was leading with great coolness. At the same time Lieutenant and Adjutant J G Lowndes, whilst rendering valuable assistance to Lieutenant Colonel Murray, was also wounded.

24. At 1.15 pm, whilst the Infantry was detraining, Lieutenant Colonel Turner had completed the collection of his force at the point Q, and in order to assist the Infantry under Lieutenant Colonel Murray, commenced a flank movement across the open ground south-west of the haystack at E, so as to cut the enemy off from the gully, G.

25. Lieutenant Colonel Murray continued his advance, driving the enemy before him under somewhat difficult circumstances, as the Boers were practically invisible in the bush, P. About 2 pm Lieutenant Colonel Turner, dismounting his men, again came into action against a body of the enemy east of Macfarlane's farm.

26. As soon as Lieutenant Colonel Murray had left Kimberley Station, a second train was got ready to proceed if necessary to the scene of the fight, and one company of the Kimberley Regiment was also ordered to "fall in."

27. At 2 pm Lieutenant Colonel Finlayson was directed to move off one company Kimberley Regiment to the station and to entrain his men. Additional ammunition for the guns was also trucked on this train, and further two saloon coaches provided with stretchers were attached to this train for the conveyance of the wounded men back to Kimberley. The men of the Kimberley Regiment were rapidly entrained, and at 2.15 pm the train was steaming out of the station.

28. At 2.10 pm I noticed that our guns were retiring slowly southwards towards Kimberley, and at 2.35 pm the guns were again observed to come into action at T; the fire of the guns on this occasion was directed against a distant body of the enemy retiring from Pringle's ridge towards Koodoes Dam.

29. At 3.30 pm the trains conveying the wounded and the Infantry were observed to leave their position south of Dronfield Siding for the return journey to Kimberley.

30. Commandant Petrus Botha, in command of the enemy's force engaged this day, was killed during the fight, and from papers found on his body it transpired that he had received instructions from Head Commandant Wessels (of the Western Division Burgher Force, Orange Free State) to capture and drive off our livestock from Kenilworth. There can be little doubt that the force under Commandant Botha was in the act of attempting to execute this task when it was surprised and defeated by the force sent out by me from Kimberley. The numbers of the enemy engaged this day are estimated at 800 men; no information is obtainable as to the loss the enemy incurred.

31. Lieutenant Colonel Turner has brought the conduct of Lieutenant R L McClintock to my special notice. This Officer had given his horse to Lieutenant Colonel Turner (who had already mounted a wounded man on his own horse), and it was while Lieutenant McClintock was retiring on foot, carrying blasting gelatine and detonators in his haversack, that he was wounded in the side. Captains R G Scott, VC, and H J Bowen, and Lieutenant W Newdigate, Kimberley Light Horse, ably assisted Lieutenant Colonel Turner, and showed great pluck in retaining their positions under a very heavy fire. The conduct of Major F A Eliott, Cape Police, was particularly praiseworthy. This Officer during this day on two occasions advanced to meet the enemy's flags of truce, although previous experience (during the present war) in connection with the performance of a similar duty had shown him that in all probability he would be fired upon by the Boers.

Appendices

32. I wish to record my appreciation of the conduct of all the troops engaged with the enemy this day. I regret the loss of the brave men killed in the fight.

33. A return showing strength of corps which took part in the engagement, and a sketch map of the neighbourhood where the fighting occurred on the 24th October, are attached.

34. I wish to place on record the valuable assistance afforded me by my Staff Officers: - Captain (local Major) W A J O'Meara, RE (Intelligence Officer, Kimberley), and Lieutenant (local Captain) D S MacInnes, RE (Staff Officer, Kimberley). They carried out my orders in connection with the arrangements made for the conveyance of reinforcements to the scene of the fight, &c., in a rapid and careful manner.

35. The following Officers in command of the troops actually engaged with the enemy deserve special mention: -

    - Major (local Lieutenant Colonel) W H E Murray, 1st Battalion Loyal North Lancashire Regiment, for the able manner in which he handled his men.
    - Major (local Lieutenant Colonel) H S Turner, Royal Highlanders, for the judgment and dash with which he handled the mounted troops.
    - Captain S May, Diamond Fields Artillery, for the great coolness displayed by him in handling his guns in action in an unfavourable situation.
    - Dr A J Ortlepp, who accompanied the Artillery, also showed great coolness. His horse was shot.

36. Lastly, I wish to record my appreciation of the very plucky conducts of Gunner F D Payne, Diamond Fields Artillery, who, although severely wounded in the foot early in the action, continued to lay his gun until the "cease fire" sounded.

I have the honour to be,
Sir,
Your obedient Servant,
R G Kekewich, Lieutenant Colonel, Commanding Griqualand West and Bechuanaland.

Appendix 15 – Proclamation of the state of siege

V R PROCLAMATION

Proclamation by Lieut Col R. G. Kekewich, Commanding the Troops at Kimberley.

1. Whereas a state of grave public danger exists at Kimberley and in the territories of Griqualand West and Bechuanaland.
2. In virtue of my office as Commander of the Forces in the said territories—
3. I hereby proclaim that a state of siege exists within the said territories of Griqualand West and Bechuanaland.
4. All persons resident within the said District who are not members of the Imperial Forces, The Colonial Forces, The Kimberley and Beaconsfield Town Guard, are hereby ordered to register and to produce for registration to the Commissioner of Police or other duly authorized Officer any rifle, shot gun, revolver, or other firearm, and any ammunition that may be their property or in their keeping in Kimberley and Beaconsfield within 24 hours, and in the Country District within 72 hours, from the time of issuing this Proclamation, and any person failing to do so, or failing to give good and satisfactory reason for failing to do so, shall be deemed to have contravened the provisions of this Proclamation, and to be liable to such pains and penalties as the Court of Summary Jurisdiction here-inafter mentioned shall award.
5. All persons residing in Kimberley and Beaconsfield other than Members of the Forces mentioned in paragraph No. 4 of this Proclamation are prohibited from leaving their houses between the hours of 9 pm and 6 am except with the written permission of an Officer of the above-mentioned forces.
6. All canteens, bars, and eating houses shall be closed between the hours of 9 pm and 6 am.
7. In case of the alarm signal sounding, all persons except members of the Defensive Forces are hereby ordered to proceed at once to their own houses and there to remain until orders to the contrary are issued.
8. Any person or persons suspected of in any way aiding or abetting or supplying or conveying information to, or in any way whatsoever assisting the Queen's enemies, may be summarily arrested on the order of any Officer, and failing to give a satisfactory account of himself, herself, or themselves, shall be dealt with according to the customs and usages of martial law.
9. Any person who shall in any way interfere with the troops-shall be liable to summary punishment on the spot
10. Any act of treason shall be punishable by forfeiture of goods and by death.
11. Any person found guilty of any act which is contrary to the accepted customs and usages of war between civilised nations shall suffer the punishment of death, and to this sentence there is no alternative.
12. Any person contravening any of the preceding sections or committing any act calculated in any way to be detrimental to the interests of Her Majesty, shall be summarily dealt with according to this Proclamation and shall suffer such pains and penalties as the Court of Summary Jurisdiction or other competent Court shall award.
13. The following gentlemen are hereby nominated as Members of the Special Court of Summary Jurisdiction, and of them any two shall form a quorum:— Hon. Mr. Justice LANGE, E A JUDGE, Esq, Civil Commissioner, G C BAYNE, Esq, Resident Magistrate, Kimberley, W MUNGEAM, Esq, Resident Magistrate, Beaconsfield, Commissioner M B ROBINSON, Cape Police, Maj. HENRY SCOTT-TURNER, Royal Highlanders, Capt. W A J O'MEARA, Royal Engineers, Lieut. DUNCAN MACINNES, Royal Engineers.

    And such other members as shall from time to time be appointed by the Commandant of the Forces in Griqualand West and Bechuanaland for the time being.
14. Nothing in this Proclamation shall be deemed to interfere with any other penalties or prosecutions or confiscations of property to which the said persons who shall offend against the provisions of this Proclamation shall be liable, by reason of any civil or criminal law enforced in the feretories aforesaid.
15. Nothing in this Proclamation shall be deemed to interfere with the ordinary course of business in the Civil Courts of the Colony.
16. Given under my hand at Kimberley, at noon, this 15th day of October, in the year of our Lord, One Thousand Eight Hundred and Ninety-nine.

God Save the Queen!
R. G. KEKEWICH,
Lieut.-Col. Commanding the Forces in Griqualand West and Bechuanaland.

Appendix 16 – Kimberley Town Guard

The KTG was raised to defend the town. It was called out for permanent service on 10th October 1899 and served throughout the siege.

The Memorandum forming the KTG set out its roll and structure. It said the "Kimberley and Beaconsfield Town Guard is organised solely for local defence in case of attack from without. The radius of service is within eight miles from the Market Square, Kimberley."

"Whatever is worth doing at all, is worth doing well."

"Had there been 12 ships of the enemy, and we had taken 11 and allowed 1 to escape when we could have taken her, I should never have called that well done."

Nelson's despatches.

Memorandum

Re FORMATION AND ORGANIZATION OF PROPOSED TOWN GUARD FOR KIMBERLEY AND BEACONSFIELD.

Kimberley and Beaconsfield Town Guard is organised solely for local defence in case of attack from without.

The radius of service is within eight miles from the Market Square, Kimberley.

The organisation is divided into two heads :—

1st—MILITARY.
Able-bodied men who are capable of active service in the defence.

2nd—CIVIL.
In connection with a Special Constable, and Medical duties. Men for this part of the work need not necessarily be of sound health. Again, there will probably be a number who are willing to undertake civil duties through inability to shoot, dependance upon them of relations, &c., &c., cannot join the military class.

Facsimile of the first page of the Memorandum announcing the formation of the Town Guards

---

I do promise and swear that I will be faithful and bear true allegiance to Her Majesty Queen Victoria and her heirs and successors according to law; and that I will serve in the Kimberley and Beaconsfield Town Guard for such period as my services may be required; provided that I shall not be called on to serve outside an area formed by a circle drawn with a radius of eight miles from the Town Hall, Kimberley, except with my own consent; and that I will faithfully, honestly, and soberly carry out whatever duties may be assigned to me to the best of my ability, and obey whatever orders shall be given me by my superior officers.
SO HELP ME GOD

The Town Guard Oath

Kimberley Siege Account and Medal Roll

The organisation was divided into two main sections:

"1st Class — Military. Able-bodied men who are capable of active service in the defence.

2nd Class — Civil. In connection with a Special Constable, and Medical duties. Men for this part of the work need not necessarily be of sound health. Again, there will probably be a number who are willing to undertake civil duties through inability to shoot, dependence upon them of relations, &c., &c, cannot join the military class."

It is suggested, firstly, that a number of rallying posts be selected where the Companies may assemble and be armed.

1st Class – Military

De Beers Workshops	1st Division	R G Scott VC	330
Rock Shaft, De Beers	2nd Division	H J Ap O Bowen	300
Ordnance Store, Transvaal Road	3rd Division	J T Lucas	300
Kimberley Mine	4th Division	Major Peakman	300
Veterans, Kimberley Club	5th Division	Captain Mandy	100
Beaconsfield	6th Division	Captain Nelson	200
Premier Mine	7th Division	Capt J Swanson	150
			1680

2nd Class – Civilian

Special Constables, Town Hall	8th Division	HW the Mayor	120
Medical Corps, Hospital	9th Division	HW the Mayor	100
			220
			1900

Organisation of a Division: Commander of a Division commands also a Company. Staff Officer of a Division either commands a Company or is a Lieutenant in one of the Companies. Strength of a Division, 300: i.e., three Companies of 100 each.

Organisation of a Company: One Captain commands a Company, having under him four Lieutenants, each of whom commands a section, consisting of one Lieutenant, one Sergeant, one Corporal, twenty-one or twenty Privates. Company Staff consists of in addition to the Captain, a Quartermaster, a Colour Serjeant, a Clerk, an Issuer and a Bugler. Total strength of Company: Six Staff, four Lieutenants, four Sergeants, four Corporals, eighty-two Privates.

Pay for volunteers was given at the standard Colonial rate.

Lieutenant Colonel R G Kekewich was appointed Commandant of the Forces. Lieutenant Colonel Harris was appointed as second in command. Major Peakman was to act as Staff Officer. The Town Guard was raised as an Imperial Force and was supposed to be under Imperial officers but there were not enough officers to achieve this. In his diary entry of 22nd October 1899, Kekewich expressed his frustrations at the administrative burden associated with imperial and colonial units:

"The Town Guard in accordance with the High Commissioner's order is an Imperial Force, but I am the only Imperial Officer in it; other Imperial Officers for it have not been available and I could not spare officers for it from the half battalion 1/Loyal North Lan Regt which is very short of officers. I have done my best to separate Imperial from Colonial charges, and to make arrangements as to the pay of the Town Guard, Volunteers, Kimberley Light Horse, etc, and the Standard Bank has authorized me to draw the amount I require for this. I fear however that with my small staff and no proper arrangements of books, clerks, etc which are not available that many difficulties may arise hereafter; as previously stated I have been so fully occupied with arrangements for the defence of this place that it has been quite out of my power to supervise many matters as I should have wished. I have had to make pay lists to suit the different Corps, and I hope things will work out all right eventually, but with these rapid transfers from one corps to another there must I fear be confusion as to accounts, etc and it is most difficult in many cases to separate what is chargeable against Imperial and what from Colonial Funds."

Appendices

In the Memorandum, the company and section arrangement was set out for some of the divisions[69]:

Division	Company	Section
1st (Capt R G Scott)	A (Capt W Newdigate)	Lt T L Angel, Lt C D Lucas, Lt Harris, Lt H McDonald
	B (Capt I Grimmer)	Lt (to be appointed), Lt Archibald, Lt N Crosby, Lt W D Fynn
	C (Capt R B Carnegy)	Lt D K Sinclair, Lt S Dallas, Lt W McHardy, Lt Stewart
2nd (H J Ap O Bowen)	D (Capt W S Elkin)	Lt G Lambourne, Lt G Saunders, Lt G Paley, Lt W J Wilcox
	E (Capt R Brand)	Lt P Waldek, Lt W Hornby, Lt W Hayston, Lt J Anderson
	F (Capt E H Moseley)	Lt F C Rogers, Lt C J Walters, Lt H A Ziegenbein, Lt E A Penny
3rd (J T Lucas)	G (Capt C Holliday)	Lt F Haidler, Lt T Rattey, Lt R Percy, Lt B E A O'Meara
	H (Capt J Pooley)	Lt J D Tyson, Lt J M Saddler, Lt J W Gentleman, Lt J R Booth
	K (Capt G White)	Lt G H Johnson, Lt S Johns, Lt H Schmidt, Lt S Tait
4th (Major Peakman)	L (Capt W H Faulkner)	Lt T Stratten, Lt F White, Lt J Cox,
	M (Capt P W Mallett)	Lt D P Hearn, Lt C Coghlan, Lt K C Elliot, Lt J B Sheasby
	N (Capt J Stevenson)	Lt T Woodbourne, Lt J Druce, Lt T Hulley, Lt C E Cleaver

Kekewich's figures for the strength of the KTG on 21st October 1899 show how effective the recruiting had been. The force totalled 2,248 (2,164 all ranks and 84 reserves).

Division	All ranks	Reserves	Division	All ranks	Reserves
Staff	9		6th	338	
1st	213		7th	194	
2nd	351	61	8th	153	
3rd	291	23	9th	97	
4th	320		Kamfers Dam	42	
5th	135		Civil Service	21	

Another update on 25th November 1899 shows an increase in the size of the KTG:

Unit	Officers	Men	All ranks
KTG	94	1,784	1,878
Premier Mine	7	219	226
Beaconsfield	20	368	388
Kenilworth	4	53	57
De Beers Rock Staff	1	60	61
Kimberley Mine	4	35	39
Total	130	2,319	2,649

A weekly breakdown of the size of the KTG appears on page 287.

---

[69] The original list has been amended to align with the medal roll. For example, Capt J Stephenson should be Capt J Stevenson. Not all names appear on the medal roll, for example Lt T Rattey. Initials have been added where these can be identified but this is not always the case, for example Lt Harris and Lt Stewart.

Kimberley Siege Account and Medal Roll

Municipal Sect.

KIMBERLEY TOWN GUARD.

SECTION "C."

Rallying Post:—Town Hall, Kimberley.

WE HEREBY agree to have our names entered on Section "C" of the Town Guard of Kimberley, and should it be found necessary to sound the alarm, we undertake at once to proceed to the Rallying Post mentioned above and join the Town Guard already enrolled.

ALARM SIGNAL:—Sounding of Hooters from De Beers, Kimberley, and Wesselton Mines.

SIGNATURE	ADDRESS
H. A. Oliver	6 Belgravia Road
Hugh Rugg	55 Currey St.
H. Allen	Currey St.
T. W. Alexander	14 Knight St.
J. Savage	4 Compound St.
C. H. Betteridge	59 Stockdale St.
J. E. Powrie	139 Transvaal Rd.
James Edgar	13 Carr Street
L. W. Hyppant	56 Currey St
A. J. Moore	33 Thompson Street
H. Parker	13 Saul Street
J. M. Veksey	Fire Station Stockdale Street
J. Smith	11 Braud street, Newton
L. Hartley	56 Warren St. De Beers
W. J. Read	52 Stockdale St
E. J. Beddome	7 Goodrum St.
W. Townsend	114 Transvaal Road
F. Ware	Adair Street
H. L. Rawlinson	23 Thompson St.

The attestation sheet for C Section. Note the first signature, H A Oliver

Appendix 17 – Nominal roll by location

In his diary of 25th November 1899, Kekewich recorded the positions of the troops and this provides a useful breakdown of the defensive troops:

Location	Unit	Officers	Men	All ranks
Botanical Garden Camp	23rd Co RGA	1	28	29
	1st LNLR	8	263	271
	RAMC	1	4	5
	ASC	1	8	9
	DFA	4	104	108
	Maxim Battery	-	34	34
Sanatorium	1st LNLR	1	67	68
	Kimberley Regt	8	228	236
Reservoir	23rd Co RGA	1	19	20
Newton	Kimberley Regt	7	158	165
Premier Mine	23rd Co RGA	1	23	24
	1st LNLR	1	72	73
	RAMC	-	1	1
Kimberley Mine No 1	7th Co RE	1	50	51
	Cape Police Maxim Detachment	-	6	6
Mounted Corps Workshops	Cape Police	18	327	345
	DFH	8	157	165
	KLH	18	343	361
	1st LNLR	1	20	21
	Cape Police Maxim Detachment	-	6	6
	Ambulance	1	13	14
	Transport	-	1	1
	Staff	4	3	7
Crusher Mill	23rd Co RGA	1	20	21
Kimberley Mine No 2	Cape Police 8 pounder Detachment	1	22	23
South Circular Road	Cape Police Maxim Detachment	-	6	6
Total		87	1,983	2,070

At the end of the book *Siege of Kimberley*, there is an excellent breakdown of the troops by location. In this list, the men are named but sometimes their numbers and initial are omitted making it a very difficult task to cross-reference this nominal roll against the medal roll. Where possible, the location information has been incorporated into the medal roll. Where there is no matching name in the medal roll (eg Pte J M Schneider of the Cape Police who was not issued with the QSA) or the name cannot be uniquely matched (eg A Sutherland of which there are several on the medal roll), the name is displayed in italic, grey text.

The majority of the list is presented at it appears in the *Siege of Kimberley*. The reproduction of this list must be accompanied by a number of caveats:

- Where a large number of men in a unit are at one location, their names have not been reproduced. For example the 252 LNLR men at the HQ Camp are not listed but the other men from this unit are listed. In this way, it can still be determined where a men served during the siege.

- It is not identified on what date in the siege the list was put together or the remit for the list. It would appear to be a complete list of who served in the different units. Most men appear only once in the list but there are a few instances where a man appears to have served at a maximum of three locations.

- While it was not identified within the book, the *Siege of Kimberley* went through a number of editions. The list that follows contains information taken from the third and last edition of the book.

In the lists, officers are sorted by rank and then alphabetically by surname. These are followed by NCOs and men who are sorted alphabetically by surname.

Kimberley Siege Account and Medal Roll

Headquarters' Staff 424
Loyal North Lancashire Regiment 426
Army Service Corps 427
Royal Artillery 427
Royal Engineers 428
Cape Police 428
Kimberley Regiment of Volunteers 431
Diamond Fields Artillery 431
De Beers Maxim Battery 431
Kimberley Light Horse 431
Town Guard
    Pickering's Redoubt, No 1 432
    Pickering's Redoubt, No 2 432
    No 3 Redoubt, (8 & 9 Machine) 432
    No 4 Redoubt (No 1 Machine De Beers) 433
    Mostert's Redoubt 434
    No 6 Redoubt 434
    Civil Service Redoubt 435
    Otto's Kopje 435
    Cyclist Corps 436
    No 1 Company, Medical Corps 436
    Kimberley Mine Ambulance Company 436
    No 2 Schmidt's Breastworks 437
    No 3 Redoubt 438
    Belgravia Fort 438
    Mandy Fort 438
    No 4 Redoubt, De Beers Floors 439
    No 2 Redoubt, Kimberley Mine 442
    No 1 Redoubt, Kimberley Mine 443
    Kamfersdam Company 443
    No 2 Redoubt, No 1 location 444
    Premier Mine 444
    Municipal Guard 445
    Beaconsfield Town Guard 446
    Kenilworth Defence Force 448
Miscellaneous 449
Errata queries 449

Headquarters' Staff

    Lt Col R G Kekewich, 1st LNLR
    Major (Local Lt Col) Henry Scott-Turner, Royal Highlanders
    Capt (local Major) W A J O'Meara, Royal Engineers
    Lt (Local Capt) D S MacInnes, Royal Engineers

Royal Army Medical Corps

    Capt O'Gorman, in command
    S Sgt William Cooper
    Sgt Mark Benson
    Ptes John Hughes, George Jefferies and George Taylor

Army Pay Corps

    Sgt A W Saunders

Army Service Corps

    A E Mawby, G Stoney

Cape Police Division II

    Acting Sub Inspectors: S J H Brink; *J Clear; A N de Kock;* E C J Brand. Sgt A Piercy

Appendices

Colonial Ordnance Department

    Capt (Local Major) C Langworthy Ricketts, Assistant Commissary of Ordnance
    Sgt J L Squire (Cape Mounted Rifles), Ordnance Storekeeper
    T Rothwell and *E W Bates*, Clerks

Kimberley Town Guard – Headquaters' Staff

    Lt Col D Harris VD
    Major S Richards, SO
    Capt S Dallas, ASO
    Capt C E Hertog, Paymaster
    Capt J Morton, QM
    Capt B E A O'Meara, Garrison Adjutant and QM
    Lt F W Smith, ASO
    Lt A Tidd-Pratt, ASO
    Lt G E Whiley, Assistant Paymaster
    Armourer Sgt A W Walshe
    Ptes R S Jones and *W Craven*

Medical Officers and their stations

    Dr Ashe and Dr Watkins (Kimberley Hospital)
    Dr Mackenzie (Kimberley Mine Compound)
    Dr Symonds (Workshops)
    Dr Mathias (Rock Shaft, De Beers Mine)
    Dr Westerfield (Sanatorium)
    Dr Stoney (Reservoir)

Supply Depots

    Head Office: Bennie, A, Paymaster; *Jones, R H, Clerk*

    No 1 Depot Guards: Dugmore, J F; Staff, George E; Snedden, W; Hill, R; McKenzie, J; McNaughton, W; McKenzie, E; File, A C; Jones, H W; Staff, R F; Dixon, P; Pope, W

    No 2 Depot Guards: Stewart, D C; Bristow, S A; Doherty, M; Green, G H; Lawrence, Wm; Calder, G W; Heynes, J F; Joslin, V; Dobbin, F J; Fillis, H; Durrell, J H; Van Der Merwe, A

    No 3 Depot Guards: Nothard, H; Brown; H A; Nothard, Tom; Poulton, P; Beavis, E; Philp, S Y

    No 4 Depot Guards: Jackson, J; Clucas, A B; Voges, P J; Pritchard, T H; Nicholls, E F; Birkley, R

    No 5 Depot Guards: Key, J G; Foster, A W; McEvoy, B; *Meinaber, W;* Millar, W; Smyth, J J

    No 6 Depot Guards: Mendelssohn, M; Villet, G; Climpson, C; Green, Ben; Owen, L M; Hunter, G M

Staff of black and Asian food supply stores

    Controller: Cundill, T J

    Managers: *Swords, G B;* **Cotty, A F;** *White, H B; Green, E J; Rawson, H; McEwen, E G; MacKenzie, J R; Oates, E;* **Vines, C G;** *Solomon, R*

    Assistants: *Alexander, C; Thompson, J; Caine, T J; Ward, R;* **Davis, C R;** *Harris, S;* **Lee, E J;** *Griffin, J W; Maberley, A L*

Telegraph signallers

    Symons, J E; Osman, F; Jubber, C D B; Bevan, W; Upfold, J; Backman, W A; Lunnon, W C; Foster, C H; Stephen, W W; White, J W; Simpson, C J; Wilson, A; Rankin, D

Kimberley Siege Account and Medal Roll

Loyal North Lancashire Regiment

Location – The Botanical Gardens Camp

Lt Col Kekewich, R G, commanding troops Kimberley
Maj Fraser, J R, commanding Town Guard, Beaconsfield
Maj Murray, W H E
Capt O'Brien, T H, commanding troops, Premier Mine
Lt Wallace, A R, Sanatorium
Lt Bingham, C H M
Lt Woodward, F W
Lt de Putron, C
Lt Clifford, W R, mounted infantry
2nd Lt Hewett, A W
2nd Lt Webster, A McW, Armoured train
Lt & Adjutant Lowndes, J G
Lt & QM Gill, H J

In addition to the officers, 252 NCOs and men were stationed at the Botanical Gardens Camp.

Location - Sanatorium Camp

Allen, 5187 Pte W	Fitzsimmons, 4357 Pte W	Kay, 4340 Pte J	Riley, 4705 Pte T
Allinson, 4372 Pte J	Forbes, 4989 Pte W	Kennedy, 3667 Pte B	Rolf, 4611 Pte W
Ascott, 4958 Pte H	Geldard, 3729 Pte W	Macken, 3713 Pte J	Ryan, 4202 Pte M
Bolling, 4844 Pte A	Gibson, 5103 Pte R	Maguire, 5232 Pte T	Shelton, 5579 Pte F
Bray, 996 Band Sgt G	Godfrey, 5586 Pte H	Malamphy, 4686 Pte J	Smith, 3828 Pte W
Britton, 4345 Pte N	Gray, 5340 Pte J W	Martin, 2709 Sgt R	Smith, 5321 Pte C
Brown, 5540 Pte R	Gunning, 5240 Pte J	McGreavy, 5015 Pte J	Starkie, 5150 Pte J
Butler, 4348 Pte A	Haley, 5309 Pte T	Milne, 3763 Pte W	Tarpey, 4306 Pte J
Cottrill, 5364 Pte W	Hallett, 5208 Pte C	Murray, 4854 Pte J	Tattersall, 4276 Cpl A
Curtis, 4796 Cpl C	Harrison, 4762 Pte E	Murray, 4902 Pte D	Taylor, 4496 Pte W
Davenport, 5438 Pte J	Hayward, 4320 Pte W	Nightingale, 4630 Drum B	Thornhill, 3960 Pte S
Dean, 4878 Pte C	Heffernan, 5466 Pte W	Nixon, 4661 Pte D	Tomlinson, 4673 Pte W
Driscoll, 4086 Pte H	Hilditch, 3781 Pte E	O'Connor, 4968 Pte J T	Walker, 4472 Pte H
Duerdon, 3665 Pte R	Hinchon, 4933 Pte J	O'Hara, 5257 Pte W	Weall, 3886 Sgt H
Elliot, 3974 Pte J	Hindle, 4728 Pte J	Parrington, 4310 Pte G	Whitehead, 4028 Pte E
Elliott, 3731 Pte J	Hobbs, 5222 Pte J	Partington, 4038 Pte J	Whittaker, 5062 Pte W
Entwistle, 5386 Pte J	Hughes, 3771 Pte C	Pomfret, 5011 Pte D	Whitworth, 4092 Pte S
Fagan, 3773 Pte J	Johnson, 5031 Pte E	Poole, 5562 Pte J	Wilson, 3693 Pte R
Faulkner, 4518 Pte G	Jones, 5174 Pte T	Rees, 5451 Pte F	
Fisher, 5301 Pte W	Kavanagh, 4009 Drum J	Reynolds, 3366 L Sgt J	

Location - Premier Mine, Wesselton

Almond, 3816 Pte W	Cherry, 4351 Pte S	Ingram, 4192 Pte H	Pownall, 3849 Pte J
Ansell, 3290 Col Sgt A	Cosgrove, 4254 Pte T	Jamieson, 4156 Cpl G	Randall, 4587 Pte J
Ashcroft, 4657 Pte T	Craig, 5531 Pte J	Jones, 4174 Pte J	Reeves, 5581 Pte G
Atherton, 3935 Pte J	Dillion, 5278 Pte E	Knowles, 3973 Pte T	Rourke, 3901 Drum T
Atkinson, 4859 Pte J	Ditchfield, 4718 Pte J	Levi, 4529 Pte W	Sayers, 4521 Pte H
Bailey, 4061 Pte R	Eatock, 5550 Pte W	Marsden, 2960 Sgt J	Slattery, 3858 Pte R
Baker, 5495 Pte R	Ellis, 5572 Pte G	McCreary, 3361 Pte G	Smith, 2269 Pte W
Beer, 2567 L Sgt F	Firth, 5474 Pte W	McDonagh, 3917 Pte J	Smith, 3679 Pte J
Belfield, 5029 Pte W	Foy, 5454 Pte J	McKearnan, 4062 Pte E	Sutcliffe, 3760 Pte W
Bell, 4565 Pte J	Greary, 5065 Pte W	Measure, 4621 Pte G	Taylor, 3791 Pte G
Bentley, 4675 Pte N	Green, 4539 Pte J	Murphy, 4733 Pte J	Tedder, 5468 Pte G
Blakeley, 4013 Pte J	Green, 5431 Pte R	Murray, 3481 Pte M	Walker, 5303 Pte J
Bowers, 4508 Pte W	Gregson, 4628 Pte R	Neeley, 2880 Cpl H	Ward, 5068 Pte E T
Brindle, 4093 Pte W	Hall, 3738 Pte W	Nutting, 4365 Pte P	Wardley, 4711 Pte J
Brown, 3842 Pte T	Hall, 5234 Pte S	Parkins, 4189 Pte W	Waterhouse, 4929 Pte W
Brown, 3968 Pte J	Hampson, 4203 Pte W	Pilkington, 4315 Pte W	Whalley, 3866 Pte J
Cannon, 5142 Pte C	Holt, 5443 Pte W	Porter, 5157 Pte C	Willis, 5123 Pte E
Carroll, 4940 Drum G	Houghton, 3862 Pte J	Porter, 5482 Pte J	Woods, 5489 Pte W

Mounted Infantry Detachment

Anderson, 4769 Pte J M	Bagnall, 4775 Pte T	Barker, 5184 Pte J	Cooper, 5339 Pte H
Ashmead, Cond R (att'd)	Bamber, 4305 Pte A	Cooper, 4045 Pte A	Didsbury, 4516 Pte T

Appendices

Farnworth, 4741 Pte H
Fisher, 5004 Pte C
George, 4246 Pte D
Hagger, 4625 Pte W

Hellard, 3892 Cpl E
Holmes, 4568 Pte G
Hopwood, 3705 Pte J
Morley, 4074 Pte E

Nelson, 1261 L Sgt J
Neville, 4649 Pte J
Overall, 4480 Pte G
Reed, 4152 Pte J

Tunney, 4757 Pte J T
Waring, 4740 Pte P

B Company, 1st LNLR. Location - Premier Mine

O'Brien, Capt T H
Almond, Pte W
Ansell, Col Sgt A
Ashcroft, Pte T
Atherton, Pte J
Atkinson, Pte J
Bailey, Pte R
Baker, Pte R
Beer, L Sgt F
Belfield, Pte W
Bell, Pte J
Bentley, Pte N
Blakeley, Pte J
Bowers, Pte W
Brindle, Pte W
Brown, Pte J
Brown, Pte T
Cannon, Pte C
Carroll, Drum G

Cherry, Pte S
Clare, Pte P
Cosgrove, Pte T
Craig, Pte J
Crofts, Pte T
Dillon, Pte E
Ditchfield, Pte S
Eatock, Pte W
Ellis, Pte G
Firth, Pte W
Foy, Pte J
Greary, Pte W
Green, Pte J
Green, Pte J
Gregson, Pte R
Hall, Pte S
Hall, Pte W
Hampton, Pte W
Holt, Pte W

Houghton, Pte J
Ingram, Pte H
Jamieson, Cpl G
Jones, Pte J
Knowles, Pte S
Levi, Pte W
Marsden, Sgt J
McCreary, Pte G
McKernan, Pte E
Measure, Pte G
Murphy, Pte J
Murray, Pte M
Neely, Cpl H
Nutting, Pte P
Parkins, Pte W
Pilkington, Pte W
Porter, Pte C
Porter, Pte J
Pownall, Pte J

Randall, Pte J
Redfern, Pte O
Reeves, Pte J
Rourke, Drum T
Sayers, Pte H
Slattery, L Cpl R
Smith, Pte W
Sutcliffe, Pte W
Taylor, Pte G
Tedder, Pte G
Walker, Pte G
Ward, Pte T
Wardley, Pte J
Waterhouse, L Cpl W
Whalley, Pte J
Willis, Pte E
Willoughby, Pte J
Woods, Pte

Army Service Corps

Gorle, Maj H V
Benwell, Sgt F
Edmonds, L Cpl J

Ferris, Pte W
Ford, L Cpl E
Lewis, Pte W

Noble, Dvr W H
Pratt, Pte C
Sohami, Pte J

Royal Artillery

Location - The Gardens

Chamier, Lt Col G D
Ellis, 90622 Gnr A
Gilbert, 10650 Gnr H
Gilmore, 67858 Gnr R
Gilvary, 10631 Gnr D
Greenwood, 90145 Bomb J
Jones, 17597 CSM C H

Jones, 2547 Gnr U W
Jones, 7183 Gnr W G
Jordan, 93922 Bombdr W
Kilpin, 15893 Gnr G
Land, 3770 Gnr G
Lewis, 70013 Gnr A
Lock, 3625 Bombdr E

Lofts, 7426 Bombdr G
Lonergraw, 25965 Gnr R
Maud, 13532 Gnr G
Nelson, 9088 Gnr G
Parker, 95390 Gnr T
Parry, 9706 Gnr J
Rudkin, 15465 Gnr J

Smith, 24719 Tmptr F
Swift, 97887 Gnr C
Theaker, 24401 Tmptr G
Trodd, 59807 CQS H S
Williams, 9147 Gnr J J

Location - Premier Mine Redoubt

Rynd, 2nd Lt F F
Arthurs, 4278 Gnr J
Bennett, 8926 Gnr W
Borner, 91597 Bombdr H
Butler, 7293 Gnr J
Clements, 89023 Cpl H

Drinkhill, 98126 Gnr J
Edwards, 64847 Gnr J
Farrelly, 62457 Gnr P J
Fennelly, 94126 Gnr M
Gorham, 94797 Gnr E
Johns, 96166 Gnr T

Johnson, 7577 Gnr J J
Jones, 22231 Gnr A
Keast, 3477 Gnr G
Knott, 94947 Gnr L C
Manning, 64748 Gnr H
Murphy, 9286 Gnr P

O'Neil, 9337 Bombdr A
Raynos, 79312 Sgt G H
Richardson, 6008 Bomb W
Scannell, 10835 Gnr E
Tauser, 10904 Gnr F
Vickers, 10135 Gnr S

Location - Crusher Redoubt

Close, Lt H M
Beale, 97797 Gnr T
Bullock, 74703 Gnr W
Butterfield, 6674 Gnr E
Cairns, 95635 Gnr H
Campion, 1478 Gnr W

Chamberlain, 93525 Gnr J
Cox, 1903 Gnr R
Eyre, 68853 Sgt E
Hogan, 26238 Gnr M
Hooper, 79575 Cpl T
Hunter, 7199 Gnr W

Laing, 132 Gnr C T
Marshall, 77147 Bomb F G
Mason, 7766 Gnr J
Revell, 7171 Bombdr C
Roberts, 80503 Gnr S
Smedley, 14062 Gnr A

Stenson, 93644 Gnr E
Thompson, 22071 Gnr W
Trigg, 97344 Gnr J H
Tucker, 85120 Gnr W
Wheatley, 6961 Gnr E

Location - Reservoir Redoubt

Johnston, Lt H B H
Appleford, 78670 Gnr H
Bull, 7091 Gnr C

Gard, 980 Gnr A
Gilbert, 90431 Sgt J M
Knight, 11410 Gnr J H

McGrath, 1538 Gnr J
Mills, 73894 Gnr W H
Mitchell, 94316 Gnr R

Moss, 95207 Gnr J J
Pickwell, 97526 Gnr J
Purcell, 74499 Gnr W

Kimberley Siege Account and Medal Roll

Rees, 97360 Gnr T
Sach, 94375 Gnr H
Smith, 1763 Gnr R
Thomas, 977 Gnr E
Torrington, 94004 Bombd A
Wedgbury, 37857 Sgt H F
Welsh, 8661 Gnr J
Wheatley, 98076 Gnr R
Wilkinson, 90568 Gnr H

Royal Engineers

McClintock, Lt R L
Allen, 1234 Sapr S
Archer, 2186 Sapr P
Atkins, 27010 L Cpl F
Bardin, 27688 2C G
Barton, 52 Sapr W
Bilton, 2758 Sapr L
Brennan, 2145 Dvr M
Broe, 1680 Sapr P
Butcher, 281 Sapr M
Carr, 27551 Sapr A
Clark, 20559 Cpl G
Coulter, 27395 Sapr R

Crick, 1214 Sapr H
Cullum, 27209 Sapr H
Dalziel, 2262 Sapr R
Davis, 24579 Dvr A
Dawe, 2326 Sapr S
Dester, 28374 L Cpl V
Donohoe, 22962 Sapr F
Dooley, 1259 Sapr J
Duff, 2173 Sapr D
Field, 28228 L Cpl G
Foster, 1306 Sapr J
Hackett, 28224 L Cpl K
Hackett, 29893 Sapr J

Hall, 1203 Sapr J
Hall, 26783 Sapr C
Hannell, 29805 Dvr W
Hobbs, 17297 Sgt G
Hughes, 2255 Sapr J
Hyland, 2171 Sapr L
Long, 2302 Sapr M
McDonald, 700 Sapr D
McDougall, 2178 Sapr P
McIntosh, 2190 Sapr J
McMahon, 29256 Sapr J
Moore, 1202 Sapr J
Morgan, 1660 Sapr W

Mullins, 28361 L Cpl G
Olver, 2062 Sapr W
Pearce, 2197 Sapr F
Redman, 27770 Sapr J
Reed, 27578 Sapr F
Reid, 97530 Sapr T
Ross, 29829 Dvr G
Sharp, 1147 Sapr W
Smith, 27547 L Cpl C
Stubbs, 2296 Sapr W
Togwell, 2235 Sapr A
Wilson, 29429 Sapr W

Cape Police

Headquarters Staff and Depot Mounted Branch

Robinson, Town Cmdt M B
Shutte, Capt R F
Brauns, Pte H
Campbell, A/Sgt Signaller L
Castles, Pte T
Corbett, Pte G
Cullinan, Sgt Maj J C
Edwards, Pte E H S

Fielding, Cpl W C D
Foxcroft, Pte R J
Hipwell, Pte W
Jolly, Sgt Maj J B
MacLachlan, Pte W M
Martin, Pte S E
Montleo, Pte G L
O'Connor, Pte J

Penning, Pte A W
Preston, Pte J A S
Rutherford, Pte G
Ryan, A Cpl F K
Scannell, Pte D
Schneider, Pte J M
Smith, Pte C N
Taylor, Pte J M

Walker, Pte R
Williams, Pte W
Wood, Pte F
Wooding, Pte H
Young, Pte A R

Dismounted Branch (on barrier and redoubt duties)

Lorimer, Maj S
Cowieson, Capt D
Donohoe, Lt W
Moorhead, Lt J
Alexander, Sgt D
Asquith, Pte H
Bartholemew, Sgt W
Bateman, Pte C J
Beck, QMS J
Beckett, Pte E G
Beckhilling, Pte C
Blaine, Pte H R
Bonsor, Pte M W
Brady, Pte H
Bridges, Pte A
Cameron, Sgt A
Carter, Pte T R
Crook, Pte I
Cullen, Pte G
Deacon, Pte W C
Dinwoodie, Sgt S

Donohoe, Sgt W
Egley, Pte J
Ericksen, Pte J
Falcon, Pte G
Fisher, Pte A H
Foley, Pte W P
Forshaw, Pte R
Franklin, Pte S
Gardiner, Pte C
Geldenhuis, Pte D
Gordon, Pte F
Graham, A Cpl H W
Gray, Pte W
Griffin, Pte F T
Hall, Pte C
Hanlon, Pte R
Harris, Pte W
Hearn, Sgt H A
Hicks, Pte A E
Hicks, Pte H H
Hooper, Pte F

Hynes, Pte W
Johnstone, Pte J
Kennedy, Sgt W
Kingsbury, Pte F H
Kingston, A Cpl G G
Kingston, Pte F H
Leigh, Pte J
Lock, Pte W
MacGregor, Pte F
Maguire, Sgt G
Malarkey, Pte P
Malarkey, Pte T F
Merry, Pte C
Molloy, Sgt A
Morris, Pte C J
Mulholland, Pte J
Murphy, Pte J
Neilmayer, Pte J E
Newman, Pte A
O'Brien, Pte J
Phillips, Pte F

Raath, Pte C
Ramsay, Pte F W
Rawlinson, Pte W J
Red, Pte W J
Rogers, Pte G
Ross, Pte J
Russel, Pte D
Sadler, Pte W
Scott, Sgt W H
Sharrock, A Cpl W
Sheriff, Pte J J
Smith, Pte J
Smith, Pte W J
Storer, Pte E
Swiss, Pte C W
Trueman, Pte T J
Venables, Pte A E
Walker, Sgt H C
Wardle, Pte W G J
Watson, Pte E
Wilson, Pte A

Beaconsfield (Dismounted)

Bester, Pte B J
Halling, Pte A C
Headon, Pte C F

Hennessy, Sgt P
Houston, Pte W A
Lotter, Pte M J

McCarthy, Pte J
Meldrum, Pte W
Piper, Pte P

Reabow, Pte F
White, Sgt J
Wilcox, Sgt G A

Intelligence and Detective Staff

Baxter, Pte W C F
Beatty, Pte A
Brennan, Sgt A

Brown, Pte S
Cotton, Pte H S L
Hambly, Pte W J

Hill, Pte G
Nelson, Sgt D
O'Connell, Pte T

White, Pte E

428

Appendices

7-pounder Detachment

White, Capt J T	De Smidt, Pte A	Rogers, Pte W	Thornley, Pte G
Beale, Pte R J	Dunk, Cpl C H	Schæfer, Pte F E	White, Pte F E W
Bewsher, Pte J	Fabling, Pte L M	*Scholtz, Pte C F*	Wilson, Pte G
Blasspoles, Pte A	Hills, Pte W H	Short, Pte W W	
Bowden, Pte S V	*Munro, Sgt Maj D*	St Quinton, Pte A	
Campbell, Pte H	Procter, Tmptr W	Sutherland, Pte G W	

No 1 Maxim Gun Detachment

Gregory, Pte G L	O'Neill, Cpl P L	*Waterford, Pte C S*	
Jennings, Pte H	*Smithwick, Pte M S*		

No 2 Maxim Gun Detachment

Baxter, Pte F	Gibbs, Pte E A	Moberley, Cpl D H	
Downing, Pte H K	Gore, Pte W	*Riky, Pte G R*	

No 3 Maxim Gun Detachment

Blair, Pte J C	Harding, Pte J E	Spencer, Cpl C H W	Ward, Pte F E
Dillon, Arm Pte W C	Mair, Pte J	Voules, Pte T A	Woon, Sgt E W

1st Division, Cape Mounted Police Camp

Eliott, Maj F A H; Foy, Maj L A

A Squadron

Snow, Maj A B	Dickason, L Cpl J H	Howell, Pte J H	Perry, Pte J J
Cumming, Capt J R	Dodd, Pte G H	*Hunt, Cpl G*	Poole, Pte F H
Halse, Capt G B	*Dowd, Pte M*	Jack, Pte C M	*Quinn, Pte C M*
Hayes, Capt H	*Drake, Pte W*	Jenkins, Camp SM W H	*Read, Pte F J*
Allcock, Pte N G	*Duran, Pte H J*	Jones, Pte E R	*Rix, Pte R J*
Allnutt, Cpl A	Edy, Pte N H	Kukard, Pte F F G	*Robertson, Pte G G*
Bagley, Pte J C	Elliott, Pte H J L	*Keitz, Pte O T*	Ryan, Cpl M
Bailey, Sgt H	*Emslie, Pte K G*	*Kinnear, Pte W J*	Sadler, Pte E C
Barber, Pte H S	Erasmus, Pte J C	Kitching, Pte J	Salkeld, Pte P D'O
Barton, Pte D	Finn, Pte W B	Kurton, Pte H	*Sampson, L Cpl S A*
Bayes, Pte S H	Fitzgerald, Pte E D	Lambe, QM Sgt H	*Scott, Pte J A*
Bonet, Mess Sgt G C	Fitzpatrick, Cpl E W	Lawrence, Cpl G	Seidel, Pte N O
Bovey, Sgt E	Fleischer, Pte S W	Leppan, Pte V	Spilsbury, Pte W G
Brain, Pte F S	Foster, Pte E	Leversage, Pte F	Stassen, Pte J N
Brown, Pte P	Frederick, Cpl W	Levis, Pte J G	Symington, Pte J
Burnette, Pte F	Garde, Pte T W	*Lill, Pte A E*	Taylor, Pte J F
Burrows, Cpl M	Geldenhuis, Pte J	Loder, Pte J O	Vallaney, Pte W B
Canny, L Cpl J	Gradwell, L Cpl G W	Mahon, Sgt G	Van der Merwe, Pte J J
Chadborne, Pte J A	Gratton, Pte R J	Malcolm, Pte A N	Van der Schyff, Pte L H
Clague, Pte E	Griffin, Pte M	McDonough, Pte P	Van Wyk, Pte A J
Clancy, Pte J W	Grindrod, Pte J H	McNay, Pte C G	Volkebron, Pte C H
Clinkenberry, Sgt P	*Grobellaar, Pte J H*	*Meade, Pte W*	Von Witt, Pte W J
Coetzee, Pte C J	Hammond, Pte E	Meintjies, Pte A G	Walter, Pte P G
Crosbie, Sgt P	Hansen, Pte H	Merry, Pte H C	Welsh, Pte G B
Davidson, SSM T M	Hastings, Sgt G	Misdall, Pte A H	Williams, Pte J E
Deacon, Pte E E	Hennes, Pte M C	Morrison, Cpl S	Wood, Pte W F
Deane, Pte C	Hennessy, Pte J	Mulligan, Pte J H	
Delport, Pte B	Hillier, Pte H W	Nosworthy, Pte F T	
Dennison, Pte C D	Hoskins, Pte C H	Parker, Pte A	

B Squadron

Ayliff, Maj W E	O'Brien, Capt P	*Boltmann, Pte P S*	*Campbell, Pte J*
Crawford, Capt R M	*Agnew, Pte G*	Bowles, Pte A O	Carlyle, Pte T
Colvin, Capt & QM J W	Amos, Pte E J	Bown, Pte S H	Carson, Cpl F R
Crozier, Capt M K	*Banks, Pte A J*	*Brole, Pte W E P*	Clark, Pte W
Davis, Capt W H	Bell, Pte J	*Brummer, Pte A*	Cloete, Pte H
Gerrard, Capt J H	Birks, Sgt R	*Calder, Pte V*	*Coetzee, Pte E*

429

Kimberley Siege Account and Medal Roll

Colbeck, Pte T M
Coleman, Pte W R
Cottle, Pte F W
Cowan, Pte F T
Creagh, Pte J
Davies, Pte J D
Dawson, Pte E E
de Reuck, Pte S P
Dickason, Pte R
Dickenson, Pte W
Dryden, Cpl W J
Dye, L Cpl J B
Else, Pte H
Fagan, Pte W
Fawcett, Pte A
Fivaz, Pte C F
Garrett, Pte G H
Gould, Pte B P
Grace, Pte J J
Green, Pte E R A
Greyling, Pte J C
Grobler, Pte J
Growden, Pte J
Hambly, L Cpl R

Hasenjäger, Pte A E
Hassett, Cpl P
Hatton, L Cpl H
Hayes, Pte M
Hayes, Pte P C
Hearns, L Cpl W
Henderson, Pte A E
Herbert, Pte J J
Hillstrom, Pte F
Hopewill, Pte C
Humphreys, Pte S R
Jennings, Pte A
Jennings, SS Maj S
Johnston, Pte M K
Jones, Sgt T
Jubilees, Pte J
Laing, Pte P
Leishman, Pte O S
Liebenberg, Pte J S
Lockhart, Pte H
Lubbe, Pte J J
Lucas, Sgt J J
MacKenzie, Pte R S
Maggs, L Cpl C E

Marsden, Cpl A E
Martin, Pte A W H
Maskovitz, Pte J
McDougall, Pte P R
Meere, Pte A C
Metrovich, Pte J
Mildred, Pte C
Murphy, Pte T
Narroway, Pte H G
Nell, Pte L F
Nicholas, Pte F
Okes, Pte H T
Oosthuizen, Pte J
Otto, Sgt J H
Parker, Pte R C
Peacock, Pte C W
Petersen, Pte J B
Phillips, Pte H W
Rowe, Pte E
Schley, Pte G T
Schoeman, Pte H
Shepherd, Sgt G
Smith, L Cpl L C
Smith, Pte J G

Spangenberg, Pte D F
Spangenberg, Pte J P
Sprong, Cpl J L
Stone, Pte C A
Swart, Pte M D B
Tarr, Pte G
Tee, Pte R
Tetley, Pte F J
Thompson, Pte A H
Thompson, Pte R A
Tucker, Pte A
Van Breda, Pte K
Van der Gryp, Pte F
Van Rensburg, Pte J
Wall, Pte T W J
Wheeler, Cpl H W
Whittaker, Cpl P J
Wilkie, Pte H M
Willis, Pte P
Wilson, L Cpl C D
Yates, Pte T J
Young, Pte W A

C Squadron

Berrange, Maj C A
MacGregor, Maj C F M
Fisher, Capt E M
Gillward, Capt F
Moony, Capt J H O E
Rush, Capt W W
Arundale, Pte F R
Atkins, Pte A
Attwood, Sgt A J
Ball, Sq Sgt Maj J
Beatty, Sgt J
Beckett, Pte D M
Benadie, Pte G F
Bezuidenhout, Pte G P
Bourke, Pte W P
Bovey, L Cpl H
Brady, Sq Sgt Maj G C
Brick, Pte T
Brown, Pte C
Brown, Pte H P
Burgher, Pte A P
Burgher, Pte G P
Burt, Pte F S
Carr, Pte A
Carswell, Pte I C
Clack, L Cpl G F
Cook, Pte W G
Coomer, Pte F A
Corrie, Pte J
Cousins, Pte H

Davis, Pte E
Deere, Pte R H
Donovan, Pte C F
Douglas, Pte J
Downes, Pte F T
Dye, Pte W T
Ehlers, Pte J F M S
Eliott, Pte H G
Else, Pte J G
Ewes, Cpl J A D
Farrel, Pte J H
Ferreira, Pte C J
Fielding, L Cpl R C
Goldswain, Sgt C
Gow, Pte J
Graves, Pte A S
Halpin, L Cpl J
Hanekom, Pte D J T
Hannibal, L Cpl H
Hastie, Pte J A
Helfrich, Pte G
Henderson, Pte F S
Henley, Pte F J
Holland, Pte J R
Holliday, Cpl W
Holloway, Pte E D
Hooper, Cpl D H
Humbly, Pte A
Jacobs, Pte W D
Jamieson, Pte C

Jansen, Pte J T
Judge, Pte E
Keen, Pte W G
Kellett, Cpl T Y
Leslie, Pte J D
Lewis, Pte G de B
McIntosh, Sgt E M
Maloney, Pte J
Mathieson, Pte G R
Matthews, Cpl J
McKinley, Sgt F D
McLennan, L Cpl W J
Mey, Pte C
Mitcham, Pte P H
Moorcroft, Pte G
Mostert, Pte G
Munro, Pte S C
Naude, Pte G J
Oakes, Pte F H A
O'Dell, Pte D
Oosthuizen, Pte J A
Orpen, Pte C
Packet, Pte W
Pinnock, Pte R
Raath, Pte D J P
Ralph, Sgt J
Rathbone, Pte G H
Reed, L Cpl T E
Reeland, Pte C J
Reynolds, Pte W H

Schroeder, Pte E A
Seed, Pte F H
Shaw, Pte T
Shepherd, Pte J H
Simpson, Pte F D
Skinner, Pte R L
Smith, Pte W B
Smith, Sgt G
Stanford, Pte E R
Stolz, Pte J J
Stouffer, Pte W H
Stranch, Pte L
Sweeney, Pte A
Taylor, Pte W H C
Tee, Pte A E
Toke, Pte G W
Turner, Pte D
Venter, Pte J P
Venter, Pte P J
Villiers, Pte J H S de
Voekins, L Cpl H J
Von Buddenbock, Pte W
Von der Venter, Pte J L
Wagenaar, Pte J C
Wallace, Pte E H
Warr, Pte H
Watermeyer, Sgt F E
Wilson, Pte R
Wilson, Pte R

Special Location Police, O'Molony, Lt S, commanding
Location - Kimberley

Africa, Pte J
Batting, Sgt G
Calvert, Pte J
Charles, Pte M
Crittel, Sgt A

De Jong, Pte R
Du Plessis, Pte J
Fick, Pte F
Foster, Pte A
Fredericks, Pte C

Heuvel, Pte C
Lalako, Pte F
Leone, Pte O
Martin, Pte A
Martin, Pte G

Peterson, Pte A
Price, Pte T
Stricker, Pte J
Thomas, Pte G
Walker, Pte G

Location - Beaconsfield

Appendices

Abrahams, Pte J	*Johnstone, Pte T*	*Munick, Pte H*	*Stollenkamp, Pte A*
Appol, Pte P	*Joshua, Pte J*	*Oliver, Pte D*	*Sullivan, Pte J*
Bautrey, Pte J	*Joubert, Pte F*	*Paulse, Pte P*	*Tobin, Pte A*
Booth, Pte W	*Karstem, Pte M*	*Sampson, Pte C*	*Tonke, Pte W*
Carls, Pte P	*Knight, Sgt C*	*Simpson, Pte J*	*Waters, Pte J*
De Vos, Pte W	*McArthur, Sgt J*	*Smith, Pte A*	*Williams, Pte C*
Gray, Sgt G	*McBride, Pte R*	*Stollenkamp, Pte P*	*Williams, Pte T F*

Kimberley Regiment of Volunteers

Rhodes, Hon Col C J	Braine, Lt W	Duncan, Pipe Maj W G	McDonald, Sgt Inst J L
Finlayson, Lt Col R A	Cramp, Lt R S	Ferraro, Sgt Inst E T	Monk, Sgt Cook W A
Black, Maj A O	Harrison, Lt F	Freeman, CSM J T	Petrie, CSM J
Rodger, Maj T H	Hollingworth, Lt R H	Freeman, Sgt Sadl W L	Rynbnikar, Bandmst G
Bodley, Capt J H	Howie, Lt C	Fyvie, CSM L C	Selling, Sgt Inst W G
Bridge, Capt J M	Martin, Lt A H	Glover, Band Sgt F W	Smith, Drum Maj A F
Church, Capt G	Matthews, Lt T H	Goodwin, Sgt Farr A	Smith, Pay Sgt W H
Duirs, Capt M	Salaman, Lt S	Hayes, Band Sgt W	Thompson, CSM W J
Green, Capt A J	Smith, Lt H W	Haygarth, SM Tlr H	Thwaites, Bugl Maj A H
Humphrys, Capt E T	Tillemans, Lt A A	Horn, Arm Sgt F	Tozer, RSM E E M
Shackleton, Capt C C	Wilcox, Lt W J	Keogan, CSM P	Tutt, SM Tlr W B
Waldek, Capt TO S P	Smith, Surg Maj J A J	Macfarlane, OR Sgt D K	Wooding, CSM G
Wright, Capt A J	Davie, SSIG R T	McArthur, Sgt Inst R	

In addition to these members of the regiment, there are a further 533 NCOs and men.

Diamond Fields Artillery

Location – Botanical Gardens

May, Maj T J	Faulkner, Lt T J	Ortlepp, Surg Lt A J	Cramp, QM HT
White, Capt	Cramp, Lt R S	Moss, BSM A	Needhan, Farr Sgt G

In addition, there are 105 NCOs and men.

De Beers Maxim Battery

Headquarters - Botanical Gardens

Adams, Dvr W T	Glanville, Dvr G	*Jeffrey, Cpl G*	Stanley, Gnr J
Akenhead, BQMS A	Gleave, Gnr J	*Leans, Sgt W*	Wilkins, Dvr H J
Bower, Dvr W	Glover, Dvr E	Osborne, BSM J P	Winteridge, Dvr J
Domper, Dvr C	Howell, Dvr J R	Skuse, Dvr W	

Headquarters and Searchlight

Beer, Gnr H	Foules, Sgt C	Henderson, Gnr R
Bunn, Cpl D	Hardman, Gnr W	

Reservoir Redoubt

Glennie, Sgt J T	Hardware, Gnr W	Hines, Gnr W	McTavish, Cpl D

Crusher Redoubt

Bissett, Gnr W	Gilmore, Gnr G	Hone, Cpl W

Armoured Train

Adcock, Cpl H W A	Bray, Cpl W J	Duke, Cpl H	Mickle, Sgt W
Armstrong, Cpl J	Buchannan, Cpl T	Jagger, Cpl T J	Poole, Cpl A W

Kimberley Light Horse

437 officers, NCOs and men are listed.

Kimberley Siege Account and Medal Roll

Town Guard

Pickerings Redoubt No.1

Pickering, Capt W

Tidd-Pratt, Capt S	Hogg, Lt J C	Lyon, QMS D M	
Webster, Lt R	Kirsten, Bugler C J G	Marshall, OR Clerk Walker	

No I Section, C Company

Webbstock, Lt H J	Freislich, Pte H W	Long, Pte W J	Tomlin, Pte H
Collard, Cpl T J	Gallow, Pte A H	Parker, Pte A	Townsend, Desp Rider G H
Croft, Pte C T	Innes, Pte W A	Pinnock, Sgt G	
Everill, Pte S F H	Jackson, Sgt G W	Power, Pte P T	
Fishpool, Pte J	King, Pte W S	Snell, Pte W	

No II Section, C Company

Stewart, Lt J	Harford, Pte C J	Kenniford, Pte W J	Pearson, Pte A
Bellingham, Pte O B C	Hawkins, Pte F D	Kenny, Col Sgt E	Prentice, Pte J
Blue, Pte C	Henry, Pte J	Kingston, Pte P A	Walsh, Pte T
Burnard, Cpl J A	Innes, Sgt J D	Maconachie, Pte W R	West, Pte E G
Egan, Pte M W	Johnston, Pte W	Oostermeyer, Pte J J	Whitter, Pte W

No III Section, C Company

Orr, Lt J	Holmes, Pte L S	Morse, Sgt F A	Truter, Pte J J
Bullen, Pte H	Kelly, Pte J J	Sprong, Pte J R	*Van Der Hayden, Pte H F*
Cundill, Pte J W	Markgraaff, Pte A	Sprong, Pte P D	Wilson, Cpl G
Dowrick, Pte A	McEwen, Pte D	Switzer, Pte R E	Wyngaard, Pte J J
Hinks, Pte C G	Meeks, Pte W	Thompson, Pte W	

Pickerings Redoubt No 2

No II Section, C Company

McHardy, Lt W	Eliott, Pte G A	Parker, Pte E	Sutherland, Pte J
Anderson, Pte G	Fletcher, Pte A C	Ross, Cpl G C	Topp, Pte J B
Armstrong, Pte W	Gibbs, Pte J	Rowlands, Pte H	Uren, Pte W M
Barnes, Pte H	Halloran, Pte J J	Ryan, Pte J	Ward, Pte H
Broderick, Pte M I	Jackson, Pte C H	Sharpe, Pte E J	Warren, Pte J W
Clarke, Sgt J	Johnson, Pte C W	*Smith, Pte A de S*	
Cramond, Pte A	Leddy, Pte H W	Sprong, Pte J R	

No IV Section, C Company

Sinclair, Lt D K	Ellis, Pte C	Hocking, Pte W J H	Rinkquest, Pte D G
Bennett, Pte J D	Evert, Pte W J	Holman, Pte T C	Siebert, Pte James
Boyd, Sgt R	Frond, Pte D	Jessiman, Pte W	Siebert, Pte John
Burton, Pte F H	Fryar, Pte J	*King, Pte W*	Sinclair, Pte H M L
Davidson, Cpl J	Guild, Pte F R	*Marten, Pte H W C*	White, Pte W J
Eales, Pte W J	Hobson, Pte J	Neilson, Pte J C	Whitter, Pte T R

No 3 Redoubt (8 and 9 Machine)

Dallas, Capt S

No 1 Section, B2 Company

Todd, Lt C W	Howell, Cpl E T	Pascual, Pte E	Stuart, Pte D
Bird, Pte J	Jennings, Pte J	Pickering, Pte F	Timm, Pte R
Boult, Pte S E	King, Pte G F	Plank, Pte G	White, Pte P
Bryant, Dispatch Rider J	Marnitz, Pte H J	Scott, Pte C J	Wilson, Pte A C
Carnegy, Pte P	McDonald, Pte F	Sinclair, Pte J	
Cleator, Pte R J	*McGregor, Pte J*	Snell, Pte T	
Ebdon, Pte A	Pappin, Sgt H	Stephens, Pte J G	

432

No II Section, B2 Company

Chester, Lt F
Armstrong, Pte J
Berryman, Pte J
Campbell, Pte A
Carey, Pte C
Condell, Pte R

Heneke, Pte P
Hooper, Pte W E
Kenny, Pte M
Leckie, Pte J A
Long, Pte J
May, Sgt A J

McCloskey, Pte A
McIvor, Pte J
McNeil, Pte J
Pryra, Pte B
Robson, Cpl P
Roslee, Pte W

Switzer, Pte H A
Van der Heyden, Pte C
Whitworth, Pte A
Wilding, Pte J

No III Section, F Company

Zeigenbein, Lt H A
Abrahamse, Pte C J
Adams, Pte J
Cayford, Pte F
Clarke, Pte R J E
Flack, Pte E
Giles, Pte J G
Glover, Pte W

Howe, Pte H
Lawrence, Pte H J
Longcake, Pte N W
Lown, Pte D E
Mackintosh, Pte J
Marwick, Pte J
Murray, Pte J
Porter, Pte C

Raper, Pte J
Sealey, Pte W J
Shepherd, Pte R A
Stanner, Pte W G S
Stewart, Pte R
Tinson, Pte J B
Topper, Pte H P
Venables, Pte W E

Warder, Cpl R
Watts, Pte J L
White, Sgt S
Wright, Pte T W
Zeigenbein, Pte H A

B Line of defence
(Most of these men are a duplicate of the three sections already listed for No 3 Redoubt)

Tabuteau, Capt H
Kearns, Lt F
Todd, Lt C W
Ziegenbein, Lt H A
Abrahamse, Pte C J
Adams, Pte J
Armstrong, L Cpl J
Berryman, Pte J
Bird, Pte J
Boult, Pte T
Bryant, Despatch Rider P J
Campbell, Pte A
Carey, L Cpl C
Carnegy, Pte P
Cayford, Pte F
Clarke, Pte R J E
Cleator, Pte R J
Condell, Pte R
Eatenlowe, (Amb) Pte F V
Ebdon, Pte A
Everington, Pte J
Floyd, Pte E
Giles, Pte

Glover, Sgt W
Heneke, Pte P
Hillman, Pte J
Hooper, Pte W E
Howe, Pte H
Howell, Cpl E T
James, Pte J
Jennings, Pte J
Jolly, Pte J
Kenny, Pte M
King, Pte G F
Law, Pte C
Lawrence, Pte H J
Leckie, Pte J A
Longcake, Pte N W
Lowden, Pte H
Lown, Cpl D E
Mackintosh, Pte J
Marnitz, Pte H J
Marwick, Pte J
McCloskey, Pte A
McDonald, Pte D
McDonald, QMS F

McGregor, Pte J
McIvor, Pte J
McNeil, Pte J
Murray, Pte J
Nicholls, Pte J
Pappin, Sgt H
Park, Pte J
Pascual, Pte E
Plank, Pte G
Porter, Pte C
Pryra, Pte B
Raper, Pte J
Robson, Cpl P
Roslee, Pte W
Rowe, Pte J
Scheibe, Pte J
Scott, Pte C J
Sealey, Pte W J
Shepherd, Pte R A
Snell, Pte F
Stanner, Pte W G S
Stephens, L Cpl J G
Statzkowski, Pte C

Stewart, Pte R
Stuart, Pte D
Sullivan, Pte J
Switzer, Pte H A
Timm, Pte R
Tinson, Sgt J B
Topper, Pte H P
Trembath, Pte R
Van der Heyden, Pte C
Venables, Pte W E
Warder, Sgt R
Watts, Pte J L
White, Col Sgt W
White, Pte P
Whitworth, Pte A
Wilding, Pte J
Wilkins, (Amb) Pte F E
Willock, Pte J
Wilson, Pte A C
Wright, Pte T W

Redoubt No 4 (No 1 Machine De Beers)

B Company

Pim, Capt H; Reid, QM Sgt W

Section I

Watson, Lt J W
Berry, Pte J
Dyason, Pte J
Elliot, Pte G C
Fry, Pte H W

Gibson, Pte R J
Gibson, Pte R T
Johns, Cpl H T
Lawrence, Pte D
Lawrence, Pte W

May, Pte W
Taylor, Pte A
Taylor, Pte T N
Timmann, Pte W
Vicary, Pte A

Webber, Pte W
Webber, Pte W J
Weir, Pte G
Wilkinson, Pte J
Worrall, Sgt W

Section II

Townsend, Lt G
Alexander, Pte J
Cundill, Pte A E
Hopley, Pte C E
Irving, Pte R
Kirkman, Pte W

Megaw, Pte T
Marshall, Pte H
McEwen, Pte J W
McLaren, Cpl G A
McLoughlin, Sgt M
Morton, Pte R

Moult, Pte T M
Murdoch, Pte W
Nicholson, Pte J R
O'Regan, Pte M
Smith, Pte A F
Stewart, Pte D

Strachan, Pte J
Sutton, Pte E C
Swan, Pte J A
Webb, Pte H J

433

Kimberley Siege Account and Medal Roll

Section III

Tabuteau, Lt H
Corrigan, Pte W
Coxen, Pte W C
Harris, Sgt W
Hasler, Pte G

Hockey, Pte C H
Lee, Pte G T
Leonard, Pte E
McDonald, Pte W H
McKinnon, Pte D

Pringle, Pte J
Shepherd, Pte W
Short, Pte J
Stevens, Pte J
Stewart, Pte S A

Veale, Pte C H
Vicary, Pte W A
Vincent, Cpl E
Wolstenholme, Pte H

Section IV

Harris, Lt L W H
Baker, Pte L
Berry, Pte J
Boyd, Pte J H
Carroll, Pte C
Cass, Pte H

Croft, Pte J H
Flemming, Pte J
Greenless, Pte J
Hendry, Pte G S
Hobson, Pte W S
Jenkins, Pte E C

Jenkins, Pte E
Ladyson, Pte W
Maloney, Pte C
Meiklejohns, Pte M
Palmer, Sgt G
Patrick, Pte H

Russell, Pte J P
Searle, Cpl R
Van Eyssen, Pte H

Mostert's Redoubt

F Company

Mosely, Capt E H
Grieves, Col Sgt R

Stewart, QMS W M
Watters, QMS C J

Watts, Issuer Geo

Section I

Carstairs Rogers, Lt F
Anderson, Pte J E
Aplin, Pte H H
Carr, Pte C
Clark, Pte J
Crowther, Pte A

Cummings, Cpl J
Davidson, Pte D
Gibbs, Pte J
Hill, Pte P J
Johnston, Pte M A
Kemp, Pte J M

Knowles, Pte W
Lean, Pte J J
Lee, Pte J
Motherwell, Sgt D
Pearson, Pte L
Quincey, Pte E B

Rand, L Cpl E J
Raper, Pte G A
Rearden, Pte J
Sweeney, Pte W
Upstill, Pte P
Wightman, Pte F

Section II

Harris, Lt W S
Ainsley, Pte G
Allison, Cpl H A
Deith, Pte G
Grimmer, L Cpl H A
Hauptfleish, Pte J

Howie, Pte T S
Humphreys, Pte T
Hutchins, Sgt F
Innes, Pte
Kennedy, Pte P
Lee, Pte R M

Mends, Pte J G
Nicolson, Pte M N
Petrie, Pte R L
RoyL, Pte W H
Rugen, Pte A
Saunders, Pte G

Skelden, Pte P
Taylor, Pte W
Wells, Pte E T
Williams, Pte D L

Section IV

Penny, Lt E A
Abrahams, Pte J
Brown, Pte
Busst, Cpl A
Carruthers, Pte
Graham, Pte E

Gunning, Pte E R
Harrison, Pte A J
Harrison, Pte A T
Harvey, Pte J
Hill, L Cpl J
Jackson, Pte J W

Johnstone, Pte J
Kendall, Pte A
Lezard, Pte H
Lezard, Pte L F
Long, Pte C F
Main, Sgt W

Nurton, Pte W H
Rayner, Pte A E
Swift, Pte H
Wallace, Pte C

No 6 Redoubt

Hornby, Capt W
Channer, Lt R
Hayston, Lt W
Nicholson, Lt N
Waldek, Lt P
Alexander, Cpl W
Alexander, Pte F
Allisse, Pte J
Angwin, Pte A
Barnes, Pte N
Barnes, Pte W
Barrass, Pte James
Barrass, Pte Jno
Batten, Pte G
Bellas, Pte E

Bowes, Pte T
Bredenkamp, Pte M
Buckley, Pte J W
Clemo, Pte F
Close, Pte J
Cook, Pte L
Cox, Pte J
Cross, Pte W
Davidson, Pte E
De Melker, Pte J R
Dennis, Pte R
Dixon, Pte F
Dixon, Pte G
Dobson, Cpl J E
Dunstan, Pte W

Ede, Pte W
Edwards, Pte B
Ellis, Pte J
Ellis, Pte W H
Everington, Pte A
Ewing, Pte P
Folley, Pte G
Foster, Pte W B
Freel, Pte J
Gartrell, Pte J
Giles, Pte J G
Gouldie, Pte J
Gouldie, Pte W H
Graham, Col Sgt T
Grigg, Pte A

Hardman, Pte J W
Harvey, Pte G
Haynes, Pte E
Hickman, Pte W
Hocking, Pte J
Hodgson, Pte T
Horn, Pte J
Hurst, Pte J
Ivison, Pte R
James, Pte J H
Jenkins, Pte W P
Lovenson, Pte J
Lowden, Pte J H
Lowden, Pte T
Mahoney, Pte M

434

Marnitz, Bugler G
McConochi, Pte D
McDonald, Pte G
Mitchell, Pte A
Mitchell, Sgt D
Moore, Cpl B
Mulcaster, QMS W W
Napier, Pte W
Nelson, Cpl W
Nichol, Pte W
Nicholas, Pte R G
Nicholls, Pte R J
Nicholls, Pte T

Nicholls, Pte W J
Nixon, Pte J
Noonan, Pte I J
Oats, Pte J
O'Brien, Pte T
Park, Pte E
Polworth, Pte W
Poulton, Pte C
Prince, Pte E
Prince, Pte J
Quaile, Pte W
Richards, Pte J P
Rogers, Pte T

Rowe, Pte A
Rowe, Pte H
Rowe, Pte J
Rundle, Pte C
Sanders, Pte W A
Sefton, Sgt T
Shepherd, Pte R
Small, Pte J J
Smith, Pte F
Spence, Pte A
Spence, Pte N
Sullivan, Sgt P
Taylor, Issuer C

Tippett, Pte W H
Tregonning, Pte H
Van Blerk, Pte C
Van Blerk, Pte C H
Veale, Pte P H
Waddington, Sgt J
Walker, Clerk T
Walker, Pte T W
Whitburn, Pte W
Young, Pte J T

Civil Service Redoubt

Wright, Lt W G
Adamson, Pte G D
Carmichael, Pte W
Coller, Pte F W
Day, Pte E
Eadie, Sgt D
Gardiner, Pte T J G

Gill, Pte L W J
Gillett, Pte J L
Hudson, Pte
Keytal, Pte H B
Mallett, Pte
Metelerkamp, Pte F W
Morley, Pte G H

Paterson, Pte R C
Radloff, Pte J C
Reid, Pte E J A
Shand, Pte W B
Shaw, Pte B
Strong, Pte W
Swan, Pte R

Tennant, Pte J
Thomas, Pte
Tidmarsh, Pte J F
Tinley, Cpl E
Tuck, Pte F L

Otto's Kopje

Otto's Kopje Scouts

Dunbar, Capt J B
Damant, Lt F H
Harford, Lt C J
Anderson, Tpr
Arnold, Tpr A D
Barber, Tpr C M
Bayne, Tpr H P
Berry, Tpr
Brady, Tpr
Busby, Tpr H
Byrne, Tpr J F
Chaplin, Tpr G S

Chapin, Tpr C H
Collins, Tpr T
Creed, Tpr H
Davidson, Tpr J F
Duke, Tpr H P
Giddes, Tpr
Glover, Paymtr E
Gordon, QMS J E
Hartley, Cpl D R
Hartley, Sgt J W
Hartz, Tpr
Hay, Tpr H W

Hayes, Tpr C
Hodgkins, Tpr
Hopkins, Tpr D
Johnston, Sgt W P
Jones, Sgt
Jubilee, Tpr
Kallenborn, Tpr J B
Kilroe, Tpr R
King, Cpl
Lord, Tpr E S
Martin, Tpr J
Matheus, Cpl

McArthy, Tpr
Pierson, Tpr
Sampson, Tpr A W
Scott, Troop Sgt Maj
Stone, Tpr W A
Sutherland, Tpr J
Tarrant, Tpr
Trembath, Tpr J
Van Musik, Tpr S
White, Tpr C W J
Williams, Tpr
Zeedeberg, Tpr W

Otto's Kopje Company

Chapman, Capt W E
Byrne, J F
Drury, D J
Geddes, W
Gilbert, J
Glover, Evelyn
Gordon, J E
Gunders, J

Hannam, W H
Hart, O C
Hartley, D R
Hartley, J W
Haupt, R
Hutchinson, A T
Kallenborn, J B
Lockhart, H T

Martin, J
Meiring, G
Mitchell, J
Nabal, D C
O'Mara, J
Perks, C E
Pucker, S
Reynhardt, A

Russell, J
Halstead, S
Staunton, G H
Stewart, J
Stewart, M
Vass, H
Ward, Percy
Wright, G C

Royal Artillery

Beale, Gnr T
Butterfield, Gnr E
Campion, Gnr W

Eyre, SM Instructor E
Laing, Gnr C T
Revel, Bombdr C

Roberts, Gnr S
Smedley, Gnr A
Thompson, Gnr W

Cape Police

Campbell, Tpr H
Dunk, Cpl C H

Schaefer, Tpr F E
Shortt, Tpr

St Quinton, Tpr A
Stewart, Tpr

Whyte, Cpl
Woon, Sgt Maj E W

Maxim

Adams, Gnr W T

Bissett, Gnr W

Hone, Cpl W

Kimberley Siege Account and Medal Roll

Army Medical Corps

Armstrong, Bearer	*Bartholomew, Bearer T*	Fisher, Bearer J A	Lezard, Bearer J

Cycle Corps

A Company

Angel, Capt T L	Curgenven, Pte B	Hobson, Pte J (Jnr)	Reid, Sgt J L
Eliot, Lt A E	*Davies, Pte D*	Hobson, Pte J A	*Reynolds, Pte M*
McDonald, Lt H	Dickens, Pte J	Jarvis, Pte R	Reynolds, Pte N
Rowland, Lt A	Dixon, Pte H	Kearns, Pte C	Richardson, Cpl J
Smith, Lt D W	Dodd, Pte W	Keers, Pte R	Robertson, Pte A
Solomon, Lt R	Dold, Pte C	Kelly, Cpl E	Robertson, Pte J
Addison, Pte H	Drysdale, Cpl G	Kelly, Pte F	Rose, Sgt H
Archibald, Pte P	Eddy, Pte W	Kelly, Pte J	Russell, Sgt J
Boscombe, Pte M	Estment, Pte E W	Kimble, Pte M	Shepherd, Pte J
Bourhill, Pte R	Etherington, Pte E W H	*Landison, Sgt C*	Sneddon, Pte D
Brophy, Pte R	Evert, Pte G	Litkie, Pte C	Solomon, Clerk E
Bryant, Pte J	Farquhar, Pte W	Maclachlan, Sgt J	Solomon, Pte B
Bush, Pte F	Gallow, Pte J	Markgraaff, Pte G	Spence, Pte J E
Bush, Pte R	Gardner, Pte G	Marvell, Pte H	Stack, Cpl G
Byrne, Pte J	Good, Pte W A	Mathews, Pte J	Sterley, Pte W
Campbell, Pte I	Gore, Pte R	McCarthy, Pte D	Sutton, Col Sgt H
Cato, Pte J	Greenway, Pte J	McKay, Pte G G	Trevithick, Pte A
Cawood, Pte R H	Griffiths, Pte E	McLean, Pte D	Van Eyssen, Pte F
Channer, Pte E W	Hammond, Pte G	Mulder, Pte M	Walker, Pte H P
Chapman, Pte G	Harrison, Pte J H	Munford, Pte G	Warner, Pte E A
Charles, Pte W	Harvett, Pte A	Nicholls, Pte D J	*Wilson, Pte J*
Cornwall, Pte J	Hemsworth, Cpl H	Nicholson, Pte A	Windsor, Pte D
Crabtree, Pte S	Hemsworth, Pte F	Parker, Pte R	Wolstenholme, Pte H
Craven, Pte L S	Henry, Pte S	Powell, QMS H	Wright, Pte A J
Crawford, Pte R	Hinks, Pte O W	Rattham, Pte W	Wright, Pte E H

No 1 Company, Medical Corps

C Section

Drew, Capt G B	Elliott, Pte J	Middleton, Pte J	Sandham, Cpl R
Wilkins, Lt A	Hayston, Sgt John	Murray, Pte G	Shillaw, Pte C
Bennetto, Pte J	Leck, Pte J	Richardson, Pte J	Woodlands, Cyclist H
Brown, Pte M	Leck, Pte W	Rigg, Cpl J	

D Section

Bugler, Pte J	Foster, Pte J	McCartney, Cpl G	*Smith, Pte W*
Carlyon, Pte C	Hayston, Sgt Jos	Polworth, Pte R	Thompson, Cyclist J
Early, Pte W	Holton, Sgt Maj H	Saundry, Cpl J	Tippett, Pte H

F Section

Cronin, Cpl A M	Kalkschmidt, Pte H	Montgomery, Pte J	Smith, Pte T F
Indge, Cyclist W J	Kearns, Sgt B C	O'Brien, Pte B	*Swords, Pte G*
James, Pte R C	Mackay, Pte H C	Rhodocanachi, Pte G	Whitehead, Cpl A R

Rontgen Ray Operators at the Hospital

Hancox, F H	*McCracken, W*

Kimberley Mine Ambulance Company

Cruichshank, Capt Alex	Raynham, Pte E F	Taylor, Cpl D C
Hornby, Sgt J H	Stephens, Cyclist P	

Section with Mounted Forces

Abbott, Co Sgt Maj H J	Blakemore, Pte J M	English, Sgt J T	Hardy, Pte Geo
Beeman, Pte T J	De Villiers, Pte H	Gluyas, Pte J	Hunt, Pte G

Appendices

Miles, Pte F E
Robins, Pte F

Thomas, Pte J A
Watts, Pte Geo

Woodruff, Cpl C

A Section

Anderson, Pte J A
Armstrong, Cpl H G
Barnes, Cpl G W
Bartholomew, Pte H

Botha, Pte C C
Fisher, Pte J A
Lezard, Pte J
Luxon, Pte T H

MacBeath, Pte J W
Nelson, Pte R D
Pyall, Pte S P
Ralph, Pte J

Scott, Pte A
Snape, Pte W
Street, Pte S C

B Section

Bodley, Pte P
Coxwell, Cpl P D
Dacres, Pte T M
Davis, Pte A

Dixon, Pte R
Eatonlowe, Pte F A St V
Geyer, Pte W
Hauptfleisch, Pte G S

Marriott, Cyclist C E
Mellett, Pte T B
Quayle, Pte T
Smith, Sgt G

Spooner, Pte H
Wilkins, Pte F E

E Section

Blakemore, Cpl A
Cilliers, Pte J
Fairgrieve, Pte R
Hansen, Pte M P

Heale, Pte J
Hendrikz, Pte L
Johnson, Pte A
Law, Pte E G

Meyer, Pte E
Odendaal, Pte D C
Pope, Pte A E
Rigg, Cyclist W J

Thompson, Pte J
Turner, Pte C

Food Supply Staff

Birt, Controller Lt A G
Amm, Assistant Richd
Apsey, Assistant H
Beet, Assistant George
Briscoe, Assistant F
Brown, Assistant H A
Cahill, Issuer J H

Currey, Issuer C C
Eland, Assistant A
Ellison, Issuer J W
Fletchar, Assistant J
Heubner, Assistant C
Hudson, Assistant H W
King, Issuer T A

Liebenberg, Assistant W J
Lodge, Issuer W A
Millar, Assistant W
Nothard, Assistant T
Richardson, Clerk S
Roberts, Assistant T A L
Robinson, Scrutineer A M

Sheppard, Issuer Ernst
Smuts, Assistant H M
Sutherland, Messenger W
Trevor-Smith, Assistant C
Truter, Assistant D
Wedderburn, Issuer G
Wyatt, Clerk A A

No 2 Schmidt's Breastwork

No 1 Permanant Guard

Ellis, Capt G K
Poole, Lt W F
Rawson, Lt T G
Banks, Pte H
Barlow, Sgt Maj W J
Batting, Pte F C
Benson, Sgt O P
Berrier, Pte T
Bock, Cpl R C
Bowness, Pte J
Brill, Pte F G
Brown, Pte C H
Brown, Pte C
Button, QMS A
Campbell, Pte G
Chapin, Pte C H
Charlton, Pte E
Clark, Pte C
Cole, Pte A
Condon, Pte P
Crowther, Pte C F
Daisley, Pte W
De Lacey, Pte J M
Delamere, Pte E
Denvers, Pte H J
Dickson, L Cpl J
Dold, Pte J H
Doyle, Pte D

Duff, Pte R
Eilbeck, Pte W
Farren, Pte J
Forsyth, L Cpl D
Foster, Pte W B
Friend, Sgt F
Goldie, Pte J
Goldie, Pte R
Grieves, Pte W
Halverson, Pte C
Harding, Pte Jas
Harding, Pte John
Harvey, Pte G
Hatcher, Pte W
Henderson, Pte J A
Hocking, Pte W
Hodgson, Pte J
Howard, Cpl Martin
Irving, Pte C E J
Jackson, Pte W
James, Pte Henry
Jamieson, Pte W
Jeffrey, Pte C
Johns, Pte T
Joice, Pte H
Kent, Pte C L
Kideon, Pte J
Kideon, Pte W

Kilroe, Pte G
King, Pte R
Krine, Pte T S
Larney, Pte J
Law, Pte A
Leach, Pte B W
Lyle, Pte J
Mason, Bugler J F
McCaffery, Pte T
McDonald, Pte A R
McQueen, Pte W
Miller, Pte W D
Montgomery, L Cpl J B
Montgomery, Pte G
Montgomery, Pte J
Oates, Pte J
Osner, Cpl W
Parkin, Orderly Rm Sgt D C
Parkin, Pte E D
Patterson, Pte G
Peat, Pte W H
Phillips, Cpl B
Phillipson, L Cpl J A
Pomeroy, Pte T C
Porter, Pte H J
Raaff, Sgt T H
Rafferty, Pte J
Ratcliffe, L Cpl J

Ring, Pte G
Roberts, Pte J H
Robertson, Pte T
Rook, Pte W
Rowe, Pte W
Sandham, Pte J
Southward, Pte I
Sparkes, Pte W
Strong, Sgt P
Taylor, L Cpl J
Taylor, Pte G W
Taylor, Pte W J
Thomas, Pte W
Thompson, Pte A W
Treadwell, L Cpl W
Tretheway, Pte Jos
Turner, Pte E
Vialoux, Pte Alf
Watson, Pte G
Wheatman, Cpl W
Whitehorn, Pte J A
Williams, Pte H
Williams, Pte T
Wright, Pte T
Yule, Pte C
Zeederberg, Pte W

437

Kimberley Siege Account and Medal Roll

No 3 Redoubt

Permanant Guard
No 2 Company

Blum, Capt A	Franklin, Pte J J	Keddie, Pte A C	Skrine, Pte T
Nettelton, Lt T	Garner, Pte F	Kilroe, Pte T	Stenson, Cpl W
Bartho, Pte J P	Gilling, Pte G W	Kilroe, QMS Sgt R	Stewart, Pte J K
Bottley, Pte G	Gordon, Pte W	Kingwell, Pte H J	Stone-Raper, Sgt R J
Bushell, Pte B E	Granger, Pte R	Lewis, Pte C	Stratford, Pte J A
Clark, Pte R	Hawley, Pte C T	Maile, Pte P R	Stuart, Pte J
Dodds, Pte J C	Hocking, Pte N H	Marsh, Pte W G	Summers, Cpl A
Donaldson, Cpl J	Holman, Pte J	Massey, L Cpl W	Tanner, Pte A
Drake, Pte P E	*Hughes, Pte R*	Meadows, Pte J	*Thomas, Pte J*
Duck, Pte J	Jameson, Pte H	Miles, Pte J W	Turner, Pte H R
Dyer, Pte C	Jameson, Pte T R	Millar, Sgt E J	Ward, Pte P R
Emanuel, Pte H	Jebb, Pte A C	Nelson, Pte W G	Whitehead, Pte J G
Finch, Col Sgt G	Jessett, Sgt G	Partridge, L Cpl J	Wilkins, Pte A
Forbes, Pte J M	Judd, Pte G M	Roberts, Pte W	Wiseman, Pte H

Belgravia Fort, Belgravia Mine

"Kimberley Buffs", 5th Division
Mandy, Capt Frank

Section I

Coghlan, Lt J J	Hayston, Pte W	Olds, Pte H F	Sunde, Pte K
Aaronson, Pte M M	Howard, Pte H W	Philip, Pte G H	*Sutherland, Pte A*
Brink, Pte A	Kershaw, Pte C	Quentrall, Pte T	Trevor-Smith, Pte C W
Byrne, Pte J F	Lawn, Pte J G	Ramsay, Pte A	Tyson, Pte T G
Farquhar, Cpl J	Lawrance, Pte W	Ricketts, Pte A W	Vyall, Pte G H
Ford, Pte H F	Lineham, Pte T G	Salisbury, Pte P	Wright, L Cpl O D
Fraser, Pte J L	Lynch, Pte F	Salmon, Pte G H	
Grassie, Pte P	Moir, Sgt J	Stokes, Pte S	

Section II

Stead, Lt B	Davies, Pte J E M	Hartley, Pte J	Oliver, Pte H A
Amm, Pte R G	Deary, Pte P	Henderson, Sgt D H	Reyersbach, Pte L
Bennie, Pte A	Diederich, Pte H W	Jones, Pte T L	Skelding, Pte R A
Bourhill, Pte H	Ford, Pte J E	Kellett, Pte W	Smith, Cpl J J
Bradford, Pte W K	Frames, Pte L G	MacGill, Pte D	Stonnill, Pte R E
Clark, Col Sgt H E	Gardiner, Pte F J	Mendelssohn, Pte I	Sutherland, Pte G W
Compton, Pte G W	Gasson, Pte W	Montague, Pte H S	Thorn, Pte D T
Cornwall, Pte Moses	Greatbatch, Pte D W	Morton, Pte W D	
Cundill, Pte T J	Hampson, Pte B	Munro, Pte D	

Section III

Young, Lt D R	Hudson, Pte W M	Morgan, Pte G A	Solomon, Pte W H
Adams, Pte J	Hull, Pte G H	Mutton, Pte T W	Storey, Pte J
Atkinson, Pte W J	Jessup, Pte A	Percy, Pte G	Towell, Pte F
Bell, Pte T	Law, L Cpl J	Redpath, Pte W O D	Vigne, Cpl J T
Brice, Pte A E	McBean, Pte L	Ricketts, Pte W A	Vines, Pte C G
Carlyon, Pte E J	McBean, Sgt D M	Roberts, Pte E R	White, Pte F
Fisher, Pte W A	Moir, Pte R H	Rutherford, Pte C G	
Hazell, Pte A J	Moir, Pte W G	Smyth, Pte H W	

Mandy Fort, Boshof Road

Section I

Wells, Lt W H	Chappell, Pte C A	Day, Pte W D	English, Pte T R
Beadle, Pte C	Cranswick, Pte W F	Dietrich, Pte M	Furmidge, Pte S
Bell, Pte D	Currey, Pte C C	Donnelly, Pte W T	Greatbatch, Pte R
Brown, Pte S A	Davidson, Pte W	Dorward, Pte A G	Haile, Pte T
Brown, Pte T A	Dawkins, Pte T J	Eastwood, Pte W	Harris, Pte B
Burns, Pte J	Day, Cpl B W	Edington, Pte T D	Hopper, Pte T

Appendices

Ling, Pte W J
Maltmann, Pte W

Metelercamp, L Cpl P W
Roberts, Sgt H J G

Skirving, QMS Sgt D
Stoney, Pte G H

Section II

Oats, Lt F
Adams, A SM A W
Beet, Pte G
Eland, Pte A
Gould, Pte F
Jeffreys, Pte S
Johnson, Pte W P
Kewley, Pte C

McLeod, Sgt H
Milborrow, Pte R H
Munro, Pte J
Murphy, Pte J
Newby, Pte W G
Orr, Pte J
Parkin, Pte E D
Parkins, Pte T

Pinnock, Pte E W
Ruffel, Pte N O
Shepherd, Pte B B
Smith, Cpl F R H
Stewart, Pte S
Store, Pte A
Tredrea, Pte T B
Turner, Pte B

Turner, Pte J C
Vincent, Pte E
Ward, Pte C
Whitehead, Pte W B
Whyte, Pte Tom

No 4 Redoubt, De Beers Floor

B Company

Tabuteau, Capt C
Harris, Lt L
Townshend, Lt G H
Watson, Lt J W
Watters, Lt
Alexander, Pte J
Baker, Pte L
Berry, Pte J
Boyd, Pte J H
Brown, Pte E T
Carroll, Pte C
Cass, Pte H
Charles, Pte J
Corrigan, Pte W
Coxen, Pte W C
Croft, Pte J H
Cundill, Pte A E
Dyason, Pte J
Elliott, Pte G C
Flemming, Pte J
Fry, Pte H W

Gibson, Pte R T
Greenlees, Sgt J
Harris, Sgt W
Haslar, Pte G
Hendry, Pte G S
Hobson, Despatch Rider J
Hockey, Pte C H
Hoply, Pte C
Jenkins, Pte E
Jennings, Pte J
Johns, Sgt H T
Kirkmam, Pte W
Ladyson, Pte W
Laurance, Pte D
Lee, Pte G T
Leonard, Pte E
Maloney, Pte C
Maloney, Pte J H
Marshall, Pte H
May, Cpl W
McCarthy, Pte D

McDonald, Pte W C
McEwen, Pte J
McEwen, Pte J W
McKinnon, Pte D
McLaren, Cpl A
McLoughlin, Col Sgt M
Megaw, Pte T
Miklejohn, Pte M
Morton, Pte R
Moult, Pte T M
Murdoch, Pte W
Nicholson, Pte J R
O'Regan, Pte M
Palmer, Sgt G
Pringle, Pte J
Reid, Issuer of Stores W
Searle, Cpl R
Shepherd, Pte W
Short, Pte J
Smith, OR Clk A F
Stevens, Pte J

Stewart, Pte S
Strachen, Pte J
Sutton, Pte E C
Swan, Pte J A
Taylor, Pte A
Taylor, Pte T F N
Timman, Pte W
Van Eyssen, Pte H
Veale, Pte C H
Vicary, Pte A
Vicary, Pte W A
Vincent, Cpl E
Webb, Pte H J
Webber, Pte W
Weir, Pte G
Wilkinson, Pte J
Williamson, Pte G
Worrall, Sgt W

D Company
Division II

Saunders, Capt G A
Elkin, Capt W S

Gardner, Bugler W
Neal, Issuer G

Peat, QM R C
Sharpe, Orderly Rm Clk R

Wustman, Col Sgt F R

Section I

Lambourne, Lt G
Atkinson, Pte J
Bell, Pte J T
Betteridge, Pte W
Bowman, Pte A
Briggs, Pte M

Briscoe, Pte R
Charles, Pte J
Gattrell, Pte H
Grant, Pte C
Grant, Pte J
Kendall, Pte J

Kendall, Pte R
Kitto, Pte J H
Rowe, Pte T
Rundle, Pte C
Stephens, Pte F
Stone, Pte G

Symons, Sgt H
Taylor, Cpl W
Walker, Pte E (jnr)
Williams, Pte C
Wright, Pte W J

Section II

Johnston, Lt J
Bawden, Pte F W
Bawden, Pte G
Clarke, Pte N E
De Villiers, Pte W

Everington, Pte H
Fawkes, Pte R
Harrison, Pte J
Hodgson, Pte H
Ingram, Pte H

Jorey, Pte S
Key, Pte J H
Kinsman, Pte W
Spriddell, Pte W
Stopforth, Pte P

Thorburn, Pte W
Vincent, Pte F
Wallace, Pte H
Wilkinson, Pte W
Woodend, Cpl W

Section III

Paley, Lt G
Fawkes, Pte J
Gartrell, Pte R
Good, Pte W

Kitto, Sgt E J
Knowles, Pte J
Lowden, Cpl J W
Milne, Pte H

Rabe, Pte H
Robinson, Pte J
Robson, Pte T
Scoble, Pte T

Seaton, Pte J
Shorter, Pte T
Smith, Pte R E
Snaith, Pte H

439

Kimberley Siege Account and Medal Roll

Steele, Pte J
Stockenstroom, Pte F

Thomas, Pte W
Thomas, Pte W H

Watterson, Pte R
Wilcock, Pte W

Section IV

Wilson, Lt J F
Barrass, Pte C
Barrass, Pte W
Bellas, Pte J
Bellas, Pte W

Edgar, Pte G
Ellis, Pte W
Gray, Pte A
Griffin, Sgt W
Hill, Pte C

Hocking, Pte J
James, Pte B
Mathews, Pte F
Porter, Pte W D
Rowe, Pte H

Smith, Pte A
Thomas, Pte B
Vipond, Pte J
Van Blerk, Pte H
Wills, Cpl J

Reserve

Addison, Pte J
Alemandro, Pte J
Bailey, Pte E
Beckerley, Pte T
Ferry, Pte P
George, Pte J

Gerans, Pte J
Howieson, Pte J
Jackson, Pte W
Jacobson, Pte A
Jones, Pte W H
Lees, Pte J

McFarlane, Pte P
McMillan, Pte D S
McVittie, Pte J
Rigg, Pte J
Roberts, Pte J H
Rowe, Pte S

Rowe, Pte W
Schiebe, Pte J (snr)
Scott, Pte T
Taylor, Pte T N
Trengrove, Pte E
Walker, Pte E (snr)

G Company

Holliday, Capt C
Bayman, Lt W
Fitzgerald, Lt P F
Haddock, Lt R S
Percy, Lt R J
Aaronson, Pte M
Aston, Pte H
Attwell, Pte R A H
Backman, Sgt J
Bacon, Pte J
Bands, Pte E
Bartenback, Pte H
Bicker-Caarten, L Cpl A G
Bodley, Cpl A
Bottom, Pte W
Bowness, Pte G H
Braden, Pte F
Budde, Pte J
Bunyard, Pte A B
Burge, Pte J M
Cann, Sgt J
Cator, Pte A
Chauncey, Pte P B
Clark, Pte A
Clark, Pte T G

Clarke, Pte A J
Cook, Col Sgt A G
Cranswick, Pte W F
Creen, Pte G B
Crosbie, Pte J
Cunningham, Pte G
Dashwood, Pte F
Davidson, Pte H W
Dolman, Clerk F
Dremer, L Cpl E A
Engledoe, Pte R J H
Ettling, Pte M H C
Foley, Pte F W
Furmidge, Pte E R
Goose, Pte A
Gray, Pte C W
Grierson, Pte D
Griffin, Pte P
Haddock, Cpl W L
Harrison, Pte A E
Hescroff, Pte R
Hinsch, Pte R
Howard, Pte A E
Jackson, Pte C
Jackson, Pte H

James, Pte P
Kennett, Pte H
Lewis, Pte J
Lewis, Pte M
Liether, Pte H
Maris, Pte L
Martin, Pte R H
McDonald, Pte M
McKenzie, Pte J
Mellett, Pte C
Millar, Pte N J
Mulder, Cpl J L
Munks, Cpl A G
Munnick, Pte J A
Northcote, Pte S J
Pearson, Pte G T
Pocock, Pte W
Pooley, Pte E
Popham, Pte H T
Porter, Pte W
Raaff, Pte J
Reader, Pte J H
Ronaldson, Sgt G S
Rose, Pte A
Rowe, Pte T

Rutherford, L Cpl L
Scott, Pte J C
Shalders, Pte W A
Silson, Pte R
Smith, Pte H W
Smith, Pte S J
Solomon, QMS J
Stockhill, Pte F
Tangney, Pte M
Tarrant, Pte J
Taylor, Sgt J
Thomas, Pte T
Thompson, Pte H J
Tirbitt, Pte S A
Voaden, Pte W
Voegt, Pte H D
Walker, Pte E
Wearne, Pte S F
Westley, L Cpl P
Westley, Pte A
Wilding, Pte T
Willey, L Cpl E E
Wilson, Pte A
Wright, Pte W J

H Company

Pooley, 1250 Capt J
Booth, 1322 Lt J R
Croxford, 1323 Lt P G
Field, 1322 Lt H G
Gentleman, 1298 Lt J W
Sadler, 1275 Lt J M
Tyson, 1251 Lt J D
Abram, 1321 Pte J
Alexander, 1318 Pte J
Anderson, 1262 Pte J
Airth, 1312 Pte J
Ashford, 1325A Pte A J
Ashton, 1266 Pte W
Baker, 1272 Pte G H
Bayers, 1279 Pte H M
Bentley, 1297A Pte W M
Bergstrom, 1258 Pte H
Bishop, 1296 Pte R
Brandt, 1257 Pte F J

Breda, 1333A Pte H A
Browning, 1277 Sgt J
Browning, 1346 CS R B
Bryce, 1328 Pte W G
Burge, 1290 Pte F
Butler, 1336 Pte T W
Campbell, 1261 Pte W J
Campbell, Pte J
Cargill, 1278 Pte J H
Chinner, 1309 Pte A
Cohen, 1345 QMS A A
Cook, 1281 Pte H
Cox, 1276 Sgt W S
Crook, 1347 Pte R
Crouch, 1311 Pte T G
Dalgleish, 1256 Pte J
Deary, 1295 Pte J E
Desconde, 1302A Pte P C
Dvig, 1338 Pte J A

Easton, 1343 Pte A J
Evert, 1337 Pte J B
Flood, 1287 Pte F
Franklin, 1271 Cpl A O
Gallow, 1326 Pte W F
Gilbert, 1251A Pte J
Goldstucker, 1277 Cpl W
Gove, 1264 Pte W E
Gunders, 1276A Pte F C
Hamilton, 1305 Pte T
Hammond, 1331 Pte J E
Hannam, 1253A Pte W H
Harrington, 1284 Pte J L
Harrison, 1288 Pte H S
Hartley, 1332 Pte K
Heeney, 1252A Pte E
Henderson, 1285 Pte E C
Herridge, 1330 Pte A J
Hillier, 1259 Pte F J

Hitchman, 1314 Pte G E
Hitchman, 1304 Pte W
Hodgson, 1273 Pte G
Humberstone, 1265 Pte W
Husband, 1306 Pte P L
Jordan, 1253 Sgt O R
Kenyon, 1308 Pte P H
Lamont, 1339 Pte A
Lee, 1331A Pte St J
Lewis, 1289 Pte R
McCormick, 1348 Pte W
McCurdy, 1324 Cpl J
McLean, 1270 Pte G D
Mering, 1300 Cpl F
Minch, 1286 Pte P
Mitchell, 1335 Pte J S
Morgan, 1327A Pte E
Murray, 1282 Pte D
Murray, Pte P

Appendices

Nicholls, 1313 Pte S
Parker, 1291 Pte J K
Paulic, 1344 Pte A
Payne, 1341 Pte G
Paynter, 1299 Sgt J
Phillip, 1329 Pte J
Poole, 1332A Pte H C
Puckers, 1275A Pte S G
Raaff, 1394A Pte A
Reed, 1316 Pte C

Richards, 1329A Pte D
Richardson, 1280 Pte J
Rouse, 1279 Pte W D
Samuel, 1302 Pte J
Samuel, 1325 Pte W
Savage, 1299A Pte A H
Schriner, 1299A Pte J
Shelley, 1263 Pte P
Silbert, 1330A Pte P
Sladdon, 1301 Pte C

Smith, 1268 Pte W
Stewart, 1320 Pte G
Strickland, 1292 Pte C
Swain, 1349 Pte W W
Taylor, 1279 Pte R L
Tredrea, 1274 Cpl W J
Ulrichsen, 1328A Pte O A
Waterworth, 1326 Pte C
White, 1317 Pte S
White, 1342 Pte E H

Wightman, 1327 Pte J S
Williams, 1255 Pte G W
Williams, 1269 Pte D
Wills, 1307 Pte J
Wilson, 1283 Pte A
Wollenschlager, 1319 Pt H
Wyngard, 1254 Pte J J
Wyngard, 1260 Pte J J

K Company

White, Capt Greenwood
Harper, Col Sgt T W

Hutchinson, QM Alexr
Ott, Bugler C S

Robertson, Issuer J
Watson, Clerk J

Section I

Johnston, Lt G H
Andrews, Pte C
Andrews, Pte J
Baker, Pte J
Bawden, Pte C
Bawden, Pte F W

Bayly, L Cpl J B
Blake, Cpl J
De Melker, Pte S
Edwards, Pte H
Fyfe, Pte D
Hill, Pte S W

Judge, Pte P
Key, L Cpl C W
Koen, Pte P
Lodge, Pte H
Moyes, Pte J
Reed, Pte R

Rusher, Pte C J
Strouch, Pte S
Thomas, Pte L J
Tillemans, Pte H P
Webster, Sgt J R H

Section II

Johns, Lt S
Addicks, Pte A N
Coleman, Pte P J
Davis, Pte H F
De Witt, Pte J G
Farren, Pte J

Gowie, Pte T S
Green, L Cpl W H
Hatton, Pte A J
Harper, Cpl L J J
Kempner, Pte L
Kershaw, Sgt J H

Konigsberg, Pte A
Minaar, Pte J
Page, Pte E C
Page, Pte K
Phillips, Pte R
Polsue, Pte E A

Rask, Pte A W L
Reeler, Pte E G
Stouppe, Pte R
Taylor, Pte J
Taylor, Pte W

Section III

Schmidt, Lt H
Colin, Pte P
Davidson, Pte J
Dickens, Pte W
Eden, Pte D R
Ettwein, Pte G

Fairley, Pte H W
Fitzpatrick, Pte J A
Fraser, Cpl A M
Hannan, Pte D
Hyland, Pte F
Ives, Pte J A

Jeffrey, Pte A G
Keat, Pte H
Mileham, Pte E
Niven, L Cpl C K
Philips, Pte A R
Richards, Pte T

Schmidt, Sgt W A
Smith, Pte W
Sparks, Pte A
Spence, Pte J
Wickham, Pte F
Wyngard, Pte A

Section IV

Tait, Lt S
Ash, Pte F C
Bain, Pte H
Davey, Pte E G
De Melker, Pte H G
Duncan, Pte W G

Eaton, Pte G W
Garden, Sgt F
Gates, Pte H C
Hoare, L Cpl A J
Hughes, Pte P R
Jacobs, Pte H

Johnson, Pte J J
Luman, Pte H M
McColl, Pte J C
Page, Cpl J
Richards, Pte T
Robertson, Pte W

Roger, Pte A
Scott, Pte R W
Seaton, Pte C
Spooner, Pte F
Woodward, Pte F J
Wright, Pte L S

L Company

Faulkner, OC Capt W H
Buxton, Clerk W A
Cooper, Col Sgt G S

Crawford, Des Rider R
Hartley, Clerk C V
Lindsay, QMS J

Mitchell, Issuer T
Ralph, Medical Section J
Scott, Medical Section A

Watcham, Col Sgt J H
Wolstenholme, Des Rider H

Section I

Stratten, Lt T
Armstrong, Pte J W
Brunton, Pte R J
Butler, Pte T
Carstens, Pte H
Cooke, Pte E

Daly, Pte W R
Dempster, Pte W
Dexter, Pte H C
Druce, Pte W G
Eddy, L Cpl J
Feeney, Cpl E

Graham, Pte W
Kiddle, Pte W
Lawry, Pte E
Munks, Pte H G
O'Callaghan, Pte C
O'Connor, Pte G

O'Malley, Pte W
Reynolds, Pte A
Rule, Sgt J
Timby, Pte W
Varrie, Pte A S
Wills, Pte W

Kimberley Siege Account and Medal Roll

Section II

White, Lt F	Cowell, Pte J W	Jones, Pte W A	Stephenson, Pte M
Allen, Pte H	Dixon, Pte W	Martindale, Pte A	Thomas, Pte R B
Bennett, Pte R	Franklin, Pte M W	McNeil, Sgt C	Twigg, Pte J
Borrill, Cpl T	Hancock, Pte C	Rucastle, Pte J	Twigg, Pte W J
Boyd, Pte F	Harris, Pte R	Skeldon, Pte J	Wallace, Pte W
Boyd, Pte R W	Head, Pte J	Smith, Pte T	
Coughlan, Pte J	Hortop, Pte J	Spry, L Cpl J	

Section III

Johnston, Lt J	Craig, Pte R M	Kelly, Pte F	Twigg, Cpl J
Benson, Pte J	Cron, Pte M	Lloyd, Pte J P	Vandergryp, Pte S W
Beynon, Pte G	Daly, Pte J E	McGuiness, Pte F	Vass, Pte H
Brophy, Pte F	Doherty, Pte T	McMullen, Pte H	Walker, Pte J
Brown, Pte A S	Faull, Pte W	Morcom, Pte J H	
Campbell, Sgt D	Gouldie, Pte J	Simpson, Pte H	
Collister, Pte J	Kelly, L Cpl R	Stavers, Pte W A	

Section IV

Marshall, Lt H	Hillies, Pte W	McCurrie, Pte J (jnr)	Phieffer, Pte L
Alexander, Pte J	Hodgson, L Cpl H	McCurrie, Pte J (snr)	Savage, Pte H
Alexander, Pte R	Hodgson, Pte T	Murphy, Pte W	Shaw, Pte J
Coles, Pte E	Jones, Pte E	Murphy, Pte W H	Smith, Pte H
Coward, Cpl J W	Keevy, Pte J M	Norris, Pte C E	Stead, Sgt A W C
Devlin, Pte T	Lawson, Pte P	*Owens, L Cpl E A*	Wells, Pte A

No 2 Redoubt, Kimberley Mine

M Company

Mallett, Staff Capt P W	Benjamin, Clerk to staff L H	Oatley, Col Sgt W H	Sydney, Clerk to staff E J
Coghlan, Capt C P J	Dickens, Bugler W	Reunert, QMS T	Wright, Issuer L O

Section I

Hearn, Lt D P	Bottomley, Pte R H	Lovegrove, Sgt F R	Reynolds, Sgt W R
Alexander, Pte H M	*Bouwer, Pte L*	Maxwell, Pte R F T	Robb, Pte F W
Alexander, Pte S	Connell, Pte G	MacKenzie, Sgt J R	Robinson, Pte E A
Amm, Pte R	Dickson, Pte J W	Nixon, Pte J	Robinson, Pte G M
Andries, Pte C	Dutoit, Pte S F	Packer, Pte F W	*Roslie, Pte S P*
Bodley, Cpl C	Lancaster, Pte H J	Parker, Pte S A	Shoobert, Pte A
Borcher, Pte H	Lawler, Pte M	Parker, Pte T	Turner, Pte J

Section II

Franceys, Lt A L	Hadlow, Pte J	Montague, Pte J F V	Sundien, Pte J
Alderson, Pte A W	Harrison, Sgt H	Morgan, Pte R S	Thompson, Pte C M
Anders, Pte P C	Hudson, Sgt W H	Noonan, Pte J	Viljoen, Pte C
Bellows, Pte N	Jullien, Pte G	Parker, Pte J K	Woleck, Pte E
Brun, Pte A	Lyall, Cpl A F	Persson, Pte L	
Dlugadz, Pte D	Macaulay, Pte J H	Sampson, Pte A W	
Egan, Pte T	Marks, Pte S J	Sherman, Pte S	

Section III

Elliott, Lt K C	George, Pte P H	Mapp, Pte J	Van Niekerk, Pte H
Blaiberg, Pte B	Gilbert, Pte F	Mason, Pte H F	Verheyen, Cpl G
Brookes, Pte T	Hennesey, Pte B	McDonald, Sgt A R	Verheyen, Pte J
Carpenter, Pte A V	Jackson, Pte R	Pugh, Pte W J	Wedderburn, Sgt G R
Cook, Pte S	Kipling, Pte H S	Robson, Pte C E	Wehmeyer, Pte W
Dempster, Pte J	Manning, Pte F R	Smyth, Sgt J J	
Evert, Pte M	Manning, Pte F S	Tobin, Pte E J	

Section IV

Lawrence, Lt W
Sheasby, Lt J B
Abrahamse, Pte A J
Barnes, Pte G R
Brooks, Pte H
Brown, Sgt C H
Farquhar, Pte C J

Hammond, Pte J
Hayston, Pte R B
Holroyd, Pte A J
Hosking, Pte H J
Hunter, Pte G M
Lanz, Pte F
McCracken, Pte S

McGregor, Pte R W
McHardy, Pte D
Mitchell, Cpl J
Norris, Pte W B
Palmer, Pte K
Pattenden, Pte E
Rossam, Pte G

Thompson, Pte R
Walshe, Pte G
Watson, Pte R
Weston, Pte E E
Weston, Pte E W
Wiley, Pte T S

No 1 Redoubt, Kimberley Mine

N Company

Grimmer, Capt I
Stevenson, Capt J
Cleaver, Lt C E
Druce, Lt J C
Hulley, Lt T H
Woodbourne, Lt T J
Alexander, Pte T
Atkinson, Pte W
Barnes, Cpl J B
Blakemore, Pte D
Blakemore, Pte W
Bradford, Pte J
Burden, Pte W
Byrne, Pte D
Cameron, Pte T
Carnell, Pte C
Corbett, Pte F
Crellin, Sgt J J
Cross, Cpl J J
Cross, Pte J
Cudlipp, Pte J B
Dexter, Issuer F C E
Dunbar, Pte M
Eales, Pte A
Eden, Pte A
Eden, Pte T A

Erskine, Pte C
Etherington, Cpl T
Etherington, Pte C
Eyre, Bugler E
Fairweather, Pte C
Fairweather, Pte E
Finnerty, Pte R
Fitzpatrick, Pte J
Francis, Pte A
Gordon, Pte T
Hall, Pte W S
Hannan, Pte C
Hartley, Sgt W H
Hawkins, Pte B A
Hawkins, Pte J H
Head, Pte J
Heath, Pte A
Heffer, Pte C
Hellegren, Pte A
Howard, Sgt C H
Ivey, Pte T
Johnson, Pte H
Kelly, Pte B
Kelly, Pte J P
Kelly, Pte W J
Kerr, Cpl E

Kitchin, Pte D
Laing, QM R C
Longhurst, Sgt A
Lowther, Pte J
Luscombe, Pte W
Marriott, Pte J
Marriott, Pte W C
Mashford, Pte F
McCurrie, Pte J
McKay, Pte C C
McKay, Pte D J
McKay, Pte R C
McNish, Pte D
McNish, Pte W
McNish, Pte W
Mitchell, Pte P
Mitchell, Pte W
Nicholson, Pte R G
Norris, Pte G M
Northey, Pte J
Olivier, Pte C
Oxford, Pte S
Partridge, Pte G T
Powrie, Col Sgt J E
Pratley, Pte G
Revell, OR Cpl D G

Richardson, Pte W
Roberts, Pte R
Rouse, Pte A E
Rudman, Pte J J
Sealey, Pte T
Skelton, Pte T
Smith, Pte T
Southward, Pte B
Stewart, Pte C W
Stewart, Pte J N
Sumner, Pte F
Sumner, Pte J
Sumner, Pte R
Tatters, Pte J
Todd, Pte H
Turner, Pte J
Twigg, Pte T
Uren, Pte L
Ward, Pte J W
Watridge, Pte C
Wills, Pte G L
Wright, Pte J
Young, Pte J W

Attached

Mumford, Cyclist G

Nelson, Ambulance R D

Wright, Cyclist A J

Kimberley Mine searchlight and telephone section

Franklin, Pte M
Hansen, Pte M P

Jones, Pte W A
Kelly, Pte E C

McCrackem, Pte E W
Owens, Pte W

Kamfersdam Company

Armstrong, OC Capt J
Birt, Lt A G
Goate, Lt E W C
Bawden, Pte N
Bernhardi, Pte J
Brooks, Pte W
Brooks, Pte W T
Carroll, Pte J
Carroll, Pte M
Clark, Pte W
Cumming, Pte C
Dakers, Pte W

Douglas, Pte W
Duggan, Pte C
Duggan, Pte G H
Duggan, Pte G V
Elkington, Pte F
Francis, Sgt H
Furness, Pte J
Furness, Pte J B
Grant, Pte J
Hunt, Pte G
Hunt, Pte W
Kelly, Pte J D

Kirby, Pte W
Livingstone, Cpl J
Lorrie, Pte J
Lund, Pte T
Lunt, Pte W H
Martin, Pte C
Martin, Pte F
McCallum, Pte C
McCallum, Pte J
Mitchell, Pte J
Pitcher, Pte M
Renfree, Pte H

Rennie, Sgt G
Ringrove, Pte H
Seaward, Pte H
Smith, Pte C
Strugnell, Pte H
Townsend, Cpl G
Tull, Pte W
Webster, Pte C
Williams, Pte J
Wilson, Pte R

443

Kimberley Siege Account and Medal Roll

No 2 Redoubt, No 1 Location
C Company

Section III (this list is very similar to No II Section, Pickering's Redoubt No 2)

McHardy, Lt W	Elliot, 347A Pte G A	Morphy, 335 Pte J	*Spring, 334 Pte T*
Anderson, 342 Pte G	Fletcher, 341 Pte A C	Parker, 340 Pte E	Sutherland, 336 Pte J
Armstrong, 344 Pte W	Gibbs, 347 Pte J	Ross, 327 Cpl G	Topp, 343 Pte J B
Barnes, Pte H	Halloran, 330 Pte J J	Rowlands, Pte H	Uren, 332 Pte W M
Broderick, 345 Pte M	Jackson, 337 Cpl C H	Ryan, 333 Pte J	Ward, 324B Pte H
Clark, 326 Sgt J	Johnston, 338 Pte C W	Sharpe, 329 Pte E J	Warren, 339 Pte J
Cramond, 328 Pte A	Leddy, 331 Pte H W	Smith, 346 Pte A D	

Section IV

Hogg, 396 Lt J C	Ellis, 377 Pte C	Holman, 393 Pte F C	Rinkquest, 395B Pte D
Sinclair, 371 Lt D K	Evert, 395A Pte W	Jessiman, 381 Pte W	Siebert, 388 Pte Jno
Bennett, 374 Pte J	Frond, 378 Pte D	*King, 324 Pte W*	Siebert, 395 Pte Jas
Boyd, 372 Sgt R	Fryar, 379 Pte J	Lyon, 385 Pte D M	Sinclair, 387 Pte H M L
Burton, 375 Pte F H	Guild, 394 Pte F R	Marshall, 367 Pte W	White, 381 Pte W J
Davidson, 373 Cpl J	Hobson, 380 Pte J	Martin, 383 Pte H	Whitter, 390 Cpl R
Eales, 395C Pte W	Hocking, 382 Pte W J	Neilson, 384 Pte J	

Premier Mine

Jones, T M (Manager)
5th Division

Swanson, Capt J	Conley, Cpl M	Harris, Pte W J	Lorimer, Pte G
Curry, Lt A W	Cooke, Pte E	Harris, Sgt J R	Lowrie, Pte J
Drew, Lt P J V	Cotton, Pte J L	Hartley, Pte E	*Lynton, Pte C E*
Madoc, Lt H W	Cotty, Pte C T A	Hartley, Pte H T	MacNamara, Pte G
McKay, Lt G G	Curgenven, QMS F	Harty, Pte W	Marrillier, Pte F R
Smith, Lt R A L	Curtis, Pte W	Henning, Pte W R	Masencamp, Pte F
Macpherson, LT QM A B	Cutting, Pte R	Hewitson, A L Cpl T	Mason, Pte A
Booth, Capt (SMO) R D	Daniel, Pte J N	Haylett, Pte A H	Maude, Pte S
King, Lt (JMO) G C	David, Pte T J	Hopkirk, Pte J R	Mayston, Pte W H D
Acker, Pte J	Davies, Sgt H	Hunter, Pte W	McAdam, Pte A (jnr)
Addison, Pte A	Davis, Pte G	Huntington, Pte T W	McAdam, Pte A (snr)
Alexander, Pte J	Davis, Pte L	Hyde, Pte A J	McCallum, Pte J D
Andrews, Pte H R	Dexter, Pte A E	*Irwin, Pte J*	McCarthy, Pte G
Arlt, Pte A E	Dicker, Pte W R	Jackson, Pte C L	McCarthy, Pte J
Ayrton, Pte G H	Dubois, Pte F	Jackson, Pte C M	McEvoy, Pte P
Babb, Pte C	Early, Pte T K	Jackson, Pte F	McGuiness, Pte C A
Barker, Pte H J	Edgecombe, Pte H	Jenkins, Pte A	McLaughlin, Sgt W
Barnes, Pte G D	Edgell, Pte H	Johnston, Pte W J	McTavish, Pte D
Braske, Pte A	Edwards, Pte A G	Johnstone, Pte W	Mennie, Pte J G
Bayne, A L Cpl H P	Ellis, Pte C	Jones, A L Cpl E P	Mercer, Pte H T
Billett, Pte E G	Else, Pte H	Kermeen, Pte W J	Morgan, Pte S H
Birtley, Pte W	Evans, Pte E J	Kieser, Pte D F	Munn, Cpl G J
Blundell, Pte T C	Exter, Pte H G	Kieser, Pte W P	Munro, Pte J D
Bould, Pte J	Fitzpatrick, Pte P D	Keith, Pte A C	*Murdoch, Pte E J*
Bowden, Pte W J	Forrester, Pte Q	Kelly, Pte G	Murray, Pte J
Bradshaw, Pte T	Franke, Pte A K R	Kennedy, Pte W	Neal, Pte G H
Bugler, Pte C F	Freeman, Pte J	Kennett, Pte H J W	Newton, Pte C R
Button, Pte H	Freeman, Pte W F	Keogh, Pte M	Norvall, Pte F A
Cahill, Pte T	Freestone, Pte G W	Kernick, Pte G S	Nutzhorn, Pte E C
Carlos, Pte J	Fry, Pte I	Laing, Pte J	O'Brien, Pte J D
Chavasse, Pte S	Gainsford, A L Cpl R F	Lange, Pte W F	O'Brien, Pte J W
Clack, Pte A M	Gainsford, Pte E R	Langmaid, Pte C C	O'Halloran, Pte H F N
Clack, Pte T	Gibbon, Pte R (jnr)	Lawrence, Pte C G	Olive, Pte W A
Clarence, Pte W J	Gibbon, Pte R (snr)	Leeson, Pte F J	Olver, Pte R
Clark, Pte O G	Gillbee, Pte G F	Leggatt, Pte W	Owen, Pte R E
Clarke, Pte A	Gouldie, Pte H	Liesching, Pte C F	Packer, Pte F W
Clarke, Pte F R	Grindlay, Pte D	Liesching, Pte F	Page, Pte G
Clements, Pte J	Grunig, Pte F C J H	Liesching, Pte P	Page, Pte H E
Close, Pte R	Hamer, Pte H	Lewis, Pte A	Parr, QMS (Staff Clerk) J B
Cock, Pte H	Hammond, Pte J B	Logan, Pte J R	*Payne, Sgt J L*
Cole, A L Cpl C A	Harris, Pte J J	Long, Pte A H	Pearson, Pte C A

444

Appendices

Peddle, Pte E J J	*Russell, Pte T*	*Stewart, Pte J J*	*Webber, Pte W*
Pitchers, Pte V	Sandilands, Pte J	Still, Pte E S L	Weir, Pte A
Pole, Pte H	Sangster, Pte D K	Striker, Pte H	Wells, Pte F G S
Poulton, Pte W N J	Schultz, Pte W C	*Stuart, Pte D*	Westley, Pte H J
Radcliffe, Pte L	Seeley, Pte W	*Sutherland, Pte A*	*White, Pte F J*
Rainsford, Pte A A	Shingler, Pte W J	Taylor, Pte J	White, Pte J H M
Renney, Pte R J	Short, Pte A G	Taylor, Pte W H	White, Pte P
Robertson, Pte T	Skutnas, Pte A	Terras, Pte J	Whitebeard, Pte T A
Robinson, Pte C G	Smith, Cpl P R	Terras, Pte W G	Wilder, Pte W
Robinson, Pte G H	Smith, Pte F J	Thomas, Pte C B	*Williams, Pte A*
Roffey, Pte C	Smith, Pte H J	Thomson, Pte W	Williams, Pte E
Rogers, Cpl H W	Smith, Pte J	Tiernay, A L Cpl J M	Williams, Pte E J
Rogers, Pte A	Solomon, Cpl H S	Truran, Pte J H	*Williams, Pte S*
Rogers, Pte A E	Solomon, Pte P	Urquhart, Pte D	Wilson, Pte D E
Ross, Pte H S	Spence, A L Cpl J W	Veroghan, Pte L	Wilson, Pte W
Ross, Pte S E M	Spence, Pte H	Walshe, Pte M R	*Wood, Pte H T*
Rouse, Pte J C	Stables, Pte J	Walton, Pte R W	Woolmer, Pte T
Rule, Pte G	Stannard, Pte F C	Warren, Pte R	Wylam, Pte J
Rule, Pte T H	Stephenson, Pte W J	Waterston, Pte A A	Yelland, Pte F P

Detchment 23rd Company Western Division, RGA

Rynd, Lt F F	Drinkhill, Gnr J	Johnson, Gnr J	O'Neil, Bombdr A
Arthur, Gnr J	Edwards, Gnr J	Jones, Gnr A S F	Raynor, Sgt G H
Bennett, Gnr W	Farelly, Gnr P J	Keast, Gnr G	Richardson, Bombdr W
Borner, Bombdr H	Fennelly, Gnr M	Knott, Gnr L C	Scannell, Gnr E
Butler, Gnr J	Gorham, Gnr E	Manning, Gnr H	Tanser, Gnr F
Clements, Cpl H	Johns, Gnr T	Murphy, Gnr P	Vickers, Gnr S

Municipal Guard

Location - Reservoir

Henderson, Div Cmdr R H	O'Molony, Sgt S	Savage, Clerk & Issuer W J	Wells, QMS E R
Rugg, Capt H	Ross, Look-out C	Welch, Col Sgt A T	

Section A
No I Company

Callen, Lt T	Crittell, Pte A	Irving, Pte C E J	Riches, Pte F H
Baxter, Pte C	Crosthwaite, Pte W	Johnston, Pte T	Sheehan, Pte T
Betteridge, Cpl C	Drummond, Pte W	Little, Pte A	Ubsdell, Pte G
Burton, Sgt C L	Eva, Pte H M	McMorrin, Pte T	Westbrook, Pte E J
Callister, Pte J S	Hughes, Pte H	*Nicolson, Pte K*	Willis, Pte J
Compton, Pte R	Ingleton, Pte H	Page, Pte C	

No II Company

Beddome, Lt E I	Eales, Pte R	Konigsberg, Pte A	Partridge, Pte J F
Anthony, Pte D	Evans, Pte J J	Lawrence, Pte J R	Phillips, Pte W
Bergmann, Pte V	Fraser, Pte D	Ling, Pte B	*Rodgers, Pte A*
Black, Pte W O	Gartrell, Pte H	McCann, Cpl P	Simpson, Pte J
Colchester, Pte E J	James, Pte E H	Myers, Pte W	Smith, Pte M C
Delaney, Pte W P	James, Pte V	Newton, Pte J	Viggers, Sgt W

No III Company

Bird, Lt I	Hay, Pte G	*Mourse, Pte A G*	Thirer, Pte C
Bailey, Pte J (jnr)	Hay, Pte H W	Pierce, Pte W	Thompson, Pte P
Bands, Pte H	Kelley, Pte G	Pike, Pte D	Thomson, Pte J
Cloete, Pte J H	Knowles, Pte W	Roffe, Pte H	Tideswell, Pte J
Crosslands, Pte J	Lawson, Pte T H	Rowell, Pte J	*Trotter, Pte R J*
Cutting, Pte H	Louw, Pte W J	Sheriff, Sgt E J	
Dutoit, Pte D	Matthews, Cpl J L	Teare, Pte T	

No IV Company

Brennan, Lt H J	Carr, Pte J M	Davies, Pte D	Graham, Pte W
Blacklock, Pte J	Chalmers, Pte J	Droste, Pte T	Gray, Pte R

Kimberley Siege Account and Medal Roll

Hobson, Pte H E	*King, Pte J C*	Raper, Pte D	Suttie, Pte D
Hobson, Pte H L	Loudon, Sgt J	Sandford, Pte G	Thompson, Cpl R
Hocking, Pte J	McLean, Pte L C	Saunders, Pte W S	Van der Gryp, Pte A
Hogg, Pte J W	McLeod, Pte G D	*Stuart, Pte W*	
Irwin, Pte T	Partridge, Pte S W	*Sutherland, Pte Alex*	

Section B
No I Company

Alexander, Lt W W	Darvall, Pte H	*Korster, Pte J A*	Riches, Pte T
Allen, Pte W	Davis, Pte W H	Lane, Pte C	Robb, Pte G
Backhouse, Pte J E	*De Baisieux, Pte E*	Langley, Pte J H	Robertson, Pte J
Baillie, Pte J	De Melker, Pte A	Lee, Pte J	Shackleton, Pte T F
Bernhard, Pte C P	Delamere, Pte T H	Levey, Pte G J	Simmons, Pte M
Blumenthal, Pte H	Doig, Pte D	Mackie, Pte H	Smith, Pte C
Blumenthal, Pte M	Dougherty, Pte J	McCaffery, Pte T	Smith, Pte J J
Bodley, Pte G	Doyle, Pte B	Mitchell, Pte J	Starkey, Pte R
Botha, Pte J A	Dyer, Pte J	Moore, Pte J P	Staton, Pte H J
Boxall, Pte G	England, Pte J	Moore, Pte W	*Steinberg, Pte B*
Breda, Pte H A	Everleigh, Pte T	Morphy, Pte J	*Sutherland, Pte A*
Bumford, Cpl W	Gibson, Pte P	Moseley, Pte A	Taylor, Pte R
Butcher, Sgt W	Gietzmann, Pte C	Neale, Pte G	Townsend, Pte W
Cartright, Pte C T	Grainger, Pte W	*Nicoll, Pte W*	Turner, Pte W
Clark, Pte A	Greer, Pte V	O'Connor, Pte M	Verncenil, Pte S H
Clark, Pte F	Hamilton, Pte G	Parker, Pte H	Von Brandis, Pte J
Clark, Pte G W	Harsant, Pte S W	Phelan, Pte J	Walsh, Pte T
Clear, Pte D	Hendry, Cpl D	Phillips, Pte G	Ware, Pte F
Cloete, Pte F P	Hewitt, Pte J B	Pienaar, Pte J W	Wearne, Pte J
Close, Pte W H	Hill, Pte A B	Pirzenthal, Pte H F	Webster, Pte J W
Conradie, Pte D	*How, Pte H*	Price, Pte H	Williams, Pte L J
Croal, Pte G T	Irving, Pte C	Raaff, Pte J	Wilson, Pte A C
Crumplin, Pte A	*Jones, Pte G J*	Raaff, Pte T	Wilson, Pte H
Cutting, Pte J H	Kellsey, Pte A	Rae, Pte C	Woodward, Pte W
Cutting, Pte R	Kent, Pte C	Read, Pte W	

Beaconsfield Town Guard

Fraser, Maj J R	Cheetham, Staff Clerk F G	Hyde, OR Sgt A W	
Blackbeard, Capt C A	Cuthbertson, OR Sgt W M	Keathley, OR Clerk W	
Thorpe, Paymaster Lt J H	Ferns, QM H C	Van Reenen, OR Clk W D	

A Company
Section I

Blacking, Lt E	Duncan, Pte C	Jenkinson, Pte E D	McKay, Pte C H
Adamson, Pte J	Glen, Pte Jas	Jose, Pte W	Osselair, Pte F
Adendorff, Pte W L A	Green, Pte G	Joshua, Pte P	Pryra, Pte E
Arundel, Pte H	Green, Pte J J	Kerby, Pte A S	Soderblom, Pte A
Blackbeard, Pte L	Gregory, Pte E	Langford, Sgt R E	Tomlinson, Pte J
Christie, Pte J R	Hassett, Cpl J B	Locker, Pte H E	Zederick, Pte R
Conn, Pte R	Jenkins, Pte H J	McCarthy, Pte C	

Section II

Troup, Lt Jos	Clark, Pte H J	Klein, Pte A	Stanley, Pte J
Belcher, Pte W A	Cogle, Pte C J	McIntyre, Pte C	Swan, Pte C M
Bennette, Pte A	Ford, Cpl J J	Nutzhorn, Pte E C	Thompson, Pte G
Boffey, Pte G	Hardacre, Pte W (jnr)	Palmer, Pte T	Whitebeard, Pte T
Borcher, Pte A	Hassett, Pte F	Parker, Pte T H	
Carter, Pte W C	Jeffreys, Sgt W	Schouw, Pte T	
Clark, Pte A C	Kemm, Pte H R	Scott, Pte H	

Section, III

Britton, Lt W D	Clack, Cpl A M	Faulds, Pte Alf	Hobbs, Pte P
Austin, Pte C H	De Wyers, Pte J	Hale, Pte R C	Hunter, Pte W
Brooks, Pte J	Exter, Pte J J	Heldsinger, Pte F	Jeyes, Pte C
Bushney, Pte G	Farquharson, Pte P H	Heldsinger, Pte P	Kinnear, Pte G

Appendices

Kinnear, Pte H
Kinnear, Pte J
Kurten, Pte H

McCreath, Pte Jas
Palm, Pte W
Pratley, Sgt J M

Tarr, Pte M G
Tarr, Pte W C
Van der Linde, Pte B

Ward, Pte W G
Wolveck, Pte E

Section IV

Peake, Lt S
Booth, Sgt Thos
Brown, Pte A F
Carmichael, Pte P
Carter, Pte W
Donnelly, Pte R D

Duggan, Pte R H
Fivaz, Pte F J
Hall, Cpl H
Hardacre, Pte W (snr)
Jenkinson, Pte R
Kensit, Pte A

Klein, Pte J
Klein, Pte W
McCarthy, Pte D
McClusky, Pte W
McLaren, Pte J
McLeod, Pte F W

Ortell, Pte J
Palmer, Pte J
Pitchers, Pte J
Scott, Pte W A
Streak, Pte M A

B Company
Section I

Nelson, Capt W
Irwin, Lt G
Barrand, Pte M
Bolitho, Pte J
Boscombe, Pte W
Came, Pte R
Coates, Pte H

Coxen, Pte H
Dale, Cpl J W
Dale, Pte Geo H
Davidson, Pte A
Dohse, Pte C
Early, Pte A
Exner, Pte F

Geyer, Pte J H
Jennings, Pte W S
Mather, Pte R A
McAdam, Sgt J
Parkin, Pte J M
Petrazzas, Pte P
Sathas, Pte N

Selzer, Pte F
Selzer, Pte G
Taylor, Pte S
Theys, Pte F

Section II

Osborne, Lt C
Champion, Pte H B
Chapman, Pte C R
Clifford, Pte H
Crawford, Pte H
Field, Pte G

Hartley, Pte F
Hartley, Pte G
Hellyer, Pte H
James, Pte R C
Jensen, Pte R P
Osborne, Pte A

Viljoen, Pte J
Wakeford, Pte E V
Ward, Pte F
Webber, Pte G A
West, Pte F
Whitfield, Pte D

Wilson, Cpl W
Wilson, Pte G
Wilson, Sgt T A

Section III

Devenish, Lt F A R
Barton, Pte H
Clarke, Pte W J
Crawford, Pte G H
Glen, Cpl G H
Glen, Sgt J W

Hickson-Mahoney, Pte S
Holing, Pte S
Holing, Pte W
Holtzhousen, Pte D
Jenkins, Pte A R
Le Cordeur, Pte A P

McCarthy, Pte J
Nelson, Pte W (jnr)
Penniall, Pte A
Richter, Pte A
Smith, Pte C
Swanvelder, Pte C J

Tennant, Pte R D
Topp, Pte R C
Wade, Pte A W
Wallace, Pte E
Webster, Pte S

Section IV

Keating, Lt E W
Allende, Pte J R
Austin, Pte H R
Bird, Sgt T
Bishop, Pte H T
Bridger, Pte H

Clark, Pte W R
Coxen, Pte E H
Crawford, Pte T
Dodds, Pte W W
Greenspan, Pte S
Hassett, Pte M

Kelly, Cpl T
Liddall, Pte L B
Murray, Pte F
Ross, Pte L G
Scrad, Pte J
Smith, Pte G

Willis, Pte J
Wilson, Pte A T
Wilson, Pte S J

Mounted Section

Plane, Lt F W
Bradley, Sgt F J
Busschan, Pte J

Dodd, Pte H
Dodd, Pte J
Hale, Pte S W R

Knight, Cpl H J
Langsley, Pte S
Meder, Pte J

Nelson, Pte J
Topp, Pte A B
Wright, Pte E O

C Company
Section I

Sandham, Capt J
Prior, Lt C E
Albrice, Pte J
Andrews, Pte F
Assor, Pte D
Austin, Pte A
Bendixon, Sgt H A
Bridger, Pte W

Bussinne, Pte W
Cathey, Sgt Thos
Clayton, Pte W
Donelly, Pte J
Hill, Pte J
Kelly, Pte W E
Klein, Pte B
Knight, Pte P

Knight, Pte W A
McIntosh, Pte D
McGuiness, Pte C H
Molyneaux, Pte J
Morris, Pte P
Murray, Pte W
Presow, Pte G
Reddie, Pte A

Scott, Pte W J
Southern, Pte F
Spargo, Pte J
Stanton, Pte B
Walker, Cpl T
Whammond, Pte A E
White, Pte A

447

Kimberley Siege Account and Medal Roll

Section II (Location – Gibraltar Fort, Davis's Heap)

Jones, Lt E	Demas, Pte J	Langford, A Sgt R E	Sherbourne, Pte G
Adamson, A Cpl J	*Ginghello, Pte J*	Leeson, Pte F S	*Shingler, Pte O E*
Andrews, Pte H R	Gobey, Pte J	Liebenberg, Pte C	*Shingler, Pte P W*
Black, Cpl J	Hemming, Pte F H	McMasters, Sgt J	Spence, Pte D J
Blunden, Pte C	Hobbs, Pte P	McMinn, Pte J	*Thomas, Pte*
Breda, Pte H	Hogg, Cpl J	Nagel, Pte F	Thompson, Pte A
Brophy, Pte M T	Horne, Pte G	Nagel, Pte J A	*Turner, Pte A*
Chambers, Pte A J	Jensen, Pte W	Nankervis, Pte T	Walker, Pte W
Christie, Pte J	Jones, Pte C P	Neal, Pte R P	Walton, Pte R
Coxs, Pte T W	Kube, Pte C	Rogers, Pte J	Winter, Pte A

Section III

Chilman, Lt H R	Gavera, Pte J	Klein, Pte J	Sharland, Sgt G
Bann, Pte J	Geduld, Pte D	Levy, Pte Thos	*Simms, Pte J*
Bawden, Pte W J	Hogg, Cpl J	McDermott, Pte E	Stevens, Pte J
Coutts, Pte J	Hunter, Pte W G	McMinn, Pte J	Thomas, Pte G
Dennis, Pte J	Jenkins, Pte W J	Nankervis, Pte T	Tregonning, Pte F
England, Pte R	Johnson, Pte A	Owen, Pte H	Woolgar, Pte H
Erasmus, Pte L	Jones, Pte J E	Presow, Pte R	
Fraser, Pte D	Keown, Pte J	Rogers, Pte J	
Freeman, Pte H	Kinley, Pte J	Rogers, Pte T	

Section IV

Yates, Lt F G	Hunt, Sgt A C	Perdica, Pte C	Sherborn, Pte G
Antill, Pte H	Laing, Pte J	Quinn, Pte P	Smith, Pte G
Baggs, Pte C	Lawson, Pte E R	Richardson, Pte W	Strong, Pte W
Fitzpatrick, Pte J	McGuiness, Pte C	Rowlands, Pte D	*Taylor, Pte R*
George, Pte W	Pate, Pte A	Salo, Pte P	Van Niekerk, Pte C A
Harris, Pte H	Peel, Pte W	Salt, Pte J	Walton, Pte R W
Humphries, Pte W	Pepper, Cpl E	Scott, Pte C H	Weetman, Pte F

D Company (Veterans)

Blacking, Capt F	Edwards, Pte C	Marks, Pte J	Smith, Pte S W
Hockey, Lt S	Faulds, Pte A (snr)	Matthews, Pte T M	Spence, Pte H (snr)
Amunsen, Pte A	Keating, Pte S	O'Sullivan, Sgt J P	Steines, Pte W O
Augury, Pte B	Kelly, Pte J	Prince, Pte F C	Tait, Pte T A
Brandham, Pte T	*Kimp, Pte G M*	Purchase, Pte A	Young, Cpl S
Buckingham, Pte J	Lawson, Pte J	Reynolds, Pte T	
Claude, Pte A J	Luscombe, Pte J	Rudlin, Pte F	
Crawford, Pte G W	Lyons, Pte L H	Schouw, Pte C	

Ambulance Corps

Booth, Capt Dr R	*Edge, Pte J*	Laverack, Pte (Rev)	Senier, Pte P
Woodman, Lt (Rev) T	Engledoe, Cpl R G	McAdam, Pte W S	*Sharp, Pte A T*
Anderson, Pte H J	*Green, Pte F*	Milne, Pte (Rev) P	Smith, Cpl J J
Barker, Pte H E	Hine, Cpl T A	Molloy, Pte E	Swanepoel, Pte H
Braske, Pte W	Howe, Sgt H W	Morris, Cpl (Rev) J S	Van der Merwe, Pte W
Beck, Pte F	Hussey, Cpl M	Munnik, Pte G	Venter, Pte G R M
Burns, Pte J H	Jacobs, Pte C	Olsen, Pte J	Venter, Pte J M
Christie, Pte C R	Jacobs, Pte D	Olver, Pte H	Warren, Instructor E M
Damon, Pte D	Jansen, Pte J	Peters, Pte C	Williams, Pte D
Devenish, Pte L I	Keating, Pte G C	Peters, Pte W F	

Kenilworth Defence Force

Adams, Capt H J Goold-	Carr, Lt J R	Grant, Lt W G	
Flynn, Lt & QM J F	Grant, Lt D	Hayles, Lt F	

Mounted Men

Brooks, Tpr	Clay, Tpr W	*Deury, Tpr*	*Gonns, Tpr*
Cannon, Cpl T	*Croft, Tpr*	Devenish, Tpr A E	Healy, Tpr M

Appendices

Jennings, Tpr G H	McIntyre, Cpl K G	Steele, Tpr H	Wingrove, Tpr H
John, Tpr W O	Peasland, Tpr S F	*Stewart, Tpr*	Wingrove, Tpr W B
Kearns, Tpr J J	Poulton, Sgt C	Trenwick, Tpr J S	
Kennedy, Tpr	Skinner, TSM C	Vicary, Tpr J	
Martin, Tpr	*Smith, Tpr*	*Warren, Tpr*	

Infantry

Artman, Pte L	Douglas, Pte W	Jones, Pte J C	Peachey, Sgt S
Barrie, Pte G	*Duff, Pte*	Jordan, Pte G	Pennett, Cpl A
Behrens, Pte T W	*Dyson, Cpl*	Kallenborn, Pte J B	Ricketts, Pte A E
Bowness, Pte	Fisher, Pte T B	*Kennedy, Pte*	Ross, A Cpl J T
Brampton, Pte H H	Gouldie, Pte H	*Ladder, Pte*	Rutherford, Pte R
Brown, Sgt W A	Gouws, Pte A E S	*Lauder, Pte*	*Sims, Pte G*
Bruce, Pte A	*Graham, Pte*	Lawrie, Pte A J	Smith, Pte T
Bryant, Pte	Griffiths, Pte D	Makin, Pte G	Stern, Pte L
Bush, Pte J	Grose, Pte T	McAlister, Pte T	*Stone, Pte A*
Capes, Sgt S	*Harrison, Pte*	McClucas, Pte	Sutherland, A Cpl A
Carter, Pte R	Hauptfleisch, Pte P	McDermot, Pte	Thompson, Cpl C
Cartmale, Pte J C	*Hobson, Pte*	McGrath, Pte J	Thompson, Pte H B
Cheen, Pte G	Hobson, Pte W S	McKenzie, Pte A	Waldek, Pte I
Clark, Pte	Holder, Pte H J	*Miller, Pte*	Walters, Pte G
Clarke, Pte	Holman, Pte J	Mitchell, Pte A	*Wheeler, Pte J*
Corless, Pte	Hudson, Cpl P M	Muir, Sgt A J	*Williams, Pte*
Coughlan, Pte W	Hunter, Pte E	*Murray, Pte*	*Woolf, Pte J*
Davidson, Cpl A	*Jameson, Pte*	Nelson, Pte B	
Dickinson, A Cpl G R	Johnson, Pte G	Patterson, Pte F H	

Miscellaneous

There are two lists of miscellaneous men. These appear to be men who have been missed off the original list. As their section numbers are not given, it is not possible to locate them in their correct positions and they are therefore presented as in the *Siege of Kimberley*.

Haider, Capt F R, H Co	Cowen, Pte M, Buffs	Lunt, Pte T, Kamfers	*Randall, Pte J M, B Co*
Stewart, Lt W M, F Co	Dedusey, Pte G, B Co	MacKenzie, Sgt J R, M Co	Russell, SSM J P
Arnold, Pte H, A Co	Dever, Pte M, B Co	*Manning, Pte J F, F Co*	Shackell, QMS J H, F Co
Barnsley, Cpl J R, Amb	Glyn-Cuthbert, Sgt W, H Co	*McLeod, Pte S, B Co*	Ward, Pte R A, Buffs
Beck, Pte C, B Co	Hall, Sgt A N, N Co	Miles, Pte J W, B Co	Westerman, Pte F, F Co
Bennett, Pte T, F Co	Hickens, Pte J J, K Co	*Misselbrook, Pte P W, F Co*	Whitton, Pte R, N Co
Cameron, CS F, N Co	Hodgson, Pte J, F Co	Nomell, Pte E F, Cyclist	*Wonfor, Pte J E, A Co*
Carr, Pte J L, F Co	*Holmes, Pte H G, A Co*	Notcutt, Pte H C, A Co	Zapp, Pte C, D Co
Clarkson, Pte W J, Buffs	*Knight, Pte H E, C Co*	Petersson, Sgt E, N Co	
Coetze, Pte M H, F Co	*Lawrence, Issuer J W*	Porter, Pte C, F Co	

Errata queries

There are 25 men listed in the Errata. While it is not stated why there are listed there, most of the names are to do with initials or surnames spelled incorrectly. Where this is the case, the correction has been made to the lists above. There are however some names that either cannot be reconciled or they belong to a section which is not identified and to choose a section would not be appropriate. The anomalies are listed here:

Kimberley Town Guard	*Pte Ueberle Grasman, I Company*
	Pte C A Chappell, Buffs
Cape Police, Division II	Sgt G Cecil Boult
Army Service Corps	*Pte C Platts (ASC Supply Depot)*
De Beers Maxim Battery	*Gnr A L Hind*

Appendix 18 – Unit photographs

This appendix contains photographs of the main units that served during the siege. Unfortunately, many of the group pictures are not named but, where possible, names have been given where they are available.

Loyal North Lancashire Regiment 451
Army Service Corps 453
Royal Artillery 454
Royal Engineers 456
Cape Police 456
Kimberley Regiment of Volunteers 459
Diamond Fields Artillery 462
De Beers Maxim Battery 465
Kimberley Light Horse 465
Diamond Fields Horse 466
Town Guard 468
Miscellaneous 491

The Eden Family who were represented in several of the local units: DFH, KRV and KTG.
Back row, left to right: W E Eden, G A Eden
Front row: T E Eden, J C Eden, Mr Joseph Eden and youngest son Walter, D R Eden

Mr Eden received a telegram from King Edward VII congratulating him on having so many sons fighting for King and country.

Loyal North Lancashire Regiment

Officers of the 1st Battalion
(pictured in front of the Mess in the Main Barracks, Cape Town, 1899. Not all were involved in the siege)
Back row, left to right: Capt Jourdain, Lt Bingham, __, __, Lt Webster, Capt Wylde-Browne
Middle row: Capt Gill, Capt Lowndes, Maj Jackson, Lt Col Kekewich, Maj Murray, Maj Fielden
Front row: Lt Clifford, Capt Woodward

The Sergeant's Mess at the Main Barracks, Cape Town, 1899 (Not all were involved in the siege)
Standing: Col Sgt Wilkinson, Sgts Brennan, Hodgson, Cpl Rathbone, Sgts Richardson, Mitchell, Ennis
3rd row: Sgts Mossop, Bowman, Dorey, Bray, Moffat, Jeffreys, Atkinson, Col Sgt Porter, Sgts Davis, Holohan, Burton, Col Sgt Still, Sgts Coles, Passmore, Wilson, Messent, Hellard, Nelson
2nd row: Sgt O'Donnell, Col Sgt Heald, Bd Mr Frayling, RSM Mudge, Maj Jackson, Col Kekewich, Lt Lowndes, RQMS Hill, Sgt Langton, Col Sgt Miller, Sgt O'Brien
Front row: Sgts Herbert, Dwyer, Watts, Morgan, Morley, Beer, Col Sgt Carey

Kimberley Siege Account and Medal Roll

LNLR on parade

LNLR at breakfast

Men of the LNLR

Army Service Corps

Gorle and the many men who assisted the ASC

Royal Army Medical Corps

This picture is dated 1900 and may have been taken during the siege

Kimberley Siege Account and Medal Roll
Royal Artillery

Officers and NCOs of the RA and DFA

Men of the RA

Appendices

The RA gun at Premier Mine

Cleaning their 7-pounder field gun at No 1 Searchlight

Kimberley Siege Account and Medal Roll

Royal Engineers

A company of the Royal Engineers under Lt McClintock

Cape Police

Officers

Appendices

Officers of CPD2
Back row, left to right: Lt Currie, Lt T M Davidson, Lt D Monro, Lt Hemsworth, Lt W W Rush
Front row: Capt Murray, Maj F A H Eliott, Lt Col M B Robinson, Capt C A L Berrange, Capt A S Legg

Men of CPD2 stationed at Camp Redoubt

Headquarters staff

Officers and NCOs

Kimberley Regiment of Volunteers

Headquarters section

D Section

Lt Col Finalyson with officers and NCOs

The KRV camp at the Sanatorium

Signallers

Officers and NCOs of Capt Church's Company

Kimberley Siege Account and Medal Roll
Diamond Fields Artillery

Right Section

DFA at the Intermediate Pumping Station

Sub-Section No 4

Sub-Section No 5

Passing through Main Street

The gun limber captured by the DFA on 28th November 1899

Appendices

De Beers Maxim Battery

De Beers Maxim Battery

Kimberley Light Horse

Back row, left to right: E Joyce, J Roberston, D Fenn, A Williams, R Chatfield, G Heberden, J Cox, C Hawker, M Crosbie
Seated: G Harris, R Scott, C Rhodes, W Clifford, R Brand, W Rickman
Front row: J Anderson, J Hickson-Mahoney, A Craven

Kimberley Siege Account and Medal Roll
Diamond Fields Horse

Officers

Officers of the DFH
Back row, left to right: W H Tiller, Capt C C Shackleton, Lt F L Soames, Capt G A Ettling, Mr J Kayne
Front row, left to right: Capt P B Crause, Capt J Lucas, Maj J Peakman, Capt R Brand, Capt T Rodger

Tiller worked for the *Morning News* and Kayne for the *Diamond Fields Advertiser*
This photograph was taken before the siege commenced

Appendices

The DFH at Kenilworth

Back row, left to right, C Jourdan, O P Powell, J J Rogers
Middle row: P Douglass, P Leipoldt
Front row: H L Johnson

Kimberley Siege Account and Medal Roll

Town Guard

Capt Pickering's Redoubt

Officers from No 6 and No 7 Redoubts

Appendices

Officers of Moseley's Redoubt

Mostert's Redoubt. Capt E H Moseley in command

Kimberley Siege Account and Medal Roll

Lt D P Hearn and men of No 2 Redoubt

No 2 Redoubt

Appendices

No IV Section, L Company at No 1 Redoubt

No I Section, N Company at No 1 Redoubt

Kimberley Siege Account and Medal Roll

No III Section, L Company at No 1 Redoubt

No IV Section, N Company at No 1 Redoubt

Appendices

Officers and men of the Permanent Guard at No 3 Redoubt

Kenilworth Defence Force at No 2 Searchlight Redoubt (Fort Rhodes)

Kimberley Siege Account and Medal Roll

A section from No 6 Redoubt at De Beers Mine

Men from Schmidt's Drift Road defences

Appendices

Part of the Permanent Guard at Kimberley Mine

A Section of the Permanent Guard

Kimberley Siege Account and Medal Roll

Officers and NCOs of the Permanent Guard

Officers and NCOs of No 7 Redoubt. Capt G K Ellis in command

No 6 Redoubt. Capt Hornby in command

No 7 and 8 Redoubt

Officers and staff of M Company at No 2 Redoubt
Back row, left to right: Col Sgt N Lawrence, Lt K C Elliot, QM T Reunert, Lt E J Sydney, Mr Weatherby
Front row: Lt C P J Coghlan, Capt P W Mallett, Capt White (Cape Police), Lt D P Hearn

No IV Section, C Company, Pickering's Redoubt No 2

No 4 Redoubt. Capt H Pim in command

Kamfersdam Redoubt. Capt J Armstrong in command

Officers at Premier Mine

Civil Service Corps

Appendices

G Company at Camp Redoubt

H Company at the Reservoir

Municipal Town Guard

Officers of D Section at the Sanatorium

Appendices

Staff despatch riders

Wesselton Mine despatch riders

Kimberley Siege Account and Medal Roll

Cycle despatch riders. Capt Angel in command

De Beers Mine Ambulance. Capt Drew in command

Kimberley Mine Ambulance Corps

Appendices

The fort at No 4 machine, Kenilworth
Standing, left to right: Lt W Grant, Lt H Hayes, Lt D Grant
Seated, left to right: Lt J Carr, Capt H J G-Adams, Lt J F Flynn

The Town Guard at one of the searchlights

The Buffs at Belgravia Fort

The Buffs on lookout in one of their trenches

Appendices

The Buffs at Boshof Redan

Officers and NCOs of Belgravia Fort
Back row, left to right: J Law, J Farquhar, B Stead, F Mandy, D Young, J Moir, D H Henderson, J J Smith
Front row: D M McBean, O D Wright, J J Coghlan, C G Vines, W D Redpath, J T Vigne

Kimberley Siege Account and Medal Roll

No I Sectrion, Belgravia Fort
Back row, left to right: M M Aronson, A Brink, A Ramsay, F Lynch, C W Trevor-Smith, G H Philip,
G H Vyall, P Salisbury, H W Howard
Middle row: T Quentrall, H F Ford, T G Lineham J Farquhar, O D Wright, F Mandy, J J Coghlan, J Moir,
A W Ricketts, G H Salmon, (unknown)
Front row: J L Fraser, P Grassie, W Lawrence, C Kershaw, K Sunde

No 2 Section Belgravia Fort
Back row: I Mendelssohn, E Stonnill, J Davies, J Ford, J Hartley, W Kellet, B Hampson, T Jones
Middle row: R A Skelding, W K Bradford, T J Cundill, R G Arum, M Cowen, H A Oliver, D H Henderson,
W D Morton, F J Gardiner, M Cornwall, (unknown)
Front row: F Mandy, B Stead

Appendices

Beaconsfield Town Guard

Major Fraser and officers

Beaconsfield Town Guard

Captain Blackbeard and officers

Dr R Booth and the members of the Beaconsfield Town Guard Ambulance Corps

Miscellaneous

Lt Col Scott-Turner and officers from the mounted units of the CP, DFH, KLH and LNLR MI

Lt Col Peakman and staff officers from the Mounted Corps

Col Harris and men of the LNLR. Note the two scale models of the Honoured Dead Memorial that were presented by the LNLR to the citizens of Kimberley. The picture post-dates the siege as the men are now wearing their QSAs and KSAs

Officers of the DFH in 1893

Appendix 19 – Photographs of the defences

This appendix contains photographs of the defences. See page 293 for plan diagrams of the defences.

Fort Kumo

Fort Methuen

493

Mostert's Redoubt

Fort Nelson, manned by the Beaconsfield Town Guard

Appendices

The barricade at Kenilworth

Kenilworth Redoubt

Men of No 7 Redoubt standing at arms

No 2 Redoubt, Kimberley Mine

Appendices

Otto's Kopje Mine

The view from Kimberley Mine searchlight

Kimberley Siege Account and Medal Roll

Four views of the Reservoir

Appendix 20 – Queen's South Africa medals

This appendix contains pictures of QSA medals with the Defence of Kimberley clasp as either single items or in groups. Standard Kimberley QSAs, that is medals with the single clasp or in combination with other common clasps, are featured in this appendix.

The details of the naming of the QSA are also included to show the various styles that appear on these medals. The appendix that follows on page 508 discusses non-standard QSAs and the one after that, on page 516, contains information about the Kimberley Star which is often seen with Defence of Kimberley QSAs.

The Defence of Kimberley clasp was one of 26 clasps issued for the QSA. The order of wearing the clasps was defined and this is shown on the right. The clasps at the bottom of the list appear closest to the suspender of the QSA.

This order of wearing explains why the Defence of Kimberley is usually the first clasp on a QSA. Only where the recipient subsequently served in the Relief of Mafeking[70] would the Defence of Kimberley clasp not appear first[71].

QSA with clasp Defence of Kimberley

Order of clasps
South Africa 1902
South Africa 1901
Belfast
Wittebergen
Diamond Hill
Laing's Nek
Johannesburg
Transvaal
Defence of Mafeking
Wepener
Driefontein
Relief of Ladysmith
Orange Free State
Paardeberg
Relief of Kimberley
Tugela Heights
Modder River
Belmont
Defence of Ladysmith
Elandslaagte
Talana
Defence of Kimberley
Relief of Mafeking
Rhodesia
Natal
Cape Colony

Qualification for the Defence of Kimberley clasp

The Army Order 94 of 1901 defined the criteria for the award of all the clasps. For the Defence of Kimberley, the criterion was "A clasp inscribed 'Defence of Kimberley' will be granted to all troops in the garrison of Kimberley between October 14th, 1899 and February 15th, 1900, both dates inclusive."

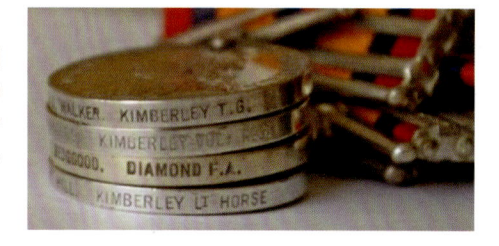

This appendix is arranged in unit order:

Loyal North Lancashire Regiment 500
Army Service Corps 501
Royal Army Medical Corps 501
Royal Engineers 502
Royal Artillery 502
De Beers Maxim Battery 503
Cape Police 503
Kimberley Regiment of Volunteers 505
Kimberley Light Horse 505
Kimberley Town Guard 506
Diamond Fields Artillery 507
Post Office Corps 507

---

[70] The criterion for the Relief of Mafeking clasp states 'A clasp inscribed "Relief of Mafeking" will be granted to all troops under the command of Colonel Mahon, who marched from Barkly West on May 4th, 1900, and all troops who were under Colonel Plumer's command between October 11th, 1899, and May 17th, 1900, both dates inclusive, and who were south of an east and west line drawn through Palachwe.' It is the start date of 11th October, preceding Kimberley by 3 days, that forces this clasp ahead of the Defence of Kimberley clasp.

[71] Excepting the 4 men who received the Rhodesia clasp and further 4 men who received the Natal clasp.

Kimberley Siege Account and Medal Roll

Loyal North Lancashire Regiment

The medals to Major General Robert George Kekewich. His biography can be seen on page 346.

The medals to Colonel F W Woodward. His biography appears on page 358.

The medals to 5004 Private C Fisher. Christopher Fisher joined the 1st Battalion LNLR from the 3rd Battalion LNLR aged just over 18 years on a short service basis on 28th December 1895. He measured 5 feet 5 inches and had brown hair. He received good conduct pay in December 1897 but had to forfeit this in July 1899 until it was restored in November 1900. He transferred to the Army Reserve on completion of 12 years of service. In addition to home service, he was posted to Ceylon for a year and Canada for three years. His service in South Africa was from 11th February 1899 to 17th September 1902. During the siege, he was part of the mounted infantry detachment which had a very busy time, particularly in the early part of the siege. The Boer War was Fisher's only campaign service and the three medals shown here his sole entitlement.

Appendices

Army Service Corps
The naming of the medal to 4875 Private W Ferris who died of wounds 16 January 1901. His medal is engraved as is often seen to the ASC.

Below is the extensive service group of nine medals to J J Edmonds. Note the large ring suspender on the Kimberley Star in place of the usual floriated suspension bar and smaller ring.

Royal Army Medical Corps
The medals to Captain O'Gorman. His biography can be seen on page 350.

The medals to Sergeant Major, later Captain and Quartermaster William Cooper.

501

Kimberley Siege Account and Medal Roll

Royal Engineers

To the left the group to Major W A J O'Meara. His biography can be seen on page 351. Below, the group of medals to Sapper W E Barton.

The 7th Field Company Royal Engineers was posted to the Curragh, County Kildare, Ireland early in 1896 and was serving there in 1899. On 14th July 1899 the 7th Company left the Curragh bound for Southampton. The strength of the company was 6 officers, 180 NCOs and men, and 30 horses. The company embarked on board the Braemar Castle on 15th July 1899 for Cape Town. They arrived on 5th August and were immediately sent to Wynberg Camp where their task was to build accommodation for the troops who were en route to South Africa. The need for Imperial Troops in Kimberley led to No 1 Section under Lieutenant McClintock being sent there on 18th September 1899. The Engineers were heavily involved in the construction of the defensive works in the early part of the siege and also took part in the reconnaissances. The remainder of the 7th Company were in the relieving force and the companies were re-united after the siege. The 7th Company moved to Bloemfontein on 1st March 1900 where it was employed on camp duties. On 10th March the company took part in the battle of Driefontein and then remained at Bloemfontein until 25th April 1900 when it joined the 9th Division for the march to Pretoria. On 29th May the 7th Company supported the attack on the Boer position at Doornkop and entered Pretoria on 5th June 1900. They served through the remainder of the Boer War and did not set foot back in England until 28th September 1902. Barton subsequently saw service in the East Yorks Regiment during the Great War.

Royal Artillery

The DSO and medals to Lieutenant Francis Rynd. His biography can be seen on page 354.

On the next page is the medal to 78260 Gunner John Campbell.

John Campbell joined the Royal Artillery on 11th March 1890 at Leith Fort. He had been born in Dundee and was aged 24. He gave his occupation as labourer and he had served in the Farfar and Kincardine Artillery prior to enlistment. Despite his military experience he took a dislike to the RA and deserted within 6 months being absent for 30 days and his subsequent punishment was imprisonment for 42 days. He joined the 23rd RGA in January 1891. He received

Appendices

good conduct pay in December 1892 but had for forfeit this within a year. He transferred to the Army Reserve but rejoined the Colours in May 1898 and was posted back to the 23rd Company. After the Boer War he re-engaged with the intention of completing 21 years of service but was discharged within two years on 28th May 1904. In addition to service at home, he was posted to Mauritius and South Africa. His two tours in South Africa totalled just less than 9 years. He was awarded a 3rd Class Education Certificate in June 1890 and passed courses in gunnery, telephony and position finding. In addition to his QSA, he received the KSA with two clasps.

De Beers Maxim Battery
The QSA named to Gunner D Bunn who served in the DBMB.

Cape Police
The medals to Commissioner Macleod Robinson. His biography can be seen on page 354.

The medals awarded to Sub Inspector E C J Brand. He had served as a Lieutenant in the DFA in 1892 being promoted Captain and Adjutant in DFH 1895 to 1899. He took part in the Bechuanaland campaign of 1897. He served in the Diamond Detective Department before and on night patrol during the siege. In January 1900 when taking letters to the Boer lines from Boer prisoners, he was himself taken prisoner and sent to Pretoria. He was released on 6th June 1900 and returned to Kimberley as a Detective Officer. He enlisted in 1916 as a Conductor in the South African Service Corps and was discharged in January 1917.

On the top ribbon clasp of the Kimberley Star, note the engraving. It is not uncommon to see, as here 'Siege of Kimberley' or the dates of the siege.

Kimberley Siege Account and Medal Roll

The medals to Captain Robert Crawford. His biography can be seen on page 341.

The medals below were awarded to Lieutenant Colonel W W Rush. See page 354 for his biography. Note the miniature, gold Kimberley Star at the end of the group.

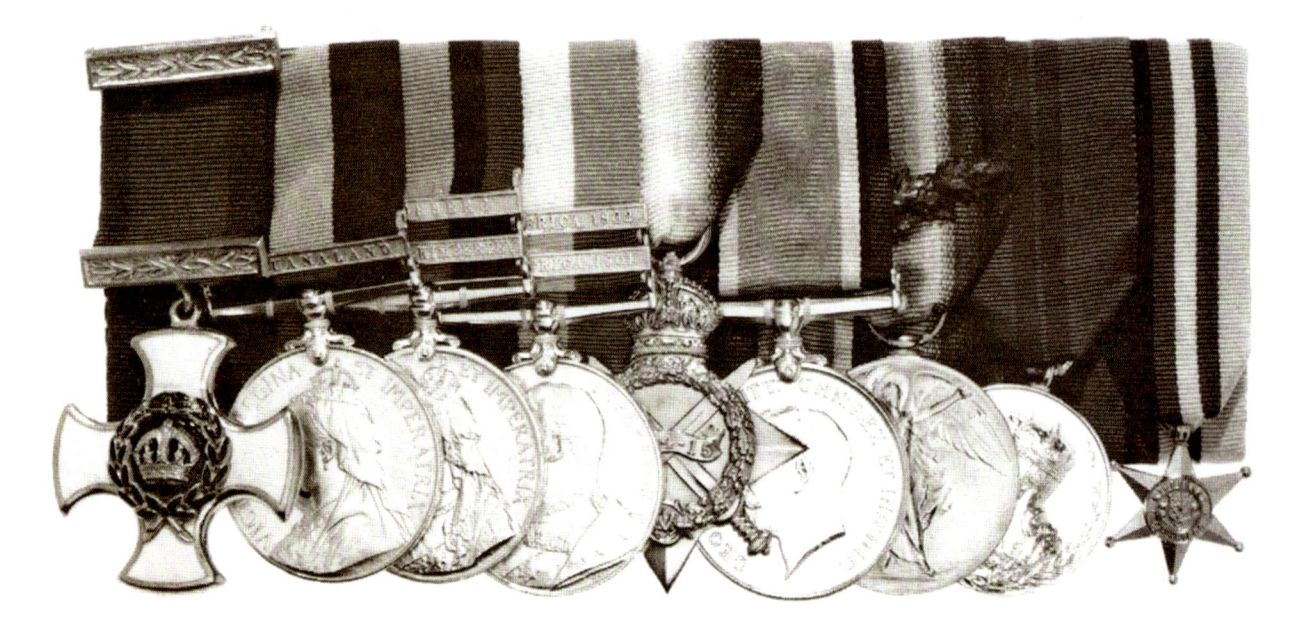

The medals and reverse of the Kimberley Star awarded to Pte Ernest Storer. He served in the dismounted branch of the Cape Police and was engaged in barrier and redoubt duties. The style of naming is typical of that found on the Kimberley Star.

Appendices

The medals to Francis J Henley. Born 1877, he arrived in Kimberley in 1896. He served with the Cape Police, C Squadron, during the siege and was discharged 18 May 1904. Transvaal Town Police 1906. Head Constable, South African Police.

Kimberley Regiment of Volunteers

The medals to Lieutenant Colonel Robert Finlayson. His biography appears on page 343.

The QSA naming to Private R Saunders, KRV. He was killed in action 17 May 1900. The casualty roll says he was wounded at Mafeking 16 May 1900 and died the same day. He possibly served in the Bechuanaland Rebellion 1897 with the DFH earning CGHGSM (1) Bech.

Kimberley Light Horse,

1048 Trooper William Charles Hill served in the KLH between 18th October 1899 and 10th November 1900. He then joined the Cape Police Special Contingent between 18th December 1900 and 25th March 1902 earning the KSA (2).

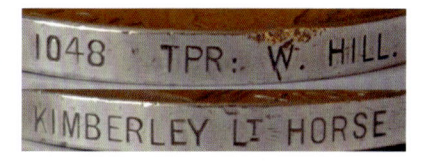

505

Kimberley Siege Account and Medal Roll

Kimberley Town Guard

On the left is the miniature group to Mayor Oliver. His biography can be seen on page 351. On the right is the group to Lieutenant K C Elliot. This group is very unusual because of the inclusion of a Kimberley Medal.

Medals to the Town Guard are usually inscribed 'Kimberley Town Gd:' or 'Kimberley T.G.' It is notable that some medals, for example the ones issued to the doctors, are named to 'Kimb. Town Guard'. However, the two doctors' medals that are known are both renamed and it is likely that they were presented to the recipients at a later date and using QSAs that had been returned as unclaimed.

Officers' medals were either engraved or impressed. The naming of the medal to Captain J Morton is shown to the right. In this case the abbreviation is 'Kimberley Tn: Gd:'

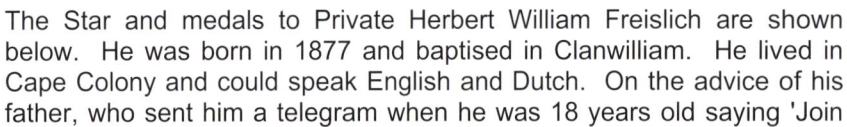

The Star and medals to Private Herbert William Freislich are shown below. He was born in 1877 and baptised in Clanwilliam. He lived in Cape Colony and could speak English and Dutch. On the advice of his father, who sent him a telegram when he was 18 years old saying 'Join Cape Police you will regret not following my advice', he duly enlisted in the Cape Police on 26th March 1895 and with that unit he earned the CGHGSM. In the rank of Pte, his pay amounted to 7 Shillings per day. His service was not without its disciplinary problems leading to his dismissal for neglect of duty on 10th May 1899. It is also recorded that he was twice absent without leave, fined for using abusive language (10 Shillings) and fined for insubordination (20 Shillings). During the siege he served in the Town Guard. His brother was killed in action 25th November 1899.

Appendices

The group below was awarded to Private William Henry Hannam of the KTG. Born in England, he worked at Otto's Kopje Mine before the siege and at Wesselton Mine afterwards, He was admitted to hospital 19th March 1901 and died 28th August 1901. His SAGS Medal is unusual because of the attachment of the unofficial clasp '1880-81'.

Diamond Fields Artillery

The exceptional long service group to Major Thomas May. His biography can be seen on page 349.

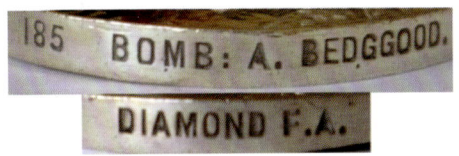

The QSA named to 185 Bombardier A Bedggood. He was born 20th May 1875 in Camden New Town, London. His father worked as a butler. He served with the Kimberley Rifles from the 4th July 1895 to 13th June 1898, receiving the Cape of Good Hope Medal with Bechuanaland clasp. He enrolled in the DFA 14th September 1899 at the onset of the Boer War in Kimberley where he was a fitter at De Beers. His name appears in the Diamond Fields Orders twice during the siege; once for being absent from roll call and the second time for 'irregularities on Guard' for which he was fined 10 Shillings. He resigned from the DFA on 6th January 1903. He is also entitled to the KSA (2).

Post Office Corps

The QSA named to W J Gardiner. He served as acting postmaster during the siege and was mentioned in despatches for this work.

Appendix 21 – Non-standard Kimberley QSAs

While most of the QSAs awarded for the siege carried the clasp Defence of Kimberley either on its own or in combination with other clasps such as Transvaal and Orange Free State, this was not always the case. Due to reasons that are not always wholly clear, not all the people who should or should not have received the medal and clasp did do. In addition, some other anomalies with the Defence of Kimberley clasp are also discussed. This appendix explores the twelve main areas of deviation from the standard practice:

Served but not in the forces and received no clasp 508
Served but not in the forces and received no award 510
Served but not in the forces and received a different award 510
Served in the relief of Kimberley and received the Defence of Kimberley clasp in error 511
Served in the relief of Mafeking and received the Defence of Mafeking clasp in error 511
Served in the defence of Kimberley and received the Defence of Mafeking clasp in error........... 511
Defence of Kimberley and Paardeberg combination 512
Defence of Kimberley and Cape Colony combination 512
Defence of Kimberley and Relief of Kimberley combination 512
QSAs named to units that were served in after the siege 514
Did not serve in the siege 515
QSA forfeited 515

Served but not in the forces and received no clasp

There were 75 QSAs that were awarded to men of the Town Guard but who did not receive a clasp. The reason given is that the men were 'not enrolled in the forces during the siege'. The roll on which this information is based is dated 10th June 1904 and shows the continuing desire for recognition for the work they carried out. Some men on the 1904 roll had been missed off the original KTG roll and were awarded the QSA clasp, but the men in the following table were only awarded the medal:

Name	Nature of work carried out (as described on the medal roll)
Abbot, G B	Ambulance work in connection with scurvy outbreak
Airth, W	Guarding Natives on construction work or trenches
Annetts, E	Construction of barricades and trenches
Ashton, S	Construction of shelters for women and children
Barnes, H	In charge of native guards
Barron, C	Searchlight maintenance
Batten, C F S	Electrical work in connection with searchlight
Berry, W	Gun construction, repairs to Maxims and rifles
Brand, J G	Construction of forts, trenches, barricades etc
Brooks, R H	Chief Electrical Department in charge of searchlights, telephones and dynamite mines
Brown, J	In charge of natives on sanitary works
Bussell, E H	Maintenance of telephones in redoubts
Byrnes, J H	Guarding natives on construction works
Calmeyer, J	Construction of forts, barricades etc
Cheffins, F W	Clearing bushwood, making entanglements etc
Cole, W C	Guarding natives on construction work
Da Fonseca, G T	Construction works, trenches, barricades etc
Daniel, F A	Guarding natives on construction works
Denyer, J	Guarding natives on construction works
Du Toit, G J	Construction of trenches, removing bushes etc
Ebdon, W	Driving pumping engine for the town water supply
Flesch, J A	Removing and burying dead horses
Fletcher, W	Electrical work, searchlights and telephones
Floyd, J	Construction of shelters for women and children
Foster, H	Gun construction, repairing rifles and Maxims
Gallow, E	Guarding natives on construction works
Giddy, B H	In charge of alarm signals
Gilchrist, W	Signaller at alarm post
Glass, W B	In charge of natives (scurvy patients)
Gordon, W	Chief carpenter. In charge of all woodwork erected at the suggestion of the RE Officer
Grant, J	In charge of pump for the town water supply

Name	Nature of work carried out (as described on the medal roll)
Heath, H H	Electrical work; dynamite mines and telephones
Hendry, G	Repairing gun limbers, wheels etc
Hickman, W	Fireman searchlight engine
Humphries, W H	Relief man at pump for the town water supply
Humphries, W J	Clerical assistant to Paymaster
Hunter, G	Casting shells and repairing locomotives
Hutchison, J	In charge of cattle kraals
Jamieson, W	Electrical work; searchlights and dynamite mines
Kirsten, F B A	Construction of forts and barricades. See his biography page 347
Laird, W	Carpentering general work and repairing wagons
Leslie, J	Electrical work; dynamo room
Loriston, A	Water pump. Engine driver
Loudon, A H	Construction of forts, barricades etc
Massey, C E	Ambulance work in connection with scurvy outbreak
McArthur, J H	Telephone and searchlight construction
McIvor, M	Electrical work; dynamo room and mines
McKerrow, A	Repairing gun carriages and carpentering
McKimmie, G	In charge of natives on construction works
McLoughlin, W	In charge of natives acting as despatch carriers
Mierke, F	Construction of forts and barricades
Morkel, P L	Construction of forts and barricades
Morrison, J	Carpentering work under direction of RE Officer
Munro, J	Guarding natives on construction work
O'Brien, J M	Manufacturing shells and loading cartridges
Oostermeyer, H G	Manufacturing shells and repairing Maxims
Outram, E H	Electrical work; searchlights etc
Palm, B	In charge of natives employed on forts
Palvie, S C	Ambulance work in connection with scurvy outbreak
Pine, J	Construction of forts and barricades
Robertson, G M	Electrical work; dynamite mines
Robinson, C H	Construction of shelters for women and children
Smith, T F	Ambulance work in connection with scurvy outbreak
Stouppe, J	Manufacturing shells and ammunition
Sumpton, J	Electrical work; searchlights and telephones
Sutherland, S	Wood work generally under the RE Officer
Taylor, J	Guarding natives on construction works
Timms, E M	Electrical work; dynamos and mines
Trobridge, G	Carpentering for shelters and redoubts
Van Blerk, C H	Engine driver for dynamos
Van Blerk, C J	Telephone exchange for redoubts
Van Breda, G H	Clerical work; Paymaster's office
Vicary, J	Construction works; redoubts, trenches etc
Williams, J G	Repairing tents and making tent pegs
Wright, W O	In charge of guard over scurvy patients

This is the naming of the medal to W Hickman. It is notable that even though none of these men were enrolled, their medals were still named with a rank and the unit was given as the KTG. The lack of a clasp must have rankled with some men as a few examples of no clasp QSAs containing the clasp are known.

Naming of the no clasp QSA to W Hickman

During the Boer War, many town guards[72] were raised to assist in the defence against Boer attack. By far the largest was Kimberley's but there were also town guards in Mafeking, Ladysmith and Dundee as well as a multitude of smaller towns. The medals to the KTG are the only ones issued to the larger town guards without a clasp.

---

[72] Approximately 125 town guards, ranging from Aberdeen to Zeerust.

Served but not in the forces and received no reward

Many people provided assistance during the siege but, as they were not enrolled in any of the military units, their service was not rewarded with either the medal or clasp.

While there were many people in this predicament, the case of J Denoon Duncan is a good case in point. His role in the siege is described in his biography on page 342. Disappointed that there was no recognition beyond his own MID, Kekewich raised his and the case of four other civilians to Sir Ian Hamilton, then at the War Office, in January 1901. The application was considered by the Commander in Chief in August 1901 at the time when a number of awards were being made. However, he was unable to make any award because his allocation of rewards had been expended and he argued the number of recommendations far exceeded his limited allocation. Unable to do anything himself, he transferred the case to the Colonial Office later that month. Kekewich was still pursuing the matter in 1903 but nothing came of this and the case for these rewards was never brought to a successful conclusion.

Served but not in the forces and received a different award

John William Spencer was in Kimberley during the siege, working for the *Diamond Fields Advertiser* as a compositor. As such he did not receive the QSA with the DoK clasp. However, after the siege, he joined the ASC as a Civil Conductor and so earned the clasp for Cape Colony. He died in Kimberley on 26th September 1901. His obituary read: "It is with much regret that we have to record the death of Mr J W Spencer, which occurred on the 26th September at Kimberley Hospital, at the age of 28 years. He will be remembered as the son of ex-Police Sergeant Spencer, late of the Richmond Police Force. The deceased was formerly employed by Mr R W Simpson at the Herald office, first as an apprentice at Richmond and subsequently in a more prominent position at Barnes, but owing to ill-health and under medical advice he went to South Africa, and there found employment on the *Diamond Fields Advertiser*. He was in Kimberley throughout the siege, and the privation he then experienced told upon his somewhat weak constitution. After the siege he returned to England for a time, but went back to South Africa about twelve months ago and to his old employment as a compositor. After a time he was obliged to leave this confined sphere of labour, and found work with the Army Service Corps, in charge of military stores, up to the time of his death. He was much respected by all who knew him. He was accorded a military funeral, the escort being formed of Paget's Horse."

He wrote a letter to his brother on 24th May 1900 about his siege experience: "No doubt you would like to hear from me as to how I passed through the trying and nerve-shattering tumult of the siege of Kimberley. There is one thing about it - I don't want any more siege during the rest of my life ... I saw the military balloon and the Lyddite shells bursting on the kopjes at six o'clock in the morning of that dark day [the battle of Magersfontein] from Reservoir Camp. Anybody who knew the country between the Modder River and Kimberley would condemn any move as disastrous against an enemy such as the Boers ... Some time after communication was cut off the Boers brought "Silent Susan" into operation from Wimbledon Ridge and was sending them into the Reservoir Camp wholesale sometimes, very often early in the morning. Then after a while they got a large gun, with about a 20lb shell at Carter's Ridge, later on another at Susannah Otto's Ridge (a hundred pounder) five miles off. That fairly took the cake and often the whole lot would be sending them in at the same time. What ho! She bumps. Yes, they bumped in to the Market Place to a pretty tune - setting stores on fire, completely wrecking other parts of the Town, and all the women and children were sent down the mines for safety - and there remained until relief came and Boer shells were no more. It was an awful time for every one concerned in the last six weeks or so. Our very small force of mounted troops were

QSA with clasp
Cape Colony

reduced to an almost useless degree, and sickness began to be felt both amongst soldiers and civilians alike. Hospitals were over crowded with the wounded and sick of all nationalities, and things were generally speaking, as serious as they could possibly be. Every day, and sometimes twice a day, military funerals were the only active bodies moving, and these more often than not when there was a heavy bombardment going on. Very often by the silvery moonlight of that starry African sky, I have known twenty being buried at one service - including a Colonel shot dead at Shelby's Nek on reconnaissance. In all conscience this was bad enough to endure - when you could not get away from it - but add to that short rations, very little water and the trying heat of summer in those parts. It was too much for me. Although I managed to escape everything in the shape of shells and bullets, I was caught with camp fever and diarrhoea and laid in the hospital for a month, and was nearly reduced to a shadow ... Now I think this is a rattling good historical letter for modem times, don't you?"

Served in the relief of Kimberley and received the Defence of Kimberley clasp in error

There are nine examples in the medal rolls of the Defence of Kimberley clasp being issued in error. Five of these awards were to the Royal Navy[73], two the Royal Engineers and the remaining two to the cavalry.

1. Trumpeter Frank Yule Garrard, 14th Hussars. He was born in January 1882 and, at the time of his attestation, lived in Newington, Surrey. He was 14 years and 11 months when he joined and give his 'occupation' as Band Boy. His apparent age was recorded to be 15 years and 6 months and he was 5 feet tall, weighed 95 lbs and had brown hair and blue eyes. He was posted to the 14th Hussars on 14th December 1896 and appointed a bandsman on 1st April 1898. His appointment to Trumpeter was on 1st August 1899 and he served at home and in South Africa from 22nd December 1899 to 3rd May 1903. He was discharged at his own request on 4th September 1904 on payment of £18. At discharge his conduct was noted to be 'Very good, thoroughly sober, steady and trustworthy and an excellent soldier before the enemy and in peace a good trombone player in the band for two years'. His service papers show his medal entitlement to be QSA (4) Paar, Drief, RoK and Tr and KSA (2). The medal roll however has the Defence of Kimberley clasp clearly marked and this was attached to his QSA.

The group to Trumpeter Garrard

2. Pte Thomas Wilson, 2nd Dragoons. He attested for the Royal Scots Greys on 4th February 1895 and gave his occupation as tinsmith. He was just less than 19. The majority of his service was at home although he was in South Africa between 6th November 1899 and 1st March 1900. His discharge papers record the award of the QSA but not the clasps. Many men in the 2nd Dragoons received the clasp combination Relief of Kimberley and Paardeberg and this should have been earned by Wilson before he returned to England. However, the medal roll shows he was awarded the clasps Defence of Kimberley and Paardeberg. There is no reason to suggest he was in Kimberley during the siege and he only departed for South Africa after the siege had commenced. For these reasons, it is believed the Defence of Kimberley clasp was recorded in error.

Served in the relief of Mafeking and received the Defence of Mafeking clasp in error

After the siege of Kimberley was lifted, a body of men took part in the relief of Mafeking and received the clasp. However, there are two men who appear to have received the Defence of Mafeking[74] clasp in addition to their Defence of Kimberley clasp. The two men are:

1. Hogg, Corporal J, KTG
2. Ingleton, Sergeant H, KTG

These men should have received the Relief of Mafeking clasp. However, the roll clearly shows the award of the Defence clasp. It is possible that these men were also despatch riders (see page 547) but there is no evidence to support this.

Served in the defence of Kimberley and received the Defence of Mafeking clasp in error

There are two such men:

1. Gainsford, Pte E R, KTG. The DoM clasp is recorded on the CRSS roll.
2. Lodge, Pte J A, KRV. The error was spotted at some point and a correction made to the roll.

---

[73] The men listed are 122290 Petty Officer W Milford, HMS Doris; 171020 Able Seaman H Evans, HMS Doris; 154420 Able Seaman J Grimaldi, HMS Monarch; 169446 Able Seaman E A Harvey, HMS Monarch; 6512 Gunner W H Hughes, HMS Monarch.

[74] A clasp inscribed "Defence of Mafeking" will be granted to all troops in the garrison of Mafeking between October 13th, 1899 and May 17th, 1900, both days inclusive.

Defence of Kimberley and Paardeberg combination

This is less an anomaly and more an unusual combination. The chase of Cronje had advanced faster than the supply lines could support, leaving the troops with very little to live on other than what they carried. As the siege of Kimberley had just been lifted, a message we sent into Kimberley asking for a delivery of bread. The bread was duly baked by De Beers and packed into wagons for the short journey to Paardeberg. Accompanying the wagons was a guard of men taken from the Kimberley garrison. The bread was delivered without incident and the guard stayed overnight in Paardeberg before returning to Kimberley the next day. Their presence entitled them to the Paardeberg[75] clasp. Aside from the supplies requirement, it is possible that some of these men left Kimberley to go to Paardeberg and gained entitlement to the clasp in this way.

The following table lists the units that supplied men for the guard or that were awarded the Paardeberg clasp.

Unit	All ranks
14th Hussars	1
2nd Dragoons	1
Army Service Corps	1
Army Veterinary Corps	1
Command in Chief's Bodyguard	2
Cape Police, District 1	3
Cape Police, District 2	9
Diamond Fields Artillery	1
Damant's Horse	21
Kitchener's Horse	1
Kimberley Light Horse	75
Kimberley Regiment of Vols	12
Kimberley Town Guard	17
Loyal North Lancs Regiment	20
Royal Engineers	6
South African Constabulary	1
Scott's Railway Guards	2
Total	174

QSA with clasps
DoK and Paardeberg

Defence of Kimberley and Cape Colony combination

In Army Order 94 (April 1901) which defined the QSA clasps there was a rule that affected the Defence of Kimberley clasp. It was defined that anyone who was issued with a clasp for an engagement within a state was not thereafter eligible for the clasp for that state. Thus, as Kimberley was in Cape Colony, no one could gain eligibility to the clasps Cape Colony and Defence of Kimberley on the same medal. There are examples in the medal rolls however of recipients being given the Cape Colony clasp in addition to their Defence of Kimberley clasp.

This situation normally happened when the recipient changed units after the siege and then went on to serve in Cape Colony with his new unit. The new unit would correctly record the Cape Colony clasp entitlement but what should have happened, is that the Cape Colony clasp would be crossed through when the Defence of Kimberley entitlement became known. In most cases, this did happen but there are many examples where the Cape Colony clasp was not expunged.

Unless the actual medal has been seen, it is impossible to say whether the medal was made up with this incorrect combination. It is possible that the compositor spotted the error and left off the Cape Colony clasp when the medal and clasps were made up.

Defence of Kimberley and Relief of Kimberley combination

It was further defined in the Army Order that no individual can have both the defence and relief clasps for the Kimberley, Mafeking, or Ladysmith sieges. Thus, a QSA with both the Defence of Kimberley and Relief of Kimberley clasps would be an impossible combination. However, here are two examples of groups with this combination.

---

[75] A clasp inscribed "Paardeberg" will be granted to all troops within 7,000 yards of General Cronje's final laager between midnight of February 17th and midnight of February 26th, 1900, and to all troops within 7,000 yards of Koodoe'e Rand Drift between those dates.

Appendices

The group to Trooper Thomas Blundell, Damant's Horse.

This QSA is interesting because it contains both clasps. This was because the Damant's Horse roll incorrectly shows RoK against his name. He earned his DoK with KTG and it is DoK not RoK that should have been shown on the medal roll. As it stands, this is an impossible but verified combination.

The medals below were awarded to Arthur Cumming, Field Intelligence Department.

See page 341 for his biography. This is a most unusual medal because of the inclusion of the Belmont clasp. Note also the addition of the Relief of Kimberley clasps which has been added later and is not attached to his other clasps.

513

Kimberley Siege Account and Medal Roll

QSAs named to units served in after the siege was lifted

Here are three examples of QSAs named to units that the recipient served in after the siege.

Pte Francis Sturge Brain, Frontier Light Horse. He was a member of A Squadron, Cape Police during the siege. He subsequently joined G Squadron of the Cape Colonial Forces as a QMS. He attested in the Frontier Light Horse on 2nd January 1902 in King Williamstown. The defined area of service for the FLH was the town itself and rail duty in the surrounding area. The pay for troopers was 5 Shilling per day but this did include rations. This is the only known Defence of Kimberley named to the FLH.

The group to Lieutenant William Bray, Scott's Railway Guards. He served during the siege in the De Beers Maxim Battery where he was one of 8 men who served aboard the armoured train. After the siege he saw service with the KLH (185) 9th March to 3rd June 1900 and then with SRG between 18th May 1901 and 30th April 1902. His QSA was issued off the roll for SRG and his KSA from WLH with the rank of Lieutenant. It is unusual to see a Defence of Kimberley issued to this unit.

The group below belongs to William Roberts. It is believed that Roberts was issued with two QSAs, one by the Kimberley Town Guard and another by Damant's Horse. The various papers that relate to him do not present an absolutely clear picture of whether this is one man or two. There is evidence to say that this is two different Welsh men and contradicting information to say the person must be one and the same. His DCM (awarded for gallantry at Boschbult on 31st March 1902) and KSA are not with the two QSAs. The picture below therefore shows how his completed group might look. To date, the two QSAs and Kimberley Star have been acquired from three separate sources.

514

Appendices

Did not serve in the siege

Occasionally there appears on the market, QSAs that include the DoK clasp but where the recipient was not in the siege at all. One such example is the single clasp QSA to 3618 Cpl G Dickenson LNLR that was sold at Glendining's auction in April 1978. This man's actual entitlement was CC and OFS. In November 2005, Spink offered for sale a QSA with 3 clasps DoK, OFS and Tr to 3191 Pte T O'Malley and his KSA (2). His entitlement was again to CC and OFS and the KSA (2). Medals have been seen to regiments that were not part of the siege, for example, QSA (1) DoK to Pte E Jennings of the Liverpool Regiment   The problem is not confined to the QSA. There are examples of Kimberley Stars named to people who appear not to have been part of the garrison during the siege. It is interesting to speculate how these anomalies arose.

QSA forfeited

For misdemeanours, men could forfeit clasps or the entire medal. Where this happened, the men have been removed from this medal roll as the medal should no longer exist. The medals do sometimes resurface either because they are not destroyed or because an issue was subsequently made to the man. An example is the QSA to 5104 Pte B Hope LNLR with clasps DoK, OFS, Tr, SA01 was 'forfeited and returned 30 May 03'. His QSA with clasps DoK, OFS, Tr was sold at Glendining in March 1989. It is not know how many forfeited medals are on the market but this is the only one that is so far known.

The medals awarded to
General P A Cronje

Appendix 22 – Commemorative medals and awards

The commemorative medals will be dealt with in chronological order. The first description will be of the ill-fated Siege Medal. This will be followed by the Mayor's Siege Medal, more popularly known as the Kimberley Star, partly to differentiate it from the first commemorative award. This appendix also contains an account of the sword received by Colonel Kekewich and finishes with a description of the Children's siege medal.

Kimberley Medal

Soon after the siege was lifted, the civic authorities decided they wanted to commemorate the siege by the issuing of a medal. Lord Roberts wrote back to the Mayor on 21st March 1900 saying he thought a commemorative medal would not be appropriate. He said "I doubt if soldiers could be allowed to wear any war medal, other than those presented by Her Majesty or a Foreign Power." Despite this, the authorities pressed on with their ideas and produced the Kimberley Medal. Little is known about this medal and much of what follows about its history is conjecture.

The medal was designed and manufactured, possibly both activities taking place in England. Unusually, the silver medal bears no hallmarks. As the picture of the medal shows, the reverse included the Royal monogram VRI and Imperial crown. While there is no evidence to support this hypothesis, it is believed that the medal was manufactured before authorisation to include these official royal symbols was either requested or obtained. When the English authorities became aware of this medal, the issue was immediately stopped. While it is not known who produced the medal, it is presumed that an order was given that the medals be melted back down to their base silver. Some medals survived the furnace and are today much prized by collectors. The number of surviving medals is not known but, from their occasional appearance in museums and dealers' catalogues, the number must be small, probably less than 50. These 50 could have been the proofs that were to be evaluated by the Kimberley authorities or, alternatively, a small initial batch that was manufactured and sent to Kimberley.

Another hypothesis for the suppression of the medal is that the start date of the siege on the reverse is incorrect. However, the date of 15th October 1899 is perfectly acceptable and this therefore seems an unlikely explanation.

Kimberley Medal reverse

Kimberley Medal obverse

Kimberley Town Hall on the obverse

Kimberley Medal suspender

How the medal was attached to the ribbon and what ribbon was intended are also unclear. The usual suspension is a claw and loop leading to a small silver ring. Occasionally, the medal is presented with a straight suspender similar to the QSA but this is not thought to have been the intention. The ribbon normally used with the medal is the same as for the Kimberley Star but examples are known with a central blue strip with white and then red on either side.

Most of the surviving medals are unnamed although a few examples have been privately engraved.

516

Kimberley Star

Despite the initial commemorative medal failing to come to fruition, the desire to mark the siege was unabated. Under the title 'The Mayor's Medal – Offer gratefully accepted – Meeting last night', the *Diamond Fields Advertiser* reported a meeting that took place on 25th October 1900 to discuss the feasibility of issuing a medal:

> "Last night there was a large gathering of officers of the Kimberley siege garrison, Volunteers and Town Guard – Lieutenant Colonel Harris MLA and Lieutenant Colonel Finlayson being among the number, in the Council Chamber. The meeting was called by the Mayor to decide as the advisability or otherwise of presenting a medal to those who took part in the defence of the town, His Worship being the would-be donor.
>
> The matter was very fully discussed and the matter that has passed between the Governor and the Mayor on the subject read. Eventually, a resolution was unanimously adopted to the effect that the Mayor's offer of presenting a medal be accepted, and that such medal be given to all members of the garrison who served for a period of 90 days between October 1, 1899 and February 28, 1900, with the exception of those discharged for misconduct. It was further recommended that the medal be issued on the first anniversary of the raising of the siege (February, 15).
>
> A board of officers, consisting of Colonels Harris, Finlayson and Peakman, the officer commanding the Cape Police, Dr Mackenzie and the Mayor, was appointed to arrange the necessary details relative to the distribution &c.
>
> A vote of thanks to the Mayor for his generosity was proposed by Mr Mandy, seconded by Dr Mackenzie, and carried with acclamation."

The Mayor's Siege Medal

The Mayor's Minutes for the year ending 31 Dec 1900 contain Oliver's intention to award a siege medal. The article said:

> "As the Council is aware, it is my intention to present a siege medal to our gallant defenders in commemoration of the now historical siege of Kimberley. My original idea was to make the date for the presentation on the anniversary of the relief of the town by General French, but I am afraid that I cannot have things all ready by that date. I shall, however, endeavour to carry out this plan, although I fear the unexpected and unavoidable delay which has occurred in England, occasioned through the medals having to be restamped after being hall-marked, will prevent me from doing so. However, there will be no delay on my part in completing the arrangements for the distribution of the medal. I trust that all who took part in any way in the defence of the town will also receive some recognition of their services at the hands of the Imperial Government, for if Kimberley and Mafeking had fallen the condition of affairs in this portion of the territory would have been most alarming, and serious in its consequences for the whole of the Colony, and these towns were practically saved by the devotion of volunteers, police, and citizens, a devotion which I feel confident will not be allowed to be lost sight of by Lord Roberts."

In the Minute, Oliver alludes to delays caused by the medals 'having to be restamped after being hall-marked'. Here, he must be referring to the Star as the Kimberley Medal was not hallmarked. Perhaps he is glossing over the transition from medal to star but this seems unlikely.

The criteria for awarding the Star was a minimum of 90 days of service during the siege. It is presumed that there was one Star awarded for each qualifying person. It is not possible to say whether awards were made to people who did not receive the QSA, for example unattached civilians. While it is usually the case that the Kimberley Star appears alongside the QSA with clasp for the Defence, as no roll exists of the recipients of the Star, it is not possible to assume that all recipients of the Defence of Kimberley clasp were also recipients of the Star. QSAs with the Defence of Kimberley clasp are seen without the Kimberley Star and vice versa.

As an unofficial award, the Star could not be worn in uniform. The award was produced in miniature, possibly on a private basis and a few examples have survived.

Kimberley Siege Account and Medal Roll

In the Records of the Adjutant General's Office at the National Archives (WO 162/96) the Decision Book for the Boer War contains two entries relating to the Kimberley Star:

    1 Jun 1900   Medal for Kimberley. Request by Mayor of Kimberley to present a medal to all who took part in the defence of that town, not acceded to.

    17 Jul 1901   Kimberley Siege Medal. Cannot be worn but can be distributed.

There is no intervening record to explain why the decision was taken to allow the Siege Medal to be manufactured. Perhaps for commemorative medals that were locally manufactured and funded, the Adjutant General was less concerned. Interestingly, the date of the permission to distribute the Siege Medal was over two months after the first batch of medals were presented in Kimberley. It is intriguing to consider whether the office of the Kimberley Mayor coupled with the backing of De Beers made it a fait accompli for the Adjutant General. Immediately preceding the entry of 1 Jun 1900 in the Decision Book, but dated 6 Jun 1900, is a request from the Ladysmith Town Council to issue a bronze star to all women and children who took part in that siege. The response recorded was 'not entertained'. The civil powers in Kimberley certainly had more cause to want to mark the siege than did their opposite numbers in Ladysmith and for this reason, their resolve was justifiably stronger.

The Star is 6 pointed. On the obverse, the word 'Kimberley' appears at the top of the central design and the dates '1899 – 1900' at the bottom. Beneath the Kimberley coat of arms is the motto *Spero Meliora* which means 'I promise better things'. The reverse displays the words 'Mayor's Siege Medal 1900'.

Obverse centre    Reverse of the Star

The reverse is also hallmarked with the assay year of manufacture and the maker's initials, AHD[76]. The most common hallmark is 'a' which was the main year of manufacture but there are also Stars with hallmarks 'b', 'c' and 'd'. There is one recorded with hallmark 'm'[77]. The Star was not named but many were privately engraved. More than one die was used to produce the Star with variations in the size of lettering, shield and even whether the coat of arms was convex or concave.

Birmingham mark	⚓
Silver mark	🦁
Assay year 1900	a
Assay year 1901	b
Assay year 1902	c
Assay year 1903	d

Birmingham hallmarks

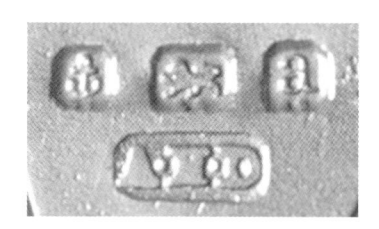

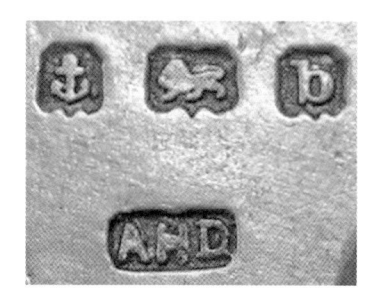

[76] Alfred Horatio Darby. Operated from 51 Caroline Street, Birmingham.
[77] Sotheby, November 1978, Second part of the Lovell sale, lot 911.

The *Diamond Fields Advertiser* reported on the issue of the Kimberley Star on 16th April 1901.

"Mayor's Siege Medal - Distribution last night

The distribution of the medals presented by the Mayor of Kimberley (Councillor H A Oliver JP) to the members of the Siege Garrison took place in the Public Gardens last night. The various forces who took part in the defence of Kimberley during the Siege, so far as they could be got together, assembled at the appointed places under their respective officers and marched to the Gardens, where, in front of the bandstand, a platform had been erected for the distribution ceremony. In addition to those who had served in the defence forces, there was a dense crowd of spectators, the gathering being altogether one of the largest ever seen in Kimberley. The electric light, aided by the search light, which was appropriately directed on to the scene of operations, revealed the different sections of the Siege Garrison, many of them in khaki, drawn up in the centre of the ground, while the raised platform, the surroundings of the bandstand (where the band of the Kimberley Regiment, under Bandmaster Rybnikar, played martial music) and all other available space, was occupied by the general public. On a table in front of the platform were the boxes (as yet unopened) containing the medals as received from the manufacturers, together with a number of flower-baskets intended to facilitate the distribution. In all some 2,700 medals had been brought down to the grounds, for last night's ceremony, and of these considerably over 2,000 found recipients, the remainder being left over for those who, from one reason or another, could not fall in with their companies for the formal ceremony, and for the representatives of those who lost their lives during the siege, the distribution on this occasion being necessarily confined to the organised detachments present.

The medal is a six-pointed star, surmounted by a chased bar, the colours of the ribbon being dark blue, red, white, blue and orange. On the obverse is the Kimberley coat-of-arms with the motto "Spero Meliora" with the word "Kimberley" above, and the date 1899-1900 beneath. On the reverse the words "Mayor's Siege medal, 1900" are engraved. The souvenir is chaste and unique, and well worthy of Kimberley's leading citizen.

The proceedings were opened by the band playing the National Anthem, followed, at the Mayor's request, by three cheers for the King.

The Mayor then briefly addressed the assembly. He said: Officers and men of the Kimberley Siege Garrison. It is my pleasant duty tonight to fulfil the promise I made to you some months ago, that if I could obtain permission I would present each member of the Siege Garrison with a medal in commemoration of the defence of Kimberley. I may in the first instance explain that I have made arrangements to provide a medal for every man who took part in the defence of the town, but I have requested a board of officers to sit and decide all cases wherein men only served for a short period, or in some instances, while not actually taking part in the work of defence, did good service in other respects. I take no responsibility personally as to who receive medals and who do not. I have provided medals for the whole garrison, and it is my personal desire that every man who deserves the medal should receive it. (Hear, hear). The decision on that point, however, I have left entirely in the hands of the board of officers. I know that several hundred applications have come in from men who did not serve for the specified time, and that, as their excuses or reasons were considered satisfactory, a great proportion of these have been awarded the medal. It was the Mayoress's great pleasure this afternoon to hand the first medal that has been presented, to Mr Rhodes (applause) - who took so great an interest in the welfare of the citizens during the siege, and did so much towards defending the town by raising a mounted force. (Applause). I would like to take this opportunity of expressing my gratification, as the Mayor of this town, with reference to the manner in which the Kimberley Siege Garrison acquitted itself during the trying period of the investment, and it affords me very great pleasure now to show that appreciation by requesting the Mayoress, and the ladies appointed with her, to hand the siege medal to the members of the Siege Garrison who are present to-night. There are some 2,000 men who served in the Siege Garrison but who are now away from Kimberley, and on their return, whether it be soon or late, the medal will be there ready for them. I have had a number of requests for medals from the relatives of those who fell in the defence of Kimberley, on account of husbands, sons or other who laid down their lives in defence of the town. In every one of these cases, a medal will in due course be handed to the next-of-kin of the deceased. I will now ask the officers to first step to the front and receive their medals, and call upon the Mayoress to make the presentations. (Applause).

The officers of the various sections of the late Town Guard then assembled in front of the platform, and the Mayoress fastened the medal to the breast of each recipient.

Kimberley Siege Account and Medal Roll

The officers having been decorated, a number of hospital nurses, who had charge of the wounded during the siege, received medals, and the distribution was then made to the men of the various detachments. The officer in charge having reported the number of men present in each case, the required number of medals were handed over, and were distributed to the men by lady residents who kindly undertook the duty, one lady officiating for each detachment present.

The medals for the Kimberley Regiment were handed by the Mayor to Colonel Finlayson. In doing so, the Mayor said: A number of the men of the Kimberley Regiment, under Colonel Finlayson, are on duty, and unable to be here to receive their medals, so I wish publicly to present them to Colonel Finlayson, who has promised to distribute them to the men of the regiment. I have great pleasure in presenting these medals to the Kimberley Regiment. (Applause).

The Mayor then called for three cheers for the Kimberley Regiment, which were heartily given.

Colonel Finlayson: On behalf of the Kimberley Regiment, I beg to tender to you, Mr Mayor, our hearty thanks for this most generous gift, and I trust that the Kimberley Regiment, by continuing to do their duty as they have done in the past, will show themselves worthy of the distinction you have so kindly conferred upon those who took part in the defence of Kimberley during the siege. (Applause).

The Mayor subsequently announced that any member of the Siege Garrison entitled to the medal, who had been unable to assemble with their companies on this occasion, could obtain their medals on application at the Town Hall between 10 and 12 am today and following days.

The Mayor then called for three cheers for the late Kimberley Town Guard, which were given with enthusiasm, and on the request of Captain Pooley, hearty cheers were given for the Mayor and Mayoress, this bringing the formal proceedings to a close.

The band contributed a series of patriotic marches, the selections including the ever popular "Soldiers of the Queen", "Sons of the Empire" and other equally well known."

Kimberley Stars in gold

While most stars were in silver, two were manufactured in gold; one to Mayor Oliver and the other to Robert Archibald.

- Mayor Oliver. As the person funding the issue of the Kimberley Star, it was fitting that he should receive something special in reward. The obverse of his star is very similar to the silver version. On the plain reverse is engraved "FROM / THE CITIZEN / SIEGE GARRISON / TO / THE MAYOR". The reverse is marked 18 ct and is believed to have been manufactured in Kimberley by W A Rayner. The star was presented to him on the occasion of a visit to England in 1901.

- Robert Archibald. His star is different to Oliver's and the general pattern for silver stars which again suggests it was an individual manufacture. The reverse is again plain and has the inscription "BOER WAR / SOUVENIER / FROM THE EMPLOYEES / OF THE / DE BEERS CONS. MINES LD / TO / ROBT. ARCHIBALD ESQ / FOR SERVICES / RENDERED".[78] The star is again in 18 ct gold.

---

[78] One has to feel sympathy for the engraver who chiselled 'souvenier' in error.

520

Archibald was a De Beers' floors manager. The story of how he came to receive a gold star is told in the *Diamond Fields Advertiser* of 29th July 1901:

> **Presentation at Kenilworth**
>
> The evening of Saturday, July 27, 1901 will be a red letter day in the annuls of the village of Kenilworth, for the villagers – most of whom are floor employees – hearing of the departure of Mr Robert Archibald, floor manager, for the Old Country, made up their minds to do him honour, and so, although his intention was to have slipped away quietly, they thwarted this intention by inviting him to the Club on Saturday evening, and presenting him with a beautiful illuminated address and a very handsome gold medal – a replica of that presented to the Mayor of Kimberley. …
>
> There was a large attendance. The chair was occupied by Mr J F Flynn, the club manager, who said that Mr Archibald had very nearly got away without any notice being taken of his departure, which he (the speaker) was aware was his desire, but he was the victim of his friends' goodwill that evening. They were all well aware of the series of unfortunate circumstances which led to Mr Archibald being unable to take a conspicuous part in the defence of Kimberley. Circumstances over which he had not the least control but which all the same deprived him of the Mayor's medal. Well, for that they tried to make amends that evening. When the speaker first remembered Mr Archibald, it was as an officer in the Diamond Fields Horse – one of the framed pictures on the Club walls bore testimony to that fact. He was forced to resign his commission through pressure of ever increasing work in his department, but that he did not lose interest in all that was most useful in the Volunteer movement was fully evinced by the manner he had carried out the construction of the local range a year before the war broke out, the range being formally opened by Mrs Archibald. The date of the investment of Kimberley by the Boers found Mr Archibald on a bed of sickness, with a temperature of 103 degrees. After six weeks' illness he recovered sufficiently to get about again but his ardour for making himself useful led to an accident by which he narrowly escaped death. Trying to mount his horse while he was still feeble from the effects of recent illness, it bolted, and he escaped death almost by a miracle. Towards the close of the siege they found him, however, in the front of the enemy, axe in hand, encouraging on the chopping down of the corn from which the enemy 'sniped' the cattle guards on the confines of this village. His devotion to the welfare of the water supply for Kimberley – which lay in his department – was well known to them all, and for which they, in common with the people of Kimberley, owed him much. Mr Flynn went on to say that it was as citizen of the village they were most indebted to Mr Archibald. …
>
> Mr Flynn then called on Captain Braine, of the Village Town Guard, who read the address as follows: Dear Sir, We the undersigned employees of the De Beers Consolidated Mines Limited, representing various departments, hearing of your departure for the Old Country, desire to take advantage of the event by placing on record our appreciation of the services rendered by you under very trying circumstances during the Siege, and we beg you to accept the accompanying medal as a souvenir of these trying times. …
>
> Mr Archibald suitably and feelingly replied. He said it was quite true he did not receive the Mayor's medal. It could not be expected that the Mayor and others could understand his case as did his friends and neighbours, and as long as they did not misunderstand him he felt quite satisfied. He felt strongly, however, for others who had not as many friends as himself in this matter of medals, and he intended lending his voice on their behalf at a later date as their case had been brought home to him …"

Miniature Kimberley Stars in gold

Examples of the miniature Kimberley Star in both silver and gold are sometimes seen in groups and as individual items. Much rarer are a number of miniature stars that were struck in gold for the men at De Beers who worked on the production of Long Cecil. As such, there are probably less than 50 in existence but the exact number is not known. They were made of 9 ct gold and were engraved on the back "NAME / LONG CECIL / 99 – 1900". They were probably manufactured because the workmen, who made this significant contribution to the siege effort, would otherwise not have been rewarded as they were not eligible for the QSA.

Sword of Honour for Colonel Kekewich

The Mayor had the idea of making a special presentation to Kekewich in March 1900. He approached Lord Roberts and received a positive response in which Roberts replied "I fully appreciate and will support the wish of inhabitants of Kimberley to present a sword of honour to Colonel Kekewich." In the Mayor's Minutes for the year ending 31st December 1900, there is a record of the intention to reward Kekewich for his pivotal role in the siege:

Kimberley Siege Account and Medal Roll

"We have also had in hand the matter of the subscriptions for obtaining a sword of honour for presentation to Colonel (now Major-General) R. G. Kekewich as a mark of appreciation by the citizens of this town of his services during the siege. I do not propose to panegyrise the gallant general. We all know how well he defended the town and how indefatigably he worked for our benefit. His attention was everywhere. Night and day in the conning tower, the mark for the enemy's shells; and at headquarters always ready and willing to co-operate with the citizens for the good of the town, always courteous amidst all his cares. We owe him a debt of gratitude for his untiring and ever watchful efforts in our defence. I am pleased to be able to say that we have obtained a sword of honour that will be worthy of his acceptance, and we are looking forward to the day when he will be able to pay us a visit, when I shall be proud to place this token of our regard and esteem in his hands.

In this connection I would like to bear testimony to the cordial relations that have been the feature of all our dealings with the Commandant and other military authorities both during the siege and after our relief when General Kekewich left us for duties elsewhere in the war's wide field of operations. Closely associated as I have been, as representing the Council and the town, with the military authorities, and in touch with them in the many matters connected with the good government and welfare of a town of 50,000 inhabitants under Martial Law, I think I may truthfully state that the untiring efforts of the gallant Colonel in our behalf won the gratitude and esteem of all classes of the community. This speaks volumes for the tact and ability displayed by those in military authority. We had a little trouble at first in the matter of transport of passengers and supplies by rail, but on representation our views have invariably been endeavoured to be met, and I should like to place on record here my thanks to the military authorities for the assistance they have always been ready to render us, and for the manner in which our suggestions in reference to the affairs of the town have been met. Perhaps I cannot pay a higher compliment than to say no British loyalist need ever have any fear when under Martial Law with such officers to administer it as it has been our good fortune to have with us."

The sword was described in the *Illustrated London News*. It was made by Mappin and Webb and the scabbard, hilt and mounting were of 18 ct gold, studded with precious stones. The picture accompanying the description does not do the sword justice:

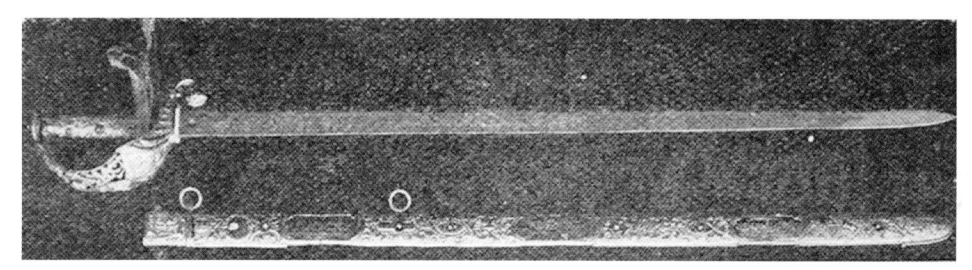

The Sword of Honour

The sword was presented to Kekewich on Thursday 10th July 1902. An article in the *Diamond Fields Advertiser* recorded the presentation:

"Yesterday's immense gathering on the Eclectic Ground adds one more to the series of historic events connected with the late war which it is safe to say will be treasured in the memory of the inhabitants as long as Kimberley exists. Colonel Kekewich was deeply touched, as well he might be, by the warmth of his greeting – a proof, as he well put it, that he made hosts of friends and well-wishers during the period of his command in beleaguered Kimberley. Those who seek popularity do not always attain it; it was Colonel Kekewich's good fortune to win the esteem and gratitude of the public of the Diamond Fields, not by playing to the gallery or by meretricious devices of any description, but by plain, unselfish, and unwearying devotion to duty. It is only too true that the real character of the siege of Kimberley is still imperfectly realised by the outside world. Because the Boers refrained from pressing home their attacks with the same reckless gallantry that they displayed at Ladysmith, it is too often assumed that the task devolving upon the officer in command was comparatively an easy one. Nothing could be further removed from the truth. At Mafeking and Ladysmith the non-combatant population was extremely small. Here the purely military problem was complicated by the presence of a civilian population of 50,000, and the question of supplies alone added enormously to the difficulties with which Colonel Kekewich had to deal. Again, while Ladysmith was garrisoned by 13,000 troops, almost the pick of the British Army, with a large and extremely able military staff, the defence of Kimberley, with its enormous perimeter, devolved chiefly on its own citizens, with a mere stiffening of trained Imperial soldiers. No better body of men than those belonging to Colonel Kekewich's own distinguished corps have ever come to South Africa, but all told they mustered a half battalion, and the remaining companies forming part of Lord Methuen's famous First Division, took part in the relief operations, greatly distinguishing themselves on many occasions, notably at Modder River, where they were largely instrumental in forcing the passage and compelling the Boers to retreat from their positions on the north bank. Colonel Kekewich's splendid tribute to the mounted troops, including of course the Cape Police, will be heartily endorsed by the people of Kimberley. There is little doubt that we owed our safety not merely to the Boer distrust of the dynamite which has been so often cited in explanation of their reluctance to attack, but to the ceaseless activity, the magnificent bravery, and above all, the straight shooting of the Kimberley Mounted Corps, at first commanded by the late Colonel Scott-Turner, and afterwards by Colonel Peakman. If the nature of the siege itself has never been quite fully understood, it is equally true that full justice has not been done to the influence of the successful defence of this town on the fortunes of the campaign as a whole. Colonel Kekewich referred yesterday to the belief which is entertained by many that the taking of Kimberley and Ladysmith were to be the signals for a general rising of the Cape Colony. Whether this was the case or not, it is certain that the unexpected resistance offered by Kimberley detained large numbers of Boers who might otherwise have been free to penetrate far into the Cape Colony, and that if Kimberley had fallen at an early stage of the war, Lord Robert on his arrival in Cape Town would have found himself confronted with the tremendous task of reconquering the whole country from the Hex River Mountain northward. Viewed in this light, Colonel Kekewich's successful defence of Kimberley must be reckoned as not the least among the factors which have contributed to the ultimate success of the British arms."

Beasonsfield Children's Medal

The Mayor of Beaconsfield decided to issue a commemorative medal to the children who had gone through the siege. Parents were required to fill in an application form to obtain the medal for their children. The majority of awards were presented at a special ceremony in October 1901.

The medal takes the form of a circular medallion with a diameter of 38 mm. It was manufactured in silver (though not hallmarked) and white metal.

The reverse depicts Peace and the wording 'Children's medal presented by the Town Council 1900'. The centre of the obverse contains the Beaconsfield coat of arms. The motto below the shield reads 'Forti nihil difficile' which translates to 'Nothing is difficult for the strong'. Around the edge is the wording 'Siege of Beaconsfield - 14 October 1899 – 15 February 1900'.

Most of the examples that are known are unnamed but some have been privately engraved.

Beaconsfield Municipality.

MUNICIPAL NOTICE No 1901, L.

Distribution of Children's Siege Medals.

NOTICE is hereby given that the Medals presented by the Town Council will be handed to those persons whose names are registered as being entitled thereto, on production of the certified forms previously issued, at the TOWN HALL, BEACONSFIELD, on WEDNESDAY MORNING next, the 23rd instant, commencing at 9.30 prompt.

Medals will NOT be issued after 12 noon, as the programme of the Mayor's Treat to the Children of the Township will be started at 1.30 p.m.

The Pupils of the various Schools, and also unattached Children are requested to assemble on the Market Square, Beaconsfield, not later than 1.15 p.m.

By order of the Mayor and Council,

J. HOPWOOD THORP,
Town Clerk.

Town Office, Beaconsfield,
17th October, 1901.

Appendix 23 – De Beers Consolidated Mines Limited

The De Beers Company made an enormous contribution to the siege effort. This appendix highlights this contribution and shows how poorly they were compensated for their expenses. It is notable that the rapidity with which De Beers took the decisions to release, allocate and consume funds, resources and men was in stark contrast to the bureaucracy that fettered military decision-making of the period.

October 1899. The local troops were called out. Rhodes reached Kimberley by train and lived at the Sanatorium. A request to the High Commissioner for guns, rifles, ammunition and food was sent but did not arrive. Coal store amounted to 8,000 tons.

November 1899. The directors in Kimberley were Cecil Rhodes, David Harris, Francis Oats, G W Compton and L Reyersbach. The Boers blew up 1,500 cases of dynamite at Dronfield magazine. 800 horses were purchased for the KLH and DFA.

> **The role of De Beers**
> "It strikes me, that this Company, which owes its great success and strength to its eminent Chairman, has performed a very great service. In the first place, the defences of Kimberley and Mafeking in this tremendous war have been for long the only bright spots in our military operations. In the second place, the defence of Kimberley has, I believe, beyond doubt been the means of saving the Cape Colony. I believe that if the Republican force engaged in the investment of Kimberley had been free at first to move southward to make a dash on the Orange River—a most vital strategical position, which was for some time guarded only by three companies—and to move still farther southward and carry out what was undoubtedly the Republican military plan—to extend their military control down to the Hex River Mountains—I very much fear the Boers would have been successful (Hear, hear). And therefore the defence of Kimberley was not merely the defence of yourselves, but it has also played a great part in the history of the Cape Colony."
> Sir Ellis Ashmead-Bartlett MP
> Comments made at the special meeting of De Beers, held in Kimberley on 23 February 1900.

December 1899. The diminution of supplies meant that plans were made to cease working the mines. The Company funded the KLH. The uncertainty surrounding the siege and its impact on the company led to the decision not to declare a dividend. In his book on De Beers, Chilvers remarks on Rhodes' opportunism for keeping the business running: "Rhodes's amazing opportunism was never more clearly exemplified than when, during the siege, he used a powerful De Beers' searchlight-helio and despatch riders to advance negotiations with the New Bultfontein Company. For a decade Rhodes had been anxious to acquire the one block of this Company's claims that was outstanding. De Beers owned all the other claims in the five local diamond mines. Rhodes made his proposals through the searchlight and despatch riders. The proposals reached London and were considered by the Company's directors there. The purchase of the New Bultfontein Mining Company was completed on June 21, 1900."

February 1900. On 23rd February 1900, Rhodes presided at the 11th AGM for the year ending 30th June 1899. He reported that the profit was around £2,000,000. He also said that during the siege their workmen had received their usual pay, but instead of carrying out De Beers' business they has been defending the town. Rhodes also paid tribute to George Labram, chief mechanical engineer, to Major Scott-Turner and the contribution of Generals French, Roberts and Kitchener. He said "I would offer a suggestion to Mr. Rudyard Kipling that he should devote his thoughts to a lay of the Citizen Soldier." About the effect of the siege on De Beers, Rhodes said "During the last four months we have not been working our mines, while our expenditure was continued at almost the same rate; as against the natives who have been paid off there has been the relief work. The only saving there has been is in fuel, and against this there has been no return of diamonds. We owe the bank to-day £213,000; our liabilities in London for debenture interest and sinking fund amount to £270,000; our expenses for the balance of February and March total £65,000; dynamite factory, £25,000; provisions and coal ordered — we have ordered large shipments of coal from England, as we believe it will be some time before an adequate supply can be obtained from the mines in the Cape Colony — £100,000; and the cash balance of the New Bultfontein Company — the negotiations regarding which are practically finished and will give us the whole of the four mines — £125,000. These liabilities show a total of £798,000, against which we have

> "I beg to bear tribute to the loyal support of our employes in the defence of Kimberley during the trying time of the siege, most of whom joined the various military organizations, and were obliged to subsist on the poor and scanty diet of their various camps and redoubts, while their families were left alone during all those memorable days when Boer shells were being constantly thrown into the residential parts of the town. I regret to record that nine of our employes lost their lives in action, while a large number succumbed to the ravages of typhoid fever."
> Gardner Williams in the 12th Annual Report

diamonds valued at £167,000, thus giving us a debit balance of £631,000. Against this we have a reserve fund of about £1,200,000, so that we renew work with an asset of about £600,000."

The pumps in both mines were kept going until near the very end of the siege. They were restarted before the water had filled the tunnels and thus no damage was done to the underground works. In spite of the Boer shelling, De Beers suffered no damage to any machinery. This was remarkable given the scale and size of the De Beers operations. The conning tower, on top of the pit-head frame at No 1 shaft, De Beers Mine was frequently targeted but never hit.

Casting shells in the De Beers Workshops

March 1900. De Beers contributed £10,000 to the Widows' and Orphans' Fund. The decision was taken to pay George Labram's widow an annuity and a grant for the education of her son. Coal store at the end of the siege 800 tons. The military were on the point of commandeering all the De Beers mules to take part in the relief of Mafeking but this necessity was avoided by the work of the Remount Department who sourced mules from elsewhere. With regard to mules, the Annual Report said 'It may seem strange that a great industry like ours should depend for its output of diamonds on a few hundred mules." For its part in the siege, the company received letters of thanks from the Beaconsfield Council, the Ministers' Association, Lord Methuen and Lord Roberts:

> Osfontein Camp, 5th March, 1900.
>
> Dear Mr Pickering,
>
> I beg you will convey to the Directors of the De Beers Company my best thanks for the assistance they have afforded us in the matter of transport. We were in great difficulties in this respect, and the timely help given by the Company is most valuable.
>
> I am sure the timely aid will be continued, for we must depend upon Kimberley for some days yet for our supplies, and without De Beers' help Lord Methuen would be quite unable to meet our wants.
>
> I note with pleasure that the Company do not propose to make any charge for the transport they have so kindly put at our disposal.
>
> Believe me, Yours very truly,
> Roberts

Kimberley Siege Account and Medal Roll

August 1900. A special commission was appointed to investigate claims by De Beers against the Government in London for damage to farms, stock and fences during the Boer War. De Beers claimed £32,435 in addition to the account for siege expenses amounting to £274,685. On 23rd October 1902, the Under Secretary of State for War offered De Beers £30,000 in full settlement of the claim and this was accepted.

December 1900. Francis Oats presided at the 12th AGM. He said in the year to 30th June 1900 revenue had fallen from £4,000,000 to £2,000,000. He mentioned the siege as a major factor. No dividend was to be paid again.

January 1901. Rhodes suggested raising a force of 600 men to patrol the railway line from De Aar to Mafeking. De Beers would raise, equip and maintain 200 of the men. The unit would be known as Scott's Railway Guards.

The Directors of De Beers in 1900, some of whom served in the siege
Back row, left to right: W Pickering, I R Grimmer, Alpheus F Williams, H P Rudd
Front row: F Hirschhorn, Capt H M Penfold, C E Nind, Gardner F Williams, Lt Col D Harris

Expense details

De Beers separated the costs they incurred during the siege into two schedules in the 1903 Annual Report. Schedule A contained costs for which they sought reparation from the Government and Schedule B listed other expenses for which no claim was made. There is no explanation of the rationale of how expenditure items were placed in the two schedules.

In Schedule A, the introductory note says "Summary of Account rendered to Imperial Government for Expenditure incurred in connection with the Siege of Kimberley, amounting to £54,641 9s 9d, in settlement of which only £30,000 was allowed. No interest was charged, and all charges were made at absolute cost. The expenditure was incurred during period 15th September, 1899, to 31st March, 1900." Note that the figures in all the accounts have been shown in whole Pounds.

Appendices

The costs were:

Item	£
Erecting fortifications under military instructions and supervision, also barbed wire fences and wiring bushes round forts	25,116
Repairing railway line	134
Making shelter trenches	1,384
Cleaning ground for camps, equipment, etc.	876
Laying mines	359
Hire of transport for Lord Roberts to Paardeberg: purchase of oxen, mules, wagons, and wages of drivers, etc ... Exclusive of the company's own transport supplied on this occasion for which no charge was made.	4,104
Kimberley Light Horse: equipment, rations, etc. ,	5,818
Maxim Battery: equipment, rations, wages of drivers, etc.	3,036
Royal Artillery: Diamond Fields Artillery, wages of native drivers and conductors, equipments, etc	1,875
Ambulance wagons: wages, equipment, etc.	1,149
Firemen: wages and equipment of special firemen advertised for by Colonel Kekewich, 18th October, 1899	1,264
Cost making shells	1,445
Scouts, despatch carriers, etc.	1,168
Running searchlights and supplying current generally	2,847
General stores	1,732
Repairs to guns, etc	598
Telephonic communication between defences	67
Armouring trains	576
Guarding cattle, etc.	72
Removal of buildings and stores out of line of fire	76
Sundry hospital expenses	92
Sundries	841
Total	54,641
Horses supplied during the siege (NB the Government did pay for these)	20,836

Schedule B was introduced with the statement "Summary of Direct Losses incurred by De Beers Consolidated Mines, Limited, consequent on the War, for which no claim has been made on the Imperial Government." The table shows that De Beers incurred the full cost of the manufacture of Long Cecil and also demonstrates the philanthropy of the Company.

Item	£
Defence:	
Erection of forts, redoubts, and equipment of same	3,436
Purchase of rifles, repairs to guns, gun carriages, etc.	1,019
Cost drilling company's employees, Town Guard, prior to siege	74
Shoeing horses, mules, and branding, etc.	28
Company's ammunition supplied to Town Guard	1,327
Intelligence, scouting, despatch riders, etc.	844
Preparing and clearing Kimberley Light Horse Mounted Camps	3,623
Protecting company's pumping machinery at Premier Mine, and guarding water supply for townships Kimberley and Beaconsfield	4,384
Town Guard (pay of company's employees after deduction of military pay received by the company)	73,329
Extra rations and stores issued to Town Guard and mounted troops, and cost of distribution	8,615
Demolition of buildings within line of fire by order of military	444
Cost of cycles and repairs for cycle corps	648
Cost of constructing "Long Cecil" and making shells	2,015
General:	
Cost of public soup depot	537
Hospital expenses in connection with company's native labourers	350
Ambulance corps	314

Kimberley Siege Account and Medal Roll

Item	£
Refugee fund	1,480
Guarding Premier Mine boys sent out of compounds under authority of military	105
Charges putting women and children down Company's Mines	193
Comforts for Boer prisoners in gaol	297
Guarding and distributing food	161
Kimberley Mine Fire Service	90
Relief work—wages of non-combatants and aged men (white and black) employed in making and repairing town roads to enable them to earn a wage to keep themselves and families from starving	41,286
Sundry payments	2,786
Total	147,395

The direct siege expenses detailed in Schedules A and B were not the only ones incurred by De Beers. Overall, their liability totalled just less than £275,000. The total of expenses was set out in the 1903 Annual Report:

Item	£
Schedule A (these are the siege costs detailed above)	75,477
Less cash paid for horses	- 20,838
Less Government settlement for siege costs	- 30,000
Schedule B (Direct losses incurred in connection with the siege for which no claim was made on the Government)	147,395
Schedule C (Loss and damage sustained to the Company's farms and property in Griqualand West)	28,925
Less settlement made by Colonial Government	- 16,924
Schedule D (Loss and damage sustained to the Company's farms in ORC)	8,497
Colonial Defence Force (Company contribution to SRG and expenses incurred in defending Company's farms and live stock)	80,367
Total	272,904

Kekewich's Despatch said: "I wish to record the fact that the officials of the De Beers Consolidated Mines Limited placed most unreservedly at my disposal the immense resources and establishments at their command. A great many of the structural works in connection with observation, electric searchlights etc were designed and erected by officials of the company. The company's telephone system was placed at my disposal, and even a gun and artillery ammunition were manufactured at a time when relief did not appear to be near at hand."

The base of a shell manufactured by De Beers

Appendix 24 – Long Cecil

The design, construction and manufacture of 'Long Cecil', a 100 mm breach-loading rifled siege gun, must rate as one of the most notable engineering feats of the Boer War. It stemmed from the need for long range artillery for the defenders of the beleaguered garrison and the most fortunate mix of materials, human resourcefulness, entrepreneurial enthusiasm and the undeniable talent of George Labram. For his biography, see page 347.

The Kimberley garrison's muster of artillery in October 1899 amounted to twelve 2.5 in (64 mm) guns; two of these were obsolete rifled muzzle loaders (RML) brought into the town by the Cape Police. These guns fired a 7 lb (3.1 kg) shrapnel shell and had an effective range of 3,300 yards (3,000 m) and, in the environment of Kimberley,

> "One of the most notable engineering feats of the Boer War"

5,000 yards (600 m) when ring shell was used. Kimberley's elevation and high summer temperatures actually helped increased the guns' range. The investing forces had nine field guns and eight of these were 75 mm Krupp guns with a range of 6,600 yards (6,035 m) and were placed out of reach of Kekewich's artillery. Hence there was an urgent need for a gun which could actually strike the Boer emplacements.

It is not recorded who first suggested the making of a gun, but Labram discovered a large, 10 foot (3m) long steel billet, 10.5 inches (26.8 cm) in diameter and weighing 2,800 lbs (1,270 kg), which had been ordered by De Beers as shafting from the Cannon Steel Works of Sheffield. From this raw material it was envisioned that a barrel could be fashioned with a 4 inch (100 mm) bore and thus a gun of this size should have the desired range capable of reaching the Boer lines.

Having received Cecil Rhodes' sanction, Labram began immediately to collate all the information available within Kimberley on the construction of an artillery piece. This resulted in a surprising amount of information and ranged from the Encyclopaedia Britannica to a 'Treatise on Ammunition'. The resources of De Beers Consolidated Mines were made available and Labram called upon the expertise of some exceptionally competent individuals, namely Edward Goffe, the Chief Draughtsman and Workshop Foreman William Barry. The work was undertaken enthusiastically by the De Beers labour force that though they had never built a piece of ordnance before, they set to with a will and they were fortunate that several artisans were found who had worked previously in the Royal Gun Factory at Woolwich. The attitude of the Imperial officers of the garrison present is recorded as 'cool and indifferent', in contrast to Rhodes driving enthusiasm.

Long Cecil under construction

Work began on 26th December 1899 when the billet was brought in and boring commenced. The construction was organised so that work, wherever possible proceeded in tandem and while the steel billet was on the lathe, work also began on creating the carriage and the manufacture of the shells. It was quickly deduced that to endure successive firings the barrel would have to be strengthened as the carbon content of the steel was considerably below that needed for gun barrel construction. So the workshop blacksmiths fashioned 13 strengthening rings or hoops, forged, heat shrunk and fitted in two overlapping rows across the entire length of the billet from available Low Moor iron.

The barrel was progressively bored to 4.1 inches (approx 100 mm) and then rifled using an increasing twist of 32 spiral grooves from breech to muzzle, an intricate procedure requiring ingenuity given the paucity of experience and materials. The firing chamber was capped with a full screw breech block and obturator to prevent the loss of gasses on combustion. The trunnion ring was forged from a single piece of steel, to create two x 5 inch (12.8 cm) trunnions, 24 inches (61 cm) across and then heat shrunk onto the barrel. The final touches were the fitting of a clinometer and a fore and back sight which was offset by 2 degrees to allow for drift and this, in the test firing, proved extremely accurate.

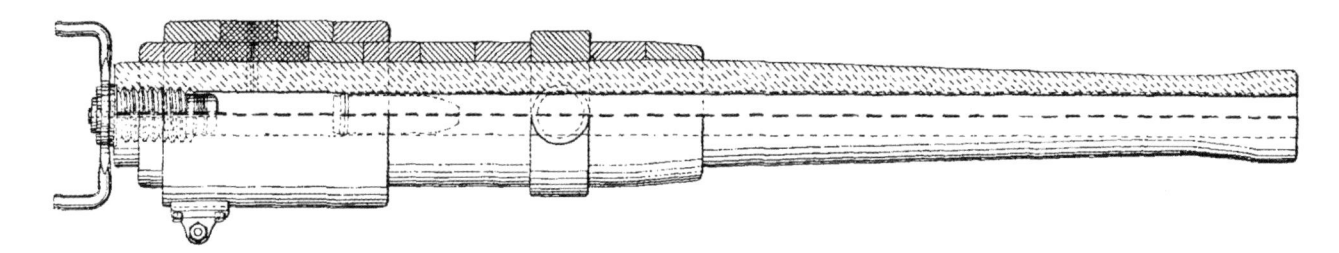

Firing was by means of a radial vent and a Mark III friction tube, drilled through the strengthening hoops to the chamber and then copper lined. This initially proved successful until the gun suffered damage on 23rd January due to the loading of a larger charge than previous and during the repair the radial vent was sealed and a new axial vent was created which functioned perfectly.

The carriage was constructed from available materials and the wheels were found and adapted from a portable engine and fitted with gun metal blocks. An elevating screw was fitted beneath the barrel which allowed an elevation of 0 – 26 degrees. Wheel brakes were later fitted to absorb some of the recoil when the gun went into service.

The men who created Long Cecil. George Labram can be seen holding the end of the barrel and to his left is Goffe. On the far left is Barry (Head Fitter) and to his left is Paley (Assistant Engineer)

Meanwhile, construction of two types of shell, common and ringed, the latter contained serrated rings of cast iron which split into small pieces on impact, had been undertaken in the adjoining workshop. The shell cases were cast in iron, 32 cm high and then steam pressure tested to 8.6 Bar to ensure gas tightness, this proved to be a notable achievement and no 'prematures' were recorded at any time during firings. The shells were fitted with a percussion fuse devised by Labram using a plunger with retaining wires and spring to prevent accidental discharge and a percussion cap. These proved extremely successful. Each shell was marked with a diamond logo and 'De Beers' and some were additionally marked 'With Compts. CJR', Rhodes' initials. The complete shell weighed 29 lbs (13 kg).

The gun was completed in a just 24 days, a further feat given that the Boers regularly shelled the town and on several occasions scored direct hits on and close to the workshops. There was an ample supply of large-grain black blasting powder within De Beers store to produce the shells. Some of this powder had been stored for over ten years and was found to be in excellent condition. Each shell was propelled with a charge of 5 lbs (2.2 kg) of gun powder sewn into wool-serge bags with silk tapes and were made by a local draper.

Appendices

Limbered up at the De Beers workshops

The test firing was arranged for Friday 19th January 1900. The occasion drew a large crowd and the honour of firing the first shot was given to and declined by the senior gunner present, Lieutenant Colonel Chamier. Undeterred, Mr Rhodes then called on Mrs Pickering, the wife of De Beers Secretary and offered her the firing lanyard of the gun, which had been named 'Long Cecil' in his honour. One may only guess at her stalwart courage at stepping forward to fire the first shot of this home-made and untried gun.

The gunners who worked Long Cecil

The first shot ran swift and true and fell to the utter surprise of the Boers amongst their hitherto safe laager at the Intermediate Pumping Station, 7,800 yards (7,200 m) away. After this success a further 15 rounds were fired, including several by Rhodes himself, while calibration, fall of shot and muzzle velocities were calculated by De Beers' staff to produce a set of range tables. Following a thorough evaluation and a few minor adjustments in the workshop 'Long Cecil' was handed over to the Diamond Fields Artillery on 21st January 1900 and based at the No 1 Searchlight Redoubt under the command of Lieutenant H M Close RA.

During the siege 'Long Cecil' fired 255 shells at varying ranges of 5,000 – 8000 yards (4,500 - 7,300 m). Only one significant and several minor incidents interrupted this rate of fire and on each occasion repairs were promptly affected by De Beers' workshops. A reduction in the size of the firing charge was instigated by Lieutenant Colonel Chamier and after this no further faults were recorded. Similarly, tests after firing showed no appreciable wear down of the gun's bore, a testament to the skill of the gun's constructors.

Firing Long Cecil

On 6th February 1900 and in response to this notable addition to the garrison's armament, the Boers brought in a 'Long Tom'. See page 533 for more information. At 6 pm on 9th February, the final shot of the day from this gun and on what was to be the heaviest day of shelling during the siege, fell on the second floor of the Grand Hotel, where Labram was dressing for dinner and killed him instantly. Ironically, his African servant in the room with him at the time was unhurt.

His funeral, with full military honours was held the following night at 8 pm, a Saturday and a huge crowd congregated from the hospital to follow the gun-carriage cortege, draped in the Union Jack to Gladstone cemetery. The Boers chose this occasion to shell the town and so the solemn procession was held in silence for fear the music of the band would create a target and in complete darkness. To Colonel Kekewich goes the deserved epithet 'The Defender' but to George Labram, 'The Saviour of Kimberley' is justly deserved. De Beers awarded his widow an annuity and a grant for his son's education in the United States. Subsequently a grateful Kimberley named a suburb after him and these were his only rewards.

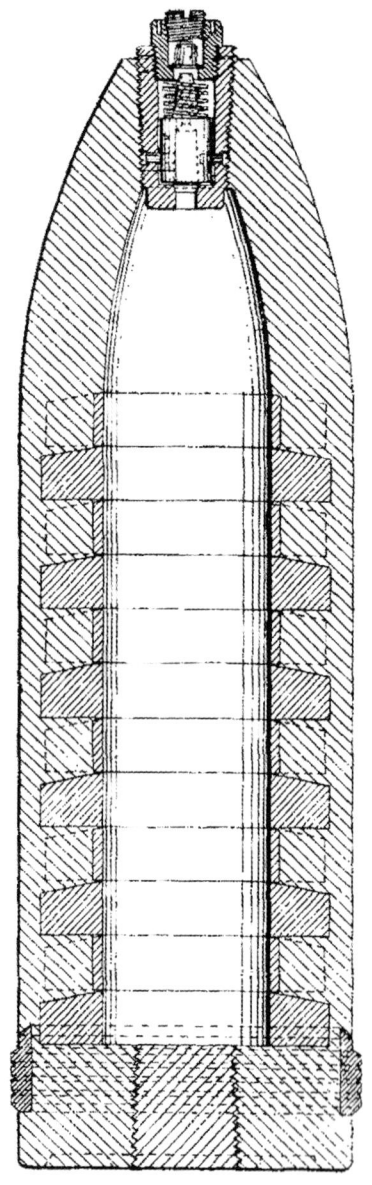

Plan of the shell

After the siege was lifted 'Long Cecil' was used twice, but for ceremonial and not for warlike purposes. The first as an exhibit for the visiting Duke and Duchess of Cornwall and York (future King George V and Queen Mary) at Cape Town in August 1901, where it created great interest. The second was more poignant and was as the gun carriage for Cecil Rhodes funeral in March 1902, firstly at Cape Town for the procession to the railway station and then to his grave site in the Matopo Hills drawn by twelve gleaming oxen.

Afterwards, the gun was returned to Kimberley and placed at the Honoured Dead Memorial where it remains to this day.

Appendix 25 – Long Tom

'Long Tom' was the name given to the 6 inch (155 mm) breech loading Creusot gun used by the Boers. The gun fired a 94 lb (43 kg) shell and had a range of 11,000 yards (10,060 m).

In total, there were four such guns. They were originally purchased with the intention of using them in the forts of Pretoria and Johannesburg. The forts had been designed after the Jameson Raid and the Long Toms were to be mounted on wooden platforms within them.

Long Tom in transport mode en route to Kimberley

Probably because the British blockade prevented further deliveries of guns, the Boers took the decision to carry their Long Toms into the field. The weight of the pieces made this a bold decision and the Boers must be commended for manoeuvring the guns across the landscape by sheer human and animal force. The oxen teams could be 12, 16 or more depending on the terrain to be covered. Manoeuvrability was aided by the fact that an additional set of wheels helped to spread the load and because the 4.2 m barrel could be repositioned on the carriage when the gun was being transported.

The Long Tom easily outranged any gun in use by the British but this advantage was somewhat hampered in the early days by a lack of experience amongst the Boer gunners and by problems with fuzes. The use of black powder meant that its firing could be identified and this fact was used by the Kimberley garrison.

The move into the guerrilla phase meant the Long Toms, in spite of the manoeuvrability were too much of a burden for the mobile Boers. All four of the Long Toms were destroyed to prevent them from falling into the hands of the British. The first was destroyed at Komati Poort on 22nd September 1900. The second ended it days on 18th October 1900, the third on 16th April 1901 and the final Long Tom on 30th April 1901.

94 lb shell and the De Beers 9 lb shell

The Long Tom that was used at Kimberley had earlier been damaged at Ladysmith

Kimberley Siege Account and Medal Roll

during the raid on Gun Hill on the night of 6th December 1899. The gun was taken back to Johannesburg where it was repaired. A new breech block was made and the damaged barrel was shortened leading to it being nicknamed 'die Jood' or 'the Jew'. This work was carried out at Begbie's Foundry in Doornfontein, which had been commandeered by the Transvaal Government.

From its location at Kamfersdam, the Long Tom could deliver shells to most parts of the Kimberley garrison. Only Wesselton Mine and Premier Mine were outside its range.

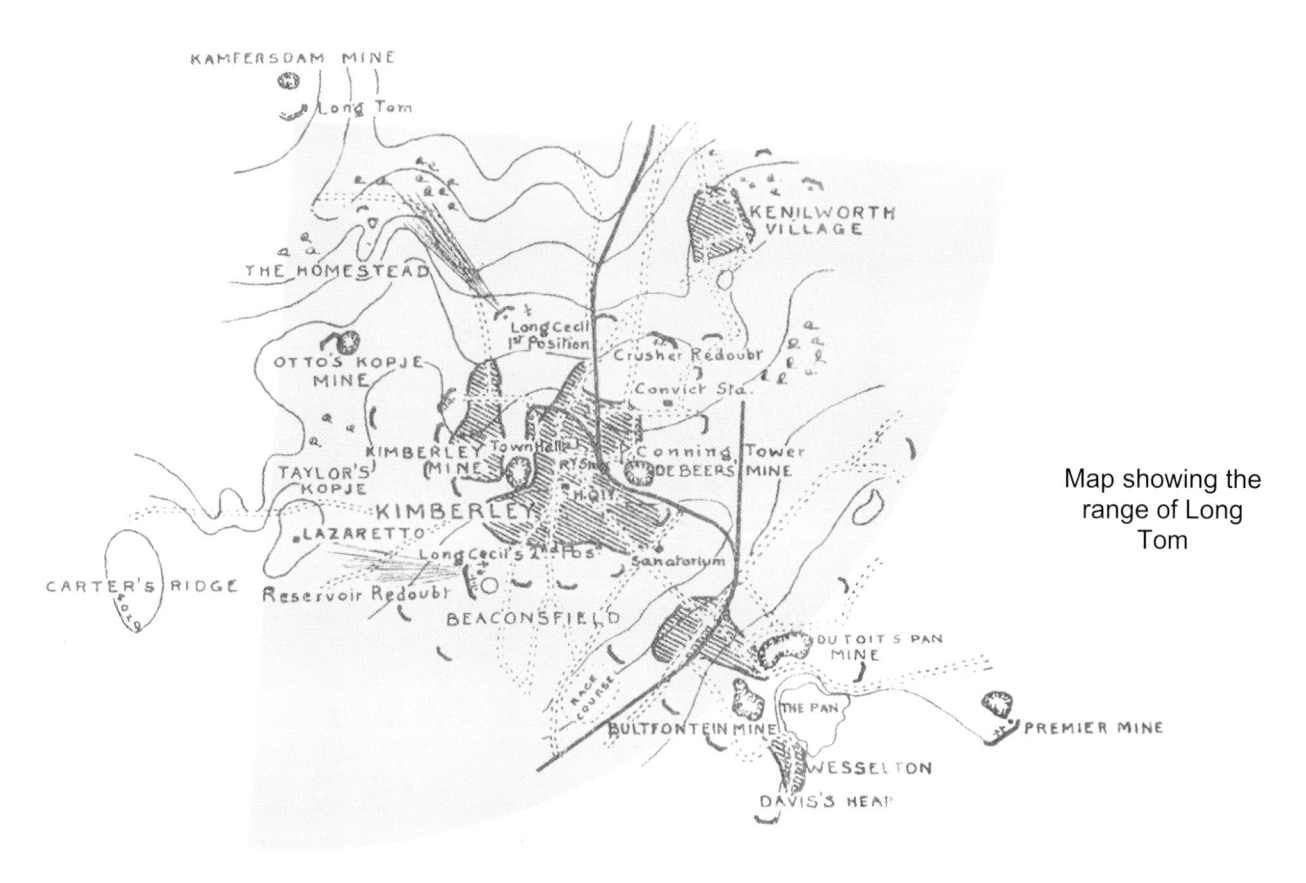

Map showing the range of Long Tom

Two photographs showing the effect of Long Tom's shells. The first shows a house and the second the stock exchange

Appendix 26 – The armoured train

Rather fortuitously, the De Beers workshops were building an armoured train for the Rhodesian Railway just prior to the siege beginning. Kekewich inspected it on 26th September 1899. This train was used throughout the siege and arrangements were put in hand on the 22nd November 1899 for a second train to be armoured. The cost of armouring an engine was £400 and for a truck £200.

Lieutenant A McC Webster[79], LNLR, commanded the armoured train and he was frequently deployed outside the garrison limits to harass the Boers, reconnoitre and support a sortie. Webster wrote an account of his time with the train but only part of this has survived. This appendix is based on the surviving fragment.

The armoured train with two trucks

Webster described the train: "The Armoured Train consisted of an engine and tender completely armoured, except for the funnel, to within nine inches of the ground together with two armoured trucks, one coupled in front and the other behind the engine and tender. These trucks had loopholes 18" long and 3" high with a steel covering flap outside which was opened and closed at will by the simple expedient of a piece of wire passing through a small hole in the armour above the loophole. At the other end of each truck a maxim gun on a swivel mounting on a horizontal slide was fixed to fire through a port hole which was similarly covered when not in use. There were wooden benches around both sides of the trucks and elevated portholes with a seat above and on either side of each maxim gun for observation purposes."

18th September 1899	Orders received to send half a Battalion from Cape Town (to Kimberley).
20th September 1899	Arrived in Kimberley and Kekewich told me I was to have charge of the Armoured Train and directed me to learn to drive the engine in case anything happened to the regular driver. Warned me not to let anyone know about it as the steps then being taken were secret and only precautionary as War had not yet been declared. I accordingly took lessons in driving on the engine of a goods train and was always in mufti. I had several trips learning to drive and also practised whistle signals for communication from the trucks to the engine driver who in his cabin had no means of observation. After about twenty such trips either in the direction of Graspan or the Modder River we managed to perfect these. Of course I always had to travel in the leading truck according to which direction we were travelling in.
10th October 1899	Kekewich received news from Cape Town that Kruger had issued an ultimatum which expired at 4 p.m. on the 11th calling on all [to] leave the Transvaal, OFS and Natal.
11th October 1899	Two 7lb guns intended for Mafeking arrived in Kimberley about noon and were handed over to the Armoured Train who had orders to take them to Vryburg, and hand them over there to a detachment from Mafeking, returning the next day.
	We arrived at Vryburg about 5 p.m. but found no party from Mafeking. There being nothing to do but wait I went to the Hotel and whilst having dinner there received a message stating that the railway line from Mafeking had been destroyed at Kraaipan, a few miles north of Vryburg.

---

[79] For his biography, see page 357.

Kimberley Siege Account and Medal Roll

12th October 1899	At 4 a.m. I received a second message that the Armoured Train had been derailed at this point and that its crew captured by the Boers. We left Vryburg at 6 a.m. escorting a passenger train, which was stranded there, and proceeding cautiously at about five miles per hour in case the Boers had interfered with the line or tampered with any of the many culverts between there and Fourteen Streams.

About noon just about a mile from the bridge at Fourteen Streams we were fired at several times from a kopje about half a mile East of the railway but only a few hit us and no damage was done.

We crossed the Fourteen Streams' bridge soon after noon and as soon as we were over I released a carrier pigeon saying we were safely across. Col Kekewich told me later that he was very relieved to get this message and as it intimated that the line to Vryburg was still open he telegraphed there to them to send their sick, their rolling stock and all the provisions they could spare into Kimberley at once. This they did the same evening. |
15th October 1899	At daybreak the Armoured Train was sent out to make a reconnaissance a few miles South of Spytfontein siding. We reported by carrier pigeon that we had located a Boer Commando. A good many shells were fired at the train but no serious damage was done and we got our forward maxim gun going for the first time making a party of mounted Boers on the railway about 600 yards away "skidaddle" beautifully. After about ten minutes we retired, as Kekewich had instructed us not to run any risk of damage to the train, and picked up the station-master of Spytfontein siding, some gangers and their belongings and brought them in with us.
20th October 1899	For the past four days we had only had our routine daily patrols North and South to find out if the Boer guns were still in their same positions by drawing their fire. We frequently got them to waste a dozen or more shells from each of their positions but none of them ever came too near. We soon got to know the regular places where they would fire at us and if they did not do so we used to stop the Armoured Train and blow off steam or turn some of the men out to fuss about. This was generally successful, especially when they had changed their positions, and then our job was over.
24th October 1899	At 4.30 a.m. Scott-Turner who was in command of all the mounted troops in Kimberley (670) was ordered to reconnoitre North with 300 men in the direction of Riverton Road station, some 16 miles North of Kimberley, and the Armoured Train followed him to Dronfield siding (7 miles from Kimberley) arriving there at 6.45 a.m. as soon as we arrived Scott-Turner moved on and at a culvert just North of the siding was held up by the enemy. We remained where we were and about two hours later Scott-Turner withdrew to the siding, closely followed by the enemy, and sent a helio message to Kekewich asking for reinforcements. These had already been entrained and about 200 men of the battalion under Major Murray came along together with two of the guns from Kimberley. Two mounted maxims were also sent out by road. The Armoured Train was unable to use its maxim guns so really had little part in the subsequent action which drove the Boers out of Dronfield.
24th November 1899	A month of monotonous daily patrolling to give target practice to the Boers, brought us to daybreak on this day. We then discovered that the enemy had destroyed the culverts South of Spytfontein siding and took the news back to Kimberley.
27th November 1899	The Armoured Train made three excursions North harassing Boers at the Intermediate Pumping Station.
15th February 1900	The Relief Column entered Kimberley and the crew returned to ordinary duty.

The only casualty the crew of the Armoured Train had during the whole siege occurred at the Spytfontein siding on 15th Oct 99[80]. A L Corporal and myself were both looking through the same porthole on the left side of the leading maxim gun when a 12-pounder shell burst about 50 yards away and a small splinter about 1" long and ½" each way passed between our heads and buried itself in the woodwork at the other end of the carriage. It just scratched me and made a two inch cut in the L/Cpl's cheek which he had to have stitched.

---

[80] The name of the Lance Corporal does not appear on the official casualty list. Also, Kekewich's despatch for this day says "the armoured train … returned to Kimberley without having sustained any damage or loss". See page 397.

Appendix 27 – Diamond Fields Advertiser

In the early years of Kimberley, the town was well supplied with newspapers. There were six in the 1870s. The very first was *The Diamond Field* which was launched in 1870. *The Diamond Fields Advertiser and Commercial Guide* was born a few years later on 22nd March 1878. Initially, it was published twice a week and was free of charge. It was sold for the first time on 18th September 1878. On 10th February 1879 the name was changed to the *Diamond Fields Advertiser*.

From May 1882, the paper was printed daily. In the early years, compositors were used to create the text and it was not until 1910 that linotype machines were installed.

The editor during the siege was George Green[81]. He had accepted the editorship in 1898 on the advice of his friend, Edmund Garrett. He was a good friend of Rhodes and earned the nickname 'The Prince of Journalists'.

The privations of the siege affected the paper badly. There was not enough news to print so the paper was reduced to a daily edition of four pages. News brought in by the despatch riders was eagerly sought as were copies of other newspapers that were taken from the Boers. Rhodes would loan newspapers that he acquired from his despatch riders but always asked for their return so that they could be loaned out again. One paper that had cost Rhodes £200 was cut up by Green and his staff to use as copy. In his search for material for the paper, Green was struck by the idea of reprinting patriotic accounts from history to sustain and encourage the inhabitants of Kimberley during the siege. From the Public Library, he obtained a copy of Napier's history of the Peninsular War and started producing special articles under the heading 'Historical Achievements of the British Army by a local student of military history'. The articles were very successful and were reported to be much read by the members of the Town Guard.

Producing a paper daily placed demands on their limited printing supplies. As neither the military nor De Beers would supply any paper, it took the intervention of Rhodes to relieve the problem and allow publication to continue.

In the closing says of the siege, Green and Rhodes discussed the slowness of the military approach and Rhodes suggested that an article in the DFA would help. The article 'Why Kimberley cannot wait' appeared the next day on 10th February 1900. The response from the military can be seen on page 75. Unwilling to submit to censorship, Green decided against publishing the DFA from that date until 16th February 1900 when news of the relief forced a resumption of printing. The paper re-started normal production on the 17th.

The tale of the siege pig

---

[81] For his biography see page 345.

There was some discussion with General French about arresting Green and sending him to trial by a military court for the content of his leader on 10th February. Rhodes again intervened on Green's behalf. He reputedly said to French "Just let me point out that you can't arrest Green because, if you do, you will have to arrest me. And you can't arrest me because you are my guest!". French agreed and the matter was dropped.

When important events occurred during the siege, the DFA would issue 'Extras'. Kekewich also used the paper as a way of promulgating his proclamations to the inhabitants.

V.R.

PROCLAMATION.

PROCLAMATION by Lieut.-Col. R. G. Kekewich, Commanding the Troops at Kimberley.

The remainder of this appendix contains three famous articles from the DFA. The first describing the funeral of Scott-Turner, the second about the slowness of relief entitled 'An impossible rumour' and the third the infamous 'Why Kimberley cannot wait'.

The funeral of Scott-Turner - 30th November 1899

"As the time for the funeral drew near, the streets, other than those on the line of route to the cemetery, became deserted, practically the whole of the inhabitants wending their way in the direction of the thoroughfares through which the cortege was to pass. Long before the hour fixed for the procession to leave the hospital—where the dead were lying—Dutoitspan Road was lined on either side by sorrowful crowds of spectators, and it was the same all along the deep line of route. Even nature seemed to join in the general mourning, a welcome shower being followed by a dark and lowering sky, in keeping with the solemnity of the passing hour. During the day the Hospital had been the scene of many a pitiful outburst of grief on the part of bereaved relatives, over which it was well to draw a veil. Unfortunately two of the bodies could not be identified.

Shortly after five the mournful procession started. A deeper silence than that which had gone before pervaded the assemblage as the Lancashire Regiment, headed by Lieut.-Col. Murray, marched out through the hospital gates with arms reversed. Next came ambulance wagons containing one, two or more coffins, preceding two gun carriages furnished by the Diamond Fields Artillery, on the first of which rested the remains of Lieut. O. Wright, while the second carried the coffin containing the corpse of Lieut.-Col. Scott-Turner, followed by the deceased officer's charger. The last two coffins were covered with beautiful wreaths, while the majority of the rank and file had not been forgotten by their comrades in the matter of floral tributes.

Bearers, drawn from the Ambulance Corps and the Lancashire Regiment, marched by the side of the various vehicles. Following the gun-carriages came representatives of the various forces composing the garrison, these being succeeded by vehicles containing relatives and friends of the deceased. Along Bean Street and De Beers Road into Warren Street slowly passed the sad procession, men baring their heads and women shedding furtive tears at every step. At the Mounted Camp practically the whole of the men turned out and joined the procession, now of enormous length. The Lancashire Regiment, Royal Artillery, Diamond Fields Artillery, Cape Police, Diamond Fields Horse, Kimberley Light Horse, Kimberley Regiment, and Town Guard were all there, and, on the latter portion of the journey, the dead were followed by the whole of the available men of the Kimberley garrison. Had the men been engaged in the more congenial task of a march past, the spectacle would have been of a most soul-stirring character. Under the circumstances, it was one the like of which Kimberley has never seen before, and which it will probably be many a long day 'ere it witnesses again.

Slowly and sadly the procession wended its way to the gates of the cemetery, around which many hundreds of spectators thronged, and at which the Venerable Archdeacon Holbech waited, in company with Col. Kekewich (the officer commanding Griqualand West and Bechuanaland) and Capt. MacInnes, staff officer. As each coffin was borne from the vehicle on which it had been conveyed to the cemetery by its quartet of bearers, the military guarding the approaches saluted, the spectators meanwhile preserving an awe-stricken silence, only broken by the orders of the officer in charge. The ambulance wagons having been relieved one by one of their burdens, the gun-carriages came up, and the bodies of the officers followed those of the men they had led so well in life, through the ranks of sorrowful onlookers, then through those of the firing party, and so on to the graves, Archdeacon Holbech preceding the final coffin, and commencing the solemn but comforting words of the Church of England Burial Service.

Slowly pacing on either side of the coffin were the pallbearers — Col. Kekewich; Lieut.-Col. Chamier, R.A.; Lieut.-Col. Robinson, Cape Police; Lieut.-Col. Harris, M.L.A., commanding Kimberley Town Guard; Lieut.-Col. Finlayson, commanding the Kimberley Regiment; and Lieut.-Col. Peakman, commanding the mounted forces.

Grouped around the open graves were the Right Hon. C. J. Rhodes, Mr. and the Hon. Mrs Rochfort Maguire, Dr. Smartt, M.L.A., the Mayor of Kimberley (Mr. R. H. Henderson, J.P.), the Rev. Father Morley, representing Bishop Gaughran, the Revs. James Scott, W. H. Richards, John Gifford, Joseph Ward, and C. Meyer, Messrs. A. Stead, M.L.A., Gardner F. Williams (General Manager, De Beers Consolidated Mines, Limited), W. Pickering (Secretary, De Beers Consolidated Mines, Limited), W. T. Anderson (President of the Kimberley Chamber of Commerce), and many other prominent citizens, in addition to every officer of the forces able to attend.

It was an impressive scene; the day slowly drawing to a close and night commencing to descend upon the earth, the sky leaden and overcast, the hundreds of uniformed men with the little knot of black-coated civilians showing up more plainly by contrast, the crowd in the distance, the debris heaps even having their complement of spectators, and the solemn silence all around, broken only by the quiet voice of the Archdeacon as he slowly recited the words telling of the sure and certain hope of the resurrection of the dead—all combined to make the scene one not easily to be forgotten, even by the most callous.

The Burial Service concluded, the orders to the firing party rang out sharp and clear on the still air, followed by the crack of many rifles and the loud blast of several bugles, six volleys and six blasts in all. Thus was laid to rest the mortal remains of Lieut.-Col. Scott-Turner, a soldier to the backbone, and as fearless a one as ever donned Queen's uniform. His epitaph might with advantage be confined to five words: 'An officer and a gentleman.'

Next was buried Lieut. Wright, the first of the local officers to fall in the present campaign, another brave man, and one whose loss is deeply deplored by his comrades. Then followed the remainder of the honoured dead, two by two, until the Burial Service had been read over nineteen in all. In another portion of the cemetery Sergt.-Maj. Brady was laid to rest, the Burial Service in his case being read by the Rev. Father Varnat. By this time the shades of night had fallen, but not a man stirred until the whole ceremony was concluded, and every man laid to rest—brave men all. May they rest in peace!"

An impossible rumour - 13th December 1899

"The fact, to which all can testify, that an unmistakable wave of depression is passing over Kimberley at the very-moment when, with relief slowly but surely drawing nearer, brightness and optimism should reign supreme, constitutes so strange a social and metaphysical phenomenon that, as honest chroniclers of the times in which we live, it is impossible for us to pass it over in silence. No doubt the unexampled and wholly unaccountable dearth of reliable news, which is so peculiarly exasperating to many of us, is well calculated to produce a "crisis of nerves" in a modern and up-to-date community, but this is not the fons et origo of the uneasy feeling to which we refer. We may state quite frankly that the real cause is to be found in the extraordinary and, of course, purely conjectural interpretation placed by the public upon the Mayor's announcement regarding the grant of free passes to persons desirous of leaving Kimberley as soon as railway communication is established.

It is darkly hinted that this innocent announcement is merely a sort of official feeler, and that it will be followed in due course by a military ukase banishing from their homes for an indefinite period all women and children, as well as every male inhabitant not actually bearing arms in defence of the place. There can be no possible object in concealing the existence of a rumour which has been widely diffused and anxiously discussed for days past, the more so as, in the absence of the slightest official hint or "communique" upon the subject, we scarcely hesitate to dismiss it as a mischievous and preposterous canard invented, possibly, by the enemy. For our part, we do not regard the Mayor's announcement with even the faintest tinge of suspicion. According to our view of the matter, it is natural that the authorities should wish to offer inducements for people to voluntarily leave Kimberley so as to reduce the number of mouths to feed in the possible contingency of communication being temporarily interrupted at any future time; and we are inclined, in some measure, to regard the offer of free passes as a very acceptable and practical acknowledgment of the sacrifices which the people of Kimberley—poor as well as rich—have made in so cheerful and uncomplaining fashion during this unexpectedly protracted siege. All who are able will doubtless avail themselves of the privilege, and the exodus to the seaside, which always begins at this time of the year, will be unusually large. But such a measure as rumour basely suggests would be a very different matter.

To speak plainly, it would mean not merely banishment for an indefinite period, but bankruptcy for many a struggling shopkeeper and professional man—abject penury and ruin for thousands of humble wage earners and their families who, away from Kimberley, would be quite unable to discover a means of livelihood. The terrible journey to the coast in densely overcrowded trains and over congested lines of railway—and most of us appreciate what that would mean for delicate women and children, with recollections of Glencoe and the more recent harrowing stories of the hegira from the Transvaal fresh in our memories—would perhaps be the least among the hardships to be faced. The coast towns where our unhappy refugees would presumably be dumped down and left to shift for themselves, are overcrowded already, and hundreds, if not thousands, find it hard to procure shelter and food to eat. The distress among these people is notoriously great, far greater than the exertions of philanthropy can hope to cope with, and no sensible person can desire to see that misery added to or intensified by an enforced exodus from Kimberley.

In deliberately asserting our opinion that this hideous and disturbing rumour must be and is wholly and absurdly untrue, we take, however, higher ground. Kimberley, the most important inland town of the Colony and as a great industrial centre where thirty millions of British capital are invested, occupies a position of wholly exceptional importance, and its claim for adequate protection in time of war cannot be disregarded without grievous loss of prestige in the eyes of the world. Admitting that the question of keeping open the communications is a difficult one, we would point out that there are always difficulties of this kind to be accepted and faced in planning out a modern campaign, and they have always been quite successfully surmounted without resorting to any such an anomalous expedient as rumour talks about—viz., that a friendly and victorious army should proceed upon its arrival as a "relieving" column to paralyse and impoverish the entire community and metamorphose a busy industrial city, which has escaped, largely through its own exertions, unscathed from the worst that an enemy could do after a protracted siege, into the semblance of one of the dead cities of the Zuyder Zee. Such an unprecedented proceeding, following upon successful military operations, would cause doubt to be cast upon our victories and, as we have said, be ruinous to British prestige in the eyes of the whole world: and therefore, guided rather by pure reason and common sense than by any knowledge of what is passing in the official mind in Capetown, we have no hesitation in reiterating our entire disbelief in a rumour which we regard as mischievous and preposterous in an equal degree."

Why Kimberley cannot wait - 10th February 1900

"After the disturbing developments of the last three days, we think it must have been brought home to Lord Roberts and to the whole world that, in the interests of humanity, the relief of this beleaguered city can no longer be delayed. In putting the case of the inhabitants plainly, we cannot be accused of want of patience. Not since the siege began, four months ago, has a single exclamation of restlessness or disquiet, so far as we are aware, appeared in these columns; on the contrary, the gravity of the situation has been constantly understated with the object of allaying public uneasiness, even at the risk of conveying a misleading impression of the situation to the outside world. We now find that that risk was more serious than we foresaw. How utterly the public and the authorities have failed to grasp the claim which Kimberley, by the heroic exertions of her citizens, has established upon the British Empire is only too apparent upon reading the callous comments of some of the English papers, and the utter indifference with which our fate appears to be regarded by the military hierarchy.

Yet what are the facts? We have withstood a siege which is rapidly approaching the duration of the siege of Paris; we have practically defended ourselves with citizen soldiers (for, thankful as we are to the Imperial garrison, their numbers have condemned them to play a secondary role); we have raised a large body of mounted troops, who have on two occasions attacked the enemy's strongholds with the most magnificent gallantry; and, through the genius of Mr. Labram—whose tragic death yesterday has sent a thrill of sorrow through the whole community—we have been able not merely to supply ammunition for the military pop-guns sent to Kimberley, but also to produce in our own workshops the only weapon capable of minimising the terrible havoc and destruction caused by the enemy's 6-inch gun throwing a projectile weighing 100 lbs. broadcast over the town at a range of three miles. And if the bravery and resourcefulness of the men of Kimberley are not appreciated at their true worth, still less has justice been done to the sufferings borne so patiently and uncomplainingly by the whole civil population, including women and children. There can be no harm in saying that for nearly six weeks past many have been mainly living on bread and horseflesh, nor need we disguise the ravages of typhoid and other diseases among the Kimberley population to which the unpublished statistics of the medical officer of health bear eloquent testimony. These facts have been made widely known through the Boer press agencies—the only agencies through which the British public gets any real idea of what is taking place in this beleaguered city.

WHY KIMBERLEY CANNOT WAIT.

"After the disturbing developments of the last three days, we think it must have been brought home to Lord Roberts and to the whole world that, in the interests of humanity, the relief of this beleaguered city can no longer be delayed. In putting the case of the inhabitants plainly, we cannot be accused of want of patience. The siege has now lasted nearly four months, and during that long and trying period not a single indication of restlessness or disquiet has, so far as we are aware, appeared in these columns; while facts have been consistently understated with the object of allaying public uneasiness, even at the risk—which has proved far more serious than we ever foresaw—of conveying a misleading impression of the situation to the outer world. How utterly the public and the authorities have failed to grasp the claim which Kimberley, by the heroic exertions of her citizens, has established upon the British Empire is only too apparent upon reading the callous comments of some of the English papers and the utter indifference with which our fate appears to be regarded by the military hierarchy. Yet what are the facts? We have stood a siege which is enough to vie with the siege of Paris, it is enough that in asking for prompt relief we are not asking for anything that we do not deserve, nor for anything that it is not in the power of the British army to give. Although the difficulties of getting news have been well nigh insuperable, we are aware at this moment that there are 120,000 British troops in South Africa, and of these, between 30,000 and 35,000 landed between January 10 and February 10. Arrayed against this vast Army — the largest by far that England has ever got together since the Napoleonic wars — are the burghers of two small Republics who, in the opinion of men who ought to know, like Mr. Rhodes and Mr. J. B. Robinson, do not muster more than 30,000 burghers between them, with perhaps 10,000 recruits in the shape of Colonial rebels and hired European mercenaries. In Natal we have 9,000 men shut up in Ladysmith and nearly 30,000 more marching to relieve them; and as the Boer Army cannot exceed 16,000 men between Ladysmith and the Tugela, we may fairly assume that an army of nearly 40,000 British soldiers, under men like White and Buller, and with every modern military equipment, will be fully able to cope with the immediate task which lies before them in Natal. What, therefore, becomes of the balance of the 110,000 troops now in South Africa?

We need not dilate further on the circumstances of our position, or attempt to draw pictures which would very fairly vie with those of the siege of Paris, it is enough that in asking for prompt relief we are not asking for anything that we do not deserve, nor for anything that it is not in the power of the British army to give. Although the difficulties of getting news have been well nigh insuperable, we are aware at this moment that there are 120,000 British troops in South Africa, and of these, between 30,000 and 35,000 landed between January 10 and February 10. Arrayed against this vast Army — the largest by far that England has ever got together since the Napoleonic wars — are the burghers of two small Republics who, in the opinion of men who ought to know, like Mr. Rhodes and Mr. J. B. Robinson, do not muster more than 30,000 burghers between them, with perhaps 10,000 recruits in the shape of Colonial rebels and hired European mercenaries. In Natal we have 9,000 men shut up in Ladysmith and nearly 30,000 more marching to relieve them; and as the Boer Army cannot exceed 16,000 men between Ladysmith and the Tugela, we may fairly assume that an army of nearly 40,000 British soldiers, under men like White and Buller, and with every modern military equipment, will be fully able to cope with the immediate task which lies before them in Natal. What, therefore, becomes of the balance of the 110,000 troops now in South Africa?

It is asserted in some quarters that all the available reinforcements are being employed in the Cape Colony, and that this population of 45,000 loyal British subjects; must continue to suffer in silence while the whole resources of the British Army are employed to remove a Dutch Landdrost and re-instal an English one in his place in the notoriously disloyal distinct of Colesberg. Yet even supposing that the fall of Colesberg is intended as the prelude of other important developments—and, of course, on this point we know nothing—the potentialities of delay and disappointment are so great that in all probability we should benefit as little by the fall of Colesberg as we should by the fall of Paris or St. Petersburg. Why, therefore, in the name of common sense, should Kimberley wait? Look at the matter as we may, the Dutch have decided that the war shall be fought to an issue at Ladysmith in the east and Kimberley in the west, and, having brought our troops into the field late, we have no alternative but to accept the situation. According to the Federal plan, the surrender of Ladysmith is to be the triumph of the Transvaal, and the Free State is to rejoice over the fall of Kimberley. Military men may make maps at the War Office, and may chatter in Capetown; they may continue to evolve the most wonderful schemes to take the place of those which one by one have had to be abandoned, but they cannot, save at the risk of jeopardising the whole campaign, evade the task of relieving Kimberley. Spytfontein is said to be an impregnable position, but what of that? There is a way into Kimberley over perfectly flat country where a large force of British troops could more than hold its own against an inferior number of Boers drawn from their kopjes to attack them.

We quite agree as to the necessity of relieving Ladysmith; but if troops are being wasted at Colesberg while Kimberley is exposed to the horrors of a bombardment, we can only say what we have long ago suspected, that, owing to a triple Press censorship, only the most erroneous impressions of the state of Kimberley have reached the outer world. We have held our tongues for long, believing that relief was merely a question of days, or at most, of weeks. It seems that we were mistaken. We have now reached a situation when either a newspaper must speak out or it has no raison d'etre, and should cease to exist. They shout to us 'Have patience.' Will they remember that we have fought alone and unaided for four long months? Will they remember that we are situated practically in the centre of a desert 600 miles from the coast; that we have been from the beginning dependent upon our own resources? Will they remember that our lives are now daily and hourly exposed to danger; that our women and children are being slaughtered and our buildings fired? Will they deny that we have a right in these circumstances to expect something better than that a large British army should remain inactive in the presence of eight or ten thousand peasant soldiers? The time has come to put in plain English the plain truths of the situation. We have been influenced in the past by various considerations, notably a desire to avoid compromising what is called the military situation. We have now come to the conclusion that respect for the military situation merely means deceiving our own people, and if only for the sake of future record, we take this opportunity of placing the naked truth before our readers."

Facsimile of the original article (SATURDAY, FEBRUARY 10, 1900.)

Appendix 28 – The Kimberley Club

Ernest Oppenheimer said of the Club in 1935 "Kimberley Club is not just a club in the ordinary sense - it has a tradition all of its own. The memory of the men who made the new and greater South Africa is enshrined in this building." It is certainly true that the Club has held an important place in the history of South Africa and Kimberley both before and after the siege.

The Club traces its history to the early days of Kimberley. The *Diamond Fields Advertiser* carried an advertisement in 1881 asking for designs for the Kimberley Club with costs not to exceed £6,000. The club was ready for business on 14th August 1882. The original Articles of Association for the club were signed by 74 people including J H Lange, Theodore Reunet, Leander Starr Jameson and Cecil Rhodes. In was in the Club that Rhodes hatched and developed his plans for Rhodesia and the Jameson Raid.

The Kimberley Club

During the siege, the Club served as Kekewich's headquarters and provided accommodation for the headquarters staff with an overspill at 44 Currey Street. The Military Press Censor was stationed at the Club.

The Club provided a company of the Town Guard from amongst its members. They were called 'The Buffs' after Kekewich's old regiment and were commanded by Captain Mandy. They were about 100 in number and were stationed at Belgravia Redoubt for some 120 days. Belgravia Fort was rumoured to be one of the more comfortable of the posts.

Despite the paucity of food available during the siege, the Club advertised an extraordinary menu for its 'Siege Dinner Menu, Xmas Day, 1899'. The menu consisted of anchovies and olives, turtle soup, mutton cutlets and peas, aspic of foie gras, roast turkey and ham, asparagus, boiled potatoes, plum pudding, preserved ginger, stilton cheese and unspecified dessert. The menu is still in existence but what is in some doubt is whether this array of food was offered up to the diners. In his diary, Kekewich, who would have been one of the diners, does not even mention the meal so perhaps it was a myth after all.

Secretary of the Club, Captain Tim Tyson, used their resources to provide the famous soup kitchen.

Green in '*An editor looks back*' says the Club did well out of the Boer War. "During the South African War the Kimberley Club made huge profits, for the officers of crack British Regiments and of the Imperial Yeomanry, who were constantly turning up, spent lavishly and emptied the extensive wine cellars which were largely the relic of more prosperous days."

It was no idle boast that there were more millionaires to the square foot in the club than anywhere else in the world. Chilvers said of the Club "Go into the Kimberley Club, identified for so many years particularly with De Beers men, where have foregathered Jameson, Barnato, the Rudds, Beit, the Stows, the Joels and Oppenheimers, Gardner and Alpheus Williams, Sir John Lange, Sir William Solomon, Sir David Harris, Sir Lewis Mitchell, Sir Julius Wernher, Klisser; also, Scott-Turner, Koch, Lord Roberts, Kitchener, Baden Powell and Alverstone, General Kekewich, Justices Bigham and Lawrence, Joe Chamberlain, Sir John Ardach, the Rothschilds, Smuts, Mark Twain, Sir Charles Warren and a host of other notables."

Amongst the most prominent 'other notables' were King George VI, Queen Elizabeth and the two princesses, Elizabeth and Margaret, who dined at the Club on 18th April 1947.

Appendix 29 – The Sanatorium

The Sanatorium was build and opened in 1897 as a health resort and has served many purposes during its time. In 1902, it was renamed the Hotel Belgrave. Afterwards it was used as a convent school and, since 1971, it has housed the McGregor Museum.

The Sanatorium in peace time

During the siege it was Rhodes' quarters. He occupied two modest rooms on the ground floor. The Sanatorium was also home to Dr Smartt and Mr and Mrs Maguire. The presence of Rhodes there meant that the Sanatorium was one of the two favourite targets for the Boer gunners. But, like the other target, the conning tower, it was never hit. A lookout was built on top of the Sanatorium and a gong was sounded as soon as the person stationed there saw the Boers fire. The lookout was also able to see the shells from the battle of Magersfontein.

The Sanatorium in war time. Note the sandbags, reinforcements to the structure of the building, screening and the maxim machine gun over the doorway.
Seated from left to right: J R Maguire, C J Rhodes, H Scott-Turner, Mrs Maquire.
Standing: Dr T W Smartt and G M C Luard.

Appendix 30 – The Town Hall

This building was only constructed in 1899 and opened just before the start of the Boer War. It is frequently referred to as both the City and Town Hall. Its central location and civil importance gave it a high profile during the siege, not least to the Boer gunners who used to target it and managed to damage it.

The Town Hall under construction

A ticket to the opening

The Town Guard marching past the Town Hall

There were several events to mark the opening of the Town Hall. One of these involved the coloured children of Kimberley who met in the Hall for a speech by Mayor Henderson followed by some sports and games. The mayor said their parents were a very important part of the community and that they should not be left out. At the end of the day they each received a commemorative medal and this is shown on the right. The obverse of the medal shows a picture of the Town Hall and the words 'Town Hall – Kimberley'.

Appendix 31 – The Postal Telegraph Department

The members of the Postal Telegraph, like all civil servants were not permitted to take part in military operations. In spite of this and due to the cutting of the telegraph lines, many did volunteer their services. On 15th October, 40 men reported to the De Beers Rock Shaft, where they formed the 'Telegraph Squad', under Mr J E Symons of the KTG. They were assigned a position near No 7 Fort. Some telegraphists also worked as signallers for the military authorities.

The Telegraphists who worked as signallers:
Back row, left to right: C Jubber, J Upfold, W Lunnon, C Foster, J White, Wilson
Middle row: W Bevan, F Osman, J Symons, Simpson, D Rankin
Front row: W Backman, W Stephens
(There were two signallers with the surname Simpson and two with the surname Wilson)

The *Siege of Kimberley* takes up the story:

> "Exceedingly good work was done by the Telegraph Engineering Staff under Inspector Gilbert, who erected telephone lines in a remarkably smart manner to many different points, including the redoubts. These lines have since been maintained in such a manner that complaints as to bad working have been conspicuously absent. A telephone was fitted up in the armoured train, and whenever it went out, which was often during the early days of the siege, telephonic communication was established with the Conning Tower.
>
> The number of telephone wires erected and the urgent need for skilled attention to the telephones at the Headquarter Office, Lennox Street, the Drill Hall, Conning Tower, Mounted Camp, Reservoir, Exchange, &c, and the necessity for relieving many of the officers, whose duties were interrupted by the numerous telephone calls, prompted the military authorities to recall the "Telegraph Squad" from the trenches and caused them to take up duties at the various points mentioned.
>
> The most awkward part of the telephone operator's duties occurred when there was an alarm on. All of those who were not actually on duty at the time, had to fall in at once and march down to the Drill Hall: many of the men had to run a considerable distance for their rifles and ammunition; at the Drill Hall they were included with the Reserve. Arrangements had to be made to relieve the operators at the different points, who, instead of going home, came on to the Drill Hall. Throughout the night and day men were constantly arriving and leaving, from or to other duties.

Kimberley Siege Account and Medal Roll

A corps of signallers was asked for later on, and a number of telegraphists were detached for instructional purposes under Mr J. E Symons, who instructed them in a few details such as the adjustment of the heliograph instrument, &c. After mastering these details, which occupied three days, they naturally became competent signallers.

The "telegraph signallers" were Messrs. Symons, Osman, Lunnon, Rankin, Bevan, Upfold, Simpson, Backman, Henman, Stephens, Foster, White, Jubber, Wilson and Dennison. The "Telegraph Signallers" manned the Conning Tower, the Reservoir and No 1 Searchlight, assisting the hard worked North Lancashire Regimental signallers. Everybody knows how difficult it is to get a "show in" where the military are concerned, and although telegraphists are essentially signallers, they did not get a chance of distinguishing themselves until the work was too heavy for the Regulars to cope with. There was signalling to be done of course, but nothing very great. During the last week of the siege, however, and especially after Gen. French arrived, there was a tremendous lot of signalling work, and the Telegraph Signallers rose to the occasion. On Friday morning, the 16th February, helios were flashing all over the country. Our local men, who had occupied the Intermediate Station, Diebel's Vlei, &c, flashed in their morning state and asked for orders, &c. Col. Broadwood's Cavalry Brigade at Benaauwdheidsfontein kept in touch with us, while Gen. French's column began early, on its way to Dronfield, sending an occasional short message and asking for information. Our one helio was not sufficient for all this, although we managed with it until 10 am. Three Lancashire signallers and two helios were then sent to the Conning Tower to cope with the work, and very soon all the instruments were engaged. The Telegraph Signallers had the honour of retaining the line of communication to Gen. French's column the whole of the day, occasionally turning round to assist in other directions when there was a "rush" on.

During the existence of the 6-inch gun at Kamfersdam the life of the signallers and telephone operators on the Conning Tower was somewhat interesting. Everyone in Kimberley knows how persistently the Boers tried to demolish the Tower; few, however, know how close they got to it though. One shell passed under the canvas awning of the Tower, another between the bars, lower down (one of these while Col. Kekewich was there). A great splinter struck about 5 feet below the signalling platform and made the whole structure quiver. Splinters and bullets from shrapnel were found all around and under the Tower. One shrapnel was timed about half a second too late, and exploded with a terrific bang over the open mine just behind. Shells which struck in a line for the Tower but short, sent splinters whizzing angrily past.

This brief account will show that the members of the Postal-Telegraph Department were of distinct use to the military authorities during the siege of Kimberley."

Col. Kekewich (on the Conning Tower): "Drill Hall, please."
Exchange: "Through."
Col.: "Send two guns to the railway station at once."
Col.: "Mounted Camp, please."
"Through."
"Send two mounted orderlies to the Conning Tower, sharp."
Col.: "Traffic Manager's office."
"Through."
"Get two engines under steam and arrange for a number of carriages to be sent, with one to bring in the wounded: the other engine to be ready to take out reinforcements. Advise when they are ready."
Col.: "Armoured train."
"Through."
Col.: "How many wounded men are there?"
Lieutenant Webster: "Twenty odd, sir."
Col.: "And how many Boers killed?"
Lieutenant: "Don't know, sir, will go and count'"
Col.: "Delaney's."
"Through."
Col.: "Send your ambulance wagon down to the Railway Station to convey the wounded to the Hospital"

After finishing this, the Colonel turned round and said "This is a regular telephone siege."

Appendix 32 – Despatch riders

'Despatch riders' was the term given to those men who tried to go in and out of Kimberley while the siege was in place to carry despatches and other information of a military, commercial or personal nature. While some were indeed mounted, many proceeded on foot to and from their destination. There is no definitive list of the despatch riders and most of what is known of them must be pieced together from numerous sources but even then the picture that is revealed lacks clarity. While some information is known of the white despatch riders, there is generally very little documented about the far more numerous black despatch carriers. Their story is very little heard.

Regardless of colour, the carrying of despatches was a profitable but hazardous business. Ashe used them twice to convey a financial transactions. He says:

> "I went to the bank and got a draft in duplicate just in the usual way, and then I got the military people to let me send the duplicate drafts off by their despatch-riders, with a short letter, on two different nights, hoping that at least one of them would manage to get through. … About a month afterwards, the military told me that neither of the despatch-riders had got through, and neither of them had returned, so they were either dead or prisoners."

Harris relates the story of how Rhodes employed a runner to go to Mafeking:

> "Rhodes was very anxious during the siege to get into communication with Baden-Powell at Mafeking. He asked one of the De Beers Compound Managers if he had a reliable native who knew that part of the country, and would take a message through the Boer lines to Mafeking. Shortly afterwards the Compound Manager brought into De Beers office a native who assured Rhodes that he knew the country well; that he came from Bechuanaland and Mafeking, and that he would get the message through for him. Rhodes warned him that he would have to avoid the roads and make his way across the hills. The native replied that it was the nearest way, and that he would go over the hills. Producing fifty sovereigns and a letter, Rhodes told the native that if he took the letter to Baden-Powell and brought an answer back from him, he would be given the fifty sovereigns. Rhodes put the gold into a bag and placed it in the safe, and said to the native "If I am not here, this gentleman (indicating the secretary), or someone else, will give you this money when you return with the answer." Rhodes gave the boy a few pounds to help him during the journey. The boy did the double journey all right; he brought an answer, and was paid the £50."

In his book *An Editor Looks Back,* Green says '..we had to depend on the news that was brought from the south, first by Rhodes's European despatch riders, of whom Cumming and Baron were the most daring and successful..'

It is possible to identify a few of the despatch riders from the casualty rolls but the task is not an easy one. Lt H G Field can be clearly identified because he returned to Kimberley after escaping imprisonment. Others can be identified because they happened to fall within the issue conditions for clasps to the QSA and thus have proof they were in and out of Kimberley during the siege. A third case is exemplified by Cpl Nicholetts and Pte S Brown who are proven despatch riders but this is not reflected on their QSAs.

It is known that the despatch riders went north to Mafeking and south to communicate with Methuen. Should a person have been in Mafeking while that siege was taking place, they would have been eligible for the Defence of Mafeking clasp to the QSA. The medal roll do list three people who have both the DoK and DoM clasps. It is not believed these are despatch riders but, instead, recording errors. See page 511 for more details.

Medals to Despatch Riders

There are 6 people whose QSAs confirm they were despatch riders and were present at either Belmont, Modder River or both engagements. They were:

Barron, R B. See page 104
Buxton, J. See page 119
Carson, J. See page 122
Cumming, A W. See page 132
Fairbrass, W. See page 146
Von Witt, W S. See page 264

Harris paid tribute to the work of these intrepid despatch riders:

> "Throughout the days of ceaseless vigil, regular communication was maintained with the military by means of white despatch riders and native runners, very few of whom were captured by the enemy. Towards the end of 1900, however, this method of getting messages through became very risky, so much so that the natives were unavailable for this particular service. Notwithstanding this fact, the

white men, to their everlasting credit, stuck to their duty manfully. There were some who had hairbreadth escapes. One of them was captured, but a Mr. Milrais and Captain Cummings (now Colonel) did what was expected of them to the very end. I was present when Rhodes thanked them warmly for the services they had rendered. They were fearless men, for, if captured, they would probably have been shot."

The despatch riders' story

The *Diamond Fields Advertiser* carried an extensive article on despatch riders in their Christmas 1899 edition:

"…perhaps it may be a surprise to some people to learn that to a great extent despatch riding, so-called, is not riding at all, but getting through the enemy's lines on foot, which Mr. Cumming[82] has found by experience to be the best, and, in fact, the only way to perform that ticklish operation with reasonable hope of success. Of the several journeys which he made between Kimberley and Orange River during the siege, only one, and that the first, was done on horseback throughout. If a horseman got into too close touch with the enemy's lines, he could hardly escape being seen and heard. He might make a bolt for it, but bullets travel faster than horses anyway. If he is on foot, and accidentally stumbles across a Boer patrol in the darkness—well, down he drops behind whatever cover the place affords, and either keeps still until the coast is clear, or crawls away to a safer distance when he gets the chance, as circumstances may suggest. An enterprising Home journal, which recently depicted Mr. Cumming in the act of groping his way along behind a rock, while a bow-legged Boer sentry in a wide sombrero stared conveniently in a contrary direction, also spoke of him as crawling on his hands and knees for thirty miles! When he read this, and saw this fancy sketch, Mr Cumming laughed. He has no recollection of crawling thirty miles, although he had to crawl a bit now and then.

On his first journey, shortly after the siege began, he was accompanied by — Beddie. They went on horseback, and took the route via Schmidt's Drift, but when they reached Radloff's farm, Secretaris, they found that they were just on the top of Commandant Greyling and 150 men. This altered their course, and they went down to Rooidam instead. The Boer commando, which they had so nearly struck, was on its way to the De Beers farms. On getting to Rooidam, the despatch riders were informed that a military guard had been stopped at the gates, within 150 yards of the house, by a party of Boers, 300 of whom were stationed in the kopjes, about twenty minutes' riding distance from the spot. On hearing this, Messrs. Cumming and Beddie lost no time in making tracks, and in due course found themselves at Pohl's farm, Kameelfontein. There they off-saddled, and procured a change of steeds, their horses being done up. They then rode to Barron's farm, on the Riet River, which at that early stage of the war was beyond the Boer lines, and knowing that the rest of the journey was perfectly safe, completed it in a cart. On this occasion only, they travelled by day as well as by night. Mr. Barron joined the travellers at his farm, and accompanied them to Orange River, returning with Mr. Cumming to Kimberley a few days afterwards.

Private Samuel Brown, CP, carried the first despatches from Kimberley to Methuen on the night of 14th October 1899

Messrs. Cumming and Barron then agreed that in the event of any further employment as despatch riders being obtainable, they would run together, and on Mr. Cumming's subsequent journeys, Mr. Barron, a staunch friend and comrade, was his companion. In returning from Orange River the first time, they retained their horses as far as Pohl's farm, about 18 miles distance, by road, from Kimberley. Here they found that the enemy's cordon round Kimberley had been considerably increased and that it would be madness to attempt to come in on horseback. So they lay at the farm for that day, and walked in at night, taking a route which carefully skirted houses, kopjes, &c. At one point they came on the Boer fires, and saw and heard the Boer horses hobbled near, but by making a detour they got safely past without observation, and eventually struck the four-mile-post, from whence they were not long in getting into town.

A few days later Messrs. Cumming and Barron went out again, selecting a very dark night for the enterprise, and taking a course which skirted Carter's Ridge, leaving it on the left. Again they got among the Boer lines,

---

[82] See page 341 for his biography.

and made a detour, experiencing some difficulty in regaining the right course. They passed a farm and some dwellings just as the occupants were getting up, and caught sight of a man moving about with a candle, but did not think it prudent to stop for breakfast. Some time after this they heard shots fired, and men shouting, in the direction of a big kopje ahead. This was in the neighbourhood of Koodoosberg Drift. Presently they met a native and asked him if there were any Boers about. It was a lucky meeting, for there were Boers, and plenty of them. The Bloemfontein laager was immediately ahead, and 300 or 400 cattle were grazing not far away. Right about face and quick match became the order, and the despatch-carriers soon left Bloemfontein laager, with the unsuspecting commandoes, considerably in the rear. They went through Koppiesdam, and over Van Jaarveld's farm, where they ran against the farmer's son, bringing in horses. An attempt to evade observation was unsuccessful, so they put a bold face on it, the result being that the young Dutchman no sooner caught sight of them than he made himself scarce in double quick time, no doubt thinking they belonged to some British patrol. From thence they went on to Pohl's farm, and lay there a whole day, after which they felt themselves in safer regions, and took to the saddle for the remainder of the journey. There was, however, still a certain amount of risk, chiefly from the rebels of the district, who, although they might not have personally interfered, were liable at any time to give information, which might have led to the despatch riders being overtaken and captured before they could have accomplished another hour's distance. There was the additional risk, too, that by some of these Colonial rebels one or other of them might be recognised. As a matter of fact, £300 was offered by the Boers in Douglas for Mr. Cumming's capture, and at one farm house at which he stopped a pretence was made, by way of a joke, that it was the intention of the occupier to give him up. From several quarters, in the course of his journeys, he heard of the anxiety of the Boers to secure his arrest.

Black runners arriving at Modder River under cover of night. The Kimberley searchlight is visible in the background.

Having safely reached Orange River and transacted their business, Messrs. Cumming and Barron proceeded to return, and on the way had more than one very narrow escape. They got to Bernstein's (Tafelberg) and lay there for a day. At night they resumed their course, and got to Pohl's. The day of their arrival turned out very hot, and, being fagged, they were glad of a bath and a rest. They accordingly lay down in an outside room. All went well until about three o'clock in the afternoon, when their host came rushing out to the room in a very excited state, exclaiming, "Here they come!" The sleepers awoke without needing a second call, and quickly slipping on jacket and boots, Mr. Cumming took a survey of the surroundings from the window. Sure enough, there was a Boer commando, in a cloud of dust, a few hundred yards away. The two despatch riders made their exit by the back door about the same time as 27 armed burghers dismounted at the front! For about an hour they lay hidden in some convenient bushes not far from the back of the premises, meanwhile taking the precaution to deposit their despatches in mother earth, in view of possible eventualities. The Boers had merely come to make enquiries, and were not particularly in search of the Kimberley messengers, though doubtless they would have been very glad to find them. But not being gifted with the discernment of Sherlock Holmes, they saw nothing unusual, and went away no wiser than they had come, passing at a distance of about fifty yards the concealed despatch riders, who lay there and counted them as they went by. When the coast seemed clear, they came out of their retreat, and went into the house. Shortly afterwards, however, while they were sitting on the verandah talking to their friends, a Boer armed with Mauser and bandolier passed close to the house. This time there was no opportunity of concealment, but fortunately it was not needed. The burgher took no notice of the party, probably knowing that enquiries had already been made at the house, and went on to a bywoner's cottage some distance away. A little boy was sent out to look round, but reported that there were no more in sight. The idea was suggested of making a prisoner of this solitary patrol, and bringing him into Kimberley, but it was not seriously entertained. It might have been possible to capture him, but his presence would have given increased trouble later on.

As it turned out, Messrs. Cumming and Barron had quite enough to do that night in getting in themselves. They left Pohl's farm by night, on foot. It was slightly moonlight, which fact, while it made travelling easier, rendered it more difficult to escape being seen. Somewhere in the neighbourhood of the Riet River they found

Kimberley Siege Account and Medal Roll

themselves in the midst of about 150 horses, and promptly took cover again until the moon had gone down, when they made a fresh start. This time they got within about eight miles of Kimberley, and were proceeding cautiously through the gloom, when Mr. Cumming became aware that some hundred yards away, to the right, was an undefined patch which seemed to be darker than its surroundings. He quietly called his companion's attention to it, and they stopped, uncertain what to do. There was no movement, and whether the shadowy outline ahead was inanimate or otherwise they could not at first tell. Presently, however, they made out the presence of a Boer party of probably some 25 men, who were coming up on the right, and had called a halt. There was not a scrap of cover near, and as they were almost certain to be discovered as soon as the patrol advanced, Mr. Cumming and his friend made a bolt for it, and did the next few hundred yards at their very best speed. Reaching cover, they lay down for a breather, and then went ahead again, tumbling over rocks and boulders in the darkness, until the sound of horses' hoofs in their vicinity sent them to ground once more, with the uncomfortable thought that this time they were going to be captured, sure enough. But no, the patrol had no sooner got near enough to discover them than they bore round, and went off in another direction. Had they gone straight on for a little longer, there would have been no despatches for Kimberley on that journey. After this narrow shave, Messrs Cumming and Barron had a clear course, and made the best of it. They crossed Carter's Ridge close to the spot where the Boer artillery were stationed, struck the two-milestone, and having got their bearings found themselves some time later safely recuperating, after their fatigues and anxieties, at Kimberley Club, where an officer of the Town Guard, who had been out in the same direction that morning, and had sighted no less than three Boer patrols, was not a little surprised to learn that they had come in the way they did.

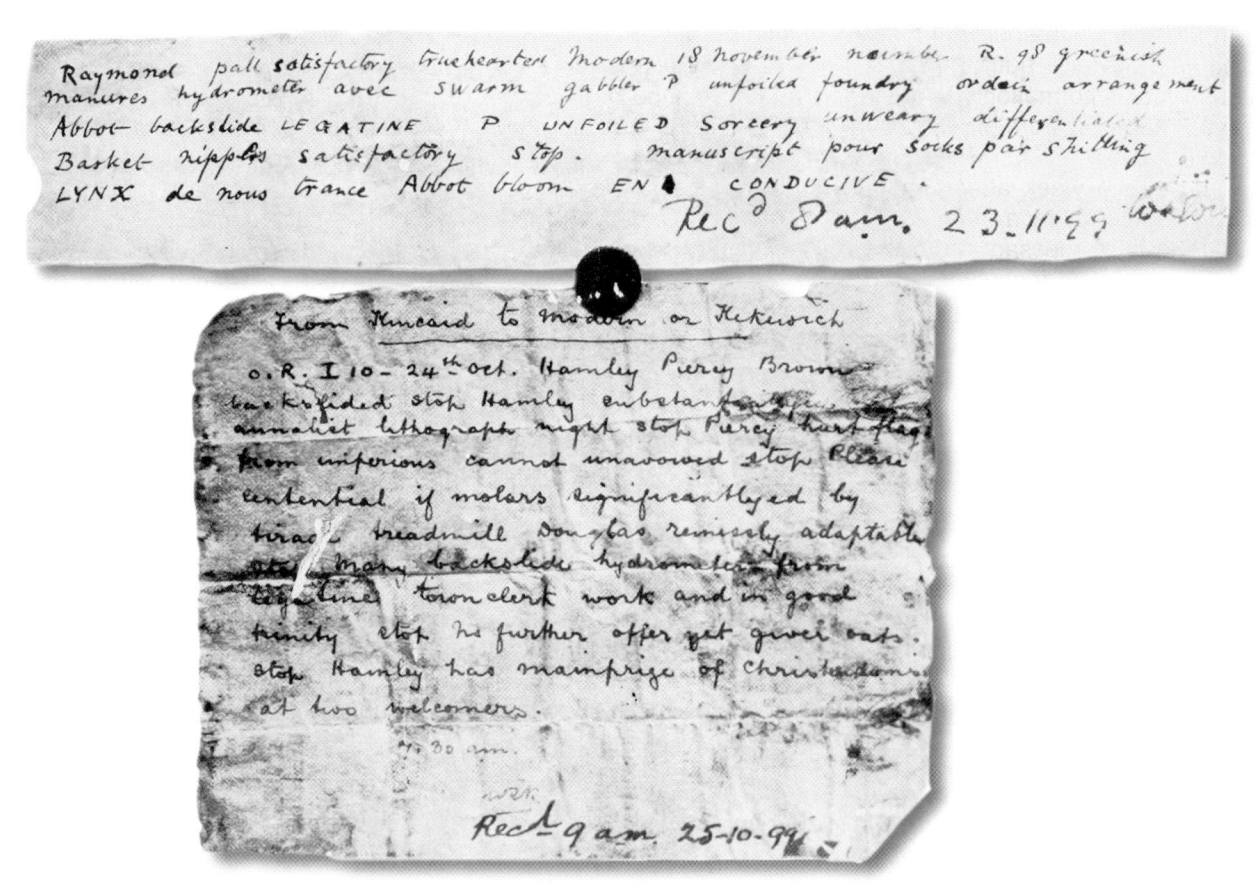

An example of a despatch received in Kimberley during the siege

On his next journey Mr. Cumming's instructions were to meet the relief column at Belmont or Orange River. On the way down, with Mr. Barron, they heard that the Boers had been boasting how on the last occasion they nearly caught Cumming. On this trip they swam the Riet River. They had some difficulty in finding the troops, and owing to this took a different route to that which they had previously followed. It afterwards transpired that had they not done this, they would almost certainly have been captured, the Boers having posted five men at a spot near the farm Weltevrede, where they would have had to pass. At Wolvepan they found the pan occupied by about thirty of the enemy, but skirted the laager successfully. In due course they found the relief column, and delivered their despatches. They saw something of the Belmont fight, and as some of the readers of this article may remember, called at the Advertiser office on their return to Kimberley, and gave an outline of the progress of the column up to that date.

Messrs. Cumming and Barron went out once after that, when they took out the news of the fight on November 28th, on which occasion, by the way, they had been present, having charge of the ammunition. They did not return again to Kimberley until after the siege. Mr. Cumming became attached to the cavalry brigade, and did a good deal of work in riding despatches for the military, both before and after Kimberley's relief, going on with the troops into the Transvaal. He was present at the battle of Magersfontein, and had a narrow escape from being caught in a Boer trap at Paardeberg, where the enemy artfully put out a number of horses as a lure, with some of their men concealed within range. Cumming and others went to get the horses, and had to beat a hasty retreat under a cross fire, out of which they were extremely lucky to escape without injury, the bullets coming, as Mr. Cumming modestly put it, quite near enough. While in the performance of duties of this description he was sniped at continually, and he has certainly been fortunate in having come through safely. Mr. Cumming subsequently received a commission as lieutenant in the Army Service Corps, and accompanied Lord Roberts' army to Bloemfontein and thence on the long march to Pretoria. He has suffered serious damage at the hands of looting rebels, who plundered his hotel and store, near Douglas, appropriating furniture, cattle and other property, and, considering the valuable services which he rendered at a critical period of the war, it is to be hoped that the substantial claim which he has felt himself justified in making on the imperial authorities for compensation will he liberally dealt with."

A divisive tool

The use of despatch riders and runners provided much needed information about the outside world. However, this information was not combined to give as complete a picture as possible because it was not seen as a central resource. The picture that comes through is that the military shared what information they could with the civil authorities but Rhodes and De Beers appear to have kept their information largely to themselves. Information of a commercial nature need not be shared with the military authorise but Rhodes strayed well away from purely business communication as this extract from O'Meara demonstrates:

> "Just a week after Kimberley was isolated, a despatch, addressed to Kekewich, was brought into Kimberley by a "runner"; it was in military cipher. After the document had been decoded, it was found to be a message from the High Commissioner to Rhodes. The tone of the communication was in every way friendly; in it could be detected a spirit of good-humoured chaff. It seemed obvious that H.E.'s message was in reply to one which he had received. As censorship had been put in force on the Diamond Fields, as has already been stated, as soon as war was declared, and, strictly, a permit was required by every one who wished to go beyond the barriers erected at the roadways passing through the lines of defence. Rhodes had not said anything to Kekewich concerning any desire on his part to communicate with the High Commissioner, although they met every day; and he did not apply to the military authorities for the necessary permits for his despatch-riders. From a remark dropped by Rhodes in Kekewich's presence, it appeared that the former had formed the intention to communicate at the earliest opportunity with Lord Rothschild (in London), in order that pressure might be brought to bear on the Cabinet at home so that instructions should be issued to the military authorities at the Cape, ordering them to deal with the relief of Kimberley as of the first importance. But it was not then known at Kekewich's Headquarters what, if any, action had been taken in the matter by Rhodes—it is, of course, now known that Rhodes began communicating with the High Commissioner on 16th October, that is to say, within 48 hours of the telegraph wire being cut, and that three days later he apparently succeeded in getting another message sent out of Kimberley, a paragraph relating to which was published in London. It should perhaps be stated that Kekewich would have placed no obstacle In Rhodes' way had he informed him that he desired to communicate with the High Commissioner.
>
> The High Commissioner's reply having come into his hands, Kekewich thought it right, although Rhodes did not seem to have behaved well in the matter, to let him know how it was that the message was reaching him through military Headquarters. A transcript of the High Commissioner's message was typed out and a staff officer was sent to the Sanatorium Hotel (where Rhodes was staying) with instructions to hand the document to Rhodes personally and to explain that the message had reached Kekewich in military cipher and had, consequently, to be decoded in his office. A staff officer, accordingly, at once rode up to the Sanatorium Hotel and, finding Rhodes in, handed him the envelope; Rhodes tore it open and glanced hastily through the message, and then flew into a violent passion and became most abusive. He took a little time to calm down and then, turning to the bearer of the message, said: "I intend to have my way, and as I can't get it by other means, I shall now send Milner an insulting message." On his return to Headquarters, the staff officer reported to Kekewich what had taken place at the hotel. Kekewich naturally did not wish to be a party in any way to the transmission of an offensive message to the Sovereign's representative, and was therefore unwilling to allow the use of the military cipher to Rhodes. He, however, wished to avoid a rupture with Rhodes, and therefore sent the staff officer back to the Sanatorium Hotel with instructions to tell Rhodes, that the Commandant had no objection to a message being sent by him to the High

Commissioner in the Chartered Company's code, and that he did not wish to see the text of the message, or to be informed of its contents. At the same time, Rhodes was also told that, if he so desired, his message for the High Commissioner could be sent south by the military despatch-rider, who would be leaving Kimberley in the evening with despatches for the Orange River.

Rhodes did not avail himself of Kekewich's offer, and, consequently, the military authorities continued to remain in the dark as to what was being done by Rhodes and his friends in Kimberley in the matter of the representations, which it is now known were being made not only to the High Commissioner, but apparently also to some influential person or persons in London. Under the sensational headlines, "KIMBERLEY WANTS TROOPS," "Gradually being surrounded by a large Boer force," the following announcement appeared in the *Daily Mail* of 24th October, 1899:

"The Daily Mail has reason to know that a message was received in London from Mr. Rhodes yesterday, dated Kimberley, 19th October, stating that the inhabitants of Kimberley desire to call the attention of the Secretary of State for War to the need for sending as speedily as possible reinforcements for the protection of the town, which is being surrounded by increasing numbers of Transvaal and Free State Boers. The matter has been placed before several members of the Cabinet, and is receiving due attention."

Kekewich tried to funnel the information coming into Kimberley through one point but this was not a success:

"Jan 2nd No 68. Strict law in Kimberley that all persons wishing to enter town must do so at authorized barriers only, punishment follows evasion of this law; also all communications entering Kimberley not censored at Modder River confiscated. Kindly instruct Cummings and Harding and others dealing with natives journeying between us accordingly, and ensure directions being given natives that they must on arrival at Barrier ask to be taken to Transvaal Rd Police Station where everything coming into town is registered before delivery."

Given this situation, it is easy to empathise with the plight of Kekewich in his dealings with Rhodes.

Staff of the Intelligence Department

Appendix 33 – The involvement of Black people in the siege

The black population was the largest racial element within the siege community. The estimated total of 55,000 included approximately 21,000 blacks. Some suggest the total to be closer to 30,000. Of these, De Beers employed some 12,000 'in and around the mines'. The remainder worked in small businesses, as domestic help, were unemployed or were family members, both women and children.

The blacks employed by De Beers were housed in compounds close to the five mines. The others were in areas around the town of Kimberley.

A census was carried out by Robinson on 2nd January 1900 and this showed the total population of 6,802 in the non-mine locations. Adding these to the 12,000 employed by De Beers and thus living in the compounds makes a total of less than 19,000. The discrepancy between the two population figures needs to be explained. There are a few possible explanations:

- There was certainly a push to encourage the blacks to leave Kimberley. Estimates of how many did so vary but are thought to be around 8,000
- The October 1899 population estimate could have over stated the true numbers
- Robinson's count could have been inaccurate
- There were deaths amongst the black population. For example, there were nearly 500 deaths from scurvy.
- But there would also have been an increase in the population at the start of the siege caused by an influx of refugees

At the beginning of the siege, advertisements appeared asking for volunteers for the locally-raised forces. Being a predominantly 'white man's war', the decision had to be taken to restrict participation in the fighting forces. This was also the view of the military authorities in Kimberley but Kekewich did not want to alienate the applicants as this response to the Town Clerk shows: "It is not possible to consider the question of arming the coloured men. Colonel Kekewich however suggests that you take their names and if an opportunity arises he will gladly avail himself of their services, and he highly appreciates the spirit of their offer." Despite this formal rejection, blacks did take part in the military aspects of the siege. They formed a unit of police in the Town Guard, acted as drivers and conductors with the RGA, guarded cattle and acted as despatch runners throughout the siege. Money was also offered for any cattle that were driven in to Kimberley. This was risky business but very beneficial to the garrison. Some 187 cattle were collected in this way.

No QSAs are known to have been issued to any of these men.

Scout McLaughlin and three black scouts (including Jacob Gout)

Away from the military roles, there was much civic work to be undertaken. This affected both the employees of De Beers and any other able blacks. The extensive defensive preparations were largely constructed by the De Beers' men, who guarded convicts and provided labourers and relief work boys. MacInnes' report on page 389 explains how the labour force that constructed the defences was composed.

A relief committee was set up to help those in need in the city. Ashe, in his diary, is disparaging about the people who applied to the committee for relief, "One day over one hundred and sixty natives were told that if they wanted help they must work for it, and stone-breaking work was offered them. Three accepted it, and that was about the style of most of the people who applied for relief."

Kimberley Siege Account and Medal Roll

By far the greatest assistance for the black community came in the shape of the relief works established by Cecil Rhodes. Ashe describes the work they carried out: "They were started by Mr. Rhodes quite early in the siege. The roads of one part of the town, which had only been acquired by the De Beers Company a few months ago, were shockingly bad, so when it became necessary to find something for natives, and others who had 'got no work to do,' to make a living wage at, they were turned on to these roads, and several thousands of them have been working ever since, and besides making a living for themselves, have wonderfully improved that part of the town." The workers constructed and repaired over 7 miles (11 km) of roads. Five of the reads met at the highest point in Kimberley, the site of the Honoured Dead Monument. The work consumed the labour of 904 white worker shifts, 3,690 coloured and Indian shifts and 4,997 black shifts. Meyer notes a complication with the work: "There is a great dearth of spades, so that only those that can provide their own tools get work."

Towards the end of the siege when Long Tom heightened the need for shelter, many blacks worked on their construction. See page 76 for Ashe's description of this work.

While there was work for those who could take it, there was paucity of food to go around. The tiered system saw the greatest share going to the whites, next share to the coloureds and least of all to the black community. Ration amounts are described on page 60. The food allowance was progressively lowered as the siege dragged on. At one point, there was a near mutiny in one of the compounds caused by the paucity of food being issued.

The poor and sparse diet inevitably led to disease. It is very noticeable that disease struck the black community much more so than the other ethnic groups. Nearly 600 deaths from scurvy were recorded from a total, albeit under-recorded, of 1,648. Illnesses suffered by the blacks included dysentery, pneumonia, tuberculosis and diarrhoea. The rate of infant mortality was 935 in every 1000 births, a staggering figure.

One of the least worrying aspects of the siege for the black community was the Boer shelling. This accounted for two deaths and an unrecorded number of people wounded.

While the records from the period record very few names of prominent blacks, a few can be identified:

- Jacob Gout. The *Diamond Fields Advertiser* reports that, "He was one of two natives who after sundry others had failed were selected to try to reach Lord Methuen's column with despatches from Kimberley. They left Kimberley at nine o'clock at night, marching via Cook's Farm, Rooidam and Modder River. At the break of dawn they espied a commando of Boers. They had to be low the whole of that day until after dark, when Jacob's companion refused to face further danger and returned. Jacob took his despatches from him and set off by himself, evading the Boers and after five days and nights he reached the relief column near Belmont. Alter resting two days he started with Lord Methuen's despatch for Col. Kekewich, and, slipping through the Boer cordon, reached Kimberley safely on the third night. He afterwards made two trips to Modder River, and on each occasion delivered his despatch safely."

Jacob Gout

- David. He was a Basuto who worked for a while for the Boers at Jacobsdal hospital before returning to Kimberley with much useful information.
- Moosie. He led the delegation to General Cronje to negotiate the safe passage of blacks through the Boer lines and into Bechuanaland. In addition, he regularly carried despatches. De Beers rewarded him with a payment of 100 sovereigns and a pension.

After the siege, the De Beers mines returned to production capacity and many blacks were able to return to work. Others were able to gain work with the British forces in a logistics capacity. Reports also say that some continued to raid cattle from the Boers.

The part played by the black community in the siege and the suffering they endured is under played and not given due credit in the contemporary publications. It is therefore important that today we do not forget their sacrifice and contribution in this important aspect of the siege.

Appendix 34 – A Supply Officer's view

Captain Gorle[83] wrote 'A brief account of the method of administrating Supplies during the Siege of Kimberley, 15th October, 1899, to 15th February, 1900' from his perspective as the supply officer. The account was intended to explain what actions he had taken so that the information could be of use to others who found themselves in a similar position. The account was published in *The Army Service Corps Journal* in November 1902.

The first detachment of regular troops arrived in Kimberley on the 21st September, 1899, under command of Major Chamier, CMG, Royal Garrison Artillery. I was with this party. Shortly after arrival instructions were received from the Director of Supplies and Transport (Colonel Bridge, CB) at Cape Town to take stock of all supplies in the hands of the merchants of Kimberley. This was done, and careful records kept. I collected all information that I thought would be of use in the way of Supplies and Transport on the spot, and what Transport could be got within about seven days.

Captain Gorle

On the evening of the 15th October, 1899, the line was cut north and south of Kimberley, and we were isolated. I was out early next morning arranging about sending ammunition and supplies to the different points of defence, the quantities of supplies to be sent to each place had already been worked out, and all the forts were rationed for seven days by about 11 am. I cannot remember the exact number of forts, but there were some fourteen or fifteen in all, the total line of defence being about eleven miles in circumference. These supplies were issued from the reserve that had been sent up from Cape Town. The following morning, 17th October, I brought up all the preserved meat and biscuit there was in the town, and had it sent to my reserve store. The number of live cattle fit for slaughter, ie, not actually in milk, were noted, and the number to be slaughtered limited to twenty-five per diem, this gave an average of about one pound per diem for adults and a half-pound for each child under fourteen, and I took steps to have the cattle brought into a place of safety. The only exception to this was a number of trek oxen used on sanitary work, which were allowed to go out to the sanitary pits, and were taken by the Boers a few days after the siege commenced. The price of paraffin oil went up with a run from seventeen shillings per case for eight gallons to thirty-four shillings, as some of the dealers tried to make a corner in it, but the then Mayor, Mr R H Henderson, got Colonel Kekewich's approval to fix the price at seventeen shillings, and the dealers who had bought in at thirty-four shillings hoping to sell at three pounds were badly left. This system of fixing the price of supplies at the usual rate existing before we were cut off was adapted throughout.

The next few days were taken up in arranging various details in connection with the formation of a supply committee fixing up about weekly states from the dealers, and arranging for their sales being checked against the numbers of inhabitants, etc. The numbers at the beginning of the siege were, roughly: — Europeans 14,000, coloured people 6,000, Asiatics 1,000, natives in De Beers compound 10,000, in the locations 15,000, making a grand total of 46,000 of all nationalities. I found on comparing the flour and Boer meal, (ie, ground wheat with the bran removed) that the proportion was about one to three respectively, orders were accordingly issued that bread was to be made of these proportions. The result was very good brown bread, but we got very tired of it before the end of the siege. White bread was issued to the Hospital and to sick people on a doctor's certificate. It was found that the consumption of meat actually drawn amounted to about a half-pound per adult, and a quarter-pound per child below fourteen, and this was fixed as the ration. About the end of October the consumption of other supplies worked out at about the ordinary soldier's rations.

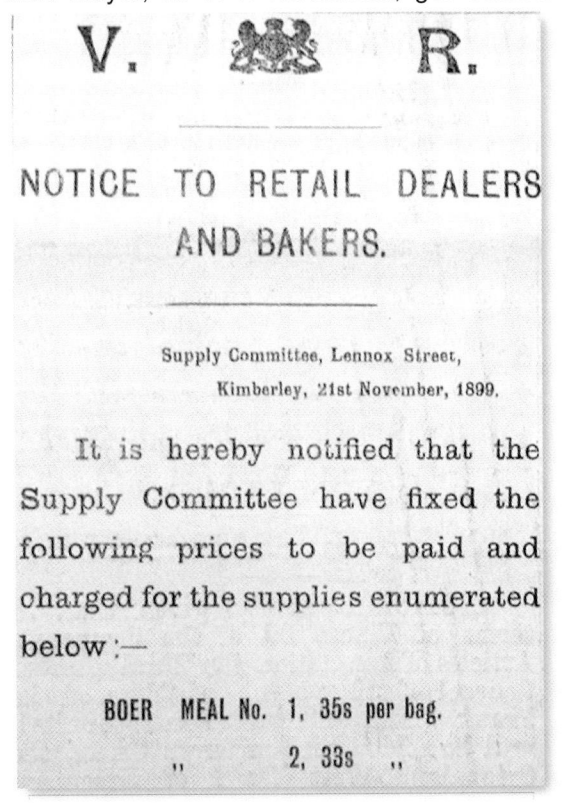

V. R.

NOTICE TO RETAIL DEALERS AND BAKERS.

Supply Committee, Lennox Street,
Kimberley, 21st November, 1899.

It is hereby notified that the Supply Committee have fixed the following prices to be paid and charged for the supplies enumerated below:—

BOER MEAL No. 1, 35s per bag.
  "   "   2, 33s "

Newspaper notice about the fixing of prices

---

[83] See page 344 for his biography.

Kimberley Siege Account and Medal Roll

The Supply Committee was originally composed of myself as president and three members and a secretary; five more members were added afterwards. This addition to the Committee was a mistake, as it made it unwieldy.

A Supply Committee should include the Mayor of the town, two commission agents, and the leading medical man, the smaller the better, but the commission agents are necessary to fix prices, of course the officer in charge supplies should be in addition to the four members, and should be president of the Committee. By Commission Agents I mean men whose business it is to buy all kinds of produce on commission, and who therefore know the ruling prices that should be paid for supplies. On the 15th November all bread-stuffs, sugar, and rice, were taken over and placed in six stores or depots, and a clerk was appointed to each depot, he had to keep proper records of all transactions in connection with the receipt and issue of all supplies placed under his charge. He made issues in bulk only, to retail dealers on production of a permit signed by the secretary of the Supply Committee. These permits were issued according to the amount of trade done by the dealer, who was required to forward a statement showing the approximate number of customers dealing with him. The money for the supplies was paid to the secretary at the time the permit was obtained, no cash was received by the clerk at the depot where the issues were made.

Permit supply staff

This system worked well, and the supplies issued agreed with the quantities that should have been consumed according to my calculations, but as it seemed very uncertain as to how long we were to hold out Colonel Kekewich directed me to organise a system by which we could control the actual issue to the consumers.

I drew up a scheme which was discussed, improved upon in Committee, and passed, and the following arrangements came into force in December, 1899:—Coffee, tea, etc., were taken over and placed in the six depots in addition to the supplies already there. Every householder was required to get a permit before he could be supplied. For this purpose the town was divided up into municipal wards, and a permit staff appointed for each ward, whose duty it was to enquire into the matter, and, if satisfied, to issue a permit. When making the first application for a permit the householder was required to make a declaration stating the numbers in the household, and also the quantities if any of the following supplies that were in his possession, viz.:— flour, Boer meal, mealie meal, samps (split mealies), sugar, tea, coffee.

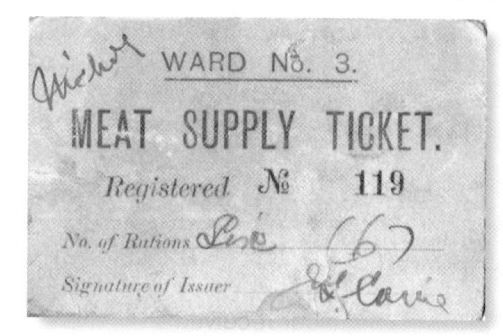

Meat supply ticket

A record was made of the quantities so declared, and permits were not issued to get fresh supplies until these quantities had lasted their allotted time according to scales fixed by proclamation. These permits were taken by the householder to the retail dealer, who sold the supplies enumerated on permit, viz; —one week's supply for the numbers set forth in the declaration. The permits were filed by the dealer, and at the end of each week the total sold was made out with the permits in support, and presented to the secretary of the Supply Committee, who gave the dealer a permit to draw sufficient to replace the quantities sold. The secretary took possession of the permits. This system was adapted with regard to the Europeans and coloured people.

For the supply of Natives a retail shop was established in east location, where mealie meal, unsifted Boer meal, Kaffir corn meal, sugar, tea, and coffee were sold direct to the consumer, a special shop being set aside for Asiatics, ie Indians, Malays, Chinese, etc.

To keep a check on the numbers and to see that they did not purchase more than the quantities laid down by scale, each location (there were six in all) had a different coloured ticket, and each ticket bore a number. When making the first purchase the native declared how many there were in each hut; this was registered, and a ticket bearing the same register number was given him, the numbers in the hut being also shewn on the ticket. Natives were allowed to purchase a week's supply at a time. In making subsequent purchases the native would produce his ticket and this would be compared with the register. If it agreed, and it was a week since the last issue as shewn by the date on the register, a further issue for one week was made, and the quantity and date entered in the places left for them in the register. Daily issues were made if desired. The numbers said to be in each hut were checked against the numbers as shewn in the police returns, but the Natives gave no trouble, and I found them very easy to deal with and quite truthful as to the numbers in their huts. In this way complete control was maintained until the supplies were actually issued to the consumer.

The meat supply was left in the hands of the butchers, each being allowed to kill so many cattle per diem according to the numbers in his possession at the beginning of the siege. A clerk was placed in charge of each shop to see that the meat was issued fairly and according to scale. This system worked well until all the smaller butchers having slaughtered their stock, the business of supplying the consumers fell on one man, and it was impossible for him to compete with the increase of custom. This being the case the supply of meat was taken over by the Supply Committee on the 3rd January, 1900.

For this purpose a slaughter-house was rented, a staff of butchers and clerks engaged, and the whole thing placed under the management of Mr Clarkson (the chief clerk in the Managing Director's Office, De Beers Consolidated Mines Ltd). This gentleman did excellent work. The Wards of the Town were again taken as a unit, and each Ward was supplied from a separate table, with a special staff told off to make the issues.

Siege butchers

Each householder received a numbered ticket, on which was shewn the numbers in the house and the rations to which the household were entitled, ie, full rations for adults, half for children under fourteen. The Market Hall was taken over for the purpose of making issues, and the people of each Ward were formed up in a line two deep opposite the entrance set aside for that Ward as they assembled, those coming first being served first. They were let in four per Ward at a time. On reaching the table they presented their ticket to the clerk in charge, who satisfied himself as to the identity of the person by referring to his register kept for that purpose, and the issue was made by the issuer. The person served then moved on and passed out of the building through the exit door.

Kimberley Siege Account and Medal Roll

The morning queue for meat

It was found on comparing the Wards that numbers two and six together equalled the other four Wards, so I decided to make issues on alternate days, numbers two and six drawing one day, and numbers one, three, four, and five, drawing on the next. This reduced the time, besides enabling the meat to be drawn in larger joints, two days' supply being drawn at once. The issue on the first day took some four hours, but by making the change about, the Wards drawing on alternate days, and other slight alterations suggested by Mr Clarkson, the time of issue was reduced to about an hour. This was of great moment, as standing about in the sun was very trying. The issue began each morning at six am.

A separate place of issue was established for the coloured people, and also for the natives; these latter only drew the offal, ie, heads, livers, etc. After the first few days in January the ration consisted of half cow-beef and half horse, mule, and donkey meat. The latter is quite good, and if in good condition, is as good eating as beef, and certainly better than the wretched stuff we had in the cow line, which consisted of very young stock and thin cows. The rains not coming early enough, there was very little grass for the poor beasts to eat within the limited grazing areas, and there was no hay to spare for them.

Cows that were giving any milk were kept for that purpose, but the milk supply was far too small. There was a fair supply of condensed milk in the different depots, but as I was afraid of having to slaughter all the cows, and not knowing how long we were likely to be shut up, I kept a tighter hold of this than was necessary; it was unfortunate, and had I been more liberal it might, as things turned out, have reduced the suffering of the children, but as it was not at all unlikely that we should have to hang on until April, and I knew that we should have to slaughter everything by the end of February, I did not like to recommend a big increase in the issue. I had bought up everything I could in the way of infant and invalid foods about the middle of November, but there was very little to be got. There were a good many supplies, jam, condensed milk, etc, lying at the station in transit, these I took over, and they were sold at a retail store on the order of the different medical men, countersigned by myself.

It is rather funny to think of bacon and cheese being prescribed by doctors in doses, though it was anything but funny at the time, and to get up from every meal feeling hungry may have been good for one, but it was not at all pleasant. Breakfast was the worst meal; some samp porridge, tea, without milk in either case, about a cubic inch of horse, and a couple of slices of brown bread dry and chippy. This, possibly after a ride from 6.30 am to about 8 am looking after my vegetable garden, which the locusts fell on and devoured when I was just hoping to gather the crop. It was a frightful year for locusts, they used to march down the streets in droves.

The Natives suffered worse than anyone else, as the scale of 12 oz meal, 2 oz sugar, ½ oz coffee, ½ oz salt, was very small, but they were wonderfully contented, and did not grumble. There was a good deal of scurvy, but it was worse in the De Beers Compounds—where the boys were only fed on meat and salt—than in the locations. This was done with a view to make the boys go; finally they were all turned out of the Compounds except about two thousand. Of those that were turned out a few went to their homes, but the greater number simply went into the locations, as the Boers did not let them go through their lines if they could help it. The native population increased from about fifteen thousand to twenty-six thousand in the locations, and decreased to about two thousand in De Beers Compounds, or a net increase of about three thousand between the time we were shut up and the 31st January, 1900.

The troops were rationed in the ordinary way, with the exception of the Town Guard. As only a certain number of the Town Guard were employed by day, and this was changed at night, it was impossible for me to

Appendices

check the numbers drawing, and to obviate this it was arranged that the men should receive the value of the ration (10½ d) in addition to their pay, and any rations they wanted were issued on payment.

The scale of rations for troops was 1 lb bread, ½ lb meat, 1/3 oz coffee, 1/6 oz tea, 2 ozs sugar, ½ oz. salt, 1/36 oz pepper. Civilians, ie, Europeans and coloured people, drew ½ lb bread, ½ lb meat, 2 ozs sugar, ½ oz coffee, ¼ oz tea. The meat ration was reduced to 4 ozs about the second week in January. More horse meat could have been issued, but a great many of the people would not eat it, and I had the number of horses slaughtered reduced accordingly. Children under fourteen drew half meat ration in every case. I have already given the scale of groceries issued to natives.

Towards the end of January the late Mr Rhodes started a soup kitchen, which was a great success. He used to draw a certain amount of cow beef, and this was taken to the Convict Station, where large cauldrons were fixed, and made into soup mangels, and any other vegetables that could be got being put into it. Grapes were also added, and the result was quite good.

The method of issuing the soup was as follows:—On drawing meat in the morning each person stated the number of rations of meat and soup required respectively. The meat was issued and a card stating numbers of rations of soup to which such household was entitled was given to the person drawing, who paid for the total number of rations of soup and meat drawn, at the time of the meat issue. This card was then presented to the issuer told off for the purpose of issuing the soup who took the necessary action.

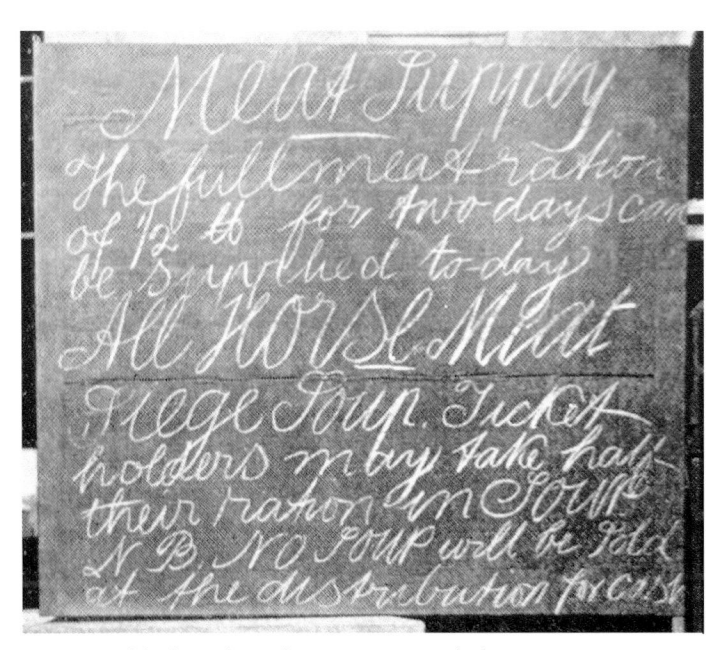

Notice about horse meat and siege soup

Receptacles for taking soup away in had to be provided by the person drawing. A pint of soup was equal to a ration of beef, and charged for at the same rate, beef was sold at 1s per lb, horse meat 9d per lb. Only the total number of rations according to numbers in household were allowed to be drawn. These could be partly in meat and partly in soup, or all in one or other of the two classes of rations. The issue of soup began about 11 am each day.

Wood was very scarce and was supplied from the Stores held by De Beers. For this purpose a printed indent was signed by me, the name of the person drawing being inserted which was taken to the Secretary of the Company, who gave the necessary order for the issue. The quantity was limited to ½ lb per diem for each member of a household, and one week's supply issued at a time. The money was collected by De Beers, 2s per 100 lbs being the price charged.

A certain amount of wood was collected by me and sold but it did not amount to very much, and only consisted of small mimosa thorn trees.

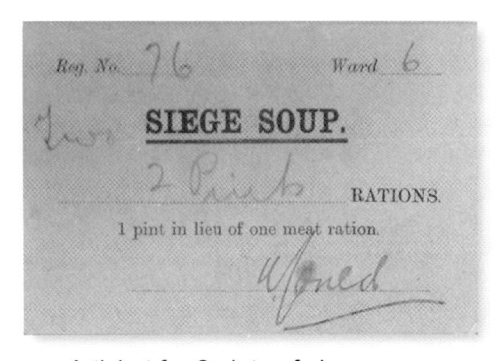

A ticket for 2 pints of siege soup

Mr Rhodes had a small cold store built, this was completed about the middle of December, and all the fattest cattle and goats were slaughtered and placed in it, where they kept in thoroughly good condition and were issued as the other supplies diminished. The Cold Store was designed by the late Mr Labram, who also constructed "Long Cecil". It answered very well and would have been invaluable had the siege lasted into March, as all the stock would have to have been slaughtered and placed in this store. It consisted of a small ante-chamber where the meat was cooled off and two inner chambers where the temperature could be reduced below freezing point.

One of my greatest difficulties was to get vegetables and it was a terrible blow when the Dutchman from whom I used to get them was imprisoned for communicating with the enemy, and no persuasion could get his wife to carry on the garden. I tried one of my own, but as I have already stated the locusts disputed, or rather

Kimberley Siege Account and Medal Roll

took forcible possession of it. Mr Rhodes got one in train on a large scale, but it was only just beginning to grow when we were relieved. For the greater part of the siege I was able to issue to the Troops, but the civil population came off rather badly.

There were generally a small quantity to go round every morning and these used to be issued at the same time as the meat. The day before we were relieved we got possession of Alexandersfontein about 8 miles out, where I got a fine supply of onions, custard marrows, etc, also two enormously fat pigs. There were some fowls but I only knew of their presence at the farm, through a head or a leg projecting from some of the men's pockets or by seeing a wretched hen running for all it was worth, and dodging behind bushes, pursued by a hungry looking gentleman in khaki; but as there were only a few they would have been of no use to me, so I didn't bother about them. When you've got about 45,000 people to feed it takes at least 4,000 hens to make you enthusiastic.

I took over all the imported wine and spirits, such as port, brandy, whisky, &c, that I could get, also anything in the way of cornflour, bacon, cheese, ham, &c, for use of the sick and children, but there was not much in the town, and my chief supply of these things was from the supplies lying at the station in transit, and of which I took possession. I bought a certain quantity of lime but I could only get it slaked so that it was not of much use except as a deodorizer.

There were small quantities of carbolic powder, chloride of lime, etc, which I got about December. Possibly I could have got more, earlier, but when I asked the Medical Officer what supplies he wanted me to hold, he said he didn't want any. At first I held all the supplies I had taken over as medical comforts myself, and did not allow any to be issued except on a doctor's certificate which I countersigned or initialled. This did not please some of the medical men, who, though they had taken no steps to tell me what supplies they would like me to take over, wished to have control of them when they were in my possession. Had they come to me and said that they wanted certain supplies early in the siege it would have made all the difference, as until about November I only got such things as I thought would be needed for the men who were sick, and when I took in the sick civilians requiring to be fed too, a great deal of the supplies had been sold. Of course no one realized the length of time that the siege would last, and the medical men having so much to do, it was hardly to be expected that they should look forward and think what their patients would require in the way of invalid foods to keep them going for two or three months.

The signing of certificates threw a great deal of work on to them, and finally it was arranged to have a permit office, where orders for medical comforts could be obtained on a Doctor's recommendation and this office was more or less directly under the Medical Men. Lt O'Gorman, RAMC, formed a Committee for its administration, a store for the sale of milk was started and this was placed under the control of Dr Stoney, Medical Officer of Health for the town.

The supply of forage was really the most serious of all, as the number of animals was increased from about 400 horses and mules before the siege to about 1,500 after we had been shut up. This increase was due to the raising of the Kimberley Light Horse, and the Police coming in from the outlying districts. I knew nothing about the raising of the Kimberley Light Horse until we had been shut up, when the Corps was actually formed and demanded rations. Had I known before, I possibly might not have been able to get the extra supply of forage up in time, still I should have had the satisfaction of knowing that I had made the attempt. As it was, directly I knew about it, I bought all the oat-Hay, chaff, and oats that I could lay hands on, and started gradually to reduce the forage ration from 20 lbs (ie, 10 Grain, 10 Hay) to 10 lbs. I found that though there was a good supply of mealies, the quantity of oats was small, and, to avoid changing abruptly from oats to mealies, I knocked off 1 lb oats and replaced it by mealies until the final grain ration was 4 lbs mealies, 2 lbs oats, 2 lbs chaff, and 2 lbs hay. Hay and chaff were very short and there was hardly any bran, the little there was I kept for sick animals. They did very well on the ration though some more hay or chaff could have been given with advantage. The forage would have lasted until the 28th February had we not been relieved, but the Relief Column took large quantities, and the last lot of hay was issued on the same day that the line was repaired and a fresh consignment received.

Only certain civilians, doctors, and those whose duties made it necessary for them to keep horses, were allowed to draw forage. All supplies were paid for by the consumer and no free issues made. All others had to hand their horses over to a special guard told off for this purpose, and the animals were grazed on certain areas. These horses were sold by their owners to the Supply Committee and slaughtered for food as required.

The siege was raised by General French on the 15th February, 1900. I hope that if any of my brother Officers find themselves alone in the same position, the above lines may be of use to them.

Appendix 35 – How Kimberley was relieved

The siege of Kimberley began on 15th October 1899, before the gathering might of the British Army Corps, under the command of General Sir Redvers Buller, had fully assembled in the Cape and before it had determined its priorities and strategies for the ensuing campaign.

Sir Alfred Milner, the British High Commissioner for South Africa was a resolute imperialist, who had in many ways instigated the unfolding war as a means of cementing the two colonies and the two republics into a unified South Africa under the British flag. Now as the storm clouds gathered he began to receive daily reports of the rapidly deteriorating situation within the country. Mafeking and Kimberley were encircled in October and General White was besieged in Ladysmith with over 13,000 men in November 1899. While the loyalty of Natal was never called into question, Cape Colony with its high Afrikaner population was a very different proposition and caused him great concern.

General Buller was under intense pressure from Milner to proceed with the plan to march on Bloemfontein and not to split the Army Corps which would, at all cost, defend the Cape. Buller achieved much in his short time at Cape Town and he was widely respected by Milner. He understood the nature of the country, the Boers and the need for mobile forces and mounted troops. It was Buller who envisaged the formation of local units of mounted men who understood the lie of the land, could ride, shoot and in many cases spoke Afrikaans.

Lord Methuen

On 4th November, General Buller came to his decision and casting aside Milner's assertions that Natal could be sacrificed, split his force and taking one third of the Army Corps, some 12,000 men and himself at their head of the Natal Field Force, sailed for Durban to the relief of Ladysmith. He left behind Lieutenant General Lord Methuen in command of the Cape. Paul Sanford, Third Baron Methuen, was the youngest Lieutenant General in the British Army, however his only field experience was in Bechuanaland in 1885. He was professional and conscientious but was not considered very clever. Methuen had a strong overall force of three infantry brigades (Grenadiers, Coldstream and Scots) supplemented by an armoured train and a Naval brigade of 400 but he was weak in mounted units. Based at Orange River Station some 50 miles from Kimberley, on the rail route from Cape Town to Mafeking, his instructions from Buller were to relieve Kimberley.

The situation in Kimberley at this time was stable. In spite of this, Rhodes began sending alarming messages in November 1899, demanding that Kimberley be relieved and implying that its loss to the Boers would have catastrophic consequences for the prestige of the Empire. These claims were perhaps more egocentric than true. In a cable dated 5th November 1899, Rhodes to the High Commissioner, 'My opinion is that if you do not advance at once from Orange River you will lose Kimberley'.

On 21st November 1899 Methuen began his march. Ahead of him lay the short distance to Kimberley and he sent Colonel Kekewich the optimistic signal, '...would arrive 26th, unless delayed at Modder River'. On the 21st and 22nd, he managed 10 miles a day.

Battle of Belmont, 23rd November 1899.
On the 23rd he engaged the first line of Boers and fought a sharp engagement at Belmont. Methuen was unaware of the Boers' strength and proposed a head-on attack. The troops left camp early in the morning and followed a rough map which brought them well short of the Boers. The band of the Scots Guards was playing as the first Mauser bullets found their target. The men fixed bayonets and prepared to ascend the kopje from where the Boers were firing down on them. As the British reached the summit, the Boers were already departing. The British were elated by the result.

Methuen told the Guards 'With troops like you, no General can fear the results of his plan'. The British suffered 232 casualties while inflicting only about 70 casualties from a total Boer force of approximately 2,000.

Kimberley Siege Account and Medal Roll

Battle of Rooilaagte, 25th November 1899

The next engagement took place two days later at Rooilaagte, between Graspan and Enslin. The Naval Brigade lead the assault and, just as at Belmont, reached the crest of the hill to find the Boers had gone. The frontal assault by the British and the fact that the Boers did not intend to engage the overwhelming force meant that disproportionately heavy casualties were again suffered by the attackers. The Boer losses were estimated at 21. It was here that some of the disillusionments of war were first felt and that rumours began to circulate of the Boer use of dum-dum bullets and their misuse of the white flag.

Battle of Modder River, 28th November 1899

Undeterred, Methuen resumed his advance on the Modder River, 25 miles south of Kimberley, believing this to be lightly held by the enemy and he arrived there on the 28th November to a very rude awakening. The Boer forces that lay in wait, up to 9,000 strong, were well camouflaged and commanded by two extremely competent Boer generals, Piet Cronje and Koos De La Rey. Based on his experience at Belmont and Rooilaagte, Methuen initially proposed a flanking attack via Jacobsdal, 10 miles to the east.

However, his tactical decisions were swayed by the recent news of victories using frontal attacks at Talana and Elandslaagte and it was this form of attack that was to be used. The fusillade and artillery barrage lasted 10 hours and rarely were the enemy sighted, so effective were their river-side defences. At one point, Methuen made the comment that there are 'probably no Boers at all' and Lieutenant Colonel A Codrington noted how he had been in three battles with the Boers and only seen three of them! In the bitter fighting and mounting casualties that ensued, Methuen's men pressed forward across the drift and overwhelmed the Boer lines. Lord Methuen was wounded in this engagement as was De La Rey, whose son Adriaan was mortally injured. Some of Cronje's men were reported to have fled the battlefield thereby crippling the Boer's counter-attack and bitter recriminations and accusations of cowardice flew back and forth.

The next morning the Boers withdrew. Of the battle, Methuen said it was 'one of the hardest and most trying fights in the annals of the British Army'.

In the days after the battle, Methuen stayed at Modder River to regroup and resupply. He received supplies and reinforcements of infantry, cavalry, guns and a war balloon. He repaired the bridge over the Modder River but did not scout for Boers believing them to be on the next area of high ground at Magersfontein, the last defensive ridge before Kimberley.

In the 10 days that elapsed after the engagement at Modder River to the movement of Methuen's force north from Modder River, the Boers had put the time to good use in building a series of concealed trenches across the railway line and a formidable line of defence at the base of the ridge.

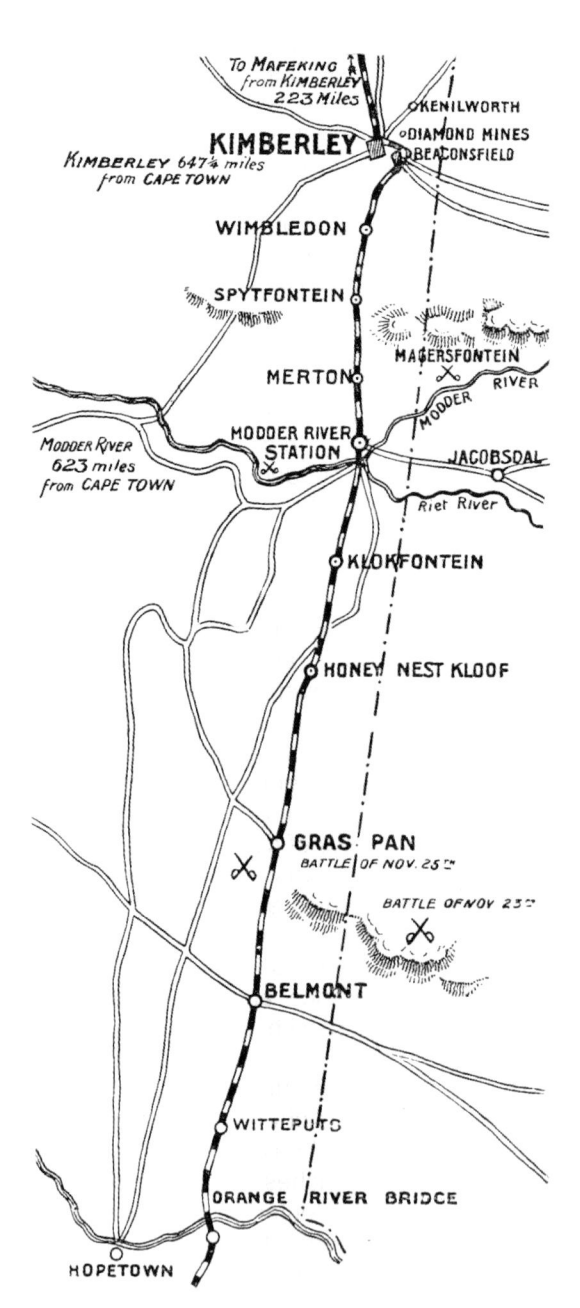

Map showing the relief route

The battle of Magersfontein, 11th December 1899

The engagement opened on the 10th December in a 'softening-up operation' with a massive artillery barrage of Methuen's field guns and howitzers, prior to the frontal attack and included the Royal Navy's 4.7 inch gun 'Joe Chamberlain' which had newly arrived while Methuen was at Modder River. The artillery was aimed at where the Boers were though to be but not where they were. The effect of the bombardment was the wounding of just three of the defenders.

Appendices

At the break of dawn on 11th December 1899 and after an exhausting night march, the unsuspecting Highland Brigade under Major General Andrew Wauchope and led by the Brigade Major, Major G E Benson, advanced towards the ridge and into a veritable hail of lead. The surprise was complete and the effect of smokeless Mauser fire at short range on the massed ranks of Highlanders was devastating. The advancing lines of soldiers were perfectly silhouetted against the morning sky, making an easy target for the Boers who lay patiently in their superbly designed and camouflaged trenches. The British could not see the enemy before them, even at close range. In swathes they fell killed, wounded or to seek cover behind the smallest stones or needle-sharp bushes which covered the area. Wauchope, a veteran of many campaigns and beloved of his men, had been an early casualty, struck down in the initial fusillade.

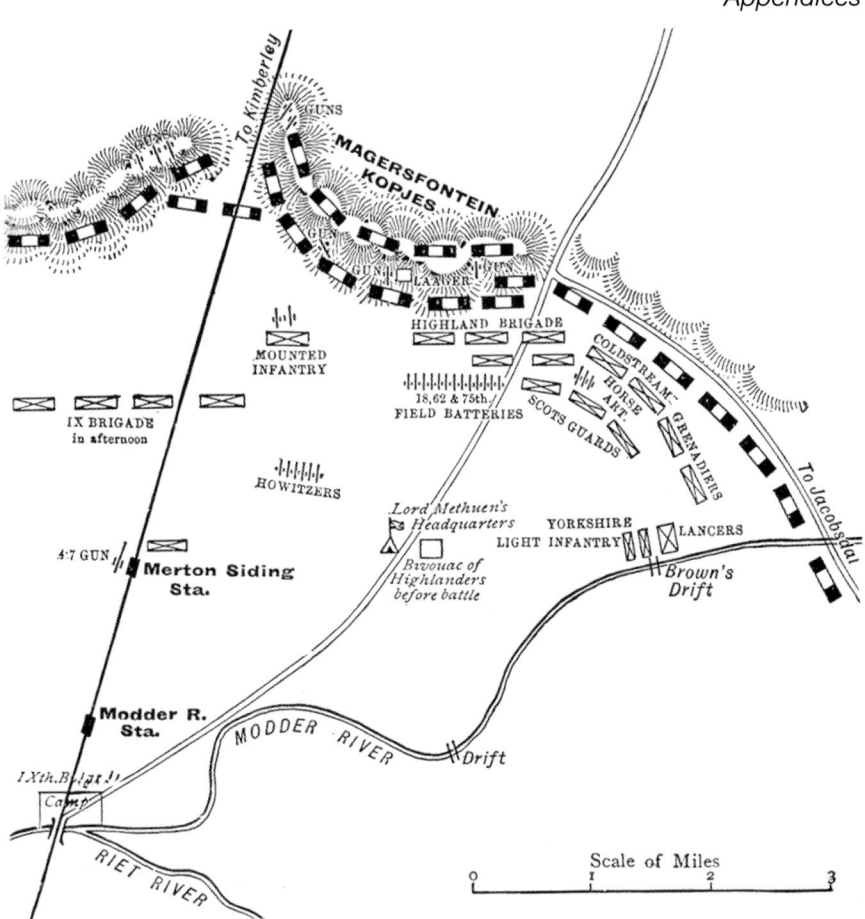

Map of the battle of Magersfontein

The front line troops remained pinned down for many hours and the slightest movement, under the burning sun, brought an instant Boer response. Methuen did not exploit his advantage and could still have snatched victory from the jaws of defeat but he was at a loss as to the true disposition of the Boer lines. Methuen's one chance to succeed was the discovery of a weakness in the Boer's left flank. But as the time passed, the Boers sent in reserves and Methuen failed to send in substantial reinforcements, so his opportunities waned and finally withered. Eventually, the inevitable occurred and the men lying close to the Boer trenches, exposed and exhausted, could take no more and breaking cover they stood and ran to the rear. It was a humiliating experience and despite their officers' entreaties and threats, a rout ensued which the Boer marksmen exploited with deadly effect.

Unlike previous encounters, the Boers did not withdraw after inflicting this painful blow on Methuen's force and the next morning's flight of the observation balloon revealed the trenches were still manned. It was not until 12th December that the British forced through the opposition and barbed wire entanglements, as the remaining Boers left their trenches and rode away. De La Rey accrued much of the credit for the ingenuity of the defences at Magersfontein, which despite suffering the intense artillery barrage had inflicted few casualties on the Boers, while General Wauchope suffered the ultimate ignominy and became the scapegoat for this British reverse. The total British casualties were just less than 1,000, some four times the estimate of Boer losses.

This defeat coming within days of the debacle at Colenso in Natal and the surrender at Stormberg led to the banner headline 'Black Week' in the British newspapers of the day.

Casualties during the relief operations

These were the casualties sustained:

Action	Killed / DOW Officers	Killed / DOW Men	Wounded Officers	Wounded Men	Missing / Prisoner Officers	Missing / Prisoner Men	Total Officers	Total Men
Belmont	4	71	11	138	-	1	23	209
Rooilaagte	4	18	5	158	-	9	9	185
Modder River	4	98	20	361	-	2	24	461
Magersfontein	26	218	42	609	-	76	68	903

Kimberley Siege Account and Medal Roll

A pause in the relief effort

In December 1899, Field Marshall Lord Roberts was appointed Commander in Chief in South Africa and Lieutenant General Lord Kitchener was appointed his Chief of Staff. Roberts immediately ordered Methuen to cease operations to relieve Kimberley, to withdraw to the Modder River Station and to await his assumption of command.

The strategic plan of the campaign under Lord Robert's command in January and early February 1900, now changed direction away from Kimberley and a march directly on Johannesburg and Pretoria, the seat of government of the Transvaal Republic through Bloemfontein the capital of the Orange Free State and thereby annexing both republics under British rule.

However, Rhodes continued to agitate for Kimberley's relief and Robert's decided this would have to be affected by a relief column rather than the whole Army Corps which had now built to five divisions, including a cavalry division under Lieutenant General John French.

French's flying column

General French was given instructions to form a 'flying column' comprising 5,000 men to relieve Kimberley on 11th February 1900. French was beset with transport difficulties and so it was only after considerable hardship that the column made its preparations for the dash to outflank the Boers. The risks en route were great and included a charge across the Abon Dam dust flats which could have proven fatal to the large cavalry horses in the summer heat of South Africa. In effect the dash virtually ruined French's cavalry, although as a manoeuvre it was described as a 'Master stroke' by the observing German Military Attaché.

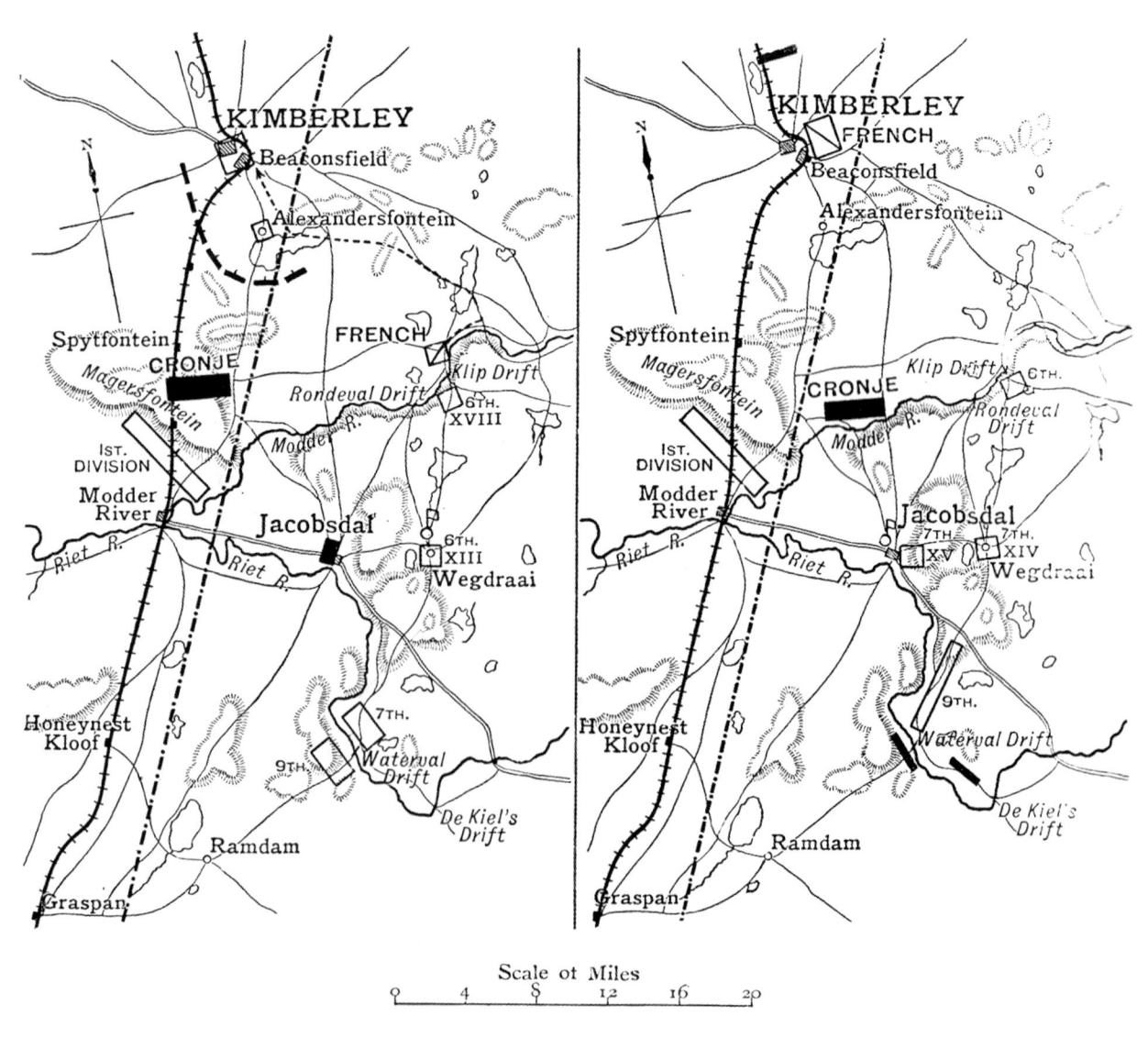

The position on the night of
Wednesday 14th February 1900

The position on the night of
Thursday 15th February 1900

Appendices

On 15th February after a 124 day siege the dust raised by the approaching column was sighted from the Conning Tower in Kimberley. By 15:30 the first of the relief column, Rimington's Guides entered Kimberley to be greeted by the disbelieving and exhausted townsfolk. General French arrived shortly afterwards and went straight to the Sanatorium where he had a meeting with Rhodes.

The siege of Kimberley had been lifted after a punishing yet masterly dash. The Boers withdrew and took with them their artillery. Many of the besieging Boer commandos went to the relief of their compatriots to join Cronje at Paardeberg, where the next saga in the war was unfolding.

The 10th Hussars crossing Klip Drift

Queen's South Africa Medal with Clasp 'Relief of Kimberley'

This clasp was "granted to all troops in the relief column under Lieutenant General French who marched from Klip Drift on February 15th 1900, and all the 6th Division under Lieutenant General Kelly-Kenny who were within 7,000 yards of Klip Drift on February 15th 1900."

The units that were eligible for this clasp and approximate numbers of clasps issued (where known) are listed below:

Australian Horse, 1st; Cape Garrison Artillery; Cape Medical Staff Corps; Cheshire Regiment; Damant's Horse (Rimington's Guides); Dragoon Guards, 1st (3), 3rd (2), 4th (2), 6th (445), 7th (2); Dragoons, 1st (2), 2nd (363), 6th (67); Duke of Edinburgh's Own Volunteer Regiment; East Kent Regiment; Essex Regiment; Field Intelligence Department; French's Scouts; Gloucester Regiment; Hussars, 3rd (10), 7th (8), 8th (4), 10th (458), 11th (3), 14th (159), 15th (4), 18th (7); Kitchener's Horse; Lancers, 5th (3), 9th (419), 12th (381), 16th (459), 17th (4), 21st (7); Life Guards, 1st (153) and 2nd (155); New South Wales Lancers; New Zealand Mounted Rifles; Norfolk Regiment; Northamptonshire Regiment; Oxford Light Infantry; Queensland Mounted Infantry, 1st; Roberts' Horse; Royal Dublin Fusiliers; Royal Horse Guards (136); Royal Irish Regiment; Royal Navy; South African Constabulary; Welsh Regiment; West Riding Regiment; Yorkshire Regiment.

QSA with clasp for the Relief of Kimberley

565

Kimberley Siege Account and Medal Roll

Natal Mercury Souvenir Special.

PRICE 1d.] **WEDNESDAY, JUNE 6, 1900.** [PRICE 1d.

THE WAR.
A CROWNING EVENT.
PRETORIA TAKEN.

Occupied by British Troops.

Capetown, June 5 (Reuter).—Lord Roberts reports:—

We are now in possession of Pretoria. The official entry will be made at 2 o'clock this afternoon.

MARCHING ON PRETORIA.
Lord Roberts's Report.

Capetown, June 5 (Reuter's Special).—The following is officially communicated:—

Lord Roberts to High Commissioner:

Six Mile Spruit, June 4.—We started this morning at daybreak, and marched ten miles to Six Mile Spruit. Both flanks engaged the enemy. Colonels Henry and Ross's Mounted Infantry, with the West Somersets, Bedford, Dorset, and Sussex companies of Yeomanry quickly dislodged the enemy from the south bank and pursued them nearly a mile, when they found themselves under a very heavy fire from guns which the Boers had placed on a well-concealed commanding position.

Our heavy guns, Naval and Horse Artillery, which had purposely been placed in the front of the column, were hurried to the assistance of the mounted infantry as fast as oxen and mules could travel over great rolling hills, by which Pretoria is surrounded.

The guns were supported by Stephenson's Brigade and Pole-Carew's Division, and, after a few rounds, drove the enemy out of their positions.

The Boers then attempted to turn our left flank. In this they were again foiled by the mounted infantry and Yeomanry, supported by Maxwell's Brigade and Tucker's Division. As, however, they still kept pressing on our left rear, I sent word to Ian Hamilton, who was advancing three miles on our left, to incline towards us, and fill up a gap between the two columns. This finally checked the enemy, who were driven back towards Pretoria. The Guards' Brigade are quite near the most southern of the five forts by which Pretoria is defended, and less than four miles from the town.

French, with the 3rd and 4th Cavalry Brigades and Hutton's Mounted Infantry are to the north of Pretoria. Broadwood's Brigade is between French's and Hamilton's Columns. Gordon is watching the right flank of the main force, not far from the only bridge at Irene Station, which has been destroyed by the enemy.

Our casualties, I hope, are very few. I have only heard of two officers—Commandant Dehorkey, who is slightly wounded in the foot, and the Duke of Norfolk, whose right hip was dislocated, owing to his horse falling. Fortunately, the doctor was handy, and reduced the dislocation on the field. The Duke is now comfortably settled in the Irish ambulance.

KIMBERLEY (124 Days).
Siege commenced October 14, 1899
Relieved February 15, 1900

MAFEKING (216 Days).
Siege commenced October 13, 1899
Relieved May 17, 1900

LADYSMITH (119 Days).
Siege commenced November 2, 1899
Relieved February 28, 1900

JOHANNESBURG
Surrendered May 31, 1900

A celebration from the *Natal Witness* of the lifting of the three sieges of Kimberley, Ladysmith and Mafeking, the capture of Johannesburg and Pretoria and the general belief that the war would soon be over.

Bibliography

Books

Abbott, P E, *Recipients of the Distinguished Conduct Medal, 1855–1909*, J B Hayward & Son, Suffolk, 1987

Ashe, E O, *Besieged by the Boers*, Hutchison & Co, London, 1900

Beet, A J and Harris, C B, *Kimberley Under Siege – Fiftieth Anniversary – An Illustrated Survey*, Diamond Fields Advertiser, Kimberley, 1950

Birch, J H and Northrop, H D, *History of the War in South Africa*, Canada c 1900

Boer War Services of Military Officers, 1899 – 1902, Savannah Publications, London, 1998

Bradley, J, *A Pottery Man's Journal of the Siege of Kimberley*, J C Looney, Kimberley, 1900

Brown, H, *War with the Boers*, Virtue and Company Ltd, London, 1901

Chilvers, H A, *The Story of De Beers*, Cassell and Company Ltd, 1940

Conan Doyle, A, *The Great Boer War: A Two-Years' Record, 1899-1901*, Smith, Elder & Co, London, 1901

Creswicke, L, *South Africa and the Transvaal War*, T C & E C Jack, Edinburgh, 1900

Crockford's Clerical Dictionary for 1907, Horace Cox, London, 1907

Cunliffe, F H E, *The History of the Boer War*, Volume II, Methuen and Co, London, 1904

Davitt, M, *The Boer fight for freedom*, Funk & Wagnalls Company, New York and London, 1902

De Villebois-Mareuil, G, *War Notes – the Diary of Colonel De Villebois-Mareuil from November 24, 1899 to April 4 1900*, Methuen & Co, London, 1902

De Wet, C R, *Three Years War*, Charles Scribner, New York, 1902

Donaldson, K, *South African Who's Who, 1910*, Bemrose & Sons Ltd, Derby, 1910

Dooner, M, *The Last Post*, J B Hayward and Son, Suffolk, 1980

Downham, J, *Red Roses on the Veldt*, Carnegie Publishing, Lancaster, 2000

Forsyth, D, *Defenders of Kimberley*, Roberts Publications Ltd

Green, G A L, *An Editor looks back: South African and other memories, 1883-1946*, Juta & Co, Cape Town, 1947

Hall, D, *The Hall handbook of the Boer War 1899 - 1902*, University of Natal Press, Pietermaritzburg, 1999

Hayward & Son, J B, *The South African War Casualty Roll for the South African Field Force, 11th October 1899 to June 1902*, Suffolk, 1982

Henderson, R H, *An Ulsterman in Africa*, Unie-Volkspers Beperk, Cape Town, 1945

Hibbard, M G, *Boer War Tribute Medals*, Constantia Classics Publications, Sandton, South Africa, 1982

Hornby, G, *Medal Roll of the Corps of Royal Engineers, Volume 5*, Institution of Royal Engineers, Chatham, Kent, 2004

Khaki in South Africa – an album of pictures and photographs illustrating the chief events of the War under Lord Roberts, George Newnes Ltd, London, 1900

Lighton, C and Harris, C B, *Details Regarding the Diamond Fields Advertiser (1878-1968)*, Northern Cape Printers Ltd, Kimberley, 1968

List of Officers of the Royal Regiment of Artillery, 1862 – 1914, Sheffield, 1914

Lunderstedt, S and Duminy, K, *Summer of 1899*, Kimberley Africana Library, Kimberley, 1999

Marix Evans, M, *Encyclopaedia of the Boer War*, ABC-CLIO, London, 2000

Maurice, F, *History of the War in South Africa 1899 – 1902*, Hurst & Blackett 1906-10

Kimberley Siege Account and Medal Roll

    Meyer, C, *Days of Horror*, Swiftprint, Kimberley, 1999

    O'Meara, Lt Col W A G, *Kekewich in Kimberley*, Medici Society Ltd, London, 1926

    Robinson, Commander C, *Celebrities of the Army*, London, 1902

    South African Honours and Awards, 1899 – 1902, Arms and Armour Press in association with J B Hayward & Son, London, 1971

    Stirling, J, *British Regiments in South Africa, 1899 – 1902*, J B Hayward and Son, London, 1994

    Stirling, J, *The Colonials in South Africa, 1899 – 1902*, J B Hayward and Son, London, 1990

    The Prominent men of Cape Colony, South Africa, The Lakeside Press, Portland Maine, 1902

    The Siege of Kimberley 1899-1900, author unknown, c 1900

    The Times History of the War in South Africa, edited by L S Amery, Sampson Low, Marston and Company Ltd, London, 1900-06

    The War in South Africa, The Battery Press, Nashville, 1998

    Wilson, H W, *After Pretoria: The Guerilla War*, Amalgamated Press ltd, London, 1902

    Wilson, H W, *With the Flag to Pretoria*, Harmsworth Brothers, London, 1900

Internet sites

    www.angloboerwar.com

    www.gazettes-online.co.uk

Manuscripts, journals, newspapers and diaries

    Black and White, Black and White Publishing Company Ltd, London, 1900

    De Beers Consolidated Mines Limited, Annual Reports, 1900 – 1903

    Gorle, Captain H V, *A brief account of the method of administrating Supplies during the Siege of Kimberley, 15th October, 1899, to 15th February, 1900*, The Army Service Corps Journal, November 1902

    Illustrated London News from 1899 and 1900

    Lucas, C D, *Notes on the siege of Kimberley*, St Andrew's College Magazine, May 1900

    Lunderstedt, S, *The role of black people during the siege of Kimberley and its aftermath*, Anglo-Boer South African War Conference, 29-31 August 2000

    Newspapers: *The Times, Diamond Fields Advertiser, Natal Witness*

    Orders and Medals Research Society Journals

    South African Military History Society, volume 3, number 4, *The Diary of a Doctor's Wife*

National Archives

    Medal rolls, Army Lists and documents from the National Archives, London

Index

A

Abrams, Loius 337
Adams, Hamilton J G 291, 335, 337, 485
Adamson, J 81
Adler, Henry M 54, 331, 368
Alberts, J J P 374
Alexandersfontein.....31, 44, 57, 59, 60, 81, 82, 83, 281, 283, 372, 373, 393, 401, 402, 403, 404, 405, 411, 412, 413
Altham, Edward A......................................6, 7, 337
Anderson, Edward............................60, 332, 368
Anderson, J M 368
Anderson, James M 421, 465
Anderson, W T 539
Angel, Thomas L 291, 335, 336, 337, 359, 421, 484
Archibald, Robert....................................520, 521
Armaments
  Boer
    Artillery
      75mm Krupp 529
      9-pounder 84
      Long Tom 64, 70, 72, 73, 74, 76, 81, 83, 87, 532, 533
    Rifle
      Mauser 35, 53, 281, 549, 561, 563
  British
    Artillery
      15-pounder 15
      7-pounder ..7, 8, 11, 14, 15, 60, 67, 68, 280, 395, 396
      Long Cecil 67, 68, 70, 73, 87, 378, 527, 529, 559
    Machine gun
      Maxim ..7, 14, 15, 16, 26, 34, 38, 44, 50, 52, 281, 391, 403, 404, 405, 407, 410, 411, 413, 535, 536
    Rifle
      Lee-Metford 7, 9, 15, 53
      Martini-Henry 14, 15
      Snider 14
Armoured train....15, 26, 33, 34, 37, 46, 48, 50, 51, 280, 281, 282, 323, 324, 325, 328, 330, 333, 347, 357, 386, 394, 396, 397, 404, 405, 406, 407, 409, 414, 415, 431, 535
Armstrong, Arthur H 44, 334, 368
Armstrong, J 61, 291, 335, 479
Army Service Corps .... See Units
Aronson, M M 488
Arum, R G 488
Arundale, Francis R 54, 331, 368
Ashe, Evelyn O ..21, 29, 33, 35, 41, 48, 49, 68, 72, 82, 291, 335, 337, 359, 547, 553
Ashe, Mrs 335
Ashmead-Bartlett, Ellis 86, 524
Atkinson, J...451
Attwood, Arthur, J 291, 337
Ayliff, William E....38, 291, 333, 337, 344, 368, 398

B

Backman, W A... 545, 546
Baden-Powell, Robert S S................. 15, 542, 547
Bailey, H 48, 328, 368
Bainbridge, C 335
Baker, William J 54, 331, 368
Banham, W C 291
Bankier, A A 35, 324, 368
Barkly West 15, 33, 37, 280
Barnard, M 374
Barron, Robert B 48, 329, 337, 368, 547, 548, 549, 550
Barton, W E 502
Bayman, W 291
Bayne, George C 335, 337
Beaconsfield...7, 16, 17, 19, 57, 72, 76, 79, 81, 87, 281, 334, 387, 388, 390, 391, 392, 396, 399, 400, 401, 402, 404, 418
Beaconsfield Town Guard .... See Units
Beale, H 374
Bechuanaland 5
Beddome, Edward I 291
Bedggood, A 507
Beer, F 451
Beet, George 338, 359
Belk, Samuel W 291, 338
Belmont
  Battle of.....................49, 281, 341, 550, 561, 562
  Casualties 563
Benaauwheidsfontein 411, 412, 546
Benade, H 374
Benade, J 374
Benjamin, Lionel H 338, 359
Bennett, G 291
Bennie, A 291
Benson, George E 563
Berg, C G 368
Berlin Conference... 5
Berrange, Christian A L 38, 280, 291, 336, 338, 359, 407, 457
Bester, J 374
Bester, W 374
Bevan, Ernest Henry 338
Bevan, W 545, 546
Bezuidenhout, C J 374
Bezuidenhout, G 374
Billing, G 48, 329, 368
Bingham, Charles H M 35, 291, 324, 338, 368, 416, 451
Biographies 337
Bird, I 291
Birt, A G 291
Bishop, R 291
Black, Andrew O 291, 334, 338, 359
Blackaller 374
Blackbeard, Charles A 291, 334, 338, 490
Blacking, E 291

Kimberley Siege Account and Medal Roll

Blacking, F 339, 359
Blacks 19, 27, 57, 524, 553
    Population 553
Blake, Alfred 34, 368
Blankenberg's Vlei 19, 85
Bloemfontein 1, 56, 70, 551, 561, 564
Blum, A 291, 335, 339
Blundell, Thomas 513
Bodley, Joseph H 44, 281, 291, 327, 339, 368, 404, 415
Bolton, P W J 374
Booth, J R 291, 421
Booth, R D 291, 490
Boshof 11, 35, 37, 396, 415
Bosman, John 33
Botes, A L 374
Botha, J H 374
Botha, N J 374
Botha, Petrus J 35, 36, 37, 280, 339, 367, 383, 416
Bowden, Sidney V 339
Bowen, Harry J Ap O..48, 291, 329, 334, 336, 339, 368, 406, 416, 420, 421
Bradford, W K 488
Brady, Claude 35, 324, 368
Brady, George C 54, 331, 368, 539
Brain, Francis S 514
Braine, W 52, 291, 521
Brand, E C J 503
Brand, F R 374
Brand, Reginald 291, 421, 465, 466
Bray, G 451
Bray, William 514
Bredinand, P 374
Brice, F 335
Brick, T 368
Bridge, Charles H 555
Bridge, J M 291, 339
Brink, A 488
Brits, T 374
Britton, W D 291
Britz, Dolf 374
Broese, J H 374
Brooks, J L 368
Brown, Henry P 368, 372
Brown, Samuel 33, 334, 547, 548
Brunton, Walter G 339, 359
Buller, Redvers 45, 46, 56, 58, 87, 561
Bultfontein 385
Bunn, D 503
Burger, A 374
Burger, J 374
Butler, T 369
Butler, William 8, 339
Buxton, John 547

C

Callen, Thomas 291, 335, 339
Campbell, James N 44, 326, 369
Campbell, John 502
Canut, R C 60, 332, 369
Cape Colonial Ordnance Department ..... See Units

Cape Police .... See Units
Cape Town 1, 5, 7, 8, 9, 14, 58, 62, 66, 74, 283, 397, 523, 532, 535, 555, 561
Carlyle, Thomas 48, 328, 339, 369
Carnegy, R B 421
Carr, Albert 334
Carr, John R 335, 485
Carson, Francis R 334
Carson, James 547
Carstairs-Rogers, Fergus 291, 340, 421
Carter's Farm ... 38, 44, 51, 52, 282, 372, 404, 406, 407, 409
Carter's Ridge 17, 31, 44, 46, 47, 48, 50, 51, 52, 59, 60, 64, 281, 282, 283, 346, 355, 368, 369, 370, 371, 372, 380, 392, 510, 548, 550
Casualties
    Boer 373, 374
    British 368, 372
    Portraits 367
Cawood, Barrett N 48, 329, 369
Chadborn, John Arthur 340
Chamberlain, Joseph 5, 542
Chambers, J 369
Chamier, George D ..14, 15, 16, 21, 34, 46, 48, 50, 51, 54, 61, 81, 282, 291, 333, 336, 340, 359, 405, 406, 407, 408, 409, 410, 531, 539, 555
Channer, R W 291
Chapman, George E 35, 324, 369
Chatfield, Robert 291, 334, 465
Child, Jane C 335
Chilman, H R 291
Chronology of the siege 280
Church, George 360, 461
Churcher, Joseph H 44, 326, 369
Clark, William 48, 328, 369
Clarke, E P 44, 326, 369
Cleaver, Charles E 421
Clifford, Wigram R 46, 52, 53, 54, 330, 333, 336, 340, 369, 408, 409, 451, 465
Close, Hugh M 291, 340, 531
Cochrane, L H 335
Codrington, A 562
Coetser, J 374
Coetzer, J 374
Coghlan, Charles P J 7, 291, 340, 360, 421, 478
Coghlan, J J 291, 335, 487, 488
Colesberg Kopje 3
Colin, P 369
Collier, Herbert I 48, 329, 367, 369
Colvin, James W 291, 333
Commando
    Bloemfontein 373
    Bloemhof 31, 33, 47, 48, 52, 373
    Boshof 31, 64, 373
    Brandfort 373
    Gordonia 373
    Griqualand 31
    Griqualand West 373
    Hoopstad 373
    Jacobsdal 31, 64, 373
    Kroonstad 31, 373
    Ladybrand 373
    Lichtenburg 31, 64, 373

Potchefstroom 373
Schweizer-Reneke 373
Warrenton 31
Wesselton 373
Winburg 373
Wolmaransstad 31, 48, 64
Committee, J 369
Communication
Heliograph 34, 36, 51, 63, 83, 283, 407, 408, 412, 414, 415, 546
Searchlight 46, 404, 406, 524
Telephone 21, 36, 335, 391, 545, 546
Conning tower 11, 21, 59, 63, 72, 347, 369, 522, 525, 543
Connolly, J 369
Cooper, A J 48, 328, 369
Cooper, William 501
Cornwall, Henry 54, 331, 369
Cornwall, Moses 340, 488
Cornwall, Mrs 335
Corrie, James 48, 328, 369
Couch, C 335
Court of Summary Jurisdiction ...33, 280, 335, 337, 346, 347, 418
Cowen, M 488
Cowieson, David 291
Cox, J 421, 465
Crause, P B 466
Craven, Archibald K 465
Crawford, Robert M 341, 504
Cronje, Pietrus Arnoldus 31, 48, 341, 343, 353, 512, 554, 562, 565
Crosbie, Michael J 465
Crosby, N 421
Croxford, P G 291
Crozier, M K 333, 341
Cruickshank, Alex 291
Cullinan, John C 33, 341, 369
Cumming, Arthur W..341, 360, 513, 547, 548, 549, 550, 552
Cundill, T J 488
Curry, A W 291

D

Dallas, Seymour 291, 360, 421
Damant, Frederick H 291, 341, 360
Darby, Alfred Horatio 518
Dare, Arthur S 54, 331, 369
Davidson, Thomas M 457
Davies, J E 488
Davies, R T 369
Davis, F 451
Davis, Valfrid E 341, 360
Davis, William H 291
Day, Frederick H 54, 331, 369
De Beer, J 374
De Beers Consolidated Mines Limited .3, 7, 12, 14, 17, 19, 21, 27, 29, 36, 38, 45, 57, 62, 67, 69, 76, 87, 518, 524, 525, 529, 530, 531, 537, 548, 555, 559
Expenses 526

Appendices

De Beers Maxim Battery .... *See* Units
De Klerk, A P J 374
De La Rey, Adriaan 562
De La Rey, Jacobus H ...31, 41, 64, 281, 341, 562, 563
De Lange, G 374
De Putron, Cyril 60, 291, 333, 342, 413
De Villebois-Mareuil, Georges.66, 70, 74, 342, 360
De Wet, J 374
Deere, R H 48, 328, 369
Defences 384
1898 report 384
1899 report 385
Belgravia Redoubt 19, 43, 281, 388, 438, 486, 487, 488, 542
Boshof Redan 19, 387, 438, 487
Breastworks 311
Camp Redoubt 19, 300, 388, 389, 457, 481
Civil Service Redoubt 19, 310, 388, 435
Crusher Redoubt ... 18, 26, 27, 41, 423, 427, 431
Davis's Heap 19, 61, 81
De Beers Redoubt 19, 308, 388
Fort Gibraltar 61, 448
Fort Methuen 493
Fort Nelson 494
Kamfersdam Redoubt 443, 479
Kenilworth Redoubt ..18, 19, 306, 388, 391, 448, 495
Kumo House 19, 493
Mostert's Redoubt 434, 469, 494
New Kimberley Redoubt 18, 320, 388
No 1 Searchlight Redoubt.18, 20, 312, 388, 390, 401, 443, 455, 471, 472, 531, 546
No 2 De Beers Redoubt 19, 20, 314, 388
No 2 Redoubt 27, 442, 444, 470, 496
No 2 Searchlight Redoubt.18, 67, 410, 423, 473, 478
No 3 Redoubt 432, 438, 473
No 4 Redoubt 433, 439, 479, 485
No 6 Redoubt 434, 468, 474, 477, 480, 497
No 7 Redoubt 468, 476, 496
Old Kimberley Redoubt 18, 302, 388, 423, 475
Otto's Kopje Redoubt27, 61, 316, 342, 388, 435, 497
Pickering's Redoubt No 1 432
Pickering's Redoubt No 2 .... 432, 478
Premier Mine Redoubt..20, 26, 27, 63, 304, 388, 398, 401, 402, 403, 423, 426, 427, 444, 455, 480
Reservoir Redoubt..19, 20, 26, 27, 50, 298, 385, 387, 388, 390, 394, 401, 404, 405, 406, 407, 423, 427, 431, 445, 481, 498, 510, 546
Rinderpest Redoubt 19, 20, 294, 388, 390
Sanatorium .... *See Kimberley* Sanatorium
Schmidt's Drift Redoubt 19, 388, 437, 474
Smith's Redoubt 18, 388
St Augustine's Redoubt 318, 388
Stables Redoubt 18, 296, 388
Transvaal Road Breastworks 387, 388
Work schedule 388
Deile, H T 374
Dennison, Clifford D 54, 331, 369
Dennison, F W 546

571

Kimberley Siege Account and Medal Roll

Despatch riders 547
Devenish, Ferdinand A R 291
Diamond Fields Advertiser ... 13, 28, 36, 40, 54, 58, 62, 74, 76, 281, 283, 510, 517, 519, 522, 537, 548, 554
    History 537
    Proclamations 538
Diamond Fields Artillery .... *See* Units
Diamond Fields Horse .... *See* Units
Dickinson, Arthur F 35, 82, 324, 369
Dodds, J C 35, 324, 369
Dorey, J 451
Douglas 549, 551
Douglass, P 467
Drew, G B 484
Drew, Percy J V 291
Dronfield . 17, 34, 38, 64, 66, 84, 85, 280, 283, 379, 398, 413, 414, 415, 416, 524, 536, 546
Druce, James C 291, 421
Du Plessis, J 374
Du Plessis, S I 374
Du Plooy, A 374
Du Toit, Herklaas 374
Du Toit, J 374
Dunbar, J Brander 291, 335, 342
Duncan, James D 83, 335, 342, 510
Durban 1, 339, 341, 343, 561
Dye, W T 35, 324, 369

E

Eden, D R 450
Eden, G A 450
Eden, J C 450
Eden, Joseph 450
Eden, T E 450
Eden, W E 369, 450
Edkins, George 54, 330, 369
Edmonds, J J 501
Edy, Norman H 54, 331, 369
Elandslaagte, battle of 562
Eliot, Algernon E A 291, 342
Eliott, Francis A H ... 34, 52, 54, 291, 333, 342, 360, 414, 416, 457
Elkin, W S 291, 335, 421
Elliot, K C 291, 421, 478, 506
Elliott, G 369
Elliott, Hugh J L 35, 324, 367, 369
Ellis, G K 291, 476
Elphinstone, Frederick S 343, 360
Engagement
    Alexandersfontein
        14 Feb 00 82
        17 Nov 99 .... 44, 327, 404
    Carter's Farm
        16 Nov 99 .... 44, 326, 404
            Casualties 44, 372
        3 Nov 99 38
            Casualties 372
    Carter's Ridge
        25 Nov 99 .... 46, 328
            Casualties 48, 372

        28 Nov 99 .... 50, 330
            Casualties 54, 372
    Kamfersdam
        9 Dec 99 .... 60, 332
            Casualties 60
    Kenilworth
        22 Nov 99 44
        3 Nov 99 .... 38, 398
            Casualties 372
    Macfarlane's Siding
        24 Oct 99 .... 34, 323, 397, 414
            Casualties 35, 372
    Otto's Kopje
        11 Nov 99 .... 44, 325, 404
            Casualties 372
    Riverton
        20 Oct 99 34
Ettling, G A 466
Eyre, Edwin 343

F

Fabling, Laucelot M 343
Fairbrass, William M 547
Farquhar, J 487, 488
Farr, Leo G 48, 329, 369
Faulkner, T J 291
Faulkner, W H 291, 335, 421
Fenn, Dudley B 334, 465
Ferguson, Fergus 54, 331, 369
Ferreira, Ignatius S 64, 66, 282, 343, 361
Ferris, W 501
Field, H G 291, 343, 369, 547
Fielden, Ramsay R 451
Finlayson, Robert A .. 291, 334, 336, 343, 361, 413, 416, 460, 505, 517, 520, 539
Fisher, Christopher 500
Fisher, Edward M 291, 343
Fletcher, Walter J C 33, 291, 344, 367, 369, 383
Flynn, J F 291, 485, 521
Ford, H F 488
Ford, J E 488
Ford, Thurston J 291
Forestier-Walker, W F E F 9
Foster, C H 545, 546
Foster, Ernest 369
Fourie 374
Fourie, L 374
Fourie, L C G 374
Fourie, N D 374
Fourteen Streams 15, 280, 356, 396, 397, 536
Foy, Louis A 344
Franceys, A L 291
Fraser, J L 488
Fraser, John R .. 48, 50, 81, 83, 291, 334, 336, 344, 392, 405, 406, 409, 411, 489
Freislich, Charles E 48, 329, 367, 369, 506
Freislich, Herbert W 506
French, John D P ... 83, 84, 85, 283, 404, 412, 413, 524, 538, 546, 564, 565
Fuller, Arthur 7
Fynn, W D 14, 41, 291, 335, 421

572

Fyvie, L C 82, 369

G

Gagiano, J J 374
Gainsford, E R 511
Gardiner, F J 488
Gardiner, W J 335, 507
Garrard, Frank Y 511
Garrett, Edmund 537
Gentleman, J W 291, 421
Geoghegan, John P 48, 329, 369
Gibson, William M 344
Gifford, John 335, 539
Gifford, Sophie C 344
Gilbert, J 335, 545
Gill, H J 291, 451
Gill, Lionel W J 344
Gillett, John L 344, 361
Gladstone, William 5
Glover, E 369, 403
Glover, Louis S 344
Glyn, Charles 54, 331, 369
Goate, E W C 291
Goffe, Edward 291, 361, 529
Goodall, Thomas J 44, 326, 369
Goodenough, William H 6, 7, 337, 339, 344
Gordon Sprigg, John 7, 8, 344, 355, 361
Gordon, Harry J 54, 331, 369
Gordon, J 335
Gorle, Harry V 26, 29, 291, 333, 336, 344, 361, 395, 555
Gout, Jacob 554
Gouws, M G 374
Gow, James 35, 324, 369
Gradwell, G W 35, 324, 369
Grahamstown 3, 14
Grant, Douglas 485
Grant, William G 485
Grassie, P 488
Greeff, G P 374
Green, Arthur J 291, 345
Green, George A L 345, 361, 537, 542, 547
Gregory, Edward P 48, 329, 369
Grimmer, Irvine 335, 421, 526
Grindrod, John H 54, 331, 369

H

Haddock, R S 291
Haidler, F 291, 421
Hall, S 369
Hallett, W A 374
Hambly, R 370
Hambly, William J 345
Hampson, B 488
Hannam, William H 507
Harmse, C J H 374
Harper, Henwood G 54, 331, 370
Harris, David 7, 8, 12, 14, 291, 334, 336, 345, 361, 420, 492, 517, 524, 526, 539, 542, 547

Appendices

Harris, G 334
Harris, George H F 370, 465
Harris, L W H 291
Harris, Roy J R 35, 324, 370
Harris, Wilfrid S 291
Harrison, Fred 291, 345
Hartigan, Marcus M 35, 324, 345, 370
Hartley, J 488
Hasenjäger, August E 48, 328, 370
Hastings, John W 54, 331, 367, 370
Hauptfleisch, J 370
Hawker, Charles H 44, 334, 370, 465
Hayes, H 291, 485
Hayston, W 291, 421
Heald, A 54, 330, 370, 451
Health
    Disease 69, 88, 510
    Mortality rates 69, 88, 554
Hearn, D P 291, 421, 470, 478
Heberden, George A ... 15, 291, 334, 336, 345, 465
Hellard, H 451
Henderson, D H 487, 488
Henderson, H P 82, 370
Henderson, Mark 335
Henderson, Robert H 8, 68, 291, 335, 336, 345, 351, 361, 420, 539, 544, 555
Henley, Francis J 505
Henman, R A 546
Henning, F H 374
Henrietta, Sister 335
Hertog, Charles E 291, 335, 345, 362
Hewett, Arthur W 82, 346, 407
Hickman, W 509
Hickson-Mahoney, J C 48, 291, 329, 334, 346, 370, 406, 465
Hill, William C 505
Hillier, H W 54, 331, 370
Hirschhorn, F 526
Hiscock, Herbert 54, 331, 370
Hobson, Charles H 291
Hodgson, C 451
Hogg, J 511
Hogg, J C 291
Holbech, William A 335, 346, 538
Holliday, C 421
Hollingworth, R H 291
Holton, H 291
Honoured Dead Memorial 377
    Inscription 378
Hope, B 515
Hornby, W 291, 421, 477
Hoskins, C H 35, 324, 370
Howard, H W 488
Howell, James H 54, 331, 370
Howell, Richard 52, 54, 331, 367, 370
Howie, C 346, 362
Hughes, D T 370
Hulley, T H 291, 421
Human, John L 370
Humphrys, Edward T 291, 334, 346
Hurley, L 374

573

I

Ibberson 374
Idebski, William M 291, 346, 362
Ingleton, H..511
Intelligence Department 552
Ironstone Kopje 46, 406, 407, 409
Irwin, G 291
Isaacs, M 335

J

Jacobs, D 375
Jacobs, J 375
Jacobs, L M D 375
Jacobsdal 27, 411, 554, 562
Jameson Raid 5, 6, 7, 352, 355, 533, 542
  Participants ...338, 339, 340, 343, 344, 347, 350, 351, 352, 354, 358
Jameson, Leander S 356, 542
Jennings, E 515
Jewell, S 335
Johannesburg 1, 4, 533, 534, 564
Johns, S 291, 421
Johnson, G H 291, 421
Johnson, H L 44, 326, 370, 467
Johnston, Hugh B H 291, 346
Johnston, J W 291
Johnstone's Kopje 46, 50, 51
Jones, Arthur S F 370
Jones, Ernest 81, 291
Jones, T J M 291
Jones, T L 488
Jones, Thomas (CP) 48, 328, 367, 370
Jones, Thomas (LNLR) 370, 403
Joubert, C J 375
Joubert, F J 375
Jourdain, Charles E 451
Jourdan, C 467
Joyce, Edward W 291, 465
Jubber, C D B 545, 546
Judge, Edward A 68, 69, 291, 335, 346

K

Kamfersdam ...48, 60, 70, 282, 283, 393, 400, 401, 402, 403, 405, 407, 410, 534, 546
Kayne, J 466
Kearns, F 291
Keating, E W 291
Kekewich, Robert G ...9, 10, 11, 12, 13, 14, 15, 16, 17, 19, 21, 26, 28, 29, 31, 33, 34, 35, 37, 40, 44, 45, 46, 48, 49, 50, 51, 53, 54, 55, 56, 57, 58, 59, 60, 63, 67, 69, 70, 74, 75, 76, 80, 81, 83, 84, 85, 86, 87, 280, 281, 282, 291, 323, 333, 335, 336, 346, 362, 372, 381, 420, 423, 451, 500, 510, 516, 522, 523, 532, 535, 536, 538, 542, 546, 551, 552, 553, 555, 556, 561
  Despatch 15 Feb 1900 395
  Siege proclamation 418
  Sword of Honour 521
  Ultimatum response 40
Keller, Joseph A 54, 331, 370
Kellet, W 488
Kelly, George 282, 370
Kenilworth.17, 18, 19, 27, 36, 38, 40, 60, 281, 283, 372, 388, 390, 392, 393, 398, 400, 402, 403, 413, 416, 521
Kenilworth Defence Force ....See Units
Kenton, James 54, 330, 370
Kershaw, C 488
Kidd, William E 60, 332, 370
Kilpin, G C 370
Kimberley
  Benevolent Society 335
  History 3
    First diamond find 3
    Founding of Kimberley 3
    Life in the 1880s 4
  Kimberley Club 70, 83, 409, 542, 550
  Medal ....See Medals
  Population breakdown 3, 4, 14, 27, 69, 74, 85, 522, 541
  Sanatorium 19, 26, 56, 72, 83, 283, 385, 387, 388, 390, 398, 423, 426, 460, 482, 524, 543, 551, 565
  Star ....See Medals
  Town Hall 70, 72, 86, 340, 516, 520, 544
  Town Hall Medal 544
Kimberley Light Horse ....See Units
Kimberley Regiment of Volunteers ....See Units
Kimberley Town Guard ....See Units
King Williamstown ..8, 15, 339, 340, 341, 343, 357, 514
King, Charles W 53, 54, 331, 370
King, G C 291
Kipling, Lockwood 378
Kipling, Rudyard 378
Kirsten, Frederick B A 347, 362
Kitchener, Horatio H 86, 335, 524, 542, 564
Kleinhans, T 375
Klokfontein 55, 282
Klopper 375
Knight, Frank S 54, 331, 370
Koffyfontein 27, 353
Kok, W J 375
Kok, W L 375
Kolbe, Willem J 347
Koodoosberg Drift 549
Koppiesdam 549
Kotzee, H G 375
Kraai Pan 11, 14, 15, 31, 394, 396, 535
Krieg, C J 375
Kruger, Stephen J 5, 31, 535

L

Labram, George F 16, 60, 67, 73, 87, 283, 291, 347, 362, 378, 383, 385, 386, 394, 403, 524, 525, 529, 530, 532, 540, 559
Lace, E 370
Ladysmith 1, 45, 64, 72, 87, 393, 509, 512, 518, 522, 523, 533, 541, 561

Lambourne, G 291, 421
Land mines...21, 41, 386, 388, 390, 391, 393, 508, 509, 527
Lange, Johannes H 33, 45, 347, 542
Lanigan, D J 48, 329, 370
Law, J 487
Lawrence, N 478
Lawrence, W 488
Lawrence, William 291
Lawson, Charles F 347
Lazaretto ..46, 51, 52, 61, 400, 401, 404, 405, 406, 407, 408, 409
Lee, H 35, 324, 330, 370
Lefevre, Charles 60, 332, 370
Legg, Archer S 457
Legward, Charles 48, 329, 370
Leipoldt, Peter 35, 324, 370, 467
Leon, M 70, 403
Leon, S 375
Lester, Charles R 44, 326, 347, 370
Liddiard, Eaben J 348, 362
Liebenberg, C 375
Liebenberg, G P 375
Lineham, T G 488
Litkie, E M 370
Lock, H 375
Lodge, J A 511
Lombaard, W 375
Lorimer, S 36, 291, 333
Lowndes, John G35, 291, 324, 333, 348, 362, 370, 416, 451
Loyal North Lancashire Regiment .... See Units
Luard, G M C..348, 543
Lubbe, J P S...375
Lubbe, Johannes J 38, 370, 398
Lucas, Claude D........................335, 348, 362, 421
Lucas, J T 420, 421, 466
Lunnon, W C 545, 546
Lutner, T 54, 330, 370
Lynch, F 488

M

MacDougall, Ewan A 291
Macfarlane's Farm..34, 38, 85, 280, 398, 404, 413, 414, 415, 416
Macfarlane's Station 414, 415
MacInnes, Duncan S 9, 10, 26, 291, 293, 333, 336, 348, 363, 384, 395, 396, 397, 553
Mackenzie, John E 68, 82, 335, 348, 517
MacKenzie, Roderick 35, 324, 370
Macpherson, A B..291
Madoc, Henry W..291, 349
Mafeking.1, 7, 9, 15, 31, 44, 45, 48, 393, 394, 396, 517, 522, 525, 526, 535, 561
Magersfontein 8, 33, 59, 64, 562
  Battle of 14, 38, 59, 282, 341, 510, 543, 551, 562, 563
  Casualties 563
Maguire, James R 14, 349, 363, 539, 543
Maguire, Julia B...................................14, 349, 539, 543
Mair, George 349, 363

Appendices

Mallett, Percy W 7, 291, 349, 421, 478
Mandy, Frank ...291, 335, 349, 420, 487, 488, 517, 542
Marais, E J 375
Mare, J 375
Maree, J J..375
Maribogo 15
Marshall, H 291
Marshall, John T 54, 331, 370
Martin, A H 291
Mathias, J 335
Mathieson, George R 48, 328, 334, 370
Matthews, T H 291, 363
May, A J 370
May, Thomas J.......34, 46, 60, 291, 334, 336, 349, 363, 415, 417, 507
Mayor's Siege Star ....See Medals
Mayston, W H D 48, 329, 370
McBean, D M... 487
McBeath, J W 357
McCallum, S H 334, 336
McCaskill, Ronald.............................35, 324, 370
McClintock, Robert L 34, 35, 291, 324, 333, 336, 348, 370, 388, 405, 412, 416, 456, 502
McDermott, A 371
McDonald, H 421
McDonald, John R..............................54, 331, 371
McDonald, Walter.........................52, 54, 331, 371
McHardy, Donald.. 348
McHardy, William 348, 421
McKay, G G 291
McNay, Charles G 54, 331, 371
Medal roll
  Caveats.. 96
  Explanation of format.. 96
  Surname A 97
  Surname B 102
  Surname C 119
  Surname D 133
  Surname E 142
  Surname F 146
  Surname G 153
  Surname H 161
  Surname I 178
  Surname J 178
  Surname K 184
  Surname L 190
  Surname M 197
  Surname N.. 214
  Surname O 217
  Surname P 221
  Surname Q 229
  Surname R.. 229
  Surname S 238
  Surname T 254
  Surname U 261
  Surname V 261
  Surname W 264
  Surname Y 278
  Surname Z 278
Medals
  Beaconsfield Children's Medal..................... 523
  Kimberley Medal 506, 516

575

Kimberley Star 517, 518
    Distribution on 15 Apr 01 519
    Gold 520
    Gold miniature 521
    Hallmark 518
King's South Africa Medal 95
Queen's South Africa Medal 91, 493, 499
    Clasp issue error 511
    Clasps awarded 92
    Clasps by state 94
    Defence of Kimberley and Cape Colony 512
    Defence of Kimberley and Paardeberg 512
    Defence of Kimberley and Relief of Kimberley
    512
    Defence of Kimberley entitlement 499
    Defence of Mafeking entitlement 511, 547
    Extant medals 95
    No clasp medals 508
    Non-standard 508
    Order of clasps 499
    Relief of Kimberley entitlement 565
    Relief of Mafeking entitlement 499
Meijer, G H 375
Meijer, J 375
Meijer, W 375
Mendelssohn, I 488
Methuen, Paul Sanford ...31, 38, 46, 48, 50, 55, 56, 57, 59, 63, 69, 86, 87, 282, 283, 342, 406, 522, 525, 547, 554, 561, 562, 563
Metrovitch, Joseph G 54, 331, 371
Meyer, Carl 349, 539
Meyer, J G 375
Meyer, J P 375
Meyer, S 375
Meyer, S F 375
Mildred, Charles A 349, 363
Meyer, S F 375
Milne, W G 291, 349, 363
Milner, A 35, 324, 371
Milner, Alfred 8, 9, 11, 13, 14, 15, 31, 44, 45, 57, 58, 339, 349, 551, 561
Mine
    Bultfontein 3, 16, 19
    De Beers 3, 16, 21, 26, 67, 87, 283, 387, 525
    Du Toit's Pan 3, 16
    Kimberley 3, 16, 18, 27, 281, 282, 283, 370, 384, 385, 386, 400
    Otto's Kopje 16, 18, 38, 44, 66, 281, 404, 405, 406, 410
    Premier16, 17, 26, 27, 29, 37, 41, 281, 282, 283, 385, 388, 397, 398, 400, 534
    Wesselton 16, 18, 280, 282, 391, 534
Mitchell, Walter 44, 326, 371
Modder River....27, 28, 46, 55, 57, 59, 74, 87, 280, 282, 394, 395, 399, 404, 406, 411, 510, 535, 552, 554, 561, 562, 564
    Battle of 282, 522, 562
    Casualties 563
Moir, Jimmy 363, 487, 488
Monro, David 457
Montleo, G L 33, 371
Monument
    Cape Police 379
    Carter's Ridge 380
    Honoured Dead Memorial 377
    Loyal North Lancashire Regiment 381
Moosie 554
Morice, Father 335
Morley, G H 371
Morris, J S 335
Morton, J 335, 506
Morton, W D 488
Moseley, E H 291, 335, 421, 469
Moss, Alfred 60, 282, 332, 371, 410
Mudge, Ernest C 333, 336, 451
Mungeam, William 350
Murphy, Daniel J 350
Murray, William H E 34, 83, 84, 291, 333, 350, 363, 412, 413, 414, 415, 417, 451

N

Namaqualand 5
Neale-Shutte, Richard F 291, 350
Nel, H J 375
Nelson, J 451
Nelson, W 291, 334, 364, 420
Neville, J 54, 330, 371
New Rush 3
Newdigate, William 334, 416, 421
Nicholas, Benjamin L 54, 331, 371
Nicholetts, Ashley B 52, 53, 334, 547
Nicholson, Christina A 335
Nicholson, N 291
Nieuwoudt, J H 375
Nieuwoudt, S F 375
Nind, C E 526
Noonan, Joseph D 350, 364
Notcutt, Henry C 350, 364

O

O'Dell, David 48, 328, 371
O'Malley, T O 515
O'Molony, S 291, 335
Oatley, William H 48, 329, 334, 336, 371
Oats, Francis 291, 351, 524, 526
O'Brien, Thomas H 82, 291, 333, 350, 411
O'Gorman, Charles J . 291, 333, 336, 350, 501, 560
Olifantsfontein ..31, 39, 64, 66, 280, 283, 401, 402, 403, 411
Oliver, Henry A 68, 83, 85, 291, 335, 336, 351, 364, 422, 488, 506, 517, 519, 520
O'Meara, Bulkeley E A 291, 334, 336, 351, 421
O'Meara, Walter A J ...9, 10, 11, 15, 26, 38, 40, 46, 56, 70, 75, 81, 83, 85, 291, 333, 336, 351, 364, 395, 396, 409, 417, 502, 551
O'Molony, Chidley K 335, 351
Opperman, H J P 375
Orange River ..9, 12, 15, 33, 45, 46, 281, 395, 398, 406, 548, 549, 550, 552, 561
Orr, John 44, 326, 351, 371
Ortlepp, Albert J 291, 334, 351, 364, 417
Osborne, Alfred 371
Osborne, C 291

Osman, F 545, 546

P

Paardeberg 64, 85, 343, 512, 551, 565
   Bread convoy 512
Paley, George 291, 421
Parker, Algernon 44, 325, 371, 404
Parkin, Julius M 351
Parsons, D 44, 326, 371
Passmore, S 451
Payne, Fred W 35, 324, 371, 417
Peake, S 291
Peakman, Tom C12, 38, 44, 51, 52, 53, 54, 60, 61, 68, 281, 282, 283, 291, 326, 334, 336, 352, 364, 371, 404, 406, 408, 409, 411, 420, 421, 466, 517, 523, 539
Peddiefontein 398, 404, 405, 406, 407, 408
Peiser, John 48, 329, 371
Penfold, Hugh M 352, 526
Penny, E A 421
Percy, R J 291, 421
Pescod, William 335
Petersen, John B 35, 324, 371
Philip, G H 488
Pickering, William 291, 335, 336, 352, 364, 526, 539
Pienaar, W 375
Pieterse 375
Pim, H 291, 335, 479
Plane, F W 291
Pool, Frank H 54, 331, 371
Pooley, J 291, 421, 520
Port Elizabeth 14
Post Office Corps .... See Units
Powell, Frank 52, 54, 331, 371
Powell, O P 467
Presow, R 291
Pretoria 64, 533, 551, 564
Pretorius, J L J 375
Pretorius, M 375
Pretorius, S J 375
Prince, E 371
Prinsloo 375
Pritchard, Matthew J 48, 329, 371
Putter, D 375
Putter, J C 375
Putter, J D J 375
Putter, N J 375

Q

QSA .... See Medals
Quentrall, T 488

R

Ramsay, A 488
Rankin, D 545, 546
Ras, M 375

Ras, P 375
Raynham, Eustace F 335, 336, 352
Reade, Raymond N R 46
Redpath, W D 487
Reeland, Charles J H 352
Reinecke, D J 375
Reinecke, J G 375
Relief operations 561
   Celebration 83
   French's Flying Column 564
   Methuen's view 56
   Plans 46, 59, 66, 67, 74, 394, 551, 564
   Removal of citizens 56, 57, 58
   Rhodes' view 44, 45, 57, 74, 75
Reunert, Theodore 352, 478
Reyersbach, Louis J 352, 364, 524
Rhodes, Cecil J 6, 14, 17, 40, 44, 45, 48, 54, 56, 57, 58, 62, 67, 68, 74, 76, 80, 83, 85, 86, 87, 281, 282, 283, 291, 335, 349, 352, 355, 365, 397, 465, 519, 524, 526, 529, 530, 531, 532, 537, 539, 541, 542, 543, 547, 548, 551, 552, 554, 559, 560, 561, 564, 565
Richards, Sidney 334, 336, 353
Richards, T B 45
Richards, W H 335, 539
Richardson, Henry 54, 331, 371
Richardson, J 371
Ricketts, C L 334
Ricketts, W A 488
Rickman, William E 291, 334, 336, 353, 465
Riet River 548, 549
Ring, George 48, 329, 371
Riverton ... 17, 33, 34, 372, 391, 398, 413, 414, 536
Roberts, Frederick S 66, 67, 74, 75, 76, 81, 86, 283, 353, 365, 400, 516, 517, 521, 524, 525, 540, 542, 551, 564
Roberts, William 514
Robertson, James W 334, 353, 465
Robinson, McLeod B 9, 10, 26, 291, 333, 336, 354, 365, 395, 457, 503, 539, 553
Rodger, Thomas H 60, 82, 291, 334, 336, 354, 365, 371, 466
Rogers, J J 467
Rooidam 548, 554
Rooilaagte
   Battle of 281, 562
   Casualties 563
Rossiter, W 44, 326, 371
Royal Army Medical Corps .... See Units
Royal Engineers .... See Units
Royal Garrison Artillery .... See Units
Rudd, H P 526
Rugg, H 291, 335
Rush, William W .48, 291, 328, 354, 365, 371, 406, 457, 504
Russell, J P 335, 336
Russell, W 335
Ryan, Francis K 354
Rybnikar, G C 519
Rynd, Francis F 291, 354, 502

S

Saddler, J M 421
Sadler, J M 291
Salaman, Sam 291, 354, 365
Salisbury, Philip 355, 488
Salkeld, Phillip D'O 54, 331, 371
Salmon, G H 488
Sandham, J 291
Saunders, G A 291, 421
Saunders, R 505
Schmidt, H 291, 421
Schreiner, William P 8, 15, 355, 365
Schultz, W 375
Scott, Herbert Thring 31, 280, 355, 395
Scott, James 335, 539
Scott, Robert G 291, 334, 336, 355, 365, 408, 409, 412, 416, 420, 421, 465
Scott, William 291, 355
Scott-Turner, Henry....9, 10, 12, 26, 34, 37, 44, 46, 48, 50, 51, 52, 53, 54, 280, 281, 282, 291, 331, 333, 355, 367, 371, 382, 395, 397, 398, 404, 405, 406, 409, 414, 417, 418, 491, 523, 524, 536, 538, 539, 542, 543
Screech, Charles 331, 371
Searchlights 20, 53, 64, 390, 393, 401
Seaward, H 61
Shackleton, C C 52, 291, 356, 466
Sharpe, Frederick 54, 331, 371
Sheasby, James B 291, 421
Shepherd, Daniel D 54, 331, 371
Shiels, T L 335
Simpson (POC) 545, 546
Simpson, F D 35, 324, 371
Sinclair, D K 421
Skelding, R A 488
Skelton, Henry 371, 383
Skill, N C 48, 329, 371
Skinner, R L 48, 328, 371
Smartt, Thomas W 14, 68, 291, 335, 356, 365, 539, 543
Smit, B G 375
Smith, D W 291
Smith, F W 291
Smith, H W 44, 326, 371
Smith, J J 487
Smith, James A J 291, 334, 336, 356, 366
Smith, Robert A L 291, 356
Smith, Samuel H 371
Smith's farm 401, 402, 403
Snipers 71, 281
Snow, A B 61, 356, 408, 411
Snyman, C R P 375
Soames, F L 466
Solomon, Richard 7
Sonnekus W F 375
Sonnekus, R H 375
Spencer, John W 510
Spilsbury, W G 54, 331, 371
Spitzkop 51, 400, 405, 406, 407, 408, 412
Spytfontein ...31, 33, 37, 57, 74, 81, 280, 282, 397, 405, 406, 536, 541
Stacpole, Henry F 54, 331, 371

Stassen, John N 371
Stead, A 539
Stead, B 291, 487, 488
Stearns, Charles C 54, 331, 371
Steenkamp, G A 375
Stenson, W 371
Stephens, W W 545, 546
Stevenson, J 291, 421
Stewart, A W 60, 332, 371
Stewart, J 291
Steyn, C J 375
Steyn, J J 375
Steyn, Martinus T 33, 280, 356, 366
Steyn, P J 376
Stolz, J J 48, 328, 371
Stoney, William W 68, 335, 560
Stonnill, E 488
Storer, Ernest 504
Stratten, T 421
Strickland, E 335
Strugnell, H 61
Stumke, John C A 44, 325, 371, 404
Sunde, K 488
Supplies 27, 45, 57, 58, 59, 555, 556
   Cattle 60, 282, 559
   Cattle guarding 391
   Cold store 559
   Gorle's account 555
   Medical 69, 560
   Mining 27, 57, 69, 87, 524
   Permits 556
   Pricing 28, 29, 30, 555
   Rations 60, 68, 69, 282
   Soup kitchen 68, 283, 527, 542, 559
   Supply Committee 29, 60, 68, 280, 555, 557, 560
   Water 17, 19, 29, 60, 82, 391, 393, 521
Swanepoel, C J 376
Swanepoel, D J 376
Swanson, J 291, 420
Sydney, E J 478
Symons, J E 335, 545, 546

T

Tabuteau, Charles 291, 335
Tabuteau, Henry 291, 335
Tait, S 291, 421
Talana, battle of 562
Tarr, G 48, 328, 371
Taungs 11, 396, 397
Taylor, Herbert 54, 331, 371
Taylor, John F 54, 371
Theron, A H L 376
Thomas, Kenneth R 356, 366
Thompson, Joseph 54, 331, 372
Thorpe, J H 291
Tidd-Pratt, S 291
Tillard, Max O 356
Tillemans, A A 291
Tiller, W H 466
Trevor-Smith, C W 488
Trotter, James K 8, 15, 17, 356, 384, 386

Troup, J 291
Turner, Alfred E 357, 366
Tyldesley, T 54, 330, 372
Tyson, John D 291, 357, 421
Tyson, Thomas G 68, 291, 334, 335, 357, 366, 542

U

Units
  Army Pay Corps 424
  Army Service Corps 9, 395, 424, 427, 510
    Medals 501
    MID 333
    Photographs 453
    Strength 287
  Beaconsfield Town Guard .. 44, 50, 81, 327, 328, 330, 396, 404, 405, 406, 407, 411, 418, 419, 446
    MID 334
    Photographs 489
  Boer .... See Commando
  Cape Colonial Ordnance Department 425
    MID 334
  Cape Police 9, 10, 11, 14, 15, 33, 34, 44, 46, 52, 53, 60, 81, 84, 280, 323, 324, 325, 326, 327, 328, 330, 331, 332, 391, 395, 396, 398, 404, 406, 409, 411, 424, 428, 429, 430, 523, 538
    Artillery 27
    Casualties 368
    Maxim 26, 325, 326
    Medals 503
    MID 333
    Monument 379
    Photographs 456
    Strength 287
  De Beers Maxim Battery 323, 324, 328, 330, 332, 391, 431
    Casualties 368
    Expenses 527
    Maxim 26
    Medals 503
    Photographs 465
    Strength 287
  Diamond Fields Artillery 8, 15, 34, 46, 50, 51, 52, 60, 61, 67, 82, 280, 323, 324, 326, 327, 328, 330, 332, 394, 398, 401, 403, 404, 405, 406, 407, 408, 409, 410, 411, 412, 413, 415, 431, 531, 538
    Artillery 27
    Casualties 368
    Medals 507
    MID 334
    Photographs 462
    Strength 13, 287, 395
  Diamond Fields Horse 7, 8, 14, 44, 50, 52, 60, 323, 324, 325, 326, 327, 330, 331, 368, 391, 398, 406, 408, 409, 410, 411, 412, 538
    Casualties 368
    MID 334
    Photographs 466, 492
    Strength 13, 287, 395
  Kenilworth Defence Force 448
    Strength 421
  Kimberley Light Horse. 14, 34, 44, 46, 50, 52, 53, 60, 76, 323, 324, 325, 326, 327, 328, 329, 330, 331, 332, 398, 399, 406, 408, 409, 410, 411, 413, 420, 431, 524, 538, 560
    Casualties 368
    Expenses 527
    Medals 505
    MID 334
    Photographs 465
    Raised 14, 280, 391, 397
    Strength 287
  Kimberley Regiment of Volunteers . 35, 323, 328, 329, 330, 391, 392, 394, 395, 405, 406, 411, 412, 413, 416, 431, 538
    Casualties 368
    Medals 505
    MID 334
    Photographs 459
    Strength 13, 287
  Kimberley Town Guard 11, 12, 13, 14, 26, 45, 50, 76, 328, 330, 332, 391, 392, 394, 405, 406, 410, 419, 420, 421, 425, 432, 508, 520, 537, 538, 542, 550, 553, 558
    Casualties 368
    Expenses 527
    Medals 506
    MID 334
    Photographs 468
    Strength 13, 287
  Loyal North Lancashire Regiment ... 9, 13, 15, 26, 34, 50, 51, 52, 53, 56, 323, 324, 328, 330, 332, 389, 391, 392, 394, 395, 396, 404, 406, 407, 408, 410, 411, 412, 413, 414, 415, 416, 426, 427, 538
    Casualties 368
    Maxim 26
    MID 333
    Monument 381, 382
    Mounted Infantry . 10, 46, 50, 52, 60, 325, 326, 327, 328, 330, 332, 333, 340, 391, 395, 406, 426, 500
    Photographs 451
    Strength 287
  Post Office Corps 328, 425, 545
    Medals 507
  Royal Army Medical Corps 9, 323, 324, 395, 424
    Medals 501
    MID 333
    Photographs 453
    Strength 287
  Royal Engineers ... 9, 46, 51, 328, 330, 332, 385, 388, 389, 390, 391, 392, 394, 395, 405, 406, 407, 408, 410, 411, 428
    Casualties 368
    Medals 502
    MID 333
    Photographs 456
    Strength 287
  Royal Garrison Artillery 9, 26, 27, 60, 62, 280, 332, 391, 394, 395, 398, 400, 401, 402, 404, 406, 407, 408, 410, 427, 445
    Casualties 368

579

Kimberley Siege Account and Medal Roll

    Maxim 26
    Medals 502
    MID 333
    Photographs 454
    Strength 287
Upfold, J 545, 546

V

Vaal River 3, 280, 391, 394, 396, 413
Van Aswegen 31
Van der Merwe 376
Van der Merwe, J F 376
Van der Merwe, N J S 376
Van der Westhuizen, H 376
Van Heerden, A 376
Van Niekerk, A A 376
Van Niekerk, C 376
Van Niekerk, Chris 376
Van Niekerk, J A 376
Van Niekerk, S R 376
Van Rensburg, A 376
Van Rensburg, J J D P 376
Van Vrede, P 376
Van Wyk, G 376
Varivis 376
Venter, W 376
Vigne, J T 487
Viljoen, A J J 376
Vines, C G 487
Von Witt, William S 547
Vosloo, J P 376
Vryburg 1, 11, 15, 31, 280, 395, 396, 397, 535

W

Wahldat, W 376
Walcroft, J 48, 328, 372
Waldek, P 421
Waldek, S P 54, 291, 331, 372, 409
Wallace, A 335
Wallace, Augustus R 291, 357
Wallace, Charles O 291
Walters, C J 421
Ward, Joseph 539
Warren, Charles 542
Warrenton 33, 37
Waterboer, Nicholas 3
Watermeyer, F E 38, 372, 398
Watkins, Arthur H 68, 291, 335, 357
Watkins, Mrs 335
Watkins, Nurse 335
Watson, H G 54, 331, 372, 409
Watson, J W 291
Wauchope, Andrew G 563
Waugh, F J 47
Weatherby, Mr 478

Webbstock, Horace J 291
Webster, Alexander McC..33, 48, 50, 51, 291, 333, 357, 397, 405, 406, 409, 414, 451, 535
Wells, E R 291
Wells, William H 291, 357
Wessels, Cornelius J 31, 36, 40, 64, 281, 282, 357, 366, 416
    Ultimatum 39, 40, 398
Wessels, G 376
Wesselton 16, 19, 61
Westerfield, W J 335
Whale, Harry 82, 372
Whiley, G E 291
White, F 421
White, Greenwood 291, 335, 357, 366, 421
White, J 545, 546
White, James T ...60, 291, 332, 334, 357, 372, 410
Wilcox, W J 291, 421
Wild, F 372
Wilkins, A 291
Wilkinson, E 451
Williams, A E 48, 329, 372
Williams, Albert S 291, 465
Williams, Alpheus F 357, 366, 526, 542
Williams, Gardner F 80, 291, 357, 366, 524, 526, 539, 542
Williams, James E 54, 331, 372
Williams, W 45
Willmore, Albert E 48, 329, 372
Wilson (POC) 545, 546
Wilson, Thomas 511
Wimbledon Ridge 17, 46, 48, 50, 51, 61, 64, 82, 398, 401, 402, 403, 407, 411, 412, 510
Winburg 11
Winter, Alexander 82, 372
Wood, Alfred 54, 331, 372
Woodbourne, T J 291, 421
Woodman, Thomas 291, 335
Woodward, Francis W 291, 333, 358, 451, 500
Woon, E W 358
Wright, A J 291, 358
Wright, O D 487, 488
Wright, Stephen O 53, 54, 331, 358, 372, 409, 538, 539
Wright, W G 335
Wylde-Browne, Gerald H 451

Y

Yates, F G 291
Young, Antony R 358
Young, D 487

Z

Ziegenbein, H A 421
Zybel, C J 376

Also by David J. Biggins

ELANDSLAAGTE
Account and Medal Roll

This major work takes a detailed look at the Battle of Elandslaagte, often using eye-witness accounts. Includes many previously unpublished photos and a comprehensive Medal Roll of all the British and Colonial Officers and men entitled to the Elandslaagte clasp for the QSA.

Now includes a FREE full up-date on CD-Rom

Order your copy today! £24.95 (+£3.00 P&P)
Call 01404 44166, log on to www.tokenpublishing.com
or write to Token Publishing, Orchard House, Duchy Road,
Heathpark, Honiton, Devon EX14 1YD

From the man who signed the banknotes!
INSIDE MAFEKING
The diary of
Captain Herbert Greener
Edited by Robin Droogleever

Step inside the walls of Mafeking with this exciting publication from Token Publishing Ltd.

- The fascinating story of the famous stamps and banknotes produced under the noses of the Boer enemy, by Captain Greener, the man who helped design, print them and actually signed the originals.

The personal diary of Herbert Greener the Paymaster General for Baden-Powell during the famous siege of Mafeking. Illustrated with numerous photographs taken during the siege. An outstanding factual account of an exciting, dramatic and sometimes harrowing period in British Colonial history where the idea for the foundation of the Boy Scout Movement first became a reality.

A not to be missed publication for anyone interested in the story of the siege.

Order your copy today! £29.95 FREE P&P FOR UK!
Call 01404 44166, log on to www.tokenpublishing.com
or write to Token Publishing, Orchard House, Duchy Road,
Heathpark, Honiton, Devon EX14 1YD